The
National Electrical Code® Handbook

The
National Electrical Code® Handbook

Based on the 1981 Edition of the *National Electrical Code*

JOSEPH A. ROSS, Editor

WILFORD I. SUMMERS, Technical Consultant

Second Edition

National Fire Protection Association
Quincy, Massachusetts

This is the second edition of *The National Electrical Code® Handbook* published by the National Fire Protection Association. The National Fire Protection Association formerly sponsored a handbook which was published by the McGraw-Hill Book Company and based on the *National Electrical Code.®* This publication, *The National Electrical Code® Handbook,* does not emanate from and is not in any way connected with or associated with the McGraw-Hill Book Company.

®Registered trademarks of the National Fire Protection Association
Life Safety Code® is a registered trademark of the National Fire Protection Association.

NFPA No. SPP-6C
ISBN 0-87765-186-8
Library of Congress No. 80-83269
Printed in the United States of America

First Printing, October 1980
Second Printing, January 1981
Third Printing, April 1981
Fourth Printing, June 1981

Contents

Chapter 4. Equipment for General Use

Chapter 5. Special Occupancies

Chapter 6. Special Equipment

Chapter 7. Special Conditions

Chapter 8. Communications Systems

Chapter 9. Tables and Examples

Appendix

Preface

The *National Electrical Code* is the most widely adopted code in the world. The combined sales of the 1975 and 1978 editions totaled nearly two million copies. The *National Electrical Code* is a nationally accepted guide to the safe installation of electrical conductors and equipment and is, in fact, the basis for all electrical codes used in the United States.

The National Electrical Code Handbook is an official publication of the National Fire Protection Association and is published in order to assist those concerned with electrical safety to understand the intent of the 1981 edition of the *Code*. A verbatim reproduction of the 1981 *National Electrical Code* is included and added where necessary are comments, diagrams, and illustrations that are intended to clarify further some of the intricate requirements of the *National Electrical Code*.

The editor has worked very closely with members of the National Electrical Code Panels in discussions that have led to the various revisions that have been incorporated in the 1981 edition of the *Code*. The assistance and cooperation of the Code-Making Panel Chairmen and various committee members are herein gratefully acknowledged.

The editor acknowledges with thanks the many manufacturers and their representatives who generously supplied photographs, drawings, and data upon request. Special thanks, too, go to Richard Biermann and Jay Stewart for their major contributions in the areas of special conditions and emergency systems. The editor also recognizes the contributions of Arel Sessions and Wilford I. Summers.

Appreciation is expressed to the NFPA staff members who attended to the countless details that went into the preparation of this *Handbook* and especially to Charles A. Tuck, Jr., Managing Editor; Carol Albanese, typing; Elizabeth Carmichael and Melissa Evans, composition; Ann Coughlin and Mary Strother, proofreading; and Donald McGonagle, production.

Finally, the editor wishes to express his sincere appreciation to his associate Peter Schram, Chief Electrical Engineer, NFPA, and to Mr. Schram's former colleagues at UL—George Schall, Jr., Gene Bockmier, Norman Davis, C. B. Schram, and R. W. Eckardt—for their help in preparing illustrations and text for the commentary portion of this *Handbook*.

Joseph A. Ross, *Editor*

Concise History of the
National Electrical Code

In 1881, the National Association of Fire Engineers met in Richmond, Virginia. From this meeting came a proposal that served as a basis for the first *National Electrical Code,* covering items such as the use of insulated conduit, the use of single disconnect devices, and the identification of the white wire. The first nationally recommended electrical code was published by the National Board of Fire Underwriters (now the American Insurance Association) in 1895. (The National Board of Fire Underwriters continued to publish the *National Electrical Code* until 1962, thus contributing greatly to its current universality.) With this 1895 code as a basis, in 1897 the *National Electrical Code* was drafted, the product of the combined labors of architectural, electrical, insurance, and allied interests which, through the National Conference on Standard Electrical Rules, composed of delegates from various national associations, unanimously voted to recommend it to their respective associations for approval or adoption.

In 1911, the National Fire Protection Association (NFPA) assumed sponsorship and control of the *National Electrical Code,* the National Conference on Standard Electrical Rules having disbanded in that very same year. Since 1920, the *National Electrical Code* has also been officially endorsed by the American National Standards Institute (formerly the United States of America Standards Institute and the American Standards Association), and the NFPA has maintained its capacity as Administrative Sponsor. Since that date, the Committee has been identified as "ANSI Standards Committee C1" (formerly "USAS C1" or "ASA C1").

In 1923, the *National Electrical Code* was rearranged and rewritten; in 1937 it was editorially revised so that all of the general rules would appear in the first chapters followed by supplementary rules in the following chapters; and, in 1959, it was editorially revised again, this time in order to incorporate a new numbering system under which each section of each article is identified by the article number preceding the section number. The National Fire Protection Association has been publishing and distributing the *National Electrical Code* since 1951. It does so through its own office and through the American National Standards Institute. In addition, the *National Electrical Code* is found in Volume Six of the NFPA's annual *National Fire Codes®*. The *National Electrical Code* is acknowledged to be the most widely adopted code of standard practices in the U.S.A.

1981 Edition of the *National Electrical Code*

This 1981 Edition of the *National Electrical Code* (NFPA 70-1981) was adopted by the National Fire Protection Association on May 21, at its 1980 Annual Meeting held in Boston, MA. It was approved by the American National Standards Institute on June 25, 1980, and it will be known as ANSI/NFPA 70-1981. It supersedes all previous editions of the *National Electrical Code,* the most recent previous edition being 1978.

This *Code* is purely advisory as far as the NFPA and ANSI are concerned but is offered for use in law and for regulatory purposes in the interest of life and property protection. Anyone noticing any errors should please notify the NFPA Executive Office, the Chairman and the Secretary of the Committee.

Development of the *National Electrical Code*

In accordance with the provisions of the NFPA Regulations Governing Committee Projects, a National Electrical Code Committee Report containing proposed amendments to the 1978 *National Electrical Code* was published by the NFPA in August 1979. This report recorded the actions of the various Code-Making Panels and the Correlating Committee of the National Electrical Code Committee on each proposal that had been made to revise the 1978 *Code*. The report was circulated to all members of the National Electrical Code Committee, and was made available to other interested NFPA members and to the public for review and comment. Following the close of the public comment period, the Code-Making Panels met, acted on each comment and reported their action to the Correlating Committee. The NFPA published the National Electrical Code Technical Committee Documentation in March, 1980, which recorded the actions of the Code-Making Panels and the Correlating Committee on each public comment to the National Electrical Code Committee Report. The NFPA also published the Advanced Printing of the Proposed 1981 *National Electrical Code* in March 1980 to permit the study and evaluation by those interested, prior to formal action on the Committee Report by the 1980 NFPA Annual Meeting. The National Electrical Code Committee Report and National Electrical Code Committee Documentation were presented to the 1980 NFPA Annual Meeting for adoption. The proceedings of that adoption are published in the September 1980 issue of the NFPA *Fire Journal* ®.

Coincident with the above processing procedures, each of the Code-Making Panels and the Chairman of the Correlating Committee reported their recommendations to meetings of the Electrical Section at the 1980 NFPA Annual Meeting. The Electrical Section thus had opportunity to discuss and review the report of the National Electrical Code Committee prior to the adoption of this edition of the *Code* by the Association.

The *Electrical Code for One- and Two-Family Dwellings*, NFPA 70A-1981, is an abridged version of the 1981 text, edited only as dictated to eliminate extraneous material not of concern to this type of occupancy, and to place in the text only the more popular types of wiring methods, not to exclude any other type authorized by the complete *Code*.

Summary of Code Changes

Art. 90 — Introduction
New. 90-2(b)(5) fine print note; 90-8, Metric Units of Measurement.
Revised. 90-1(a), (b), and (c), Titles; 90-2(a)(1) and 90-2(b)(1), Floating Dwelling Units; 90-2(a)(1), (2), and (3); 90-3; 90-6.

Art. 100 — Definitions
New. Identified; In Sight From; Interrupting Rating; fine print note to Dust-Tight.
Revised. Accessible (As applied to Equipment); Circuit Breaker, fine print note; Dust-Tight; Ground-Fault Circuit-Interrupter; Labeled; Listed; Raceway; Rainproof; Raintight; Volatile Flammable Liquid; Voltage, Nominal, fine print note reference; Watertight.
Deleted. Appliances, Fixed; Appliances, Portable; Appliances, Stationary; Approved for the Purpose; Identified (as applied to a grounding conductor or terminal;

Art. 110 — Requirements for Electrical Installations. *New.* SI Unit Footnotes to Tables 110-16(a), 110-34(a), and 110-34(e).
Revised. 110-2; 110-2, fine print note; 110-3(a); 110-11, 110-12; 110-14(a); 110-16; 110-16(a); 110-16(a), Exception No. 2; 110-17; 110-17(a); 110-30; 110-31(b)(1); 110-31(c); 110-34(a)(3), Exception; 110-34(b); 110-34(c); Table 110-34(e), Title.

Art. 200 — Use and Identification of Grounded Conductors. *Revised.* 200-2; 200-10(b); 200-10(b), Exception; 200-10(e).

Art. 210 — Branch Circuits
New. 210-1, Exception; 210-7(a), Exception No. 2.
Revised. 210-4; 210-5(a); 210-6(a), Exception No. 1b.; 210-6(b); 210-6(c)(1); 210-8(a); 210-8(b); 210-19(b); 210-23(b); 210-25(a) and renumbered 210-50; 210-25(b) and renumbered 210-52; 210-25(c), renumbered 210-60; 210-25(d) and renumbered 210-62; 210-26 and renumbered 210-70.

Art. 215 — Feeders
New. 215-1, Exception.
Revised. 215-2; 215-2(a); 215-2(b); 215-6; 215-8; 215-9.
Deleted. 215-2(c).1

Art. 220 — Branch-Circuit and Feeder Calculations *New.* 220-1, Exception; 220-2(c)(3); Table 220-2(b), SI Unit Footnote and double asterisk (**) Footnote; Table 220-34, SI Unit Footnote.
Revised. Table 220-2(b), Banks and Office Buildings; 220-3(d); 220-20; 220-30(a)(b), and (c); Table 220-30; 220-31; 220-32(a), (b), and (c); 220-32(a)(2), Exception; 220-34, last paragraph.
Deleted. 220-3(b)(1) and 220-16(a), "Family Room."

Art. 225 — Outside Branch Circuits and Feeders *New.* 225-1, Exception.
Revised. 225-6(a); 225-10; 225-14(a); 225-14(b); 225-18; 225-19.

Art. 230 — Services
New. 230-2, second paragraph; 230-24(d); 230-46, Exception No. 5; Table 230-51(c), SI Unit Footnote; 230-56; 230-95(a), Exception No. 2; 230-201, Exception; 230-202(b)(7), Busways; 230-205(b).
Revised. 230-2; 230-2, Exception No. 2; 230-2, Exception No. 3; 230-22; 230-24(a) and (b); 230-27; 230-28; 230-30, Exception c. and d.; 230-40; 230-40, Exception c. and d.; 230-43; 230-48; 230-50(b), "10 feet"; 230-54(d); 230-71(a); 230-72(a), (b), and (d); 230-82, Exception Nos. 1, 2, and 4; 230-83; 230-83, Exception; 230-84(a), second paragraph; 230-90(a), Exception No. 4; 230-91; 230-95(a); 230-200; 230-201(b); 230-202(b); 230-202(c); 230-202(g); 230-208(a)(1); 230-208(b)(1).

Art. 240 — Overcurrent Protection
New. 240-21, Exception Nos. 9 and 10.
Revised. 240-3, Exception No. 4; 240-8, Exception; 240-21, Exception No. 3d.; 240-24(a), Exception No. 1; 240-24(d); 240-32; 240-40, Exception No. 1; 240-52; 240-61; 240-61, Exception No. 2; 240-83(d).

Art. 250 — Grounding
New. 250-23(a), Exception No. 5; 250-26(a), Exception; 250-26(b), Exception; 250-57, Exception; 250-71(b).

Revised. Added Titles, throughout article; 250-2; 250-5(c) 250-23; 250-23(a); 250-23(a), Exception No. 1; 250-23(b); 250-25; 250-26(a) and (b); 250-42(d); 250-42(f), Exception No. 2; 250-43(g); 250-44(d); 250-45(a) and (b); 250-50; 250-50(a); 250-53(a); 250-57; 250-57(b); 250-57(b), Exception Nos. 1 and 3; 250-59(a) and (b); 250-60; 250-60(a) and (b); 250-61(a); 250-71(a); 250-72(e); 250-75; 250-77; 250-78; 250-81; 250-81(c), delete word "solid"; 250-83(c)(3); 250-84; 250-86; 250-91(a) and (b); 250-91(b), Exception Nos. 1 and 2; 250-92(a); 250-92(b)(2); 250-93(c); Table 250-94, column headings; 250-94, Exception Nos. 1 and 2; 250-95; Table 250-95; 250-97; 250-99, Title; 250-99(b); 250-115; 250-121, Exception; 250-123; 250-124; 250-125; 250-154; 250-154(d) and (f); 250-155.

Deleted. Part M, reletter Part N to become Part M; 250-1(g); 250-57(c); 250-61(b), Exception No. 4; 250-81(c), delete the word "solid"; 250-98; 250-111.

Art. 280 — Lightning Arresters
Revised. Complete article.

Art. 300 — Wiring Methods
New. 300-1, Titles; 300-1(c); 300-15(b), Exception No. 6; 300-20(a), Exception No. 2; 300-22(b), fine print note; 300-22(c), fine print note; 300-22(c), Exception No. 4; 300-22(c), Exception No. 5.

Revised. 300-2; 300-4(b); Table 300-5; 300-5(a); 300-5(d); 300-5(e); 300-15(a), Exception Nos. 1 and 2; 300-15(b), Exception No. 3; 300-15(b), Exception No. 5; 300-18(b) and (d); 300-21; 300-22(b); 300-22(c); 300-22(c), Exception No. 2.

Art. 305 — Temporary Wiring
Revised. 305-1; 305-2(b); 305-2(c); 305-2(d); 305-2(g).

Deleted. 305-2(e); Part B (305-10, 305-11, 305-12, and 305-13), to consolidate duplicated provisions (above and below 600 volts).

Art. 310 — Conductors for General Wiring
New. 310-2(b); 310-4, Exception No. 2; Table 310-5; 310-5 Exception Nos. 8, 9, and 10; 310-6; 310-7; 310-10, fine print note; 301-13; 310-14; 310-15; Correction factors (41-45°C and 46-50°C) to Tables 310-16 and 310-17; SI Unit Footnotes to Tables.

Revised. 310-2; 310-5; existing 310-7 becomes 310-8; existing 310-8 becomes 310-9; existing 310-9 becomes 310-10; existing 310-10 becomes 310-12; existing 310-11 (Marking) remains 310-11; 310-8(a) and (b); 310-9; 310-10; 310-11(a)(1); 310-11(b)(2), Exception No. 4; 310-12(b); Table 310-13 (add references); Tables 310-16 and 310-17 (revise ampacities and obelisk (†) note; Tables 310-18 and 310-19, Headings; Notes 3, 8, 10, and 11 to Tables 310-16 through 310-19; Note 2 of Tables 310-39 through 310-54 becomes 310-15(b) and Notes 3 and 4 are renumbered 2 and 3. Existing 310-61 becomes 310-6; Table 310-32, second Note.

Deleted. 310-30; 310-31; 310-38; Table 310-13, Footnote (aluminum and copper-clad aluminum, minimum size); Table 310-32, Footnote (aluminum and copper-clad aluminum, minimum size).

Art. 318 — Cable Trays
New. SI Unit Footnotes to Tables; Titles to paragraphs throughout article; 318-12(a), Exception No. 2.

Revised. 318-2(b)(1); 318-4; 318-6(b)(1); 318-6(b)(4); 318-7; 318-8; 318-9; 318-10(b); 318-12(b).

Art. 320 — Open Wiring on Insulators
Revised. 320-3; 320-14.

Art. 321 — Messenger Supported Wiring
New. Complete article.

Art. 324 — Concealed Knob-and-Tube Wiring
Revised. 324-8.

Art. 326 — Medium Voltage Cable
New. 326-6, Exception.
Revised. 326-3; 326-4.

Art. 328 — Flat Conductor Cable
New. Complete article (formerly a T.I.A. to the 1978 *NEC*).

Art. 330 — Mineral Insulated, Metal-Sheathed Cable
Revised. 330-14.

Art. 333 — Armored Cable
Revised. 333-6(3), (third paragraph); 333-12(a) and (b), Titles.

Art. 334 — Metal-Clad Cable
New. 334-13.
Revised. 334-2; 334-3(10); 334-10, Titles; 334-11(c); 334-12; 334-21(a) and (b).

Art. 336 — Nonmetallic-Sheathed Cable
New. 336-13.
Revised. 336-2, second paragraph; 336-3, second sentence; 336-4; 336-5, Exception No. 2.

Art. 337 — Shielded Nonmetallic-Sheathed Cable
Revised. 337-6.

Art. 338 — Service-Entrance Cable
Revised. 338-1(a), (b), and (c), Titles; 338-1(b); 338-4(a), (b), and (c), Titles.
Deleted. 338-4(b), delete the word "applicable."

Art. 339 — Underground Feeder and Branch-Circuit Cable
Revised. 339-1(a); 339-3(b)(7) and (b)(9).

Art. 340 — Power and Control Tray Cable
Revised. 340-3; 340-4; 340-4(1); 340-5.

Art. 342 — Nonmetallic Extensions
Revised. 342-4, Titles; 342-6.

Art. 344 — Underplaster Extensions
Revised. 344-2.

Art. 345 — Intermediate Metal Conduit
Revised. 345-3(a) and (b), Titles; 345-5; 345-8; 345-9(a) and (b), Titles; 345-16(a) and (b), Titles.

Art. 346 — Rigid Metal Conduit
New. Tables 346-10, 346-10, Exception, and 346-12, SI Unit Footnotes to Tables.
Revised. 346-1(a), (b), and (c), Titles; 346-1(b), Exception; 346-4; 346-7(a); 346-7(a) and (b), Titles; 346-9(a) and (b), Titles.

Art. 347 — Rigid Nonmetallic Conduit
New. Table 347-8, SI Unit Footnote to Table.
Revised. 347-1, fine print note, add "fiberglass epoxy"; 347-2; 347-2(a), (b), (c), (d), (e), (f), and (g), Titles; 347-2(f); 347-3(a), (b), (c), (d), and (e), Titles; 347-3(c); 347-6; 347-9; 347-17(a) and (b), Titles.

Art. 348 — Electrical Metallic Tubing
Revised. 348-4; 348-11.

Art. 349 — Flexible Metallic Tubing
New. Tables 349-20(a) and 349-20(b), SI Unit Footnotes to Tables.
Revised. 349-12(a) and (b), Titles; 349-18; 349-20(a) and (b) Titles; Tables 349-20(a) and 349-20(b), Titles.

Art. 350 — Flexible Metallic Conduit
Revised. 350-3, Exception No. 3; 350-5; 350-5, Exception; 350-6, Title and text, delete "concealed."

Art. 351 — Liquidtight Flexible Conduit
New. Article heading; Part A heading; Part B, Liquidtight Flexible Nonmetallic Conduit.
Revised. 351-1; 351-4(a) and (b), Titles; 351-4(a)(2); 351-6(a) and (b), Titles; 351-7; 351-9; 351-9, Exception; 351-10.

Art. 352 — Surface Raceways
Revised. 352-1; 352-1, Exception; 352-8, second paragraph; 352-22(2).

Art. 353 — Multioutlet Assembly
Revised. 353-2(2) and (6).

Art. 354 — Underfloor Raceways
Revised. 354-2(2); 354-15.

Art. 356 — Cellular Metal Floor Raceways *Revised.* 356-2(2); 356-11.

Art. 358 — Cellular Concrete Floor Raceways *Revised.* 358-2(2); 358-4.

Art. 362 — Wireways
Revised. 362-5; 362-10.

Art. 363 — Flat Cable Assemblies
Revised. 363-1; 363-4(1) and (3); 363-5; 363-9; 363-10; 363-11, first and second paragraphs; 363-12; 363-14; 363-15; 363-18; 363-20.

Art. 364 — Busways
Revised. 364-4(b)(3) and (b)(4); 364-5; 364-8
Deleted. 364-5, Exception Nos. 1 and 2.

Art. 365 — Cablebus
Revised. 365-2; 365-6(a), (b), (c), and (d), Titles; 365-7, style; 365-8.

Art. 366 — Electrical Floor Assemblies
Revised. 366-6; 366-20(a) and (b), Titles.

Art. 370 — Outlet, Switch and Junction Boxes, and Fittings *New.* 370-20(d).
Revised. 370-3, first and second paragraphs; 370-5; 370-6(a)(1); 370-7(c); 370-11; 370-13; first and second paragraphs; 370-15(a), (b), and (c), Titles; 370-15(a), fine print note; 370-17(b) and Exception; 370-18(c); 370-18(d), Title; 370-19, Exception; 370-20, Reference; 370-51(c), Title; 370-52(a), (b), (c), (d), (e), and (f), Titles.

Art. 373 — Cabinets and Cutout Boxes
New. Table 373-6(a), SI Unit Footnote to Table; 373-6(b)(1), Exception, and (b)(2); Table 373-6(b).
Revised. 373-1; 373-6(b); 373-10(a); 373-11(a)(3).

Art. 374 — Auxiliary Gutters
Revised. 374-8(a), (b), (c), and (d), Titles; 374-9(a), (b), (c), (d), and (e), Titles.

Art. 380 — Switches
New. 380-14(c); 380-17, fine print note; 380-18.
Revised. 380-3; 380-6(b); 380-8(a); 380-8(a) and (b), Titles; 380-13(a); 380-13(b); 380-13(a), (b), (c), and (d), Titles; 380-16.

Art. 384 — Switchboards and Panelboards *New.* 384-2 and four Exceptions; 384-3(a), Exception; 384-25 and two Exceptions; Table 384-26, SI Unit Footnote to Table; 384-27, Exception No. 2.
Revised. 384-3(f); 384-3(a), (b), (c), (d), (e), (f), and (g), Titles; 384-9; 384-16(a), Exception No. 2; 384-16(a), (b), (c), (d), and (e), Titles; 384-18; 384-21; Table 384-26 (nominal).

Art. 400 — Flexible Cords and Cables
New. Table 400-4, (Types SPE-1, SPE-2, SPE-3, SVOO, SVTOO, SJOO, SJTOO, SOO, STOO); 400-5; Maximum Allowable Load Current Table; Table 400-5, Triple asterisk (***) Note; 400-14.
Revised. Table 400-4; Table 400-4, Note 6; 400-5; Table 400-5; 400-7(a) and (b), Titles; 400-9; 400-31(a).

Art. 402 — Fixture Wires
Revised. 402-3; Table 402-3 (impregnated asbestos, KF-2, KFF-2, HF, HFF); 402-11, Exception.

Art. 410 — Lighting Fixtures, Lampholders, Lamps, Receptacles, and Rosettes
New. 410-4(d); 410-20 and Exception; 410-56(e) and (g); 410-58(e); 410-65(c) and two Exceptions, 410-73(f) and Exception.
Revised. 410-2; 410-4; 410-4(c)(1); 410-8(a)(2), second paragraph; 410-11, second paragraph; 410-14(a) and (b), and Titles; 410-16(a) through (g); 410-18(a) and (b), Titles; 410-19(a) and (b), Titles; 410-24(a) and fine print note; 410-27(a), (b), and (c), Titles; 410-28(c), (d), fine print note, (e), and (f); 410-29(a), (b), (c), and (d), Titles; 410-29(e); 410-30(c); 410-42(a); 410-42(b)(2); 410-56(c); 410-57(b); 410-64; 410-66; 410-72; 410-73(b); 410-73(a), (b), (c), (d), and (e), Titles; 410-75(a) and (b), Titles; 410-80(b); 410-80(a), (b), and (c), Titles; 410-85(a) and (b), Titles; 410-86(a), (b), and (c), Titles.

Art. 422 — Appliances
Revised. 422-1; 422-3, 422-5(a); 422-8(d)(1) and (d)(2); 422-14(a), Exception; 422-14(b); 422-15(a); 422-15(b), Exception; 422-15(a), (b), and (c), Titles; 422-16; 422-17(a) and (b), Titles; 422-21(a) and (b), Titles; 422-22(a), (b), (c), and (d), Titles; 422-27(a); 422-27(f), Exception No. 2b. 422-27(a), (b), (c), (d), (e), and (f), Titles; 422-30(a) and (b), Titles; 422-32(a) and (b), Titles.
Deleted. 422-16, Exception.

Art. 424 — Fixed Electric Space Heating Equipment *New.* 424-13, Exception.
Revised. 424-1; 424-2; 424-3(b); 424-12(a) and (b), Titles; 424-14; 424-20(a) and (b), Titles; 424-22(b); 424-22(e); 424-35(a); 424-38(a), (b), and (c), Titles; 424-41(e); 424-41(f), Exception; 424-41(a) through (i), Titles; 424-43(a), (b), (c), and (d), Titles; 424-44(a) through (f), Titles; 424-44(e); 424-58; 424-60; 424-71; 424-72(a), (b), (c), and (e); 424-72(a), (b), (c), and (d), Titles; 424-80; 424-81; 424-85.

Art. 426 — Fixed Outdoor Electric De-Icing and Snow-Melting Equipment *New.*
426-1(b); Definitions.

Revised. Complete Article has been rewritten and expanded.

Art. 427 — Fixed Electric Heating Equipment for Pipelines and Vessels. *Revised.*
Complete Article has been rewritten and expanded.

Art. 430 — Motors, Motor Circuits, and Controllers *New.* 430-10(b); Table 430-10(b); 430-12(e) and Exception; Table 430-12(b), SI Unit Footnotes to Table; 430-22, Exception No. 2; 430-113, Exception No. 2; 430-145(a), fine print note; Table 430-151, Footnote.

Revised. 430-2; Diagram 430-1; 430-3, second paragraph; 430-6(a), (b), and (c); 430-7(b), second paragraph; 430-7(d); 430-8; 430-10(a); Table 430-12(b); 430-32(b)(1) and Exception; 430-35(a), Title; 430-36; 430-51; 430-52, second paragraph, Exception to second paragraph, and fifth paragraph; 430-53(a), (a)(2), (b), and (d); 430-72, complete Section; 430-86(a) and (b), Titles; 430-87, Exception; 430-89(a), (b), and (c), Titles; 430-109, Exception No. 5; 430-100(c)(1), Exception; 430-111(a), (b), and (c), Titles; 430-125(a); 430-132(a), (b), and (c), Titles.

Deleted. Throughout the Article, the word "running" has been deleted from the phrases "motor running overloads" and "motor running overcurrent"; 430-71(a), second paragraph; Table 430-149, delete four columns and the heading for Synchronous Type Unity Power Factor Amperes and the Footnote at the bottom of Table.

Art. 440 — Air-Conditioning and Refrigerating Equipment. *New.* 440-14, Exception.

Revised. 440-2(a), (b), (c), and (d), Titles; 440-3(a), (b) and (c), Titles; 440-5(a) and (b), Titles; 440-12(a), (b), (c), and (d), Titles; 440-12(b), Exception; 440-21; 440-22(b), (b)(1)1 (b)(2), (b) Exception; 440-22(c), Title; 440-41(a) and (b), Titles; 440-54(a) and (b), Titles; 440-55(a), (b), and (c), Titles; 440-62(a), (b), and (c), Titles.

Art. 445 — Generators
Revised. 445-1; 445-2; 445-5; 445-6.

Art. 450 — Transformers and Transformer Vaults *New.* 450-2, second paragraph and first fine print note; 450-23, two fine print notes; 450-24; 450-45(e), fine print note.

Revised. 450-1, last paragraph; 450-2, Exception Nos. 1 and 2; 450-3(a), (a)(1), and (a)(2); Table 450-3(a)(2); 450-3(b)(1) and (b)(2); 450-5; 450-8; 450-21(a), (b), and (c); 450-22, second paragraph; 450-23; 450-26, Exception No. 2; 450-27 (formerly 450-26 — 1978 *NEC*); 450-42, Exception; 450-43(a), Exception; 450-45(e).

Art. 460 — Capacitors
Revised. 460-1, second paragraph; 460-2(a) and (b), Titles; 460-7(a) and (b); 460-8(c)(2); 460-25(a), (b), (c), and (d), Titles; 460-28(a) and (b), Titles.

Art. 470 — Resistors and Reactors
Revised. 470-18(a), (b), (c), (d), and (e), Titles.

Art. 480 — Storage Batteries
Revised. 480-5(b), (nominal).

Art. 500 — Hazardous (Classified) Locations *Revised.* 500-1, Exception, fourth paragraph, second, third, and eighth fine print notes, and sixth paragraph; 500-2, second, third, fourth, fifth, sixth, and seventh fine print notes; Table 500-2; 500-2(a); 500-2(a), fine print note; 500-2(b); 500-2(b), Exception Nos. 3 and 4; 500-2(b), fine print note; 500-2(c), fine print note; 500-4(a) and fine print note; 500-2(b) and two fine print notes; 500-5(a) and fine print note; 500-5(b); 500-6(a), two fine print notes.

Art. 501 — Class I Locations
New. 501-5(a)(1); 501-11, last paragraph.

Revised. 501-2(a)(1) and (2); 501-3(a)(1), second paragraph; 501-3(b)(1), Exception c.; 501-3(b)(6)(2); 501-4(b), Exception and second paragraph; 501-5(a)(1) Exception; 501-5(a)(4); 501-5(b)(2); 501-5(c)(2); 501-5(d) second paragraph; 501-5(e)(2), fine print note, (e)(3), and (e)(4); 501-6(b)(3) and (b)(5); 501-9(a)(3) and (a)(4); 501-9(b)(3); 501-10(b)(1)a.; 501-11 (New), last paragraph; 501-14(b)(1), Exception c.; 501-16; 501-16(b), (c), (d), and (e).

Art. 502 — Class II Locations
Revised. 502-1, last paragraph; 502-2(a)(1) and (b)(3); 502-3; 502-5 (New), second paragraph; 502-6(a)(1); 502-6(b); 502-7(b)(1); 502-8(b) and Exception b.; 502-10(b)(3); 502-11(a)(3) and (a)(4); 502-11(b)(4); 502-16(b), (c), and (d).

Delete. 502-16(c); 502-16(e).

Art. 503 — Class III Locations
Revised. 503-1, fine print note; 503-9(c) and (d).

Art. 510 — Hazardous (*Classified) Locations — Specific. No Change.

Art. 511 — Commercial Garages, Repair and Storage. *Revised.* 511-2; 511-2(c), (d), and (f); 511-3; 511-4; 511-5(a), (c), and (d); 511-6; 511-7; 511-8(b) and (c).

Art. 513 — Aircraft Hangars
Revised. 513-3; 513-4; 513-4(a); 513-5; 515-5(c); 513-6(a) and (b); 513-7; 513-9; 513-10(a); 513-11(a).

Art. 514 — Gasoline Dispensing and Service Stations *New.* Table 514-2.
Revised. 514-2; 514-3; 514-4; 514-6(b); 514-8.

Art. 515 — Bulk Storage Plants
New. Table 515-2.
Revised. 515-2; 515-3; 515-4; 515-5(a); 515-6.

Art. 516 — Finishing Processes
New. Figures 1, 2, and 3, SI Unit Footnotes.
Revised. 516-1, fine print note; 516-2; 516-2(b)(5); 516-2(c); Figures 1, 2, and 3; 516-3(a), (c), and (d); 516-4(a) and Exception; 516-5(a) and (b); 516-5(b), Exception; 516-6(a); 516-7(a) and (b).

Art. 517 — Health Care Facilities
New. 517-1, second paragraph; 517-2, definition, Selected Receptacles; 517-11(a) Exception Nos. 1 and 2; 517-13; Part C and Part D, fine print notes; Diagrams 517-44(3) and 517-60(3); 517-83(b), Exception No. 2; 517-90(b); 517-90(c), fine print note; 517-104(a)(5), second paragraph; 517-120, fine print note; Part K, X-ray Installations.

Revised. 517-2, definitions: Alternate Power

Source, Critical Branch, Emergency System, Essential Electrical Systems, Exposed Conductive Surfaces, Health Care Facilities, and Patient Equipment Grounding Point; 517-11(b); 517-40; 517-41; 517-44, complete section; 517-45, complete section; 517-46(a) and (b); 517-46(b), Exception and fine print note; 517-46(b)(2) and (b)(3); 517-47, complete section; 517-Part E, 517-58 through 517-65; 517-80(b) (b)(1), (b)(2), and (b)(3); 517-81(b); 517-83(a); 517-83(c); (c)(1), (c)(4), and (c)(5); 517-90(a) and (a)(2); 517-100(a)(1); 517-100(b)(1) and (b)(2); 517-101(a)(3); 517-101(b)(6); 517-101(c)(1) and (c)(2); 517-103; 517-104(b)(1) and (b)(3); 517-104(c), (c)(2), (c)(3), (c)(4), and (c)(5); 517-106(a) (b), and (c).
Deleted. 517-45(b); 517-62(b); 517-122(c).

Art. 518 — Places of Assembly
Revised. 518-1; 518-2(a).

Art. 520 — Theaters and Similar Locations
Revised. 520-21; 520-22; 520-45; 520-53(f); 520-65.

Art. 530 — Motion Picture and Television Studios and Similar Locations
Revised. 530-12; 530-18(d); 530-31; 530-61; 530-62.

Art. 540 — Motion Picture Projectors
Revised. 540-10 (Classified).

Art. 545 — Manufactured Building
Revised. 545-9(b); 545-12 (change "attachment of" to "attachment to").

Art. 547 — Agricultural Buildings
New. 547-1(c).
Revised. 547-1; 547-3; 547-4.

Art. 550 — Mobile Homes and Mobile Home Parks
New. 550-2, definitions: Appliance Fixed, and Appliance Stationary.
Revised. 550-1(d); 550-3(i); 550-21; 550-23(d).

Art. 551 — Recreational Vehicles and Recreational Vehicle Parks
New. 551-2, definitions: Appliance Fixed, Appliance Portable, and Appliance, Stationary; 551-3(c)(5); 551-4(b), Exception; 551-4(c); 551-8(c), second fine print note; 551-14(e), Exception No. 2.
Revised. 551-1(b) and (c); 551-3(e)(2); 551-5(e); 551-6(a); 551-6(b); 551-7(c)(1); 551-8(c); 551-11(b) and (c); 551-12(d); 551-13(a)(1); 551-13(b); 551-14(a); 551-48(a); 551-50(a) and fine print note; 551-50(b); 551-51(a).
Deleted. 551-14(n), delete parenthesis enclosing the word "nominal"; 551-15(a), Exception.

Art. 555 — Marinas and Boatyards
New. 555-1, fine print note; 555-9(b), fine print note; Part B, Floating Dwelling Units.
Revised. 555-1; 555-6; 555-6, Exception No. 1.

Art. 600 — Electric Signs and Outlet Lighting
New. 600-6(c); 600-11 and Exception.
Revised. 600-2(b); 600-4; 600-5, Exception No. 2; 600-21(b), Exception Nos. 1 and 2; 600-21(e); 600-31(a) and (b); 600-31(b), Exception; 600-32(b); 600-32(d), Exception No. 2; 600-34(a), (c), and (h); 600-35.

Art. 604 — Manufactured Wiring Systems
New. Complete Article.

Art. 610 — Cranes and Hoists
New. 610-2(c); Footnote for SI Units to Chart for Distances between Supports [following 610-14(d)].
Revised. 610-31.

Art. 620 — Elevators, Dumbwaiters, Escalators, and Moving Walks.
Revised. 620-1, fine print note; 620-12(b); 620-21; 620-42; 620-53(a) and (b); 620-91.

Art. 630 — Electrical Welders
No changes.

Art. 640 — Sound Recording and Similar Equipment
Revised. 640-7; 640-11(a); 640-12.

Art. 645 — Data Processing Systems
Revised. 645-1; 645-2(c)(2); 645-3.

Art. 650 — Organs
No changes.

Art. 660 — X-Ray Equipment
Revised. 660-3; 660-4(c); 660-5.

Art. 665 — Induction and Dielectric Heating Equipment
New. 665-1, third fine print note.
Revised. 665-1, 665-3; 665-4 and Exception; 665-61(a) and (b), Titles.
Deleted. 665-64(c).

Art. 668 — Electrolytic Cells
Revised. 668-30(c)(1).

Art. 669 — Electroplating
New. Complete Article.

Art. 670 — Metalworking Machine Tools
No changes.

Art. 675 — Electrically Driven or Controlled Irrigation Machines
New. 675-9, last sentence.
Revised. 675-4(b); 675-9; 675-13; 675-22(a) and (b); 675-23(b); 675-25(a).

Art. 680 — Swimming Pools, Fountains, and Similar Installations
New. 680-1, fine print note; 680-4, definition: Spa or Hot Tub; 680-8, Exception No. 2; 680-8 Chart, Column C; 680-10; 680-21(e); 680-25(d); 680-27, (a), (b) and (c); Part D, Spas and Hot Tubs; Part F, Therapeutic Pools and Tubs in Health Care Facilities.
Revised. 680-1; 680-3; 680-4, definitions: Dry-Niche Lighting Fixture, Forming Shell, Permanently Installed Decorative Fountains and Reflection Pools, Storable Swimming or Wading Pool, Wet-Niche Lighting Fixture; 680-6(a)(1), (a)(2), (a)(3), and Exception to (a)(1); 680-6(b)(1), Exception; Figure 680-8, Exception No. 1; 680-11, Title (formerly 680-47); 680-20(a)(3), Exception and (a)(4); 680-20(c), second paragraph; 680-21(a) and (d); 680-22(a)(5); 680-22(c); 680-23; 680-25(a); 680-25(b), (b)(1), Exception Nos. 1 and 2 to (b)(1), (b)(2), and (b)(3); 680-25(c), Exception Nos. 1 and 2; 680-25(e); 680-30; 680-31; 680-50 and Exception; 680-51(b); 680-52(a) and (b).

Art. 685 — Integrated Electrical Systems
New. Complete Article.

Art. 700 — Emergency Systems
New. 700-1, first, second, and third fine print

notes; 700-5(b); 700-6; 700-7(d); 700-9, Exception Nos. 4 and 5; 700-12, third paragraph; 700-12(b)(3), Exception and (b)(5); 700-12(c); 700-26.

Revised. 700-1; 700-4(a), (b), (c), (d), and (e), Titles; 700-5(a) and (b); 700-7(a), (b), (c); 700-9; 700-12; 700-12(a); 700-12(b)(1), (b)(2), (b)(3); 700-12(d) and (e); 700-16, second paragraph; 700-17; 700-22.

Deleted. 700-11; 700-19(b) and Exception.

Art. 701 — Legally Required Standby Systems *New*. Complete Article.

Art. 702 — Optional Standby Systems

New. Complete Article.

Art. 710 — Over 600 Volts, Nominal, General. *New*. 710-3(b), Exception Nos. 1 and 2; 710-3(c); Tables 710-3(b) and 710-33, SI Unit Footnotes.

Revised. 710-2; 710-3(a) and (b); 710-9; 710-21(b)(1), (c)(1), and (d)(6), Title; 710-41(a), Title; 710-51, Title; 710-54(a) and (b), Titles; 710-70; 710-72(a), (b), (c), (d), and (e), Titles; 710-72(d).

Art. 720 — Circuits and Equipment Operating at Less than 50 Volts *Revised*. 720-2.

Art. 725 — Class 1, Class 2, and Class 3 Remote-Control, Signaling, and Power-Limited Circuits. *New*. 725-2(e); 725-3(b), fine print note; 725-12(a) and (b), Exception Nos. 2 and 3; 725-12(c); 725-40(b)(3), Exception; Tables 725-31(a) and 725-31(b), Notes 2 and 5.

Revised. 725-2; 725-2(a), (b), (c), and (d), Titles; 725-11(a); 725-16; 725-17(a), (b), and (c), Titles; 725-18; 725-31; 725-32; 725-35; 725-39(a), (b), and (c), Titles; 725-40(a), Exception and (b), Exception; 725-40(b)(2), Exception; 725-40(b)(3).

Deleted. 725(a) and (b), Exception.

Art. 760 — Fire Protective Signaling Systems. *New*. 760-7, Exception and first fine print note; 760-22, Exception and fine print note; 760-30(c), Exception No. 3; 760-30(f).

Revised. 760-1; 760-4(a), (b), (c), and (d), Titles; 760-11; 760-16(a) and (b); 760-17; 760-18(a), (b), and (c), Titles; 760-21; 760-25; 760-28 (complete section); 760-29 (complete section); 760-30; 760-30(a), (b), (c), (d), and (e), Titles; 760-31(a) and (b).

Art. 800 — Communication Circuits

New. 800-2(c)(1)e.

Revised. 800-2; 800-2(b); 800-2(c)(1)c.; 800-2(c)(1)d., fine print note; 800-3(c); 800-11(c)(1), (c)(3), (c)(3) Exception, and (c)(4); 800-31(b)(1), (b)(5), and (b)(6).

Art. 810 — Radio and Television Equipment *New*. Tables 810-16(a) and 810-52, SI Unit Footnotes.

Revised. 810-4; 810-15; 801-19; 810-20(a) and (c); 810-21(f), (f)(1), (f)(2), (f)(3), (f)(4), (f)(5), and Exception.

Art. 820 — Community Antenna Television and Radio Distribution Systems

Revised. 820-7(a) and (b); 820-14; 820-22(f), (f)(1), (f)(2), (f)(3), (f)(4), and (f)(5).

Deleted. 820-12.

Chapter 9, Tables

Revised. Notes to Tables, Note 4 and Note 5; Table 6 and Footnotes; Table 7 and Footnotes; Table 8

Chapter 9, Examples

Revised. SI Units Note to Examples; Example No. 2; Example No. 3; Example No. 4(a), (Feeder neutral load for main feeder); Example No. 8.

Tables

XX TABLES

The
National Electrical Code®
Handbook

NOTE: The text and illustrations that make up the commentary on the various sections of the *National Electrical Code* are printed in color. The text of the *Code* itself is printed in black.

National Electrical Code

NFPA 70

ARTICLE 90 — INTRODUCTION

Contents

90-1. Purpose.

(a) Practical Safeguarding. The purpose of this Code is the practical safeguarding of persons and property from hazards arising from the use of electricity.

The *National Electrical Code* (*NEC*) is the most widely adopted set of electrical safety requirements in the world and is offered for use in law and for regulatory purposes in the interest of life and property protection.

(b) Adequacy. This Code contains provisions considered necessary for safety. Compliance therewith and proper maintenance will result in an installation essentially free from hazard, but not necessarily efficient, convenient, or adequate for good service or future expansion of electrical use.

Hazards often occur because of overloading of wiring systems by methods or usage not in conformity with this Code. This occurs because initial wiring did not provide for increases in the use of electricity. An initial adequate installation and reasonable provisions for system changes will provide for future increases in the use of electricity.

Consideration should always be given to future expansion of electrical uses, i.e., plan an initial installation comprising service-entrance conductors and equipment, feeder conductors, and panelboards that will allow for future additions, alterations, designs, etc.

(c) Intention. This Code is not intended as a design specification nor an instruction manual for untrained persons.

The *National Electrical Code* is intended for use by capable engineers and electrical contractors for the basic design and/or installation of electrical equipment; by inspection authorities exercising legal jurisdiction over electrical installations; by property insurance inspectors; by qualified industrial, commer-

1

cial, and residential electricians; and by instructors teaching electrical apprentices or students.

90-2. Scope.

(a) Covered.   This Code covers:

(1) Installations of electric conductors and equipment within or on public and private buildings or other structures, including mobile homes, recreational vehicles, and floating dwelling units; and other premises such as yards, carnival, parking and other lots, and industrial substations.

The requirements for floating dwelling units as they appear in Part B of Article 555 were introduced in the 1981 *NEC*.

(2) Installations of conductors that connect to the supply of electricity.

(3) Installations of other outside conductors on the premises.

(b) Not Covered.   This Code does not cover:

(1) Installations in ships, watercraft other than floating dwelling units, railway rolling stock, aircraft, or automotive vehicles other than mobile homes and recreational vehicles.

(2) Installations underground in mines.

(3) Installations of railways for generation, transformation, transmission, or distribution of power used exclusively for operation of rolling stock or installations used exclusively for signaling and communication purposes.

(4) Installations of communication equipment under the exclusive control of communication utilities, located outdoors or in building spaces used exclusively for such installations.

(5) Installations under the exclusive control of electric utilities for the purpose of communication, or metering; or for the generation, control, transformation, transmission, and distribution of electric energy located in buildings used exclusively by utilities for such purposes or located outdoors on property owned or leased by the utility or on public highways, streets, roads, etc., or outdoors by established rights on private property.

It is the intent of this section that this Code covers all premises' wiring or wiring other than utility owned metering equipment, on the load side of the service point of buildings, structures, or any other premises not owned or leased by the utility. Also, it is the intent that this Code cover installations in buildings used by the utility for purposes other than listed in (b)(5) above, such as office buildings, warehouses, garages, machine shops, and recreational buildings which are not an integral part of a generating plant, substation, or control center.

This fine print note was added to the 1981 *NEC* to clarify the intent of Sections 90-1 and 90-2. See Figure 90-1.

(c) Special Permission.   The authority having jurisdiction for enforcing this Code may grant exception for the installation of conductors and equipment, not under the exclusive control of the electric utilities and used to connect the electric utility supply system to the service-entrance conductors of the premises served, provided such installations are outside a building or terminate immediately inside a building wall.

90-3. Code Arrangement.
This Code is divided into the Introduction and nine chapters. Chapters 1, 2, 3, and 4 apply generally; Chapters 5, 6, and 7 apply to special occupancies, special

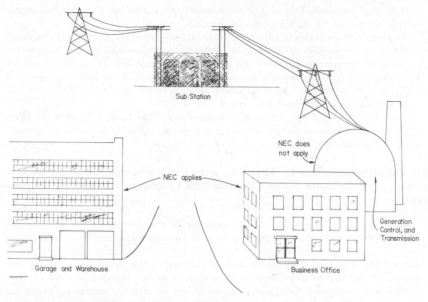

Figure 90-1. A typical electric utility complex indicating those facilities subject to the provisions of the *NEC*.

equipment, or other special conditions. These latter chapters supplement or modify the general rules. Chapters 1 through 4 apply except as amended by Chapters 5, 6, and 7 for the particular conditions.

Chapter 8 covers communications systems and is independent of the other chapters except where they are specifically referenced therein.

Chapter 9 consists of tables and examples.

The reference to the "Introduction" in the first sentence is made with the intention that Article 90 be included in the application of this *Code*.

Chapters 1 through 4 apply generally, except "as amended" or "specifically referenced therein." For example, Section 300-22 (Chapter 3) is modified by Sections 725-2 and 760-4 (Chapter 7) and specifically referenced in Section 800-3 (Chapter 8).

90-4. Enforcement. This Code is intended to be suitable for mandatory application by governmental bodies exercising legal jurisdiction over electrical installations and for use by insurance inspectors. The authority having jurisdiction of enforcement of the Code will have the responsibility for making interpretations of the rules, for deciding upon the approval of equipment and materials, and for granting the special permission contemplated in a number of the rules.

Section 90-4 advises that an authority must grant approval for all materials and equipment used under the requirements of the *Code* in its area of jurisdiction. Text of Sections 90-6, 110-2, and 110-3, along with the definitions of "Approved," "Identified," "Listed," and "Labeled," are intended to provide a basis for the authority having jurisdiction to make necessary judgments that are its responsibility.

The authority having jurisdiction may waive specific requirements in this Code or permit alternate methods, where it is assured that equivalent objectives can be achieved by establishing and maintaining effective safety.

It is the responsibility of the local authority enforcing the *Code* to make interpretations of the specific rules of the *Code*.

The second paragraph to Section 90-4 is included to allow the authority having jurisdiction the option of making an individual judgment to permit alternative methods where specific rules are not established in the *Code*. This also allows the local authority to waive specific requirements in industrial occupancies, research and testing laboratories, and other occupancies where such installations were not contemplated in the original *Code* rules.

Some localities do not adopt the *National Electrical Code*, but, even in those localities, installations meeting the current *Code* are prima facie evidence that the electrical installation is safe.

90-5. Formal Interpretations.   To promote uniformity of interpretation and application of the provisions of this Code, the National Electrical Code Committee has established interpretation procedures.

The procedures for formal interpretations of the provisions of the *National Electrical Code* are outlined in the Regulations Governing Committee Projects that may be obtained from the V.P.-Standards of the National Fire Protection Association. The formal interpretations procedure can be found in Section 16 and has been reprinted in its entirety in the appendix to this Handbook.

The Interpretations Committee is made up of five or more members or alternates of the Technical Committee(s) having primary jurisdiction of the *Code* covering the subject under consideration. The members are to be selected by the Correlating Committee or the V.P.-Standards if the Chairman is not available. No member or alternate is to be eligible for appointment to an Interpretation Subcommittee if he or she is directly involved in the particular case prompting the request for the Interpretation. The Interpretation Subcommittee should include Committee members or alternates representing the same interest categories as the requester and the other parties involved as well as representatives of other parties. The personnel of Interpretation Subcommittees may be varied for each request.

The Committee cannot be responsible for subsequent actions by authorities enforcing the *NEC* as to whether they accept or reject the findings. The authority having jurisdiction has the responsibility of interpreting the *Code* rules and should attempt to resolve all disagreements at the local level.

Two general forms of Formal Interpretations are recognized: (1) those making an interpretation of the literal text and (2) those making an interpretation of the intent of the Technical Committee when the particular text was adopted.

Interpretations not subject to processing are those that (1) do not involve a determination of compliance of a design, installation, or product or equivalency of protection, (2) do not involve a review of plans or specifications or require judgment or knowledge that can only be required as a result of on-site inspection, and (3) do not involve texts that clearly and decisively provide the requested information.

Formal Interpretations of *Code* rules are published in the NFPA *Fire News* and sent to interested trade publications.

90-6. Examination of Equipment for Safety.   For specific items of equipment and materials referred to in this Code, examinations for safety made under standard conditions will provide a basis for approval where the record is made generally available through promulgation by organizations properly equipped and qualified for experimental testing, inspections of the run of goods at factories, and service-value determination through field inspections. This avoids the necessity for repetition of examinations by different examiners, frequently with inadequate facilities for such work, and the confusion that would result from conflicting reports as to the suitability of devices and materials examined for a given purpose.

It is the intent of this Code that factory-installed internal wiring or the construction of equipment need not be inspected at the time of installation of the equipment, except to detect alterations or damage, if the equipment has been listed by a qualified electrical testing laboratory which is recognized as having the facilities described above and which requires suitability for installation in accordance with this Code.

See Examination of Equipment, Section 110-3.

See definition of "Listed," Article 100.

Qualified testing laboratories, inspection agencies, or other organizations concerned with product evaluation publish lists of equipment or materials that have been tested and meet nationally recognized standards or that have been found suitable for use in a specified manner. The *Code* does not contain detailed information on equipment or materials, but refers to the products as "Listed," "Labeled," or "Identified." See Article 100, "Definitions," for explanation of these terms.

It is not the intent of the *Code* to apply to the internal factory-installed wiring, or to the construction of listed equipment at the time of installation, unless damage or alterations are detected.

90-7. Wiring Planning.

(a) Plans and specifications that provide ample space in raceways, spare raceways, and additional spaces will allow for future increases in the use of electricity. Distribution centers located in readily accessible locations will provide convenience and safety of operation. See Sections 110-16 and 240-24 for clearances and accessibility.

(b) It is elsewhere provided in this Code that the number of wires and circuits confined in a single enclosure be varyingly restricted. Limiting the number of circuits in a single enclosure will minimize the effects from a short-circuit or ground fault in one circuit.

Distribution centers should contain additional spaces and capacity for future additions and should be conveniently located for accessibility.

Where easy access is not achieved, a spare raceway(s) or "pull line(s)" should be run to specific areas. See Figure 90-2.

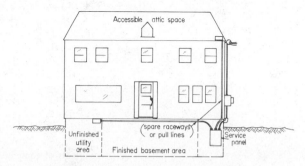

Figure 90-2. Spare raceways or pull lines provide additional capacity for future additions to the distribution system.

90-8. Metric Units of Measurement.
For the purpose of this Code metric units of measurement are in accordance with the modernized metric system known as the International System of Units (SI).

Values of measurement in the Code text will be followed by an approximate equivalent value in SI units. Tables will have a footnote for SI conversion units used in the table.

Conduit size, wire size, horsepower designation for motors, and trade sizes that do not reflect actual measurements, e.g., box sizes, will not be assigned dual designation SI units.

For metric conversion practices, see ANSI Z210.1-1976, Standard for Metric Practice.

An example of an application of SI conversion units as used in Table 110-16(a) is as follows:

$$3 \text{ ft} = 36 \text{ in.} \times 25.4 \text{ mm} = 914 \text{ mm}$$
$$3\frac{1}{2} \text{ ft} \times 0.3048 \text{ m} = 1.07 \text{ m}$$
$$4 \text{ ft} \times 0.3048 \text{ m} = 1.22 \text{ m}$$

Generally, dimensions up to 36 inches are expressed in millimeters, and those over 36 inches are expressed in meters. Footnotes to tables are expressed as "one foot = 0.3048 meter"; however, throughout the text the metric equivalent has been converted to millimeters and rounded off to 305 millimeters.

1 GENERAL

ARTICLE 100 — DEFINITIONS

Scope. Only definitions of terms peculiar to and essential to the proper use of this Code are included. In general, only those terms used in two or more articles are defined in Article 100. Other definitions are included in the article in which they are used but may be referenced in Article 100.

Other definitions are included in Articles 210 (bathroom), 225 (festoon lighting), 230 (service point), 440 (branch-circuit selection current) 502 (dust-ignition-proof) 517, 550, 551, and 680, for example.

Part A of this article contains definitions intended to apply wherever the terms are used throughout this Code. Part B contains definitions applicable only to the parts of articles covering specifically installations and equipment operating at over 600 volts, nominal.

Contents

A. General
B. Over 600 Volts, Nominal

A. General

AC General-Use Snap Switch: See under "Switches."

AC-DC General-Use Snap Switch: See under "Switches."

Accessible: (As applied to wiring methods.) Capable of being removed or exposed without damaging the building structure or finish, or not permanently closed in by the structure or finish of the building. (See "Concealed" and "Exposed.")

Wiring methods located behind removable panels designed to allow access are not considered permanently enclosed. See Figure 100-1.

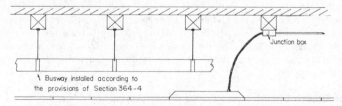

Figure 100-1. Busways and junction boxes are considered accessible when located above hung ceilings having lift-out panels.

Accessible: (As applied to Equipment.)   Admitting close approach: not guarded by locked doors, elevation, or other effective means. (See "Readily Accessible.")

"Readily accessible" means capable of being reached quickly for operation, renewal, or inspections, without requiring those to whom ready access is requisite to climb over or remove obstacles or to resort to portable ladders, chairs, etc. See Figure 100-2.

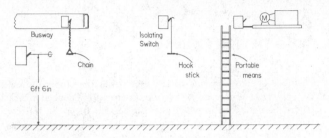

Figure 100-2. This figure illustrates the provisions of Section 380-8. Section 364-12 permits ropes, chains, or hook sticks as suitable for operating disconnecting means mounted on busways.

Ampacity: Current-carrying capacity of electric conductors expressed in amperes.

Anesthetizing Location: See Section 517-2.

Appliance: Utilization equipment, generally other than industrial, normally built in standardized sizes or types, which is installed or connected as a unit to perform one or more functions such as clothes washing, air conditioning, food mixing, deep frying, etc.

The definitions of fixed, portable, and stationary appliances were deleted from the 1981 *NEC*. A technical subcommittee (TSC) found that some requirements for fixed appliances, portable appliances, and stationary appliances were based on different meanings of the terms. These differences arise from the intent of the authors of the requirements at the time the text is adopted. In some cases, the requirements are based on the means of electrical connection of the appliance to the supply circuit. In other instances, the requirements involve the physical location of the appliance. The TSC noted some requirements that appeared to involve both meanings and still others where it was not clear from the wording what the concerned code-making panel intended.

As an aid to clarifying the intent of the requirements, the TSC suggests that, as required, the following terms or phrases be employed: permanently connected, cord- and plug-connected, fastened in place, or located to be on a specific circuit.

The definitions were reviewed by Code-Making Panel 19 (Article 550, Mobile Homes and Mobile Home Parks, and Article 551, Recreational Vehicles and Recreational Vehicle Parks). Panel 19 reviewed the deletion intended by Code-Making Panel 1. Due to the securing of appliances for over-the-road movement, Panel 19 felt that the definitions of "appliances, fixed, stationary, and portable" were pertinent and voted to retain them. The definitions will appear in Articles 550 and 551.

Appliance Branch Circuit: See "Branch Circuit, Appliance."

Approved: Acceptable to the authority having jurisdiction.

The phrase "authority having jurisdiction" is used in NFPA standards in a broad manner since jurisdiction and "approval" agencies vary as do their responsibilities. Where public safety is primary, the "authority having jurisdiction" may be a federal, state, local, or other regional department or individual such as a fire chief, fire marshal, chief of a fire prevention bureau, labor department, health department, building official, electrical inspector, or others having statutory authority. For insurance purposes, an insurance inspection department, rating bureau, or other insurance company representative may be the "authority having jurisdiction." In many circumstances the property owner or his delegated agent assumes the role of the "authority having jurisdiction"; at government installations, the commanding officer or departmental official may be the "authority having jurisdiction."

Askarel: A generic term for a group of nonflammable synthetic chlorinated hydrocarbons used as electrical insulating media. Askarels of various compositional types are used. Under arcing conditions the gases produced, while consisting predominantly of noncombustible hydrogen chloride, can include varying amounts of combustible gases depending upon the askarel type.

Attachment Plug (Plug Cap) (Cap):   A device which, by insertion in a receptacle, establishes connection between the conductors of the attached flexible cord and the conductors connected permanently to the receptacle.

Automatic: Self-acting, operating by its own mechanism when actuated by some impersonal influence, as for example, a change in current strength, pressure, temperature, or mechanical configuration. (See "Nonautomatic.")

Bare Conductor: See under "Conductor."

Block (City, Town, or Village):   See Section 800-2.

Bonding: The permanent joining of metallic parts to form an electrically conductive path which will assure electrical continuity and the capacity to conduct safely any current likely to be imposed.

Bonding Jumper: A reliable conductor to assure the required electrical conductivity between metal parts required to be electrically connected.

See Figure 100-3.

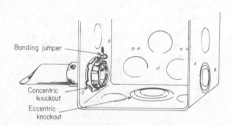

Bonding jumper

Concentric knockout

Eccentric knockout

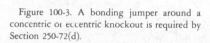

Figure 100-3. A bonding jumper around a concentric or eccentric knockout is required by Section 250-72(d).

Bonding Jumper, Circuit: The connection between portions of a conductor in a circuit to maintain required ampacity of the circuit.

Bonding Jumper, Equipment: The connection between two or more portions of the equipment grounding conductor.

Bonding Jumper, Main: The connection between the grounded circuit conductor and the equipment grounding conductor at the service.

See Figure 100-4.

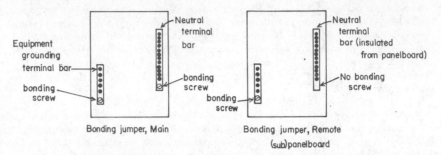

Bonding jumper, Main   Bonding jumper, Remote
                                        (sub)panelboard

Figure 100-4. The equipment grounding terminal bar is to be bonded to the panelboard (or cabinet) frame and is not to be connected to the neutral bar in other than service equipment. Bonding method may be by bonding screws or bonding jumpers.

Branch Circuit: The circuit conductors between the final overcurrent device protecting the circuit and the outlet(s).

See Section 240-9 for thermal cutouts, thermal relays, and other devices.

See Figure 100-5.

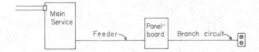

Figure 100-5. Conductors between the overcurrent device in the panelboard and the duplex receptacle are branch-circuit conductors.

Branch Circuit, Appliance: A branch circuit supplying energy to one or more outlets to which appliances are to be connected; such circuits to have no permanently connected lighting fixtures not a part of an appliance.

Receptacle outlets as required in Section 220-3(b) for the kitchen, pantry, etc. and Section 220-3(c) for laundry areas are not to have any other outlets or permanently connected lighting fixtures connected to them. See comments following Section 220-3(b).

Branch Circuit, General Purpose: A branch circuit that supplies a number of outlets for lighting and appliances.

Branch Circuit, Individual: A branch circuit that supplies only one utilization equipment.

An individual branch circuit is a circuit that supplies "only" one utilization equipment, that is, one range, or one space heater, or one motor. See Section 210-23.

It may supply "only" one single receptacle for the connection of a single attachment plug. See Section 210-21(b).

A branch circuit may be installed to supply one duplex receptacle which can accommodate two cord- and plug-connected appliances or similar equipment and therefore this circuit would not be considered an individual branch circuit. See Figure 100-6.

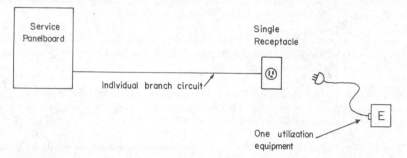

Figure 100-6. Illustrated is a single receptacle, which is intended for the connection of one utilization equipment.

Branch Circuit, Multiwire: A branch circuit consisting of two or more ungrounded conductors having a potential difference between them, and a grounded conductor having equal potential difference between it and each ungrounded conductor of the circuit and which is connected to the neutral conductor of the system.

See Sections 210-4, 210-6(c), and 240-20(b).

Branch-Circuit Selection Current: See Section 440-3(c), Definition.

Building: A structure which stands alone or which is cut off from adjoining structures by fire walls with all openings therein protected by approved fire doors.

A building is a structure used or intended for supporting or sheltering any use or occupancy. Definitions of the terms "fire walls" and "fire doors" are the responsibility of the municipal and/or state building codes and interpretations of "building terms" have been avoided by *NEC* committees. Fire-resistance rating is defined as the time, in minutes or hours, that materials or assemblies have withstood a fire exposure.

Cabinet: An enclosure designed either for surface or flush mounting and provided with a frame, mat, or trim in which a swinging door or doors are or may be hung.

Both cabinets and cutout boxes are covered in Article 373. Cabinets are designed for surface or flush mounting with a trim to which a swinging door(s) is hung. Cutout boxes are designed for surface mounting with a swinging door(s) secured directly to the box.

Cell (As applied to Raceways):   See Sections 356-1 and 358-1.

Circuit Breaker: A device designed to open and close a circuit by nonautomatic means and to open the circuit automatically on a predetermined overcurrent without injury to itself when properly applied within its rating.

The automatic opening means can be integral, direct acting with the circuit breaker or remote from the circuit breaker. See definition of "Switching Devices" in Part B of this article for definition applying to circuits and equipment over 600 volts, nominal.

Adjustable: (As applied to Circuit Breakers.) A qualifying term indicating that the circuit breaker can be set to trip at various values of current and/or time within a predetermined range.

Instantaneous Trip: (As applied to Circuit Breakers.) A qualifying term indicating that no delay is purposely introduced in the tripping action of the circuit breaker.

Inverse Time: (As applied to Circuit Breakers.) A qualifying term indicating there is purposely introduced a delay in the tripping action of the circuit breaker, which delay decreases as the magnitude of the current increases.

Nonadjustable: (As applied to Circuit Breakers.) A qualifying term indicating that the circuit breaker does not have any adjustment to alter the value of current at which it will trip or the time required for its operation.

Setting: (of Circuit Breaker.) The value of current and/or time at which an adjustable circuit breaker is set to trip.

Communication Circuit: See Section 800-1.

Concealed: Rendered inaccessible by the structure or finish of the building. Wires in concealed raceways are considered concealed, even though they may become accessible by withdrawing them. [See "Accessible — (As applied to wiring methods)."]

Raceways and cables supported within the hollow frames or permanently closed in by the finish of buildings are considered "concealed." Open-type work, such as raceways and cables in open areas, for example, in unfinished basements, in accessible underfloor areas or attics, or attached to the surface of finished areas, which may be removed without damage to the building structure or finish is not considered "concealed." See definition of "Exposed (as applied to wiring methods)."

Conductor:

Bare: A conductor having no covering or electrical insulation whatsoever. (See "Conductor, Covered.")

Covered: A conductor encased within material of composition or thickness that is not recognized by this Code as electrical insulation. (See "Conductor, Bare.")

Insulated: A conductor encased within material of composition and thickness that is recognized by this Code as electrical insulation.

Conduit Body: A separate portion of a conduit or tubing system that provides access through a removable cover(s) to the interior of the system at a junction of two or more sections of the system or at a terminal point of the system.
Boxes such as FS and FD or larger cast or sheet metal boxes are not classified as conduit bodies. See Table 370-6(a).

This definition is intended to clarify that conduit bodies are a portion of a raceway system with removable covers to allow access to the interior of the system.
In the past, conduit bodies have been commonly referred to in the trade as condulets of the LB, LL, LR, C, and T conduit fittings. Sections 300-15, 345-14, 346-14, 346-15, 347-16, 348-14, 348-15, 370-1, 370-6(c), and 370-18(a) Exception may be referred to for the rules on the usage of conduit bodies.

Type FS or FD boxes are not classified as conduit bodies and they are listed with boxes in Table 370-6(a).

Connector, Pressure (Solderless):   A device that establishes a connection between two or more conductors or between one or more conductors and a terminal by means of mechanical pressure and without the use of solder.

Continuous Duty: See under "Duty."

Continuous Load: A load where the maximum current is expected to continue for three hours or more.

Control Circuit: See Section 430-71.

Controller: A device or group of devices that serves to govern, in some predetermined manner, the electric power delivered to the apparatus to which it is connected. See also Section 430-81(a).

A "controller" is any switch, circuit breaker, or device normally used to start and stop motors and other apparatus and, in the case of motors, is to be capable of interrupting the stalled-rotor current of the motor.

Cooking Unit, Counter-Mounted: A cooking appliance designed for mounting in or on a counter and consisting of one or more heating elements, internal wiring, and built-in or separately mountable controls. (See "Oven, Wall-Mounted.")

Copper-Clad Aluminum Conductors: Conductors drawn from a copper-clad aluminum rod with the copper metallurgically bonded to an aluminum core. The copper forms a minimum of 10 percent of the cross-sectional area of a solid conductor or each strand of a stranded conductor.

Covered Conductor: See under "Conductor."

Current-Limiting Overcurrent Protective Device: See Section 240-11.

Cutout Box: An enclosure designed for surface mounting and having swinging doors or covers secured directly to and telescoping with the walls of the box proper. (See "Cabinet.")

Damp Location: See under "Location."

Dead Front: Without live parts exposed to a person on the operating side of the equipment.

Demand Factor: The ratio of the maximum demand of a system, or part of a system, to the total connected load of a system or the part of the system under consideration.

Device: A unit of an electrical system which is intended to carry but not utilize electric energy.

Units, such as switches, circuit breakers, receptacles, and lampholders, that distribute or control, but do not consume, electricity are termed devices.

Disconnecting Means: A device, or group of devices, or other means by which the conductors of a circuit can be disconnected from their source of supply.

For disconnecting means for service equipment, see Part H of Article 230; for fuses and thermal cutouts, see Part D of Article 240; for circuit breakers, see Part

G of Article 240; for appliances, see Part D of Article 422; for space heating equipment, see Part C of Article 424; for motors and controllers, see Part H of Article 430; and for air-conditioning and refrigerating equipment, see Part B of Article 440. See also references for "Disconnecting Means" in Index.

See definition in Part B of this article for definition applying to circuits and equipment over 600 volts, nominal.

Dry Location: See under "Location."

Dust-Ignitionproof: See Section 502-1.

Dustproof: So constructed or protected that dust will not interfere with its successful operation.

Dusttight: So constructed that dust will not enter the enclosing case under specified test conditions.

For test conditions other than for rotating equipment, see ANSI/NEMA ICS6-1978, Enclosures for Industrial Controls and Systems, Paragraph ICS6-110.54.

Reference to the ANSI/NEMA Standard will permit the user to evaluate the enclosure with regard to actual conditions of use.

Duty:

Continuous Duty: Operation at a substantially constant load for an indefinitely long time.

Intermittent Duty: Operation for alternate intervals of (1) load and no load; or (2) load and rest; or (3) load, no load, and rest.

Periodic Duty: Intermittent operation in which the load conditions are regularly recurrent.

Short-Time Duty: Operation at a substantially constant load for a short and definitely specified time.

Varying Duty: Operation at loads, and for intervals of time, both of which may be subject to wide variation.

See Table 430-22(a), Exception for illustration of various types of duty.

For the protection of intermittent, periodic, short-time, and varying-duty motors against overload, see Section 430-33.

Duty Cycle (Welding):   See Section 630-31(b), Fine Print Note.

Dwelling:

Dwelling Unit: One or more rooms for the use of one or more persons as a housekeeping unit with space for eating, living, and sleeping, and permanent provisions for cooking and sanitation.

Where dwelling units are referenced throughout the *Code*, it is important to note that rooms of motels, hotels, and similar occupancies may be classified as dwelling units. See Figure 100-7.

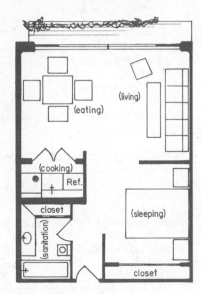

Figure 100-7. A motel or hotel room with eating, living, and sleeping areas and areas having permanent provisions for cooking and sanitation meets the definition of a "dwelling unit."

Multifamily Dwelling: A building containing three or more dwelling units.

One-Family Dwelling: A building consisting solely of one dwelling unit.

Two-Family Dwelling: A building consisting solely of two dwelling units.

Electric Sign: A fixed, stationary, or portable self-contained, electrically illuminated utilization equipment with words or symbols designed to convey information or attract attention.

Enclosed: Surrounded by a case, housing, fence, or walls which will prevent persons from accidentally contacting energized parts.

Enclosure: The case or housing of apparatus, or the fence or walls surrounding an installation to prevent personnel from accidentally contacting energized parts, or to protect the equipment from physical damage.

Equipment: A general term including material, fittings, devices, appliances, fixtures, apparatus, and the like used as a part of, or in connection with, an electrical installation.

Equipment Grounding Conductor: See "Grounding Conductor, Equipment."

See Section 250-91(b) for types of equipment grounding conductors.

Explosionproof Apparatus: Apparatus enclosed in a case that is capable of withstanding an explosion of a specified gas or vapor which may occur within it and of preventing the ignition of a specified gas or vapor surrounding the enclosure by sparks, flashes, or explosion of the gas or vapor within, and which operates at such an external temperature that a surrounding flammable atmosphere will not be ignited thereby.

Exposed: (As applied to live parts.) Capable of being inadvertently touched or approached nearer than a safe distance by a person. It is applied to parts not suitably guarded, isolated, or insulated. (See "Accessible" and "Concealed.")

See Section 110-17. See also comments following definition of "Guarded."

Exposed: (As applied to wiring methods.) On or attached to the surface or behind panels designed to allow access. [See "Accessible — (As applied to wiring methods)."]

See Figure 100-1.

Externally Operable: Capable of being operated without exposing the operator to contact with live parts.

Feeder: All circuit conductors between the service equipment, or the generator switchboard of an isolated plant, and the final branch-circuit overcurrent device.

See Figure 100-5.

Festoon Lighting: See Section 225-6(b).

Fitting: An accessory such as a locknut, bushing, or other part of a wiring system that is intended primarily to perform a mechanical rather than an electrical function.

The term "fitting" as defined in Article 100 is not intended to apply to the use of "fitting" as it appears in Section 300-15. See also Section 370-1.

Garage: A building or portion of a building in which one or more self-propelled vehicles carrying volatile flammable liquid for fuel or power are kept for use, sale, storage, rental, repair, exhibition, or demonstrating purposes, and all that portion of a building which is on or below the floor or floors in which such vehicles are kept and which is not separated therefrom by suitable cutoffs.

See Section 511-1.

General-Purpose Branch Circuit: See "Branch Circuit, General Purpose."

General-Use Snap Switch: See under "Switches."

General-Use Switch: See under "Switches."

Ground: A conducting connection, whether intentional or accidental, between an electrical circuit or equipment and the earth, or to some conducting body that serves in place of the earth.

Grounded: Connected to earth or to some conducting body that serves in place of the earth.

Grounded (Effectively Grounded Communication System):   See Section 800-2(c)(1).

Grounded Conductor: A system or circuit conductor that is intentionally grounded.

Grounding Conductor: A conductor used to connect equipment or the grounded circuit of a wiring system to a grounding electrode or electrodes.

Grounding Conductor, Equipment: The conductor used to connect the noncurrent-carrying metal parts of equipment, raceways, and other enclosures to the system grounded conductor and/or the grounding electrode conductor at the service equipment or at the source of a separately derived system.

Grounding Electrode Conductor: The conductor used to connect the grounding electrode to the equipment grounding conductor and/or to the grounded conductor of the circuit at the service equipment or at the source of a separately derived system.

The grounding electrode conductor is to be of copper, aluminum, or copper-clad aluminum and is used to connect the equipment grounding conductor and/or the grounded conductor (at the service equipment or at the separately derived system) to the grounding electrode for either grounded or ungrounded systems.
It is sized by using Table 250-94. See also Article 250, Parts H and J.

Ground-Fault Circuit-Interrupter: A device intended for the protection of personnel that functions to de-energize a circuit or portion thereof within an established period of time when a current to ground exceeds some predetermined value that is less than that required to operate the overcurrent protective device of the supply circuit.

Guarded: Covered, shielded, fenced, enclosed, or otherwise protected by means of suitable covers, casings, barriers, rails, screens, mats, or platforms to remove the likelihood of approach or contact by persons or objects to a point of danger.

See Sections 110-17, 110-34, 430-133, 450-7, and Article 710.

Hazardous (Classified) Locations: See Article 500.

Header: See Sections 356-1 and 358-1.

Hermetic Refrigerant Motor-Compressor: See Section 440-1.

Hoistway: Any shaftway, hatchway, well hole, or other vertical opening or space in which an elevator or dumbwaiter is designed to operate.

See Article 620 for the installation of electric equipment and wiring methods in hoistways.

Identified: (As applied to Equipment.)   Recognizable as suitable for the specific purpose, function, use, environment, application, etc., where described in a particular Code requirement. (See "Equipment.")

Suitability of equipment for a specific purpose, environment, or application may be determined by a qualified testing laboratory, inspection agency, or other organization concerned with product evaluation. Such identification may include labeling or listing: see "Labeled," "Listed," and Section 90-6.

Definitions of "Approved for the Purpose" and "Identified" (as applied to the grounded terminal or conductor) have been deleted from the 1981 *NEC*.
A technical subcommittee on the uses of the term "Approved for the Purpose" found that this term seemed to be used as a substitute for "Listed" or "Labeled." The Correlating Committee instructed all code-making panels to remove the term "Approved for the Purpose" as a part of the revision of the 1981 *NEC*.
The definition of the term "Identified" has been deleted, and the code-making panels have reviewed their sections of the *Code* to ensure that the term "Identified" is no longer used to refer to a conductor or terminal that is grounded.
"Identified" (as applied to equipment) was recommended as a substitute for the term "Approved for the Purpose" with no change in concept from its definition in the 1978 *NEC*. Code-Making Panel 1 felt that the use of this term would more readily permit the code-making panels to include the function, use, environment,

specific purpose, etc., in the text of the *Code* requirements — for example: identified for use in wet locations; identified as suitable for Class I, Division 1 locations; identified as weatherproof.

By stating the specific conditions of use, the equipment can be marked to show its suitability for the intended application. Further, it overcomes the inference that the authority having enforcement jurisdiction has sole responsibility for the decision as to acceptability for the purpose, but rather implies that the manufacturer, installer, user, testing laboratory, etc., have an obligation to convey to the inspection authority their concurrence with such intended use.

Individual Branch Circuit: See "Branch Circuit, Individual."

In Sight From (Within Sight From, Within Sight.):   Where this Code specifies that one equipment shall be "in sight from," "within sight from," or "within sight," etc., of another equipment, one of the equipments specified shall be visible and not more than 50 feet (15.24 m) distant from the other.

The terms "in sight from," "within sight from," "within sight," "out of sight," "not within sight," and "not in sight from" are used in six articles (16 sections — see listings below) of the *NEC*.

Most of the sections of the *NEC* that use the subject terms deal with equipments where motors and motor equipment are involved. Other sections using these terms deal with fixtures, duct heaters, controllers supplementary overcurrent devices, and signs.

410-81	424-19(a)(2) a.	424-65
422-26	424-19(a)(2) b.	430-4
422-26 Exception	424-19(a)(2) c.	430-86
424-19(a)	424-19(a)(2) d.	430-102
424-19(a)(1)	424-19(b) 2.	440-63
		600-2(a)

Insulated Conductor: See under "Conductor."

Intermittent Duty: See under "Duty."

Interrupting Rating: The highest current at rated voltage that an overcurrent protective device is intended to interrupt under specified test conditions.

Equipment intended to break current at other than fault levels may have its interrupting rating implied in other ratings, such as horsepower or locked rotor current.

This definition was included in Article 100 as the term appears, for example, in Sections 110-9, 240-60(c), and 240-83(c).

Interrupting ratings are essential to coordinating electrical systems so that available fault currents can be properly controlled.

Isolated: Not readily accessible to persons unless special means for access are used.

See Sections 110-31, 110-34, and 710-22. See definition of "Switch, Isolating" in Article 100.

Labeled: Equipment or materials to which has been attached a label, symbol, or other identifying mark of an organization acceptable to the authority having jurisdiction and concerned with product evaluation, that maintains periodic inspection of production of labeled equipment or materials and by whose labeling the manufacturer indicates compliance with appropriate standards or performance in a specified manner.

Equipment and conductors required or permitted by this *Code* are acceptable only when approved for a specific environment or application by the authority having jurisdiction. See Section 110-2.

"Listing" or "Labeling" by a qualified testing laboratory will provide a basis for approval. See Section 90-6.

Lighting Outlet: An outlet intended for the direct connection of a lampholder, a lighting fixture, or a pendant cord terminating in a lampholder.

Listed: Equipment or materials included in a list published by an organization acceptable to the authority having jurisdiction and concerned with product evaluation, that maintains periodic inspection of production of listed equipment or materials, and whose listing states either that the equipment or material meets appropriate standards or has been tested and found suitable for use in a specified manner.

The means for identifying listed equipment may vary for each organization concerned with product evaluation, some of which do not recognize equipment as listed unless it is also labeled. The authority having jurisdiction should utilize the system employed by the listing organization to identify a listed product.

See comments that follow the definition of "Labeled."

Location:

Damp Location: Partially protected locations under canopies, marquees, roofed open porches, and like locations, and interior locations subject to moderate degrees of moisture, such as some basements, some barns, and some cold-storage warehouses.

Dry Location: A location not normally subject to dampness or wetness. A location classified as dry may be temporarily subject to dampness or wetness, as in the case of a building under construction.

Wet Location: Installations underground or in concrete slabs or masonry in direct contact with the earth, and locations subject to saturation with water or other liquids, such as vehicle washing areas, and locations exposed to weather and unprotected.

See Sections 300-6(c) and 410-4.

Low-Energy Power Circuit: A circuit that is not a remote-control or signaling circuit but has its power supply limited in accordance with the requirements of Class 2 and Class 3 circuits. (See Article 725.)

Multioutlet Assembly: A type of surface or flush raceway designed to hold conductors and receptacles, assembled in the field or at the factory.

In dry locations, metallic and nonmetallic multioutlet assemblies are permitted; however, they are not to be installed where concealed. See Article 353 for details of recessing these assemblies.

Multiwire Branch Circuit: See "Branch Circuit, Multiwire."

Neutral Conductor: See Note 10 to Tables 310-16 through 310-19.

Nonautomatic: Action requiring personal intervention for its control. (See "Automatic.")

As applied to an electric controller, nonautomatic control does not necessarily imply a manual controller, but only that personal intervention is necessary.

Outlet: A point on the wiring system at which current is taken to supply utilization equipment.

For example, a lighting outlet or a receptacle outlet.

Outline Lighting: An arrangement of incandescent lamps or electric discharge tubing to outline or call attention to certain features such as the shape of a building or the decoration of a window.

See Article 600, Part B (600 volts or less) and Part C (over 600 volts).

Oven, Wall-Mounted: An oven for cooking purposes designed for mounting in or on a wall or other surface and consisting of one or more heating elements, internal wiring, and built-in or separately mountable controls. (See "Cooking Unit, Counter-Mounted.")

Overcurrent: Any current in excess of the rated current of equipment or the ampacity of a conductor. It may result from overload (see definition), short circuit, or ground fault.

A current in excess of rating may be accommodated by certain equipment and conductors for a given set of conditions. Hence the rules for overcurrent protection are specific for particular situations.

Overload: Operation of equipment in excess of normal, full-load rating, or of a conductor in excess of rated ampacity which, when it persists for a sufficient length of time, would cause damage or dangerous overheating. A fault, such as a short circuit or ground fault, is not an overload. (See "Overcurrent.")

For motor apparatus applications, see Section 430-31.

Panelboard: A single panel or group of panel units designed for assembly in the form of a single panel; including buses, automatic overcurrent devices, and with or without switches for the control of light, heat, or power circuits; designed to be placed in a cabinet or cutout box placed in or against a wall or partition and accessible only from the front. (See "Switchboard.")

See Article 384.

Periodic Duty: See under "Duty."

Power Outlet: An enclosed assembly which may include receptacles, circuit breakers, fuseholders, fused switches, buses, and watt-hour meter mounting means; intended to supply and control power to mobile homes, recreational vehicles, or boats; or to serve as a means for distributing power required to operate mobile or temporarily installed equipment.

Premises Wiring (System):   That interior and exterior wiring, including power, lighting, control, and signal circuit wiring together with all of its associated hardware, fittings, and wiring devices, both permanently and temporarily installed, which extends from the load end of the service drop, or load end of the service lateral conductors to the outlet(s). Such wiring does not include wiring internal to appliances, fixtures, motors, controllers, motor control centers, and similar equipment.

Projector, Nonprofessional: See Section 540-3.

Projector, Professional: See Section 540-2.

Qualified Person: One familiar with the construction and operation of the equipment and the hazards involved.

Raceway: An enclosed channel designed expressly for holding wires, cables, or busbars, with additional functions as permitted in this Code.

Raceways may be of metal or insulating material, and the term includes rigid metal conduit, rigid nonmetallic conduit, intermediate metal conduit, liquidtight flexible metal conduit, flexible metallic tubing, flexible metal conduit, electrical metallic tubing, underfloor raceways, cellular concrete floor raceways, cellular metal floor raceways, surface raceways, wireways, and busways.

Rainproof: So constructed, protected, or treated as to prevent rain from interfering with the successful operation of the apparatus under specified test conditions.

The phrase "under specified test conditions" was added to the definition since "rain" is not clearly described. Testing laboratories have tests which are used to evaluate equipment and these tests are well known to manufacturers of electrical products as well as to large users of this type of equipment. Users of the *NEC* should be alerted to the existence of these tests.

Raintight: So constructed or protected that exposure to a beating rain will not result in the entrance of water under specified test conditions.

Raceways on exterior surfaces of buildings are to be made raintight. See Sections 225-22 and 230-53.
For boxes and cabinets, see Section 300-6.
See comments following definition of "Rainproof."

Rated-Load Current: See Section 440-3(a), Definition.

Readily Accessible: Capable of being reached quickly for operation, renewal, or inspections, without requiring those to whom ready access is requisite to climb over or remove obstacles or to resort to portable ladders, chairs, etc. (See "Accessible.")

Overcurrent devices are to be readily accessible. See Section 240-24(a). There is considered to be a high degree of safety when switches or circuit breakers can be disconnected quickly without being hindered by obstacles. See Section 230-72(c) for services. See also the exceptions to this rule for busways, Section 364-12; and for supplementary overcurrent protection, Section 240-10.

Receptacle: A receptacle is a contact device installed at the outlet for the connection of a single attachment plug.

A single receptacle is a single contact device with no other contact device on the same yoke. A multiple receptacle is a single device containing two or more receptacles.

The basic receptacle is a single contact device for the connection of a single attachment plug. A multiple receptacle is a contact device containing two or more receptacles for the connection of two or more attachment plugs. See Figure 100-8.

Receptacle Outlet: An outlet where one or more receptacles are installed.

See Figure 100-8.

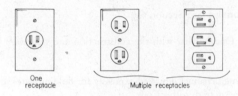

One receptacle   Multiple receptacles

Figure 100-8. When calculating other loads—all occupancies [Section 220-2(c)], loads for additions to existing dwelling units [Section 220-2(d)(1)], and other dwelling units [Section 220-2(d)(2)] each single or multiple receptacle is to be considered at not less than 180 volt-amperes.

Remote-Control Circuit: Any electric circuit that controls any other circuit through a relay or an equivalent device.

See Figure 100-9.

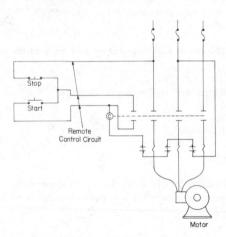

Figure 100-9. A remote control circuit for starting and stopping an electric motor.

Sealable Equipment: Equipment enclosed in a case or cabinet that is provided with a means of sealing or locking so that live parts cannot be made accessible without opening the enclosure. The equipment may or may not be operable without opening the enclosure.

Service: The conductors and equipment for delivering energy from the electricity supply system to the wiring system of the premises served.

Service Cable: Service conductors made up in the form of a cable.

Service Conductors: The supply conductors that extend from the street main or from transformers to the service equipment of the premises supplied.

Service conductors from an overhead distribution system originate at the utility pole, or wires attached to it, and terminate at the service equipment.
Service conductors from an underground distribution system originate at the utility manhole and terminate at the service equipment. When primary conductors are extended to outdoor pad-mounted or underground transformers on private

property, the service conductors originate at the secondary connections of the transformers.

See Article 230, Part K for service conductors exceeding 600 V.

Service Drop: The overhead service conductors from the last pole or other aerial support to and including the splices, if any, connecting to the service-entrance conductors at the building or other structure.

See Figure 100-10.

Service-Entrance Conductors, Overhead System: The service conductors between the terminals of the service equipment and a point usually outside the building, clear of building walls, where joined by tap or splice to the service drop.

See Figure 100-10.

Figure 100-10. Illustration of an overhead system showing a service drop from a utility pole to attachment on the house and service entrance conductors from point of attachment (spliced to service drop conductors), down the side of the house, through the meter socket, and terminating within the service equipment.

Service-Entrance Conductors, Underground System: The service conductors between the terminals of the service equipment and the point of connection to the service lateral.

See Figure 100-11.

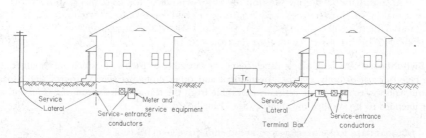

Figure 100-11. Service laterals (underground systems) may be run from poles or from transformers and with or without terminal boxes.

Where service equipment is located outside the building walls, there may be no service-entrance conductors, or they may be entirely outside the building.

Service Equipment: The necessary equipment, usually consisting of a circuit breaker or switch and fuses, and their accessories, located near the point of entrance of supply conductors to a building or other structure, or an otherwise defined area, and intended to constitute the main control and means of cutoff of the supply.

Service equipment consists of a circuit breaker or a fused switch provided to disconnect all conductors in a building or other structure from the service-entrance conductors.

The disconnecting means is to consist of not more than six circuit breakers or six switches and is to be readily accessible, either inside or outside the building or structure nearest the point of entrance of the service-entrance conductors.

See Article 230, Part H.

Service Lateral: The underground service conductors between the street main, including any risers at a pole or other structure or from transformers, and the first point of connection to the service-entrance conductors in a terminal box or meter or other enclosure with adequate space, inside or outside the building wall. Where there is no terminal box, meter, or other enclosure with adequate space, the point of connection shall be considered to be the point of entrance of the service conductors into the building.

See Figure 100-11.

Service Raceway: The raceway that encloses the service-entrance conductors.

Setting (of Circuit Breaker):   The value of the current at which it is set to trip.

Short-Time Duty: See under "Duty."

Show Window: Any window used or designed to be used for the display of goods or advertising material, whether it is fully or partly enclosed or entirely open at the rear and whether or not it has a platform raised higher than the street floor level.

Sign: See "Electric Sign."

Signaling Circuit: Any electric circuit that energizes signaling equipment.

Special Permission: The written consent of the authority having jurisdiction.

The authority having jurisdiction for enforcement of the *Code* has responsibility for making interpretations and granting special permission contemplated in a number of the rules. Examples: see Section 110-16(a), Exception No. 2; Section 230-2, Exception Nos. 3 and 4; or Section 426-14.

Switchboard: A large single panel, frame, or assembly of panels on which are mounted, on the face or back or both, switches, overcurrent and other protective devices, buses, and usually instruments. Switchboards are generally accessible from the rear as well as from the front and are not intended to be installed in cabinets. (See "Panelboard.")

Busbars are to be arranged to avoid inductive overheating.

Service busbars are to be isolated by barriers from the remainder of the switchboard.

Most modern switchboards are totally enclosed to reduce to a minimum the probability of communicating fire to adjacent combustible materials and to guard live parts.

Switches:

General-Use Switch: A switch intended for use in general distribution and branch circuits. It is rated in amperes, and it is capable of interrupting its rated current at its rated voltage.

General-Use Snap Switch: A form of general-use switch so constructed that it can be installed in flush device boxes or on outlet box covers, or otherwise used in conjunction with wiring systems recognized by this Code.

AC General-Use Snap Switch: See Section 380-14(a).

AC-DC General-Use Snap Switch: See Section 380-14(b).

Isolating Switch: A switch intended for isolating an electric circuit from the source of power. It has no interrupting rating, and it is intended to be operated only after the circuit has been opened by some other means.

Motor-Circuit Switch: A switch, rated in horsepower, capable of interrupting the maximum operating overload current of a motor of the same horsepower rating as the switch at the rated voltage.

Thermal Cutout: An overcurrent protective device that contains a heater element in addition to and affecting a renewable fusible member which opens the circuit. It is not designed to interrupt short-circuit currents.

Thermally Protected: (As applied to motors.) The words "Thermally Protected" appearing on the nameplate of a motor or motor-compressor indicate that the motor is provided with a thermal protector.

Thermal Protector: (As applied to motors.) A protective device for assembly as an integral part of a motor or motor-compressor and which, when properly applied, protects the motor against dangerous overheating due to overload and failure to start.

The thermal protector may consist of one or more sensing elements integral with the motor or motor-compressor and an external control device.

Utilization Equipment: Equipment which utilizes electric energy for mechanical, chemical, heating, lighting, or similar purposes.

Varying Duty: See under "Duty."

Ventilated: Provided with a means to permit circulation of air sufficient to remove an excess of heat, fumes, or vapors.

Volatile Flammable Liquid: A flammable liquid having a flash point below 38°C (100°F), or a flammable liquid whose temperature is above its flash point, or a Class II combustible liquid having a vapor pressure not exceeding 40 psia (276 kPa) at 38°C (100°F) whose temperature is above its flash point.

Flash point of the liquid is the minimum temperature at which it gives off sufficient vapor to form an ignitible mixture with the air near the surface of the liquid or within the vessel used. By "ignitible mixture" is meant a mixture within the explosive range (between upper and lower limits) that is capable of the propagation of flame away from the source of ignition when ignited. Some evaporation takes place below the flash point but not in sufficient quantities to form an ignitible mixture.

Voltage (of a Circuit): The greatest root-mean-square (effective) difference of potential between any two conductors of the circuit concerned.

Some systems, such as 3-phase 4-wire, single-phase 3-wire, and 3-wire direct-current may have various circuits of various voltages.

A 3-phase, 4-wire wye system has two voltages (277/480, 120/208). The "voltage of the circuit" is the highest voltage between any two conductors, that is, 480 V and 208 V. The "voltage of the circuit" of a 2-wire feeder or branch circuit (one phase and the grounded conductor) derived from the above systems would be the voltage between the two wires of the lower voltage, that is, 277 V and 120 V.

The same applies to dc or single-phase, 3-wire systems where there are two voltages.

Voltage, Nominal: A nominal value assigned to a circuit or system for the purpose of conveniently designating its voltage class (as 120/240, 480Y/277, 600, etc.).

The actual voltage at which a circuit operates can vary from the nominal within a range that permits satisfactory operation of equipment.

See "Voltage Ratings for Electric Power Systems and Equipment (60 Hz)," ANSI C84.1-1977.

Voltage to Ground: For grounded circuits, the voltage between the given conductor and that point or conductor of the circuit that is grounded; for ungrounded circuits, the greatest voltage between the given conductor and any other conductor of the circuit.

The "voltage to ground" of a 277/480 V wye system would be 277 V; of a 120/208 V wye system, 120 V; and of a 3-phase, 3-wire ungrounded 480 V system, 480 V.

Watertight: So constructed that moisture will not enter the enclosure under specified test conditions.

For test conditions other than for rotating equipment, see ANSI/NEMA, ICS6-1978, Enclosures for Industrial Controls and Systems, Paragraph ICS6-110.56.

Unless the enclosure is hermetically sealed, it is possible for moisture to enter the enclosure. The ANSI/NEMA Standard alerts the user to the possibility of condensation in the enclosure and contains widely used testing procedures for enclosures for electrical equipment.

Weatherproof: So constructed or protected that exposure to the weather will not interfere with successful operation.

Rainproof, raintight, or watertight equipment can fulfill the requirements for weatherproof where varying weather conditions other than wetness, such as snow, ice, dust, or temperature extremes, are not a factor.

Welder, Electric:

Actual Primary Current: See Section 630-31(b).

Rated Primary Current: See Section 630-31(b).

Wet Location: See under "Location."

X-ray:

Long-Time Rating: See Sections 517-40 and 660-2.

Momentary Rating: See Sections 517-40 and 660-2.

B. Over 600 Volts, Nominal

Whereas the preceding definitions are intended to apply wherever the terms are used throughout this Code, the following ones are applicable only to the parts of articles specifically covering installations and equipment operating at over 600 volts, nominal.

Circuit Breaker: See under "Switching Devices."

Cutout: See under "Switching Devices."

Disconnect (Isolator): See under "Switching Devices."

Disconnecting Means: See under "Switching Devices."

Fuse: An overcurrent protective device with a circuit opening fusible part that is heated and severed by the passage of overcurrent through it.

A fuse comprises all the parts that form a unit capable of performing the prescribed functions. It may or may not be the complete device necessary to connect it into an electrical circuit.

Expulsion Fuse Unit (Expulsion Fuse): A vented fuse unit in which the expulsion effect of gases produced by the arc and lining of the fuseholder, either alone or aided by a spring, extinguishes the arc.

Power Fuse Unit: A vented, nonvented or controlled vented fuse unit in which the arc is extinguished by being drawn through solid material, granular material, or liquid, either alone or aided by a spring.

Vented Power Fuse: A fuse with provision for the escape of arc gases, liquids, or solid particles to the surrounding atmosphere during circuit interruption.

Nonvented Power Fuse: A fuse without intentional provision for the escape of arc gases, liquids, or solid particles to the atmosphere during circuit interruption.

Controlled Vented Power Fuse: A fuse with provision for controlling discharge circuit interruption such that no solid material may be exhausted into the surrounding atmosphere. The discharge gases shall not ignite or damage insulation in the path of the discharge, nor shall these gases propagate a flashover to or between grounded members or conduction members in the path of the discharge when the distance between the vent and such insulation or conduction members conforms to manufacturer's recommendations.

Grounded, Effectively: Permanently connected to earth through a ground connection of sufficiently low impedance and having sufficient ampacity that ground-fault current which may occur cannot build up to voltages dangerous to personnel.

Interrupter Switch: See under "Switching Devices."

Multiple Fuse: An assembly of two or more single-pole fuses.

Oil (Filled) Cutout: See under "Switching Devices."

Power Fuse: See under "Fuse."

Regulator Bypass Switch: See under "Switching Devices."

Switching Device: A device designed to close and/or open one or more electric circuits.

Switching Devices:

Circuit Breaker: A switching device capable of making, carrying, and breaking currents under normal circuit conditions, and also making, carrying for a specified time, and breaking currents under specified abnormal circuit conditions, such as those of short circuit.

Cutout: An assembly of a fuse support with either a fuseholder, fuse carrier, or disconnecting blade. The fuseholder or fuse carrier may include a conducting element (fuse link), or may act as the disconnecting blade by the inclusion of a nonfusible member.

Disconnecting (or Isolating) Switch (Disconnector, Isolator): A mechanical switching device used for isolating a circuit or equipment from a source of power.

Disconnecting Means: A device, group of devices, or other means whereby the conductors of a circuit can be disconnected from their source of supply.

Interrupter Switch: A switch capable of making, carrying, and interrupting specified currents.

Oil Cutout (Oil-Filled Cutout): A cutout in which all or part of the fuse support and its fuse link or disconnecting blade are mounted in oil with complete immersion of the contacts and the fusible portion of the conducting element (fuse link), so that arc interruption by severing of the fuse link or by opening of the contacts will occur under oil.

Oil Switch: An oil switch is a switch having contacts which operate under oil (or askarel or other suitable liquid).

Regulator Bypass Switch: A specific device or combination of devices designed to bypass a regulator.

ARTICLE 110 — REQUIREMENTS FOR
ELECTRICAL INSTALLATIONS

Contents

A. General

110-1. Mandatory Rules and Explanatory Material. Mandatory rules of this Code are characterized by the use of the word "shall." Explanatory material is in the form of fine print notes.

110-2. Approval. The conductors and equipment required or permitted by this Code shall be acceptable only if approved.

See Examination of Equipment for Safety, Section 90-6 and Examination, Identification, Installation, and Use of Equipment, Section 110-3. See definitions of "Approved," "Identified," "Labeled," and "Listed."

Section 110-2 of the *Code* requires that all equipment be approved and, as such, be acceptable to the authority having jurisdiction. Section 110-3 provides guidance for the judging of equipment and recognizes listing or labeling as a means of establishing suitability.

Approval of equipment is the responsibility of the electrical inspection authority and many such "approvals" are based on tests and listings of testing laboratories such as Underwriters Laboratories Inc. (UL) or Factory Mutual (FM), etc.

110-3. Examination, Identification, Installation, and Use of Equipment.

  (a) Examination. In judging equipment, considerations such as the following shall be evaluated:

    (1) Suitability for installation and use in conformity with the provisions of this Code. Suitability of equipment use may be identified by a description marked on or provided with a product to identify the suitability of the product for a specific purpose, environment, or application. Suitability of equipment may be evidenced by listing or labeling.

    (2) Mechanical strength and durability, including, for parts designed to enclose and protect other equipment, the adequacy of the protection thus provided.

    (3) Wire-bending and connection space.

(4) Electrical insulation.

(5) Heating effects under normal conditions of use and also under abnormal conditions likely to arise in service.

(6) Arcing effects.

(7) Classification by type, size, voltage, current capacity, specific use.

(8) Other factors which contribute to the practical safeguarding of persons using or likely to come in contact with the equipment.

For wire-bending and connection space see Sections 300-8 and 373-6, Tables 373-6(a) and 373-6(b), and Sections 373-7, 373-9, and 373-11.

(b) Installation and Use.   Listed or labeled equipment shall be used or installed in accordance with any instructions included in the listing or labeling.

It is very important to consider the listing or labeling installation instructions. For example, Section 210-52(a), Exception permits permanently installed electric baseboard heaters to be equipped with receptacle outlets that are the required receptacle outlets for the wall space utilized by such heaters. Installation instructions for such permanent baseboard heaters indicate that these heaters should not be mounted beneath a receptacle. In dwelling units, it is very common to use low-density heat units which may measure in excess of 12 ft in length; therefore, to meet the provisions of Section 210-52(a) first paragraph and also the installation instructions, a receptacle must be part of the heating unit as it should not be placed above it. See Figures 210-24 and 210-25.

110-4. Voltages.   Throughout this Code the voltage considered shall be that at which the circuit operates.

See definitions of "Voltage (of a Circuit)," "Voltage, Nominal," and "Voltage to Ground" in Article 100.
See also Sections 300-2 and 300-3.

110-5. Conductors.   Conductors normally used to carry current shall be of copper unless otherwise provided in this Code. Where the conductor material is not specified, the sizes given in this Code shall apply to copper conductors. Where other materials are used, the size shall be changed accordingly.

For aluminum and copper-clad aluminum conductors, see Tables 310-16 through 310-19.

See Section 310-14 for aluminum conductor material.

110-6. Conductor Sizes.   Conductor sizes are expressed in American Wire Gage (AWG) or in circular mils.

For copper, aluminum, or copper-clad aluminum conductors up to size No. 0000(4/0), this *Code* uses the American Wire Gage (AWG) for size identification, which is the same as the Brown and Sharpe Gage (BS).
Conductors larger than 4/0 are sized in circular mils, beginning with 250,000 circular mils (or 250 MCM). See Tables 310-16 through 310-19.
The circular mil (CM) area of a conductor is equal to its diameter, in mils, squared (1 in. equals 1,000 mils).
Example: The diameter of a No. 8 solid conductor is 0.1285 in.

$$0.1285 \text{ in.} \times 1,000 = 128.5 \text{ mils}$$
$$128.5 \times 128.5 \quad\quad = 16512.25 \text{ CM}$$

or 16510 'CM, as rounded off by Table 8 of Chapter 9.

This represents the circular mil area for one conductor. Where stranded conductors are used, the resulting figure must be multiplied by the number of strands (see Table 8 of Chapter 9).

110-7. Insulation Integrity. All wiring shall be so installed that when completed the system will be free from short circuits and from grounds other than as permitted in Article 250.

Insulation is the material between points of different potential in an electrical system preventing the flow of electricity between those points. Failure of the insulation system is one of the most common causes of problems in electrical installations. This is true on both high-voltage and low-voltage systems.

Insulation tests are performed on new or existing installations to determine the quality or condition of the insulation of conductors and/or equipment.

The principal causes of insulation failures are heat, moisture, and dirt. Insulation can also fail due to chemical attack, mechanical damage, sunlight, and excessive voltage stresses.

In an insulation resistance test, an applied voltage from 100 to 5,000 V (usually 500 to 1,000 V for systems of 600 V or less), supplied from a source of constant potential, is applied across the insulation. A hand-generated megohmmeter is the usual potential source, and it indicates the insulation resistance directly on a scale calibrated in megohms. The quality of the insulation is evaluated based on the level of the insulation resistance.

The insulation resistance of many types of insulation is quite variable with temperature, so the data obtained should be corrected to the standard temperature for the class of equipment under test. Some published charts are available for this purpose.

The megohm value of insulation resistance obtained will be inversely proportional to the volume of insulation being tested. As an example, a cable 1,000 ft long would be expected to have one-tenth the insulation resistance of a cable 100 ft long if all other conditions were identical.

The insulation resistance test is relatively easy to perform and is useful on all types and classes of electrical equipment. Its main value lies in the charting of data from periodic tests, corrected for temperature, over the life of the equipment so that deteriorative trends might be detected.

Excellent manuals on this subject are available from instrument manufacturers, such as the James G. Biddle Co., Plymouth Meeting, PA. Thorough knowledge in the use of insulation testers is essential if the test results are to be meaningful.

See Figure 110-1 for a typical megohmmeter insulation tester.

110-8. Wiring Methods. Only wiring methods recognized as suitable are included in this Code. The recognized methods of wiring shall be permitted to be installed in any type of building or occupancy, except as otherwise provided in this Code.

The scope of Article 300 applies generally to all wiring methods, except as amended, modified, or supplemented by Chapter 5 (Special Occupancies), Chapter 6 (Special Equipment), and Chapter 7 (Special Conditions).

Chapter 8 (Communications Systems) is independent of the other chapters except where it is specifically referenced by the *Code*.

110-9. Interrupting Rating. Equipment intended to break current at fault levels shall have an interrupting rating sufficient for the system voltage and the current which is available at the line terminals of the equipment.

Figure 110-1. Multivoltage multirange insulation tester. (*James G. Biddle Co.*)

Equipment intended to break current at other than fault levels shall have an interrupting rating at system voltage sufficient for the current that must be interrupted.

Section 110-9 states that all fuses and circuit breakers intended to break the circuit at fault levels must have an adequate interrupting rating wherever they are used in the electrical system. Fuses or circuit breakers which do not have adequate interrupting ratings could rupture while attempting to clear a short circuit.

Instructions for calculating available short-circuit currents are provided in ANSI Std. C37.010-1972, Application Guide for AC High-Voltage Circuit Breakers Rated on a Symmetrical Current Basis (IEEE Std. 3KA.520-1972). Additional details are provided in IEEE Std. 141-1976, Recommended Practice for Electric Power Distribution for Industrial Plants, Chapter 4; and IEEE Std. 241-1974, Recommended Practice for Electric Power Systems in Commercial Buildings, Chapter 9.

110-10. Circuit Impedance and Other Characteristics.   The overcurrent protective devices, the total impedance, the component short-circuit withstand ratings, and other characteristics of the circuit to be protected shall be so selected and coordinated as to permit the circuit protective devices used to clear a fault without the occurrence of extensive damage to the electrical components of the circuit. This fault shall be assumed to be either between two or more of the circuit conductors, or between any circuit conductor and the grounding conductor or enclosing metal raceway.

The basic purpose of overcurrent protection is to open the circuit before conductors or conductor insulation are damaged when an overcurrent condition exists. An overcurrent condition can be the result of an overload or a short circuit and must be removed before the conductor insulation damage point is reached.

Overcurrent protective devices (such as fuses and circuit breakers) should be selected in such a manner that the short-circuit rating of the system components will not be exceeded should a short circuit occur. System components include wire, bus structures, starters, etc., all of which have limited short-circuit ratings and would be damaged or destroyed if these short-circuit ratings are exceeded. Merely providing overcurrent protective devices with sufficient interrupting capacity will not assure short-circuit protection for the system components to be protected. When the available short-circuit current exceeds the withstand rating of an electrical component, the overcurrent protective device must limit the let-through energy to within the rating of that electrical component.

Utility companies usually determine and provide information on available short-circuit current at the service equipment. Literature on calculating short-circuit currents can be obtained by contacting representatives of manufacturers of overcurrent protective devices.

See Sections 230-98, 240-1, and 430-52.

The following information on cartridge fuses has been extracted from the UL Electrical Construction Materials List:

Fuses designated as Class K1, K5, K9 (0-600 A, 250 V, ac or 600 V, ac) are classified as to interrupting capacity and in terms of maximum clearing ampere squared seconds and maximum peak let-through current. They incorporate dimensional features equivalent to, and are interchangeable with, other nonrenewable cartridge fuses intended for installation in conventional designs of equipment recognized by the *Code* for branch circuit, service, and motor overload use. They are not marked "Current Limiting."

Fuses designated as Class RK1 and RK5 (0-600 A, 250 V, ac or 600 V, ac) are high interrupting capacity types and are marked "Current Limiting." They have maximum peak let-through currents and maximum clearing ampere squared seconds at 50,000, 100,000, and 200,000 rms symmetrical amperes.

They incorporate features that permit their insertion into holders for other nonrenewable cartridge fuses intended for installation in conventional designs of equipment recognized by the *NEC* for branch circuits, service, and motor overload use. They are provided with a feature that allows their insertion into rejection-type fuseholders designed to accept only Class RK1 or RK5 fuses.

The rejection-type fuseholders are used in equipment as covered in the *NEC*.

Fuses designated as Class G (0-60 A, 300 V, ac) are high interrupting capacity types and are marked "Current Limiting." They are not interchangeable with other fuses mentioned above and below.

Fuses designated as Class J (0-600 A, 600 V, ac) or Class L (601-6000 A, 600 V, ac) are high interrupting capacity types and are marked "Current Limiting." They are not interchangeable with other fuses such as those mentioned above.

Fuses designated as Class T (0-600 A, 250 and 600 V, ac) are high interrupting capacity types and are marked "Current Limiting." They are not interchangeable with other fuses mentioned above.

The term "Current Limiting" indicates that a fuse, when tested on a circuit capable of delivering a specific short-circuit current (rms amperes symmetrical) at rated voltage, will start to melt within 90 electrical degrees and will clear the circuit within 180 electrical degrees (1/2 cycle).

Because the time required for a fuse to melt is dependent on the available current of the circuit, a fuse which may be current limiting when subjected to a specific short-circuit current (rms amperes symmetrical) may not be current limiting on a circuit of lower maximum available current.

The performance of a fuse, as it is determined by the ability of the fuse to open and clear a circuit, is indicated by the following maximum permissible let-through values which are obtained when fuses of the Class K designs are connected to circuits having an available current of up to 100,000 A maximum (rms symmetrical) but not greater than the marked interrupting rating of the fuse if it is less than 100,000 A, when fuses of the Class G design are connected to circuits having an available current of 100,000 A maximum (rms symmetrical), and when fuses of the Class J, L, RK, and T designs are connected to circuits having available currents of 50,000, 100,000 and 200,000 A maximum (rms symmetrical).

Class K1, K5, and K9 fuses are marked, in addition to their regular voltage and current ratings, with an interrupting rating of 200,000, 100,000, or 50,000 A (rms symmetrical).

Class RK1, RK5, J, L, and T fuses are marked, in addition to their regular voltage and current ratings, with an interrupting rating of 200,000 A (rms symmetrical).

Equipment (switches, motor starters, panelboards, etc.) which has been investigated and found suitable for use with these fuses is marked with the class of fuse intended to be used in the equipment and an available current rating applicable to that piece of equipment.

The equipment, when so marked, with these fuses installed, is considered to be suitable for use on circuits which can deliver currents under short-circuit conditions up to the available current rating of the equipment or the interrupting rating of the fuse, whichever is lower.

An interrupting rating on a fuse included in a piece of equipment does not automatically qualify the equipment in which the fuses are installed for use on circuits with higher available currents than the rating of the equipment itself.

Class L fuses are designed for use in equipment to which line and load connections are made by means of solid busbars. For this reason temperature rises on Class L fuse blades may exceed those observed in connection with other cartridge fuse designs. Terminal connections for wires in such equipment must be designed to avoid excessive temperatures on the wire insulation.

Some manufacturers are in a position to provide fuses which are advertised and marked indicating they have "time delay" characteristics. In the case of Class G, Class H, Class K, and Class RK fuses, time delay characteristics of fuses (minimum blowing time) have been investigated. Class G fuses, which can carry 200 percent of rated current for 12 seconds or more, and Class H, Class K, or Class RK fuses, which can carry 500 percent of rated current for 10 seconds or more, may be marked with "D," "Time Delay," or some equivalent designation. Class L fuses are permitted to be marked "Time Delay" but have not been evaluated for such performance. Class J and T fuses are not permitted to be marked "Time Delay."

110-11. Deteriorating Agents.   Unless identified for use in the operating environment, no conductors or equipment shall be located in damp or wet locations; where exposed to gases, fumes, vapors, liquids, or other agents having a deteriorating effect on the conductors or equipment; nor where exposed to excessive temperatures.

See Section 300-6 for protection against corrosion.

Control equipment, utilization equipment, and busways approved for use in dry locations only shall be protected against permanent damage from the weather during building construction.

110-12. Mechanical Execution of Work.   Electric equipment shall be installed in a neat and workmanlike manner.

Unused openings in boxes, raceways, auxiliary gutters, cabinets, equipment cases or housings shall be effectively closed to afford protection substantially equivalent to the wall of the equipment.

Many *Code* conflicts or violations have been cited by the authority having jurisdiction based on his interpretation of "neat and workmanlike manner."

Many electrical inspection authorities use their own experience or precedents in their local areas as the basis for their judgments but they should realize that any ruling should be based on uniformity as intended by the National Electrical Code Committee.

Examples of installations that are considered not to be "neat and in a workmanlike manner" are exposed runs of cables or raceways that are improperly supported, that is, sagging between supports or using unapproved methods for supports; field-bent and kinked, flattened, or poorly measured raceways; or cabinets, cutout boxes, and enclosures that are not plumb or that are not properly secured.

110-13. Mounting and Cooling of Equipment.

(a) Mounting.   Electric equipment shall be firmly secured to the surface on which it is mounted. Wooden plugs driven into holes in masonry, concrete, plaster, or similar materials shall not be used.

(b) Cooling.   Electrical equipment which depends upon the natural circulation of air and convection principles for cooling of exposed surfaces shall be installed so that room air flow over such surfaces is not prevented by walls or by adjacent installed equipment. For equipment designed for floor mounting, clearance between top surfaces and adjacent surfaces shall be provided to dissipate rising warm air.

See Sections 430-14(a) and 430-16 for motor locations, and Sections 450-8 and 450-45 for transformer locations.

Electrical equipment provided with ventilating openings shall be installed so that walls or other obstructions do not prevent the free circulation of air through the equipment.

For example, a ventilated busway must be located where there are no walls, or other objects, that might interfere with the natural circulation of air and convection principles for cooling.

110-14. Electrical Connections.
Because of different characteristics of copper and aluminum, devices such as pressure terminal or pressure splicing connectors and soldering lugs shall be suitable for the material of the conductor and shall be properly installed and used. Conductors of dissimilar metals shall not be intermixed in a terminal or splicing connector where physical contact occurs between dissimilar conductors (such as copper and aluminum, copper and copper-clad aluminum, or aluminum and copper-clad aluminum), unless the device is suitable for the purpose and conditions of use. Materials such as solder, fluxes, inhibitors, and compounds, where employed, shall be suitable for the use and shall be of a type which will not adversely affect the conductors, installation, or equipment.

(a) Terminals.   Connection of conductors to terminal parts shall ensure a thoroughly good connection without damaging the conductors and shall be made by means of pressure connectors (including set-screw type), solder lugs, or splices to flexible leads.

Exception: Connection by means of wire binding screws or studs and nuts having upturned lugs or equivalent shall be permitted for No. 10 or smaller conductors.

Terminals for more than one conductor and terminals used to connect aluminum shall be so identified.

(b) Splices.   Conductors shall be spliced or joined with splicing devices suitable for the use or by brazing, welding, or soldering with a fusible metal or alloy. Soldered splices shall first be so spliced or joined as to be mechanically and electrically secure without solder and then soldered. All splices and joints and the free ends of conductors shall be covered with an insulation equivalent to that of the conductors or with an insulating device suitable for the purpose.

Field observations and trade magazine articles indicate that failures of electrical connections are the cause of many equipment burn-outs and fires. Many of these failures are attributable to improper terminations, poor workmanship, different characteristics of dissimilar metals, and improper binding screws or splicing devices.

Recent revisions in Underwriters Laboratories Inc. requirements for listing solid aluminum conductors in sizes No. 12 and No. 10 AWG and for listing snap switches and receptacles for use on 15- and 20-A branch circuits incorporate stringent tests which take the factors listed in the previous paragraph into account. See Sections 380-14(c) and 410-56(g).

Screwless pressure terminal connectors of the conductor push-in type are for use with copper and copper-clad aluminum conductors only.

Instructions describing proper installation techniques and emphasizing the need to follow these techniques and practice good workmanship are required to be included with each coil of No. 12 and No. 10 AWG insulated aluminum wire or cable.

New product and material designs which provide for increased levels of safety of aluminum wire terminations have recently been developed by the electrical industry.

To assist all concerned parties in the proper and safe use of solid aluminum wire in making connections to wiring devices used on 15- and 20-A branch circuits, the following information is presented. Understanding and utilizing this information is essential to proper application of materials and devices now available.

For New Installations

The following was prepared by the Ad Hoc Committee on Aluminum Terminations: Comply with Section 110-14(a) of the 1981 *NEC* when aluminum wire is used in new installations.

New Materials and Devices
   a.   For direct connection use only 15- and 20-A receptacles and switches marked "CO/ALR" and connected as described under "Installation Method."

The "CO/ALR" marking is on the device mounting strap. The "CO/ALR" marking means the devices have been tested to stringent heat cycling requirements to determine their suitability for use with UL labeled aluminum, copper, or copper-clad aluminum wire.

1. Strip wires ⅝" 2. Pretwisting unnecessary. Hold stripped wires together with ends even. (Lead stranded wires slightly.) 3. Screw on connector—push wires firmly into connector when starting. COPPER TO COPPER ALUMINUM TO ALUMINUM	Typical connector carton marking
COPPER TO ALUMINUM (dry locations only)	
Temperature rating: 150°C. (302°F.) Max. Listed as a PRESSURE TYPE wire connector on the following solid and/or stranded wire combinations.	

2 or 3 #8	3 #10 with 1 or 2 #14
2 #8 with 1 or 2 #10	→2 #10 with 1,2,3, or 4 #12
2 #8 with 1,2, or 3 #12	2 #10 with 1,2, or 3 #14
1 #8 with 1,2,3, or 4 #10	1 #10 with 1,2,3,4, or 5 #12
1 #8 with 1,2,3,4, or 5 #12	1 #10 with 1,2,3, or 4 #14
3 #8 with 1 #12	2,3,4,5, or 6 #12
2,3,4, or 5 #10	4 #12 with 1 or 2 #14
5 #10 with 1 #12	3 #12 with 1,2, or 3 #14
4 #10 with 1 or 2 #12	→2 #12 with 1,2, or 3 #14
4 #10 with 1 #14	1 #12 with 2,3, or 4 #14
3 #10 with 1,2, or 3 #12	

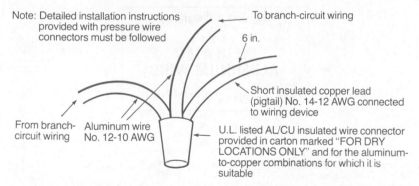

Note: Detailed installation instructions provided with pressure wire connectors must be followed

To branch-circuit wiring

6 in.

Short insulated copper lead (pigtail) No. 14-12 AWG connected to wiring device

From branch-circuit wiring   Aluminum wire No. 12-10 AWG

U.L. listed AL/CU insulated wire connector provided in carton marked "FOR DRY LOCATIONS ONLY" and for the aluminum-to-copper combinations for which it is suitable

Figure 110-2. Pigtailing copper to aluminum conductor. (*Underwriters Laboratories Inc.*)

Note. Pigtailing, either field- or factory-wired, as illustrated in Figure 110-2, is recognized by the *NEC.*

b.   Use solid aluminum wire, No. 12 or No. 10 AWG, marked with the Underwriters Laboratories' new aluminum insulated wire label, as shown in Figure 110-3. Follow the installation instructions packaged with the wire. Conductor bearing this UL label is judged under the requirements for the chemistry, physical properties, and processing of the conductor which became effective September 20, 1972.

Installation Method

1.   Wrap the freshly stripped end of the wire two-thirds to three-quarters of the distance around the wire-binding screw post, as shown in Step A of Figure 110-3.

The loop is made so that rotation of the screw in tightening will tend to wrap the wire around the post rather than unwrap it.

2.   Tighten the screw until the wire is snugly in contact with the underside of the screw head and with the contact plate on the wiring device, as shown in Step B of Figure 110-3.

3.   Tighten the screw an additional one-half turn, thereby providing a firm connection. Where torque screwdrivers are used, tighten to 12 pound inches. See Step C of Figure 110-3.

4.   Position the wires behind the wiring device so as to decrease the likelihood of the terminal screws loosening when the device is positioned into the outlet box.

Figure 110-4 illustrates incorrect methods for connection and should not be used.

Existing Inventory

When UL-labeled solid aluminum wire No. 12 and No. 10 AWG not bearing the new aluminum wire label is used, it should be used with wiring devices marked "CO/ALR" and connected as described in "Installation Method." This is the preferred and recommended method for using such wire.

Note. Pigtailing, either field- or factory-wired, as illustrated in Figure 110-2, is recognized by the *NEC.*

In the following types of devices the terminals shall not be directly connected to

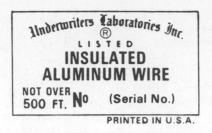

PRINTED IN U.S.A.

Correct method of terminating aluminum wire at wire-binding-screw terminals of receptacles and snap switches

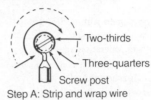

Two-thirds

Three-quarters

Screw post

Step A: Strip and wrap wire

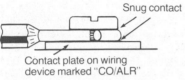

Snug contact

Contact plate on wiring device marked "CO/ALR"

Step B: Tighten screw to full contact

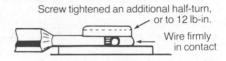

Screw tightened an additional half-turn, or to 12 lb-in.

Wire firmly in contact

Step C: Complete connection

Figure 110-3. Correct method of terminating aluminum wire at wire-binding screw terminals of receptacles and snap switches. (*Underwriters Laboratories Inc.*)

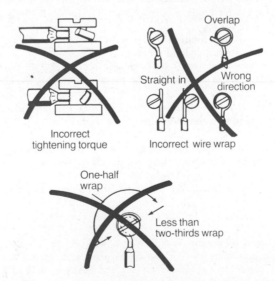

Overlap

Straight in

Wrong direction

Incorrect tightening torque

Incorrect wire wrap

One-half wrap

Less than two-thirds wrap

Figure 110-4. Incorrect methods of terminating aluminum wire at wire-binding screw terminals of receptacles and snap switches. (*Underwriters Laboratories Inc.*)

aluminum conductors but may be used with UL-labeled copper or copper-clad conductors:

Receptacles and snap switches marked "AL-CU"

Receptacles and snap switches having no conductor marking
Receptacles and snap switches having backwired terminals or screwless terminals of the push-in type.

For Existing Installations

If examination discloses overheating or loose connections the recommendations described under "For New Installations Existing Inventory" should be followed.

110-16. Working Space About Electric Equipment (600 Volts, Nominal, or Less). Sufficient access and working space shall be provided and maintained about all electric equipment to permit ready and safe operation and maintenance of such equipment.

(a) Working Clearances. Except as elsewhere required or permitted in this Code, the dimension of the working space in the direction of access to live parts operating at 600 volts, nominal, or less and likely to require examination, adjustment, servicing, or maintenance while alive shall not be less than indicated in Table 110-16(a). Distances shall be measured from the live parts if such are exposed or from the enclosure front or opening if such are enclosed. Concrete, brick, or tile walls shall be considered as grounded.

In addition to the dimensions shown in Table 110-16(a), the work space shall not be less than 30 inches (762 mm) wide in front of the electric equipment.

Note that the 30-in. wide dimension is intended to be clear all the way to the floor. See Figures 110-5 and 110-6.

Table 110-16(a). Working Clearances

Voltage to Ground, Nominal		Minimum Clear Distance (feet)		
	Condition:	1	2	3
0-150		3	3	3
151-600		3	3½	4

For SI units: one inch = 25.4 millimeters; one foot = 0.3048 meter.

Where the "Conditions" are as follows:

1. Exposed live parts on one side and no live or grounded parts on the other side of the working space, or exposed live parts on both sides effectively guarded by suitable wood or other insulating materials. Insulated wire or insulated busbars operating at not over 300 volts shall not be considered live parts.

2. Exposed live parts on one side and grounded parts on the other side.

3. Exposed live parts on both sides of the work space (not guarded as provided in Condition 1) with the operator between.

Exception No. 1: Working space shall not be required in back of assemblies such as dead-front switchboards, or motor control centers where there are no renewable or adjustable parts such as fuses or switches on the back and where all connections are accessible from locations other than the back.

Exception No. 2: By special permission smaller spaces may be permitted (1) where it is judged that the particular arrangement of the installation will provide adequate accessibility, or (2) where all uninsulated parts are at a voltage no greater than 30 volts RMS or 42V dc.

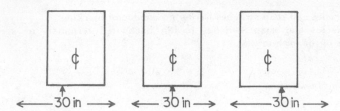

Figure 110-5. The 30-inch wide front work space need not be directly centered on the electrical equipment where it is assured that the space is sufficient for safe operation and maintenance of such equipment.

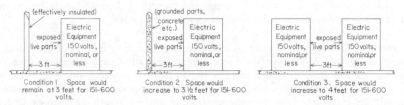

Figure 110-6. Distances are measured from the live parts if such are exposed or from the enclosure front if live parts are enclosed. If any assemblies, such as switchboards or motor-control centers, are accessible from the back and expose live parts, the working clearance dimensions would be required at the rear of the equipment as illustrated above.

(b) Clear Spaces.   Working space required by this section shall not be used for storage. When normally enclosed live parts are exposed for inspection or servicing, the working space, if in a passageway or general open space, shall be suitably guarded.

(c) Access and Entrance to Working Space.   At least one entrance of sufficient area shall be provided to give access to the working space about electric equipment. For switchboards and control panels rated 1200 amperes or more and over 6 feet (1.83 m) wide, there shall be one entrance not less than 24 inches (610 mm) wide at each end where reasonably practicable.

(d) Front Working Space.   In all cases where there are live parts normally exposed on the front of switchboards or motor control centers, the working space in front of such equipment shall not be less than 3 feet (914 mm).

(e) Illumination.   Illumination shall be provided for all working spaces about service equipment, switchboards, panelboards, or motor control centers installed indoors.

Exception: Service equipment or panelboards, in dwelling units, that do not exceed 200 amperes.

(f) Headroom.   The minimum headroom of working spaces about service equipment, switchboards, panelboards, or motor control centers shall be 6¼ feet (1.91 m).

Exception: Service equipment or panelboards, in dwelling units, that do not exceed 200 amperes.

For higher voltages, see Article 710.

As used in this section, a motor control center is an assembly of one or more enclosed sections having a common power bus and principally containing motor control units.

110-17. Guarding of Live Parts (600 Volts, Nominal, or Less).

(a) Except as elsewhere required or permitted by this Code, live parts of electric equipment

Figure 110-7. A switchgear in a NEMA 3R walk-in enclosure with two entry doors to meet the requirements of 110-16(c) and overhead illumination to meet the intent of 110-16(e). (*Square D Co.*)

operating at 50 volts or more shall be guarded against accidental contact by approved enclosures or by any of the following:

(1) By location in a room, vault, or similar enclosure that is accessible only to qualified persons.

(2) By suitable permanent, substantial partitions or screens so arranged that only qualified persons will have access to the space within reach of the live parts. Any openings in such partitions or screens shall be so sized and located that persons are not likely to come into accidental contact with the live parts or to bring conducting objects into contact with them.

(3) By location on a suitable balcony, gallery, or platform so elevated and arranged as to exclude unqualified persons.

(4) By elevation of 8 feet (2.44 m) or more above the floor or other working surface.

For example, see the requirements of Sections 610-13, Exception No. 2 and 610-21(a). Although contact conductors obviously need to be bare in order for contact shoes on the moving member to make contact with the conductor, it is also possible to place guards near the conductor to prevent accidental contact with it by persons and yet have slots or spaces through which the moving contacts can operate. Note that the *Code* also recognizes the guarding of live parts by elevation.

(b) In locations where electric equipment would be exposed to physical damage, enclosures or guards shall be so arranged and of such strength as to prevent such damage.

(c) Entrances to rooms and other guarded locations containing exposed live parts shall be marked with conspicuous warning signs forbidding unqualified persons to enter.

For motors, see Sections 430-132 and 430-133. For over 600 volts, see Section 110-34.

Live parts of electric equipment should be covered, shielded, enclosed, or otherwise protected by covers, barriers, mats, or platforms to remove the likelihood of contact by persons or objects. See definitions for "Dead Front," "Guarded," and "Isolated" in Article 100.

110-18. Arcing Parts.   Parts of electric equipment which in ordinary operation produce arcs, sparks, flames, or molten metal shall be enclosed or separated and isolated from all combustible material.

For hazardous (classified) locations, see Articles 500 through 517. For motors, see Section 430-14.

An example of electric equipment that in "ordinary" operation produces sparks is an open motor having commutators or collection rings. Adequate separation from combustible material is necessary where open motors are used.

110-19. Light and Power from Railway Conductors.   Circuits for lighting and power shall not be connected to any system containing trolley wires with a ground return.

Exception: Car houses, power houses, or passenger and freight stations operated in connection with electric railways.

110-21. Marking.   The manufacturer's name, trademark, or other descriptive marking by which the organization responsible for the product may be identified shall be placed on all electric equipment. Other markings shall be provided giving voltage, current, wattage, or other ratings as are specified elsewhere in this Code. The marking shall be of sufficient durability to withstand the environment involved.

The *Code* requires that the rating of equipment be marked on the equipment and that such markings be located so as to be visible or easily accessible, during or after installation.

110-22. Identification of Disconnecting Means.   Each disconnecting means required by this Code for motors and appliances, and each service, feeder, or branch circuit at the point where it originates shall be legibly marked to indicate its purpose unless located and arranged so the purpose is evident. The marking shall be of sufficient durability to withstand the environment involved.

Note that proper identification is to be specific. For example, it is not merely to indicate "motor," but rather "motor, water pump"; not merely "lights," but rather "lights, front lobby."

B. Over 600 Volts, Nominal

110-30. General.   Conductors and equipment used on circuits over 600 volts, nominal, shall comply with all applicable provisions of the preceding sections of this article and with the following sections, which supplement or modify the preceding sections. In no case shall the provisions of this part apply to equipment on the supply side of the service conductors.

110-31. Enclosure for Electrical Installations.   Electrical installations in a vault, room, or closet or in an area surrounded by a wall, screen, or fence, access to which is controlled by lock and key or other approved means, shall be considered to be accessible to qualified persons only. The type of enclosure used in a given case shall be designed and constructed according to the nature and degree of the hazard(s) associated with the installation.

A wall, screen, or fence less than 8 feet (2.44 m) in height shall not be considered as preventing access unless it has other features that provide a degree of isolation equivalent to an 8-foot (2.44-m) fence.

Article 450 covers minimum construction requirements for transformer vaults.
Isolation by elevation is covered in paragraph (b) of this section and in Section 110-34.

(a) Indoor Installations.

(1) In Places Accessible to Unqualified Persons.   Indoor electrical installations that are open to unqualified persons shall be made with metal-enclosed equipment or shall be enclosed in a vault or in an area access to which is controlled by a lock. Metal-enclosed switchgear, unit substations, transformers, pull boxes, connection boxes, and other similar associated equipment shall be marked with appropriate caution signs. Openings in ventilated dry-type transformers or similar openings in other equipment shall be designed so that foreign objects inserted through these openings will be deflected from energized parts.

(2) In Places Accessible to Qualified Persons Only.   Indoor electrical installations considered accessible to qualified persons only in accordance with this section shall comply with Sections 110-34, 710-32, and 710-33.

(b) Outdoor Installations.

(1) In Places Accessible to Unqualified Persons.   Outdoor electrical installations that are open to unqualified persons shall comply with Article 225.

For clearances of conductors for system voltages over 600 volts, nominal, see National Electrical Safety Code (ANSI C2-1977).

(2) In Places Accessible to Qualified Persons Only.   Outdoor electrical installations having exposed live parts shall be accessible to qualified persons only in accordance with the first paragraph of this section and shall comply with Sections 110-34, 710-32, and 710-33.

(c) Metal-Enclosed Equipment Accessible to Unqualified Persons.   Ventilating or similar openings in equipment shall be so designed that foreign objects inserted through these openings will be deflected from energized parts. When exposed to physical damage from vehicular traffic suitable guards shall be provided. Metal-enclosed equipment located outdoors accessible to the general public shall be designed so that exposed nuts or bolts cannot be readily removed, permitting access to live parts. Where metal-enclosed equipment is accessible to the general public and the bottom of the enclosure is less than 8 feet (2.44 m) above the floor or grade level, the enclosure door or hinged cover shall be kept locked.

110-32. Workspace about Equipment.   Sufficient space shall be provided and maintained about electric equipment to permit ready and safe operation and maintenance of such equipment. Where energized parts are exposed, the minimum clear workspace shall not be less than 6½ feet (1.98 m) high (measured vertically from the floor or platform), or less than 3 feet (914 mm) wide (measured parallel to the equipment). The depth shall be as required in Section 110-34(a). In all cases, the workspace shall be adequate to permit at least a 90-degree opening of doors or hinged panels.

110-33. Entrance and Access to Workspace.

(a) At least one entrance not less than 24 inches (610 mm) wide and 6½ feet (1.98 m) high shall be provided to give access to the working space about electric equipment. On switchboard and control panels exceeding 48 inches (1.22 m) in width, there shall be one entrance at each end of such board where reasonably practicable. Where bare energized parts at any voltage or insulated energized parts above 600 volts, nominal, are located adjacent to such entrance, they shall be suitably guarded.

(b) Permanent ladders or stairways shall be provided to give safe access to the working space around electric equipment installed on platforms, balconies, mezzanine floors, or in attic or roof rooms or spaces.

110-34. Work Space and Guarding.

(a) Working Space.   The minimum clear working space in front of electric equipment such as switchboards, control panels, switches, circuit breakers, motor controllers, relays, and similar equipment shall not be less than specified in Table 110-34(a) unless otherwise specified in this Code. Distances shall be measured from the live parts if such are exposed, or from the enclosure front or opening if such are enclosed.

Table 110-34(a)

Minimum Depth of Clear Working Space in Front of Electric Equipment

Nominal	Conditions		
Voltage to Ground	1	2	3
	(Feet)	(Feet)	(Feet)
601-2500	3	4	5
2501-9000	4	5	6
9001-25,000	5	6	9
25,001-75 kV	6	8	10
Above 75 kV	8	10	12

For SI units: one foot = 0.3048 meter.

Where the "Conditions" are as follows:

1.   Exposed live parts on one side and no live or grounded parts on the other side of the working space or exposed live parts on both sides effectively guarded by suitable wood or other insulating materials. Insulated wire or insulated busbars operating at not over 300 volts shall not be considered live parts.

2.   Exposed live parts on one side and grounded parts on the other side. Concrete, brick, or tile walls will be considered as grounded surfaces.

3.   Exposed live parts on both sides of the work space (not guarded as provided in Condition 1) with the operator between.

Exception: Working space is not required in back of equipment such as dead-front switchboards or control assemblies where there are no renewable or adjustable parts (such as fuses or switches) on the back and where all connections are accessible from locations other than the back. Where rear access is required to work on de-energized parts on the back of enclosed equipment, a minimum working space of 30 inches (762 mm) horizontally shall be provided.

(b) Separation from Low-Potential Equipment.   Where switches, cutouts, or other equipment operating at 600 volts, nominal, or less, are installed in a room or enclosure where there are exposed live parts or exposed wiring operating at over 600 volts, nominal, the high-potential equipment shall be effectively separated from the space occupied by the low-potential equipment by a suitable partition, fence, or screen.

Exception: Switches or other equipment operating at 600 volts, nominal, or less, and serving only equipment within the high-voltage vault, room, or enclosure may be installed in the high-voltage enclosure, room, or vault if accessible to qualified persons only.

(c) Locked Rooms or Enclosures.   The entrances to all buildings, rooms, or enclosures containing exposed live parts or exposed conductors operating at over 600 volts, nominal, shall be kept locked.

Equipment used on circuits over 600 volts, nominal, containing exposed live parts or exposed conductors is to be located in a locked room or enclosure. The provisions for locking are not required where the location is under observation at all times such as some engine rooms.

Exception: Where such entrances are under the observation of a qualified person at all times.

Where the voltage exceeds 600 volts, nominal, permanent and conspicuous warning signs shall be provided, reading substantially as follows: "Warning—High Voltage—Keep Out."

(d) Illumination.   Adequate illumination shall be provided for all working spaces about electrical equipment. The lighting outlets shall be so arranged that persons changing lamps or making repairs on the lighting system will not be endangered by live parts or other equipment.

The points of control shall be so located that persons are not likely to come in contact with any live part or moving part of the equipment while turning on the lights.

(e) Elevation of Unguarded Live Parts.   Unguarded live parts above working space shall be maintained at elevations not less than required by Table 110-34(e).

Table 110-34(e)
Elevation of Unguarded Live Parts above Working Space

Nominal Voltage Between Phases	Elevation
601-7500	8'6"
7501-35000	9'
Over 35kV	9' +0.37" per kV above 35

For SI units: one inch = 25.4 millimeters; one foot = 0.3048 meter.

2 WIRING DESIGN AND PROTECTION

ARTICLE 200 — USE AND IDENTIFICATION
OF GROUNDED CONDUCTORS

Contents

200-1. Scope. This article provides requirements for: (1) identification of terminals; (2) grounded conductors in premises wiring systems; and (3) identification of grounded conductors.

See Article 100 for definitions of "Grounded Conductor" and "Grounding Conductor."

200-2. General. All premises wiring systems shall have a grounded conductor that is identified in accordance with Section 200-6.

Exception: Circuits and systems exempted or prohibited by Sections 210-10, 215-7, 250-3, 250-5, 250-7, 503-13, and 517-104.

Isolated circuits are required in hazardous areas of hospital anesthetizing locations. The ungrounded conductors of these circuits are colored orange and brown (for 3-phase systems, the third conductor is yellow) and are provided with a continually operating "Line Isolation Monitor." See Section 517-104(d) and (e). See also NFPA 56A, Standard for the Use of Inhalation Anesthetics.

The grounded conductor, when insulated, shall have insulation: (1) which is suitable, other than color, for any ungrounded conductor of the same circuit on circuits of less than 1000 volts, or (2) rated not less than 600 volts for solidly grounded neutral systems of 1 kV and over as described in Section 250-152(a).

This paragraph is intended to correlate Section 200-2, which requires full system voltage rating for neutral conductor insulation, and Section 250-152, which only requires 600-volt rating on the insulation of high-voltage solidly grounded neutral conductors.

47

200-3. Connection to Grounded System.   Premises wiring shall not be electrically connected to a supply system unless the latter contains, for any grounded conductor of the interior system, a corresponding conductor which is grounded.

For the purpose of this section, "electrically connected" shall mean connection capable of carrying current as distinguished from connection through electromagnetic induction.

Grounded conductors of premises wiring are to be connected to the premises system grounded conductor to assure a common, continuous grounded system.

200-6. Means of Identifying Grounded Conductors.

(a) Sizes No. 6 or Smaller.   An insulated grounded conductor of No. 6 or smaller shall be identified by a continuous white or natural gray outer finish along its entire length.

Exception No. 1: The grounded conductor of a mineral-insulated, metal-sheathed cable shall be identified at the time of installation by distinctive marking at its terminations.

See Figure 200-1.

Exception No. 2: Where the conditions of maintenance and supervision assure that only qualified persons will service the installation, grounded conductors in multiconductor cables shall be permitted to be permanently identified at their terminations at the time of installation by a distinctive white marking or other equally effective means.

See Figure 200-2.

(b) Sizes Larger than No. 6.   An insulated grounded conductor larger than No. 6 shall be identified either by a continuous white or natural gray outer finish along its entire length or at the time of installation by a distinctive white marking at its terminations.

See Figure 200-3.

Exception: Where the conditions of maintenance and supervision assure that only qualified persons will service the installation, grounded conductors in multiconductor cables shall be permitted to be permanently identified at their terminations at the time of installation by a distinctive white marking or other equally effective means.

(c) Flexible Cords.   An insulated conductor intended for use as a grounded conductor, where contained within a flexible cord, shall be identified by a white or natural gray outer finish or by methods permitted by Section 400-22.

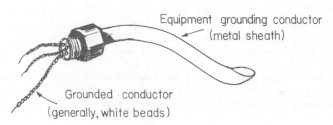

Figure 200-1. The grounded conductor of Type MI cable is identified at the time of installation by selecting a conductor, which is bare at this time, and after a continuity test, identifying it at both ends with white beads or other approved insulating material.

Article 200 contains the grounded circuit identification requirements. The grounded circuit conductor is referred to throughout the *Code* as the neutral conductor or the grounded conductor. The *NEC* formerly made recommendations for identification of ungrounded circuit conductors for branch circuits. Section 210-5, however, no longer requires or recommends an identification scheme for ungrounded branch-circuit conductors.

Section 215-8, covering 3-phase, 4-wire delta connected systems with the midpoint of one phase grounded, requires that the higher phase-to-ground conductor is to be identified by the color orange, by tagging, or by some other effective means at every point of connection where the neutral is also present. The high leg of 120/240 4-wire, 3-phase delta systems is 208 V to ground (120 V x 1.73).

Both Sections 200-6(a) and (b) contain Exceptions introducing a concept for identifying grounded conductors of multiconductor cables. These Exceptions allow the identification of conductors at the time of installation by a distinctive white marking or other equally effective means. A variety of other schemes, equally effective, include numbering, lettering, or tagging. These Exceptions are intended to apply in locations where a regulated system of maintenance and supervision assures that only qualified persons will service the installation.

For the identification of branch-circuit conductors, see Section 210-5. For the identification of the high leg (delta system) conductor, see Section 215-8. See Section 384-3(f) for the phase arrangement of 3-phase buses on switchboards and panelboards.

200-7. Use of White or Natural Gray Color.   A continuous white or natural gray covering on a conductor or a termination marking of white or natural gray color shall be used only for the grounded conductor.

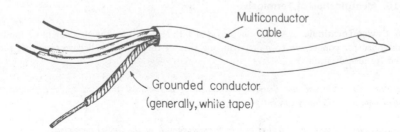

Figure 200-2. The grounded conductor of multiconductor cable is identified at the time of installation by qualified persons, generally in commercial or industrial locations, where supervision and maintenance are assured. This method is permitted for all sizes of conductors of multiconductor cables.

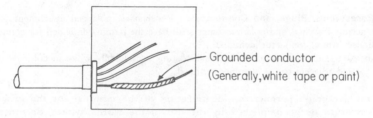

Figure 200-3. All conductors are larger than No. 6.

Exception No. 1: An insulated conductor with a white or natural gray finish shall be permitted as an ungrounded conductor where permanently reidentified to indicate its use, by painting or other effective means at its termination, and at each outlet where the conductor is visible and accessible.

Exception No. 2: A cable containing an insulated conductor with a white or natural gray outer finish shall be permitted for single-pole, 3-way, or 4-way switch loops where the white or natural gray conductor is used for the supply to the switch, but not as a return conductor from the switch to the switched outlet. In these applications, reidentification of the white or natural gray conductor shall not be required.

Exception No. 3: A flexible cord for connecting an appliance having one conductor identified with a white or natural gray outer finish, or by any other means permitted by Section 400-22, shall be permitted whether or not the outlet to which it is connected is supplied by a circuit having a grounded conductor.

Exception No. 4: A white or natural gray conductor of circuits of less than 50 volts shall be required to be grounded only as required by Section 250-5(a).

200-9. Means of Identification of Terminals.   The identification of terminals to which a grounded conductor is to be connected shall be substantially white in color. The identification of other terminals shall be of a readily distinguishable different color.

Exception: Where the conditions of maintenance and supervision assure that only qualified persons will service the installations, terminals for grounded conductors shall be permitted to be permanently identified at the time of installation by a distinctive white marking or other equally effective means.

See the comments following Section 200-6.

200-10. Identification of Terminals.

(a) Device Terminals.   All devices provided with terminals for the attachment of conductors and intended for connection to more than one side of the circuit shall have terminals properly marked for identification.

Exception No. 1: Where the electrical connection of a terminal intended to be connected to the grounded conductor is clearly evident.

Exception No. 2: Single-pole devices to which only one side of the line is connected.

Exception No. 3: The terminals of lighting and appliance branch-circuit panelboards.

Exception No. 4: Devices having a normal current rating of over 30 amperes other than polarized attachment plugs and polarized receptacles for attachment plugs as required in (b) below.

(b) Receptacles, Plugs, and Connectors.   Receptacles, polarized attachment plugs and cord connectors for plugs and polarized plugs shall have the terminal intended for connection to the grounded (white) conductor identified.
Identification shall be by a metal or metal coating substantially white in color or the word "white" located adjacent to the identified terminal.

This paragraph permits the identification of the terminal for the grounded conductor to be accomplished by the use of the word "white" or otherwise identified by a distinctive white color on all devices including those with binding head screws. These permitted methods would allow plating of all screws and terminals to meet requirements of specific applications, such as corrosion-resistant devices.

If the terminal is not visible, the conductor entrance hole for the connection shall be colored white or marked with the word "white."

The terminal for the connection of the equipment grounding conductor shall be identified by: (1) a green-colored, not readily removable terminal screw with a hexagonal head; (2) a green-colored, hexagonal, not readily removable terminal nut; or (3) a green-colored pressure wire connector. If the terminal for the grounding conductor is not visible, the conductor entrance hole shall be marked with the word "green" or otherwise identified by a distinctive green color.

Exception: Terminal identification shall not be required for 2-wire nonpolarized attachment plugs.

This Exception coordinates with Section 410-42(a) and makes it clear that two-wire "polarized" attachment plugs are to have the grounded terminal identified.

(c) Screw Shells. For devices with screw shells, the terminal for the grounded conductor shall be the one connected to the screw shell.

(d) Screw-Shell Devices with Leads. For screw-shell devices with attached leads, the conductor attached to the screw shell shall have a white or natural gray finish. The outer finish of the other conductor shall be of a solid color that will not be confused with the white or natural gray finish used to identify the grounded conductor.

(e) Appliances. Appliances that have a single-pole switch or a single-pole overcurrent device in the line or any line-connected screw-shell lampholders, and that are to be connected (1) by permanent wiring methods or (2) by field-installed attachment plugs and cords with three or more wires (including the equipment grounding conductor) shall have means to identify the terminal for the grounded circuit conductor (if any).

The "means" for identifying the terminal for the grounded conductor may be by a metal, or metal coating, substantially white in color or by the word "white" located adjacent to the terminal to be so identified.

200-11. Polarity of Connections. No grounded conductor shall be attached to any terminal or lead so as to reverse designated polarity.

ARTICLE 210 — BRANCH CIRCUITS

Contents

A. General Provisions

210-1. Scope. The provisions of this article apply to branch circuits supplying lighting or appliance loads or combinations of both. Where motors or motor-operated appliances are connected to any branch circuit that also supplies lighting or other appliance loads, the provisions of both this article and Article 430 shall apply. Article 430 applies where a branch circuit supplies motor loads only.

Exception: See Section 668-3(c), Exceptions No. 1 and No. 4 for electrolytic cells.

Section 668-3(c), Exception Nos. 1 and 4 indicate that electrolytic cell line conductors, cells, cell line attachments, and the wiring of auxiliary equipment and devices within the cell line working zone are not required to comply with the provisions of Article 210.

210-2. Other Articles for Specific-Purpose Branch Circuits. Branch circuits shall comply with this article and also with the applicable provisions of other articles of this Code. The provisions for branch circuits supplying equipment in the following list amend or supplement the provisions in this article and shall apply to branch circuits referred to therein:

	Article	Section
Air-Conditioning and Refrigerating Equipment		440-5
		440-31
		440-32
Busways		364-9
Class 1, Class 2, and Class 3 Remote Control, Signaling, and Power-Limited Circuits	725	

210-3. Classifications. Branch circuits recognized by this article shall be classified in accordance with the maximum permitted ampere rating or setting of the overcurrent device. The classification for other than individual branch circuits shall be: 15, 20, 30, 40, and 50 amperes. Where conductors of higher ampacity are used for any reason, the ampere rating or setting of the specified overcurrent device shall determine the circuit classification.

210-4. Multiwire Branch Circuits. Branch circuits recognized by this article shall be permitted as multiwire circuits. Multiwire branch circuits shall supply only line to neutral load.

Exception No. 1: A multiwire branch circuit that supplies only one utilization equipment.

Exception No. 2: Where all ungrounded conductors of the multiwire branch circuit are opened simultaneously by the branch-circuit overcurrent device.

Article 100 defines "Branch Circuit, Multiwire" as two or more ungrounded conductors having a potential difference between them, and a grounded conductor having an equal potential difference between it and each ungrounded conductor.

The circuit generally used as a multiwire branch circuit consists of two ungrounded conductors and one grounded conductor supplied from a single-phase, 3-wire system. Multiwire branch circuits have many advantages, such as three wires doing the work of four (in place of two 2-wire circuits), less conduit fill, easier balancing and phasing of a system, and less voltage drop (see comments following Section 215-2).

Other multiwire branch circuits are 3-phase, 4-wire; 2-phase, 3-wire; and 2-phase, 5-wire. It is always advisable to properly balance all multiwire branch circuits. In a 3-phase, 4-wire circuit the neutral could be called upon to carry a current equal to that carried by each of the 3-phase conductors and should, therefore, be sized the same. The neutral capacity for a 2-phase, 3-wire circuit is to be multiplied by 140 percent of the ampere rating of the circuit. See Section 220-22.

Where loads are connected "line-to-line" (utilization equipment connected between two or three phases), it requires 2-pole or 3-pole circuit breakers or switches to disconnect all ungrounded conductors simultaneously. There have been cases of multiwire branch circuits supplying a "line-to-line" load (240 V) and a "line-to-neutral" load (120 V) causing a hazard where two single-pole circuit breakers are used and the opening of one could cause the two loads (240 V and 120 V) to create a 120-V series circuit. In testing 240-V equipment, it is quite possible not to realize that the circuit is still energized with 120 V if one overcurrent device is open. See Sections 210-10 and 240-20(b).

All conductors shall originate from the same panelboard.

In dwelling units a multiwire branch circuit supplying more than one receptacle on the same yoke shall be provided with a means to disconnect simultaneously all ungrounded conductors at the panelboard where the branch circuit originated.

Many 125-volt, 15- and 20-ampere duplex receptacles have a break-off feature that permits each of the two receptacles to be supplied from a different polarity and the single grounded conductor of a three-wire (multiwire) branch circuit. This is commonly called a "split-wired" receptacle, i.e., one-half of the duplex receptacle on one circuit and the other half on another circuit. The simultaneous opening of both "hot" conductors at the panelboard will effectively protect personnel from inadvertent contact with an energized conductor or device terminal. The simultaneous disconnection can be secured by a 2-pole circuit breaker or by two single-pole circuit breakers with a handle tie. Where fuses are used, a 2-pole disconnect switch is required. See Figure 210-1.

Some homeowners have attempted to replace "split-wired" receptacles and were not aware that the break-off link must first be removed. Failure to remove this link results in a short circuit when the multiwire branch circuit is energized. It is necessary to break off the link connection between the ungrounded conductor terminals, leaving the link on the grounded side in place. The link is removed by prying and bending with a thin screwdriver and/or long-nose pliers. See Figure 210-2.

Where the duplex receptacle is supplied from a multiwire branch circuit but both receptacles are connected to the same "hot" conductor, the requirement for simultaneous disconnection does not apply.

Break-off link removed.

Double-pole circuit breaker or two single-pole circuit breakers with a "handle-tie" or a two-pole switch.

Figure 210-1. A multiwire branch circuit supplying a split-wired receptacle, i.e., a duplex receptacle with the break-off link removed.

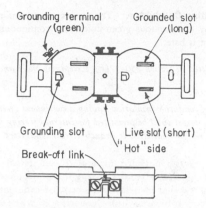

Figure 210-2. A grounding type of duplex receptacle is illustrated with the break-off link in place.

210-5. Color Code for Branch Circuits.

(a) Grounded Conductor. The grounded conductor of a branch circuit shall be identified by a continuous white or natural gray color. Where conductors of different systems are installed in the same raceway, box, auxiliary gutter, or other types of enclosures, one system neutral, if required, shall have an outer covering of white or natural gray. Each other system neutral, if required, shall have an outer covering of white with an identifiable colored stripe (not green) running along the insulation or other and different means of identification.

See Figure 210-3.

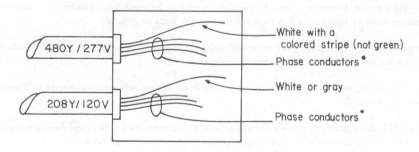

Figure 210-3. Illustrated are conductors of different systems in the same enclosure. Phase conductors may be any color other than white, gray, or green.

Exception No. 1: The grounded conductors of mineral-insulated, metal-sheathed cable shall be identified by distinctive marking at the terminals during the process of installation.

See Figure 200-1.

Exception No. 2: As permitted in Exception No. 2 of Section 200-6(a) and the Exception to Section 200-6(b).

See Figure 200-2.

(b) Equipment Grounding Conductor. The equipment grounding conductor of a branch circuit shall be identified by a continuous green color or a continuous green color with one or more yellow stripes unless it is bare.

Exception No. 1: As permitted in Section 250-57(b), Exceptions No. 1 and 3 and Section 310-12(b), Exceptions No. 1 and 2.

Exception No. 2: The use of conductor insulation having a continuous green color or a continuous green color with one or more yellow stripes shall be permitted for internal wiring of equipment if such wiring does not serve as the lead wires for connection to branch-circuit conductors.

The color-coding requirements for grounded and grounding conductors are given in Section 210-5. Section 210-5(a) covers installations where more than one grounded conductor is carried in a raceway, box, or other enclosure. It requires one grounded conductor to have an outer covering of white or natural gray, and each other system neutral in the raceway, etc., where required, is to have an outer coloring of white with an identifiable colored stripe (not green) to provide a means of identifying the grounded conductors of each different system.

Although the *Code* no longer recommends the use of black, red, and blue for phase conductors of a circuit, it is extremely important that multiwire branch circuits and their grounded circuit conductors (neutral) be identified in the course of installation to assure that the phase conductors are connected to the proper circuit breakers so that the grounded circuit conductors (neutral) will not be overloaded. This can be accomplished by taping all the circuit conductors together or any other process whereby the electrician can keep the conductors of a multiwire circuit together to properly connect the phase conductors to opposite phases of the circuit.

210-6. Maximum Voltage.

(a) Voltage to Ground. Branch circuits supplying lampholders, fixtures, or standard receptacles rated 15 amperes or less shall not exceed 150 volts to ground.

Exception No. 1: The voltage shall not exceed 300 volts to ground on branch circuits in industrial establishments where all the following conditions are met:

a. The conditions of maintenance and supervision indicate that only qualified persons will service the lighting fixtures.

b. The branch circuits supply only lighting fixtures that are equipped with mogul-base, screw-shell lampholders or with lampholders of other types applied within their voltage rating.

c. Incandescent lamp fixtures, if used, shall be mounted not less than 8 feet (2.44 m) above the floor. Where conditions do not permit 8 feet (2.44 m), the incandescent fixtures shall be permitted at the available height.

See Section 110-17.

d. Integral lighting switch, if used, shall not be readily accessible.

The provisions of Exception No. 1 permit the connection of lighting fixtures line to line on a four-wire, 3-phase neutral grounded system of 480 Y/277 volts or 240 V delta, grounded or ungrounded, with conditions that need to be met in order to apply this Exception. The judgment of the local authority having jurisdiction of enforcement of the *Code* is involved in determining the conditions of maintenance and supervision. See Figure 210-4.

Exception No. 2: The voltage shall not exceed 300 volts to ground on branch circuits in stores, health care facilities, office buildings, schools, or public and commercial areas of other buildings, such as hotels or transportation terminals, where all of the following conditions are met:

a. The branch circuits only supply the ballasts for permanently installed electric-discharge lamp fixtures.

b. Integral lighting switch, if used, shall not be readily accessible.

c. Lampholders of the screw shell type, if used, shall be mounted not less than 8 feet (2.44 m) from the floor.

Exception No. 3: For lampholders of infrared industrial heating appliances as provided in Section 422-15(c).

Exception No. 4: The railway properties as described in Section 110-19.

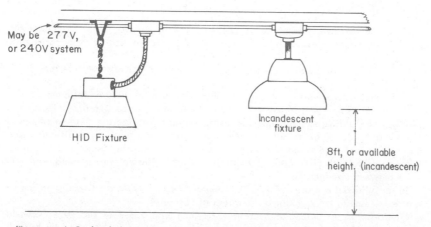

Figure 210-4. Cord-and-plug connected high-intensity discharge fixtures or incandescent fixtures (mogul-base screw-shell lampholders) at over 150 volts but not to exceed 300 volts to ground are permitted in industrial locations only. Permanently installed HID fixtures are permitted in other locations. See Exception No. 2 and comments.

In industrial establishments where the enforcing authority for the *Code* is assured that the conditions of maintenance and supervision are such that only qualified persons will service the light fixtures, the voltage to ground on lighting circuits may be as much as 300 V. This permits a 3-phase, 4-wire, 277/480 V wye system to supply electric-discharge ballasts at line-to-line or line-to-neutral hookups. Under these conditions, incandescent fixtures must be mounted 8 ft or more above the floor or at the available height, where conditions do not permit 8 ft, and, if integral lighting switches are used, they are not to be readily accessible. In addition, the branch circuits are to supply only lighting fixtures that are equipped with mogul-base screw-shell lampholders or with other lampholders that have been examined by a qualified testing laboratory and found to be suitable for the purpose. In Exception No. 2, electric-discharge lamps may be supplied by voltages not exceeding 300 V to ground in the listed occupancies. Where lampholders of the screw-shell type are used, they are to be mounted not less than 8 ft from the floor, and where integral lighting switches are provided, they are not to be readily accessible. See Figure 210-5.

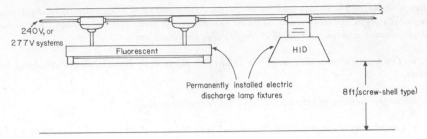

Figure 210-5. Permanently installed electric-discharge lamp fixtures not exceeding 300 volts to ground are permitted in stores, health care facilities, office buildings, schools, etc.

(b) Voltage Between Conductors—Poles, Tunnels, and Similar Structures. The voltage shall not exceed 600 volts between conductors on branch circuits supplying only the ballasts for electric-discharge lamps mounted in permanently installed fixtures where the fixtures are mounted as follows:

(1)   Not less than a height of 22 feet (6.71 m) on poles or similar structures for the illumination of outdoor areas, such as highways, roads, bridges, athletic fields, or parking lots.

(2)   Not less than a height of 18 feet (5.49 m) on other structures, such as tunnels.

A Formal Interpretation 78-2 was released in October 1979 as follows:
Statement: The 1971 *National Electrical Code* in Sections 210-6(a), Exception No. 5, and 730-7(c) established mounting heights for lighting fixtures mounted outside of buildings or on poles or other structures and used for area illumination. These Sections contained the requirements for mounting heights of lighting fixtures for branch circuits of 150 volts to ground, 300 volts to ground, and 500 volts between conductors.
In the editorial rewrite of the 1971 *National Electrical Code*, the literal wording of the text seems to have changed the intent of the rules.
Question: Is the intent of Sections 210-6(b) and 225-7 of the 1978 *National Electrical Code* to require electric-discharge lighting fixtures, supplied by branch circuits of 150 volts to ground or 300 volts to ground, to be mounted no less than 22 feet on poles or similar structures?
Answer: No.

(c) Voltage Between Conductors.

(1)   The voltage shall not exceed 150 volts between conductors on branch circuits supplying screw-shell lampholder(s), receptacle(s), or appliance(s) in dwelling unit(s) and guest rooms in hotels, motels, and similar occupancies.

See comments following Section 210-4.

Exception No. 1: Permanently connected appliances.

Exception No. 2: Cord- and plug-connected loads of more than 1380 watts or ¼ horsepower or greater rating.

See Article 100 for definition of Receptacle.

(2)   The voltage shall not exceed 150 volts between conductors on branch circuits supplying one or more medium-base, screw-shell lampholders in occupancies other than those specified in (c) (1).

See Exception No. 1 to (a) above for 300-volt limitation for mogul-base, screw-shell lampholders under specific conditions in industrial establishments.

In dwelling units, 240 V circuits may supply permanently connected appliances (such as water heaters, electric heat), cord- and plug-connected appliances of more than 1380 W (such as electric ranges or clothes dryers), or lampholders for fluorescent lamps as they are not of the screw-shell type.

210-7. Receptacles and Cord Connectors.

(a) Grounding Type. Receptacles installed on 15- and 20-ampere branch circuits shall be of the grounding type. Grounding-type receptacles shall be installed only on circuits of the voltage class and current for which they are rated, except as provided in Tables 210-21(b)(2) and (b)(3).

A single receptacle installed on an individual branch circuit is to have an ampere rating of not less than that of the branch circuit. That is, a single receptacle on a 20-ampere circuit must be rated at 20 amperes; however, two or more 15-ampere receptacles would be permitted on a 20-ampere circuit.

Exception No. 1: Grounding-type receptacles of the type that reject nongrounding-type attachment plugs or which are of the locking type shall be permitted for specific purposes or in special locations. Receptacles required in Sections 517-101(a)(3) and 517-101(c) shall be considered as meeting the requirements of this section.

Exception No. 2: Nongrounding-type receptacles installed in accordance with Section 210-7(d), Exception.

(b) To Be Grounded. Receptacles and cord connectors having grounding contacts shall have those contacts effectively grounded.

Exception: Receptacles mounted on portable and vehicle-mounted generators in accordance with Section 250-6.

(c) Methods of Grounding. The grounding contacts of receptacles and cord connectors shall be grounded by connection to the equipment grounding conductor of the circuit supplying the receptacle or cord connector.

For installation requirements for the reduction of electrical noise, see Section 250-74, Exception No. 4.

The branch circuit or branch-circuit raceway shall include or provide a grounding conductor to which the grounding contacts of the receptacle or cord connector shall be connected.

Section 250-91(b) describes acceptable grounding means.

For extensions of existing branch circuits, see Section 250-50.

(d) Replacements. Grounding-type receptacles shall be used as replacements for existing nongrounding types and shall be connected to a grounding conductor installed in accordance with (c) above.

Exception: Where a grounding means does not exist in the receptacle enclosure a nongrounding type of receptacle shall be used.

Requiring grounding-type receptacles and grounding-type cord connectors came about because of the work of a technical subcommittee representing all the major affected interests using the *National Electrical Code.* The subcommittee concluded that the proper grounding of portable hand-held tools and appliances was necessary for safety.

Grounding is not required on all cord- and plug-connected equipment, such as toasters and other types of heating appliances having exposed or nonsheathed elements. These appliances are subject to physical contact of the heating elements by insertion of knives, forks, or other objects. It is a common occurrence for a householder to insert a fork in a toaster to remove a slice of toast, and additional hazards are thereby introduced by grounding such appliances.

When existing nongrounding-type receptacles are replaced, it is necessary to use only grounding-type receptacles where a grounding means exists in the receptacle enclosure. Where a grounding means does not exist, a nongrounding-type receptacle is permitted, thereby indicating to the user that a grounding means for an appliance is not available.

For an extension of a branch circuit, see the Exception to Section 250-50.

(e) Cord-and Plug-Connected Equipment.   The installation of grounding-type receptacles shall not be used as a requirement that all cord- and plug-connected equipment be of the grounded type.

See Section 250-45 for type of cord-and plug-connected equipment to be grounded.

Over the years there has been a requirement that grounding-type receptacles be used as replacements for nongrounding types. See Section 210-7(d). It is intended that grounding-type receptacles be conveniently located for use with utilization equipment that is required to be grounded. For cord- and plug-connected equipment that is to be grounded, see Section 250-45.

Many appliances are not required to be grounded, for example, toasters, flat irons, and some heating equipment, and there are many nongrounding-type receptacles in use. The use of an adapter or other approved means is necessary where grounding is required. Distinctively marked, listed, double-insulated tools and appliances are not required to be grounded.

(f) Noninterchangeable Types.   Receptacles connected to circuits having different voltages, frequencies, or types of current (ac or dc) on the same premises shall be of such design that the attachment plugs used on these circuits are not interchangeable.

210-8. Ground-Fault Protection for Personnel.

(a) Dwelling Units.

(1)   All 125-volt, single-phase, 15- and 20-ampere receptacles installed in bathrooms shall have ground-fault circuit-interrupter protection for personnel.

The requirement for ground-fault circuit-interrupters for receptacles in bathrooms was originally inserted in the *Code* because data supplied with the *Code* proposal for GFCIs indicated that a number of accidents occurring in bathrooms could be prevented by GFCIs.

Article 100 defines a dwelling unit as having one or more rooms for the use of one or more persons as a housekeeping unit with space for eating, living, sleeping, and permanent provisions for cooking and sanitation.

Thus, the usual guest room in a motel which does not have permanent provisions for cooking is not a dwelling unit and thus would not be judged under Section

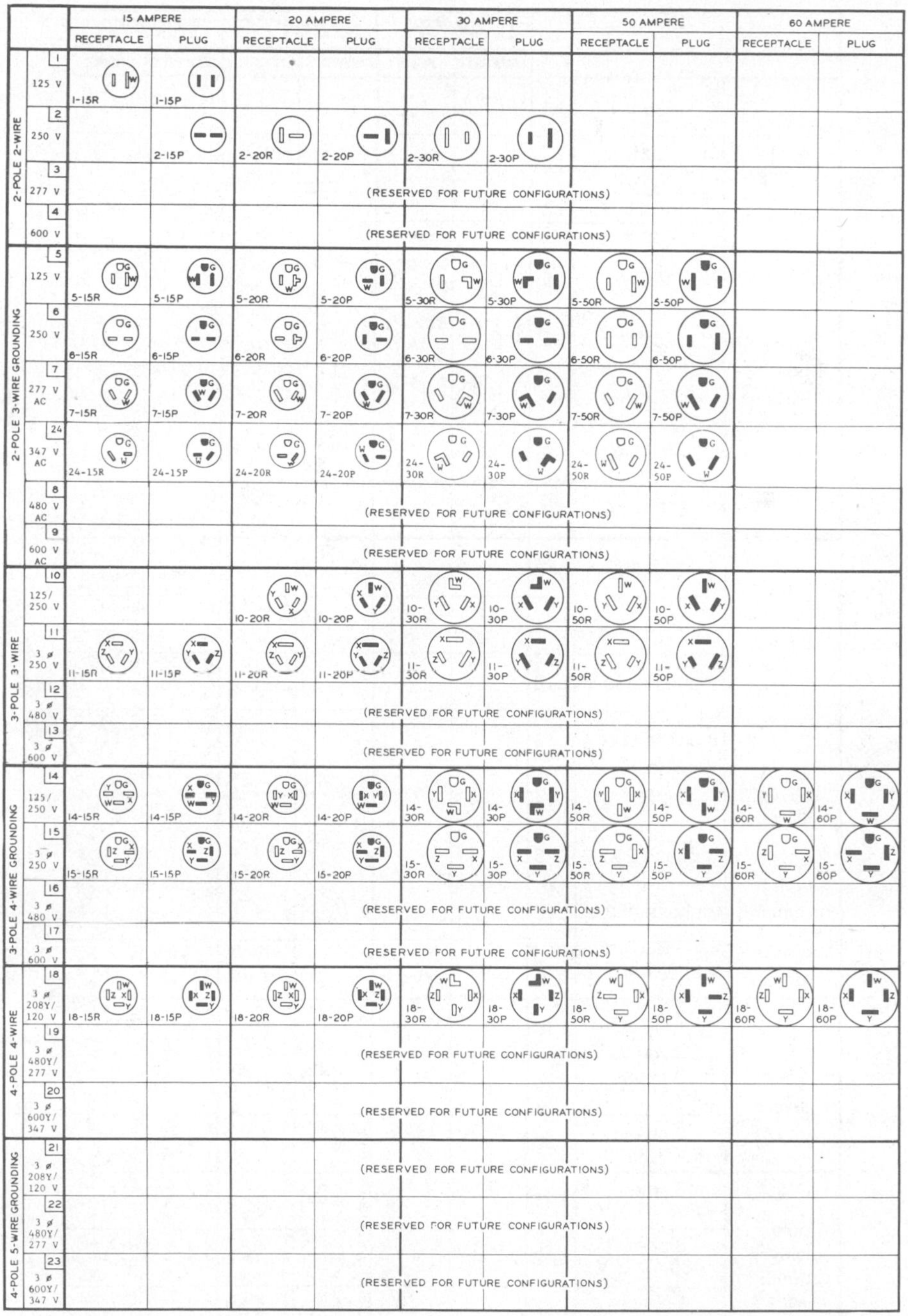

Figure 210-6. Configuration chart for general-purpose nonlocking plugs and receptacles; taken from ANSI C73 Standard.

			15 AMPERE		20 AMPERE		30 AMPERE	
			RECEPTACLE	PLUG	RECEPTACLE	PLUG	RECEPTACLE	PLUG
2-pole 2-wire	125 V	L1	L1-15R	L1-15P				
	250 V	L2			L2-20R	L2-20P		
	277 V AC	L3	F	U	T	U	R	E
	600 V	L4	F	U	T	U	R	E
2-pole 3-wire grounding	125 V	L5	L5-15R	L5-15P	L5-20R	L5-20P	L5-30R	L5-30P
	250 V	L6	L6-15R	L6-15P	L6-20R	L6-20P	L6-30R	L6-30P
	277 V AC	L7	L7-15R	L7-15P	L7-20R	L7-20P	L7-30R	L7-30P
	480 V AC	L8			L8-20R	L8-20P	L8-30R	L8-30P
	600 V AC	L9			L9-20R	L9-20P	L9-30R	L9-30P
3-pole 3-wire	125/250 V	L10			L10-20R	L10-20P	L10-30R	L10-30P
	3 phase 250 V	L11	L11-15R	L11-15P	L11-20R	L11-20P	L11-30R	L11-30P
	3 phase 480 V	L12			L12-20R	L12-20P	L12-30R	L12-30P
	3 phase 600 V	L13					L13-30R	L13-30P
3-pole 4-wire grounding	125/250 V	L14			L14-20R	L14-20P	L14-30R	L14-30P
	3 phase 250 V	L15			L15-20R	L15-20P	L15-30R	L15-30P
	3 phase 480 V	L16			L16-20R	L16-20P	L16-30R	L16-30P
	3 phase 600 V	L17					L17-30R	L17-30P
4-pole 4-wire	3 phase 208Y/120 V	L18			L18-20R	L18-20P	L18-30R	L18-30P
	3 phase 480Y/277 V	L19			L19-20R	L19-20P	L19-30R	L19-30P
	3 phase 600Y/347 V	L20			L20-20R	L20-20P	L20-30R	L20-30P
4-pole 5-wire grounding	3 phase 208Y/120V	L21			L21-20R	L21-20P	L21-30R	L21-30P
	3 phase 480Y/277 V	L22			L22-20R	L22-20P	L22-30R	L22-30P
	3 phase 600Y/347 V	L23			L23-20R	L23-20P	L23-30R	L23-30P

Figure 210-7. Configuration chart for specific-purpose locking plugs and receptacles; taken from ANSI C73 Standard.

210-8(a). If, however, a guest room in a motel had permanent provisions for cooking and sanitation and otherwise conformed with the definition of a dwelling unit, it would need to have the bathroom receptacles conform with Section 210-8(a). See Figure 210-8.

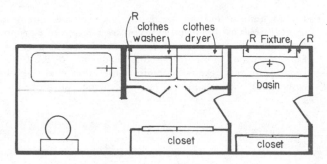

R=125-V, 15-A or 20-A Receptacle

Figure 210-8. Section 210-8(a)(1) indicates that all receptacles in bathrooms are to have GFCI protection for personnel including any located for a clothes washer, clothes dryer (gas), or integral with the lighting fixture, and, of course, the one wall-mounted adjacent to the basin. The definition of bathroom refers to an area that includes the entire area shown above, whether a separating door (as illustrated) is present or not.

(2) All 125-volt, single-phase, 15- or 20-ampere receptacles installed in garages shall have ground-fault circuit-interrupter protection for personnel.

Exception No. 1 to (a)(2): Receptacles which are not readily accessible.

Exception No. 2 to (a)(2): Receptacles for appliances occupying dedicated space which are cord- and plug-connected in accordance with Section 400-7(a)(6), (a)(7), or (a)(8).

Receptacles installed under Exceptions to Section 210-8(a)(2) shall not be considered as meeting the requirements of Section 210-52(f).

The purpose of GFCIs in garages is to provide a degree of safety for persons using portable hand-held tools. GFCIs are not needed for appliances such as freezers or refrigerators, and these appliances should not be subject to tripping caused by other appliances. See Figure 210-9.

(3) All 125-volt, single-phase, 15- and 20-ampere receptacles installed outdoors where there is direct grade level access to the dwelling unit and to the receptacles shall have ground-fault circuit-interrupter protection for personnel.

Installation of GFCIs for outdoor receptacles requires that care be taken to assure that the receptacle faceplate rests securely on the supporting surface to prevent moisture from entering the enclosure. Where brick, stone, or stucco are encountered, it may be necessary to patch openings with caulking compound or mastic. See Section 410-57. See Figure 210-10.

Bathroom: A bathroom is an area including a basin with one or more of the following: a toilet, a tub, or a shower.

Such ground-fault circuit-interrupter protection may be provided for other circuits, locations, and occupancies, and, where used, will provide additional protection against line-to-ground shock hazard.

See Section 215-9 for feeder protection.

With regard to information on need for ground-fault circuit-interrupter protection for receptacles used in dwellings, you are referred to a proposal to add a new Section 442-X to the 1971 *National Electrical Code* which appeared on Pages 144 to 151 of the "Preprint" of the Proposed Amendments for the 1971 *NEC*. The supporting comment for this proposal contains tables, text, charts and bar graphs depicting number and percentage of fatal accidents in areas of dwelling occupancies.

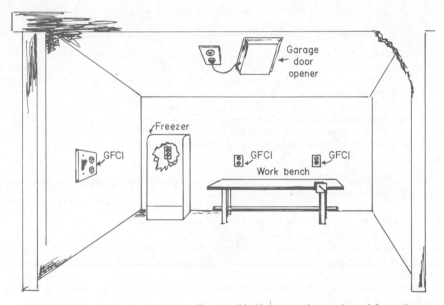

Figure 210-9. Receptacles that are not readily accessible (door opener) or are located for appliances occupying dedicated space (food freezer) are not required to have GFCI protection for personnel.

Figure 210-10. The three receptacles located outdoors at a dwelling unit are considered to be at direct grade level access and must have GFCI protection for personnel.

(b) Construction Sites. All 125-volt single-phase, 15- and 20-ampere receptacle outlets which are not a part of the permanent wiring of the building or structure, and which are in use by employees shall have ground-fault circuit-interrupter protection for personnel.

Receptacle outlets that are a part of the permanent wiring of the building are not required to have GFCI protection; however, it is intended that they be used with portable GFCIs or meet the provisions of Exception No. 2.

Ground-fault circuit-interrupters may be of the portable type (Figure 210-12), receptacle type (Figure 210-13), or circuit-breaker type (Figure 210-12). A commonly used temporary power unit is shown in Figure 305-1.

Exception No. 1: Receptacles on a portable or vehicle-mounted generator rated not more than 5 kW, where the circuit conductors are insulated from the generator frame as permitted in Section 250-6.

Exception No. 2: Where a written procedure, acceptable to the authority having jurisdiction, is continuously enforced by a designated individual at the construction site to indicate that equipment grounding conductors for 125-volt, single-phase, 15- and 20-ampere receptacles, flexible cord sets, and equipment connected by cord and plug are installed and maintained in accordance with the applicable requirements of Sections 210-7(c), 250-45, 250-59, and 305-2(d). The procedure shall include electrical continuity tests of all required equipment, grounding conductors and their connections. These tests shall be conducted as follows:

a. Fixed receptacles shall be tested where there is evidence of damage.

b. Flexible cord sets (extension cords) shall be tested before first use on the construction site. All flexible cord sets shall be tested where there is evidence of damage, and after any repairs.

c. Equipment connected by cord and plug shall be tested: (1) before first use on the construction site; (2) where there is evidence of damage; (3) after any repairs; and (4) at intervals not exceeding 3 months.

The requirement to provide GFCIs for construction sites originally appeared in the 1971 *NEC* and its enforcement was held in abeyance by order of the Department of Labor (OSHA). Other enforcing agencies adopting the 1971 *NEC* enforced all the *Code* requirements. After a lengthy public hearing, OSHA issued an alternative assured equipment grounding program on construction sites. The *NEC* panels accepted a new Exception No. 2, and the most substantial difference between it and that offered by OSHA was the requirement that the written procedure must be acceptable to the authority having jurisdiction.

Figure 210-11 shows a typical circuit arrangement of a GFCI for personnel protection. The line conductors are passed through a toroidal coil and connected to a shunt-trip device.

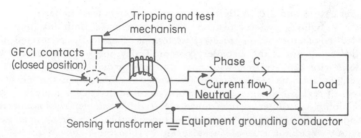

Figure 210-11. The circuitry and components for a typical ground-fault circuit-interrupter.

As long as the current in each conductor remains equal, the device remains in a closed position. If one of the conductors comes in contact with a grounded object, some of the current returns by an alternative path and an unbalanced current results. The unbalanced current is sensed by the toroidal coil and a circuit is established to the shunt-trip which opens the circuit. Ground-fault circuit-interrupters operate on currents of 5 mA with a plus or minus (±) value of 1 mA. Evaluation standards permit a differential of 4 to 6 mA. At trip levels of 5 mA (the instantaneous current could be much higher), a shock can be felt during the time of the fault, leading to involuntary reactions that may cause secondary accidents, such as falls. GFCIs will not sense phase-to-phase faults.

After several years of experience and reports made available by numerous public hearings, it has become evident that certain precautions must be taken to ensure efficient operation of GFCIs on construction sites. It has been shown that long lengths of portable cords strung on construction sites where moisture is present lead to leakage currents affecting the satisfactory operation of GFCIs. Moisture at cord caps and improper maintenance of portable hand-held tools invariably lead to trouble. Equipment intended for dry locations should not be used on construction sites and a number of manufacturers offer receptacles, panelboards, cord caps, etc., intended to keep electrical connections dry. The location of GFCIs should be such that runs of wiring can be kept to a minimum. Sufficient numbers of GFCIs should be supplied to keep the number of tools on any given circuit at a minimum. See Section 305-2(d).

A variety of GFCIs are available, including plug-in circuit breaker types and duplex receptacle types. These also come in portable units and each has a test switch so that the unit can be checked periodically to ensure continuous proper operation.

It should be pointed out that the use of GFCIs on construction sites does not absolve employers from meeting the *Code* requirement that all electric tools be properly grounded.

210-9. Circuits Derived from Autotransformers.   Branch circuits shall not be supplied by autotransformers.

Exception No. 1: Where the system supplied has a grounded conductor that is electrically connected to a grounded conductor of the system supplying the autotransformer.

Exception No. 2: An autotransformer used to extend or add an individual branch circuit in an existing installation for an equipment load without the connection to a similar identified grounded conductor when transforming from a nominal 208 volts to a nominal 240-volt supply or similarly from 240 volts to 208 volts.

An autotransformer is a transformer in which a part of the winding is common to both primary and secondary circuits.

Figures 210-15 and 210-16 illustrate autotransformers used to derive 110 V and 110/220 V lighting systems from a 220 V system. In both installations the grounded conductor of the primary system is electrically connected to the grounded conductor of the secondary system. Today, the single-phase 220 V and 3-phase, 3-wire 220 V system with one conductor grounded is not widely used; however, the autotransformer starter (manual or automatic) is the most widely used type of reduced-voltage starter for polyphase squirrel-cage motors.

Exception No. 2 allows an autotransformer (without an electrical connection to a grounded conductor) to extend or add an individual branch circuit in an existing installation when, for example, transforming (boosting) 208 V to 240 V or transforming (bucking) 240 V to 208 V for use with appliances, for example,

Figure 210-12. A portable plug-in-type ground-fault circuit-interrupter. (*Square D Co.*)

ranges, air-conditioners, heating elements, and motors. It is common also to increase 240 V to 277 V for lighting systems. A single unit is used to boost or buck single-phase voltage, but two or three units are used to boost or buck 3-phase voltage. An autotransformer requires little physical spacing, is economical, and, above all, efficient.

A buck-boost transformer is a means of raising or lowering (boosting or bucking) a supply line voltage by a small amount—usually no more than ± 20 percent. It is an insulating transformer with two primary (input) windings, both rated at 120 V or 240 V and two secondary (output) windings, both rated at either 12 V, 16 V, or 24 V. Its primary and secondary windings can be connected together so that the electrical characteristics are changed from an insulating transformer to those of a "boosting" or "bucking" autotransformer correcting voltage up to ± 20 percent.

Literature is available from manufacturers containing diagrams for connection and application of autotransformers.

210-10. Ungrounded Conductors Tapped from Grounded Systems.   Two-wire dc circuits and ac circuits of two or more ungrounded conductors shall be permitted to be tapped from the ungrounded conductors of circuits having a grounded neutral conductor. Switching devices in each tapped circuit shall have a pole in each ungrounded conductor. All poles of multipole switching devices shall manually switch together where such switching devices also serve as a disconnecting means as required by Section 422-21(b) for an appliance; Section 424-20 for a fixed electric space heating unit; Section 426-21 for electric de-icing and snow-melting equipment; Section 430-85 for a motor controller; and Section 430-103 for a motor.

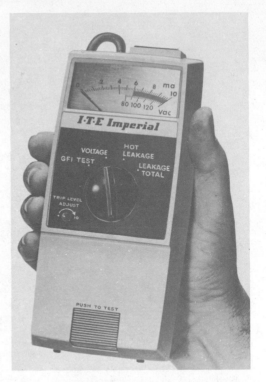

Figure 210-13. A 15-A duplex receptacle with integral ground-fault circuit-interrupter, which also protects downstream loads. (*Pass & Seymour, Inc.*)

Figure 210-14. Leakage of the neutral conductor to ground and ground-fault leakage current from the hot conductor can be measured by this GFCI tester. (*Gould Inc.*)

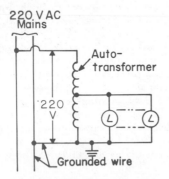

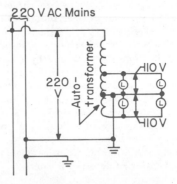

Figure 210-15. The circuitry for an autotransformer used to derive a 2-wire, 110-V system for lighting from a 220-V power system.

Figure 210-16. The circuitry for an autotransformer used to derive a 3-wire 110/220-V system for lighting from a 220-V system.

Two-wire ungrounded branch circuits may be tapped from ac or dc circuits of two or more ungrounded conductors having a grounded neutral conductor. Figure 210-19 illustrates ungrounded 2-wire branch circuits tapped from the ungrounded conductors of a dc or single-phase system to supply a small motor. Figure 210-20 illustrates a 3-phase, 4-wire wye system.

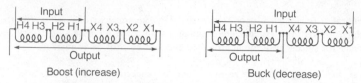

Boost (increase)   Buck (decrease)

Figure 210-17. Typical hookups for buck or boost transformers connected as autotransformers to change 240-V single-phase to 208 V or vice versa.

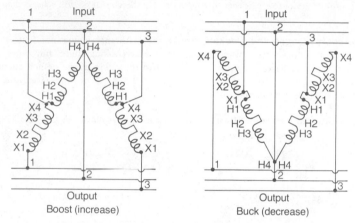

Boost (increase)   Buck (decrease)

Figure 210-18. Typical hookups for buck or boost transformers connected in 3-phase open delta as autotransformers to change 240 V to 208 V or vice versa.

Circuit breakers or switches used as the disconnecting means for a branch circuit are to open all poles simultaneously. This requirement involves only the manual operation of the disconnecting means; thus, where switches and fuses are used and one fuse blows, or where circuit breakers (two single-pole circuit breakers with a "handle-tie") are used and one breaker trips, one pole could remain closed. The intention is not to provide a common trip of fuses or circuit breakers, but to disconnect "manually" the ungrounded conductors of the branch circuit with one manual operation.

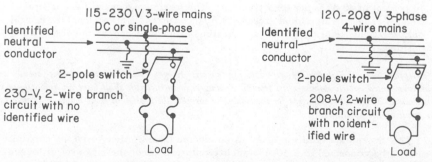

Figures 210-19 and 210-20. Branch circuits tapped from ungrounded conductors of multiwire systems.

B. Branch-Circuit Ratings

210-19. Conductors—Minimum Ampacity and Size.

(a) General. Branch-circuit conductors shall have an ampacity of not less than the rating of the branch circuit and not less than the maximum load to be served. Cable assemblies with the neutral conductor smaller than the ungrounded conductors shall be so marked.

See Tables 310-16 through 310-19 for ampacity ratings of conductors.
See Part B of Article 430 for minimum rating of motor branch-circuit conductors.
Conductors for branch circuits as defined in Article 100, sized to prevent a voltage drop exceeding 3 percent at the farthest outlet of power, heating, and lighting loads, or combinations of such loads and where the maximum total voltage drop on both feeders and branch circuits to the farthest outlet does not exceed 5 percent, will provide reasonable efficiency of operation. See Section 215-2 for voltage drop on feeder conductors.

(b) Household Ranges and Cooking Appliances. Branch-circuit conductors supplying household ranges, wall-mounted ovens, counter-mounted cooking units, and other household cooking appliances shall have an ampacity not less than the rating of the branch circuit and not less than the maximum load to be served. For ranges of 8 3/4 kW or more rating, the minimum branch-circuit rating shall be 40 amperes.

For a minimum 40-ampere branch-circuit rating, for example:

> No. 8 AWG copper, Type TW = 40A.
> No. 6 AWG aluminum, Type TW = 40A.

See Table 310-16 for other applications.

Exception No. 1: The neutral conductor of a 3-wire branch circuit supplying a household electric range, a wall-mounted oven, or a counter-mounted cooking unit shall be permitted to be smaller than the ungrounded conductors where the maximum demand of a range of 8 3/4 kW or more rating has been computed according to Column A of Table 220-19, but shall have an ampacity of not less than 70 percent of the ampacity of the ungrounded conductors and shall not be smaller than No. 10.

Column A of Table 220-19 indicates that the maximum demand for one range (not over 12 kW rating) is 8 kW (8 kW = 8000 watts; 8000 watts divided by 230 V = 34.8 A). The allowable ampacity of a No. 8 TW copper conductor is 40 A (see Table 310-16) and may be used for the range branch circuit. According to this computation, the neutral of this 3-wire circuit can be smaller than No. 8 but not smaller than No. 10 which has an allowable ampacity of 30 A (30 A is more than 70 percent of 40 A, as per the Exception). The maximum demand for a neutral of an 8 kW range circuit seldom exceeds 25 A since current is drawn from the neutral only for lights, clocks, timers, and heating elements when in the low-heating position.

Exception No. 2: Tap conductors supplying electric ranges, wall-mounted electric ovens, and counter-mounted electric cooking units from a 50-ampere branch circuit shall have an ampacity of not less than 20 and shall be sufficient for the load to be served. The taps shall be no longer than necessary for servicing the appliance.

This Exception permits a 20-A tap conductor from a range, oven, or cooking unit to be connected to a 50-A branch circuit provided: the taps are no longer than necessary for servicing or to allow accessibility to the junction box; the taps to each unit are properly spliced; the junction box is adjacent to each unit; and the taps are of sufficient size for the load to be served. See Figure 210-21.

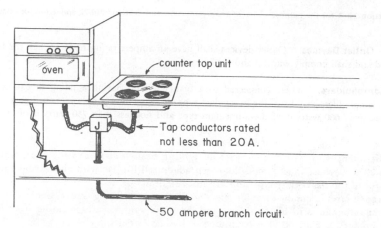

Figure 210-21. Tap conductors are permitted to be sized smaller than the branch-circuit conductors, but they are to be no longer than necessary for servicing.

(c) Other Loads.   Branch-circuit conductors supplying loads other than cooking appliances as covered in (b) above and as listed in Section 210-2 shall have an ampacity sufficient for the loads served and shall not be smaller than No. 14.

Exception No. 1: Tap conductors for such loads shall have an ampacity not less than 15 for circuits rated less than 40 amperes and not less than 20 for circuits rated at 40 or 50 amperes and only where these tap conductors supply any of the following loads:

a. Individual lampholders or fixtures with taps extending not longer than 18 inches (457 mm) beyond any portion of the lampholder or fixture.

b. A fixture having tap conductors as provided in Section 410-67.

c. Individual outlets with taps not over 18 inches (457 mm) long.

d. Infrared lamp industrial heating appliances.

e. Nonheating leads of de-icing and snow-melting cables and mats.

Exception No. 2: Fixture wires and cords as permitted in Section 240-4.

Tap conductors are to be suitable for the temperature encountered and, where the conductors supply loads as specified in subparts a. through e. of Exception No. 1, they are to have an ampacity of 15 A or more (No. 14 wire) for circuits rated less than 40 A, and an ampacity of 20 A or more (No. 12 wire) for circuits rated 40 or 50 A.

210-20. Overcurrent Protection.

(a) General.   Branch-circuit conductors and equipment shall be protected by overcurrent protective devices having a rating or setting (1) not exceeding that specified in Section 240-3 for conductors; (2) not exceeding that specified in the applicable articles referenced in Section 240-2 for equipment; and (3) as provided for outlet devices in Section 210-21.

Exception: Tap conductors, fixture wire, and cords as permitted in Section 210-19(c) shall be considered as being protected by the circuit overcurrent device.

See Section 240-1 for the purpose of overcurrent protection and Sections 210-22 and 220-2 for continuous loads.

210-21. Outlet Devices.   Outlet devices shall have an ampere rating not less than the load to be served and shall comply with (a) and (b) below.

(a) Lampholders.   Where connected to a branch circuit having a rating in excess of 20 amperes, lampholders shall be of the heavy-duty type. A heavy-duty lampholder shall have a rating of not less than 660 watts if of the admedium type and not less than 750 watts if of any other type.

The intent is to restrict a fluorescent lighting branch-circuit rating to not more than 20 A, because most lampholders manufactured for use with fluorescent lights are not of the heavy-duty type and are not rated at 750 W.

Branch-circuit conductors for electric-discharge lighting are connected to a ballast rather than to lampholders, and, by specifying a wattage rating for these lampholders, a limit of 20 A is applied to ballast circuits.

It is only the admedium lampholder that is recognized as heavy duty at the rating of 660 W. The medium-base lampholder rated 660 W is required to have a rating of not less than 750 watts to be recognized as heavy duty and, therefore, is not heavy duty. The requirement stated in Section 210-21(a) prohibits the use of medium-base lampholders on branch circuits in excess of 20 amperes.

(b) Receptacles.

(1)   A single receptacle installed on an individual branch circuit shall have an ampere rating of not less than that of the branch circuit.

See Comment following Section 210-7.

See definition of Receptacle in Article 100.

(2)   Where connected to a branch circuit supplying two or more receptacles or outlets, a receptacle shall not supply a total cord- and plug-connected load in excess of the maximum specified in Table 210-21(b)(2).

(3)   Where connected to a branch circuit supplying two or more receptacles or outlets, receptacle ratings shall conform to the values listed in Table 210-21(b)(3).

See Comment following Section 210-7.

(4)   It shall be acceptable to base the ampere rating of a range receptacle on a single range demand load specified in Table 220-19.

210-22. Maximum Loads.   The total load shall not exceed the rating of the branch circuit, and it shall not exceed the maximum loads specified in (a) through (c) below under the conditions specified therein.

(a) Motor-Operated and Combination Loads.   Where a circuit supplies only motor-operated loads, Article 430 shall apply. Where a circuit supplies only air-conditioning and/or refrigerating equipment, Article 440 shall apply. For circuits supplying loads consisting of motor-operated utilization equipment that is fastened in place and that has a motor larger than ⅛ horsepower in combination with other loads, the total computed load shall be based on 125 percent of the largest motor load plus the sum of the other loads.

Table 210-21(b)(2)
Maximum Cord- and Plug-Connected Load to Receptacle

Circuit Rating Amperes	Receptacle Rating Amperes	Maximum Load Amperes
15 or 20	15	12
20	20	16
30	30	24

Table 210-21(b)(3)
Receptacle Ratings for Various Size Circuits

Circuit Rating Amperes	Receptacle Rating Amperes
15	Not over 15
20	15 or 20
30	30
40	40 or 50
50	50

(b) Inductive Lighting Loads. For circuits supplying lighting units having ballasts, transformers, or autotransformers, the computed load shall be based on the total ampere ratings of such units and not on the total watts of the lamps.

(c) Other Loads. Continuous loads, such as store lighting and similar loads, shall not exceed 80 percent of the rating of the branch circuit.

Exception No. 1: Motor loads having demand factors computed in accordance with Article 430.

Exception No. 2: Circuits that have been derated in accordance with Note 8 to Tables 310-16 through 310-19.

Exception No. 3: Circuits supplied by an assembly together with its overcurrent devices that is listed for continuous operation at 100 percent of its rating.

It shall be acceptable to apply demand factors for range loads in accordance with Table 220-19, including Note 4.

Article 100 defines a "Continuous Load" as a load where the maximum current is expected to continue for three hours or more. Continuous loads, such as lighting in mercantile occupancies, restaurants, etc., must not exceed 80 percent of the branch-circuit rating. Exception Nos. 1 and 2 prevent a "double" derating of circuits. Exception No. 3 provides a 100 percent rating of a circuit if supplied by an overcurrent device and assembly, listed by a qualified testing laboratory, for continuous operation.

210-23. Permissible Loads. In no case shall the load exceed the branch-circuit ampere rating. It shall be acceptable for an individual branch circuit to supply any load for which it is rated. A branch circuit supplying two or more outlets shall supply only the loads specified according to its size in (a) through (c) below and summarized in Section 210-24 and Table 210-24.

(a) 15- and 20-Ampere Branch Circuits. A 15- or 20-ampere branch circuit shall be permitted to supply lighting units, appliances, or a combination of both. The rating of any one cord- and plug-connected appliance shall not exceed 80 percent of the branch-circuit ampere rating. The total rating of appliances fastened in place shall not exceed 50 percent of the branch-circuit ampere rating where lighting units, cord- and plug-connected appliances not fastened in place, or both, are also supplied.

Exception: The small appliance branch circuits required in a dwelling unit(s) by Section 220-3(b) shall supply only the receptacle outlets specified in that section.

This permits a 15- or 20-A branch circuit for lighting to also supply an appliance fastened in place, such as an air-conditioner rated not to exceed 50 percent of the branch circuit ampere rating, that is, 7.5 A on a 15-A circuit and 10 A on a 20-A circuit. Such appliances, fastened in place, are not to be installed on the small-appliance branch circuits required in the kitchen, dining room, etc., as per Section 220-3(b).

(b) 30-Ampere Branch Circuits.   A 30-ampere branch circuit shall be permitted to supply fixed lighting units with heavy-duty lampholders in other than dwelling unit(s) or appliances in any occupancy. A rating of any one cord- and plug-connected appliance shall not exceed 80 percent of the branch-circuit ampere rating.

(c) 40- and 50-Ampere Branch Circuits.   A 40- or 50-ampere branch circuit shall be permitted to supply fixed lighting units with heavy-duty lampholders or infrared heating units in other than dwelling units or cooking appliances that are fastened in place in any occupancy.

A branch circuit supplying two or more outlets is to supply only the loads specified according to its size as per Section 210-23(a) through (c) and summarized in Section 210-24 and Table 210-24. Any other circuit is not permitted to have more than one outlet and would be an individual branch circuit. However, individual branch circuits are not required for portable, mobile, and transportable medical X-ray equipment requiring a capacity of not over 60 A (see Sections 517-141(b) and 660-4).

210-24. Branch-Circuit Requirements—Summary.   The requirements for circuits having two or more outlets, other than the receptacle circuits of Section 220-3(b) as specifically provided for above, are summarized in Table 210-24.

Table 210-24 summarizes branch-circuit requirements of conductors, overcurrent protection, outlet devices, maximum load, and permissible loads where two or more outlets are supplied.

Where the branch circuit serves a fixture load and supplies two or more outlets, Section 210-23 requires the branch circuit to have a specific ampere rating which is also the rating of the overcurrent device as stated in Section 210-3. Thus, if the circuit breaker protecting the branch circuit is rated 20 A, the conductors supplying this circuit must have a 20-A load current rating after applying any derating factor required by Note 8 to Tables 310-16 through 310-19. See also Table 210-24 and the single asterisk note following the table. Where 7 to 24 such conductors are in one conduit, a No. 12 AWG THHN copper conductor with an ampacity of 30 A derated to 70 percent would be suitable for a load of 20 A and thus would be acceptable for use on the 20-A multioutlet branch circuit.

C. Required Outlets

210-50. General.   Receptacle outlets shall be installed as specified in Sections 210-52 through 210-62.

Table 210-24

Summary of Branch-Circuit Requirements

(Type FEP, FEPB, RUW, SA, T, TW, RH, RUH, RHW, RHH, THHN, THW, THWN, and XHHW conductors in raceway or cable.)

CIRCUIT RATING	15 Amp	20 Amp	30 Amp	40 Amp	50 Amp
CONDUCTORS (Min. Size)					
Circuit Wires*	14	12	10	8	6
Taps	14	14	14	12	12
Fixture Wires and Cords			Refer to Section 240-4		
OVERCURRENT PROTECTION	15 Amp	20 Amp	30 Amp	40 Amp	50 Amp
OUTLET DEVICES:					
Lampholders Permitted	Any Type	Any Type	Heavy Duty	Heavy Duty	Heavy Duty
Receptacle Rating**	15 Max. Amp	15 or 20 Amp	30 Amp	40 or 50 Amp	50 Amp
MAXIMUM LOAD	15 Amp	20 Amp	30 Amp	40 Amp	50 Amp
PERMISSIBLE LOAD	Refer to Section 210-23(a)	Refer to Section 210-23(a)	Refer to Section 210-23(b)	Refer to Section 210-23(c)	Refer to Section 210-23(c)

* These ampacities are for copper conductors where derating is not required. See Tables 310-16 through 310-19.

** For receptacle rating of cord-connected electric-discharge lighting fixtures, see Section 410-30(c).

(a) Cord Pendants. A cord connector that is supported by a permanently installed cord pendant shall be considered a receptacle outlet.

(b) Cord Connections. A receptacle outlet shall be installed wherever flexible cords with attachment plugs are used. Where flexible cords are permitted to be permanently connected, it shall be permitted to omit receptacles for such cords.

Flexible cords may be permitted to be permanently connected to boxes or fittings where specifically permitted by the *Code*. However, plugging a cord into a lampholder by inserting a screw-plug adapter is not permissible (see Section 410-47).

(c) Laundry Outlet. Appliance outlets installed in a dwelling unit for specific appliances, such as laundry equipment, shall be installed within 6 feet (1.83 m) of the intended location of the appliance.

See Sections 210-52(e) and (f) and 220-3(c).

210-52. Dwelling Unit Receptacle Outlets.

(a) General Provisions. In every kitchen, family room, dining room, living room, parlor, library, den, sun room, bedroom, recreation room, or similar rooms of dwelling units, receptacle outlets shall be installed so that no point along the floor line in any wall space is more than 6 feet (1.83 m), measured horizontally, from an outlet in that space, including any wall space 2 feet (610 mm) or more in width and the wall space occupied by sliding panels in exterior walls. The wall space afforded by fixed room dividers, such as free-standing bar-type counters, shall be included in the 6-foot (1.83-m) measurement.

See Figure 210-22.

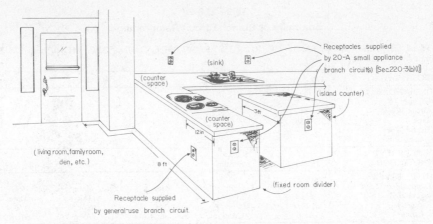

Figure 210-22. Section 210-52(a) requires the wall space afforded by fixed room dividers to be included in the 6-ft measurement. Section 210-52(b) requires a receptacle at each counter space wider than 12 in.

As used in this section a "wall space" shall be considered a wall unbroken along the floor line by doorways, fireplaces, and similar openings. Each wall space 2 or more feet (610 mm or more) wide shall be treated individually and separately from other wall spaces within the room. A wall space shall be permitted to include two or more walls of a room (around corners) where unbroken at the floor line.

The purpose of this requirement is to minimize the use of cords across doorways, fireplaces, and similar openings.

Receptacle outlets shall, insofar as practicable, be spaced equal distances apart. Receptacle outlets in floors shall not be counted as part of the required number of receptacle outlets unless located close to the wall.

Receptacles are to be located so that no "point" in any wall space is more than 6 ft from a receptacle. This rule intends that an appliance or lamp with a flexible cord attached may be placed anywhere in the room and be within 6 ft of a receptacle, thus eliminating the need for extension cords.

A "wallspace" is a wall unbroken along the floor line by doorways, fireplaces, archways and similar openings, and may include two or more walls of a room (around corners, as illustrated in Figure 210-23).

Fixed room dividers, including bar-type counters, are to be included in the 6-ft measurement. Isolated, individual wall spaces 2 ft or more in width are considered usable for the location of a lamp or appliance and a receptacle outlet must be provided. This also applies to counter spaces 12 in. or more in width in kitchen or dining areas. Receptacles are required to be located at these spaces, thereby eliminating probable hazards caused by running cords across doorways or passageways or across sinks or range tops, etc. Sliding panels in exterior walls are counted as regular wall space, and a floor-type receptacle can be used to meet the required spacing.

The receptacle outlets required by this section shall be in addition to any receptacle that is part of any lighting fixture or appliance, located within cabinets or cupboards, or located over 5½ feet (1.68 m) above the floor.

Exception: Permanently installed electric baseboard heaters equipped with factory-installed receptacle outlets or outlets provided as a separate assembly by the manufacturer shall be permitted as the required

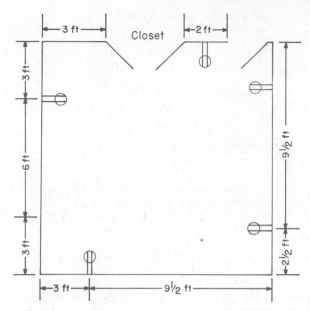

Figure 210-23. Plan view of the location of receptacles in a typical room. Receptacles are spaced to permit a lamp or appliance equipped with 6-ft cords to be located anywhere in the room.

outlet or outlets for the wall space utilized by such permanently installed heaters. Such receptacle outlets shall not be connected to the heater circuits.

According to listing instructions [see Section 110-3(b)], permanent electric baseboard heaters are not to be located beneath wall receptacles. Where the receptacle is a part of the heater, cords of appliances or lamps are less apt to be exposed to the heating elements, such as falling into convector slots. See Figures 210-24 and 210-25.

Figure 210-24. An electric baseboard heater with a receptacle outlet provided as the required receptacle outlet for the wall space. (*Square D Co.*)

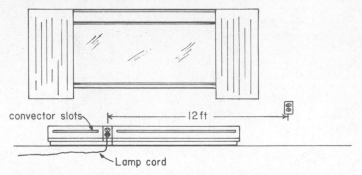

convector slots

|← ———— 12 ft ————→|

Lamp cord

Figure 210-25. Many electrical baseboard heaters are of the low-density type and are designed to be longer than 12 ft. To meet the spacing requirements of Section 210-52(a), it is necessary that the required receptacle be located as a part of the heater unit.

(b) Counter Tops.   In kitchen and dining areas of dwelling units a receptacle outlet shall be installed at each counter space wider than 12 inches (305 mm). Counter top spaces separated by range tops, refrigerators, or sinks shall be considered as separate counter top spaces. Receptacles rendered inaccessible by appliances fastened in place or appliances occupying dedicated space shall not be considered as these required outlets.

Receptacles rendered inaccessible by appliances fastened in place or by appliances occupying dedicated space, such as dishwashers, garbage disposal units, built-in gas ovens, waste compactors, etc., are not to be considered as the required receptacles.

(c) Bathrooms.   In dwelling units at least one wall receptacle outlet shall be installed in the bathroom adjacent to the basin location. See Section 210-8(a)(1).

In bathrooms of a dwelling unit, one wall receptacle is to be installed adjacent to the wash basin and this receptacle is required in addition to any receptacle that may be part of any lighting fixture or medicine cabinet. All 125-V single-phase, 15- and 20-A receptacles installed in bathroom areas are to have ground-fault circuit-interrupter protection for personnel.

(d) Outdoor Outlets.   For one-and two-family dwellings at least one receptacle outlet shall be installed outdoors. See Section 210-8(a)(3).

It is mandatory for two-family dwellings to have at least one outdoor receptacle. This applies to both duplex and two-tenement (one-over-one) types. It is the intent that a two-family dwelling have two receptacles, one for each family. See Figure 210-26.

(e) Laundry Areas.   In dwelling units at least one receptacle outlet shall be installed for the laundry.

Exception No. 1: In a dwelling unit that is an apartment or living area in a multifamily building where laundry facilities are provided on the premises that are available to all building occupants, a laundry receptacle shall not be required.

Exception No. 2: In other than one-family dwellings where laundry facilities are not to be installed or permitted, a laundry receptacle shall not be required.

Figure 210-26. Illustration of the intended number of outdoor receptacles for a two-family dwelling. Two are shown; only one is required.

(f) Basements and Garages.   For a one-family dwelling at least one receptacle outlet in addition to any provided for laundry equipment shall be installed in each basement and in each attached garage. See Section 210-8(a)(2).

It is mandatory in a one-family dwelling to install a receptacle in each basement (in addition to the laundry receptacle, which is also mandatory), and in each attached garage. The *Code* intends that it is not mandatory to install a receptacle in unattached garages. However, if receptacles are installed in this location, GFCIs must be provided.

210-60. Guest Rooms.   Guest rooms in hotels, motels, and similar occupancies shall have receptacle outlets installed in accordance with Section 210-52.

Exception: In rooms of hotels and motels, receptacle outlets may be located convenient for the permanent furniture layout.

210-62. Show Windows.   At least one receptacle outlet shall be installed directly above a show window for each 12 linear feet (3.66 m) or major fraction thereof of show window area measured horizontally at its maximum width.

Show windows are usually designed from floor to ceiling for maximum display. To discourage floor receptacles and unsightly extension cords likely to cause physical injury, receptacles must be installed "directly above" a show window and one receptacle is required for every 12 linear feet or "major (more than 6 ft) fraction" thereof.

210-70. Lighting Outlets Required.   Lighting outlets shall be installed where specified in (a) and (b) below.

(a) Dwelling Unit(s).   At least one wall switch-controlled lighting outlet shall be installed in every habitable room; in bathrooms, hallways, stairways, and attached garages; and at outdoor entrances.

A vehicle door in an attached garage is not considered as an outdoor entrance.

At least one lighting outlet shall be installed in an attic, underfloor space, utility room and basement only where these spaces are used for storage or containing equipment requiring servicing.

Exception No. 1: In habitable rooms, other than kitchens, one or more receptacles controlled by a wall switch shall be permitted in lieu of lighting outlets.

Exception No. 2: In hallways, stairways, and at outdoor entrances remote, central, or automatic control of lighting shall be permitted.

(b) Guest Rooms.   At least one wall switch-controlled lighting outlet or wall switch-controlled receptacle shall be installed in guest rooms in hotels, motels, or similar occupancies.

This section points out that adequate lighting and proper control and location of switching is as essential to the safety of occupants of dwelling units(s), hotels, motels, etc., as are proper wiring requirements. Proper illumination assures safe movement for persons of all ages and many accidents are avoided.

Installation of lighting outlets in attics, under floor space or crawl areas, utility rooms or basements are required "only" where these spaces are used for storage (Christmas decorations, luggage, etc.) or where such spaces contain equipment requiring servicing (air-handling units, cooling and heating equipment, water pumps, sump pumps, etc.).

Remote, central, or automatic control of lighting for hallways, stairways, and outdoor entrances is practical in multifamily dwellings where it is desirable to use time clocks or to locate switches where they may not be intentionally or inadvertently turned "off."

Although the requirement calls for a lighting outlet at outdoor entrances, it does not prohibit a single lighting outlet, if suitably located, from serving more than one door.

A wall switch controlled lighting outlet is required in the kitchen and bathroom.

ARTICLE 215 — FEEDERS

Contents

215-1. Scope.   This article covers the installation requirements and minimum size and ampacity of conductors for feeders supplying branch-circuit loads as computed in accordance with Article 220. The requirements of Section 215-8 shall apply to feeders and other applications where identification is equally necessary.

Exception: See Section 668-3(c), Exception Nos. 1 and 4 for electrolytic cells.

A thorough calculation of the total connected load to be supplied by the feeder is required to determine accurately feeder conductor ampacity. The sum of the connected loads supplied by a feeder is multiplied by the "demand factor" to determine the load which the feeder conductors must be sized to serve. (See Article 100 for definition of "Demand Factor.")

When the total connected load is operated simultaneously, the demand factor is 100 percent; that is, the maximum demand is equal to the total connected load. Due to diversity, the maximum operating load ever carried may be ¾ of the total connected load; the demand factor is thus 75 percent.

On a new installation, a minimum value for the demand factor can be determined by applying the requirements and tables of Article 220 (Branch Circuit and Feeder Calculations).

Feeder conductor sizes are determined by calculating the total wattage of the feeder load at the voltage of the feeder circuit:

<table>
<tr><td align="center">Single Phase</td><td align="center">Three Phase</td></tr>
<tr><td align="center">$I = \dfrac{\text{watts load}}{E}$</td><td align="center">$I = \dfrac{\text{watts load}}{E \times 1.73}$</td></tr>
</table>

where I = current in amperes
E = volts

See Tables of Article 310 for allowable ampacities and sizes of insulated conductors.

Feeder circuits are to have sufficient ampacity for safety. Overloading of a wiring system that does not provide for increases in the use of electricity often creates hazards. It is good practice to allow for future increases.

215-2. Minimum Rating and Size. Feeder conductors shall have an ampacity not lower than required to supply the load as computed in Parts B, C, and D of Article 220. The minimum sizes shall be as specified in (a) and (b) below under the conditions stipulated. Feeder conductors for a dwelling unit or a mobile home need not be larger than service-entrance conductors. Note 3 of Table 310-16 shall be permitted to be used for conductor size.

This section correlates with Note 3 of Table 310-16. For example, Table 310-16 allows 200 amperes for a No. 3/0 THW copper wire. But for a three-wire, single-phase dwelling service, Note 3 permits 200 amperes for a 2/0 copper conductor or 200 amperes for a 4/0 aluminum conductor. It stands to reason that feeder conductors carrying the total load supplied by the service-entrance conductors should not be required to be sized larger than the service-entrance conductors. See Figure 215-1.

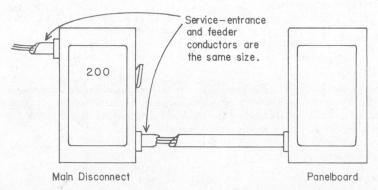

Figure 215-1. For a 3-wire, single-phase dwelling service, Note 3 of Table 310-16 permits an ampacity of 200 A for 2/0 copper conductors for use as service-entrance conductors and for feeder conductors.

(a) For Specified Circuits.   The ampacity of feeder conductors shall not be less than 30 where the load supplied consists of the following number and types of circuits: (1) two or more 2-wire branch circuits supplied by a 2-wire feeder; (2) more than two 2-wire branch circuits supplied by a 3-wire feeder; and (3) two or more 3-wire branch circuits supplied by a 3-wire feeder.

(b) Ampacity Relative to Service-Entrance Conductors.   The feeder conductor ampacity shall not be lower than that of the service-entrance conductors where the feeder conductors carry the total load supplied by service-entrance conductors with an ampacity of 55 or less.

See Examples 1 through 8 in Chapter 9.
Conductors for feeders as defined in Article 100, sized to prevent a voltage drop exceeding 3 percent at the farthest outlet of power, heating, and lighting loads, or combinations of such loads and where the maximum total voltage drop on both feeders and branch circuits to the farthest outlet does not exceed 5 percent, will provide reasonable efficiency of operation.
See Section 210-19(a) for voltage drop for branch circuits.

Total voltage drop consists of the voltage drop in the feeder plus the voltage drop in the branch circuit. Reasonable operating efficiency will be achieved where the maximum voltage drop of a feeder and a branch circuit does not exceed 5 percent. Conductors of a feeder should be sized to prevent a voltage drop exceeding 3 percent and conductors of a branch circuit should be sized to prevent a voltage drop exceeding 2 percent. See Article 100 for definition of "Feeder" and "Branch Circuit."

The 5 percent voltage drop value is a recommended practice, and, as such, it appears as a fine print note. Fine print notes are explanatory and not mandatory (see Section 110-1).

The resistance or impedance of conductors may cause a substantial difference between voltage values at service equipment and voltage values at the point of utilization equipment. Excessive voltage drop impairs the starting and operation of electrical equipment. In addition to reactance or impedance, length, size, and type of conductor, type of raceway or cable enclosure, type of circuit ac, dc, single-phase, 3-phase and power factor are to be considered to determine voltage drop.

The basic formula for determining voltage drop in a 2-wire dc circuit, a 2-wire ac circuit, or a 3-wire ac single-phase circuit with a balanced load at 100 percent power factor and where reactance can be neglected is:

$$VD = \frac{2 \times r \times L \times I}{\text{circular mils}}$$

where VD = voltage drop
    r = resistivity of conductor material (12 ohms per CM ft for copper and 18 ohms per CM ft for aluminum or copper-clad)
    L = one-way length of circuit (feet)
    I = current in conductor (amperes)

For 3-phase circuits (at 100 percent power factor) the voltage drop between any two phase conductors is 0.866 times the voltage drop calculated by this formula.

Example: 230-V 2-wire heating circuit. Load is 50 A. Circuit size is No. 6 AWG THHN copper and the one-way circuit length is 100 ft.

$$VD = \frac{2 \times r \times L \times I}{CM} = \frac{2 \times 12 \times 100 \times 50}{26,240 \text{ (Table 8, Chapter 9)}}$$

$$VD = \frac{120,000}{26,240} = 4.57\text{-V drop}$$

An 11.5-V drop on a 230-V circuit is approximately a 5-percent drop; therefore, a 4.57-V drop falls within this percentage.

Should the voltage drop exceed 5 percent then a larger size conductor should be used, or the circuit length shortened, or the circuit load should be reduced.

Voltage drop tables and calculations are available from various manufacturers.

215-3. Overcurrent Protection.   Feeders shall be protected against overcurrent in accordance with the provisions of Part A of Article 240.

215-4. Feeders with Common Neutral.

(a) Feeders with Common Neutral.   Feeders containing a common neutral shall be permitted to supply two or three sets of 3-wire feeders, or two sets of 4-wire or 5-wire feeders.

(b) In Metal Raceway or Enclosure.   Where installed in a metal raceway or other metal enclosure, all conductors of all feeders using a common neutral shall be enclosed within the same raceway or other enclosure as required in Section 300-20.

Where feeder conductors carrying ac current, including the neutral, are installed in metal raceways, they are to be grouped together to avoid induction heating of the surrounding metal.

A 3-phase, 4-wire (208 wye/120 V, 480 wye/277 V) system is often used to supply both lighting and motor loads. The 3-phase motor loads will cause no current to flow in the neutral conductor. Therefore, the maximum current the neutral will carry is from lighting loads, or circuits where the neutral is used. On this type of system (3-phase, 4-wire), a demand factor of 70 percent is to be permitted for that portion of the neutral load in excess of 200 A. See Section 220-22. Thus, if the maximum possible load is 500 A, the neutral would need to be large enough to carry 200 A plus 70 percent of 300 A, or 410 A. There is to be no reduction of the neutral capacity for that portion of the load consisting of electric-discharge lighting. See Section 220-22 for other systems to which the 70 percent demand factor may be applied. The maximum unbalanced load for feeders supplying household ranges, wall-mounted ovens, and counter-mounted cooking units is to be considered as 70 percent of the load of the ungrounded conductors. See Example Nos. 1 through 5 of Chapter 9.

The following calculation for feeders is for instances where the main service is 3-phase, 4-wire, 120/208 V and the supply to the individual apartments is from two phase conductors and the neutral. A sample calculation has been made for Example 4(a) (Chapter 9, Part B, Examples) for both 20 and 40 apartments.

This sample calculation follows the method given in Example 7 (Chapter 9, Part B, Examples) that avoids having to add out-of-phase currents together.

Although the neutral will carry full current from two phase conductors for a single apartment, the basis for providing capacity for this neutral is the same as for single-phase systems.

Example: (For a 3-phase load using Example 4(a) in Chapter 9, tables and examples):

Minimum size feeder required from service equipment to meter bank for 20 apartments.

(20 apartments — 14 connected to two phase conductors)

Total computed load

Lighting and small appliance load	14 × 5,400 =	75,600 watts
Water and space heating	14 × 8,500 =	119,000 watts
Range load	14 × 8,000 =	112,000 watts
	Net computed load	306,600 watts

Net computed load using optional calculation (Table 220-32)

306,600 × 0.40 .... 122,640 watts

122,640 × 0.5 ÷ 120 V......................... 511 amperes (each phase conductor)

Minimum size main feeder required (less house load) for 40 apartments.

Total computed load

Lighting and small appliance load	28 × 5,400 =	151,200 watts
Water and space heating	28 × 8,500 =	238,000 watts
Range load	28 × 8,000 =	224,000 watts
Net computed load		613,200 watts

Net computed load using optional calculation (Table 220-32)

613,200 × 0.33 .... 202,356 watts

202,356 × 0.5 ÷ 120 V......................... 843 amperes (each phase conductor)

Feeder neutral load for feeder from service equipment to meter bank for 20 apartments.

Lighting and small appliance load	14 × 5,400 watts =	75,600 watts
First 3,000 watts at 100%	=	3,000 watts
72,600 watts at 35%	=	25,410 watts
Subtotal		28,410 watts
14 ranges = 29,000 watts at 70%	=	20,300 watts
(see Table 220-19 and Section 220-19)		
Total		48,710 watts
48,710 watts × 0.5 ÷ 120 V		= 203 A
Further demand factor (Section 220-19)		
First 200 amperes at 100%		= 200 A
Balance: 3 amperes at 70%		= 2 A
Total		202 A

215-5. Diagrams of Feeders.   If required by the authority having jurisdiction, a diagram showing feeder details shall be provided prior to the installation of the feeders. Such a diagram shall show the area in square feet of the building or other structure supplied by each feeder, the total connected load before applying demand factors, the demand factors used, the computed load after applying demand factors, and the size and type of conductors to be used.

215-6. Feeder Conductor Grounding Means.   Where a feeder supplies branch circuits in which equipment grounding conductors are required, the feeder shall include or provide a grounding means in accordance with the provisions of Section 250-57 to which the equipment grounding conductors of the branch circuits shall be connected.

215-7. Ungrounded Conductors Tapped from Grounded Systems.   Two-wire dc circuits and ac circuits of two or more ungrounded conductors may be tapped from the ungrounded conductors of circuits having a grounded neutral conductor. Switching devices in each tapped circuit shall have a pole in each ungrounded conductor.

It is not intended to provide a common trip of fuses or circuit breakers but to disconnect "manually" the ungrounded conductors of the feeder. See Section 210-10.

215-8. Means of Identifying Conductor with the Higher Voltage to Ground.   On a 4-wire, delta-connected secondary where the midpoint of one phase is grounded to supply lighting and similar loads, the phase conductor having the higher voltage to ground shall be identified by an outer finish that is orange in color or by tagging or other effective means. Such identification shall be placed at each point where a connection is made if the neutral conductor is also present.

It is permitted to ground the midpoint of one phase to supply (120 V) lighting and similar loads on a delta-connected secondary. This results in one phase conductor having a higher voltage to ground and it is identified by an orange finish at any point, such as junction or pull boxes, panelboards, etc., where connections may be made and the neutral is also present. The orange high-leg of a 3-phase, 4-wire (120/240 V) delta system is 208 V to ground (120 V x 1.73 = 208 V) and should obviously not be used for 120-V circuits. See Sections 230-56, and 384-3(e) and (f). See Figure 215-2.

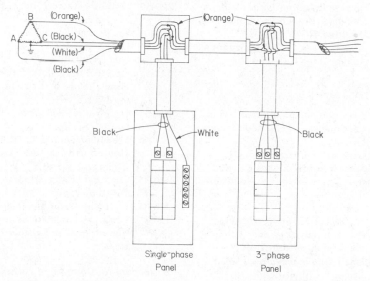

Figure 215-2. With a 4-wire, delta-connected secondary in which the midpoint of one phase is grounded, one phase conductor has a higher voltage to ground than the other two. It is identified in this illustration as having an "orange" finish. The identification must be visible at every point where a connection is made if a neutral is present.

215-9. Ground-Fault Protection for Personnel. Feeders supplying 15- and 20-ampere receptacle branch circuits shall be permitted to be protected by a ground-fault circuit-interrupter in lieu of the provisions for such interrupters as specified in Section 210-8.

Several manufacturers offer double-pole 120/240-V ground-fault circuit-interrupters for application to a feeder, thereby protecting all branch circuits supplied by that feeder. This installation is in lieu of provisions of Section 210-8 for outdoor, bathroom, garage, and construction-site receptacles.

It may be more economical or convenient to install ground-fault circuit-interrupters for feeders. However, it will be monitoring several branch circuits and, in response to a line-to-ground fault from one branch circuit, it will de-energize all of the branch circuits.

ARTICLE 220 — BRANCH-CIRCUIT AND
FEEDER CALCULATIONS

Contents

A. General

220-1. Scope.   This article provides requirements for determining the number of branch circuits required and for computing branch-circuit and feeder loads.

For uniform application of the provisions of Articles 210, 215 and 220, a nominal voltage of 115 and 230 volts is to be used in computing the ampere load on the conductor.

See Chapter 9, Examples 1 through 7. The results of these Examples are generally expressed in amperes. Except where the computations result in a major fraction of an ampere (larger than 0.5), such fractions may be dropped.

To select conductor sizes, refer to Tables 310-16 through 310-19 and the Notes that pertain to such tables.

Exception: See Section 668-3(c), Exceptions No. 1 and No. 4 for electrolytic cells.

This Exception also appears after Sections 210-1, 215-1, 220-1, and 225-1.

220-2. Computation of Branch Circuits. Branch-circuit loads shall be computed as shown in (a) through (d) below.

(a) Continuous Loads. The continuous load supplied by a branch circuit shall not exceed 80 percent of the branch-circuit rating.

See Figure 220-1.

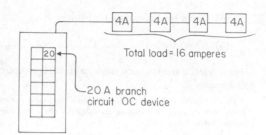

Total load = 16 amperes

20 A branch circuit OC device

Figure 220-1. Continuous loads, such as store lighting, must not exceed 80 percent of the branch-circuit rating.

Exception No. 1: Where branch-circuit conductors have been derated in accordance with Note 8 to Tables 310-16 through 310-19.

Where branch-circuit conductors have been derated according to the provisions of Note 8 to Tables 310-16 through 310-19 because of the number of conductors in a raceway, cable, or stacked bundle, it is not necessary to apply the derating provisions of Section 220-2(a), i.e., "double-derating" is not required.

Exception No. 2: Where the assembly, including overcurrent devices, is listed for continuous operation of 100 percent of its rating.

(b) Lighting Load for Listed Occupancies. A unit load of not less than that specified in Table 220-2(b) for occupancies listed therein shall constitute the minimum lighting load for each square foot (0.093 sq m) of floor area. The floor area for each floor shall be computed from the outside dimensions of the building, apartment, or other area involved. For dwelling unit(s), the computed floor area shall not include open porches, garages, or unused or unfinished spaces not adaptable for future use.

Examples of "unused or unfinished" spaces are some attics or some crawl spaces.

The unit values herein are based on minimum load conditions and 100 percent power factor, and may not provide sufficient capacity for the installation contemplated.

(c) Other Loads — All Occupancies. In all occupancies the minimum load for each outlet for general-use receptacles and outlets not used for general illumination shall be not less than the following, the loads shown being based on nominal branch-circuit voltages.

(1) Outlet for a specific appliance or other load except for a motor load .... ampere rating of appliance or load served.

(2) Outlet for motor load .... See Sections 430-22 and 430-24 and Article 440.

(3) An outlet supplying recessed lighting fixture(s) shall be the maximum volt-ampere rating of the equipment and lamps for which the fixture(s) is rated.

The rating of 180 volt-amperes is not required for outlets for recessed lighting fixtures that do not accept lamps of that wattage. To apply the 180 VA requirement, in this case, would be unrealistic as it would restrict the number of lighting outlets on a branch circuit unnecessarily. That is, lighting fixture outlets should not be rated more than the largest lamp for which the fixture is rated.

(4) Outlet for heavy-duty lampholder .... 600 volt-amperes.

(5) *Other outlets .... 180 volt-amperes per outlet.

For receptacle outlets, each single or multiple receptacle shall be considered at not less than 180 volt-amperes.

* This provision shall not be applicable to receptacle outlets connected to the circuit specified in Section 220-3(b) nor to receptacle outlets provided for the connection of cord- and plug-connected equipment as provided for in Section 400-7.

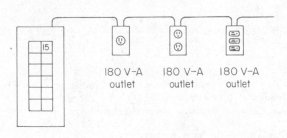

180 V-A outlet   180 V-A outlet   180 V-A outlet

Figure 220-2. The 180 volt-ampere rating is applied to the outlet, regardless of whether a single, duplex, or triplex receptacle is connected to that outlet.

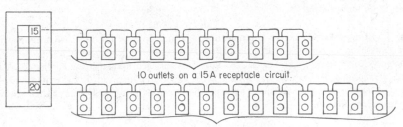

10 outlets on a 15A receptacle circuit.

13 outlets on a 20A receptacle circuit.

15 amperes x 115 volts = 1725 VA ÷ 180 VA = 9.6 or 10 receptacle outlets.
20 amperes x 115 volts = 2300 VA ÷ 180 VA = 12.8 or 13 receptacle outlets.

Figure 220-3. Computation of the maximum number of outlets permitted on 15- and 20-A branch circuits. In some areas, enforcing authorities may permit only 9 receptacle outlets on a 15-A branch circuit and 12 receptacle outlets on a 20-A branch circuit.

Exception No. 1: Where fixed multioutlet assemblies are employed, each 5 feet (1.52 m) or fraction thereof of each separate and continuous length shall be considered as one outlet of not less than 1½ ampere capacity, except in locations where a number of appliances are likely to be used simultaneously, when each 1 foot (305 mm) or fraction thereof shall be considered as an outlet of not less than 1½ amperes. The requirements of this section shall not apply to dwelling unit(s) or the guest rooms of hotels or motels.

See Figure 220-4.

Exception No. 2: Table 220-19 shall be considered as an acceptable method of computing the load for a household electric range.

Exception No. 3: A load of not less than 200 watts per linear foot (305 mm) of show window, measured horizontally along its base, shall be permitted instead of the specified unit load per outlet.

See Figure 220-5.

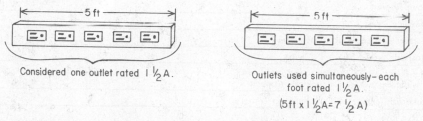

Considered one outlet rated 1 ½ A.

Outlets used simultaneously—each
foot rated 1 ½ A.
(5ft x 1 ½ A = 7 ½ A)

Figure 220-4. Fixed multi-outlet assemblies are commonly used in commercial or industrial locations and may have been selected for a number of receptacles along a given work area (light use) or for the simultaneous connection and use of a number of appliances (heavy use).

200 watts per linear foot.
200 W x 10 ft = 2000 watts.

Figure 220-5. The linear foot calculation method is permitted in lieu of the specified unit load per outlet.

Exception No. 4: The loads of outlets serving switchboards and switching frames in telephone exchanges shall be waived from the computations.

(d) Loads for Additions to Existing Installations.

(1) Dwelling Units. Loads for structural additions to an existing dwelling unit or to a previously unwired portion of an existing dwelling unit, either of which exceeds 500 square feet (46.5 sq m), shall be computed in accordance with (b) above. Loads for new circuits or extended circuits in previously wired dwelling units shall be computed in accordance with either (b) or (c) above.

(2) Other than Dwelling Units. Loads for new circuits or extended circuits in other than dwelling units shall be computed in accordance with either (b) or (c) above.

Table 220-2(b).   General Lighting Loads by Occupancies

Type of Occupancy	Unit Load per Sq. Ft. (Watts)
Armories and Auditoriums	1
Banks	3½**
Barber Shops and Beauty Parlors	3
Churches	1
Clubs	2
Court Rooms	2
*Dwelling Units	3
Garages — Commercial (storage)	½
Hospitals	2
*Hotels and Motels, including apartment houses without provisions for cooking by tenants	2
Industrial Commercial (Loft) Buildings	2
Lodge Rooms	1½
Office Buildings	3½**
Restaurants	2
Schools	3
Stores	3
Warehouses (storage)	¼
In any of the above occupancies except one-family dwellings and individual dwelling units of multifamily dwellings:	
Assembly Halls and Auditoriums	1
Halls, Corridors, Closets	½
Storage Spaces	¼

For SI units: one square foot = 0.093 square meter.

* All receptacle outlets of 20-ampere or less rating in one-family and multifamily dwellings and in guest rooms of hotels and motels [except those connected to the receptacle circuits specified in Section 220-3(b)] shall be considered as outlets for general illumination, and no additional load calculations shall be required for such outlets.

** In addition a unit load of 1 watt per square foot shall be included for general purpose receptacle outlets when the actual number of general purpose receptacle outlets is unknown.

220-3. Branch Circuits Required.   Branch circuits for lighting and for appliances, including motor-operated appliances, shall be provided to supply the loads computed in accordance with Section 220-2. In addition, branch circuits shall be provided for specific loads not covered by Section 220-2 where required elsewhere in this Code; for small appliance loads as specified in (b) below; and for laundry loads as specified in (c) below.

(a) Number of Branch Circuits.   The minimum number of branch circuits shall be determined from the total computed load and the size or rating of the circuits used. In all installations the number of circuits shall be sufficient to supply the load served. In no case shall the load on any circuit exceed the maximum specified by Section 210-22.

(b) Small Appliance Branch Circuits — Dwelling Unit.

(1) In addition to the number of branch circuits determined in accordance with (a) above, two or more 20-ampere small appliance branch circuits shall be provided for all receptacle outlets specified by Section 210-52 for the small appliance loads, including refrigeration equipment, in the kitchen, pantry, breakfast room, and dining room of a dwelling unit. Such circuits, whether two or more are used, shall have no other outlets.

See Figure 220-6.

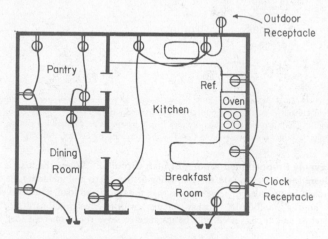

Figure 220-6. This figure illustrates the requirements of Section 220-3(b)(1) and (2). Though these small appliance branch circuits may serve certain outlets in other specified areas, they are not permitted to serve any other outlets such as might be connected to exhaust hoods or fans, disposal units, or dishwashers.

Exception: A receptacle installed solely for the electric supply to and support of an electric clock in any of these stipulated rooms or outdoor receptacle outlets shall be supplied either by a small appliance branch circuit or by a general purpose branch circuit.

(2) Receptacle outlets installed in the kitchen shall be supplied by not less than two small appliance branch circuits, either or both of which shall also be permitted to supply receptacle outlets in the other rooms specified in (b)(1) above. Additional small appliance branch circuits shall be permitted to supply receptacle outlets in such other rooms.

Two or more 20-A circuits are to be provided for all receptacle outlets for the small appliance loads, including refrigeration equipment, in the kitchen, dining room, pantry, and breakfast room of a dwelling unit. Receptacle outlets in kitchens are to be supplied by no fewer than two small appliance branch circuits. These circuits may also supply receptacle outlets in the pantry, dining room, and breakfast room as well as to supply an electric clock receptacle or outdoor receptacles, but are to have no other outlets.

At least one additional 20-A branch circuit is to be provided to supply the laundry receptacle outlet(s) required, and this circuit is to have no other outlets. See Figures 220-6 and 220-7.

(c) Laundry Branch Circuits — Dwelling Unit. In addition to the number of branch circuits determined in accordance with (a) and (b) above, at least one additional 20-ampere branch circuit shall be provided to supply the laundry receptacle outlet(s) required by Section 210-52(e). This circuit shall have no other outlets.

See Figure 220-7.

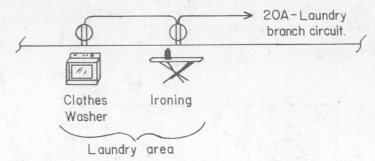

Figure 220-7. At least one 20-A branch circuit is required to supply the laundry receptacle outlet(s). Lighting outlets in laundry areas must not be connected to the laundry branch circuit. If the laundry area is in a basement or an attached garage, this receptacle outlet is not to be considered as that required by Section 210-52(f).

(d) Load Evenly Proportioned Among Branch Circuits.   Where the load is computed on a watts-per-square-foot (0.093 sq m) basis, the wiring system up to and including the branch-circuit panelboard(s) shall be provided to serve not less than the calculated load. This load shall be evenly proportioned among multioutlet branch circuits within the panelboard(s). Branch-circuit overcurrent devices and circuits need only be installed to serve the connected load.

See Examples 1, 1(a), 1(b), 1(c), and 4, Chapter 9.

B. Feeders

220-10. General.

(a) Ampacity and Computed Loads.   Feeder conductors shall have sufficient ampacity to supply the load served. In no case shall the computed load of a feeder be less than the sum of the loads on the branch circuits supplied as determined by Part A of this article after any applicable demand factors permitted by Parts B, C, or D have been applied.

See Examples 1 through 8, Chapter 9. See Section 210-22(b) for maximum load in amperes permitted for lighting units operating at less than 100 percent power factor.

(b) Continuous and Noncontinuous Loads.   Where a feeder supplies continuous loads or any combination of continuous and noncontinuous load, neither the ampere rating of the overcurrent device nor the ampacity of the feeder conductors shall be less than the noncontinuous load plus 125 percent of the continuous load.

Exception: Where the assembly including the overcurrent devices protecting the feeder(s) are listed for operation at 100 percent of their rating, neither the ampere rating of the overcurrent device nor the ampacity of the feeder conductors shall be less than the sum of the continuous load plus the noncontinuous load.

Sections 220-10 through 220-22, which are included in Part B, give the requirements for calculating feeder load. Sections 220-30 and 220-32 give optional methods for calculating feeder load in dwelling units and multifamily dwellings.

220-11. General Lighting.   The demand factors listed in Table 220-11 shall apply to that portion of the total branch-circuit load computed for general illumination. They shall not be applied in determining the number of branch circuits for general illumination.

See Section 220-16 for application of demand factors to small appliance and laundry loads in dwellings.

Table 220-11.   Lighting Load Feeder Demand Factors

Type of Occupancy	Portion of Lighting Load to Which Demand Factor Applies (wattage)	Demand Factor Percent
Dwelling Units	First 3000 or less at	100
	Next 3001 to 120,000 at	35
	Remainder over 120,000 at	25
*Hospitals	First 50,000 or less at....................................	40
	Remainder over 50,000 at.................................	20
*Hotels and Motels — Including Apartment Houses without Provision for Cooking by Tenants	First 20,000 or less at....................................	50
	Next 20,001 to 100,000 at...............................	40
	Remainder over 100,000 at	30
Warehouses (Storage)	First 12,500 or less at....................................	100
	Remainder over 12,500 at.................................	50
All Others	Total Wattage	100

* The demand factors of this table shall not apply to the computed load of feeders to areas in hospitals, hotels, and motels where the entire lighting is likely to be used at one time, as in operating rooms, ballrooms, or dining rooms.

220-12. Show-Window Lighting. For show-window lighting, a load of not less than 200 watts shall be included for each linear foot (305 mm) of show window, measured horizontally along its base.

See Section 220-2(c), Exception No. 3, for branch circuits supplying show windows.

See Figure 220-5.

220-13. Receptacle Loads — Nondwelling Units. In other than dwelling units, the use of the demand factors for lighting loads in Table 220-11 or those shown in Table 220-13 shall be permitted for receptacle loads computed at not more than 180 volt-amperes per outlet in accordance with Section 220-2(c)(5).

Table 220-13

Demand Factors for Nondwelling Receptacle Loads

Portion of Receptacle Load to which demand factor applies (wattage)	Demand Factor Percent
First 10 kW or less	100
Remainder over 10 kW at	50

220-14. Motors. Motor loads shall be computed in accordance with Sections 430-24, 430-25, and 430-26.

220-15. Fixed Electric Space Heating. Fixed electric space heating loads shall be computed at 100 percent of the total connected load.

Exception No. 1: Where reduced loading of the conductors results from units operating on duty-cycle, intermittently, or from all units not operating at one time, the authority having jurisdiction may grant permission for feeder conductors to have an ampacity less than 100 percent, provided the conductors have an ampacity for the load so determined.

Exception No. 2: The use of the optional calculations in Sections 220-30 and 220-31 shall be permitted for fixed electric space heating loads in a dwelling unit. In a multifamily dwelling the use of the optional calculation in Section 220-32 shall be permitted.

220-16. Small Appliance and Laundry Loads — Dwelling Unit.

(a) Small Appliance Circuit Load. In each dwelling unit the feeder load shall be computed at 1500 watts for each 2-wire small appliance branch circuit required by Section 220-3(b) for small appliances supplied by 15- or 20-ampere receptacles on 20-ampere branch circuits in the kitchen, pantry, dining room, and breakfast room. Where the load is subdivided through two or more feeders, the computed load for each shall include not less than 1500 watts for each 2-wire branch circuit for small appliances. These loads shall be permitted to be included with the general lighting load and subjected to the demand factors permitted in Table 220-11 for the general lighting load.

(b) Laundry Circuit Load. A feeder load of not less than 1500 watts shall be included for each 2-wire laundry branch circuit installed as required by Section 220-3(c). It shall be permissible to include this load with the general lighting load and subjected to the demand factors provided in Section 220-11.

In each dwelling unit, the feeder load is to be calculated at 1500 watts for each of the two or more (two-wire) small appliance branch circuits and 1500 watts for each (2-wire) laundry branch circuit. It is permissible to total these loads and add them to the general lighting load and subject the total load (small appliance, laundry, plus general lighting) to the demand factors provided in Table 220-11.

220-17. Fixed Appliance Load — Dwelling Unit(s). It shall be permissible to apply a demand factor of 75 percent to the nameplate-rating load of four or more appliances fastened in place served by the same feeder in a one-family, two-family, or multifamily dwelling.

Exception: This demand factor shall not be applied to electric ranges, clothes dryers, space heating equipment, or air-conditioning equipment.

Example: 115/230 V Fixed appliance load — Dwelling unit(s)

water heater	4,000 W	230 V	17.3 A
kitchen disposal	½ hp	115 V	9.8 A
dishwasher	1,200 W	115 V	10.4 A
furnace motor	¼ hp	115 V	5.8 A
attic fan	¼ hp	115 V	5.8 A
water pump	½ hp	230 V	4.9 A
Ampere load on each ungrounded leg —		Total	54.0 A

For appliances fastened in place (other than ranges, clothes dryers, space heating equipment, and air-conditioning equipment), feeder capacity must be provided for the sum of these loads, and the total load of four or more such appliances may be reduced by a demand factor of 75 percent.

Seventy-five percent of 54 A = 41 A, which is the load to be added to the other determined loads for calculating the size of service and/or feeder conductors.

See Table 430-148 for the full-load current in amperes of single-phase ac motors.

220-18. Electric Clothes Dryers — Dwelling Unit(s). The load for household electric clothes dryers in a dwelling unit(s) shall be 5000 watts or the nameplate rating, whichever is larger, for each dryer served. The use of the demand factors in Table 220-18 shall be permitted.

This requirement provides a minimum demand of 5 kW for the calculation of feeder conductors to compute the load of household electric dryers. Where the nameplate rating is known, and exceeds 5 kW, the larger rating is to be applied.

Table 220-18
Demand Factors for Household Electric Clothes Dryers

Number of Dryers	Demand Factor Percent
1	100
2	100
3	100
4	100
5	80
6	70
7	65
8	60
9	55
10	50
11-13	45
14-19	40
20-24	35
25-29	32.5
30-34	30
35-39	27.5
40 & over	25

Table 220-19.   Demand Loads for Household Electric Ranges, Wall-Mounted Ovens, Counter-Mounted Cooking Units, and Other Household Cooking Appliances over 1¾ kW Rating. Column A to be used in all cases except as otherwise permitted in Note 3 below.

NUMBER OF APPLIANCES	Maximum Demand (See Notes) COLUMN A (Not over 12 kW Rating)	Demand Factors Percent (See Note 3) COLUMN B (Less than 3½ kW Rating)	COLUMN C (3½ kW to 8¾ kW Rating)
1	8 kW	80%	80%
2	11 kW	75%	65%
3	14 kW	70%	55%
4	17 kW	66%	50%
5	20 kW	62%	45%
6	21 kW	59%	43%
7	22 kW	56%	40%
8	23 kW	53%	36%
9	24 kW	51%	35%
10	25 kW	49%	34%
11	26 kW	47%	32%
12	27 kW	45%	32%
13	28 kW	43%	32%
14	29 kW	41%	32%
15	30 kW	40%	32%
16	31 kW	39%	28%
17	32 kW	38%	28%
18	33 kW	37%	28%
19	34 kW	36%	28%
20	35 kW	35%	28%
21	36 kW	34%	26%
22	37 kW	33%	26%
23	38 kW	32%	26%
24	39 kW	31%	26%
25	40 kW	30%	26%
26-30	15 kW plus 1 kW for each range	30%	24%
31-40		30%	22%
41-50	25 kW plus ¾ kW for each range	30%	20%
51-60		30%	18%
61 & over		30%	16%

Note 1. Over 12 kW through 27 kW ranges all of same rating. For ranges individually rated more than 12 kW but not more than 27 kW, the maximum demand in Column A shall be increased 5 percent for each additional kW of rating or major fraction thereof by which the rating of individual ranges exceeds 12 kW.

The size of the conductors is to be determined by the rating of the range. By reference to Table 220-19, it can be seen that, for a range not over 12 kW, the demand load is 8 kW and a No. 8 AWG copper conductor, with 60°C insulation, would suffice.

Note 2. Over 12 kW through 27 kW ranges of unequal ratings. For ranges individually rated more than 12 kW and of different ratings but none exceeding 27 kW, an average value of rating shall be computed by adding together the ratings of all ranges to obtain the total connected load (using 12 kW for any range rated less than 12 kW) and dividing by the total number of ranges; and then the maximum demand in Column A shall be increased 5 percent for each kW or major fraction thereof by which this average value exceeds 12 kW.

Note 2 provides for ranges larger than 12 kW, and Note 4 covers situations in which the range consists of several components.

Note 3. Over 1¾ kW through 8¾ kW. In lieu of the method provided in Column A, it shall be permissible to add the nameplate ratings of all ranges rated more than 1¾ kW but not more than 8¾ kW and multiply the sum by the demand factors specified in Column B or C for the given number of appliances.

Note 4. Branch-Circuit Load. It shall be permissible to compute the branch-circuit load for one range in accordance with Table 220-19. The branch-circuit load for one wall-mounted oven or one counter-mounted cooking unit shall be the nameplate rating of the appliance. The branch-circuit load for a counter-mounted cooking unit and not more than two wall-mounted ovens, all supplied from a single branch circuit and located in the same room, shall be computed by adding the nameplate rating of the individual appliances and treating this total as equivalent to one range.

It is permissible to compute the branch-circuit load for one range, one counter-mounted cooking unit, or one wall-mounted oven, by the nameplate rating of the appliance or in accordance with Table 220-19. Where a single branch circuit supplies a counter-mounted cooking unit and not more than two wall-mounted ovens, all of which are located in the same room, it is permissible to add the nameplate ratings of these appliances and treat this total as equivalent to one range.

Example: a single branch circuit for

one counter-mounted cooking unit	8 kW
one wall-mounted oven	7 kW
one wall-mounted oven	6 kW
Total	21 kW

The maximum demand from Column A of Table 220-19 for one range not over 12 kW is 8 kW.

21 kW is less than 27 kW and exceeds 12 kW by 9 kW (see Note 1). The maximum demand in Column A (8 kW) is to be increased 5 percent for each additional kW exceeding 12 kW (9 kW).

5 percent $\times$ 9 = 45 percent
8 kW $\times$ 45 percent = 3.6 kW increase
8 kW + 3.6 kW = 11.6 kW load to calculate single branch circuit
11,600 watts $\div$ 230 V = 50.4 A

Note 5. This table also applies to household cooking appliances rated over 1¾ kW and used in instructional programs.

See Table 220-20 for commercial cooking equipment.

220-19. Electric Ranges and Other Cooking Appliances — Dwelling Unit(s). The feeder demand load for household electric ranges, wall-mounted ovens, counter-mounted cooking units, and other household cooking appliances individually rated in excess of 1¾ kW shall be permitted to be computed in accordance with Table 220-19. Where two or more single-phase ranges are supplied by a 3-phase, 4-wire feeder, the total load shall be computed on the basis of twice the maximum number connected between any two phases.

See Example 7, Chapter 9.

It is permissible to add the nameplate ratings of all household cooking appliances rated more than 1¾ kW, but not more than 8¾ kW, and multiply the sum by the demand factors specified in Column B or C for the given number of appliances.

For feeder demand factors other than for dwelling unit(s), that is, commercial electric cooking equipment, dishwasher booster heaters, water heaters, etc., see Table 220-20.

Demand factors of this *Code* are based on the diversified use of appliances since it is unlikely that all appliances will be energized simultaneously or that all cooking units and the oven of a range will be at maximum heat for any length of time.

220-20. Kitchen Equipment — Other than Dwelling Unit(s). It shall be permissible to compute the load for commercial electric cooking equipment, dishwasher booster heaters, water heaters, and other kitchen equipment in accordance with Table 220-20; however, in no case shall a feeder load current rating be less than the rating of the largest branch circuit supplied.

Table 220-20
Feeder Demand Factors for Kitchen Equipment —
Other than Dwelling Unit(s)

Number of Units of Equipment	Demand Factors Percent
1	100
2	100
3	90
4	80
5	70
6 & over	65

220-21. Noncoincident Loads. Where it is unlikely that two dissimilar loads will be in use simultaneously, it shall be permissible to omit the smaller of the two in computing the total load of a feeder.

220-22. Feeder Neutral Load. The feeder neutral load shall be the maximum unbalance of the load determined by this article. The maximum unbalanced load shall be the maximum connected load between the neutral and any one ungrounded conductor, except that the load thus obtained shall be multiplied by 140 percent for 5-wire, 2-phase systems. For a feeder supplying household electric ranges, wall-mounted ovens, and counter-mounted cooking units, the maximum unbalanced load shall be considered as 70 percent of the load on the ungrounded conductors, as determined in accordance with Table 220-19. For 3-wire dc or single-phase ac, 4-wire, 3-phase, and 5-wire, 2-phase systems, a further demand factor of 70 percent shall be permitted for that portion of the unbalanced load in excess of 200 amperes. There shall be no reduction of the neutral capacity for that portion of the load which consists of electric-discharge lighting.

See Examples 1, 1(a), 1(b), 1(c), 2, 3, 4, and 5, Chapter 9.

Section 220-22 of the *Code* describes the basis for calculating the neutral load as the maximum unbalanced load that can occur between the neutral and any other ungrounded conductor.

For a household electric range, the maximum unbalanced load may be assumed at 70 percent so the neutral may be sized on this basis. Section 250-60 of the *Code* allows the grounded circuit conductor of not less than No. 10 AWG to ground the frame of a range, except for ranges in mobile homes and travel trailers. The supply cable to the range may be service-entrance cable with an uninsulated grounded conductor, if the branch circuit to the range originates at the service equipment. If the range is supplied with a three-conductor branch circuit, a receptacle and attachment plug, if used, may be of the three-pole type without an equipment ground. If nonmetallic sheathed cable is used to supply the range, the conductor provided for equipment grounding purposes cannot be used for the grounded circuit conductor, as stated in Section 336-2.

Where the system supplies electric discharge lighting, the neutral is considered to be a current carrying conductor if the electric discharge lighting load on the feeder neutral consists of more than half of the total load. Electric discharge lighting will have harmonic current in the neutral which may approximate the load current, and it would be appropriate to require a full size feeder neutral conductor.

C. Optional Calculations for Computing Feeder and Service Loads

220-30. Optional Calculation — Dwelling Unit.

(a) **Feeder and Service Load.**   For a dwelling unit having the total connected load served by a single 3-wire, 120/240-volt or 208Y/120-volt set of service-entrance or feeder conductors with an ampacity of 100 or greater, it shall be permissible to compute the feeder and service loads in accordance with Table 220-30 instead of the method specified in Part B of this article. Feeder and service-entrance conductors whose demand load is determined by this optional calculation shall be permitted to have the neutral load determined by Section 220-22.

The optional method given in Section 220-30 is applicable to a single-dwelling unit, whether it is a separate building or located in a multifamily dwelling.

Examples of the optional calculation for a dwelling unit are given in Chapter 9, Example Nos. 1(b) and (c).

See Article 100 for definition of "Dwelling Unit."

(b) **Loads.**   The loads identified in Table 220-30 as "other load" and as "remainder of other load" shall include the following:

(1) 1500 watts for each 2-wire, 20-ampere small appliance branch circuit and each laundry branch circuit specified in Section 220-16.

(2) 3 watts per square foot (0.093 sq m) for general lighting and general-use receptacles.

(3) The nameplate rating of all fixed appliances, ranges, wall-mounted ovens, counter-mounted cooking units, and including four or more separately controlled space heating units.

(4) The nameplate ampere or kVA rating of all motors and of all low-power-factor loads.

Table 220-30
Optional Calculation for Dwelling Unit

Load (in kW or kVA)	Demand Factor Percent
Largest of [see Section 220-30(c)]	
Air conditioning and cooling, including heat pump compressors	100
Central electric space heating including integral supplemental heating in heat pumps...	65
Less than four separately controlled electric space heating units.................................	65
Plus:	
First 10 kW of all other load	100
Remainder of other load	40

(c) Largest Load. When applying Section 220-21 to Table 220-30 use the largest of the following:

(1) Air-conditioning load.

(2) The 65 percent diversified demand of the central electric space heating load including integral supplemental heating in heat pumps.

(3) The 65 percent diversified demand of the load of less than four separately controlled electric space heating units.

(4) The connected load of four or more separately controlled electric space heating units.

Section 220-30(c) states that, when considering noncoincident loads, you are to use the largest of those being considered. While the air-conditioning load is considered at 100 percent, the central electric space heating load is considered at 65 percent. If the air-conditioning equipment is also a heat pump, it is added to the heating load at 100 percent.

220-31. Optional Calculation for Additional Loads in Existing Dwelling Unit. For an existing dwelling unit presently being served by an existing 120/240 volt or 208Y/120, 3-wire, 60-ampere service, it shall be permissible to compute load calculations as follows:

Load (in kW or kVA)	Percent of Load
First 8 kW of load at	100%
Remainder of load at	40%

Load calculation shall include lighting at 3 watts per square foot (0.093 sq m); 1500 watts for each 20-ampere appliance circuit; range or wall-mounted oven and counter-mounted cooking unit, and other appliances that are permanently connected or fastened in place, at nameplate rating.

If air-conditioning equipment or electric space heating equipment is to be installed the following formula shall be applied to determine if the existing service is of sufficient size.

Air-conditioning equipment* 100%
Central electric space heating* 100%
Less than four separately controlled space heating units* 100%
First 8 kW of all other load 100%
Remainder of all other load 40%

Other loads shall include:

1500 watts for each 20-ampere appliance circuit.

Lighting and portable appliances at 3 watts per square foot (0.093 sq m)

Household range or wall-mounted oven and counter-mounted cooking unit.

All other appliances fastened in place, including four or more separately controlled space heating units, at nameplate rating.

* Use larger connected load of air conditioning and space heating, but not both.

This optional method would permit the maximum possible load that can be connected to an existing 115/230 V or 120/208 V, 3-wire, 60-A service to be 22,500 W, which is based on the following calculation:

$$230 \text{ V} \times 60 \text{ A} = 13,800 \text{ W}$$
$$13,800 \text{ W} - 8,000 \text{ W} \text{ (first 8 kW at 100\%)} = 5,800 \text{ W}$$
$$5,800 \text{ W} = 0.4 \text{ (Remainder at 40\%)} \times X$$
$$5,800 \text{ W} \div 0.4 = X$$
$$X = 14,500 \text{ W}$$
$$8,000 \text{ W} + 14,500 \text{ W} = 22,500 \text{ W}$$

Recheck, based on following:
$$22,500 \text{ W} - 8,000 \text{ W} \text{ (first 8 kW at 100\%)} = 14,500 \text{ W}$$
$$14,500 \times 0.4 \text{ (Remainder at 40\%)} = 5,800 \text{ W}$$
$$8,000 \text{ W} + 5,800 \text{ W} = 13,800 \text{ W} (230 \text{ V} \times 60 \text{ A})$$

Therefore, an existing 30 ft by 40 ft dwelling unit with a 60-A service would have a total load as follows:

1,200 sq. ft (30 × 40) × 3 W/sq. ft	=	3,600 W
two 20-A appliance circuits (at 1,500 W)	=	3,000 W
one electric range	=	10,400 W
furnace circuit	=	700 W
total watts		17,700 W

Since 22,500 W is the maximum permitted total load, an appliance(s) load not exceeding 4,800 W could be added (22,500 W − 17,700 W = 4,800 W). However, air-conditioning equipment or electric space heating equipment is to be calculated at 100 percent demand (where it is unlikely air conditioning and electric space heating will be in use simultaneously, the smaller load is omitted from computing the additional load). From the 17,700 W total load, deduct first 8,000 W at 100 percent demand as follows:

17,700 W − 8,000 W	=	9,700 W
9,700 W × 0.4 (40%)	=	3,880 W

$$8,000 \text{ W} + 3,880 \text{ W} = 11,880 \text{ W}$$
$$13,800 \text{ W} \ (230 \text{ V} \times 60 \text{ A}) - 11,880 = 1,920 \text{ W}$$

The addition of air-conditioning or electric space heating equipment (the larger load of the two) at 100 percent demand could not exceed 1,920 W.

220-32. Optional Calculation — Multifamily Dwelling.

(a) Feeder or Service Load.   It shall be permissible to compute the feeder or service load of a multifamily dwelling in accordance with Table 220-32 instead of Part B of this article where all the following conditions are met:

(1) No dwelling unit is supplied by more than one feeder.

(2) Each dwelling unit is equipped with electric cooking equipment.

It should be recognized that the method of calculation of load under Section 230-32 is optional and only applies where the feeder supplies all of the load of a dwelling unit and has the other limitations that are intended to provide appropriate diversity. It should be understood that where all of the stated conditions prevail, it is intended that the optional calculations in Section 230-32 may be used instead of those in Part B of Article 220 and this is stated in Paragraph (a).

Exception: When the computed load for multifamily dwellings without electric cooking in Part B of this article exceeds that computed under Part C for the identical load plus electric cooking (based on 8 kW per unit), the lesser of the two loads may be used.

Section 220-32(a)(2) requires each dwelling unit to be equipped with electric cooking in order to use this method of calculation. This Exception permits calculation under this Section for dwelling units which do not have electric cooking.

(3) Each dwelling unit is equipped with either electric space heating or air conditioning or both.
Feeders and service-entrance conductors whose demand load is determined by this optional calculation shall be permitted to have the neutral load determined by Section 220-22.

(b) House Loads.   House loads shall be computed in accordance with Part B of this article and shall be in addition to the dwelling unit loads computed in accordance with Table 220-32.

(c) Connected Loads.   The connected load to which the demand factors of Table 220-32 apply shall include the following:

(1) 1500 watts for each 2-wire, 20-ampere small appliance branch circuit and each laundry branch circuit specified in Section 220-16.

(2) 3 watts per square foot (0.093 sq m) for general lighting and general-use receptacles.

(3) The nameplate rating of all appliances that are fastened in place, permanently connected or located to be on a specific circuit, ranges, wall-mounted ovens, counter-mounted cooking units, clothes dryers, water heaters, and space heaters.

If water heater elements are so interlocked that all elements cannot be used at the same time, the maximum possible load shall be considered the nameplate load.

(4) The nameplate ampere or kVA rating of all motors and of all low-power-factor loads.

(5) The larger of the air-conditioning load or the space heating load.

Table 220-32

Optional Calculation — Demand Factors for Three or More Multifamily Dwelling Units

Number of Dwelling Units	Demand Factor Percent
3–5	45
6–7	44
8–10	43
11	42
12–13	41
14–15	40
16–17	39
18–20	38
21	37
22–23	36
24–25	35
26–27	34
28–30	33
31	32
32–33	31
34–36	30
37–38	29
39–42	28
43–45	27
46–50	26
51–55	25
56–61	24
62 & over	23

220-33. Optional Calculation — Two Dwelling Units. Where two dwelling units are supplied by a single feeder and the computed load under Part B of this article exceeds that for three identical units computed under Section 220-32, the lesser of the two loads shall be permitted to be used.

220-34. Optional Method — Schools. The calculation of a feeder or service load for schools shall be permitted in accordance with Table 220-34 in lieu of Part B of this article where equipped with electric space heating, or air conditioning, or both. The connected load to which the demand factors of Table 220-34 apply shall include all of the interior and exterior lighting, power, water heating, cooking, other loads, and the larger of the air-conditioning load or space heating load within the building or structure.

Feeders and service-entrance conductors whose demand load is determined by this optional calculation shall be permitted to have the neutral load determined by Section 220-22. Where the building or structure load is calculated by this optional method, feeders within the building or structure shall have ampacity as permitted in Part B of this article; however, the ampacity of an individual feeder need not be larger than the ampacity for the entire building.

This section shall not apply to portable classroom buildings.

Many schools are adding portable buildings of a small square foot area. The air-conditioning load is to comply with Article 440 and the lighting load is to be considered as continuous. To allow the demand factors of Table 220-34 to be applied to a portable classroom would decrease the feeder or service size to below that required for the connected continuous load.

Table 220-34

**Optional Method — Demand Factors for Feeders
and Service-Entrance Conductors for Schools**

Connected Load Watts per Square Foot	Demand Factors Percent
Connected load up to and including 3, plus	100
Connected load over 3 and including 20, plus	75
Connected load over 20 at	25

For SI units: one square foot = 0.093 square meter.

220-35. Optional Calculations for Additional Loads to Existing Installations. For the purpose of allowing additional loads to be connected to existing feeders and services, it shall be permitted to use actual maximum kVA demand figures to determine the existing load on a service or feeder when all the following conditions are met:

(1) The maximum demand data is available in kVA for a minimum of a one-year period.

(2) The existing demand at 125 percent plus the new load does not exceed the ampacity of the feeder or rating of the service.

(3) The feeder or service has overcurrent protection in accordance with Sections 230-90 and 240-3.

Where existing installations have been checked and the maximum demand kVA data for a minimum of a one-year period is available and the installation complies with (2) and (3), it is to be permitted to connect additional loads to existing services and feeders.

D. Method for Computing Farm Loads

220-40. Farm Loads — Buildings and Other Loads.

(a) Dwelling Unit. The feeder or service load of a farm dwelling unit shall be computed in accordance with the provisions for dwellings in Part B or C of this article.

(b) Other than Dwelling Unit. For each farm building or load supplied by two or more branch circuits the load for feeders, service-entrance conductors, and service equipment shall be computed in accordance with demand factors not less than indicated in Table 220-40.

See Section 230-21 for overhead conductors from a pole to a building or other structure.

Section 230-21 requires such overhead conductors to be considered as a service drop and installed accordingly.

220-41. Farm Loads — Total. The total load of the farm for service-entrance conductors and service equipment shall be computed in accordance with the farm dwelling unit load and demand factors specified in Table 220-41. Where there is equipment in two or more farm equipment buildings or for loads having the same function, such loads shall be computed in accordance with Table 220-40 and may be combined as a single load in Table 220-41 for computing the total load.

See Section 230-21 for overhead conductors from a pole to a building or other structure.

Table 220-40

Method for Computing Farm Loads for Other Than Dwelling Unit

Ampere Load at 230 Volts	Demand Factor Percent
Loads expected to operate without diversity, but not less than 125 percent full-load current of the largest motor and not less than the first 60 amperes of load...............	100
Next 60 amperes of all other loads	50
Remainder of other load..	25

Table 220-41

Method for Computing Total Farm Load

Individual Loads Computed in Accordance with Table 220-40	Demand Factor Percent
Largest load	100
Second largest load	75
Third largest load	65
Remaining loads	50

To this total load, add the load of the farm dwelling unit computed in accordance with Part B or C of this article.

ARTICLE 225 — OUTSIDE BRANCH CIRCUITS

AND FEEDERS

Contents

225-1. Scope. This article covers electric equipment and wiring for the supply of utilization equipment located on or attached to the outside of public and private buildings, or run between buildings, other structures or poles on other premises served.

Exception: See Section 668-3(c), Exceptions No. 1 and No. 4 for electrolytic cells.

For additional information on wiring over 600 volts, see the National Electrical Safety Code (ANSI C2-1977).

225-2. Other Articles. Application of other articles, including additional requirements to specific cases of equipment and conductors, is as follows:

	Article
Branch Circuits	210
Class 1, Class 2, and Class 3 Remote Control, Signaling, and Power-Limited Circuits	725
Communication Circuits	800
Community Antenna Television and Radio Distribution Systems	820
Conductors	310
Electrically Driven or Controlled Irrigation Machines	675
Electric Signs and Outline Lighting	600
Feeders	215
Fire Protective Signaling Systems	760
Fixed Outdoor Electric De-icing and Snow-Melting Equipment	426
Fixtures	410
Grounding	250
Hazardous (Classified) Locations	500
Hazardous (Classified) Locations, Specific	510
Marinas and Boatyards	555
Messenger Supported Wiring	321
Over 600 Volts, General	710
Overcurrent Protection	240
Radio and Television Equipment	810
Services	230
Swimming Pools, Fountains and Similar Installations	680
Use and Identification of Grounded Conductors	200

225-3. Calculation of Load.

(a) Branch Circuits. The load on outdoor branch circuits shall be as determined by Section 220-2.

(b) Feeders. The load on outdoor feeders shall be as determined by Part B of Article 220.

225-4. Conductor Covering.   Where within 10 feet (3.05 m) of any building or other structure, open wiring on insulators shall be insulated or covered. Conductors in cables or raceways, except Type MI cable, shall be of the rubber-covered type or thermoplastic type and in wet locations shall comply with Section 310-8. Conductors for festoon lighting shall be of the rubber-covered or thermoplastic type.

225-5. Size of Conductors.   The ampacity of outdoor branch-circuit and feeder conductors shall be in accordance with Tables 310-16 through 310-19 based on loads as determined under Section 220-2 and Part B of Article 220.

225-6. Minimum Size of Conductor.

   (a) Overhead Spans.   Overhead conductors shall not be smaller than the following:

   (1) For 600 volts, nominal, or less, No. 10 copper or No. 8 aluminum for spans up to 50 feet (15.2 m) in length and No. 8 copper or No. 6 aluminum for a longer span.

   (2) For over 600 volts, nominal, No. 6 copper or No. 4 aluminum where open individual conductors and No. 8 copper or No. 6 aluminum where in cable.

   The size limitation of copper or aluminum conductors is based upon an adequate mechanical strength. See Figure 225-1.

   (b) Festoon Lighting.   Overhead conductors for festoon lighting shall not be smaller than No. 12.

Exception: Where supported by messenger wires.

See Section 225-25 for outdoor lampholders.

Definition: Festoon lighting is a string of outdoor lights suspended between two points more than 15 feet (4.57 m) apart.

   See Figure 225-3.

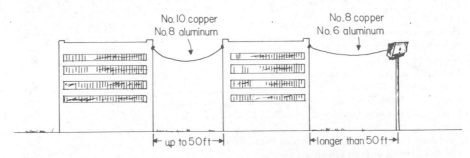

Figure 225-1. Overhead spans run between buildings, structures, or poles.

225-7. Lighting Equipment on Poles or Other Structures.

   (a) General.   For the supply of lighting equipment installed on a single pole or structure, the branch circuits shall comply with Article 210 and (c) below.

   (b) Common Neutral.   It shall be permissible to use a multiwire branch circuit consisting of

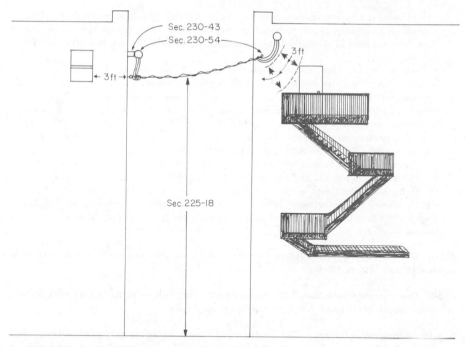

Figure 225-2. Section 225-11 references Sections 230-43 (wiring methods) and 230-54 (weather service heads, points of attachment, and drip loops). Section 225-18 covers the requirements for clearances from ground (not over 600 V), and Section 225-19 covers the requirements for clearances from buildings (not over 600 V). See Section 225-19(d) for clearances from windows, doors, fire escapes, etc.

the neutral and not more than eight ungrounded conductors. The ampacity of the neutral conductor shall not be less than the calculated sum of the currents in all ungrounded conductors connected to any one phase of the circuit.

(c) Voltage to Ground.   Branch circuits supplying lampholders or lighting fixtures mounted on the outside of buildings or on poles or structures for area illumination of residential, commercial, or industrial property shall not exceed 150 volts to ground.

Exception: The voltage shall not exceed 300 volts to ground on branch circuits supplying lighting fixtures for illumination of outdoor areas of industrial establishments, office buildings, schools, stores, and other commercial or public buildings where all of the following conditions are met:

a. The fixtures are mounted on the outside of buildings or out-of-doors on poles or other structures.

b. The fixtures are not less than 8 feet (2.44 m) above grade or other surface accessible to individuals other than those charged with fixture maintenance and supervision.

c. The fixtures are not less than 3 feet (914 mm) from windows, platforms, fire escapes, and the like.

(d) Voltage Between Conductors.   The voltage between conductors on branch circuits supplying only the ballast for permanently installed electric-discharge fixtures for area illumination shall be in accordance with Section 210-6(b).

Multiwire branch circuits consisting of a neutral and not more than eight ungrounded conductors are permissible, provided the neutral capacity is not less than the total load of all ungrounded conductors connected to any one phase of the circuit.

Branch circuits for outdoor illumination of residential, commercial, or industrial areas are not to exceed 150 V to ground. Operating a 115-V circuit at approximately 10 percent over voltage will provide increased light intensity. Many designers of outdoor light installations on poles, however, prefer a 10 percent under voltage (130-V rated lamps on 115-V circuits) thereby decreasing the light intensity, prolonging the life of the lamps, and minimizing pole lamp maintenance, which can be difficult, because longer periods of time elapse between relamping.

Exceptions to the rule of not exceeding 150 V to ground can be found in the Exception to Section 225-7(c) which allows 300 V to ground where the installation requirements of the Exception are met, and, also, Section 225-7(d) which allows 500 V between branch-circuit conductors mounted at the heights required by Section 210-6(b) and supplying only the ballasts of electric-discharge lamps.

225-8. Disconnection.   The disconnecting means for branch-circuit and feeder fuses shall be in accordance with Section 240-40.

225-9. Overcurrent Protection.   Overcurrent protection shall be in accordance with Section 210-20 for branch circuits and Part A of Article 240 for feeders.

225-10. Wiring on Buildings.   The installation of outside wiring on surfaces of buildings shall be permitted for circuits of not over 600 volts, nominal, as open wiring on insulators, as multiconductor cable, as Type MC cable, as Type MI cable, in rigid metal conduit, in intermediate metal conduit, in rigid nonmetallic conduit as provided in Section 347-2, in busways as provided in Article 364, or in electrical metallic tubing. Circuits of over 600 volts, nominal, shall be installed as provided for services in Section 230-202. Circuits for sign and outline lighting shall be installed in accordance with Article 600.

225-11. Circuit Exits and Entrances.   Where outside branch and feeder circuits leave or enter a building, the requirements of Sections 230-43, 230-52, and 230-54 shall apply.

See Figure 225-2.

225-12. Open-Conductor Supports.   Open conductors shall be supported on glass or porcelain-knobs, racks, brackets, or strain insulators.

225-13. Festoon Supports.   In spans exceeding 40 feet (12.2 m), the conductors shall be supported by a messenger wire; and the messenger wire shall be supported by strain insulators. Conductors or messenger wires shall not be attached to any fire escape, downspout, or plumbing equipment.

Festoon lighting consists of a string of outdoor lights suspended between two points more than 15 ft apart, and the conductors are not to be smaller than No. 12 unless they are supported by a messenger wire. On all spans of festoon lighting exceeding 40 ft, messenger wire is required and is to be supported by strain insulators. Where no messenger wire is required, the No. 12 or larger conductors are to be supported by strain insulators. See Figure 225-3.

Attachment to fire escapes, plumbing equipment, or drainspouts is prohibited since they could provide a path to ground. Moreover, such methods of attachment could not be relied upon for permanent or secure means of support.

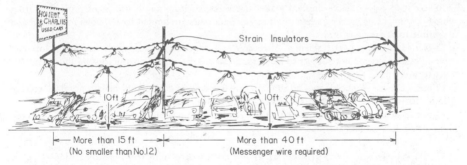

Figure 225-3. Messenger wires are required for festoon lighting conductors smaller than No. 12 or for spans exceeding 40 feet.

225-14. Open-Conductor Spacings.

(a) 600 Volts, Nominal, or Less.   Conductors of 600 volts, nominal, or less, shall comply with the spacings provided in Table 230-51(c).

(b) Over 600 Volts, Nominal.   Conductors of over 600 volts, nominal, shall comply with the spacings provided in Part D of Article 710.

(c) Separation from Other Circuits.   Open conductors shall be separated from open conductors of other circuits or systems by not less than 4 inches (102 mm).

(d) Conductors on Poles.   Conductors on poles shall have a separation of not less than 1 foot (305 mm) where not placed on racks or brackets. Conductors supported on poles shall provide a horizontal climbing space not less than the following:

Power conductors, below communication conductors .... 30 inches (762mm)
Power conductors alone or above communication conductors:
   300 volts or less .... 24 inches (610mm)
   Over 300 volts .... 30 inches (762mm)
Communication conductors below power conductors .... same as power conductors
Communication conductors alone .... no requirement

Ample space is required to enable linemen to climb over or through conductors to safely service conductors on the pole.

225-15. Supports Over Buildings.   Supports over a building shall be in accordance with Section 230-29.

225-16. Point of Attachment to Buildings.   The point of attachment to a building shall be in accordance with Section 230-26.

225-17. Means of Attachment to Buildings.   The means of attachment to a building shall be in accordance with Section 230-27.

225-18. Clearance from Ground.   Open conductors of not over 600 volts, nominal, shall conform to the following:

10 feet (3.05 m) — above finished grade, sidewalks, or from any platform or projection from which they might be reached where the supply conductors are limited to 150 volts to ground and accessible to pedestrians only.

12 feet (3.66 m) — over residential driveways and commercial areas such as parking lots and drive-in establishments not subject to truck traffic where the supply conductors are limited to 300 volts to ground.

15 feet (4.57 m) — above finished grade where the supply conductors have a nominal voltage greater than 300 volts to ground and accessible to pedestrians only.

18 feet (5.49 m) — over public streets, alleys, roads, driveways on other than residential property, and parking lots subject to truck traffic.

The clearances from ground, as given, coordinate with the National Electrical Safety Code. See Section 230-24.

Note: For clearances of conductors of over 600 volts, see National Electrical Safety Code (ANSI C2-1977).

225-19. Clearances from Buildings for Conductors of Not Over 600 Volts, Nominal.

(a) Over Roofs. Conductors not fully insulated for the operating voltage shall have a vertical or diagonal clearance of not less than 10 feet (3.05 m) from the roof surface.

Exception No. 1: Fully insulated conductors shall be permitted to have vertical or diagonal clearance of 3 feet (914 mm) or more.

Exception No. 2: Above roof space accessible to pedestrians. Vertical clearance shall be not less than 15 feet (4.57 m) for uninsulated, 8 feet (2.44 m) for insulated conductors.

Exception No. 3: Above roof space accessible to vehicular traffic, vertical clearance shall be not less than 18 feet (5.49 m).

Exception No. 4: Where the voltage between conductors does not exceed 300 and the roof has a slope of not less than 4 inches (102 mm) in 12 inches (305 mm), a reduction in clearance to 3 feet (914 mm) shall be permitted.

Exception No. 5: Where the voltage between conductors does not exceed 300, a reduction in clearance over the roof to 18 inches (457 mm) shall be permitted if:

a. They do not pass over more than 4 feet (1.22 m) of the overhang portion of the roof; and

b. They are terminated at a (through-the-roof) raceway or approved support.

(b) From Nonbuilding or Nonbridge Structures. From signs, chimneys, radio and television antennas, tanks, other nonbuilding or nonbridge structures, clearances, vertical, diagonal and horizontal, shall be not less than 5 feet (1.52 m) for uninsulated conductors, 3 feet (914 mm) for insulated conductors.

(c) Horizontal Clearances. Clearances shall be not less than 5 feet (1.52 m) for uninsulated conductors, 3 feet (914 mm) for insulated conductors.

(d) Final Spans. Final spans of feeders or branch circuits to a building they supply or from which they are fed shall be permitted to be attached to the building, but they shall be kept 3 feet (914 mm) from windows, doors, porches, fire escapes, or similar locations.

See Figure 225-2.

Conductors run above the top level of a window shall be considered out of reach from that window.

(e) Zone for Fire Ladders. Where buildings exceed three stories or 50 feet (15.2 m) in height, overhead lines shall be arranged, where practicable, so that a clear space (or zone) at least 6 feet (1.83 m) wide will be left either adjacent to the buildings or beginning not over 8 feet (2.44 m) from them to facilitate the raising of ladders when necessary for fire fighting.

Note: For clearance of conductors over 600 volts, see National Electrical Safety Code (ANSI C2-1977).

225-20. Mechanical Protection of Conductors. Mechanical protection of conductors on buildings, structures, or poles shall be as provided for services in Section 230-50.

225-21. Multiconductor Cables on Exterior Surfaces of Buildings. Multiconductor cables on exterior surfaces of buildings shall be as provided for service cable in Section 230-51.

225-22. Raceways on Exterior Surfaces of Buildings. Raceways on exterior surfaces of buildings shall be made raintight and suitably drained.

Raintight is defined as "so constructed or protected that exposure to a beating rain will not result in the entrance of water." To assure this, all conduit bodies, fittings, and boxes used in wet locations are to be provided with threaded hubs or other approved means. Threadless couplings and connectors used with metal conduit or electrical metallic tubing are to be of the raintight type (see Sections 345-9, 346-9, and 348-8).

Where exposed to weather or rain through weatherhead openings, condensation is likely to occur, causing moisture to accumulate within raceways at low points of the installation and in junction boxes. Raceways should thus be installed to permit drainage through drain holes at appropriate locations.

225-23. Underground Circuits. Underground circuits shall meet the requirements of Section 300-5.

225-24. Outdoor Lampholders. Where outdoor lampholders are attached as pendants, the connections to the circuit wires shall be staggered. Where such lampholders have terminals of a type that puncture the insulation and make contact with the conductors, they shall be attached only to conductors of the stranded type.

Splices to branch-circuit conductors for outdoor lampholders of the Edison-base type or "pig-tail sockets" are to be staggered so as not to place splices in close proximity to each other.

"Pin-type" terminal sockets are to be attached to stranded conductors only and are intended for installations for temporary lighting or decorations, signs, or specifically approved applications. See Figures 225-3 and 225-4.

225-25. Location of Outdoor Lamps. Locations of lamps for outdoor lighting shall be below all live conductors, transformers, or other electric equipment.

Exception No. 1: Where clearances or other safeguards are provided for relamping operations.

Exception No. 2: Where equipment is controlled by a disconnecting means that can be locked in the open position.

Since Section 225-18 requires a minimum clearance for open conductors of 10 ft above grade or platforms, it would be difficult to keep all electrical equipment

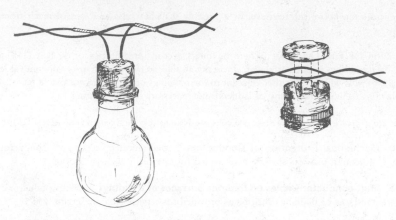

Figure 225-4. Outdoor lampholders attached as pendants showing staggered connections and pin- or puncture-type for use with standard conductors.

above the lamps. Exception No. 1, therefore, allows other clearances or safeguards to permit safe relamping, and Exception No. 2 permits the use of a disconnecting means to de-energize the circuit. It may be assumed that metal raceways would not be considered as "other electrical equipment," according to this section.

ARTICLE 230 — SERVICES

Contents

A. General

230-1. Scope.   This article covers service conductors and equipment for control and protection of services; the number, types, and sizes of services and service equipment; and the installation requirements.

230-2. Number of Services.   A building or other structure served shall be supplied by only one service.

Where more than one service is permitted by any of the following exceptions, a permanent plaque or directory shall be installed at each service drop or lateral or at each service-equipment location denoting all other services on or in that building or structure and the area served by each.

> This section states the basic requirement that a building or other structure should be supplied by only one service. A new paragraph has been added to require a permanent plaque or directory to be installed at each service drop or lateral or at each service-equipment location denoting all other services on or in that building or structure and the area served by each. See Figure 230-1.
>
> In the 1981 *NEC*, the definition and application of "sub-sets" has been deleted and also the references to multiple-occupancy buildings that do or do not have individual occupancy above the second floor have been deleted from Sections 230-72(d) and 230-90(a), Exception No. 4. The Code-Making Panel intends that the service disconnecting means for each service or for each set of service-entrance conductors permitted by Section 230-2, Exception No. 3 shall consist of not more than six switches or six circuit breakers mounted in a single enclosure, in a group of separate enclosures, or in or on a switchboard.
>
> The *Code* does continue the practice in multiple-occupancy buildings of permitting a separate service for each occupancy, provided the service-entrance conductors are installed outside of the building, or encased in concrete, to a point where the conductors enter the individual occupancy. The 1981 *NEC* removed the restriction of having to terminate within the individual occupancy.

Exception No. 1: For fire pumps where a separate service is required.

Exception No. 2: For emergency, legally required standby, or optional standby systems where a separate service is required.

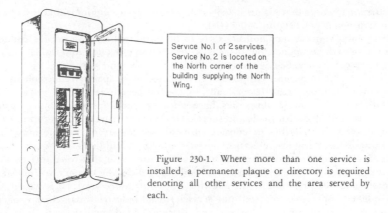

Service No.1 of 2 services. Service No. 2 is located on the North corner of the building supplying the North Wing.

Figure 230-1. Where more than one service is installed, a permanent plaque or directory is required denoting all other services and the area served by each.

Exception No. 3: Multiple-Occupancy Buildings.

a. By special permission, in multiple-occupancy buildings where there is no available space for service equipment accessible to all the occupants.

b. Buildings of multiple occupancy shall be permitted to have two or more separate sets of service-entrance conductors which are tapped from one service drop or lateral.

Exception No. 4: Capacity Requirements. Two or more services shall be permitted:

a. Where the capacity requirements are in excess of 3000 amperes at a supply voltage of 600 volts or less; or

b. Where the load requirements of a single-phase installation are greater than the serving agency normally supplies through one service; or

c. By special permission.

Exception No. 5: Buildings of Large Area. By special permission, for a single building or other structure sufficiently large to make two or more services necessary.

Exception No. 6: For different characteristics, such as for different voltages, frequencies, or phases, or for different uses, such as for different rate schedules.

Exception No. 7: For the purpose of Section 230-45 only, underground sets of conductors, size 1/0 and larger, running to the same location and connected together at their supply end but not connected together at their load end shall be considered to be one service.

The general rule is that a building or other structure is to be supplied by only one service. There are, however, several Exceptions.

Exception Nos. 1 and 2 permit separate services where necessary for fire pumps (with one to six switches or circuit breakers) or emergency, legally required standby, or optional standby electrical systems (with one to six switches or circuit breakers) in addition to the regular building service (with one to six switches or circuit breakers). The *Code* recognizes that disruption at the main building service should not disconnect fire pump equipment or emergency , legally required standby, or optional standby systems. See Section 230-72(b).

Exception No. 3 permits a separate service in multiple-occupancy buildings:

(a) By special permission (the written consent of the authority having jurisdiction), where there is no space available for service equipment accessible to all occupants as per Section 240-24(b).

(b) Multiple-occupancy buildings are to be permitted to have service conductors run to each occupancy, but there is no restriction of having to terminate in the individual occupancy. See Section 230-72(d).

Exception No. 4 permits two or more services where capacity requirements are in excess of 3,000 A or for lesser loads, by special permission.

Many electric power companies have adopted special regulations covering certain types of electrical loads and service equipment that may be energized from their lines. It is advisable to consult with the serving utility to determine line capacities when designing electrical services for large buildings.

Exception No. 5 requires special permission for more than one service to a sufficiently large building. Expansion of buildings, shopping centers, or industrial plants would often necessitate the addition of two or more services. It would, for example, be impossible to install one service for an industrial plant with capacity requirements to compensate for any and all future load requirements. It is also impractical to run feeders extremely long distances due to high costs and voltage drop problems. As in Exception No. 4, it is advisable to consult with the serving utility and the authority having jurisdiction.

Exception No. 6 allows more than one service for different characteristics, such as different voltages, single-phase and 3-phase, or different utility rate schedules for different uses. For example, different service characteristics exist between a 3-wire, 120/240 volt single-phase service and a 3-phase, 4-wire wye 480/277 volt service; and for different uses, such as different rate schedules, it is intended to allow a second service for supplying a second meter for other equipment such as an electric water heater on a different rate.

Exception No. 7 allows from two to six sets of service lateral conductors to serve up to six service disconnects, provided the conductors are 1/0 or larger and connected together at the supply end, which is normally the transformer secondary terminals. This Exception was included in the *Code* to increase the cable impedance by not paralleling the conductors, thereby lowering the available short-circuit current at the building. See Sections 110-9 and 110-10. Exception No. 7 does not require each set of conductors to be the same size, provided that each set is 1/0 or larger. See Figure 230-2.

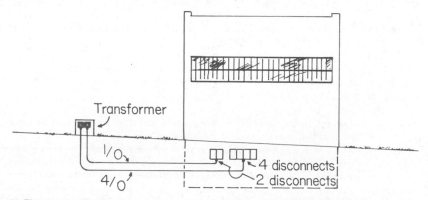

Figure 230-2. Illustrated are two sets of underground conductors, size 1/0 and larger (4/0), connected at their supply and running to the same location, not connected together at their supply end, and not more than six disconnects. It is permissible to run six such sets of conductors to six individual service disconnects.

230-3. One Building or Other Structure Not to Be Supplied Through Another. Service conductors supplying a building or other structure shall not pass through the interior of another building or other structure.

Exception: Where the buildings or other structures served are under single occupancy or management.

See Section 230-44 for masonry-encased conductors considered outside of a building.

It is permissible for service conductors to pass along the "exterior" of one building to supply another building. However, service conductors supplying a building are not to pass through the "interior" of a building unless the buildings served are under single occupancy or management. Each building served in this manner is to be provided with means for disconnecting all ungrounded conductors as per Section 230-84(a). See Figure 230-3.

Conductors are considered outside a building where installed beneath the building under 2 in. of concrete or in a raceway within the building enclosed by 2 in. of concrete or brick. See Section 230-44. See Figure 230-9.

Figure 230-3. Service conductors may pass through the interior of Building No. 1 to supply Building No. 2 where both buildings are under single occupancy or management. A disconnecting means suitable for use as service equipment is to be provided for each building. For overhead service conductors, it is common to run the service conductors along the outside of Building No. 1. See Figure 230-5.

B. Insulation and Size of Service Conductors

230-4. Insulation of Service Conductors. Service conductors shall normally withstand exposure to atmospheric and other conditions of use without detrimental leakage of current.

For Service Drops — See Section 230-22.

For Underground Services — See Section 230-30.

For Service-Entrance Conductors — See Section 230-40.

230-5. Size of Service Conductors. Service conductors shall have adequate ampacity to conduct safely the current for the loads supplied without a temperature rise detrimental to the insulation or covering of the conductors, and shall have adequate mechanical strength.

Minimum sizes are given in the following references:
    For Service Drops — See Section 230-23.
    For Underground Service Conductors — See Section 230-31.
    For Service-Entrance Conductors — See Section 230-41.
    For Farmstead Service Conductors — See Part D of Article 220.

C. Overhead Services

230-21. Overhead Supply.   Overhead conductors to a building or other structure from another building or other structure (such as a pole) on which a meter or disconnecting means is installed shall be considered as a service drop and installed accordingly.

Example: Farm loads in Part D of Article 220.

230-22. Insulation or Covering.   Individual conductors shall be insulated or covered with an extruded thermoplastic or thermosetting insulating material.

The intent is to prevent problems that are created by covered cable or covered open wiring, which over a period of years is subjected to weather, abrasion, and other deleterious effects that reduce the nonconductive properties of the covering.

Exception: The grounded conductor of a multiconductor cable shall be permitted to be bare.

Service-drop conductors in cable or open wiring and covered with an extruded thermoplastic or thermosetting insulating material have an ampacity equal to that of bare conductors of the same size as listed in Table 310-19.

230-23. Size and Rating.   Conductors shall have sufficient ampacity to carry the load. They shall have adequate mechanical strength and shall not be smaller than No. 8 copper, No. 6 aluminum or copper-clad aluminum.

Exception: For installations to supply only limited loads of a single branch circuit such as small polyphase power, controlled water heaters and the like, they shall not be smaller than No. 12 hard-drawn copper or equivalent.

The grounded conductor shall not be less than the minimum size required by Section 250-23(b).

230-24. Clearances.   The vertical clearances of all service-drop conductors shall be based on conductor temperature of 60°F, no wind, with final unloaded sag in the wire, conductor, or cable.
Service-drop conductors shall not be readily accessible and shall comply with (a) through (d) below for services not over 600 volts, nominal.

(a) Above Roofs.   Conductors shall have a vertical clearance of not less than 8 feet (2.44 m) from all points of roofs above which they pass.

Exception No. 1: Where the voltage between conductors does not exceed 300 and the roof has a slope of not less than 4 inches (102 mm) in 12 inches (305 mm), a reduction in clearance to 3 feet (914 mm) shall be permitted.

Service-drop conductors are not to be readily accessible and, passing over roofs, where not over 600 V, are to have a clearance of 8 ft. Exception No. 1 permits a clearance of 3 ft where the voltage between conductors does not exceed 300 and the roof is sloped not less than 4 in. in 12 in. It would be difficult to walk upon a sloped roof of this angle or pitch. See Figure 230-4.

Exception No. 2: Where the voltage between conductors does not exceed 300, a reduction in clearance above only the overhanging portion of the roof to not less than 18 inches (457 mm) shall be permitted if

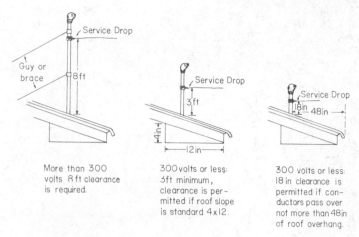

More than 300
volts 8 ft clearance
is required.

300 volts or less:
3 ft minimum,
clearance is per-
mitted if roof slope
is standard 4 x 12.

300 volts or less:
18 in clearance is
permitted if con-
ductors pass over
not more than 48 in
of roof overhang.

Figure 230-4. Clearances for service-drop conductors passing over the overhanging portion of a roof and minimum angle of roof slope permitting a 3-ft clearance
for service-drop conductors.

(1) not more than 4 feet (1.22 m) of service-drop conductors pass above the roof overhang, and (2) they
are terminated at a through-the-roof raceway or approved support.

See Section 230-28 for mast supports.

A further reduction of service-drop conductor clearances to 18 in. is permitted
by Exception No. 2 for service-mast (through-the-roof) installations where the
voltage between conductors does not exceed 300 and the mast is located within 4 ft
of the edge of the roof. See Figure 230-4. This Exception applies to either sloped
or flat roofs.

(b) Vertical Clearance from Ground.   Service-drop conductors where not in excess of 600
volts, nominal, shall have the following minimum clearance from final grade.

10 feet (3.05 m) — at the electric service entrance to buildings, or at the drip loop of the
building electric entrance, measured from final grade or other accessible surface only for
service-drop cables supported on and cabled together with a grounded bare messenger and limited
to 150 volts to ground.

12 feet (3.66 m) — for those areas listed in the 15 foot (4.57 m) classification when the voltage
is limited to 300 volts to ground.

15 feet (4.57 m) — over residential property and driveways, and those commercial areas not
subject to truck traffic.

18 feet (5.49 m) — over public streets, alleys, roads, parking areas subject to truck traffic,
driveways on other than residential property, and other land traversed by vehicles such as
cultivated, grazing, forest, and orchard.

See Figure 230-5.

(c) Clearance from Building Openings.   Service conductors shall have a clearance of not
less than 3 feet (914 mm) from windows, doors, porches, fire escapes, or similar locations.

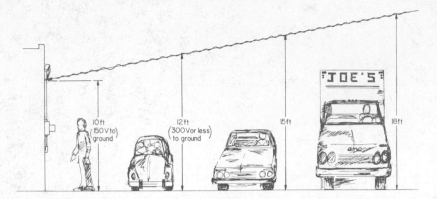

Figure 230-5. Illustrated clearances are coordinated with the National Electrical Safety Code (ANSI C2).

Conductors run above the top level of a window shall be considered out of reach from that window.

The clearance of 3 ft is applied to the conductors and not to a raceway or cable assembly approved for service conductors. The intent is to protect the conductors from physical damage and/or accidental contact. See Figure 230-6.

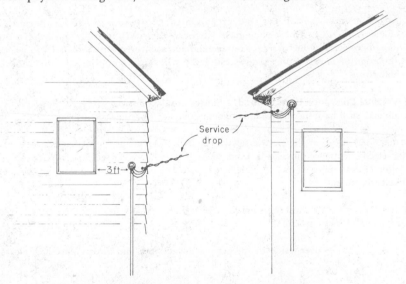

Figure 230-6. Illustration showing service conductors (raceway or cable) spaced 3 ft from a window and service conductors (raceway or cable) above the top level of a window.

(d) Clearance from Swimming Pools.   See Section 680-8.

230-26. Point of Attachment.   The point of attachment of conductors to a building or other structure shall provide the minimum clearances as specified in Section 230-24. In no case shall this point of attachment be less than 10 feet (3.05 m) above finished grade.

Minimum conductor clearances of 8 ft over flat or easily walked-upon roofs, and 10 ft above grade or any platform, and 3 ft from any window, porch or fire escape are considered to be safe distances from the reach of people. See Figures 230-4, 230-5, and 230-6.

230-27. Means of Attachment. Multiconductor cables used for service drops shall be attached to buildings or other structures by fittings identified for use with service conductors. Open conductors shall be attached to fittings identified for use with service conductors or to noncombustible, nonabsorbent insulators securely attached to the building or other structure.

See Section 230-51 for mounting and supporting of service cables or individual open service conductors.
See Section 230-54 for connections at service head.

230-28. Service Masts as Supports. Where a service mast is used for the support of service-drop conductors, it shall be of adequate strength or be supported by braces or guys to withstand safely the strain imposed by the service drop. Where raceway-type service masts are used, all raceway fittings shall be identified for use with service masts.

See Figure 230-4.

230-29. Supports Over Buildings. Service-drop conductors passing over a roof shall be securely supported by substantial structures. Where practicable, such supports shall be independent of the building.

D. Underground Services

230-30. Insulation. Service lateral conductors shall be insulated for the applied voltage.

Exception: A grounded conductor shall be permitted to be uninsulated as follows:

a. Bare copper used in a raceway.

b. Bare copper for direct burial where bare copper is judged to be suitable for the soil conditions.

c. Bare copper for direct burial without regard to soil conditions when part of a cable assembly identified for underground use.

d. Aluminum or copper-clad aluminum without individual insulation or covering when part of a cable assembly identified for underground use in a raceway or for direct burial.

See Figure 230-7.

a. Bare copper, raceway   b. Bare copper direct buried, suitable for soil conditions.   c. and d. Bare copper or aluminum, part of an identified cable assembly.

Figure 230-7. Various applications of bare grounded conductors for underground locations. Aluminum or copper-clad aluminum conductors must be insulated where run in a raceway or direct-buried.

230-31. Size and Rating.   Conductors shall have sufficient ampacity to carry the load. They shall not be smaller than No. 8 copper or No. 6 aluminum or copper-clad aluminum. The grounded conductor shall not be less than the minimum size required by Section 250-23(b).

Exception: For installations to supply only limited loads of a single branch circuit such as small polyphase power, controlled water heaters and the like, they shall not be smaller than No. 12 copper or No. 10 aluminum or copper-clad aluminum.

E. Service-Entrance Conductors

230-40. Insulation of Service-Entrance Conductors.   Service-entrance conductors entering or on the exterior of buildings or other structures shall be insulated.

Exception: A grounded conductor shall be permitted to be uninsulated as follows:

a. Bare copper used in a raceway or part of a service cable assembly.

b. Bare copper for direct burial where bare copper is judged to be suitable for the soil conditions.

c. Bare copper for direct burial without regard to soil conditions when part of a cable assembly identified for underground use.

d. Aluminum or copper-clad aluminum without individual insulation or covering when part of a cable assembly identified for underground use in a raceway or for direct burial.

230-41. Size and Rating.

(a) General.   Conductors shall be of sufficient size to carry the loads as computed in accordance with Article 220. Ampacity shall be determined from Tables 310-16 through 310-19 and all applicable notes to these tables.

(b) Ungrounded Conductors.   Ungrounded conductors shall not be smaller than:

(1) 100-ampere, 3-wire, for a one-family dwelling with six or more 2-wire branch circuits.

(2) 100-ampere, 3-wire, for a one-family dwelling with an initial computed load of 10 kW or more.

(3) 60 amperes for other loads.

See Figure 230-8.

Exception No. 1: For loads consisting of not more than two 2-wire branch circuits, No. 8 copper or No. 6 aluminum or copper-clad aluminum.

Exception No. 2: By special permission, for loads limited by demand or by the source of supply, No. 8 copper or No. 6 aluminum or copper-clad aluminum.

Exception No. 3: For limited loads of a single branch circuit, No. 12 copper or No. 10 aluminum or copper-clad aluminum, but in no case smaller than the branch-circuit conductors.

(c) Grounded Conductors.   The grounded (neutral) conductor shall not be less than the minimum size as required by Section 250-23(b).

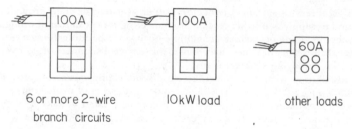

6 or more 2-wire branch circuits   10kW load   other loads

Figure 230-8. A least a 100-ampere, 3-wire service is required for a one-family dwelling if it has six or more 2-wire circuits or a computed load of 10 kW or more. Sixty amperes would be permissible for a one-family dwelling with four branch circuits and a computed load of less than 10 kW. However, many communities require a minimum service of 100 amperes for all one-family dwellings.

F. Installation of Service Conductors

230-43. Wiring Methods for 600 Volts, Nominal, or Less. Service-entrance conductors shall be installed in accordance with the applicable requirements of this Code covering the type of wiring method used and limited to the following methods: (1) open wiring on insulators; (2) rigid metal conduit; (3) intermediate metal conduit; (4) electrical metallic tubing; (5) service-entrance cables; (6) wireways; (7) busways; (8) auxiliary gutters; (9) rigid nonmetallic conduit; (10) cablebus; (11) Type MC cable; or (12) mineral-insulated, metal-sheathed cable.

Approved cable tray systems shall be permitted to support cables approved for use as service-entrance conductors. See Article 318.

230-44. Conductors Considered Outside of Building. Conductors shall be considered outside of a building or other structure under any of the following conditions: (1) where installed under not less than 2 inches (50.8 mm) of concrete beneath a building or other structure, or (2) where installed within a building or other structure in a raceway that is enclosed by concrete or brick not less than 2 inches (50.8 mm) thick.

See Figure 230-9.

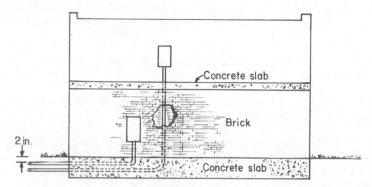

Figure 230-9. Conductors are considered outside of a building where installed under not less than 2 inches of concrete beneath a building or in a raceway enclosed by 2 inches of concrete or brick within a building.

230-45. Separate Enclosures. Where two to six service disconnecting means in separate enclosures supply separate loads from one service drop or lateral, one set of service-entrance conductors shall be permitted to supply each or several such service equipment enclosures.

One set of service-entrance conductors, either overhead or underground, is to be permitted to supply two to six service disconnecting means in lieu of a single main disconnect. A single-occupancy or multiple-occupancy building (either residential or other than residential) may have one main service disconnect or up to six main disconnects supplying separate loads.

An installation where the main service disconnecting means is rated 1200 A, 277/480 V (see Section 230-95) would require ground-fault protection. However, this same installation with two service disconnects rated at 600 A each, three service disconnects rated at 400 A each, or six rated at 200 A each would not require ground-fault protection.

Where two to six sets of fuses or circuit breakers are used, the total rating of the multiple overcurrent devices need not match the ampacities of the service-entrance conductors. The combined ratings of all switches or circuit breakers are not to be less than the rating required for a single overcurrent device and may exceed the ampacity of the service-entrance conductors.

See Section 230-2, Exception No. 7 for (underground) sets of service lateral conductors.

230-46. Unspliced Conductors.   Service-entrance conductors shall not be spliced.

Exception No. 1: Clamped or bolted connections in metering equipment enclosures shall be permitted.

Exception No. 2: Where service-entrance conductors are tapped to supply two to six disconnecting means grouped at a common location.

Exception No. 3: At a properly enclosed junction point where an underground wiring method is changed to another type of wiring method.

Where a building has a basement, an underground service raceway usually terminates at a terminal box. At this point service conductors may be spliced or run directly to service equipment. Splices are to be permitted where, for example, conduit enters a terminal box and a different wiring method, such as service cable, continues to the service equipment. See Section 230-43 for wiring methods for service conductors.

Exception No. 4: A connection shall be permitted where service-conductors are extended from a service drop to an outside meter location and returned to connect to the service-entrance conductors of an existing installation.

Splices are necessary where meters are located on the line side of service equipment as shown in Figure 230-6.

Exception No. 5: When the service-entrance conductors consist of busway, connections shall be permitted as required to assemble the various sections and fittings.

The 1981 *NEC* added Exception No. 5 to permit splicing (connecting) busway to facilitate the necessary splices required to connect the various (head "T," "L," limited length, etc.) portions of a busway service-entrance system together.

230-47. Other Conductors in Raceway or Cable.   Conductors other than service conductors shall not be installed in the same service raceway or service-entrance cable.

Exception No. 1: Grounding conductors.

Exception No. 2: Time switch conductors having overcurrent protection.

Time switch conductors are control circuit or switch leg conductors for use with special rate meters, usually for water heater circuits. See Figure 230-10.

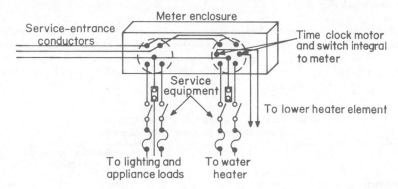

Figure 230-10. Time clock and control switch integral to a meter for use, generally, with water heaters.

230-48. Raceway Seal.   Where a service raceway enters from an underground distribution system, it shall be sealed in accordance with Section 300-5. Spare or unused raceways shall also be sealed. Sealants shall be identified for use with the cable insulation, shield, or other components.

Sealing, such as duct seal or a bushing incorporating the physical characteristics of a seal, is to be used to plug the ends of service raceways. Some sealants are known to have deleterious effects on insulations, extruded semiconducting layers, etc.

230-49. Protection Against Damage — Underground.   Underground service conductors shall be protected against physical damage in accordance with Section 300-5.

230-50. Protection of Open Conductors and Cables Against Damage — Aboveground.   Service-entrance conductors installed aboveground shall be protected against physical damage as specified in (a) or (b) below.

(a) Service-Entrance Cables.   Service-entrance cables, where subject to physical damage, such as where installed in exposed places near driveways or coal chutes, or where subject to contact with awnings, shutters, swinging signs, or similar objects, shall be protected in any of the following ways: (1) by rigid metal conduit; (2) by intermediate metal conduit; (3) by rigid nonmetallic conduit suitable for the location; (4) by electrical metallic tubing; (5) by Type MC cable; or (6) by other approved means.

(b) Other than Service-Entrance Cable.   Individual open conductors and cables other than service-entrance cables shall not be installed within 10 feet (3.05 m) of grade level or where exposed to physical damage.

230-51. Mounting Supports.   Cables or individual open service conductors shall be supported as specified in (a), (b), or (c) below.

(a) Service-Entrance Cables.   Service-entrance cables shall be supported by straps or other approved means within 12 inches (305 mm) of every service head, gooseneck, or connection to a raceway or enclosure and at intervals not exceeding 4 ½ feet (1.37 m).

(b) Other Cables.   Cables that are not approved for mounting in contact with a building or other structure shall be mounted on insulating supports installed at intervals not exceeding 15 feet (4.57 m) and in a manner that will maintain a clearance of not less than 2 inches (50.8 mm) from the surface over which they pass.

(c) Individual Open Conductors.   Individual open conductors shall be installed in accordance with Table 230-51(c). Where exposed to the weather, the conductors shall be mounted on insulators or on insulating supports attached to racks, brackets, or other approved means. Where not exposed to the weather, the conductors shall be mounted on glass or porcelain knobs.

Table 230-51(c).   Supports and Clearances for Individual Open Service Conductors

Maximum Volts	Maximum Distance In Feet Between Supports	Minimum Clearances In Inches	
		Between Conductors	From Surface
600	9	6	2
600	15	12	2
300	4½	3	2
600*	4½*	2½*	1*

For SI units: one inch = 25.4 millimeters; one foot = 0.3048 meter.
* Where not exposed to weather.

230-52. Individual Conductors Entering Buildings or Other Structures.   Where individual open conductors enter a building or other structure, they shall enter through roof bushings or through the wall in an upward slant through individual, noncombustible, nonabsorbent insulating tubes. Drip loops shall be formed on the conductors before they enter the tubes.

230-53. Raceways to Drain.   Where exposed to the weather, raceways enclosing service-entrance conductors shall be raintight and arranged to drain. Where embedded in masonry, raceways shall be arranged to drain.

Service raceways exposed to weather are to have raintight fittings and drainholes. During installation of raceways in masonry, it is nearly impossible to prevent the entrance of surface water, rain, or water from poured concrete.

230-54. Connections at Service Head.

(a) Raintight Service Head.   Service raceways shall be equipped with a raintight service head.

(b) Service Cable Equipped with Raintight Service Head or Gooseneck.   Service cables, either (1) unless continuous from pole to service equipment or meter, shall be equipped with a raintight service head, or (2) formed in a gooseneck and taped and painted or taped with a self-sealing, weather-resistant thermoplastic.

(c) Service Heads Above Service-Drop Attachment.   Service heads and goosenecks in service-entrance cables shall be located above the point of attachment of the service-drop conductors to the building or other structure.

Exception: Where it is impracticable to locate the service head above the point of attachment, the service head location shall be permitted not farther than 24 inches (610 mm) from the point of attachment.

(d) Secured.   Service cables shall be held securely in place.

(e) Opposite Polarity Through Separately Bushed Holes.   Service heads shall have conductors of opposite polarity brought out through separately bushed holes.

(f) Drip Loops.   Drip loops shall be formed on individual conductors. To prevent the entrance of moisture, service-entrance conductors shall be connected to the service-drop conductors either (1) below the level of the service head, or (2) below the level of the termination of the service-entrance cable sheath.

(g) Arranged that Water Will Not Enter Service Raceway or Equipment.   Service-drop conductors and service-entrance conductors shall be arranged so that water will not enter service raceway or equipment.

Most areas require service raceways and service cables to be equipped with a raintight service weather head. Service (SE) cables, however, may be continuous from utility pole to metering or service equipment or, where shaped in a downward direction or "gooseneck" and sealed by taping and painting, may be used without a service head. See Figure 230-11.

Wherever practical, service heads and goosenecks are to be located above the service-drop attachment. Individual conductors should extend in a downward direction, as shown in Figure 230-11, or drip loops are to be formed.

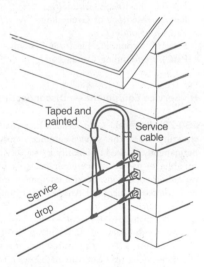

Figure 230-11. A service-entrance cable that terminates in a "gooseneck" without a raintight service weather head.

230-55. Termination at Service Equipment.   Any service raceway or cable shall terminate at the inner end in a box, cabinet, or equivalent fitting that effectively encloses all live metal parts.

Exception: Where the service disconnecting means is mounted on a switchboard having exposed busbars on the back, a raceway shall be permitted to terminate at a bushing.

230-56. Service-Entrance Conductor with the Higher Voltage-to-Ground.   On a 4-wire delta-connected service where the midpoint of one phase is grounded, the service-entrance conductor having the higher phase voltage-to-ground shall be durably and permanently marked by an outer finish that is orange in color or by other effective means.

Proper service connections cannot be made without durably marking the service conductor having the higher voltage-to-ground by an outer finish of orange, by tagging, etc. Marking should be both at the point of connection to the service-entrance conductors and the point of connection to the service disconnect. See Sections 215-8 and 384-3(e) and (f).

G. Service Equipment — Guarding and Grounding

230-62. Service Equipment — Enclosed or Guarded.   Live parts of service equipment shall be enclosed as specified in (a) below, or guarded as specified in (b) below.

(a) Enclosed.   Live parts shall be enclosed so that they will not be exposed to accidental contact or guarded as in (b) below.

(b) Guarded.   Live parts that are not enclosed shall be installed on a switchboard, panelboard, or control board and guarded in accordance with Sections 110-17 and 110-18. Such an enclosure shall be provided with means for locking or sealing doors giving access to live parts.

230-63. Grounding and Bonding.   Service equipment, raceways, cable armor, cable sheaths, etc., and any service conductor that is to be grounded shall be grounded in accordance with the following parts of Article 250.

Part B.   Circuit and System Grounding.
Part C.   Location of System Grounding Connections.
Part D.   Enclosure Grounding.
Part F.   Methods of Grounding.
Part G.   Bonding.
Part H.   Grounding Electrode Systems.
Part J.   Grounding Conductors.

H. Service Equipment — Disconnecting Means

230-70. General.   Means shall be provided to disconnect all conductors in a building or other structure from the service-entrance conductors. Each service disconnecting means shall be permanently marked to identify it as a service disconnecting means and shall be of the type that is suitable for use as service equipment. Each service disconnecting means shall be suitable for the prevailing conditions. Service equipment installed in hazardous (classified) locations shall comply with the requirements of Articles 500 through 517.

Section 230-70 requires that the disconnecting means serve to disconnect all of the conductors in the building from the service-entrance conductors.

Section 230-71(a) states that the total number of disconnecting means is not to exceed six, and Section 230-72(a) requires that all of the disconnecting means be grouped.

Each service disconnecting means is to be identified as a service disconnecting means, is to be suitable for use as service equipment, and is to be marked to indicate the load served.

230-71. Maximum Number of Disconnects.

(a) General.   The service disconnecting means for each service or for each set of service-entrance conductors permitted by Section 230-2, Exception No. 3b. shall consist of not more than six switches or six circuit breakers mounted in a single enclosure, in a group of separate enclosures, or in or on a switchboard.

(b) Single-Pole Units.   Two or three single-pole switches or breakers, capable of individual operation, shall be permitted on multiwire circuits, one pole for each ungrounded conductor, as one multipole disconnect provided they are equipped with "handle ties" or a "master handle" to disconnect all conductors of the service with no more than six operations of the hand.

See Section 384-16(a) for service equipment in panelboards.

It is the intent of this section to recognize six disconnecting means for each service. Each service permitted by Section 230-2 must be disconnected with no more than six operations of the hand.

230-72. Grouping of Disconnects.

(a) General.   The two to six disconnects for each service as permitted in Section 230-71 shall be grouped. Each disconnect shall be marked to indicate the load served.

Exception No. 1: Services as permitted in Section 230-2.

Exception No. 2: One of the two to six service disconnecting means permitted in Section 230-71, when used only for a water pump also intended to provide fire protection, shall be permitted to be located remote from the other disconnecting means.

(b) Additional Service Disconnecting Means.   The one or more additional service disconnecting means for fire pumps or for emergency, legally required standby, or optional standby services permitted by Section 230-2 shall be installed sufficiently remote from the one to six service disconnecting means for normal service to minimize the possibility of simultaneous interruption of supply.

The intent of Section 230-2, Exception Nos. 1 and 2, is to permit separate services where necessary for fire pumps (with one to six disconnects) or emergency systems (with one to six disconnects) in addition to the one to six disconnects for the normal building service. Article 230 recognizes that a disruption of the normal building service should not disconnect the fire pump or emergency systems.

See Section 700-12(d) and (e) for emergency system services.

(c) Location.   The service disconnecting means shall be installed either inside or outside of a building or other structure at a readily accessible location nearest the point of entrance of the service-entrance conductors.

No distance or footage is specified from the point of entrance of service conductors to a readily accessible location for the installation of a service disconnecting means. The authority enforcing this *Code* has the responsibility and is charged with making interpretations of specific installations. The length of service-entrance conductors should be kept to a minimum inside buildings since power utilities provide limited overcurrent protection, and, in the event of a "fault," the service conductors could ignite nearby wood construction or combustible material.
The authority may permit service conductors to bypass coal bins, oil barrels, or gas meters, etc., so as to be in a readily accessible location. However, if the authority judges the distance excessive, the disconnecting means may be required to be located outside, according to this section. See, also, Section 230-44 for conductors considered outside of buildings.

(d) Access to Occupants.   In a multiple-occupancy building, each occupant shall have access to his disconnecting means.

A multiple-occupancy building is a building that may have any number of dwelling units, offices, and the like, that are independent of each other. Unless electric service and maintenance are provided by and under continuous supervision of the building management, each occupant is to have access to his disconnecting means. See Section 240-24(b).

Multiple-occupancy buildings may have service conductors run to each occupancy and each service may have not more than six disconnects. See Section 230-2, Exception No. 3.

Multiple-occupancy buildings may have the one to six disconnecting means located and grouped in a common, readily accessible place, or it is permitted to have service conductors run to each occupancy and each occupancy may have one to six service disconnects. The 1981 *NEC* removed the restriction that the service conductors are to terminate within the occupancy. Where service conductors are run to each occupancy or to a location to service several occupancies, the service conductors are to be installed outside the building or encased in concrete (see Section 230-44).

230-73. Working Space.   Sufficient working space shall be provided in the vicinity of the service disconnecting means to permit safe operation, inspection, and repairs. In no case shall this be less than that specified by Section 110-16.

230-74. Simultaneous Opening of Poles.   Each disconnecting means shall simultaneously disconnect all ungrounded conductors.

230-75. Disconnection of Grounded Conductor.   Where the service disconnecting means does not disconnect the grounded conductor from the premises wiring, other means shall be provided for this purpose in the service equipment. A terminal or bus to which all grounded conductors can be attached by means of pressure connectors shall be permitted for this purpose.

At the service equipment, provisions are to be made to disconnect the grounded conductor from the premises wiring. This disconnection need not be by operation of the service disconnecting means. Disconnection can be, and most commonly is, accomplished by "manually" removing it from the bus or terminal bar to which it is lugged or bolted.

Manufacturers design neutral terminal bars for service equipment so that grounded conductors must be cut to be attached, that is, the grounded conductor cannot be run straight through the service equipment without means of disconnection from the premises wiring.

230-76. Manually or Power Operable.   The disconnecting means for ungrounded conductors shall consist of either (1) a manually operable switch or circuit breaker equipped with a handle or other suitable operating means, or (2) a power-operated switch or circuit breaker provided the switch or circuit breaker can be opened by hand in the event of a power supply failure.

230-77. Indicating.   The disconnecting means shall plainly indicate whether it is in the open or closed position.

230-78. Externally Operable.   An enclosed service disconnecting means shall be externally operable without exposing the operator to contact with live parts.

Exception: A power-operated switch or circuit breaker shall not be required to be externally operable by hand to a closed position.

A service disconnecting means must be capable of being operated to the "on" or "off" position without exposing the operator (generally a homeowner, custodian, or other unqualified person) to live parts. See Article 100 for definition of "Dead Front."

230-79. Rating of Disconnect. The service disconnecting means shall have a rating not less than the load to be carried, determined in accordance with Article 220. In no case shall the rating be lower than specified in (a), (b), (c), or (d) below.

(a) One-Circuit Installation. For installations to supply only limited loads of a single branch circuit, the service disconnecting means shall have a rating of not less than 15 amperes.

(b) Two-Circuit Installations. For installations consisting of not more than two 2-wire branch circuits, the service disconnecting means shall have a rating of not less than 30 amperes.

(c) One-Family Dwelling. For a one-family dwelling, the service disconnecting means shall have a rating of not less than 100 amperes, 3-wire under either of the following conditions: (1) where the initial computed load is 10 kW or more, or (2) where the initial installation consists of six or more 2-wire branch circuits.

A service disconnecting means is to have a rating not less than the load to be carried. See Example 1(b), Chapter 9. See Figure 230-8.

(d) All Others. For all other installations the service disconnecting means shall have a rating of not less than 60 amperes.

230-80. Combined Rating of Disconnects. Where the service disconnecting means consists of more than one switch or circuit breaker, as permitted by Section 230-71, the combined ratings of all the switches or circuit breakers used shall not be less than the rating required for a single switch or circuit breaker.

Section 230-71 permits up to six individual switches or circuit breakers to serve as the required service disconnecting means. Section 230-80 refers to where more than one switch or circuit breaker is used and indicates the combined rating of all the switches or circuit breakers used shall not be less than the rating required for a single switch or circuit breaker. Section 230-90 requires that overcurrent protection be provided in each ungrounded service conductor and have a rating or setting not higher than the allowable ampacity of the service conductors. Exception No. 3 of Section 230-90 allows for not more than six circuit breakers or six sets of fuses to be considered as the overcurrent device and, therefore, none of these individual overcurrent devices can have a rating or setting higher than the ampacity of the service conductors.

In complying with these rules, it is possible for the total of the six overcurrent devices to be larger than the rating of the service-entrance conductors. However, the size of the service-entrance conductors needs to be adequate for the connected load and each individual service disconnecting means needs to be large enough for the individual loads supplied.

230-81. Connection to Terminals. The service conductors shall be connected to the service disconnecting means by pressure connectors, clamps, or other approved means. Connections that depend upon solder shall not be used.

230-82. Equipment Connected to the Supply Side of Service Disconnect. Equipment shall not be connected to the supply side of the service disconnecting means.

Exception No. 1: Cable limiters or other current-limiting devices.

Exception No. 1 formerly permitted service fuses connected ahead of the service disconnecting means and the 1981 *NEC* has changed this to only allow cable limiters or other current limiting devices ahead of a service disconnecting means. Section 230-91 no longer permits service overcurrent devices to be located at the outer end of the service-entrance conductors. A required arrangement is that the overcurrent device be an integral part of the service disconnecting means. The safest practice is to disconnect the service before replacing an overcurrent device.

Exception No. 2: Fuses and disconnecting means or circuit breakers suitable for use as service equipment, in meter pedestals or otherwise provided and connected in series with the ungrounded service conductors and located away from the building supplied.

Exception No. 3: Meters nominally rated not in excess of 600 volts, provided all metal housings and service enclosures are grounded in accordance with Article 250.

Exception No. 4: Instrument transformers (current and potential), high-impedance shunts, surge-protective devices identified for use on the supply side of the service disconnect, time switches, and surge arresters.

In Exception No. 4, the word "capacitors" was replaced with the word "devices" as a number of surge-protective devices have been listed by qualified testing laboratories that are not of the capacitor type.

Exception No. 5: Taps used only to supply time switches, circuits for emergency systems, stand-by power systems, fire pump equipment, and fire and sprinkler alarms if provided with service equipment and installed in accordance with requirements for service-entrance conductors.

Systems such as emergency lighting, fire alarms, fire pumps, stand-by power, and sprinkler alarms are permitted to be connected ahead of the normal service disconnecting means where such systems are provided with a separate disconnecting means and overcurrent protection. See Section 700-12.

230-83. Transfer Equipment.   Where an alternate source is used to supply the same load conductors supplied by the normal source, transfer equipment for shifting from one source to the other shall open all ungrounded conductors of one source before connection is made to the other.

Exception: Where parallel operation is used and suitable automatic or manual control equipment is provided.

Suitable transfer equipment is required to assure that a successful shifting of load from normal power to emergency power will occur without back-feeding into utility power lines.

230-84. More than One Building or Other Structure.

(a) Disconnect Required for Each.   Where more than one building or other structure is on the same property and under single management, each building or other structure served shall be provided with means for disconnecting all ungrounded conductors.
Location shall be in accordance with Section 230-72(c) and (d).

The requirements for applying the rule of a disconnect for each building, for two buildings under single management, and for three buildings under single

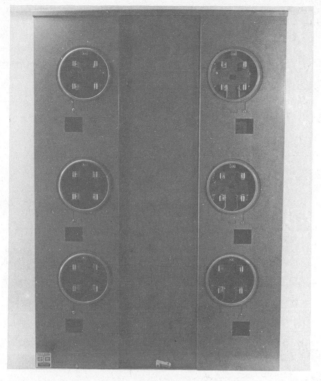

Figure 230-12. An enclosure for grouping service equipment, consisting of six circuit breakers or six fuse-switches. This arrangement does not require a main switch. Six separate enclosures would also be permitted as the service equipment. (*Anchor Electric*)

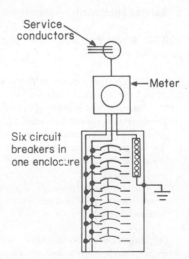

Figure 230-13. Six circuit breakers in one service equipment enclosure.

management are shown in Figures 230-14 and 230-15. The garage circuits for a detached garage supplied from a dwelling unit must be controlled by a switch and this is normally done by either single-pole or 3-way snap switches. All farm buildings must be provided with a disconnecting means to disconnect the wiring in each building.

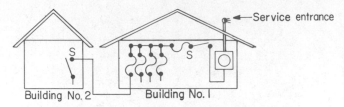

Figure 230-14. A switch (S) is required in Building No. 2.

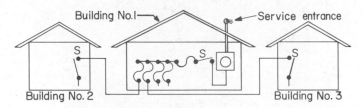

Figure 230-15. Switches are required in Building Nos. 2 and 3.

(b) Suitable for Service Equipment.   The disconnecting means specified in (a) above shall be suitable for use as service equipment.

Exception: For garages and outbuildings on residential property, a snap switch or a set of 3-way or 4-way snap switches suitable for use on branch circuits shall be permitted as the disconnecting means.

J. Service Equipment — Overcurrent Protection

230-90. Where Required.   Each ungrounded service-entrance conductor shall have overcurrent protection.

Service-entrance conductors, overhead or underground, are the supply conductors from the point of connection of service drop or service lateral conductors to the service equipment. Service equipment is intended to constitute the main control and means of cutoff of the supply to the premises wiring system. At this point an overcurrent device, which usually consists of circuit breakers or fuses, is to be provided in series with each ungrounded service conductor to protect "loadside" conductors as well as to prevent an overload on service-entrance conductors.

The basic purpose of overcurrent protection is to open the circuit before conductors are damaged by an overcurrent condition, such as a short circuit or ground fault.

(a) Ungrounded Conductor.   Such protection shall be provided by an overcurrent device in series with each ungrounded service conductor having a rating or setting not higher than the allowable ampacity of the conductor.

Exception No. 1: For motor-starting currents, ratings in conformity with Sections 430-52, 430-62, and 430-63 shall be permitted.

Where a service supplies a motor load as well as lighting or a lighting and appliance load, the overcurrent protective device is to have a rating sufficient to carry the lighting and/or appliance load as determined in accordance with Articles 210 and 220, plus, for an individual motor, the rating permitted by Section 450-52, and, for two or more motors, the rating permitted by Section 430-62.

Example: A service consisting of 100 A, lighting and appliance load, one 25-hp squirrel cage induction motor (full-voltage starting, service factor 1.15, Code letter F), and two 30-hp wound rotor induction motors (40°C rise) on a 230-V, 3-phase system is to have the service conductors and service disconnecting means calculated as follows:

Conductor Loads

The full-load current of the 25-hp motor is 69 A (Table 430-150). The full-load current of the 30-hp motor is 80 A (Table 430-150). The service-entrance conductors will be 125 percent of 80 plus 80 plus 68, or 248 A (Section 430-24).

$$
\begin{array}{rl}
& 248 \text{ A motors} \\
& \underline{100} \text{ A lighting and appliance} \\
\text{Total} & 348 \text{ A}
\end{array}
$$

Therefore, the service-entrance conductors are to be 600 MCM Type TW conductors (Table 310-16).

Overcurrent Protection

The maximum rating of the service overcurrent protection device is based on the sum of the largest branch-circuit overcurrent device [300 percent for the 25-hp motor using a nontime delay fuse (Table 430-152) = 68 x 3 = 204 A, therefore the next larger size 225 A] plus the sum of the full-load currents of the other motors plus the lighting and appliance load (see Section 430-63).

$$
\begin{array}{rl}
& 225 \text{ A 25-hp motor} \\
& 80 \text{ A 30-hp motor} \\
& 80 \text{ A 30-hp motor} \\
& \underline{100} \text{ A lighting and appliance load} \\
\text{Total} & 485 \text{ A}
\end{array}
$$

The nearest standard fuse that does not exceed this value is 450 A.

Exception No. 2: Fuses and circuit breakers with a rating or setting in conformity with Section 240-3, Exception No. 1, and Section 240-6.

Exception No. 3: Not more than six circuit breakers or six sets of fuses shall be considered as the overcurrent device.

Circuit-breaker or fuse-ampere ratings must not be greater than the ampacity of the service conductor (except for motor-starting currents), unless such conductor rating does not correspond to the standard ampere rating of a circuit breaker or fuse, whereupon the next larger size circuit breaker or fuse may be used, provided its rating does not exceed 800 A as permitted in Section 240-3, Exception No. 1. See Section 240-6 for standard ampere ratings of fuses and circuit breakers.

Example: The ampacity of a 500 MCM AWG THW copper conductor is 380 A, as per Table 310-16, and may be protected by a 400-A fuse or circuit breaker. (The rating of the fuse or circuit breaker is based on the ampacity of the service conductor and not the rating of the service disconnect switch.)

As shown in the Example, a 400-A fuse or circuit breaker may be considered as properly sized for the protection of 500 MCM service conductors. If the service disconnecting means (see Exception No. 3) is six circuit breakers or six sets of fuses, the total rating of the six disconnecting means should be as near as practicable to the ampacity of the service-entrance conductors, that is, six disconnects at 100 A each with a total rating of 600 A would not be unreasonable where the calculated load did not exceed the ampacity of the service conductors. See Section 230-80.

Exception No. 4: In a multiple-occupancy building each occupant shall have access to his overcurrent protective devices.

Exception No. 5: Fire Pumps. Where the service to the fire pump room is judged to be outside of buildings, these provisions shall not apply. Overcurrent protection for fire pump services shall be selected or set to carry locked-rotor current of the motor(s) indefinitely [see NFPA 20-1978 (ANSI), Standard for Centrifugal Fire Pumps].

Section 230-90(a), Exception 5, permits service-entrance conductors that are connected ahead of the main service disconnect and that service fire pump rooms to be installed without overload protection for the conductors. Two methods of installation are considered as meeting the intent of this section. They are (1) where the service conductors to the pump room are installed outside the building; or (2) where the conductors are installed under not less than 2 in. of concrete or in a raceway enclosed by concrete or brick not less than 2 in. thick (see Section 230-44) that terminates in a fire-resistant pump room.

Section 430-31 of the *Code* indicates that provisions for motor and branch circuit running overcurrent and overload protection are not to be interpreted as requiring overload protection in cases where it might introduce additional or increased hazards. Fire pump motors are a case in point; they are allowed much larger overcurrent protection than other motors, recognizing that fire pumps should be allowed to operate to failure rather than be removed from the line in order to prolong their usefulness under adverse fire conditions. See, also, Section 230-95, Exception No. 2.

Figure 230-9 is a diagram of the wiring and components of a fire pump circuit designed to comply with requirements of the *NEC* and NFPA 20, Standard for the Installation of Centrifugal Fire Pumps. The pump motor represented is a 100-hp, 460-V, 3-phase, squirrel-cage induction type, and its full-load current, taken from Table 430-150, is 124 A.

"The service conductors, feeder conductors, and branch-circuit conductors are sized at 125 percent of the motor full-load current rating (124 A x 125 percent = 155 A). According to Table 310-16, the next closest copper wire size for 155 A is a 3/0 TW conductor with an allowable ampacity of 165 A; therefore, all the conductors would be sized with a 3/0 TW copper conductor. (See Sections 430-22 and 430-23 for sizing of conductors.) Other conductors with an ampacity of 155 A or more would also be permitted in this instance.

The locked-rotor current of the motor in the installation illustrated is 738 A, as derived from Table 430-151, and the power supply protection may consist of either fuses or circuit breakers sized so that they will not open at locked-rotor current. In either case, the next standard ampere rating for fuses or circuit breakers is 800 A as taken from Section 240-6. This protection complies with the intent of the requirements of Section 6-3.4 of NFPA 20 and also of Section 430-31 of the *NEC*.

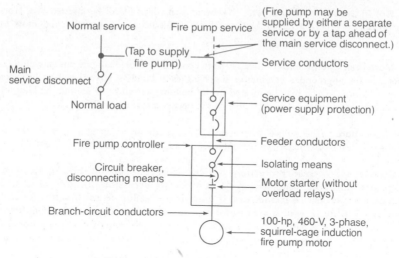

Figure 230-16. A typical fire pump installation.

The isolating means in the illustrated pump's controller could be a motor circuit switch rated in horsepower (see Section 430-109) or a suitable nonautomatic circuit breaker (molded case switch), as required by Section 7-4.1 of NFPA 20.

If a motor circuit switch were to be used for the isolating means, it would be horsepower rated at 100 hp and have an ampere rating of at least 115 percent of the full-load current rating of the motor, that is, 124 A x 115 percent = 142.6 A, to meet requirements of Section 430-110(a) of the *NEC* and Subsection 7-4.1.2 of NFPA 20.

The circuit breaker used to protect the branch circuit to the squirrel-cage induction motor would be a magnetic trip-type having a time delay of not over 20 sec at locked-rotor current, and it would be calibrated up to and set at 300 percent of the motor's full-load current [see Subsection 7-4.2.7(a) of NFPA 20]. In this particular instance it would be calibrated at 372 A (124 A x 300 percent).

Circuit breakers for dc and wound-rotor ac motors for fire pumps are of the instantaneous type, calibrated up to and set at 400 percent of the motor's full-load current. See Subsection 7-4.2.7 of NFPA 20.

UL-listed pump controllers are investigated for their ability to meet the requirements of the *NEC* and NFPA 20 for the time-current characteristics of the magnetic circuit breakers to assure the 20-sec delay at locked-rotor current and 300 percent or 400 percent trip setting, depending on the type of motor used.

The motor starter (without overload relays) is of a magnetic type with a contact in each ungrounded conductor, in accordance with Section 7-4.3 of NFPA 20.

A set of fuses shall be considered all the fuses required to protect all the ungrounded conductors of a circuit. Single-pole circuit breakers, grouped in accordance with Section 230-71(b), shall be considered as one protective device.

Two or three single-pole switches or circuit breakers on multiwire circuits and capable of individual operation are to be permitted as one protective device, provided they are equipped with "handle ties" or a "master handle" to disconnect all ungrounded conductors of a service with no more than six operations of the hand.

(b) Not in Grounded Conductor.   No overcurrent device shall be inserted in a grounded service conductor except a circuit breaker which simultaneously opens all conductors of the circuit.

(c) More than One Building.   In a property comprising more than one building under single management, the ungrounded conductors supplying each building served shall be protected by overcurrent devices, which may be located in the building served or in another building on the same property, provided they are accessible to the occupants of the building served.

230-91. Location.   The service overcurrent device shall be an integral part of the service disconnecting means or shall be located immediately adjacent thereto.

> Service overcurrent protection devices (fuses or circuit breakers), where located within a building, are to be at a readily accessible location nearest the entrance of the service conductors. If there is no readily accessible area, or if the available readily accessible area is not near the entrance of the service conductors, and the distance is judged by the authority having jurisdiction to be a potential hazard, the overcurrent devices are to be located outside of the building.

230-92. Location of Branch-Circuit Overcurrent Devices.   Where the service overcurrent devices are locked or sealed, or otherwise not readily accessible, branch-circuit overcurrent devices shall be installed on the load side, shall be mounted in an accessible location, and shall be of lower rating than the service overcurrent device.

230-93. Protection of Specific Circuits.   Where necessary to prevent tampering, an automatic overcurrent device protecting service conductors supplying only a specific load, such as a water heater, shall be permitted to be locked or sealed where located so as to be accessible.

230-94. Relative Location of Overcurrent Device and Other Service Equipment.   The overcurrent device shall protect all circuits and devices.

Exception No. 1: The service switch shall be permitted on the supply side.

Exception No. 2: High-impedance shunt circuits, lightning arresters, surge protective capacitors, and instrument transformers (current and potential) shall be permitted to be connected and installed on the supply side of the service disconnecting means as permitted in Section 230-82.

Exception No. 3: Circuits for emergency supply and time switches shall be permitted to be connected on the supply side of the service overcurrent device where separately provided with overcurrent protection.

Exception No. 4: Circuits used only for the operation of fire alarm, other protective signaling systems, or the supply to fire pump equipment shall be permitted to be connected on the supply side of the service overcurrent device where separately provided with overcurrent protection.

Exception No. 5: Meters nominally rated not in excess of 600 volts, provided all metal housings and service enclosures are grounded in accordance with Article 250.

Exception No. 6: Where service equipment is power operable, the control circuit shall be permitted to be connected ahead of the service equipment if suitable overcurrent protection and disconnecting means are provided.

230-95. Ground-Fault Protection of Equipment.   Ground-fault protection of equipment shall be provided for solidly grounded wye electrical services of more than 150 volts to ground, but not exceeding 600 volts phase-to-phase for each service disconnecting means rated 1000 amperes or more.

The impetus to require ground-fault protection of equipment on services rated 480/277 V wye was due to the unusually high number of burndowns that were being reported on this type of service. Ground-fault protection of services will not protect the conductors on the supply side of the service disconnecting means but will provide protection from line-to-ground faults occurring on the load side of the service disconnecting means rated 1,000 A or more. Rather than installing ground-fault protection, it may be desirable to provide multiple disconnects rated less than 1,000 A. For instance, six 800-A disconnecting means may be used, and, in this case, ground-fault protection would not be necessary. The fine print note recognizes that ground-fault protection may be desirable at lesser amperages on solidly grounded systems for voltages exceeding 150 V to ground, but not exceeding 600 V phase-to-phase.

In addition to providing ground-fault protection, a close study needs to be undertaken of the circuit impedance to determine the short-circuit currents that would be available at the supply terminals so that equipment and overcurrent protection of the proper interrupting rating is used. See Sections 110-9 and 110-10.

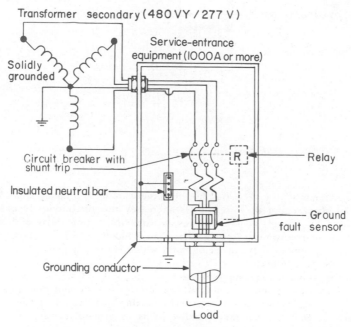

Figure 230-17. Ground-fault sensor encircling all circuit conductors, including the neutral.

There are two basic types of ground-fault equipment protectors and these are illustrated in Figures 230-17 and 230-18. In Figure 230-17, the ground-fault sensor is installed around all the circuit conductors, and a stray current on a line-to-ground fault will set up an unbalance of the currents flowing in individual conductors installed through the ground-fault sensor. When this current exceeds the setting of the ground-fault sensor, the shunt trip will operate and remove the circuit breakers from the line.

The ground-fault sensor illustrated in Figure 230-18 is installed around the grounding-conductor bonding jumper only, and when an unbalanced current from a line-to-ground fault occurs, the current will flow through the bonding jumper and the shunt trip will cause the circuit breaker to operate and remove the load from the line.

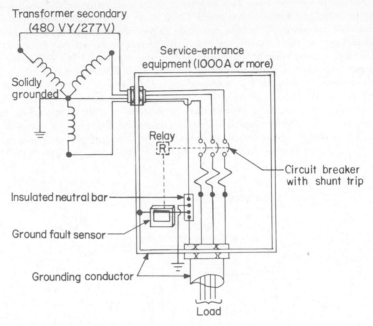

Figure 230-18. Ground-fault sensor encircling the bonding jumper conductor only.

The maximum setting is 1,200 A; however, there are no minimums, and it should be noted that setting at lower levels increases the likelihood of unwanted shutdowns. The requirements now provide a maximum time delay of 1 sec for ground-fault currents equal to or greater than 3,000 A in order to minimize the amount of damage done by an arcing fault, which is directly proportional to the time it is allowed to burn.

Where interconnection is made between multiple supply systems, care should be taken to assure proper ground-fault sensing by the ground-fault protection equipment, and, in most cases, a careful engineering study must be made to assure that fault currents do not take parallel paths to ground, causing no trip or unwanted trips on the ground-fault protected system.

(a) Setting. The ground-fault protection system shall operate to cause the service disconnecting means to open all ungrounded conductors of the faulted circuit. The maximum setting of the ground-fault protection shall be 1200 amperes and the maximum time delay shall be one second for ground-fault currents equal to or greater than 3000 amperes.

Exception No. 1: The provisions of this section shall not apply to a service disconnecting means for a continuous industrial process where a nonorderly shutdown will introduce additional or increased hazards.

Exception No. 2: The provisions of this section shall not apply to fire pumps.

Most fire pumps rated 100 hp and over would require a disconnecting means rated 1000 amperes or more; however, due to the nature of their use, fire pumps are exempt from the provisions of Section 230-95.

(b) Fuses.   If a switch and fuse combination is used, the fuses employed shall be capable of interrupting any current higher than the interrupting capacity of the switch during a time when the ground-fault protective system will not cause the switch to open.

As used in this section, the rating of the Service Disconnecting Means is considered to be the rating of the largest fuse that can be installed or the highest trip setting for which the actual overcurrent device installed in a circuit breaker is rated or can be adjusted.

It is recognized that ground-fault protection may be desirable for service disconnecting means rated less than 1000 amperes on solidly grounded systems having more than 150 volts to ground, not exceeding 600 volts phase-to-phase.

As used in this section, solidly grounded means that the grounded conductor (neutral) is grounded without inserting any resistor or impedance device.

Ground-fault protection that functions to open the service disconnecting means will afford no protection from faults on the line side of the protective element. It serves only to limit damage to conductors and equipment on the load side in the event of an arcing ground fault on the load side of the protective element.

This added protective equipment at the service equipment will make it necessary to review the overall wiring system for proper selective overcurrent protection coordination. Additional installations of ground-fault protective equipment will be needed on feeders and branch circuits where maximum continuity of electrical service is necessary.

Where ground-fault protection is provided for the service disconnecting means and interconnection is made with another supply system by a transfer device, means or devices may be needed to assure proper ground-fault sensing by the ground-fault protection equipment.

(c) Performance Testing.   The ground-fault protection system shall be performance tested when first installed. The test shall be conducted in accordance with approved instructions which shall be provided with the equipment. A written record of this test shall be made and shall be available to the authority having jurisdiction.

The requirement for ground-fault protection system "performance testing" was written as a result of numerous reports of ground-fault systems that were improperly wired and that could not perform the function for which they were intended. It is expected that qualified testing laboratories will require a set of approved performance testing instructions to be supplied with the equipment in accordance with Section 110-3(b) for installation and use of listed and labeled equipment.

230-96. Working Space.   Sufficient working space shall be provided in the vicinity of the service overcurrent devices to permit safe operation, replacements, inspection, and repairs. In no case shall this be less than that specified by Section 110-16.

230-98. Available Short-Circuit Current.   Service equipment shall be suitable for the short-circuit current available at its supply terminals.

K. Services Exceeding 600 Volts, Nominal

230-200. General.   Service conductors and equipment used on circuits exceeding 600 volts, nominal, shall comply with all applicable provisions of the preceding sections of this article and

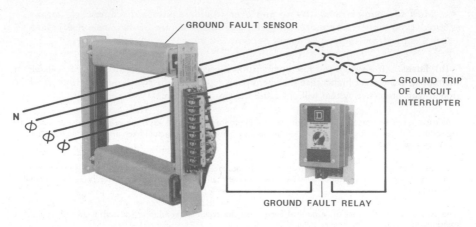

Figure 230-19. Ground-fault protection system (*Square D Co.*)

Figure 230-20. Current-limiting circuit breaker within UL Class R fuse levels and former Class K-5 levels. (*Square D Co.*)

with the following sections, which supplement or modify the preceding sections. In no case shall the provisions of this article apply to equipment on the supply side of the service-point.

Definition: Service-point is the point of connection between the facilities of the serving utility and the premises' wiring.

For clearances of conductors of over 600 volts, nominal, see National Electrical Safety Code (ANSI C2-1977).

230-201. Classification of Service Conductors.

(a) Secondary Conductors. The secondary conductors shall constitute the service conductors where the step-down transformers are located as follows: (1) outdoors; (2) in a separate building from the building or other structure served; (3) inside the building or other structure served where in a vault complying with Part C of Article 450; (4) inside the building or other structure served where in a locked room or other locked enclosure and accessible to qualified persons only; or (5) inside the building or other structure where in metal-enclosed gear.

(b) Primary Conductors. In all cases not specified in (a) above, the primary conductors shall be considered the service conductors.

Exception: Either the primary or the secondary conductors shall be permitted to constitute the service conductors for an industrial complex where both the primary and secondary voltages are over 600 volts, nominal.

For a transformer having a secondary voltage of 600 volts or less, the secondary conductors are considered the service conductors. For a transformer where both the primary and secondary voltages are over 600 volts, nominal, in an industrial complex, then either the primary or the secondary conductors are permitted to be the service conductors.

The design and installation of electrical distribution systems for large industrial complexes is done by persons highly trained in all aspects of the electrical power field. The type of distribution system, voltages selected and installation practices have been proven by many successful years of experience. The intent here is not to restrict the system designers with "hard to define and interpret" code requirements and allow an industrial design to be viewed as a whole instead of many individual small concepts.

230-202. Service-Entrance Conductors. Service-entrance conductors to buildings or enclosures shall be installed to conform to the following:

(a) Conductor Size. Service conductors shall be not smaller than No. 6 unless in cable. Conductors in cable shall not be smaller than No. 8.

(b) Wiring Methods. Service-entrance conductors shall be installed by means of one of the following wiring methods: (1) in rigid metal conduit; (2) in intermediate metal conduit; (3) in rigid nonmetallic conduit where encased in not less than 2 inches (50.8 mm) of concrete; (4) as multiconductor cable identified as service cable; (5) as open conductors where supported on insulators and where either accessible only to qualified persons or where effectively guarded against accidental contact; (6) in cablebus; or (7) in busways.

Underground service-entrance conductors shall conform to Section 710-3(b).

Cable tray systems shall be permitted to support cables identified as service-entrance conductors. See Article 318.

See Section 310-6 for shielding of solid dielectric insulated conductors.

(c) Open Work. Open wire services over 600 volts, nominal, shall be installed in accordance with the provisions of Article 710, Part D.

(d) Supports. Service conductors and their supports, including insulators, shall have strength and stability sufficient to ensure maintenance of adequate clearance with abnormal currents in case of short circuits.

(e) Guarding. Open wires shall be guarded to make them accessible only to qualified persons.

(f) Service Cable. Where cable conductors emerge from a metal sheath or raceway, the insulation of the conductors shall be protected from moisture and physical damage by a pothead or other approved means.

(g) Draining Raceways. Unless conductors identified for use in wet locations are used, raceways embedded in masonry or exposed to the weather shall be arranged to drain.

(h) Over 15,000 Volts.   Where the voltage exceeds 15,000 volts between conductors they shall enter either metal-enclosed switchgear or a transformer vault conforming to the requirements of Sections 450-41 through 450-48.

(i) Conductor Considered Outside Building.   Conductors placed under at least 2 inches (50.8 mm) of concrete beneath a building, or conductors within a building in conduit or raceway and enclosed by concrete or brick not less than 2 inches (50.8 mm) thick shall be considered outside the building.

230-203. Warning Signs.   High voltage signs with the words "High Voltage" shall be posted where unauthorized persons might come in contact with live parts.

230-204. Isolating Switches.

(a) Where Required.   Where oil switches or air or oil circuit breakers constitute the service disconnecting means, an air-break isolating switch shall be installed on the supply side of the disconnecting means and all associated service equipment.

Exception: Where such equipment is mounted on removable truck panels or metal-enclosed switchgear units, which cannot be opened unless the circuit is disconnected, and which, when removed from the normal operating position, automatically disconnect the circuit breaker or switch from all live parts.

(b) Fuses as Isolating Switch.   Where fuses are of the type that can be operated as a disconnecting switch, a set of such fuses shall be permitted as the isolating switch where: (1) the oil disconnecting means is a nonautomatic switch, and (2) the set of fuses disconnect the oil switch and all associated service equipment from the service-entrance conductors.

(c) Accessible to Qualified Persons Only.   The isolating switch shall be accessible to qualified persons only.

(d) Grounding Connection.   Isolating switches shall be provided with a means for readily connecting the load side conductors to ground when disconnected from the source of supply.
    A means for grounding the load side conductors need not be provided for any duplicate isolating switch installed and maintained by the electric supply company.

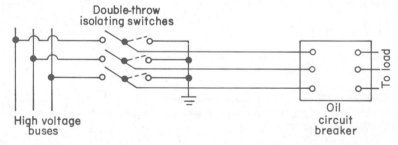

Figure 230-21. A two-position switch grounds load-side conductors when disconnected from high voltage line buses.

230-205. Disconnecting Means.

(a) Type.   The service disconnecting means shall simultaneously disconnect all ungrounded conductors and shall be capable of being closed on a fault equal to or greater than the maximum available short-circuit current in the circuit at its supply terminals.
    Where fused switches or separately mounted fuses are installed, the fuse characteristics shall be permitted to contribute to the fault-closing rating of the disconnecting means.

(b) Location.   A disconnecting means shall be available for the premises wiring system either ahead of or near the defined service point.

See definition of "service-point" in Section 230-200.

230-206. Overcurrent Devices as Disconnecting Means.   Where the circuit breaker or alternative for it specified in Section 230-208 for service overcurrent devices meets the requirements specified in Section 230-205, they shall constitute the service disconnecting means.

230-207. Equipment in Secondaries.   Where the primary service equipment supplies one or more transformers whose secondary windings connect to a common bus of bars or wires, and the primary load-interrupter switch or circuit breaker is capable of being opened and closed from a point outside the transformer vault, the disconnecting means and overcurrent protection shall not be required in the secondary circuit if the primary fuse or circuit breaker is rated or set to protect the secondary circuit.

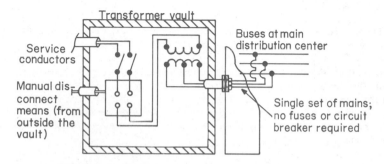

Figure 230-22. In installations where a transformer supplies a single set of secondary mains, the mains may be connected directly to the buses at the distribution center without a switch or overload protection; however, the primary breaker must be set to protect the secondary circuit.

230-208. Overcurrent Protection Requirements.   Service-entrance conductors shall have a short-circuit protective device in each ungrounded conductor, on the load side of, or as an integral part of, the service-entrance switch. The protective device shall be capable of detecting and interrupting all values of current in excess of its trip setting or melting point, which can occur at its location. A fuse rated in continuous amperes not to exceed three times the ampacity of the conductor, or a circuit breaker with a trip setting of not more than six times the ampacity of the conductors shall be considered as providing the required short-circuit protection.

Tables 310-39 through 310-54 for ampacity of high-voltage conductors.

Overcurrent devices shall conform to the following:

(a) In Vault or Consisting of Metal-Enclosed Switchgear.   Where the service equipment is installed in a transformer vault meeting the provisions of Sections 450-41 through 450-48, or consists of metal-enclosed switchgear, the overcurrent protection and disconnecting means shall be one of the following:

(1) A nonautomatic oil switch, oil fuse cutout, or air load-interrupter switch shall be permitted with fuses. The interrupting rating of this switch shall equal or exceed the continuous current rating of the fuse.

(2) An automatic trip circuit breaker of suitable current-carrying and interrupting capacity.

(3) A switch capable of interrupting the no-load current of the transformer supplied through the switch and suitable fuses shall be permitted provided the switch is interlocked with a single switch or circuit breaker on the secondary circuit of the transformer so that the primary switch cannot be opened when the secondary circuit is closed.

(b) Not in Vault or Not Consisting of Metal-Enclosed Switchgear. Where the service equipment is not in a vault or metal-enclosed switchgear, the overcurrent protection and disconnecting means shall be either of the following:

(1) An air load-interrupter switch or other switch capable of interrupting the rated circuit load shall be permitted with fuses on a pole or elevated structure outside the building provided the switch is operable by persons using the building.

(2) An automatic-trip circuit breaker of suitable ampacity and interrupting capacity. The circuit breaker shall be located outside the building as near as practicable to where the service conductors enter the building. The location shall be permitted on a pole, roof, foundation, or other structure.

(c) Fuses. Fuses shall have an interrupting rating no less than the maximum available short-circuit current in the circuit at their supply terminals.

(d) Circuit Breakers. Circuit breakers shall be free to open in case the circuit is closed on an overload. This can be accomplished by means such as trip-free circuit breakers. A service circuit breaker shall indicate clearly whether it is open or closed, and shall have an interrupting rating no less than the maximum available short-circuit current at its supply terminals.

Overcurrent relays shall be furnished in connection with current transformers in one of the following combinations:

(1) Three overcurrent relays operated from current transformers in each phase.

(2) Two overcurrent relays operated by current from current transformers in any two phases and one overcurrent relay sensitive to ground-fault current that is operated by the sum of the currents from current transformers in each phase.

(3) Two overcurrent relays operated by current from current transformers in any two phases and one overcurrent relay sensitive to ground-fault current that is operated from a current transformer which links all three phase conductors and the grounded circuit conductor (neutral), if provided.

(e) Enclosed Overcurrent Devices. The restriction to 80 percent of rating for an enclosed overcurrent device on continuous loads shall not apply to overcurrent devices installed in services operating at over 600 volts.

230-209. Surge Arresters (Lightning Arresters). Surge arresters installed in accordance with the requirements of Article 280 shall be placed on each ungrounded overhead service conductor on the supply side of the service equipment, when called for by the authority having jurisdiction.

230-210. Service Equipment-General Provisions. Service equipment including instrument transformers shall conform to Article 710, Part B.

230-211. Metal-Enclosed Switchgear. Metal-enclosed switchgear shall consist of a substantial metal structure and a sheet metal enclosure. Where installed over a wood floor, suitable protection thereto shall be provided.

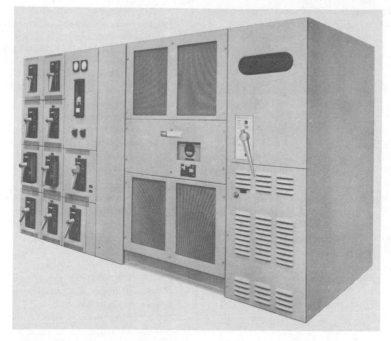

Figure 230-23. An assembly of metal-enclosed switchgear. (*Federal Pacific Electric Co.*)

ARTICLE 240 — OVERCURRENT PROTECTION

240-1. Scope. Parts A through G of this article provide the general requirements for overcurrent protection and overcurrent protective devices not more than 600 volts, nominal. Part H covers overcurrent protection over 600 volts, nominal.

Overcurrent protection for conductors and equipment is provided to open the circuit if the current reaches a value that will cause an excessive or dangerous temperature in conductors or conductor insulation. See also Sections 110-9 and 110-10 for requirements for interrupting capacity and protection against fault currents.

Contents

A. General

240-2. Protection of Equipment. Equipment shall be protected against overcurrent in accordance with the article in this Code covering the type of equipment as specified in the following list.

240-3. Protection of Conductors — Other than Flexible Cords and Fixture Wires. Conductors, other than flexible cords and fixture wires, shall be protected against overcurrent in accordance with their ampacities as specified in Tables 310-16 through 310-19 and all applicable notes to these tables.

Exception No. 1: Next Higher Overcurrent Protective Device Rating. Where the ampacity of the conductor does not correspond with the standard ampere rating of a fuse or a circuit breaker without overload trip adjustment above its rating (but which may have other trip or rating adjustments), the next higher standard device rating shall be permitted only if this rating does not exceed 800 amperes.

Table 210-24 summarizes the requirements for the size of conductors where two or more outlets are required. The first footnote also indicates that these ampacities are for copper conductors where derating is not required. Section 210-3 indicates that branch-circuit conductors rated 15, 20, 30, 40, and 50 A, with two or more outlets, must be protected at their ratings. Section 210-19(a) requires that branch-circuit conductors are to have an ampacity of not less than the rating of the branch circuit and not less than the maximum load to be served.

These are specific requirements and take precedence over Section 240-3, Exception No. 1 which applies generally. Where conductor ampacities do not correspond to standard ampere ratings of fuses or circuit breakers, the next standard device rating is to be permitted.

Exception No. 2: Tap Conductors. Tap conductors as permitted in Sections 210-19(c); 240-21, Exceptions No. 2, 3, 5, and 8; 364-10 and 364-11; and Part D of Article 430.

Exception No. 3: Motor and Motor-Control Circuits. Motor and motor-control circuit conductors protected in accordance with Parts C, D, E, and F of Article 430. Motor-operated appliance circuit conductors protected in accordance with Parts B and D of Article 422. Air-conditioning and refrigerating equipment circuit conductors protected in accordance with Parts C and F of Article 440.

Exception No. 4: Remote Control Circuits. Remote-control circuits shall comply with Article 725.

See Section 725-12(a) and (b) and Exception Nos. 2 and 3.

Exception No. 5: Transformer Secondary Conductors. Conductors supplied by the secondary side of a single-phase transformer having a 2-wire (single-voltage) secondary shall be considered as protected by overcurrent protection provided on the primary (supply) side of the transformer, provided this protection is in accordance with Section 450-3 and does not exceed the value determined by multiplying the secondary conductor ampacity by the secondary-to-primary transformer voltage ratio. Transformer secondary conductors (other than 2 wire) are not considered to be protected by the primary overcurrent protection.

The voltage ratio of a constant-potential transformer, that is, the ratio of primary-to-secondary voltage, depends primarily upon the ratio of the primary to the secondary turns. For general work, the voltage ratio can be taken equal to the turn ratio of the windings. The current ratio of a constant-potential transformer will be approximately equal to the inverse ratio of the turns in the two windings. For example, for transforming or "stepping down" from 480 V to 240 V the ratio of the turns in the windings will be 2:1. The currents in the primary and the secondary windings will be, very closely, inversely proportional to the ratio of the primary and secondary voltages, because, disregarding the small losses of transformation, the power put into a transformer will equal the power delivered by it. For example, considering a transformer with windings having a ratio of 2:1; if its secondary windings deliver 100 A at 240 V, the input to its primary winding must receive almost exactly 50 A at 480 V.

For example, a dry-type transformer that has a 2-wire, 480-V primary and a 2-wire, 240-V secondary with a primary current of 50 A would need to be protected by a 50-A fuse with a No. 6 TW copper wire which is rated at 55 A. The ratio of primary-to-secondary is a 2:1 ratio; therefore, the secondary current would be 100 A and the minimum size TW conductors would be No. 1 TW copper that is rated at 110 A. This arrangement satisfies the Exception No. 5 since the primary conductors are protected at their rated ampacities and the No. 1 secondary conductors have an ampacity of 110 A and are properly protected by the 50-A primary fuses. Therefore, the length of the secondary conductors is not limited and no overcurrent protection is required on the secondary side.

For transformers having more than two wires on the secondary, the secondary conductors must be protected on the secondary side except as permitted for tap conductors in Exception Nos. 2 and 8 of Section 240-21.

If the secondary was 3-wire, 240/120 V load, a 120-A load on the secondary (line-to-neutral with no load on the other 120-V winding) the 50-A primary fuse would only see a 30-A load. This is a result of the 4:1 ratio and the 120-V secondary winding plus two of the three secondary conductors would be seriously overloaded.

Also, in analyzing the current ratios for a three-phase transformer, unbalanced loading of the secondary circuit must be considered. Power to a single-phase secondary load will be delivered by all three transformers but the load is not shared equally. The ratio of the currents in the primary and secondary feeder conductors will not be in accordance with the transformer turns ratio.

Exception No. 6: Capacitor circuits which comply with Article 460.

Exception No. 7: Welders circuits which comply with Article 630.

Exception No. 8: Power Loss Hazard. Conductor overload protection shall not be required where the interruption of the circuit would create a hazard, such as in a material handling magnet circuit. Short-circuit protection shall be provided.

240-4. Protection of Fixture Wires and Cords.   Fixture wire or flexible cord, size No. 16 or No. 18, and tinsel cord shall be considered as protected by 20-ampere overcurrent devices.

Flexible cord approved for use with specific appliances shall be considered as protected by the overcurrent device of the branch circuit of Article 210 when conforming to the following:

20-ampere circuits, No. 18 cord and larger.
30-ampere circuits, cord of 10-ampere capacity and over.
40-ampere circuits, cord of 20-ampere capacity and over.
50-ampere circuits, cord of 20-ampere capacity and over.

Fixture wire shall be considered as protected by the overcurrent device of the branch circuit of Article 210 when conforming to the following:

20-ampere circuits, No. 18 and larger.
30-ampere circuits, No. 14 and larger.
40-ampere circuits, No. 12 and larger.
50-ampere circuits, No. 12 and larger.

240-6. Standard Ampere Ratings.   The standard ampere ratings for fuses and inverse time circuit breakers shall be considered 15, 20, 25, 30, 35, 40, 45, 50, 60, 70, 80, 90, 100, 110, 125, 150, 175, 200, 225, 250, 300, 350, 400, 450, 500, 600, 700, 800, 1000, 1200, 1600, 2000, 2500, 3000, 4000, 5000, and 6000.

Exception: Additional standard ratings for fuses shall be considered 1, 3, 6, 10, and 601.

240-8. Fuses or Circuit Breakers in Parallel.   Fuses, circuit breakers, or combinations thereof shall not be connected in parallel.

Exception: Circuit breakers or fuses, factory assembled in parallel, and approved as a unit.

Section 240-8 prohibits the use of fuses or circuit breakers in parallel, and Section 380-17 prohibits the use of fuses in parallel in fused switches.

It is not the intent of this Exception to restore the use of standard fuses in parallel in disconnect switches. However, this Exception gives recognition to parallel low-voltage circuit breakers or fuses and parallel high-voltage circuit breakers or fuses where tested and factory-assembled in parallel and approved as a unit.

High-voltage fuses have long been recognized in parallel where assembled in an identified common mounting as per Section 710-21(b)(1).

240-9. Thermal Devices.   Thermal cutouts, thermal relays, and other devices not designed to open short circuits shall not be used for the protection of conductors against overcurrent due to short circuits or grounds but the use of such devices shall be permitted to protect motor-branch-circuit conductors from overload if protected in accordance with Section 430-40.

Thermal cutouts are overcurrent protective devices consisting of a heater element that senses overloads on motors or motor branch-circuit conductors and opens the circuit by actuating a renewable fusible member. They are not designed to interrupt short-circuit currents.

240-10. Supplementary Overcurrent Protection.   Where supplementary overcurrent protection is used for lighting fixtures, appliances, and other equipment or for internal circuits and components of equipment, it shall not be used as a substitute for branch-circuit overcurrent devices or in place of the branch-circuit protection specified in Article 210. Supplementary overcurrent devices shall not be required to be readily accessible.

240-11. Definition of Current-Limiting Overcurrent Protective Device.   A current-limiting overcurrent protective device is a device which, when interrupting currents in its current-limiting range, will reduce the current flowing in the faulted circuit to a magnitude substantially less than that obtainable in the same circuit if the device were replaced with a solid conductor having comparable impedance.

Most electrical distribution systems can deliver large short-circuit currents to components, such as conductors, service equipment, etc. These components are not generally able to handle short-circuit currents; they can be damaged or destroyed and serious "burndowns" and fires could result. Properly selected current-limiting overcurrent protective devices will limit the let-through energy to within the rating of the components in spite of high available short-circuit currents.

See Sections 110-9 and 110-10 for interrupting ratings, circuit impedance, and other characteristics requirements.

Figure 240-1. Class R current-limiting fuse with rejection feature to prohibit the installation of noncurrent-limiting fuses. (*Bussmann Mfg. Co.*)

240-12. Electrical System Coordination.   In industrial locations where an orderly shutdown is required to minimize hazard(s) to personnel and equipment, a system of coordination based on the following two conditions shall be permitted:

(1) Coordinated short-circuit protection.

(2) Overload indication based on monitoring systems or devices.

Coordination is defined as properly localizing a fault condition to restrict outages to the equipment affected, accomplished by choice of selective fault-protective devices. The monitoring system may cause the condition to go to alarm allowing corrective action or an orderly shutdown thereby minimizing personnel hazard and equipment damage.

B. Location

240-20. Ungrounded Conductors.

(a) Overcurrent Device Required. A fuse or an overcurrent trip unit of a circuit breaker shall be connected in series with each ungrounded conductor. A combination of a current transformer and overcurrent relay shall be considered equivalent to an overcurrent trip unit.

For motor circuits, see Parts C, D, F, and J of Article 430.

(b) Circuit Breaker as Overcurrent Device. Circuit breakers shall open all ungrounded conductors of the circuit.

Exception: Individual single-pole circuit breakers shall be acceptable as the protection for each conductor of ungrounded 2-wire circuits, each ungrounded conductor of 3-wire direct-current or single-phase circuits, or for each ungrounded conductor of lighting or appliance branch circuits connected to 4-wire, 3-phase systems or 5-wire, 2-phase systems, provided such lighting or appliance circuits are supplied from a system having a grounded neutral and no conductor in such circuits operates at a voltage greater than permitted in Section 210-6.

240-21. Location in Circuit.
An overcurrent device shall be connected at the point where the conductor to be protected receives its supply.

Exception No. 1: Smaller Conductor Protected. Where the overcurrent device protecting the larger conductor also protects the smaller conductor in accordance with Tables 310-16 through 310-19.

Exception No. 1 is illustrated by Figure 240-2. A smaller 1/0 THW conductor (150 A) is tapped from a larger 3/0 THW feeder conductor (200 A) which is in turn protected by a 150-A circuit breaker that is equal to the ampacity of the 1/0 tap conductor. The circuit breaker protecting the feeder conductors is rated to protect the tap conductors.

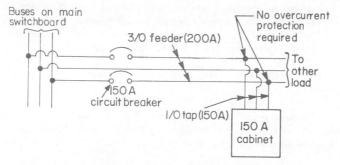

Figure 240-2. The circuit breaker protecting the feeder conductors also protects the tap conductors to the cabinet, in this case.

Exception No. 2: Feeder Taps Not Over 10 Feet (3.05 m) Long. For conductors tapped to a feeder or transformer secondary where all the following conditions are met:
  a. The length of the tap conductors does not exceed 10 feet (3.05 m).
  b. The ampacity of the tap conductors is:
    (1) not less than the combined computed loads on the circuits supplied by the tap conductors, and
    (2a) not less than the rating of the device supplied by the tap conductors, or

(2b) not less than the rating of the overcurrent protective device at the termination of the tap conductors.

c. The tap conductors do not extend beyond the switchboard, panelboard, or control devices they supply.

d. Except at the point of connection to the feeder, the tap conductors are enclosed in a raceway, which shall extend from the tap to the enclosure of an enclosed switchboard, panelboard, or control devices, or to the back of an open switchboard.

See Section 384-16(a) for lighting and appliance branch-circuit panelboards.

Exception No. 2 permits a tap from a feeder or from a transformer secondary without requiring overcurrent protection at the point where the tap conductor receives its supply, provided the tap conductor (1) is not more than 10 ft long, (2) is enclosed in a raceway, (3) does not extend beyond the switchboard, panelboard, or control devices that it supplies, and (4) has an ampacity not less than the combined computed loads supplied and not less than the ampere rating of the switchboard, panelboard, or control devices supplied, except where the tap conductor terminates in an overcurrent protective device which does not exceed the ampacity of the tap conductor.

Exception No. 3: Feeder Taps Not Over 25 Feet (7.62 m) Long. For conductors tapped to a feeder where all of the following conditions are met:

a. The length of the tap conductors does not exceed 25 feet (7.62 m).

b. The ampacity of the tap conductors is not less than ⅓ that of the feeder conductors from which they are supplied.

c. The tap conductors terminate with a single circuit breaker or a single set of fuses that will limit the load to the ampacity of the tap conductors. This single overcurrent device shall be permitted to supply any number of additional overcurrent devices on its load side.

d. The tap conductors are suitably protected from physical damage and are enclosed in a raceway.

Exception No. 3 is illustrated in Figure 240-3. A No. 3/0 THW tap conductor, protected from physical damage in a raceway and not over 25 ft long, is tapped from a 500 MCM feeder and terminates in a circuit breaker.

Note: A No. 3/0 THW conductor (200 A) is more than ⅓ the ampacity of a 500 MCM (380 A) conductor. See Table 310-16 for copper conductors.

Exception No. 4: Service Conductors. For service-entrance conductors where protected in accordance with Section 230-91.

Exception No. 5: Branch-Circuit Taps. Taps to individual outlets and circuit conductors supplying a single household electric range shall be considered as protected by the branch- circuit overcurrent devices when in accordance with the requirements of Sections 210-19, 210-20, and 210-24.

Exception No. 6: Motor Circuit Taps. For motor-branch-circuit conductors where protected in accordance with Sections 430-28 and 430-53.

Exception No. 7: Busway Taps. For busways where protected in accordance with Sections 364-10 through 364-14.

Exception No. 8: Transformer Feeder Taps with Primary Plus Secondary Not Over 25 Feet (7.62 m) Long. Where all of the following conditions are met:

a. The conductors supplying the primary of a transformer have an ampacity at least ⅓ that of the conductors or overcurrent protection from which they are tapped.

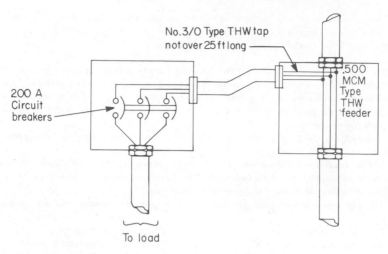

Figure 240-3. Feeder taps terminating in a single circuit breaker. See Exception No. 3.

b. The conductors supplied by the secondary of the transformer have an ampacity that, when multiplied by the ratio of the secondary-to-primary voltage, is at least ⅓ the ampacity of the conductors or overcurrent protection from which the primary conductors are tapped.

c. The total length of one primary plus one secondary conductor, excluding any portion of the primary conductor that is protected at its ampacity, is not over 25 feet (7.62 m).

d. The primary and secondary conductors are suitably protected from physical damage.

e. The secondary conductors terminate in a single circuit breaker or set of fuses which will limit the load to that allowed in Tables 310-16 through 310-19.

Exception No. 8 is illustrated in Figure 240-4.

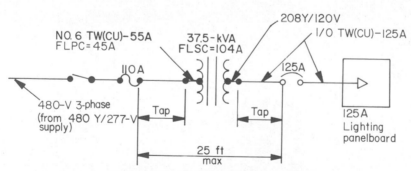

Figure 240-4. Transformer feeder taps (primary plus secondary) not over 25 ft long, as per Section 240-21, Exception No. 8. Also applies to overcurrent protection requirements of Sections 384-16(a) and 450-3(b).

Exception No. 9: Conductors from generator terminals to the first overcurrent device as covered in Section 445-5.

Exception Nos. 9 and 10 first appeared in the 1981 *NEC*. Exception No. 9 provides tap distances for generators as other Exceptions have provided tap requirements for transformers, motor circuits, etc.

Exception No. 10: Feeder Taps Over 25 Feet (7.62 m) Long. In high bay manufacturing buildings [over 35 feet (10.67 m) high at walls], where conditions of maintenance and supervision assure that only qualified persons will service the systems, conductors tapped to a feeder shall be permitted to be not over 25 feet (7.62 m) long horizontally and not over 100 feet (30.5 m) total length where all of the following conditions are met.

a. The ampacity of the tap conductors is not less than ⅓ that of the overcurrent device from which they are supplied.

b. The tap conductors terminate with a single circuit breaker or a single set of fuses that will limit the load to the ampacity of the tap conductors. This single overcurrent device shall be permitted to supply any number of additional overcurrent devices on its load side.

c. The tap conductors are suitably protected from physical damage and are installed in raceways.

d. The tap conductors are continuous from end-to-end and contain no splices.

e. The tap conductors shall be No. 6 AWG copper or No. 4 AWG aluminum or larger.

f. The tap conductors shall not penetrate walls, floors, or ceilings.

See Figure 240-5

240-22. Grounded Conductors.   No overcurrent device shall be connected in series with any conductor that is intentionally grounded.

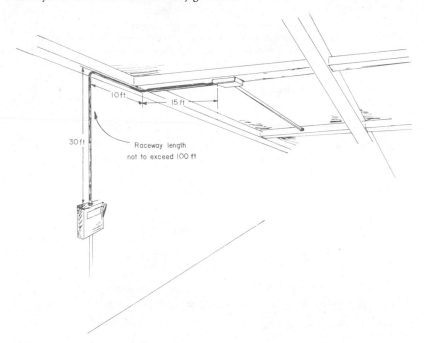

10 ft

15 ft

30 ft

Raceway length
not to exceed 100 ft

Figure 240-5. Section 240-21, Exception No. 9 permits a tap rule of 100 ft for manufacturing buildings with walls over 35 ft high, where conditions of maintenance and supervision ensure that only qualified persons will service these systems.

Exception No. 1: Where the overcurrent device opens all conductors of the circuit, including the grounded conductor, and is so designed that no pole can operate independently.

Exception No. 2: Where required by Sections 430-36 and 430-37 for motor running (overload) protection.

240-23. Change in Size of Grounded Conductor. Where a change occurs in the size of the ungrounded conductor, a similar change may be made in the size of the grounded conductor.

This section acknowledges that the size of a grounded conductor may be increased or reduced to correspond to a change made in the size of an ungrounded conductor, where all are of the same circuit.

240-24. Location in or on Premises.

(a) Readily Accessible. Overcurrent devices shall be readily accessible.

Exception No. 1: For services.

This Section is intended to correlate with Section 230-91, i.e., the service overcurrent device shall be an integral part of the service disconnecting means or shall be located immediately adjacent thereto.
Section 230-91 no longer provides that service overcurrent devices be permitted to be located at the outer end of the entrance.

Exception No. 2: For busways as provided in Section 364-12.

Exception No. 3: For supplementary overcurrent protection as described in Section 240-10.

(b) Occupant to Have Ready Access. Each occupant shall have ready access to all overcurrent devices protecting the conductors supplying his occupancy.

Exception: In a multiple-occupancy building where electric service and electrical maintenance are provided by the building management and where these are under continuous building management supervision, the service overcurrent devices and feeder overcurrent devices supplying more than one occupancy shall be permitted to be accessible to authorized management personnel only.

(c) Not Exposed to Physical Damage. Overcurrent devices shall be located where they will not be exposed to physical damage.

(d) Not in Vicinity of Easily Ignitible Material. Overcurrent devices shall not be located in the vicinity of easily ignitible material such as in clothes closets.

The 1981 *NEC* includes the words "such as in clothes closets"; however, overcurrent devices that are an integral part of a listed distribution panelboard are permitted just inside a closet entry in mobile homes as provided in Section 550-4(a).

C. Enclosures

240-30. General. Overcurrent devices shall be enclosed in cabinets or cutout boxes.

Exception No. 1: Where a part of an assembly that provides equivalent protection.

Exception No. 2: Where mounted on open-type switchboards, panelboards, or control boards that are in rooms or enclosures free from dampness and easily ignitible material and accessible only to qualified personnel.

Exception No. 3: The operating handle of a circuit breaker shall be permitted to be accessible without opening a door or cover.

Properly selected overcurrent protective devices are designed to open a circuit before an overcurrent condition can seriously damage conductor insulation, and requirements that overcurrent devices be enclosed in cabinets or cutout boxes are to ensure that electrical disturbances in the vicinity will be kept to a minimum.

Overcurrent devices mounted on open-type switchboards, panelboards, or controlboards and having exposed live parts are to be located where accessible only to qualified persons.

240-32. Damp or Wet Locations.   Enclosures for overcurrent devices in damp or wet locations shall be identified for use in such locations and shall be mounted so there is at least ¼-inch (6.35-mm) air space between the enclosure and the wall or other supporting surface.

240-33. Vertical Position.   Enclosures for overcurrent devices shall be mounted in a vertical position unless in individual instances this is shown to be impracticable.

This section indicates that a wall-mounted, vertical position is desirable to achieve easier access, natural hand-operation, normal swing or closing of doors or covers, and legibility of manufacturer's markings.

D. Disconnecting and Guarding

240-40. Disconnecting Means for Fuses and Thermal Cutouts.   Disconnecting means shall be provided on the supply side of all fuses or thermal cutouts in circuits of over 150 volts to ground and cartridge fuses in circuits of any voltage, where accessible to other than qualified persons, so that each individual circuit containing fuses or thermal cutouts can be independently disconnected from the source of electric energy.

Exception No. 1: A device provided for current limiting on the supply side of the service disconnecting means as permitted by Section 230-82.

Exception No. 2: A single disconnecting means shall be permitted on the supply side of more than one set of fuses as provided by Section 430-112 for group operation of motors and in Section 424-22 for fixed electric space heating equipment.

Plug fuses are classified at not more than 125 V and 0 to 30 A (Section 240-53).

Cartridge fuses are classified as types not more than 250-V, not more than 300-V, and not more than 600-V, and from 0 to 6,000 A (Section 240-61). A disconnecting means must be provided whenever cartridge fuses are accessible to other than qualified persons.

Note: Cartridge fuseholders have live parts openly exposed to personnel during replacement of fuses.

240-41. Arcing or Suddenly Moving Parts.   Arcing or suddenly moving parts shall comply with (a) and (b) below.

(a) Location.   Fuses and circuit breakers shall be so located or shielded that persons will not be burned or otherwise injured by their operation.

(b) Suddenly Moving Parts.   Handles or levers of circuit breakers, and similar parts which may move suddenly in such a way that persons in the vicinity are likely to be injured by being struck by them, shall be guarded or isolated.

Arcing or suddenly moving parts are usually associated with switchboards or controlboards which may be of the open-type and which should be under competent supervision and accessible only to qualified persons. Fuses or circuit breakers are to be so located or shielded that under an abnormal condition the subsequent arc across the opened device will not injure persons in the vicinity.

Guardrails may be provided in the vicinity of disconnecting means. Modern switchboards, etc., are equipped with removable handles but these sudden-moving handles may be capable of causing injury.

See Article 100 for definition of "Guarded." See also Section 110-17.

E. Plug Fuses, Fuseholders, and Adapters

240-50. General.

(a) **Maximum Voltage.**   Plug fuses and fuseholders shall not be used in circuits exceeding 125 volts between conductors.

Exception: In circuits supplied by a system having a grounded neutral and having no conductor at over 150 volts to ground.

(b) **Marking.**   Each fuse, fuseholder, and adapter shall be marked with its ampere rating.

(c) **Hexagonal Configuration.**   Plug fuses of 15-ampere and lower rating shall be identified by a hexagonal configuration of the window, cap, or other prominent part to distinguish them from fuses of higher ampere ratings.

(d) **No Live Parts.**   Plug fuses, fuseholders, and adapters shall have no exposed live parts after fuses or fuses and adapters have been installed.

(e) **Screw Shell.**   The screw shell of a plug-type fuseholder shall be connected to the load side of the circuit.

240-51. Edison-Base Fuses.

(a) **Classification.**   Plug fuses of the Edison-base type shall be classified at not over 125 volts and 0 to 30 amperes.

(b) **Replacement Only.**   Plug fuses of the Edison-base type shall be used only for replacements in existing installations where there is no evidence of overfusing or tampering.

240-52. Edison-Base Fuseholders.   Fuseholders of the Edison-base type shall be installed only where they are made to accept Type S fuses by the use of adapters.

240-53. Type S Fuses.   Type S fuses shall be of the plug type and shall comply with (a) and (b) below.

(a) **Classification.**   S fuses shall be classified at not over 125 volts and 0 to 15 amperes, 16 to 20 amperes, and 21 to 30 amperes.

(b) **Noninterchangeable.**   Type S fuses of an ampere classification as specified in (a) above shall not be interchangeable with a lower ampere classification. They shall be so designed that they cannot be used in any fuseholder other than a Type S fuseholder or a fuseholder with a Type S adapter inserted.

240-54. Type S Fuses, Adapters, and Fuseholders.

(a) **To Fit Edison-Base Fuseholders.**   Type S adapters shall fit Edison-base fuseholders.

(b) To Fit Type S Fuses Only.   Type S fuseholders and adapters shall be so designed that either the fuseholder itself or the fuseholder with a Type S adapter inserted cannot be used for any fuse other than a Type S fuse.

(c) Nonremovable.   Type S adapters shall be so designed that once inserted in a fuseholder, they cannot be removed.

(d) Nontamperable.   Type S fuses, fuseholders, and adapters shall be so designed that tampering or shunting (bridging) would be difficult.

(e) Interchangeability.   Dimensions of Type S fuses, fuseholders, and adapters shall be standardized to permit interchangeability regardless of the manufacturer.

F. Cartridge Fuses and Fuseholders

240-60. General.

(a) Maximum Voltage — 300-Volt Type.   Cartridge fuses and fuseholders of the 300-volt type shall not be used in circuits of over 300 volts between conductors.

Exception: In circuits supplied by a system having a grounded neutral and having no conductor at over 300 volts to ground.

(b) Noninterchangeable — 0-6000 Ampere Cartridge Fuseholders.   Fuseholders shall be so designed that it will be difficult to put a fuse of any given class into a fuseholder that is designed for a current lower, or voltage higher, than that of the class to which it belongs. Fuseholders for current-limiting fuses shall not permit insertion of fuses that are not current limiting.

(c) Marking.   Fuses shall be plainly marked, either by printing on the fuse barrel or by a label attached to the barrel, showing the following: (1) ampere rating; (2) voltage rating; (3) interrupting rating where other than 10,000 amperes; (4) "current limiting" where applicable; (5) the name or trademark of the manufacturer.

Exception: Interrupting rating marking shall not be required on fuses used for supplementary protection.

240-61. Classification.   Cartridge fuses and fuseholders shall be classified as follows:

Not Over 250 Volts	Not Over 300 Volts	Not Over 600 Volts
0- 30	0- 30	0- 30
31- 60	31- 60	31- 60
61- 100	61- 100	61- 100
101- 200	101- 200	101- 200
201- 400	201- 400	201- 400
401- 600	401- 600	401- 600
601- 800	601- 800	601- 800
801-1200	801-1200	801-1200
1201-1600	1201-1600	1201-1600
1601-2000	1601-2000	1601-2000
2001-2500	2001-2500	2001-2500
2501-3000	2501-3000	2501-3000
3001-4000	3001-4000	3001-4000
4001-5000	4001-5000	4001-5000
5001-6000	5001-6000	5001-6000

Fuses rated 600 volts, nominal, or less, shall be permitted to be used for voltages at or below their voltage ratings.

See Section 710-21(b)(3) for application of high-voltage fuses.

Exception No. 1: Fuses and fuseholders larger than 6000 amperes shall be permitted.

Exception No. 2: Fuses and fuseholders of other voltages not over 600 volts, nominal, shall be permitted.

G. Circuit Breakers

240-80. Method of Operation.   Circuit breakers shall be trip free and capable of being closed and opened by manual operation. Their normal method of operation by other than manual means such as electrical or pneumatic shall be permitted if means for manual operation is also provided.

240-81. Indicating.   Circuit breakers shall clearly indicate whether they are in the open "off" or closed "on" position.

Where circuit breaker handles on switchboards are operated vertically rather than rotationally or horizontally, the up position of the handle shall be the "on" position.

240-82. Nontamperable.   A circuit breaker shall be of such design that any alteration of its trip point (calibration) or the time required for its operation will require dismantling of the device or breaking of a seal for other than intended adjustments.

240-83. Marking.

(a) Durable and Visible.   Circuit breakers shall be marked with their rating in a manner that will be durable and visible after installation. Such marking shall be required to be visible after removal of a trim or cover.

(b) Location.   Circuit breakers rated at 100 amperes or less and 600 volts or less shall have the ampere rating molded, stamped, etched, or similarly marked into their handles or escutcheon areas.

(c) Interrupting Rating.   Every circuit breaker having an interrupting rating other than 5000 amperes shall have its interrupting rating shown on the circuit breaker.

Exception: Interrupting rating marking shall not be required on circuit breakers used for supplementary protection.

(d) Circuit Breakers Used as Switches.   Where used as switches in 120-volt, fluorescent lighting circuits, circuit breakers shall be approved for such switching duty and shall be marked "SWD."

The marking of cartridge fuses, as per Section 240-60(c), with regard to interrupting capacity (IC) requires that the rating for other than 10,000 A be plainly marked on the fuse barrel. Class H type cartridge fuses have a rating (IC) of 10,000 A, and this rating need not be marked on the fuse. However, Class G, J, K, L, R, and T cartridge fuses have over 10,000 A (IC) rating and must be marked.

The marking of circuit breakers, as shown in Section 240-83(c), with regard to interrupting capacity (IC) requires that the rating for other than 5,000 A be indicated on the circuit breaker.

Fuses or circuit breakers used for supplementary protection of fluorescent fixtures, semiconductor rectifiers, motor-operated appliances, etc., need not be marked for IC.

Switching duty circuit breakers (SWD) are required where the breakers are used as switches for 120-V fluorescent lighting. Switching duty circuit breakers generally have heavier-duty contacts such as those used on 277-V circuit breakers.

H. Overcurrent Protection Over 600 Volts, Nominal

240-100. Feeders.   Feeders shall have a short-circuit protective device in each ungrounded conductor or comply with Section 230-208(d)(2) or (d)(3). The protective device(s) shall be capable of detecting and interrupting all values of current which can occur at their location in excess of their trip setting or melting point. In no case shall the fuse rating in continuous amperes exceed three times, or the long-time trip element setting of a breaker six times, the ampacity of the conductor.

The operating time of the protective device, the available short-circuit current, and the conductor used will need to be coordinated to prevent damaging or dangerous temperatures in conductors or conductor insulation under short-circuit conditions.

240-101. Branch Circuits.   Branch circuits shall have a short-circuit protective device in each ungrounded conductor or comply with Section 230-208(d)(2) or (d)(3). The protective device(s) shall be capable of detecting and interrupting all values of current which can occur at their location in excess of their trip setting or melting point.

ARTICLE 250—GROUNDING

Contents

A. General

250-1. Scope.   This article covers general requirements for grounding and bonding of electrical installations, and specific requirements in (a) through (f) below.

The term "identified" no longer is applicable to terminals and conductors intended to be recognized as grounded.

The 1981 *NEC*, Article 100-Definitions, recognizes the term "identified" as a substitute for the phrase "approved for the purpose" with no change in concept. The phrase "approved for the purpose" has been deleted throughout the 1981 *NEC*.

(a) Systems, circuits, and equipment required, permitted, or not permitted to be grounded.

(b) Circuit conductor to be grounded on grounded systems.

(c) Location of grounding connections.

(d) Types and sizes of grounding and bonding conductors and electrodes.

(e) Methods of grounding and bonding.

(f) Conditions under which guards, isolation, or insulation may be substituted for grounding.

Systems and circuit conductors are grounded to limit voltages due to lightning, line surges, or unintentional contact with higher voltage lines, and to stabilize the voltage to ground during normal operation. Systems and circuit conductors are solidly grounded to facilitate overcurrent device operation in case of ground faults.

Conductive materials enclosing electrical conductors or equipment, or forming part of such equipment, are grounded to limit the voltage to ground on these materials and to facilitate overcurrent device operation in case of ground faults. See Section 110-10.

250-2. Application of Other Articles.   In other articles applying to particular cases of installation of conductors and equipment, there are requirements that are in addition to those of this article or are modifications of them:

	Article	Section
Appliances		422-16
Branch Circuits		210-5
		210-6
		210-7
Cablebus		365-9
Circuits and Equipment Operating at Less Than 50 Volts	720	
Class 1, Class 2, and Class 3 Circuits		725-20
		725-42
Communications Circuits	800	
Community Antenna Television and Radio Distribution Systems		820-7
		820-22
		820-23
Conductors	310	
Conductors (Grounded)	200	
Cranes and Hoists	610	
Data Processing Systems		645-4
Electrically Driven or Controlled Irrigation Machines		675-8
		675-9
		675-10
		675-11
Electrical Floor Assemblies		366-14
Electric Signs and Outline Lighting	600	
Electrolytic Cells	668	
Elevators, Dumbwaiters, Escalators, and Moving Walks	620	
Fire Protective Signaling Systems		760-6
Fixed Electric Heating Equipment for Pipelines and Vessels		427-21
		427-29
		427-48
Fixed Electric Space Heating Equipment		424-14
Fixed Outdoor Electric De-icing and Snow-Melting Equipment		426-27
Fixtures and Lighting Equipment		410-17
		410-18
		410-19
		410-21
Flexible Cords		400-22
		400-23
Generators		445-8
Grounding-Type Receptacles (Outlets)		210-7
Hazardous (Classified) Locations	500-517	
Health Care Facilities	517	
Induction and Dielectric Heating Equipment	665	
Lighting Fixtures, Lampholders, Lamp Receptacles, and Rosettes	410	
Marinas and Boatyards		555-7
Metalworking Machine Tools	670	
Mobile Homes and Mobile Home Parks	550	
Motion Picture and Television Studios and Similar Locations		530-20
		530-66

B. Circuit and System Grounding

250-3. Direct-Current Systems.

(a) **Two-Wire Direct Current Systems.** Two-wire dc systems supplying premises wiring shall be grounded.

Exception No. 1: A system equipped with a ground detector and supplying only industrial equipment in limited areas.

Exception No. 2: A system operating at 50 volts or less between conductors.

Exception No. 3: A system operating at over 300 volts between conductors.

Exception No. 4: A rectifier-derived dc system supplied from an ac system complying with Section 250-5.

Exception No. 5: DC fire protective signaling circuits having a maximum current of 0.030 amperes as specified in Article 760, Part C.

(b) **Three-Wire Direct-Current Systems.** The neutral conductor of all 3-wire dc systems supplying premises wiring shall be grounded.

250-5. Alternating-Current Circuits and Systems to Be Grounded. AC circuits and systems shall be grounded as provided for in (a), (b), (c), or (d) below. Other circuits and systems shall be permitted to be grounded.

(a) **Alternating-Current Circuits of Less than 50 Volts.** AC circuits of less than 50 volts shall be grounded under any of the following conditions:

(1) Where supplied by transformers if the transformer supply system exceeds 150 volts to ground.

(2) Where supplied by transformers if the transformer supply system is ungrounded.

(3) Where installed as overhead conductors outside of buildings.

(b) Alternating-Current Systems of 50 Volts to 1000 Volts.   AC systems of 50 volts to 1000 volts supplying premises wiring and premises wiring systems shall be grounded under any of the following conditions:

(1) Where the system can be so grounded that the maximum voltage to ground on the ungrounded conductors does not exceed 150 volts.

(2) Where the system is nominally rated 480Y/277-volt, 3-phase, 4-wire in which the neutral is used as a circuit conductor.

(3) Where the system is nominally rated 240/120-volt, 3-phase, 4-wire in which the midpoint of one phase is used as a circuit conductor.

(4) Where a service conductor is uninsulated in accordance with Section 230-4.

Exception No. 1: Electric systems used exclusively to supply industrial electric furnaces for melting, refining, tempering, and the like.

Exception No. 2: Separately derived systems used exclusively for rectifiers supplying only adjustable speed industrial drives.

Exception No. 3: Separately derived systems supplied by transformers that have a primary voltage rating less than 1000 volts provided that all of the following conditions are met:
a. The system is used exclusively for control circuits.
b. The conditions of maintenance and supervision assure that only qualified persons will service the installation.
c. Continuity of control power is required.
d. Ground detectors are installed on the control system.

Exception No. 4: Isolated systems as permitted in Article 517.

The proper use of suitable ground detectors on ungrounded systems can provide additional protection.

(c) Alternating-Current Systems of 1 kV and Over.   AC systems of 1 kV and over supplying mobile or portable equipment shall be grounded as specified in Section 250-154. Where supplying other than portable equipment, such systems shall be permitted to be grounded. Where such systems are grounded, they shall comply with the applicable provisions of this article.

(d) Separately Derived Systems.   A premises wiring system whose power is derived from generator, transformer, or converter windings and has no direct electrical connection, including a solidly connected grounded circuit conductor, to supply conductors originating in another system, if required to be grounded as in (a) or (b) above, shall be grounded as specified in Section 250-26.

Figures 250-1(A) and (B) depict a 480/277 V wye electrical service supplying a building with a feeder to a dry-type transformer that transforms the 480/277 V system to a 208/120 V wye system. The 208/120 V system is fed through a transfer switch that is connected to a generator intended to provide power for emergency or standby systems.

Figure 250-1(A) does not have the neutral conductor connected to the 3-pole transfer switch; thus there is a direct electrical connection of the grounded circuit conductor (neutral) to the generator. Therefore, the system supplied by the generator is not a separately derived system, and there are no requirements for grounding the neutral at the generator. Under these conditions it would be necessary to carry an equipment grounding conductor from the dry-type transformer to the 3-pole transfer switch and from there to the generator.

Figure 250-1(B) has a neutral conductor connected to a 4-pole transfer switch and, consequently, the generator system does not have a direct electrical connection of the grounded circuit conductor (neutral). Therefore, the generator is a separately derived system and is grounded in accordance with Section 250-26 for separately derived systems.

Note that each of the dry-type transformers in Figures 250-1(A) and (B) qualifies as a separately derived system since they have no direct electrical connections, including the solidly connected grounded circuit conductor (neutral) to the supply conductors originating from the service disconnect.

Section 250-26 requires a bonding jumper connected from the generator frame to the grounded circuit conductor (neutral). The grounding electrode conductor from the generator is to be connected to a grounding electrode as near to the generator as is practical. The preferred grounding electrode is the nearest effectively grounded structural metal member; in descending order of preference, the next choice is the nearest available effectively grounded metal water pipe or other electrodes specified in Sections 250-81 and 250-83 that can be used where an effectively grounded structural metal member or a grounded metal water pipe is not available.

250-6. Portable and Vehicle-Mounted Generators.

(a) **Portable Generators.**   Under the following conditions the frame of a portable generator shall not be required to be grounded and shall be permitted to serve as the grounding electrode for a system supplied by the generator:

(1) The generator supplies only equipment mounted on the generator and/or cord- and plug-connected equipment through receptacles mounted on the generator, and

(2) The noncurrent-carrying metal parts of equipment and the equipment grounding conductor terminals of the receptacles are bonded to the generator frame.

(b) **Vehicle-Mounted Generators.**   Under the following conditions the frame of a vehicle shall be permitted to serve as the grounding electrode for a system supplied by a generator located on the vehicle:

(1) The frame of the generator is bonded to the vehicle frame, and

(2) The generator supplies only equipment located on the vehicle and/or cord- and plug-connected equipment through receptacles mounted on the vehicle or on the generator, and

(3) The noncurrent-carrying metal parts of equipment and the equipment grounding conductor terminals of the receptacles are bonded to the generator frame, and

(4) The system complies with all other provisions of this article.

(c) **Neutral Conductor Bonding.**   A neutral conductor shall be bonded to the generator frame when the generator is a component of a separately derived system. The bonding of any conductor other than a neutral within the generator to its frame shall not be required.

For grounding of portable generators supplying fixed wiring systems, see Section 250-5(d).

250-7. Circuits Not to Be Grounded.   The following circuits shall not be grounded:

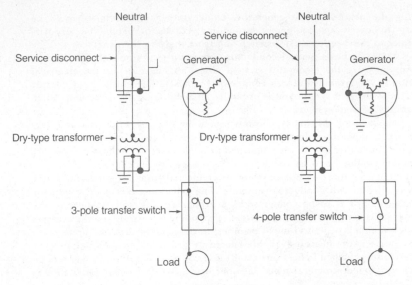

Generator *not* a separately derived system   Generator a separately derived system

A   B

Figure 250-1. Installation A (left) has a direct electrical connection of the grounded circuit conductor (neutral) to the generator; therefore, the generator is not a separately derived system and there are no requirements for grounding the neutral. Installation B (right) does not have a direct electrical connection of the grounded circuit conductor (neutral); therefore, the generator is a separately derived system and is grounded in accordance with Section 250-26.

(a) Cranes.   Circuits for electric cranes operating over combustible fibers in Class III locations, as provided in Section 503-13.

(b) Health Care Facilities.   Circuits as provided in Article 517.

C. Location of System Grounding Connections

250-21. Objectionable Current over Grounding Conductors.

(a) Arrangement to Prevent Objectionable Current.   The grounding of electric systems, circuit conductors, surge arresters, and conductive noncurrent-carrying materials and equipment shall be installed and arranged in a manner that will prevent an objectionable flow of current over the grounding conductors or grounding paths.

(b) Alterations to Stop Objectionable Current.   If the use of multiple grounding connections results in an objectionable flow of current, one or more of the following alterations shall be made:

(1) Discontinue one or more such grounding connections.

(2) Change the locations of the grounding connections.

(3) Interrupt the continuity of the conductor or conductive path interconnecting the grounding connections.

(4) Take other suitable remedial action satisfactory to the authority having jurisdiction.

(c) Temporary Currents Not Classified as Objectionable Currents.   Temporary currents resulting from accidental conditions, such as ground-fault currents, that occur only while the grounding conductors are performing their intended protective functions shall not be classified as objectionable current for the purposes specified in (a) and (b) above.

250-22. Point of Connection for Direct-Current Systems.   DC systems to be grounded shall have the grounding connection made at one or more supply stations. A grounding connection shall not be made at individual services nor at any point on premises wiring.

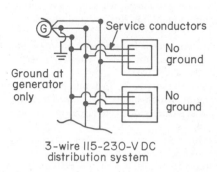

3-wire 115-230-V DC distribution system

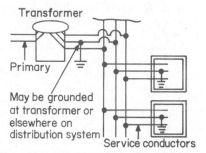

3-wire 115-230-V AC single-phase secondary distribution system

Figure 250-2. The neutral is shown grounded at the generator site in this 3-wire dc distribution system. Grounding of a 2-wire dc system would be accomplished in the same manner.

Figure 250-3. On a 2-wire or 3-wire single-phase ac secondary distribution system, grounding connections are made on the secondary side of the transformer and on the supply side of the service disconnecting means.

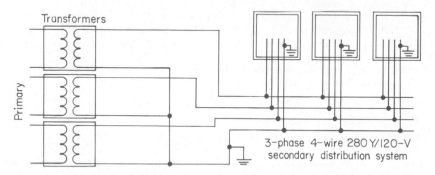

3-phase 4-wire 280 Y/120-V secondary distribution system

Figure 250-4. The neutral is grounded at each service and on the secondary side of the transformer on a 4-wire, 3 phase, 208 Y/120-V secondary distribution system. When 3-wire, 3-phase service equipment is installed for power purposes on such an ac system, the grounded (neutral) conductor must run to the service equipment. See Section 250-23(b).

250-23. Grounding Service-Supplied Alternating-Current Systems.

(a) System Grounding Connections.   A premises wiring system that is supplied by an ac service and is required to be grounded by Section 250-5 shall have at each service a grounding electrode conductor connected to a grounding electrode which complies with Part H of Article

250. The grounding electrode conductor shall be connected to the grounded service conductor at any accessible point from the load end of the service drop or service lateral to and including the terminal or bus to which the grounded service conductor is connected at the service disconnecting means. Where the transformer supplying the service is located outside the building, at least one additional grounding connection shall be made from the grounded service conductor to a grounding electrode, either at the transformer or elsewhere outside the building. A grounding connection shall not be made to any grounded circuit conductor on the load side of the service disconnecting means.

The power for ac premises wiring systems is either separately derived in accordance with Section 250-5(d), or is supplied by the service (see definition of "Service" in Article 100). Section 250-26 covers grounding for separately derived ac systems. Section 250-23(a) covers system grounding for service-supplied ac systems.

This section covers a premises wiring system that is supplied by an ac service and the system is required to be grounded by Section 250-5. This statement is similar to the leading statement in Section 250-26.

Such a system is required to have at each service a grounding electrode conductor connected to a grounding electrode which meets the requirements in Part H. Note the grounding electrode for a separately derived system is specified in Section 250-26(c).

The grounding electrode conductor connection to the grounded conductor is accurately specified. First, the connection should be made to the grounded service conductor. Second, the text more accurately describes where the connection is permitted to be made to the grounded service conductor.

Where the transformer supplying the service is located outside the building, the additional grounding connection to the grounded service conductor should be made outside the building. It is unnecessary to specify that the connection is to be made on the secondary side of the transformer because by definition a grounded service conductor extends "from the street main or from transformers to the service equipment of the premises supplied."

A grounding connection shall not be made to any grounded circuit conductor on the load side of the service disconnecting means.

See definition of Service Drop and Service Lateral; also Section 230-21.

Exception No. 1: A grounding electrode conductor shall be connected to the grounded conductor of a separately derived system in accordance with the provisions of Section 250-26(b).

Where a separately derived system is required to be grounded, a grounding electrode conductor is required to be connected to the grounded conductor of the derived system as specified in Section 250-26(b).

Exception No. 2: A grounding conductor connection shall be made at each separate building where required by Section 250-24.

Exception No. 3: For ranges, counter-mounted cooking units, wall-mounted ovens, clothes dryers, and meter enclosures as permitted by Section 250-61.

Exception No. 4: For services that are dual fed (double ended) in a common enclosure or grouped together in separate enclosures and employing a secondary tie, a single grounding electrode connection to the tie point of the grounded circuit conductors from each power source shall be permitted.

Exception No. 5: Where the main bonding jumper specified in Sections 250-53(b) and 250-79 is a wire or busbar, and is installed from the neutral bar or bus to the equipment grounding terminal bar or bus in the service equipment, the grounding electrode conductor shall be permitted to be connected to the equipment grounding terminal bar or bus to which the main bonding jumper is connected.

Where a ground-return type sensor is used for ground-fault protection equipment, the sensor must be installed on the main bonding jumper and the grounding electrode conductor must be connected to the equipment grounding bus or terminal bar in order for ground-fault current to be accurately sensed. Where the service equipment is power switchgear, it is often more practical to connect the grounding electrode conductor to the ground bus in the switchgear.

(b) Grounded Conductor Brought to Service Equipment.   Where an ac system operating at less than 1000 volts is grounded at any point, the grounded conductor shall be run to each service. This conductor shall be routed with the phase conductors and shall not be smaller than the required grounding electrode conductor specified in Table 250-94 and, in addition, for service phase conductors larger than 1100 MCM copper or 1750 MCM aluminum, the grounded conductor shall not be smaller than 12½ percent of the area of the largest phase conductor.

Exception: The grounded conductor shall not be required to be larger than the largest ungrounded service conductor.

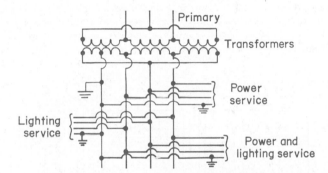

Figure 250-5. On a 4-wire, 3-phase, 230-V delta secondary system, a mid-phase tap is made at one transformer to provide a neutral for a 3-wire, 115/230-V system for lighting and 115-V receptacles. This neutral is grounded at the transformer and at each individual service. This neutral is also to be run to service equipment supplied from the above-mentioned secondary system, even though installed for 3-wire, 3-phase power purposes. Also, on a 3-wire, 3-phase, 220-V distribution system without a neutral, but with one phase conductor grounded, it is required to ground that phase conductor at each individual service.

250-24. Two or More Buildings Supplied from Single Service Equipment.

(a) Grounded Systems.   Where two or more buildings are supplied by a grounded system from a single service equipment, each building shall have a grounding electrode connected to the ac system grounded circuit conductor on the supply side of the building disconnecting means.

The following is a Formal Interpretation of Sections 250-23 and 250-24 of the 1978 edition of the *National Electrical Code.*
Statement: A building is supplied by an ac grounded system operating at less than 1,000 volts. It is intended to install electrical conductors within a grounded rigid metal conduit system from overcurrent protection located on the load side of the service-entrance equipment of this building and run to a second building, not

containing livestock, on the same property and under the same management to supply a 3-phase motor load and/or other loads not requiring a grounded conductor. The second building is provided with a means for disconnecting all ungrounded conductors in accordance with Section 230-84.

Consider Sections 230-3, 230-40, 230-41(c), 230-84, 230-90(c), 250-23, 250-24, 250-91(b)(2), and any other pertinent parts of Articles 230 or 250. Also consider definitions in Article 100.

Question No. 1: Are the conductors to the second building defined as a feeder? Answer: Yes.

Question No. 2: Under the conditions specified in the statement, is a grounded conductor required from the first building to the second building? Answer: No.

(b) Ungrounded Systems. Where two or more buildings are supplied by an ungrounded system from a single service equipment, each building shall have a grounding electrode connected to the metal enclosure of the building disconnecting means.

Exception for (a) and (b) above: A grounding electrode at a separate building shall not be required where the conditions of either a. or b. below are met:

a. Only one branch circuit is supplied and there is no equipment in the building that requires grounding.

b. No livestock is housed in the building, an equipment grounding conductor is run with the circuit conductors for grounding any noncurrent-carrying equipment, interior metal piping systems or building metal frames and the equipment grounding conductor is bonded to grounding electrodes described in Sections 250-81 and 250-83 which exist at the building.

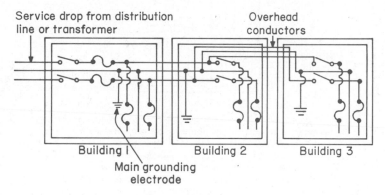

Figure 250-6. Where a single service (grounded system) supplies three buildings, each building is required to have a grounding electrode installed, unless conditions prevail as described in the Exception to Section 250-24.

250-25. Conductor to Be Grounded—Alternating-Current Systems. For ac premises wiring systems, the conductor to be grounded shall be as specified in (1) through (5) below.

(1) Single-phase, 2-wire: one conductor.

(2) Single-phase, 3-wire: the neutral conductor.

(3) Multiphase systems having one wire common to all phases: the common conductor.

(4) Multiphase systems requiring one grounded phase: one phase conductor.

(5) Multiphase systems in which one phase is used as in (2) above: the neutral conductor. Grounded conductors shall be identified by the means specified in Article 200.

250-26. Grounding Separately Derived Alternating-Current Systems. A separately derived ac system that is required to be grounded by Section 250-5 shall be grounded as specified in (a) through (d) below.

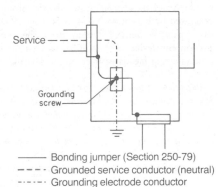

——— Bonding jumper (Section 250-79)
– – – – Grounded service conductor (neutral)
– – – – · Grounding electrode conductor

Figure 250-7. Grounding and bonding at an individual service.

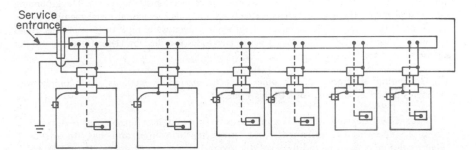

Figure 250-8. The grounding and bonding arrangement for six switches that serve as the service disconnecting means for an individual service.

(a) Bonding Jumper. A bonding jumper, sized in accordance with Section 250-79(c) for the derived phase conductors, shall be used to connect the equipment grounding conductors of the derived system to the grounded conductor. Except as permitted by Exception No. 4 of Section 250-23(a), this connection shall be made at any point on the separately derived system from the source to the first system disconnecting means or overcurrent device; or it shall be made at the source of a separately derived system which has no disconnecting means or overcurrent devices.

It is the intention to permit this connection at the transformer, etc., or at the first disconnecting means or overcurrent device where there is likely to be more standard arrangements incorporated (as in a panelboard suitable for service equipment).

Exception: The size of the bonding jumper for a system that supplies a Class 1 remote control or signaling circuit, and is derived from a transformer rated not more than 1000 volt-amperes, shall not be smaller than the derived phase conductors and shall not be smaller than No. 14 copper or No. 12 aluminum.

Section 250-79(c) requires the bonding jumper to be not smaller than the sizes given in Table 250-94, i.e., not smaller than No. 8 AWG. This Exception permits a bonding jumper for a Class 1 remote control or signaling circuit to be not smaller than No. 14 AWG.

(b) Grounding Electrode Conductor.   A grounding electrode conductor, sized in accordance with Section 250-94 for the derived phase conductors, shall be used to connect the grounded conductor of the derived system to the grounding electrode as specified in (c) below. Except as permitted by Exception No. 4 of Section 250-23(a), this connection shall be made at any point on the separately derived system from the source to the first system disconnecting means or overcurrent device; or it shall be made at the source of a separately derived system which has no disconnecting means or overcurrent devices.

Exception: A grounding electrode conductor shall not be required for a system that supplies a Class 1 remote control or signaling circuit, and is derived from a transformer rated not more than 1000 volt amperes, provided the system grounded conductor is bonded to the transformer frame or enclosure by a jumper sized in accordance with the Exception for (a), above, and the transformer frame or enclosure is grounded by one of the means specified in Section 250-57.

See comments following Section 250-26(a), Exception.

(c) Grounding Electrode.   The grounding electrode shall be as near as practicable to and preferably in the same area as the grounding conductor connection to the system. The grounding electrode shall be: (1) the nearest available effectively grounded structural metal member of the structure; or (2) the nearest available effectively grounded metal water pipe; or (3) other electrodes as specified in Sections 250-81 and 250-83 where electrodes specified by (1) or (2) above are not available.

(d) Grounding Methods.   In all other respects, grounding methods shall comply with requirements prescribed in other parts of this Code.

A separately derived system is a premises wiring system where power is derived from a generator, a transformer, or converter windings and has no direct electrical connection, including a solidly grounded circuit conductor (neutral), to supply conductors originating in another system. See comments following Section 250-5(d).

The requirements of Section 250-26 are most commonly applied to 480/277 V transformers which are used to transform a 480 V supply to a 208/120 V wye system to supply lighting and appliance loads.

These requirements provide for a low impedance path to ground so that line-to-ground faults from ungrounded conductors will create sufficient current to operate the overcurrent devices. These requirements also apply to generators or systems derived from converter windings, but do not have the same wide use as dry-type transformers.

Figure 250-9 shows a typical diagram of a dry-type transformer supplied from a 480-V, 3-phase feeder to derive a 208/120 V wye secondary. As indicated in Section 250-26(a), the bonding jumper connection sized according to Section 250-79(c) is to be made at the source of the separately derived system or the first system disconnecting means or overcurrent device and, as illustrated, would be the transformer enclosure. With the grounding electrode conductor, the bonding jumper, and the bonding of the grounded circuit conductor (neutral) connected at the transformer enclosure, line-to-ground fault currents are permitted to return to the supply source rather than going through the earth. In this way, a path of low impedance is provided which facilitates the operation of fuses and circuit breakers in accordance with Section 250-51(c).

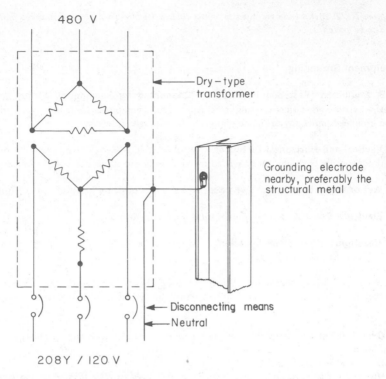

Figure 250-9. A grounding arrangement for a separately derived system. The bonding jumper connection is permitted at the transformer, as illustrated, or at the first system disconnecting means.

The grounding electrode conductor from the secondary grounded circuit conductor is sized according to Section 250-94.

D. Enclosure Grounding

250-32. Service Raceways and Enclosures. Metal enclosures for service conductors and equipment shall be grounded.

250-33. Other Conductor Enclosures. Metal enclosures for other than service conductors shall be grounded.

This section requires bonding, grounding, and electrical continuity of metal raceways and thus requires connectors, couplings, or other fittings that provide bonding and grounding continuity between the fitting and the raceway metal (such as would be required for liquidtight flexible metal conduit). Metal enclosures are required to be grounded, so that any fault between a live conductor and the metal enclosure would not allow the enclosure to become energized and remain so and thus present a shock hazard to persons.

Exception No. 1: Metal enclosures for conductors added to existing installations of open wire, knob-and-tube wiring, and nonmetallic-sheathed cable, if in runs of less than 25 feet (7.62 m), if free from probable contact with ground, grounded metal, metal lath, or other conductive material, and if guarded against contact by persons shall not be required to be grounded.

Exception No. 2: Metal enclosures used to protect cable assemblies from physical damage shall not be required to be grounded.

E. Equipment Grounding

250-42. Equipment Fastened in Place or Connected by Permanent Wiring Methods (Fixed).   Exposed noncurrent-carrying metal parts of fixed equipment likely to become energized shall be grounded under any of the conditions in (a) through (f) below.

(a) Vertical and Horizontal Distances.   Where within 8 feet (2.44 m) vertically or 5 feet (1.52 m) horizontally of ground or grounded metal objects and subject to contact by persons.

(b) Wet or Damp Locations.   Where located in a wet or damp location and not isolated.

(c) Electrical Contact.   Where in electrical contact with metal.

(d) Hazardous (Classified) Locations.   Where in a hazardous (classified) location as covered by Articles 500 through 517.

(e) Metallic Wiring Methods.   Where supplied by a metal-clad, metal-sheathed, or metal-raceway wiring method, except as permitted by Section 250-33 for short sections of raceway.

(f) Over 150 Volts to Ground.   Where equipment operates with any terminal at over 150 volts to ground.

Exception No. 1: Enclosures for switches or circuit breakers used for other than service equipment and accessible to qualified persons only.

Exception No. 2: Metal frames of electrically heated appliances, exempted by special permission, in which case the frames shall be permanently and effectively insulated from ground.

Exception No. 3: Distribution apparatus, such as transformer and capacitor cases, mounted on wooden poles, at a height exceeding 8 feet (2.44 m) above ground or grade level.

250-43. Fastened in Place or Connected by Permanent Wiring Methods (Fixed)— Specific.   Exposed, noncurrent-carrying metal parts of the kinds of equipment described in (a) through (j) below, regardless of voltage, shall be grounded.

(a) Switchboard Frames and Structures.   Switchboard frames and structures supporting switching equipment.

Exception: Frames of dc, single-polarity switchboards where effectively insulated.

(b) Organs.   Generator and motor frames in an electrically operated organ.

Exception: Where the generator is effectively insulated from ground and from the motor driving it.

(c) Motor Frames.   Motor frames, as provided by Section 430-142.

(d) Enclosures for Motor Controllers.   Enclosures for motor controllers.

Exception: Lined covers of snap switches.

(e) Elevators and Cranes.   Electric equipment for elevators and cranes.

(f) Garages, Theaters, and Motion Picture Studios. Electric equipment in garages, theaters, and motion picture studios.

Exception: Pendant lampholders supplied by circuits not over 150 volts to ground.

(g) Electric Signs. Electric signs and associated equipment.

Exception: Where insulated from ground and from other conductive objects and accessible only to qualified persons.

(h) Motion Picture Projection Equipment. Motion picture projection equipment.

(i) Class 1, Class 2, and Class 3 Circuits. Equipment supplied by Class 1, Class 2, and Class 3 remote-control and signaling circuits where required to be grounded by Part B of this article.

(j) Lighting Fixtures. Lighting fixtures as provided in Part E of Article 410.

250-44. Nonelectric Equipment. The metal parts of nonelectric equipment described in (a) through (e) below shall be grounded.

(a) Cranes. Frames and tracks of electrically operated cranes.

(b) Elevator Cars. Frames of nonelectrically driven elevator cars to which electric conductors are attached.

(c) Electric Elevators. Hand-operated metal shifting ropes or cables of electric elevators.

(d) Metal Partitions. Metal partitions, grill work, and similar metal enclosures around equipment of 1 kV and over between conductors except substations or vaults under the sole control of the supply company.

(e) Mobile Homes and Recreational Vehicles. Mobile homes and recreational vehicles as required in Articles 550 and 551.

Where extensive metal in or on buildings may become energized and is subject to personal contact, adequate bonding and grounding will provide additional safety.

250-45. Equipment Connected by Cord and Plug. Under any of the conditions described in (a) through (d) below, exposed noncurrent-carrying metal parts of cord- and plug-connected equipment likely to become energized shall be grounded.

(a) In Hazardous (Classified) Locations. In hazardous (classified) locations (see Articles 500 through 517).

(b) Over 150 Volts to Ground. Where operated at over 150 volts to ground.

Exception No. 1: Motors, where guarded.

Exception No. 2: Metal frames of electrically heated appliances, exempted by special permission, in which case the frames shall be permanently and effectively insulated from ground.

See Section 422-16.

(c) In Residential Occupancies. In residential occupancies: (1) refrigerators, freezers, and air conditioners; (2) clothes-washing, clothes-drying, dish-washing machines, sump pumps, electrical aquarium equipment; (3) hand-held motor-operated tools; (4) motor-operated appliances of the following types: hedge clippers, lawn mowers, snow blowers, and wet scrubbers; (5) portable handlamps.

Exception: Listed tools and listed appliances protected by a system of double insulation, or its equivalent, shall not be required to be grounded. Where such a system is employed, the equipment shall be distinctively marked.

(d) In Other than Residential Occupancies. In other than residential occupancies: (1) refrigerators, freezers, and air conditioners; (2) clothes-washing, clothes-drying, dish-washing machines, sump pumps, electrical aquarium equipment; (3) hand-held motor-operated tools; (4) motor-operated appliances of the following types: hedge clippers, lawn mowers, snow blowers, and wet scrubbers; (5) cord- and plug-connected appliances used in damp or wet locations or by persons standing on the ground or on metal floors or working inside of metal tanks or boilers; (6) tools likely to be used in wet and conductive locations; and (7) portable handlamps.

Exception No. 1: Tools likely to be used in wet and conductive locations shall not be required to be grounded where supplied through an isolating transformer with an ungrounded secondary of not over 50 volts.

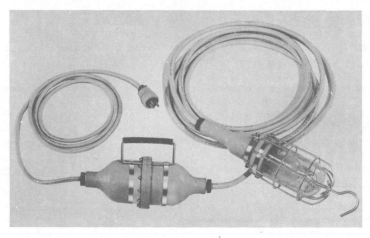

Figure 250-10. Lighting equipment supplied through an isolating transformer operating at 6 or 12 volts provides safe illumination for work inside of boilers, tanks, and similar locations that may be metallic and/or wet. (*Daniel Woodhead Co.*)

Exception No. 2: Listed portable tools and listed appliances protected by an approved system of double insulation, or its equivalent, shall not be required to be grounded. Where such a system is employed, the equipment shall be distinctively marked.

With reference to (c) and (d), portable tools or appliances not provided with special insulating or grounding protection are not intended to be used in damp, wet, or conductive locations.

Tools should be grounded by an equipment grounding conductor in a cord or cable supplying the tool except where supplied by an isolating transformer as permitted by Exception No. 1. Portable tools and appliances protected by an approved system of double insulation should be listed by a qualified laboratory as being suitable for the purpose, and the equipment should be distinctively marked as double insulated as indicated by Exception No. 2.

Cord-connected portable tools or appliances are not intended to be used in damp, wet, or conductive locations unless supplied by an isolation transformer or protected by an approved system of double insulation.

250-46. Spacing from Lightning Rods. Metal raceways, enclosures, frames, and other noncurrent-carrying metal parts of electric equipment shall be kept at least 6 feet (1.83 m) away from lightning rod conductors, or they shall be bonded to the lightning rod conductors.

See Sections 250-86 and 800-31(b)(5). For further information see the Lightning Protection Code, NFPA 78-1977 (ANSI), which contains detailed information on grounding lightning protection systems.

F. Methods of Grounding

250-50. Equipment Grounding Conductor Connections. Equipment grounding conductor connections at the source of separately derived systems shall be made in accordance with Section 250-26(a). Equipment grounding conductor connections at service equipment shall be made as indicated in (a) or (b) below.

(a) For Grounded System. The connection shall be made by bonding the equipment grounding conductor to the grounded service conductor and the grounding electrode conductor.

(b) For Ungrounded System. The connection shall be made by bonding the equipment grounding conductor to the grounding electrode conductor.

Exception for (a) and (b) above: For branch-circuit extensions only in existing installations that do not have an equipment grounding conductor in the branch circuit, the grounding conductor of a grounding-type receptacle outlet shall be permitted to be grounded to a grounded cold water pipe near the equipment.

250-51. Effective Grounding Path. The path to ground from circuits, equipment, and conductor enclosures shall: (1) be permanent and continuous; (2) have capacity to conduct safely any fault current likely to be imposed on it; and (3) have sufficiently low impedance to limit the voltage to ground and to facilitate the operation of the circuit protective devices in the circuit.

250-53. Grounding Path to Grounding Electrode at Services.

(a) Grounding Electrode Conductor. A grounding electrode conductor shall be used to connect the equipment grounding conductors, the service-equipment enclosures and, where the system is grounded, the grounded service conductor to the grounding electrode.

See Section 250-23(a).

The fine print note reference to Section 250-23(a) directs the reader to more detailed specifications for connecting the grounding electrode conductor.

(b) Main Bonding Jumper. For a grounded system, an unspliced main bonding jumper shall be used to connect the equipment grounding conductor and the service-equipment enclosure to the grounded conductor of the system within the service equipment or within the service conductor enclosure. A main bonding jumper shall be a wire, bus, screw, or similar suitable conductor.

250-54. Common Grounding Electrode. Where an ac system is connected to a grounding electrode in or at a building as specified in Sections 250-23 and 250-24, the same electrode shall be used to ground conductor enclosures and equipment in or on that building.

Two or more electrodes that are effectively bonded together shall be considered as a single electrode in this sense.

250-55. Underground Service Cable. Where served from a continuous underground metal-sheathed cable system, the sheath or armor of underground service cable metallically connected to the underground system, or underground service conduit containing a metal-sheathed cable bonded to the underground system, shall not be required to be grounded at the building and shall be permitted to be insulated from the interior conduit or piping.

250-56. Short Sections of Raceway. Isolated sections of metal raceway or cable armor, where required to be grounded, shall be grounded in accordance with Section 250-57.

250-57. Equipment Fastened in Place or Connected by Permanent Wiring Methods (Fixed)—Grounding. Noncurrent-carrying metal parts of equipment, raceways, and other enclosures, where required to be grounded, shall be grounded by one of the methods indicated in (a) or (b) below.

Exception: Where equipment, raceways, and enclosures are grounded by connection to the grounded circuit conductor as permitted by Sections 250-24, 250-60, and 250-61.

This Exception eliminates any possible conflict between Section 250-57, which requires an equipment grounding conductor to be used for equipment grounding, and Sections 250-24, 250-60, and 250-61, which permit the grounded circuit conductor to be used for equipment grounding if certain specified conditions are met.

(a) Equipment Grounding Conductor Types. By any of the equipment grounding conductors permitted by Section 250-91(b).

(b) With Circuit Conductors. By an equipment grounding conductor contained within the same raceway, cable, or cord or otherwise run with the circuit conductors. Bare, covered or insulated equipment grounding conductors shall be permitted. Individually covered or insulated equipment grounding conductors shall have a continuous outer finish that is either green, or green with one or more yellow stripes.

Exception No. 1: An insulated conductor larger than No. 6 copper or aluminum shall, at the time of installation, be permitted to be permanently identified as an equipment grounding conductor at each end and at every point where the conductor is accessible. Identification shall be accomplished by one of the following:

    a. Stripping the insulation from the entire exposed length,
    b. Coloring the exposed insulation green, or
    c. Marking the exposed insulation with green colored tape or green colored adhesive labels.

Exception No. 2: For direct-current circuits only, the equipment grounding conductor shall be permitted to be run separately from the circuit conductors.

Exception No. 3: Where the conditions of maintenance and supervision assure that only qualified persons will service the installation, an insulated conductor in a multiconductor cable shall, at the time of installation, be permitted to be permanently identified as an equipment grounding conductor at each end and at every point where the conductor is accessible by one of the following means:

    a. Stripping the insulation from the entire exposed length,
    b. Coloring the exposed insulation green, or
    c. Marking the exposed insulation with green tape or green colored adhesive labels.

See Section 250-79 for equipment bonding jumper requirements.

See Section 400-7 for use of cords for fixed equipment.

250-58. Equipment Considered Effectively Grounded. Under the conditions specified in (a) and (b) below, the noncurrent-carrying metal parts of the equipment shall be considered effectively grounded.

(a) Equipment Secured to Grounded Metal Supports. Electric equipment secured to and in electrical contact with a metal rack or structure provided for its support and grounded by one of the means indicated in Section 250-57. The structural metal frame of a building shall not be used as the required equipment grounding conductor for ac equipment.

(b) Metal Car Frames. Metal car frames supported by metal hoisting cables attached to or running over metal sheaves or drums of elevator machines which are grounded by one of the methods indicated in Section 250-57.

250-59. Cord- and Plug-Connected Equipment. Noncurrent-carrying metal parts of cord- and plug-connected equipment, where required to be grounded, shall be grounded by one of the methods indicated in (a), (b), or (c) below.

(a) By Means of the Metal Enclosure. By means of the metal enclosure of the conductors supplying such equipment if a grounding-type attachment plug with one fixed grounding contact is used for grounding the metal enclosure, and if the metal enclosure of the conductors is secured to the attachment plug and to equipment by approved connectors.

Exception: A self-restoring grounding contact shall be permitted on grounding-type attachment plugs used on the power supply cord of portable hand-held, hand-guided, or hand-supported tools or appliances.

(b) By Means of a Grounding Conductor. By means of an equipment grounding conductor run with the power supply conductors in a cable assembly or flexible cord properly terminated in grounding-type attachment plug with one fixed grounding contact. An uninsulated equipment grounding conductor shall be permitted but, if individually covered, the covering shall have a continuous outer finish that is either green or green with one or more yellow stripes.

Exception: A self-restoring grounding contact shall be permitted on grounding-type attachment plugs used on the power supply cord of portable hand-held, hand-guided, or hand-supported tools or appliances.

(c) Separate Flexible Wire or Strap. By means of a separate flexible wire or strap, insulated or bare, protected as well as practicable against physical damage, where part of equipment.

250-60. Frames of Ranges and Clothes Dryers. Frames of electric ranges, wall-mounted ovens, counter-mounted cooking units, clothes dryers, and outlet or junction boxes which are part of the circuit for these appliances shall be grounded in the manner specified by Section 250-57 or 250-59; or except for mobile homes or recreation vehicles shall be permitted to be grounded to the grounded circuit conductor if all of the conditions indicated in (a) through (d) below are met.

(a) The supply circuit is 120/240-volt, single-phase, 3-wire; or 208Y/120-volt derived from a 3-phase, 4-wire, wye-connected system.

(b) The grounded conductor is not smaller than No. 10 copper or No. 8 aluminum.

(c) The grounded conductor is insulated; or the grounded conductor is uninsulated and part of a service-entrance cable and the branch circuit originates at the service equipment.

(d) Grounding contacts of receptacles furnished as part of the equipment are bonded to the equipment.

The grounded circuit conductor (neutral) may be used to ground the frames of an electric range, wall-mounted oven or counter-mounted cooking units, provided all the conditions of (a) through (d) are met. The grounded circuit conductor may also be used to ground any junction boxes in the circuit supplying the appliance and a 3-wire pigtail and range receptacle may be used regardless of whether or not the circuit to the receptacle contains a separate grounding conductor.

The use of the grounded circuit conductor (neutral) for grounding purposes is counter to other requirements of the *Code*; however, it has been allowed for many years because of the good safety record of appliances that are grounded through the grounded circuit (neutral) conductor and because a break in the grounded circuit conductor would normally render the appliance inoperable.

Where service-entrance cable with an uninsulated neutral is used, it is necessary that the circuit originate from the service equipment in order to avoid multiple grounding from downstream panelboards.

250-61. Use of Grounded Circuit Conductor for Grounding Equipment.

(a) Supply-Side Equipment. A grounded circuit conductor shall be permitted to ground noncurrent-carrying metal parts of equipment, raceways, and other enclosures on the supply side of the service disconnecting means, and on the supply side of the main disconnecting means for separate buildings as provided in Section 250-24.

(b) Load-Side Equipment. A grounded circuit conductor shall not be used for grounding noncurrent-carrying metal parts of equipment on the load side of the service disconnecting means or on the load side of a separately derived system disconnecting means or the overcurrent devices for a separately derived system not having a main disconnecting means.

Exception No. 1: The frames of ranges, wall-mounted ovens, counter-mounted cooking units, and clothes dryers under the conditions specified by Section 250-60.

Exception No. 2: As permitted in Section 250-24 for separate buildings.

Exception No. 3: It shall be permissible to ground meter enclosures by connection to the grounded circuit conductor on the load-side of the service disconnect if:
a. No service ground-fault protection is installed; and
b. All meter enclosures are located near the service disconnecting means.

250-62. Multiple Circuit Connections. Where equipment is required to be grounded, and is supplied by separate connection to more than one circuit or grounded premises wiring system, a means for grounding shall be provided for each such connection as specified in Sections 250-57 and 250-59.

G. Bonding

250-70. General. Bonding shall be provided where necessary to assure electrical continuity and the capacity to conduct safely any fault current likely to be imposed.

250-71. Service Equipment.

(a) Bonding of Service Equipment. The noncurrent-carrying metal parts of equipment indicated in (1), (2) and (3) below shall be effectively bonded together.

(1) Except as permitted in Section 250-55, the service raceways, cable trays, or service cable armor or sheath.

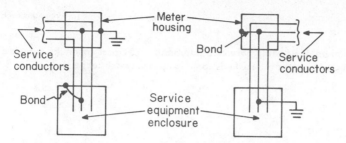

Figures 250-11 and 250-12. Two different types of grounding and bonding arrangements. Figure 250-11 shows a grounding electrode conductor at the meter housing with the service equipment enclosure bonded to the grounded service conductor. Figure 250-12 shows the grounding electrode conductor at the service equipment and the meter housing bonded to the grounded service conductor.

(2) All service equipment enclosures containing service-entrance conductors, including meter fittings, boxes, or the like, interposed in the service raceway or armor.

(3) Any conduit or armor enclosing a grounding electrode conductor.

(b) Bonding to Other Systems.   At dwellings, an accessible means external to enclosures for connecting intersystem bonding and grounding conductors shall be provided at the service by at least one of the following means:

(1) Exposed metallic service conduit.

(2) Exposed grounding electrode conductor.

(3) Approved means for the external connection of a bonding, or grounding conductor to the service raceway or equipment.

Section 250-71(b) shall become effective August 1, 1981.

The *Code* requires separate systems to be bonded together to reduce differences of potentials between them, which can result from lightning or power contacts. Interconnection is required for lightning rod systems (Section 250-46), communications systems [Section 800-31(b)(5)] and CATV systems [Section 800-22(f)]. Lack of interconnection can result in severe shock and fire hazard.

It is becoming difficult for communications installers to comply with *Code* grounding and bonding requirements, particularly in residences, because of the increasing use of plastic for water pipe, fittings, water meters and service conduit. In the past the bond between communications and power systems was usually achieved by connecting the communications protector grounds to an interior water pipe, because this was most likely used for the power grounding electrode. Thus, the requirement that the power, communications and water piping systems be bonded together was easily satisfied. In the event that the power was grounded to one of the other electrodes permitted by the *Code*, usually a ground rod, the bond was connected to the power grounding electrode conductor or to metallic service conduit since at least one of these was usually accessible. With the growing proliferation of plastic water pipe, the increasing tendency for the service equipment to be installed in finished areas where the grounding electrode conductor is often concealed (and flush-mounted service equipment installed), as well as the use of plastic entrance conduit, communications installers no longer have an easily identifiable point for connecting bonds or grounds. See Figure 250-14.

See Sections 800-31 and 820-22 for bonding and grounding requirements for communication and CATV circuits.

250-72. Method of Bonding Service Equipment. Electrical continuity at service equipment shall be assured by one of the methods specified in (a) through (e) below.

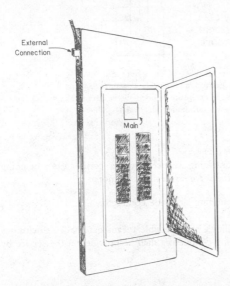

Figure 250-13. An external accessible means for connecting intersystem bonding and grounding conductors for dwellings to provide a bonding point for such systems as communication and CATV circuits.

Figure 250-14. A grounding bushing used to connect a copper bonding or grounding wire to a conduit. (*The Thomas & Betts Co., Inc.*)

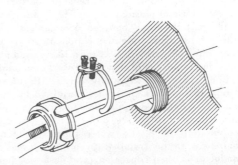

Figures 250-15 and 250-16. Figure 250-15 (left) shows a grounding wedge lug for providing an electrical connection between a conduit and a box. Figure 250-16 (right) shows the manner in which the lug is installed (*The Thomas & Betts Co., Inc.*)

Figure 250-17. A threaded grounding bushing showing openings for set screws to assure electrical and mechanical connection. (*General Electric Co.*)

(a) Pressure Connectors, Clamps, etc.   Bonding equipment to the grounded service conductor in a manner provided in Section 250-113.

(b) Threaded Couplings.   Threaded couplings and threaded bosses on enclosures with joints shall be made up wrenchtight where rigid metal conduit and intermediate metal conduit are involved.

(c) Threadless Couplings.   Threadless couplings made up tight for rigid metal conduit, intermediate metal conduit and electrical metallic tubing.

(d) Bonding Jumpers.   Bonding jumpers meeting the other requirements of this article. Bonding jumpers shall be used around concentric or eccentric knockouts that are punched or otherwise formed so as to impair the electrical connection to ground.

(e) Other Devices.   Other approved devices, such as bonding-type locknuts and bushings.

Note that paragraph (e) requires bonding-type locknuts to be used, and that standard locknuts or sealing locknuts are not acceptable for bonding at service equipment.

Bonding bushings for use with rigid metal conduit are provided with means (usually one or more setscrews) for reliably bonding the bushing (and the conduit on which it is threaded) to the metal equipment enclosure or box. Means for connecting a grounding or bonding wire are not provided, and if there is need for such a conductor a grounding bushing should be used.

Grounding bushings for use with rigid metal conduit have provision for the connection of a bonding or grounding wire or have means for mounting a wire connector available from the manufacturer. Such a bushing may also have means (usually one or more setscrews) for reliably bonding the bushing to the metal equipment enclosure or box in the same manner that is accomplished by a bonding bushing.

250-73. Metal Armor or Tape of Service Cable.   The metal covering of service cable having an uninsulated grounded service conductor in continuous electrical contact with its metallic armor or tape shall be considered to be grounded.

250-74. Connecting Receptacle Grounding Terminal to Box.   An equipment bonding jumper shall be used to connect the grounding terminal of a grounding-type receptacle to a grounded box.

Exception No. 1: Where the box is surface mounted, direct metal-to-metal contact between the device yoke and the box shall be permitted to ground the receptacle to the box.

Exception No. 2: Contact devices or yokes designed and listed for the purpose shall be permitted in conjunction with the supporting screws to establish the grounding circuit between the device yoke and flush-type boxes.

Exception No. 3: Floor boxes designed for and listed as providing satisfactory ground continuity between the box and the device.

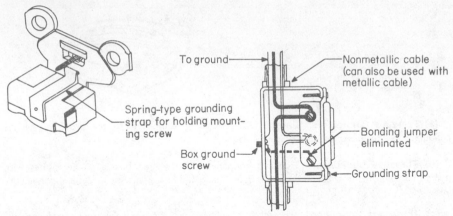

To ground

Spring-type grounding strap for holding mounting screw

Box ground screw

Nonmetallic cable (can also be used with metallic cable)

Bonding jumper eliminated

Grounding strap

Figure 250-18. Receptacle designed with spring-type grounding strap which holds mounting screw captive and eliminates a bonding jumper to box in accordance with Exception No. 2 of Section 250-74.

Exception No. 4: Where required for the reduction of electrical noise (electromagnetic interference) on the grounding circuit, a receptacle in which the grounding terminal is purposely insulated from the receptacle mounting means shall be permitted. The receptacle grounding terminal shall be grounded by an insulated equipment grounding conductor run with the circuit conductors. This grounding conductor shall be permitted to pass through one or more panelboards without connection to the panelboard grounding terminal as permitted in Section 384-27, Exception, so as to terminate directly at the applicable derived system or service grounding terminal.

250-75. Bonding Other Enclosures.   Metal raceways, cable trays, cable armor, cable sheath, enclosures, frames, fittings, and other metal noncurrent-carrying parts that are to serve as grounding conductors shall be effectively bonded where necessary to assure electrical continuity and the capacity to conduct safely any fault current likely to be imposed on them. Any nonconductive paint, enamel, or similar coating shall be removed at threads, contact points, and contact surfaces or be connected by means of fittings so designed as to make such removal unnecessary.

The addition of cable trays is consistent with the bonding requirements for cable trays in Section 318-6(b)(4).

250-76. Bonding for Over 250 Volts.   For circuits of over 250 volts to ground, the electrical continuity of metal raceways and cables with metal sheaths that contain any conductor other than service conductors shall be assured by one or more of the methods specified for services in Section 250-72(b) through (e); or by (a) or (b) below.

(a) Threadless Fittings.   Threadless fittings made up tight, with conduit or metal-clad cable.

(b) Two Locknuts.   Two locknuts, one inside and one outside of boxes and cabinets.

It is intended that fittings, such as EMT connectors, cable connectors, etc., having shoulders that seat against the box or cabinet meet the intent of Section 250-76 and only one locknut located on the inside of the box is required.

250-77. Bonding Loosely Jointed Metal Raceways.   Expansion joints and telescoping sections of raceways shall be made electrically continuous by equipment bonding jumpers or other means.

250-78. Bonding in Hazardous (Classified) Locations. Regardless of the voltage of the electrical system, the electrical continuity of noncurrent-carrying metal parts of equipment, raceways, and other enclosures in any hazardous (classified) location as defined in Article 500 shall be assured by any of the methods specified for services in Section 250-72(b) through (e) that are approved for the wiring method used.

250-79. Main and Equipment Bonding Jumpers.

(a) **Material.** Main and equipment bonding jumpers shall be of copper or other corrosion-resistant material.

(b) **Attachment.** Main and equipment bonding jumpers shall be attached in the manner specified by the applicable provisions of Section 250-113 for circuits and equipment and by Section 250-115 for grounding electrodes.

(c) **Size—Equipment Bonding Jumper on Supply Side of Service and Main Bonding Jumper.** The bonding jumper shall not be smaller than the sizes given in Table 250-94 for grounding electrode conductors. Where the service-entrance phase conductors are larger than 1100 MCM copper or 1750 MCM aluminum, the bonding jumper shall have an area not less than 12½ percent of the area of the largest phase conductor except that where the phase conductors and the bonding jumper are of different materials (copper or aluminum), the minimum size of the bonding jumper shall be based on the assumed use of phase conductors of the same material as the bonding jumper and with an ampacity equivalent to that of the installed phase conductors. Where the service- entrance conductors are paralleled in two or more raceways, the size of the bonding jumper for each raceway shall be based on the size of service conductors in each raceway.

The size of the equipment bonding jumper on the supply side of the service and the main bonding jumper is the same as that required for the grounding electrode conductor taken from Table 250-94 (including the 12½ percent requirement for phase conductors larger than 1,100 MCM copper or 1,750 MCM aluminum).

Example: In applying the bonding requirements of Figure 250-8, if one of the switches is rated 100 A and the supply conductor ampacity is 95 A (No. 2 TW), Table 250-94 would require a grounding electrode conductor of No. 8 copper or No. 6 aluminum. The bonding jumper would also be No. 8 copper or No. 6 aluminum.

If another switch is rated 200 A and the conductors supplying it are rated 200 A (No. 3/0 THW), the grounding electrode conductor and the bonding jumper would be a minimum of No. 4 copper or No. 2 aluminum.

To apply the bonding jumper requirements, each switch should be treated as a separate service equipment and Table 250-94 should be used to derive the bonding jumper size.

In some instances the bonding jumper may be larger than the grounding electrode conductor. Section 250-79(c) indicates that, where the service-entrance conductors are larger than 1,100 MCM copper or 1,750 MCM aluminum, the bonding jumper is to have an area not less than 12½ percent of the area of the largest phase conductor. If a service is supplied by 2,000 MCM conductors for each phase, the minimum bonding jumper size would be 250 MCM (2,000 MCM x 0.125).

(d) **Size—Equipment Bonding Jumper on Load Side of Service.** The equipment bonding jumper on the load side of the service overcurrent devices shall not be smaller than the sizes listed by Table 250-95 for equipment grounding conductors.

(e) **Installation—Equipment Bonding Jumper.** The equipment bonding jumper shall be permitted to be installed inside or outside of a raceway or enclosure. Where installed on the outside, the length of the equipment bonding jumper shall not exceed 6 feet (1.83 m) and shall be routed with the raceway or enclosure.

In many applications it is necessary to install equipment bonding jumpers on the outside of raceways and enclosures. For example, it would be impractical to install the bonding jumper for a conduit expansion joint on the inside of the conduit. For some rigid conduit systems and systems in hazardous (classified) locations, it is desirable to have the bonding jumper visible and accessible for inspection and maintenance. An external bonding jumper will have a higher impedance than an internal bonding jumper. However, by limiting the length to 6 ft and routing with the raceway, there will not be a significant increase in the total impedance of the equipment grounding circuit. This rule permits an exterior bonding jumper around sections of flexible metal conduit.

250-80. Bonding of Piping Systems.

(a) Metal Water Piping.   The interior metal water piping system shall always be bonded to the service equipment enclosure, the grounded conductor at the service, the grounding electrode conductor where of sufficient size, or to the one or more grounding electrodes used. The bonding jumper shall be sized in accordance with Table 250-94.

This Section requires a single connection to the metal water piping system. However, some judgment must be exercised in each case, and where it cannot reasonably be concluded that the hot and cold pipes are reliably interconnected, then an electrical bond would be required to assure this connection.

(b) Other Metal Piping.   Interior metal piping which may become energized shall be bonded to the service equipment enclosure, the grounded conductor at the service, the grounding electrode conductor where of sufficient size, or to the one or more grounding electrodes used. The bonding jumper shall be sized in accordance with Table 250-95 using the rating of the circuit which may energize the piping.

The equipment grounding conductor for the circuit which may energize the piping shall be permitted to serve as the bonding means.

Bonding all piping and metal air ducts within the premises will provide additional safety.

H. Grounding Electrode System

250-81. Grounding Electrode System.   If available on the premises at each building or structure served, each item (a) through (d) below shall be bonded together to form the grounding electrode system. The bonding jumper shall be sized in accordance with Section 250-94 and shall be connected in the manner specified in Section 250-115. The unspliced grounding electrode conductor shall be permitted to run to any convenient grounding electrode available in the grounding electrode system. It shall be sized for the largest grounding electrode conductor required among all the available electrodes.

(a) Metal Underground Water Pipe.   A metal underground water pipe in direct contact with the earth for 10 feet (3.05 m) or more (including any metal well casing effectively bonded to the pipe) and electrically continuous (or made electrically continuous by bonding around insulating joints or sections or insulating pipe) to the points of connection of the grounding electrode conductor and the bonding conductors. Continuity of the grounding path or the bonding connection to interior piping shall not rely on water meters. A metal underground water pipe shall be supplemented by an additional electrode of a type specified in Section 250-81 or in

Section 250-83. The supplemental electrode shall be permitted to be bonded to the grounding electrode conductor, the grounded service-entrance conductor, the grounded service raceway or the interior metal water piping at any convenient point.

The requirement to supplement the metal water pipe is based on the practice of using a plastic pipe for replacement when the original metal water pipe fails from corrosion, which would then leave the system without a grounding electrode where the supplementary electrode is not provided.

(b) Metal Frame of the Building.   The metal frame of the building, where effectively grounded.

(c) Concrete-Encased Electrode.   An electrode encased by at least 2 inches (50.8 mm) of concrete, located within and near the bottom of a concrete foundation or footing that is in direct contact with the earth, consisting of at least 20 feet (6.1 m) of one or more steel reinforcing bars or rods of not less than ½ inch (12.7 mm) diameter, or consisting of at least 20 feet (6.1 m) of bare copper conductor not smaller than No. 4 AWG.

(d) Ground Ring.   A ground ring encircling the building or structure, in direct contact with the earth at a depth below earth surface not less than 2½ feet (762 mm), consisting of at least 20 feet (6.1 m) of bare copper conductor not smaller than No. 2 AWG.

Section 250-81 requires the metal underground water pipe, the metal frame of the building, a concrete encased electrode, and a ground ring electrode (where these electrodes are present) to be bonded together to form the grounding electrode system. Where a metal underground water pipe is the only grounding electrode available, it must be supplemented by one of the grounding electrodes specified in Section 250-81 or Section 250-83.

There has always been a degree of misunderstanding as to whether metal water piping systems should be used as a grounding electrode, and a number of years ago the electrical industry and the water works industry formed a committee of all the affected interests to evaluate the use of metal underground water piping systems as the grounding electrode. Based on their findings, the committee issued an authoritative report on this subject. The International Association of Electrical Inspectors published the "Interim Report of the American Research Committee on Grounding" in January 1944 and had reprints made in March 1949.

The National Bureau of Standards in Washington, D.C. has monitored the electrolysis of metal systems because a flow of current at a grounding electrode on dc systems can cause displacement of metal. The results of this monitoring have shown that problems are minimal.

250-83. Made and Other Electrodes.   Where none of the electrodes specified in Section 250-81 is available, one or more of the electrodes specified in (a) through (d) below shall be used. Where practicable, made electrodes shall be embedded below permanent moisture level. Made electrodes shall be free from nonconductive coatings, such as paint or enamel. Where more than one electrode system is used (including those used for lightning rods), each electrode of one system shall not be less than 6 feet (1.83 m) from any other electrode of another system.

Two or more electrodes that are effectively bonded together are to be treated as a single electrode system in this sense.

(a) Metal Underground Gas Piping System.   An electrically continuous metal underground gas piping system that is uninterrupted with insulating sections or joints and without an outer nonconductive coating, and then only if acceptable to and expressly permitted by both the serving gas supplier and the authority having jurisdiction.

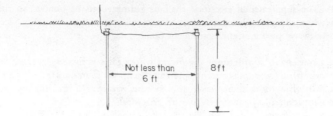

Figure 250-19. Section 250-83 presently requires a spacing of 6 ft between electrodes of different systems. Revised Section 250-84 requires a 6-ft spacing between electrodes of the same system.

(b) Other Local Metal Underground Systems or Structures. Other local metal underground systems or structures, such as piping systems and underground tanks.

(c) Rod and Pipe Electrodes. Rod and pipe electrodes shall not be less than 8 feet (2.44 m) in length and shall consist of the following materials, and shall be installed in the following manner:

(1) Electrodes of pipe or conduit shall not be smaller than ¾-inch trade size and, where of iron or steel, shall have the outer surface galvanized or otherwise metal-coated for corrosion protection.

(2) Electrodes of rods of steel or iron shall be at least ⅝ inch (15.87 mm) in diameter. Nonferrous rods or their equivalent shall be listed and shall be not less than ½ inch (12.7 mm) in diameter.

(3) The electrode shall be installed such that at least 8 feet (2.44 m) of length is in contact with the soil. It shall be driven to a depth of not less than 8 feet (2.44 m) except that where rock bottom is encountered, the electrode shall be driven at an oblique angle not to exceed 45 degrees from the vertical or shall be buried in a trench that is at least 2½ feet (762 mm) deep. The upper end of the electrode shall be flush with or below ground level unless the aboveground end and the grounding electrode conductor attachment are protected against physical damage as specified in Section 250-117.

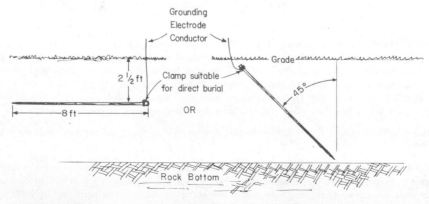

Figure 250-20. All pipe and rod electrodes must have 8 ft of length in contact with soil regardless of rock bottom and to provide that the upper end of the electrode be flush with or below ground level unless the above ground portion is protected against physical damage.

(d) Plate Electrodes.   Each plate electrode shall expose not less than 2 square feet (0.186 sq m) of surface to exterior soil. Electrodes of iron or steel plates shall be at least ¼ inch (6.35 mm) in thickness. Electrodes of nonferrous metal shall be at least 0.06 inch (1.52 mm) in thickness.

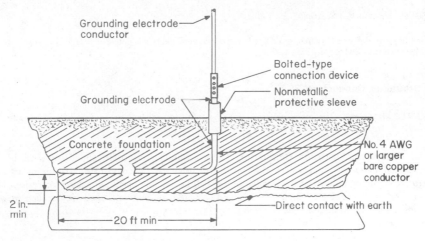

Figure 250-21. A concrete-encased grounding electrode known as the "Ufer system."

250-84. Resistance of Made Electrodes.   A single electrode consisting of a rod, pipe, or plate which does not have a resistance to ground of 25 ohms or less shall be augmented by one additional electrode of any of the types specified in Section 250-81 or 250-83. Where multiple rod, pipe, or plate electrodes are installed to meet the requirements of this section, they shall be not less than 6 feet (1.83 m) apart.

The paralleling efficiency of rods longer than 8 feet (2.44 m) is improved by spacing greater than 6 feet (1.83 m).

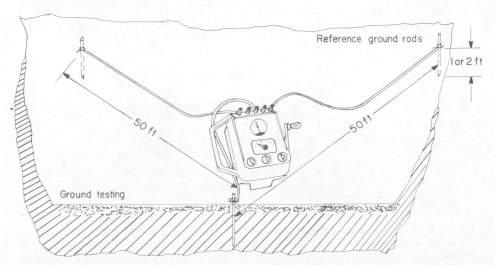

Figure 250-22. The resistance to ground of a driven grounding electrode can be measured by a ground tester used in this manner.

250-86. Use of Lightning Rods.   Lightning rod conductors and driven pipes, rods, or other made electrodes used for grounding lightning rods shall not be used in lieu of the made grounding electrodes required by Section 250-83 for grounding wiring systems and equipment. This provision shall not prohibit the required bonding together of grounding electrodes of different systems.

See Sections 250-46, 800-31(b)(7), and 820-22(h).

Bonding together of all separate grounding electrode systems will limit potential differences between them and between their associated wiring systems.

J. Grounding Conductors

250-91. Material.   The material for grounding conductors shall be as specified in (a) and (b) below.

(a) Grounding Electrode Conductor.   The grounding electrode conductor shall be of copper, aluminum, or copper-clad aluminum. The material selected shall be resistant to any corrosive condition existing at the installation or shall be suitably protected against corrosion. The conductor shall be solid or stranded, insulated, covered, or bare and shall be installed in one continuous length without a splice or joint.

Exception No. 1: Splices in busbars shall be permitted.

Exception No. 2: Where a service consists of more than a single enclosure as permitted in Section 230-45, it shall be permissible to connect taps to the grounding electrode conductor. Each such tap conductor shall extend to the inside of each such enclosure. The grounding electrode conductor shall be sized in accordance with Section 250-94, but the tap conductors shall be permitted to be sized in accordance with the grounding electrode conductors specified in Section 250-94 for the largest conductor serving the respective enclosures.

This requirement to allow taps to the common grounding electrode conductor was inserted in the *Code* due to the problems associated from looping the grounding electrode conductor from one enclosure to another. The grounding electrode tap conductors are to be sized from Table 250-94 and are based on the size of the largest conductors serving each enclosure. The grounding electrode conductor is determined by the size of the largest service-entrance conductor or equivalent area for parallel conductors as per Table 250-94. See Figure 250-23.

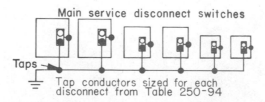

Figure 250-23. The tap method eliminates the difficulties found in looping grounding electrode conductors from one enclosure to another.

(b) Types of Equipment Grounding Conductors.   The equipment grounding conductor run with or enclosing the circuit conductors shall be one or more or a combination of the following: (1) a copper or other corrosion-resistant conductor. This conductor shall be solid or stranded; insulated, covered, or bare; and in the form of a wire or a busbar of any shape; (2) rigid metal conduit; (3) intermediate metal conduit; (4) electrical metallic tubing; (5) flexible metal conduit where both the conduit and fittings are approved for grounding; (6) armor of Type AC cable; (7) the sheath of mineral-insulated, metal-sheathed cable; (8) the metallic sheath or the combined metallic sheath and grounding conductors of Type MC cable; (9) cable trays as permitted in Sections 318-2(c) and 318-6; (10) other electrically continuous metal raceways approved for grounding.

Exception No. 1: Flexible metal conduit and flexible metallic tubing shall be permitted for grounding if all the following conditions are met:

a. The length in any ground return path does not exceed 6 feet (1.83 m).

b. The circuit conductors contained therein are protected by overcurrent devices rated at 20 amperes or less.

c. The conduit or tubing is terminated in fittings approved for grounding.

Exception No. 2: Liquidtight flexible metal conduit shall be permitted for grounding in the 1¼ -inch and smaller trade sizes if the total length in any ground return path does not exceed 6 feet (1.83 m) and the conduit is terminated in fittings approved for grounding.

Exception No. 3: For direct-current circuits only, the equipment grounding conductor shall be permitted to be run separately from the circuit conductors.

The various types of conductors, armored or metal-sheathed cables, or metal raceways that are suitable for use as equipment grounding conductors are described in Section 250-91 (b).

Flexible metal conduit and flexible metallic tubing are recognized in Exception No. 1 as equipment grounding conductors, where termination fittings approved for grounding are used, if the total length is not over 6 ft in any ground return path, and the contained circuit conductors are protected by overcurrent devices rated at 20 amperes or less.

Liquidtight flexible metal conduit is recognized as an equipment grounding conductor by Exception No. 2 where used with termination fittings approved for grounding in sizes not over 1¼ inches, and in lengths not over 6 ft in any ground return path.

Termination fittings that are approved for grounding may be determined by a qualified testing laboratory, inspection agency, or other organization concerned with product evaluation as part of its listing and labeling program. See the definition for "Approved, Identified, Listed and Labeled" in Article 100. For grounding requirements, see also Sections 349-16, 350-5, and 351-9.

(c) Supplementary Grounding. Supplementary grounding electrodes shall be permitted to augment the equipment grounding conductors specified in Section 250-91(b), but the earth shall not be used as the sole equipment grounding conductor.

250-92. Installation. Grounding conductors shall be installed as specified in (a) and (b) below.

(a) Grounding Electrode Conductor. A grounding electrode conductor or its enclosure shall be securely fastened to the surface on which it is carried. A No. 4, copper or aluminum, or larger conductor shall be protected if exposed to severe physical damage. A No. 6 grounding conductor that is free from exposure to physical damage shall be permitted to be run along the surface of the building construction without metal covering or protection where it is rigidly stapled to the construction; otherwise, it shall be in rigid metal conduit, intermediate metal conduit, rigid nonmetallic conduit, electrical metallic tubing, or cable armor. Grounding conductors smaller than No. 6 shall be in rigid metal conduit, intermediate metal conduit, rigid nonmetallic conduit, electrical metallic tubing, or cable armor.

Metal enclosures for grounding conductors shall be electrically continuous from the point of attachment to cabinets or equipment to the grounding electrode, and shall be securely fastened to the ground clamp or fitting. Metal enclosures that are not physically continuous from cabinet or equipment to the grounding electrode shall be made electrically continuous by bonding each end to the grounding conductor. Where intermediate metal conduit is used for protection for a grounding conductor, the installation shall comply with the requirements of Article 345. Where rigid metal conduit is used as protection for a grounding conductor, the installation shall comply with the requirements of Article 346. Where rigid nonmetallic conduit is used as protection for a grounding conductor, the installation shall comply with the requirements of Article 347. Where electrical metallic tubing is used, the installation shall comply with the requirements of Article 348.

Aluminum or copper-clad aluminum grounding conductors shall not be used where in direct contact with masonry or the earth or where subject to corrosive conditions. Where used outside, aluminum or copper-clad aluminum grounding conductors shall not be installed within 18 inches (457 mm) of the earth.

(b) Equipment Grounding Conductor.   An equipment grounding conductor shall be installed as follows:

(1) Where it consists of a raceway, cable tray, cable armor, or cable sheath or where it is a wire within a raceway or cable, it shall be installed in accordance with the applicable provisions in this Code using fittings for joints and terminations approved for use with the type raceway or cable used. All connections, joints, and fittings shall be made tight using suitable tools.

(2) Where it is a separate grounding conductor as provided in the Exception for Section 250-50(a) and (b), it shall be installed in accordance with (a) above in regard to restrictions for aluminum and also in regard to protection from physical damage.

Exception: Sizes smaller than No. 6 shall not be required to be enclosed in a raceway or armor where run in the hollow spaces of a wall or partition or where otherwise installed so as not to be subject to physical damage.

250-93. Size of Direct-Current System Grounding Conductor.   The size of the grounding conductor for a dc system shall be as specified in (a) through (c) below.

(a) Not Be Smaller than the Neutral Conductor.   Where the dc system consists of a 3-wire balancer set or a balancer winding with overcurrent protection as provided in Section 445-4(d), the grounding conductor shall not be smaller than the neutral conductor.

(b) Not Be Smaller than the Largest Conductor.   Where the dc system is other than as in (a) above, the grounding conductor shall not be smaller than the largest conductor supplied by the system.

(c) Not Be Smaller than No. 8.   In no case shall the grounding conductor be smaller than No. 8 copper or No. 6 aluminum.

250-94. Size of Alternating-Current Grounding Electrode Conductor.   The size of the grounding electrode conductor of a grounded or ungrounded ac system shall not be less than given in Table 250-94.

Exception No. 1: Grounded Systems.   Where connected to made electrodes as in Section 250-83 (c) or (d), that portion of the grounding electrode conductor which is the sole connection between the grounding electrode and the grounded system conductor shall not be required to be larger than No. 6 copper wire or No. 4 aluminum wire.

Exception No. 2: Ungrounded Systems.   Where connected to made electrodes as in Section 250-83 (c) or (d), that portion of the grounding electrode conductor which is the sole connection between the grounding electrode and the service equipment shall not be required to be larger than No. 6 copper wire or No. 4 aluminum wire.

Table 250-94
Grounding Electrode Conductor for AC Systems

Size of Largest Service-Entrance Conductor or Equivalent Area for Parallel Conductors		Size of Grounding Electrode Conductor	
Copper	Aluminum or Copper-Clad Aluminum	Copper	*Aluminum or Copper-Clad Aluminum
2 or smaller	0 or smaller	8	6
1 or 0	2/0 or 3/0	6	4
2/0 or 3/0	4/0 or 250 MCM	4	2
Over 3/0 thru 350 MCM	Over 250 MCM thru 500 MCM	2	0
Over 350 MCM thru 600 MCM	Over 500 MCM thru 900 MCM	0	3/0
Over 600 MCM thru 1100 MCM	Over 900 MCM thru 1750 MCM	2/0	4/0
Over 1100 MCM	Over 1750 MCM	3/0	250 MCM

Where there are no service-entrance conductors, the grounding electrode conductor size shall be determined by the equivalent size of the largest service-entrance conductor required for the load to be served.

* See installation restrictions in Section 250-92(a).

See Section 250-23(b).

250-95. Size of Equipment Grounding Conductors.   The size of copper, aluminum, or copper-clad aluminum equipment grounding conductors shall not be less than given in Table 250-95.

Where conductors are run in parallel in multiple raceways, as permitted in Section 310-4, the equipment grounding conductor, where used, shall be run in parallel. Each parallel equipment grounding conductor shall be sized on the basis of the ampere rating of the overcurrent device protecting the circuit conductors in the raceway in accordance with Table 250-95.

When conductors are adjusted in size to compensate for voltage drop, equipment grounding conductors, where required, shall be adjusted proportionately in size.

Where a single equipment grounding conductor is run with multiple circuits in the same raceway, it shall be sized for the largest overcurrent device protecting conductors in the raceway.

It is intended that a single equipment grounding conductor be sized for the largest overcurrent device and not be sized for the composite of all the circuits in the raceway.

Exception No. 1: An equipment grounding conductor not smaller than No. 18 copper and not smaller than the circuit conductors if an integral part of a listed flexible cord assembly shall be permitted for grounding cord-connected equipment where the equipment is protected by overcurrent devices not exceeding 20-ampere rating.

Exception No. 2: The equipment grounding conductor shall not be required to be larger than the circuit conductors supplying the equipment.

Exception No. 3: Where a raceway or a cable armor or sheath is used as the equipment grounding conductor, as provided in Sections 250-57(a) and 250-91(b).

250-97. Outline Lighting.   Isolated noncurrent-carrying metal parts of outline lighting systems shall be permitted to be bonded together by a No. 14 copper or No. 12 aluminum conductor protected from physical damage, where a conductor complying with Section 250-95 is used to ground the group.

250-99. Equipment Grounding Conductor Continuity.

(a) Separable Connections.   Separable connections such as those provided in draw-out equipment or attachment plugs and mating connectors and receptacles shall provide for first-make, last-break of the equipment grounding conductor.

Exception: Interlocked equipment, plugs, receptacles and connectors which preclude energization without grounding continuity.

(b) Switches.   No automatic cutout or switch shall be placed in the equipment grounding conductor of a premises wiring system.

Exception: Where the opening of the cutout or switch disconnects all sources of energy.

K. Grounding Conductor Connections

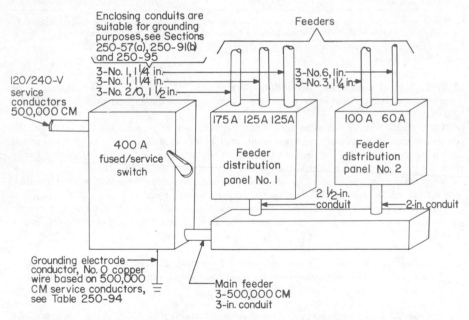

Figure 250-24. Various sizes of enclosing conduits used as equipment grounding conductors are shown as they apply to a service and feeder system.

250-112. To Grounding Electrode.   The connection of a grounding electrode conductor to a grounding electrode shall be accessible and made in a manner that will assure a permanent and effective ground. Where necessary to assure this for a metal piping system used as a grounding electrode, effective bonding shall be provided around insulated joints and sections and around any equipment that is likely to be disconnected for repairs or replacement.

Exception: A connection to a concrete-encased, driven, or buried grounding electrode shall not be required to be accessible.

250-113. To Conductors and Equipment. Required grounding conductors and bonding jumpers shall be connected by pressure connectors, clamps, or other approved means. Connection devices or fittings that depend on solder shall not be used.

Table 250-95. Minimum Size Equipment Grounding Conductors for Grounding Raceway and Equipment

Rating or Setting of Automatic Overcurrent Device in Circuit Ahead of Equipment, Conduit, etc., Not Exceeding (Amperes)	Size	
	Copper Wire No.	Aluminum or Copper-Clad Aluminum Wire No.*
15	14	12
20	12	10
30	10	8
40	10	8
60	10	8
100	8	6
200	6	4
300	4	2
400	3	1
500	2	1/0
600	1	2/0
800	0	3/0
1000	2/0	4/0
1200	3/0	250 MCM
1600	4/0	350 "
2000	250 MCM	400 "
2500	350 "	600 "
3000	400 "	600 "
4000	500 "	800 "
5000	700 "	1200 "
6000	800 "	1200 "

* See installation restrictions in Section 250-92(a).

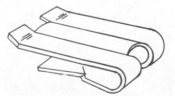

Figure 250-25. A clip used to connect a copper grounding conductor to a box.

250-114. Continuity and Attachment of Branch-Circuit Equipment Grounding Conductors to Boxes. Where more than one equipment grounding conductor of a branch circuit enters a box, all such conductors shall be in good electrical contact with each other and the arrangement shall be such that the disconnection or removal of a receptacle, fixture, or other device fed from the box will not interfere with or interrupt the grounding continuity.

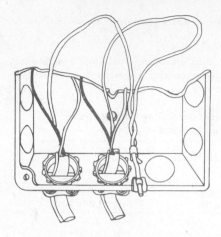

Figure 250-26. An application of a grounding clip.

(a) Metal Boxes. A connection shall be made between the one or more equipment grounding conductors and a metal box by means of a grounding screw which shall be used for no other purpose, or an approved grounding device.

(b) Nonmetallic Boxes. One or more equipment grounding conductors brought into a nonmetallic outlet box shall be so arranged that a connection can be made to any fitting or device in that box requiring grounding.

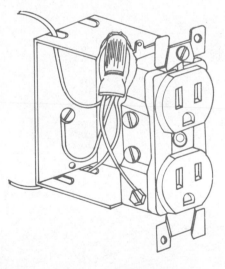

Figure 250-27. Grounding conductors may be attached to a box by a variety of methods, such as a screw, as shown, or such as shown in Figures 250-25 and 250-26.

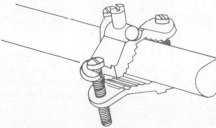

Figure 250-28. A ground clamp generally used with No. 8 through No. 4 grounding electrode conductors.

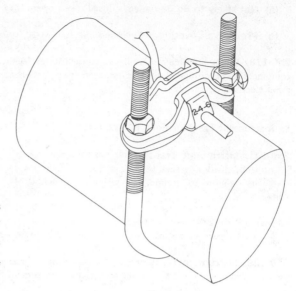

Figure 250-29. U-bolt ground clamps are available for all pipe sizes and all grounding electrode conductor sizes. Where grounding electrode conductors are run in conduits, conduit hubs may be bolted to the threaded portion of the U-bolt.

250-115. Connection to Electrodes. The grounding conductor shall be connected to the grounding fitting by suitable lugs, pressure connectors, clamps, or other approved means. Connections depending on solder shall not be used. Ground clamps shall be suitable for the materials of the grounding electrode and the grounding electrode conductor and where used on pipe, rod or other buried electrodes shall also be suitable for direct soil burial. Not more than one conductor shall be connected to the grounding electrode by a single clamp or fitting unless the clamp or fitting is approved for multiple conductors. One of the methods indicated in (a), (b), (c), or (d) below shall be used.

(a) An Approved Bolted Clamp. An approved bolted clamp of cast bronze or brass or plain or malleable iron.

(b) Pipe Fitting, Pipe Plug, etc. A pipe fitting, pipe plug, or other approved device screwed into a pipe or pipe fitting.

(c) Sheet-Metal-Strap Type Ground Clamp. A sheet-metal-strap type ground clamp having a rigid metal base that seats on the electrode and having a strap of such material and dimensions that it is not likely to stretch during or after installation.

(d) An Equally Substantial Approved Means. An equally substantial approved means.

Consideration is to be given to the suitability for direct soil burial of ground clamps used on ground rod or pipe electrodes or other buried electrodes, as many of the ground clamps advertised and recognized for use on ground rods are not suitable for soil burial since they are made of aluminum or steel or are held together with steel screws.

See Section 250-83(c)(3) requiring rod and pipe electrodes to be completely buried or protected against damage.

250-117. Protection of Attachment. Ground clamps or other fittings shall be approved for general use without protection or shall be protected from ordinary physical damage as indicated in (a) or (b) below.

(a) **Not Likely to Be Damaged.**   Installations where they are not likely to be damaged.

(b) **Protective Covering.**   Enclosing in metal, wood, or equivalent protective covering.

250-118. Clean Surfaces.   Nonconductive coatings (such as paint, lacquer, and enamel) on equipment to be grounded shall be removed from threads and other contact surfaces to assure good electrical continuity.

L. Instrument Transformers, Relays, etc.

250-121. Instrument Transformer Circuits.   Secondary circuits of current and potential instrument transformers shall be grounded where the primary windings are connected to circuits of 300 volts or more to ground, and where on switchboards, shall be grounded irrespective of voltage.

Exception: Circuits where the primary windings are connected to circuits of less than 1000 volts with no live parts or wiring exposed or accessible to other than qualified persons.

250-122. Instrument Transformer Cases.   Cases or frames of instrument transformers shall be grounded where accessible to other than qualified persons.

Exception: Cases or frames of current transformers, the primaries of which are not over 150 volts to ground and which are used exclusively to supply current to meters.

250-123. Cases of Instruments, Meters, and Relays—Operating at Less than 1000 Volts.   Instruments, meters, and relays operating with windings or working parts at less than 1000 volts shall be grounded as specified in (a), (b), or (c) below.

(a) **Not on Switchboards.**   Instruments, meters, and relays not located on switchboards, operating with windings or working parts at 300 volts or more to ground, and accessible to other than qualified persons, shall have the cases and other exposed metal parts grounded.

(b) **On Dead-Front Switchboards.**   Instruments, meters, and relays (whether operated from current and potential transformers, or connected directly in the circuit) on switchboards having no live parts on the front of the panels shall have the cases grounded.

(c) **On Live-Front Switchboards.**   Instruments, meters, and relays (whether operated from current and potential transformers, or connected directly in the circuit) on switchboards having exposed live parts on the front of panels shall not have their cases grounded. Mats of insulating rubber or other suitable floor insulation shall be provided for the operator where the voltage to ground exceeds 150.

250-124. Cases of Instruments, Meters, and Relays—Operating Voltage 1 kV and Over.   Where instruments, meters, and relays have current-carrying parts of 1 kV and over to ground, they shall be isolated by elevation or protected by suitable barriers, grounded metal or insulating covers or guards. Their cases shall not be grounded.

Exception: Cases of electrostatic ground detectors where the internal ground segments of the instrument are connected to the instrument case and grounded and the ground detector is isolated by elevation.

250-125. Instrument Grounding Conductor.   The grounding conductor for secondary circuits of instrument transformers and for instrument cases shall not be smaller than No. 12 copper or No. 10 aluminum. Cases of instrument transformers, instruments, meters, and relays which are mounted directly on grounded metal surfaces of enclosures or grounded metal switchboard panels shall be considered to be grounded and no additional grounding conductor will be required.

M. Grounding of Systems and Circuits of 1 kV and Over (High Voltage)

250-150. General. Where high-voltage systems are grounded, they shall comply with all applicable provisions of the preceding sections of this article and with the following sections which supplement and modify the preceding sections.

250-151. Derived Neutral Systems. A system neutral derived from a grounding transformer shall be permitted to be used for grounding a high-voltage system.

250-152. Solidly Grounded Neutral Systems.

(a) Neutral Conductor. The neutral of a solidly grounded neutral system shall comply with (1) and (2) below.

(1) The minimum insulation level for neutral conductors of solidly grounded systems shall be 600 volts.

Exception No. 1: Bare copper conductors shall be permitted to be used for the neutral of service entrances and the neutral of direct buried portions of feeders.

Exception No. 2: Bare conductors shall be permitted for the neutral of overhead portions installed outdoors.

(2) The neutral grounding conductor shall be permitted to be a bare conductor if isolated from phase conductors and protected from physical damage.

(b) Multiple Grounding. The neutral of a solidly grounded neutral system shall be permitted to be grounded at more than one point for:

(1) Services.

(2) Direct buried portions of feeders employing a bare copper neutral.

(3) Overhead portion installed outdoors.

250-153. Impedance Grounded Neutral Systems. Impedance grounded neutral systems shall comply with the provisions of (a) through (d) below.

(a) Location. The grounding impedance shall be inserted in the grounding conductor between the grounding electrode of the supply system and the neutral point of the supply transformer or generator.

(b) Identified and Insulated. Where the neutral conductor of an impedance grounded neutral system is used, it shall be identified, as well as fully insulated with the same insulation as the phase conductors.

(c) System Neutral Connection. The system neutral shall not be connected to ground, except through the neutral grounding impedance.

(d) Equipment Grounding Conductors. Equipment grounding conductors shall be permitted to be bare and shall be connected to the ground bus and grounding electrode conductor at the service-entrance equipment and extended to the system ground.

250-154. Grounding of Systems Supplying Portable or Mobile Equipment. Systems supplying portable or mobile high-voltage equipment, other than substations installed on a temporary basis, shall comply with (a) through (e) below.

Portable means easily carried, while mobile means easily movable, as on wheels, treads, etc.

(a) Portable or Mobile Equipment. Portable or mobile high-voltage equipment shall be supplied from a system having its neutral grounded through an impedance. Where a delta-connected high-voltage system is used to supply portable or mobile equipment, a system neutral shall be derived.

(b) Exposed Noncurrent-Carrying Metal Parts. Exposed noncurrent-carrying metal parts of portable or mobile equipment shall be connected by an equipment grounding conductor to the point at which the system neutral impedance is grounded.

(c) Ground-Fault Current. The voltage developed between the portable or mobile equipment frame and ground by the flow of maximum ground-fault current shall not exceed 100 volts.

(d) Ground-Fault Detection and Relaying. Ground-fault detection and relaying shall be provided to automatically de-energize any high-voltage system component which has developed a ground fault. The continuity of the equipment grounding conductor shall be continuously monitored so as to de-energize automatically the high-voltage feeder to the portable or mobile equipment upon loss of continuity of the equipment grounding conductor.

(e) Isolation. The grounding electrode to which the portable or mobile equipment system neutral impedance is connected shall be isolated from and separated in the ground by at least 20 feet (6.1 m) from any other system or equipment grounding electrode, and there shall be no direct connection between the grounding electrodes, such as buried pipe, fence, etc.

(f) Trailing Cable and Couplers. High voltage trailing cable and couplers for interconnection of portable or mobile equipment shall meet the requirements of Part C of Article 400 for cables and Section 710-45 for couplers.

250-155. Grounding of Equipment. All noncurrent-carrying metal parts of fixed, portable, and mobile equipment and associated fences, housings, enclosures, and supporting structures shall be grounded.

Exception No. 1: Where isolated from ground and located so as to prevent any person who can make contact with ground from contacting such metal parts when the equipment is energized.

Exception No. 2: Pole-mounted distribution apparatus as provided in Section 250-42, Exception No. 3.

Grounding conductors not an integral part of a cable assembly shall not be smaller than No. 6 copper or No. 4 aluminum.

ARTICLE 280 — SURGE ARRESTERS

Contents

This Article was completely revised for the 1981 *NEC*, and these results are from the work of a Subcommittee which included representation from Code-Making Panel 5, ANSI C62, the insurance industry, manufacturers, telephone group and a qualified testing laboratory. The charge to the Subcommittee was to: (1) Determine if a basis exists for requiring surge arresters; (2) Recognize current practices, including the use of surge arresters at locations other than "Industrial Stations"; (3) Re-examine installation, connection and grounding requirements; (4) Revise any unenforceable requirements; and (5) Update wording to current nomenclature.

The committee has functioned within this charge and has produced new wording which it believes will be as durable as that in the present Article 280 which has stood essentially unchanged since circa 1940.

Part M, "Connecting Lightning Arresters," has been deleted from Article 250. The concurrent rewrite of Article 280 moves the wording of Article 250, Part M into Article 280.

A. General

280-1. Scope.   This article covers general requirements, installation requirements, and connection requirements for surge arresters installed on premises wiring systems.

280-2. Definition.   A surge arrester is a protective device for limiting surge voltages by discharging or bypassing surge current, and it also prevents continued flow of follow current while remaining capable of repeating these functions.

280-3. Number Required.   Where used at a point on a circuit, a surge arrester shall be connected to each ungrounded conductor. A single installation of such surge arresters shall be permitted to protect a number of interconnected circuits provided that no circuit is exposed to surges while disconnected from the surge arresters.

Means must be provided to protect circuits that may be disconnected from the generating station bus. A switch with a double-throw action disconnecting the outside circuits from the station generator and alternatively connecting these circuits to ground would satisfy the condition of a single set of arresters protecting more than one circuit.

280-4. Surge Arrester Selection.

(a) On Circuits of Less than 1000 Volts. The rating of the surge arrester shall be equal to or greater than the maximum continuous phase-to-ground power frequency voltage available at the point of application.

(b) On Circuits of 1 kV and Over. The rating of the surge arrester shall be not less than 125 percent of the maximum continuous phase-to-ground voltage available at the point of application.

For further information on selection of surge arresters, see Guide for Application of Valve Type Lightning Arresters for Alternating-Current Systems (ANSI C62.2-1969).

B. Installation

280-11. Location.
Surge arresters shall be permitted to be located indoors or outdoors and shall be made inaccessible to unqualified persons.

Exception: Surge arresters listed for installation in accessible locations.

280-12. Routing of Surge Arrester Connections.
The conductor used to connect the surge arrester to line or bus and to ground shall not be any longer than necessary and shall avoid unnecessary bends.

Arrester conductors should be as short and straight as practicable, avoiding sharp bends and turns which would increase the impedance to lightning discharges and tend to reduce the effectiveness of a grounding conductor.

C. Connecting Surge Arresters

280-21. Installed at Services of Less than 1000 Volts.
Line and ground connecting conductors shall not be smaller than No. 14 copper or No. 12 aluminum. The arrester grounding conductor shall be connected to one of the following: (1) the grounded service conductor; (2) the grounding electrode conductor; (3) the grounding electrode for the service; or (4) the equipment grounding terminal in the service equipment.

Single-phase or 3-phase grounded or ungrounded services may have the surge arrester grounded to the equipment grounding terminal in the service equipment. Figure 280-1 shows three methods of grounding the ground terminals of surge arresters at service entrances.

280-22. Installed on the Load Side of Services of Less than 1000 Volts.
Line and ground connecting conductors shall not be smaller than No. 14 copper or No. 12 aluminum. A surge arrester shall be permitted to be connected between any two conductors (ungrounded conductor(s), grounded conductor, grounding conductor). The grounded conductor and the grounding conductor shall be interconnected only by the normal operation of the surge arrester during a surge.

280-23. Circuits of 1 kV and Over — Surge-Arrester Conductors.
The conductor between the surge arrester and the line and surge arrester and the grounding connection shall not be smaller than No. 6 copper or aluminum.

280-24. Circuits of 1 kV and Over — Interconnections.
The grounding conductor of a surge arrester protecting a transformer that supplies a secondary distribution system shall be permitted to be interconnected as specified in (a) and (b) below.

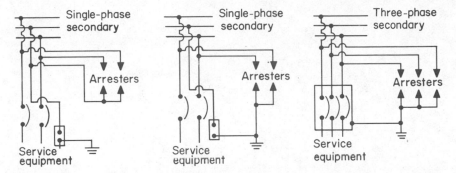

Figure 280-1. Three locations of grounding surge arresters at service entrances. Left, arrester connected to a neutral service conductor; center, arrester connected to a grounding electrode conductor; and right, arrester connected to a grounding electrode conductor of an ungrounded system.

(a) **Metallic Interconnections.** A metallic interconnection shall be permitted to be made to the secondary neutral provided that, in addition to the direct grounding connection at the surge arrester:

(1) The grounded conductor of the secondary has elsewhere a grounding connection to a continuous metal underground water piping system. However, in urban water-pipe areas where there are at least four water-pipe connections on the neutral and not less than four such connections in each mile of neutral, the metallic interconnection shall be permitted to be made to the secondary neutral with omission of the direct grounding connection at the surge arrester.

(2) The grounded conductor of the secondary system is a part of a multiground neutral system of which the primary neutral has at least four ground connections in each mile of line in addition to a ground at each service.

(b) **Through Spark Gap.** Where the secondary is not grounded as in (a) above, but is otherwise grounded as in Sections 250-81 and 250-83, such interconnections, where made, shall be through a spark gap having a 60-hertz breakdown voltage of at least twice the primary circuit voltage but not necessarily more than 10 kV, and there shall be at least one other ground on the grounded conductor of the secondary not less than 20 feet (6.1 m) distant from the surge arrester grounding electrode.

(c) **By Special Permission.** An interconnection of the surge arrester ground and the secondary neutral, other than as provided in (a) or (b) above, shall be permitted to be made only by special permission.

280-25. Grounding. Except as indicated in this article, surge arrester grounding connections shall be made as specified in Article 250. Grounding conductors shall not be run in metal enclosures unless bonded to both ends of such enclosure.

3 WIRING METHODS AND MATERIALS

ARTICLE 300 — WIRING METHODS

Contents

B. Requirements for Over 600 Volts, Nominal

300-31. Covers Required.
300-32. Conductors of Different Systems.

300-33. Inserting Conductors in Raceways.
300-34. Conductor Bending Radius.
300-35. Protection Against Induction Heating.
300-36. Grounding.

A. General Requirements

300-1. Scope.

(a) All Wiring Installations. The provisions of this article shall apply to all wiring installations.

Exception No. 1: Only those sections referenced in Article 725 shall apply to Class 1, Class 2, and Class 3 circuits.

Exception No. 2: Only those sections referenced in Article 760 shall apply to fire protective signaling circuits.

Exception No. 3: Only those sections referenced in Article 800 shall apply to communication systems.

The three Exceptions clearly indicate that Article 300 applies generally to Articles 725, 760, and 800. However, as specified in Section 90-3, these latter articles may supplement, modify, or amend Article 300. Such is the case, for example, where the Exceptions to Section 725-2(b), 760-4(d), or 800-3(d) amend the provisions of Section 300-22.

(b) Integral Parts of Equipment. The provisions of this article are not intended to apply to the conductors which form an integral part of equipment, such as motors, controllers, motor control centers, or factory-assembled control equipment.

(c) Single Conductors. Single conductors specified in Table 310-13 shall only be permitted to be installed where part of a recognized wiring method of Chapter 3.

The *Code* recognizes the use of single conductors as a wiring method and Paragraph (c) is added to the 1981 *NEC* to give coverage to this recognition.

300-2. Voltage Limitations.
Wiring methods specified in Chapter 3 shall be used for voltages 600 volts, nominal, or less where not specifically limited in some section of Chapter 3. They shall be permitted for voltages over 600 volts, nominal, where specifically permitted elsewhere in this Code.

300-3. Conductors of Different Systems.

(a) 600 Volts, Nominal, or Less. Conductors of 600 volts, nominal, or less shall be permitted to occupy the same equipment wiring enclosure, cable, or raceway, without regard to whether the individual circuits are alternating current or direct current, where all conductors are insulated for the maximum voltage of any conductor within the enclosure, cable, or raceway.

(b) Over 600 Volts, Nominal. Conductors of over 600 volts, nominal, shall not occupy the same equipment wiring enclosure, cable, or raceway with conductors of 600 volts, nominal, or less.

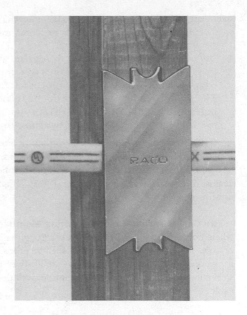

Figure 300-1. Steel plate to protect nonmetallic-sheathed cables within 1¼ in. of the edge of a stud. (*RACO*)

See Section 300-32, Conductors of Different Systems — over 600 volts, nominal.

Exception No. 1: Secondary wiring to electric-discharge lamps of 1000 volts or less, if insulated for the secondary voltage involved, shall be permitted to occupy the same fixture enclosure as the branch-circuit conductors.

Exception No. 2: Primary leads of electric-discharge lamp ballasts, insulated for the primary voltage of the ballast, when contained within the individual wiring enclosure, shall be permitted to occupy the same fixture enclosure as the branch-circuit conductors.

Exception No. 3: Excitation, control, relay, and ammeter conductors used in connection with any individual motor or starter shall be permitted to occupy the same enclosure as the motor circuit conductors.

The conductors of a 3-phase, 4-wire, 120/208-V ac circuit; a 3-phase, 4-wire, 277/480-V ac circuit; and a 3-wire, 120/240-V dc circuit may occupy the same equipment wiring enclosure, cable, or raceway where all conductors are insulated for the maximum voltage of any conductor. In this case the maximum voltage would be 480 V, and 600-V insulation would be required for all of the conductors.

300-4. Protection Against Physical Damage. Where subject to physical damage, conductors shall be adequately protected.

(a) Cables Through Wood Framing Members.

(1) Bored Holes. In both exposed and concealed locations, where a cable or raceway-type wiring method is installed through bored holes in joists, rafters, or similar structural wood members, holes shall be bored at the approximate center of the face of the member. Holes in studs for cable-type wiring methods shall be bored so that the edge of the hole is not less than 1¼ inches (31.8 mm) from the nearest edge of the stud or shall be protected from nails and screws by either a steel plate or bushing at least ¹⁄₁₆ inch (1.59 mm) thick and of appropriate length and width installed to cover the area through which nails or screws might penetrate the installed cable.

The intent of this section is to prevent wallboard or sheetrock nails from being driven into cables. By keeping the edge of the drilled hole 1¼ in. from the nearest edge of the stud, nails would not penetrate the stud far enough to injure the cables. The model building codes provide maximum requirements for bored or notched holes in studs and Paragraph (a)(2) indicates that consideration should be given to the size of notches in studs so as not to affect the strength of the structure.

(2) **Notches in Wood.**   Where there is no objection because of weakening the building structure, in both exposed and concealed locations, cables shall be permitted to be laid in notches in wood studs, joists, rafters, or other wood members where the cable at those points is protected against nails or screws by a steel plate at least ¹⁄₁₆ inch (1.59 mm) thick installed before the building finish is applied.

(b) **Cables Through Metal Framing Members.**   In both exposed and concealed locations where nonmetallic-sheathed cables pass through either factory or field punched, cut or drilled slots or holes in metal members, the cable shall be protected by bushings or grommets securely fastened in the opening. Where nails or screws are likely to penetrate the cable, a steel sleeve, steel plate or steel clip not less than ¹⁄₁₆ inch (1.59 mm) in wall thickness shall be used to protect the nonmetallic cable.

Exception: When the slots or holes are so formed that no metal edge can cut or tear cable insulation, bushings or grommets shall not be required.

300-5. Underground Installations.

(a) **Minimum Cover Requirements.**   Direct buried cable or conduit or other raceways shall be installed to meet the minimum cover requirements of Table 300-5.

Exception No. 1: The minimum cover requirements shall be permitted to be reduced by 6 inches (152 mm) for installations where a 2-inch (50.8-mm) thick concrete pad or equivalent in physical protection is placed in the trench over the underground installation.

Exception No. 2: The minimum cover requirements shall not apply to conduits or other raceways which are located under a building or exterior concrete slab not less than 4 inches (102 mm) in thickness and extending not less than 6 inches (152 mm) beyond the underground installation.

Exception No. 3: Areas subject to heavy vehicular traffic, such as thoroughfares, shall have a minimum cover of 24 inches (610 mm).

Exception No. 3 applies to all wiring methods listed in Table 300-5, i.e., rigid metal conduit, intermediate metal conduit, rigid nonmetallic conduit, etc. Areas subject to heavy vehicular traffic include, for example, thoroughfares, gasoline service stations, and commercial parking lots.

Exception No. 4: Residential branch circuits rated 300 volts or less and provided with overcurrent protection of not more than 30 amperes shall be permitted with a cover requirement of 12 inches (305 mm).

For example, a Type UF cable used for a 125-V, 15-A branch circuit for a lamp post on residential property is permitted to be buried 12 in. deep.

Exception No. 5: Lesser depths are permitted where cables and conductors rise for terminations or splices or where access is otherwise required.

The authority having jurisdiction for enforcing this *Code* may require supplementary protection, such as sleeves or running boards, to prevent physical damage where cables or conductors rise for termination to accessible junction or splice boxes. See Figure 300-2.

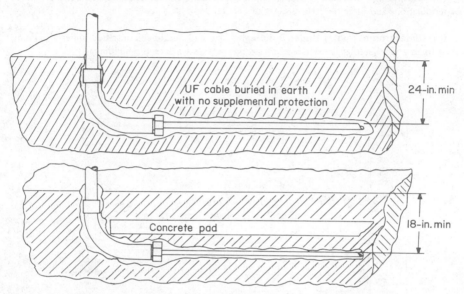

Figure 300-2. Type UF cable buried in compliance with Section 300-5. Note the protective bushing where the cable is used with metal conduit.

Table 300-5
Minimum Cover Requirements, 0 to 600 Volts, Nominal

(Cover is defined as the distance between the top surface of direct buried cable, conduit, or other raceways and the finished grade.)

Wiring Method	Minimum Burial (Inches)
Direct Buried Cables	24
Rigid Metal Conduit	6
Intermediate Metal Conduit	6
Rigid Nonmetallic Conduit Approved for Direct Burial without Concrete Encasement	18
Other Approved Raceways*	18

For SI units: one inch = 25.4 millimeters.
* Note: Raceways approved for burial only when concrete encased shall require a concrete envelope not less than 2 inches (50.8 mm) thick.

Exception No. 6: In airport runways, including adjacent defined areas where trespass is prohibited, cable shall be permitted to be buried not less than 18 inches (457 mm) deep and without raceways, concrete encasement or equivalent.

Exception No. 7: Raceways installed in solid rock shall be permitted to be buried at a lesser depth when covered by 2 inches (50.8 mm) or more of concrete over the installation and extending down to the rock surface.

Exception No. 8: Circuits for the control of irrigation and landscape lighting systems which are limited to not more than 30 volts and are installed with Type UF or other approved cable shall be permitted with a minimum cover of 6 inches (152 mm).

(b) Grounding.   Metallic shielding, sheath, or metallic conduit shall be effectively grounded at terminations and meet the requirements of Section 250-51.

(c) Underground Cables Under Buildings.   Underground cable installed under a building shall be in a raceway that is extended beyond the outside walls of the building.

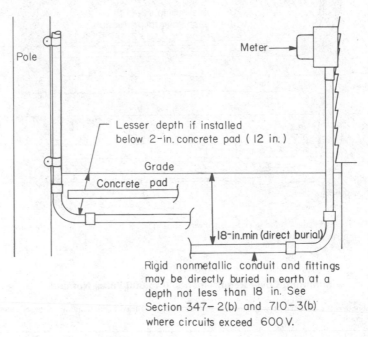

Figure 300-3. PVC rigid nonmetallic conduit buried in compliance with Section 300-5.

(d) Protection from Damage.   Conductors emerging from the ground shall be protected by enclosures or raceways extending from below grade to a point 8 feet (2.44 m) above finished grade.

> Note that Section 230-50(b) requires service conductors and cables, other than service-entrance cables, to be protected to a height of 10 ft above grade level.

Conductors entering a building shall be protected to the point of entrance.
Where subject to physical damage, the conductors shall be installed in rigid metal conduit, intermediate metal conduit, Schedule 80 rigid nonmetallic conduit, or equivalent.

(e) Splices and Taps.   Underground cables in trenches shall be permitted to be spliced or tapped without the use of splice boxes. The splices or taps shall be made by methods and with material identified for the purpose.

Figure 300-4. Electrical splicing kit for nonshielded single cables up to 5 kV and multiconductor cables up to 600 V. (*3M Company*)

(f) Backfill. Backfill containing large rock, paving materials, cinders, large or sharply angular substance, or corrosive material shall not be placed in an excavation where materials may damage raceways, cables, or other substructures or prevent adequate compaction of fill or contribute to corrosion of raceways, cables or other substructures.

Where necessary to prevent physical damage to the raceway or cable, protection shall be provided in the form of granular or selected material, suitable running boards, suitable sleeves, or other approved means.

(g) Raceway Seals. Conduits or raceways through which moisture may contact energized live parts shall be sealed or plugged at either or both ends.

Figure 300-5. Conduit sealing bushing to prevent the entrance of gas or moisture. See Section 230-48 for sealing service raceways. (*O.Z./Gedney Co.*)

(h) Bushing. A bushing shall be used at the end of a conduit which terminates underground where cables leave the conduit as a direct burial wiring method. A seal incorporating the physical protection characteristics of a bushing shall be permitted to be used in lieu of a bushing.

See Figure 300-2.

(i) Single Conductors. All conductors of the same circuit including the grounding conductor where required shall be installed in the same raceway or shall be installed in close proximity in the same trench.

Note that the use of the words "same raceway" intends that all phase conductors, and, where used, the neutral, and the equipment grounding conductor are all to be installed within the same raceway regardless whether the raceway is rigid metal conduit, intermediate metal conduit, or rigid nonmetallic conduit, etc.

300-6. Protection Against Corrosion.   Metal raceways, cable armor, boxes, cable sheathing, cabinets, elbows, couplings, fittings, supports, and support hardware shall be of materials suitable for the environment in which they are to be installed.

(a) General.   Ferrous raceways, cable armor, boxes, cable sheathing, cabinets, metal elbows, couplings, fittings, supports, and support hardware shall be suitably protected against corrosion inside and outside (except threads at joints) by a coating of approved corrosion-resistant material such as zinc, cadmium, or enamel. Where protected from corrosion solely by enamel, they shall not be used out-of-doors or in wet locations as described in (c) below. When boxes or cabinets have an approved system of organic coatings and are marked "Raintight," "Rainproof" or "Outdoor Type," they shall be permitted out-of-doors.

(b) In Concrete or in Direct Contact with the Earth.   Ferrous or nonferrous metal raceways, cable armor, boxes, cable sheathing, cabinets, elbows, couplings, fittings, supports, and support hardware shall be permitted to be installed in concrete or in direct contact with the earth, or in areas subject to severe corrosive influences when made of material judged suitable for the condition, or when provided with corrosion protection approved for the condition.

Section 300-6(a) and (b) applies generally. For specific applications, see the particular article covering the various cables, raceways, or enclosures, such as Sections 333-6, 336-3(a), 345-3, 345-5, 346-1(c), 346-3, 346-4, 347-2, 348-1, 348-4, and 370-5.

(c) Indoor Wet Locations.   In portions of dairies, laundries, canneries, and other indoor wet locations, and in locations where walls are frequently washed or where there are surfaces of absorbent materials, such as damp paper or wood, the entire wiring system, including all boxes, fittings, conduits, and cable used therewith, shall be mounted so that there is at least ¼-inch (6.35-mm) air space between it and the wall or supporting surface.

In general, areas where acids and alkali chemicals are handled and stored may present such corrosive conditions, particularly when wet or damp. Severe corrosive conditions may also be present in portions of meat-packing plants, tanneries, glue houses, and some stables; installations immediately adjacent to a seashore and swimming pool areas; areas where chemical de-icers are used; and storage cellars or rooms for hides, casings, fertilizer, salt, and bulk chemicals.

Ferrous or nonferrous metal conduit may be installed in concrete, in contact with the earth, or in areas exposed to severe corrosive influences where protected by corrosion protection and judged suitable for the condition. Special precautions are normally necessary for installing aluminum conduits in concrete, and specific approval by the authority having jurisdiction may be necessary.

To avoid deterioration, all metal raceways installed in the earth should be coated with an asphalt compound, plastic sheath, or other equivalent protection.

300-7. Raceways Exposed to Different Temperatures.

(a) Sealing.   Where portions of an interior raceway system are exposed to widely different temperatures, as in refrigerating or cold-storage plants, circulation of air from a warmer to a colder section through the raceway shall be prevented.

Where a raceway is used to enclose the lighting and refrigeration branch-circuit conductors within a walk-in chest, for example, the circulation of air from a warmer to a colder section through the raceway would cause condensation within the raceway. This can be prevented by sealing the raceway with a suitable, pliable compound at a conduit body or junction box, usually installed in the raceway before it enters the colder section. Special sealing fittings are not necessary.

(b) Expansion Joints.   Raceways shall be provided with expansion joints where necessary to compensate for thermal expansion and contraction.

300-9. Grounding Metal Enclosures.   Metal raceways, boxes, cabinets, cable armor, and fittings shall be grounded as required in Article 250.

300-10. Electrical Continuity of Metal Raceways and Enclosures.   Metal raceways, cable armor, and other metal enclosures for conductors shall be metallically joined together into a continuous electric conductor, and shall be so connected to all boxes, fittings, and cabinets as to provide effective electrical continuity. Raceways and cable assemblies shall be mechanically secured to boxes, fittings, cabinets, and other enclosures, except as provided for nonmetallic boxes in Section 370-7(c).

Metal raceways, metal armor or sheaths of cable, metal outlet or junction boxes, and fittings, such as connectors, couplings, locknuts, bushings, etc., must form an effective path to ground at low resistance, to conduct safely any fault current, and facilitate the operation of overcurrent devices protecting the enclosed circuit conductors.

300-11. Secured in Place.   Raceways, cable assemblies, boxes, cabinets, and fittings shall be securely fastened in place, unless otherwise provided for specific purposes elsewhere in this Code.

See Article 318 for cable trays.

300-12. Mechanical Continuity — Raceways and Cables.   Metal or nonmetallic raceways, cable armors, and cable sheaths shall be continuous between cabinets, boxes, fittings, or other enclosures or outlets.

300-13. Mechanical and Electrical Continuity — Conductors.

(a) General.   Conductors shall be continuous between outlets, devices, etc., and there shall be no splice or tap within a raceway itself.

Exception No. 1: As provided in Section 374-8 for auxiliary gutters.

Exception No. 2: As provided in Section 362-6 for wireways.

Exception No. 3: As provided in Section 300-15(a), Exception No. 1 for boxes or fittings.

Exception No. 4: As provided in Section 352-7 for metal surface raceways.

Splices or taps are prohibited within a raceway, unless the raceways are equipped with hinged or removable covers according to the four Exceptions.

(b) Device Removal.   In multiwire circuits the continuity of a grounded conductor shall not be dependent upon device connections, such as lampholders, receptacles, etc., where the removal of such devices would interrupt the continuity.

Grounded (neutral) conductors of multiwire branch circuits supplying receptacles, lampholders, etc., are not to be dependent upon terminal connections for continuity. For such installations (3- or 4-wire circuits), a splice is made and a jumper is connected to the terminal unless "looped" (see comments to Section 300-14); that is, a receptacle or lampholder could be replaced without interrupting the continuity of energized downstream line-to-neutral loads. Opening the neutral could cause unbalanced voltages and a considerably higher voltage would be impressed on one part of a multiwire branch circuit, especially if the downstream line-to-neutral loads are appreciably unbalanced. This requirement does not apply to individual 2-wire circuits or to other circuits that do not contain a grounded neutral conductor. See Figure 370-1.

300-14. Length of Free Conductors at Outlets and Switch Points.   At least 6 inches (152 mm) of free conductor shall be left at each outlet and switch point for splices or the connection of fixtures or devices.

Exception: Conductors that are not spliced or terminated at the outlet or switch point.

A conductor looping through an outlet box and intended for connection to receptacles, switches, lampholders, etc., requires enough slack so that terminal connections may be made easily.

Conductors running through a box should have sufficient slack to prevent physical injury from the insertion of devices or from the use of fixture studs, hickeys, or other fixture supports within the box.

300-15. Boxes or Fittings — Where Required.

(a) Box or Fitting.   A box or fitting shall be installed at each conductor splice connection point, outlet, switch point, junction point, or pull point for the connection of conduit, electrical metallic tubing, surface raceway, or other raceways.

Exception No. 1: A box or fitting shall not be required for a conductor splice connection in surface raceways, wireways, header-ducts, multi-outlet assemblies, auxiliary gutters, cable trays, and conduit bodies having removable covers which are accessible after installation.

Conduit bodies (Types "T," "L," etc.) are a part of the conduit or tubing system and should not contain more conductors than permitted for the raceway. Conduit bodies having provisions for less than three conduit entries are not to contain splices, taps, or devices unless they are durably and legibly marked with their cubic inch capacity and the maximum number of conductors that are permitted to be enclosed is to be computed as per Table 370-6(b). See Section 370-6(b) and (c).

For the use of conductors No. 4 or larger, see Section 370-18(a).

Exception No. 2: As permitted in Section 410-31 where a fixture is used as a raceway.

(b) Box Only.   A box shall be installed at each conductor splice connection point, outlet, switch point, junction point, or pull point for the connection of Type AC cable, Type MC cable, mineral-insulated, metal-sheathed cable, nonmetallic-sheathed cable, or other cables, at the connection point between any such cable system and a raceway system and at each outlet and switch point for concealed knob-and-tube wiring.

Exception No. 1: As permitted by Section 336-11 for insulated outlet devices supplied by nonmetallic-sheathed cable.

Exception No. 2: As permitted by Section 410-62 for rosettes.

Exception No. 3: Where accessible fittings are used for straight-through splices in mineral-insulated, metal-sheathed cable.

Exception No. 4: Where cables enter or exit from conduit or tubing which is used to provide cable support or protection against physical damage.

Exception No. 4 was inserted in the *Code* to permit conduit or tubing to be used as support and protection against physical damage without terminating in a box at such places as boilers or furnaces where nonmetallic-sheathed cables would dangle in free air for 5 or 6 ft. This Exception also permits conduit or tubing to be used as physical protection for underground cables exiting from buildings or outdoors on poles, without a box being required on the end of the conduit.

Exception No. 5: A device having brackets that securely fasten the device to a structural member in walls or ceilings of conventional on-site frame construction for use with nonmetallic-sheathed cable shall be permitted without a separate box.

Exception No. 5 applies to a device with an integral enclosure (boxless device) and indicates the mounting requirements for such devices.

See Sections 336-5, Exception No. 2; 545-10; 550-8(j); and 551-14(e), Exception No. 1.

Exception No. 6: Where metallic manufactured wiring systems are used.

See Article 604 — Manufactured Wiring Systems.

300-16. Raceway or Cable to Open or Concealed Wiring.

(a) Box or Fitting. A box or terminal fitting having a separately bushed hole for each conductor shall be used wherever a change is made from conduit, electrical metallic tubing, nonmetallic-sheathed cable, Type AC cable, Type MC cable, or mineral-insulated, metal-sheathed cable and surface raceway wiring to open wiring or to concealed knob-and-tube wiring. A fitting used for this purpose shall contain no taps or splices and shall not be used at fixture outlets.

(b) Bushing. A bushing shall be permitted in lieu of a box or terminal fitting at the end of a conduit or electrical metallic tubing where the raceway terminates behind an open (unenclosed) switchboard or at an unenclosed control and similar equipment. The bushing shall be of the insulating type for other than lead-sheathed conductors.

300-17. Number and Size of Conductors in Raceway.   The number and size of conductors in any raceway shall not be more than will permit dissipation of the heat and ready installation or withdrawal of the conductors without damage to the conductors or to their insulation.

See the following sections of this Code: conduit, 345-7 and 346-6; electrical metallic tubing, 348-6; rigid nonmetallic conduit, 347-11; flexible metallic tubing, 349-12; flexible metal conduit, 350-3; liquidtight flexible metal conduit, 351-6; liquidtight nonmetallic flexible conduit, 351-25; surface raceways, 352-4 and 352-25; underfloor raceways, 354-5; cellular metal floor raceways, 356-5; cellular concrete floor raceways, 358-9; wireways, 362-5; auxiliary gutters, 374-5; fixture wire, 402-7; theaters, 520-5; signs, 600-21(d); elevators, 620-33; sound recording, 640-3 and 640-4; Class 1, Class 2, and Class 3 circuits, Article 725; and fire protective signaling circuits, Article 760.

300-18. Inserting Conductors in Raceways.

(a) Installation. Raceways shall first be installed as a complete raceway system without conductors.

Exception: Exposed raceways having a removable cover or capping.

(b) Pull Wires.   Pull wires, if to be used, shall not be installed until the raceway system is in place.

(c) Lubricants.   Cleaning agents or materials used as lubricants that have a deleterious effect on conductor coverings shall not be used.

300-19. Supporting Conductors in Vertical Raceways.

(a) Spacing Intervals — Maximum.   Conductors in vertical raceways shall be supported. One cable support shall be provided at the top of the vertical raceway or as close to the top as practical, plus a support for each additional interval of spacing as specified in Table 300-19(a).

Exception No. 1: If the total vertical riser is less than 25 percent of the spacing specified in Table 300-19(a), no cable support shall be required.

Exception No. 2: Steel wire armor cable shall be supported at the top of the riser with a cable support that clamps the steel wire armor. A safety device shall be permitted at the lower end of the riser to hold the cable in the event there is slippage of the cable in the wire armored cable support. Additional wedge-type supports shall be permitted to relieve the strain on the equipment terminals caused by expansion of the cable under load.

Table 300-19(a).   Spacings for Conductor Supports

	Conductors	
	Aluminum or Copper-Clad Aluminum	Copper
No. 18 thru No. 8.............................Not greater than ....100 feet	100 feet	100 feet
No. 6 thru No. 0.............................. " " " ....200 feet	100 feet	
No. 00 thru No. 0000 .... " " " ....180 feet	80 feet	
211,601 CM thru 350,000 CM .... " " " ....135 feet	60 feet	
350,001 CM thru 500,000 CM .... " " " ....120 feet	50 feet	
500,001 CM thru 750,000 CM .... " " " .... 95 feet	40 feet	
Above 750,000 CM......................... " " " .... 85 feet	35 feet	

For SI units: one foot = 0.3048 meter.

(b) Support Methods.   One of the following methods of support shall be used:

(1) By clamping devices constructed of or employing insulating wedges inserted in the ends of the conduits. Where clamping of insulation does not adequately support the cable, the conductor also shall be clamped.

(2) By inserting boxes at the required intervals in which insulating supports are installed and secured in a satisfactory manner to withstand the weight of the conductors attached thereto, the boxes being provided with covers.

(3) In junction boxes, by deflecting the cables not less than 90 degrees and carrying them horizontally to a distance not less than twice the diameter of the cable, the cables being carried on two or more insulating supports, and additionally secured thereto by tie wires if desired. When this method is used, cables shall be supported at intervals not greater than 20 percent of those mentioned in the preceding tabulation.

(4) By a method of equal effectiveness.

Conductors in long vertical runs are to be supported to prevent the weight of the conductors from damaging the insulation where leaving the conduit and to prevent the conductors from being pulled out of the terminals. Supports like those shown in Figures 300-6 and 300-7 may be used in addition to many other types of grips manufactured for this purpose.

Example: A vertical raceway contains 1/0 copper conductors. One cable support near the top of the run would be required if the vertical run is from 25 to 100 ft. If the vertical run in this example is less than 25 ft, no cable supports are required.

Figure 300-6. A support bushing located at the top of a vertical conduit at a cabinet or pull box, which prevents the weight of the conductors from damaging the insulation or placing a strain on termination points. (*O.Z./Gedney Co.*)

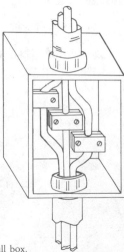

Figure 300-7. Vertical conductors supported by cleats in a pull box.

300-20. Induced Currents in Metal Enclosures or Metal Raceways.

(a) Conductors Grouped Together.   Where conductors carrying alternating current are installed in metal enclosures or metal raceways, they shall be so arranged as to avoid heating the surrounding metal by induction. To accomplish this, all phase conductors and, where used, the neutral and all equipment grounding conductors shall be grouped together.

See comments following Section 300-5(i).

Exception No. 1: As permitted in Section 250-50, Exception for equipment grounding connections.

Exception No. 2: As permitted in Section 427-47 for skin effect heating.

By its very nature, skin effect heating uses induced currents in metal raceways to heat pipelines. Importantly, the temperature of the raceway is known and bears a definite relationship to the pipeline temperature and the overall thermal parameters of the system.

(b) Individual Conductors.   When a single conductor of a circuit passes through metal with magnetic properties the inductive effect shall be minimized by: (1) cutting slots in the metal between the individual holes through which the individual conductors pass, or (2) passing all the conductors in the circuit through an insulating wall sufficiently large for all of the conductors of the circuit.

Exception: In the case of circuits supplying vacuum or electric-discharge lighting systems or signs, or X-ray apparatus, the currents carried by the conductors are so small that the inductive heating effect can be ignored where these conductors are placed in metal enclosures or pass through metal.

Because aluminum is not a magnetic metal, there will be no heating due to hysteresis; however, induced currents will be present. They will not be of sufficient magnitude to require grouping of conductors or special treatment in passing conductors through aluminum wall sections.

300-21. Spread of Fire or Products of Combustion.   Electrical installations in hollow spaces, vertical shafts, and ventilation or air-handling ducts shall be so made that the possible spread of fire or products of combustion will not be substantially increased. Openings around electrical penetrations through fire resistance rated walls, partitions, floors, or ceilings shall be firestopped using approved methods.

It is the intent of this section that electrical equipment, raceways, cables, etc., be installed in such a manner that they will not contribute to the spread of fire or the products of combustion through the specified component parts of a building. See Figure 300-8.

Figure 300-8. Fire seals used to maintain the integrity of fire-rated walls, floors, partitions, or ceilings as required by Section 300-21. (O.Z./ Gedney Co.)

300-22. Wiring in Ducts, Plenums, and Other Air-Handling Spaces.   The provisions of this section apply to the installation and uses of electric wiring and equipment in ducts, plenums, and other air-handling spaces.

See Article 424, Part F for Electric Duct Heaters.

(a) Ducts for Dust, Loose Stock, or Vapor Removal.   No wiring systems of any type shall be installed in ducts used to transport dust, loose stock, or flammable vapors. No wiring system of any type shall be installed in any duct, or shaft containing only such ducts, used for vapor removal or for ventilation of commercial-type cooking equipment.

(b) Ducts or Plenums Used for Environmental Air.   Only wiring methods consisting of mineral-insulated, metal-sheathed cable, Type MC cable employing a smooth or corrugated impervious metal sheath without an overall nonmetallic covering, electrical metallic tubing, flexible metallic tubing, intermediate metal conduit, or rigid metal conduit shall be installed in ducts or plenums used for environmental air. Flexible metal conduit and liquidtight flexible metal conduit shall be permitted, in lengths not to exceed 4 feet (1.22 m), to connect physically adjustable equipment and devices permitted to be in these ducts and plenum chambers. The connectors used with flexible metal conduit shall effectively close any openings in the connection. Equipment and devices shall be permitted within such ducts or plenum chambers only if necessary for their direct action upon, or sensing of, the contained air. Where equipment or devices are installed and illumination is necessary to facilitate maintenance and repair, enclosed gasketed-type fixtures shall be permitted.

The above applies to ducts and plenums specifically fabricated to transport environmental air.

The intent of this section is to limit the materials that would contribute smoke and products of combustion during a fire in an area that handles environmental air, and, in the case of Paragraph (b), to provide an effective barrier against the excursion of products of combustion into the duct or plenum.

Paragraph (b) applies to ducts and plenums specifically constructed to transport environmental air, such as sheet metal ducts. Equipment and devices such as lighting fixtures and motors are not normally permitted in ducts or plenums and, for this reason, Paragraph (b) wiring methods are different from the wiring methods permitted in Paragraph (c).

(c) Other Space Used for Environmental Air.   Only mineral-insulated, metal-sheathed cable, Type MC cable without an overall nonmetallic covering, and Type AC cable, and other factory-assembled multiconductor control or power cable which is specifically listed for the use shall be used for wiring in systems installed in other space used for environmental air. Other type cables and conductors shall be installed in electrical metallic tubing, flexible metallic tubing, intermediate metal conduit, rigid metal conduit, metal surface raceway or wireway with metal covers where accessible, or flexible metal conduit. Electric equipment that is permitted within a building concealed space shall be permitted to be installed in other space used for environmental air if the associated wiring material and fixtures are suitable for the ambient temperature.

The above applies to other spaces such as spaces over hung ceilings which are used for environmental air-handling purposes.

Paragraph (c) applies to other spaces used to transport environmental air that are not specifically manufactured as a duct or plenum, such as hung ceilings. Most hung ceilings are intended to transport return air. However, some are also used for supply air, but this use is not nearly so common as those used for return air. Due to the fact that spaces above "hung-type" ceilings contain lighting fixtures, motors, and other equipment and devices, the wiring methods permitted in Paragraph (c) are different from those contained in Paragraph (b).

Exception No. 1: Liquidtight flexible metal conduit in single lengths not exceeding 6 feet (1.83 m).

Exception No. 2: Integral fan systems specifically identified for such use.

Exception No. 3: This section does not include habitable rooms or areas of buildings, the prime purpose of which is not air handling.

Exception No. 3 applies to rooms and hallways being used as portions of air-return systems in buildings. It is not intended that the limitation of wiring methods be applied to these parts of a building.

Exception No. 4: Listed prefabricated cable assemblies of metallic manufactured wiring systems without nonmetallic sheath shall be permitted where listed for this use.

Note that the cable assembly must be listed for use in space used for environmental air. See Article 604.

Exception No. 5: This section does not include the joist or stud spaces in dwelling units when wiring or equipment passes through such spaces perpendicular to the long dimension of such spaces.

See Figure 300-9.

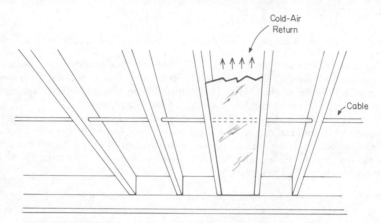

Figure 300-9. Illustrated is a cable passing through joist spaces of a dwelling unit. It is common to enclose a joist space with a sheet metal covering and use this space as a cold-air return for a forced warm-air central heating system.

(d) Data Processing Systems.   Electric wiring in air-handling areas beneath raised floors for data processing systems shall comply with Article 645.

B. Requirements for Over 600 Volts, Nominal

300-31. Covers Required.   Suitable covers shall be installed on all boxes, fittings, and similar enclosures to prevent accidental contact with energized parts or physical damage to parts or insulation.

300-32. Conductors of Different Systems.   Conductors of high-voltage and low-voltage systems shall not occupy the same wiring enclosure or pull and junction boxes.

Exception No. 1: In motors, switchgear and control assemblies and similar equipment.

Exception No. 2: In manholes, if low-voltage conductors are separated from high-voltage conductors.

300-33. Inserting Conductors in Raceways.   Raceways, except those used for exposed work and having a removable cover, shall first be installed as a complete raceway system without the conductors. Pull wires, if used, shall not be installed until the raceway system is in place. Approved pulling compound may be used as a lubricant in inserting conductors in raceways. Cleaning agents or lubricants having a deleterious effect on conductor coverings shall not be used.

300-34. Conductor Bending Radius.   The conductor shall not be bent to a radius less than eight times the overall diameter for nonshielded conductors or twelve times the diameter for shielded or lead-covered conductors during or after installation.

300-35. Protection Against Induction Heating. Metallic raceways and associated conductors shall be so arranged as to avoid heating of the raceway by induction.

300-36. Grounding. Wiring and equipment installations shall be grounded in accordance with the applicable provisions of Article 250.

ARTICLE 305 — TEMPORARY WIRING

Contents

305-1. Scope. The provisions of this article apply to temporary electrical power and lighting wiring methods which may be of a class less than would be required for a permanent installation. Except as specifically modified in this article, all other requirements of this Code for permanent wiring shall apply to temporary wiring installations.

The 1981 *NEC* clarifies the intent of the article and consolidates duplicated provisions for temporary wiring circuits rated above or below 600 V, nominal.

(a) During the Period of Construction. Temporary electrical power and lighting installations shall be permitted during the period of construction, remodeling, maintenance, repair, or demolition of buildings, structures, equipment, or similar activities.

Where temporary wiring is used for construction, remodeling, maintenance, repair, or demolition of buildings, ground-fault circuit-interrupters or assured equipment grounding procedures are to be used on all 125-V, single-phase, 15- and 20-A receptacle outlets where portable tools and equipment are used. See Section 210-8(b).

(b) 90 Days. Temporary electrical power and lighting installations shall be permitted for a period not to exceed 90 days for Christmas decorative lighting, carnivals, and similar purposes.

Note that the temporary wiring applications of Paragraphs (a) and (c) are not restricted to 90 days.

(c) Emergencies and Tests. Temporary electrical power and lighting installations shall be permitted during emergencies and for tests, experiments, and developmental work.

(d) Removal. Temporary wiring shall be removed immediately upon completion of construction or purpose for which the wiring was installed.

305-2. General.

(a) Services. Services shall be installed in conformance with Article 230.

(b) Feeders. Feeders shall be protected as provided in Article 240. They shall originate in an approved distribution center. The conductors shall be permitted within multiconductor cord or cable assemblies or where not subject to physical damage; they shall be permitted to be run as open conductors on insulators not more than 10 feet (3.05 m) apart.

(c) Branch Circuits.   All branch circuits shall originate in an approved power outlet or panelboard. Conductors shall be permitted within multiconductor cord or cable assemblies or as open conductors. All conductors shall be protected by overcurrent devices at their rated ampacity. Runs of open conductors shall be located where the conductors will not be subject to physical damage, and the conductors shall be fastened at intervals not exceeding 10 feet (3.05 m). No branch-circuit conductors shall be laid on the floor. Each branch circuit that supplies receptacles or fixed equipment shall contain a separate equipment grounding conductor when run as open conductors.

> The 1981 *NEC* deleted the requirement that temporary wiring be "fastened at ceiling height." Many temporary branch circuits are needed in locations where there is no ceiling or for other locations, such as high-bay structures.
> The basic requirement for safety is that temporary wiring be required to be located where it will not be subject to physical damage.
> Note that extension cords are permitted to be laid on the floor.

(d) Receptacles.   All receptacles shall be of the grounding type. Unless installed in a complete metallic raceway all branch circuits shall contain a separate equipment grounding conductor and all receptacles shall be electrically connected to the grounding conductor. Receptacles on construction sites shall not be installed on branch circuits which supply temporary lighting. Receptacles shall not be connected to the same ungrounded conductor of multiwire circuits which supply temporary lighting.

> The intent of this paragraph is to require installations so that the operation of a fuse or circuit breaker or a ground-fault circuit-interrupter due to a fault or overload of equipment will not de-energize the lighting circuit.

See Section 210-8 for receptacles installed on construction sites.

(e) Disconnecting Means.   Suitable disconnecting switches or plug connectors shall be installed to permit the disconnection of all ungrounded conductors of each temporary circuit.

(f) Lamp Protection.   All lamps for general illumination shall be protected from accidental

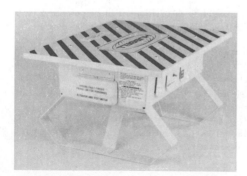

Figure 305-1. Temporary power outlet units commonly used on construction sites with a variety of configurations. Some are available with ground-fault interrupter protection. (*Hubbell*)

Figure 305-2. Nuisance tripping of ground-fault interrupter protective devices by wet or damp weather conditions can be avoided by using watertight plugs and connectors. (*Hubbell*)

contact or breakage. Protection shall be provided by elevation of at least 7 feet (2.13 m) from normal working surface or by a suitable fixture or lampholder with a guard.

Brass shell, paper-lined sockets, or other metal-cased sockets shall not be used unless the shell is grounded.

(g) Splices.   On construction sites a box shall not be required for splices or junction connections where the circuit conductors are multiconductor cord or cable assemblies or open conductors. See Sections 110-14(b) and 400-9. A box shall be used wherever a change is made to a raceway system or a cable system which is metal clad or metal sheathed.

(h) Protection from Accidental Damage.   Flexible cords and cables shall be protected from accidental damage. Sharp corners and projections shall be avoided. When passing through doorways or other pinch points, protection shall be provided to avoid damage.

> Note that unlike Section 400-8, Section 305-2(h) permits flexible cords and cables, because of the nature of their use, to pass through doorways.

305-3. Grounding.   All grounding shall conform with Article 250.

305-5. Guarding.   For temporary wiring over 600 volts, nominal, suitable fencing, barriers, or other effective means shall be provided to prevent access of other than authorized and qualified personnel.

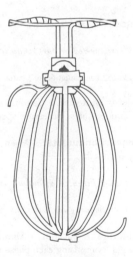

Figure 305-3. Temporary lighting can be supplied by factory-assembled lighting strings or by field-assembled units such as the type illustrated.

ARTICLE 310 — CONDUCTORS FOR GENERAL WIRING

Contents

310-1. Scope. This article covers general requirements for conductors and their type designations, insulations, markings, mechanical strengths, ampacity ratings, and uses. These requirements do not apply to conductors that form an integral part of equipment, such as motors, motor controllers, and similar equipment, or to conductors specifically provided for elsewhere in this Code.

The 1981 *NEC* revised Article 310 for editorial clarification to integrate the information on "over 600-V" conductors with that of 600-V conductors, to revise certain ampacities in Tables 310-16 and 310-17, to clarify Notes 3, 8, 10, and 11 of those tables and to add an explanatory note to Section 310-10.

For flexible cords and cables, see Article 400. For fixture wires, see Article 402.

310-2. Conductors.

(a) Insulated.   Conductors shall be insulated.

Exception: Where covered or bare conductors are specifically permitted elsewhere in this Code.

See Section 250-152 for insulation of neutral conductors of a solidly grounded high-voltage system.

(b) Conductor Material.   Conductors in this article shall be of aluminum, copper-clad aluminum, or copper unless otherwise specified.

310-3. Stranded Conductors.   Where installed in raceways, conductors of size No. 8 and larger shall be stranded.

Exception No. 1: When used as busbars or in mineral-insulated, metal-sheathed cable.

Exception No. 2: Bonding conductors as required in Sections 680-20(b)(1) and 680-22(b).

310-4. Conductors in Parallel.   Aluminum, copper-clad aluminum, or copper conductors of size 1/0 and larger, comprising each phase or neutral, shall be permitted to be connected in parallel (electrically joined at both ends to form a single conductor) only if all of the following conditions are met: all of the parallel conductors shall be of the same length, of the same conductor material, same circular-mil area, same insulation type, and terminated in the same manner. Where run in separate raceways or cables, the raceways or cables shall have the same physical characteristics.

Exception No. 1: As permitted in Section 620-12(a)(1), Exception.

Exception No. 2: Conductors in sizes smaller than No. 1/0 AWG shall be permitted to be run in parallel to supply control power to indicating instruments, contactors, relays, solenoids, and similar control devices provided: (a) they are contained within the same raceway or cable; (b) the ampacity of each individual conductor is sufficient to carry the entire load current shared by the parallel conductors; and (c) the overcurrent protection is such that the ampacity of each individual conductor will not be exceeded if one or more of the parallel conductors become inadvertently disconnected.

For example, in control work it is sometimes found necessary to reduce cable capacitance effect or voltage drop over long lengths of wire. If a No. 14 AWG conductor is more than enough to carry the load, yet two No. 14 conductors in parallel will reduce the voltage drop to acceptable limits, this should be permissible providing the safeguards indicated in Exception No. 2 are taken.

When metallic equipment grounding conductors are used with conductors in parallel, they shall comply with the requirements of this section except that they shall be sized as per Section 250-95.

When conductors are used in parallel, space in enclosures shall be given consideration (see Articles 370 and 373).

Conductors installed in parallel shall be subject to ampacity reduction factors as required in Note 8 to Tables 310-16 through 310-19.

This section permits a practical means of installing large capacity conductors for feeders or services. The paralleling of two or more conductors in place of one large conductor relies on a number of factors to ensure equal division of current; therefore, several conditions must be satisfied so as not to overload any of the individual paralleled conductors. Other than as permitted in Section 250-95 and the Exceptions to Section 310-4, there does not appear to be any practical need to parallel conductors smaller than size 1/0.

To avoid excessive voltage drop and also to ensure equal division of current, it is essential that separate phase conductors be located close together and that each phase conductor and the neutral and grounding conductors, if used, be grouped together in each conduit.

The impedance of a circuit in an aluminum raceway will be different from the impedance of the same circuit in a steel raceway, hence it is required that separate raceways have the same physical characteristics. See Section 300-20.

Note that all of the conductors are to be of the same conductor material, i.e., if twelve conductors are to be paralleled for a 3-phase, 4-wire, 480Y/277 ac circuit, four conductors could be installed in each of three raceways, and the *Code* intends that "all" twelve conductors be of copper or all twelve conductors be of aluminum, but not a mixture of, for example, eight copper and four aluminum. Also, it is intended that the three raceways have the same physical characteristics, i.e., three rigid metal conduits or three IMC conduits or three EMTs or three nonmetallic conduits, and, again, not a mixture of, for example, two rigid metal conduits and one EMT.

It is neither economical nor practical to use conductors larger than 1,000,000 CM in raceways unless the conductor size is governed by voltage drop. The ampacity of larger sizes would increase very little in proportion to the increase in the size of the conductor. Therefore, when the size of a conductor increases 50 percent, for example, from 1,000,000 to 1,500,000 CM, a Type THW conductor increases 80 A (less than 15 percent). An increase from 1,000,000 to 2,000,000 CM (100 percent increase) causes an increase of only 120 A (approximately 20 percent). Generally speaking, in situations that call for the use of single conductors larger than 500,000 CM, determining the cost of the entire installation using single conductors rather than two (or more) conductors in parallel is beneficial.

310-5. Minimum Size of Conductors.   The minimum size of conductors shall be as given in Table 310-5.

Section 310-5 was revised to add minimum sizes for conductors for cables rated over 600 V. The added information correlates with present Tables 310-32 through 310-37.

Table 310-5

Voltage Rating of Conductor—Volts	Minimum Conductor Size—AWG
Up to 2000	14 Copper
	12 Aluminum or
	Copper-Clad Aluminum
2001 to 5000	8
5001 to 8000	6
8001 to 15000	2 100% Insulation Level*
	1 133% Insulation Level*
15001 to 28000	1
28001 to 35000	1/0

* See Table 310-34, Definitions.

Exception No. 1: For flexible cords as permitted by Section 400-12.

Exception No. 2: For fixture wire as permitted by Section 410-24.

Exception No. 3: For fractional horsepower motors as permitted by Section 430-22.

Exception No. 4: For cranes and hoists as permitted by Section 610-14.

Exception No. 5: For elevator control and signaling circuits as permitted by Section 620-12.

Exception No. 6: For Class 1, Class 2, and Class 3 circuits as permitted by Sections 725-16, 725-37, and 725-40.

Exception No. 7: For fire protective signaling circuits as permitted by Sections 760-16, 760-27, and 760-30.

Exception No. 8: For 2001-5000 volt for Types AVA, AVB, and AVL cables, the minimum conductor size is No. 14 AWG copper or No. 12 AWG aluminum or copper-clad aluminum.

Exception No. 9: For Type V cables, the minimum conductor sizes are: No. 12 AWG for 2000-volt rating, No. 10 AWG for 3000-volt rating, and No. 8 AWG for 4000-volt rating.

Exception No. 10: For motor control circuits as permitted by Section 430-72.

This Exception was added to correlate the requirements for motor control circuits and control circuit protection. See Section 430-72(a) and (b).

310-6. Shielding. Solid dielectric insulated conductors operated above 2000 volts in permanent installations shall have ozone-resistant insulation and shall be shielded. Shielding shall be for the purpose of confining the voltage stresses to the insulation.

Section 310-6 integrates higher voltage conductors. Text clarifies the intent and correlates with Section 710-3(b).

Exception: Nonshielded insulated conductors listed by a qualified testing laboratory shall be permitted for use up to 8000 volts under the following conditions:

a. Conductors shall have insulation resistant to electric discharge and surface tracking, or the insulated conductor(s) shall be covered with a material resistant to ozone, electric discharge, and surface tracking.

b. Where used in wet locations the insulated conductor(s) shall have an overall nonmetallic jacket or a continuous metallic sheath.

c. Where operated at 5001 to 8000 volts, the insulated conductor(s) shall have a nonmetallic jacket over the insulation. The insulation shall have a specific inductive capacity no greater than 3.6 and the jacket shall have a specific inductive capacity no greater than 10 and no less than 6.

d. Insulation and jacket thicknesses shall be in accordance with Table 310-33.

Permanently installed solid dielectric insulated conductors operated above 2,000 V are to have ozone-resistant insulation and are to be shielded (note Exception).

Shielding is the application of a metallic or nonmetallic semiconducting tape (which is grounded during installation) around the conductor surface and which will prevent corona from forming and will reduce high-voltage stresses. Corona is a faint glow adjacent to the surface of the electrical conductor at high voltage. If there are high-voltage stresses and a charging current flowing between the conductor and ground (usually due to moisture), the surrounding atmosphere is ionized and ozone (which is generated by an electric discharge in ordinary oxygen or air) is formed, which will attack the conductor jacket and insulation and may eventually break them down. The (grounded) shield is at ground potential; therefore, no voltage above ground is present on the jacket outside of the shield, thus preventing a discharge from the jacket and the subsequent formation of ozone.

Figure 310-1 shows a three-conductor cable of the shielded type.

Figure 310-2 illustrates a stress relief cone for an indoor cable terminator.

Figure 310-3 illustrates a stress cone on a single-conductor shielded cable terminating inside a pothead. Notice that a clamping ring provides a grounding connection between the copper shielding tape and shield to the metallic base of the pothead.

Specialized training and close adherence to manufacturer's instructions are absolutely essential for high-voltage cable installations.

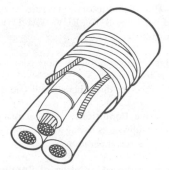

Figure 310-1. Three-conductor cable of the shielded type.

310-7. Direct Burial Conductors. Cables rated above 2000 volts shall be shielded. Conductors used for direct burial applications shall be of a type identified for such use.

Exception: Nonshielded multiconductor cables rated 2001-5000 volts shall be permitted if the cable has an overall metallic sheath or armor.

The metallic shield, sheath or armor shall be grounded through an effective grounding path meeting the requirements of Section 250-51.

See Sections 300-5 and 710-3(b).

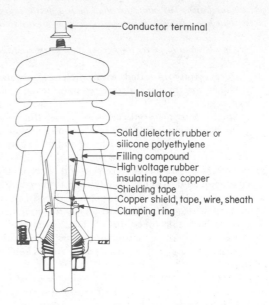

Conductor terminal

Insulator

Solid dielectric rubber or
silicone polyethylene
Filling compound
High voltage rubber
insulating tape copper
Shielding tape
Copper shield, tape, wire, sheath
Clamping ring

Figure 310-2. One-piece, premolded stress relief cone is for indoor cable terminations of up to 35 kV phase-to-phase. (*ITT Blackburn Co.*)

Figure 310-3. A stress cone on a single-conductor shielded cable terminating inside a pothead.

310-8. Wet Locations.

(a) Insulated Conductors. Insulated conductors used in wet locations shall be (1) lead-covered; (2) Types RHW, RUW, TW, THW, THWN, XHHW; or (3) of a type listed for use in wet locations.

(b) Cables. Cables of one or more conductors used in wet locations shall be of a type listed for use in wet locations.

Conductors used for direct burial applications shall be of a type listed for such use.

310-9. Corrosive Conditions. Conductors exposed to oils, greases, vapors, gases, fumes, liquids, or other substances having a deleterious effect upon the conductor or insulation shall be of a type suitable for the application.

310-10. Temperature Limitation of Conductors. No conductor shall be used in such a manner that its operating temperature will exceed that designated for the type of insulated conductor involved. In no case shall conductors be associated together in such a way with respect to type of circuit, the wiring method employed, or the number of conductors that the limiting temperature of any conductor is exceeded.

Most terminations are designed only for 60°C (140°F) or 75°C (167°F) maximum temperatures; therefore, the higher rated ampacities for conductors of 90°C (194°F), 110°C (230°F), etc., cannot be utilized unless the terminations have comparable ratings.

Tables 310-16 through 310-19 have correction factor tables for ambient temperatures that exceed 30°C (86°F). To assign the proper allowable load current to a conductor in an ambient above 30°C (86°F), the appropriate correction factors must be used to determine the maximum allowable load permitted on any given conductor.

Example: A No. 2 TW copper conductor is to be installed in a raceway in an ambient temperature of 50°C (122°F). According to Table 310-16, the ampacity of the conductor is 95 A which is multiplied by 0.58 (taken from the correction factors at the bottom of the table); thus the maximum allowable load current of the No. 2 conductor is reduced to 55.1 A (95 A x 0.58 = 55.1 A).

If six of these conductors were run in a raceway, Note 8 to the Tables would require the maximum allowable load current to be reduced to 80 percent, which, in this case, would be 55.1 A x 0.8 = 44.08 A. Under these conditions the No. 2 conductor would be suitable for a 40-A circuit.

The basis for determining the ampacities of conductors for Tables 310-16 through 310-19 was the "NEMA Report of Determination of Maximum Permissible Current-Carrying Capacity of Code Insulated Wires and Cables for Building Purposes" dated June 27, 1938.

The temperature rating of a conductor (see Table 310-13) is the maximum temperature, at any location along its length, that the conductor can withstand over a prolonged time period without serious degradation. The principal determinants of operating temperature are (1) the ambient temperature (which may vary along the length as well as from time to time), (2) the heat generated internally by load current flow, and (3) the rate at which the internally generated heat dissipates into the ambient medium (air, earth, etc.). Cognizance must also be taken of adjacent load-carrying conductors which will both raise the temperature of the conductors and partially impede dissipation of heat.

Conductors that have a rating above the anticipated maximum ambient temperature should be chosen. The operating temperature of conductors should be controlled at or below its rating by coordinating conductor size, number of associated conductors, and allowable load current for the particular conductor rating and ambient temperature. Tables 310-17 and 310-19 give ampacities, or allowable load currents, for isolated conductors (not in contact with other conductors). Tables 310-16 and 310-18 give ampacities where up to three conductors are closely associated (in contact). All tabulations are based on a 30°C (86°F) ambient temperature condition and should be corrected for the anticipated ambient using the correction factors at the bottom of the tables. Where more than three conductors are associated together, the additional correction given in Note 8 to the Tables is to be applied.

The temperature rating of a conductor (see Tables 310-13 and 310-31) is the maximum temperature, at any location along its length, that the conductor can withstand over a prolonged time period without serious degradation. Tables 310-16 through 310-19 and 310-39 through 310-54, the correction factors at the bottom of these tables, and the notes to the tables provide guidance for coordinating conductor sizes, types, allowable load currents, ambient temperatures, and number of associated conductors.

The principal determinants of operating temperature are:

1. Ambient temperature. Ambient temperature may vary along the conductor length as well as from time to time.

2. Heat generated internally in the conductor as the result of load current flow.

3. The rate at which generated heat dissipates into the ambient medium. Thermal insulation which covers or surrounds conductors will affect the rate of heat dissipation.

4. Adjacent load-carrying conductors. Adjacent conductors have the dual effect of raising the ambient temperature and impeding heat dissipation.

The Fine Print Note is intended to focus attention to the necessity for derating conductors where high ambient temperatures are encountered and to provide users with helpful information in coordinating ampacities, ambient temperatures, conductor size and number, etc., to assure operation at or below rating.

310-11. Marking.

(a) Required Information.   All conductors and cables shall be marked to indicate the following information, using the applicable method described in (b) below.

(1) The maximum rated voltage for which the conductor was listed.

(2) The proper type letter or letters for the type of wire or cable as specified elsewhere in this article, in Tables 310-13 and 310-31, and in Articles 336, 337, 338, 339, 340, and Section 725-40(b)(3).

(3) The manufacturer's name, trademark, or other distinctive marking by which the organization responsible for the product can be readily identified.

(4) The AWG size or circular-mil area.

(b) Method of Marking.

(1) Surface Marking.   The following conductors and cables shall be durably marked on the surface at intervals not exceeding 24 inches (610 mm):

    (a) Single- and multiconductor rubber- and thermoplastic- insulated wire and cable.
    (b) Nonmetallic-sheathed cable.
    (c) Service-entrance cable.
    (d) Underground feeder and branch-circuit cable.
    (e) Tray cable.
    (f) Irrigation cable.
    (g) Power-limited tray cable

(2) Marker Tape.   Metal-covered multiconductor cables shall employ a marker tape located within the cable and running for its complete length.

Exception No. 1: Mineral-insulated, metal-sheathed cable.

Exception No. 2: Type AC cable.

Exception No. 3: The information required in Section 310-11(a)(1), (2), and (4) above shall be permitted to be durably marked on the outer nonmetallic covering of Type MC or Type PLTC cables at intervals not exceeding 24 inches (610 mm).

Exception No. 4: The information required in Section 310-11(a) shall be permitted to be durably marked on a nonmetallic covering under the metallic sheath of Type PLTC cable at intervals not exceeding 24 inches (610 mm).

Type PLTC cable is permitted to have a metallic sheath or armor over a nonmetallic jacketed cable. A second nonmetallic jacket is optional over the metallic sheath. Exception Nos. 2 and 3 will define the marking requirements for either case.

Included in the group of metal-covered cables are: Type AC cable (Article 333), Type MC cable (Article 334) and lead-sheathed cable.

(3) Tag Marking.   The following conductors and cables shall be marked by means of a printed tag attached to the coil, reel, or carton:

(a) Mineral-insulated, metal-sheathed cable.
(b) Switchboard wires.
(c) Metal-covered, single-conductor cables.
(d) Conductors having outer surface of asbestos.
(e) Type AC cable.

(4) Optional Marking of Wire Size.   For the following multiconductor cables, the information required in (a) (4) above shall be permitted to be marked on the surface of the individual insulated conductors:

(a) Type MC cable.
(b) Tray cable.
(c) Irrigation cable.
(d) Power-limited tray cable.

(c) Suffixes to Designate Number of Conductors.   A type letter or letters used alone shall indicate a single insulated conductor. The following letter suffixes shall indicate the following:

D — for two insulated conductors laid parallel within an outer nonmetallic covering.

M — for an assembly of two or more insulated conductors twisted spirally within an outer nonmetallic covering.

310-12. Conductor Identification.

The 1981 Edition revised Section 310-12 to editorially combine 1978 *NEC* versions of Sections 310-12, 310-13, 310-30 and 310-31, integrating the information to include conductors of all voltages.

(a) Grounded Conductors.   Insulated conductors of No. 6 or smaller, intended for use as grounded conductors of circuits, shall have an outer identification of a white or natural gray color. Multiconductor flat cable No. 4 or larger shall be permitted to employ an external ridge on the grounded conductor.

Exception No. 1: Multiconductor varnished-cloth-insulated cables.

Exception No. 2: Fixture wires as outlined in Article 402.

Exception No. 3: Mineral-insulated, metal-sheathed cable.

Exception No. 4: A conductor identified as required by Section 210-5(a) for branch circuits.

Exception No. 5: Where the conditions of maintenance and supervision assure that only qualified persons will service the installation, grounded conductors in multiconductor cables shall be permitted to be permanently identified at their terminations at the time of installation by a distinctive white marking or other equally effective means.

For aerial cable the identification shall be as above, or by means of a ridge so located on the exterior of the cable as to identify it.

Wires having their outer covering finished to show a white or natural gray color but having colored tracer threads in the braid, identifying the source of manufacture, shall be considered as meeting the provisions of this section.

For identification requirements for conductors larger than No. 6, see Section 200-6.

(b) Equipment Grounding Conductors.   Bare, covered or insulated grounding conductors shall be permitted. Individually covered or insulated grounding conductors shall have a continuous outer finish that is either green, or green with one or more yellow stripes.

Exception No. 1: An insulated conductor larger than No. 6 shall, at the time of installation, be permitted to be permanently identified as a grounding conductor at each end and at every point where the conductor is accessible. Identification shall be accomplished by one of the following means:

a. Stripping the insulation from the entire exposed length;

b. Coloring the exposed insulation green; or

c. Marking the exposed insulation with green colored tape or green colored adhesive labels.

Exception No. 2: Where the conditions of maintenance and supervision assure that only qualified persons will service the installation, an insulated conductor in a multiconductor cable shall, at the time of installation, be permitted to be permanently identified as a grounding conductor at each end and at every point where the conductor is accessible by one of the following means:

a. Stripping the insulation from the entire exposed length;

b. Coloring the exposed insulation green; or

c. Marking the exposed insulation with green tape or green colored adhesive labels.

(c) Ungrounded Conductors.   Conductors which are intended for use as ungrounded conductors, whether used as single conductors or in multiconductor cables, shall be finished to be clearly distinguishable from grounded and grounding conductors. Ungrounded conductors shall be distinguished by colors other than white, natural gray, or green; or by a combination of color plus distinguishing marking. Distinguishing markings shall also be in a color other than white, natural gray, or green, and shall consist of a stripe or stripes or a regularly spaced series of identical marks. Distinguishing markings shall not conflict in any manner with the surface markings required by Section 310-11(b)(1).

310-13. Conductor Constructions and Applications.   Insulated conductors shall comply with the applicable provisions of one or more of the following: Tables 310-13, 310-31, 310-32, 310-33, 310-34, 310-35, 310-36, and 310-37.

These conductors shall be permitted for use in any of the wiring methods recognized in Chapter 3 and as specified in their respective tables.

Thermoplastic insulation may stiffen at temperatures colder than minus 10°C (plus 14°F), requiring care be exercised during installation at such temperatures. Thermoplastic insulation may also be deformed at normal temperatures where subjected to pressure, requiring care be exercised during installation and at points of support.

Table 310-13 lists the various types of insulated conductors as covered by the requirements of this *Code*. More detailed wire classification information from sizes Nos. 14 through 2,000 MCM may be obtained from standards or directories, such as those published by the Underwriters Laboratories Inc.

Table 310-13 also includes conductor applications and maximum operating temperatures. Some conductors have dual ratings, such as Type XHHW, rated 90°C (194°F) for dry locations and 75°C (167°F) for wet locations, or Type THW, 75°C (167°F) for dry and wet locations and 90°C (194°F) for special applications within electric-discharge lighting equipment. In no case are conductors to be associated together in such a way, with respect to type of circuit, the wiring method employed, or the number of conductors, that the limiting temperature of any conductor is exceeded (see Section 310-10). Most terminals of wiring devices, switches, and panelboards have not been tested for use with conductors whose maximum insulation temperature exceeds 75°C (167°F).

The maximum continuous ampacities for copper, copper-clad aluminum, and aluminum are listed in Tables 310-16 through 310-19 and accompanying Notes 1 through 12.

Receptacles and snap switches rated 20 A or less, not marked "CO/ALR," are for use with copper and copper-clad aluminum conductors only. Devices marked "CO/ALR" are for use with aluminum, copper, and copper-clad aluminum conductors. Screwless pressure terminal connectors of the conductor push-in type are for use only with copper and copper-clad aluminum conductors.

Receptacles rated 30 A or more and not marked "AL-CU" are for use with copper and copper-clad aluminum conductors only. Receptacles rated 30 A or more and marked "AL-CU" are for use with aluminum, copper, and copper-clad aluminum conductors.

Copper-clad aluminum conductors are drawn from a copper clad aluminum rod with the copper metallurgically bonded to an aluminum core. The copper forms a minimum of 10 percent of the cross-sectional area of a solid conductor or each strand of a stranded conductor. See also comments following Section 110-14.

The following table compares the characteristics of copper-clad aluminum with copper and aluminum conductors.

Conductor Characteristics

	Copper	Cu/Al	Aluminum
Density lbs/in^3	0.323	0.121	0.098
Density gm/cm^3	8.91	3.34	2.71
Resistivity ohms/CMF	10.37	16.08	16.78
Resistivity Microhm-CM	1.724	2.673	2.790
Conductivity (IACS%)	100	61-63	61
Weight % Copper	100	26.8	. . . .
Tensile K psi-Hard	65.0	30.0	27.0
Tensile kg/mm^2-Hard	45.7	21.1	19.0
Tensile K psi-Annealed	35.0	17.0	17.0*
Tensile kg/mm^2-Annealed	24.6	12.0	12.0
Specific Gravity	8.91	3.34	2.71

*Semi-annealed

310-14. Aluminum Conductor Material.   Solid aluminum conductors No. 8, 10, and 12 AWG shall be made of an aluminum alloy conductor material.

As the *Code* recognizes CO/ALR devices, this section is to provide proper recognition of approved aluminum alloy conductor material.

310-15. Ampacity.

(a) Applications Covered by Tables.   Ampacities for conductors rated 0-2000 volts shall be as specified in Tables 310-16 through 310-19 and their accompanying notes. The ampacity for Types V, AVA, AVB, and AVL conductors rated 2001-5000 volts shall be the same as for those conductor types rated 0-2000 volts. The ampacities for solid dielectric insulated conductors rated 2001 to 35000 volts shall be as specified in Tables 310-39 through 310-54 and their accompanying notes.

(b) Applications Not Covered by Tables. Ampacities for cable insulations, cable configurations, voltage levels, or thermal resistivities not included in the tables shall be permitted to be calculated, under engineering supervision, by means of the following general formula:

$$I = \sqrt{\frac{TC - (TA + DELTA\ TD)}{RDC\ (1 + YC)\ RCA}}$$

TC = Conductor temperature in degrees C

TA = Ambient temperature in degrees C

DELTA TD = Dielectric loss temperature rise

RDC = DC resistance of conductor at temperature TC

YC = Component ac resistance resulting from skin effect and proximity effect

RCA = Effective thermal resistance between conductor and surrounding ambient.

Table 310-13.   Conductor Application and Insulations

Trade Name	Type Letter	Max. Operating Temp.	Application Provisions	Insulation	AWG or MCM	Thickness of Insulation Mils	Outer Covering
Heat-Resistant Rubber	RH	75°C 167°F	Dry locations.	Heat-Resistant Rubber	**14-12 .... 30 10 .... 45 8-2 .... 60 1-4/0 .... 80 213-500 .... 95 501-1000 .... 110 1001-2000 .... 125 For 601-2000 volts, see Table 310-32.		*Moisture-resistant, flame-retardant, non-metallic covering
Heat-Resistant Rubber	RHH	90°C 194°F	Dry locations.				
Moisture and Heat-Resistant Rubber	RHW	75°C 167°F	Dry and wet locations. For over 2000 volts insulation shall be ozone-resistant.	Moisture and Heat-Resistant Rubber	14-10 .... 45 8-2 .... 60 1-4/0 .... 80 213-500 .... 95 501-1000 .... 110 1001-2000 .... 125 For 601-2000 volts, see Table 310-32.		*Moisture-resistant, flame-retardant, non-metallic covering
Heat-Resistant Latex Rubber	RUH	75°C 167°F	Dry locations.	90% Un-milled, Grainless Rubber	14-10 .... 18 8-2 25		Moisture resistant, flame-retardant, non-metallic covering

* Some rubber insulations do not require an outer covering.
** For 14-12 sizes RHH shall be 45 mils thickness insulation.

Table 310-13 (Continued)

Trade Name	Type Letter	Max. Operating Temp.	Application Provisions	Insulation	AWG or MCM	Thickness of Insulation Mils	Outer Covering
Moisture-Resistant Latex Rubber	RUW	60°C 140°F	Dry and wet locations.	90% Un-milled, Grainless Rubber	14-10 8-2	.18 .25	Moisture-resistant, flame-retardant, non-metallic covering
Thermoplastic	T	60°C 140°F	Dry locations.	Flame-Retardant, Thermoplastic Compound	14-10 8 6-2 1-4/0 213-500 501-1000 1001-2000	30 45 60 80 95 110 125	None
Moisture-Resistant Thermoplastic	TW	60°C 140°F	Dry and wet locations.	Flame-Retardant, Moisture-Resistant Thermoplastic	14-10 8 6-2 1-4/0 213-500 501-1000 1001-2000	30 45 60 80 95 110 125	None
Heat-Resistant Thermoplastic	THHN	90°C 194°F	Dry locations.	Flame-Retardant, Heat-Resistant Thermoplastic	14-12 10 8-6 4-2 1-4/0 250-500 501-1000	15 20 30 40 50 60 70	Nylon jacket or equivalent

Table 310-13 (Continued)

Trade Name	Type Letter	Max. Operating Temperature	Application Provisions	Insulation	(Sizes / Thickness)	Outer Covering
Moisture- and Heat-Resistant Thermoplastic	THW	75°C 167°F 90°C 194°F	Dry and wet locations. Special applications within electric discharge lighting equipment. Limited to 1000 open-circuit volts or less. (Size 14-8 only as permitted in Section 410-31.)	Flame-Retardant, Moisture- and Heat-Resistant Thermoplastic	14-10........45 8-2........60 1-4/0........80 213-500........95 501-1000........110 1001-2000........125	None
Moisture- and Heat-Resistant Thermoplastic	THWN	75°C 167°F	Dry and wet locations.	Flame-Retardant, Moisture- and Heat-Resistant Thermoplastic	14-12........15 10........20 8-6........30 4-2........40 1-4/0........50 250-500........60 501-1000........70	Nylon jacket or equivalent
Moisture- and Heat-Resistant Cross-Linked Synthetic Polymer	XHHW	90°C 194°F 75°C 167°F	Dry locations. Wet locations.	Flame-Retardant Cross-Linked Synthetic Polymer	14-10........30 8-2........45 1-4/0........55 213-500........65 501-1000........80 1001-2000........95	None
Moisture-, Heat- and Oil-Resistant Thermoplastic	MTW	60°C 140°F 90°C 194°F	Machine tool wiring in wet locations as permitted in NFPA Standard No. 79. (See Article 670.) Machine tool wiring in dry locations as permitted in NFPA Standard No. 79. (See Article 670.)	Flame-Retardant, Moisture-, Heat- and Oil-Resistant Thermoplastic	(A) (B) 22-12 30 15 10 30 20 8 45 30 6 60 30 4-2 60 40 1-4/0 80 50 213-500 95 60 501-1000 110 70	(A) None (B) Nylon jacket or equivalent

Table 310-13 (Continued)

Trade Name	Type Letter	Max. Operating Temp.	Application Provisions	Insulation	AWG or MCM	Thickness of Insulation	Mils	Outer Covering
Perfluoro-alkoxy	PFA	90°C 194°F 200°C 392°F	Dry locations. Dry locations — special applications.	Perfluoro-alkoxy	14-10 8-2 1-4/0		20 30 45	None
Perfluoro-alkoxy	PFAH	250°C 482°F	Dry locations only. Only for leads within apparatus or within raceways connected to apparatus. (Nickel or nickel-coated copper only.)	Perfluoro-alkoxy	14-10 8-2 1-4/0		20 30 45	None
Extruded Polytetra-fluoroethylene	TFE	250°C 482°F	Dry locations only. Only for leads within apparatus or within raceways connected to apparatus, or as open wiring. (Nickel or nickel-coated copper only.)	Extruded Polytetra-fluoro-ethylene	14-10 8-2 1-4/0		20 30 45	None
Thermoplastic and Asbestos	TA	90°C 194°F	Switchboard wiring only.	Thermo-plastic and Asbestos	14-8 6-2 1-4/0	Th'pl. 20 30 40	Asb. 20 25 30	Flame-retardant, nonmetallic covering
Thermoplastic and Fibrous Outer Braid	TBS	90°C 194°F	Switchboard wiring only.	Thermo-plastic	14-10 8 6-2 1-4/0		30 45 60 80	Flame-retardant, nonmetallic covering
Synthetic Heat-Resistant	SIS	90°C 194°F	Switchboard wiring only.	Heat-Resistant Rubber	14-10 8 6-2 1-4/0		30 45 60 80	None

Table 310-13 (Continued)

Trade Name	Type	Max. Operating Temperature	Application Provisions	Insulation	Size	Ampacity	Outer Covering
Mineral Insulation (Metal Sheathed)	MI	85°C 185°F 250°C 482°F	Dry and wet locations. For special application.	Magnesium Oxide	16-10 9-4 3-250	36 50 55	Copper
Underground Feeder & Branch-Circuit Cable-Single Conductor. (For Type UF cable employing more than one conductor, see Article 339.)	UF	60°C 140°F 75°C** 167°F	See Article 339	Moisture-Resistant / Moisture- and Heat-Resistant	14-10 8-2 1-4/0	*60 *80 *95	Integral with insulation
Underground Service-Entrance Cable-Single Conductor. (For Type USE cable employing more than one conductor, see Article 338.)	USE	75°C 167°F	See Article 338	Heat- and Moisture-Resistant	12-10 8-2 1-4/0 213-500 501-1000 1001-2000	45 60 **80 ***95 110 125	Moisture-resistant nonmetallic covering [See 338-1 (2).]

* Includes integral jacket.

** For ampacity limitation, see Section 339-1(a).

*** Insulation thickness shall be permitted to be 80 mils for listed Type USE conductors that have been subjected to special investigations.

The nonmetallic covering over individual rubber-covered conductors of aluminum-sheathed cable and of lead-sheathed or multiconductor cable shall not be required to be flame retardant. For Type MC cable, see Section 334-20. For nonmetallic-sheathed cable, see Section 336-2. For Type UF cable, see Section 339-1.

Table 310-13 (Continued)

Trade Name	Type Letter	Max. Operating Temp.	Application Provisions	Insulation	AWG or MCM	Thickness of Insulation Mils	Outer Covering
Silicone-Asbestos	SA	90°C 194°F	Dry locations.	Silicone Rubber	14-10	45	Asbestos or glass
					8-2	60	
		125°C 257°F	For special application.		1-4/0	80	
					213-500	95	
					501-1000	110	
					1001-2000	125	
Fluorinated Ethylene Propylene	FEP or FEPB	90°C 194°F	Dry locations.	Fluorinated Ethylene Propylene	14-10	20	None
		200°C 392°F	Dry locations—special applications.		8-2	30	
				Fluorinated Ethylene Propylene	14-8	14	Glass braid
					6-2	14	Asbestos braid
Modified Fluorinated Ethylene Propylene	FEPW	75°C 90°C	Wet locations. Dry locations.	Modified Fluorinated Ethylene Propylene	14-10	20	None
					8-2	30	
Modified Ethylene Tetrafluoroethylene	Z	90°C 194°F 150°C 302°F	Dry locations. Dry locations—special applications.	Modified Ethylene Tetrafluoroethylene	14-12	15	None
					10	20	
					8-4	25	
					3-1	35	
					1/0-4/0	45	
Modified Ethylene Tetrafluoroethylene	ZW	75°C 167°F 90°C 194°F 150°C 302°F	Wet locations. Dry locations. Dry locations—special applications.	Modified Ethylene Tetrafluoroethylene	14-10	30	None
					8-2	45	

Table 310-13 (Continued)

Trade Name	Type Letter	Max Operating Temp	Application Provisions	Insulation	Thickness of Insulation (mils)	Outer Covering
Varnished Cambric	V	85°C 185°F	Dry locations only. Smaller than No. 6 by special permission.	Varnished Cambric	14-8 ...... 45 6-2 ...... 60 1-4/0 ...... 80 213-500 ...... 95 500-1000 ...... 110 1001-2000 ...... 125 For 1000-5000 volts, see Table 310-35 or 310-36.	Nonmetallic covering or lead-sheath
Asbestos and Varnished Cambric	AVA	110°C 230°F	Dry locations only.	Impregnated Asbestos and Varnished Cambric	*(see thickness table below)*	AVA-asbestos braid or glass
Asbestos and Varnished Cambric	AVL	110°C 230°F	Dry and wet locations.			AVL-lead sheath

Thickness of insulation (mils) for AVA / AVL:

```
                        1st         AVA      AVL
                        Asb.  VC    2nd      2nd
                                    Asb.     Asb.
14-8 (solid only)       —     30    30       25
6-2 ......              10    30    15       25
1-4/0 ......            15    30    20       25
213-500 ......          20    30    30       30
501-1000 ......         25    40    40       40
1001-2000 ......        30    50    50       50
For 1000-5000 volts, see Table 310-37.
```

Flame-retardant cotton braid (switchboard wiring):

```
                        VC   Asb.
                  Asb.  VC
18-8 ......        30    30   20
6-2 ......         40    40   30
1-4/0 ......       40    40   40
```

Trade Name	Type Letter	Max Operating Temp	Application Provisions	Insulation	Thickness of Insulation (mils)	Outer Covering
Asbestos and Varnished Cambric	AVB	90°C 194°F	Dry locations only.	Impregnated Asbestos and Varnished Cambric	*(see thickness table below)*	Flame-retardant, cotton braid

Thickness of insulation (mils) for AVB:

```
                              2nd
                  Asb.  VC    Asb.
14-8 ......        10    30    15
6-2 ......         15    30    20
1-4/0 ......       20    30    30
213-500 ......     25    40    40
501-1000 ......    30    50    40
1001-2000 ......   30    50    50
For 1000-5000 volts, see Table 310-37.
```

Table 310-13 (Continued)

Trade Name	Type Letter	Max. Operating Temp.	Application Provisions	Insulation	AWG or MCM	Thickness of Insulation Mils	Outer Covering
Asbestos	A	200°C 392°F	Dry locations only. Only for leads within apparatus or within raceways connected to apparatus. Limited to 300 volts.	Asbestos	14 12-8	30 40	Without asbestos braid
Asbestos	AA	200°C 392°F	Dry locations only. Only for leads within apparatus or within raceways connected to apparatus or as open wiring. Limited to 300 volts.	Asbestos	14 12-8 6-2 1-4/0	30 30 40 60	With asbestos braid or glass
Asbestos	AI	125°C 257°F	Dry locations only. Only for leads within apparatus or within raceways connected to apparatus. Limited to 300 volts.	Impregnated Asbestos	14 12-8	30 40	Without asbestos braid
Asbestos	AIA	125°C 257°F	Dry locations only. Only for leads within apparatus or within raceways connected to apparatus or as open wiring.	Impregnated Asbestos	14 12-8 6-2 1-4/0 213-500 501-1000	Sol. Str. 30 30 30 40 40 60 60 75 90 105	With asbestos braid or glass
Paper		85°C 185°F	For underground service conductors, or by special permission.	Paper			Lead sheath

Table 310-16.   Allowable Ampacities of Insulated Conductors Rated 0-2000 Volts, 60° to 90°C

Not More Than Three Conductors in Raceway or Cable or Earth (Directly Buried), Based on Ambient Temperature of 30°C (86°F)

Size	Temperature Rating of Conductor, See Table 310-13								Size
	60°C (140°F)	75°C (167°F)	85°C (185°F)	90°C (194°F)	60°C (140°F)	75°C (167°F)	85°C (185°F)	90°C (194°F)	
AWG MCM	TYPES †RUW, †T, †TW, †UF	TYPES †FEPW, †RH, †RHW, †RUH, †THW, †THWN, †XHHW, †USE, †ZW	TYPES V, MI	TYPES TA, TBS, SA, AVB, SIS, †FEP, †FEPB, †RHH †THHN, †XHHW*	TYPES †RUW, †T, †TW, †UF	TYPES †RH, †RHW, †RUH, †THW, †THWN, †XHHW, †USE	TYPES V, MI	TYPES TA, TBS, SA, AVB, SIS, †RHH, †THHN, †XHHW*	AWG MCM
	COPPER				ALUMINUM OR COPPER-CLAD ALUMINUM				
18	....	....	....	14	....	....	....	....	....
16	....	....	18	18	....	....	....	....	....
14	20†	20†	25	25†	....	....	....	....	....
12	25†	25†	30	30†	20†	20†	25	25†	12
10	30†	35†	40	40†	25†	30†	30	35†	10
8	40	50	55	55	30	40	40	45	8
6	55	65	70	75	40	50	55	60	6
4	70	85	95	95	55	65	75	75	4
3	85	100	110	110	65	75	85	85	3
2	95	115	125	130	75	90	100	100	2
1	110	130	145	150	85	100	110	115	1
0	125	150	165	170	100	120	130	135	0
00	145	175	190	195	115	135	145	150	00
000	165	200	215	225	130	155	170	175	000
0000	195	230	250	260	150	180	195	205	0000
250	215	255	275	290	170	205	220	230	250
300	240	285	310	320	190	230	250	255	300
350	260	310	340	350	210	250	270	280	350
400	280	335	365	380	225	270	295	305	400
500	320	380	415	430	260	310	335	350	500
600	355	420	460	475	285	340	370	385	600
700	385	460	500	520	310	375	405	420	700
750	400	475	515	535	320	385	420	435	750
800	410	490	535	555	330	395	430	450	800
900	435	520	565	585	355	425	465	480	900
1000	455	545	590	615	375	445	485	500	1000
1250	495	590	640	665	405	485	525	545	1250
1500	520	625	680	705	435	520	565	585	1500
1750	545	650	705	735	455	545	595	615	1750
2000	560	665	725	750	470	560	610	630	2000

CORRECTION FACTORS

Ambient Temp. °C	For ambient temperatures over 30°C, multiply the ampacities shown above by the appropriate correction factor to determine the maximum allowable load current.								Ambient Temp. °F
31-40	.82	.88	.90	.91	.82	.88	.90	.91	86-104
41-45	.71	.82	.85	.87	.71	.82	.85	.87	105-113
46-50	.58	.75	.80	.82	.58	.75	.80	.82	114-122
51-60	....	.58	.67	.71	....	.58	.67	.71	123-141
61-70	....	.35	.52	.58	....	.35	.52	.58	142-158
71-80	....	....	.30	.41	....	....	.30	.41	159-176

† The load current rating and the overcurrent protection for conductor types marked with an obelisk (†) shall not exceed 15 amperes for 14 AWG, 20 amperes for 12 AWG, and 30 amperes for 10 AWG copper; or 15 amperes for 12 AWG and 25 amperes for 10 AWG aluminum and copper-clad aluminum.

* For dry locations only. See 75°C column for wet locations.

Table 310-17.   Allowable Ampacities of Insulated Conductors Rated 0-2000 Volts, 60° to 90°C

Single conductors in free air, based on ambient temperature of 30°C (86°F).

Size	Temperature Rating of Conductor, See Table 310-13								Size
	60°C (140°F)	75°C (167°F)	85°C (185°F)	90°C (194°F)	60°C (140°F)	75°C (167°F)	85°C (185°F)	90°C (194°F)	
AWG MCM	TYPES †RUW, †T, †TW	TYPES †FEPW, †RH, †RHW, †RUH, †THW, †THWN, †XHHW, †ZW	TYPES V, MI	TYPES TA, TBS, SA, AVB, SIS, †FEP, †FEPB, †RHH †THHN, †XHHW*	TYPES †RUW, †T, †TW	TYPES †RH, †RHW, †RUH, †THW, †THWN, †XHHW	TYPES V, MI	TYPES TA, TBS, SA, AVB, SIS, †RHH, †THHN, †XHHW*	AWG MCM
	COPPER				ALUMINUM OR COPPER-CLAD ALUMINUM				
18	....	....	....	18	....	....	....	....	....
16	....	....	23	24	....	....	....	....	....
14	25†	30†	30	35†	....	....	....	....	
12	30†	35†	40	40†	25†	30†	30	35†	12
10	40†	50†	55	55†	35†	40†	40	40†	10
8	60	70	75	80	45	55	60	60	8
6	80	95	100	105	60	75	80	80	6
4	105	125	135	140	80	100	105	110	4
3	120	145	160	165	95	115	125	130	3
2	140	170	185	190	110	135	145	150	2
1	165	195	215	220	130	155	165	175	1
0	195	230	250	260	150	180	195	205	0
00	225	265	290	300	175	210	225	235	00
000	260	310	335	350	200	240	265	275	000
0000	300	360	390	405	235	280	305	315	0000
250	340	405	440	455	265	315	345	355	250
300	375	445	485	505	290	350	380	395	300
350	420	505	550	570	330	395	430	445	350
400	455	545	595	615	355	425	465	480	400
500	515	620	675	700	405	485	525	545	500
600	575	690	750	780	455	540	595	615	600
700	630	755	825	855	500	595	650	675	700
750	655	785	855	885	515	620	675	700	750
800	680	815	885	920	535	645	700	725	800
900	730	870	950	985	580	700	760	785	900
1000	780	935	1020	1055	625	750	815	845	1000
1250	890	1065	1160	1200	710	855	930	960	1250
1500	980	1175	1275	1325	795	950	1035	1075	1500
1750	1070	1280	1395	1445	875	1050	1145	1185	1750
2000	1155	1385	1505	1560	960	1150	1250	1335	2000
CORRECTION FACTORS									
Ambient Temp. °C	For ambient temperatures over 30°C, multiply the ampacities shown above by the appropriate correction factor to determine the maximum allowable load current.								Ambient Temp. °F
31-40	.82	.88	.90	.91	.82	.88	.90	.91	86-104
41-45	.71	.82	.85	.87	.71	.82	.85	.87	105-113
46-50	.58	.75	.80	.82	.58	.75	.80	.82	114-122
51-60	....	.58	.67	.71	....	.58	.67	.71	123-141
61-70	....	.35	.52	.58	....	.35	.52	.58	142-158
71-80	....	....	.30	.41	....	....	.30	.41	159-176

† The load current rating and the overcurrent protection for conductor types marked with an obelisk (†) shall not exceed 20 amperes for 14 AWG, 25 amperes for 12 AWG, and 40 amperes for 10 AWG copper, or 20 amperes for 12 AWG and 30 amperes for 10 AWG aluminum and copper-clad aluminum.

* For dry locations only. See 75°C column for wet locations.

Table 310-18. Allowable Ampacities for Insulated Conductors Rated 0-2000 Volts, 110 to 250°C

Not More Than Three Conductors in Raceway or Cable
Based on Ambient Temperature of 30°C (86°F).

Size AWG MCM	Temperature Rating of Conductor. See Table 310-13								Size AWG MCM
	110°C (230°F) TYPES AVA, AVL	125°C (257°F) TYPES AI, AIA	150°C (302°F) TYPE Z	200°C (392°F) TYPES A, AA, FEP, FEPB, PFA	250°C (482°F) TYPES PFAH, TFE	110°C (230°F) TYPES AVA, AVL	125°C (257°F) TYPES AI, AIA	200°C (392°F) TYPES A, AA	
	COPPER				NICKEL OR NICKEL-COATED COPPER	ALUMINUM OR COPPER-CLAD ALUMINUM			
14	30	30	30	30	40	....	....	....	....
12	35	40	40	40	55	25	30	30	12
10	45	50	50	55	75	35	40	45	10
8	60	65	65	70	95	45	50	55	8
6	80	85	90	95	120	60	65	75	6
4	105	115	115	120	145	80	90	95	4
3	120	130	135	145	170	95	100	115	3
2	135	145	150	165	195	105	115	130	2
1	160	170	180	190	220	125	135	150	1
0	190	200	210	225	250	150	160	180	0
00	215	230	240	250	280	170	180	200	00
000	245	265	275	285	315	195	210	225	000
0000	275	310	325	340	370	215	245	270	0000
250	315	335	....	....	....	250	270	....	250
300	345	380	....	....	....	275	305	....	300
350	390	420	....	....	....	310	335	....	350
400	420	450	....	....	....	335	360	....	400
500	470	500	....	....	....	380	405	....	500
600	525	545	....	....	....	425	440	....	600
700	560	600	....	....	....	455	485	....	700
750	580	620	....	....	....	470	500	....	750
800	600	640	....	....	....	485	520	....	800
1000	680	730	....	....	....	560	600	....	1000
1500	785	....	....	....	....	650	....	....	1500
2000	840	....	....	....	....	705	....	....	2000

CORRECTION FACTORS

Ambient Temp. °C	For ambient temperatures over 30°C, multiply the ampacities shown above by the appropriate correction factor to determine the maximum allowable load current.								Ambient Temp. °F
31-40	.94	.95	.96	....	....	.94	.95	....	87-104
41-45	.90	.92	.94	....	....	.90	.92	....	105-113
46-50	.87	.89	.91	....	....	.87	.89	....	114-122
51-55	.83	.86	.89	....	....	.83	.86	....	123-131
56-60	.79	.83	.87	.91	.95	.79	.83	.91	132-141
61-70	.71	.76	.82	.87	.91	.71	.76	.87	142-158
71-75	.66	.72	.79	.86	.89	.66	.72	.86	159-167
76-80	.61	.68	.76	.84	.87	.61	.69	.84	168-176
81-90	.50	.61	.71	.80	.83	.50	.61	.80	177-194
91-100	....	.51	.65	.77	.80	....	.51	.77	195-212
101-120	....	....	.50	.69	.72	....	....	.69	213-248
121-140	....	....	.29	.59	.59	....	....	.59	249-284
141-160	....	....	....	....	.54	....	....	....	285-320
161-180	....	....	....	....	.50	....	....	....	321-356
181-200	....	....	....	....	.43	....	....	....	357-392
201-225	....	....	....	....	.30	....	....	....	393-437

Table 310-19.   Allowable Ampacities for Insulated Conductors
Rated 0-2000 Volts, 110 to 250°C, and for Bare and Covered Conductors

Single Conductors in Free Air,
Based on Ambient Temperature of 30°C (86°F).

Size	Temperature Rating of Conductor. See Table 310-13.										Size
	110°C (230°F) TYPES AVA, AVL	125°C (257°F) TYPES AI, AIA	150°C (302°F) TYPE Z	200°C (392°F) TYPES A, AA, FEP, FEPB, PFA	Bare and covered conductors	250°C (482°F) TYPES PFAH, TFE	110°C (230°F) TYPES AVA, AVL	125°C (257°F) TYPES AI, AIA	200°C (392°F) TYPES A, AA	Bare and covered conductors	
AWG MCM	COPPER					NICKEL OR NICKEL-COATED COPPER	ALUMINUM OR COPPER-CLAD ALUMINUM				AWG MCM
14	40	40	40	45	30	60	....	....	....	....	....
12	50	50	50	55	40	80	40	40	45	30	12
10	65	70	70	75	55	110	50	55	60	45	10
8	85	90	95	100	70	145	65	70	80	55	8
6	120	125	130	135	100	210	95	100	105	80	6
4	160	170	175	180	130	285	125	135	140	100	4
3	180	195	200	210	150	335	140	150	165	115	3
2	210	225	230	240	175	390	165	175	185	135	2
1	245	265	270	280	205	450	190	205	220	160	1
0	285	305	310	325	235	545	220	240	255	185	0
00	330	355	360	370	275	605	255	275	290	215	00
000	385	410	415	430	320	725	300	320	335	250	000
0000	445	475	490	510	370	850	345	370	400	290	0000
250	495	530	....	....	410	....	385	415	....	320	250
300	555	590	....	....	460	....	435	460	....	360	300
350	610	655	....	....	510	....	475	510	....	400	350
400	665	710	....	....	555	....	520	555	....	435	400
500	765	815	....	....	630	....	595	635	....	490	500
600	855	910	....	....	710	....	675	720	....	560	600
700	940	1005	....	....	780	....	745	795	....	615	700
750	980	1045	....	....	810	....	775	825	....	640	750
800	1020	1085	....	....	845	....	805	855	....	670	800
900	....	....	....	....	905	....	....	....	....	725	900
1000	1165	1240	....	....	965	....	930	990	....	770	1000
1500	1450	....	....	....	1215	....	1175	....	....	985	1500
2000	1715	....	....	....	1405	....	1425	....	....	1165	2000

CORRECTION FACTORS

Ambient Temp. °C	For ambient temperatures over 30°C, multiply the ampacities shown above by the appropriate correction factor to determine the maximum allowable load current.										Ambient Temp. °F
31-40	.94	.95	.96	....		....	.94	.95	....		87-104
41-45	.90	.92	.94	....		....	.90	.92	....		105-113
46-50	.87	.89	.91	....		....	.87	.89	....		114-122
51-55	.83	.86	.89	....		....	.83	.86	....		123-131
56-60	.79	.83	.87	.91		.95	.79	.83	.91		132-141
61-70	.71	.76	.82	.87		.91	.71	.76	.87		142-158
71-75	.66	.72	.79	.86		.89	.66	.72	.86		159-167
76-80	.61	.68	.76	.84		.87	.61	.69	.84		168-176
81-90	.50	.61	.71	.80		.83	.50	.61	.80		177-194
91-100	....	.51	.65	.77		.80	....	.51	.77		195-212
101-120	....	....	.50	.69		.72	....	....	.69		213-248
121-140	....	....	.29	.59		.59	....	....	.59		249-284
141-160	....	....	....	....		.54	....	....	....		285-320
161-180	....	....	....	....		.50	....	....	....		321-356
181-200	....	....	....	....		.43	....	....	....		357-392
201-225	....	....	....	....		.30	....	....	....		393-437

Notes to Tables 310-16 through 310-19

1. Explanation of Tables. For explanation of Type Letters, and for recognized size of conductors for the various conductor insulations, see Section 310-13. For installation requirements, see Sections 310-1 through 310-10, and the various articles of this Code. For flexible cords, see Tables 400-4 and 400-5.

2. Application of Tables. For open wiring on insulators and for concealed knob-and-tube wiring, the allowable ampacities of Tables 310-17 and 310-19 shall be used. For all other recognized wiring methods, the allowable ampacities in Tables 310-16 and 310-18 shall be used, unless otherwise provided in this Code.

3. Three-Wire, Single-Phase Dwelling Services. In dwelling units, conductors, as listed below, shall be permitted to be utilized as three-wire, single-phase, service-entrance conductors and the three-wire, single-phase feeder that carries the total current supplied by that service.

See Section 215-2.

Conductor Types and Sizes
RH-RHH-RHW-THW-THWN-THHN-XHHW

Copper	Aluminum and Copper-Clad AL	Service Rating in Amps
AWG	AWG	
4	2	100
3	1	110
2	1/0	125
1	2/0	150
1/0	3/0	175
2/0	4/0	200

4. Type MC Cable. The ampacities of Type MC cables are determined by the temperature limitation of the insulated conductors incorporated within the cable. Hence the ampacities of Type MC cable may be determined from the columns in Tables 310-16 and 310-18 applicable to the type of insulated conductors employed within the cable.

5. Bare Conductors. Where bare conductors are used with insulated conductors, their allowable ampacities shall be limited to that permitted for the insulated conductors of the same size

6. Mineral-Insulated, Metal-Sheathed Cable. The temperature limitation on which the ampacities of mineral-insulated, metal-sheathed cable are based is determined by the insulating materials used in the end seal. Termination fittings incorporating unimpregnated, organic, insulating materials are limited to 85°C operation.

7. Type MTW Machine Tool Wire. The ampacities of Type MTW wire are specified in Table 11-1(b) of the Standard for Electrical Metalworking Machine Tools and Plastics Processing Machinery (NFPA 79-1980).

8. More than Three Conductors in a Raceway or Cable. Where the number of conductors in a raceway or cable exceeds three, the ampacity shall be as given in Tables 310-16 and 310-18, but the maximum allowable load current of each conductor shall be reduced as shown in the following table:

Number of Conductors	Percent of Values in Tables 310-16 and 310-18
4 thru 6	80
7 thru 24	70
25 thru 42	60
43 and above	50

Where single conductors or multiconductor cables are stacked or bundled without maintaining spacing and are not installed in raceways, the maximum allowable load current of each conductor shall be reduced as shown in the above table.

Exception No. 1: When conductors of different systems, as provided in Section 300-3, are installed in a common raceway the derating factors shown above shall apply to the number of power and lighting (Articles 210, 215, 220, and 230) conductors only.

Exception No. 2: The derating factors of Sections 210-22(c), 220-2(a) and 220-10(b) shall not apply when the above derating factors are also required.

Exception No. 3. For conductors installed in cable trays, the provisions of Section 318-10 shall apply.

9. Overcurrent Protection. Where the standard ratings and settings of overcurrent devices do not correspond with the ratings and settings allowed for conductors, the next higher standard rating and setting shall be permitted.

Exception: As limited in Section 240-3.

10. Neutral Conductor.

(a) A neutral conductor which carries only the unbalanced current from other conductors, as in the case of normally balanced circuits of three or more conductors, shall not be counted when applying the provisions of Note 8.

(b) In a 3-wire circuit consisting of 2-phase wires and the neutral of a 4-wire, 3-phase wye-connected system, a common conductor carries approximately the same current as the other conductors and shall be counted when applying the provisions of Note 8.

(c) On a 4-wire, 3-phase wye circuit where the major portion of the load consists of electric-discharge lighting, data processing, or similar equipment, there are harmonic currents present in the neutral conductor and the neutral shall be considered to be a current-carrying conductor.

Third harmonic currents in 3-phase power systems are capable of causing the current in the neutral to exceed that in the phase conductor.

Third harmonics in the equipment mentioned are a result of the use of diodes charging capacitors on the input of power supplies. The current waveforms characteristic of such a load are very high in third harmonics. Third harmonics, in contrast to the fundamental, are

not reduced by balancing the load. As a result, the neutral, in areas of concentrated electronic loads such as computer installations, production test areas, etc., should not have its current capacity reduced.

11. Grounding Conductor. A grounding conductor shall not be counted when applying the provisions of Note 8.

12. Voltage Drop. The allowable ampacities in Tables 310-16 through 310-19 are based on temperature alone and do not take voltage drop into consideration.

Note 2 indicates that the provisions of Table 310-16 are for not more than three conductors in a raceway, cable, or earth. Table 310-18 is based on conductors with higher temperature ratings [110°C (230°F) to 250°C (482°F)] and provides for not more than three conductors in a raceway or cable. For more than three conductors, Note 8 would apply.

Note 3 provides special ampacity allowances for the listed conductor types and sizes. This allowance is limited to 3-wire, single-phase dwelling service-entrance conductors and to the 3-wire, single-phase feeder that carries the "total" current supplied by that service.

The derating factors for "allowable load currents" of more than three conductors in a raceway or cable, or conductors stacked or bundled are covered in Note 8. Exception No. 2 indicates that "double" derating of conductors is not required, pertaining to the sections listed.

Table 310-31.   Conductor Application and Insulation

Trade Name	Type Letter	Maximum Operating Temperature	Application Provision	Insulation	Outer Covering
Medium voltage solid dielectric	MV-75 MV-85 MV-90	75C 85C 90C	Dry or wet locations rated 2001 volts and higher	Thermoplastic or Thermosetting	Jacket, Sheath or Armor

Table 310-32. Thickness of Insulation for 601-2000 Volt Nonshielded Types RHH and RHW, in Mils

Conductor Size AWG-MCM	A	B
14-10	80	60
8	80	70
6-2	95	70
1-2/0	110	90
3/0-4/0	110	90
213-500	125	105
501-1000	140	120

Note: Column A insulations are limited to natural, SBR, and butyl rubbers.
Note: Column B insulations are materials such as cross-linked polyethylene, ethylene propylene rubber, and composites thereof.

Table 310-33. Thickness of Insulation and Jacket for Nonshielded Solid Dielectric Insulated Conductors Rated 2001 to 8000 Volts, in Mils

Conductor Size AWG-MCM	2001-5000 Volts						5001-8000 Volts 100 Percent Insulation Level Wet or Dry Locations		
	Dry Locations Single Conductor			Wet or Dry Locations			Single Conductor		Multi-Conductor*
	Without Jacket	With Jacket		Single Conductor		Multi-Conductor*			
	Insulation	Insulation	Jacket	Insulation	Jacket	Insulation	Insulation	Jacket	Insulation
8	110	90	30	125	80	90	180	80	180
6	110	90	30	125	80	90	180	80	180
4-2	110	90	45	125	80	90	180	95	180
1-2/0	110	90	45	125	80	90	180	95	180
3/0-4/0	110	90	65	125	95	90	180	110	180
213-500	120	90	65	140	110	90	210	110	210
501-750	130	90	65	155	125	90	235	125	235
751-1000	130	90	65	155	125	90	250	140	250

* Note: Under a common overall covering such as a jacket, sheath or armor.

Table 310-34.   Thickness of Insulation for Shielded Solid Dielectric
Insulated Conductors Rated 2001 to 35,000 Volts, in Mils

Conductor Size AWG-MCM	2001-5000 Volts	5001-8000		8001-15,000		15,001-25,000		25,001-28,000	28,001-35,000
		100* Percent Insulation level	133* Percent Insulation level	100* Percent insulation level	133* Percent insulation level	100* Percent insulation level	133* Percent insulation level	100* Percent insulation level	100* Percent insulation level
8	90	—	—	—	—	—	—	—	—
6-4	90	115	140	—	—	—	—	—	—
2	90	115	140	175	—	—	—	—	—
1	90	115	140	175	215	260	345	280	—
1/0-1000	90	115	140	175	215	260	345	280	345

*Definitions:

100 Percent Insulation Level.   Cables in this category shall be permitted to be applied where the system is provided with relay protection such that ground faults will be cleared as rapidly as possible, but in any case within 1 minute. While these cables are applicable to the great majority of cable installations which are on grounded systems, they shall be permitted to be used also on other systems for which the application of cables is acceptable provided the above clearing requirements are met in completely de-energizing the faulted section.

133 Percent Insulation Level.   This insulation level corresponds to that formerly designated for ungrounded systems. Cables in this category shall be permitted to be applied in situations where the clearing time requirements of the 100 percent level category cannot be met, and yet there is adequate assurance that the faulted section will be de-energized in a time not exceeding 1 hour. Also they shall be permitted to be used when additional insulation strength over the 100 percent level category is desirable.

Table 310-35.   Thickness of Varnished-Cambric Insulation for
Single-Conductor Cable, in Mils

Conductor Size AWG or MCM	For Voltages Not Exceeding				
	1000	2000	3000	4000	5000
14	60	—	—	—	—
12	60	80	—	—	—
10	60	80	95	—	—
8-2	60	80	95	110	140
1-4/0	80	95	95	110	140
213-500	95	95	110	125	155
501-1000	110	110	110	125	155
1001-2000	125	125	125	140	155

Table 310-36.   Thickness of Varnished-Cambric Insulation for Multiconductor Cable, in Mils

Conductor Size AWG or MCM	For Voltages Not Exceeding									
	1000		2000		3000		4000		5000	
	C	B	C	B	C	B	C	B	C	B
14	60	0	—	—	—	—	—	—	—	—
12	60	0	80	0	—	—	—	—	—	—
10	60	0	80	0	80	30	—	—	—	—
8-2	60	0	80	0	80	30	95	45	95	60
1-4/0	80	0	95	0	95	30	95	45	95	60
213-500	95	0	95	0	95	30	95	45	110	60
501-1000	95	30	95	30	95	45	95	60	110	60
1001-2000	110	30	110	30	110	45	110	60	110	80

The thickness given in columns headed "C" are for the insulation on the individual conductors. Those given in the columns headed "B" are for the thickness of the overall belt of insulation.

Table 310-37

Thickness of Asbestos and Varnished-Cambric Insulation for Single-Conductor Cable, Types AVA, AVB, and AVL, in Mils

Conductor AWG or MCM	Asbestos 1st Wall	Varnished Cambric					Asbestos 2nd Wall
		For Voltages Not Exceeding					
	1000-5000	1000	2000	3000	4000	5000	1000-5000
14-2	15	45	60	80	100	120	25
1-4/0	20	45	60	80	100	120	30
213-500	25	45	60	80	100	120	40
501-1000	30	45	60	80	100	120	40
1001-2000	30	55	75	95	115	140	50

Table 310-39

Allowable Ampacities for Insulated Single Copper
Conductor Isolated in Air

Based on Conductor Temperature of 90°C and Ambient
Air Temperature of 40°C

Conductor Size AWG-MCM	2001-5000 Volts Ampacity	5001-15,000 Volts Ampacity	15,001-35,000 Volts Ampacity
8	83	—	—
6	110	110	—
4	145	150	—
2	190	195	—
1	225	225	225
1/0	260	260	260
2/0	300	300	300
3/0	345	345	345
4/0	400	400	395
250	445	445	440
350	550	550	545
500	695	685	680
750	900	885	870
1000	1075	1060	1040
1250	1230	1210	1185
1500	1365	1345	1315
1750	1495	1470	1430
2000	1605	1575	1535

Table 310-40

Allowable Ampacities for Insulated Single Aluminum Conductor
Isolated in Air

Based on Conductor Temperature of 90°C and Ambient
Air Temperature of 40°C

Conductor Size AWG-MCM	2001-5000 Volts Ampacity	5001-15,000 Volts Ampacity	15,001-35,000 Volts Ampacity
8	64	—	—
6	85	87	—
4	115	115	—
2	150	150	—
1	175	175	175
1/0	200	200	200
2/0	230	235	230
3/0	270	270	270
4/0	310	310	310
250	345	345	345
350	430	430	430
500	545	535	530
750	710	700	685
1000	855	840	825
1250	980	970	950
1500	1105	1085	1060
1750	1215	1195	1165
2000	1320	1295	1265

Table 310-41

Allowable Ampacities of an Insulated Three Conductor Copper
Cable Isolated in Air

Based on Conductor Temperature of 90°C and Ambient
Air Temperature of 40°C

Conductor Size AWG-MCM	2001-5000 Volts Ampacity	5001-35,000 Volts Ampacity
8	59	—
6	79	93
4	105	120
2	140	165
1	160	185
1/0	185	215
2/0	215	245
3/0	250	285
4/0	285	325
250	320	360
350	395	435
500	485	535
750	615	670
1000	705	770

Table 310-42

Allowable Ampacities of an Insulated Three Conductor
Aluminum Cable Isolated in Air

Based on Conductor Temperature of 90°C and Ambient
Air Temperature of 40°C

Conductor Size AWG-MCM	2001-5000 Volts Ampacity	5001-35,000 Volts Ampacity
8	46	—
6	61	72
4	81	95
2	110	125
1	125	145
1/0	145	170
2/0	170	190
3/0	195	220
4/0	225	255
250	250	280
350	310	345
500	385	425
750	495	540
1000	585	635

Table 310-43
Allowable Ampacities of an Insulated Triplexed or Three Single Conductor Copper Cables in Isolated Conduit in Air
Based on Conductor Temperature of 90°C and Ambient Air Temperature of 40°C

Conductor Size AWG-MCM	2001-5000 Volts Ampacity	5001-35,000 Volts Ampacity
8	55	—
6	75	83
4	97	110
2	130	150
1	155	170
1/0	180	195
2/0	205	225
3/0	240	260
4/0	280	295
250	315	330
350	385	395
500	475	480
750	600	585
1000	690	675

Table 310-44
Allowable Ampacities of Insulated Triplexed or Three Single Conductor Aluminum Cables in Isolated Conduit in Air
Based on Conductor Temperature of 90°C and Ambient Air Temperature of 40°C

Conductor Size AWG-MCM	2001-5000 Volts Ampacity	5001-35,000 Volts Ampacity
8	43	—
6	58	65
4	76	84
2	100	115
1	120	130
1/0	140	150
2/0	160	175
3/0	190	200
4/0	215	230
250	250	255
350	305	310
500	380	385
750	490	485
1000	580	565

Table 310-45
Allowable Ampacities of an Insulated Three Conductor Copper Cable in Isolated Conduit in Air
Based on Conductor Temperature of 90°C and Ambient Air Temperature of 40°C

Conductor Size AWG-MCM	2001-5000 Volts Ampacity	5001-35,000 Volts Ampacity
8	52	—
6	69	83
4	91	105
2	125	145
1	140	165
1/0	165	195
2/0	190	220
3/0	220	250
4/0	255	290
250	280	315
350	350	385
500	425	470
750	525	570
1000	590	650

Table 310-46
Allowable Ampacities of an Insulated Three Conductor Aluminum Cable in Isolated Conduit in Air
Based on Conductor Temperature of 90°C and Ambient Air Temperature of 40°C

Conductor Size AWG-MCM	2001-5000 Volts Ampacity	5001-35,000 Volts Ampacity
8	41	—
6	53	64
4	71	84
2	96	115
1	110	130
1/0	130	150
2/0	150	170
3/0	170	195
4/0	200	225
250	220	250
350	275	305
500	340	380
750	430	470
1000	505	550

Table 310-47
Allowable Ampacities of an Insulated Triplexed or Three Single Conductor Copper Cables in Underground Raceways
Based on Conductor Temperature of 90°C, Ambient Earth Temperature of 20°C, 100% Load Factor and Thermal Resistance (RHO) of 90

One Circuit Size AWG-MCM	2001-5000 Volts Ampacity	5001-35,000 Volts Ampacity
8	64	—
6	85	90
4	110	115
2	145	155
1	170	175
1/0	195	200
2/0	220	230
3/0	250	260
4/0	290	295
250	320	325
350	385	390
500	470	465
750	585	565
1000	670	640
Three Circuit Size		
8	56	—
6	73	77
4	95	99
2	125	130
1	140	145
1/0	160	165
2/0	185	185
3/0	210	210
4/0	235	240
250	260	260
350	315	310
500	375	370
750	460	440
1000	525	495
Six Circuit Size		
8	48	—
6	62	64
4	80	82
2	105	105
1	115	120
1/0	135	135
2/0	150	150
3/0	170	170
4/0	195	190
250	210	210
350	250	245
500	300	290
750	365	350
1000	410	390

Table 310-48
Allowable Ampacities of Insulated Triplexed or Three Single Conductor Aluminum Cables in Underground Raceways

Based on Conductor Temperature of 90°C, Ambient Earth Temperature of 20°C, 100% Load Factor and Thermal Resistance (RHO) of 90

One Circuit Size AWG-MCM	2001-5000 Volts Ampacity	5001-35,000 Volts Ampacity
8	50	—
6	66	70
4	86	91
2	115	120
1	130	135
1/0	150	155
2/0	170	175
3/0	195	200
4/0	225	230
250	250	250
350	305	305
500	370	370
750	470	455
1000	545	525
Three Circuit Size		
8	44	—
6	57	60
4	74	77
2	96	100
1	110	110
1/0	125	125
2/0	145	145
3/0	160	165
4/0	185	185
250	205	200
350	245	245
500	295	290
750	370	355
1000	425	405
Six Circuit Size		
8	38	—
6	48	50
4	62	64
2	80	80
1	91	90
1/0	105	105
2/0	115	115
3/0	135	130
4/0	150	150
250	165	165
350	195	195
500	240	230
750	290	280
1000	335	320

Table 310-49
Allowable Ampacities of an Insulated Three Conductor Copper Cable in Underground Raceways
Based on Conductor Temperature of 90°C, Ambient Earth Temperature of 20°C, 100% Load Factor and Thermal Resistance (RHO) of 90

One Circuit Size AWG-MCM	2001-5000 Volts Ampacity	5001-35,000 Volts Ampacity
8	59	—
6	78	88
4	100	115
2	135	150
1	155	170
1/0	175	195
2/0	200	220
3/0	230	250
4/0	265	285
250	290	310
350	355	375
500	430	450
750	530	545
1000	600	615
Three Circuit Size		
8	53	—
6	69	75
4	89	97
2	115	125
1	135	140
1/0	150	160
2/0	170	185
3/0	195	205
4/0	225	230
250	245	255
350	295	305
500	355	360
750	430	430
1000	485	485
Six Circuit Size		
8	46	—
6	60	63
4	77	81
2	98	105
1	110	115
1/0	125	130
2/0	145	150
3/0	165	170
4/0	185	190
250	200	205
350	240	245
500	290	290
750	350	340
1000	390	380

Table 310-50
Allowable Ampacities of an Insulated Three Conductor Aluminum Cable in Underground Raceways
Based on Conductor Temperature of 90°C, Ambient Earth Temperature of 20°C, 100% Load Factor and Thermal Resistance (RHO) of 90

One Circuit Size AWG-MCM	2001-5000 Volts Ampacity	5001-35,000 Volts Ampacity
8	46	—
6	61	69
4	80	89
2	105	115
1	120	135
1/0	140	150
2/0	160	170
3/0	180	195
4/0	205	220
250	230	245
350	280	295
500	340	355
750	425	440
1000	495	510
Three Circuit Size		
8	41	—
6	54	59
4	70	75
2	90	100
1	105	110
1/0	120	125
2/0	135	140
3/0	155	160
4/0	175	180
250	190	200
350	230	240
500	280	285
750	345	350
1000	400	400
Six Circuit Size		
8	36	—
6	46	49
4	60	63
2	77	80
1	87	90
1/0	99	105
2/0	110	115
3/0	130	130
4/0	145	150
250	160	160
350	190	190
500	230	230
750	280	275
1000	320	315

Table 310-51

Allowable Ampacities for Insulated Single Copper Conductor, Direct Buried

Based on Conductor Temperature of 90°C, Ambient Earth Temperature of 20°C, 100% Load Factor, Thermal Resistance (RHO) of 90, and 7½ Inch Spacing Between Conductor Center Lines, and 24 Inch Spacing Between Circuits

Conductor Size AWG-MCM	2001-5000 Volts Ampacity	5001-35,000 Volts Ampacity
One Circuit- 3 Conductors		
8	110	—
6	140	130
4	180	170
2	230	210
1	260	240
1/0	295	275
2/0	335	310
3/0	385	355
4/0	435	405
250	470	440
350	570	535
500	690	650
750	845	805
1000	980	930
Two Circuits- 6 Conductors		
8	100	—
6	130	120
4	165	160
2	215	195
1	240	225
1/0	275	255
2/0	310	290
3/0	355	330
4/0	400	375
250	435	410
350	520	495
500	630	600
750	775	740
1000	890	855

For SI units: one inch = 25.4 millimeters.

Table 310-52
Allowable Ampacities of an Insulated Single Aluminum Conductor, Direct Buried

Based on Conductor Temperature of 90°C, Ambient Earth
Temperature of 20°C, 100% Load Factor, Thermal Resistance (RHO)
of 90, and 7½ Inch Spacing Between Conductor Center Lines,
and 24 Inch Spacing Between Circuits

Conductor Size AWG-MCM	2001-5000 Volts Ampacity	5001-35,000 Volts Ampacity
One Circuit- 3 Conductors		
8	85	—
6	110	100
4	140	130
2	180	165
1	205	185
1/0	230	215
2/0	265	245
3/0	300	275
4/0	340	315
250	370	345
350	445	415
500	540	510
750	665	635
1000	780	740
Two Circuits- 6 Conductors		
8	80	—
6	100	95
4	130	125
2	165	155
1	190	175
1/0	215	200
2/0	245	225
3/0	275	255
4/0	310	290
250	340	320
350	410	385
500	495	470
750	610	580
1000	710	680

For SI units: one inch = 25.4 millimeters.

Table 310-53

Allowable Ampacities of an Insulated Three Conductor Copper Cable, Direct Buried

Based on Conductor Temperature of 90°C, Ambient Earth Temperature of 20°C, 100% Load Factor, Thermal Resistance (RHO) of 90, and 24 Inch Spacing Between Cable Center Lines

Conductor Size AWG-MCM	2001-5000 Volts Ampacity	5001-35,000 Volts Ampacity
One Circuit		
8	85	—
6	105	115
4	135	145
2	180	185
1	200	210
1/0	230	240
2/0	260	270
3/0	295	305
4/0	335	350
250	365	380
350	440	460
500	530	550
750	650	665
1000	730	750
Two Circuits		
8	80	—
6	100	105
4	130	135
2	165	170
1	185	195
1/0	215	220
2/0	240	250
3/0	275	280
4/0	310	320
250	340	350
350	410	420
500	490	500
750	595	605
1000	665	675

For SI units: one inch = 25.4 millimeters.

Table 310-54
Allowable Ampacities of an Insulated Three Conductor Aluminum Cable, Direct Buried
Based on Conductor Temperature of 90°C, Ambient Earth Temperature of 20°C, 100% Load Factor, Thermal Resistance (RHO) of 90, and 24 Inch Spacing Between Cable Center Lines

Conductor Size AWG-MCM	2001-5000 Volts Ampacity	5001-35,000 Volts Ampacity
One Circuit		
8	65	—
6	80	90
4	105	115
2	140	145
1	155	165
1/0	180	185
2/0	205	210
3/0	230	240
4/0	260	270
250	285	300
350	345	360
500	·420	435
750	520	540
1000	600	620
Two Circuits		
8	60	—
6	75	80
4	100	105
2	130	135
1	145	150
1/0	165	170
2/0	190	195
3/0	215	220
4/0	245	250
250	265	275
350	320	330
500	385	395
750	480	485
1000	550	560

For SI units: one inch = 25.4 millimeters.

Notes To Tables 310-39 Through 310-54

Ampacities calculated in accordance with the following Notes 1 and 2 will require reference to AIEE/IPCEA "Power Cable Ampacities" Vols. I and II (IPCEA Pub. No. P-46-426) and "The References" therein for availability of all factors and constants.

1. *Ambients Not in Tables.* Ampacities at ambient temperatures other than those shown in the tables shall be determined by means of the following formula:

$$I_2 = I_1 \sqrt{\frac{TC - TA_2 - DELTA\ TD}{TC - TA_1 - DELTA\ TD}}$$

Where,

I_1 = Ampacity from tables at ambient TA_1 TA_1 = Surrounding ambient from tables in degrees C
I_2 = Ampacity at desired ambient TA_2 TA_2 = Desired ambient in degrees C
TC = Conductor temperature in degrees C   DELTA TD = Dielectric loss temperature rise

2. *Grounded Shields.* Ampacities shown in Tables 310-39, 310-40, 310-51 and 310-52 are for cable with shields grounded at one point only. When shields are grounded at more than one point, ampacities shall be adjusted to take into consideration the heating due to shield currents.

3. *Duct Bank Configuration.* Ampacities shown in Tables 310-47, 310-48, 310-49 and 310-54 shall apply only when the cables are located in the outer ducts of the duct bank. Ampacities for cables located in the inner ducts of the duct bank will have to be determined by special calculations.

ARTICLE 318 — CABLE TRAYS

Contents

318-1. Scope.   A cable tray system is a unit or assembly of units or sections, and associated fittings, made of metal or other noncombustible materials forming a rigid structural system used to support cables. Cable tray systems include ladders, troughs, channels, solid bottom trays, and other similar structures.

It is not the intent of this article to require that cables be installed in cable tray systems or to recognize the use of all conductors described in Article 310 in cable tray systems for general wiring.

318-2. Uses Permitted.

(a) Wiring Methods.   The following shall be permitted to be installed in cable tray systems under the conditions described in the article for each:

1. Mineral-insulated, metal-sheathed cable (Article 330); 2. armored cable (Article 333); 3. metal-clad cable (Article 334); 4. power-limited tray cable (Section 725-40); 5. nonmetallic-sheathed cable (Article 336); 6. shielded, nonmetallic-sheathed cable (Article 337); 7. multiconductor

service-entrance cable (Article 338); 8. multiconductor underground feeder and branch-circuit cable (Article 339); 9. power and control tray cable (Article 340); 10. other factory-assembled, multiconductor control, signal, or power cables, which are specifically approved for installation in cable trays; or 11. any approved conduit or raceway with its contained conductors.

(b) In Industrial Establishments. In industrial establishments only, where conditions of maintenance and supervision assure that only qualified persons will service the installed cable tray system, any of the cables in (1) and (2) below shall be permitted to be installed in ladder, ventilated trough, or 4-inch (102-mm) ventilated channel-type cable trays.

(1) Single Conductor. Single conductor cables shall be 250 MCM or larger, and shall be Type RHH, RHW, MV, USE, or THW. Other 250 MCM or larger copper or aluminum single conductor cables shall be permitted if such cables are specifically approved for installation in cable trays. Where exposed to direct rays of the sun, cables shall be sunlight-resistant.

(2) Multiconductor. Multiconductor cables Type MV (Article 326) where exposed to direct rays of the sun shall be sunlight-resistant.

(c) Equipment Grounding Conductors. Metal in cable trays, as defined in Table 318-6(b) (2), shall be permitted to be used as equipment grounding conductors in commercial and industrial establishments only, where continuous maintenance and supervision assure that only qualified persons will service the installed cable tray system.

(d) Hazardous (Classified) Locations. Cable trays in hazardous (classified) locations shall contain only the cable types permitted in Sections 501-4, 502-4, and 503-3.

318-3. Uses Not Permitted. Cable tray systems shall not be used in hoistways or where subjected to severe physical damage.

318-4. Construction Specifications. Cable trays shall comply with the following:

(a) Strength and Rigidity. Shall have suitable strength and rigidity to provide adequate support for all contained wiring.

(b) Smooth Edges. Shall not present sharp edges, burrs, or projections injurious to the insulation or jackets of the wiring.

(c) Corrosion Protection. If made of metal, shall be adequately protected against corrosion or shall be made of corrosion-resistant material.

(d) Side Rails. Shall have side rails or equivalent structural members.

(e) Fittings. Shall include fittings or other suitable means for changes in direction and elevation of runs.

318-5. Installation.

(a) Complete System. Cable trays shall be installed as a complete system. Field bends or modifications shall be so made that the electrical continuity of the cable tray system and support for the cables shall be maintained.

Cable tray is to be installed as a complete system, i.e., unconnected sections are not permitted to support conductors, cables, etc. Manufactured sections or field-adapted sections are to be used for angle turns or for elevated directions.

(b) Completed Before Installation.   Each run of cable tray shall be completed before the installation of cables.

(c) Supports.   Supports shall be provided to prevent stress on cables where they enter another raceway or enclosure from cable tray systems.

(d) Noncombustible Covers.   In portions of runs where additional protection is required, noncombustible covers or enclosures providing the required protection shall be used.

(e) Multiconductor Cables Rated 600 Volts or Less.   Multiconductor cables rated 600 volts or less shall be permitted to be installed in the same cable tray.

(f) Cables Rated Over 600 Volts.   Cables rated over 600 volts shall not be installed in the same cable tray with cables rated 600 volts or less.

Exception No. 1: Where separated by solid noncombustible fixed barriers.

Exception No. 2: Where cables are Type MC.

Figure 318-1. A cable tray installation. The trays are installed as complete systems; any field modifications made must not interfere with the electrical continuity of the system. (*Husky Trough and Ladder*)

(g) Through Partitions and Walls.   Cable trays shall be permitted to extend transversely through partitions and walls or vertically through platforms and floors in wet or dry locations where the installations, complete with installed cables, are made in accordance with the requirements of Section 300-21.

See Figure 300-8.

(h) Exposed and Accessible. Cable trays shall be exposed and accessible except as permitted by Section 318-5 (g).

(i) Adequate Access. Sufficient space shall be provided and maintained about cable trays to permit adequate access for installing and maintaining the cables.

> No specific clearance distance is given. Sufficient spacing is to be provided for cable installation and maintenance.

318-6. Grounding.

(a) Metallic Cable Trays. Metallic cable trays which support electrical conductors shall be grounded as required for conductor enclosures in Article 250.

> Much the same as the *Code* requires metal raceways and metal enclosures to be grounded, cable trays must also be grounded.

(b) Steel or Aluminum Cable Tray Systems. Where steel or aluminum cable tray systems are used as equipment grounding conductors, all of the following provisions shall be complied with:

(1) The cable tray sections and fittings shall be identified for grounding purposes.

(2) The minimum cross-sectional area of cable trays shall conform to the requirements in Table 318-6(b) (2).

(3) All cable tray sections and fittings shall be legibly and durably marked to show the cross-sectional area of metal in channel-type cable trays or cable trays of one-piece construction, and the total cross-sectional area of both side rails for ladder or trough-type cable trays.

Table 318-6(b) (2)

**Metal Area Requirements for Cable Trays
Used as Equipment Grounding Conductors**

Ampere Rating or Setting of Largest Automatic Overcurrent Device Protecting Any Circuit in the Cable Tray System	Minimum Cross-Sectional Area of Metal* in Square Inches	
	Steel Cable Trays	Aluminum Cable Trays
0— 60	0.20	0.20
61— 100	0.40	0.20
101— 200	0.70	0.20
201— 400	1.00	0.40
401— 600	1.50**	0.40
601— 1000	—	0.60
1001— 1200	—	1.00
1201— 1600	—	1.50
1601— 2000	—	2.00**

For SI units: one square inch = 645 square millimeters.

* Total cross-sectional area of both side rails for ladder or trough-type cable trays; or the minimum cross-sectional area of metal in channel-type cable trays or cable trays of one-piece construction.

** Steel cable trays shall not be used as equipment grounding conductors for circuits protected above 600 amperes. Aluminum cable trays shall not be used for equipment grounding conductors for circuits protected above 2000 amperes.

(4) Cable tray sections, fittings, and connected raceways shall be bonded in accordance with Section 250-75 using bolted mechanical connectors or bonding jumpers sized and installed in accordance with Section 250-79.

318-7. Cable Installation.

(a) Cable Splices.   Cable splices made and insulated by approved methods shall be permitted to be located within a cable tray provided they are accessible and do not project above the side rails.

(b) Fastened Securely.   In other than horizontal runs, the cables shall be fastened securely to transverse members of the cable trays.

(c) Bushed Conduit.   A box shall not be required where cables or conductors are installed in bushed conduit used for support or for protection against physical damage.

(d) Connected in Parallel.   Where single conductor cables comprising each phase or neutral of a circuit are connected in parallel as permitted in Section 310-4, the conductors shall be installed in groups consisting of not more than one conductor per phase or neutral, to prevent current unbalance in the paralleled conductors due to inductive reactance.

Single conductors shall be securely bound in circuit groups to prevent excessive movement due to fault-current magnetic forces.

Exception: Where single conductors are cabled together, such as triplexed assemblies.

318-8. Number of Multiconductor Cables, Rated 2000 Volts, Nominal, or Less, in Cable Trays.   The number of multiconductor cables, rated 2000 volts, nominal, or less, permitted in a single cable tray shall not exceed the requirements of this section. The conductor sizes herein apply to both aluminum and copper conductors.

(a) Any Mixture of Cables.   Where ladder or ventilated trough cable trays contain multiconductor power or lighting cables, or any mixture of multiconductor power, lighting, control, and signal cables, the maximum number of cables shall conform to the following:

(1) Where all of the cables are 4/0 AWG or larger, the sum of the diameters of all cables shall not exceed the cable tray width, and the cables shall be installed in a single layer.

(2) Where all of the cables are smaller than 4/0 AWG, the sum of the cross-sectional areas of all cables shall not exceed the maximum allowable cable fill area in Column 1 of Table 318-8, for the appropriate cable tray width.

(3) Where 4/0 AWG or larger cables are installed in the same cable tray with cables smaller than 4/0 AWG, the sum of the cross-sectional areas of all cables smaller than 4/0 AWG shall not exceed the maximum allowable fill area resulting from the computation in Column 2 of Table 318-8, for the appropriate cable tray width. The 4/0 AWG and larger cables shall be installed in a single layer and no other cables shall be placed on them.

(b) Multiconductor Control and/or Signal Cables Only.   Where a ladder or ventilated trough cable tray, having a usable inside depth of 6 inches (152 mm) or less, contains multiconductor control and/or signal cables only, the sum of the cross-sectional areas of all cables at any cross section shall not exceed 50 percent of the interior cross-sectional area of the cable tray. A depth of 6 inches (152 mm) shall be used to compute the allowable interior cross-sectional area of any cable tray which has a usable inside depth of more than 6 inches (152 mm).

(c) Solid Bottom Cable Trays Containing Any Mixture.   Where solid bottom cable trays contain multiconductor power or lighting cables, or any mixture of multiconductor power, lighting, control, and signal cables, the maximum number of cables shall conform to the following:

(1) Where all of the cables are 4/0 AWG or larger, the sum of the diameters of all cables shall not exceed 90 percent of the cable tray width, and the cables shall be installed in a single layer.

(2) Where all of the cables are smaller than 4/0 AWG, the sum of the cross-sectional areas of all cables shall not exceed the maximum allowable cable fill area in Column 3 of Table 318-8, for the appropriate cable tray width.

(3) Where 4/0 AWG or larger cables are installed in the same cable tray with cables smaller than 4/0 AWG, the sum of the cross-sectional areas of all cables smaller than 4/0 AWG shall not exceed the maximum allowable fill area resulting from the computation in Column 4 of Table 318-8, for the appropriate cable tray width. The 4/0 AWG and larger cables shall be installed in a single layer and no other cables shall be placed on them.

(d) Solid Bottom Cable Tray Multiconductor Control and/or Signal Cables Only.   Where a solid bottom cable tray, having a usable inside depth of 6 inches (152 mm) or less, contains multiconductor control and/or signal cables only, the sum of the cross-sectional areas of all cables at any cross section shall not exceed 40 percent of the interior cross-sectional area of the cable tray. A depth of 6 inches (152 mm) shall be used to compute the allowable interior cross-sectional area of any cable tray which has a usable inside depth of more than 6 inches (152 mm).

(e) Ventilated Channel-type Cable Trays.   Where ventilated channel-type cable trays contain multiconductor cables of any type, the combined cross-sectional area of all cables shall not exceed 1.3 square inches (839 sq mm) in 3-inch (76-mm) wide channel trays, or 2.5 square inches (1613 sq mm) in 4-inch (102-mm) wide channel trays.

Exception: Where only one multiconductor cable is installed in a ventilated channel-type tray the cross-sectional area of the cable shall not exceed 2.3 square inches (1484 sq mm) in a 3-inch (76-mm) wide channel tray, or 4.5 square inches (2903 sq mm) in a 4-inch (102-mm) wide channel tray.

Cable trays may be ladder or ventilated trough, solid bottom, ventilated channel-type, solid unventilated covered, etc., and various widths and depths of cable trays may be used. Therefore, inspectors or contractors are not expected to compute the various combinations of cable tray fill in the field. Installation handbooks for cable tray applications are available from various manufacturers.

318-9. Number of Single Conductor Cables, Rated 2000 Volts or Less, in Cable Trays.   The number of single conductor cables, nominally rated 2000 volts or less, permitted in a single cable tray section shall not exceed the requirements of this section. The single conductors, or conductor assemblies, shall be evenly distributed across the cable tray. The conductor sizes herein apply to both aluminum and copper conductors.

(a) Ladder or Ventilated Trough Cable Trays.   Where ladder or ventilated trough cable trays contain single conductor cables, the maximum number of single conductors shall conform to the following:

(1) Where all of the cables are 1000 MCM or larger, the sum of the diameters of all single conductor cables shall not exceed the cable tray width.

**Table 318-8.   Allowable Cable Fill Area for Multiconductor Cables
in Ladder, Ventilated Trough, or Solid Bottom Cable Trays
for Cables Rated 2000 Volts or Less**

| | Maximum Allowable Fill Area in Square Inches for Multiconductor Cables | | | |
| | Ladder or Ventilated Trough Cable Trays, Section 318-8(a) | | Solid Bottom Cable Trays, Section 318-8(c) | |
Inside Width of Cable Tray (Inches)	Column 1 Applicable for Section 318-8(a) (2) Only (Square Inches)	Column 2* Applicable for Section 318-8(a) (3) Only (Square Inches)	Column 3 Applicable for Section 318-8(c) (2) Only (Square Inches)	Column 4* Applicable for Section 318-8(c) (3) Only (Square Inches)
6	7	7—(1.2 Sd)**	5.5	5.5—Sd**
12	14	14—(1.2 Sd)	11.0	11.0—Sd
18	21	21—(1.2 Sd)	16.5	16.5—Sd
24	28	28—(1.2 Sd)	22.0	22.0—Sd
30	35	35—(1.2 Sd)	27.5	27.5—Sd
36	42	42—(1.2 Sd)	33.0	33.0—Sd

For SI units: one square inch = 645 square millimeters.

* The maximum allowable fill areas in Columns 2 and 4 shall be computed. For example, the maximum allowable fill, in square inches, for a 6-inch (152-mm) wide cable tray in Column 2 shall be: 7 minus (1.2 multiplied by Sd).

** The term Sd in Columns 2 and 4 is equal to the sum of the diameters, in inches, of all 4/0 AWG and larger multiconductor cables in the same cable tray with smaller cables.

(2) Where all of the cables are smaller than 1000 MCM, the sum of the cross-sectional areas of all single conductor cables shall not exceed the maximum allowable cable fill area in Column 1 of Table 318-9, for the appropriate cable tray width.

(3) Where 1000 MCM or larger single conductor cables are installed in the same cable tray with single conductor cables smaller than 1000 MCM, the sum of the cross-sectional areas of all cables smaller than 1000 MCM shall not exceed the maximum allowable fill area resulting from the computation in Column 2 of Table 318-9, for the appropriate cable tray width.

(b) 4-Inch (102-mm) Ventilated Channel-type Cable Trays.   Where 4-inch (102-mm) wide ventilated channel-type cable trays contain single conductor cables, the sum of the diameters of all single conductors shall not exceed the inside width of the channel.

318-10. Ampacity of Cables Rated 2000 Volts or Less in Cable Trays.   The derating factors of Note 8 to Tables 310-16 through 310-19 do not apply to the ampacity of cables in cable trays.

(a) Multiconductor Cables.   The ampacity of multiconductor cables, nominally rated 2000 volts or less, installed according to the requirements of Section 318-8 shall comply with the allowable ampacities of Tables 310-16 and 310-18.

Exception: Where cable trays are continuously covered for more than 6 feet (1.83 m) with solid unventilated covers, not more than 95 percent of the allowable ampacities of Tables 310-16 and 310-18 shall be permitted for multiconductor cables.

(b) Single Conductor Cables.   The ampacity of single conductor cables, or single conductors cabled together (triplexed, quadruplexed, etc.), nominally rated 2000 volts or less, shall comply with the following:

(1) Where installed according to the requirements of Section 318-9, the ampacities for 600 MCM and larger single conductor cables in uncovered cable trays shall not exceed 75 percent of

**Table 318-9.   Allowable Cable Fill Area for Single Conductor
Cables in Ladder or Ventilated Trough Cable Trays
for Cables Rated 2000 Volts or Less**

Inside Width of Cable Tray (Inches)	Maximum Allowable Fill Area in Square Inches for Single Conductor Cables in Ladder or Ventilated Trough Cable Trays	
	Column 1 Applicable for Section 318-9(a) (2) Only (Square Inches)	Column 2* Applicable for Section 318-9(a) (3) Only (Square Inches)
6	6.50	6.50—(1.1 Sd)**
12	13.0	13.0 —(1.1 Sd)
18	19.5	19.5 —(1.1 Sd)
24	26.0	26.0 —(1.1 Sd)
30	32.5	32.5 —(1.1 Sd)
36	39.0	39.0 —(1.1 Sd)

For SI units: one square inch = 645 square millimeters.

* The maximum allowable fill areas in Column 2 shall be computed. For example, the maximum allowable fill, in square inches, for a 6-inch (152-mm) wide cable tray shall be: 6.5 minus (1.1 multiplied by Sd).

** The term Sd in Column 2 is equal to the sum of the diameters, in inches, of all 1000 MCM and larger single conductor cables in the same ladder or ventilated trough cable tray with smaller cables.

the allowable ampacities in Tables 310-17 and 310-19. Where cable trays are continuously covered for more than 6 feet (1.83 m) with solid unventilated covers, the ampacities for 600 MCM and larger cables shall not exceed 70 percent of the allowable ampacities in Tables 310-17 and 310-19.

(2) Where installed according to the requirements of Section 318-9, the ampacities for 250 MCM through 500 MCM single conductor cables in uncovered cable trays shall not exceed 65 percent of the allowable ampacities in Tables 310-17 and 310-19. Where cable trays are continuously covered for more than 6 feet (1.83 m) with solid unventilated covers, the ampacities for 250 MCM through 500 MCM cables shall not exceed 60 percent of the allowable ampacities in Tables 310-17 and 310-19.

(3) Where single conductors are installed in a single layer in uncovered cable trays, with a maintained space of not less than one cable diameter between individual conductors, the ampacity of 250 MCM and larger cables shall not exceed the allowable ampacities in Tables 310-17 and 310-19.

318-11. Number of Type MV and Type MC Cables (2001 Volts or Over) in Cable Trays.   The number of cables, nominally rated 2001 volts or over, permitted in a single cable tray shall not exceed the requirements of this section.

The sum of the diameters of single conductor and multiconductor cables shall not exceed the cable tray width, and the cables shall be installed in a single layer. Where single conductor cables are triplexed, quadruplexed, or bound together in circuit groups, the sum of the diameters of the single conductors shall not exceed the cable tray width, and these groups shall be installed in single layer arrangement.

318-12. Ampacity of Type MV and Type MC Cables (2001 Volts or Over) in Cable Trays.   The ampacity of cables, rated 2001 volts, nominal, or over, installed according to Section 318-11 shall not exceed the requirements of this section.

(a) Multiconductor Cables (2001 Volts or Over).   The ampacity of multiconductor cables shall comply with the allowable ampacities of Tables 310-45 and 310-46.

Exception No. 1: Where cable trays are continuously covered for more than 6 feet (1.83 m) with solid unventilated covers, not more than 95 percent of the allowable ampacities of Tables 310-45 and 310-46 shall be permitted for multiconductor cables.

Exception No. 2: Where multiconductor cables are installed in a single layer in uncovered cable trays, with a maintained spacing of not less than one cable diameter between cables, the ampacity shall not exceed the allowable ampacities of Tables 310-41 and 310-42.

(b) Single Conductor Cables (2001 Volts or Over).   The ampacity of single conductor cables, or single conductors cabled together (triplexed, quadruplexed, etc.), shall comply with the following:

(1) The ampacities for 250 MCM and larger single conductor cables in uncovered cable trays shall not exceed 75 percent of the allowable ampacities in Tables 310-39 and 310-40. Where the cable trays are covered for more than 6 feet (1.83 m) with solid unventilated covers, the ampacities for 250 MCM and larger single conductor cables shall not exceed .70 percent of the allowable ampacities in Tables 310-39 and 310-40.

(2) Where single conductor cables are installed in a single layer in uncovered cable trays, with a maintained space of not less than one cable diameter between individual conductors, the ampacity of 250 MCM and larger cables shall not exceed the allowable ampacities in Tables 310-39 and 310-40.

ARTICLE 320 — OPEN WIRING ON INSULATORS

Contents

320-1. Definition.   Open wiring on insulators is an exposed wiring method using cleats, knobs, tubes, and flexible tubing for the protection and support of single insulated conductors run in or on buildings, and not concealed by the building structure.

Open wiring on insulators is an exposed wiring method and is not to be concealed by the structure or finish of the building. It is permitted indoors or outdoors, in dry or wet locations, and where subject to corrosive vapors. Open wiring may be any of the general-use conductors listed in Table 310-13, such as Types RH, T, TW, XHHW; the selection, of course, is dependent upon whether the location is wet or dry, temperature considerations, ampacities, etc.

This method of wiring may be used for temporary lighting and power circuits on construction sites, lighting and power circuits in agricultural buildings, and services, and is commonly used for feeders in industrial locations. See Sections 230-43, 305-2, and 547-3.

320-2. Other Articles.   Open wiring on insulators shall comply with this article and also with the applicable provisions of other articles in this Code, especially Articles 225 and 300.

320-3. Uses Permitted.   Open wiring on insulators shall be permitted on systems of 600 volts, nominal, or less, only for industrial or agricultural establishments, indoors or outdoors, in wet or dry locations, where subject to corrosive vapors, and for services.

320-5. Conductors.

(a) Type.   Conductors shall be of a type specified by Article 310.

(b) Ampacity.   The ampacity shall comply with Tables 310-17 and 310-19 and all applicable notes to those tables.

320-6. Conductor Supports.   Conductors shall be rigidly supported on noncombustible, nonabsorbent insulating materials and shall not contact any other objects. Supports shall be installed as follows: (1) within 6 inches (152 mm) from a tap or splice; (2) within 12 inches (305 mm) of a dead-end connection to a rosette, lampholder, or receptacle; (3) at intervals not exceeding 4½ feet (1.37 m) and at closer intervals sufficient to provide adequate support where likely to be disturbed.

Exception No. 1: Supports for conductors No. 8 or larger installed across open spaces shall be permitted up to 15 feet (4.57 m) apart if noncombustible, nonabsorbent insulating spacers are used at least every 4½ feet (1.37 m) to maintain at least 2½ inches (64 mm) between conductors.

Exception No. 2: Where not likely to be disturbed in buildings of mill construction, No. 8 and larger conductors shall be permitted to be run across open spaces if supported from each wood cross member on approved insulators maintaining 6 inches (152 mm) between conductors.

Exception No. 3: In industrial establishments only, where conditions of maintenance and supervision assure that only qualified persons will service the system, conductors of size 250 MCM and larger shall be permitted to be run across open spaces where supported on intervals up to 30 feet (9.1 m) apart.

Mill construction is generally considered to be a building where the floors and ceilings are supported on wooden beams or wooden cross members spaced approximately 15 ft apart. No. 8 and larger conductors may safely span this distance, where the ceilings are high and the conductors are unable to contact other objects and are free from obstructions.

It is common practice in industrial buildings to install open feeders on insulators which are mounted on the bottom of roof trusses at every bay location. Many times bay locations are in excess of 15-ft spacing; therefore, Exception No. 3 permits size 250 MCM and larger conductors to be supported at 30-ft intervals where it is assured that qualified persons will service the system.

In addition to the ease and economy of installations or alterations of open wiring, it is to be noted that by close spacing of conductors the reactance of a circuit is reduced; hence, the voltage drop is reduced.

320-7. Mounting of Conductor Supports.   Where nails are used to mount knobs, they shall not be smaller than 10 penny. Where screws are used to mount knobs, or where nails or screws are used to mount cleats, they shall be of a length sufficient to penetrate the wood to a depth equal to at least one-half the height of the knob and fully the thickness of the cleat. Cushion washers shall be used with nails.

320-8. Tie Wires. No. 8 or larger conductors supported on solid knobs shall be securely tied thereto by tie wires having an insulation equivalent to that of the conductor.

320-10. Flexible Nonmetallic Tubing. In dry locations where not exposed to severe physical damage, conductors shall be permitted to be separately enclosed in flexible nonmetallic tubing. The tubing shall be in continuous lengths not exceeding 15 feet (4.57 m) and secured to the surface by straps at intervals not exceeding 4½ feet (1.37 m).

320-11. Through Walls, Floors, Wood Cross Members, etc. Open conductors shall be separated from contact with walls, floors, wood cross members, or partitions through which they pass by tubes or bushings of noncombustible, nonabsorbent insulating material. Where the bushing is shorter than the hole, a waterproof sleeve of noninductive material shall be inserted in the hole and an insulating bushing slipped into the sleeve at each end in such a manner as to keep the conductors absolutely out of contact with the sleeve. Each conductor shall be carried through a separate tube or sleeve.

320-12. Clearance from Piping, Exposed Conductors, etc. Open conductors shall be separated at least 2 inches (50.8 mm) from metal conduit, piping, or other conducting material, and from any exposed lighting, power, or signaling conductor, or shall be separated therefrom by a continuous and firmly fixed nonconductor in addition to the insulation of the conductor. Where any insulating tube is used, it shall be secured at the ends. Where practicable, conductors shall pass over rather than under any piping subject to leakage or accumulations of moisture.

The provision for additional protective insulation on open wiring is to prevent contact with metal piping, metal objects, or exposed conductors of other circuits.

320-13. Entering Spaces Subject to Dampness, Wetness, or Corrosive Vapors. Conductors entering or leaving locations subject to dampness, wetness, or corrosive vapors shall have drip loops formed on them and shall then pass upward and inward from the outside of the buildings, or from the damp, wet, or corrosive location, through noncombustible, nonabsorbent insulating tubes.

See also Section 230-52.

320-14. Protection from Physical Damage. Conductors within 7 feet (2.13 m) from the floor shall be considered exposed to physical damage. Where open conductors cross ceiling joists and wall studs and are exposed to physical damage, they shall be protected by one of the following methods: (1) by guard strips not less than ⅞ inch (22 mm) in thickness and at least as high as the insulating supports, placed on each side of and close to the wiring; (2) by a substantial running board at least ½ inch (12.7 mm) thick back of the conductors with side protections. Running boards shall extend at least 1 inch (25.4 mm) outside the conductors, but not more than 2 inches (50.8 mm), and the protecting sides shall be at least 2 inches (50.8 mm) high and at least ⅞ inch (22 mm) thick; (3) by boxing made as above and furnished with a cover kept at least 1 inch (25.4 mm) away from the conductors within. Where protecting vertical conductors on side walls, the boxing shall be closed at the top and the holes through which the conductors pass shall be bushed; (4) by rigid metal conduit, intermediate metal conduit, rigid nonmetallic conduit, or electrical metallic tubing, in which case the rules of Article 345, 346, 347, or 348 shall apply; or by metal piping, in which case the conductors shall be encased in continuous lengths of approved flexible tubing. The conductors passing through metal enclosures shall be so grouped that current in both directions is approximately equal.

320-15. Unfinished Attics and Roof Spaces. Conductors in unfinished attics and roof spaces shall comply with (a) or (b) below.

(a) Accessible by Stairway or Permanent Ladder. Conductors shall be installed along the side of or through bored holes in floor joists, studs, or rafters. Where run through bored holes, conductors in the joists and in studs or rafters to a height of not less than 7 feet (2.13 m) above the floor or floor joists shall be protected by substantial running boards extending not less than 1 inch (25.4 mm) on each side of the conductors. Running boards shall be securely fastened in place. Running boards and guard strips shall not be required for conductors installed along the sides of joists, studs, or rafters.

(b) Not Accessible by Stairway or Permanent Ladder. Conductors shall be installed along the sides of or through bored holes in floor joists, studs, or rafters.

Exception: In buildings completed before wiring is installed and having head room at all points of less than 3 feet (914 mm).

320-16. Switches. Surface-type snap switches shall be mounted in accordance with Section 380-10(a), and boxes shall not be required. Other type switches shall be installed in accordance with Section 380-4.

ARTICLE 321 — MESSENGER SUPPORTED WIRING

Contents

321-1. Definition. Messenger supported wiring is an exposed wiring support system using a messenger wire to support insulated conductors by any one of the following: (1) a messenger with rings and saddles for conductor support; (2) a messenger with a field-installed lashing material for conductor support; (3) factory-assembled aerial cable; (4) multiplex cables utilizing a bare conductor, factory assembled and twisted with one or more insulated conductors, such as duplex, triplex, or quadruplex type of construction.

The 1981 *NEC* introduced Article 321 to recognize the requirements for "messenger supported wiring" as, by tradition and practice, messenger supported wiring systems are approved systems.

Messenger supported wiring systems have been manufactured and have been used successfully for many years in industrial installations. They have also been used for many years as service drops by utilities for commercial and residential installations.

See reference in Section 225-6, Exception.

321-2. Other Articles. Messenger supported wiring shall comply with this article and also with the applicable provisions of other articles in this Code, especially Articles 225 and 300.

321-3. Uses Permitted.

(a) Cable Types. The following shall be permitted to be installed in messenger supported wiring under the conditions described in the article for each: (1) mineral-insulated, metal-sheathed cable (Article 330); (2) metal-clad cable (Article 334); (3) multiconductor service-entrance cable (Article 338); (4) multiconductor underground feeder and branch-circuit cable (Article 339); (5) power and control tray cable (Article 340); (6) other factory-assembled, multiconductor control, signal, or power cables which are identified for the use.

(b) In Industrial Establishments. In industrial establishments only, where conditions of maintenance and supervision assure that only competent individuals will service the installed messenger supported wiring, any of the following sizes and types of cables shall be permitted: (1) single conductor, Type MV, Types RHH and RHW without outer braids, and THW, where exposed to direct rays of the sun, cables shall be sunlight-resistant; (2) multiconductor, Type MV cable (Article 326), where exposed to direct rays of the sun, cables shall be sunlight-resistant.

(c) Hazardous (Classified) Locations. Messenger supported wiring shall be permitted to be used in hazardous (classified) locations where the contained cables are permitted for such use in Sections 501-4, 502-4, and 503-3.

321-4. Uses Not Permitted. Messenger supported wiring shall not be used in hoistways or where subjected to severe physical damage.

321-5. Ampacity. The ampacity shall comply with Table 310-16, 310-18, 310-41, or 310-42 and all notes to those tables as applicable.

321-6. Messenger Support. The messenger shall be supported at dead ends and at intermediate locations so as to eliminate tension on the conductors. The conductors shall not be permitted to come into contact with the messenger supports or any structural members, walls, or pipes.

321-7. Grounding. The messenger shall be grounded as required by Sections 250-32 and 250-33 for enclosure grounding.

321-8. Conductor Splices and Taps. Conductor splices and taps made and insulated by approved methods shall be permitted in messenger supported wiring.

ARTICLE 324 — CONCEALED KNOB-AND-TUBE
WIRING

Contents

324-1. Definition.   Concealed knob-and-tube wiring is a wiring method using knobs, tubes, and flexible nonmetallic tubing for the protection and support of single insulated conductors concealed in hollow spaces of walls and ceilings of buildings.

Open wiring on insulators (Article 320) is an "exposed" wiring method, whereas knob-and-tube wiring is a "concealed" method. Conductors used for knob-and-tube work may be of any general-use type specified by Article 310.

324-2. Other Articles.   Concealed knob-and-tube wiring shall comply with this article and also with the applicable provisions of other articles in this Code, especially Article 300.

324-3. Uses Permitted.   Concealed knob-and-tube wiring shall be permitted to be used only for extensions of existing installations and elsewhere only by special permission under the following conditions:

(1) In the hollow spaces of walls and ceilings.

(2) In unfinished attic and roof spaces as provided in Section 324-11.

Knob-and-tube wiring is permitted to be installed "only" for extensions of existing installations and "only" if special permission is granted by the authority having jurisdiction of enforcement of the *Code*.

324-4. Uses Not Permitted.   Concealed knob-and-tube wiring shall not be used in commercial garages, theaters and similar locations, motion picture studios, or hazardous (classified) locations.

324-5. Conductors.

(a) Type.   Conductors shall be of a type specified by Article 310.

(b) Ampacity.   The ampacity shall comply with Tables 310-17 and 310-19 and all applicable notes to those tables.

324-6. Conductor Supports.   Conductors shall be rigidly supported on noncombustible, nonabsorbent insulating materials and shall not contact any other objects. Supports shall be installed as follows: (1) within 6 inches (152 mm) of each side of each tap or splice, and (2) at intervals not exceeding 4½ feet (1.37 m).

Exception: If it is not practicable to provide supports in dry locations it shall be permissible to fish conductors through hollow spaces if each conductor is individually enclosed in flexible nonmetallic tubing. The tubing shall be in continuous lengths between supports, between boxes, or between a support and a box.

324-7. Tie Wires.   Where solid knobs are used, conductors shall be securely tied thereto by tie wires having insulation equivalent to that of the conductor.

324-8. Conductor Clearances.   A clearance of not less than 3 inches (76 mm) shall be maintained between conductors and of not less than 1 inch (25.4 mm) between the conductor and the surface over which it passes.

Exception: Where space is too limited to provide the above minimum clearances, such as at meters, panelboards, outlets, and switch points, the conductors shall be individually enclosed in flexible nonmetallic tubing, which shall be in continuous lengths between the last support or box and the terminal point.

324-9. Through Walls, Floors, Wood Cross Members, etc.   Conductors shall comply with Section 320-11 where passing through holes in structural members. Where passing through wood cross members in plastered partitions, conductors shall be protected by noncombustible, nonabsorbent, insulating tubes extending not less than 3 inches (76 mm) beyond the wood member.

The provision for insulated tubes for use with knob-and-tube wiring where passing through wood cross members in plastered partitions is to protect the wire from contact with plaster that is likely to accumulate on horizontal wood members.

324-10. Clearance from Piping, Exposed Conductors, etc.   Conductors shall comply with Section 320-12 for clearances from other exposed conductors, piping, etc.

324-11. Unfinished Attics and Roof Spaces.   Conductors in unfinished attics and roof spaces shall comply with (a) or (b) below.

(a) Accessible by Stairway or Permanent Ladder.   Conductors shall be installed along the side of or through bored holes in floor joists, studs, or rafters. Where run through bored holes, conductors in the joists and in studs or rafters to a height of not less than 7 feet (2.13 m) above the floor or floor joists shall be protected by substantial running boards extending not less than 1 inch (25.4 mm) on each side of the conductors. Running boards shall be securely fastened in place. Running boards and guard strips shall not be required where conductors are installed along the sides of joists, studs, or rafters.

(b) Not Accessible by Stairway or Permanent Ladder.   Conductors shall be installed along the sides of or through bored holes in floor joists, studs, or rafters.

Exception: In buildings completed before wiring is installed and having head room at all points of less than 3 feet (914 mm).

Figure 324-1 illustrates the "running board" method of protecting open-type conductors in an accessible attic. This method is applied in attics that are accessible by stairways or permanent ladders and where such spaces are generally used for storage.

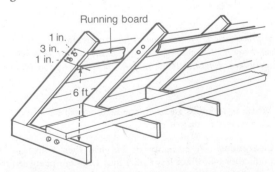

Figure 324-1. Open wiring in accessible attic. Wires run through rafters and through joists where there is no floor.

324-12. Splices.   Splices shall be soldered unless approved splicing devices are used. In-line or strain splices shall not be used.

324-13. Boxes.   Outlet boxes shall comply with Article 370.

324-14. Switches.   Switches shall comply with Sections 380-4 and 380-10(b).

ARTICLE 326 — MEDIUM VOLTAGE CABLE

Type MV

Contents

326-1. Definition.
326-2. Other Articles.
326-3. Uses Permitted.
326-4. Uses Not Permitted.

326-5. Construction.
326-6. Ampacity.
326-7. Marking.

326-1. Definition.   Type MV is a single or multiconductor solid dielectric insulated cable rated 2001 volts or higher.

Medium voltage cables are rated 2001 to 35,000 V. Cables rated 2001 to 8000 V may be shielded or nonshielded. All insulated conductors 8001 V and higher have electrostatic shielding.

326-2. Other Articles.   In addition to the provisions of this article, Type MV cable shall comply with the applicable provisions of this Code, especially Articles 300, 305, 310, 318, 501, and 710.

326-3. Uses Permitted.   Type MV cables shall be permitted for use on power systems rated up to 35,000 volts, nominal, in wet or dry locations, in raceways, or directly buried in accordance with Section 710-3(b) and in messenger supported wiring.

326-4. Uses Not Permitted.   Type MV cable shall not be used unless identified for the use (1) where exposed to direct sunlight, and (2) in cable trays.

Cables intended for installation in cable trays in accordance with Article 318 are marked "for CT Use" or "for use in cable trays."

326-5. Construction.   Type MV cables shall have copper, aluminum, or copper-clad aluminum conductors and shall be constructed in accordance with Sections 310-6 and 310-13.

Cables with aluminum conductors are marked with the word "aluminum" or the letters "AL."

326-6. Ampacity.   The ampacity of Type MV cable shall be in accordance with Section 310-15.

Exception: The ampacity of Type MV cable installed in cable tray shall be in accordance with Section 318-12.

This Exception is required to provide the correct ampacities for conductors and multiconductor cables where installed in cable tray.

326-7. Marking. Medium voltage cable shall be marked as required in Section 310-11.

Cables are marked with their conductor size, voltage rating, and insulation level (100 percent or 133 percent).

ARTICLE 328 — FLAT CONDUCTOR CABLE TYPE FCC

Contents

A. General

328-1. Scope. This article covers a field-installed wiring system for branch circuits incorporating Type FCC cable and associated accessories as defined by the article. The wiring system is designed for installation under carpet squares.

This article first appeared in the 1981 *NEC* and covers the design and installation requirements of this undercarpet wiring method.

The technical basis for this article is a comprehensive Fact-Finding Report on Under Carpet Flat Conductor Cable Systems by Underwriters Laboratories.

The Flat Conductor Cable System is designed to provide a completely accessible, flexible power system. It also provides an easy method for reworking obsolete wiring systems currently in use in many office facilities.

328-2. Definitions.

Type FCC Cable. Type FCC cable consists of three or more flat copper conductors placed edge-to-edge and separated and enclosed within an insulating assembly.

FCC System. A complete wiring system for branch circuits that is designed for installation under carpet squares. The FCC system includes Type FCC cable and associated shielding, connectors, terminators, adapters, boxes, and receptacles.

Cable Connector. A connector designed to join Type FCC cables without using a junction box.

Insulating End. An insulator designed to electrically insulate the end of a Type FCC cable.

Top Shield. A grounded metal shield covering undercarpet components of the FCC system for the purposes of providing protection against physical damage.

Bottom Shield. A shield mounted on the floor under the FCC system to provide protection against physical damage.

Transition Assembly. An assembly to facilitate connection of the FCC system to other approved wiring systems, incorporating (1) a means of electrical interconnection, and (2) a suitable box or covering for providing electrical safety and protection against physical damage.

Metal Shield Connections. Means of connection designed to electrically and mechanically connect a metal shield to another metal shield, to a receptacle housing or self-contained device, or to a transition assembly.

328-3. Other Articles. The FCC systems shall conform with applicable provisions of Articles 210, 220, 240, 250 and 300.

328-4. Uses Permitted.

(a) Branch Circuits. Use of FCC systems shall be permitted both for general purpose and appliance branch circuits, and for individual branch circuits.

(b) Floors. Use of FCC systems shall be permitted on hard, sound, smooth, continuous floor surfaces made of concrete, ceramic, or composition flooring, wood, and similar materials.

(c) Walls. Use of FCC systems shall be permitted on wall surfaces in surface metal raceways.

(d) Damp Locations. Use of FCC systems in damp locations shall be permitted.

(e) Heated Floors. Materials used for floors heated in excess of 30°C (86°F) shall be identified as suitable for use at these temperatures.

328-5. Uses Not Permitted. FCC systems shall not be used: (1) outdoors or in wet locations; (2) where subject to corrosive vapors; (3) in any hazardous (classified) location; or (4) in residential, school, and hospital buildings.

328-6. Branch-Circuit Ratings.

(a) Voltage. Voltage between ungrounded conductors shall not exceed 300 volts. Voltage between ungrounded conductors and grounded conductor shall not exceed 150 volts.

(b) Current. General purpose and appliance branch circuits shall have ratings not exceeding 20 amperes. Individual branch circuits shall have ratings not exceeding 30 amperes.

B. Installation

328-10. Coverings. Floor-mounted Type FCC cable, cable connectors, and insulating ends shall be covered with carpet squares. Those carpet squares that are adhered to the floor shall be attached with release-type adhesives.

328-11. Cable Connections and Insulating Ends. All Type FCC cable connections shall use connectors identified for their use, installed such that electrical continuity, insulation, and sealing against dampness and liquid spillage are provided. All bare cable ends shall be insulated and sealed against dampness and liquid spillage using listed insulating ends.

328-12. Shields.

(a) Top Shield.   A metal top shield shall be installed over all floor-mounted Type FCC cable, connectors, and insulating ends. The top shield shall completely cover all cable runs, corners, connectors, and ends.

(b) Bottom Shield.   A bottom shield shall be installed beneath all Type FCC cable, connectors, and insulating ends.

328-13. Enclosure and Shield Connections.   All metal shields, boxes, receptacle housings, and self-contained devices shall be electrically continuous to the equipment grounding conductor of the supplying branch circuit. All such electrical connections shall be made with connectors identified for this use. The electrical resistivity of such shield system shall not be more than that of one conductor of the Type FCC cable used in the installation.

328-14. Receptacles.   All receptacles, receptacle housings, and self-contained devices used with the FCC system shall be identified for this use and shall be connected to the Type FCC cable and metal shields. Connection from any grounding conductor of the Type FCC cable shall be made to the shield system at each receptacle.

328-15. Connection to Other Systems.   Power feed, grounding connection, and shield system connection between the FCC system and other wiring systems shall be accomplished in a transition assembly identified for this use.

328-16. Anchoring.   All FCC system components shall be firmly anchored to the floor or wall using an adhesive or mechanical anchoring system identified for this use. Floors shall be prepared to assure adherence of the FCC system to the floor until the carpet squares are placed.

328-17. Crossings.   Crossings of two Type FCC cable runs shall be permitted. Crossings of a Type FCC cable over or under a flat telephone cable shall be permitted. In each case, a grounded layer of metal shielding shall separate the two cables.

328-18. System Height.   Any portion of an FCC system with a height above floor level exceeding 0.090 inches (2.29 mm) shall be tapered or feathered at the edges to floor level.

328-19. FCC Systems Alterations.   Alterations to FCC systems shall be permitted. New cable connectors shall be used at new connection points to make alterations. It shall be permitted to leave unused cable runs and associated cable connectors in place and energized. All cable ends shall be covered with insulating ends.

328-20. Polarization of Connections.   All receptacles and connections shall be constructed and installed so as to maintain proper polarization of the system.

C. Construction

328-30. Type FCC Cable.   Type FCC cable shall be approved for use with the FCC system and shall consist of three, four, or five flat copper conductors, one of which shall be an equipment grounding conductor. The insulating material of the cable shall be moisture-resistant and flame-retardant.

328-31. Markings.   Type FCC cable shall be clearly and durably marked on both sides at intervals of not more than 24 inches (610 mm), with the information required by Section 310-11(a) and with the following additional information: (1) material of conductors; (2) maximum temperature rating; and (3) ampacity.

328-32. Conductor Identification.

(a) **Colors.** Conductors shall be clearly and durably marked on both sides throughout their length as specified in Section 310-12.

(b) **Order.** For a two-wire FCC system with grounding, the grounding conductor shall be central.

328-33. Corrosion Resistance. Metal components of the system shall be either: (1) corrosion-resistant; (2) coated with corrosion-resistant materials; or (3) insulated from contact with corrosive substances.

328-34. Insulation. All insulating materials in the FCC systems shall be identified for their use.

328-35. Shields.

(a) **Materials and Dimensions.** All top and bottom shields shall be of designs and materials identified for their use. Top shields shall be metal. Both metallic and nonmetallic materials shall be permitted for bottom shields.

(b) **Resistivity.** Metal shields have cross-sectional areas that provide for electrical resistivity of not more than that of one conductor of the Type FCC cable used in the installation.

(c) **Metal-Shield Connectors.** Metal shields shall be connected to each other and to boxes, receptacle housings, self-contained devices, and transition assemblies using metal-shield connectors.

328-36. Receptacles and Housings. Receptacle housings and self-contained devices designed either for floor mounting or for in- or on-wall mounting shall be permitted for use with the FCC system. Receptacle housings and self-contained devices shall incorporate means for facilitating entry and termination of Type FCC cable, and for electrically connecting the housing or device with the metal shield. Receptacles and self-contained devices shall comply with Section 210-7. Power and communications outlets installed together in common housing shall be permitted in accordance with Section 800-3(a)(2), Exception No. 1.

328-37. Transition Assemblies. All transition assemblies shall be identified for their use. Each assembly shall incorporate means for facilitating entry of the Type FCC cable into the assembly, for connecting the Type FCC cable to grounded conductors, and for electrically connecting the assembly to the metal cable shields and to equipment grounding conductors.

ARTICLE 330 — MINERAL-INSULATED,
METAL-SHEATHED CABLE

Type MI

Contents

A. General

330-1. Definition.   Type MI mineral-insulated, metal-sheathed cable is a factory assembly of one or more conductors insulated with a highly compressed refractory mineral insulation and enclosed in a liquidtight and gastight continuous copper sheath.

330-2. Other Articles.   Type MI cable shall comply with this article and also with the applicable provisions of other articles in this Code, especially Article 300.

Mineral-insulated, metal-sheathed cable consists of one or more solid copper conductors insulated with highly compressed magnesium oxide and enclosed in a continuous copper sheath. It is labeled in sizes 16 AWG to 250 MCM one conductor, 16 to 4 AWG two and three conductor, 16 to 6 AWG four conductor and 16 to 10 AWG seven conductor. The cable is rated 600 V.

Terminations especially investigated for use with this cable are listed by Underwriters Laboratories Inc. as Mineral Insulated Cable Fittings.

Supplementary nonmetallic coatings presently used have not been investigated for resistance to corrosion.

The Listing Mark of Underwriters Laboratories Inc. affixed to the reel supporting the cable or tag attached to the cable is the only method provided by UL to identify products manufactured under its Listing and Follow-Up Service. The Listing Mark for these products includes the name and/or symbol of Underwriters Laboratories Inc. together with the word "Listed," a control number, and the following product name: "Mineral-Insulated Metal-Sheathed Cable."

· Fittings for use on Mineral-Insulated Cable Type MI and small-diameter mineral-insulated cable are suitable for use at a maximum operating temperature of 85°C (185°F) in dry locations and 60°C (140°F) in wet locations. A complete box connector consists of a connector body and a screw-on potting fitting.

The screw-on potting fitting to be used with the connector may be used separately as an end fitting for change to open wiring. The screw-on potting fitting is to be assembled with a special tool and consists of a screw-on pot, insulating cap, insulating sleeving, anchoring bead, and sealing compound.

330-3. Uses Permitted.   Type MI cable shall be permitted as follows: (1) for services, feeders, and branch circuits; (2) in dry, wet, or continuously moist locations; (3) indoors or outdoors; (4) where exposed or concealed; (5) embedded in plaster, concrete, fill or other masonry, whether above or below grade; (6) in any hazardous (classified) location; (7) where exposed to oil and gasoline; (8) where exposed to corrosive conditions not deteriorating to its sheath; (9) in underground runs where suitably protected against physical damage and corrosive conditions.

Mineral-insulated, metal-sheathed cable (Type MI) is suitable for all power and control circuits up to 600 V and may be used for services, feeders, and branch circuits in exposed and concealed work; in dry and wet locations; for underplaster extensions and embedment in plaster; in masonry, concrete, or fill; for underground runs; or where exposed to weather, continuous moisture, oil in any hazardous (classified) location, or other conditions not having a deteriorating effect on the metallic sheath.

330-4. Uses Not Permitted.   Type MI cable shall not be used where exposed to destructive corrosive conditions.

Exception: Where protected by materials suitable for the conditions.

B. Installation

330-10. Wet Locations.   Where installed in wet locations, Type MI cable shall comply with Section 300-6(c).

330-11. Through Joists, Studs, or Rafters.   Type MI cable shall comply with Section 300-4 where installed through studs, joists, rafters, or similar wood members.

330-12. Supports.   Type MI cable shall be securely supported at intervals not exceeding 6 feet (1.83 m) by straps, staples, hangers, or similar fittings so designed and installed as not to damage the cable.

Exception: Where cable is fished in.

330-13. Bends.   Bends in Type MI cable shall be so made as not to damage the cable. The radius of the inner edge of any bend shall not be less than five times the cable diameter.

330-14. Fittings.   Fittings used for connecting Type MI cable to boxes, cabinets, or other equipment shall be identified for such use. Where single-conductor cables enter ferrous metal boxes or cabinets, the installation shall comply with Section 300-20 to prevent inductive heating.

330-15. Terminal Seals.   Where Type MI cable terminates, an approved seal shall be provided immediately after stripping to prevent the entrance of moisture into the insulation. The conductors extending beyond the sheath shall be individually provided with an approved insulating material.

C. Construction Specifications

330-20. Conductors.   Type MI cable conductors shall be of solid copper with a cross-sectional area corresponding to standard AWG sizes.

330-21. Insulation.   The conductor insulation in Type MI cable shall be a highly compressed refractory mineral that will provide proper spacing for the conductors.

330-22. Outer Sheath.   The outer sheath shall be of a continuous copper construction to provide mechanical protection, a moisture seal, and an adequate path for grounding purposes.

ARTICLE 333 — ARMORED CABLE

Type AC Cable

Contents

333-12. In Accessible Attics.
  (a) Where Run Across the Top of
    Floor Joists.

(b) Where Carried along the Sides
of Floor Joists.

333-1. Definition. Type AC cable is a fabricated assembly of insulated conductors in a flexible metallic enclosure. See Section 333-4.

Armored cable is listed in sizes No. 14 through No. 1 AWG copper and No. 12 through No. 1 AWG aluminum and is rated at 600 V or less.

333-2. Other Articles. Type AC cable shall comply with this article and also with the applicable provisions of other articles in this Code, especially Article 300.

333-3. Marking. The provisions of Section 310-11 shall apply, except that Type AC cable shall have ready identification of the maker by distinctive external markers on the cable sheath throughout its entire length.

333-4. Construction. Type AC cable shall be an approved cable with acceptable metal covering. The insulated conductors shall conform with Section 333-5.
   Type AC cables are branch-circuit and feeder cables with armor of flexible metal tape. Cables of the AC type, except ACL, shall have an internal bonding strip of copper or aluminum, in intimate contact with the armor for its entire length.

The armor of Type AC cable is recognized as an equipment grounding conductor by Section 250-91(b). The required internal bonding strip is simply cut off at the termination of the armored cable; its use is to supplement the effectiveness of the spiral armor as an equipment grounding means.

333-5. Conductors. Insulated conductors shall be of a type listed in Table 310-13. In addition, the conductors shall have an overall moisture-resistant and fire-retardant fibrous covering. For Type ACT, a moisture-resistant fibrous covering shall be required only on the individual conductors.

UL data refers to the marking of cables as follows. ACT indicates an armored cable employing conductors having thermoplastic insulation. AC indicates an armored cable employing conductors having thermosetting insulation. No suffix indicates 60°C (140°F) rating. H indicates 75°C (167°F) rating. HH indicates 90°C (194°F) rating.

333-6. Use. Except where otherwise specified elsewhere in this Code, and where not subject to physical damage, Type AC cable shall be permitted for branch circuits and feeders in both exposed and concealed work.
   Type AC cable shall be permitted in dry locations; for underplaster extensions as provided in Article 344; and embedded in plaster finish on brick or other masonry, except in damp or wet locations. It shall be permissible to run or fish this cable in the air voids of masonry block or tile walls; where such walls are exposed or subject to excessive moisture or dampness or are below grade line, Type ACL cable shall be used. This cable shall contain lead-covered conductors (Type ACL) if used where exposed to the weather or to continuous moisture; for underground runs in raceways and embedded in masonry, concrete, or fill in buildings in course of construction; or where exposed to oil, or other conditions having a deteriorating effect on the insulation.
   Type AC cable shall not be used where prohibited elsewhere in this Code, including (1) in theaters and similar locations, except as provided in Article 518, Places of Assembly; (2) in motion picture studios; (3) in any hazardous (classified) locations; (4) where exposed to corrosive fumes or vapors; (5) on cranes or hoists, except as provided in Section 610-11, Exception No. 3; (6) in storage

battery rooms; (7) in hoistways or on elevators, except as provided in Section 620-21; or (8) in commercial garages where prohibited in Article 511.

Exception: See Section 501-4(b), Exception.

The Exception permits Type AC cable and other wiring methods, including nonmetallic-sheathed cable, for the wiring of intrinsically safe equipment. See Sections 500-1 (4th paragraph) and 501-4(b), Exception.

Type ACL cable shall not be used for direct burial in the earth.

The designation "L" indicates that a lead covering has been applied over the conductor assembly.

333-7. Supports.   Type AC cable shall be secured by approved staples, straps, hangers, or similar fittings so designed and installed as not to injure the cable at intervals not exceeding 4½ feet (1.37 m) and within 12 inches (305 mm) from every outlet box or fitting.

Exception No. 1: Where cable is fished.

Exception No. 2: Lengths of not more than 2 feet (610 mm) at terminals where flexibility is necessary.

333-8. Bends.   All bends shall be made so that the cable will not be injured, and the radius of the curve of the inner edge of any bend shall not be less than five times the diameter of the Type AC cable.

333-9. Boxes and Fittings.   At all points where the armor of AC cable terminates, a fitting shall be provided to protect wires from abrasion, unless the design of the outlet boxes or fittings is such as to afford equivalent protection, and, in addition, an approved insulating bushing or its equivalent approved protection shall be provided between the conductors and the armor. The connector or clamp by which the Type AC cable is fastened to boxes or cabinets shall be of such design that the insulating bushing or its equivalent will be visible for inspection. This bushing shall not be required with lead-covered cables where so installed that the lead sheath will be visible for inspection. Where change is made from Type AC cable to other cable or raceway wiring methods, a box shall be installed at junction points as required in Section 300-15.

Armored cable connectors are considered suitable for grounding.

333-10. Through Studs, Joists, and Rafters.   Type AC cable shall comply with Section 300-4 where installed through studs, joists, rafters, or similar wood members.

333-11. Exposed Work.   Exposed runs of cable shall closely follow the surface of the building finish or of running boards.

Exception No. 1: Lengths of not more than 24 inches (610 mm) at terminals where flexibility is necessary.

Exception No. 2: On the underside of floor joists in basements where supported at each joist and so located as not to be subject to physical damage.

It is to be noted that this Exception is not to be applied to Type NM or NMC cables.

333-12. In Accessible Attics.   Type AC cables in accessible attics or roof spaces shall be installed as specified in (a) and (b) below.

(a) Where Run Across the Top of Floor Joists.   Where run across the top of floor joists, or within 7 feet (2.13 m) of floor or floor joists across the face of rafters or studding, in attics and roof spaces which are accessible, the cable shall be protected by substantial guard strips which are at least as high as the cable. Where this space is not accessible by permanent stairs or ladders, protection shall only be required within 6 feet (1.83 m) of the nearest edge of the scuttle hole or attic entrance.

(b) Where Carried Along the Sides of Floor Joists.   Where cable is carried along the sides of rafters, studs, or floor joists, neither guard strips nor running boards shall be required.

ARTICLE 334 — METAL-CLAD CABLE

Contents

A. General

334-1. Definition.   Type MC cable is a factory assembly of one or more conductors, each individually insulated and enclosed in a metallic sheath of interlocking tape, or a smooth or corrugated tube.

    Type MC cable is of three designs: (1) interlocked metal type, (2) corrugated tube, and (3) smooth tube, and all are intended for aboveground use, except when marked for direct burial. Cables which are suitable for use in cable trays, directly buried, or in direct sunlight are so marked. Type MC cables include Type CS (copper sheath) and Type ALS (aluminum sheath).

334-2. Other Articles.   Metal-clad cable shall comply with this article and also with the applicable provisions of other articles in this Code, especially Article 300.
  Type MC cable shall be permitted for systems in excess of 600 volts, nominal. See Section 300-2.

    Type MC cable is rated for use up to 5000 V and listed in sizes No. 18 AWG and larger for copper and No. 12 AWG and larger for aluminum and employs thermoset (rubber), varnished cloth or composite varnished cloth-thermoplastic insulated conductors. The latter is designated as Type VT and rated 85°C (185°F).

334-3. Uses Permitted.   Except where otherwise specified in this Code and where not subject to physical damage, Type MC cables shall be permitted as follows: (1) for services, feeders, and branch circuits; (2) for power, lighting, control, and signal circuits; (3) indoors or outdoors; (4) where exposed or concealed; (5) direct buried; (6) in cable tray; (7) in any approved raceway; (8) as open runs of cable; (9) as aerial cable on a messenger; (10) in hazardous (classified) locations as permitted in Articles 501, 502, and 503; (11) in dry locations; and (12) in wet locations when any of the following conditions are met:

(1) The metallic covering is impervious to moisture.

(2) A lead sheath or moisture impervious jacket is provided under the metal covering.

(3) The insulated conductors under the metallic covering are approved for use in wet locations.

Exception: See Section 501-4(b), Exception.

See Section 300-6 for protection against corrosion.

334-4. Uses Not Permitted.   Type MC cable shall not be used where exposed to destructive corrosive conditions, such as direct burial in the earth, in concrete, or where exposed to cinder fills, strong chlorides, caustic alkalis, or vapors of chlorine or of hydrochloric acids.

Exception: Where the metallic sheath is suitable for the conditions or is protected by material suitable for the conditions.

B. Installation

334-10. Installation.   Type MC cable shall be installed in compliance with Articles 300, 710, and 725 as applicable.

(a) Support.   Type MC cable shall be supported and secured at intervals not exceeding 6 feet (1.83 m).

(b) Cable Tray.   Type MC cable installed in cable tray shall comply with Article 318.

(c) Direct Buried.   Direct buried cable shall comply with Section 300-5 or 710-3, as appropriate.

(d) Installed as Service-Entrance Cable.   Type MC cable installed as service-entrance cable shall comply with Article 230.

(e) Installed Outside of Buildings or as Aerial Cable.   Type MC cable installed outside of buildings or as aerial cable shall comply with Article 225.

334-11. Bending Radius.   All bends shall be so made that the cable will not be injured, and the radius of the curve of the inner edge of any bend shall not be less than shown below.

(a) Smooth Sheath.

(1) Ten times the external diameter of the metallic sheath for cable not more than ¾ inch (19 mm) in external diameter

(2) Twelve times the external diameter of the metallic sheath for cable more than ¾ inch (19 mm) but not more than 1½ inches (38 mm) in external diameter; and

(3) Fifteen times the external diameter of the metallic sheath for cable more than 1½ inches (38 mm) in external diameter.

(b) Interlocked-type Armor or Corrugated Sheath.   Seven times the external diameter of the metallic sheath.

(c) Shielded Conductors.   Twelve times the overall diameter of one of the individual conductors or seven times the overall diameter of the multiconductor cable, whichever is greater.

The minimum bending radius of twelve times the overall diameter of a single shielded conductor is consistent with IPCEA requirements and good engineering practice; however, the same minimum on a multiconductor cable would be excessive.

For example, consider 5000 kcmil, 15 kV, 100 percent insulation level (0.175 in. insulation):

	O.D.	12 × O.D.	7 × O.D.
Single Conductor	1.50 in.	18 in.	—
Three Conductor	3.15—3.50 in.	38—42 in.	22—24 in.

334-12. Fittings.   Fittings used for connecting Type MC cable to boxes, cabinets, or other equipment shall be identified for such use. Where single-conductor cables enter ferrous metal boxes or cabinets, the installation shall comply with Section 300-20 to prevent inductive heating.

Connectors should be selected in accordance with the size and type of cable for which they are designed. Bronze connectors are intended for use only with cable employing corrugated copper armor.

334-13. Ampacity.   The ampacity of Type MC cable rated 2000 volts or less shall be determined from Tables 310-16 through 310-19 and their accompanying notes. The ampacities of Type MC cable rated over 2000 volts shall be determined from Section 310-15.

This section is required to correctly identify the allowable ampacities for Type MC cable depending on the installation, i.e., isolated in air, direct buried, in conduit, or in cable tray.

Exception: The ampacities for Type MC cable installed in cable tray shall be determined in accordance with Sections 318-10 and 318-12.

C. Construction Specifications

334-20. Conductors.   The conductors shall be of copper, aluminum, or copper-clad aluminum, solid or stranded.
The minimum conductor size shall be No. 18 copper and No. 12 aluminum or copper-clad aluminum.

334-21. Insulation.   The insulated conductors shall comply with (a) or (b) below.

(a) 600 Volts.   Insulated conductors in sizes No. 18 and 16 shall be of a type listed in Table

402-3, with a maximum operating temperature not less than 90°C, and as permitted by Section 725-16. Conductors larger than No. 16 shall be of a type listed in Table 310-13 or of a type identified for use in MC cable.

(b) Over 600 Volts.   Insulated conductors shall be of a type listed in Tables 310-31 through 310-37.

334-22. Metallic Sheath.   The metallic covering shall be one of the following types: smooth metallic sheath, welded and corrugated metallic sheath, interlocking metal tape armor. The metallic sheath shall be continuous and close fitting.

Supplemental protection of an outer covering of corrosion-resistant material shall be permitted, and shall be required where such protection is needed. The sheath shall not be used as a current-carrying conductor.

See Section 300-6 for protection against corrosion.

334-23. Grounding.   Type MC cable shall provide an adequate path for equipment grounding as required by Article 250.

334-24. Marking.   The provisions of Section 310-11 shall apply.

Type MC cable is required to be marked with the maximum working voltage, proper type letter or letters for the type of wire, and the AWG size or circular mil area. This marking may be on a marker tape located within the cable running for its complete length, or, if the metallic covering is of smooth construction which permits surface marking, the MC cable may be durably marked on the outer covering at intervals not exceeding 24 in. See Section 310-11 for marking requirements.

ARTICLE 336 — NONMETALLIC-SHEATHED CABLE

Types NM and NMC

Contents

336-1. Definition.   Nonmetallic-sheathed cable is a factory assembly of two or more insulated conductors having an outer sheath of moisture-resistant, flame-retardant, nonmetallic material.

Nonmetallic-sheathed cable may be used for either exposed or concealed wiring and is a common substitute for concealed knob-and-tube wiring (Article 324) and open wiring on insulators (Article 320). The basic advantages of Nonmetallic-sheathed cable may be used for either exposed or concealed wiring and is a common substitute for concealed knob-and-tube wiring (Article 324) and open wiring on insulators (Article 320). The basic advantages of nonmetallic-sheathed cable (Type NM and Type NMC) are that the outer sheath provides continuous protection in addition to the rubber-covered or thermoplastic insulation applied to the conductors; the cable is easily fished in partitions of finished buildings; no insulating supports are required; and only one hole need be bored and can accommodate more than one cable passing through a wooden cross member.

Where the cable passes through factory or field-punched holes in metal studs or similar members, it is to be protected by bushings or grommets securely fastened in the opening. See Section 300-4(b).

336-2. Construction.   Nonmetallic-sheathed cable shall be an approved Type NM or NMC in sizes No. 14 through 2 with copper conductors and in sizes No. 12 through 2 with aluminum or copper-clad aluminum conductors. In addition to the insulated conductors, the cable may have an approved size of insulated or bare conductor for equipment grounding purposes only.

Conductors of Types NM and NMC shall be one of the types listed in Table 310-13 which is suitable for branch-circuit wiring or one which is identified for use in these cables. The ampacity of Types NM and NMC cable shall be that of 60°C (140°F) conductors in Table 310-16.

Types NM and NMC may have conductors rated 60°C (140°F), 75°C (167°F), or 90°C (194°F) for use in different ambient temperatures. Cables with conductors rated at 75°C (167°F) are designated Type NMH or NMCH, and those with conductors rated 90°C (194°F) are designated Type NMHH or NMCHH. The ampacities of nonmetallic-sheathed cable types, regardless of the conductor temperature rating, are those of 60°C (140°F) conductors.

(a) Type NM.   The overall covering shall have a flame-retardant and moisture-resistant finish.

(b) Type NMC.   The overall covering shall be flame-retardant, moisture-resistant, fungus-resistant, and corrosion-resistant.

(c) Marking.   In addition to the provisions of Section 310-11, the cable shall have a distinctive marking on the exterior for its entire length specifying the cable type.

336-3. Uses Permitted or Not Permitted.   Type NM and Type NMC cables shall be permitted to be used in one- and two-family dwellings, or multifamily dwellings and other structures not exceeding three floors above grade. For the purpose of this article, the first floor of a building shall be that floor which is designed for human habitation and which has 50 percent or more of its perimeter level with or above finished grade of the exterior wall line.

It is to be noted that Type NM and Type NMC cables are to be permitted for multifamily dwellings and other structures such as stores, professional offices, motels, etc., providing these dwellings or structures do not exceed three floors above grade. See Figure 336-1.

Also, Types NM and NMC cables are permitted in one- and two-family dwellings that exceed three floors above grade.

(a) Type NM.   This type of nonmetallic-sheathed cable shall be permitted to be installed for both exposed and concealed work in normally dry locations. It shall be permissible to install or fish Type NM cable in air voids in masonry block or tile walls where such walls are not exposed or subject to excessive moisture or dampness.

Type NM cable shall not be installed where exposed to corrosive fumes or vapors; nor shall it be imbedded in masonry, concrete, adobe, fill, or plaster; nor run in a shallow chase in masonry, concrete, or adobe and covered with plaster, adobe, or similar finish.

(b) Type NMC.   Type NMC cable shall be permitted for both exposed and concealed work in dry, moist, damp, or corrosive locations, and in outside and inside walls of masonry block or tile.

(c) Uses Not Permitted for Either Type NM or NMC.   Types NM and NMC cables shall not be used: (1) as service-entrance cable; (2) in commercial garages; (3) in theaters and similar locations, except as provided in Article 518, Places of Assembly; (4) in motion picture studios; (5) in storage battery rooms; (6) in hoistways; (7) in any hazardous (classified) location; or (8) embedded in poured cement, concrete, or aggregate.

Exception: See Section 501-4(b), Exception.

Type NMC (corrosion resistant) cable has proven very beneficial for installations in dairy barns and similar farm buildings (see Article 547) where extremely cold temperatures are experienced and ordinary types of nonmetallic cables have in some cases deteriorated rapidly due to the growth of fungus or mold.

In addition to the insulated conductors, nonmetallic-sheathed cable may have an approved size of insulated or bare conductor for equipment grounding purposes only. See Section 250-57 and Table 250-95.

336-4. Other Articles.   In addition to the provisions of this article, installations of nonmetallic-sheathed cable shall comply with the other applicable provisions of this Code, especially Article 300 and Note 8 to Tables 310-16 through 310-19.

The second paragraph of Note 8 to Tables 310-16 through 310-19 states "Where single conductors or multiconductor cables are stacked or bundled without maintaining spacing and are not installed in raceways, the maximum allowable load current of each conductor shall be reduced as shown in the above Table."

Failure to comply with the appropriate ampacity derating called for by Note 8, where Types NM and NMC cables may be stacked or bundled, can lead to overheating of conductors.

The requirements of Note 8 apply to other wiring methods as they do to nonmetallic-sheathed cables.

336-5. Supports.   Nonmetallic-sheathed cable shall be secured by staples, straps, or similar fittings so designed and installed as not to injure the cable. Cable shall be secured in place at intervals not exceeding 4½ feet (1.37 m) and within 12 inches (305 mm) from every cabinet, box, or fitting.

Exception No. 1: For concealed work in finished buildings, or finished panels for prefabricated buildings where such supporting is impracticable, it shall be permissible to fish the cable between access points.

Exception No. 2: A wiring device identified for the use, without a separate outlet box, incorporating an integral cable clamp shall be permitted when the cable is secured in place at intervals not exceeding 4½ feet (1.37 m) and within 12 inches (305 mm) from the wiring device wall opening, and there shall be at least a 12-inch (305-mm) loop of unbroken cable or 6 inches (152 mm) of a cable end available on the interior side of the finished wall to permit replacement.

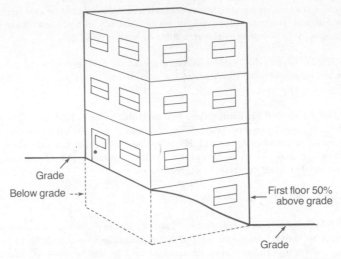

Figure 336-1. A representation of a first floor of a building which is level with or above finished grade of the exterior wall line of 50 percent or more of its perimeter.

For concealed work, nonmetallic cable should be installed in such a way as to be adequately protected from the physical damage that could be caused by nails or screws. Where practical, care should be taken to avoid areas where trim, door and window casings, baseboards, picture moldings, etc., may be nailed. See Section 300-4.

336-6. Exposed Work—General.   In exposed work, except as provided in Sections 336-8 and 336-9, the cable shall be installed as specified in (a) and (b) below.

(a) To Follow Surface.   The cable shall closely follow the surface of the building finish or of running boards.

(b) Protection from Physical Damage.   The cable shall be protected from physical damage where necessary by conduit, pipe, guard strips, or other means. Where passing through a floor the cable shall be enclosed in rigid metal conduit, intermediate metal conduit, or metal pipe extending at least 6 inches (152 mm) above the floor.

336-7. Through Studs, Joists, and Rafters.   The cable shall comply with Section 300-4 where installed through studs, joists, rafters, and similar members.

336-8. In Unfinished Basements.   Where the cable is run at angles with joists in unfinished basements, it shall be permissible to secure cables not smaller than two No. 6 or three No. 8 conductors directly to the lower edges of the joists. Smaller cables shall either be run through bored holes in joists or on running boards. Where run parallel to the joists, cable of any size shall be secured to the sides or faces of the joists.

336-9. In Accessible Attics.   The installation of cable in accessible attics or roof spaces shall also comply with Section 333-12.

336-10. Bends.   Bends in cable shall be so made, and other handling shall be such, that the protective coverings of the cable will not be injured, and no bend shall have a radius less than five times the diameter of the cable.

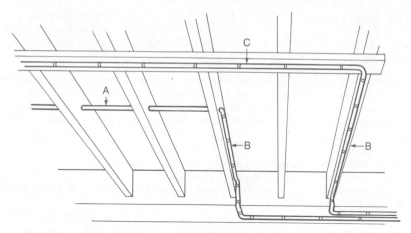

Figure 336-2. Nonmetallic-sheathed cable as installed in an unfinished basement. The cable can be run through joists (A), and attached to the side or face of joists or beams (B) and to the underside of running boards (C).

336-11. Devices of Insulating Material.   Switch, outlet, and tap devices of insulating material shall be permitted to be used without boxes in exposed cable wiring, and for rewiring in existing buildings where the cable is concealed and fished. Openings in such devices shall form a close fit around the outer covering of the cable, and the device shall fully enclose that part of the cable from which any part of the covering has been removed.

Where connections to conductors are by binding-screw terminals, there shall be available as many terminals as conductors.

Exception: Where cables are clamped within the structure, and terminals are of a type approved for multiconductors.

336-12. Boxes of Insulating Material.   Nonmetallic outlet boxes shall be permitted as provided in Section 370-3.

Nonmetallic boxes and nonmetallic wiring systems are desired in corrosive atmospheres; however, nonmetallic boxes sized over 100 cu in. (for instance, 5 in. x 5 in. x 5 in. = 125 cu in.) with bonding means between all metal raceways and metal enclosed cables are permitted. See Sections 370-3, 370-7(c), and Article 547.

336-13. Devices with Integral Enclosures.   Wiring devices with integral enclosures identified for such use shall be permitted as provided in Section 300-15(b), Exception No. 5.

The *Code* recognizes wiring devices with integral enclosures in conventional on-site frame construction at the time of initial installation of the wiring system.

ARTICLE 337 — SHIELDED NONMETALLIC-
SHEATHED CABLE

Type SNM

Contents

337-1. Definition.   Type SNM shielded nonmetallic-sheathed cable is a factory assembly of two or more insulated conductors in an extruded core of moisture-resistant, flame-resistant nonmetallic material, covered with an overlapping spiral metal tape and wire shield and jacketed with an extruded moisture-, flame-, oil-, corrosion-, fungus-, and sunlight-resistant nonmetallic material.

Type SNM cables are multiconductor cables in an extruded core of nonmetallic material covered with an overlapping spiral metal tape and wire shield with an overall nonmetallic material jacketing and is basically used in cable trays or in raceways. See Section 337-3.

Figure 337-1 depicts a fragmentary perspective illustration of a Type SNM cable, and Figure 337-2 is a sectional view illustrating fittings for connecting such a cable to a rigid metal conduit or intermediate metal conduit.

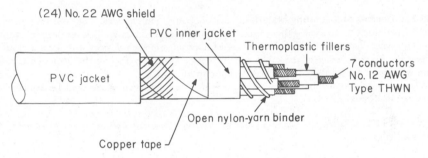

Figure 337-1. A seven-conductor No. 12 Type SNM cable typical for use in cable trays or raceways.

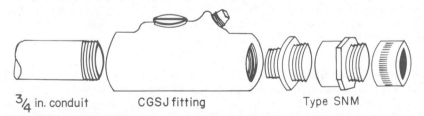

Figure 337-2. Connection-type fitting used where Type SNM cable enters a ¾-in. rigid metal conduit in Class I and Class II, Division 2 hazardous (classified) locations.

337-2. Other Articles.   In addition to the provisions of this article, installation of Type SNM cable shall conform to other applicable provisions, such as Articles 300, 318, 501, and 502.

337-3. Uses Permitted.   Type SNM cable shall be used only as follows: (1) where operating temperatures do not exceed the rating marked on the cable; (2) in cable trays or in raceways; or (3) in hazardous (classified) locations where permitted in Articles 500 through 516.

337-4. Bends.   Bends in Type SNM cable shall be so made as not to damage the cable or its covering. The radius of the inner edge shall not be less than five times the cable diameter.

337-5. Handling.   Type SNM cable shall be handled in such a manner as not to damage the cable or its covering.

337-6. Fittings.   Fittings for connecting Type SNM cable to enclosures or equipment shall be identified for this use.

337-7. Bonding.   The wire shield shall be bonded to the frame or enclosure of the utilization equipment and to the ground bus or connection at the power supply point. This bonding shall be accomplished using fittings (Section 337-6) or by other Code-approved bonding methods [Section 501-16(b)].

337-8. Construction.   The conductors of Type SNM cable shall be Type TFN, TFFN, THHN or THWN in sizes No. 18 through No. 2 copper and No. 12 through No. 2 in aluminum or copper-clad aluminum. Conductor sizes may be mixed in individual cables. The flat overlapping metal tapes shall be spiraled with a long lay. The shield wires shall have a total cross-sectional area as required by Article 250 and not less than the largest circuit conductor in the cable.

The outer jacket shall be water-, oil-, flame-, corrosion-, fungus-, and sunlight-resistant, and suitable for installation in cable trays.

337-9. Marking.   Type SNM cable shall have a distinctive marking on its exterior surface for its entire length indicating its type and maximum operating temperature. It shall comply with the general marking requirements of Section 310-11.

The conductors shall each be numbered for identification from each other by durable marking on two sides 180 degrees apart every 6 inches (152 mm) of length, with alternate legends inverted to facilitate reading from both sides.

ARTICLE 338 — SERVICE-ENTRANCE CABLE

Types SE and USE

Contents

338-1. Definition.   Service-entrance cable is a single conductor or multiconductor assembly provided with or without an overall covering, primarily used for services and of the following types:

(a) Type SE.   Type SE, having a flame-retardant, moisture-resistant covering, but not required to have inherent protection against mechanical abuse.

(b) Type USE.   Type USE, identified for underground use, having a moisture-resistant covering, but not required to have a flame-retardant covering or inherent protection against mechanical abuse.

Cabled single-conductor Type USE constructions recognized for underground use may have a bare copper conductor cabled with the assembly. Type USE single, parallel, or cabled conductor assemblies recognized for underground use may have a bare copper concentric conductor applied. These constructions do not require an outer overall covering.

See Section 230-40, Exception b.

(c) One Uninsulated Conductor. If Type SE or USE cable consists of two or more conductors, one shall be permitted to be uninsulated.

> Service-entrance cable is labeled in sizes No. 12 AWG and larger for copper and No. 10 AWG and larger for aluminum or copper-clad aluminum with Types RH, THW, THH or XHHW conductors. If the type designation for the conductors is marked on the outside surface of the cable, the temperature rating of the cable corresponds to the rating of the individual conductors. When this marking does not appear, the temperature of the cable is 75°C (167°F).
> The cables are classified as follows:
> Type SE—Cable for aboveground installation.
> Type USE—Cable for underground installation including burial directly in the earth. Cable in sizes No. 4/0 AWG and smaller and having all conductors insulated is suitable for all of the underground uses for which Type UF cable is permitted.

338-2. Uses Permitted as Service-Entrance Conductors.   Service-entrance cable used as service-entrance conductors shall be installed as required by Article 230.

338-3. Uses Permitted as Branch Circuits or Feeders.

(a) Grounded Conductor Insulated.   Type SE service-entrance cables shall be permitted in interior wiring systems where all of the circuit conductors of the cable are of the rubber-covered or thermoplastic type.

(b) Grounded Conductor Not Insulated.   Type SE service-entrance cables without individual insulation on the grounded circuit conductor shall not be used as a branch circuit or as a feeder within a building, except a cable that has a final nonmetallic outer covering and is supplied by alternating current at not over 150 volts to ground shall be permitted: (1) as a branch circuit to supply only a range, wall-mounted oven, counter-mounted cooking unit, or clothes dryer as covered in Section 250-60, or (2) as a feeder to supply only other buildings on the same premises.

Service-entrance cable shall be permitted for interior use where the fully insulated conductors are used for circuit wiring and the uninsulated conductor is used for equipment grounding purposes.

> According to the UL Electrical Construction Materials Directory, based upon tests which have been made involving the maximum heating that can be produced, an uninsulated conductor employed in a service cable assembly is considered to have the same current-carrying capacity as the insulated conductors even though it may be smaller in size.

(c) Temperature Limitations.   Type SE service-entrance cable used to supply appliances shall not be subject to conductor temperatures in excess of the temperature specified for the type of insulation involved.

338-4. Installation Methods.

(a) Interior Wiring.   In addition to the provisions of this article, Type SE service-entrance cable used for interior wiring shall comply with the applicable provisions of Article 300.

(b) Unarmored Cable.   Unarmored cable shall be installed in accordance with the provisions of Article 336.

Section 336-3 prohibits the use of nonmetallic-sheathed cables in multifamily dwellings and other structures exceeding three floors above grade. Likewise, Type SE cable (unarmored), which is similar in construction to Types NM and NMC, where used for interior branch circuits and feeders, should also meet the provisions of Section 336-3.

The same restriction is to be applied to Type UF where used for interior wiring. See Section 339-3(a)(4).

(c) Through Studs, Joists, Rafters, or Similar Members.   Cables shall comply with Section 300-4 where installed through studs, joists, rafters, or similar members.

338-5. Marking.   Service-entrance cable shall be marked as required in Section 310-11. Cable with the neutral conductor smaller than the ungrounded conductors shall be so marked.

ARTICLE 339 — UNDERGROUND FEEDER AND
BRANCH-CIRCUIT CABLE

Type UF

Contents

339-1. Description and Marking.

(a) Description.   Underground feeder and branch-circuit cable shall be an approved Type UF cable in sizes No. 14 copper or No. 12 aluminum or copper-clad aluminum through No. 4/0. The conductors of Type UF shall be one of the moisture-resistant types listed in Table 310-13 which is suitable for branch-circuit wiring or one which is identified for such use. The ampacity of Type UF cable shall be that of 60°C (140°F) conductors in Table 310-16. In addition to the insulated conductors, the cable shall be permitted to have an approved size of insulated or bare conductor for equipment grounding purposes only. The overall covering shall be flame-retardant, moisture-, fungus-, and corrosion-resistant, and suitable for direct burial in the earth.

(b) Marking.   In addition to the provisions of Section 310-11, the cable shall have a distinctive marking on the exterior for its entire length specifying the cable type.

339-2. Other Articles.   In addition to the provisions of this article, installations of underground feeder and branch-circuit cable (Type UF) shall comply with other applicable provisions of this Code, especially Article 300 and Section 310-13.

Underground feeder and branch-circuit cable is rated for use at 60°C (140°F), 600 V, and is labeled in sizes Nos. 14 to 4/0 AWG, copper, and Nos. 12 to 4/0 AWG, aluminum or copper-clad aluminum, for single and multiple conductor cables.

Submersible Water Pump Cable indicates a multiconductor cable in which 2, 3, or 4 single-conductor Type UF cables are twisted together without an outer covering. The cable is labeled in sizes from 14 AWG to 2 AWG, copper, and from 12 AWG to 2 AWG, aluminum or copper-clad aluminum. The cable is tag marked: For use within the well casing for wiring deep-well water pumps where the cable is not subject to repetitive handling caused by frequent servicing of the pump units. The insulation may also be surface-marked "Pump Cable."

This cable may employ copper, or aluminum, or copper-clad aluminum conductors. Cables with copper-clad aluminum conductors are surface printed "AL (CU-CLAD)."

If single conductor Type UF cable is terminated with a fitting not specifically recognized for use with single conductor cable, special care should be taken to assure it is properly secured and not subject to damage.

339-3. Use.

(a) Uses Permitted.

(1) Type UF cable shall be permitted for use underground, including direct burial in the earth, as feeder or branch-circuit cable where provided with overcurrent protection of the rated ampacity as required in Section 339-4.

(2) Where single-conductor cables are installed, all cables of the feeder circuit, subfeeder circuit, or branch circuit, including the neutral conductor, if any, shall be run together in the same trench or raceway.

(3) For underground requirements, see Section 300-5.

(4) Type UF cable shall be permitted for interior wiring in wet, dry, or corrosive locations under the recognized wiring methods of this Code, and where installed as nonmetallic-sheathed cable, the installation shall comply with the provisions of Article 336 and shall be of the multiconductor type.

See commentary following Sections 336-3 and 338-4(b).

Exception: Single-conductor cables shall be permitted as the nonheating leads for heating cables as provided in Section 424-43.

Type UF cable supported by cable trays shall be of the multiconductor type.

(b) Uses Not Permitted.   Type UF cable shall not be used: (1) as service-entrance cables; (2) in commercial garages; (3) in theaters; (4) in motion picture studios; (5) in storage battery rooms; (6) in hoistways; (7) in any hazardous (classified) location; (8) embedded in poured cement, concrete, or aggregate, except where embedded in plaster as nonheating leads as provided in Article 424; (9) where exposed to direct rays of the sun, unless identified as sunlight-resistant.

Exception: See Section 501-4(b), Exception.

Type UF cables suitable for exposure to the direct rays of the sun are indicated by tag marking and marking on the surface of the cable with the designation "Sunlight Resistant."

339-4. Overcurrent Protection.   Overcurrent protection shall be provided in accordance with provisions of Section 240-3.

339-5. Rated Ampacity.   The ampacities of conductors in Type UF cable shall be according to Table 310-16.

ARTICLE 340 — POWER AND CONTROL TRAY CABLE

Type TC

Contents

340-1. Definition.   Type TC power and control tray cable is a factory assembly of two or more insulated conductors, with or without associated bare or covered grounding conductors under a nonmetallic sheath, approved for installation in cable trays, in raceways, or where supported by a messenger wire.

340-2. Other Articles.   In addition to the provisions of this article, installations of Type TC tray cable shall comply with other applicable articles of this Code, especially Articles 300 and 318.

340-3. Construction.   The insulated conductors of Type TC tray cable shall be in sizes 18 AWG through 1000 MCM copper and sizes 12 AWG through 1000 MCM aluminum or copper-clad aluminum. Insulated conductors of size 14 AWG and larger copper and size 12 AWG and larger aluminum or copper-clad aluminum shall be one of the types listed in Table 310-13, which is suitable for branch circuit and feeder circuits or one which is identified for such use. Insulated conductors of size No. 18 and No. 16 AWG copper shall be in accordance with Section 725-16. The outer sheath shall be a flame-retardant, nonmetallic material. Where installed in wet locations, Type TC cable shall be resistant to moisture and corrosive agents.

340-4. Use Permitted.   Type TC tray cable shall be permitted to be used: (1) for power, lighting, control, signal, and communication circuits; (2) in cable trays, or in raceways, or where supported in outdoor locations by a messenger wire; (3) in cable trays in hazardous (classified) locations as permitted in Articles 318 and 501 in industrial establishments where the conditions of maintenance and supervision assure that only qualified persons will service the installation; (4) for Class 1 circuits as permitted in Article 725.

> The restriction that requires the condition of maintenance and supervision to ensure that only qualified persons will service the installation of Type TC cable applies only where the cable is to be used in a hazardous (classified) location.

340-5. Uses Not Permitted.   Type TC tray cable shall not be: (1) installed where they will be exposed to physical damage; (2) installed as open cable on brackets or cleats; (3) used where exposed to direct rays of the sun, unless identified as sunlight-resistant; (4) direct buried, unless identified for such use.

> Where identified for the use, Type TC cable is permitted to be direct buried. See definition of "Identified" in Article 100.

340-6. Marking.   The cable shall be marked in accordance with Section 310-11.

340-7. Ampacity.   The ampacities of the conductors of Type TC tray cable shall be determined from Table 400-5 and Section 318-10.

ARTICLE 342 — NONMETALLIC EXTENSIONS

Contents

342-1. Definition.   Nonmetallic extensions are an assembly of two insulated conductors within a nonmetallic jacket or an extruded thermoplastic covering. The classification includes both surface extensions, intended for mounting directly on the surface of walls or ceilings, and aerial cable, containing a supporting messenger cable as an integral part of the cable assembly.

342-2. Other Articles.   In addition to the provisions of this article, nonmetallic extensions shall be installed in accordance with the applicable provisions of this Code.

342-3. Uses Permitted.   Nonmetallic extensions shall be permitted only where all of the following conditions are met:

(a) From an Existing Outlet.   The extension is from an existing outlet on a 15- or 20-ampere branch circuit in conformity with the requirements of Article 210.

(b) Exposed and in a Dry Location.   The extension is run exposed and in a dry location.

(c) Nonmetallic Surface Extensions.   For nonmetallic surface extensions, the building is occupied for residential or office purposes.

Nonmetallic surface extensions are limited to residential or office locations. However, it is permitted as an aerial cable in industrial occupancies where a highly flexible means for connecting equipment is necessary. See Sections 342-4(a) and 342-7(b).

(c1) [Alternate to (c)]   For aerial cable, the building is occupied for industrial purposes, and the nature of the occupancy requires a highly flexible means for connecting equipment.

A nonmetallic extension is an assembly of two insulated circuit conductors with or without a grounding conductor within a nonmetallic jacket or extruded thermoplastic covering. Assemblies without a grounding conductor are marked "intended for replacement use only."

342-4. Uses Not Permitted.   Nonmetallic extensions shall not be used:

(a) Aerial Cable.   As aerial cable to substitute for one of the general wiring methods specified by this Code.

(b) Unfinished Areas.   In unfinished basements, attics, or roof spaces.

(c) Voltage Between Conductors.   Where the voltage between conductors exceeds 150 volts for nonmetallic surface extension and 300 volts for aerial cable.

(d) Corrosive Vapors.   Where subject to corrosive vapors.

(e) Through a Floor or Partition.   Where run through a floor or partition, or outside the room in which it originates.

342-5. Splices and Taps.   Extensions shall consist of a continuous unbroken length of the assembly, without splices, and without exposed conductors between fittings. Taps shall be permitted where approved fittings completely covering the tap connections are used. Aerial cable and its tap connectors shall be provided with an approved means for polarization. Receptacle-type tap connectors shall be of the locking-type.

342-6. Fittings.   Each run shall terminate in a fitting that covers the end of the assembly. All fittings and devices shall be of a type identified for the use.

342-7. Installation.   Nonmetallic extensions shall be installed as specified in (a) and (b) below.

(a) Nonmetallic Surface Extensions.

(1) One or more extensions shall be permitted to be run in any direction from an existing outlet, but not on the floor or within 2 inches (50.8 mm) from the floor.

(2) Nonmetallic surface extensions shall be secured in place by approved means at intervals not exceeding 8 inches (203 mm).

Exception: Where connection to the supplying outlet is made by means of an attachment plug, the first fastening shall be permitted 12 inches (305 mm) or less from the plug.

There shall be at least one fastening between each two adjacent outlets supplied. An extension shall be attached only to woodwork or plaster finish, and shall not be in contact with any metal work or other conductive material other than with metal plates on receptacles.

(3) A bend that reduces the normal spacing between the conductors shall be covered with a cap to protect the assembly from physical damage.

(b) Aerial Cable.

(1) Aerial cable shall be supported by its messenger cable, securely attached at each end with approved clamps and turnbuckles. Intermediate supports shall be provided at not more than 20-foot (6.1-m) intervals. Cable tension shall be adjusted to eliminate excessive sag. The cable shall have a clearance of not less than 2 inches (50.8 mm) from steel structural members or other conductive material.

(2) Aerial cable shall have a clearance of not less than 10 feet (3.05 m) above floor areas accessible to pedestrian traffic, and not less than 14 feet (4.27 m) above floor areas accessible to vehicular traffic.

(3) Cable suspended over work benches, not accessible to pedestrian traffic, shall have a clearance of not less than 8 feet (2.44 m) above the floor.

(4) Aerial cables shall be permitted as a means to support lighting fixtures when the total load on the supporting messenger cable does not exceed that for which the assembly is intended.

(5) The supporting messenger cable, when installed in conformity with the applicable provisions of Article 250 and when properly identified as an equipment grounding conductor, shall be permitted to ground equipment. The messenger cable shall not be used as a branch-circuit conductor.

342-8. Marking.   Nonmetallic extensions shall be marked in accordance with Section 110-21.

ARTICLE 344 — UNDERPLASTER EXTENSIONS

Contents

344-1. Use.   An underplaster extension installed as permitted by this article shall be permitted only for extending an existing branch circuit in a building of fire-resistive construction.

Many times workers have found it impossible to fish cables into voids or hollow spaces of fire-resistive construction, and in these instances underplaster extensions have been a suitable alternative. An underplaster extension, as specified in Sections 344-2 and 344-5, is buried in the plaster finish of ceilings and walls.

344-2. Materials.   Such extension shall be run in rigid or flexible conduit, Type AC cable, intermediate metal conduit, rigid nonmetallic conduit, electrical metallic tubing, Type MI cable, or metal raceways. Standard sizes of conduit, cable, tubing, and raceways shall be used.

Exception: For a single conductor only, conduit or tubing having not less than 5/16 inch inside diameter, single-conductor Type AC cable, or single-conductor Type MI cable shall be permitted.

344-3. Boxes and Fittings.   Boxes and fittings shall comply with the applicable provisions of Article 370.

344-4. Installation.   An underplaster extension shall be laid on the face of masonry or other material and buried in the plaster finish of ceilings or walls. The methods of installation of the raceway or cable for such extension shall be as specified elsewhere in this Code for the particular type of material used.

344-5. Extension to Another Floor.   No such extension shall extend beyond the floor on which it originates unless installed in a standard size of rigid metal conduit, intermediate metal conduit, electrical metallic tubing, Type AC cable, or Type MI cable.

Underplaster extensions are permitted in buildings of fire-resistive construction, such as concrete and brick buildings, where fishing cables in hollow spaces is virtually impossible.

This type of installation is permitted only for extending an existing branch circuit and is limited to the wiring methods specified in Sections 344-2 and 344-5.

ARTICLE 345 — INTERMEDIATE METAL CONDUIT

Contents

A. General

345-1. Definition.   Intermediate metal conduit is a metal raceway of circular cross section with integral or associated couplings, connectors and fittings approved for the installation of electrical conductors.

> Intermediate metal conduit (IMC) is a thinner walled rigid metal conduit and is satisfactory for use in all locations where rigid metal conduit may be used. Also, threaded and unthreaded fittings, couplings, connectors, etc., are interchangeable for either IMC or rigid metal conduit.
> Galvanized IMC installed in concrete does not require supplementary corrosion protection. Wherever ferrous metal conduit runs directly from concrete encasement to soil burial, severe corrosive effects are likely to occur on the metal in contact with the soil. In the absence of specific local experience, soils producing severe corrosive effects are generally characterized by low resistivity, less than 2000 ohm-centimeters.

345-2. Other Articles.   Installations for intermediate metal conduit shall comply with the provisions of the applicable sections of Article 300.

345-3. Uses Permitted.

(a) All Atmospheric Conditions and Occupancies.   Use of intermediate metal conduit shall be permitted under all atmospheric conditions and occupancies. Where practicable, dissimilar metals in contact anywhere in the system shall be avoided to eliminate the possibility of galvanic action. Intermediate metal conduit shall be permitted as an equipment grounding conductor.

See Section 250-91.

Exception: Aluminum fittings and enclosures shall be permitted to be used with steel intermediate metal conduit.

(b) Corrosion Protection.   Intermediate metal conduit, elbows, couplings, and fittings shall be permitted to be installed in concrete, in direct contact with the earth, or in areas subject to severe corrosive influences when protected by corrosion protection and judged suitable for the condition.

See Section 300-6.

(c) Cinder Fill.   Intermediate metal conduit shall be permitted to be installed in or under cinder fill where subject to permanent moisture when protected on all sides by a layer of noncinder concrete not less than 2 inches (50.8 mm) thick; when the conduit is not less than 18 inches (457 mm) under the fill; or when protected by corrosion protection and judged suitable for the condition.

See Section 300-6.

B. Installation

345-5. Wet Locations.   All supports, bolts, straps, screws, etc., shall be of corrosion-resistant materials or protected against corrosion by corrosion-resistant materials.

See Section 300-6 for protection against corrosion.

345-6. Size.

(a) **Minimum.**   Conduit smaller than ½-inch electrical trade size shall not be used.

(b) **Maximum.**   Conduit larger than 4-inch electrical trade size shall not be used.

345-7. Number of Conductors in Conduit.   The number of conductors in a single conduit shall not exceed that permitted by the percentage fill specified in Table 1, Chapter 9, using the conduit dimensions of Table 4, Chapter 9.

345-8. Reaming and Threading.   All cut ends of conduits shall be reamed or otherwise finished to remove rough edges. Where conduit is threaded in the field, an electrical conduit thread cutting die with a taper shall be used.

345-9. Couplings and Connectors.

(a) **Threadless.**   Threadless couplings and connectors used with conduit shall be made tight. Where buried in masonry or concrete, they shall be the concretetight type. Where installed in wet locations, they shall be the raintight type.

(b) **Running Threads.**   Running threads shall not be used on conduit for connection at couplings.

345-10. Bends—How Made.   Bends of intermediate metal conduit shall be so made that the conduit will not be injured, and that the internal diameter of the conduit will not be effectively reduced. The radius of the curve of the inner edge of any field bend shall not be less than indicated in Table 346-10.

Exception: For field bends for conductors without lead sheath and made with a single operation (one shot) bending machine designed for the purpose, the minimum radius shall not be less than that indicated in Table 346-10 Exception.

345-11. Bends—Number in One Run.   A run of conduit between outlet and outlet, between fitting and fitting, or between outlet and fitting, shall not contain more than the equivalent of four quarter bends (360 degrees, total), including those bends located immediately at the outlet or fitting.

345-12. Supports.   Intermediate metal conduit shall be installed as a complete system as provided in Article 300 and shall be securely fastened in place. Conduit shall be firmly fastened within 3 feet (914 mm) of each outlet box, junction box, cabinet, or fitting. Conduit shall be supported at least every 10 feet (3.05 m).

345-13. Boxes and Fittings.   See Article 370.

345-14. Splices and Taps.   Splices and taps shall be made only in junction, outlet boxes or conduit bodies. Conductors, including splices and taps, shall not fill a conduit body to more than 75 percent of its cross-sectional area at any point. All splices and taps shall be made by approved methods.

345-15. Bushings.   Where a conduit enters a box or fitting, a bushing shall be provided to protect the wire from abrasion unless the design of the box or fitting is such as to afford equivalent protection. See Section 373-6(c) for the protection of conductors at bushings.

C. Construction Specifications

345-16. General.   Intermediate metal conduit shall comply with (a) through (c) below.

   (a) Standard Lengths.   Intermediate metal conduit as shipped shall be in standard lengths of 10 feet (3.05 m) including coupling, one coupling to be furnished with each length. For specific applications or use, it shall be permissible to ship lengths shorter or longer than 10 feet (3.05 m), with or without couplings.

   (b) Corrosion-Resistant Material.   Nonferrous conduit of corrosion-resistant material shall have suitable markings.

   (c) Marking.   Each length shall be clearly and durably identified at 2½-foot (762-mm) intervals with the letters IMC. Each length shall be marked as required in the first sentence of Section 110-21.

ARTICLE 346 — RIGID METAL CONDUIT

Contents

346-1. Use.   The use of rigid metal conduit shall be permitted under all atmospheric conditions and occupancies subject to the following:

   (a) Protected by Enamel.   Ferrous raceways and fittings protected from corrosion solely by enamel shall be permitted only indoors and in occupancies not subject to severe corrosive influences.

(b) Dissimilar Metals.   Where practicable, dissimilar metals in contact anywhere in the system shall be avoided to eliminate the possibility of galvanic action.

Exception: Aluminum fittings and enclosures shall be permitted to be used with steel rigid metal conduit, and also, steel fittings and enclosures shall be permitted to be used with aluminum rigid metal conduit.

(c) Corrosion Protection.   Ferrous or nonferrous metal conduit, elbows, couplings, and fittings shall be permitted to be installed in concrete, in direct contact with the earth, or in areas subject to severe corrosive influences where protected by corrosion protection and judged suitable for the condition.

See Section 300-6.

This section indicates the permitted uses for ferrous and nonferrous conduit, including their use in concrete, in direct contact with the earth, and in corrosive areas. The fine print note references Section 300-6 for additional information on protecion against corrosion and specific types of corrosion-resistant materials.

The Exception to Section 346-1(b) has been revised in the 1981 *Code* to make it clear that aluminum rigid conduit can be used with steel fittings and enclosures as well as aluminum fittings and enclosures with steel rigid conduit. It has been shown by test that the galvanic corrosion at steel and aluminum interfaces is minor in comparison to the natural corrosion on the combination of steel and steel or aluminum and aluminum.

It is advisable to consult with the authority enforcing this *Code* for the approval of corrosion-resistant materials and/or for requirements prior to the installation of nonferrous metal (aluminum) in concrete since chloride additives in the concrete mix have caused corrosion.

346-2. Other Articles.   Installations of rigid metal conduit shall comply with the applicable provisions of Article 300.

A. Installation

346-3. Cinder Fill.   Conduit shall not be used in or under cinder fill where subject to permanent moisture.

Exception No. 1: Where of corrosion-resistant material suitable for the purpose.

Exception No. 2: Where protected on all sides by a layer of noncinder concrete at least 2 inches (50.8 mm) thick.

Exception No. 3: Where the conduit is at least 18 inches (457 mm) under the fill.

Although cinder fill is not commonly used in modern construction, it is still encountered in older building basement slabs and care should be taken to install metallic conduits as per the Exceptions because cinders contain sulphur, and sulfuric acid is formed which can corrode metal raceways.

346-4. Wet Locations.   All supports, bolts, straps, screws, etc., shall be of corrosion-resistant materials or protected against corrosion by corrosion-resistant materials.

See Section 300-6 for protection against corrosion.

346-5. Minimum Size.   Conduit smaller than ½ inch electrical trade size shall not be used.

Exception No. 1: For underplaster extensions as permitted in Section 344-2.

Exception No. 2: For enclosing the leads of motors as permitted in Section 430-145(b).

346-6. Number of Conductors in Conduit.   The number of conductors permitted in a single conduit shall not exceed the percentage fill specified in Table 1, Chapter 9.

Tables 3A, 3B, and 3C in Chapter 9 are based on the allowable percentages of Table 1, Chapter 9, for conduit or tubing fill, that is, 53 percent for 1 conductor, 31 percent for 2 conductors, and 40 percent for 3 or more. Percentages for lead-covered conductors vary, somewhat, from other conductor types (see Table 1).

346-7. Reaming and Threading.

(a) Reamed.   All cut ends of conduits shall be reamed or otherwise finished to remove rough edges.

(b) Threaded.   Where conduit is threaded in the field, a standard conduit cutting die with a ¾-inch (19-mm) taper per foot (305 mm) shall be used.

346-8. Bushings.   Where a conduit enters a box or other fitting, a bushing shall be provided to protect the wire from abrasion unless the design of the box or fitting is such as to afford equivalent protection.

See Section 373-6(c) for the protection of conductors at bushings.

346-9. Couplings and Connectors.

(a) Threadless.   Threadless couplings and connectors used with conduit shall be made tight. Where buried in masonry or concrete, they shall be of the concretetight type. Where installed in wet locations, they shall be of the raintight type.

(b) Running Threads.   Running threads shall not be used on conduit for connection at couplings.

Figure 346-1 illustrates a threadless connection integral to a conduit body, FS box, etc. This type of connection may be separate from the conduit body or box as an individual fitting of the compression type (raintight) suitable for wet locations or of the set-screw type (concrete tight).

Figure 346-2 illustrates an Erickson coupling which is used to join two lengths of conduit where it is impossible to turn either length such as in underground or concrete-slab construction (bolted split couplings may also be used). Running threads are not permitted to join two conduits; but may be permitted to join two boxes where electrical and mechanical connections are assured (locknuts and bushings).

346-10. Bends—How Made.   Bends of rigid metal conduit shall be so made that the conduit will not be injured, and that the internal diameter of the conduit will not be effectively reduced. The radius of the curve of the inner edge of any field bend shall not be less than shown in Table 346-10.

Exception: For field bends for conductors without lead sheath and made with a single operation (one shot) bending machine designed for the purpose, the minimum radius shall not be less than indicated in Table 346-10 Exception.

Figure 346-1. Conduit body with threadless connector. (*Appleton Electric Co.*)

Figure 346-2. Erickson or union-type coupling. (*Appleton Electric Co.*)

The term "field bend" means any bend or offset made by workmen during the installation of a run of conduit.

346-11. Bends—Number in One Run.   A run of conduit between outlet and outlet, fitting and fitting, or outlet and fitting shall not contain more than the equivalent of four quarter bends (360 degrees, total), including those bends located immediately at the outlet or fitting.

Limiting the number of bends in a conduit run ensures easy inserting or removal of conductors during later phases of construction when the conduit may be permanently enclosed by the finish of the building and adjustments at that time may be impossible.

Table 346-10
Radius of Conduit Bends (Inches)

Size of Conduit (In.)	Conductors Without Lead Sheath (In.)	Conductors With Lead Sheath (In.)
½	4	6
¾	5	8
1	6	11
1¼	8	14
1½	10	16
2	12	21
2½	15	25
3	18	31
3½	21	36
4	24	40
4½	27	45
5	30	50
6	36	61

For SI units: (Radius) one inch = 25.4 millimeters.

346-12. Supports.   Rigid metal conduit shall be installed as a complete system as provided in Article 300 and shall be securely fastened in place. Conduit shall be firmly fastened within 3 feet (914 mm) of each outlet box, junction box, cabinet, or fitting. Conduit shall be supported at least every 10 feet (3.05 m).

Exception No. 1: If made up with threaded couplings, it shall be permissible to support straight runs of rigid metal conduit in accordance with Table 346-12, provided such supports prevent transmission of stresses to termination where conduit is deflected between supports.

Exception No. 2: The distance between supports may be increased to 20 feet (6.1 m) for exposed vertical risers from machine tools and the like, provided the conduit is made up with threaded couplings, is firmly supported at the top and bottom of the riser, and no other means of intermediate support is readily available.

Table 346-10.   Exception
Radius of Conduit Bends (Inches)

Size of Conduit (In.)	Radius to Center of Conduit (In.)
½	4
¾	4½
1	5¾
1¼	7¼
1½	8¼
2	9½
2½	10½
3	13
3½	15
4	16
4½	20
5	24
6	30

For SI units: (Radius) one inch = 25.4 millimeters.

Table 346-12.   Supports for Rigid Metal Conduit

Conduit Size (Inches)	Maximum Distance Between Rigid Metal Conduit Supports (Feet)
½–¾	10
1	12
1¼–1½	14
2–2½	16
3 and larger	20

For SI units: (Supports) one foot = 0.3048 meter.

346-13. Boxes and Fittings.   Boxes and fittings shall comply with the applicable provisions of Article 370.

346-14. Splices and Taps.   Splices and taps shall be made only in junction, outlet boxes or conduit bodies. Conductors, including splices and taps, shall not fill a conduit body to more than 75 percent of its cross-sectional area at any point. All splices and taps shall be made by approved methods.

B. Construction Specifications

346-15. General.   Rigid metal conduit shall comply with (a) through (d) below.

(a) Standard Lengths.   Rigid metal conduit as shipped shall be in standard lengths of 10 feet (3.05 m) including coupling, one coupling to be furnished with each length. Each length shall be reamed and threaded on each end. For specific applications or uses, it shall be permissible to ship lengths shorter or longer than 10 feet (3.05 m), with or without couplings.

(b) Corrosion-Resistant Material.   Nonferrous conduit of corrosion-resistant material shall have suitable markings.

(c) Durably Identified.   Each length shall be clearly and durably identified in every 10 feet (3.05 m) as required in the first sentence of Section 110-21.

(d) Conduit Bodies.   Conduit bodies shall have a cross-sectional area at least twice that of the largest conduit to which they are connected.

ARTICLE 347 — RIGID NONMETALLIC CONDUIT

Contents

347-1. Description.   This article shall apply to a type of conduit and fittings of suitable nonmetallic material that is resistant to moisture and chemical atmospheres. For use aboveground, it shall also be flame-retardant, resistant to impact and crushing, resistant to distortion from heat under conditions likely to be encountered in service, and resistant to low temperature and sunlight effects. For use underground, the material shall be acceptably resistant to moisture and corrosive agents and shall be of sufficient strength to withstand abuse, such as by impact and crushing, in handling and during installation. Where intended for direct burial, without encasement in concrete, the material shall also be capable of withstanding continued loading that is likely to be encountered after installation.

Materials that have been recognized as having suitable physical characteristics when properly formed and treated include fiber, asbestos cement, soapstone, rigid polyvinyl chloride, fiberglass epoxy, and high-density polyethylene for underground use, and rigid polyvinyl chloride for use aboveground.

Unless marked for a higher temperature, rigid nonmetallic conduit (Schedule 40 and Schedule 80) in this category is intended for use with wires rated 75°C (167°F) or less (1) aboveground, (2) for direct burial underground, (3) where encased in concrete within buildings, and (4) where ambient temperature is 50°C (122°F) or less. When encased in concrete in trenches outside of buildings it is suitable for use with wire rated 90°C (194°F) or less.

Direct burial conduit is suitable for cables rated over 600 V when it is buried to a depth in accordance with Table 710-3(b). Rigid nonmetallic conduit is listed in sizes ½ to 6 in. inclusive.

Listed PVC conduit is inherently resistant to atmosphere containing common industrial corrosive agents and will also withstand vapors or mist of caustic, pickling acids, plating baths and hydrofluoric and chromic acids.

PVC conduit is designed for connection to couplings, fittings and boxes by the use of a suitable solvent-type cement. Instructions supplied by the manufacturer describe the method of assembly and precautions to be followed.

Fiberglass epoxy conduit was added to the recognized materials mentioned in the fine print note in the 1981 *Code*.

For use of Schedule 80, see Sections 300-5(d), 551-51(b), and 710-3(b)(1).

347-2. Uses Permitted.   The use of rigid nonmetallic conduit and fittings shall be permitted under the following conditions:

(a) Concealed.   In walls, floors, and ceilings.

(b) Corrosive Influences.   In locations subject to severe corrosive influences as covered in Section 300-6 and where subject to chemicals for which the materials are specifically approved.

(c) Cinders.   In cinder fill.

(d) Wet Locations.   In portions of dairies, laundries, canneries, or other wet locations and in locations where walls are frequently washed, the entire conduit system including boxes and fittings used therewith shall be so installed and equipped as to prevent water from entering the conduit. All supports, bolts, straps, screws, etc., shall be of corrosion-resistant materials or be protected against corrosion by approved corrosion-resistant materials.

(e) Dry and Damp Locations.   In dry and damp locations not prohibited by Section 347-3.

(f) Exposed.   For exposed work where not subject to physical damage if identified for such use.

(g) Underground Installations.   For underground installations, see Sections 300-5 and 710-3(b).

The requirement for concrete encasement if the potential exceeds 600 V in Section 347-2(b) of the 1978 and previous editions of the *Code* has been deleted in the 1981 edition.

347-3. Uses Not Permitted.   Rigid nonmetallic conduit shall not be used:

(a) Hazardous (Classified) Locations.   In hazardous (classified) locations, except as covered in Sections 514-8 and 515-5; and Class I, Division 2 locations as permitted in the Exception to Section 501-4(b).

(b) Support of Fixtures.   For the support of fixtures or other equipment.

(c) Physical Damage.   Where subject to physical damage unless identified for such use.

(d) Ambient Temperatures.   Where subject to ambient temperatures exceeding those for which the conduit is approved.

(e) Insulation Temperature Limitations.   For conductors whose insulation temperature limitations would exceed those for which the conduit is approved.

Nonmetallic conduits are not permitted in ducts, plenums, and other air-handling spaces.

In addition, nonmetallic conduits are not to be used where it would aid the possible spread of fire or products of combustion through fire-rated, fire-resistant or fire-stopped walls, partitions, ceilings and floors, hollow spaces, vertical shafts, and ventilating or air-handling ducts. See Section 300-21 for prevention of fire spread or products of combustion.

347-4. Other Articles. Installation of rigid nonmetallic conduit shall comply with the applicable provisions of Article 300. Where equipment grounding is required by Article 250, a separate equipment grounding conductor shall be installed in the conduit.

A. Installations

347-5. Trimming. All cut ends shall be trimmed inside and outside to remove rough edges.

347-6. Joints. All joints between lengths of conduit, and between conduit and couplings, fittings, and boxes, shall be made by an approved method.

347-8. Supports. Rigid nonmetallic conduit shall be supported as required in Table 347-8. In addition, there shall be a support within 3 feet (914 mm) of each box, cabinet, or other conduit termination.

The requirement in Section 347-8 for a support within 3 ft of each conduit termination is consistent with the minimum support spacing in Table 347-8.

It is recognized that these requirements are fairly stringent because they are based on ambient temperatures much higher than normally encountered and utilize horizontal support tests only.

Table 347-8. Support of Rigid Nonmetallic Conduit

Conduit Size (Inches)	Maximum Spacing Between Supports (Feet)
½-1	3
1¼-2	5
2½-3	6
3½-5	7
6	8

For SI units: (Supports) one foot = 0.3048 meter.

347-9. Expansion Joints. Expansion joints for rigid nonmetallic conduit shall be provided to compensate for thermal expansion and contraction.

Expansion joints or expansion couplings are generally provided in exposed runs of nonmetallic rigid conduit where (1) the run is long, (2) the run is subjected to hot and cold changing temperatures, and (3) expansion and contraction measures are provided for the building structure.

The normal expansion range of most larger sizes of nonmetallic rigid conduit expansion couplings is generally 6 in. Information concerning installation and application of this type of coupling may be obtained from manufacturer's instructions.

Expansion couplings are seldom used underground. Where the conduit is buried or covered immediately, expansion and contraction are not problems.

347-10. Minimum Size. No conduit smaller than ½-inch electrical trade size shall be used.

347-11. Number of Conductors. The number of conductors permitted in a single conduit shall not exceed the percentage fill specified in Table 1, Chapter 9.

See comments following Section 346-6.

347-12. Bushings.   Where a conduit enters a box or other fitting, a bushing or adapter shall be provided to protect the wire from abrasion unless the design of the box or fitting is such as to provide equivalent protection.

See Section 373-6(c) for the protection of conductors at bushings.

347-13. Bends—How Made.   Bends of rigid nonmetallic conduit shall be so made that the conduit will not be injured and that the internal diameter of the conduit will not be effectively reduced. Field bends shall be made only with bending equipment intended for the purpose, and the radius of the curve of the inner edge of such bends shall not be less than shown in Table 346-10.

347-14. Bends—Number in One Run.   A run of conduit between outlet and outlet, fitting and fitting, or outlet and fitting shall not contain more than the equivalent of four quarter bends (360 degrees, total), including those bends located immediately at the outlet or fitting.

347-15. Boxes and Fittings.   Boxes and fittings shall comply with the applicable provisions of Article 370.

347-16. Splices and Taps.   Splices and taps shall be made only in junction, outlet boxes or conduit bodies. Conductors, including splices and taps, shall not fill a conduit body to more than 75 percent of its cross-sectional area at any point. All splices and taps shall be made by approved methods.

B. Construction Specifications

347-17. General.   Rigid nonmetallic conduit shall comply with (a) below.

     (a) Marking.   Each length of nonmetallic conduit shall be clearly and durably marked at least every 10 feet (3.05 m) as required in the first sentence of Section 110-21. The type of material shall also be included in the marking unless it is visually identifiable. For conduit recognized for use aboveground these markings shall be permanent. For conduit limited to underground use only, these markings shall be sufficiently durable to remain legible until the material is installed.

     (b) Conduit Bodies.   Conduit bodies shall have a cross-sectional area at least twice that of the largest conduit to which they are connected.

ARTICLE 348 — ELECTRICAL METALLIC TUBING

Contents

348-1. Use. The use of electrical metallic tubing shall be permitted for both exposed and concealed work. Electrical metallic tubing shall not be used: (1) where, during installation or afterward, it will be subject to severe physical damage; (2) where protected from corrosion solely by enamel; (3) in cinder concrete or cinder fill where subject to permanent moisture unless protected on all sides by a layer of noncinder concrete at least 2 inches (50.8 mm) thick or unless the tubing is at least 18 inches (457 mm) under the fill. Where practicable, dissimilar metals in contact anywhere in the system shall be avoided to eliminate the possibility of galvanic action.

Exception: Aluminum fittings and enclosures shall be permitted to be used with steel electrical metallic tubing.

Ferrous or nonferrous electrical metallic tubing, elbows, couplings, and fittings shall be permitted to be installed in concrete, in direct contact with the earth, or in areas subject to severe corrosive influences when protected by corrosion protection and judged suitable for the condition.

Galvanized steel electrical metallic tubing installed in concrete on grade or above grade generally requires no supplementary corrosion protection. EMT installed in concrete below grade level or installed in contact with soil generally requires supplementary corrosion protection.

See Section 300-6.

348-2. Other Articles. Installations of electrical metallic tubing shall comply with the applicable provisions of Article 300.

A. Installation

348-4. Wet Locations. All supports, bolts, straps, screws, etc., shall be of corrosion-resistant materials or protected against corrosion by corrosion-resistant materials.

See Section 300-6 for protection from corrosion.

348-5. Size.

(a) **Minimum.** Tubing smaller than ½-inch electrical trade size shall not be used.

Exception No. 1: For underplaster extensions as permitted in Section 344-2.

Exception No. 2: For enclosing the leads of motors as permitted in Section 430-145(b).

(b) **Maximum.** The maximum size of tubing shall be the 4-inch electrical trade size.

348-6. Number of Conductors in Tubing. The number of conductors permitted in a single tubing shall not exceed the percentage fill specified in Table 1, Chapter 9.

348-7. Threads. Electrical metallic tubing shall not be threaded. Where integral couplings are utilized, such couplings shall be permitted to be factory threaded.

348-8. Couplings and Connectors. Couplings and connectors used with tubing shall be made up tight. Where buried in masonry or concrete, they shall be concretetight type. Where installed in wet locations, they shall be of the raintight type.

Fittings that are suitable for use (UL listed) in poured concrete or where exposed to rain are so indicated on the fitting or carton. The term "raintight" or the equivalent on the carton indicates suitability for use where directly exposed to rain. The term "concrete-tight" or equivalent on the carton indicates suitability for use in poured concrete. See Sections 225-22 and 230-53.

Fittings have been tested for use only with steel tubing unless marked on the device or carton to indicate suitability for use with aluminum or other material.

Indentor-type fittings are for use with metallic-coated electrical metallic tubing only and require a special tool supplied by the manufacturer for proper installation. Diametrically opposed indentor-type tools require two sets of indentations nominally 90 degrees apart. Triple indent tools require one set of indentations.

348-9. Bends—How Made.   Bends in the tubing shall be so made that the tubing will not be injured and that the internal diameter of the tubing will not be effectively reduced. The radius of the curve of the inner edge of any field bend shall not be less than shown in Table 346-10.

Exception: For field bends made with a bending machine designed for the purpose, the minimum radius shall not be less than indicated in Table 346-10 Exception.

348-10. Bends—Number in One Run.   A run of electrical metallic tubing between outlet and outlet, fitting and fitting, or outlet and fitting shall not contain more than the equivalent of four quarter bends (360 degrees, total), including those bends located immediately at the outlet or fitting.

See comments following Section 346-11.

348-11. Reaming.   All cut ends of electrical metallic tubing shall be reamed or otherwise finished to remove rough edges.

In addition to a reamer, a file or a knife has proven more practicable to remove rough edges with excellent results.

348-12. Supports.   Electrical metallic tubing shall be installed as a complete system as provided in Article 300 and shall be securely fastened in place at least every 10 feet (3.05 m) and within 3 feet (914 mm) of each outlet box, junction box, cabinet, or fitting.

348-13. Boxes and Fittings.   Boxes and fittings shall comply with the applicable provisions of Article 370.

348-14. Splices and Taps.   Splices and taps shall be made only in junction, outlet boxes or conduit bodies. Conductors, including splices and taps, shall not fill a conduit body to more than 75 percent of its cross-sectional area at any point. All splices and taps shall be made by approved methods.

B. Construction Specifications

348-15. General.   Electrical metallic tubing shall comply with (a) through (c) below.

(a) Cross Section.   The tubing, and elbows and bends for use with the tubing, shall have a circular cross section. Conduit bodies shall have a cross-sectional area at least twice that of the largest conduit to which they are connected.

(b) Finish. Tubing shall have such a finish or treatment of outer surfaces as will provide an approved durable means of readily distinguishing it, after installation, from rigid metal conduit.

(c) Connectors. Where the tubing is coupled together by threads, the connector shall be so designed as to prevent bending of the tubing at any part of the thread.

ARTICLE 349 — FLEXIBLE METALLIC TUBING

Contents

A. General

349-1. Scope. The provisions of this article apply to a raceway for electrical conductors which is circular in cross section, flexible, metallic, liquidtight without a nonmetallic jacket and intended for use where not subject to physical damage such as above suspended ceilings.

Flexible metallic tubing is a product developed by the Anaconda Co. for certain specific applications, particularly for use under the requirements of Section 300-22(b) and (c) for wiring in ducts, plenums, and air-handling spaces. Flexible metallic tubing is a material that is readily flexed and is barely affected by conditions of vibration or other movement. It is an effective barrier to gases and products of combustion when installed with matching fittings and is of adequate mechanical strength for use where not exposed to physical damage. Similarly, flexible metallic tubing has the necessary properties for use as required for tap conductors for lighting fixtures where outlet boxes are placed 1 ft from the fixture. Flexible metallic tubing has advantages over the use of liquidtight flexible metal conduit in ducts and plenums because it does not have a nonmetallic (PVC) outer sheath that would introduce a probable source of smoke and products of combustion into the ventilation system in the event of a fire situation.

349-2. Other Articles. Installations of flexible metallic tubing shall comply with the provisions of the applicable sections of Article 300.

349-3. Uses Permitted. Flexible metallic tubing shall be permitted to be used: (1) in dry locations; (2) in accessible locations when protected from physical damage or concealed; (3) for 1000 volts maximum; and (4) in branch circuits.

A common application of flexible metallic tubing is as a wiring method for equipment or lighting fixtures mounted on, or above, suspended ceilings.

349-4. Uses Not Permitted. Flexible metallic tubing shall not be used: (1) in hoistways; (b) in storage battery rooms; (3) in hazardous (classified) locations; (4) underground for direct earth burial, or embedded in poured concrete or aggregate; and (5) in lengths over 6 feet (1.83 m).

Unlike flexible metal conduit or liquidtight flexible metal conduit, flexible metallic tubing is limited to 6 ft in length. It is to be noted that flexible nonmetallic conduit is also limited to 6 ft in length. See Section 351-23(b)(3).

B. Construction and Installation

349-10. Size.

(a) Minimum. Flexible metallic tubing smaller than ½-inch electrical trade size shall not be used.

Exception No. 1: ⅜-inch trade size shall be permitted to be installed in accordance with Section 300-22(b) and (c).

Exception No. 2: ⅜-inch trade size shall be permitted in lengths not in excess of 6 feet (1.83 m) as part of an approved assembly or for lighting fixtures. See Section 410-67(c).

(b) Maximum. The maximum size of flexible metallic tubing shall be the ¾-inch trade size.

349-12. Number of Conductors.

(a) ½-Inch and ¾-Inch Flexible Metallic Tubing. The number of conductors permitted in ½-inch and ¾-inch trade sizes of flexible metallic tubing shall not exceed the percentage of fill specified in Table 1, Chapter 9.

(b) ⅜-Inch Flexible Metallic Tubing. The number of conductors permitted in ⅜-inch trade size flexible metallic tubing shall not exceed that permitted in Table 350-3.

349-16. Grounding. See Section 250-91(b), Exception No. 1.

349-18. Fittings. Flexible metallic tubing shall be used only with approved terminal fittings. Fittings shall effectively close any openings in the connection.

See Section 300-22(b) and (c).

349-20. Bends.

(a) Infrequent Flexing Use. Where the flexible metallic tubing shall be infrequently flexed in service after installation, the radii of bends measured to the inside of the bend shall not be less than specified in Table 349-20(a).

(b) Fixed Bends. Where the flexible metallic tubing is bent for installation purposes and is not flexed or bent as required by use after installation, the radii of bends measured to the inside of the bend shall not be less than specified in Table 349-20(b).

Table 349-20(a). Minimum Radii for Flexing Use

Trade Size	Minimum Radii
⅜ inch	10 inches
½ inch	12½ inches
¾ inch	17½ inches

For SI units: (Radii) one inch = 25.4 millimeters.

Table 349-20(b).   Minimum Radii for Fixed Bends

Trade Size	Minimum Radii
⅜ inch	3½ inches
½ inch	4 inches
¾ inch	5 inches

For SI units: (Radii) one inch = 25.4 millimeters.

ARTICLE 350 — FLEXIBLE METAL CONDUIT

Contents

350-1. Other Articles.
350-2. Use.
350-3. Minimum Size.

350-4. Supports.
350-5. Grounding.
350-6. Bends.

350-1. Other Articles.   Installations of flexible metal conduit shall comply with the applicable provisions of Articles 300, 333, and 346.

350-2. Use.   Flexible metal conduit shall not be used: (1) in wet locations, unless conductors are of the lead-covered type or of other type approved for the specific conditions; (2) in hoistways, other than provided in Section 620-21; (3) in storage-battery rooms; (4) in any hazardous (classified) location other than permitted in Section 501-4(b); (5) where rubber-covered conductors are exposed to oil, gasoline, or other materials having a deteriorating effect on rubber; nor (6) underground or embedded in poured concrete or aggregate.

350-3. Minimum Size.   Flexible metal conduit less than ½-inch electrical trade size shall not be used.

Exception No. 1: For underplaster extensions as permitted in Section 344-2.

Exception No. 2: For enclosing the leads of motors as permitted in Section 430-145(b).

Exception No. 3: Flexible metal conduit of ⅜-inch nominal trade size shall be permitted in lengths not in excess of 6 feet (1.83 m) as a part of an approved assembly, or for tap connections to lighting fixtures as required in Section 410-67(c), or for lighting fixtures.

This Exception makes it clear that flexible metal conduit may be used as the factory- or field-installed metal raceway (4 to 6 ft in length) to enclose tap conductors from the outlet box to the fixture terminal housing of recessed lighting fixtures.

Also, flexible metal conduit may be used, for example, as a 6-ft "whip" from an outlet box to a lighting fixture mounted on a suspended ceiling.

350-4. Supports.   Flexible metal conduit shall be secured by an approved means at intervals not exceeding 4½ feet (1.37 m) and within 12 inches (305 mm) on each side of every outlet box or fitting.

Exception No. 1: Where flexible metal conduit is fished.

Exception No. 2: Lengths of not more than 3 feet (914 mm) at terminals where flexibility is necessary.

Table 350-3. **Maximum Number of Insulated Conductors in ⅜-Inch Flexible Metal Conduit.***

Col. A = With fitting inside conduit.
Col. B = With fitting outside conduit.

Size AWG	Types RFH-2, SF-2		Types TF, T, XHHW, AF, TW, RUH, RUW		Types TFN, THHN, THWN		Types FEP, FEPB, PF, PGF	
	A	B	A	B	A	B	A	B
18	..	3	3	7	4	8	5	8
16	..	2	2	4	3	7	4	8
14	..	..	..	4	3	7	3	7
12	..	..	..	3	..	4	..	4
10	..	..	..	..	..	2	..	3

* In addition, one uninsulated grounding conductor of the same AWG size shall be permitted.

Exception No. 3: Lengths of not more than 6 feet (1.83 m) from a fixture terminal connection for tap connections to lighting fixtures as required in Section 410-67(c).

Flexible metal conduit is permitted to be concealed or rendered inaccessible by the finish of a building. However, unlike other raceways, such as rigid metal conduit, intermediate metal conduit, or electrical metallic tubing, that are required to be supported every 10 ft and within 3 ft of every box or fitting, flexible metal conduit must be supported at least every 4½ ft and within 12 in. of every box or fitting. See Sections 345-12, 346-12, and 348-12. Similar to other raceways, a run of flexible metal conduit run between boxes, conduit bodies, etc. is to contain no more than the equivalent of four quarter bends. Adequate shaping and support of this flexible wiring method will assure that conductors can be easily installed or withdrawn at any time.

350-5. Grounding. Flexible metal conduit shall be permitted as a grounding means where both the conduit and the fittings are approved for grounding. Where an equipment bonding jumper is required around flexible metal conduit, it shall be installed in accordance with Section 250-79.

Where flexible metal conduit and fittings have not been specifically approved as a grounding means, a separate grounding conductor (insulated or bare) is to be run inside or outside the conduit. Where run outside, the grounding conductor is to be 6 ft or less in length, routed with the raceway or enclosure, and bonded at each end of the flexible metal conduit to which it is connected.

Exception: Flexible metal conduit shall be permitted as a grounding means if the total length in any ground return path is 6 feet (1.83 m) or less, the conduit is terminated in fittings approved for grounding, and the circuit conductors contained therein are protected by overcurrent devices rated at 20 amperes or less.

Flexible metal conduit is to be permitted as a grounding means installed in 6-ft lengths so that a fault to ground anywhere on this circuit will not have to traverse through more than 6 ft of flexible metal conduit before the fault current returns to the overcurrent device protecting the circuit. See the comments following Section 250-91(b). See Figure 350-1.

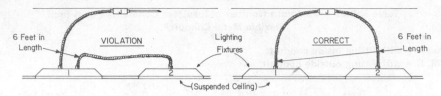

Figure 350-1. The sketch on the right shows the proper application of flexible metal conduit where the total length of any ground return path is limited to 6 ft. The sketch on the left shows an application that is in violation, as the ground return for fixture No. 2 is 12 ft.

350-6. Bends. A run of conduit between outlet and outlet, fitting and fitting, or outlet and fitting shall not contain more than the equivalent of four quarter bends (360 degrees, total), including those bends located immediately at the outlet or fitting.

Angle connectors shall not be used for concealed raceway installations.

ARTICLE 351 — LIQUIDTIGHT FLEXIBLE CONDUIT

Contents

A. Liquidtight Flexible Metal Conduit

351-1. Scope. Part A of this article covers use and installation requirements for liquidtight flexible metal conduit.

Liquidtight flexible metal conduit is intended for use in wet locations or where exposed to mineral oil, both at a maximum temperature of 60°C (140°F). It is not intended for use where exposed to gasoline or similar light petroleum solvents nor for use in hazardous (classified) locations unless so marked on the product.

351-2. Definition. Liquidtight flexible metal conduit is a raceway of circular cross section having an outer liquidtight, nonmetallic, sunlight-resistant jacket over an inner flexible metal core with associated couplings, connectors, and fittings and approved for the installation of electric conductors.

351-3. Other Articles. Installations of liquidtight flexible metal conduit shall comply with the applicable provisions of Article 300 and with the specific sections of Articles 350, 501, 502, and 503 referenced below.

351-4. Use.

(a) Permitted.   The use of liquidtight flexible metal conduit shall be permitted for both exposed and concealed work:

(1) Where conditions of installation, operation, or maintenance require flexibility or protection from liquids, vapors, or solids.

(2) As permitted by Sections 501-4(b), 502-4, and 503-3, and in other hazardous (classified) locations where specifically approved.

(b) Not Permitted.   Liquidtight flexible metal conduit shall not be used:

(1) Where subject to physical damage.

(2) Where any combination of ambient and/or conductor temperature will produce an operating temperature in excess of that for which the material is approved.

351-5. Size.

(a) Minimum.   Liquidtight flexible metal conduit smaller than ½-inch electrical trade size shall not be used.

Exception: ⅜-inch size shall be permitted as covered in Section 350-3.

(b) Maximum.   The maximum size of liquidtight flexible metal conduit shall be the 4-inch trade size.

351-6. Number of Conductors.

(a) Single Conduit.   The number of conductors permitted in a single conduit, ½- through 4-inch trade sizes, shall not exceed the percentage of fill specified in Table 1, Chapter 9.

(b) ⅜-Inch Liquidtight Flexible Metal Conduit.   The number of conductors permitted in ⅜-inch liquidtight flexible metal conduit shall not exceed that permitted in Table 350-3.

351-7. Fittings.   Liquidtight flexible metal conduit shall be used only with approved terminal fittings.

See the comments following Sections 250-91(b) and 350-5.

351-8. Supports.   Where liquidtight flexible metal conduit is installed as a fixed raceway, it shall be secured at intervals not exceeding 4½ feet (1.37 m) and within 12 inches (305 mm) on each side of every outlet box or fitting.

Exception No. 1: Where liquidtight flexible metal conduit is fished.

Exception No. 2: Lengths of not more than 3 feet (914 mm) at terminals where flexibility is desired.

351-9. Grounding.   Liquidtight flexible metal conduit shall be permitted as a grounding conductor where both the conduit and the fittings are approved for grounding. Where an equipment bonding jumper is required around liquidtight flexible metal conduit, it shall be installed in accordance with Section 250-79.

Exception: Liquidtight flexible metal conduit shall be permitted as a grounding means in the 1¼-inch and smaller trade sizes if the total length in any ground return path is 6 feet (1.83 m) or less and the conduit is terminated in fittings approved for grounding.

351-10. Bends. A run of conduit between outlet and outlet, fitting and fitting, or outlet and fitting shall not contain more than the equivalent of four quarter bends (360 degrees, total), including those bends located immediately at the outlet or fitting.

Angle connectors shall not be used for concealed raceway installations.

B. Liquidtight Flexible Nonmetallic Conduit

351-21. Scope. Part B of this article covers use and installation requirements for liquidtight flexible nonmetallic conduit for industrial application.

> Part B first appeared in the 1981 *NEC*. Unlike liquidtight flexible metallic conduit, liquidtight flexible nonmetallic conduit is limited to industrial applications only.

351-22. Definition. Liquidtight flexible nonmetallic conduit is a raceway of circular cross section having a smooth seamless inner core and cover bonded together and having one or more reinforcement layers between the core and cover. This conduit is flame-resistant and with fittings is approved for the installation of electrical conductors.

351-23. Use.

(a) Permitted. Liquidtight flexible nonmetallic conduit shall be permitted to be used in exposed locations:

(1) Where flexibility is required for installation, operation, or maintenance;

(2) Where protection of the contained conductors is required from vapors, liquids, or solids.

> Liquidtight flexible nonmetallic conduit has been used extensively in the machine tool industry.

(b) Not Permitted. Liquidtight flexible nonmetallic conduit shall not be used:

(1) Where subject to physical damage;

(2) Where any combination of ambient and conductor temperatures is in excess of that for which the liquidtight flexible nonmetallic conduit is approved;

(3) In lengths longer than 6 feet (1.83 m);

Exception: Where approved for special installations.

(4) Where voltage of the contained conductors is in excess of 600 volts, nominal.

351-24. Size. The sizes of liquidtight flexible nonmetallic conduit shall be electrical trade sizes ½ inch to 1½ inch inclusive.

351-25. Number of Conductors. The number of conductors permitted in a single conduit shall be in accordance with the percentage fill specified in Table 1, Chapter 9.

351-26. Fittings. Liquidtight flexible nonmetallic conduit shall be used only with terminal fittings identified for such use.

351-27. Grounding. Where a grounding conductor is required for the circuits installed in liquidtight flexible nonmetallic conduit, it shall be contained in the conduit with the circuit conductors. Fittings and boxes shall be bonded or grounded in accordance with Article 250.

ARTICLE 352 — SURFACE RACEWAYS

Contents

A. Metal Surface Raceways

B. Nonmetallic Surface Raceways

A. Metal Surface Raceways

352-1. Use. The use of surface raceways shall be permitted in dry locations. They shall not be used: (1) where subject to severe physical damage unless otherwise approved; (2) where 300 volts or more between conductors unless the metal has a thickness of not less than .040 inch (1.02 mm); (3) where subject to corrosive vapors; (4) in hoistways; (5) in any hazardous (classified) location except Class I, Division 2 locations as permitted in the Exception to Section 501-4(b); nor (6) concealed except as follows:

Exception No. 1: Metal surface raceways shall be permitted for underplaster extensions where identified for such use.

Exception No. 2: As permitted in Section 645-2(c)(2).

See definition of "Exposed — (As applied to wiring methods)" in Article 100.

352-2. Other Articles. Metal surface raceways shall comply with the applicable provisions of Article 300.

The number, type, and size of conductors that may be installed in a listed raceway is marked on the raceway or on the package in which it is shipped.

Raceways, which have been listed for use with lighting fixtures and/or other devices, are marked to this effect on the raceway or on the package in which it is shipped.

The UL Listing Mark is applied to each length or package of complete raceway, raceway cover, or raceway base.

Some lighting fixtures covered under the UL categories of Fixtures and Recessed-Type Fixtures are suitable for use as raceways. See Section 250-91(b)(10).

352-3. Size of Conductors. No conductor larger than that for which the raceway is designed shall be installed in metal surface raceway.

See Figures 352-1 through 352-4.

352-4. Number of Conductors in Raceways. The number of conductors installed in any raceway shall be no greater than the number for which the raceway is designed.

The derating factors in Note 8 to Tables 310-16 through 310-19 shall not apply to conductors installed in surface raceways when all of the following conditions are met: (1) the cross-sectional area of the raceway exceeds 4 square inches (2580 sq mm); (2) the current-carrying conductors do not exceed thirty in number; (3) the sum of the cross-sectional area of all contained conductors does not exceed 20 percent of the interior cross-sectional area of the surface raceway.

352-5. Extension Through Walls and Floors. It shall be permissible to extend unbroken lengths of metal surface raceways through dry walls, dry partitions, and dry floors.

See Section 353-3 for multioutlet assemblies.

352-6. Combination Raceways. Where combination metal surface raceways are used both for signaling and for lighting and power circuits, the different systems shall be run in separate compartments identified by sharply contrasting colors of the interior finish, and the same relative position of compartments shall be maintained throughout the premises.

352-7. Splices and Taps. Splices and taps shall be permitted in metal surface raceway having a removable cover that is accessible after installation. The conductors, including splices and taps, shall not fill the raceway to more than 75 percent of its area at that point. Splices and taps in metal surface raceways without removable covers shall be made only in junction boxes. All splices and taps shall be made by approved methods.

352-8. Construction. Metal surface raceways shall be of such construction as will distinguish them from other raceways. Metal surface raceways and their elbows, couplings, and similar fittings shall be so designed that the sections can be electrically and mechanically coupled together without subjecting the wires to abrasion. Holes for screws or bolts inside the raceway shall be so designed that when screws or bolts are installed the heads will be flush with the metal surface.

Where covers and accessories of nonmetallic materials are used on metal raceways, they shall be identified for such use.

B. Nonmetallic Surface Raceways

352-21. Description. Part B of this article shall apply to a type of nonmetallic surface raceway and fittings of suitable nonmetallic material that is resistant to moisture and chemical atmospheres. It shall also be flame-retardant, resistant to impact and crushing, resistant to distortion from heat under conditions likely to be encountered in service, and resistant to low-temperature effects.

352-22. Use. The use of nonmetallic surface raceways shall be permitted in dry locations. They shall not be used (1) where concealed; (2) where subject to severe physical damage; (3) where 300 volts or more between conductors; (4) in hoistways; (5) in any hazardous (classified) location except Class I, Division 2 locations as permitted in the Exception to Section 501-4(b); (6) where subject to ambient temperature exceeding 50°C; nor (7) for conductors whose insulation temperature exceeds 75°C.

352-23. Other Articles. Nonmetallic surface raceways shall comply with the applicable provisions of Article 300.

352-24. Size of Conductors. No conductor larger than that for which the raceway is designed shall be installed in nonmetallic surface raceway.

352-25. Number of Conductors in Raceways. The number of conductors installed in any raceway shall be no greater than the number for which the raceway is designed.

Type of Raceway	Wire Size Gage No.	Types RHH, RHW	Type THW	Type TW	Types THHN, THWN
No. 200 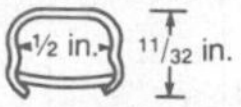	12		2	3	3
	14		2	3	3
No. 500 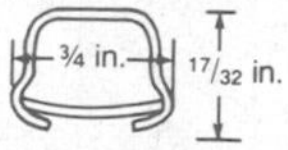	8			2	2
	10	2	2	3	4
	12	2	3	4	7
	14	2	4	6	9
No. 700 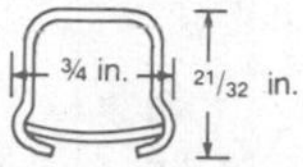	6				2
	8		2	2	3
	10	2	3	4	5
	12	2	4	6	8
	14	3	5	7	11
No. 5700 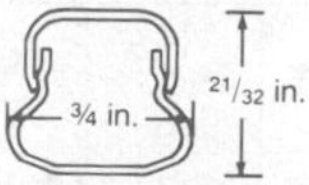	8		2	2	3
	10	2	3	5	6
	12	2	4	6	9
	14	3	5	8	12
No. 1000 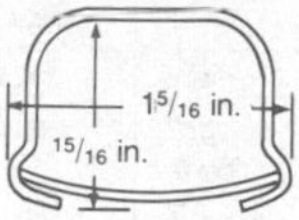	6	2	3	3	5
	8	4	5	7	9
	10	6	9	13	16
	12	7	12	17	25
	14	9	14	22	34
No. 1500 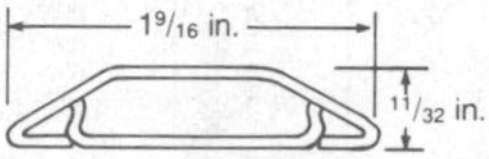	6				2
	8			2	3
	10	2	3	4	5
	12	2	3	5	7
	14	2	4	6	10
No. 1900 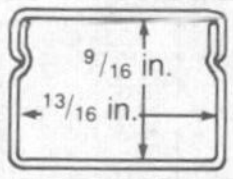	12			3	3
	14			3	3
No. 2000† 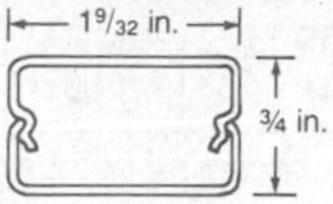	12			3* 3	3
	14			3* 3	3
No. 2100† 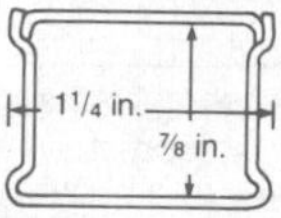	6	2	4	4	6
	8	4	6	8	10
	10	7	10	14	17
	12	8	13	19	28
	14	10	15	24	37
No. 2200† 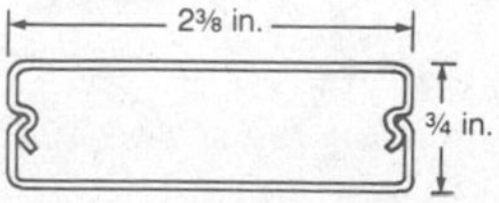	6	5	7	3* 7	11
	8	8	11	7* 14	19
	10	13	19	10* 26	32
	12	15	23	10* 34	51
	14	18	29	10* 44	69
No. 2600 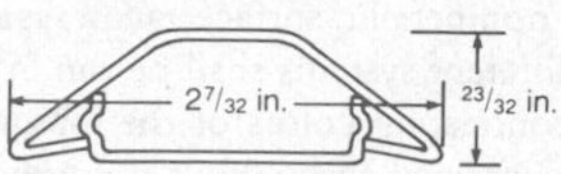	6	2	3	3	5
	8	4	5	7	9
	10	6	9	12	15
	12	7	11	16	24
	14	9	14	21	33

†Figures for Nos. 2000, 2100, and 2200 are *without receptacles,* except where noted.
*With receptacles.

Figure 352-1. Wiremold metal surface raceway. (*The Wiremold Co.*)

Type of Raceway	Wire Size Gage No.	Number of Wires in One Raceway				
		Types RHH, RHW	Type RH	Type THW	Types T, TW	Types THHN, THWN
No. 111	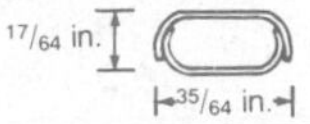 12				2	3
	14				2	3
No. 222	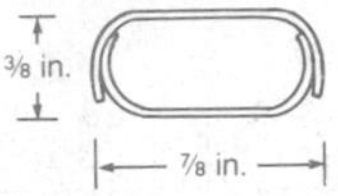 8				2	2
	10	2		2	4	4
	12	2		3	5	7
	14	3		4	6	10
No. 333	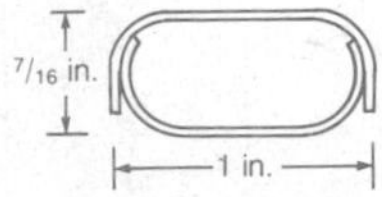 7					2
	8			2	2	3
	10	2	2	3	5	6
	12	2	4	4	6	9
	14	3	4	5	8	12
No. 888	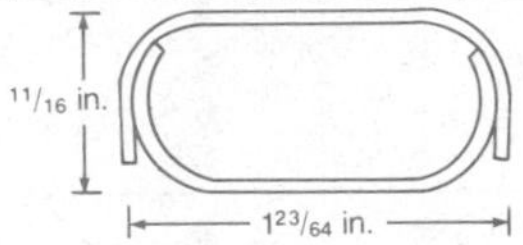 6	2	2	3	3	5
	8	3	3	5	7	9
	10	6	6	9	13	16
	12	7	10	11	17	25
	14	9	12	14	22	34
No. 711	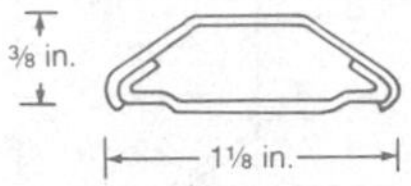 8				2	2
	10			2	3	4
	12	2	2	3	4	7
	14	2	3	4	6	9
No. 733	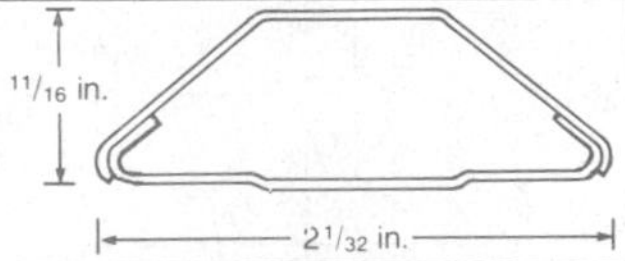 6	3	3	4	4	7
	8	4	4	7	9	11
	10	8	8	11	16	20
	12	9	13	14	21	31
	14	11	16	17	27	42

Type of Raceway	Wire Size Gage No.	Types RHH, RHW		Type RH		Type THW		Types T, TW		Types THHN, THWN	
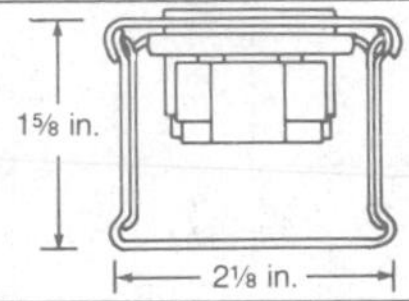 No. 1700†	6	3*	18	3*	18	5*	13	5*	13	8*	21
	8	5*	14	5*	14	8*	21	10*	27	13*	34
	10	9*	24	9*	24	13*	35	19*	49	23*	60
	12	11*	28	15*	39	17*	43	24*	64	36*	94
	14	13*	33	18*	48	20*	53	31*	81	49*	126

No. 3400	Catalog No. 3400 is a raceway consisting of two No. 1700 housings in a common cover. Each channel has the same wire fill as 1700.
No. 5100	Catalog No. 5100 is a raceway consisting of three No. 1700 housings in a common cover. Each channel has the same wire fill at 1700.

†Figures for No. 1700 are *without devices,* except where noted.
*With devices.

Figure 352-2. Types of metal surface raceways. (*Walker Parkersburg Div. of Textron Inc.*)

352-26. Combination Raceways. Where combination nonmetallic surface raceways are used both for signaling and for lighting and power circuits, the different systems shall be run in separate compartments, identified by printed legend or by sharply contrasting colors of the interior finish, and the same relative position of compartments shall be maintained throughout the premises.

352-27. General. Nonmetallic surface raceways shall be of such construction as will distinguish them from other raceways. Nonmetallic surface raceways and their elbows, couplings,

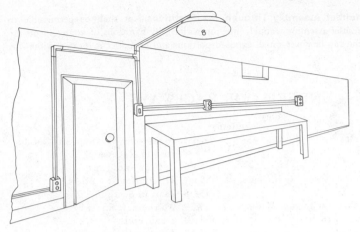

Figure 352-3. Metal surface raceway used as an extension from an existing receptacle. This installation is typical of how surface raceways can be used.

Figure 352-4. A shallow switch box used with a surface raceway.

and similar fittings shall be so designed that the sections can be mechanically coupled together without subjecting the wires to abrasion. Holes for screws or bolts inside the raceway shall be so designed that when screws or bolts are installed the heads will be flush with the nonmetallic surface.

ARTICLE 353 — MULTIOUTLET ASSEMBLY

Contents

353-1. Other Articles. A multioutlet assembly shall comply with applicable provisions of Article 300.

See definition in Article 100.

Multioutlet assemblies are metal raceways that are usually surface mounted and designed to contain branch-circuit conductors and receptacles. Receptacles may be spaced at desired intervals and may be assembled at the factory or in the field. See Section 220-2(c), Exception No. 1.

353-2. Use. The use of multioutlet assembly shall be permitted in dry locations. It shall not be installed: (1) where concealed, except that it shall be permissible to surround the back and sides of a metal multioutlet assembly by the building finish or recess a nonmetallic multioutlet assembly in a baseboard; (2) where subject to severe physical damage; (3) where 300 volts or more between conductors unless the assembly is of metal having a thickness of not less than .040 inch (1.02 mm); (4) where subject to corrosive vapors; (5) in hoistways; nor (6) in any hazardous (classified) locations except Class I, Division 2 locations as permitted in the Exception to Section 501-4(b).

353-3. Metal Multioutlet Assembly Through Dry Partitions. It shall be permissible to extend a metal multioutlet assembly through (not run within) dry partitions, if arrangements are made for removing the cap or cover on all exposed portions and no outlet is located within the partitions.

ARTICLE 354 — UNDERFLOOR RACEWAYS

Contents

354-1. Other Articles. Underfloor raceways shall comply with the applicable provisions of Article 300.

354-2. Use. The installation of underfloor raceways shall be permitted beneath the surface of concrete or other flooring material or in office occupancies, where laid flush with the concrete floor and covered with linoleum or equivalent floor covering. Underfloor raceways shall not be installed (1) where subject to corrosive vapors, nor (2) in any hazardous (classified) location except Class I, Division 2 locations as permitted in the Exception to Section 501-4(b). Unless made of a material judged suitable for the condition or unless corrosion protection approved for the condition is provided, ferrous or nonferrous metal underfloor raceways, junction boxes, and fittings shall not be installed in concrete, or in areas subject to severe corrosive influences.

An underfloor raceway is a practical means of bringing light, power, and signal systems to desks or tables that are not located adjacent to wall space. This wiring method offers great flexibility in layout when used with movable partitions and is commonly used in large retail stores for connection to display cases at any desired location.

Underfloor raceways are to be permitted beneath the surface of concrete, wood, or other flooring material. The wiring method between cabinets, raceway junction boxes, and outlet boxes may be metal conduit and EMT. Flexible metal conduit may be used when not installed in concrete.

354-3. Covering. Raceway coverings shall comply with (a) through (d) below.

(a) Raceways Not Over 4 Inches (102 mm) Wide. Half-round and flat-top raceways not over 4 inches (102 mm) in width shall have not less than ¾ inch (19 mm) of concrete or wood above the raceway.

Exception: As permitted in (c) below for flat-top raceways.

(b) Raceways Over 4 Inches (102 mm) Wide but Not Over 8 Inches (203 mm) Wide. Flat-top raceways over 4 inches (102 mm) but not over 8 inches (203 mm) wide with a minimum of 1 inch (25.4 mm) spacing between raceways shall be covered with concrete to a depth of not less than 1 inch (25.4 mm). Raceways spaced less than 1 inch (25.4 mm) apart shall be covered with concrete to a depth of 1½ inches (38 mm).

Approved flush-type underfloor raceways may be installed flush with the floor surface provided they have reasonable covers at least equal to those of junction box covers. Coverings for underfloor raceways are illustrated in Figures 354-1, 354-2, and 354-3.

(c) Trench-type Raceways Flush with Concrete. Trench-type flush raceways with removable covers shall be permitted to be laid flush with the floor surface. Such approved raceways shall be so designed that the cover plates will provide adequate mechanical protection and rigidity equivalent to junction box covers.

(d) Other Raceways Flush with Concrete. In office occupancies, approved metal flat-top raceways, if not over 4 inches (102 mm) in width, shall be permitted to be laid flush with the concrete floor surface provided they are covered with substantial linoleum not less than ¹⁄₁₆ inch (1.59 mm) in thickness or with equivalent floor covering. Where more than one and not more than three single raceways are each installed flush with the concrete, they shall be contiguous with each other and joined to form a rigid assembly.

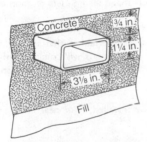

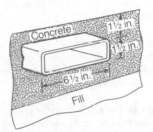

Figure 354-1. A ¾-in. wood or concrete covering is required over underfloor raceways, except for trench-type flush raceways. See Section 354-3(a). (*Walker Parkersburg Div. of Textron Inc.*)

Figure 354-2. Flat-top underfloor raceways over 4 in. in width and spaced less than 1 in. apart must be covered with at least 1½ in. of concrete. See Section 354-3(b). (*Walker Parkersburg Div. of Textron Inc.*)

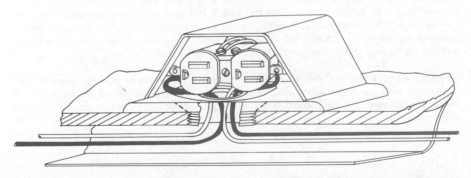

Figure 354-3. A receptacle outlet supplied from an underfloor raceway by the "loop" method of wiring.

354-4. Size of Conductors.   No conductor larger than that for which the raceway is designed shall be installed in underfloor raceways.

354-5. Maximum Number of Conductors in Raceway.   The combined cross-sectional area of all conductors or cables shall not exceed 40 percent of the interior cross-sectional area of the raceway.

354-6. Splices and Taps.   Splices and taps shall be made only in junction boxes.

For the purposes of this section, so-called loop wiring (continuous, unbroken conductor connecting the individual outlets) shall not be considered to be a splice or tap.

> Loop wiring (continuous, unbroken conductors) is recognized when it runs from the underfloor raceway up to the terminals of attached receptacles, back into the raceway, and then on to the next device. See Figure 354-3.
>
> When an outlet is removed, the sections of conductors supplying the outlet must be removed from the raceway as well. As would be the case with abandoned outlets on loop wiring, reinsulated conductors are not to be allowed in the raceways. See Section 354-7.

354-7. Discontinued Outlets.   When an outlet is abandoned, discontinued, or removed, the sections of circuit conductors supplying the outlet shall be removed from the raceway. No splices or reinsulated conductors, such as would be the case with abandoned outlets on loop wiring, shall be allowed in raceways.

354-8. Laid in Straight Lines.   Underfloor raceways shall be laid so that a straight line from the center of one junction box to the center of the next junction box will coincide with the center line of the raceway system. Raceways shall be firmly held in place to prevent disturbing this alignment during construction.

354-9. Markers at Ends.   A suitable marker shall be installed at or near each end of each straight run of raceways to locate the last insert.

354-10. Dead Ends.   Dead ends of raceways shall be closed.

354-13. Junction Boxes.   Junction boxes shall be leveled to the floor grade and sealed to prevent the free entrance of water or concrete. Junction boxes used with metal raceways shall be metal and shall be electrically continuous with the raceways.

354-14. Inserts.   Inserts shall be leveled and sealed to prevent the entrance of concrete. Inserts used with metal raceways shall be metal and shall be electrically continuous with the raceway. Inserts set in or on fiber raceways before the floor is laid shall be mechanically secured to the raceway. Inserts set in fiber raceways after the floor is laid shall be screwed into the raceway. In cutting through the raceway wall and setting inserts, chips and other dirt shall not be allowed to remain in the raceway, and tools shall be used that are so designed as to prevent the tool from entering the raceway and injuring conductors that may be in place.

354-15. Connections to Cabinets and Wall Outlets.   Connections between raceways and distribution centers and wall outlets shall be made by means of flexible metal conduit when not installed in concrete, rigid metal conduit, intermediate metal conduit, electrical metallic tubing, or approved fittings.

ARTICLE 356 — CELLULAR METAL FLOOR RACEWAYS

Contents

356-1. Definitions. For the purposes of this article, a "cellular metal floor raceway" shall be defined as the hollow spaces of cellular metal floors, together with suitable fittings, which may be approved as enclosures for electric conductors. A "cell" shall be defined as a single, enclosed tubular space in a cellular metal floor member, the axis of the cell being parallel to the axis of the metal floor member. A "header" shall be defined as a transverse raceway for electric conductors, providing access to predetermined cells of a cellular metal floor, thereby permitting the installation of electric conductors from a distribution center to the cells.

Cellular metal floor raceways are a form of metal floor deck construction, designed for use in steel frame buildings, and consist of sheet metal formed into shapes combining to form cells or raceways. The cells extend across the building and, depending on the structural strength required, can have various shapes and sizes.

A cross-sectional view of one type of cellular metal floor is illustrated in Figure 356-1. See Figure 356-2 for installation of header ducts (one for power conductors and one for telephone conductors) prior to the concrete being applied.

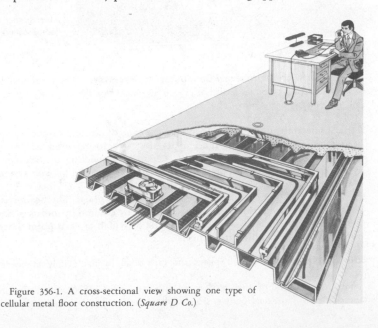

Figure 356-1. A cross-sectional view showing one type of cellular metal floor construction. (*Square D Co.*)

356-2. Use.   Conductors shall not be installed in cellular metal floor raceways (1) where subject to corrosive vapor; (2) in any hazardous (classified) location except Class I, Division 2 locations as permitted in the Exception to Section 501-4(b); nor (3) in commercial garages, other than for supplying ceiling outlets or extensions to the area below the floor but not above. No electric conductors shall be installed in any cell or header that contains a pipe for steam, water, air, gas, drainage, or any service other than electrical.

356-3. Other Articles.   Cellular metal floor raceways shall comply with the applicable provisions of Article 300.

A. Installation

356-4. Size of Conductors.   No conductor larger than No. 1/0 shall be installed, except by special permission.

Figure 356-2. Telephone and power header ducts feeding Cellu-floor distribution system. (*Square D Co.*)

356-5. Maximum Number of Conductors in Raceway.   The combined cross-sectional area of all conductors or cables shall not exceed 40 percent of the interior cross-sectional area of the cell or header.

Connections to the cells are made by means of headers extending across the cells and connecting only to those cells that are to be used as raceways for the conductors. Two or three separate headers, connecting to different sets of cells, may be used for different systems, such as light and power systems, signaling systems, and communication systems.

Figure 356-3 shows the cells with a header in place. The header is extended up to a cabinet or distribution center on a wall or column by means of a special elbow fitting. A junction box or access fitting is provided at each point where the header crosses a cell to which it connects.

356-6. Splices and Taps.   Splices and taps shall be made only in header access units or junction boxes.

For the purposes of this section, so-called loop wiring (continuous unbroken conductor connecting the individual outlets) shall not be considered to be a splice or tap.

Figure 356-3. A typical cellular metal floor raceway installation showing cells, header ducts, junction boxes, and special elbow fittings. (*Square D Co.*)

See Figure 354-3 and comments following Section 354-6.

356-7. Discontinued Outlets.   When an outlet is abandoned, discontinued, or removed, the sections of circuit conductors supplying the outlet shall be removed from the raceway. No splices or reinsulated conductors, such as would be the case with abandoned outlets on loop wiring, shall be allowed in raceways.

356-8. Markers.   A suitable number of markers shall be installed for the future locating of cells.

Markers are brass flat-head screws set into the top side of the cells and so adjusted that their heads, flush with the floor finish, are exposed to locate cells for future installations.

356-9. Junction Boxes.   Junction boxes shall be leveled to the floor grade and sealed against the free entrance of water or concrete. Junction boxes used with these raceways shall be of metal and shall be electrically continuous with the raceway.

356-10. Inserts.   Inserts shall be leveled to the floor grade and sealed against the entrance of concrete. Inserts shall be of metal and shall be electrically continuous with the raceway. In cutting through the cell wall and setting inserts, chips and other dirt shall not be allowed to remain in the raceway, and tools shall be used that are designed to prevent the tool from entering the cell and injuring the conductors.

Figure 356-3 illustrates cells connected to "headers" with junction boxes for future access and a special elbow fitting for connecting the "header" to a cabinet. Connections to wall outlets are to be made with metal raceways (see Section 356-11).

Installation instructions are supplied by the manufacturer for the use of the general contractor, erector, electrical contractor, inspector, and others concerned with the installation.

Figure 356-4 illustrates a preset dual insert, installed prior to concrete being applied, used with cellular metal floor raceways. To install an insert after concrete has been applied, markers should be checked to locate a cell (see Section 356-8). Then a properly sized concrete-boring drill is used to the top of the cell. At this point a properly sized metal-cutting hole saw is used to cut through the cell wall. The saw is preset to prevent the tool from entering the cell and injuring the conductors. The metal insert threads into the hole providing an electrical, mechanical, and bushed connection.

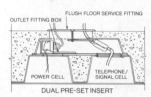

Figure 356-4. A preset dual insert used with a cellular metal floor raceway to provide access to the power and telephone/signal cells in the floor. Note separation. (*Square D Co.*)

356-11. Connection to Cabinets and Extensions from Cells. Connections between raceways and distribution centers and wall outlets shall be made by means of flexible metal conduit when not installed in concrete, rigid metal conduit, intermediate metal conduit, electrical metallic tubing, or approved fittings.

B. Construction Specifications

356-12. General. Cellular metal floor raceways shall be so constructed that adequate electrical and mechanical continuity of the complete system will be secured. They shall provide a complete enclosure for the conductors. The interior surfaces shall be free from burrs and sharp edges, and surfaces over which conductors are drawn shall be smooth. Suitable bushings or fittings having smooth rounded edges shall be provided where conductors pass.

ARTICLE 358 — CELLULAR CONCRETE FLOOR
RACEWAYS

Contents

358-1. Scope. Approved precast cellular concrete floor raceways shall comply with the applicable provisions of Article 300. For the purpose of this article, "precast cellular concrete floor raceways" shall be defined as the hollow spaces in floors constructed of precast cellular concrete slabs, together with suitable metal fittings designed to provide access to the floor cells in an approved manner. A "cell" shall be defined as a single, enclosed tubular space in a floor made of precast cellular concrete slabs, the direction of the cell being parallel to the direction of the floor member. A "header" shall be defined as transverse metal raceways for electric conductors, providing access to predetermined cells of a precast cellular concrete floor, thereby permitting the installation of electric conductors from a distribution center to the floor cells.

Cellular concrete floor raceways are a form of floor deck construction and are commonly used in high-rise office buildings. This method is very similar in design, application, and adaptation to cellular metal floor raceways. See Figure 358-1.

Basically, this wiring method consists of floor cells (which are part of the structural floor system); header ducts, laid at right angles to the cells and which are used to carry conductors from cabinets to cells; and junction boxes as shown in Figure 358-1.

Figure 358-1. Standard underfloor duct used on precast cellular concrete floor raceway. (*Square D Co.*)

358-2. Use. Conductors shall not be installed in precast cellular concrete floor raceways (1) where subject to corrosive vapor; (2) in hazardous (classified) locations except Class I, Division 2 locations as permitted in the Exception to Section 501-4(b); nor (3) in commercial garages, other than for supplying ceiling outlets or extensions to the area below the floor but not above. No electric conductors shall be installed in any cell or header that contains a pipe for steam, water, air, gas, drainage, or any service other than electrical.

358-3. Header. The header shall be installed in a straight line, at right angles to the cells. The header shall be mechanically secured to the top of the precast cellular concrete floor. The end joints shall be closed by a metallic closure fitting and sealed against the entrance of concrete. The header shall be electrically continuous throughout its entire length and shall be electrically bonded to the enclosure of the distribution center.

358-4. Connection to Cabinets and Other Enclosures. Connections from headers to cabinets and other enclosures shall be made by means of metal raceways and approved fittings.

358-5. Junction Boxes. Junction boxes shall be leveled to the floor grade and sealed against the free entrance of water or concrete. Junction boxes shall be of metal and shall be mechanically and electrically continuous with the header.

Figure 358-2 illustrates a trench-type raceway with a rigid cover plate extending at a right angle across the cells, with access to predetermined cells.

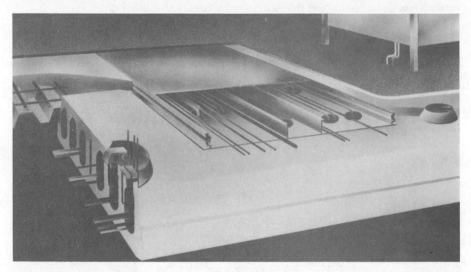

Figure 358-2. Trench-type raceway with removable cover shown extending at right angles across the cells of cellular concrete floor construction. (*Bargar Metal Fabricating Co.*)

358-6. Markers.   A suitable number of markers shall be installed for the future location of cells.

358-7. Inserts.   Inserts shall be leveled and sealed against the entrance of concrete. Inserts shall be of metal and shall be fitted with receptacles of the grounded type. A grounding conductor shall connect the insert receptacles to a positive ground connection provided on the header. In cutting through the cell wall for setting inserts or other purposes (such as providing access openings between header and cells), chips and other dirt shall not be allowed to remain in the raceway, and the tool used shall be so designed as to prevent the tool from entering the cell and injuring the conductors.

358-8. Size of Conductors.   No conductor larger than No. 1/0 shall be installed, except by special permission.

358-9. Maximum Number of Conductors.   The combined cross-sectional area of all conductors or cables shall not exceed 40 percent of the cross-sectional area of the cell or header.

358-10. Splices and Taps.   Splices and taps shall be made only in header access units or junction boxes.

For the purposes of this section, so-called loop wiring (continuous unbroken conductor connecting the individual outlets) shall not be considered to be a splice or tap.

358-11. Discontinued Outlets.   When an outlet is abandoned, discontinued, or removed, the sections of circuit conductors supplying the outlet shall be removed from the raceway. No splices or reinsulated conductors, such as would be the case with abandoned outlets on loop wiring, shall be allowed in raceways.

ARTICLE 362 — WIREWAYS

Contents

362-1. Definition. Wireways are sheet-metal troughs with hinged or removable covers for housing and protecting electric wires and cable and in which conductors are laid in place after the wireway has been installed as a complete system.

Wireways are sheet-steel enclosures equipped with hinged or removable covers and are manufactured in lengths from 1 to 10 ft and various widths and depths. Couplings, elbows, end plates, and accessories, such as "T" and "X" fittings, are available.

Unlike auxiliary gutters, which are not permitted to extend more than 30 ft from the equipment they supplement, wireways may be run throughout an entire area, as shown in Figure 362-1.

Conductors are not to exceed 20 percent of the interior cross-sectional area of the wireway and where not more than thirty conductors are installed, the derating factors of Note 8 of Tables 310-16 through 310-19 are not applied.

Example: a wireway contains twenty-four TW conductors, eight No. 3/0 (8 x 0.3288 = 2.6304), three No. 6 (3 x 0.0819 = 0.2457), three No. 8 (3 x 0.0471 = 0.1413), and ten No. 12 (10 x 0.0172 = 0.172) which totals 3.1894 sq in. (dimensions of conductors are from Table 5, Chapter 9). Five x 3.19 (equal to 20 percent) = 15.95 sq in., or 16 sq in. Thus a 4-in. x 4-in. wireway can contain these conductors and no derating factors are to be applied (less than 30).

362-2. Use. Wireways shall be permitted only for exposed work. Wireways intended for outdoor use shall be of approved raintight construction. Wireways shall not be installed (1) where subject to severe physical damage or corrosive vapor, nor (2) in any hazardous (classified) location, except Class II, Division 2 locations as permitted in Section 502-4(b).

362-3. Other Articles. Installations of wireways shall comply with the applicable provisions of Article 300.

362-4. Size of Conductors. No conductor larger than that for which the wireway is designed shall be installed in any wireway.

362-5. Number of Conductors. Wireways shall not contain more than thirty current-carrying conductors at any cross section. Conductors for signaling circuits or controller conductors between a motor and its starter and used only for starting duty shall not be considered as current-carrying conductors.

The sum of cross-sectional areas of all contained conductors at any cross section of the wireway shall not exceed 20 percent of the interior cross-sectional area of the wireway.

The derating factors specified in Note 8 to Tables 310-16 through 310-19 shall not be applicable to the thirty current-carrying conductors at 20 percent fill specified above.

Exception No. 1: Where the derating factors specified in Note 8 to Tables 310-16 through 310-19 are applied, the number of current-carrying conductors shall not be limited but the sum of the cross-sectional area of all contained conductors at any cross section of the wireway shall not exceed 20 percent of the interior cross-sectional area of the wireway.

Exception No. 2: As provided in Section 520-5, the thirty conductor limitation does not apply for theaters and similar locations.

Figure 362-1. A worker installing conductors in a sheet metal wireway after the complete wireway has been installed. (*Square D Co.*)

Exception No. 3: As provided in Section 620-32, the 20 percent fill limitation does not apply for elevators and dumbwaiters.

362-6. Splices and Taps.   Splices and taps shall be permitted within a wireway provided they are accessible. The conductors, including splices and taps, shall not fill the wireway to more than 75 percent of its area at that point.

Conductors in wireways are accessible through hinged or removable covers, and circuits, taps, or splices may be added or altered, if necessary.
See Section 362-5 and, also, Table 5, Chapter 9, for the dimensions of all common sizes of conductors.

362-7. Supports.   Wireways shall be securely supported at intervals not exceeding 5 feet (1.52 m), unless specially approved for supports at greater intervals, but in no case shall the distance between supports exceed 10 feet (3.05 m).

Exception: Vertical runs of wireways shall be securely supported at intervals not exceeding 15 feet (4.57 m) and shall have not more than one joint between supports. Adjoining wireway sections shall be securely fastened together to provide a rigid joint.

362-8. Extension Through Walls.   Unbroken lengths of wireway shall be permitted to pass transversely through walls if in unbroken lengths where passing through.

362-9. Dead Ends.   Dead ends of wireways shall be closed.

362-10. Extensions from Wireways.   Extensions from wireways shall be made with rigid or flexible metal conduit, intermediate metal conduit, rigid nonmetallic conduit, electrical metallic tubing, metal surface raceway, or metal-clad cable. Where rigid nonmetallic conduit is used, connection of equipment grounding conductors in the rigid nonmetallic conduit to the wireway shall comply with Sections 250-113 and 250-118.

Extensions are to be made from metal raceways or metal-clad cables through knockouts which are provided on the wireway or which may be field-punched. Rigid nonmetallic conduit may also be used. In this case, the equipment grounding conductor in the rigid nonmetallic conduit is to be connected to the metal wireway in accordance with Sections 250-113 and 250-118.

Sections of wireways, including accessory fittings (elbows, endplates, flanges, etc.) are bolted together assuring a rigid mechanical and electrical connection.

See Section 250-91 (b).

362-11. Marking.   Wireways shall be marked so that their manufacturer's name or trademark will be visible after installation.

ARTICLE 363 — FLAT CABLE ASSEMBLIES

Type FC

Contents

363-1. Definition.   Type FC, a flat cable assembly, is an assembly of parallel conductors formed integrally with an insulating material web specifically designed for field installation in metal surface raceway.

Type FC cable is an assembly of two, three, or four parallel No. 10 AWG special stranded copper wires formed integrally with an insulating material web. The cable is marked with the size of the maximum branch circuit to which it may be connected, the cable type designation, manufacturer's identification, maximum working voltage, conductor size, and temperature rating. A marking accompanying the cable on a tag or reel indicates the special metal raceways and specific type of FC cable fittings with which the cable is intended to be used.

Figures 363-1 and 363-2 show the basic components of this wiring method.

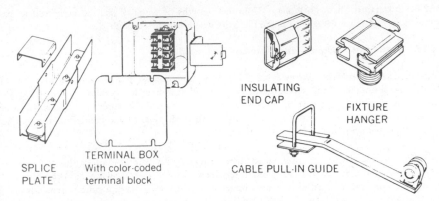

INSULATING
END CAP

FIXTURE
HANGER

TERMINAL BOX
With color-coded
terminal block

SPLICE
PLATE

CABLE PULL-IN GUIDE

Figure 363-1. The basic components and accessories used for an installation of Type FC (flat) cable assembly. (*The Wiremold Co.*)

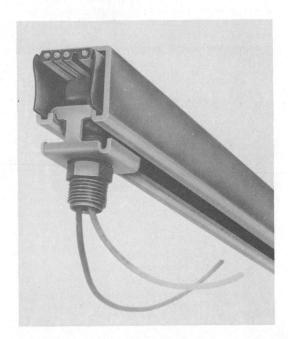

Figure 363-2. Fixture hanger used with Type FC cable assembly. (*The Wiremold Co.*)

363-2. Other Articles.   In addition to the provisions of this article, installation of Type FC cable shall conform with the applicable provisions of Articles 210, 220, 250, 300, 310, and 352.

363-3. Uses Permitted.   Flat cable assemblies shall be permitted only as branch circuits to supply suitable tap devices for lighting, small appliances, or small power loads. Flat cable assemblies shall be installed for exposed work only. Flat cable assemblies shall be installed in locations where they will not be subjected to severe physical damage.

363-4. Uses Not Permitted. Flat cable assemblies shall not be installed: (1) where subject to corrosive vapors unless suitable for the application; (2) in hoistways; (3) in any hazardous (classified) location; or (4) outdoors or in wet or damp locations unless identified for use in wet locations.

363-5. Installation. Flat cable assemblies shall be installed in the field only in metal surface raceways identified for the use. The channel portion of the metal surface raceway systems shall be installed as complete systems before the flat cable assemblies are pulled into the raceways.

363-6. Number of Conductors. The flat cable assemblies shall consist of either two, three, or four conductors.

363-7. Size of Conductors. Flat cable assemblies shall have conductors of No. 10 special stranded copper wires.

363-8. Conductor Insulation. The entire flat cable assembly shall be formed to provide a suitable insulation covering all of the conductors and using one of the materials recognized in Table 310-13 for general branch-circuit wiring.

363-9. Splices. Splices shall be made in approved junction boxes using approved wiring methods.

363-10. Taps. Taps shall be made between any phase conductor and the neutral or any other phase conductor by means of devices and fittings identified for the use. Tap devices shall be rated at not less than 15 amperes or more than 300 volts and they shall be color-coded in accordance with the requirements of Section 363-20.

363-11. Dead Ends. Each flat cable assembly dead end shall be terminated in an end-cap device identified for the use.

The dead-end fitting for the enclosing metal surface raceway shall be identified for the use.

363-12. Fixture Hangers. Fixture hangers installed with the flat cable assemblies shall be identified for the use.

363-13. Fittings. Fittings to be installed with flat cable assemblies shall be designed and installed to prevent physical damage to the cable assemblies.

363-14. Extensions. All extensions from flat cable assemblies shall be made by approved wiring methods, within the junction boxes, installed at either end of the flat cable assembly runs.

363-15. Supports. The flat cable assemblies shall be supported by means of their special design features, within the metal surface raceways.

The metal surface raceways shall be supported as required for the specific raceway to be installed.

363-16. Rating. The rating of the branch circuit shall not exceed 30 amperes.

363-17. Marking. In addition to the provisions of Section 310-11, Type FC cable shall have the temperature rating durably marked on the surface at intervals not exceeding 24 inches (610 mm).

363-18. Protective Covers. When a flat cable assembly is installed less than 8 feet (2.44 m) from the floor, it shall be protected by a metal cover identified for the use.

363-19. Identification.   The neutral conductor shall be identified throughout its length by means of a distinctive and durable white or natural gray marking.

363-20. Terminal Block Identification.   Terminal blocks identified for the use shall have distinctive and durable markings for color or word coding. The neutral section shall have a white marking or other suitable designation. The next adjacent section of the terminal block shall have a black marking or other suitable designation. The next section shall have a red marking or other suitable designation. The final or outer section, opposite the neutral section of the terminal block, shall have a blue marking or other suitable designation.

ARTICLE 364 — BUSWAYS

Contents

A. General Requirements

364-1. Scope.   This article covers service-entrance, feeder, and branch-circuit busways and associated fittings.

364-2. Definition.   For the purpose of this article a busway is considered to be a grounded metal enclosure containing factory mounted, bare or insulated conductors which are usually copper or aluminum bars, rods, or tubes.

For cablebus, refer to Article 365.

The maximum rating of UL listed busway is 600 V.

A busway that has been investigated to determine its suitability for installation in a specified position, or for use in vertical runs, or for support at intervals greater than 5 ft, or for outdoor use is so marked.

A busway that is intended to supply and support industrial and commercial lighting fixtures is classified as "Lighting Busway" and is so marked. Trolley Busway is marked "Trolley Busway" and is additionally marked "Lighting Busway" if intended to supply and support industrial and commercial lighting fixtures. A busway with provision for insertion of plug-in devices at any point along the length of the busway and intended for general use is classified as "Continuous Plug-In Busway" and is so marked.

A busway marked "Lighting Busway" and protected by overcurrent devices rated in excess of 20 A is intended for use only with fixtures employing heavy-duty lampholders unless additional overcurrent protection is provided for the fixture in accordance with this *Code*.

A "Trolley Busway" should be installed out of the reach of persons or it should be otherwise installed to prevent accidental contact with exposed conductors. See Figures 364-1 and 364-2.

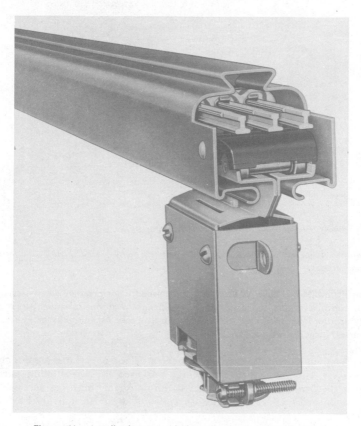

Figure 364-1. A trolley busway with the trolley in place. (*Midland Ross*)

364-3. Other Articles.   Installations of busways shall comply with the applicable provisions of Article 300.

364-4. Use.

 (a) Use Permitted.   Busways may be installed only where located in the open and are visible.

Exception: Busways shall be permitted to be installed behind panels if means of access are provided and if all the following conditions are met.

 a. No overcurrent devices are installed on the busway other than for an individual fixture.

 b. The space behind the access panels is not used for air-handling purposes.

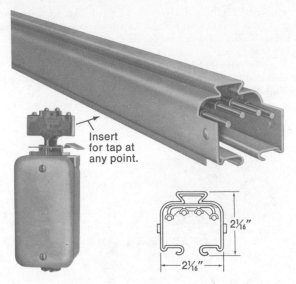

Figure 364-2. A plug-in device for stationary use on a trolley busway. (*Midland Ross*)

c. The busway is totally enclosed, nonventilating type.

d. Busway is so installed that the joints between sections and fittings are accessible for maintenance purposes.

(b) Use Prohibited. Busways shall not be installed: (1) where subject to severe physical damage or corrosive vapors; (2) in hoistways; (3) in any hazardous (classified) location, unless specifically approved for such use [see Section 501-4(b)]; nor (4) outdoors or in wet or damp locations unless identified for such use.

> The Exception permits busways to be located behind panels that are designed to allow access, such as suspended ceilings not used for air-handling purposes, provided the busway is totally enclosed, joints and fittings are accessible for maintenance, and no overcurrent device (other than for an individual fixture) is installed.
>
> Busways are commonly used as feeders, mounted horizontally in industrial buildings, or mounted vertically in high-rise buildings.
>
> Where busways are employed for ungrounded systems, an abnormal potential may build up on one of the conductors and could cause a "flashover" on the system. Figure 364-3 is a diagram of a "potentializer plug" and its connection to a busway. This device is a complete assembly in a metal enclosure designed to plug into a busway. It consists of three 18,000-ohm resistors which serve to maintain each of the conductors at a normal potential to ground. A tap is connected to each resistor, providing 120 V to three 7.5-W lamps which serve as ground detectors.

364-5. Support. Busways shall be securely supported at intervals not exceeding 5 feet (1.52 m) unless otherwise designed and marked.

364-6. Through Walls and Floors. It shall be permissible to extend unbroken lengths of busway through dry walls. It shall be permissible to extend busways vertically through dry floors if totally enclosed (unventilated) where passing through and for a minimum distance of 6 feet (1.83 m) above the floor to provide adequate protection from physical damage.

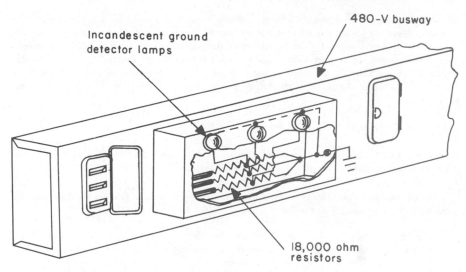

Figure 364-3. A schematic of a "potentializer plug" and its connections to a busway.

364-7. Dead Ends. A dead end of a busway shall be closed.

364-8. Branches from Busways. Branches from busways shall be made with busways, rigid metal conduit, intermediate metal conduit, rigid nonmetallic conduit, flexible metal conduit, electrical metallic tubing, metal surface raceway or metal-clad cable; or with suitable cord assemblies approved for hard usage for the connection of portable equipment or for the connection of stationary equipment to facilitate their interchange. Flexible cord assembly connections shall be permitted to be made directly to the load end terminals of a busway plug-in device, providing the connection includes a suitable tension take-up device on the cord. Where rigid nonmetallic conduit is used, connection of equipment grounding conductors in the rigid nonmetallic conduit to the busway shall comply with Sections 250-113 and 250-118.

364-9. Overcurrent Protection. Overcurrent protection shall be provided in accordance with Sections 364-10 through 364-14.

364-10. Rating of Overcurrent Protection — Feeders and Subfeeders. Where the allowable current rating of the busway does not correspond to a standard rating of the overcurrent device, the next higher rating shall be permitted.

The rated ampacity of a busway is based on the allowable temperature rise of the conductors and can be determined in the field only by reference to the nameplate data.

364-11. Reduction in Size of Busway. Omission of overcurrent protection shall be permitted at points where busways are reduced in size, provided that the smaller busway does not extend more than 50 feet (15.2 m) and has a current rating at least equal to ⅓ the rating or setting of the overcurrent device next back on the line, and provided further that such busway is free from contact with combustible material.

Where the smaller busway is kept within the specified limits, the additional cost of providing overcurrent protection at the point where the size is changed is not warranted. For example, a 1,200-A busway may be reduced in size, provided the smaller busway has a current rating of 400 A (⅓ of 1,200 A) and does not extend more than 50 ft. In this case overcurrent protection would be required if the smaller busway were rated less than 400 A, that is, 200 A, 300 A, etc.

364-12. Subfeeder or Branch Circuits.   Where a busway is used as a feeder, devices or plug-in connections for tapping off subfeeder or branch circuits from the busway shall contain the overcurrent devices required for the protection of the subfeeder or branch circuits. The plug-in device shall consist of an externally operable circuit breaker or an externally operable fusible switch. Where such devices are mounted out of reach and contain disconnecting means, suitable means such as ropes, chains, or sticks shall be provided for operating the disconnecting means from the floor.

Exception No. 1: As permitted in Section 240-21 for taps.

Exception No. 2: For fixed or semi-fixed lighting fixtures, where the branch-circuit overcurrent device is part of the fixture cord plug on cord-connected fixtures.

Exception No. 3: Where fixtures without cords are plugged directly into the busway and the overcurrent device is mounted on the fixture.

Externally operated fused switches and circuit breakers plugged into busways, which are mounted out of reach, are to be considered accessible when operated by means such as ropes, chains, or hooksticks.

An appliance, without individual overcurrent protection, may be connected directly to a busway as permitted in Section 210-23; however, a motor-driven appliance must also meet all of the applicable requirements of Article 430.

364-13. Rating of Overcurrent Protection — Branch Circuits.   A busway shall be permitted as a branch circuit of any one of the types described in Article 210. When so used, the rating or setting of the overcurrent device protecting the busway shall determine the ampere rating of the branch circuit, and the circuit shall in all respects conform with the requirements of Article 210 that apply to branch circuits of that rating.

364-14. Length of Busways Used as Branch Circuits.   Busways which are used as branch circuits and which are so designed that loads can be connected at any point shall be limited to such lengths as will provide that in normal use the circuits will not be overloaded.

364-15. Marking.   Busways shall be marked with the voltage and current rating for which they are designed, and with the manufacturer's name or trademark in such manner as to be visible after installation.

B. Requirements for Over 600 Volts, Nominal

364-21. Identification.   Each bus run shall be provided with a permanent nameplate on which the following information shall be provided: (1) rated voltage; (2) rated continuous current; if bus is forced-cooled, both the normal forced-cooled rating and the self-cooled (not forced-cooled) rating for the same temperature rise shall be given; (3) rated frequency; (4) rated impulse withstand voltage; (5) rated 60-Hz withstand voltage (dry); (6) rated momentary current; and (7) manufacturer's name or trademark.

Metal-enclosed buses shall be constructed and tested in accordance with ANSI C37.20 1974, Switchgear Assemblies.

364-22. Grounding.   Metal-enclosed bus shall be grounded in accordance with Article 250.

364-23. Adjacent and Supporting Structures.   Metal-enclosed busways shall be installed so that temperature rise from induced circulating currents in any adjacent metallic parts will not be hazardous to personnel or constitute a fire hazard.

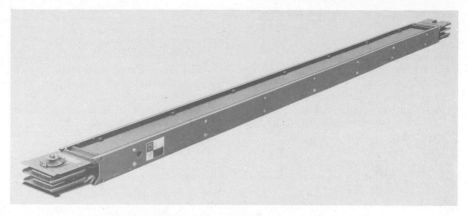

Figure 364-4. A 10-ft section of feeder busway. (*Square D Co.*)

364-24. Neutral.   Neutral bus, where required, shall be sized to carry all neutral load current, including harmonic currents, and shall have adequate momentary and short-circuit rating consistent with system requirements.

364-25. Barriers and Seals.   Bus runs having sections located both inside and outside of buildings shall have a vapor seal at the building wall to prevent interchange of air between indoor and outdoor sections.

Exception: Vapor seals not required in forced-cooled bus. Fire barriers shall be provided where fire walls, floors, or ceilings are penetrated.

364-26. Drain Facilities.   Drain plugs, filter drains, or similar methods shall be provided to remove condensed moisture from low points in bus run.

364-27. Ventilated Bus Enclosures.   Ventilated bus enclosures shall be installed in accordance with Article 710, Part D, unless designed so that foreign objects inserted through any opening will be deflected from energized parts.

364-28. Terminations and Connections.   Where bus enclosures terminate at machines cooled by flammable gas, seal-off bushings, baffles, or other means shall be provided to prevent accumulation of flammable gas in the bus enclosures.

Flexible or expansion connections shall be provided in long, straight runs of bus to allow for temperature expansion or contraction, or where the bus run crosses building vibration insulation joints.

All conductor termination and connection hardware shall be accessible for installation, connection, and maintenance.

364-29. Switches.   Switching devices or disconnecting links provided in the bus run shall have the same momentary rating as the bus. Disconnecting links shall be plainly marked to be removable only when bus is de-energized. Switching devices which are not load break shall be interlocked to prevent operation under load, and disconnecting link enclosures shall be interlocked to prevent access to energized parts.

364-30. Low-Voltage Wiring.   Secondary control devices and wiring which are provided as part of the metal-enclosed bus run shall be insulated by fire-retardant barriers from all primary circuit elements with the exception of short lengths of wire, such as at instrument transformer terminals.

ARTICLE 365 — CABLEBUS

365-1. Definition.   Cablebus is an approved assembly of insulated conductors with fittings and conductor terminations in a completely enclosed, ventilated protective metal housing. The assembly is designed to carry fault current and to withstand the magnetic forces of such current. Cablebus shall be permitted at any voltage or current for which the spaced conductors are rated.

Cablebus consists of a metal structure or framework which is installed in a manner similar to a cable tray support system. Insulated conductors, No. 1/0 or larger, are field-installed within the framework on special insulating blocks at specified intervals to provide controlled spacing between conductors. To completely enclose the conductors, a ventilated top cover is attached to the framework. See Figure 365-1.

Figure 365-1. A section of cablebus with conductors in place and the ventilated top cover ready to be attached to the busway frame. (*Husky Cabl-Bus*)

Cablebus is ordinarily assembled at the point of installation from components furnished or specified by the manufacturer in accordance with instructions for the specific job.

365-2. Use.   Cablebus shall be installed only for exposed work. Cablebus installed outdoors or in corrosive, wet, or damp locations shall be identified for such use. Cablebus shall not be installed in hoistways or in hazardous (classified) locations unless specifically approved for such use. Cablebus may be used for branch circuits, feeders, and services.

Cablebus framework, where adequately bonded, shall be permitted as the equipment grounding conductor for branch circuits and feeders.

365-3. Conductors.

(a) **Types of Conductors.** The current-carrying conductors in cablebus shall have an insulation rating of 75°C or higher of an approved type and suitable for the application in accordance with Articles 310 and 710.

(b) **Ampacity of Conductors.** The ampacity of conductors in cablebus shall be in accordance with Tables 310-17 and 310-19.

(c) **Size and Number of Conductors.** The size and number of conductors shall be that for which the cablebus is designed, and in no case smaller than No. 1/0.

(d) **Conductor Supports.** The insulated conductors shall be supported on blocks or other mounting means designed for the purpose.

The individual conductors in a cablebus shall be supported at intervals not greater than 3 feet (914 mm) for horizontal runs and 1½ feet (457 mm) for vertical runs. Vertical and horizontal spacing between supported conductors shall not be less than one conductor diameter at the points of support.

365-5. Overcurrent Protection.
When the allowable ampacity of cablebus conductors does not correspond to a standard rating of an overcurrent device, the next higher ampere rated overcurrent device shall be permitted.

365-6. Support and Extension Through Walls and Floors.

(a) **Support.** Cablebus shall be securely supported at intervals not exceeding 12 feet (3.66 m).

Exception: Where spans longer than 12 feet (3.66 m) are required, the structure shall be specifically designed for the required span length.

(b) **Transversely Routed.** It shall be permissible to extend cablebus transversely through partitions or walls, other than fire walls, provided the section within the wall is continuous, protected against physical damage, and unventilated.

(c) **Through Dry Floors and Platforms.** Except where fire stops are required, it shall be permissible to extend cablebus vertically through dry floors and platforms, provided the cablebus is totally enclosed at the point where it passes through the floor or platform and for a distance of 6 feet (1.83 m) above the floor or platform.

(d) **Through Floors and Platforms in Wet Locations.** Except where fire stops are required, it shall be permissible to extend cablebus vertically through floors and platforms in wet locations where (1) there are curbs or other suitable means to prevent waterflow through the floor or platform opening, and (2) where the cablebus is totally enclosed at the point where it passes through the floor or platform and for a distance of 6 feet (1.83 m) above the floor or platform.

365-7. Fittings.
A cablebus system shall include approved fittings for: (1) changes in horizontal or vertical direction of the run; (2) dead ends; (3) terminations in or on connected apparatus or equipment or the enclosures for such equipment; and (4) additional physical protection where required, such as guards for severe mechanical exposure.

365-8. Conductor Terminations.
Approved terminating means shall be used for connections to cablebus conductors.

365-9. Grounding.   Sections of cablebus shall be electrically bonded either by inherent design of the mechanical joints or by applied bonding means.

See Section 250-75 for bonding of metal noncurrent-carrying parts.

A cablebus installation shall be grounded in accordance with Sections 250-32 and 250-33.

365-10. Marking.   Each section of cablebus shall be marked with the manufacturer's name or trade designation and the maximum diameter, number, voltage rating, and ampacity of the conductors to be installed. Markings shall be so located as to be visible after installation.

ARTICLE 366 — ELECTRICAL FLOOR ASSEMBLIES

Contents

A. General

366-1. Scope.   This article covers a field-installed wiring system using electrically conductive panels and receptacle housing units for branch circuits, signaling circuits, and communication circuits. The wiring system provides access into the panels and simultaneous conduction of power, signaling, and communication.

This article covers a field-installed wiring system using laminated panels containing sheets of electrical conducting material, separated by insulating material, that forms a modular panel (outside dimensions 1 5/16 in. thick x 4 ft wide x 8 ft long). These panels are located beneath the floor covering to carry both power and signal and contain four conductive planes: two ground planes, a neutral plane, and a phase (hot) plane, insulated from each other in the form of a "sandwich." The panels, sealed on all sides by a metallic, electrically grounded sheet, are connected to a standard 120-V, 20-A, 60-Hz branch-circuit panelboard power source through a panel input unit located at the start of the string of panels.

Panels are electrically interconnected to form "power areas." Each power area is protected by a standard 20-A fuse or circuit breaker. The power areas typically are from 200 to 1,000 sq ft each, depending on individual needs.

The features of this total system's package provide power (120 V, 20 A, 60 Hz) and signal (telephone, audio, data control) on a random basis, as required. Flexibility is the biggest advantage of this system since receptacle units can be installed or removed as desired, using special tools approved for the purpose.

366-2. Other Articles.   In addition to the provisions of this article, installation of the assembly shall conform with the applicable provisions of Articles 210, 220, 250, and 310.

The signaling and communication circuits used in conjunction with this assembly shall also conform to Article 725 and to Article 800.

366-3. Definitions.

(a) Panels.   Laminated panels containing sheets of electrical conducting material separated by insulating material(s).

(b) Receptacle Housing Unit.   A special housing designed for insertion into the panels and containing power and/or signaling/communication outlets and filtering as required.

(c) Signaling/Communications Receptacle Outlet.   An outlet whose use is specifically limited to signaling and/or communications circuits.

(d) Termination Unit.   A special unit which presents the proper impedance to the high-frequency signaling and communication circuits within the electrical floor assemblies without affecting the 60-hertz power.

(e) Base Unit.   That portion of the receptacle housing unit which contains terminal probes and means for terminating the various receptacle outlets.

(f) Terminal Probe.   A special probe which makes contact only with the conductive sheet(s) with which it is designed to do so.

(g) Inter-Panel Connector.   Connectors specifically designed with three conductors, one each for phase, neutral, and grounding connections to interconnect the panels, and/or panel input units to panels, and/or termination units to panels.

(h) Panel Input Unit.   A unit specifically designed to permit connections between panels and the power branch circuit and the signaling/communication circuits or for only power branch circuits whenever signaling/communications circuits are not used.

(i) Holddown Bar.   A bar designed specifically to secure the floor panels in place on the floor.

366-4. Uses Permitted.   Electrical floor assemblies shall be used only: (1) as branch circuits to supply lighting, small appliances, and small power loads; (2) to supply signaling circuits; and (3) to supply communication circuits.

366-5. Uses Not Permitted.   Electrical floor assemblies shall not be installed: (1) where subject to corrosive vapors; (2) outdoors or in a wet or damp location; or (3) in any hazardous (classified) location.

366-6. Branch Circuit.   The rating of the branch circuit shall not exceed 20-amperes, 120-volts, nominal, 2-wire, single-phase.

B. Installation

366-10. Panels.   The panels shall be installed on surfaces which are flat and smooth. The panels shall be installed in a secure fashion. The holddown bar shall be permitted for this purpose.

366-11. All Circuits.

   (a) From the Distribution Panelboards.   All 15- and 20-ampere branch circuits shall be extended from their respective branch-circuit panelboards.

   (b) From Signaling and/or Communication Equipment.   All circuits for signaling and/or communication shall be extended from Class 2 sources.

   (c) Wiring.   The branch-circuit conductors shall be installed in rigid metal conduit, intermediate metal conduit, or raceways specifically approved for grounding purposes.

   (d) Terminations.   Termination for combination of 15- or 20-ampere branch circuits and signaling and/or communications circuits shall be within a panel input unit.

366-12. Circuits.

   (a) Branch Circuits.   A maximum length of 200 feet (61 m) of panels shall be permitted to be connected in series. Any number of panels shall be permitted to be connected to form a single branch circuit provided the total area does not exceed 1024 square feet (95 sq m).

   (b) Signaling/Communication Circuits.   Signaling/communication circuits shall be permitted to feed any number of panels. A termination unit shall be permitted at the end of each series set of panels.

366-13. Receptacle Units.   All receptacle units shall be installed or removed using suitable tools.

366-14. Grounding.   The section of the branch circuit extended from the branch-circuit panelboard to the panel input unit shall have an equipment grounding conductor. This shall be a separate, continuous, copper equipment grounding conductor, not smaller than No. 12. This equipment grounding conductor shall be installed with the branch-circuit conductors in the approved metal raceway. The equipment grounding conductor shall be connected to a properly identified terminal screw in the panel input unit and in the branch-circuit panelboard.

C. Construction

366-20. Marking.

   (a) Durable.   All markings shall be durable and shall be placed on the surface of all components in a readily recognizable location.

   (b) Information.   All panels, receptacle housing units, base units, panel input units, and tools shall be marked to indicate the following information:

   (1) The maximum working voltage and current.

   (2) The manufacturer's name, trademark, or other distinctive marking by which the organization responsible for the component can be readily identified.

366-21. Identification.

(a) **Neutral.** All neutral connection points and terminations shall be identified by means of a distinctive, durable white or natural gray marking.

(b) **Grounding.** All grounding connection points and terminations shall be identified as required by Section 200-10.

ARTICLE 370 — OUTLET, SWITCH AND JUNCTION BOXES, AND FITTINGS

Contents

A. Scope and General

370-1. Scope. This article covers the installation and use of boxes containing outlets, receptacles, switches or devices and junction or pull boxes and conduit bodies as required by Section 300-15. Fittings referred to in Section 300-15 used as outlet, junction or pull boxes shall conform with the provisions of this article depending on their use.

Installations in hazardous (classified) locations shall conform to Articles 500 through 517.

For systems over 600 volts, nominal, see Part D of this article.

370-2. Round Boxes. Round boxes shall not be used where conduits or connectors requiring the use of locknuts or bushings are to be connected to the side of the box.

This rule requires the use of rectangular or octagonal boxes having a flat bearing surface at each knockout for locknuts and bushings to ensure an adequate mechanical connection and effective electrical continuity.

370-3. Nonmetallic Boxes. Nonmetallic boxes shall be permitted only with open wiring on insulators, concealed knob-and-tube wiring, nonmetallic-sheathed cable, and with rigid nonmetallic conduit.

In addition thereto, nonmetallic boxes over 100 cubic inches manufactured with bonding means between all raceway and cable entries shall also be permitted to be used with metal raceways and metal-sheathed cable.

The revision of this section in the 1981 *Code* clarifies the revision made in the 1978 *Code*. The 1978 revision permitted nonmetallic boxes over 100 cu in. to be used with metal raceways and metal-sheathed cable when the box is manufactured with bonding means between all raceway and cable entries. The *Code* was silent on boxes over 100 cu in. which were not manufactured with bonding means. The new revision clarifies that these boxes, although not usable with metal raceway, can still be used with nonmetallic wiring methods the same as permitted for boxes not over 100 cu in. in volume.

370-4. Metal Boxes. Where used with knob-and-tube wiring or nonmetallic-sheathed cable, and mounted on or in contact with metal or metal lath ceilings, walls, or metallic surfaces, metal boxes shall be grounded.

Years ago, the use of metal boxes with knob-and-tube wiring or nonmetallic sheathed cable (without a grounding wire) was quite common. Good practice was to ground the metal box by means of a separate grounding conductor, usually to a cold water pipe. This grounding connection would protect against the energization of conductive thermal insulation or metal lath or any metal objects should a "hot" wire accidentally become grounded through the metal box.

B. Installation

370-5. Damp or Wet Locations. In damp or wet locations, boxes and fittings shall be so placed or equipped as to prevent moisture from entering or accumulating within the box or fitting. Boxes and fittings installed in wet locations shall be listed for use in wet locations.

For boxes in floors, see Section 370-17(b).

For protection against corrosion, see Section 300-6.

Article 100 defines "Weatherproof" as, "so constructed or protected that exposure to the weather will not interfere with successful operation." Rainproof, raintight, or watertight equipment can fulfill the requirements for weatherproof where varying weather conditions other than wetness, such as snow, ice, dust, or temperature extremes, are not a factor.

A "weatherhead" fitting is considered weatherproof because the openings for the conductors are placed in a downward position so that rain or snow cannot enter the fitting.

See definition of "Wet and Damp Locations" and "Weatherproof" in Article 100.

370-6. Number of Conductors in Switch, Outlet, Receptacle, Device, and Junction Boxes. Boxes shall be of sufficient size to provide free space for all conductors enclosed in the box.

The provisions of this section shall not apply to terminal housings supplied with motors. (See Section 430-12.)

Boxes and conduit bodies containing conductors, size No. 4 or larger, shall also comply with the provisions of Section 370-18.

(a) Standard Boxes. The maximum number of conductors, not counting fixture wires, permitted in standard boxes shall be as is listed in Table 370-6(a). See Section 370-18 where boxes or conduit bodies are used as junction or pull boxes.

Table 370-6(a). Metal Boxes

Box Dimension, Inches Trade Size or Type	Min. Cu. In. Cap.	Maximum Number of Conductors				
		No. 14	No. 12	No. 10	No. 8	No. 6
4 x 1¼ Round or Octagonal	12.5	6	5	5	4	0
4 x 1½ Round or Octagonal	15.5	7	6	6	5	0
4 x 2⅛ Round or Octagonal	21.5	10	9	8	7	0
4 x 1¼ Square	18.0	9	8	7	6	0
4 x 1½ Square	21.0	10	9	8	7	0
4 x 2⅛ Square	30.3	15	13	12	10	6*
4¹¹⁄₁₆ x 1¼ Square	25.5	12	11	10	8	0
4¹¹⁄₁₆ x 1½ Square	29.5	14	13	11	9	0
4¹¹⁄₁₆ x 2⅛ Square	42.0	21	18	16	14	6
3 x 2 x 1½ Device	7.5	3	3	3	2	0
3 x 2 x 2 Device	10.0	5	4	4	3	0
3 x 2 x 2¼ Device	10.5	5	4	4	3	0
3 x 2 x 2½ Device	12.5	6	5	5	4	0
3 x 2 x 2¾ Device	14.0	7	6	5	4	0
3 x 2 x 3½ Device	18.0	9	8	7	6	0
4 x 2⅛ x 1½ Device	10.3	5	4	4	3	0
4 x 2⅛ x 1⅞ Device	13.0	6	5	5	4	0
4 x 2⅛ x 2⅛ Device	14.5	7	6	5	4	0
3¾ x 2 x 2½ Masonry Box/Gang	14.0	7	6	5	4	0
3¾ x 2 x 3½ Masonry Box/Gang	21.0	10	9	8	7	0
FS— Minimum Internal Depth 1¾ Single Cover/Gang	13.5	6	6	5	4	0
FD—Minimum Internal Depth 2⅜ Single Cover/Gang	18.0	9	8	7	6	3
FS— Minimum Internal Depth 1¾ Multiple Cover/Gang	18.0	9	8	7	6	0
FD—Minimum Internal Depth 2⅜ Multiple Cover/Gang	24.0	12	10	9	8	4

* Not to be used as a pull box. For termination only.

(1) Table 370-6(a) shall apply where no fittings or devices, such as fixture studs, cable clamps, hickeys, switches, or receptacles, are contained in the box and where no grounding conductors are part of the wiring within the box. Where one or more of these types of devices, such as fixture studs, cable clamps, or hickeys are contained in the box, the number of conductors shown in the table shall be reduced by one for each type of device; an additional deduction of one conductor shall be made for each strap containing one or more devices; and a further deduction of one conductor shall be made for one or more grounding conductors entering the box. A conductor running through the box shall be counted as one conductor, and each conductor originating outside of the box and terminating inside the box is counted as one conductor. Conductors, no part of which leaves the box, shall not be counted. The volume of a wiring enclosure (box) shall be the total volume of the assembled sections, and, where used, the space provided by plaster rings, domed covers, extension rings, etc., that are marked with their volume in cubic inches, or are made from boxes the dimensions of which are listed in Table 370-6(a).

(2) For combinations of conductor sizes shown in Table 370-6(a), the volume per conductor listed in Table 370-6(b) shall apply. The maximum number and size of conductors listed in Table 370-6(a) shall not be exceeded.

Table 370-6(a) lists the maximum number of conductors in a "metal" box before the deductions provided for in Section 370-6(a)(1). Figure 370-1 illustrates one 14/2 and one 14/3 nonmetallic-sheathed cables with bare grounding conductors installed in a device box, and would be counted as:

Two nonmetallic-sheathed cables (circuit conductors)	5
Two grounding conductors	1
Internal clamp(s) (hickeys or studs)	1
Receptacle (strap containing one or more devices)	1
Total	8

Column No. 14, Table 370-6(a) lists a device box (3 x 2 x 3½ in.) which is adequate for nine No. 14 conductors, but may be too deep for shallower partitions; thus, a smaller device box (3 x 2 x 2½ in.) is permitted with a domed side bracket (marked with its volume in cubic inches) and the maximum number of conductors is to be computed as per Table 370-6(b). A 4-in. square box with plaster ring would also be permitted.

The following phrase was added to the last sentence of Section 370-6(a)(1) in the 1981 *Code*: "or are made from boxes the dimensions of which are listed in Table 370-6(a)." This means that extension rings made from boxes having the dimensions tabulated in Table 370-6(a) do not have to be marked with their cubic inch volume to be considered as having volume.

Extension rings or boxes, domed covers or plaster rings, etc., that are marked with their volume in cubic inches are to be considered as usable conductor space.

(b) Other Boxes. Boxes 100 cubic inches or less other than those described in Table 370-6(a), conduit bodies having provision for more than two conduit entries and nonmetallic boxes shall be durably and legibly marked by the manufacturer with their cubic inch capacity and the maximum number of conductors permitted shall be computed using the volume per conductor listed in Table 370-6(b) and the deductions provided for in Section 370-6(a)(1). Boxes described in Table 370-6(a) that have a larger cubic inch capacity than is designated in the table shall be permitted to have their cubic inch capacity marked as required by this section and the maximum number of conductors permitted shall be computed using the volume per conductor listed in Table 370-6(b).

Where No. 6 conductors are installed the minimum wire bending space required in Table 373-6(a) shall be provided.

Table 370-6(a) lists the cubic inch capacities and the maximum number of conductors (No. 14 through No. 6) permitted for metal boxes, most commonly used.

14/2 nonmetallic
with ground

14/3 nonmetallic
with ground

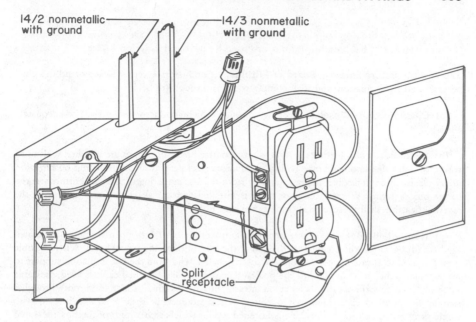

Split
receptacle

Figure 370-1. Device box, with a domed side, providing sufficient space for all conductors, clamp, and receptacle in compliance with Section 370-6(a)(1).

Table 370-6(b) lists the volume that is required for conductors (No. 14 through No. 6) used in boxes less than 100 cu in., other than those described in Table 370-6(a). Such boxes are to be marked with their cubic inch capacity. These provisions assure that free space for all conductors will be provided. A conductor running through the box without a splice or tap is counted as one conductor.

Table 370-6(b).   Volume Required per Conductor

Size of Conductor	Free Space Within Box for Each Conductor
No. 14	2. cubic inches
No. 12	2.25 cubic inches
No. 10	2.5 cubic inches
No. 8	3. cubic inches
No. 6	5. cubic inches

(c) Conduit Bodies. Conduit bodies enclosing No. 6 conductors or smaller shall have a cross-sectional area not less than twice the cross-sectional area of the largest conduit to which it is attached. The maximum number of conductors permitted shall be the maximum number permitted by Table 1, Chapter 9, for the conduit to which it is attached.

Conduit bodies having provisions for less than three conduit entries shall not contain splices, taps, or devices unless they comply with the provisions of Section 370-6(b) and are supported in a rigid and secure manner.

The intent of this section is to provide that conduit bodies are to be supported in a rigid and secure manner so that the conduit body will not turn in place. Where the conduit bodies have provisions for two or less conduit entries and contain splices, taps, or devices, they are to be durably and legibly marked with the cubic inch capacity. The maximum number of conductors permitted is to be computed using the volume for conductors listed in Table 370-6(b). See Section 370-18 for requirements when conduit bodies are used as pull and junction boxes.

370-7. Conductors Entering Boxes or Fittings. Conductors entering boxes or fittings shall be protected from abrasion, and shall comply with (a) through (d) below.

 (a) **Openings to Be Closed.** Openings through which conductors enter shall be adequately closed.

 (b) **Metal Boxes and Fittings.** Where metal outlet boxes or fittings are installed with open wiring or concealed knob-and-tube wiring, conductors shall enter through insulating bushings or, in dry places, through flexible tubing extending from the last insulating support and firmly secured to the box or fitting. Where raceway or cable is installed with metal outlet boxes or fittings, the raceway or cable shall be secured to such boxes and fittings.

 (c) **Nonmetallic Boxes.** Where nonmetallic boxes are used with open wiring or concealed knob-and-tube wiring, the conductors shall enter the box through individual holes. Where flexible tubing is used to encase the conductors, the tubing shall extend from the last insulating support to no less than ¼ inch (6.35 mm) inside the box. Where nonmetallic-sheathed cable is used, the cable assembly, including the sheath, shall extend into the box no less than ¼ inch (6.35 mm) through a nonmetallic-sheathed cable knockout opening. Where nonmetallic-sheathed cable is used with single gang boxes and where the cable is fastened within 8 inches (203 mm) of the box measured along the sheath and where the sheath extends into the box no less than ¼ inch (6.35 mm), securing the cable to the box shall not be required. In all other instances all permitted wiring methods shall be secured to the boxes.

 (d) **Conductors No. 4 AWG or Larger.** Installation shall comply with Section 373-6(c).

370-8. Unused Openings. Unused openings in boxes and fittings shall be effectively closed to afford protection substantially equivalent to that of the wall of the box or fitting. Metal plugs or plates used with nonmetallic boxes or fittings shall be recessed at least ¼ inch (6.35 mm) from the outer surface.

370-9. Boxes Enclosing Flush Devices. Boxes used to enclose flush devices shall be of such design that the devices will be completely enclosed on back and sides, and that substantial support for the devices will be provided. Screws for supporting the box shall not be used in attachment of the device contained therein.

370-10. In Wall or Ceiling. In walls or ceilings of concrete, tile, or other noncombustible material, boxes and fittings shall be so installed that the front edge of the box or fitting will not set back of the finished surface more than ¼ inch (6.35 mm). In walls and ceilings constructed of wood or other combustible material, outlet boxes and fittings shall be flush with the finished surface or project therefrom.

370-11. Repairing Plaster and Drywall or Plasterboard. Plaster, drywall or plasterboard surfaces that are broken or incomplete shall be repaired so there will be no gaps or open spaces at the edge of the box or fitting.

 Exception: On walls or ceilings of concrete, tile, or other noncombustible material.

 Sections 370-10 and 370-11 require that boxes installed in walls or ceilings of combustible materials be flush with the finished surface and any open spaces at the edge of the box be repaired.

Many inspection authorities require "mud rings" for use with square or octagonal boxes for proper installation.

"Drywall" and "Plasterboard" were added to Section 370-11 in the 1981 *Code* to indicate that these materials are to be treated the same as plaster.

370-12. Exposed Surface Extensions. In making an exposed surface extension from an existing outlet of concealed wiring, a box or an extension ring shall be mounted over the original box and electrically and mechanically secured to it.

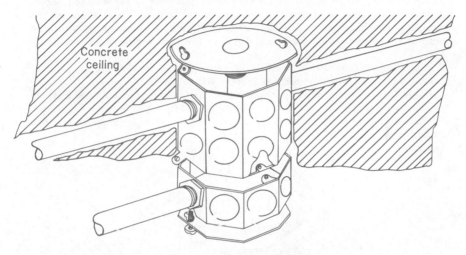

Figure 370-2. Extension boxes are secured to existing boxes in concealed construction for additions or alterations to the wiring system.

Figure 370-2 illustrates an extension box that is to be mounted to an existing box, assuring mechanical and electrical continuity.

370-13. Supports. Boxes shall be securely and rigidly fastened to the surface upon which they are mounted, or securely and rigidly embedded in concrete or masonry. Where nails are used as a mounting means and pass through the interior of the box, they shall be located within ¼ inch (6.35 mm) of the back or ends of the box. Boxes shall be supported from a structural member of the building either directly or by using a substantial and approved metal or wooden brace, or shall be supported as is otherwise provided in this section. If of wood, the brace shall not be less than nominal 1-inch (25.4-mm) thickness. If of metal it shall be corrosion-resistant and shall not be less than No. 24 MSG.

The second sentence of the first paragraph of Section 370-13 was revised for the 1981 *Code* to permit nailholes within ¼ in. of the ends of the box as well as within ¼ in. of the back of the box. The common 2 x 4 used in frame buildings has been reduced in size, and nails run into the stud ¼ in. from the back of the box have caused splitting of the stud and resulted in poor support for the box. Nails within ¼ in. of the ends give better support for the box.

Boxes installed in walls of previously occupied buildings or in walls in which there are no structural members shall be supported by the use of devices, clamps, or anchors which will provide the secure and rigid installation required by this section of the Code.

Threaded boxes or fittings not over 100 cubic inches in size that do not contain devices or support fixtures shall be considered adequately supported if two or more conduits are threaded into the box wrenchtight and are supported within 3 feet (914 mm) of the box on two or more sides as is required by this section.

Threaded boxes or fittings not over 100 cubic inches in size shall be considered to be adequately supported if two or more conduits are threaded into the box wrenchtight and are supported as required by this section within 18 inches (457 mm) of the box.

Boxes may be securely and rigidly embedded in masonry or concrete, as shown in Figure 370-3, or be supported by a structural member of the building, either directly or by using substantial wooden or metal braces. Where there are no structural members, or in existing walls, boxes may be secured by approved hold-its or clamps which may be integral to the box, as illustrated in Figure 370-5.

Figure 370-4 illustrates a method of supporting a box where the ceiling construction affords no support. See Section 410-16(a).

Boxes are not permitted to be supported by conduits using locknut and bushing connections nor is a box permitted to be supported by a single conduit. The last two paragraphs of Section 370-13 indicate the requirements for supporting a box from two or more conduits.

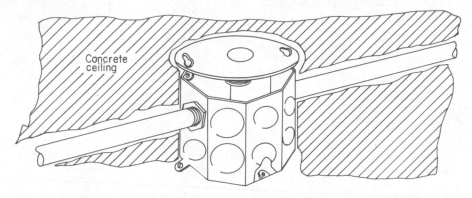

Figure 370-3. A "mud" box installed in a concrete ceiling. Additional support is not required.

370-14. Depth of Outlet Boxes.   No box shall have an internal depth of less than ½ inch (12.7 mm). Boxes intended to enclose flush devices shall have an internal depth of not less than 15⁄16 inch (23.8 mm).

Many times, usually in old work or existing construction, the use of a shallow box becomes necessary because of very narrow partitions, plumbing pipes, or duct-work encountered in the partition, etc. However, the selection of the box should be based on its having sufficient cubic inch capacity.

370-15. Covers and Canopies.   In completed installations each outlet box shall have a cover, faceplate, or fixture canopy.

(a) Nonmetallic or Metal Covers and Plates.   Nonmetallic or metal covers and plates shall be permitted with nonmetallic outlet boxes. Where metal covers or plates are used, they shall comply with the grounding requirements of Section 250-42.

See Sections 410-18(a) and 410-56(b) for metal faceplates.

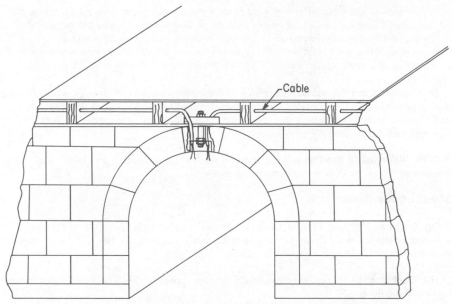

Box rod and plate hanger used when a fixture
weighing more than 50 lbs. is to be installed, or
when a box is installed in a large opening
of a tile ceiling.

Figure 370-4. A plate and threaded-rod hanger used to support an outlet box in a tile arch ceiling.

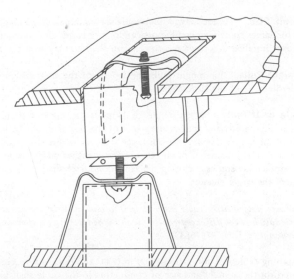

Figure 370-5. Top view of inserting and securing a box with a mounting
bracket through an opening cut in an existing wall finish.

(b) Exposed Combustible Wall or Ceiling Finish. Where a fixture canopy or pan is used,
any combustible wall or ceiling finish exposed between the edge of the canopy or pan and the
outlet box shall be covered with noncombustible material.

Because of the possibility that heat from a fixture canopy or pan could create a fire hazard, any exposed combustible wall or ceiling space between the edge of the outlet box and the perimeter of the fixture is to be covered with noncombustible material. Where the wall or ceiling finish is plaster or other noncombustible material, the requirement does not apply. See Section 370-11.

(c) Flexible Cord Pendants.   Covers of outlet boxes having holes through which flexible cord pendants pass shall be provided with bushings designed for the purpose or shall have smooth, well-rounded surfaces on which the cords may bear. So-called hard-rubber or composition bushings shall not be used.

370-16. Fastened to Gas Pipes.   Outlet boxes used where gas outlets are present shall be so fastened to the gas pipes as to be mechanically secure.

370-17. Outlet Boxes.

(a) Boxes at Lighting Fixture Outlets.   Boxes used at lighting fixture outlets shall be designed for the purpose. At every outlet used exclusively for lighting, the box shall be so designed or installed that a lighting fixture may be attached.

(b) Floor Boxes.   Boxes listed specifically for this application shall be used for receptacles located in the floor.

Exception: Boxes located in elevated floors of show windows and similar locations where the authority having jurisdiction judges them to be free from physical damage, moisture, and dirt.

370-18. Pull and Junction Boxes.   Boxes and conduit bodies used as pull or junction boxes shall comply with (a) through (d) of this section.

(a) Minimum Size.   For raceways ¾ inch trade size or larger, containing conductors of No. 4 or larger, and for cables containing conductors of No. 4 or larger, the minimum dimensions of pull or junction boxes installed in a raceway or cable run shall comply with the following:

(1) Straight Pulls.   In straight pulls the length of the box shall not be less than eight times the trade diameter of the largest raceway.

(2) Angle or U Pulls.   Where angle or U pulls are made, the distance between each raceway entry inside the box and the opposite wall of the box shall not be less than six times the trade diameter of the largest raceway. This distance shall be increased for additional entries by the amount of the sum of the diameters of all other raceway entries on the same wall of the box. The distance between raceway entries enclosing the same conductor shall not be less than six times the trade diameter of the larger raceway.

Exception: Where a conduit or cable entry is in the wall of a box or conduit body opposite to a removable cover and where the distance from that wall to the cover is in conformance with the column for one wire per terminal in Table 373-6(a).

When transposing cable size into raceway size in (a)(1) and (a)(2) above, the minimum trade size raceway required for the number and size of conductors in the cable shall be used.

(3) Boxes of dimensions less than those required in (a)(1) and (a)(2) above shall be permitted for installations of combinations of conductors that are less than the maximum conduit fill (of conduits being used) permitted by Table 1, Chapter 9, provided the box has been approved for and is permanently marked with the maximum number and maximum size of conductors permitted.

Exception: Terminal housings supplied with motors which shall comply with the provisions of Section 430-12.

(b) Conductors in Pull or Junction Boxes. In pull boxes or junction boxes having any dimension over 6 feet (1.83 m), all conductors shall be cabled or racked up in an approved manner.

See Section 373-6(c) for insulation of conductors at bushings.

(c) Covers. All pull boxes, junction boxes, and fittings shall be provided with covers compatible with the box or fitting construction and suitable for the conditions of use. Where metal covers are used, they shall comply with the grounding requirements of Section 250-42.

(d) Permanent Barriers. Where permanent barriers are installed in a box, each section shall be considered as a separate box.

This section applies to minimum dimensions of pull or junction boxes used with raceways (¾ in. or larger) or cables, where either contains No. 4 conductors or larger.

For straight pulls, for example, a 2-in. conduit containing four 4/0 THWN conductors (see Table 3B, Chapter 9) would require a 16-in. length pull box [8 x 2 in. = 16 in. as per Paragraph (a)(1)]. It is to be considered that 16 in. is to be the minimum length; however, for maximum ease of handling this size of conductor, an approximate length of 20 in. may be desired.

For angle pulls or U pulls, Paragraph (a)(2) indicates two methods for computing the box dimensions and the largest dimension computed by either of the two methods is, of course, the one to be used.

First method:

$$
\begin{array}{rl}
6 \times 4 \text{ in.} = & 24 \text{ in.} \\
2 \times 3 \text{ in.} = & 6 \\
4 \times 2\frac{1}{2} \text{ in.} = & \underline{10} \\
\text{Total} & 40 \text{ in.}
\end{array}
$$

Second method:

Figure 370-6 illustrates a box in which the conduits enter and leave in the same order, that is, there is no crossover of conductors. The 2½-in. conduit in the top, left corner must be spaced not less than 15 in. (6 x 2½ in. = 15 in.) (dimension A, measured center to center). By calculation, or by sketching the layout of the box and conduits on paper, it is determined that distance C is approximately 10½ in. and, by practical working methods for the spacing of conduits, distance B is approximately 32½ in. (10½ in. + 32½ in. = 43 in.); hence, the second method determining the larger box would be applied in this case.

The box illustrated in Figure 370-6 would be required to be approximately 7 in. deep; a double row of conduits of the same sizes would require a box approximately 14 in. deep.

Large conductors are generally formed in circuit groups and tied together with twine, or sufficient space should be allowed to provide for insulated racks to support conductors in an orderly manner. Conductors are to be prevented from resting directly on metal inside the box and insulating bushings are to be provided as required by Section 373-6(c).

370-19. Junction, Pull and Outlet Boxes to Be Accessible. Junction, pull and outlet boxes shall be so installed that the wiring contained in them can be rendered accessible without removing

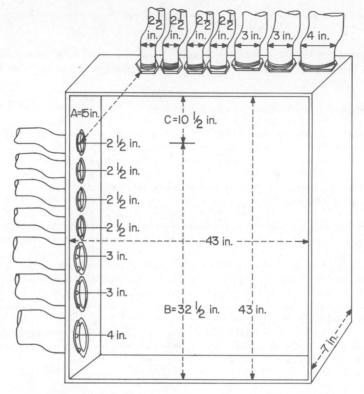

Figure 370-6. Raceways in a right-angle turn with no crossover of conductors within the pull box.

any part of the building or in underground circuits without excavating sidewalks, paving, earth, or other substance that is to be used to establish the finished grade.

Exception: Listed boxes shall be permitted where covered by gravel, light aggregate, or noncohesive granulated soil if their location is effectively identified and accessible for excavation.

A covered box may be used at any point for the connection of conduit, tubing, or cable, provided it is not rendered inaccessible. See Article 100 for definition of "Accessible (as applied to wiring methods)." See also Section 300-15.

C. Construction Specifications

370-20. Metal Outlet, Switch and Junction Boxes, and Fittings. Metal outlet, switch and junction boxes, and fittings shall comply with (a) through (d) below.

(a) Corrosion-Resistant. Metal boxes and fittings shall be corrosion-resistant or shall be well galvanized, enameled, or otherwise properly coated inside and out to prevent corrosion.

See Section 300-6 for limitation in the use of boxes and fittings protected from corrosion solely by enamel.

(b) Thickness of Metal. Sheet steel boxes and fittings not over 100 cubic inches in size shall be made from steel not less than 0.0625 inches (1.59 mm) thick. The wall of a malleable iron box and a die-cast or permanent-mold cast aluminum, brass or bronze box shall not be less than ³⁄₃₂ inch (2.38 mm) thick. Other cast metal boxes shall have a wall thickness not less than ⅛ inch (3.17 mm).

(c) Metal Boxes Over 100 Cubic Inches. Metal boxes over 100 cubic inches in size shall comply with the provisions of Section 373-10(a) and (b).

Exception: It shall be permissible for covers to consist of single flat sheets secured to the box proper by screws or bolts instead of hinges. Boxes having covers of this form shall be used only for enclosing joints in conductors or to facilitate the drawing in of wires and cables. They shall not be used to enclose switches, cutouts, or other control devices.

(d) Grounding Provisions. A means shall be provided in each metal box, designed for use with nonmetallic raceways and nonmetallic cable systems, for the connection of an equipment grounding conductor.

370-21. Covers. Metal covers shall be of a thickness not less than that specified for the walls of the box or fitting of the same material and with which they are designed to be used, or shall be lined with firmly attached insulating material not less than ¹⁄₃₂ inch (0.79 mm) in thickness. Covers of porcelain or other approved insulating material shall be permitted if of such form and thickness as to afford the required protection and strength.

370-22. Bushings. Covers of outlet boxes and outlet fittings having holes through which flexible cord pendants may pass shall be provided with approved bushings or shall have smooth, well-rounded surfaces, upon which the cord may bear. Where conductors other than flexible cord may pass through a metal cover, a separate hole equipped with a bushing of suitable insulating material shall be provided for each conductor.

370-23. Nonmetallic Boxes. Provisions for supports or other mounting means for nonmetallic boxes shall be outside of the box, or the box shall be so constructed as to prevent contact between the conductors in the box and the supporting screws.

370-24. Marking. All boxes and conduit bodies, covers, extension rings, plaster rings, and the like shall be durably and legibly marked with the manufacturer's name or trademark.

**D. Pull and Junction Boxes for Use on Systems
Over 600 Volts, Nominal**

370-50. General. In addition to the generally applicable provisions of Article 370, the rules in Sections 370-51 and 370-52 shall apply.

370-51. Size of Pull and Junction Boxes. Pull and junction boxes shall provide adequate space and dimensions for the installation of conductors in accordance with the following:

(a) For Straight Pulls. The length of the box shall be not less than forty-eight times the outside diameter, over sheath, of the largest conductor or cable entering the box.

(b) For Angle or U Pulls. The distance between each cable or conductor entry inside the box and the opposite wall of the box shall not be less than thirty-six times the outside diameter, over sheath, of the largest cable or conductor. This distance shall be increased for additional entries by the amount of the sum of the outside diameters, over sheath, of all other cables or conductor entries through the same wall of the box.

The distance between a cable or conductor entry and its exit from the box shall be not less than thirty-six times the outside diameter, over sheath, of that cable or conductor.

Exception No. 1: Where a conductor or cable entry is in the wall of a box opposite to a removable cover and where the distance from that wall to the cover is in conformance with the provisions of Section 300-34.

Exception No. 2: Terminal housings supplied with motors which shall comply with the provisions of Section 430-12.

(c) Removable Sides.   One or more sides of any pull box shall be removable.

370-52. Construction and Installation Requirements.

(a) Corrosion Protection.   Boxes shall be made of material inherently resistant to corrosion or shall be suitably protected, both internally and externally, by enameling, galvanizing, plating, or other means.

(b) Passing Through Partitions.   Suitable bushing, shields, or fittings having smooth rounded edges shall be provided where conductors or cables pass through partitions and at other locations where necessary.

(c) Complete Enclosure.   Boxes shall provide a complete enclosure for the contained conductors or cables.

(d) Wiring Is Accessible.   Boxes shall be so installed that the wiring is accessible without removing any part of the building. Working space shall be provided in accordance with Section 110-34.

(e) Suitable Covers.   Boxes shall be closed by suitable covers securely fastened in place. Underground box covers that weigh over 100 pounds (43.6 kg) shall be considered as meeting this requirement. Covers for boxes shall be permanently marked "HIGH VOLTAGE." The marking shall be on the outside of the box cover and shall be readily visible. Letters shall be block type at least ½ inch (12.7 mm) in height.

(f) Suitable for Expected Handling.   Boxes and their covers shall be capable of withstanding the handling to which they may be subjected.

ARTICLE 373 — CABINETS AND CUTOUT BOXES

Contents

373-1. Scope.   This article covers the installation of cabinets and cutout boxes. Installations in hazardous (classified) locations shall comply with Articles 500 through 517.

Cabinets and cutout boxes are designed with swinging door(s) to enclose switches, overcurrent devices, or control equipment. They are required to be of sufficient size to accommodate all devices and conductors without crowding or jamming. Overcrowding can be prevented by the use of auxiliary gutters (see Article 374).

A. Installation

373-2. Damp or Wet Locations.   In damp or wet locations, cabinets and cutout boxes of the surface type shall be so placed or equipped as to prevent moisture or water from entering and accumulating within the cabinet or cutout box, and shall be mounted so there is at least ¼-inch (6.35-mm) air space between the enclosure and the wall or other supporting surface. Cabinets or cutout boxes installed in wet locations shall be weatherproof.

For protection against corrosion, see Section 300-6.

373-3. Position in Wall.   In walls of concrete, tile, or other noncombustible material, cabinets shall be so installed that the front edge of the cabinet will not set back of the finished surface more than ¼ inch (6.35 mm). In walls constructed of wood or other combustible material, cabinets shall be flush with the finished surface or project therefrom.

373-4. Unused Openings.   Unused openings in cabinet or cutout boxes shall be effectively closed to afford protection substantially equivalent to that of the wall of the cabinet or cutout box. Where metal plugs or plates are used with nonmetallic cabinets or cutout boxes, they shall be recessed at least ¼ inch (6.35 mm) from the outer surface.

373-5. Conductors Entering Cabinets or Cutout Boxes.   Conductors entering cabinets or cutout boxes shall be protected from abrasion and shall comply with (a) through (c) below.

(a) Openings to Be Closed.   Openings through which conductors enter shall be adequately closed.

(b) Metal Cabinets and Cutout Boxes.   Where metal cabinets or cutout boxes are installed with open wiring or concealed knob-and-tube wiring, conductors shall enter through insulating bushings or, in dry places, through flexible tubing extending from the last insulating support and firmly secured to the cabinet or cutout box.

(c) Cables.   Where cable is used, each cable shall be secured to the cabinet or cutout box.

373-6. Deflection of Conductors.   Conductors at terminals or conductors entering or leaving cabinets or cutout boxes and the like shall comply with (a) through (c) below.

(a) Width of Wiring Gutters.   Conductors shall not be deflected within a cabinet or cutout box unless a gutter having a width in accordance with Table 373-6(a) is provided. Conductors in parallel in accordance with Section 310-4 shall be judged on the basis of the number of conductors in parallel.

**Table 373-6(a).   Minimum Wire Bending Space at Terminals and
Minimum Width of Wiring Gutters in Inches**

AWG or Circular-Mil Size of Wire	Wires per Terminal				
	1	2	3	4	5
14-10	Not Specified	—	—	—	—
8-6	1½	—	—	—	—
4-3	2	—	—	—	—
2	2½	—	—	—	—
1	3	—	—	—	—
0-00	3½	5	7	—	—
000-0000	4	6	8	—	—
250 MCM	4½	6	8	10	—
300-350 MCM	5	8	10	12	—
400-500 MCM	6	8	10	12	14
600-700 MCM	8	10	12	14	16
750-900 MCM	8	12	14	16	18
1,000-1,250 MCM	10	—	—	—	—
1,500-2,000 MCM	12	—	—	—	—

For SI units: one inch = 25.4 millimeters.

Bending space at terminals shall be measured in a straight line from the end of the lug or wire connector (in the direction that the wire leaves the terminal) to the wall, barrier, or obstruction.

(b) Wire Bending Space at Terminals.   Wire bending space at each terminal shall be provided in accordance with (1) or (2) below:

(1) Table 373-6(a) shall apply where the conductor does not enter or leave the enclosure through the wall opposite its terminal.

Exception: A conductor shall be permitted to enter or leave an enclosure through the wall opposite its terminal provided the conductor enters or leaves the enclosure at a point where the wire bending space conforms to Table 373-6(b) for that conductor.

(2) Table 373-6(b) shall apply where the conductor enters or leaves the enclosure through the wall opposite its terminal.

Section 373-6 has been revised for the 1981 *Code* and Table 373-6(b) was added to increase wire bending space where straight-in wiring or offset (double bends) are employed at terminals. Table 373-6(a) remains for use where only 90° bends are involved. See Figure 373-1.

(c) Insulated Bushings.   Where ungrounded conductors of No. 4 or larger enter a raceway in a cabinet, pull box, junction box, or auxiliary gutter, the conductors shall be protected by a substantial bushing providing a smoothly rounded insulating surface, unless the conductors are separated from the raceway fitting by substantial insulating material securely fastened in place. Where conduit bushings are constructed wholly of insulating material, a locknut shall be installed both inside and outside the enclosure to which the conduit is attached. The insulating bushing or insulating material shall have a temperature rating not less than the insulation temperature rating of the installed conductors.

Where No. 4 or larger (ungrounded) conductors enter a cabinet or box from metal conduit, EMT, etc., Paragraph (c) requires a smoothly rounded insulating bushing to protect the conductors from abrasion.

Conduit bushings or fittings provided with insulated sleeves or linings are commonly used. See Figure 373-2. It is also possible to use a separate insulating sleeve or lining to separate the conductors from the raceway fitting.

Table 373-6(b).   Minimum Wire Bending Space at Terminals for
Section 373-6(b)(2) in Inches

Wire Size	Wires per Terminal			
	1	2	3	4 or More
14-10	Not Specified	—	—	—
8	1½	—	—	—
6	2	—	—	—
4	3	—	—	—
3	3	—	—	—
2	3½	—	—	—
1	4½	—	—	—
0	5½	5½	7	—
2/0	6	6	7½	—
3/0	6½	6½	8	—
4/0	7	7½	8½	—
250	8½	8½	9	10
300	10	10	11	12
350	12	12	13	14
400	13	13	14	15
500	14	14	15	16
600	15	16	18	19
700	16	18	20	22
750	17	19	22	24
800	18	20	22	24
900	19	22	24	24
1000	20	—	—	—
1250	22	—	—	—
1500	24	—	—	—
1750	24	—	—	—
2000	24	—	—	—

For SI units: one inch = 25.4 millimeters.

Bending space at terminals shall be measured in a straight line from the end of the lug or wire connector (in the direction that the wire leaves the terminal) to the wall, barrier, or obstruction.

373-7. Space in Enclosures.   Cabinets and cutout boxes shall have sufficient space to accommodate all conductors installed in them without crowding.

373-8. Enclosures for Switches or Overcurrent Devices.   Enclosures for switches or overcurrent devices shall not be used as junction boxes, auxiliary gutters, or raceways for conductors feeding through or tapping off to other switches or overcurrent devices.

Exception: Where adequate space is provided so that the conductors do not fill the wiring space at any cross section to more than 40 percent of the cross-sectional area of the space, and so that the conductors, splices, and taps do not fill the wiring space at any cross section to more than 75 percent of the cross-sectional area of the space.

The design of most enclosures is intended to accommodate only those conductors that are to be connected to terminals for switches or overcurrent devices within the enclosures themselves. Where adequate space is provided that will permit additional conductors, such as control circuits, then the total conductor fill should not exceed 40 percent of the cross section of the wiring space; no more than 75 percent if splices are permitted.

An example would be, if an enclosure had a wiring space of 4 in. x 3 in., the cross-sectional area would be 12 sq in. Thus, the total conductor fill (see Table 5, Chapter 9 for dimensions of conductors) at any cross section could not exceed 4.8 sq in. (40 percent of 12 sq in.), and the maximum space for conductors and splices at any cross section could not exceed 9 sq in. (75 percent of 12 sq in.).

In general, the most satisfactory way to avoid overcrowding enclosures is to use properly sized auxiliary gutters (Sections 374-5 and 374-8) or junction boxes (Sections 370-6 and 370-18).

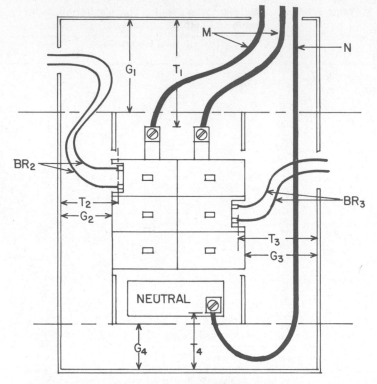

Figure 373-1. The following rules apply when wiring as shown.

T1, Section 373-6(b)(2): Table 373-6(b) applies for conductors M.

T2, Section 373-6(b)(2): Table 373-6(b) applies for conductors BR2 unless in accordance with Section 373-6(b)(1), Exception. Conductors enter a second wiring space G, conforming to Table 373-6(b) for conductors BR2.

T3, Section 373-6(b)(2): Table 373-6(b) applies for conductors BR3.

T4, Section 373-6(b)(1): Table 373-6(a) applies for conductor N.

G1, Section 373-6(a): Table 373-6(a) applies for conductors M. Table 373-6(b) applies for conductors BR2 when T2 does not comply with Table 373-6(b).

G2, Section 373-6(a): Table 373-6(a) applies for conductors BR2.

G3, Section 373-6(a): Table 373-6(a) applies for conductors BR3.

G4, Section 373-6(a): Table 373-6(a) applies for conductor N.

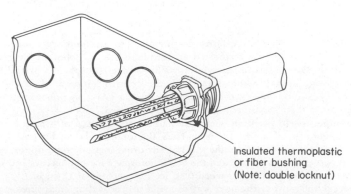

Insulated thermoplastic
or fiber bushing
(Note: double locknut)

Figure 373-2. An insulating bushing to protect conductors from chafing against a metal conduit fitting.

373-9. Side or Back Wiring Spaces or Gutters.   Cabinets and cutout boxes shall be provided with back wiring spaces, gutters, or wiring compartments as required by Section 373-11(c) and (d).

B. Construction Specifications

373-10. Material.   Cabinets and cutout boxes shall comply with (a) through (c) below.

(a) Metal Cabinets and Cutout Boxes.   Metal cabinets and cutout boxes shall be protected both inside and outside against corrosion.

For protection against corrosion, see Section 300-6.

(b) Strength.   The design and construction of cabinets and cutout boxes shall be such as to secure ample strength and rigidity. If constructed of sheet steel, the metal shall not be less than No. 16 MSG.

(c) Nonmetallic Cabinets.   Nonmetallic cabinets shall be submitted for approval prior to installation.

373-11. Spacing.   The spacing within cabinets and cutout boxes shall comply with (a) through (d) below.

(a) General.   Spacing within cabinets and cutout boxes shall be sufficient to provide ample room for the distribution of wires and cables placed in them, and for a separation between metal parts of devices and apparatus mounted within them as follows:

(1) Base.   Other than at points of support, there shall be an air space of at least $\frac{1}{16}$ inch (1.59 mm) between the base of the device and the wall of any metal cabinet or cutout box in which the device is mounted.

(2) Doors.   There shall be an air space of at least 1 inch (25.4 mm) between any live metal part, including live metal parts of enclosed fuses, and the door.

Exception: Where the door is lined with an approved insulating material or is of a thickness of metal not less than No. 12 MSG, the air space shall not be less than ½ inch (12.7 mm).

(3) Live Parts.   There shall be an air space of at least ½ inch (12.7 mm) between the walls, back, gutter partition, if of metal, or door of any cabinet or cutout box and the nearest exposed current-carrying part of devices mounted within the cabinet where the voltage does not exceed 250. This spacing shall be increased to at least 1 inch (25.4 mm) for voltages 251 to 600, nominal.

Exception: As permitted in (2) above.

(b) Switch Clearance.   Cabinets and cutout boxes shall be deep enough to allow the closing of the doors when 30-ampere branch-circuit panelboard switches are in any position; when combination cutout switches are in any position; or when other single-throw switches are opened as far as their construction will permit.

(c) Wiring Space.   Cabinets and cutout boxes that contain devices or apparatus connected within the cabinet or box to more than eight conductors, including those of branch circuits, meter loops, subfeeder circuits, power circuits, and similar circuits, but not including the supply circuit or a continuation thereof, shall have back-wiring spaces or one or more side-wiring spaces, side gutters, or wiring compartments.

(d) Wiring Space — Enclosure. Side-wiring spaces, side gutters, or side-wiring compartments of cabinets and cutout boxes shall be made tight enclosures by means of covers, barriers, or partitions extending from the bases of the devices, contained in the cabinet to the door, frame, or sides of the cabinet.

Exception: Where the enclosure contains only those conductors that are led from the cabinet at points directly opposite their terminal connections to devices within the cabinet.

Partially enclosed back-wiring spaces shall be provided with covers to complete the enclosure. Wiring spaces that are required by (c) above, and that are exposed when doors are open, shall be provided with covers to complete the enclosure. Where adequate space is provided for feed-through conductors and for splices as required in Section 373-8, Exception, additional barriers shall not be required.

ARTICLE 374 — AUXILIARY GUTTERS

Contents

374-1. Use. Auxiliary gutters shall be permitted to supplement wiring spaces at meter centers, distribution centers, switchboards, and similar points of wiring systems and may enclose conductors or busbars, but shall not be used to enclose switches, overcurrent devices, appliances, or other similar equipment.

Auxiliary gutter sections and associated fittings are identical to those of wireways, and each bears the single Underwriters Laboratories Inc. Listing Mark "Listed Wireway or Auxiliary Gutter." They differ only in their intended use. See comments following Section 362-1. Gutters (and wireways) are to be constructed and installed to assure adequate electrical and mechanical continuity of the complete system. See Section 250-91(b)(10).

Auxiliary gutters for outdoor use are to be "raintight" construction. See Section 620-35 for elevator uses and Section 640-4 for sound-recording equipment uses.

374-2. Extension Beyond Equipment. An auxiliary gutter shall not extend a greater distance than 30 feet (9.14 m) beyond the equipment which it supplements.

Exception: As provided in Section 620-35 for elevators.

For wireways, see Article 362. For busways, see Article 364.

374-3. Supports. Gutters shall be supported throughout their entire length at intervals not exceeding 5 feet (1.52 m).

374-4. Covers. Covers shall be securely fastened to the gutter.

374-5. Number of Conductors. Auxiliary gutters shall not contain more than thirty current-carrying conductors at any cross section. The sum of the cross-sectional areas of all contained conductors at any cross section of an auxiliary gutter shall not exceed 20 percent of the interior cross-sectional area of the auxiliary gutter.

Exception No. 1: As provided in Section 620-35 for elevators.

Exception No. 2: Conductors for signaling circuits or controller conductors between a motor and its starter and used only for starting duty shall not be considered as current-carrying conductors.

Exception No. 3: Where the correction factors specified in Note 8 to Tables 310-16 through 310-19 are applied, there shall be no limit on the number of current-carrying conductors, but the sum of the cross-sectional area of all contained conductors at any cross section of the auxiliary gutter shall not exceed 20 percent of the interior cross-sectional area of the auxiliary gutter.

The dimensions of rubber-covered and thermoplastic-covered conductors given in Table 5, Chapter 9 may be used to compute the size of gutters required to contain a given combination of such conductors.

Where auxiliary gutters contain thirty or less current-carrying conductors, the correction factors of Note 8 (Tables 310-16 through 310-19) do not apply. There is no limit on the number of current-carrying conductors if Note 8 is applied; however, the contained conductors are not to exceed 20 percent of the interior cross-sectional area of the gutter.

No limit is placed on the size of conductors that may be installed in an auxiliary gutter; however, see Section 374-6 for limitations of bare copper or aluminum busbars enclosed in gutters.

374-6. Ampacity of Conductors. Where the number of current-carrying conductors contained in the auxiliary gutter is thirty or less, the correction factors specified in Note 8 to Tables 310-16 through 310-19 shall not apply. The current carried continuously in bare copper bars in auxiliary gutters shall not exceed 1000 amperes per square inch (645 sq mm) of cross section of the conductor. For aluminum bars, the current carried continuously shall not exceed 700 amperes per square inch (645 sq mm) of cross section of the conductor.

374-7. Clearance of Bare Live Parts. Bare conductors shall be securely and rigidly supported so that the minimum clearance between bare current-carrying metal parts of opposite polarities mounted on the same surface will not be less than 2 inches (50.8 mm), nor less than 1 inch (25.4 mm) for parts that are held free in the air. A clearance not less than 1 inch (25.4 mm) shall be secured between bare current-carrying metal parts and any metal surface. Adequate provisions shall be made for the expansion and contraction of busbars.

374-8. Splices and Taps. Splices and taps shall comply with (a) through (d) below.

(a) **Within Gutters.** Splices or taps shall be permitted within gutters when they are accessible by means of removable covers or doors. The conductors, including splices and taps, shall not fill the gutter to more than 75 percent of its area.

(b) **Bare Conductors.** Taps from bare conductors shall leave the gutter opposite their terminal connections and conductors shall not be brought in contact with uninsulated current-carrying parts of opposite polarity.

(c) **Suitably Identified.** All taps shall be suitably identified at the gutter as to the circuit or equipment which they supply.

(d) **Overcurrent Protection.** Tap connections from conductors in auxiliary gutters shall be provided with overcurrent protection as required in Section 240-21.

Precautions must be taken to provide suitable bushings, shields, etc., where conductors pass around bends, or between gutters and cabinets and other locations to prevent abrasion of the insulation. Also, conductors are to be shaped or formed in a permanent manner so as not to be in contact with bare busbars within the gutter.

Paragraphs (c) and (d) provide that all taps from gutters be identified (as to circuits or equipment) and be protected with overcurrent devices as required in Section 240-21.

374-9. Construction and Installation.   Auxiliary gutters shall comply with (a) through (e) below.

(a) Electrical and Mechanical Continuity.   Gutters shall be so constructed and installed that adequate electrical and mechanical continuity of the complete system will be secured.

(b) Substantial Construction.   Gutters shall be of substantial construction and shall provide a complete enclosure for the contained conductors. All surfaces, both interior and exterior, shall be suitably protected from corrosion. Corner joints shall be made tight and, where the assembly is held together by rivets or bolts, these shall be spaced not more than 12 inches (305 mm) apart.

(c) Smooth Rounded Edges.   Suitable bushings, shields, or fittings having smooth rounded edges shall be provided where conductors pass between gutters, through partitions, around bends, between gutters and cabinets or junction boxes, and at other locations where necessary to prevent abrasion of the insulation of the conductors.

(d) Deflected Insulated Conductors.   Where insulated conductors are deflected within an auxiliary gutter, either at the ends or where conduits, fittings, or other raceways enter or leave the gutter, or where the direction of the gutter is deflected greater than 30 degrees, dimensions corresponding to Section 373-6 shall apply.

(e) Outdoor Use.   Auxiliary gutters intended for outdoor use shall be of approved raintight construction.

ARTICLE 380 — SWITCHES

Contents

A. Installation

380-1. Scope. The provisions of this article shall apply to all switches, switching devices, and circuit breakers where used as switches.

380-2. Switch Connections.

(a) Three-Way and Four-Way Switches. Three-way and four-way switches shall be so wired that all switching is done only in the ungrounded circuit conductor. Where in metal enclosures, wiring between switches and outlets shall be run with both polarities in the same enclosure.

(b) Grounded Conductors. Switches or circuit breakers shall not disconnect the grounded conductor of a circuit.

Exception No. 1: Where the switch or circuit breaker simultaneously disconnects all conductors of the circuit.

Exception No. 2: Where the switch or circuit breaker is so arranged that the grounded conductor cannot be disconnected until all the ungrounded conductors of the circuit have been disconnected.

380-3. Enclosure. Switches and circuit breakers shall be of the externally operable type mounted in an enclosure listed for the intended use. The minimum wire bending space at terminals and minimum gutter space provided in switch enclosures shall be as required in Section 373-6.

Exception: Pendant- and surface-type snap switches and knife switches mounted on an open-face switchboard or panelboard.

380-4. Wet Locations. A switch or circuit breaker in a wet location or outside of a building shall be enclosed in a weatherproof enclosure or cabinet that shall comply with Section 373-2.

380-5. Time Switches, Flashers, and Similar Devices. Time switches, flashers, and similar devices need not be of the externally operable type. They shall be enclosed in metal boxes or cabinets.

Exception No. 1: Where mounted in switchboards, control panels, or enclosures and so located that any live terminals, located within 6 inches (152 mm) of the manually adjustable clock dial or "on-off" switch, are covered by suitable barriers.

Exception No. 2: Where enclosed in approved individual housings with no live parts exposed to the operator.

Time-clock switches, flashers, etc., are required to be mounted in metal enclosures. Proper enclosures will prevent sparks or thermal energy from the natural operation of such automatic switching devices from contacting any combustible material in the area.

380-6. Position of Knife Switches.

(a) Single-Throw Knife Switches. Single-throw knife switches shall be so placed that gravity will not tend to close them. Single-throw knife switches, approved for use in the inverted position, shall be provided with a locking device that will ensure that the blades remain in the open position when so set.

(b) Double-Throw Knife Switches. Double-throw knife switches shall be permitted to be mounted so that the throw will be either vertical or horizontal. Where the throw is vertical, a locking device shall be provided to hold the blades in the open position when so set.

380-7. Connection of Knife Switches. Single-throw knife switches shall be so connected that the blades are dead when the switch is in the open position.

380-8. Accessibility and Grouping.

(a) Location. All switches and circuit breakers used as switches shall be so located that they may be operated from a readily accessible place. They shall be so installed that the center of the grip of the operating handle of the switch or circuit breaker, when in its highest position, will not be more than 6½ feet (1.98 m) above the floor or working platform.

Exception No. 1: On busway installations, fused switches and circuit breakers shall be permitted to be located at the same level as the busway. Suitable means shall be provided to operate the handle of the device from the floor.

Exception No. 2: Switches installed adjacent to motors, appliances, or other equipment which they supply shall be permitted to be located higher than specified in the foregoing and to be accessible by portable means.

Exception No. 3: Hookstick operable isolating switches shall be permitted at heights of more than 6½ feet (1.98 m).

(b) Voltage Between Adjacent Switches. Snap switches shall not be grouped or ganged in outlet boxes unless they can be so arranged that the voltage between adjacent switches does not exceed 300, or unless they are installed in boxes equipped with permanently installed barriers between adjacent switches.

380-9. Faceplates for Flush-Mounted Snap Switches. Flush snap switches, that are mounted in ungrounded metal boxes and located within reach of conducting floors or other conducting surfaces, shall be provided with faceplates of nonconducting, noncombustible material. Metal faceplates shall be of ferrous metal not less than 0.030 inch (0.762 mm) in thickness or of nonferrous metal not less than 0.040 inch (1.016 mm) in thickness. Faceplates of insulating material shall be noncombustible and not less than 0.10 inch (2.54 mm) in thickness but they shall be permitted to be less than 0.10 inch (2.54 mm) in thickness if formed or reinforced to provide adequate mechanical strength. Faceplates shall be installed so as to completely cover the wall opening and seat against the wall surface.

Switch plates attached to outlets supplied by a wiring method which does not provide a ready means for grounding are to be made of insulating material and are to have no exposed conductive parts.

380-10. Mounting of Snap Switches.

(a) Surface-type. Snap switches used with open wiring on insulators shall be mounted on insulating material that will separate the conductors at least ½ inch (12.7 mm) from the surface wired over.

(b) Box Mounted. Flush-type snap switches mounted in boxes that are set back of the wall surface as permitted in Section 370-10 shall be installed so that the extension plaster ears are seated against the surface of the wall. Flush-type snap switches mounted in boxes that are flush with the wall surface or project therefrom shall be so installed that the mounting yoke or strap of the switch is seated against the box.

Cooperation is necessary among the building trades (carpenters, dry-wall installers, plasterers, etc.) in order for electricians to properly set device boxes flush with the finish surface, thereby ensuring a secure seating of the switch yoke and permitting the maximum **projection** of switch handles through the installed switch plate.

380-11. Circuit Breakers as Switches. A hand-operable circuit breaker equipped with a lever or handle, or a power-operated circuit breaker capable of being opened by hand in the event of a power failure, shall be permitted to serve as a switch if it has the required number of poles.

Circuit breakers capable of being hand-operated are to clearly indicate whether they are in the open "off" or closed "on" position. See Section 240-81.

See also Section 240-83(d) for marking (SWD) for circuit breakers used in 120-V, fluorescent lighting circuits.

380-12. Grounding of Enclosures. Enclosures for switches or circuit breakers on circuits of over 150 volts to ground shall be grounded as specified in Article 250. Where nonmetallic enclosures are used with metal-sheathed cables or metallic conduits, provision shall be made for grounding continuity.

380-13. Knife Switches.

(a) Isolating Switches. Knife switches rated at over 1200 amperes at 250 volts or less, and at over 600 amperes at 251 to 600 volts, shall be used only as isolating switches and shall not be opened under load.

(b) To Interrupt Currents. To interrupt currents over 1200 amperes at 250 volts, nominal, or less, or over 600 amperes at 251 to 600 volts, nominal, a circuit breaker or a switch of special design listed for such purpose shall be used.

(c) General-Use Switches. Knife switches of ratings less than specified in (a) and (b) above shall be considered general-use switches.

See definition of general-use switch in Article 100.

(d) Motor-Circuit Switches. Motor-circuit switches shall be permitted to be of the knife-switch type.

See definition of a motor-circuit switch in Article 100.

380-14. Rating and Use of Snap Switches. Snap switches shall be used within their ratings and as follows:

(a) AC General-Use Snap Switch. A form of general-use snap switch suitable only for use on alternating-current circuits for controlling the following:

(1) Resistive and inductive loads, including electric-discharge lamps, not exceeding the ampere rating of the switch at the voltage involved.

(2) Tungsten-filament lamp loads not exceeding the ampere rating of the switch at 120 volts.

(3) Motor loads not exceeding 80 percent of the ampere rating of the switch at its rated voltage.

(b) AC-DC General-Use Snap Switch.   A form of general-use snap switch suitable for use on either ac or dc circuits for controlling the following:

(1) Resistive loads not exceeding the ampere rating of the switch at the voltage applied.

(2) Inductive loads not exceeding 50 percent of the ampere rating of the switch at the applied voltage. Switches rated in horsepower are suitable for controlling motor loads within their rating at voltage applied.

(3) Tungsten-filament lamp loads not exceeding the ampere rating of the switch at the applied voltage if "T" rated.

For switches on signs and outline lighting, see Section 600-2.

For switches controlling motors, see Sections 430-83, 430-109, and 430-110.

(c) CO/ALR Snap Switches.   Snap switches rated 20 amperes or less directly connected to aluminum conductors shall be listed and marked CO/ALR.

B. Construction Specifications

380-15. Marking.   Switches shall be marked with the current and voltage and, if horsepower rated, the maximum rating for which they are designed.

380-16. 600-Volt Knife Switches.   Auxiliary contacts of a renewable or quick-break type or the equivalent shall be provided on all knife switches rated 600 volts designed for use in breaking current over 200 amperes.

380-17. Fused Switches.   A fused switch shall not have fuses in parallel.

See Section 240-8, Exception.

380-18. Wire Bending Space.   The wire bending space required by Section 380-3 shall meet Table 373-6(b) spacings to the enclosure wall opposite the line and load terminals.

ARTICLE 384 — SWITCHBOARDS AND PANELBOARDS

Contents

384-1. General.

(a) Scope. This article covers (1) all switchboards, panelboards, and distribution boards installed for the control of light and power circuits, and (2) battery-charging panels supplied from light or power circuits.

Exception: Switchboards or portions thereof used exclusively to control signaling circuits operated by batteries.

(b) Other Articles. Switches, circuit breakers, and overcurrent devices used on switchboards, panelboards, and distribution boards, and their enclosures, shall comply with the requirements of Articles 240, 250, 370, 380, and other articles that apply. Switchboards and panelboards in hazardous (classified) locations shall comply with the requirements of Articles 500 through 517.

384-2. Installation. Equipment within the scope of Article 384 shall be located in rooms or spaces dedicated exclusively to such equipment. No piping, ducts, or equipment foreign to the electrical equipment or architectural appurtenances shall be permitted to be installed in, enter or pass through such spaces or rooms.

Exception No. 1: Control equipment which by its very nature or because of other rules of this Code must be adjacent to or within sight of its operating machinery.

Exception No. 2: Ventilating, heating, or cooling equipment that serves the electrical rooms or spaces.

Exception No. 3: Equipment located throughout industrial plants which is isolated from foreign equipment by height or physical enclosures or covers which will afford adequate mechanical protection from vehicular traffic, accidental contact by unauthorized personnel, or accidental spillage or leakage from piping systems.

Exception No. 4: Outdoor electrical equipment located in weatherproof enclosures protected from accidental contact by unauthorized personnel or vehicular traffic or accidental spillage or leakage from piping systems.

Section 384-2 in the 1978 *Code* has become Section 384-1(b) in the 1981 *Code*. New material has been added as Section 384-2, which provides requirements for rooms or space dedicated exclusively to equipment covered by Article 384, with some specific exceptions.

384-3. Support and Arrangement of Busbars and Conductors.

(a) Conductors and Busbars on a Switchboard, Panelboard, or Control Board.   Conductors and busbars on a switchboard, panelboard, or control board shall be so located as to be free from physical damage and shall be held firmly in place. Other than the required interconnections and control wiring, only those conductors that are intended for termination in a vertical section of a switchboard shall be located in that section. Barriers shall be placed in all service switchboards that will isolate the service busbars and terminals from the remainder of the switchboard.

Exception: Conductors shall be permitted to travel horizontally through vertical sections of switchboards where such conductors are isolated from busbars by a barrier.

It is usually impractical to disconnect or de-energize the service conductors supplying a service switchboard. For this reason, it is a universal practice to work on these switchboards with the service bus electrically alive. Barriers are required in all service switchboards to isolate the service busbars and terminals from the remainder of the switchboard, thus providing some measure of safety during maintenance of live energized parts.

Prior to the 1981 edition of the *Code*, conductors intended for termination in a vertical section of a switchboard were not to be routed through other sections of the switchboard. This was due to the many cases on record in which switchboards were damaged by termination failures in one section which were transported to other parts of the switchboard. To meet the intent of this requirement of the *Code*, in many cases it was necessary to provide auxiliary gutters. A new exception was added in the 1981 *NEC* to permit conductors to travel through adjacent sections of a switchboard where barriers are provided to separate the conductors from the busbars.

(b) Overheating and Inductive Effects.   The arrangement of busbars and conductors shall be such as to avoid overheating due to inductive effects.

(c) Used as Service Equipment.   Each switchboard, switchboard section, or panelboard, if used as service equipment, shall be provided with a main bonding jumper sized in accordance with Section 250-79(c) or the equivalent placed within the service disconnect section for connecting the grounded service conductor on its supply side to the switchboard or panelboard frame. All sections of a switchboard shall be bonded together using an equipment grounding conductor sized in accordance with Table 250-95.

(d) Load Terminals.   Load terminals in switchboards and panelboards shall be so located that it will be unnecessary to reach across or beyond an ungrounded line bus in order to make load connections.

(e) High-Leg Marking.   On a switchboard or a panelboard supplied from a 4-wire delta-connected system, where the midpoint of one phase is grounded, that phase busbar or conductor having the higher voltage to ground shall be marked.

(f) Phase Arrangement. The phase arrangement on three-phase buses shall be A, B, C from front to back, top to bottom, or left to right, as viewed from the front of the switchboard or panelboard. The B phase shall be that phase having the higher voltage to ground on 3-phase, 4-wire delta-connected systems. Other busbar arrangements shall be permitted for additions to existing installations and shall be marked.

> The "B" phase position maintains its center position relative to the other phases (where busbars are used) whether turning left, right, or any other direction, and this standardization of location will provide basic phase identification throughout the electric system. Other arrangements are permitted for "existing" busbar installations when suitably marked.

(g) Minimum Wire Bending Space. The minimum wire bending space at terminals and minimum gutter space provided in panelboards and switchboards shall be as required in Section 373-6.

> See comments following Section 384-25.

A. Switchboards

384-4. Location of Switchboards. Switchboards that have any exposed live parts shall be located in permanently dry locations and then only where under competent supervision and accessible only to qualified persons. Switchboards shall be so located that the probability of damage from equipment or processes is reduced to a minimum.

384-5. Wet Locations. Where a switchboard is in a wet location or outside of a building, it shall be enclosed in a weatherproof enclosure or cabinet installed to comply with Section 373-2.

384-6. Location Relative to Easily Ignitible Material. Switchboards shall be so placed as to reduce to a minimum the probability of communicating fire to adjacent combustible materials.

384-7. Clearance from Ceiling. A space of 3 feet (914 mm) or more shall be provided between the top of any switchboard and any nonfireproof ceiling.

Exception No. 1: Where a fireproof shield is provided between the switchboard and the ceiling.

Exception No. 2: Totally enclosed switchboards.

384-8. Clearances Around Switchboards. Clearances around switchboards shall comply with the provisions of Section 110-16.

> Around switchboards sufficient access and working space is required to permit ready and safe operation and maintenance of such equipment. Table 110-16(a) indicates minimum working clearances from 0 to 600 V.
> For work space clearances of switchboards operating at over 600 V, see Table 110-34(a).

384-9. Conductor Insulation. An insulated conductor used within a switchboard shall be listed, flame retardant and shall be rated not less than the voltage applied to it and not less than the voltage applied to other conductors or busbars with which it may come in contact.

384-10. Clearance for Conductors Entering Bus Enclosures. Where conduits or other raceways enter a switchboard, floor standing panelboard, or similar enclosure at the bottom, sufficient space shall be provided to permit installation of conductors in the enclosure. The wiring space shall not be less than shown in the following table where the conduit or raceways enter or leave the enclosure below the busbars, their supports, or other obstructions. The conduit or raceways, including their end fittings, shall not rise more than 3 inches (76 mm) above the bottom of the enclosure.

Conductor	Minimum Spacing Between Bottom of Enclosure and Busbars, their Supports, or other Obstructions (Inches)
Insulated busbars, their supports, or other obstructions	8 (203mm)
Noninsulated busbars	10 (254mm)

384-11. Grounding Switchboard Frames. Switchboard frames and structures supporting switching equipment shall be grounded.

Exception: Frames of direct-current, single-polarity switchboards shall not be required to be grounded if effectively insulated.

384-12. Grounding of Instruments, Relays, Meters, and Instrument Transformers on Switchboards. Instruments, relays, meters, and instrument transformers located on switchboards shall be grounded as specified in Sections 250-121 through 250-125.

B. Panelboards

384-13. General. All panelboards shall have a rating not less than the minimum feeder capacity required for the load computed in accordance with Article 220. Panelboards shall be durably marked by the manufacturer with the voltage and the current rating and the number of phases for which they are designed and with the manufacturer's name or trademark in such a manner as to be visible after installation, without disturbing the interior parts or wiring.

Some panelboards are suitable for use as service equipment and are so marked.

Panelboards are for use with copper conductors unless marked to indicate which terminals are suitable for use with aluminum conductors. Such marking is to be independent of any marking on terminal connectors and is to be on a wiring diagram or other readily visible location. If all terminals are suitable for use with aluminum conductors as well as with copper conductors, the panelboard will be marked "Use Copper or Aluminum Wire." A panelboard employing terminals or main or branch circuit units individually marked "AL-CU" will be marked as noted above or "Use Copper Wire Only." The latter marking indicates that wiring space or other factors make the panelboard unsuitable for aluminum conductors.

Panelboards to which units (circuit breakers, switches, etc.) may be added in the field are marked with the name or trademark of the manufacturer and the catalog number or equivalent of those units intended for installation in the field.

Unless the panelboard is marked to indicate otherwise, the termination provisions are based on the use of 60°C (140°F) ampacities for wire sizes Nos. 14-1 AWG, and 75°C (167°F) ampacities for wire sizes Nos. 1/0 AWG and larger.

384-14. Lighting and Appliance Branch-Circuit Panelboard. For the purposes of this article, a lighting and appliance branch-circuit panelboard is one having more than 10 percent of its overcurrent devices rated 30 amperes or less, for which neutral connections are provided.

A lighting and appliance branch-circuit panelboard is a panelboard having, for example, 42 overcurrent devices (which is the maximum, see Section 384-15), and more than 10 percent of these overcurrent devices (10 percent of 42 = 4.2) [5 or more] are rated 30 A or less and for which circuit and neutral connections are provided. Lighting circuits rated 30 A or less without a neutral connection are not considered.

384-15. Number of Overcurrent Devices on One Panelboard. Not more than forty-two overcurrent devices (other than those provided for in the mains) of a lighting and appliance branch-circuit panelboard shall be installed in any one cabinet or cutout box.

A lighting and appliance branch-circuit panelboard shall be provided with physical means to prevent the installation of more overcurrent devices than that number for which the panelboard was designed, rated, and approved.

For the purposes of this article, a 2-pole circuit breaker shall be considered two overcurrent devices; a 3-pole breaker shall be considered three overcurrent devices.

Panelboards to which units (circuit breakers, switches, etc.) may be added in the field are marked with the name or trademark of the manufacturer and the catalog number or equivalent of those units that are intended to be installed in the field.

Unless the panelboard is marked to indicate otherwise, the termination provisions are based on the use of 60°C (140°F) ampacities for wire sizes Nos. 14-1 AWG and 75°C (167°F) ampacities for wire sizes Nos. 1/0 AWG and larger.

Class CTL panelboards are identified by the words "Class CTL" on the Underwriters Laboratories Inc. "Follow-up Service Listing Mark."

Class CTL panelboards incorporate physical features which, in conjunction with the physical size, configuration, or other means provided in Class CTL circuit breakers, fuseholders, or fusible switches, are designed to prevent the installation of more overcurrent protective poles than that number for which the device is designed and rated.

Class CTL is the Underwriters Laboratories Inc. designation for the code requirement for circuit limitation within a lighting and appliance branch-circuit panelboard. It means "circuit limiting."

Figure 384-1 shows a panelboard with a 200-A main circuit breaker. Figure 384-2 shows a panelboard without main overcurrent protection, but which may be protected by overcurrent protection as illustrated in Figure 384-3.

384-16. Overcurrent Protection.

(a) Lighting and Appliance Branch-Circuit Panelboard Individually Protected. Each lighting and appliance branch-circuit panelboard shall be individually protected on the supply side by not more than two main circuit breakers or two sets of fuses having a combined rating not greater than that of the panelboard.

Exception No. 1: Individual protection for a lighting and appliance panelboard shall not be required if the panelboard feeder has overcurrent protection not greater than that of the panelboard.

Main overcurrent protection may be an integral part of a panelboard or located remote from the panelboard. See Figures 384-1, 384-2, and 384-3. See also comments following Section 384-15.

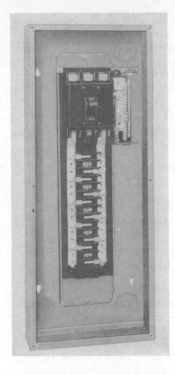

Figure 384-2. A panelboard with main lugs only. (*Square D Co.*)

Figure 384-1. A panelboard with main circuit breaker disconnect suitable for use as service equipment. (*Square D Co.*)

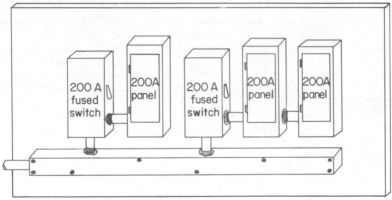

Figure 384-3. An arrangement of three individual lighting and appliance branch-circuit panelboards with main overcurrent protection remote from the panelboards. Note that the panelboard feeders have overcurrent protection not greater than the rating of the panelboard.

Exception No. 2: For existing installations, individual protection for lighting and appliance branch-circuit panelboards is not required where such panelboards are used as service equipment in supplying an individual residential occupancy.

The phrase "For existing installations" was added to Exception No. 2 for the 1981 *Code*. Therefore, this Exception is no longer applicable for new installations. This means that split-bus six disconnect panelboards are no longer permitted for new installations.

An individual residential occupancy could be a dwelling unit in a multifamily dwelling where the panelboard is used as service equipment. See the definition of "Dwelling" in Article 100. This Exception permits the use of 15- or 20-A circuits as the one to six disconnecting means permitted by Section 230-71, for existing installations only.

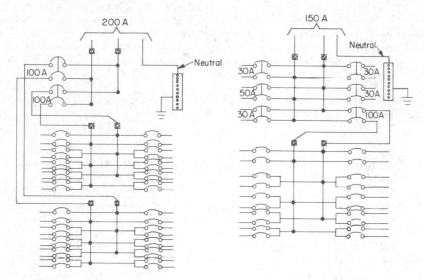

Figure 384-4. Panel on left has double 100-A main breaker disconnects and 200-A main lugs. Panel on right is a split-bus panel with 150-A main lugs and six main breaker disconnects. The panel on the right is not acceptable in new installations when used as service equipment.

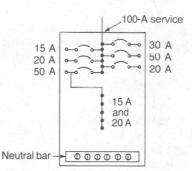

Figure 384-5. A split-bus lighting and appliance branch-circuit panelboard supplying an individual residential occupancy. This panel is acceptable only in existing installations.

(b) Snap Switches Rated at 30 Amperes or Less. Panelboards equipped with snap switches rated at 30 amperes or less shall have overcurrent protection not in excess of 200 amperes.

This requirement is limited to snap switches; it does not apply to panelboards equipped with circuit breakers.

(c) Continuous Load. The total load on any overcurrent device located in a panelboard shall not exceed 80 percent of its rating where in normal operation the load will continue for 3 hours or more.

Exception: Where the assembly including the overcurrent device is approved for continuous duty at 100 percent of its rating.

(d) Supplied through a Transformer. Where a panelboard is supplied through a transformer, the overcurrent protection required in (a) and (b) above shall be located on the secondary side of the transformer.

Exception: A panelboard supplied by the secondary side of a single-phase transformer having a two-wire (single-voltage) secondary shall be considered as protected by overcurrent protection provided on the primary (supply) side of the transformer, provided this protection is in accordance with Section 450-3(b)(1) and does not exceed the value determined by multiplying the panelboard rating by the secondary-to-primary voltage ratio.

(e) Delta Breakers. A three-phase disconnect or overcurrent device shall not be connected to the bus of any panelboard that has less than three-phase buses.

This is intended to prohibit the use of "delta breakers" in panelboards.

384-17. Panelboards in Damp or Wet Locations. Panelboards in damp or wet locations shall be installed to comply with Section 373-2.

384-18. Enclosure. Panelboards shall be mounted in cabinets, cutout boxes, or enclosures designed for the purpose and shall be dead front.

Exception: Panelboards other than of the dead front externally operable type shall be permitted where accessible only to qualified persons.

384-19. Relative Arrangement of Switches and Fuses. In panelboards, fuses of any type shall be installed on the load side of any switches.

Exception: As provided in Section 230-94 for use as service equipment.

Section 230-94 permits the service switch on either the supply side or load side of fuses. Where fuses of panelboards are accessible to other than qualified persons, such as occupants of a multifamily dwelling, Section 240-40 requires that disconnecting switches be on the supply side of all fuses. Thus, when the switch is opened, the fuses are de-energized and danger from shock is eliminated.

C. Construction Specifications

384-20. Panels. The panels of switchboards shall be made of moisture-resistant, noncombustible material.

384-21. Busbars. Insulated or bare busbars shall be rigidly mounted.

384-22. Protection of Instrument Circuits. Instruments, pilot lights, potential transformers, and other switchboard devices with potential coils shall be supplied by a circuit that is protected by standard overcurrent devices rated 15 amperes or less.

Exception No. 1: Where the operation of the overcurrent device might introduce a hazard in the operation of devices.

Exception No. 2: For ratings of 2 amperes or less, special types of enclosed fuses shall be permitted.

384-23. Component Parts.   Switches, fuses, and fuseholders used on panelboards shall comply with the applicable requirements of Articles 240 and 380.

384-24. Knife Switches.   Exposed blades of knife switches shall be dead when open.

384-25. Wire Bending Space in Panelboards.   The enclosure for a panelboard shall have the top and bottom wire bending space sized in accordance with Table 373-6(b) for the largest conductor entering or leaving the enclosure. Side wire bending space shall be in accordance with Table 373-6(a) for the largest conductor to be terminated in that space.

Exception No. 1: Either the top or bottom wire bending space shall be permitted to be sized in accordance with Table 373-6(a) for a lighting and appliance branch-circuit panelboard rated 225 amperes or less.

Exception No. 2: Either the top or bottom wire bending space for any panelboard shall be permitted to be sized in accordance with Table 373-6(a) where at least one side wire bending space is sized in accordance with Table 373-6(b) for the largest conductor to be terminated in any side wire bending space.

This section is new in the 1981 *Code*, and was generated as part of the revision of Section 373-6. This section dictates the size of the enclosure for a panelboard. With reference to Figure 373-1 (see Section 376-6), the general rule calls for wire bending space T1 and T4 to be in accordance with Table 373-6(b) for conductors M (assuming these are the largest conductors entering the enclosure). Side wire bending space T2 shall be in accordance with Table 373-6(a) for the wire size to be used with the largest rated unit facing that side space and T3 shall be similarly sized for the largest rated unit facing the right side of the enclosure. Exception No. 1 permits either T1 or T4 (not both) to be reduced to the space required by Table 373-6(a) for size M conductors for a panelboard rated 225 A or less. Exception No. 2 permits either T1 or T4 (not both) to be reduced to the space required by Table 373-6(a) for size M conductors for *any* panelboard where either T2 or T3 (or both) is sized in accordance with Table 373-6(b) for the largest conductor to be terminated in either the left or right side spaces. Under the construction rules of Section 384-25 a panelboard enclosure might not be of adequate size for all manner of wiring and Section 373-6 must be considered when wiring is planned.

384-26. Minimum Spacings.   The distance between bare metal parts, busbars, etc., shall not be less than specified in Table 384-26.

Exception No. 1: At switches or circuit breakers.

Exception No. 2: Inherent spacings in listed components.

Where close proximity does not cause excessive heating, parts of the same polarity at switches, enclosed fuses, etc., shall be permitted to be placed as close together as convenience in handling will allow.

384-27. Grounding of Panelboards.   Panelboard cabinets shall be grounded in the manner specified in Article 250 or Section 384-3(c). An approved terminal bar for equipment grounding conductors shall be provided and secured inside of the cabinet for the attachment of all the feeder and branch-circuit equipment grounding conductors, where the panelboard is used with nonmetallic raceway or cable, or where separate grounding conductors are provided. The terminal bar shall be bonded to the cabinet or panelboard frame and shall not be connected to the neutral bar in other than service equipment.

Table 384-26.   Minimum Spacings Between Bare Metal Parts

	Opposite Polarity Where Mounted on the Same Surface	Opposite Polarity Where Held Free in Air	*Live Parts to Ground
Not over 125 volts, nominal	¾ inch	½ inch	½ inch
Not over 250 volts, nominal	1¼ inch	¾ inch	½ inch
Not over 600 volts, nominal	2 inches	1 inch	1 inch

For SI units: one inch = 25.4 millimeters.
* For spacing between live parts and doors of cabinets, see Section 373-11(a) (1), (2), and (3).

A terminal bar is required to be bonded to the panelboard for the attachment of feeder and branch-circuit equipment grounding conductors, where separate grounding conductors are provided. This equipment grounding conductor terminal bar is not to be connected to the neutral (grounded conductors) bar in other than service equipment.

Exception No. 1: When an isolated ground conductor is provided as in Section 250-74, Exception No. 4, the insulated ground conductor which is run with the circuit conductors shall be permitted to pass through the panelboard without being connected to the panelboard grounding terminal bar.

Exception No. 2: The terminal bar for equipment grounding conductors shall be permitted to be connected to the neutral bar at separate buildings in accordance with the provisions of Section 250-24.

Electronic equipment, as may be used in data processing systems, hospitals, laboratories, etc., may fail to perform properly due to electromagnetic interference present in the electrical supply.

Where required for the reduction of electrical noise (electromagnetic interference) on the grounding circuit, an isolated grounding terminal is permitted. The grounding terminal is to be grounded by an insulated equipment grounding conductor that is run with the circuit conductors and is permitted to pass through one or more panelboards (without connection to the panelboard grounding terminal) so as to terminate directly at the applicable derived system or service grounding terminal.

4 EQUIPMENT FOR GENERAL USE

ARTICLE 400 — FLEXIBLE CORDS AND CABLES

Contents

A. General

400-1. Scope. This article covers general requirements, applications, and construction specifications for flexible cords and flexible cables.

400-2. Other Articles. Flexible cords and flexible cables shall comply with this article and with the applicable provisions of other articles of this Code.

400-3. Suitability. Flexible cords and cables and their associated fittings shall be suitable for the conditions of use and location.

400-4. Types. Flexible cords and flexible cables shall conform to the description in Table 400-4. Types of flexible cords and flexible cables other than those listed in the table shall be the subject of special investigations and shall not be used before being approved.

Table 400-4. Flexible Cords and Cables
(See Section 400-4)

Trade Name	Type Letter	Size AWG	No. of Conductors	Insulation	Nominal *Insulation Thickness AWG	Mils	Braid on Each Conductor	Outer Covering	Use		
Parallel Tinsel Cord	TP See Note 3	27	2	Thermoset	27	30	None	Thermoset	Attached to an Appliance	Damp Places	Not Hard Usage
	TPT See Note 3	27	2	Thermo-plastic			None	Thermo-plastic	Attached to an Appliance	Damp Places	Not Hard Usage
Jacketed Tinsel Cord	TS See Note 3	27	2	Thermoset	27	15	None	Thermoset	Attached to an Appliance	Damp Places	Not Hard Usage
	TST See Note 3	27	2	Thermo-plastic			None	Thermo-plastic	Attached to an Appliance	Damp Places	Not Hard Usage
Asbestos-Covered Heat-Resistant Cord	AFC	18-10	2 or 3	Impreg-nated Asbestos	18-14	30	Cotton or Rayon	None	Pendant	Dry Places	Not Hard Usage
	AFPD		2 / 2 or 3		12-10	45	None	Cotton, Rayon, or Saturated Asbestos			

See Notes 1 through 9.
* See Note 9.

Table 400-4 (Continued)

Trade Name	Type Letter	Size (AWG)	No. of Conductors	Insulation	AWG	Nominal Thickness	Braid on Each Conductor	Outer Covering	Use	Dry/Damp	Not Hard Usage
Cotton-Covered Heat-Resistant Cord	CFPD	18-10	2 or 3 / 2 / 2 or 3	Impregnated Cotton	18-14 / 12-10	30 / 45	Cotton or Rayon / None	None / Cotton or Rayon	Pendant	Dry Places	Not Hard Usage
All Thermoset Parallel Cord	SP-1 See Note 7.	18		Thermoset	18	30	None	None	Pendant or Portable	Damp Places	Not Hard Usage
	SP-2 See Note 7.	18-16	2 or 3		18-16	45					
	SP-3 See Note 7.	18-12		Thermoset	18-16 / 14 / 12 / 10	60 / 80 / 95 / 110		Thermoset	Refrigerators or Room Air Conditioners	Damp Places	Not Hard Usage
All Elastomer (thermoplastic) Parallel Cord	SPE-1 See Note 7.	18		Thermoplastic Elastomer	18	30	None	None	Pendant or Portable	Damp Places	Not Hard Usage
	SPE-2 See Note 7.	18-16	2 or 3		18-16	45					
	SPE-3 See Note 7.	18-12		Thermoplastic Elastomer	18-16 / 14 / 12 / 10	60 / 80 / 95 / 110		Thermoplastic Elastomer	Refrigerators or Room Air Conditioners	Damp Places	Not Hard Usage

See Notes 1 through 9.
* See Note 9.

Table 400-4 (Continued)

Trade Name	Type Letter	Size AWG	No. of Conductors	Insulation	Nominal *Insulation Thickness AWG	Nominal *Insulation Thickness Mils	Braid on Each Conductor	Outer Covering		Use	
All Plastic Parallel Cord	SPT-1 See Note 7.	18		Thermo-plastic	18	30	None	Thermoplastic	Pendant or Portable	Damp Places	Not Hard Usage
	SPT-2 See Note 7.	18-16	2 or 3		18-16	45					
	SPT-3 See Note 7.	18-10		Thermo-plastic	18-16 14 12 10	60 80 95 110	None	Thermoplastic	Refriger-ators or Room Air Condi-tioners	Damp Places	Not Hard Usage
Lamp Cord	C	18-10	2 or more	Thermoset	18-16	30	Cotton	None	Pendant or Portable	Dry Places	Not Hard Usage
Twisted Port-able Cord	PD	18-10	2 or more	Thermoset	14-10	45	Cotton	Cotton or Rayon	Pendant or Portable	Dry Places	Not Hard Usage

See Notes 1 through 9.
* See Note 9.

Table 400-4 (Continued)

Trade Name	18-17	2 or 3	Insulation	15	None (Braid)	Outer Covering	Pendant or Portable	Damp Places	Not Hard Usage
Vacuum Cleaner Cord									
SV See Note 7.			Thermoset			Thermoset			
SVE See Note 7.			Thermoplastic Elastomer			Thermoplastic Elastomer			
SVO			Thermoset			Oil-Resistant Thermoset			
SVOO			Oil-Resistant Thermoset			Oil-Resistant Thermoset			
SVT See Note 7.			Thermoset or Thermoplastic			Thermoplastic			
SVTO See Note 7.			Thermoset or Thermoplastic			Oil-Resistant Thermoplastic			
SVTOO			Oil-Resistant Thermoplastic or Thermoset			Oil-Resistant Thermoplastic			

See Notes 1 through 9.
* See Note 9.

Table 400-4 (Continued)

Trade Name	Type Letter	Size AWG	No. of Conductors	Insulation	Nominal *Insulation Thickness		Braid on Each Conductor	Outer Covering	Use		
					AWG	Mils			Pendant or Portable	Damp Places	Hard Usage
Junior Hard Service Cord	SJ	18-10	2, 3, or 4	Thermoset	10	45	None	Thermoset	Pendant or Portable	Damp Places	Hard Usage
	SJE			Thermoplastic Elastomer	18-12	30		Thermoplastic Elastomer			
	SJO			Thermoset				Oil-Resistant Thermoset			
	SJOO			Oil-Resistant Thermoset				Oil-Resistant Thermoset			
	SJT			Thermoplastic or Thermoset	18-12	30		Thermoplastic			
	SJTO			Thermoset or Thermoplastic	10	45		Oil-Resistant Thermoplastic			
	SJTOO			Oil-Resistant Thermoplastic or Thermoset				Oil-Resistant Thermoplastic			

See Notes 1 through 9.
* See Note 9.

Table 400-4 (Continued)

Trade Name	Type Letter	Size AWG	Number of Conductors	Insulation	AWG	Thickness of Insulation, Mils	Braid on Each Conductor	Outer Covering	Use		
Hard Service Cord	S See Note 5			Thermoset	18-16 (Thermoset)	30	None	Thermoset	Pendant or Portable	Damp Places	Extra Hard Usage
					18-16 (Latex)	15					
					14-10 (Thermoset)	45					
					14-10 (Latex)	18					
					8-2 (Thermoset)	60					
	SO	18-2	2 or more					Oil Resistant Thermoset			
	SE See Note 5			Thermoplastic Elastomer				Thermoplastic Elastomer			
	SOO			Oil-Resistant Thermoset				Oil-Resistant Thermoset			
	ST			Thermoplastic or Thermoset	18-16	30		Thermoplastic			
					14-10	45					
					8-2	60					
	STO							Oil Resistant Thermoplastic			
	STOO			Oil-Resistant Thermoplastic or Thermoset							
Thermoset-Jacketed Heat-Resistant Cord	AFSJ	18-16	2 or 3	Impregnated Asbestos	18-14	30	None	Thermoset	Portable Heaters	Damp Places	Hard Usage
	AFS	18-16-14									Extra Hard Usage
Heater Cord	HPD	18-12	2, 3, or 4	Thermoset or Thermoplastic with Asbestos or All Neoprene	18-16	15	None	Cotton or Rayon	Portable Heaters	Dry Places	Not Hard Usage
					14-12	30					

See Notes 1 through 9.
* See Note 9.

Table 400-4 (Continued)

Trade Name	Type Letter	Size AWG	No. of Conductors	Insulation	*Insulation Thickness AWG	Nominal Mils	Braid on Each Conductor	Outer Covering	Use		
Thermoset Jacketed Heater Cord	HSJ	18-12	2, 3 or 4	Thermoset with Asbestos	18-16 / 14-12	15 / 30	None	Cotton and Thermoset	Portable Heaters	Damp Places	Hard Usage
				All Thermoset	18-16 / 14-12	30 / 45					
Jacketed Heater Cord	HSJO	18-12	2, 3 or 4	Thermoset with Asbestos	18-16	15	None	Cotton and Oil-Resistant Compound	Portable	Damp Places	Hard Usage
	HS	14-12			14-12	30					
	HSO	14-12		All Thermoset	18-16 / 14-12	30 / 45		Cotton and Thermoset			Extra Hard Usage
								Cotton and Oil-Resistant Compound			
Parallel Heater Cord	HPN See Note 7.	18-12	2 or 3	Thermosetting	18-16 / 14 / 12	45 / 80 / 95	None	Thermosetting	Portable	Damp Places	Not Hard Usage
Range, Dryer Cable	SRD	10-4	3 or 4	Thermoset	10-4	45	None	Thermoset	Portable	Damp Places	Ranges, Dryers
	SRDE	10-4	3 or 4	Thermoplastic Elastomer			None	Thermoplastic Elastomer	Portable	Damp Places	Ranges, Dryers
	SRDT	10-4	3 or 4	Thermoplastic			None	Thermoplastic	Portable	Damp Places	Ranges, Dryers

See Notes 1 through 9.
* See Note 9.

Table 400-4 (Continued)

Trade Name	Type Letter	Size (AWG)	Number of Conductors	Insulation	AWG	No.	Braid on Each Conductor	Outer Covering	Data Processing Systems	Dry Places	Power and Signaling Circuits
Data Processing Cable	DP See Note 2.	32 Min.	2 or More	Thermoplastic, Thermoset or Crosslinked Synthetic Polymer	32-27 (50V), 26-23 (50V), 22-20 (50V), 32-16 (300V), 14-10 (300V), 8- 2 (300V)	8, 12, 16, 20, 30, 50	None	Thermoplastic, Thermoset or Crosslinked Synthetic Polymer			
Elevator Cable	E See Note 6.	20-14	2 or More		20-16	20	Cotton	Three Cotton, Outer one Flame-Retardant & Moisture-Resist. See Note 4.	Elevator Lighting and Control	Nonhazardous Locations	
	EO See Note 6.			Thermoset	14	30	Cotton	One Cotton and a Neoprene Jacket See Note 4.	Elevator Lighting and Control	Hazardous Locations	
Elevator Cable	EN See Note 6.	20-14	2 or More	Thermoset	20-16	20	Flexible Nylon Jacket	Three Cotton, Outer one Flame-Retardant & Moisture-Resist. See Note 4.	Elevator Lighting and Control	Nonhazardous Locations	
								One Cotton and a Neoprene or Thermoplastic Jacket See Note 4.		Hazardous Locations	

See Notes 1 through 9.
* See Note 9.

Table 400-4 (Continued)

Trade Name	Type Letter	Size AWG	No. of Conductors	Insulation	Nominal *Insulation Thickness		Braid on Each Conductor	Outer Covering		Use
					AWG	Mils				
Elevator Cable	ET See Note 6.	20-14	2 or More	Thermoplastic	20-16	20	Rayon	Three Cotton, Outer one Flame-Retardant & Moisture-Resist. See Note 4.		Nonhazardous Locations
	ETLB See Note 6.				14	30	None			
	ETP See Note 6.			Thermoplastic			Rayon	Thermoplastic		Hazardous Locations
	ETT See Note 6.			Thermoplastic			None	One Cotton and a Thermoplastic jacket		

See Notes 1 through 9.
* See Note 9.

Notes to Table 400-4

1. Except for Types SP-1, SP-2, SP-3, SPT-1, SPT-2, SPT-3, HPN, TP, TPT, SRD (3-conductor) and SRDT (3-conductor), individual conductors are twisted together.

2. Cables constructed differently than specified herein and listed as component parts of a data processing system shall be permitted.

3. Types TP, TPT, TS, and TST shall be permitted in lengths not exceeding 8 feet (2.44 m) when attached directly, or by means of a special type of plug, to a portable appliance rated at 50 watts or less and of such nature that extreme flexibility of the cord is essential.

4. Rubber-filled or varnished cambric tapes shall be permitted as a substitute for the inner braids.

5. Types S, SO, ST, and STO shall be permitted for use on theater stages, in garages, and elsewhere where flexible cords are permitted by this Code.

6. Elevator traveling cables for operating control and signal circuits shall contain nonmetallic fillers as necessary to maintain concentricity. Cables exceeding 100 feet (30.5 m) between supports shall have steel supporting members. In locations subject to excessive moisture or corrosive vapors or gases, supporting members of other materials shall be permitted. Where steel supporting members are used, they shall run straight through the center of the cable assembly and shall not be cabled with the copper strands of any conductor.

In addition to conductors used for control and signaling circuits, Types E, EO, EN, ET, ETP, ETLB and ETT elevator cables shall be permitted to incorporate in the construction one or more No. 20 AWG telephone conductor pairs and/or one or more coaxial cables. The No. 20 AWG conductor pairs may be covered with suitable shielding for telephone, audio or higher frequency communication circuits; the coaxial cables consist of a center conductor, insulation and shield for use in video or other radio frequency communication circuits. The insulation of the conductors shall be rubber or thermoplastic of thickness not less than specified for the other conductors of the particular type of cable. Metallic shields shall have their own protective covering. Where used, these components shall be permitted to be incorporated in any layer of the cable assembly but shall not run straight through the center.

7. A third conductor in these cables is for grounding purposes only.

8. The individual conductors of all cords, except those of heat-resistant cords (Types AFC, AFPD, AFS, AFSJ, and CFPD), shall have a thermoset or thermoplastic insulation, except that the grounding conductor where used shall be in accordance with Section 400-23(b). Unvulcanized rubber compounds shall be permitted to be used for heater cords Types HPD, HSJ, HSJO, HS, and HSO.

9. Where the voltage between any two conductors exceeds 300, but does not exceed 600, flexible cord of No. 10 and smaller shall have thermoset or thermoplastic insulation on the individual conductors at least 45 mils in thickness, unless Type S, SO, ST, or STO cord is used.

400-5. Ampacity of Flexible Cords and Cables.   Table 400-5 gives the allowable ampacity for not more than three current-carrying copper conductors in a cord. If the number of current-carrying conductors in a cord exceeds three, the maximum allowable load current of each conductor shall be reduced as shown in the following table:

Number of Conductors	Percent of Values in Table 400-5
4 through 6	80
7 through 24	70
25 through 42	60
43 and above	50

A conductor used for equipment grounding and a neutral conductor which carries only the unbalanced current from other conductors, as in the case of normally balanced circuits of three or more conductors, shall not be considered as current-carrying conductors.

Where a single conductor is used for both equipment grounding and to carry unbalanced current from other conductors, as provided for in Section 250-60 for electric ranges and electric clothes dryers, it shall not be considered as a current-carrying conductor.

Table 400-5. Ampacity of Flexible Cords and Cables

[Based on Ambient Temperature of 30° C (86°F). See Section 400-13 and Table 400-4.]

Size AWG	Thermoset Types TP, TS / Thermoplastic Types TPT, TST	Thermoset Types C, PD, E, EO, EN, S SO, SRD, SJ, SJO, SV, SVO, SP / Thermoplastic Types ET, ETT, ETLB, ETP, ST, STO, SRDT, SJT, SJTO, SVT, SVTO, SPT		Types AFS, AFSJ, HPD, HSJ, HSJO, HS, HSO, HPN	Cotton Types CFPD* / Asbestos Types AFC* AFPD*
		A†	B†		
27**	0.5	..	..	..	..
20	..	5***	7***	..	..
18	..	7	10	10	6
17	..	..	12	..	..
16	..	10	13	15	8
15	..	..	..	17	..
14	..	15	18	20	17
12	..	20	25	30	23
10	..	25	30	35	28
8	..	35	40	..	..
6	..	45	55	..	..
4	..	60	70	..	..
2	..	80	95	..	..

* These types are used almost exclusively in fixtures where they are exposed to high temperatures and ampere ratings are assigned accordingly.

** Tinsel cord.

*** Elevator cables only.

† The ampacities under sub-heading A apply to 3-conductor cords and other multiconductor cords connected to utilization equipment so that only 3 conductors are current carrying. The ampacities under sub-heading B apply to 2-conductor cords and other multiconductor cords connected to utilization equipment so that only 2 conductors are current carrying.

NOTE. Ultimate Insulation Temperature. In no case shall conductors be associated together in such a way with respect to the kind of circuit, the wiring method used, or the number of conductors that the limiting temperature of the conductors will be exceeded.

400-6. Marking. Flexible cords and cables shall be marked by means of a printed tag attached to the coil reel or carton. The tag shall contain the information required in Section 310-11(a).

Types SJ, SJO, SJT, SJTO, S, SO, ST, and STO flexible cords shall be durably marked on the surface at intervals not exceeding 24 inches (610 mm) with the type designation, size, and number of conductors.

400-7. Uses Permitted.

(a) Uses. Flexible cords and cables shall be used only for (1) pendants; (2) wiring of fixtures; (3) connection of portable lamps or appliances; (4) elevator cables; (5) wiring of cranes and hoists;

(6) connection of stationary equipment to facilitate their frequent interchange; (7) prevention of the transmission of noise or vibration; (8) appliances where the fastening means and mechanical connections are designed to permit removal for maintenance and repair; or (9) data processing cables as permitted by Section 645-2.

(b) Attachment Plugs. Where used as permitted in subsections (a)(3), (a)(6), and (a)(8) of this section, each flexible cord shall be equipped with an attachment plug and shall be energized from an approved receptacle outlet.

The flexible cords and cables referred to in this article are the ones that are attached to appliances and similar equipment. The reference is not to extension cords. See Article 305 for the applicable provisions covering the use of extension cords.

400-8. Uses Not Permitted. Unless specifically permitted in Section 400-7 flexible cords and cables shall not be used (1) as a substitute for the fixed wiring of a structure; (2) where run through holes in walls, ceilings, or floors; (3) where run through doorways, windows, or similar openings; (4) where attached to building surfaces; or (5) where concealed behind building walls, ceilings, or floors.

400-9. Splices. Flexible cord shall be used only in continuous lengths without splice or tap when initially installed in applications permitted by Section 400-7(a). The repair of hard service cord (see Column 1, Table 400-4) No. 12 and larger shall be permitted if conductors are spliced in accordance with Section 110-14(b) and the completed splice retains the insulation, outer sheath properties, and usage characteristics of the cord being spliced.

400-10. Pull at Joints and Terminals. Flexible cords shall be so connected to devices and to fittings that tension will not be transmitted to joints or terminal screws. This shall be accomplished by a knot in the cord, winding with tape, by a special fitting designed for that purpose, or by other approved means which will prevent a pull on the cord from being directly transmitted to joints or terminal screws.

400-11. In Show Windows and Show Cases. Flexible cords used in show windows and show cases shall be Type S, SO, SJ, SJO, ST, STO, SJT, SJTO, or AFS.

Exception No. 1: For the wiring of chain-supported lighting fixtures.

Exception No. 2: As supply cords for portable lamps and other merchandise being displayed or exhibited.

Flexible cords listed for "hard usage" or "extra hard usage" should be used in show windows and show cases and precautions should be taken to ensure that these approved cords are maintained in good condition because of possible contact with combustible materials usually present at these locations and because of the wear and tear they are exposed to by continuous housekeeping and display changes.

400-12. Minimum Size. The individual conductors of a flexible cord or cable shall not be smaller than the sizes in Table 400-4.

400-13. Overcurrent Protection. Flexible cords not smaller than No. 18, and tinsel cords or cords having equivalent characteristics of smaller size approved for use with specific appliances, shall be considered as protected against overcurrent by the overcurrent devices described in Section 240-4.

400-14. Protection from Damage.   Flexible cords and cables shall be protected by bushings or fittings where passing through holes in covers, outlet boxes, or similar enclosures.

This section is new in the 1981 *Code.* There are a variety of bushings and fittings available for this purpose, both insulated and noninsulated, some including strain relief means as required in Section 400-10. Many insulating bushings are listed by Underwriters Laboratories Inc. in the product categories Conduit Fittings (bushings and fittings for use on the ends of conduit in boxes, gutters, etc.); Insulating Devices and Materials, Bushings (bushings for the protection of cords where they pass through walls or barriers of metal); Outlet Bushings and Fittings (bushings and fittings for use on the ends of conduit, EMT, or armored cable where a change to open wiring is made.

B. Construction Specifications

400-20. Labels.   Flexible cords shall be examined and tested at the factory and labeled before shipment.

400-21. Nominal Insulation Thickness.   The nominal thickness of insulation for conductors of flexible cords and cables shall not be less than specified in Table 400-4.

400-22. Grounded-Conductor Identification.   One conductor of flexible cords which is intended to be used as a grounded circuit conductor shall have a continuous marker readily distinguishing it from the other conductor or conductors. The identification shall consist of one of the methods indicated in (a) through (f) below.

(a) Colored Braid.   A braid finished to show a white or natural gray color and the braid on the other conductor or conductors finished to show a readily distinguishable solid color or colors.

(b) Tracer in Braid.   A tracer in a braid of any color contrasting with that of the braid and no tracer in the braid of the other conductor or conductors. No tracer shall be used in the braid of any conductor of a flexible cord which contains a conductor having a braid finished to show white or natural gray.

Exception: In the case of Types C and PD, and cords having the braids on the individual conductors finished to show white or natural gray. In such cords the identifying marker shall be permitted to consist of the solid white or natural gray finish on one conductor, provided there is a colored tracer in the braid of each other conductor.

(c) Colored Insulation.   A white or natural gray insulation on one conductor and insulation of a readily distinguishable color or colors on the other conductor or conductors for cords having no braids on the individual conductors.

For jacketed cords furnished with appliances, one conductor having its insulation colored light blue, with the other conductors having their insulation of a readily distinguishable color other than white or natural gray.

Exception: Cords which have insulation on the individual conductors integral with the jacket.

It shall be permissible to cover the insulation with an outer finish to provide the desired color.

(d) Colored Separator.   A white or natural gray separator on one conductor and a separator of a readily distinguishable solid color on the other conductor or conductors of cords having insulation on the individual conductors integral with the jacket.

(e) Tinned Conductors.   One conductor having the individual strands tinned and the other conductor or conductors having the individual strands untinned for cords having insulation on the individual conductors integral with the jacket.

(f) Surface Marking.   One or more stripes, ridges, or grooves so located on the exterior of the cord as to identify one conductor for cords having insulation on the individual conductors integral with the jacket.

400-23. Grounding-Conductor Identification.   A conductor intended to be used as a grounding conductor shall have a continuous identifying marker readily distinguishing it from the other conductor or conductors. Conductors having a continuous green color or a continuous green color with one or more yellow stripes shall not be used for other than grounding purposes. The identifying marker shall consist of one of the methods in (a) or (b) below.

(a) Colored Braid.   A braid finished to show a continuous green color or a continuous green color with one or more yellow stripes.

(b) Colored Insulation or Covering.   For cords having no braids on the individual conductors, an insulation of a continuous green color or a continuous green color with one or more yellow stripes.

400-24. Attachment Plugs.   Where a flexible cord is provided with a grounding conductor and equipped with an attachment plug, the attachment plug shall comply with Section 250-59(a) and (b).

C. Portable Cables Over 600 Volts, Nominal

400-30. Scope.   This part applies to multiconductor portable cables used to connect mobile equipment and machinery.

400-31. Construction.

(a) Conductors.   The conductors shall be No. 8 AWG copper or larger and shall employ flexible stranding.

(b) Shields.   Cables operated at over 2000 volts shall be shielded. Shielding shall be for the purpose of confining the voltage stresses to the insulation.

(c) Grounding Conductor(s).   Grounding conductor(s) shall be provided. The total area shall be not less than that of the size of the conductor required in Section 250-95.

400-32. Shielding.   All shields shall be grounded.

400-33. Grounding.   Grounding conductors shall be connected in accordance with Part K of Article 250.

400-34. Minimum Bending Radii.   The minimum bending radii for portable cables during installation and handling in service shall be adequate to prevent damage to the cable.

400-35. Fittings.   Connectors used to connect lengths of cable in a run shall be of a type which lock firmly together. Provisions shall be made to prevent opening or closing these connectors while energized. Suitable means shall be used to eliminate tension at connectors and terminations.

400-36. Splices and Terminations.   Portable cables shall not be operated with splices unless the splices are of the permanent molded, vulcanized, or other approved type. Terminations on high-voltage portable cables shall be accessible only to authorized and qualified personnel.

ARTICLE 402 — FIXTURE WIRES

Contents

402-1. Scope.   This article covers general requirements and construction specifications for fixture wires.

402-2. Other Articles.   Fixture wires shall comply with this article and also with the applicable provisions of other articles of this Code.

For application in lighting fixtures, see Article 410.

402-3. Approved Types.   Fixture wires shall be of a type listed in Table 402-3, and they shall comply with all requirements of that table. The fixture wires listed in Table 402-3 are all suitable for service at 600 volts, nominal, unless otherwise specified.

Thermoplastic insulation may stiffen at temperatures colder than minus 10°C (plus 14°F), requiring care be exercised during installation at such temperatures. Thermoplastic insulation may also be deformed at normal temperatures where subjected to pressure, requiring care be exercised during installation and at points of support.

402-5. Ampacity of Fixture Wires.   The ampacity of fixture wire shall not exceed the following:

Table 402-5

Size (AWG)	Ampacity
18	6
16	8
14	17
12	23
10	28

No conductor shall be used under such conditions that its operating temperature will exceed the temperature specified in Table 402-3 for the type of insulation involved.

402-6. Minimum Size.   Fixture wires shall not be smaller than No. 18.

Table 402-3.   Fixture Wire

Trade Name	Type Letter	Insulation	AWG	Thickness of Insulation (Mils)	Outer Covering	Max. Operating Temp.	Application Provisions
Heat-Resistant Rubber-Covered Fixture Wire Solid or 7-Strand	RFH-1	Heat-Resistant Rubber	18	15	Nonmetallic Covering	75°C 167°F	Fixture wiring. Limited to 300 volts.
	RFH-2	Heat-Resistant Rubber	18-16	30	Nonmetallic Covering	75°C 167°F	Fixture wiring, and as permitted in Sections 725-16 and 760-16.
		Heat-Resistant Latex Rubber	18-16	18			
Heat-Resistant Rubber-Covered Fixture Wire Flexible Stranding	FFH-1	Heat-Resistant Rubber	18	15	Nonmetallic Covering	75°C 167°F	Fixture wiring. Limited to 300 volts.
	FFH-2	Heat-Resistant Rubber	18-16	30	Nonmetallic Covering	75°C 167°F	Fixture wiring, and as permitted in Sections 725-16 and 760-16.
		Heat-Resistant Latex Rubber	18-16	18			
Thermoplastic-Covered Fixture Wire —Solid or Stranded	TF	Thermoplastic	18-16	30	None	60°C 140°F	Fixture wiring, and as permitted in Sections 725-16 and 760-16.
Thermoplastic-Covered Fixture Wire —Flexible Stranding	TFF	Thermoplastic	18-16	30	None	60°C 140°F	Fixture wiring, and as permitted in Sections 725-16 and 760-16.

Table 402-3 (Continued)

Trade Name	Type Letter	Insulation	AWG	Thickness of Moisture-Resistant Insulation Mils	Thickness of Asbestos Mils	Outer Covering	Max. Operating Temperature	Application Provisions
Heat-Resistant Thermoplastic-Covered Fixture Wire—Solid or Stranded	TFN	Thermoplastic	18-16 15			Nylon Jacketed or equivalent	90°C 194°F	Fixture wiring, and as permitted in Sections 725-16 and 760-16.
Heat-Resistant Thermoplastic-Covered Fixture Wire—Flexible Stranded	TFFN	Thermoplastic	18-16 15			Nylon Jacketed or equivalent	90°C 194°F	Fixture wiring, and as permitted in Sections 725-16 and 760-16.
Cotton-Covered, Heat-Resistant, Fixture Wire	CF	Impregnated Cotton	18-14 30			None	90°C 194°F	Fixture wiring. Limited to 300 volts.
Asbestos Covered Heat-Resistant Fixture Wire	AF	Impregnated Asbestos or Moisture-Resistant Insulation and Impregnated Asbestos	18-14	— 20	30 10	None	150°C 302°F	Fixture wiring. Limited to 300 volts and indoor dry locations.
			12-10	— 25	45 20			

Table 402-3 (Continued)

Trade Name	Type Letter	Insulation	Thickness of Insulation AWG	Mils	Outer Covering	Max. Operating Temp.	Application Provisions
Silicone Insulated Fixture Wire Solid or 7-Strand	SF-1	Silicone Rubber	18	15	Nonmetallic Covering	200°C 392°F	Fixture wiring. Limited to 300 volts.
	SF-2	Silicone Rubber	18-14	30	Nonmetallic Covering	200°C 392°F	Fixture wiring, and as permitted in Sections 725-16 and 760-16.
Silicone Insulated Fixture Wire Flexible Stranding	SFF-1	Silicone Rubber	18	15	Nonmetallic Covering	150°C 302°F	Fixture wiring. Limited to 300 volts.
	SFF-2	Silicone Rubber	18-14	30	Nonmetallic Covering	150°C 302°F	Fixture wiring, and as permitted in Sections 725-16 and 760-16.
Fluorinated Ethylene Propylene Fixture Wire Solid or 7-Strand	PF	Fluorinated Ethylene Propylene	18-14	20	None	200°C 392°F	Fixture wiring, and as permitted in Sections 725-16 and 760-16.
	PGF		18-14	14	Glass Braid		
Fluorinated Ethylene Propylene Fixture Wire Flexible Stranding	PFF	Fluorinated Ethylene Propylene	18-14	20	None	150°C 302°F	Fixture wiring, and as permitted in Sections 725-16 and 760-16.
	PGFF		18-14	14	Glass Braid		

Table 402-3 (Continued)

Tape Insulated Fixture Wire	KF-1	Aromatic Polyimide Tape	18-10..........5.5	None	200°C 392°F	Fixture wiring. Limited to 300 volts.
Solid or 7-Strand	KF-2	Aromatic Polyimide Tape	18-10..........8.4	None	200°C 392°F	Fixture wiring, and as permitted in Sections 725-16 and 760-16.
Tape Insulated Fixture Wire	KFF-1	Aromatic Polyimide Tape	18-10..........5.5	None	200°C 392°F	Fixture wiring. Limited to 300 volts.
Flexible Stranding	KFF-2	Aromatic Polyimide Tape	18-10..........8.4	None	200°C 392°F	Fixture wiring, and as permitted in Sections 725-16 and 760-16.
ECTFE Solid or 7-Strand	HF	Ethylene Chloro Trifluoro Ethylene	18-14..........15	None	150°C 302°F	Fixture wiring, and as permitted in Section 725-16.
ECTFE Flexible Stranding	HFF	Ethylene Chloro Trifluoro Ethylene	18-14..........15	None	150°C 302°F	Fixture wiring, and as permitted in Section 725-16.
Modified ETFE Solid or 7-Strand	ZF	Modified Ethylene Tetrafluoro-ethylene	18-14..........15	None	150°C 302°F	Fixture wiring, and as permitted in Sections 725-16 and 760-16.
Flexible Stranding	ZFF	Modified Ethylene Tetrafluoro-ethylene	18-14..........15	None	150°C 302°F	Fixture wiring, and as permitted in Sections 725-16 and 760-16.

Table 402-3 (Continued)

Trade Name	Type Letter	Insulation	AWG	Thickness of Insulation — Mils	Outer Covering	Max. Operating Temp.	Application Provisions
Extruded Polytetra-fluoroethylene Solid or 7-Strand (Nickel or Nickel Coated Copper)	PTF	Extruded Polytetra-fluoro-ethylene	18-14	...20	None	250°C 482°F	Fixture wiring, and as permitted in Sections 725-16 and 760-16. (Nickel or nickel-coated copper)
Extruded Polytetra-fluoroethylene Flexible Stranding (No. 26-36 AWG Silver or Nickel Coated Copper)	PTFF	Extruded Polytetra-fluoro-ethylene	18-14	...20	None	150°C 302°F	Fixture wiring, and as permitted in Sections 725-16 and 760-16. (Silver or nickel-coated copper)
Perfluoro-alkoxy Solid or 7-strand (Nickel or Nickel-Coated Copper)	PAF	Perfluoro-alkoxy	18-14	...20	None	250°C 482°F	Fixture wiring, and as permitted in Sections 725-16 and 760-16. (Nickel or nickel-coated copper)
Perfluoro-alkoxy Flexible Stranding	PAFF	Perfluoro-alkoxy	18-14	...20	None	150°C 302°F	Fixture wiring, and as permitted in Sections 725-16 and 760-16.

402-7. Number of Conductors in Conduit.   The number of fixture wires permitted in a single conduit shall be as given in Table 2 of Chapter 9.

402-8. Grounded-Conductor Identification.   One conductor of fixture wires which is intended to be used as a grounded conductor shall be identified by means of stripes or by the means described in Section 400-22(a) through (e).

402-9. Marking.

   (a) Required Information.   All fixture wires shall be marked to indicate the information required in Section 310-11(a).

   (b) Method of Marking.   Thermoplastic-insulated fixture wire shall be durably marked on the surface at intervals not exceeding 24 inches (610 mm). All other fixture wire shall be marked by means of a printed tag attached to the coil, reel, or carton.

402-10. Uses Permitted.   Fixture wires shall be permitted: (1) for installation in lighting fixtures and in similar equipment where enclosed or protected and not subject to bending or twisting in use, or (2) for connecting lighting fixtures to the branch-circuit conductors supplying the fixtures.

402-11. Uses Not Permitted.   Fixture wires shall not be used as branch-circuit conductors.

   Exception: As permitted by Section 725-16 for Class 1 circuits and Section 760-16 for fire protective signaling circuits.

402-12. Overcurrent Protection.   Overcurrent protection for fixture wires shall be as specified in Section 240-4.

ARTICLE 410 — LIGHTING FIXTURES, LAMPHOLDERS, LAMPS, RECEPTACLES, AND ROSETTES

Contents

A. General

410-1. Scope. This article covers lighting fixtures, lampholders, pendants, receptacles, and rosettes, incandescent filament lamps, arc lamps, electric-discharge lamps, the wiring and equipment forming part of such lamps, fixtures and lighting installations which shall conform to the provisions of this article.

Exception: As otherwise provided in this Code.

410-2. Application to Other Articles. Equipment for use in hazardous (classified) locations shall conform to Articles 500 through 517.

410-3. Live Parts. Fixtures, lampholders, lamps, rosettes, and receptacles shall have no live parts normally exposed to contact. Exposed accessible terminals in lampholders, receptacles, and switches shall not be installed in metal fixture canopies or in open bases of portable table or floor lamps.

Exception: Cleat-type lampholders, receptacles, and rosettes located at least 8 feet (2.44 m) above the floor shall be permitted to have exposed contacts.

B. Fixture Locations

410-4. Fixtures in Specific Locations.

(a) Wet and Damp Locations. Fixtures installed in wet or damp locations shall be so constructed or installed that water cannot enter or accumulate in wireways, lampholders, or other electrical parts. All fixtures installed in wet locations shall be marked, "Suitable for Wet Locations." All fixtures installed in damp locations shall be marked, "Suitable for Wet Locations" or "Suitable for Damp Locations."

Installations underground or in concrete slabs or masonry in direct contact with the earth, and locations subject to saturation with water or other liquids, such as locations exposed to weather and unprotected, vehicle washing areas, and like locations, shall be considered to be wet locations with respect to the above requirement.

Interior locations protected from weather but subject to moderate degrees of moisture, such as some basements, some barns, some cold-storage warehouses and the like, the partially protected locations under canopies, marquees, roofed open porches, and the like, shall be considered to be damp locations with respect to the above requirement.

See Article 680 for lighting fixtures in swimming pools, fountains, and similar installations.

Fixtures marked "Suitable for Wet Locations" are to be used where exposed to the weather or where subject to water saturation. Construction, design, and installation are to be such as to prevent the entrance of rain, snow, ice, and dust. Outdoor parks and parking lots, outdoor recreational areas (tennis, golf, baseball, etc.), car wash areas, and building exteriors are areas which would be considered "wet locations."

Areas protected from the weather and not subject to water saturation, but exposed to moisture, such as the underside of store or gasoline station canopies, or theater marquees, some cold-storage warehouses, some agricultural buildings, some basements, and roofed open porches and carports may be considered "damp locations" and fixtures are to be marked "Suitable for Damp Locations."

Fixtures suitable for wet or damp locations are to function under the effects of temperature changes, that is, operate efficiently during periods of extreme cold or high humidity. See Article 100, Definitions, Location: "Damp, Dry, and Wet."

(b) Corrosive Locations.   Fixtures installed in corrosive locations shall be of a type approved for such locations.

See Section 210-7 for receptacles in fixtures.

(c) In Ducts or Hoods.   Fixtures shall be permitted to be installed in cooking hoods of nonresidential occupancies where all of the following conditions are met:

(1) The fixture shall be identified for use within commercial cooking hoods and installed so that the temperature limits of the materials used are not exceeded.

(2) The fixture shall be so constructed that all exhaust vapors, grease, oil or cooking vapors are excluded from the lamp and wiring compartment. Diffusers shall be resistant to thermal shock.

(3) Parts of the fixture exposed within the hood shall be noncorrosive or protected against corrosion and the surface shall be smooth so as not to collect deposits and facilitate cleaning.

(4) Wireways supplying the fixture shall not be exposed within the cooking hood.

The requirements for this section were initially taken from NFPA 96, Removal of Smoke and Grease-Laden Vapors from Commercial Cooking Equipment. NFPA 96 covers the basic requirements for the design, installation, and use of exhaust system components including (1) hoods, (2) grease-removal devices, (3) exhaust ducts, (4) dampers, (5) air-moving devices, (6) auxiliary equipment, and (7) fire extinguishing equipment for the exhaust system and the cooking equipment used therewith in commercial, industrial, institutional, and similar cooking applications. This standard does not apply to installations for normal residential family use.

Grease can cause short circuits or grounds in wiring, hence the requirement prohibiting raceways within ducts or hoods. Conventional enclosed and gasketed fixtures located in the path of travel of exhaust products are not acceptable because a fire could result from high temperatures of lamps enclosed within glass bowls coated with grease on the outer surface. Recessed or surface fixtures intended for location within hoods must be approved for the purpose.

(d) Pendants.   Hanging fixtures and pendants where located directly above any part of the bathtub shall be so installed that the fixture is not less than 8 feet (2.44 m) above the top of the bathtub.

Section 410-4(d) is new in the 1981 *Code* and responds to the growing trend to install hanging fixtures in bathrooms. The 8-ft minimum height is measured from the top (rim) of the bathtub. The intent is to keep the fixture out of reach of a person even when standing on the bathtub rim.

410-5. Fixtures Near Combustible Material.   Fixtures shall be so constructed, or installed, or equipped with shades or guards that combustible material will not be subjected to temperatures in excess of 90°C (194°F).

410-6. Fixtures Over Combustible Material.   Lampholders installed over highly combustible material shall be of the unswitched type. Unless an individual switch is provided for each fixture, lampholders shall be located at least 8 feet (2.44 m) above the floor, or shall be so located or guarded that the lamps cannot be readily removed or damaged.

This refers to pendants and fixed lighting equipment installed above highly combustible material. Where the lamp cannot be located out of reach, the requirement can be met by equipping the lamp with a suitable guard. This section does not refer to portable lamps.

410-7. Fixtures in Show Windows.   Externally wired fixtures shall not be used in a show window.

Exception: Fixtures of the chain-supported type may be externally wired.

410-8. Fixtures in Clothes Closets.

   (a) Location.   A fixture in a clothes closet shall be permitted to be installed:

   (1) On the wall above the closet door, provided the clearance between the fixture and a storage area where combustible material may be stored within the closet is not less than 18 inches (457 mm), or

   (2) On the ceiling over an area which is unobstructed to the floor, maintaining an 18-inch (457-mm) clearance horizontally between the fixture and a storage area where combustible material may be stored within the closet.
A flush recessed fixture with a solid lens or a ceiling-mounted fluorescent fixture shall be permitted to be installed provided there is a 6-inch (152-mm) clearance, horizontally, between the fixture and the storage area.

   (b) Pendants.   Pendants shall not be installed in clothes closets.

   It is not mandatory to install a lighting fixture in a clothes closet; if one is installed, however, the conditions of installation are as required by this section.
   The requirements here apply to lighting, incandescent and fluorescent, in various kinds of occupancies. The intent is to prevent hot lamps from coming in contact with cartons, blankets, etc., stored on shelves and clothing hung in closets which would, of course, constitute a fire hazard.
   From Figure 410-1 it is quite obvious that fixtures other than flush recessed types with solid lens and small fluorescent types cannot be located in small clothes closets because proper clearances are not provided.
   Proper lighting may be achieved in small clothes closets by locating fixtures on the outside ceiling in front of the closet door, especially in hallways where such fixtures can serve a dual function. Flush recessed fixtures with a solid lens and ceiling-mounted fluorescent fixtures are to be installed with at least a 6-in. clearance.

410-9. Space for Cove Lighting.   Coves shall have adequate space and shall be so located that lamps and equipment can be properly installed and maintained.

   Adequate space permits easy access for relamping fixtures or replacing sockets, ballasts, etc., and also improves ventilation.

C. Provisions at Fixture Outlet Boxes, Canopies, and Pans

410-10. Space for Conductors.   Canopies and outlet boxes taken together shall provide adequate space so that fixture conductors and their connecting devices can be properly installed.

410-11. Temperature Limit of Conductors in Outlet Boxes.   Fixtures shall be of such construction or so installed that the conductors in outlet boxes shall not be subjected to temperatures greater than that for which the conductors are rated.

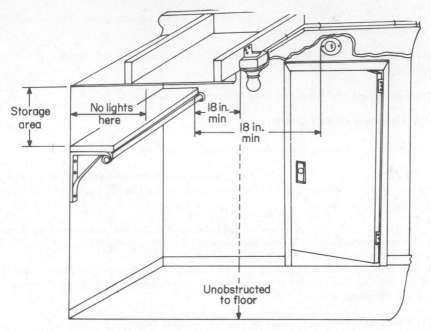

Figure 410-1. Lighting fixtures (other than recessed types with solid lens and surface-mounted fluorescents) in closets must observe the clearances shown above. The intent is to prevent combustibles from coming in contact with the lamps.

Branch-circuit wiring shall not be passed through an outlet box that is an integral part of an incandescent fixture unless the fixture is identified for through wiring.

Branch-circuit conductors run to a lighting outlet box are not to be subjected to greater temperatures than those for which they are rated. For example, the conductors of a nonmetallic-sheathed cable are rated 60°C (140°F) (see Section 336-2) and are to supply a ceiling outlet box for the connection of a surface-mounted incandescent fixture or attached outlet box of a recessed fixture. The design and installation of the fixture should be such that the heat of the incandescent lamps does not subject the conductors to a greater temperature than 60°C (140°F). These types of fixtures are listed by Underwriters Laboratories Inc. based on the heat-contributing factor of the supply conductors at not more than the maximum permitted lamp wattage of the fixture.

Figure 410-2 illustrates a recessed fixture listed by UL for one set of supply conductors, and Figure 410-3 illustrates a fixture listed for a "feed through" installation.

The following paragraph is an excerpt from the Underwriters Laboratories Inc. Electrical Construction Materials List:

With the exception of fluorescent-lamp fixtures, recessed fixtures are marked with the required minimum temperature rating of wiring supplying the fixture. Unless marked in combination with the listing mark "Maximum of _____ No. _____ AWG branch-circuit conductors suitable for at least _____°C (_____°F) permitted in junction box," no allowance has been made for any heat contributed by branch-circuit conductors which pass through, or supply and pass through, an outlet box or other splice compartment which is part of the fixture.

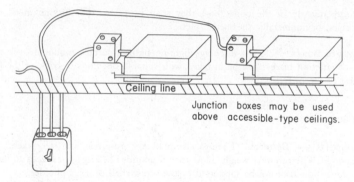

Junction boxes may be used
above accessible-type ceilings.

Figure 410-2. Branch-circuit conductors terminating at each fixture (no feed-through).

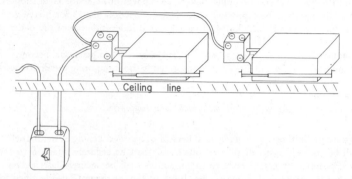

Figure 410-3. Lighting fixtures that are designed for "feed-through" branch-circuit conductors.

410-12. Outlet Boxes to Be Covered. In a completed installation, each outlet box shall be provided with a cover unless covered by means of a fixture canopy, lampholder, receptacle, rosette, or similar device.

Lighting fixtures are to be designed and installed not only to prevent overheating of conductors but also to prevent overheating of adjacent combustible wall or ceiling finishes. Hence, the requirement that any combustible finish between the edge of a fixture canopy and an outlet box be covered with a noncombustible material or fixture accessory. See Section 370-11 for requirements covering noncombustible finishes.

Where lighting fixtures are not directly mounted on outlet boxes, suitable outlet box covers are to be provided.

410-13. Covering of Combustible Material at Outlet Boxes. Any combustible wall or ceiling finish exposed between the edge of a fixture canopy or pan and an outlet box shall be covered with noncombustible material.

See comments following Section 410-12.

410-14. Connection of Electric-Discharge Lighting Fixtures.

(a) Independently of the Outlet Box. Where electric-discharge lighting fixtures are supported independently of the outlet box, they shall be connected through metal raceways, metal-clad cables, or nonmetallic-sheathed cables.

(b) Access to Boxes.   Electric discharge lighting fixtures surface mounted over concealed outlet, pull, or junction boxes shall be installed with suitable openings in back of the fixture to provide access to the boxes.

D. Fixture Supports

410-15. Supports — General.   Fixtures, lampholders, rosettes, and receptacles shall be securely supported. A fixture that weighs more than 6 pounds (2.72 kg) or exceeds 16 inches (406 mm) in any dimension shall not be supported by the screw shell of a lampholder.

410-16. Means of Support.

(a) Outlet Boxes.   Where the outlet box or fitting will provide adequate support, a fixture shall be attached thereto or be supported as required by Section 370-13 for boxes. A fixture that weighs more than 50 pounds (22.7 kg) shall be supported independently of the outlet box.

(b) Inspection.   Fixtures shall be so installed that the connections between the fixture conductors and the circuit conductors can be inspected without requiring the disconnection of any part of the wiring.

Exception: Fixtures connected by attachment plugs and receptacles.

(c) Suspended Ceilings.   Framing members of suspended ceiling systems used to support fixtures shall be securely fastened to each other and shall be securely attached to the building structure at appropriate intervals. Fixtures so supported shall be securely fastened to the ceiling framing member by mechanical means, such as bolts, screws, or rivets. Clips identified for use with the type of ceiling framing member(s) and fixture(s) shall also be permitted.

(d) Fixture Studs.   Fixture studs that are not a part of outlet boxes, hickeys, tripods, and crowfeet shall be made of steel, malleable iron, or other approved material.

(e) Insulating Joints.   Insulating joints that are not designed to be mounted with screws or bolts shall have an exterior metal casing, insulated from both screw connections.

(f) Raceway Fittings.   Raceway fittings used to support lighting fixtures shall be suitable to support the fixture(s).

Whether a lighting fixture is attached to an outlet box or supported independently of the outlet box, care should be taken to securely and rigidly fasten the outlet box or support the independent rod or pipe hanger (as shown in Figure 370-4).

So-called drop-in fixtures or surface mounted fixtures are to be securely fastened to the framing members of "hung" or suspended ceilings by mechanical means, such as bolts, screws, or rivets, or clips identified for use with the type of ceiling framing member(s) and fixture(s), and no other support of the fixture is necessary. However, the suspended ceiling framing members must be securely attached to each other and to the building structure and, also, additional supporting wires, rods, etc., may be necessary to provide ample support of the ceiling in areas where fixtures are installed.

(g) Busways.   Fixtures shall be permitted to be connected to busways in accordance with Section 364-12.

E. Grounding

410-17. General.   Fixtures and lighting equipment shall be grounded as provided in Part E of this article.

410-18. Exposed Fixture Parts.

(a) With Exposed Conductive Parts.   The exposed conductive parts of lighting fixtures and equipment directly wired or attached to outlets supplied by a wiring method which provides an equipment ground shall be grounded.

(b) Made of Insulating Material.   Fixtures directly wired or attached to outlets supplied by a wiring method which does not provide a ready means for grounding shall be made of insulating material and shall have no exposed conductive parts.

410-19. Equipment Over 150 Volts to Ground.

(a) Metal Fixtures, Transformers, and Transformer Enclosures.   Metal fixtures, transformers, and transformer enclosures on circuits operating at over 150 volts to ground shall be grounded.

(b) Other Exposed Metal Parts.   Other exposed metal parts shall be grounded or insulated from ground and other conducting surfaces and inaccessible to unqualified persons.

Exception: Lamp tie wires, mounting screws, clips, and decorative bands on glass lamps spaced not less than 1½ inches (38 mm) from lamp terminals shall not be required to be grounded.

410-20. Equipment Grounding Conductor Attachment.   Fixtures with exposed metal parts shall be provided with a means for connecting an equipment grounding conductor for such fixtures.

Exception: This requirement shall become effective April 1, 1982.

This section was added in the 1981 *Code.* To permit time for the industry to react, a future "effective date" was established.

410-21. Methods of Grounding.   Equipment shall be considered grounded where mechanically connected in a permanent and effective manner to metal raceway, the armor of armored cable, mineral-insulated, metal-sheathed cable, and the continuous sheath of Type MC cable, the grounding conductor in nonmetallic-sheathed cable, or to a separate grounding conductor sized in accordance with Table 250-95, provided that the raceway, armor, or grounding conductor is grounded in a manner specified in Article 250.

F. Wiring of Fixtures

410-22. Fixture Wiring — General.   Wiring on or within fixtures shall be neatly arranged and shall not be exposed to physical damage. Excess wiring shall be avoided. Conductors shall be so arranged that they shall not be subjected to temperatures above those for which they are rated.

410-23. Polarization of Fixtures. Fixtures shall be so wired that the screw shells of lampholders will be connected to the same fixture or circuit conductor or terminal. The identified grounded conductor, where connected to a screw-shell lampholder, shall be connected to the screw shell.

410-24. Conductors.

(a) **Insulation.** Fixtures shall be wired with conductors having insulation suitable for the environmental conditions, current, voltage, and temperature to which the conductors will be subjected.

(b) **Conductor Size.** Fixture conductors shall not be smaller than No. 18.

For ampacity of fixture wire, see Table 402-5.

For maximum operating temperature and voltage limitation of fixture wires, see Section 402-3.

410-25. Conductors for Certain Conditions.

(a) **Mogul-Base Lampholders.** Fixtures provided with mogul-base, screw-shell lampholders and operating at not over 300 volts between conductors shall be wired with Type AF, SF-1, SF-2, SFF-1, SFF-2, PF, PGF, PFF, PGFF, PTF, PTFF, PAF, PAFF, ZF or ZFF fixture wire.

(b) **Other than Mogul-Base, Screw-Shell Lampholders.** Fixtures provided with other than mogul-base, screw-shell lampholders and operating at not over 300 volts between conductors shall be wired with Type AF, SF-1, SF-2, PF, PGF, PFF, PGFF, PTF, PTFF, PAF, PAFF, ZF or ZFF fixture wire or Type AFC or AFPD flexible cord.

Exception No. 1: Where temperatures do not exceed 90°C (194°F), Types CF, TFN and TFFN fixture wire or Type CFPD flexible cord shall be permitted.

Exception No. 2: Where temperatures exceed 60°C (140°F) but are not higher than 75°C (167°F), Types RH and RHW rubber-covered wire and Types RFH-1, RFH-2, FFH-1, and FFH-2 fixture wires shall be permitted.

Exception No. 3: Where temperatures do not exceed 60°C (140°F), Type T thermoplastic wire, Types TF and TFF fixture wires shall be permitted, including fixtures of decorative types on which lamps of not over 60-watt rating are used in connection with imitation candles.

See Table 402-3 and Section 402-3 for fixture wires and conductors; and Table 400-5 for flexible cords.

410-27. Pendant Conductors for Incandescent Filament Lamps.

(a) **Support.** Pendant lampholders with permanently attached leads, where used for other than festoon wiring, shall be hung from separate stranded rubber-covered conductors that are soldered directly to the circuit conductors but supported independently thereof.

(b) **Size.** Such pendant conductors shall not be smaller than No. 14 for mogul-base or medium-base screw-shell lampholders, nor smaller than No. 18 for intermediate or candelabra-base lampholders.

Exception: Approved Christmas tree and decorative lighting outfits shall be permitted to be smaller than No. 18.

(c) **Twisted or Cabled.** Pendant conductors longer than 3 feet (914 mm) shall be twisted together where not cabled in an approved assembly.

410-28. Protection of Conductors and Insulation.

(a) Properly Secured.   Conductors shall be secured in a manner that will not tend to cut or abrade the insulation.

(b) Protection Through Metal.   Conductor insulation shall be protected from abrasion where it passes through metal.

(c) Fixture Stems.   Splices and taps shall not be located within fixture arms or stems.

(d) Splices and Taps.   No unnecessary splices or taps shall be made within or on a fixture.

For approved means of making connections, see Section 110-14.

(e) Stranding.   Stranded conductors shall be used for wiring on fixture chains and on other movable or flexible parts.

(f) Tension.   Conductors shall be so arranged that the weight of the fixture or movable parts will not put a tension on the conductors.

410-29. Cord-Connected Showcases.   Individual showcases, other than fixed, shall be permitted to be connected by flexible cord to permanently installed receptacles, and groups of not more than six such showcases shall be permitted to be coupled together by flexible cord and separable locking-type connectors with one of the group connected by flexible cord to a permanently installed receptacle.
The installation shall comply with the following requirements:

(a) Cord Requirements.   Flexible cord shall be hard-service type, having conductors not smaller than the branch-circuit conductors, having ampacity at least equal to the branch-circuit overcurrent device, and having an equipment grounding conductor.

See Table 250-95 for size of grounding conductor.

(b) Receptacles, Connectors, and Attachment Plugs.   Receptacles, connectors, and attachment plugs shall be of an approved grounding type rated 15- or 20-amperes.

(c) Support.   Flexible cords shall be secured to the undersides of showcases so that: (1) wiring will not be exposed to mechanical damage; (2) a separation between cases not in excess of 2 inches (50.8 mm), nor more than 12 inches (305 mm) between the first case and the supply receptacle will be assured; and (3) the free lead at the end of a group of showcases will have a female fitting not extending beyond the case.

(d) No Other Equipment.   Equipment other than showcases shall not be electrically connected to showcases.

(e) Secondary Circuit(s).   Where showcases are cord connected, the secondary circuit(s) of electric discharge lighting shall be limited to one showcase.

410-30. Cord-Connected Lampholders and Fixtures.

(a) Lampholders.   Where a metal lampholder is attached to a flexible cord, the inlet shall be equipped with an insulating bushing which, if threaded, shall not be smaller than nominal ⅜-inch pipe size. The cord hole shall be of a size appropriate for the cord, and all burrs and fins shall be removed in order to provide a smooth bearing surface for the cord.

Metal (brass-shell type) lampholders used with flexible cord pendants should be equipped with smooth and permanently secured insulating bushings. Nonmetallic-type lampholders do not require a bushing because the material and design afford equivalent protection.

Bushing having holes $\frac{9}{32}$ inch (7.14 mm) in diameter shall be permitted for use with plain pendant cord and holes $\frac{13}{32}$ inch (10.3 mm) in diameter with reinforced cord.

(b) Adjustable Fixtures. Fixtures which require adjusting or aiming after installation shall not be required to be equipped with an attachment plug or cord connector provided the exposed cord is of the hard usage or extra-hard usage type and is not longer than that required for maximum adjustment. The cord shall not be subject to strain or physical damage.

(c) Electric-Discharge Fixtures. It shall be permissible to locate cord-equipped fixtures directly below the outlet box, if the cord is continuously visible for its entire length outside the fixture and is not subject to strain or physical damage. Such cord-equipped fixtures shall terminate at the outer end of the cord in a grounding-type attachment plug (cap) or busway plug.

Electric-discharge lighting fixtures provided with mogul-base, screw-shell lampholders shall be permitted to be connected to branch circuits of 50 amperes or less by cords complying with Section 240-4. Receptacles and attachment plugs shall be permitted to be of lower ampere rating than the branch circuit but not less than 125 percent of the fixture full-load current.

Electric-discharge lighting fixtures equipped with a flanged surface inlet shall be permitted to be supplied by cord pendants equipped with cord connectors. Inlets and connectors shall be permitted to be of lower ampere rating than the branch circuit but not less than 125 percent of the fixture load current.

This section permits electric-discharge lighting fixtures to be connected by means of a continuously visible cord only where such cords are not used as a supporting means and the fixture is suspended directly below the outlet boxes supplying such fixtures. Electric-discharge lighting fixtures are not permitted to be supplied by cord where installed in lift-out-type ceilings. Electric-discharge fixtures are permitted to be connected to busways by cords plugged directly into the busway or suspended from the busway as permitted in Section 364-12.

410-31. Fixtures as Raceways. Fixtures shall not be used as a raceway for circuit conductors.

Exception No. 1: Fixtures approved for use as a raceway.

Fixtures approved for use as raceways are labeled by Underwriters Laboratories Inc. as "fixtures suitable for use as raceways."

Exception No. 2: Fixtures designed for end-to-end assembly to form a continuous raceway or fixtures connected together by recognized wiring methods shall be permitted to carry through conductors of a two-wire or multiwire branch circuit supplying the fixtures.

Exception No. 3: One additional two-wire branch circuit separately supplying one or more of the connected fixtures described in Exception No. 2 shall be permitted to be carried through the fixtures.

Exception No. 3 permits an additional 2-wire circuit to be carried through the fixtures to supply switched night lighting commonly used to conserve energy.

See Article 100 for definition of multiwire branch circuit.

Branch-circuit conductors within 3 inches (76 mm) of a ballast within the ballast compartment shall be recognized for use at temperatures not lower than 90°C (194°F), such as Types RHH, THW, THHN, FEP, FEPB, SA, XHHW, and AVA.

G. Construction of Fixtures

410-34. Combustible Shades and Enclosures. Adequate air space shall be provided between lamps and shades or other enclosures of combustible material.

410-35. Fixture Rating.

(a) Marking. All fixtures requiring ballasts or transformers shall be plainly marked with their electrical rating and the manufacturer's name, trademark, or other suitable means of identification. A fixture requiring supply wire rated higher than 90°C shall be so marked, in letters ¼ inch (6.35 mm) high prominently displayed on the fixture and shipping carton or equivalent.

(b) Electrical Rating. The electrical rating shall include the voltage and frequency and shall indicate the current rating of the unit, including the ballast, transformer, or autotransformer.

410-36. Design and Material. Fixtures shall be constructed of metal, wood, or other approved material and shall be so designed and assembled as to secure requisite mechanical strength and rigidity. Wireways, including their entrances, shall be such that conductors may be drawn in and withdrawn without injury.

410-37. Nonmetallic Fixtures. In all fixtures not made entirely of metal or noncombustible material, wireways shall be lined with metal.

Exception: Where armored or lead-covered conductors with suitable fittings are used.

410-38. Mechanical Strength.

(a) Tubing for Arms. Tubing used for arms and stems where provided with cut threads shall not be less than 0.040 inch (0.1 mm) in thickness and where provided with rolled (pressed) threads shall not be less than 0.025 inch (635 micrometers) in thickness. Arms and other parts shall be fastened to prevent turning.

(b) Metal Canopies. Metal canopies supporting lampholders, shades, etc., exceeding 8 pounds (3.63 kg), or incorporating attachment-plug receptacles, shall not be less than 0.020 inch (508 micrometers) in thickness. Other canopies shall not be less than 0.016 inch (406 micrometers) if made of steel and not less than 0.020 inch (508 micrometers) if of other metals.

(c) Canopy Switches. Pull-type canopy switches shall not be inserted in the rims of metal canopies that are less than 0.025 inch (635 micrometers) in thickness unless the rims are reinforced by the turning of a bead or the equivalent. Pull-type canopy switches, whether mounted in the rims or elsewhere in sheet metal canopies, shall not be located more than 3½ inches (89 mm) from the center of the canopy. Double set-screws, double canopy rings, a screw ring, or equal method shall be used where the canopy supports a pull-type switch or pendant receptacle.

The above thickness requirements shall apply to measurements made on finished (formed) canopies.

410-39. Wiring Space. Bodies of fixtures, including portable lamps, shall provide ample space for splices and taps and for the installation of devices, if any. Splice compartments shall be of nonabsorbent, noncombustible material.

410-42. Portable Lamps.

(a) **General.**   Portable lamps shall be wired with flexible cord, recognized by Section 400-4 and an attachment plug of the polarized or grounding type. When used with Edison-based lampholders, the grounded conductor shall be identified and attached to the screw shell and the identified blade of the attachment plug.

Figure 410-4. A portable handlamp with a grounded metallic guard and reflector, and a swivel-type hook that permits positioning the lamp in any location. (*Daniel Woodhead Co.*)

(b) **Portable Handlamps.**   In addition to the provisions of Section 410-42(a), portable handlamps shall comply with the following: (1) metal shell, paperlined lampholders shall not be used; (2) handlamps shall be equipped with a handle of molded composition or other insulating material; (3) handlamps shall be equipped with a substantial guard attached to the lampholder or handle; (4) metallic guards shall be grounded by the means of an equipment grounding conductor run with circuit conductors within the power supply cord.

410-44. Cord Bushings.   A bushing or the equivalent shall be provided where flexible cord enters the base or stem of a portable lamp. The bushing shall be of insulating material unless a jacketed type of cord is used.

410-45. Tests.   All wiring shall be free from short circuits and grounds and shall be tested for these defects prior to being connected to the circuit.

410-46. Live Parts.   Exposed live parts within porcelain fixtures shall be suitably recessed and so located as to make it improbable that wires will come in contact with them. There shall be a spacing of at least ½ inch (12.7 mm) between live parts and the mounting plane of the fixture.

H. Installation of Lampholders

410-47. Screw-Shell Type.   Lampholders of the screw-shell type shall be installed for use as lampholders only. Where supplied by a circuit having a grounded conductor, the grounded conductor shall be connected to the screw shell.

In past years it was common practice to install screw-shell lampholders with screw-shell adapters in baseboards and walls for connecting cord-connected appliances and lighting equipment. This now prohibited practice permitted exposed live parts to be contacted by persons when the adapters were removed.
See Section 410-56(a) for permitted uses of receptacles.

410-48. Double-Pole Switched Lampholders.   Where used on unidentified two-wire circuits tapped from the ungrounded conductors of multiwire circuits, the switching device of lampholders of the switched type shall simultaneously disconnect both conductors of the circuit in accordance with Section 210-10.

Single-pole switching may be used to interrupt the ungrounded conductor of a 2-wire circuit having one conductor grounded. The grounded conductor must always be connected to the screw shell of the socket.
Where a 2-wire circuit is tapped from two ungrounded conductors of a multiwire circuit (3- or 4-wire system) and used with switched lampholders, the switching device must be double-pole and simultaneously disconnect both ungrounded conductors of the circuit. See Section 410-52.

410-49. Lampholders in Wet or Damp Locations.   Lampholders installed in wet or damp locations shall be of the weatherproof type.

J. Construction of Lampholders

410-50. Insulation.   The outer metal shell and the cap shall be lined with insulating material which shall prevent the shell and cap from becoming a part of the circuit. The lining shall not extend beyond the metal shell more than ⅛ inch (3.17 mm), but shall prevent any current-carrying part of the lamp base from being exposed when a lamp is in the lampholding device.

410-51. Lead Wires.   Lead wires, furnished as a part of weatherproof lampholders and intended to be exposed after installation, shall be of approved stranded, rubber-covered conductors not less than No. 14 and shall be sealed in place or otherwise made raintight.

Exception: No. 18 rubber-covered conductors shall be permitted for candelabra sockets.

410-52. Switched Lampholders.   Switched lampholders shall be of such construction that the switching mechanism interrupts the electrical connection to the center contact. The switching mechanism shall also be permitted to interrupt the electrical connection to the screw shell if the connection to the center contact is simultaneously interrupted.

K. Lamps and Auxiliary Equipment

410-53. Bases, Incandescent Lamps.   An incandescent lamp for general use on lighting branch circuits shall not be equipped with a medium base if rated over 300 watts, nor with a mogul base if rated over 1500 watts. Special bases or other devices shall be used for over 1500 watts.

410-54. Enclosures for Electric-Discharge Lamp Auxiliary Equipment. Auxiliary equipment for electric-discharge lamps shall be enclosed in noncombustible cases and treated as sources of heat.

410-55. Arc Lamps. Arc lamps used in theaters shall comply with Section 520-61, and arc lamps used in projection machines shall comply with Section 540-20. Arc lamps used on constant-current systems shall comply with the general requirements of Article 710.

L. Receptacles, Cord Connectors, and Attachment Plugs (Caps)

410-56. Rating and Type.

(a) **Receptacles.** Receptacles installed for the attachment of portable cords shall be rated at not less than 15 amperes, 125 volts, or 15 amperes, 250 volts, and shall be of a type not suitable for use as lampholders.

Exception: The use of receptacles of 10-ampere, 250-volt rating used in nonresidential occupancies for the supply of equipment other than portable hand tools, portable handlamps, and extension cords shall be permitted.

(b) **Faceplates.** Metal faceplates shall be of ferrous metal not less than 0.030 inch (762 micrometers) in thickness or of nonferrous metal not less than 0.040 inch (1 mm) in thickness. Metal faceplates shall be grounded. Faceplates of insulating material shall be noncombustible and not less than 0.10 inch (2.54 mm) in thickness but shall be permitted to be less than 0.10 inch (2.54 mm) in thickness if formed or reinforced to provide adequate mechanical strength.

(c) **Position of Receptacle Faces.** After installation, receptacle faces shall be flush with or project from faceplates of insulating material and shall project a minimum of 0.015 inch (381 micrometers) from metal faceplates. Faceplates shall be installed so as to completely cover the opening and seat against the mounting surface. Boxes shall be installed in accordance with Section 370-10.

(d) **Attachment Plugs.** All 15- and 20-ampere attachment plugs and connectors shall be so constructed that there are no exposed current-carrying parts except the prongs, blades, or pins. The cover for wire terminations shall be a part, which is essential for the operation of an attachment plug or connector (dead-front construction).

Paragraph (c) requires boxes to be properly and securely mounted to provide a solid backing for receptacles so that attachment plugs can be inserted or removed without difficulty.

The reason for requiring receptacles to project from metal faceplates is to prevent faults caused by attachment plugs with exposed bare terminal screws. The design requirements of paragraph (d) for attachment plugs (dead-front construction) should prevent such faults at metal plates; however, existing attachment plugs will be available for some time.

Mounting boxes properly (Sections 370-10 and 370-13) requires the cooperation of other crafts (plasterers, dry-wall applicators, carpenters, building designers, etc.), and the proper installation of receptacles and faceplates assures that attachment plugs can be fully inserted, thus providing a better contact.

(e) **Attachment Plug Ejector Mechanisms.** Attachment plug ejector mechanisms shall not adversely affect engagement of the blades of the attachment plug with the contacts of the receptacle.

Section 410-56(e) is new in the 1981 *Code*. It permits a device designed for use by the aged, infirm, and the blind to eliminate the yanking on the cord to remove the plug.

(f) Noninterchangeability.   Receptacles, cord connectors, and attachment plugs shall be constructed so that the receptacle or cord connectors will not accept an attachment plug with a different voltage or current rating than that for which the device is intended. Nongrounding-type receptacles and connectors shall not accept grounding-type attachment plugs.

Exception: A 20-ampere T-slot receptacle or cord connector shall be permitted to accept a 15-ampere attachment plug of the same voltage rating.

See Figures 210-6 and 210-7 for ANSI C73 configuration chart.

(g) Conductors.   Receptacles rated 20 amperes or less directly connected to aluminum conductors shall be marked CO/ALR.

This is a new requirement in the 1981 *Code* and requires 15- and 20-A receptacles directly connected to aluminum conductors to be suitable for such use. If the receptacle is not of the CO/ALR type, it can be connected with a copper pigtail to an aluminum branch-circuit conductor if a wire connector suitable for such a connection, and marked with the letters "AL" and "CU," is used.

410-57. Receptacles in Damp or Wet Locations.

(a) Damp Locations.   A receptacle installed outdoors in a location protected from the weather or in other damp locations shall have an enclosure for the receptacle that is weatherproof when the receptacle is covered (attachment plug cap not inserted and receptacle covers closed).
An installation suitable for wet locations shall also be considered suitable for damp locations.
A receptacle shall be considered to be in a location protected from the weather where located under roofed open porches, canopies, marquees, and the like, and will not be subjected to a beating rain or water run-off.

(b) Wet Locations.   A receptacle installed outdoors where exposed to weather or in other wet locations shall be in a weatherproof enclosure, the integrity of which is not affected when the receptacle is in use (attachment plug cap inserted).

Exception: An enclosure that is weatherproof only when a self-closing receptacle cover is closed shall be permitted to be used for a receptacle installed outdoors where the receptacle is not to be used with other than portable tools or other portable equipment not left connected to the outlet indefinitely.

(c) Protection for Floor Receptacles.   Standpipes of floor receptacles shall allow floor-cleaning equipment to be operated without damage to receptacles.

(d) Flush Mounting with Faceplate.   The enclosure for a receptacle installed in an outlet box flush-mounted on a wall surface shall be made weatherproof by means of a weatherproof faceplate assembly that provides a watertight connection between the plate and the wall surface.

(e) Installation.   A receptacle outlet installed outdoors shall be located so that water accumulation is not likely to touch the outlet cover or plate.

Outdoor receptacle outlets are required for one-family dwellings and for swimming pool areas and are very common at other locations, such as shopping centers for children's rides and decorative lighting, truck terminals for refrigeration units and motor warmers, marinas, mobile home and recreational vehicle sites, and various other outdoor locations.

In "wet" locations the receptacle outlet must remain weatherproof with the cover open and the attachment plug inserted, except for temporary uses of portable equipment.

The enclosure for an outdoor receptacle may be flush or surface mounted or supported by conduits and used with a variety of receptacles and covers; however, it is the installer's responsibility to achieve a watertight seal.

410-58. Grounding-type Receptacles, Adapters, Cord Connectors, and Attachment Plugs.

(a) Grounding Poles.   Grounding-type receptacles, cord connectors, and attachment plugs shall be provided with one fixed grounding pole in addition to the circuit poles.

Exception: The grounding contacting pole of grounding-type attachment plugs on the power supply cords of portable hand-held, hand-guided, or hand-supported tools or appliances shall be permitted to be of the movable self-restoring type on circuits operating at not over 150 volts between any two conductors nor over 150 volts between any conductor and ground.

(b) Grounding-Pole Identification.   Grounding-type receptacles, adapters, cord connections and attachment plugs shall have a means for connection of a grounding conductor to the grounding pole. A terminal for connection to the grounding pole shall be designated by:

(1) A green-colored hexagonal headed or shaped terminal screw or nut, not readily removable; or

(2) A green-colored pressure wire connector body (a wire barrel); or

(3) A similar green-colored connection device in the case of adapters. The grounding terminal of a grounding adapter shall be a green-colored rigid ear, lug, or similar device. The grounding connection shall be so designed that it cannot make contact with current-carrying parts of the receptacle, adapter, or attachment plug. The adapter shall be polarized.

Paragraph (b)(3) requires the grounding terminal of an adapter to be a

Figure 410-5. Weatherproof receptacle cover suitable for wet locations. (*Crouse-Hinds*)

green-colored ear, lug, or similar device, thereby removing the recognition of an adapter with an attached pigtail grounding wire.

(4) If the terminal for the equipment grounding conductor is not visible, the conductor entrance hole shall be marked with the word "Green" or otherwise identified by a distinctive green color.

(c) Grounding Terminal Use. A grounding terminal or grounding-type device shall not be used for purposes other than grounding.

(d) Grounding-Pole Requirements. Grounding-type attachment plugs and mating cord connectors and receptacles shall be so designed that the grounding connection is made before the current-carrying connections. Grounding-type devices shall be designed so grounding poles of attachment plugs cannot be brought into contact with current-carrying parts of receptacles or cord connectors.

The grounding member of the attachment plug is longer to ensure a "make-first break-last" grounding connection.

(e) Use. Grounding-type attachment plugs shall be used only where an equipment ground is to be provided.

Section 410-58(e) is new in the 1981 *Code*. It prohibits use of a grounding-type attachment plug on a two-conductor cord.

M. Rosettes

410-59. Unapproved Types.

(a) Fusible Rosettes. Fusible rosettes shall not be installed.

(b) Separable Rosettes. Separable rosettes that may change polarity shall not be used.

410-60. Rosettes in Damp or Wet Locations. Rosettes installed in damp or wet locations shall be of the weatherproof type.

410-61. Rating. Rosettes shall be rated at 660 watts, 250 volts, with a maximum current rating of 6 amperes.

410-62. Rosettes for Exposed Wiring. Rosettes for exposed wiring shall be provided with bases that shall have at least two holes for supporting screws, shall be high enough to keep the wires and terminals at least ½ inch (12.7 mm) from the surface wired over, and shall have a lug of insulating material under each terminal to prevent the rosette from being placed over projections that would reduce the separation to less than ½ inch (12.7 mm).

410-63. Rosettes for Use with Boxes or Raceways. Rosettes for use with conduit boxes or raceways shall have bases high enough to keep wires and terminals at least ⅜ inch (9.52 mm) from the surface wired over.

N. Special Provisions for Flush and Recessed Fixtures

410-64. General. Fixtures installed in recessed cavities in walls or ceilings shall comply with Sections 410-65 through 410-72.

410-65. Temperature.

(a) Combustible Material.   Fixtures shall be so installed that adjacent combustible material will not be subjected to temperatures in excess of 90°C (194°F).

(b) Fire-Resistant Construction.   Where a fixture is recessed in fire-resistant material in a building of fire-resistant construction, a temperature higher than 90°C (194°F), but not higher than 150°C (302°F), shall be considered acceptable if the fixture is plainly marked that it is approved for that service.

(c) Recessed Incandescent Fixtures.   Incandescent fixtures shall have thermal protection and shall so be identified as thermally protected.

Exception No. 1: Recessed incandescent fixtures identified for use and installed in poured concrete.

Exception No. 2: Recessed incandescent fixtures identified as suitable for installation in cavities where the thermal insulation will be in direct contact with the fixture.

The requirements of Section 410-65(c) shall become effective April 1, 1982.

Energy conservation measures have led to the installation of additional thermal insulation in attics. Many fires have been reported on recessed fixtures where thermal insulation is installed directly around the fixtures. The possibility of fire exists if the insulation is installed so as to entrap the heat of the fixture and prevent the free circulation of air. The requirement of Section 410-65(c) was added in the 1981 *Code* to address this problem.

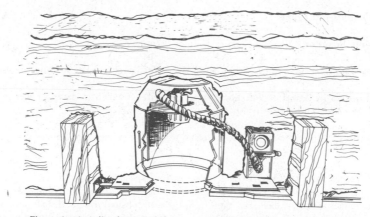

Figure 410-6. A listed recessed fixture suitable for use in insulated ceilings in direct contact with thermal insulation. (*Thomas Industries Inc.*)

410-66. Clearance.   Recessed portions of enclosures, other than at points of support, shall be spaced at least ½ inch (12.7 mm) from combustible material. Thermal insulation shall not be installed within 3 inches (76 mm) of the recessed fixture enclosure, wiring compartment, or ballast and shall not be so installed above the fixture as to entrap heat and prevent the free circulation of air unless the fixture is otherwise identified for installation within thermal insulation.

This section was not changed when Section 410-65(c) was added in the 1981 *Code.* Section 410-65(c) is intended to cover the uncontrollable abnormal condition.

410-67. Wiring.

(a) General. Conductors having insulation suitable for the temperature encountered shall be used.

(b) Circuit Conductors. Branch-circuit conductors having an insulation suitable for the temperature encountered shall be permitted to terminate in the fixture.

(c) Tap Conductors. Tap conductors of a type suitable for the temperature encountered shall be permitted to run from the fixture terminal connection to an outlet box placed at least 1 foot (305 mm) from the fixture. Such tap conductors shall be in a suitable metal raceway of at least 4 feet (1.22 m) but not more than 6 feet (1.83 m) in length.

P. Construction of Flush and Recessed Fixtures

410-68. Temperature. Fixtures shall be so constructed that adjacent combustible material will not be subject to temperatures in excess of 90°C (194°F).

410-69. Enclosure. Sheet metal enclosures shall be protected against corrosion and shall not be less than No. 22 MSG.

Exception: Where a wireway cover is within the No. 22 MSG enclosure, it shall be permitted to be of No. 24 MSG metal.

410-70. Lamp Wattage Marking. Incandescent lamp fixtures shall be marked to indicate the maximum allowable wattage of lamps. The markings shall be permanently installed, in letters at least ¼ inch (6.35 mm) high, and shall be located where visible during relamping.

410-71. Solder Prohibited. No solder shall be used in the construction of a fixture box.

410-72. Lampholders. Lampholders of the screw-shell type shall be of porcelain or other suitable insulating materials. Where used, cements shall be of the high-heat type.

Q. Special Provisions for Electric-Discharge Lighting Systems of 1000 Volts or Less

410-73. General.

(a) Open-Circuit Voltage of 1000 Volts or Less. Equipment for use with electric-discharge lighting systems and designed for an open-circuit voltage of 1000 volts or less shall be of a type intended for such service.

(b) Considered as Alive. The terminals of an electric-discharge lamp shall be considered as alive where any lamp terminal is connected to a circuit of over 300 volts.

(c) Transformers of the Oil-Filled Type. Transformers of the oil-filled type shall not be used.

(d) Additional Requirements. In addition to complying with the general requirements for lighting fixtures, such equipment shall comply with Part Q of this article.

(e) Thermal Protection. Where fluorescent fixtures are installed indoors, the ballasts shall have thermal protection integral within the ballast. Replacements for these ballasts shall also be integrally protected.

Thermal protection integral with the ballast is to be provided for fluorescent fixtures installed indoors. Ballasts not provided with integral thermal protection are not to be used as replacements for such fixtures. This type of ballast is listed and marked by Underwriters Laboratories Inc. as "Class P" and is preset at a predetermined temperature to prevent abnormal ballast heat buildup caused by a fault in one or more of the ballast components, or by some lampholder or wiring faults.

Exception to (e) above: Fluorescent fixtures with simple reactance ballasts.

Figure 410-7 illustrates a reactance-type ballast used in series with a 30 W or less preheat-type fluorescent lamp. This type ballast does not require thermal protection and the fixture may be equipped with automatic-type starters (such as used with medicine cabinet fixtures) or a manual momentary contact (such as used with desk-lamp fixtures).

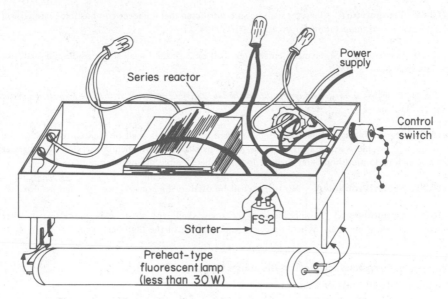

Figure 410-7. The circuitry for a simple reactance-type ballast for fluorescent lighting.

(f) Recessed High-Intensity Discharge Fixtures.   Where recessed high-intensity discharge fixtures with integral ballast are installed indoors, the ballasts shall have thermal protection integral within the ballast. Replacements for these ballasts shall also be integrally protected.

Exception: This requirement shall become effective January 1, 1982.

This section is new in the 1981 *Code.*

410-74. Direct-Current Equipment.   Fixtures installed on direct-current circuits shall be equipped with auxiliary equipment and resistors especially designed and for direct-current operation, and the fixtures shall be so marked.

410-75. Voltages — Dwelling Occupancies.

(a) Open-Circuit Voltage Exceeding 1000 Volts. Equipment having an open-circuit voltage exceeding 1000 volts shall not be installed in dwelling occupancies.

(b) Open-Circuit Voltage Exceeding 300 Volts. Equipment having an open-circuit voltage exceeding 300 volts shall not be installed in dwelling occupancies unless such equipment is so designed that there will be no exposed live parts when lamps are being inserted, are in place, or are being removed.

Fixtures intended for use in other than dwelling occupancies are so marked. This usually indicates that the fixture has maintenance features that are considered to be beyond the capabilities of the ordinary householder or involve voltages in excess of those permitted by this *Code* for dwelling occupancies. See Sections 210-6(c)(1) and (c)(2).

410-76. Fixture Mounting.

(a) Exposed Ballasts. Fixtures having exposed ballasts or transformers shall be so installed that such ballasts or transformers will not be in contact with combustible material.

(b) Combustible Low-Density Cellulose Fiberboard. Where a surface-mounted fixture containing a ballast is to be installed on combustible low-density cellulose fiberboard, it shall be approved for this condition or shall be spaced not less than 1½ inches (38 mm) from the surface of the fiberboard. Where such fixtures are partially or wholly recessed, the provisions of Sections 410-64 through 410-72 shall apply.

Combustible low-density cellulose fiberboard includes sheets, panels, and tiles that have a density of 20 pounds per cubic foot (320.36 kg/cu m) or less, and that are formed of bonded plant fiber material but does not include solid or laminated wood, nor fiberboard that has a density in excess of 20 pounds per cubic foot (320.36 kg/cu m) or is a material that has been integrally treated with fire-retarding chemicals to the degree that the flame spread in any plane of the material will not exceed 25, determined in accordance with tests for surface burning characteristics of building materials. See Method of Test for Surface Burning Characteristics of Building Materials, ANSI A2.5-1977.

Fluorescent lamp fixtures intended for mounting on combustible low-density cellulose fiberboard ceilings have been evaluated with thermal insulation above the ceiling in the vicinity of the fixture and bear the Underwriters Laboratories Inc. listing mark "Suitable for Surface Mounting on Combustible Low-Density Cellulose Fiberboard." Fluorescent lamp fixtures not so marked may be directly mounted against a ceiling surface of other than combustible low-density fiberboard or may be spaced not less than 1½ in. from the surface of the low-density fiberboard.

Further information may be obtained from the Underwriters Laboratories Inc. publication, "Building Materials Directory," and also from the American National Standards Institute publication, "Method of Test for Surface Burning Characteristics of Building Materials."

410-77. Equipment Not Integral with Fixture.

(a) Metal Cabinets. Auxiliary equipment, including reactors, capacitors, resistors, and similar equipment, where not installed as part of a lighting fixture assembly, shall be enclosed in accessible, permanently installed metal cabinets.

(b) Separate Mounting. Separately mounted ballasts that are intended for direct connection to a wiring system shall not be required to be separately enclosed.

410-78. Autotransformers. An autotransformer which is used to raise the voltage to more than 300 volts, as part of a ballast for supplying lighting units, shall be supplied only by a grounded system.

410-79. Switches.   Snap switches shall comply with Section 380-14.

R. Special Provisions for Electric-Discharge Lighting Systems of More than 1000 Volts

These sections apply to interior electric-discharge neon-tube lighting (containing neon, helium, or argon gas, with or without mercury, at low vapor pressure), long-length fluorescent tube lighting requiring more than 1,000 V, and cold-cathode fluorescent-lamp installations arranged to operate with several tubes in series.

410-80. General.

(a) **Open-Circuit Voltage Exceeding 1000 Volts.**   Equipment for use with electric-discharge lighting systems and designed for an open-circuit voltage exceeding 1000 volts shall be of a type intended for such service.

(b) **Considered as Alive.**   The terminal of an electric-discharge lamp shall be considered as alive when any lamp terminal is connected to a circuit of over 300 volts.

(c) **Additional Requirements.**   In addition to complying with the general requirements for lighting fixtures, such equipment shall comply with Part R of this article.

For signs and outline lighting, see Article 600.

410-81. Control.

(a) **Disconnection.**   Fixtures or lamp installations shall be controlled either singly or in groups by an externally operable switch or circuit breaker that opens all ungrounded primary conductors.

(b) **Within Sight or Locked Type.**   The switch or circuit breaker shall be located within sight from the fixtures or lamps, or it shall be permitted elsewhere if it is provided with a means for locking in the open position.

Providing that the switch or circuit breaker is within his view or capable of being locked "off," the serviceman assures that the disconnecting means will not be closed while he is servicing the equipment.

410-82. Lamp Terminals and Lampholders.   Parts that must be removed for lamp replacement shall be hinged or fastened by an approved means. Lamps or lampholders will be so designed that there shall be no exposed live parts when lamps are being inserted or are being removed.

410-83. Transformer Ratings.   Transformers and ballasts shall have a secondary open-circuit voltage of not over 15,000 volts with an allowance on test of 1000 volts additional. The secondary-current rating shall not be more than 120 milliamperes if the open-circuit voltage is over 7500 volts, and not more than 240 milliamperes if the open-circuit voltage is 7500 volts or less.

410-84. Transformer Type.   Transformers shall be of an approved enclosed type. Transformers of other than the askarel-insulated or dry type shall not be used.

410-85. Transformer Secondary Connections.

(a) High-Voltage Windings. The high-voltage windings of transformers shall not be connected in series or in parallel.

Exception: Two transformers, each having one end of its high-voltage winding grounded and connected to the enclosure, shall be permitted to have their high-voltage windings connected in series to form the equivalent of a midpoint grounded transformer.

(b) Grounded Ends of Paralleled Transformers. The grounded ends of paralleled transformers as permitted in (a) above shall be connected by an insulated conductor not smaller than No. 14.

410-86. Transformer Locations.

(a) Accessible. Transformers shall be accessible after installation.

(b) Secondary Conductors. Transformers shall be installed as near to the lamps as practicable to keep the secondary conductors as short as possible.

(c) Adjacent to Combustible Materials. Transformers shall be so located that adjacent combustible materials will not be subjected to temperatures in excess of 90°C (194°F).

410-87. Transformer Loading. The lamps connected to any transformer shall be of such length and characteristics as not to cause a condition of continuous overvoltage on the transformer.

Transformers should be approved for the purpose and rated to supply the proper current and voltage for the lamp or tube. See Section 600-32.

410-88. Wiring Method — Secondary Conductors. Approved gas-tube sign cable suitable for the voltage of the circuit shall be used. Conductors shall be installed in accordance with Section 600-31.

LISTED
GAS TUBE SIGN
AND IGNITION CABLE

Table 310-13, which lists various types of insulated conductors, does not include this type of cable. Underwriters Laboratories Inc., however, does have standards for this type of cable. The following information is an excerpt from the Underwriters Laboratories Inc. Electrical Construction Materials List:

Gas tube sign and ignition cable is classified as Type GTO-5 (5,000 volts), GTO-10 (10,000 volts), or GTO-15 (15,000 volts), and is labeled in sizes Nos. 18-10 AWG copper and Nos. 1210 AWG aluminum and copper-clad aluminum. This material is intended for use with gas tube signs, oil burners, and inside lighting.

L-used as a suffix in combination with any of the preceding type letter designations indicates that an outer covering of lead has been applied.

The label of Underwriters Laboratories Inc. (illustrated above) on the product is the only method provided by Underwriters Laboratories Inc. to identify Gas Tube Sign and Ignition Cable which has been produced under the Label Service.

410-89. Lamp Supports.   Lamps shall be adequately supported as required in Section 600-33.

410-90. Exposure to Damage.   Lamps shall not be located where normally exposed to physical damage.

410-91. Marking.   Each fixture or each secondary circuit of tubing having an open-circuit voltage of over 1000 volts shall have a clearly legible marking in letters not less than ¼-inch (6.35 mm) high reading "Caution....volts." The voltage indicated shall be the rated open-circuit voltage.

410-92. Switches.   Snap switches shall comply with Section 380-14.

ARTICLE 422 — APPLIANCES

Contents

(b) Household-type Appliance with Surface Heating Elements.
(c) Infrared Lamp Commercial and Industrial Heating Appliances.
(d) Open-Coil or Exposed Sheathed-Coil Types of Surface Heating Elements in Commercial-type Heating Appliances.
(e) Single Nonmotor-Operated Appliance.
(f) Electric Heating Appliances Employing Resistance-Type Heating Elements Rated More than 48 Amperes.

E. Marking of Appliances
422-30. Nameplate.
(a) Nameplate Marking.
(b) To Be Visible.
422-31. Marking of Heating Elements.
422-32. Appliances Consisting of Motors and Other Loads.
(a) Marking.
(b) Alternate Marking Method.

A. General

422-1. Scope.   This article covers electric appliances used in any occupancy.

This article covers electric appliances as found in a dwelling unit, or commercial and industrial locations, and which may be fastened in place or cord- and plug-connected, such as air-conditioning units, dishwashers, heating appliances, water heaters, infrared heating lamps, etc. See Section 422-3 for requirements of other articles.

422-2. Live Parts.   Appliances shall have no live parts normally exposed to contact.

Exception: Toasters, grills, or other appliances in which the current-carrying parts at high temperatures are necessarily exposed.

422-3. Other Articles.   All requirements of this Code shall apply where applicable. Appliances for use in hazardous (classified) locations shall comply with Articles 500 through 517.
The requirements of Article 430 shall apply to the installation of motor-operated appliances and the requirements of Article 440 shall apply to the installation of appliances containing hermetic refrigerant motor-compressor(s), except as specifically amended in this article.

B. Branch-Circuit Requirements

422-5. Branch-Circuit Sizing.   This section specifies sizes of conductors capable of carrying appliance current without overheating under the conditions specified. This section shall not apply to conductors that form an integral part of an appliance.

(a) Individual Circuits.   The rating of an individual branch circuit shall not be less than the marked rating of the appliance or the marked rating of an appliance having combined loads as provided in Section 422-32.

Exception No. 1: For motor-operated appliances not having a marked rating the branch-circuit size shall be in accordance with Part B of Article 430.

Exception No. 2: For an appliance, other than a motor-operated appliance, that is continuously loaded, the branch-circuit rating shall not be less than 125 percent of the marked rating; or not less than 100 percent if the branch-circuit device and its assembly is approved for continuous loading at 100 percent of its rating.

Exception No. 3: Branch circuits for household cooking appliances shall be permitted to be in accordance with Table 220-19.

(b) Circuits Supplying Two or More Loads.   For branch circuits supplying appliance and other loads, the rating shall be determined in accordance with Section 210-23.

422-6. Branch-Circuit Overcurrent Protection.   Branch circuits shall be protected in accordance with Section 240-3.

If a protective device rating is marked on an appliance, the branch-circuit overcurrent device rating shall not exceed the protective device rating marked on the appliance.

C. Installation of Appliances

422-7. General.   All appliances shall be installed in an approved manner.

422-8. Flexible Cords.

(a) Heater Cords.   All cord- and plug-connected smoothing irons and electrically heated appliances that are rated at more than 50 watts and produce temperatures in excess of 121°C (250°F) on surfaces with which the cord is likely to be in contact shall be provided with one of the types of approved heater cords listed in Table 400-4.

(b) Other Heating Appliances.   All other cord- and plug-connected electrically heated appliances shall be connected with one of the approved types of cord listed in Table 400-4, selected in accordance with the usage specified in that table.

(c) Other Appliances.   Flexible cord shall be permitted: (1) for connection of appliances to facilitate their frequent interchange or to prevent the transmission of noise or vibration, or (2) to facilitate the removal or disconnection of appliances, that are fastened in place, for maintenance or repair.

(d) Specific Appliances.

(1) Electrically operated kitchen waste disposers intended for dwelling unit use and provided with a Type S, SO, ST, STO, SJ, SJO, SJT, SJTO, or SPT-3, three-conductor cord terminated with a grounding-type attachment plug shall be permitted where all of the following conditions are met:

    a. The length of the cord shall not be less than 18 inches (457 mm) and not over 36 inches (914 mm).

    b. Receptacles shall be located to avoid physical damage to the flexible cord.

    c. The receptacle shall be accessible.

(2) Built-in dishwashers and trash compactors intended for dwelling unit use and provided with a Type S, SO, ST, STO, SJ, SJO, SJT, SJTO or SPT-3, three-conductor cord terminated with a grounding-type attachment plug shall be permitted where all of the following conditions are met:

    a. The length of the cord shall be 3 to 4 feet (0.914 to 1.22 m).

    b. Receptacles shall be located to avoid physical damage to the flexible cord.

    c. The receptacle shall be located in the space occupied by the appliance or adjacent thereto.

    d. The receptacle shall be accessible.

Exception: Listed kitchen waste disposers, dishwashers and trash compactors protected by a system of double insulation, or its equivalent, shall not be required to be grounded. Where such a system is employed, the equipment shall be distinctively marked.

422-9. Cord- and Plug-Connected Immersion Heaters.   Electric heaters of the cord- and plug-connected immersion type shall be so constructed and installed that current-carrying parts are effectively insulated from electrical contact with the substance in which they are immersed. The authority having jurisdiction may make exceptions for special applications of apparatus if suitable precautions are taken.

422-10. Protection of Combustible Material.   Each electrically heated appliance that is intended by size, weight, and service to be located in a fixed position shall be so placed as to provide ample protection between the appliance and adjacent combustible material.

422-11. Stands for Cord- and Plug-Connected Appliances.   Each smoothing iron and other cord- and plug-connected electrically heated appliance intended to be applied to combustible material shall be equipped with an approved stand, which shall be permitted to be a separate piece of equipment or a part of the appliance.

422-12. Signals for Heated Appliances.   In other than dwelling-type occupancies, each electrically heated appliance or group of appliances intended to be applied to combustible material shall be provided with a signal.

Exception: If an appliance is provided with an integral temperature-limiting device.

A common way to provide a signal light for electrically heated appliances in commercial or industrial locations is to use a red light so connected to and within sight of the appliance as to indicate that the appliance is energized and operating.

No signal lamp is required for an electrically heated appliance provided with a thermostat that limits it to a certain temperature.

422-13. Flatirons.   Electrically heated smoothing irons intended for use in residences shall be equipped with approved temperature-limiting means.

422-14. Water Heaters.

(a) **Storage- and Instantaneous-type Water Heaters.**   Each storage- or instantaneous-type water heater shall be equipped with a temperature-limiting means in addition to its control thermostat to disconnect all ungrounded conductors, and such means shall be: (1) installed to sense maximum water temperature and, (2) either a trip-free, manually reset type or a type having a replacement element. Such water heaters shall be marked to require the installation of a temperature and pressure relief valve.

See Listing Requirements for Relief Valves and Automatic Gas Shutoff Devices for Hot Water Supply Systems (ANSI Z21.22-1972).

Exception: Water heaters with supply water temperature of 82°C (180°F) or above and a capacity of 60 kW or above and identified as being suitable for this use; and water heaters with a capacity of 1 gallon (3.785 L) or less and identified as being suitable for such use.

(b) **Storage-type Water Heaters.**   All fixed storage-type water heaters having a capacity of 120 gallons (454.2 L) or less shall have a branch-circuit rating not less than 125 percent of the nameplate rating of the water heater.

For branch-circuit sizing, see Section 422-5(a), Exception No. 2.

422-15. Infrared Lamp Industrial Heating Appliances.

(a) 300 Watts or Less.   Infrared heating lamps rated at 300 watts or less shall be permitted with lampholders of the medium-base, unswitched porcelain type or other types identified as suitable for use with infrared heating lamps rated 300 watts or less.

(b) Over 300 Watts.   Screw-shell lampholders shall not be used with infrared lamps over 300 watts rating.

Exception: Lampholders identified as suitable for use with infrared heating lamps rated more than 300 watts.

(c) Lampholders.   Lampholders shall be permitted to be connected to any of the branch circuits of Article 210 and, in industrial occupancies, shall be permitted to be operated in series on circuits of over 150 volts to ground provided the voltage rating of the lampholders is not less than the circuit voltage.

Each section, panel, or strip carrying a number of infrared lampholders (including the internal wiring of such section, panel, or strip) shall be considered an appliance. The terminal connection block of each such assembly shall be considered an individual outlet.

Infrared (heat) radiation lamps are tungsten-filament incandescent lamps that are similar in appearance to lighting lamps; however, they are designed to operate at a lower temperature, thus transferring more heat radiation and less light intensity. Infrared lamps are used for a variety of heating and drying purposes in residential, commercial, and industrial locations.

422-16. Grounding.   Appliances required by Article 250 to be grounded shall have exposed noncurrent-carrying metal parts grounded in the manner specified in Article 250.

See Sections 250-42, 250-43 and 250-45 for equipment grounding of refrigerators and freezers and Sections 250-57 and 250-60 for equipment grounding of electric ranges, wall-mounted ovens, counter-mounted cooking units, and clothes dryers.

422-17. Wall-Mounted Ovens and Counter-Mounted Cooking Units.

(a) Permitted to Be Cord- and Plug-Connected or Permanently Connected.   Wall-mounted ovens and counter-mounted cooking units complete with provisions for mounting and for making electrical connections shall be permitted to be cord- and plug-connected or permanently connected.

(b) Separable Connector or a Plug and Receptacle Combination.   A separable connector or a plug and receptacle combination in the supply line to an oven or cooking unit used only for ease in servicing or for installation shall:

(1) Not be installed as the disconnecting means required by Section 422-20.

(2) Be approved for the temperature of the space in which it is located.

422-18. Other Installation Methods.   Appliances employing methods of installation other than covered by this article may be used only by special permission.

D. Control and Protection of Appliances

422-20. Disconnecting Means.   A means shall be provided to disconnect each appliance from all ungrounded conductors as required by the following sections of Part D. If an appliance is supplied by more than one source, the disconnecting means shall be grouped and identified.

422-21. Disconnection of Permanently Connected Appliances.

(a) **Rated at Not Over 300 Volt Amperes or ⅛ Horsepower.** For permanently connected appliances rated at not over 300 volt amperes or ⅛ horsepower, the branch-circuit overcurrent device shall be permitted to serve as the disconnecting means.

(b) **Permanently Connected Appliances of Greater Rating.** For permanently connected appliances of greater rating the branch-circuit switch or circuit breaker shall be permitted to serve as the disconnecting means where readily accessible to the user of the appliance.

For motor-driven appliances of more than ⅛ horsepower, see Section 422-26.

Exception: Appliances employing unit switches as permitted by Section 422-24.

422-22. Disconnection of Cord- and Plug-Connected Appliances.

(a) **Separable Connector or an Attachment Plug and Receptacle.** For cord- and plug-connected appliances, a separable connector or an attachment plug and receptacle shall be permitted to serve as the disconnecting means.

(b) **Connection at the Rear Base of a Range.** For cord- and plug-connected household electric ranges, an attachment plug and receptacle connection at the rear base of a range, if it is accessible from the front by removal of a drawer, shall be considered as meeting the intent of Section 422-22(a).

(c) **Rating.** The rating of a receptacle or of a separable connector shall not be less than the rating of any appliance connected thereto.

Exception: Demand factors authorized elsewhere in this Code shall be permitted to be applied.

(d) **Requirements for Attachment Plugs and Connectors.** Attachment plugs and connectors shall conform to the following:

(1) **Live Parts.** They shall be so constructed and installed as to guard against inadvertent contact with live parts.

(2) **Interrupting Capacity.** They shall be capable of interrupting their rated current without hazard to the operator.

(3) **Interchangeability.** They shall be so designed that they will not fit into receptacles of lesser rating.

422-24. Unit Switch(es) as Disconnecting Means. A unit switch(es) with a marked "off" position that is a part of an appliance and disconnects all ungrounded conductors shall be permitted as the disconnecting means required by this article where other means for disconnection are provided in the following types of occupancies:

(a) **Multifamily Dwellings.** In multifamily dwellings, the disconnecting means shall be within the dwelling unit, or on the same floor as the dwelling unit in which the appliance is installed, and shall be permitted to control lamps and other appliances.

(b) **Two-Family Dwellings.** In two-family dwellings, the disconnecting means shall be permitted to be outside the dwelling unit in which the appliance is installed. In this case an individual switch for the dwelling unit shall be permitted.

(c) One-Family Dwellings.   In one-family dwellings, the service disconnecting means shall be permitted to be used.

(d) Other Occupancies.   In other occupancies, the branch-circuit switch or circuit breaker, where readily accessible to the user of the appliance, shall be permitted for this purpose.

422-25. Switch and Circuit Breaker to Be Indicating.   Switches and circuit breakers used as disconnecting means shall be of the indicating type.

422-26. Disconnecting Means for Motor-Driven Appliances.   If a switch or circuit breaker serves as the disconnecting means for a permanently connected motor-driven appliance of more than ⅛ horsepower, it shall be located within sight from the motor controller and shall comply with Part H of Article 430.

Exception: A switch or circuit breaker that serves as the other disconnecting means as required in Section 422-24(a), (b), (c) or (d) shall be permitted to be out of sight from the motor controller of an appliance provided with a unit switch(es) with a marked "off" position and which disconnects all ungrounded conductors.

422-27. Overcurrent Protection.

(a) Appliances.   Appliances shall be considered as protected against overcurrent if supplied by branch circuits as specified in (e) and (f) below and in Sections 422-5 and 422-6.

Exception: Motors of motor-operated appliances shall be provided with overload protection in accordance with Part C of Article 430. Hermetic refrigerant motor-compressors in air-conditioning or refrigerating equipment shall be provided with overload protection in accordance with Part F of Article 440. When appliance overcurrent protective devices separate from the appliance are required, data for selection of these devices shall be marked on the appliance. The minimum marking shall be that specified in Sections 430-7 and 440-3.

(b) Household-type Appliance with Surface Heating Elements.   A household-type appliance with surface heating elements having a maximum demand of more than 60 amperes computed in accordance with Table 220-19 shall have its power supply subdivided into two or more circuits, each of which is provided with overcurrent protection rated at not over 50 amperes.

(c) Infrared Lamp Commercial and Industrial Heating Appliances.   Infrared lamp commercial and industrial heating appliances shall have overcurrent protection not exceeding 50 amperes.

(d) Open-Coil or Exposed Sheathed-Coil Types of Surface Heating Elements in Commercial-type Heating Appliances.   Open-coil or exposed sheathed-coil types of surface heating elements in commercial-type heating appliances shall be protected by overcurrent protective devices rated at not over 50 amperes.

(e) Single Nonmotor-Operated Appliance.   If the branch circuit supplies a single nonmotor-operated appliance, rated at 16.7 amperes or more, the overcurrent device rating shall not exceed 150 percent of the appliance rating.

(f) Electric Heating Appliances Employing Resistance-type Heating Elements Rated More than 48 Amperes.   Electric heating appliances employing resistance-type heating elements rated more than 48 amperes shall have the heating elements subdivided. Each subdivided load shall not exceed 48 amperes and shall be protected at not more than 60 amperes.

These supplementary overcurrent protective devices shall be: (1) factory installed within or on the heater enclosure or provided as a separate assembly by the heater manufacturer; (2) accessible, but need not be readily accessible; and (3) suitable for branch-circuit protection.

The main conductors supplying these overcurrent protective devices shall be considered branch-circuit conductors.

Exception No. 1: Household-type appliances with surface heating elements as covered in Section 422-27(b) and commercial-type heating appliances as covered in Section 422-27(d).

Exception No. 2: Commercial kitchen and cooking appliances using sheathed-type heating elements not covered in Section 422-27(d) shall be permitted to be subdivided into circuits not exceeding 120 amperes and protected at not more than 150 amperes where one of the following is met:

a. Elements are integral with and enclosed within a cooking surface;

b. Elements are completely contained within an enclosure identified as suitable for this use; or

c. Elements are contained within an ASME rated and stamped vessel.

Exception No. 3: Water heaters and steam boilers employing resistance-type immersion electric heating elements contained in an ASME rated and stamped vessel shall be permitted to be subdivided into circuits not exceeding 120 amperes and protected at not more than 150 amperes.

E. Marking of Appliances

422-30. Nameplate.

(a) Nameplate Marking. Each electric appliance shall be provided with a nameplate, giving the identifying name and the rating in volts and amperes, or in volts and watts. If the appliance is to be used on a specific frequency or frequencies, it shall be so marked.

When motor overload protection external to the appliance is required, the appliance shall be so marked.

See Section 422-27(a), Exception for overcurrent protection requirements.

(b) To Be Visible. Marking shall be located so as to be visible or easily accessible after installation.

422-31. Marking of Heating Elements.
All heating elements that are rated over one ampere, replaceable in the field, and a part of an appliance shall be legibly marked with the ratings in volts and amperes, or in volts and watts, or with the manufacturer's part number.

422-32. Appliances Consisting of Motors and Other Loads.
Appliances shall be marked in accordance with (a) or (b) below.

(a) Marking. In addition to the marking required in Section 422-30, the marking on an appliance consisting of a motor with other load(s) or motors with or without other load(s) shall specify the minimum circuit size and the maximum rating of the circuit overcurrent protective device.

Exception No. 1: Appliances factory-equipped with cords and attachment plugs, complying with Section 422-30.

Exception No. 2: An appliance where both the minimum circuit size and maximum rating of the circuit overcurrent protective device are not more than 15 amperes and complies with Section 422-30.

(b) Alternate Marking Method.   An alternate marking method shall be permitted to specify the rating of the largest motor in volts and amperes, and the additional load(s) in volts and amperes, or volts and watts in addition to the marking required in Section 422-30.

Exception No. 1: Appliances factory-equipped with cords and attachment plugs, complying with Section 422-30.

Exception No. 2: The ampere rating of a motor ⅛ horsepower or less or a nonmotor load 1 ampere or less shall be permitted to be omitted unless such loads constitute the principal load.

ARTICLE 424 — FIXED ELECTRIC SPACE
HEATING EQUIPMENT

Contents

A. General

424-1. Scope. This article covers fixed electric equipment used for space heating. For the purpose of this article, heating equipment shall include heating cable, unit heaters, boilers, central systems, or other approved fixed electric space heating equipment. This article shall not apply to process heating and room air conditioning.

424-2. Other Articles. All requirements of this Code shall apply where applicable. Fixed electric space heating equipment for use in hazardous (classified) locations shall comply with Articles 500 through 517. Fixed electric space heating equipment incorporating a hermetic refrigerant motor-compressor shall also comply with Article 440.

424-3. Branch Circuits.

(a) Branch-Circuit Requirements.   Individual branch circuits shall be permitted to supply any size fixed electric space heating equipment.

Branch circuits supplying two or more outlets for fixed electric space heating equipment shall be rated 15, 20, or 30 amperes.

Exception: In other than residential occupancies, fixed infrared heating equipment shall be permitted to be supplied from branch circuits rated not over 50 amperes.

(b) Branch-Circuit Sizing.   The ampacity of the branch-circuit conductors and the rating or setting of overcurrent protective devices supplying fixed electric space heating equipment consisting of resistance elements with or without a motor shall not be less than 125 percent of the total load of the motors and the heaters. The rating or setting of overcurrent protective devices shall be permitted in accordance with Section 240-3, Exception No. 1. A contactor, thermostat, relay, or similar device, approved for continuous operation at 100 percent of its rating, shall be permitted to supply its full-rated load as provided in Section 210-22(c), Exception No. 3.

The size of the branch-circuit conductors and overcurrent protective devices supplying fixed electric space heating equipment consisting of mechanical refrigeration with or without resistance units shall be computed in accordance with Sections 440-34 and 440-35.

The provisions of this section shall not apply to conductors which form an integral part of approved fixed electric space heating equipment.

The sizing of branch-circuit conductors supplying fixed electric space heating equipment at 125 percent (or higher if Section 240-3, Exception No. 1 is applicable) of the total load of the heaters (and motors) is predicated on the need to protect the insulation of the conductors from overheating during periods of prolonged operation.

B. Installation

424-9. General.
All fixed electric space heating equipment shall be installed in an approved manner.

424-10. Special Permission.
Fixed electric space heating equipment and systems installed by methods other than covered by this article may be used only by special permission.

424-11. Supply Conductors.
Fixed electric space heating equipment requiring supply conductors with over 60°C insulation shall be clearly and permanently marked. This marking shall be plainly visible after installation and shall be permitted to be adjacent to the field-connection box.

424-12. Locations.

(a) Exposed to Severe Physical Damage.   Fixed electric space heating equipment shall not be used where exposed to severe physical damage unless adequately protected.

(b) Damp or Wet Locations.   Heaters and related equipment installed in damp or wet locations shall be approved for such locations and shall be constructed and installed so that water cannot enter or accumulate in or on wired sections, electrical components, or duct work.

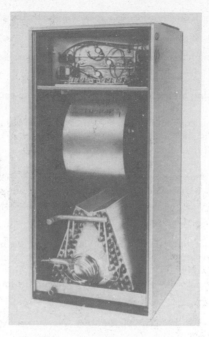

Figure 424-1. An electric furnace with cooling coils for air conditioning. (*Square D Co.*)

See Section 110-11 for equipment exposed to deteriorating agents.

424-13. Spacing from Combustible Materials. Fixed electric space heating equipment shall be installed to provide the required spacing between the equipment and adjacent combustible material, unless it has been found to be acceptable where installed in direct contact with combustible material.

424-14. Grounding. All exposed noncurrent-carrying metal parts of fixed electric space heating equipment likely to become energized shall be grounded as required in Article 250.

C. Control and Protection of Fixed Electric Space Heating Equipment

424-19. Disconnecting Means. Means shall be provided to disconnect the heater, motor controller(s), and supplementary overcurrent protective device(s) of all fixed electric space heating equipment from all ungrounded conductors. Where heating equipment is supplied by more than one source, the disconnecting means shall be grouped and identified.

   (a) Heating Equipment with Supplementary Overcurrent Protection. The disconnecting means for fixed electric space heating equipment with supplementary overcurrent protection shall be within sight from and on the supply side of the supplementary overcurrent protective device(s), and in addition shall comply with either (1) or (2) below.

   (1) Heater Containing No Motor Rated Over ⅛ Horsepower. The above disconnecting means or unit switches complying with Section 424-19(b) (3) shall be permitted to serve as the required disconnecting means for both the motor controller(s) and heater under either (a) or (b) below.

a. The disconnecting means provided is also within sight from the motor controller(s) and the heater; or

b. The disconnecting means provided shall be capable of being locked in the open position.

(2) Heater Containing a Motor(s) Rated Over ⅛ Horsepower.

a. The above disconnecting means shall be permitted to serve as the required disconnecting means for both the motor controller(s) and heater if this disconnecting means is also in sight from the motor controller(s) and the heater.

b. Where the disconnecting means is not within sight from the heater a separate disconnecting means shall be installed, or the disconnecting means shall be capable of being locked in the open position, or unit switches complying with Section 424-19(b) (3) shall be permitted.

c. Where the disconnecting means is not within sight from the motor controller location a disconnecting means complying with Section 430-102 shall be provided.

d. Where the motor is not in sight from the motor controller location, Section 430-86 shall apply.

(b) Heating Equipment Without Supplementary Overcurrent Protection.

(1) Without Motor or with Motor Not Over ⅛ Horsepower.   For fixed electric space heating equipment without a motor rated over ⅛ horsepower, the branch-circuit switch or circuit breaker shall be permitted to serve as the disconnecting means, where readily accessible for servicing.

(2) Over ⅛ Horsepower.   For motor-driven electric space heating equipment with a motor rated over ⅛ horsepower, a disconnecting means shall be located within sight from the motor controller.

Exception: As permitted by Section 424-19(a) (2).

(3) Unit Switches as Disconnecting Means.   Unit switches with a marked "off" position that are part of a fixed heater and disconnect all ungrounded conductors shall be permitted as the disconnecting means required by this article where other means for disconnection are provided in the following types of occupancies.

a. Multifamily Dwellings.   In multifamily dwellings, the other disconnecting means shall be within the dwelling unit or on the same floor as the dwelling units in which the fixed heater is installed, and shall also be permitted to control lamps and appliances.

b. Two-Family Dwellings.   In two-family dwellings, the other disconnecting means shall be permitted either inside or outside of the dwelling unit in which the fixed heater is installed.

c. One-Family Dwellings.   In one-family dwelling units the service disconnecting means shall be permitted to be the other disconnecting means.

d. Other Occupancies.   In other occupancies, the branch-circuit switch or circuit breaker, where readily accessible for servicing of the fixed heater, shall be permitted as the other disconnecting means.

424-20. Thermostatically Controlled Switching Devices.

(a) Serving as Both Controllers and Disconnecting Means.   Thermostatically controlled switching devices and combination thermostats and manually controlled switches shall be permitted to serve as both controllers and disconnecting means provided all of the following conditions are met:

(1) Provided with a marked "off" position.

(2) Directly open all ungrounded conductors when manually placed in the "off" position.

(3) Designed so that the circuit cannot be energized automatically after the device has been manually placed in the "off" position.

(4) Located as specified in Section 424-19.

(b) Thermostats that Do Not Directly Interrupt All Ungrounded Conductors.   Thermostats that do not directly interrupt all ungrounded conductors and operate remote control circuits shall not be required to meet the requirements of (a) above. These devices shall not be permitted as the disconnecting means.

424-21. Switch and Circuit Breaker to Be Indicating.   Switches and circuit breakers used as disconnecting means shall be of the indicating type.

424-22. Overcurrent Protection.

(a) Branch-Circuit Devices.   Electric space heating equipment, other than such motor-operated equipment as required by Articles 430 and 440 to have additional overcurrent protection, shall be considered as protected against overcurrent where supplied by one of the branch circuits in Article 210.

(b) Resistance Elements.   Resistance-type heating elements in electric space heating equipment shall be protected at not more than 60 amperes. Equipment rated more than 48 amperes and employing such elements shall have the heating elements subdivided, and each subdivided load shall not exceed 48 amperes. Where a subdivided load is less than 48 amperes the rating of the overcurrent protective device shall comply with Section 424-3(b).

Exception: As provided in Section 424-72(a).

(c) Overcurrent Protective Devices.   The supplementary overcurrent protective devices for the subdivided loads specified in (b) above shall be: (1) factory installed within or on the heater enclosure or supplied for use with the heater as a separate assembly by the heater manufacturer; (2) accessible, but shall not be required to be readily accessible; and (3) suitable for branch-circuit protection.

See Section 240-10.

Where cartridge fuses are used to provide this overcurrent protection, a single disconnecting means shall be permitted to be used for the several subdivided loads.

See Section 240-40.

Where subdivided loads are required, the heating manufacturer must furnish the necessary overcurrent protective devices.

The main branch-circuit conductors supplying the overcurrent protective devices for subdivided loads are considered as branch circuits to make it clear that the 125 percent requirement in Section 424-3(b) is for the branch circuit only.

(d) Branch-Circuit Conductors.   The conductors supplying the supplementary overcurrent protective devices shall be considered branch-circuit conductors.

Exception: For heaters rated 50 kW or more, the conductors supplying the supplementary overcurrent protective devices specified in (c) above shall be permitted to be sized at not less than 100 percent of the nameplate rating of the heater provided all of the following conditions are met:

a. The heater is marked with a minimum conductor size; and

b. The conductors are not smaller than the marked minimum size; and

c. A temperature-actuated device controls the cyclic operation of the equipment.

(e) Conductors for Subdivided Loads.   Field-wired conductors between the heater and the supplementary overcurrent protective devices shall be sized at not less than 125 percent of the load served. The supplementary overcurrent protective devices specified in (c) shall protect these conductors in accordance with Section 240-3.

Exception: For heaters rated 50 kW or more, the ampacity of field-wired conductors between the heater and the supplementary overcurrent protective devices shall be permitted to be not less than 100 percent of the load of their respective subdivided circuits provided all of the following conditions are met:

a. The heater is marked with a minimum conductor size; and

b. The conductors are not smaller than the marked minimum size; and

c. A temperature-activated device controls the cyclic operation of the equipment.

D. Marking of Heating Equipment

424-28. Nameplate.

(a) Marking Required.   Each unit of fixed electric space heating equipment shall be provided with a nameplate giving the identifying name and the normal rating in volts and watts, or in volts and amperes.

Electric space heating equipment intended for use on alternating current only or direct current only shall be marked to so indicate. The marking of equipment consisting of motors over ⅛ horsepower and other loads shall specify the rating of the motor in volts, amperes, and frequency, and the heating load in volts and watts, or in volts and amperes.

(b) Location.   This nameplate shall be located so as to be visible or easily accessible after installation.

424-29. Marking of Heating Elements.   All heating elements that are replaceable in the field and are a part of an electric heater shall be legibly marked with the ratings in volts and watts, or in volts and amperes.

E. Electric Space Heating Cables and Panels

424-34. Heating Cable and Heating Panel Construction. Heating cables and heating panels shall be furnished complete with factory-assembled nonheating leads at least 7 feet (2.13 m) in length.

Exception: Heating panels with junction assemblies identified as suitable for field connections.

424-35. Marking of Heating Cables and Panels. Each unit shall be marked with the identifying name or identification symbol, catalog number, ratings in volts and watts, or in volts and amperes.

(a) Heating Cables. Each unit length of heating cable shall have a permanent legible marking on each nonheating lead located within 3 inches (76 mm) of the terminal end. The lead wire shall have the following color identification to indicate the circuit voltage on which it is to be used: 120-volt nominal, yellow; 208-volt nominal, blue; 240-volt nominal, red; and 277-volt nominal, brown.

(b) Heating Panels. Heating panels shall be permanently marked in a location that is readily visible prior to application of panel finish.

424-36. Clearances of Wiring in Ceilings. Wiring located above heated ceilings shall be spaced not less than 2 inches (50.8 mm) above the heated ceiling and shall be considered as operating at an ambient of 50°C. The ampacity of conductors shall be computed on the basis of the correction factors given in Tables 310-16 through 310-19.

Exception: Wiring above heated ceilings and located above thermal insulation having a minimum thickness of 2 inches (50.8 mm) shall not require correction for temperature.

424-37. Clearances of Branch-Circuit Wiring in Walls.

(a) Exterior Walls. Where located in exterior walls, wiring shall be located outside the thermal insulation.

(b) Interior Walls. Where heating panels are located in interior walls or partitions, any wiring behind the heating panels shall be considered as operating at an ambient of 40°C (104°F) and the ampacity of conductors shall be computed on the basis of the correction factors given in Tables 310-16 through 310-19.

424-38. Area Restrictions.

(a) Shall Not Extend Beyond the Room or Area. Heating cables and panels shall not extend beyond the room or area in which they originate.

(b) Uses Prohibited. Cables and panels shall not be installed in closets, over walls or partitions that extend to the ceiling, or over cabinets whose clearance from the ceiling is less than the minimum horizontal dimension of the cabinet to the nearest cabinet edge that is open to the room or area.

Exception: Isolated single runs of cable shall be permitted to pass over partitions where they are embedded.

(c) In Closet Ceilings as Low Temperature Heat Sources to Control Relative Humidity. This provision shall not prevent the use of cable or panels in closet ceilings as low temperature heat sources to control relative humidity, provided they are used only in those portions of the ceiling that are unobstructed to the floor by shelves or other permanent fixtures.

424-39. Clearance from Other Objects and Openings. Heating elements of panels and cables shall be separated at least 8 inches (203 mm) from the edge of outlet boxes and junction boxes that are to be used for mounting surface lighting fixtures. A clearance of not less than 2 inches (50.8 mm) shall be provided from recessed fixtures and their trims, ventilating openings, and other such openings in room surfaces. Sufficient area shall be provided to assure that no heating cable or panel will be covered by any surface-mounted lighting units.

424-40. Splices. Embedded cables shall be spliced only where necessary and only by approved means, and in no case shall the length of the heating cable be altered.

424-41. Installation of Heating Cables on Dry Board, in Plaster and on Concrete Ceilings.

(a) **Shall Not Be Installed in Walls.** Cables shall not be installed in walls.

Exception: Isolated single runs of cable shall be permitted to run down a vertical surface to reach a dropped ceiling.

(b) **Adjacent Runs.** Adjacent runs of cable not exceeding 2¾ watts per foot shall be installed not less than 1½ inches (38 mm) on centers.

(c) **Surfaces to Be Applied.** Heating cables shall be applied only to gypsum board, plaster lath or other fire-resistant material. With metal lath or other electrically conductive surfaces, a coat of plaster shall be applied to completely separate the metal lath or conductive surface from the cable.

See also (f) below.

(d) **Splices.** All heating cables, the splice between the heating cable and nonheating leads, and 3-inch (76-mm) minimum of the nonheating lead at the splice shall be embedded in plaster or dry board in the same manner as the heating cable.

(e) **Ceiling Surface.** The entire ceiling surface shall have a finish of thermally noninsulating sand plaster having a nominal thickness of ½ inch (12.7 mm), or other noninsulating material identified as suitable for this use and applied according to specified thickness and directions.

(f) **Secured.** Cables shall be secured at intervals not exceeding 16 inches (406 mm) by means of approved stapling, tape, plaster, nonmetallic spreaders, or other approved means. Staples or metal fasteners that straddle the cable shall not be used with metal lath or other electrically conductive surfaces.

Exception: Cables identified to be secured at intervals not to exceed 6 feet (1.83 m).

(g) **Dry Board Installations.** In dry board installations, the entire ceiling below the heating cable shall be covered with gypsum board not exceeding ½ inch (12.7 mm) thickness. The void between the upper layer of gypsum board, plaster lath, or other fire-resistant material and the surface layer of gypsum board shall be completely filled with thermally conductive nonshrinking plaster or other approved material or equivalent thermal conductivity.

(h) **Free from Contact with Conductive Surfaces.** Cables shall be kept free from contact with metal or other electrical conductive surfaces.

(i) **Joists.** In dry board applications, cable shall be installed parallel to the joist, leaving a clear space centered under the joist of 2½ inches (64 mm) (width) between centers of adjacent runs of cable. Crossing of joist by cable shall be kept to a minimum. Surface layer of gypsum board shall be mounted so that the nails or other fasteners do not pierce the heating cable.

Where practicable, cables shall cross joists only at the ends of a room.

424-42. Finished Ceilings. Finished ceilings shall not be covered with decorative panels or beams constructed of materials which have thermal insulating properties, such as wood, fiber, or plastic. Finished ceilings shall be permitted to be covered with paint, wallpaper, or other approved surface finishes.

424-43. Installation of Nonheating Leads of Cables and Panels.

(a) Free Nonheating Leads. Free nonheating leads of cables and panels shall be installed in accordance with approved wiring methods from the junction box to a location within the ceiling. Such installations shall be permitted to be single conductors in approved raceways, single or multiconductor Type UF, Type NMC, Type MI, or other approved conductors.

(b) Leads in Junction Box. Not less than 6 inches (152 mm) of free nonheating lead shall be within the junction box. The marking of the leads shall be visible in the junction box.

(c) Excess Leads. Excess leads of heating cables shall not be cut but shall be secured to the underside of the ceiling and embedded in plaster or other approved material, leaving only a length sufficient to reach the junction box with not less than 6 inches (152 mm) of free lead within the box.

(d) Excess Nonheating Leads. Excess nonheating leads of heating panels shall be permitted to be cut to the required length. They shall meet the installation requirements of the wiring method employed in accordance with Section 424-43(a). Nonheating leads shall be considered to be an integral part of an approved fixed electric space heating panel and not subject to the ampacity requirements of Section 424-3(b) for branch circuits.

424-44. Installation of Panels or Cables in Concrete or Poured Masonry Floors.

(a) Watts per Square Foot or Linear Foot. Panels or heating units shall not exceed 33 watts per square foot (0.093 sq m) of heated area or 16½ watts per linear foot (305 mm) of cable.

(b) Spacing Between Adjacent Runs. The spacing between adjacent runs of cable shall not be less than 1 inch (25.4 mm) on centers.

(c) Secured in Place. Cables shall be secured in place by nonmetallic frames or spreaders or other approved means while the concrete or other finish is applied.
Cables, units, and panels shall not be installed where they bridge expansion joints unless protected from expansion and contraction.

(d) Spacings Between Heating Cable and Metal Embedded in the Floor. Spacings shall be maintained between the heating cable and metal embedded in the floor.

Exception: Grounded metal-clad cable shall be permitted to be in contact with metal embedded in the floor.

(e) Leads Protected. Leads shall be protected where they leave the floor by rigid metal conduit, intermediate metal conduit, rigid nonmetallic conduit, electrical metallic tubing, or by other approved means.

(f) Bushings or Approved Fittings. Bushings or approved fittings shall be used where the leads emerge within the floor slab.

424-45. Inspection and Tests. Cable installations shall be made with due care to prevent damage to the cable assembly and shall be inspected and **approved** before cables are covered or concealed.

424-46. Panels — General.   Sections 424-46 through 424-48 cover only heating panels of less than 25 watts per square foot (0.093 sq m) assembled together in the field to form a heating installation in one room or area using approved methods of interconnection. Such an installation shall be connected by a recognized wiring method.

424-47. Panels to Be Complete Units.   Panels shall be installed as complete units unless approved for field cutting in a recognized manner.

424-48. Installation.   Panels shall be installed in an approved manner. Nails, staples, or other electrically conductive fasteners shall not be used where they penetrate current-carrying parts.

Exception: Insulated fasteners shall be permitted with systems for which they are recognized.

F. Duct Heaters

424-57. General.   Part F shall apply to any heater mounted in the air stream of a forced-air system where the air moving unit is not provided as an integral part of the equipment.

Figure 424-2. An insert-type electric duct heater. (*Square D Co.*)

424-58. Identification.   Heaters installed in an air duct shall be identified as suitable for the installation.

424-59. Air Flow.   Means shall be provided to assure uniform and adequate air flow over the face of the heater.

Heaters installed within 4 feet (1.22 m) of a fan outlet, elbows, baffle plates, or other obstruction in duct work may require turning vanes, pressure plates, or other devices on the inlet side of the duct heater to assure an even distribution of air over the face of the heater.

424-60. Elevated Inlet Temperature.   Duct heaters intended for use with elevated inlet air temperature shall be identified as suitable for use at the elevated temperatures.

424-61. Installation of Duct Heaters with Heat Pumps and Air Conditioners. Heat pumps and air conditioners having duct heaters closer than 4 feet (1.22 m) to the heat pump or air conditioner shall have both the duct heater and heat pump or air conditioner approved for such installation and so marked.

424-62. Condensation. Duct heaters used with air conditioners or other air-cooling equipment that may result in condensation of moisture shall be approved for use with air conditioners.

424-63. Fan Circuit Interlock. Means shall be provided to ensure that the fan circuit is energized when the first heater circuit is energized. However, time- or temperature-controlled delay in energizing the fan motor shall be permitted.

424-64. Limit Controls. Each duct heater shall be provided with an approved, integral, automatic-reset temperature-limiting control or controllers to de-energize the circuit or circuits.

In addition, an integral independent supplementary control or controllers shall be provided in each duct heater that will disconnect a sufficient number of conductors to interrupt current flow. This device shall be manually resettable or replaceable.

424-65. Location of Disconnecting Means. Duct heater controller equipment shall be accessible with the disconnecting means installed at or within sight from the controller.

Exception: As permitted by Section 424-19(a).

424-66. Installation. Duct heaters shall be installed in accordance with the manufacturer's instructions in a manner so that operation will not create a hazard to persons or property. Furthermore, duct heaters shall be located with respect to building construction and other equipment so as to permit access to the heater. Sufficient clearance shall be maintained to permit replacement of controls and heating elements and for adjusting and cleaning of controls and other parts requiring such attention. See Section 110-16.

For additional installation information, see Air Conditioning and Ventilating Systems, NFPA 90A-1978 (ANSI) and Warm Air Heating and Air Conditioning Systems, NFPA 90B-1980 (ANSI).

G. Resistance-type Boilers

424-70. Scope. The provisions in Part G of this article shall apply to boilers employing resistance-type heating elements. Electrode-type boilers shall not be considered as employing resistance-type heating elements. See Part H of this article.

424-71. Identification. Resistance-type boilers shall be identified as suitable for the installation.

424-72. Overcurrent Protection.

(a) Boiler Employing Resistance-type Immersion Heating Elements in an ASME Rated and Stamped Vessel. A boiler employing resistance-type immersion heating elements contained in an ASME rated and stamped vessel shall have the heating elements protected at not more than 150 amperes. Such a boiler rated more than 120 amperes shall have the heating elements subdivided into loads not exceeding 120 amperes.

Where a subdivided load is less than 120 amperes, the rating of the overcurrent protective device shall comply with Section 424-3(b).

(b) Boiler Employing Resistance-type Heating Elements Rated More than 48 Amperes

and Not Contained in an ASME Rated and Stamped Vessel. A boiler employing resistance-type heating elements not contained in an ASME rated and stamped vessel shall have the heating elements protected at not more than 60 amperes. Such a boiler rated more than 48 amperes shall have the heating elements subdivided into loads not exceeding 48 amperes.

Where a subdivided load is less than 48 amperes, the rating of the overcurrent protective device shall comply with Section 424-3(b).

(c) Supplementary Overcurrent Protective Devices. The supplementary overcurrent protective devices for the subdivided loads as required by Section 424-72(a) and (b) shall be: (1) factory installed within or on the boiler enclosure or provided as a separate assembly by the boiler manufacturer; and (2) accessible, but need not be readily accessible; and (3) suitable for branch-circuit protection.

Where cartridge fuses are used to provide this overcurrent protection, a single disconnecting means shall be permitted for the several subdivided circuits. See Section 240-40.

(d) Conductors Supplying Supplementary Overcurrent Protective Devices. The conductors supplying these supplementary overcurrent protective devices shall be considered branch-circuit conductors.

Exception: Where the heaters are rated 50 kW or more, the conductors supplying the overcurrent protective device specified in (c) above shall be permitted to be sized at not less than 100 percent of the nameplate rating of the heater provided all of the following conditions are met:

a. The heater is marked with a minimum conductor size; and

b. The conductors are not smaller than the marked minimum size; and

c. A temperature or pressure-actuated device controls the cyclic operation of the equipment.

(e) Conductors for Subdivided Loads. Field-wired conductors between the heater and the supplementary overcurrent protective devices shall be sized at not less than 125 percent of the load served. The supplementary overcurrent protective devices specified in (c) shall protect these conductors in accordance with Section 240-3.

Exception: For heaters rated 50 kW or more, the ampacity of field-wired conductors between the heater and the supplementary overcurrent protective devices shall be permitted to be not less than 100 percent of the load of their respective subdivided circuits provided all of the following conditions are met:

a. The heater is marked with a minimum conductor size; and

b. The conductors are not smaller than the marked minimum size; and

c. A temperature-activated device controls the cyclic operation of the equipment.

424-73. Over-Temperature Limit Control. Each boiler designed, so that in normal operation there is no change in state of the heat transfer medium, shall be equipped with a temperature sensitive limiting means. It shall be installed to limit maximum liquid temperature and shall directly or indirectly disconnect all ungrounded conductors to the heating elements. Such means shall be in addition to a temperature regulating system and other devices protecting the tank against excessive pressure.

424-74. Over-Pressure Limit Control. Each boiler designed, so that in normal operation there is a change in state of the heat transfer medium from liquid to vapor, shall be equipped with a pressure sensitive limiting means. It shall be installed to limit maximum pressure and shall directly or indirectly disconnect all ungrounded conductors to the heating elements. Such means shall be in addition to a pressure regulating system and other devices protecting the tank against excessive pressure.

424-75. Grounding.   All noncurrent-carrying metal parts shall be grounded in accordance with Article 250. Means for connection of equipment grounding conductor(s) sized in accordance with Table 250-95 shall be provided.

H. Electrode-type Boilers

424-80. Scope.   The provisions in Part H of this article shall apply to boilers for operation at 600 volts, nominal, or less, in which heat is generated by the passage of current between electrodes through the liquid being heated.

424-81. Identification.   Electrode-type boilers shall be identified as suitable for the installation.

424-82. Branch-Circuit Requirements.   The size of branch-circuit conductors and overcurrent protective devices shall be calculated on the basis of 125 percent of the total load (motors not included). A contactor, relay or other device, approved for continuous operation at 100 percent of its rating, shall be permitted to supply its full-rated load. See Section 210-22(c), Exception No. 3. The provisions of this section shall not apply to conductors that form an integral part of an approved boiler.

Exception: For an electrode boiler rated 50 kW or more, the conductors supplying the boiler electrode(s) shall be permitted to be sized at not less than 100 percent of the nameplate rating of the electrode boiler provided all the following conditions are met:

a. The electrode boiler is marked with a minimum conductor size; and

b. The conductors are not smaller than the marked minimum size; and

c. A temperature or pressure-actuated device controls the cyclic operation of the equipment.

424-83. Over-Temperature Limit Control.   Each boiler designed, so that in normal operation there is no change in state of the heat transfer medium, shall be equipped with a temperature sensitive limiting means. It shall be installed to limit maximum liquid temperature and shall directly or indirectly interrupt all current flow through the electrodes. Such means shall be in addition to the temperature regulating system and other devices protecting the tank against excessive pressure.

424-84. Over-Pressure Limit Control.   Each boiler designed, so that in normal operation there is a change in state of the heat transfer medium from liquid to vapor, shall be equipped with a pressure sensitive limiting means. It shall be installed to limit maximum pressure and shall directly or indirectly interrupt all current flow through the electrodes. Such means shall be in addition to a pressure regulating system and other devices protecting the tank against excessive pressure.

424-85. Grounding.   For those boilers designed such that fault currents do not pass through the pressure vessel and the pressure vessel is electrically isolated from the electrodes, all exposed noncurrent-carrying metal parts including the pressure vessel, supply, and return connecting piping shall be grounded in accordance with Article 250.

For all other designs the pressure vessel containing the electrodes shall be isolated and electrically insulated from ground.

424-86. Markings. All electrode-type boilers shall be marked to show: (1) the manufacturer's name; (2) the normal rating in volts, amperes, and kilowatts; (3) the electrical supply required specifying frequency, number of phases, and number of wires; (4) the marking: "Electrode-type Boiler"; (5) a warning marking — "ALL POWER SUPPLIES SHALL BE DISCONNECTED BEFORE SERVICING INCLUDING SERVICING THE PRESSURE VESSEL."

The nameplate shall be located so as to be visible after installation.

ARTICLE 426 — FIXED OUTDOOR ELECTRIC DE-ICING AND SNOW-MELTING EQUIPMENT

Contents

A. General

Article 426 was extensively revised for the 1981 *Code* to permit resistance heating elements, impedance heating systems, or skin effect heating systems. The systems are defined in Section 426-2. In addition, specific requirements have been provided for exposed resistance heating elements of the type commonly used on residences for gutter and roof de-icing and snow melting. See Sections 426-21 and 426-23.

426-1. Scope.   The requirements of this article shall apply to electrically energized heating systems and the installation of these systems.

(a) Embedded.   Embedded in driveways, walks, steps, and other areas.

(b) Exposed.   Exposed on drainage systems, bridge structures, roofs, and other structures.

426-2. Definitions.   For the purpose of this article:

Heating System.   A complete system consisting of components such as heating elements, fastening devices, nonheating circuit wiring, leads, temperature controllers, safety signs, junction boxes, raceways, and fittings.

Resistance Heating Element.   A specific separate element to generate heat which is embedded in or fastened to the surface to be heated.

Tubular heaters, strip heaters, heating cable, heating tape, and heating panels are examples of resistance heaters.

Impedance Heating System.   A system in which heat is generated in a pipe or rod, or combination of pipes and rods, by causing current to flow through the pipe or rod by direct connection to an ac voltage source from a dual-winding transformer. The pipe or rod shall be permitted to be embedded in the surface to be heated, or constitute the exposed components to be heated.

Skin Effect Heating System.   A system in which heat is generated on the inner surface of a ferromagnetic envelope embedded in or fastened to the surface to be heated.

Typically, an electrically insulated conductor is routed through and connected to the envelope at the other end. The envelope and the electrically insulated conductor are connected to an ac voltage source from a dual-winding transformer.

426-3. Application of Other Articles.   All requirements of this Code shall apply except as specifically amended in this article. Fixed outdoor electric de-icing and snow-melting equipment for use in hazardous (classified) locations shall comply with Articles 500 through 516.

426-4. Branch-Circuit Sizing.   The ampacity of branch-circuit conductors and the rating or setting of overcurrent protective devices supplying fixed outdoor electric de-icing and snow-melting equipment shall be not less than 125 percent of the total load of the heaters. The rating or setting of overcurrent protective devices shall be permitted in accordance with Section 240-3, Exception No. 1.

B. Installation

426-10. General.   Equipment for outdoor electric de-icing and snow melting shall be identified as being suitable for:

(1) The chemical, thermal, and physical environment, and

(2) Installation in accordance with the manufacturer's drawings and instructions.

426-11. Use.   Electrical heating equipment shall be installed in such a manner as to be afforded protection from physical damage.

426-12. Thermal Protection.   External surfaces of outdoor electric de-icing and snow-melting equipment which operate at temperatures exceeding 60°C (140°F) shall be physically guarded, isolated, or thermally insulated to protect against contact by personnel in the area.

426-13. Identification.   The presence of outdoor electric de-icing and snow-melting equipment shall be evident by the posting of appropriate caution signs or markings where clearly visible.

426-14. Special Permission.   Fixed outdoor de-icing and snow-melting equipment employing methods of construction or installation other than covered by this article shall be permitted only by special permission.

C. Resistance Heating Elements

426-20. Embedded De-Icing and Snow-Melting Equipment.

   (a) Watt Density.   Panels or units shall not exceed 120 watts per square foot (0.093 sq m) of heated area.

   (b) Spacing.   The spacing between adjacent cable runs is dependent upon the rating of the cable, and shall be not less than 1 inch (25.4 mm) on centers.

   (c) Cover.   Units, panels, or cables shall be installed:

   (1) On a substantial asphalt or masonry base at least 2 inches (50.8 mm) thick and have at least 1½ inches (38 mm) of asphalt or masonry applied over the units, panels, or cables; or

   (2) They shall be permitted to be installed over other approved bases and embedded within 3½ inches (89 mm) of masonry or asphalt but not less than 1½ inches (38 mm) from the top surface; or

   (3) Equipment that has been specially investigated for other forms of installation shall be installed only in the manner for which it has been investigated.

   (d) Secured.   Cables, units, and panels shall be secured in place by frames or spreaders or other approved means while the masonry or asphalt finish is applied.

   (e) Expansion and Contraction.   Cables, units, and panels shall not be installed where they bridge expansion joints unless adequately protected from expansion and contraction.

426-21. Exposed De-Icing and Snow-Melting Equipment.

   (a) Secured.   Heating element assemblies shall be secured to the surface being heated by approved means.

   (b) Overtemperature.   Where the heating element is not in direct contact with the surface being heated, the design of the heater assembly shall be such that its temperature limitations shall not be exceeded.

   (c) Expansion and Contraction.   Heating elements and assemblies shall not be installed where they bridge expansion joints unless provision is made for expansion and contraction.

(d) Flexural Capability. Where installed on flexible structures, the heating elements and assemblies shall have a flexural capability compatible with the structure.

426-22. Installation of Nonheating Leads for Embedded Equipment.

(a) Grounding Sheath or Braid. Nonheating leads having a grounding sheath or braid shall be permitted to be embedded in the masonry or asphalt in the same manner as the heating cable without additional physical protection.

(b) Raceways. All but 1 to 6 inches (25.4 to 152 mm) of nonheating leads of Type TW and other approved types not having a grounding sheath shall be enclosed in a rigid conduit, electrical metallic tubing, intermediate metal conduit, or other raceways within asphalt or masonry; and the distance from the factory splice to raceway shall be not less than 1 inch (25.4 mm) or more than 6 inches (152 mm).

(c) Bushings. Insulating bushings shall be used in the asphalt or masonry where leads enter conduit or tubing.

(d) Expansion and Contraction. Leads shall be protected in expansion joints and where they emerge from masonry or asphalt by rigid conduit, electrical metallic tubing, intermediate metal conduit, other raceways, or other approved means.

(e) Leads in Junction Boxes. Not less than 6 inches (152 mm) of free nonheating lead shall be within the junction box.

426-23. Installation of Nonheating Leads for Exposed Equipment.

(a) Nonheating Leads. Power supply nonheating leads (cold leads) for resistance elements shall be suitable for the temperature encountered. Preassembled nonheating leads on approved heaters shall be permitted to be shortened if the markings specified in Section 426-25 are retained. Not less than 6 inches (152 mm) of nonheating leads shall be provided within the junction box.

(b) Protection. Nonheating power supply leads shall be enclosed in a rigid conduit, intermediate metal conduit, electrical metallic tubing, or other approved means.

426-24. Electrical Connection.

(a) Heating Element Connections. Electrical connections, other than factory connections of heating elements to nonheating elements embedded in masonry or asphalt or on exposed surfaces, shall be made with insulated connectors identified for the use.

(b) Circuit Connections. Splices and terminations at the end of the nonheating leads, other than the heating element end, shall be installed in a box or fitting in accordance with Sections 110-14 and 300-15.

426-25. Marking.
Each factory-assembled heating unit shall be legibly marked within 3 inches (76 mm) of each end of the nonheating leads with the permanent identification symbol, catalog number, and ratings in volts and watts, or in volts and amperes.

426-26. Corrosion Protection.
Ferrous and nonferrous metal raceways, cable armor, cable sheaths, boxes, fittings, supports, and support hardware shall be permitted to be installed in concrete or in direct contact with the earth, or in areas subject to severe corrosive influences, when made of material suitable for the condition, or when provided with corrosion protection identified as suitable for the condition.

426-27. Grounding.

(a) **Metal Parts.**   Exposed noncurrent-carrying metal parts of equipment likely to become energized shall be grounded as required in Article 250.

(b) **Grounding Braid or Sheath.**   Grounding means, such as copper braid, metal sheath, or other approved means, shall be provided as part of the heated section of the cable, panel, or unit.

(c) **Bonding and Grounding.**   All noncurrent-carrying metal parts that are likely to become energized shall be bonded together and connected to an equipment grounding conductor sized in accordance with Table 250-95, extending to the distribution panelboard.

D. Impedance Heating

426-30. Personnel Protection.   Exposed elements of impedance heating systems shall be physically guarded, isolated, or thermally insulated with weatherproof jacket to protect against contact by personnel in the area.

426-31. Voltage Limitations.   The impedance heating elements shall not operate at a voltage greater than 30 volts ac.

Exception: The voltage shall be permitted to be greater than 30 volts, but not more than 80 volts, if a ground-fault circuit-interrupter for personnel protection is provided.

426-32. Isolation Transformer.   A dual-winding transformer with a grounded shield between the primary and secondary windings shall be used to isolate the distribution system from the heating system.

426-33. Induced Currents.   All current-carrying components shall be installed in accordance with Section 300-20.

426-34. Grounding.   An impedance heating system that is operating at a voltage greater than 30, but not more than 80, shall be grounded at designated point(s).

E. Skin Effect Heating

426-40. Conductor Ampacity.   The ampacity of the electrically insulated conductor inside the ferromagnetic envelope shall be permitted to exceed the values shown in Article 310, provided it is identified as suitable for this use.

426-41. Pull Boxes.   Where pull boxes are used they shall be accessible without excavation by location in suitable vaults or above grade. Outdoor pull boxes shall be of watertight construction.

426-42. Single Conductor in Enclosure.   The provisions of Section 300-20 shall not apply to the installation of a single conductor in a ferromagnetic envelope (metal enclosure).

426-43. Corrosion Protection.   Ferromagnetic envelopes, ferrous or nonferrous metal raceways, boxes, fittings, supports, and support hardware shall be permitted to be installed in concrete or in direct contact with the earth, or in areas subjected to severe corrosive influences, where made of material suitable for the condition, or where provided with corrosion protection identified as suitable for the condition. Corrosion protection shall maintain the original wall thickness of the ferromagnetic envelope.

426-44. Grounding. The ferromagnetic envelope shall be grounded at both ends; and, in addition, it shall be permitted to be grounded at intermediate points as required by its design.

The provisions of Section 250-26 shall not apply to the installation of skin effect heating systems.

See Section 250-26(d).

F. Control and Protection

426-50. Disconnecting Means. All fixed outdoor de-icing and snow-melting equipment shall be provided with a means for disconnection from all ungrounded conductors. Where readily accessible to the user of the equipment, the branch-circuit switch or circuit breaker shall be permitted to serve as the disconnecting means. Switches used as the disconnecting means shall be of the indicating type.

426-51. Controllers.

(a) Temperature Controller with "Off" Position. Temperature controlled switching devices which indicate an "off" position and which interrupt line current shall open all ungrounded conductors when the control device is in the "off" position. These devices shall not be permitted to serve as the disconnecting means unless provided with a positive lockout in the "off" position.

(b) Temperature Controller Without "Off" Position. Temperature controlled switching devices which do not have an "off" position shall not be required to open all ungrounded conductors and shall not be permitted to serve as the disconnecting means.

(c) Remote Temperature Controller. Remote controlled temperature actuated devices shall not be required to meet the requirements of Section 426-51(a). These devices shall not be permitted to serve as the disconnecting means.

(d) Combined Switching Devices. Switching devices consisting of combined temperature actuated devices and manually controlled switches which serve both as the controller and the disconnecting means shall comply with all of the following conditions:

(1) Open all ungrounded conductors when manually placed in the "off" position; and

(2) Be so designed that the circuit cannot be energized automatically if the device has been manually placed in the "off" position; and

(3) Be provided with a positive lockout in the "off" position.

426-52. Overcurrent Protection. Fixed outdoor electric de-icing and snow-melting equipment shall be considered as protected against overcurrent where supplied by a branch circuit as specified in Section 426-4.

ARTICLE 427 — FIXED ELECTRIC HEATING EQUIPMENT FOR PIPELINES AND VESSELS

Contents

A. General

Article 427 has been extensively revised for the 1981 *Code* to include requirements for impedance heating, induction heating, and skin effect heating, in addition to resistance heating elements. Definitions of the various systems are provided in Section 427-2.

427-1. Scope.   The requirements of this article shall apply to electrically energized heating systems and the installation of these systems used with pipelines and/or vessels.

427-2. Definitions.   For the purpose of this article:

Pipeline.   A length of pipe including pumps, valves, flanges, control devices, strainers and/or similar equipment for conveying fluids.

Vessels.   A container such as a barrel, drum, or tank for holding fluids or other material.

Integrated Heating System.   A complete system consisting of components such as pipelines, vessels, heating elements, heat transfer medium, thermal insulation, moisture barrier, nonheating leads, temperature controllers, safety signs, junction boxes, raceways, and fittings.

Resistance Heating Element.   A specific separate element to generate heat which is applied to the pipeline or vessel externally or internally.

Tubular heaters, strip heaters, heating cable, heating tape, heating blankets, and immersion heaters are examples of resistance heaters.

Impedance Heating System.   A system in which heat is generated in a pipeline or vessel wall by causing current to flow through the pipeline or vessel wall by direct connection to an ac voltage source from a dual-winding transformer.

Induction Heating System.   A system in which heat is generated in a pipeline or vessel wall by inducing current and hysteresis effect in the pipeline or vessel wall from an external isolated ac field source.

Skin Effect Heating System.   A system in which heat is generated on the inner surface of a ferromagnetic envelope attached to a pipeline and/or vessel.

Typically, an electrically insulated conductor is routed through and connected to the envelope at the other end. The envelope and the electrically insulated conductor are connected to an ac voltage source from a dual-winding transformer.

427-3. Application of Other Articles.   All requirements of this Code shall apply except as specifically amended in this article. Cord-connected pipe heating assemblies intended for specific use and identified as suitable for this use shall be installed according to Article 422. Fixed electric pipeline and vessel heating equipment for use in hazardous (classified) locations shall comply with Articles 500 through 516.

427-4. Branch-Circuit Sizing.   The ampacity of branch-circuit conductors and the rating or setting of overcurrent protective devices supplying fixed electric heating equipment for pipelines and vessels shall be not less than 125 percent of the total load of the heaters. The rating or setting of overcurrent protective devices shall be permitted in accordance with Section 240-3, Exception No. 1.

B. Installation

427-10. General.   Equipment for pipeline and vessel electrical heating shall be identified as being suitable for: (1) the chemical, thermal and physical environment; and (2) installation in accordance with the manufacturer's drawings and instructions.

427-11. Use.   Electrical heating equipment shall be installed in such a manner as to be afforded protection from physical damage.

427-12. Thermal Protection.   External surfaces of pipeline and vessel heating equipment which operate at temperatures exceeding 60°C (140°F) shall be physically guarded, isolated, or thermally insulated to protect against contact by personnel in the area.

427-13. Identification.   The presence of electrically heated pipelines and/or vessels shall be evident by the posting of appropriate caution signs or markings at frequent intervals along the pipeline or vessel.

C. Resistance Heating Elements

427-14. Secured.   Heating element assemblies shall be secured to the surface being heated by means other than the thermal insulation.

427-15. Not in Direct Contact.   Where the heating element is not in direct contact with the pipeline or vessel being heated, means shall be provided to prevent overtemperature of the heating element unless the design of the heater assembly is such that its temperature limitations will not be exceeded.

427-16. Expansion and Contraction.   Heating elements and assemblies shall not be installed where they bridge expansion joints unless provisions are made for expansion and contraction.

427-17. Flexural Capability.   Where installed on flexible pipelines, the heating elements and assemblies shall have a flexural capability compatible with the pipeline.

427-18. Power Supply Leads.

(a) **Nonheating Leads.**   Power supply nonheating leads (cold leads) for resistance elements shall be suitable for the temperature encountered. Preassembled nonheating leads on approved heaters may be shortened if the markings specified in Section 427-20 are retained. Not less than 6 inches (152 mm) of nonheating leads shall be provided within the junction box.

(b) **Power Supply Leads Protection.**   Nonheating power supply leads shall be protected where they emerge from electrically heated pipeline or vessel heating units by rigid metal conduit, intermediate metal conduit, electrical metallic tubing, or other raceways identified as suitable for the application.

(c) **Interconnecting Leads.**   Interconnecting nonheating leads connecting portions of the heating system shall be permitted to be covered by thermal insulation in the same manner as the heaters.

427-19. Electrical Connections.

(a) **Nonheating Interconnections.**   Nonheating interconnections, where required under thermal insulation, shall be made with insulated connectors identified as suitable for this use.

(b) **Circuit Connections.**   Splices and terminations outside the thermal insulation shall be installed in a box or fitting in accordance with Sections 110-14 and 300-15.

427-20. Marking.   Each factory-assembled heating unit shall be legibly marked within 3 inches (76 mm) of each end of the nonheating leads with the permanent identification symbol, catalog number, and ratings in volts and watts, or in volts and amperes.

427-21. Grounding.   Exposed noncurrent-carrying metal parts of electric heating equipment which are likely to become energized shall be grounded as required in Article 250.

D. Impedance Heating

427-25. Personnel Protection.   All accessible external surfaces of the pipeline and/or vessel being heated shall be physically guarded, isolated, or thermally insulated (with weatherproof jacket for outside installations) to protect against contact by personnel in the area.

427-26. Voltage Limitations.   The pipeline or vessel being heated shall not operate at a voltage greater than 30 volts ac.

Exception: The voltage shall be permitted to be greater than 30 volts but not more than 80 volts if a ground-fault circuit-interrupter for personnel protection is provided.

427-27. Isolation Transformer.   A dual-winding transformer with a grounded shield between the primary and secondary windings shall be used to isolate the distribution system from the heating system.

427-28. Induced Currents.   All current-carrying components shall be installed in accordance with Section 300-20.

427-29. Grounding. The pipeline and/or vessel being heated which is operating at a voltage greater than 30 but not more than 80 shall be grounded at designated points.

E. Induction Heating

427-35. Scope. This part covers the installation of line frequency induction heating equipment and accessories for pipelines and vessels.

See Article 665 for other applications.

427-36. Personnel Protection. Induction coils that operate or may operate at a voltage greater than 30 volts ac shall be enclosed in a nonmetallic or split metallic enclosure, isolated or made inaccessible by location to protect personnel in the area.

427-37. Induced Current. Induction coils shall be prevented from inducing circulating currents in surrounding metallic equipment, supports, or structures by shielding, isolation, or insulation of the current paths. Stray current paths shall be bonded to prevent arcing.

F. Skin Effect Heating

427-45. Conductor Ampacity. The ampacity of the electrically insulated conductor inside the ferromagnetic envelope shall be permitted to exceed the values given in Article 310 provided it is identified as suitable for this use.

427-46. Pull Boxes. Pull boxes for pulling the electrically insulated conductor in the ferromagnetic envelope shall be permitted to be buried under the thermal insulation providing their locations are indicated by permanent markings on the insulation jacket surface and on drawings. For outdoor installations, pull boxes are to be of watertight construction.

427-47. Single Conductor in Enclosure. The provisions of Section 300-20 shall not apply to the installation of a single conductor in a ferromagnetic envelope (metal enclosure).

427-48. Grounding. The ferromagnetic envelope shall be grounded at both ends and, in addition, it shall be permitted to be grounded at intermediate points as required by its design. The ferromagnetic envelope shall be bonded at all joints to assure electrical continuity.

The provisions of Section 250-26 shall not apply to the installation of skin effect heating systems.

See Section 250-26(d).

G. Control and Protection

427-55. Disconnecting Means.

(a) Switch or Circuit Breaker. Means shall be provided to disconnect all fixed electric pipeline or vessel heating equipment from all ungrounded conductors. The branch-circuit switch or circuit breaker, where readily accessible to the user of the equipment, shall be permitted to serve as the disconnecting means. Switches used as disconnecting means shall be of the indicating type, and shall be provided with a positive lockout in the "off" position.

(b) Cord- and Plug-Connected Equipment. The factory-installed attachment plug of cord- and plug-connected equipment rated 20 amperes or less and 150 volts or less to ground shall be permitted to be the disconnecting means.

427-56. Controls.

(a) Temperature Control with "Off" Position. Temperature controlled switching devices which indicate an "off" position and which interrupt line current shall open all ungrounded conductors when the control device is in this "off" position. These devices shall not be permitted to serve as the disconnecting means unless provided with a positive lockout in the "off" position.

(b) Temperature Control Without "Off" Position. Temperature controlled switching devices which do not have an "off" position shall not be required to open all ungrounded conductors and shall not be permitted to serve as the disconnecting means.

(c) Remote Temperature Controller. Remote controlled temperature actuated devices shall not be required to meet the requirements of Section 427-56(a) and (b). These devices shall not be permitted to serve as the disconnecting means.

(d) Combined Switching Devices. Switching devices consisting of combined temperature actuated devices and manually controlled switches which serve both as the controllers and the disconnecting means shall comply with all the following conditions:

(1) Open all ungrounded conductors when manually placed in the "off" position; and

(2) Be so designed that the circuit cannot be energized automatically if the device has been manually placed in the "off" position; and

(3) Be provided with a positive lockout in the "off" position.

427-57. Overcurrent Protection. Heating equipment shall be considered as protected against overcurrent where supplied by a branch circuit as specified in Section 427-4.

ARTICLE 430 — MOTORS, MOTOR CIRCUITS,
AND CONTROLLERS

Contents

A. General

430-1. Motor Feeder and Branch Circuits. The following general requirements cover provisions for motors, motor circuits, and controllers that do not properly fall into the other parts of this article.

See Article 440 for air-conditioning and refrigerating equipment.

See Diagram 430-1.

Diagram 430-1

General	Part A
Requirements for over 600 volts, nominal	Part J
Protection of live parts all voltages	Part K
Grounding	Part L
Tables	Part M

To Supply

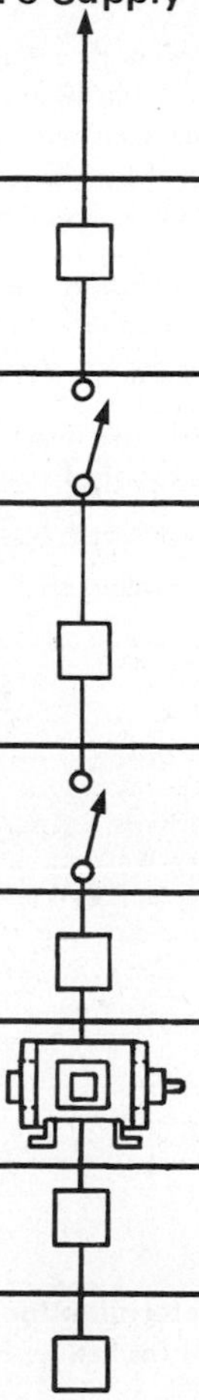

Motor Feeder	Part B Sec. 430-23 and 430-24 430-25 and 430-26
Motor Feeder	Part E
Short-Circuit and Ground-Fault Protection	Part E
Motor Disconnecting Means	Part H
Motor Branch-Circuit Short-Circuit and Ground-Fault Protection	Part D
Motor Circuit Conductor	Part B
Motor Controller	Part G
Motor Control Circuits	Part F
Motor Overload Protection	Part C
Motor	Part A
Thermal Protection	Part C
Secondary Controller Secondary Conductors	Part B Sec. 430-23
Secondary Resistor	Sec. 430-23 and Art. 470

Diagram 430-1 is intended to assist the user in following the provisions of Article 430. It is not a *Code* requirement.

430-2. Adjustable Speed Drive Systems. The incoming branch circuit or feeder to power conversion equipment included as a part of an adjustable speed drive system shall be based on the rated input to the power conversion equipment. If the power conversion equipment provides overload protection for the motor, additional overload protection is not required.

The disconnecting means shall be permitted to be in the incoming line to the conversion equipment and shall have a rating not less than 115 percent of the rated input current of the conversion unit.

430-3. Part-Winding Motors.   A part-winding-start induction or synchronous motor is one arranged for starting by first energizing part of its primary (armature) winding and, subsequently, energizing the remainder of this winding in one or more steps. The purpose is to reduce the initial values of the starting current drawn or the starting torque developed by the motor. A standard part-winding-start induction motor is arranged so that one-half of its primary winding can be energized initially and, subsequently, the remaining half can be energized, both halves then carrying equal current. A hermetic refrigerant compressor motor shall not be considered a standard part-winding-start induction motor.

Where separate overload devices are used with a standard part-winding-start induction motor, each half of the motor winding shall be individually protected in accordance with Sections 430-32 and 430-37 with a trip current one-half that specified.

Each motor-winding connection shall have branch-circuit short-circuit and ground-fault protection rated at not more than one-half that specified by Section 430-52.

Exception: A single device having this half rating shall be permitted for both windings if it will allow the motor to start. Where a time-delay (dual-element) fuse is used as a single device for both windings, it shall be permitted to have a rating not exceeding 150 percent of motor full-load current.

430-4. In Sight From.   Where this article specifies that one equipment shall be "in sight from" another equipment, one of the equipments specified shall be visible and not more than 50 feet (15.2 m) distant from the other.

430-5. Other Articles.   Motors and controllers shall also comply with the applicable provisions of the following:

Air-Conditioning and Refrigerating Equipment .... Article 440
Capacitors .... Section 460-9
Cranes and Hoists .... Article 610
Electrically Driven or Controlled Irrigation Machines .... Article 675
Elevators, Dumbwaiters, Escalators, and Moving Walks .... Article 620
Garages, Aircraft Hangars, Gasoline Dispensing and Service
    Stations, Bulk Storage Plants, Finishing Processes, and
    Flammable Anesthetics .... Articles 511, 513, 514, 515, 516, and 517-G
Hazardous (Classified) Locations .... Articles 500 thru 503
Metalworking Machine Tools .... Article 670
Motion-Picture Projectors .... Sections 540-11, 540-20
Motion-Picture and Television Studios .... Article 530
Organs .... Section 650-3
Resistors and Reactors .... Article 470
Theaters .... Section 520-48

430-6. Ampacity and Motor Rating Determination.   Conductor ampacity and motor ratings shall be determined as specified in (a) and (b) below.

(a) General Motor Applications.   Other than as specified for torque motors in (b) below, where the current rating of a motor is used to determine the ampacity of conductors or ampere ratings of switches, branch-circuit short-circuit and ground-fault protection, etc., the values given in Tables 430-147, 430-148, 430-149, and 430-150, including notes, shall be used instead of the actual current rating marked on the motor nameplate. Separate motor overload protection shall be based on the motor nameplate current rating. Where a motor is marked in amperes, but not horsepower, the horsepower rating shall be assumed to be that corresponding to the value given in Tables 430-147, 430-148, 430-149, and 430-150, interpolated if necessary.

Exception No. 1: Multispeed motors shall be in accordance with Sections 430-22(a) and 430-52.

Exception No. 2: For equipment employing a shaded-pole or permanent-split-capacitor-type fan or blower motor that is marked with the motor type, the full-load current for such motor marked on the nameplate of the equipment in which the fan or blower motor is employed shall be used instead of the horsepower rating to determine the ampacity or rating of the disconnecting means, the branch-circuit conductors, the controller, the branch-circuit short-circuit and ground-fault protection, and the separate overload protection. This marking on the equipment nameplate shall not be less than the current marked on the fan or blower motor nameplate.

(b) Torque Motors.   For torque motors the rated current shall be locked-rotor current, and this nameplate current shall be used to determine the ampacity of the branch-circuit conductors covered in Sections 430-22 and 430-24 and the ampere rating of the motor overload protection.

For motor controllers and disconnecting means, see Section 430-83, Exception No. 3 and Section 430-110.

(c) AC Adjustable Voltage Motors.   For motors used in alternating-current, adjustable voltage, variable torque drive systems, the ampacity of conductors, or ampere ratings of switches, branch-circuit short-circuit and ground-fault protection, etc., shall be based on the maximum operating current marked on the motor and/or control nameplate. If the maximum operating current does not appear on the nameplate, the ampacity determination shall be based on 150 percent of the values given in Tables 430-149 and 430-150.

430-7. Marking on Motors and Multimotor Equipment.

(a) Usual Motor Applications.   A motor shall be marked with the following information:

(1) Maker's name.

(2) Rated volts and full-load amperes. For a multispeed motor full-load amperes for each speed, except shaded-pole and permanent-split capacitor motors where amperes are required only for maximum speed.

(3) Rated frequency and number of phases, if an alternating-current motor.

(4) Rated full-load speed.

(5) Rated temperature rise or the insulation system class and rated ambient temperature.

(6) Time rating. The time rating shall be 5, 15, 30, or 60 minutes, or continuous.

(7) Rated horsepower if ⅛ horsepower or more. For a multispeed motor ⅛ horsepower or more, rated horsepower for each speed, except shaded-pole and permanent-split capacitor motors ⅛ horsepower or more where rated horsepower is required only for maximum speed. Motors of arc welders are not required to be marked with the horsepower rating.

(8) Code letter if an alternating-current motor rated ½ horsepower or more. On polyphase wound-rotor motors the code letter shall be omitted.

See (b) below.

(9) Secondary volts and full-load amperes if a wound-rotor induction motor.

(10) Field current and voltage for direct-current excited synchronous motors.

(11) Winding: straight shunt, stabilized shunt, compound, or series, if a direct-current motor. Fractional horsepower dc motors 7 inches (178 mm) or less in diameter shall not be required to be marked.

(12) A motor provided with a thermal protector complying with Section 430-32(a) (2) or (c) (2) shall be marked "Thermally Protected." Thermally protected motors rated 100 watts or less and complying with Section 430-32(c) (2) shall be permitted to use the abbreviated marking, "T.P."

(13) A motor complying with Section 430-32(c) (4) shall be marked "Impedance Protected." Impedance protected motors rated 100 watts or less and complying with Section 430-32(c) (4) shall be permitted to use the abbreviated marking "Z.P."

(b) Locked-Rotor Indicating Code Letters.   Code letters marked on motor nameplates to show motor input with locked rotor shall be in accordance with Table 430-7(b).

The code letter indicating motor input with locked rotor shall be in an individual block on the nameplate, properly designated. This code letter shall be used for determining branch-circuit short-circuit and ground-fault protection by reference to Table 430-152, as provided in Section 430-52.

(1) Multispeed motors shall be marked with the code letter designating the locked-rotor kVA per horsepower for the highest speed at which the motor can be started.

Exception: Constant-horsepower multispeed motors shall be marked with the code letter giving the highest locked-rotor kVA per horsepower.

(2) Single-speed motors starting on Y connection and running on delta connections shall be marked with a code letter corresponding to the locked-rotor kVA per horsepower for the Y connection.

(3) Dual-voltage motors that have a different locked-rotor kVA per horsepower on the two voltages shall be marked with the code letter for the voltage giving the highest locked-rotor kVA per horsepower.

(4) Motors with 60- and 50-hertz ratings shall be marked with a code letter designating the locked-rotor kVA per horsepower on 60 hertz.

(5) Part-winding-start motors shall be marked with a code letter designating the locked-rotor kVA per horsepower that is based upon the locked-rotor current for the full winding of the motor.

(c) Torque Motors.   Torque motors are rated for operation at standstill and shall be marked in accordance with (a) above.

Exception: Locked-rotor torque shall replace horsepower.

(d) Multimotor and Combination-Load Equipment.   Multimotor and combination-load equipment shall be provided with a visible nameplate marked with the maker's name, the rating in volts, frequency, number of phases, minimum supply circuit conductor ampacity, and the maximum ampere rating of the circuit short-circuit and ground-fault protective device. The conductor ampacity shall be computed in accordance with Section 430-25 and counting all of the motors and other loads that will be operated at the same time. The short-circuit and ground-fault protective device rating shall not exceed the value computed in accordance with Section 430-53. Multimotor equipment for use on two or more circuits shall be marked with the above information for each circuit.

Table 430-7(b).   Locked-Rotor Indicating Code Letters

Code Letter		Kilovolt-Amperes per Horsepower with Locked Rotor		
A		0	—	3.14
B		3.15	—	3.54
C		3.55	—	3.99
D		4.0	—	4.49
E		4.5	—	4.99
F		5.0	—	5.59
G		5.6	—	6.29
H		6.3	—	7.09
J		7.1	—	7.99
K		8.0	—	8.99
L		9.0	—	9.99
M		10.0	—	11.19
N		11.2	—	12.49
P		12.5	—	13.99
R		14.0	—	15.99
S		16.0	—	17.99
T		18.0	—	19.99
U		20.0	—	22.39
V		22.4	—	and up

Where the equipment is not factory-wired and the individual nameplates of motors and other loads are visible after assembly of the equipment, the individual nameplates shall be permitted to serve as the required marking.

The nameplate marking of the maximum ampere rating of the branch-circuit short-circuit and ground-fault protective device may limit the type of protective device to a fuse by stipulating "fuse" without reference to a circuit breaker. This means that the circuit to the equipment must be protected by fuses, such as in a fused disconnect switch. The fused switch could be supplied from a circuit breaker in a panelboard.

430-8. Marking on Controllers.   A controller shall be marked with the maker's name or identification, the voltage, the current or horsepower rating, and such other necessary data to properly indicate the motors for which it is suitable. A controller that includes motor overload protection suitable for group motor application shall be marked with the motor overload protection and the maximum branch-circuit short-circuit and ground-fault protection for such applications.

Combination controllers employing adjustable instantaneous trip circuit breakers shall be clearly marked to indicate the ampere settings of the adjustable trip element.

Where a controller is built in as an integral part of a motor or of a motor-generator set, individual marking of the controller shall not be required if the necessary data are on the nameplate. For controllers that are an integral part of equipment approved as a unit, the above marking shall be permitted on the equipment nameplate.

430-9. Marking at Terminals.   Terminals of motors and controllers shall be suitably marked or colored where necessary to indicate the proper connections.

430-10. Wiring Space in Enclosures.

(a) General.   Enclosures for motor controllers and disconnecting means shall not be used as junction boxes, auxiliary gutters, or raceways for conductors feeding through or tapping off to the other apparatus unless designs are employed which provide adequate space for this purpose.

See Section 373-8 for switch and overcurrent-device enclosures.

During the planning stages of a motor(s) installation, consideration is to be given to location and adequate work space for motor controllers and disconnects, including provisions for the use of auxiliary gutters or junction boxes to assure adequate space for conductors "feeding through" or "tapping off" to other apparatus.

For switch and overcurrent device enclosures, see Section 373-8.

(b) Wire Bending Space in Enclosures.   Minimum wire bending space within the enclosures for motor controllers shall be in accordance with Table 430-10(b) when measured in a straight line from the end of the lug or wire connector (in the direction the wire leaves the terminal) to the wall or barrier. Where alternate wire termination means is substituted for that supplied by the manufacturer of the controller, it shall be of a type identified by the manufacturer for use wth the controller and shall not reduce the minimum wire bending space.

Where the enclosure is a motor control center, the minimum wire bending space shall be in accordance with requirements of Article 373.

Table 430-10(b). Minimum Wire Bending Space at the Terminals of Enclosed Motor Controllers (in Inches)

AWG or Circular-Mil Size of Wire	*Wires per Terminal	
	1	2
14-10	Not specified	—
8-6	1½	—
4-3	2	—
2	2½	—
1	3	—
1/0	5	5
2/0	6	6
3/0-4/0	7	7
250	8	8
300	10	10
350-500	12	12
600-700	14	16
750-900	18	19

* Where provision for 3 or more wires per terminal exists the minimum wire bending space shall be in accordance with the requirements of Article 373.

See Figure 430-1 for illustration of measurement in accordance with Section 430-10(b).

430-11. Protection Against Liquids.   Suitable guards or enclosures shall be provided to protect exposed current-carrying parts of motors and the insulation of motor leads where installed directly under equipment, or in other locations where dripping or spraying oil, water, or other injurious liquid may occur, unless the motor is designed for the existing conditions.

Exposed current-carrying parts and insulated leads of motors should be suitably protected from injurious liquids (dripping oil, water, or excessive moisture) whose presence may cause an unnecessary breakdown or, in many cases, a fire.

430-12. Motor Terminal Housings.

(a) Material.   Where motors are provided with terminal housings, the housings shall be of metal and of substantial construction.

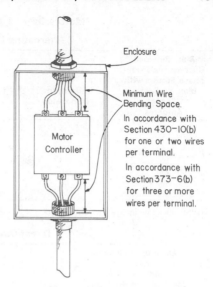

Enclosure

Minimum Wire
Bending Space.

In accordance with
Section 430-10(b)
for one or two wires
per terminal.

In accordance with
Section 373-6(b)
for three or more
wires per terminal.

Figure 430-1. Wire bending space in enclosures
for motor controllers.

*Exception: In other than hazardous (classified) locations, substantial nonmetallic, nonburning
housings shall he permitted on motors larger than 34 inches (864 mm) in diameter provided internal
grounding means between the machine frame and the conduit connection is incorporated within the
housing.*

See Method of Test for Flammability of Self-Supporting Plastics (ANSI K65.21 — 1975) for over 0.127 CM
(0.050 inch) in thickness, for nonburning test.

(b) Dimensions and Space — Wire-to-Wire Connections.   When these terminal housings
enclose wire-to-wire connections, they shall have minimum dimensions and usable volumes in
accordance with Table 430-12(b).

(c) Dimensions and Space — Fixed Terminal Connections.   Where these terminal
housings enclose rigidly mounted motor terminals, the terminal housing shall be of sufficient size
to provide minimum terminal spacings and usable volumes in accordance with Tables 430-12(c) (1)
and (c) (2).

**Table 430-12(b).   Terminal Housings — Wire-to-Wire Connections
Motors 11 Inches in Diameter or Less**

HP	Cover Opening, Minimum Dimension, Inches	Usable Volume, Minimum, Cubic Inches
1 and smaller*	1⅜	7½
1½, 2 and 3†	1¾	12
5 and 7½	2	16
10 and 15	2½	26

For SI units: one inch = 25.4 millimeters.
    * For motors rated 1 horsepower and smaller and with the terminal housing partially or wholly integral with
the frame or end shield, the volume of the terminal housing shall be not less than 0.8 cubic inch per wire-
to-wire connection. The minimum cover opening dimension is not specified.
    † For motors rated 1½, 2 and 3 horsepower and with the terminal housing partially or wholly integral with the
frame or end shield, the volume of the terminal housing shall not be less than 1.0 cubic inch per wire-to-wire
connection. The minimum cover opening dimension is not specified.

Motors Over 11 Inches in Diameter

Alternating-Current Motors

Max. Full-load Current for Three-phase Motors with Max. of Twelve Leads Amperes	Terminal Box Minimum Dimension Inches	Usable Volume Minimum Cubic Inches	Typical Maximum Horsepower Three Phase	
			230 Volt	460 Volt
45	2.5	26	15	30
70	3.3	55	25	50
110	4.0	100	40	75
160	5.0	180	60	125
250	6.0	330	100	200
400	7.0	600	150	300
600	8.0	1100	250	500

For SI units: one inch = 25.4 millimeters.

Direct-Current Motors

Maximum Full-Load Current for Motors with Maximum of Six Leads	Terminal Box Minimum Dimensions Inches	Usable Volume, Minimum Cubic Inches
68	2.5	26
105	3.3	55
165	4.0	100
240	5.0	180
375	6.0	330
600	7.0	600
900	8.0	1100

For SI units: one inch = 25.4 millimeters.

Auxiliary leads for such items as brakes, thermostats, space heater, exciting fields, etc., may be neglected if their current-carrying area does not exceed 25 percent of the current-carrying area of the machine power leads.

Table 430-12(c) (1).   Terminal Spacings — Fixed Terminals

	Minimum Spacing, Inches	
Nominal Volts	Between Line Terminals	Between Line Terminals and Other Uninsulated Metal Parts
240 or less	¼	¼
Over 250 through 600	⅜	⅜

For SI units: one inch = 25.4 millimeters.

Table 430-12(c) (2).   Usable Volumes — Fixed Terminals

Power-Supply Conductor Size, AWG	Minimum Usable Volume per Power-Supply Conductor, Cubic Inches
14	1.0
12 and 10	1¼
8 and 6	2¼

For SI units: one inch = 25.4 millimeters.

(d) Large Wire or Factory Connections.   For motors with larger ratings, greater number of leads, or larger wire sizes, or where motors are installed as a part of factory-wired equipment, without additional connection being required at the motor terminal housing during equipment installation, the terminal housing shall be of ample size to make connections, but the foregoing provisions for the volumes of terminal housings shall not be considered applicable.

(e) Equipment Grounding Connections.   A means for attachment of an equipment grounding conductor termination in accordance with Section 250-113 shall be provided at motor terminal housings for wire-to-wire connections or fixed terminal connections. The means for such connections shall be permitted to be located either inside or outside the motor terminal housing.

Exception: Where a motor is installed as a part of factory-wired equipment, which is required to be grounded and without additional connection being required at the motor terminal housing during equipment installation, a separate means for motor grounding at the motor terminal housing shall not be required.

430-13. Bushing.   Where wires pass through an opening in an enclosure, conduit box, or barrier, a bushing shall be used to protect the conductors from the edges of openings having sharp edges. The bushing shall have smooth well-rounded surfaces where it may be in contact with the conductors. If used where oils, greases, or other contaminants may be present, the bushing shall be made of material not deleteriously affected.

For conductors exposed to deteriorating agents, see Section 310-8.

430-14. Location of Motors.

(a) Ventilation and Maintenance.   Motors shall be located so that adequate ventilation is provided and so that maintenance, such as lubrication of bearings and replacing of brushes, can be readily accomplished.

(b) Open Motors.   Open motors having commutators or collector rings shall be located or protected so that sparks cannot reach adjacent combustible material, but this shall not prohibit the installation of these motors on wooden floors or supports.

430-16. Exposure to Dust Accumulations.   In locations where dust or flying material will collect on or in motors in such quantities as to seriously interfere with the ventilation or cooling of motors and thereby cause dangerous temperatures, suitable types of enclosed motors that will not overheat under the prevailing conditions shall be used. Especially severe conditions may require the use of enclosed pipe-ventilated motors, or enclosure in separate dusttight rooms, properly ventilated from a source of clean air.

For motors exposed to combustible dust or readily ignitible flying material, see the requirements of Sections 502-8 and 502-9 (Class II, Divisions 1 and 2) and Sections 503-6 and 503-7 (Class III, Divisions 1 and 2). For classification of locations, see Sections 500-5 (Class II locations) and 500-6 (Class III locations).

430-17. Highest Rated (Largest) Motor.   In determining compliance with Sections 430-24, 430-53(b), and 430-53(c), the highest rated (largest) motor shall be considered to be that motor having the highest rated full-load current. The full-load current used to determine the highest rated motor shall be the equivalent value corresponding to the motor horsepower rating selected from Tables 430-147, 430-148, 430-149, and 430-150.

430-18. Nominal Voltage of Rectifier Systems.   The nominal value of the ac voltage being rectified shall be used to determine the voltage of a rectifier derived system.

Exception: The nominal dc voltage of the rectifier shall be used if it exceeds the peak value of the ac voltage being rectified.

B. Motor Circuit Conductors

430-21. General.   Part B specifies sizes of conductors capable of carrying the motor current without overheating under the conditions specified.

Exception: The provisions of Section 430-124 shall apply over 600 volts, nominal.

The provisions of Articles 250, 300, and 310 shall not apply to conductors that form an integral part of approved equipment, or to integral conductors of motors, motor controllers, and the like.

See Sections 300-1(b) and 310-1.

430-22. Single Motor.

(a) General.   Branch-circuit conductors supplying a single motor shall have an ampacity not less than 125 percent of the motor full-load current rating.

In case of a multispeed motor, the selection of branch-circuit conductors on the line side of the controller shall be based on the highest of the full-load current ratings shown on the motor nameplate; selection of branch-circuit conductors between the controller and the motor, which are energized for that particular speed, shall be based on the current rating for that speed.

Exception No. 1: Conductors for a motor used for short-time, intermittent, periodic, or varying duty shall have an ampacity not less than the percentage of the motor nameplate current rating shown in Table 430-22(a) Exception unless the authority having jurisdiction grants special permission for conductors of smaller size.

Exception No. 2: For direct-current motors operating from a rectified single-phase power supply, the conductors between the controller and the motor shall have an ampacity of not less than the following percent of the motor full-load current rating:

a. Where a rectifier bridge of the single-phase half-wave type is used, 190 percent.

b. Where a rectifier bridge of the single-phase full-wave type is used, 150 percent.

Table 430-22(a) Exception.   Duty-Cycle Service

Classification of Service	Percentages of Nameplate Current Rating			
	5-Minute Rated Motor	15-Minute Rated Motor	30 & 60 Minute Rated Motor	Continuous Rated Motor
Short-Time Duty Operating valves, raising or lowering rolls, etc.	110	120	150	. . .
Intermittent Duty Freight and passenger elevators, tool heads, pumps, drawbridges, turntables, etc. For arc welders, see Section 630-21	85	85	90	140
Periodic Duty Rolls, ore- and coal-handling machines, etc.	85	90	95	140
Varying Duty	110	120	150	200

Any motor application shall be considered as continuous duty unless the nature of the apparatus it drives is such that the motor will not operate continuously with load under any condition of use.

See Example No. 8, Chapter 9 and Diagram 430-1.

The provision for a conductor with an ampacity of at least 125 percent of the motor full-load current rating is not a conductor derating. It is based on the need to provide for a sustained running current greater than the rated full-load current and for protection of the conductors by the motor overload protective device set above the motor full-load current rating.

(b) Separate Terminal Enclosure.   The conductors between a stationary motor rated 1 horsepower or less and the separate terminal enclosure permitted in Section 430-145(b) shall be permitted to be smaller than No. 14 but not smaller than No. 18, provided they have an ampacity as specified in (a) above.

Section 240-40 requires a disconnecting means on the supply side of cartridge fuses to disconnect the fuses from the source of electrical energy.

Figure 430-2 illustrates each motor on an individual branch circuit with branch-circuit short-circuit and ground-fault protective devices located at a distribution panel and disconnecting means, controllers, and overload protection at the motor locations.

Figure 430-3 also illustrates each motor on an individual branch circuit, but, unlike Figure 430-2, the branch circuits are tapped from a subfeeder at a convenient location such as a junction box, wireway, or from open wiring. The branch-circuit short-circuit and ground-fault protective device may be located where taps are connected to the subfeeder or may be located at any point within 25 ft of where the taps are connected to the subfeeder in accordance with Section 430-28.

Where motors or motor-operated appliances are connected to a 15- or 20-A branch circuit that also supplies lighting, or other appliance loads, as illustrated in Figure 430-4, the provisions of Articles 210 and 430 are to apply. Motors rated less than one hp may be connected to these circuits and are to be provided with overload protective devices unless the motors are not permanently installed, are started manually, and are within sight from the controller location. For additional information for the installation of motors (1 hp or less), see Sections 430-32(b) and (c), and 430-53(a).

Figure 430-5 illustrates the essential parts of a motor branch circuit: (1) the branch-circuit conductors, (2) the disconnecting means, (3) the branch-circuit short-circuit and ground-fault protective devices, and (4) the motor overload protective devices. The branch-circuit short-circuit and ground-fault protective device may be fuses or a circuit breaker and must be capable of carrying the starting current of the motor without opening the circuit. See Table 430-152.

In general, it is required that every motor be provided with overload protective devices intended to protect motors, motor-control apparatus and motor branch-circuit conductors against excessive heating due to motor overloads and failure to start. Overload in equipment is considered to be operation in excess of normal, full-load rating, which, when it persists for a sufficient length of time, will cause damage or dangerous overheating. Overload in a motor includes stalled rotor, but does not include fault currents due to short circuits or grounds. See Section 430-44 for conditions where providing automatic opening of a motor circuit due to overload may be objectionable.

A motor is considered to be for continuous duty unless the nature of the apparatus it drives is such that the motor cannot operate continuously with load under any condition of use. Conductors for a motor used for short-time, intermittent, periodic, or varying duty are to have an ampacity in accordance with Table 430-22(a) Exception. Branch-circuit conductors for a motor with a rated horsepower used for 5-minute short-time duty service are permitted to be sized smaller than for the same motor with a 60-minute rating, due to the cooling intervals between operating periods.

When selecting the smallest permissible size branch-circuit conductors for

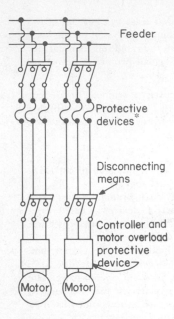

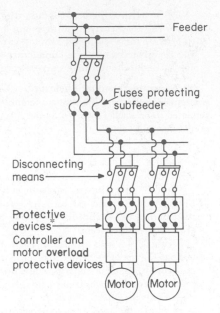

Figure 430-2. Layout showing each motor supplied by an individual branch circuit from a distribution center (*branch-circuit, short-circuit and ground-fault protective devices).

Figure 430-3. Layout showing a subfeeder supplying individual branch circuits to each motor (*branch-circuit, short-circuit and ground-fault protective devices).

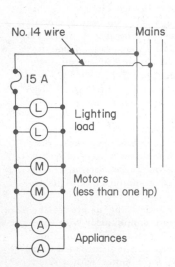

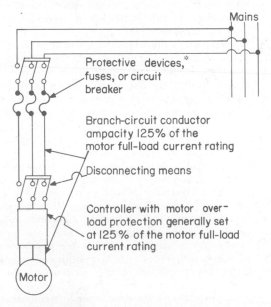

Figure 430-4. Layout showing a 15- or 20-A branch circuit supplying small motors, lamps, and appliances.

Figure 430-5. A motor branch circuit showing the three essential parts, that is, the branch-circuit conductors, branch-circuit overcurrent protection, and motor overload protection.

elevator motors, which are generally considered intermittent service motors, it is safest to be guided by the recommendations of the manufacturer of the equipment. This also applies to feeders of two or more elevator motors or other types of similar equipment.

430-23. Wound-Rotor Secondary.

(a) Continuous Duty. For continuous duty, the conductors connecting the secondary of a wound-rotor alternating-current motor to its controller shall have an ampacity not less than 125 percent of the full-load secondary current of the motor.

(b) Other than Continuous Duty. For other than continuous duty, these conductors shall have an ampacity, in percent of full-load secondary current, not less than that specified in Table 430-22(a) Exception.

(c) Resistor Separate from Controller. Where the secondary resistor is separate from the controller, the ampacity of the conductors between controller and resistor shall not be less than that given in Table 430-23(c).

Table 430-23(c).   Secondary Conductor

Resistor Duty Classification	Ampacity of Wire in Percent of Full-Load Secondary Current
Light starting duty	35
Heavy starting duty	45
Extra-heavy starting duty	55
Light intermittent duty	65
Medium intermittent duty	75
Heavy intermittent duty	85
Continuous duty	110

Wound-rotor ac motors are generally used where speed control is desired, where high-starting torque for a rapid smooth acceleration to full load is required, for frequent starting, and for low starting current. These motors are also known as slip-ring motors because three slip rings are mounted on the shaft, and brushes, which are in contact with the slip rings, are connected to field-installed external resistance units and a controller. See Figure 430-6. The resistors are a part of the rotor circuit and all of the resistance value is in the circuit when starting the motor. This value is reduced gradually until all of it is out of the circuit and the motor is at maximum speed, or until the motor is at a desired speed.

The selection of a controller used for speed regulation, usually a dial-type or a drum-type switch, is basically for two types of loads, that is, constant-torque (machine loads) and variable-torque (fan loads).

The ampacities of the conductors between the controller and the resistor units are the allowable percentages of Table 430-23(c) for the resistor classification of duty.

430-24. Conductors Supplying Several Motors.
Conductors supplying two or more motors shall have an ampacity equal to the sum of the full-load current rating of all the motors plus 25 percent of the highest rated motor in the group.

Where one or more motors of the group are used on short-time, intermittent, periodic, or varying duty, the ampacity of the conductors shall be computed as follows:

(1) Determine the needed ampere rating for each motor used for other than continuous duty from Table 430-22(a) Exception.

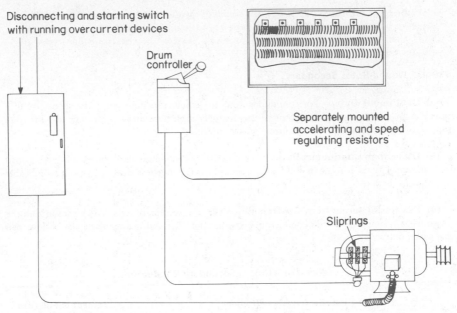

Disconnecting and starting switch
with running overcurrent devices

Drum
controller

Separately mounted
accelerating and speed
regulating resistors

Sliprings

Figure 430-6. A branch circuit to a wound-rotor induction motor showing a drum controller and separate bank of resistors for motor starting and speed regulation.

(2) Determine the needed ampere rating for each continuous-duty motor based on 100 percent motor full-load current rating.

(3) Multiply the largest single motor ampere rating determined from (1) or (2) above by 1.25. Add all other motor ampere ratings from (1) and (2) above and select the conductor ampacity for this total ampere rating.

Exception: Where the circuitry is so interlocked as to prevent the starting and running of a second motor or group of motors, the conductor size shall be determined from the larger motor or group of motors that is to be operated at a given time.

See Example No. 8, Chapter 9.

Where the conductors are feeders, the highest rating or setting of the feeder short-circuit and ground-fault protective devices for the minimum size feeder conductor permitted by this section is specified in Section 430-62.

The size of the feeder conductors is to be increased accordingly where the selection of a feeder protective device of higher rating or setting is based on the simultaneous starting of two or more motors.

These requirements, and those of Section 430-62 for the short-circuit and ground-fault protection of power feeders, are based upon the principle that a power feeder should be of such size that it will have an ampacity equal to 125 percent of the running current of the largest motor, plus the full-load running currents of all other motors supplied by the feeder. Except when two or more motors may be started simultaneously, the heaviest load that a power feeder will ever be required to carry occurs when the largest motor is started at a time when all the other motors supplied by the same feeder are running and delivering their full-rated horsepower.

Where the conductors are branch-circuit conductors to multimotor equipment, Section 430-53 specifies the maximum rating of the branch-circuit short-circuit and ground-fault protective device. Section 430-7(d) requires the maximum ampere rating of the short-circuit and ground-fault protective device to be marked on the equipment.

430-25. Conductors Supplying Motors and Other Loads.

(a) Combination Load. Conductors supplying a motor load and in addition a lighting or appliance load shall have an ampacity sufficient for the lighting or appliance load computed in accordance with Article 220 and other applicable sections plus the motor load determined in accordance with Section 430-24 or, for a single motor, in accordance with Section 430-22.

Exception: The ampacity of conductors supplying motor-operated fixed electric space heating equipment shall conform with Section 424-3(b).

(b) Multimotor and Combination-Load Equipment. The ampacity of the conductors supplying multimotor and combination-load equipment shall not be less than the minimum circuit ampacity marked on the equipment in accordance with Section 430-7(d).

To compute the load for the minimum allowable conductor size for a combination lighting (or lighting and appliance) load and motor load, the capacity for the lighting load is determined in accordance with Article 220 (and other applicable sections, Article 424, etc.) plus the sum of the motor load, determined in accordance with Section 430-22 (single motor), or Section 430-24 (two or more motors).

430-26. Feeder Demand Factor.
Where reduced heating of the conductors results from motors operating on duty-cycle, intermittently, or from all motors not operating at one time, the authority having jurisdiction may grant permission for feeder conductors to have an ampacity less than specified in Sections 430-24 and 430-25, provided the conductors have sufficient ampacity for the maximum load determined in accordance with the sizes and number of motors supplied and the character of their loads and duties.

The authority having jurisdiction may grant permission to allow a demand factor of less than 100 percent for industrial plants where operational procedures, production demands, or the nature of the work is such that all the motors are not running at one time.

430-27. Capacitors with Motors.
Where capacitors are installed in motor circuits, conductors shall comply with Sections 460-7, 460-8, and 460-9.

430-28. Feeder Taps.
Feeder tap conductors shall have an ampacity not less than that required by Part B, shall terminate in a branch-circuit protective device and, in addition, shall meet one of the following requirements: (1) be enclosed by either an enclosed controller or by a raceway and be not more than 10 feet (3.05 m) in length; or (2) have an ampacity of at least one-third that of the feeder conductors, be protected from physical damage and be not more than 25 feet (7.62 m) in length; or (3) have the same ampacity as the feeder conductors.

No short-circuit and ground-fault protection is needed at a point where a tap conductor, equal in size to the feeder conductor from which it is supplied, is used. The tap conductors will be protected by the same short-circuit and ground-fault protection (fuses or circuit breakers) protecting the feeder conductors.

In addition to the above, short-circuit and ground-fault protection may be omitted at the point of connection to a feeder where a tap conductor, which may be less than ⅓ of the feeder size, is limited to 10 ft or less in length and enclosed within a controller or raceway, and where a tap conductor, which is at least ⅓ the ampacity of the feeder, is limited to 25 ft or less in length and suitably protected from physical damage.

Tap conductors are to terminate in a branch-circuit short-circuit and ground-fault protective device and, from this point to the motor-running protective device and to the motor, conductors are run having the standard ampacity, that is, 125 percent of the full-load motor current, as specified in Section 430-22.

Example: A 15-hp 230-V 3-phase motor with autotransformer starter is to be supplied by a tap made to a 250,000 CM feeder. Assuming all conductors to be Type THW copper, the feeder has an ampacity of 255 A (see Table 310-16). Where the tap conductors are not over 25 ft long (see Figure 430-7), No. 4 AWG conductors with an ampacity of 85 A are permitted (⅓ x 255 A = 85 A).

The full-load current of the motor is 40 A and, according to Part D of Article 430, assuming that the motor is not marked with a code letter, the branch-circuit fuses should be rated at 125 A or less. With the motor overload protection set at 50 A the tap conductors are well protected from overload.

Tap conductors, connected to feeders, must never be sized smaller than the ampacity of branch-circuit conductors required by Section 430-22.

C. Motor and Branch-Circuit Overload Protection

430-31. General.   Part C specifies overload devices intended to protect motors, motor-control apparatus, and motor branch-circuit conductors against excessive heating due to motor overloads and failure to start.

Overload in electrical apparatus is an operating overcurrent which, when it persists for a sufficient length of time, would cause damage or dangerous overheating of the apparatus. It does not include short circuits or ground faults.

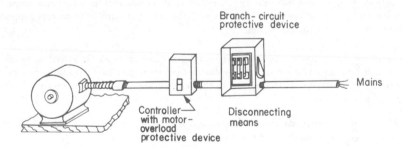

Figure 430-7. Protective devices (branch-circuit, short-circuit and ground-fault) for a branch circuit located not more than 25 ft from the point where the conductors are tapped to the main feeder.

These provisions shall not be interpreted as requiring overload protection where it might introduce additional or increased hazards, as in the case of fire pumps.

See Installation of Centrifugal Fire Pumps, NFPA 20-1978 (ANSI).

See Section 230-90(a), Exception No. 5 for the comments on centrifugal fire pumps.

The provisions of Part C shall not apply to motor circuits rated over 600 volts, nominal. See Part J.

NFPA 20-1978 contains, in general, the minimum requirements for the selection and installation of centrifugal fire pumps.

Table 430-152 gives the allowable percentages of full-load current for the selection of the maximum rating or setting of motor branch-circuit short-circuit and ground-fault protective devices. The motor branch-circuit, short-circuit and ground-fault protective device is to be capable of carrying the starting current of the motor without opening the circuit; therefore, the protective device must have a rating that is too high to provide overload protection for the motor.

Fire pump motors require circuit breakers and are allowed much larger short-circuit and ground-fault protection than other motors recognizing that the pump should be allowed to operate to failure rather than being removed from the line, under adverse fire conditions. A manually operated fuseless isolating switch is required to be connected ahead (supply side) of the circuit breaker.

For squirrel-cage induction motors, which are generally used, the circuit breaker is to be of the time-delay type and have a time delay of not over 20 seconds at locked-rotor current (approximately 600 percent of the rated full-load motor current) and is to be calibrated up to and set at 300 percent of the motor full-load current.

Combined overload protection (special-type fuses), as described in Section 430-55, is permitted as a single protective device. In most cases where motor overload protection is provided, however, the motor controller consists of a switch or contactor to control the circuit to the motor, and the motor-overload protective device is a heater coil.

For more detailed information, see the comments following Section 230-90(a), Exception No. 5.

430-32. Continuous-Duty Motors.

(a) More than 1 Horsepower.   Each continuous-duty motor rated more than 1 horsepower shall be protected against overload by one of the following means:

(1) A separate overload device that is responsive to motor current. This device shall be selected to trip or rated at no more than the following percent of the motor nameplate full-load current rating.

Motors with a marked service factor not less than 1.15 .... 125%
Motors with a marked temperature rise not over 40°C 125%
All other motors 115%

This value may be modified as permitted by Section 430-34.

For a multispeed motor, each winding connection shall be considered separately.

Where a separate motor overload device is so connected that it does not carry the total current designated on the motor nameplate, such as for wye-delta starting, the proper percentage of nameplate current applying to the selection or setting of the overload device shall be clearly designated on the equipment, or the manufacturer's selection table shall take this into account.

(2) A thermal protector integral with the motor, approved for use with the motor it protects on the basis that it will prevent dangerous overheating of the motor due to overload and failure to start. The ultimate trip current of a thermally protected motor shall not exceed the following percentage of motor full-load current given in Tables 430-148, 430-149, and 430-150.

Motor full-load current not exceeding 9 amperes 170%
Motor full-load current 9.1 to and including 20 amperes 156%
Motor full-load current greater than 20 amperes 140%

If the motor current-interrupting device is separate from the motor and its control circuit is operated by a protective device integral with the motor, it shall be so arranged that the opening of the control circuit will result in interruption of current to the motor.

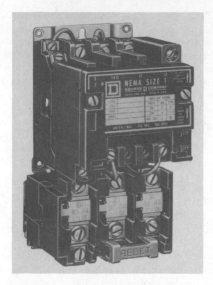

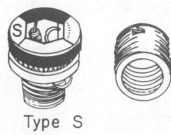

Type S

Figure 430-8. Line-voltage magnetic starter. (*Square D Co.*)

Figure 430-9. A Type S nonrenewable fuse.

(3) A motor shall be considered as being properly protected if it is a part of an approved assembly that does not normally subject the motor to overloads and if there is a protective device integral with the motor that will protect the motor against damage due to failure to start.

(4) For motors larger than 1500 horsepower, a protective device having embedded temperature detectors that cause current to the motor to be interrupted when the motor attains a temperature rise greater than marked on the nameplate in an ambient of 40°C.

(b) One Horsepower or Less, Nonautomatically Started.

(1) Each continuous-duty motor rated at 1 horsepower or less that is not permanently installed, is nonautomatically started, and is within sight from the controller location shall be considered as protected against overload by the branch-circuit short circuit and ground-fault protective device. This branch-circuit protective device shall not be larger than that specified in Part D of Article 430.

Exception: Any such motor shall be permitted on a nominal 120-volt branch circuit protected at not over 20 amperes.

(2) Any such motor that is not in sight from the controller location shall be protected as specified in Section 430-32(c). Any motor rated at 1 horsepower or less that is permanently installed shall be protected in accordance with Section 430-32(c).

(c) One Horsepower or Less, Automatically Started. Any motor of 1 horsepower or less that is started automatically shall be protected against overload by one of the following means:

(1) A separate overload device that is responsive to motor current. This device shall be selected to trip or rated at no more than the following percentage of the motor nameplate full-load current rating.

Motors with a marked service factor not less than 1.15 .... 125%
Motors with a marked temperature rise not over 40°C 125%
All other motors 115%

For a multispeed motor, each winding connection shall be considered separately. Modification of this value shall be permitted as provided in Section 430-34.

(2) A thermal protector integral with the motor, approved for use with the motor which it protects on the basis that it will prevent dangerous overheating of the motor due to overload and failure to start. Where the motor current interrupting device is separate from the motor and its control circuit is operated by a protective device integral with the motor, it shall be so arranged that the opening of the control circuit will result in interruption of current to the motor.

(3) A motor shall be considered as being properly protected if it is part of an approved assembly that does not normally subject the motor to overloads and if there is a protective device integral with the motor that will protect the motor against damage due to failure to start, or if the assembly is also equipped with other safety controls (such as the safety combustion controls of a domestic oil burner) that protect the motor against damage due to failure to start. Where the assembly has safety controls that protect the motor, it shall be so indicated on the nameplate of the assembly where it will be visible after installation.

(4) In case the impedance of the motor windings is sufficient to prevent overheating due to failure to start, the motor shall be permitted to be protected as specified in Section 430-32(b) (1) for manually started motors if the motor is part of an approved assembly in which the motor will limit itself so that it will not be dangerously overheated.

Many alternating-current motors of less than $\frac{1}{20}$ horsepower, such as clock motors, series motors, etc., and also some larger motors such as torque motors, come within this classification. It does not include split-phase motors having automatic switches that disconnect the starting windings.

(d) Wound-Rotor Secondaries.   The secondary circuits of wound-rotor alternating-current motors, including conductors, controllers, resistors, etc., shall be considered as protected against overload by the motor-overload device.

Operation of a motor in excess of its normal full-load rating for a prolonged period of time would cause damage or dangerous overheating. Overload protection is intended to protect the motor and the system components from damaging overload currents.

A continuous-duty motor with a marked service factor not less than 1.15 or with a marked temperature rise not over 40°C (104°F) can carry a 25 percent overload for an extended period of time without damage to the motor. Other types of motors, that is, those with a service factor less than 1.15 or with a marked temperature rise greater than 40°C (104°F), are not capable of withstanding a prolonged overload and the motor-overload protective device should open the circuit should the motor continue to draw 115 percent of its rated full-load current.

A thermal protector located inside the motor housing is connected in series with the motor winding. This protective device commonly consists of two contacts attached to a bimetallic disk through which the circuit is normally "closed." The thermal protector heating coil (in series with the motor winding) causes the disk to heat rapidly and the heat-actuated disk snaps "open" to protect the motor against failure to start, a sudden heavy overload, or dangerous overheating due to a prolonged overload.

After opening the circuit and after the motor has cooled to a normal temperature, the contacts will automatically close and restart the motor. In some cases this may not be desirable. For such applications the protective device is so designed that it must be returned to the closed position by a manually controlled reset button as required by Section 430-43. See Figures 430-10 and 430-11. For larger motors (usually over 1 hp) a similar device is used. This device, upon abnormal overload, acts as a relay and operates the control circuit of a motor current-interrupting device located separately from the motor, usually a motor contactor or starter. A thermal protector and circuit-interrupting device should be approved for use with the motor it protects and is to open the circuit on an overcurrent as specified in Section 430-32(a)(2).

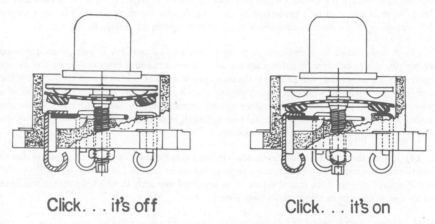

Click. . . it's off   Click. . . it's on

Figure 430-10. A thermal protector for a motor. A heat-sensitive, snap-action disk opens contacts and protects the motor against dangerous overheating. (*Texas Instruments, Inc.*)

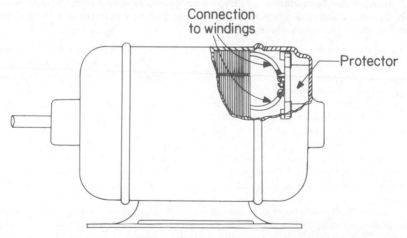

Figure 430-11. Integral mounting of the thermal protective device (Fig. 430-10) in a motor housing.

430-33. Intermittent and Similar Duty.   A motor used for a condition of service that is inherently short-time, intermittent, periodic, or varying duty, as illustrated by Table 430-22(a) Exception, shall be considered as protected against overload by the branch-circuit short-circuit and ground-fault protective device, provided the protective device rating or setting does not exceed that specified in Table 430-152.

Any motor application shall be considered to be for continuous duty unless the nature of the apparatus it drives is such that the motor cannot operate continuously with load under any condition of use.

Where a motor is selected for duty-cycle service (intermittent, short-time, periodic, or varying), it can be assumed that the motor will not operate continuously due to the nature of the apparatus or machinery it drives. Therefore, prolonged overloads are not likely to occur unless mechanical failure in the driven apparatus stalls the motor; however, in this case the branch-circuit protective device would open the circuit. The omission of overload protective devices for such motors is based upon the type of "duty" and not upon the time "rating" of the motor.

430-34. Selection of Overload Relay.   Where the overload relay selected in accordance with Section 430-32(a) (1) and (c) (1) is not sufficient to start the motor or to carry the load, the next higher size overload relay shall be permitted to be used provided the trip current of the overload relay does not exceed the following percentage of motor full-load current rating.

Motors with marked service factor not less than 1.15 .... 140%
Motors with a marked temperature rise not over 40°C 140%
All other motors 130%

If not shunted during the starting period of the motor as provided in Section 430-35, the overload device shall have sufficient time delay to permit the motor to start and accelerate its load.

430-35. Shunting During Starting Period.

(a) Nonautomatically Started.   For a nonautomatically started motor the overload protection shall be permitted to be shunted or cut out of the circuit during the starting period of the motor if the device by which the overload protection is shunted or cut out cannot be left in the starting position and if fuses or inverse time circuit breakers rated or set at not over 400 percent of the full-load current of the motor are so located in the circuit as to be operative during the starting period of the motor.

(b) Automatically Started.   The motor overload protection shall not be shunted or cut out during the starting period if the motor is automatically started.

Figure 430-12. Arrangement for across-the-line starting of a motor. When the switch is thrown momentarily to the left to start the motor, the running fuses are shunted or cut out of the circuit. The switch is then thrown to the right (running position) and must be so designed that it cannot be left in the starting position.

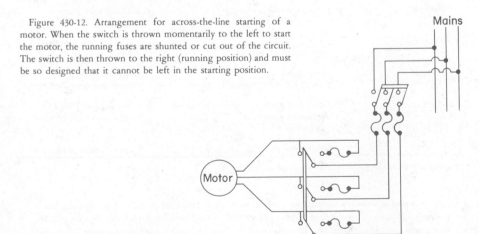

Mains

Motor

If not shunted during the starting period of the motor, the overload device is to have sufficient time delay to start and accelerate its load; whereas if shunting is employed, the overload protection is cut out of the circuit during the starting period of the motor. See Figure 430-12.

Where fuses are used as overload protection, they may be shunted or cut out of the circuit during the starting period by a device (in this case a double-throw switch designed so that it cannot be left in the starting position). Therefore, during the starting period, the motor is protected only by the branch-circuit fuses that are always rated within the limits of this section. If there are no branch-circuit fuses, as permitted by Section 430-53, then a starter (shunting) device is not allowed during the starting period unless the feeder protection is within the limits of this section (not over 400 percent of the full-load motor current).

430-36. Fuses — In Which Conductor.   Where fuses are used for motor overload protection, a fuse shall be inserted in each ungrounded conductor.

A fuse shall also be inserted in the grounded conductor if the supply system is 3-wire, 3-phase ac with one conductor grounded.

430-37. Devices Other than Fuses — In Which Conductor.   Where devices other than fuses are used for motor overload protection, Table 430-37 shall govern the minimum allowable number and location of overload units such as trip coils, relays, or thermal cutouts.

Table 430-37.   Overload Units

Kind of Motor	Supply System	Number and location of overload units, such as trip coils, relays, or thermal cutouts
1-phase ac or dc	2-wire, 1-phase ac or dc ungrounded	1 in either conductor
1-phase ac or dc	2-wire, 1-phase ac or dc, one conductor grounded	1 in ungrounded conductor
1-phase ac or dc	3-wire, 1-phase ac or dc, grounded-neutral	1 in either ungrounded conductor
2-phase ac	3-wire, 2-phase ac, ungrounded	2, one in each phase
2-phase ac	3-wire, 2-phase ac, one conductor grounded	2 in ungrounded conductors
2-phase ac	4-wire, 2-phase ac, grounded or ungrounded	2, one per phase in ungrounded conductors
2-phase ac	5-wire, 2-phase ac, grounded neutral or ungrounded	2, one per phase in any ungrounded phase wire
3-phase ac	Any 3-phase	*3, one in each phase

Exception: Where protected by other approved means.

All 3-phase motors should be provided with three-unit protection (one in each phase). The exceptions are those protected by other approved means. Specially designed or integral-type detectors with or without supplementary external protective devices are some exceptions.

430-38. Number of Conductors Opened by Overload Device. Motor overload devices other than fuses, thermal cutouts, or thermal protectors shall simultaneously open a sufficient number of ungrounded conductors to interrupt current flow to the motor.

430-39. Motor Controller as Overload Protection. A motor controller shall also be permitted to serve as an overload device if the number of overload units complies with Table 430-37 and if these units are operative in both the starting and running position in the case of a direct-current motor, and in the running position in the case of an alternating-current motor.

For the purpose of this article, a controller may be a switch, a circuit breaker, a contactor, or other device to start and stop a motor and is to be capable of interrupting the stalled-rotor current of the motor and have a hp rating not lower than the hp rating of the motor.

Dual-element fuses can be sized to provide motor overload protection. See Section 430-36. Automatically operated contactors or circuit breakers (with trip units) are to be governed by the requirements of Sections 430-37 and 430-38.

430-40. Thermal Cutouts and Overload Relays. Thermal cutouts, overload relays, and other devices for motor overload protection that are not capable of opening short circuits shall be protected by fuses or circuit breakers with ratings or settings in accordance with Section 430-52 or by a motor short-circuit protector in accordance with Section 430-52.

Exception No. 1: Where approved for group installation and marked to indicate the maximum size of fuse or inverse time circuit breaker by which they must be protected.

Exception No. 2: The fuse or circuit breaker ampere rating shall be permitted to be marked on the nameplate of approved equipment in which the thermal cutout or overload relay is used.

For instantaneous trip circuit breakers or motor short-circuit protectors, see Section 430-52.

430-42. Motors on General-Purpose Branch Circuits. Overload protection for motors used on general-purpose branch circuits as permitted in Article 210 shall be provided as specified in (a), (b), (c), or (d) below.

(a) Not Over 1 Horsepower. One or more motors without individual overload protection shall be permitted to be connected to a general-purpose branch circuit only where the installation complies with the limiting conditions specified in Section 430-53(a) (1) and (a) (2).

(b) Over 1 Horsepower. Motors of larger ratings than specified in Section 430-53(a) shall be permitted to be connected to general-purpose branch circuits only where each motor is protected by overload protection selected to protect the motor as specified in Section 430-32. Both the controller and the motor overload device shall be approved for group installation with the short-circuit and ground-fault protective device selected in accordance with Section 430-53.

(c) Cord- and Plug-Connected. Where a motor is connected to a branch circuit by means of an attachment plug and receptacle and individual overload protection is omitted as provided in (a) above, the rating of the attachment plug and receptacle shall not exceed 15 amperes at 125 volts or 10 amperes at 250 volts. Where individual overload protection is required as provided in (b) above for a motor or motor-operated appliance that is attached to the branch circuit through an attachment plug and receptacle, the overload device shall be an integral part of the motor or of the appliance. The rating of the attachment plug and receptacle shall determine the rating of the circuit to which the motor may be connected, as provided in Article 210.

(d) Time Delay. The branch-circuit short-circuit and ground-fault protective device protecting a circuit to which a motor or motor-operated appliance is connected shall have sufficient time delay to permit the motor to start and accelerate its load.

Two or more motors, or one or more motors and other loads, may be connected to the same 120-V, 15- or 20-A single-phase lighting circuit. The provision is that each motor must be rated not more than 1 hp, the full-load rating of each motor must not exceed 6 A, and the rating of the branch-circuit protective device must not be exceeded.

Motors with ratings larger than 1 hp or 6 A may be connected to general-purpose branch circuits only if the motor is protected against overload as required by Section 430-32.

It is to be noted that the requirements for overload protection as provided in Section 430-32 are to be applied in all cases regardless of the number (one or more) of motors or the type of branch circuit.

430-43. Automatic Restarting. A motor overload device that can restart a motor automatically after overload tripping shall not be installed unless approved for use with the motor it protects. A motor that can restart automatically after shutdown shall not be installed if its automatic restarting can result in injury to persons.

An integral motor overload protective device may be of the type that, after tripping and sufficiently cooling, will automatically restart the motor, or it may be of the type that, after tripping, returns to a closed position by use of a manually operated reset button. See comments following Section 430-32.

430-44. Orderly Shutdown. If immediate automatic shutdown of a motor by a motor overload protective device(s) would introduce additional or increased hazard(s) to a person(s) and continued motor operation is necessary for safe shutdown of equipment or process, a motor overload sensing device(s) conforming with the provisions of Part C of this article shall be permitted to be connected to a supervised alarm instead of causing immediate interruption of the motor circuit, so that corrective action or an orderly shutdown can be initiated.

D. Motor Branch-Circuit Short-Circuit and Ground-Fault Protection

430-51. General. Part D specifies devices intended to protect the motor branch-circuit conductors, the motor control apparatus, and the motors against overcurrent due to short circuits or grounds. They add to or amend the provisions of Article 240. The devices specified in Part D do not include the types of devices required by Sections 210-8 and 230-95.

The provisions of Part D do not apply to motor circuits rated over 600 volts, nominal. See Part J.

430-52. Rating or Setting for Individual Motor Circuit. The motor branch-circuit short-circuit and ground-fault protective device shall be capable of carrying the starting current of the motor. The required protection shall be considered as being obtained where the protective device has a rating or setting not exceeding the values given in Table 430-152.

Exception No. 1: Where the values for branch-circuit short- circuit and ground-fault protective devices determined by Table 430-152 do not correspond to the standard sizes or ratings of fuses, nonadjustable circuit breakers, or thermal protective devices, or possible settings of adjustable circuit breakers adequate to carry the load, the next higher size, rating, or setting shall be permitted.

Exception No. 2: Where the rating specified in Table 430-152 is not sufficient for the starting current of the motor:

a. The rating of a nontime-delay fuse not exceeding 600 amperes shall be permitted to be increased but shall in no case exceed 400 percent of the full-load current.

b. The rating of a time-delay (dual element) fuse shall be permitted to be increased but shall in no case exceed 225 percent of the full-load current.

c. The rating of an inverse time circuit breaker shall be permitted to be increased but shall in no case exceed (1) 400 percent for full-load currents of 100 amperes or less, or (2) 300 percent for full-load currents greater than 100 amperes.

d. The rating of a fuse of 601-6000 ampere classification shall be permitted to be increased but shall in no case exceed 300 percent of the full-load current.

Exception No. 3: Torque motor branch circuits shall be protected at the motor nameplate current rating in accordance with Section 240-3, Exception No. 1.

See Section 240-6 for standard ratings of fuses and circuit breakers.

An instantaneous trip circuit breaker shall be used only if adjustable, and if part of a combination controller having motor overload and also short-circuit and ground-fault protection in each conductor. A motor short-circuit protector shall be permitted in lieu of devices listed in Table 430-152 if the motor short-circuit protector is part of a combination controller having both motor overload protection and short-circuit and ground-fault protection in each conductor and if it will operate at not more than 1300 percent of full-load motor current. An instantaneous trip circuit breaker or motor short-circuit protector shall be used only as part of a combination motor controller which provides coordinated motor branch-circuit overload and short-circuit and ground-fault protection.

Exception: Where the setting specified in Table 430-152 is not sufficient for the starting current of the motor, the setting of an instantaneous trip circuit breaker shall be permitted to be increased but shall in no case exceed 1300 percent of the motor full-load current.

For a multispeed motor, a single short-circuit and ground-fault protective device shall be permitted for two or more windings of the motor, provided the rating of the protective device does not exceed the above applicable percentage of the nameplate rating of the smallest winding protected.

Where maximum branch-circuit short-circuit and ground-fault protective device ratings are shown in the manufacturer's overload relay table for use with a motor controller or are otherwise marked on the equipment, they shall not be exceeded even if higher values are allowed as shown above.

See Example No. 8 in Chapter 9 and Diagram 430-1.

Suitable fuses shall be permitted in lieu of devices listed in Table 430-152 for an adjustable speed drive system provided that the marking for replacement fuses is provided adjacent to the fuses.

This section defines the maximum allowable ratings or settings of devices acceptable (fuses or circuit breakers) for motor branch-circuit short-circuit and ground-fault protection and states that these devices are expected to carry the starting currents of the motor and to provide short-circuit and ground-fault protection.

For certain exceptions to the maximum rating or setting of these motor branch-circuit protective devices as specified in Table 430-152, see Sections 430-52, 430-53, and 430-54. See Figure 430-2.

Section 430-6 provides that where the current rating of a motor is used to determine the ampacity of conductors or ampere ratings of switches, branch-circuit overcurrent devices, etc., the values given in Tables 430-147 through 430-150 (including notes) are to be used instead of the actual motor nameplate current rating. Separate motor overload protection is to be based on the motor nameplate current rating.

Figure 430-5 illustrates a typical motor circuit where the branch-circuit short-circuit and ground-fault protective fuses or circuit breaker rating must carry the starting current and may be sized 150 to 300 percent of the motor full-load current (depending on the type of motor). It should be noted that it is not necessary to size the branch-circuit conductors to the percentages (150 to 300) permitted for the branch-circuit short-circuit and ground-fault protective devices.

The rules for short-circuit and ground-fault protection are specific for particular situations. A short circuit is a fault between two conductors or between phases. A ground fault is a fault to ground. During a short circuit or fault-to-ground condition, the extreme excess current would cause the protective fuses or circuit breakers to open the circuit. Excess current flow caused by an overload condition must pass through the overload protective device at the motor controller thereby causing this device to open the circuit. Branch-circuit conductors with an ampacity of 125 percent (Note: not 150 to 300 percent) of the motor full-load current are reasonably protected by motor-protective devices set to operate at nearly the same current as the ampacity of the conductors. Branch-circuit short-circuit and ground-fault protective devices will open the circuit under short-circuit conditions and thereby provide short-circuit and ground-fault protection for both the motor and overload protective device; however, the overload protective device is not intended to open short circuits or ground faults.

Section 430-7 provides for information that is to be marked on motor nameplates. AC motors, rated ½ hp or more, are to be marked with code letters in accordance with Table 430-7(b) which are used to determine the correct rating of the branch-circuit protective devices. For motors smaller than ½ hp, or for the many motors still in use without code letters, the provisions of Table 430-152 are to apply.

The rating or setting of the branch-circuit short-circuit and ground-fault protective device should be sized as low as possible for maximum protection; however, where the rating or setting specified in Table 430-152 is not sufficient for the starting current of the motor, such as in the case of severe starting conditions where the motor and its driven machinery requires an extended period of time to reach its desired speed, it is allowable to use a higher rating or setting as permitted in the Exception to Section 430-52.

The rating or setting of short-circuit and ground-fault protection for one branch circuit supplying two or more motors should not be larger than marked on the equipment in accordance with Section 430-7(d). Where not marked on the equipment, the maximum is computed in accordance with Section 430-53(c)(4).

430-53. Several Motors or Loads on One Branch Circuit.   Two or more motors or one or more motors and other loads shall be permitted to be connected to the same branch circuit under the conditions specified in (a), (b), or (c) below.

(a) Not Over 1 Horsepower.   Several motors each not exceeding 1 horsepower in rating shall be permitted on a nominal 120 volt branch circuit protected at not over 20 amperes or a branch circuit of 600 volts, nominal, or less, protected at not over 15 amperes, if all of the following conditions are met:

(1) The full-load rating of each motor does not exceed 6 amperes.

(2) The rating of the branch-circuit short-circuit and ground-fault protective device marked on any of the controllers is not exceeded.

(3) Individual overload protection conforms to Section 430-32.

(b) If Smallest Motor Protected.   If the branch-circuit short-circuit and ground-fault protective device is selected not to exceed that allowed by Section 430-52 for the motor of the smallest rating, two or more motors or one or more motors and other load(s), with each motor having individual overload protection, shall be permitted to be connected to a branch circuit where it can be determined that the branch-circuit short-circuit and ground-fault protective device will not open under the most severe normal conditions of service that might be encountered.

(c) Other Group Installation.   Two or more motors of any rating or one or more motors and other load(s), with each motor having individual overload protection, shall be permitted to be connected to one branch circuit if all of the following conditions are complied with:

(1) Each motor overload device is approved for group installation with a specified maximum rating of fuse and/or inverse time circuit breaker.

(2) Each motor controller is approved for group installation with a specified maximum rating of fuse and/or circuit breaker.

(3) Each circuit breaker is one of the inverse time type and approved for group installation.

(4) The branch circuit shall be protected by fuses or inverse time circuit breakers having a rating not exceeding that specified in Section 430-52 for the largest motor connected to the branch circuit plus an amount equal to the sum of the full-load current ratings of all other motors and the ratings of other loads connected to the circuit. Where this calculation results in a rating less than the ampacity of the supply conductors, it shall be permitted to increase the maximum rating of the fuses or circuit breaker to a value not exceeding that permitted by Section 240-3, Exception No. 1.

(5) The branch-circuit fuses or inverse time circuit breakers are not larger than allowed by Section 430-40 for the thermal cutout or overload relay protecting the smallest motor of the group.

(d) Single Motor Taps.   For group installations described above, the conductors of any tap supplying a single motor shall not be required to have an individual branch-circuit short-circuit and ground-fault protective device, provided they comply with either of the following: (1) no conductor to the motor shall have an ampacity less than that of the branch-circuit conductors, or (2) no conductor to the motor shall have an ampacity less than one-third that of the branch-circuit conductors, with a minimum in accordance with Section 430-22; the conductors to the motor overload device being not more than 25 feet (7.62 m) long and being protected from physical damage.

The following two examples describe installations permitting the omission of individual motor branch-circuit short-circuit and ground-fault protective devices. See Figures 430-13 and 430-14.

Figure 430-13 illustrates main branch-circuit conductors supplying a motor that is part of a group installation. The tap conductors have an ampacity equal to the ampacity of the main branch-circuit conductors; therefore, branch-circuit short-circuit and ground-fault protective devices, fuses or circuit breakers for the conductors in the tap are not required at the point of connection of the tap conductors to the main conductors, provided that the motor controller and motor overload protective device are approved for group installation with the size of main branch-circuit short-circuit and ground-fault protective device used.

Figure 430-14 illustrates main branch-circuit conductors supplying a motor that is part of a group installation. The tap conductors have an ampacity at least one-third the ampacity of the main branch-circuit conductors, are no more than 25 ft in length, and are suitably protected from physical damage, as shown in Figure 430-13. The motor controller and motor overload protective device must be approved for group installation with the size of main branch-circuit short-circuit and ground-fault protective device used.

In both examples, the main branch-circuit fuses or circuit breakers would operate in the event of a short circuit and the overload protective device would operate to protect the motor and the tap conductors under overload conditions.

It should be noted that the tap conductors should never be of a smaller size and ampacity than the branch-circuit conductors required by Section 430-22; that is, a tap conductor (25 ft or less) may be ⅓ the ampacity of the main branch-circuit conductor to which it is connected. However, this ampacity must be equal to or larger than 125 percent of the motor full-load current rating (see Section 430-22). For example, a feeder sized at No. 2/0 copper THW has an ampacity of 175 A and a tap conductor (25 ft or less) would be permitted to be sized at No. 6 copper THW (65 A). However, if a 25-hp, 230-V, 3-phase, squirrel-cage motor is to be supplied from this feeder, a No. 6 tap conductor would not meet the requirements of Section 430-22; that is, 125 percent of the full-load current of the motor is 85 A [1.25 x 68 A (Table 430-150) = 85 A]. Therefore, the branch-circuit tap conductors must not be smaller than a No. 4 copper THW with an ampacity of 85 A (see Table 310-16).

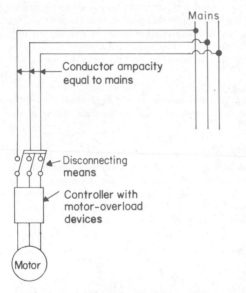

Figure 430-13. Motor branch-circuit protective devices can be omitted for tap conductors that have the same ampacity as the main branch-circuit conductors.

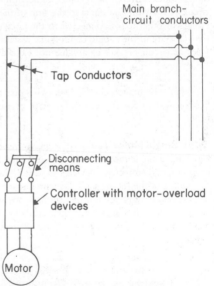

Figure 430-14. Motor branch-circuit protective devices can be omitted when the tap conductors have at least ⅓ the ampacity of the main conductors, are not over 25 ft long, and are protected from physical damage.

430-54. Multimotor and Combination-Load Equipment.   The rating of the branch-circuit short circuit and ground-fault protective device for multimotor and combination-load equipment shall not exceed the rating marked on the equipment in accordance with Section 430-7(d).

430-55. Combined Overcurrent Protection.   Motor branch-circuit short-circuit and ground fault protection and motor overload protection shall be permitted to be combined in a single protective device where the rating or setting of the device provides the overload protection specified in Section 430-32.

Either a circuit breaker with inverse time characteristics or a dual-element (time-delay) fuse may serve as both motor overload protection and also as the branch-circuit short-circuit and ground-fault protection. Figures 430-9, 430-15, and 430-16 are examples of dual-element fuses that are able to withstand the normal motor starting current when sized at or near the motor full-load rating, but open on a prolonged overload or "blow" rapidly on a short circuit or ground fault.

Figure 430-9 illustrates a dual-element Type S fuse that is available up to a 30-A rating and is designed to prevent oversize fusing. See Sections 240-51 through 240-54.

Figures 430-15 and 430-16 illustrate time-delay cartridge-type dual-element fuses. The dual-element characteristics, similar to those of the Type S fuse shown in Figure 430-9, are the "thermal cutout element," which permits harmless high inrush currents to flow for short periods (but would open the circuit during a prolonged period), and the "fuse link element," which has current limiting ability for short-circuit currents (and would "blow" rapidly). Dual-element fuses may be used in larger sizes to provide only short-circuit and ground-fault protection.

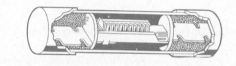

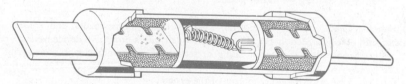

Figure 430-15. A Fusetron cartridge-type fuse. (*Bussmann Mfg. Co.*)

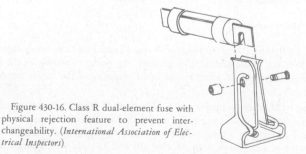

Figure 430-16. Class R dual-element fuse with physical rejection feature to prevent interchangeability. (*International Association of Electrical Inspectors*)

430-56. Branch-Circuit Protective Devices — In Which Conductor.   Branch-circuit protective devices shall comply with the provisions of Section 240-20.

430-57. Size of Fuseholder.   Where fuses are used for motor branch-circuit short-circuit and ground-fault protection, the fuseholders shall not be of a smaller size than required to accommodate the fuses specified by Table 430-152.

Exception: Where fuses having time delay appropriate for the starting characteristics of the motor are used, fuseholders of smaller size than specified in Table 430-152 shall be permitted.

Dual-element (time-delay) fuses make possible the use of sizes much smaller than with ordinary fuses and thus provide better protection because of the lower rating. This also permits a considerable saving in installation cost by using smaller size switches and panels and allows for easier arrangement of equipment where space is at a premium at motor control centers.

430-58. Rating of Circuit Breaker.   A circuit breaker for motor branch-circuit short-circuit and ground-fault protection shall have a current rating in accordance with Sections 430-52 and 430-110.

An instantaneous trip circuit breaker has no time-delay and opens only in response to currents in excess of its trip setting. Combination motor controller assemblies (see Section 430-52) are available with either interchangeable or noninterchangeable instantaneous trip units. In such a combination controller, the motor overload protective device in each conductor is relied upon to protect against excessive heating due to motor overloads and failure to start.

E. Motor Feeder Short-Circuit and Ground-Fault Protection

430-61. General.   Part E specifies protective devices intended to protect feeder conductors supplying motors against overcurrents due to short circuits or grounds.

430-62. Rating or Setting — Motor Load.

(a) Specific Load.   A feeder supplying a specific fixed motor load(s) and consisting of conductor sizes based on Section 430-24 shall be provided with a protective device having a rating or setting not greater than the largest rating or setting of the branch-circuit short-circuit and ground-fault protective device for any motor of the group (based on Table 430-152), plus the sum of the full-load currents of the other motors of the group.

Where the same rating or setting of the branch-circuit short-circuit and ground-fault protective device is used on two or more of the branch circuits of the group, one of the protective devices shall be considered the largest for the above calculations.

See Example No. 8, Chapter 9.

(b) Future Additions.   For large-capacity installations, where heavy-capacity feeders are installed to provide for future additions or changes, the rating or setting of the feeder protective devices shall be permitted to be based on the rated ampacity of the feeder conductors.

430-63. Rating or Setting — Power and Light Loads.   Where a feeder supplies a motor load, and in addition a lighting or a lighting and appliance load, the feeder protective device shall be permitted to have a rating or setting sufficient to carry the lighting or the lighting and appliance load as determined in accordance with Articles 210 and 220, plus for a single motor, the rating permitted by Section 430-52, and for two or more motors, the rating permitted by Section 430-62.

F. Motor Control Circuits

430-71. General. Part F contains modifications of the general requirements and applies to the particular conditions of motor control circuits.

Definition of Motor Control Circuit: The circuit of a control apparatus or system that carries the electric signals directing the performance of the controller, but does not carry the main power current.

430-72. Overcurrent Protection.

(a) General. A motor control circuit tapped from the load side of a motor branch-circuit short-circuit and ground-fault protective device(s) and functioning to control the motor(s) connected to that branch circuit shall be protected against overcurrent in accordance with Section 430-72. Such a tapped control circuit shall not be considered to be a branch circuit and shall be permitted to be protected by either a supplementary or branch-circuit overcurrent protective device(s). A motor control circuit other than such a tapped control circuit shall be protected against overcurrent in accordance with Section 725-12 or 725-35, as applicable.

(b) Conductor Protection.

(1) Conductors larger than No. 14 shall be protected against overcurrent in accordance with their ampacities. The ampacities shall be those given in Tables 310-16 through 310-19, without derating factors, and the limitations of Section 310-1 shall not apply.

(2) Conductors of Nos. 18, 16 and 14 shall be considered as protected by an overcurrent device(s) of not more than 20 ampere rating.

Exception No. 1 for (1) and (2): Conductors which do not extend beyond the motor control equipment enclosure shall be considered as protected by the motor branch-circuit short-circuit and ground-fault protective device(s) where the rating of the protective device(s) is not more than 400 percent of the ampacity of the control circuit conductors for conductors No. 14 and larger or not more than 25 amperes for No. 18 and 40 amperes for No. 16. The ampacities for conductors No. 14 and larger shall be the values given in Table 310-17 for 60°C conductors.

Exception No. 2 for (1) and (2): Conductors of No. 14 and larger which extend beyond the motor control equipment enclosure shall be considered as protected by the motor branch-circuit short-circuit and ground-fault protective device(s) where the rating of the protective device(s) is not more than 300 percent of the ampacity of the control circuit conductors. The ampacities shall be the values given in Table 310-16 for 60°C conductors.

Exception No. 3 for (1) and (2): Conductors supplied by the secondary side of a single-phase transformer having only a 2-wire (single-voltage) secondary shall be considered as protected by overcurrent protection provided on the primary (supply) side of the transformer, provided this protection is in accordance with Section 450-3 and does not exceed the value determined by multiplying the secondary conductor ampacity by the secondary-to-primary voltage ratio. Transformer secondary conductors (other than 2-wire) are not considered to be protected by the primary overcurrent protection.

Exception No. 4 for (1) and (2): Conductors of control circuits shall be considered as protected by the motor branch-circuit short-circuit and ground-fault protective device(s) where the opening of the control circuit would create a hazard as, for example, the control circuit of a fire pump motor, and the like.

(c) Control Circuit Transformer. Where a motor control circuit transformer is provided, the transformer shall be protected in accordance with Article 450.

Exception No. 1: Where the control circuit transformer is an integral part of the motor controller and is located within the motor controller enclosure and where an overcurrent device(s) rated or set at not more than 200 percent of the rated secondary current of the transformer is provided in the secondary circuit.

Exception No. 2: Where the transformer supplies a Class 1 power-limited, Class 2, or Class 3 remote control circuit conforming with the requirements of Article 725.

Exception No. 3: Where protection is provided by other approved means.

Exception No. 4: Overcurrent protection shall be omitted where the opening of the control circuit would create a hazard, as, for example, the control circuit of a fire pump motor and the like.

430-73. Mechanical Protection of Conductor.   Where damage to a motor control circuit would constitute a hazard, all conductors of such a remote motor control circuit that are outside the control device itself shall be installed in a raceway or be otherwise suitably protected from physical damage.

Where one side of the motor control circuit is grounded, the motor control circuit shall be so arranged that an accidental ground in the remote-control devices will not start the motor.

Where damage to the motor control circuit conductors would constitute a fire or accident hazard, physical protection of the motor control circuit conductors is necessary. Conductors are to be installed in raceways where damage to the control circuit conductors could result in an accidental ground causing the device to operate or breakage of conductors could render the device inoperative. Either condition could constitute a hazard to persons or property. Where boilers or furnaces are equipped with an automatic safety control device, damage to the conductors of the low-voltage (Article 725, Class 2) control circuit (thermostat, etc.) does not constitute a hazard.

The second paragraph of Section 430-73 requires that if one side of the motor control circuit is grounded, the circuit be arranged so that an accidental ground in the remote control devices will not start the motor. For example, if the control circuit is a 227-V single-phase circuit derived from a 480-V wye, 3-phase system supplying the motor, one side of the control circuit will be the grounded neutral. If

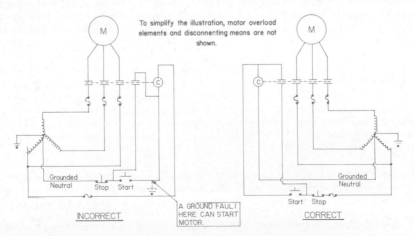

Figure 430-17. Control wiring in violation of Paragraph 2, Section 430-73 (left) and in compliance with Paragraph 2, Section 430-73 (right).

the "start" button of the motor control circuit is in the grounded neutral, a ground fault on the coil side of the "start" button can short-circuit the "start" circuit and start the motor. The same condition will exist if the ground fault is in the wiring rather than the control device itself. By locating the "start" button in the ungrounded side of the control circuit, this hazardous condition is avoided. See Figure 430-17.

Combinations of ground faults in motor and motor-control circuits can produce the same problem. If the circuit is ungrounded, the first fault may go undetected. One solution is to use double-pole control devices, one pole in each of the two control lines.

430-74. Disconnection.

(a) General.   Motor control circuits shall be so arranged that they will be disconnected from all sources of supply when the disconnecting means is in the open position. The disconnecting means shall be permitted to consist of two or more separate devices, one of which disconnects the motor and the controller from the source(s) of power supply for the motor, and the other(s), the motor control circuit(s) from its power supply. Where separate devices are used, they shall be located immediately adjacent one to each other.

Exception No. 1: Where more than twelve motor control circuit conductors are required to be disconnected, the disconnecting means shall be permitted to be located other than immediately adjacent one to each other where all of the following conditions are complied with:

a. Access to live parts is limited to qualified persons in accordance with Part K of this article.

b. A warning sign is permanently located on the outside of each equipment enclosure door or cover permitting access to the live parts in the motor control circuit(s), warning that motor control circuit disconnecting means are remotely located and specifying the location and identification of each disconnect. Where live parts are not in an equipment enclosure as permitted by Sections 430-132 and 430-133, an additional warning sign(s) shall be located where visible to persons who may be working in the area of the live parts.

Exception No. 2: Where the opening of one or more motor control circuit disconnect means may result in potentially unsafe conditions for personnel or property and the conditions a. and b. of Exception No. 1 above are complied with.

(b) Control Transformer in Controller.   Where a transformer or other device is used to obtain a reduced voltage for the motor control circuit and is located in the controller, such transformer or other device shall be connected to the load side of the disconnecting means for the motor control circuit.

G. Motor Controllers

430-81. General.   Part G is intended to require suitable controllers for all motors.

(a) Definition.   For definition of "Controller," see Article 100. For the purpose of this article, the term "Controller" includes any switch or device normally used to start and stop a motor.

(b) Stationary Motor of ⅛ Horsepower or Less.   For a stationary motor rated at ⅛ horsepower or less that is normally left running and is so constructed that it cannot be damaged by overload or failure to start, such as clock motors and the like, the branch-circuit protective device shall be permitted to serve as the controller.

(c) Portable Motor of ⅓ Horsepower or Less.   For a portable motor rated at ⅓ horsepower or less, the controller shall be permitted to be an attachment plug and receptacle.

430-82. Controller Design.

(a) Starting and Stopping.   Each controller shall be capable of starting and stopping the motor it controls, and shall be capable of interrupting the stalled-rotor current of the motor.

(b) Autotransformer.   An autotransformer starter shall provide an "off" position, a running position, and at least one starting position. It shall be so designed that it cannot rest in the starting position or in any position that will render the overload device in the circuit inoperative.

(c) Rheostats.   Rheostats shall be in compliance with the following:

(1) Motor-starting rheostats shall be so designed that the contact arm cannot be left on intermediate segments. The point or plate on which the arm rests when in the starting position shall have no electrical connection with the resistor.

(2) Motor-starting rheostats for direct-current motors operated from a constant voltage supply shall be equipped with automatic devices that will interrupt the supply before the speed of the motor has fallen to less than one-third its normal value.

430-83. Rating.   The controller shall have a horsepower rating not lower than the horsepower rating of the motor.

Exception No. 1: For a stationary motor rated at 2 horsepower or less, and 300 volts or less, the controller shall be permitted to be a general-use switch having an ampere rating not less than twice the full-load current rating of the motor.

On ac circuits, general-use snap switches suitable only for use on ac (not general-use ac-dc snap switches) shall be permitted to control a motor rated at 2 horsepower or less and 300 volts or less having a full-load current rating not more than 80 percent of the ampere rating of the switch.

Exception No. 2: A branch-circuit inverse time circuit breaker rated in amperes only shall be permitted as a controller. Where this circuit breaker is also used for overload protection, it shall conform to the appropriate provisions of this article governing overload protection.

Exception No. 3: The motor controller for a torque motor shall have a continuous-duty, full-load current rating not less than the nameplate current rating of the motor. For a motor controller rated in horsepower but not marked with the foregoing current rating, the equivalent current rating shall be determined from the horsepower rating by using Tables 430-147, 430-148, 430-149, or 430-150.

A controller, as defined in Section 430-81(a), includes any switch or device normally used to start and stop a motor. Circuit breakers are suitable for this use; however, circuit breakers used for branch-circuit short-circuit and ground-fault protection are not well adapted for motor overload protective devices.

430-84. Need Not Open All Conductors.   The controller shall not be required to open all conductors to the motor.

Exception: Where the controller serves also as a disconnecting means, it shall open all ungrounded conductors to the motor as provided in Section 430-111.

A controller that does not also serve as a disconnecting means is required to open only as many motor-circuit conductors as may be necessary to stop the motor. That is, one conductor for a dc or single-phase motor circuit; two conductors for a 3-phase motor circuit; and three conductors for a 2-phase motor circuit.

430-85. In Grounded Conductors.   One pole of the controller shall be permitted to be placed in a permanently grounded conductor, provided the controller is so designed that the pole in the grounded conductor cannot be opened without simultaneously opening all conductors of the circuit.

> Generally, one conductor of a 120-V circuit is grounded and a single-pole device must be connected in the ungrounded conductor to serve as a controller. A 2-pole controller is permitted for such a circuit, where both conductors (grounded and ungrounded) are opened simultaneously. The same requirement can be applied to other circuits, such as 230-V, 3-wire circuits with one conductor grounded.

430-86. Motor Not in Sight from Controller.   Where a motor and the driven machinery are not in sight from the controller location, the installation shall comply with one of the following conditions:

(a) Capable of Being Locked in the Open Position.   The controller disconnecting means shall be capable of being locked in the open position.

(b) Within Sight from the Motor Location.   A manually operable switch that will disconnect the motor from its source of supply shall be placed within sight from the motor location.

See Section 430-108 for type and rating.

> The basic rule is that a motor and its driven machinery should be within sight from the controller location. However, when several motors are controlled from one location, such as a motor-control center, it may be impossible to locate the control center within sight from all of the motors. Section 430-4 describes "in sight from" as one equipment visible and within 50 ft from the other equipment. Where a motor is not in sight, or more than 50 ft from its controller, the controller disconnecting means is to be capable of being locked in the "off" position or a manually operable switch in the motor circuit (not control circuit) is to be placed within sight from the motor location. Figures 430-18 through 430-20 illustrate

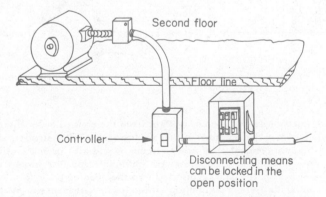

Figure 430-18. A controller disconnecting means that is not in sight of the motor installation must be designed to be locked in the "off" position.

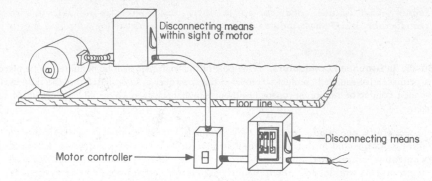

Figure 430-19. A motor installation where a disconnecting means is located within sight of the controller and another disconnecting means within sight of the motor.

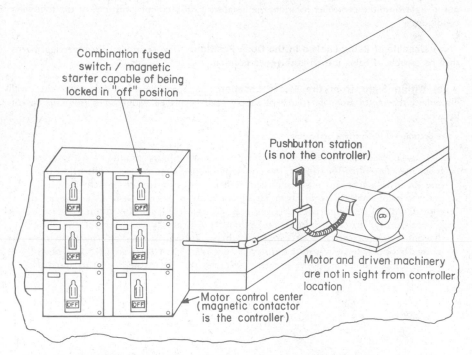

Figure 430-20. A fused switch within the motor control center has lock-open provisions. The pushbutton station at the motor location is not a controller.

installations of motors that are not in sight from the controller location.

It should be noted that a control center enclosing several controllers should not be locked because controllers of other circuits would also be inaccessible. Also, this rule does not permit the removal of "pull-out"-type fuse blocks in lieu of locking because a spare could be inserted into the opening.

Figure 430-20 illustrates a pushbutton station located adjacent to a motor. In this case the controller is a magnetic contactor located out of sight from the motor and is a separate part of a combination fused-switch unit within a control center which has individual lock-open provisions. A pushbutton station is not a controller. Its function is to operate the holding coil of the contactor. Should the control wires or the pushbutton station malfunction, the "stop" button would not release the holding coil. In this case the fused switch would disconnect the supply to the controller and de-energize the motor, hence the requirement that a disconnecting means be placed within sight from the controller. See also Section 430-102.

430-87. Number of Motors Served by Each Controller.   Each motor shall be provided with an individual controller.

Exception: For motors rated 600 volts or less, a single controller rated at not less than the sum of the horsepower ratings of all of the motors of the group shall be permitted to serve the group of motors under any one of the following conditions:

a. Where a number of motors drive several parts of a single machine or piece of apparatus, such as metal and woodworking machines, cranes, hoists, and similar apparatus.

b. Where a group of motors is under the protection of one overcurrent device as permitted in Section 430-53(a).

c. Where a group of motors is located in a single room within sight from the controller location.

These requirements for an individual controller are the same as those specified in Section 430-112 permitting the use of a single disconnecting means for a group of motors.

430-88. Adjustable-Speed Motors.   Adjustable-speed motors that are controlled by means of field regulation shall be so equipped and connected that they cannot be started under weakened field.

Exception: Where the motor is designed for such starting.

The speed of a motor will increase or decrease with variations in the amount of magnetic flux passing through the armature. Since the speed of the armature increases until the necessary counterelectromotive force is produced, it is evident that weakening the field by decreasing the current flow through the field magnets will increase the motor speed; and increasing the current flow through the field magnets will decrease the motor speed. Because of excessive starting currents, this type motor is not to be started under a weakened field condition unless the motor is designed for such starting.

430-89. Speed Limitation.   Machines of the following types shall be provided with speed limiting devices or other speed limiting means:

(a) Separately Excited DC Motors.   Separately excited direct-current motors.

(b) Series Motors.   Series motors.

(c) Motor-Generators and Converters.   Motor-generators and converters that can be driven at excessive speed from the direct-current end, as by a reversal of current or decrease in load.

Exception No. 1: When the inherent characteristics of the machines, the system, or the load and the mechanical connection thereto are such as to safely limit the speed.

Exception No. 2: When the machine is always under the manual control of a qualified operator.

DC motors are commonly used where speed control is essential such as electric railways and elevators where a smooth start, controlled acceleration, and a smooth stop are necessary.

If the load is removed from a series motor when it is running the speed of the motor will increase until it is dangerously high. To produce the necessary counterelectromotive force with a weakened field, the armature must turn correspondingly faster. Series motors are commonly used as gear-drive traction motors of electric locomotives and, thus, are continuously loaded.

The Ward Leonard speed control system is widely used to control a separately excited dc motor for the operation of electric elevators or hoists. Figure 430-21 is a simplified diagram of the speed control system where the armature of two generators (G_1 and G_2) are mounted on a shaft which is driven by a motor (not shown). M is the motor-drive for the elevator. The fields of G_1 and M are excited by G_1. By varying the rheostat R position, the voltage generated by G_2 is also varied and this in turn controls the speed of M. If the field circuit of M were to be accidently opened during a light load, the motor would reach an excessive speed; however, no speed-limiting device is required as the motor is always loaded.

Separately excited dc motors, series motors, motor (compound-wound dc) generators, and (synchronous) converters are to be provided with speed limiting devices (note Exceptions) such as a centrifugal device on the shaft of the machine or a remotely located overspeed device, which may be set at a predetermined speed to operate a set of contacts and thereby trip a circuit breaker and de-energize the machine.

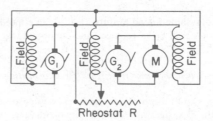

Figure 430-21. A schematic diagram of the Ward Leonard speed control system.

430-90. Combination Fuseholder and Switch as Controller.   The rating of a combination fuseholder and switch used as a motor controller shall be such that the fuseholder will accommodate the size of the fuse specified in Part C of this article for motor-running overload protection.

Exception: Where fuses having time delay appropriate for the starting characteristics of the motor are used, fuseholders of smaller size than specified in Part C of this article shall be permitted.

Time-delay (dual element) fuses can commonly be used for both motor overload and branch-circuit short-circuit and ground-fault protection and can be sized in accordance with Section 430-32. See also Sections 430-36, 430-55, and 430-57.

H. Disconnecting Means

430-101. General.   Part H is intended to require disconnecting means capable of disconnecting motors and controllers from the circuit.

See Diagram 430-1.

See Section 110-22 for identification of disconnecting means.

430-102. In Sight from Controller Location.   A disconnecting means shall be located in sight from the controller location.

Exception No. 1: For motor circuits over 600 volts, nominal, the controller disconnecting means shall be permitted to be out of sight of the controller, provided the controller is marked with a warning label giving the location and identification of the disconnecting means to be locked in the open position.

Exception No. 2: A single disconnecting means shall be permitted to be located adjacent to a group of coordinated controllers mounted adjacent one to each other on a multimotor continuous process machine.

For motors located remote from the controller location, see the comments following Section 430-86.

430-103. To Disconnect Both Motor and Controller.   The disconnecting means shall disconnect the motor and the controller from all ungrounded supply conductors and shall be so designed that no pole can be operated independently. The disconnecting means shall be permitted in the same enclosure with the controller.

See Section 430-113 for equipment receiving energy from more than one source.

The *Code* requires that a switch, circuit breaker, or other device serve as a disconnecting means for both the controller and the motor, thereby providing safety during maintenance and inspection shutdown periods. The disconnecting means also disconnects the controller; therefore, it cannot be a part of the

Figure 430-22. Heavy-duty safety switches UL listed for use on systems up to 200,000 A fault current RMS symmetrical with Class J or Class R fuses installed. (*Square D Co.*)

controller. However, separate disconnects and controllers may be mounted on the same panel or contained in the same enclosure, such as combination fused-switch, magnetic-starter units.

Depending upon the size of the motor and other conditions, the type of disconnecting means required may be a motor-circuit switch, a circuit breaker, a general-use switch, an isolating switch, an attachment plug and receptacle, or a branch-circuit short-circuit and ground-fault protective device. See Section 430-109.

If a motor is stalled, or under heavy overload, and the motor controller fails to properly open the circuit, the disconnecting means, which must be rated to interrupt locked-rotor current, can be used to open the circuit. Switches rated up to 100 hp are readily obtainable, but for motors larger than 100 hp ac or 40 hp dc, the disconnecting means are to be permitted to be a general-use or isolating switch when plainly marked "Do not operate under load." See Section 430-109, Exception No. 4.

430-104. To Be Indicating.   The disconnecting means shall plainly indicate whether it is in the open (off) or closed (on) position.

430-105. Grounded Conductors.   One pole of the disconnecting means shall be permitted to disconnect a permanently grounded conductor, provided the disconnecting means is so designed that the pole in the grounded conductor cannot be opened without simultaneously disconnecting all conductors of the circuit.

430-106. Service Switch as Disconnecting Means.   Where an installation consists of a single motor, the service switch may serve as the disconnecting means if it complies with this article and is within sight from the controller location.

430-107. Readily Accessible.   One of the disconnecting means shall be readily accessible.

430-108. Every Switch.   Every disconnecting means in the motor circuit between the point of attachment to the feeder and the point of connection to the motor shall comply with the requirements of Sections 430-109 and 430-110.

430-109. Type.   The disconnecting means shall be a motor-circuit switch rated in horsepower or a circuit breaker.

Exception No. 1: For stationary motors of ⅛ horsepower or less, the branch-circuit overcurrent device shall be permitted to serve as the disconnecting means.

Exception No. 2: For stationary motors rated at 2 horsepower or less and 300 volts or less, the disconnecting means shall be permitted to be a general-use switch having an ampere rating not less than twice the full-load current rating of the motor.

On ac circuits, general-use snap switches suitable only for use on ac (not general-use ac-dc snap switches) shall be permitted to disconnect a motor rated 2 horsepower or less and 300 volts or less having a full-load current rating not more than 80 percent of the ampere rating of the switch.

Exception No. 3: For motors of over 2 horsepower to and including 100 horsepower, the separate disconnecting means required for a motor with an autotransformer-type controller shall be permitted to be a general-use switch where all of the following provisions are met:

a. The motor drives a generator that is provided with overload protection.

b. The controller (1) is capable of interrupting the locked-rotor current of the motor; (2) is provided with a no-voltage release; and (3) is provided with running overload protection not exceeding 125 percent of the motor full-load current rating.

c. Separate fuses or an inverse time circuit breaker rated or set at not more than 150 percent of the motor full-load current are provided in the motor branch circuit.

Figure 430-23. Exception No. 1: The branch-circuit overcurrent device may serve as the disconnecting means for stationary motors of ⅛ hp or less.

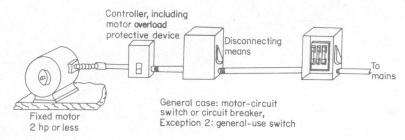

Figure 430-24. Exception No. 2: A general-use switch having an ampere rating not less than twice the motor full-load rating may serve as the disconnecting means for motors rated 2 hp or less and operating at 300 V or less.

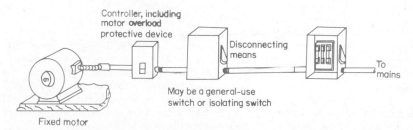

Figure 430-25. Exception No. 4: A general-use switch or isolation switch may serve as the disconnecting means for stationary motors rated more than 40 hp dc or 100 hp ac, if marked "Do not operate under load."

Exception No. 4: For stationary motors rated at more than 40 horsepower direct-current or 100 horsepower alternating-current, the disconnecting means shall be permitted to be a general-use or isolating switch when plainly marked "Do not operate under load."

Exception No. 5: For a cord- and plug-connected motor, an attachment plug and receptacle having ratings no less than the motor ratings shall be permitted to serve as the disconnecting means. A horsepower rated attachment plug and receptacle shall not be required for a cord- and plug-connected appliance in accordance with Section 422-22 or a room air conditioner in accordance with Section 440-63.

Exception No. 6: For torque motors the disconnecting means shall be permitted to be a general-use switch.

Section 430-108 requires every disconnecting means in the motor circuit to comply with Sections 430-109 and 430-110, including a manually operable switch

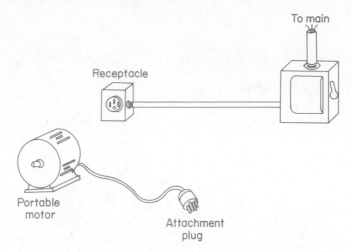

Figure 430-26. Exception No. 5: An attachment plug and receptacle of the proper rating may serve as the disconnecting means for cord- and plug-connected motors.

permitted by Section 430-86(b). See Figure 430-19.

The disconnecting means is to be a circuit breaker or a motor-circuit switch. A motor-circuit switch is a horsepower-rated switch capable of interrupting the maximum overload current of a motor (see Definitions, Article 100). Figures 430-23 through 430-26 illustrate the exceptions to this general requirement.

When horsepower-rated fused switches are required, it is to be noted that marking within the enclosure usually permits a dual horsepower rating. The "standard" horsepower rating is based on the largest nontime-delay (nondual-element) fuse rating which can be used in the switch and which will permit the motor to start. The "maximum" horsepower rating is based on the largest rated time-delay (dual-element) fuse which can be used in the switch and which will permit the motor to start. Thus, when time-delay fuses are used, smaller sized switches and fuseholders can be used. See Section 430-57, Exception.

430-110. Ampere Rating and Interrupting Capacity.

(a) **General.**   The disconnecting means for motor circuits rated 600 volts, nominal, or less, shall have an ampere rating of at least 115 percent of the full-load current rating of the motor.

(b) **For Torque Motors.**   Disconnecting means for a torque motor shall have an ampere rating of at least 115 percent of the motor nameplate current.

(c) **For Combination Loads.**   Where two or more motors are used together or where one or more motors are used in combination with other loads, such as resistance heaters, and where the combined load may be simultaneous on a single disconnecting means, the ampere and horsepower ratings of the combined load shall be determined as follows:

(1) The rating of the disconnecting means shall be determined from the summation of all currents, including resistance loads, at the full-load condition and also at the locked-rotor condition. The combined full-load current and the combined locked-rotor current so obtained shall be considered as a single motor for the purpose of this requirement as follows:
The full-load current equivalent to the horsepower rating of each motor shall be selected from

Table 430-148, 430-149, or 430-150. These full-load currents shall be added to the rating in amperes of other loads to obtain an equivalent full-load current for the combined load.

The locked-rotor current equivalent to the horsepower rating of each motor shall be selected from Table 430-151. The locked-rotor currents shall be added to the rating in amperes of other loads to obtain an equivalent locked-rotor current for the combined load. Where two or more motors and/or other loads cannot be started simultaneously, appropriate combinations of locked-rotor and full-load current shall be permitted to be used to determine the equivalent locked-rotor current for the simultaneous combined loads.

Exception: Where part of the concurrent load is resistance load, and where the disconnecting means is a switch rated in horsepower and amperes, the switch used shall be permitted to have a horsepower rating not less than the combined load of the motor(s), if the ampere rating of the switch is not less than the locked-rotor current of the motor(s) plus the resistance load.

(2) The ampere rating of the disconnecting means shall not be less than 115 percent of the summation of all currents at the full-load condition determined in accordance with (c) (1) above.

(3) For small motors not covered by Tables 430-147, 430-148, 430-149, or 430-150, the locked-rotor current shall be assumed to be six times the full-load current.

> A general-use switch, fuse, circuit breaker, or attachment plug and receptacle used as a disconnecting means must have an ampere rating of not less than 115 percent of the motor full-load current.

430-111. Switch or Circuit Breaker as Both Controller and Disconnecting Means. A switch or circuit breaker complying with Section 430-83 shall be permitted to serve as both controller and disconnecting means if it opens all ungrounded conductors to the motor, if it is protected by an overcurrent device (which may be the branch-circuit fuses) that opens all ungrounded conductors to the switch or circuit breaker, and if it is of one of the following types:

(a) Air-Break Switch. An air-break switch, operable directly by applying the hand to a lever or handle.

(b) Inverse Time Circuit Breaker. An inverse time circuit breaker operable directly by applying the hand to a lever or handle.

(c) Oil Switch. An oil switch used on a circuit whose rating does not exceed 600 volts or 100 amperes, or by special permission on a circuit exceeding this capacity where under expert supervision.

The oil switch or circuit breaker specified above shall be permitted to be both power and manually operable.

The overcurrent device protecting the controller shall be permitted to be part of the controller assembly or shall be permitted to be separate.

An autotransformer-type controller shall be provided with a separate disconnecting means.

> Where the controller consists of a manually operable air-break switch, an inverse time circuit breaker, or a 100-A maximum oil switch (higher rating by special permission), the controller is considered to be a satisfactory disconnecting means. It is the intent of this section to permit omission of an additional device to serve as a disconnecting means. See Figure 430-27.
>
> It should be noted that a separate disconnecting means must be provided if the controller is of the autotransformer or "compensator" type (this switch may be combined in the same enclosure with a motor overload protective device).

Where used as a controller, the switch or circuit breaker must meet all of the requirements for controllers and must be protected by branch-circuit short-circuit and ground-fault protective devices (fuses or a circuit breaker), which ensure that all ungrounded conductors will be opened.

430-112. Motors Served by Single Disconnecting Means.   Each motor shall be provided with an individual disconnecting means.

Exception: A single disconnecting means shall be permitted to serve a group of motors under any one of the following conditions:

a. Where a number of motors drive several parts of a single machine or piece of apparatus, such as metal and woodworking machines, cranes, and hoists.

b. Where a group of motors is under the protection of one set of branch-circuit protective devices as permitted by Section 430-53(a).

c. Where a group of motors is in a single room within sight from the location of the disconnecting means.

The single disconnecting means shall have a rating not less than is required by Section 430-110 for a single motor, the rating of which equals the sum of the horsepowers or currents of all the motors of the group.

The Exception permits a single disconnecting means to serve a group of motors. The disconnecting means is to have a rating equal to the sum of the horsepowers or currents of all the motors of the group. If the total horsepower is over 2 hp, a motor-circuit switch (horsepower-rated) is to be used. Thus, for five 2-hp motors the disconnecting means should be a motor-circuit switch rated at not less than 10 hp.

Exception a. A single disconnecting means may be used where a number of motors drive several parts of a single machine such as cranes (see Sections 610-31 and 610-32), metal or woodworking machines, steel rolling mill machinery, etc. The single disconnecting means for multimotor machinery provides a positive means of simultaneously de-energizing all motor branch circuits, including remote-control circuits, interlocking circuits, limit-switch circuits, and operator control stations.

Exception b. Section 430-53(a) permits a group of motors under the protection of the same branch-circuit device provided the device is rated not more than 20 A at 125 V or 15 A at more than 125 V but not more than 600 V. The motors must be rated one hp or less and the full-load current for each motor must be 6 A or less. A single disconnecting means is both practical and economical for a group of such small motors.

Exception c. Many times, a group of motors is located in one room, such as a pump room, compressor room, mixer room, etc. It is therefore possible to design the layout of a single disconnecting means with an unobstructed view (within 50 ft, see Section 430-4) from each motor.

These conditions are similar to the requirements in Section 430-87 that permit the use of a single controller for a group of motors.

430-113. Energy from More than One Source.   Motor and motor-operated equipment receiving electrical energy from more than one source shall be provided with disconnecting means from each source of electrical energy immediately adjacent to the equipment served. Each source shall be permitted to have a separate disconnecting means.

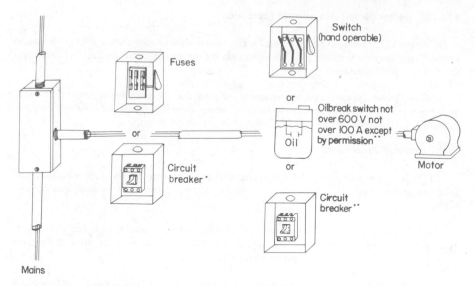

Figure 430-27. Three alternative arrangements where a switch, or circuit breaker, or oilbreak switch can serve satisfactorily as both the controller and disconnecting means (* and ** oilbreak switch or circuit breaker may be hand operated or power operated).

Exception No. 1: Where a motor receives electrical energy from more than one source, the disconnecting means for the main power supply to the motor shall not be required to be immediately adjacent to the motor provided the controller disconnecting means is capable of being locked in the open position.

Exception No. 2: A separate disconnecting means shall not be required for a Class 2 remote-control circuit conforming with Article 725, rated not more than 30 volts, and which is isolated and ungrounded.

Exception No. 1 applies to large synchronous motors that receive electrical energy from more than one source. Exception No. 2 applies to low voltage control circuits, such as thermostat circuits used with heating and air-conditioning equipment.

J. Over 600 Volts, Nominal

430-121. General. Part J recognizes the additional hazard due to the use of high voltage. It adds to or amends the other provisions of this article. Other requirements for circuits and equipment operating at over 600 volts, nominal, are in Article 710.

430-122. Marking on Controllers. In addition to the marking required by Section 430-8, a controller shall be marked with the control voltage.

430-123. Conductor Enclosures Adjacent to Motors. Flexible metal conduit not exceeding 6 feet (1.83 m) in length shall be permitted to be employed for raceway connection to a motor terminal enclosure.

430-124. Size of Conductors. Conductors supplying motors shall have an ampacity not less than the current at which the motor overload protective device(s) is selected to trip.

430-125. Motor Circuit Overcurrent Protection.

(a) General.   The high-voltage circuit for each motor shall include coordinated protection to automatically interrupt overload and fault currents in the motor, the motor circuit conductors, and the motor control apparatus.

Exception: Where a motor is vital to operation of the plant and the motor should operate to failure if necessary to prevent a greater hazard to persons, the sensing device(s) is permitted to be connected to a supervised annunciator or alarm instead of interrupting the motor circuit.

(b) Overload Protection.

(1) Each motor shall be protected against dangerous heating due to motor overloads and failure to start by a thermal protector integral with the motor of external current sensing devices, or both.

(2) The secondary circuits of wound-rotor alternating-current motors including conductors, controllers, and resistors rated for the application shall be considered as protected against overcurrent by the motor overload protection means.

(3) Operation of the overload interrupting device shall simultaneously disconnect all ungrounded conductors.

(4) Overload sensing devices shall not automatically reset after trip unless resetting of the overload sensing device does not cause automatic restarting of the motor or there is no hazard to persons created by automatic restarting of the motor and its connected machinery.

(c) Fault-Current Protection.

(1) Fault-current protection shall be provided in each motor circuit by one of the following means:

a. A circuit breaker of suitable type and rating so arranged that it can be serviced without hazard. The circuit breaker shall simultaneously disconnect all ungrounded conductors. The circuit breaker shall be permitted to sense the fault current by means of integral or external sensing elements.

b. Fuses of a suitable type and rating placed in each ungrounded conductor. Fuses shall be used with suitable disconnecting means or they shall be of a type that can also serve as the disconnecting means. They shall be so arranged that they cannot be serviced while they are energized.

(2) Fault-current interrupting devices shall not reclose the circuit automatically.

Exception: Where circuits are exposed to transient faults and where automatic reclosing of the circuit does not create a hazard to persons.

(3) Overload protection and fault-current protection shall be permitted to be provided by the same device.

430-126. Rating of Motor Control Apparatus.   Motor controllers and motor branch-circuit disconnecting means shall have a continuous ampere rating not less than the current at which the overload protective device(s) is selected to trip.

430-127. Disconnecting Means.   The controller disconnecting means shall be capable of being locked in the open position.

K. Protection of Live Parts — All Voltages

430-131. General.   Part K specifies that live parts shall be protected in a manner judged adequate to the hazard involved.

430-132. Where Required.   Exposed live parts of motors and controllers operating at 50 volts or more between terminals shall be guarded against accidental contact by enclosure or by location as follows:

(a) In a Room or Enclosure.   By installation in a room or enclosure that is accessible only to qualified persons.

(b) On a Suitable Balcony.   By installation on a suitable balcony, gallery, or platform, so elevated and arranged as to exclude unqualified persons.

(c) Elevation.   By elevation 8 feet (2.44 m) or more above the floor.

Exception: Stationary motors having commutators, collectors, and brush rigging located inside of motor-end brackets and not conductively connected to supply circuits operating at more than 150 volts to ground.

430-133. Guards for Attendants.   Where live parts of motors or controllers operating at over 150 volts to ground are guarded against accidental contact only by location as specified in Section 430-132, and where adjustment or other attendance may be necessary during the operation of the apparatus, suitable insulating mats or platforms shall be provided so that the attendant cannot readily touch live parts unless standing on the mats or platforms.

For working space, see Sections 110-16 and 110-34.

L. Grounding

430-141. General.   Part L specifies the grounding of motor and controller frames to prevent a potential above ground in the event of accidental contact between live parts and frames. Insulation, isolation, or guarding are suitable alternatives to grounding of motors under certain conditions.

430-142. Stationary Motors.   The frames of stationary motors shall be grounded under any of the following conditions: (1) where supplied by metal-enclosed wiring; (2) where in a wet location and not isolated or guarded; (3) if in a hazardous (classified) location as covered in Articles 500 through 517; (4) if the motor operates with any terminal at over 150 volts to ground.

Where the frame of the motor is not grounded, it shall be permanently and effectively insulated from the ground.

Any motor in a wet location and subject to contact by personnel constitutes a serious hazard and, unless it is isolated, elevated or guarded from reach, should be grounded.

Stationary motors are usually supplied by wiring enclosed in metal raceways (rigid metal conduit, EMT, flexible metal conduit, etc.) or by cables with metallic sheaths (Types AC, MC). Upon being effectively attached to the motor junction box or frame, the metal raceway or cable armor serves as the equipment grounding conductor. See Section 250-91(b).

430-143. Portable Motors.   The frames of portable motors that operate at over 150 volts to ground shall be guarded or grounded.

See Section 250-45(d) for grounding of portable appliances in other than residential occupancies.

See Section 250-59(b) for color of grounding conductor.

430-144. Controllers. Controller enclosures shall be grounded regardless of voltage.

Exception No. 1: Enclosures attached to ungrounded portable equipment.

Exception No. 2: Lined covers of snap switches.

430-145. Method of Grounding. Where required, grounding shall be done in the manner specified in Article 250.

(a) Grounding Through Terminal Housings. Where the wiring to fixed motors is Type AC cable or in metal raceways, junction boxes to house motor terminals shall be provided, and the armor of the cable or the metal raceways shall be connected to them in the manner specified in Article 250.

See Section 430-12(e) for grounding connection means required at motor terminal housings.

(b) Separation of Junction Box from Motor. The junction box required by (a) above shall be permitted to be separated from the motor not more than 6 feet (1.83 m), provided the leads to the motor are Type AC cable or armored cord or are stranded leads enclosed in liquidtight flexible metal conduit, flexible metal conduit, intermediate metal conduit, rigid metal conduit or electrical metallic tubing not smaller than ⅜-inch electrical trade size, the armor or raceway being connected

Table 430-147.   Full-Load Current in Amperes, Direct-Current Motors

The following values of full-load currents* are for motors running at base speed.

HP	Armature Voltage Rating*					
	90V	**120V**	**180V**	**240V**	**500V**	**550V**
¼	4.0	3.1	2.0	1.6		
⅓	5.2	4.1	2.6	2.0		
½	6.8	5.4	3.4	2.7		
¾	9.6	7.6	4.8	3.8		
1	12.2	9.5	6.1	4.7		
1½		13.2	8.3	6.6		
2		17	10.8	8.5		
3		25	16	12.2		
5		40	27	20		
7½		58		29	13.6	12.2
10		76		38	18	16
15				55	27	24
20				72	34	31
25				89	43	38
30				106	51	46
40				140	67	61
50				173	83	75
60				206	99	90
75				255	123	111
100				341	164	148
125				425	205	185
150				506	246	222
200				675	330	294

* These are average direct-current quantities.

both to the motor and to the box. Where stranded leads are used, protected as specified above, they shall not be larger than No. 10, and shall comply with other requirements of this Code for conductors to be used in raceways.

(c) Grounding of Controller Mounted Devices.   Instrument transformer secondaries and exposed noncurrent-carrying metal or other conductive parts or cases of instrument transformers, meters, instruments, and relays shall be grounded as specified in Sections 250-121 through 250-125.

Most motors are subject to vibration and good practice requires that, in nearly all cases, the wiring to motors that are fixed should be installed with a short section of liquidtight flexible metal conduit, or flexible metal conduit, to the motor terminal housing.

Table 430-148.   Full-Load Currents in Amperes
Single-Phase Alternating-Current Motors

The following values of full-load currents are for motors running at usual speeds and motors with normal torque characteristics. Motors built for especially low speeds or high torques may have higher full-load currents, and multispeed motors will have full-load current varying with speed, in which case the nameplate current ratings shall be used.

To obtain full-load currents of 208- and 200-volt motors, increase corresponding 230-volt motor full-load currents by 10 and 15 percent, respectively.

The voltages listed are rated motor voltages. The currents listed shall be permitted for system voltage ranges of 110 to 120 and 220 to 240.

HP	115V	230V
⅙	4.4	2.2
¼	5.8	2.9
⅓	7.2	3.6
½	9.8	4.9
¾	13.8	6.9
1	16	8
1½	20	10
2	24	12
3	34	17
5	56	28
7½	80	40
10	100	50

Table 430-149.   Full-Load Current
Two-Phase Alternating-Current Motors (4-Wire)

The following values of full-load current are for motors running at speeds usual for belted motors and motors with normal torque characteristics. Motors built for especially low speeds or high torques may require more running current, and multispeed motors will have full-load current varying with speed, in which case the nameplate current rating shall be used. Current in the common conductor of a 2-phase, 3-wire system will be 1.41 times the value given.

The voltages listed are rated motor voltages. The currents listed shall be permitted for system voltage ranges of 110 to 120, 220 to 240, 440 to 480, and 550 to 600 volts.

	Induction Type Squirrel-Cage and Wound-Rotor Amperes				
HP	115V	230V	460V	575V	2300V
½	4	2	1	.8	
¾	4.8	2.4	1.2	1.0	
1	6.4	3.2	1.6	1.3	
1½	9	4.5	2.3	1.8	
2	11.8	5.9	3	2.4	
3		8.3	4.2	3.3	
5		13.2	6.6	5.3	
7½		19	9	8	
10		24	12	10	
15		36	18	14	
20		47	23	19	
25		59	29	24	
30		69	35	28	
40		90	45	36	
50		113	56	45	
60		133	67	53	14
75		166	83	66	18
100		218	109	87	23
125		270	135	108	28
150		312	156	125	32
200		416	208	167	43

Table 430-150.   Full-Load Current*
Three-Phase Alternating-Current Motors

HP	Induction Type Squirrel-Cage and Wound-Rotor Amperes					Synchronous Type †Unity Power Factor Amperes			
	115V	230V	460V	575V	2300V	230V	460V	575V	2300V
½	4	2	1	.8					
¾	5.6	2.8	1.4	1.1					
1	7.2	3.6	1.8	1.4					
1½	10.4	5.2	2.6	2.1					
2	13.6	6.8	3.4	2.7					
3		9.6	4.8	3.9					
5		15.2	7.6	6.1					
7½		22	11	9					
10		28	14	11					
15		42	21	17					
20		54	27	22					
25		68	34	27		53	26	21	
30		80	40	32		63	32	26	
40		104	52	41		83	41	33	
50		130	65	52		104	52	42	
60		154	77	62	16	123	61	49	12
75		192	96	77	20	155	78	62	15
100		248	124	99	26	202	101	81	20
125		312	156	125	31	253	126	101	25
150		360	180	144	37	302	151	121	30
200		480	240	192	49	400	201	161	40

For full-load currents of 208- and 200-volt motors, increase the corresponding 230-volt motor full-load current by 10 and 15 percent, respectively.

* These values of full-load current are for motors running at speeds usual for belted motors and motors with normal torque characteristics. Motors built for especially low speeds or high torques may require more running current, and multispeed motors will have full-load current varying with speed, in which case the nameplate current rating shall be used.

† For 90 and 80 percent power factor the above figures shall be multipled by 1.1 and 1.25 respectively.

The voltages listed are rated motor voltages. The currents listed shall be permitted for system voltage ranges of 110 to 120, 220 to 240, 440 to 480, and 550 to 600 volts.

Table 430-151.   Conversion Table of Locked-Rotor Currents for Selection of Disconnecting Means and Controllers as Determined from Horsepower and Voltage Rating

For use only with Sections 430-110, 440-12 and 440-41.

| Motor Locked-Rotor Current Amperes* | | | | | | | Max. HP Rating |
| Single Phase | | Two or Three Phase | | | | | |
115V	230V	115V	200V	230V	460V	575V	
58.8	29.4	24	18.8	12	6	4.8	½
82.8	41.4	33.6	19.3	16.8	8.4	6.6	¾
96	48	43.2	24.8	21.6	10.8	8.4	1
120	60	62	35.9	31.2	15.6	12.6	1½
144	72	81	46.9	40.8	20.4	16.2	2
204	102	—	66	58	26.8	23.4	3
336	168	—	105	91	45.6	36.6	5
480	240	—	152	132	66	54	7½
600	300	—	193	168	84	66	10
—	—	—	290	252	126	102	15
—	—	—	373	324	162	132	20
—	—	—	469	408	204	162	25
—	—	—	552	480	240	192	30
—	—	—	718	624	312	246	40
—	—	—	897	780	390	312	50
—	—	—	1063	924	462	372	60
—	—	—	1325	1152	576	462	75
—	—	—	1711	1488	744	594	100
—	—	—	2153	1872	936	750	125
—	—	—	2484	2160	1080	864	150
—	—	—	3312	2880	1440	1152	200

* These values of motor locked-rotor current are approximately six times the full-load current values given in Tables 430-148 and 430-150.

Table 430-152.   Maximum Rating or Setting of Motor Branch-Circuit Short-Circuit and Ground-Fault Protective Devices

Type of Motor	Percent of Full-Load Current			
	Nontime Delay Fuse	Dual Element (Time-Delay) Fuse	Instan-taneous Trip Breaker	* Inverse Time Breaker
Single-phase, all types				
No code letter..........................	300	175	700	250
All ac single-phase and polyphase squirrel-cage and synchronous motors† with full-voltage, resistor or reactor starting:				
No code letter..........................	300	175	700	250
Code letter F to V	300	175	700	250
Code letter B to E	250	175	700	200
Code letter A	150	150	700	150
All ac squirrel-cage and synchronous motors† with autotransformer starting:				
Not more than 30 amps				
No code letter.......................	250	175	700	200
More than 30 amps				
No code letter.......................	200	175	700	200
Code letter F to V	250	175	700	200
Code letter B to E	200	175	700	200
Code letter A	150	150	700	150
High-reactance squirrel-cage				
Not more than 30 amps				
No code letter.......................	250	175	700	250
More than 30 amps				
No code letter.......................	200	175	700	200
Wound-rotor —				
No code letter..........................	150	150	700	150
Direct-current (constant voltage)				
No more than 50 hp				
No code letter.......................	150	150	250	150
More than 50 hp				
No code letter.......................	150	150	175	150

For explanation of Code Letter Marking, see Table 430-7(b).

For certain exceptions to the values specified, see Sections 430-52 through 430-54.

* The values given in the last column also cover the ratings of nonadjustable inverse time types of circuit breakers that may be modified as in Section 430-52.

† Synchronous motors of the low-torque, low-speed type (usually 450 rpm or lower), such as are used to drive reciprocating compressors, pumps, etc. that start unloaded, do not require a fuse rating or circuit-breaker setting in excess of 200 percent of full-load current.

ARTICLE 440 — AIR-CONDITIONING AND
REFRIGERATING EQUIPMENT

Contents

A. General

440-1. Scope.   The provisions of this article apply to electric motor-driven air-conditioning and refrigerating equipment, and to the branch circuits and controllers for such equipment. It provides for the special considerations necessary for circuits supplying hermetic refrigerant motor-compressors and for any air-conditioning and/or refrigerating equipment which is supplied from an individual branch circuit which supplies a hermetic refrigerant motor-compressor.

Hermetic Refrigerant Motor-Compressor: A combination consisting of a compressor and motor, both of which are enclosed in the same housing, with no external shaft or shaft seals, the motor operating in the refrigerant.

440-2. Other Articles.

(a) Article 430.   These provisions are in addition to, or amendatory of, the provisions of Article 430 and other articles in this Code, which apply except as modified in this article.

(b) Article 422, 424, or 430.   The rules of Article 422, 424, or 430, as applicable, shall apply to air-conditioning and refrigerating equipment which does not incorporate a hermetic refrigerant motor-compressor. Examples of such equipment are devices which employ refrigeration compressors driven by conventional motors, furnaces with air-conditioning evaporator coils installed, fan-coil units, remote forced air-cooled condensers, remote commercial refrigerators, etc.

(c) Article 422.   Devices such as room air conditioners, household refrigerators and freezers, drinking water coolers, and beverage dispensers shall be considered appliances and the provisions of Article 422 shall also apply.

(d) Other Applicable Articles.   Hermetic refrigerant motor-compressors, circuits, controllers, and equipment shall also comply with the applicable provisions of the following:

Capacitors .... Section 460-9
Garages, Aircraft Hangars, Gasoline Dispensing
    and Service Stations, Bulk Storage Plants,
    Finishing Processes and Flammable
    Anesthetics .... Articles 511, 513, 514, 515, 516, and 517-G
Hazardous (Classified) Locations .... Articles 500 through 503
Motion-Picture and Television Studios .... Article 530
Resistors and Reactors .... Article 470

Article 440 provides for special considerations necessary for circuits supplying hermetic refrigerant motor-compressors and is in addition to, or amendatory of, the provisions of Article 430 and other applicable articles. However, many requirements, such as disconnecting means, controllers, single or group installations, and sizing of conductors, are the same as, or very similar to, those applied in Articles 430 and 440.

Article 440 does not apply unless a hermetic refrigerant motor-compressor is supplied. Article 440 must be applied in conjunction with Article 430.

Note the term "rated load current," defined in the fine print note following

Section 440-3(a), and the term "branch-circuit selection current," defined in the fine print note following Section 440-3(c).

When a "branch-circuit selection current" is marked on a nameplate, it is to be used instead of the "rated-load current" in order to determine the size of the disconnecting means, the controller, the motor branch-circuit conductors, and the overcurrent protective devices for the branch-circuit conductors and the motor. The value of "branch-circuit selection current" will always be greater than the marked "rated-load current."

440-3. Marking on Hermetic Refrigerant Motor-Compressors and Equipment.

(a) Hermetic Refrigerant Motor-Compressor Nameplate.   A hermetic refrigerant motor-compressor shall be provided with a nameplate which shall give the manufacturer's name, trademark or symbol; identifying designation; phase; voltage; and frequency. The rated load current in amperes of the motor-compressor shall be marked by the equipment manufacturer on either or both the motor-compressor nameplate and the nameplate of the equipment in which the motor-compressor is used. The locked-rotor current of each single-phase motor-compressor having a rated-load current of more than 9 amperes at 115 volts or more than 4.5 amperes at 230 volts and each polyphase motor-compressor shall be marked on the motor-compressor nameplate. Where a thermal protector complying with Section 440-52(a)(2) and (b)(2) is used, the motor-compressor nameplate or the equipment nameplate shall be marked with the words "Thermally Protected." Where a protective system, complying with Section 440-52(a)(4) and (b)(4), is used and is furnished with the equipment, the equipment nameplate shall be marked with the words, "Thermally Protected System." Where a protective system complying with Section 440-52(a)(4) and (b)(4) is specified, the equipment nameplate shall be appropriately marked.

Definition: The rated-load current for a hermetic refrigerant motor-compressor is the current resulting when the motor-compressor is operated at the rated load, rated voltage and rated frequency of the equipment it serves.

(b) Multimotor and Combination-Load Equipment.   Multimotor and combination-load equipment shall be provided with a visible nameplate marked with the maker's name, the rating in volts, frequency and number of phases, minimum supply circuit conductor ampacity, and the maximum rating of the branch-circuit short-circuit and ground-fault protective device. The ampacity shall be calculated by using Part D and counting all the motors and other loads which will be operated at the same time. The branch-circuit short-circuit and ground-fault protective device rating shall not exceed the value calculated by using Part C. Multimotor or combination-load equipment for use on two or more circuits shall be marked with the above information for each circuit.

Exception No. 1: Multimotor and combination-load equipment which is suitable under the provisions of this article for connection to a single 15- or 20-ampere, 120-volt, or a 15-ampere, 208- or 240-volt single-phase branch circuit shall be permitted to be marked as a single load.

Exception No. 2: Room air conditioners as provided in Part G of Article 440.

(c) Branch-Circuit Selection Current.   Hermetic refrigerant motor-compressors or equipment containing such compressor(s) in which the protection system, approved for use with the motor-compressor which it protects, permits continuous current in excess of the specified percentage of nameplate rated-load current given in Section 440-52(b)(2) or (b)(4) shall also be marked with a branch-circuit selection current that complies with Section 440-52(b)(2) or (b)(4). This marking shall be provided by the equipment manufacturer and shall be on the nameplate(s) where the rated-load current(s) appears.

Definition: Branch-circuit selection current is the value in amperes to be used instead of the rated-load current in determining the ratings of motor branch-circuit conductors, disconnecting means, controllers and branch-circuit short-circuit and ground-fault protective devices wherever the running overload protective device permits a sustained current greater than the specified percentage of the rated-load current. The value of branch-circuit selection current will always be greater than the marked rated-load current.

440-4. Marking on Controllers. A controller shall be marked with the maker's name, trademark, or symbol; identifying designation; the voltage; phase; full-load and locked-rotor current (or horsepower) rating; and such other data as may be needed to properly indicate the motor-compressor for which it is suitable.

440-5. Ampacity and Rating. Ampacity of conductors and rating of equipment shall be determined as follows:

(a) Hermetic Refrigerant Motor-Compressor. For a hermetic refrigerant motor-compressor, the rated-load current marked on the nameplate of the equipment in which the motor-compressor is employed shall be used in determining the rating or ampacity of the disconnecting means, the branch-circuit conductors, the controller, the branch-circuit short-circuit and ground-fault protection, and the separate motor overload protection. Where no rated-load current is shown on the equipment nameplate, the rated-load current shown on the compressor nameplate shall be used. For disconnecting means and controllers, see also Sections 440-12 and 440-41.

Exception No. 1: When so marked, the branch-circuit selection current shall be used instead of the rated-load current to determine the rating or ampacity of the disconnecting means, the branch-circuit conductors, the controller, and the branch-circuit short-circuit and ground-fault protection.

Exception No. 2: As permitted in Section 440-22(b) for branch-circuit short-circuit and ground-fault protection of cord- and plug-connected equipment.

(b) Multimotor Equipment. For multimotor equipment employing a shaded-pole or permanent split-capacitor-type fan or blower motor, the full-load current for such motor marked on the nameplate of the equipment in which the fan or blower motor is employed shall be used instead of the horsepower rating to determine the ampacity or rating of the disconnecting means, the branch-circuit conductors, the controller, the branch-circuit short-circuit and ground-fault protection, and the separate overload protection. This marking on the equipment nameplate shall not be less than the current marked on the fan or blower motor nameplate.

440-6. Highest Rated (Largest) Motor. In determining compliance with this article and with Sections 430-24, 430-53(b) and (c), and 430-62(a), the highest rated (largest) motor shall be considered to be that motor which has the highest rated-load current. Where two or more motors have the same rated-load current, only one of them shall be considered as the highest rated (largest) motor. For other than hermetic refrigerant motor-compressors, and fan or blower motors as covered in Section 440-5(b), the full-load current used to determine the highest rated motor shall be the equivalent value corresponding to the motor horsepower rating selected from Tables 430-148, 430-149, or 430-150.

Exception: When so marked, the branch-circuit selection current shall be used instead of the rated-load current in determining the highest rated (largest) motor-compressor.

440-7. Single Machine. An air-conditioning or refrigerating system shall be considered to be a single machine under the provisions of Section 430-87, Exception and Section 430-112, Exception. The motors shall be permitted to be located remotely from each other.

B. Disconnecting Means

440-11. General. The provisions of Part B are intended to require disconnecting means capable of disconnecting air-conditioning and refrigerating equipment including motor-compressors, and controllers, from the circuit feeder. See Diagram 430-1.

440-12. Rating and Interrupting Capacity.

(a) **Hermetic Refrigerant Motor-Compressor.** A disconnecting means serving a hermetic refrigerant motor-compressor shall be selected on the basis of the nameplate rated-load current or branch-circuit selection current, whichever is greater, and locked-rotor current, respectively, of the motor-compressor as follows:

(1) The ampere rating shall be at least 115 percent of the nameplate rated-load current or branch-circuit selection current, whichever is greater.

(2) To determine the equivalent horsepower in complying with the requirements of Section 430-109, the horsepower rating shall be selected from Tables 430-148, 430-149, or 430-150 corresponding to the rated-load current or branch-circuit selection current, whichever is greater, and also the horsepower rating from Table 430-151 corresponding to the locked-rotor current. In case the nameplate rated-load current or branch-circuit selection current and locked-rotor current do not correspond to the currents shown in Tables 430-148, 430-149, 430-150, or 430-151, the horsepower rating corresponding to the next higher value shall be selected. In case different horsepower ratings are obtained when applying these tables, a horsepower rating at least equal to the larger of the values obtained shall be selected.

(b) **Combination Loads.** Where one or more hermetic refrigerant motor-compressors are used together or are used in combination with other motors and/or loads such as resistance heaters and where the combined load may be simultaneous on a single disconnecting means, the rating for the combined load shall be determined as follows:

(1) The horsepower rating of the disconnecting means shall be determined from the summation of all currents, including resistance loads, at the rated-load condition and also at the locked-rotor condition. The combined rated-load current and the combined locked-rotor current so obtained shall be considered as a single motor for the purpose of this requirement as follows:

a. The full-load current equivalent to the horsepower rating of each motor, other than a hermetic refrigerant motor-compressor, and fan or blower motors as covered in Section 440-5(b) shall be selected from Tables 430-148, 430-149, or 430-150. These full-load currents shall be added to the motor-compressor rated-load current(s) or branch-circuit selection current(s), whichever is greater, and to the rating in amperes of other loads to obtain an equivalent full-load current for the combined load.

b. The locked-rotor current equivalent to the horsepower rating of each motor, other than a hermetic refrigerant motor-compressor, shall be selected from Table 430-151, and for fan and blower motors of the shaded-pole or permanent split-capacitor type marked with the locked-rotor current, the marked value shall be used. The locked-rotor currents shall be added to the motor-compressor locked-rotor current(s) and to the rating in amperes of other loads to obtain an equivalent locked-rotor current for the combined load. Where two or more motors and/or other loads cannot be started simultaneously, appropriate combinations of locked-rotor and rated-load current or branch-circuit selection current, whichever is greater, shall be an acceptable means of determining the equivalent locked-rotor current for the simultaneous combined load.

Exception: Where part of the concurrent load is a resistance load and the disconnecting means is a switch rated in horsepower and amperes, the switch used shall be permitted to have a horsepower rating not less than the combined load to the motor-compressor(s) and other motor(s) at the locked-rotor condition, if the ampere rating of the switch is not less than this locked-rotor load plus the resistance load.

(2) The ampere rating of the disconnecting means shall be at least 115 percent of the summation of all currents at the rated-load condition determined in accordance with Section 440-12(b)(1).

(c) Small Motor-Compressors.   For small motor-compressors not having the locked-rotor current marked on the nameplate, or for small motors not covered by Tables 430-147, 430-148, 430-149, or 430-150, the locked-rotor current shall be assumed to be six times the rated-load current. See Section 440-3(a).

(d) Disconnecting Means Rated in Excess of 100 Horsepower.   Where the rated-load or locked-rotor current as determined above would indicate a disconnecting means rated in excess of 100 horsepower, the provisions of Section 430-109, Exception No. 4 shall apply.

440-13. Cord-Connected Equipment.   For cord-connected equipment such as room air conditioners, household refrigerators and freezers, drinking water coolers, and beverage dispensers, a separable connector or an attachment plug and receptacle shall be permitted to serve as the disconnecting means. See also Section 440-63.

440-14. Location.   A disconnecting means shall be located within sight from and readily accessible from the air-conditioning or refrigerating equipment.

Exception: Cord- and plug-connected appliances.

See Parts G and H of Article 430 for additional requirements.

C. Branch-Circuit Short-Circuit and Ground-Fault Protection

440-21. General.   The provisions of Part C specify devices intended to protect the branch-circuit conductors, control apparatus and motors in circuits supplying hermetic refrigerant motor-compressors against overcurrent due to short circuits and grounds. They are in addition to or amendatory of the provisions of Article 240.

Where an air conditioner is listed by a qualified testing laboratory with the nameplate stating "maximum fuse size," the listing restricts the use of this unit to fuse protection only and does not cover its use with circuit breakers. If the air conditioner has been evaluated for both fuses and circuit breakers, it may be so marked. It is the intent of Section 110-3(b) to have any restriction of listing applied to the installation of the equipment in order to comply with the *National Electrical Code.*

The UL Electrical Appliance and Utilization Equipment Directory states the following under "Air-Conditioners, Central Cooling: "This marked protective device rating is the maximum for which the equipment has been investigated and found acceptable. Where the marking specifies fuses, the equipment is intended to be protected by fuses only." (See Figure 440-1.)

440-22. Application and Selection.

(a) Rating or Setting for Individual Motor-Compressor.   The motor-compressor branch-circuit short-circuit and ground-fault protective device shall be capable of carrying the starting current of the motor. The required protection shall be considered as being obtained when this device has a rating or setting not exceeding 175 percent of the motor-compressor rated-load current or branch-circuit selection current, whichever is greater (15 amperes size minimum), provided that where the protection specified is not sufficient for the starting current of the motor, it shall be permitted to be increased, but shall not exceed 225 percent of the motor rated-load current or branch-circuit selection current, whichever is greater.

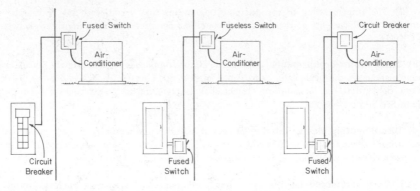

Figure 440-1. Illustrated are three correct wiring methods indicating, where the nameplate specifies fuses, that the equipment is intended to be protected by fuses only.

(b) Rating or Setting for Equipment.   The equipment branch-circuit short-circuit and ground-fault protective device shall be capable of carrying the starting current of the equipment. Where the hermetic refrigerant motor-compressor is the only load on the circuit, the protection shall conform with Section 440-22(a). Where the equipment incorporates more than one hermetic refrigerant motor-compressor or a hermetic refrigerant motor-compressor and other motors or other loads, the equipment short-circuit and ground-fault protection shall conform with Section 430-53 and the following:

(1) Where a hermetic refrigerant motor-compressor is the largest load connected to the circuit, the rating or setting of the branch-circuit short-circuit and ground-fault protective device shall not exceed the value specified in Section 440-22(a) for the largest motor-compressor plus the sum of the rated-load current or branch-circuit selection current, whichever is greater, of the other motor-compressor(s) and the ratings of the other loads supplied.

(2) Where a hermetic refrigerant motor-compressor is not the largest load connected to the circuit, the rating or setting of the branch-circuit short-circuit and ground-fault protective device shall not exceed a value equal to the sum of the rated-load current or branch-circuit selection current, whichever is greater, rating(s) for the motor-compressor(s) plus the value specified in Section 430-53(c)(4) where other motor loads are supplied, or the value specified in Section 240-3 where only nonmotor loads are supplied in addition to the motor-compressor(s).

Exception No. 1: Equipment which will start and operate on a 15- or 20-ampere 120-volt, or 15-ampere 208- or 240-volt single-phase branch circuit shall be considered as protected by the 15- or 20-ampere overcurrent device protecting the branch circuit, but if the maximum branch-circuit short-circuit and ground-fault protective device rating marked on the equipment is less than these values, the circuit protective device shall not exceed the value marked on the equipment nameplate.

Exception No. 2: The nameplate marking of cord- and plug-connected equipment rated not greater than 250 volts, single-phase, such as household refrigerators and freezers, drinking water coolers, and beverage dispensers, shall be used in determining the branch-circuit requirements, and each unit shall be considered as a single motor unless the nameplate is marked otherwise.

(c) Protective Device Rating Not to Exceed the Manufacturer's Values.   Where maximum protective device ratings shown on a manufacturer's heater table for use with a motor controller are less than the rating or setting selected in accordance with Section 440-22(a) and (b), the protective device rating shall not exceed the manufacturer's values marked on the equipment.

D. Branch-Circuit Conductors

440-31. General. The provisions of Part D and Articles 300 and 310 specify sizes of conductors required to carry the motor current without overheating under the conditions specified, except as modified in Section 440-5(a), Exception No. 1.

The provisions of these articles shall not apply to integral conductors of motors, motor controllers and the like, or to conductors which form an integral part of approved equipment.

See Sections 300-1(b) and 310-1 for similar requirements.

440-32. Single Motor-Compressor. Branch-circuit conductors supplying a single motor-compressor shall have an ampacity not less than 125 percent of either the motor-compressor rated-load current or the branch-circuit selection current, whichever is greater.

440-33. Motor-Compressor(s) With or Without Additional Motor Loads. Conductors supplying one or more motor-compressor(s) with or without additional load(s) shall have an ampacity not less than the sum of the rated-load or branch-circuit selection current ratings, whichever is larger, of all the motor-compressor(s) plus the full-load currents of the other motor(s), plus 25 percent of the highest motor or motor-compressor rating in the group.

Exception No. 1: When the circuitry is so interlocked as to prevent the starting and running of a second motor-compressor or group of motor-compressors, the conductor size shall be determined from the largest motor-compressor or group of motor-compressors that is to be operated at a given time.

Exception No. 2: Room air conditioners as provided in Part G of Article 440.

440-34. Combination Load. Conductors supplying a motor-compressor load in addition to a lighting or appliance load as computed from Article 220 and other applicable articles shall have an ampacity sufficient for the lighting or appliance load plus the required ampacity for the motor-compressor load determined in accordance with Section 440-33, or, for a single motor-compressor, in accordance with Section 440-32.

Exception: When the circuitry is so interlocked as to prevent simultaneous operation of the motor-compressor(s) and all other loads connected, the conductor size shall be determined from the largest size required for the motor-compressor(s) and other loads to be operated at a given time.

440-35. Multimotor and Combination-Load Equipment. The ampacity of the conductors supplying multimotor and combination-load equipment shall not be less than the minimum circuit ampacity marked on the equipment in accordance with Section 440-3(b).

E. Controllers for Motor-Compressors

440-41. Rating.

(a) Motor-Compressor Controller. A motor-compressor controller shall have both a continuous-duty full-load current rating, and a locked-rotor current rating, not less than the nameplate rated-load current or branch-circuit selection current, whichever is greater, and locked-rotor current, respectively (see Sections 440-5 and 440-6) of the compressor. In case the motor controller is rated in horsepower, but is without one or both of the foregoing current ratings, equivalent currents shall be determined from the ratings as follows: use Tables 430-148, 430-149, or 430-150 to determine the equivalent locked-rotor current rating.

(b) Controller Serving More than One Load. A controller, serving more than one motor-compressor or a motor-compressor and other loads, shall have a continuous-duty full-load current rating, and a locked-rotor current rating not less than the combined load as determined in accordance with Section 440-12(b).

F. Motor-Compressor and Branch-Circuit Overload Protection

440-51. General. The provisions of Part F specify devices intended to protect the motor-compressor, the motor-control apparatus, and the branch-circuit conductors against excessive heating due to motor overload and failure to start. See Section 240-3(a), Exception No. 3.

Note: Overload in electrically driven apparatus is an operating overcurrent which, when it persists for a sufficient length of time, would cause damage or dangerous overheating. It does not include short circuits or ground faults.

440-52. Application and Selection.

(a) Protection of Motor-Compressor. Each motor-compressor shall be protected against overload and failure to start by one of the following means:

(1) A separate overload relay which is responsive to motor-compressor current. This device shall be selected to trip at not more than 140 percent of the motor-compressor rated-load current.

(2) A thermal protector integral with the motor-compressor, approved for use with the motor-compressor which it protects on the basis that it will prevent dangerous overheating of the motor-compressor due to overload and failure to start. If the current-interrupting device is separate from the motor-compressor and its control circuit is operated by a protective device integral with the motor-compressor, it shall be so arranged that the opening of the control circuit will result in interruption of current to the motor-compressor.

(3) A fuse or inverse time circuit breaker responsive to motor current, which shall also be permitted to serve as the branch-circuit short-circuit and ground-fault protective device. This device shall be rated at not more than 125 percent of the motor-compressor rated-load current. It shall have sufficient time delay to permit the motor-compressor to start and accelerate its load. The equipment or the motor-compressor shall be marked with this maximum branch-circuit fuse or inverse time circuit breaker rating.

(4) A protective system, furnished or specified and approved for use with the motor-compressor which it protects on the basis that it will prevent dangerous overheating of the motor-compressor due to overload and failure to start. If the current interrupting device is separate from the motor-compressor and its control circuit is operated by a protective device which is not integral with the current-interrupting device, it shall be so arranged that the opening of the control circuit will result in interruption of current to the motor-compressor.

(b) Protection of Motor-Compressor Control Apparatus and Branch-Circuit Conductors. The motor-compressor controller(s), the disconnecting means and branch-circuit conductors shall be protected against overcurrent due to motor overload and failure to start by one of the following means which may be the same device or system protecting the motor-compressor in accordance with Section 440-52(a).

Exception: For motor-compressors and equipment on 15- or 20-ampere single-phase branch circuits as provided in Sections 440-54 and 440-55.

(1) An overload relay selected in accordance with Section 440-52(a)(1).

(2) A thermal protector applied in accordance with Section 440-52(a)(2) and which will not permit a continuous current in excess of 156 percent of the marked rated-load current or branch-circuit selection current.

(3) A fuse or inverse time circuit breaker selected in accordance with Section 440-52(a)(3).

(4) A protective system in accordance with Section 440-52(a)(4) and which will not permit a continuous current in excess of 156 percent of the marked rated-load current or branch-circuit selection current.

440-53. Overload Relays.   Overload relays and other devices for motor overload protection, which are not capable of opening short circuits, shall be protected by fuses or inverse time circuit breakers with ratings or settings in accordance with Part C unless approved for group installation or for part-winding motors and marked to indicate the maximum size of fuse or inverse time circuit breaker by which they shall be protected.

Exception: The fuse or inverse time circuit breaker size marking shall be permitted on the nameplate of approved equipment in which the overload relay or other overload device is used.

440-54. Motor-Compressors and Equipment on 15- or 20-Ampere Branch Circuits — Not Cord-and-Attachment Plug-Connected.   Overload protection for motor-compressors and equipment used on 15- or 20-ampere 120-volt, or 15-ampere 208- or 240-volt single-phase branch circuits as permitted in Article 210 shall be permitted as indicated in (a) and (b) below.

(a) Overload Protection.   The motor-compressor shall be provided with overload protection selected as specified in Section 440-52(a). Both the controller and motor overload protective device shall be approved for installation with the short-circuit and ground-fault protective device for the branch circuit to which the equipment is connected.

(b) Time Delay.   The short-circuit and ground-fault protective device protecting the branch circuit shall have sufficient time delay to permit the motor-compressor and other motors to start and accelerate their loads.

440-55. Cord-and-Attachment Plug-Connected Motor-Compressors and Equipment on 15- or 20-Ampere Branch Circuits.   Overload protection for motor-compressors and equipment that are cord-and-attachment plug-connected and used on 15- or 20-ampere 120-volt, or 15-ampere 208- or 240-volt single-phase branch circuits as permitted in Article 210 shall be permitted as indicated in (a), (b), and (c) below.

(a) Overload Protection.   The motor-compressor shall be provided with overload protection as specified in Section 440-52(a). Both the controller and the motor overload protective device shall be approved for installation with the short-circuit and ground-fault protective device for the branch circuit to which the equipment is connected.

(b) Attachment Plug and Receptacle Rating.   The rating of the attachment plug and receptacle shall not exceed 20 amperes at 125 volts or 15 amperes at 250 volts.

(c) Time Delay.   The short-circuit and ground-fault protective device protecting the branch circuit shall have sufficient time delay to permit the motor-compressor and other motors to start and accelerate their loads.

G. Provisions for Room Air Conditioners

440-60. General.   The provisions of Part G shall apply to electrically energized room air conditioners that control temperature and humidity. For the purpose of Part G, a room air conditioner (with or without provisions for heating) shall be considered as an alternating-current appliance of the air-cooled window, console, or in-wall type that is installed in the conditioned room and which incorporates a hermetic refrigerant motor-compressor(s). The provisions of Part G cover equipment rated not over 250 volts, single phase, and such equipment shall be permitted to be cord-and-attachment plug-connected.

A room air conditioner that is rated three phase or rated over 250 volts shall be directly connected to a wiring method recognized in Chapter 3, and provisions of Part G shall not apply.

440-61. Grounding. Room air conditioners shall be grounded in accordance with Sections 250-42, 250-43, and 250-45.

440-62. Branch-Circuit Requirements.

(a) Room Air Conditioner as a Single Motor Unit. A room air conditioner shall be considered as a single motor unit in determining its branch-circuit requirements when all the following conditions are met:

(1) It is cord-and-attachment plug-connected.

(2) Its rating is not more than 40 amperes and 250 volts, single phase.

(3) Total rated-load current is shown on the room air-conditioner nameplate rather than individual motor currents, and

(4) The rating of the branch-circuit short-circuit and ground-fault protective device does not exceed the ampacity of the branch-circuit conductors or the rating of the receptacle, whichever is less.

(b) Where No Other Loads Are Supplied. The total marked rating of a cord-and-attachment plug-connected room air conditioner shall not exceed 80 percent of the rating of a branch circuit where no other loads are supplied.

(c) Where Lighting Units or Other Appliances Are also Supplied. The total marked rating of a cord-and-attachment plug-connected room air conditioner shall not exceed 50 percent of the rating of a branch circuit where lighting units or other appliances are also supplied.

440-63. Disconnecting Means. An attachment plug and receptacle shall be permitted to serve as the disconnecting means for a single-phase room air conditioner rated 250 volts or less if: (1) the manual controls on the room air conditioner are readily accessible and located within 6 feet (1.83 m) of the floor, or (2) an approved manually operable switch is installed in a readily accessible location within sight from the room air conditioner.

440-64. Supply Cords. Where a flexible cord is used to supply a room air conditioner, the length of such cord shall not exceed: (1) 10 feet (3.05 m) for a nominal, 120-volt rating, or (2) 6 feet (1.83 m) for a nominal 208- or 240-volt rating.

ARTICLE 445 — GENERATORS

Contents

445-1. General.   Generators and their associated wiring and equipment shall comply with the applicable provisions of Articles 230, 250, 700, 701, and 702.

445-2. Location.   Generators shall be of a type suitable for the locations in which they are installed. They shall also meet the requirements for motors in Section 430-14. Generators installed in hazardous (classified) locations as described in Articles 500 through 503, or in other locations as described in Articles 510 through 517, and in Articles 520, 530, and 665 shall also comply with the applicable provisions of those articles.

445-3. Marking.   Each generator shall be provided with a nameplate giving the maker's name, the rated frequency, power factor, number of phases if of alternating current, the rating in kilowatts or kilovolt amperes, the normal volts and amperes corresponding to the rating, rated revolutions per minute, insulation system class and rated ambient temperature or rated temperature rise, and time rating.

445-4. Overcurrent Protection.

(a) **Constant-Voltage Generators.**   Constant-voltage generators, except alternating-current generator exciters, shall be protected from overloads by inherent design, circuit breakers, fuses, or other acceptable current-limiting means, suitable for the conditions of use.

(b) **Two-Wire Generators.**   Two-wire, direct-current generators shall be permitted to have overcurrent protection in one conductor only if the overcurrent device is actuated by the entire current generated other than the current in the shunt field. The overcurrent device shall not open the shunt field.

(c) **65 Volts or Less.**   Generators operating at 65 volts or less and driven by individual motors shall be considered as protected by the overcurrent device protecting the motor if these devices will operate when the generators are delivering not more than 150 percent of their full-load rated current.

(d) **Balancer Sets.**   Two-wire, direct-current generators used in conjunction with balancer sets to obtain neutrals for 3-wire systems shall be equipped with overcurrent devices that will disconnect the 3-wire system in case of excessive unbalancing of voltages or currents.

(e) **3-Wire, Direct-Current Generators.**   Three-wire, direct-current generators, whether compound or shunt wound, shall be equipped with overcurrent devices, one in each armature lead, and so connected as to be actuated by the entire current from the armature. Such overcurrent devices shall consist either of a double-pole, double-coil circuit breaker, or of a 4-pole circuit breaker connected in the main and equalizer leads and tripped by two overcurrent devices, one in each armature lead. Such protective devices shall be so interlocked that no one pole can be opened without simultaneously disconnecting both leads of the armature from the system.

Alternating-current generators can be designed so that, during short periods of time when the generator may carry an excessive overload, the voltage will fall off sufficiently to limit the current and power output to values that will not damage the generator.

The connection of a 2-wire generator, protected by a single-pole circuit breaker, is illustrated in Figure 445-1. Where two or more dc generators are operated in parallel or multiple, an equalizer conductor lead is connected to the positive terminal of each generator or, in effect, is the connecting of the series fields in parallel to maintain equal output voltage for each generator. The current could divide at the positive terminal, some flowing through the series field and positive lead and some flowing through the equalizer lead. The entire current generated flows through the negative lead; therefore, the fuse or circuit breaker (or at least the operating coil of a circuit breaker) must be placed in the negative lead. Overcurrent devices must be connected so as to be actuated by the entire armature output current.

An overcurrent device should not be placed in the shunt-field circuit because, if this circuit were to open when the field is at full strength, an extremely high voltage would be induced which could damage the field-winding insulation and injure the generator.

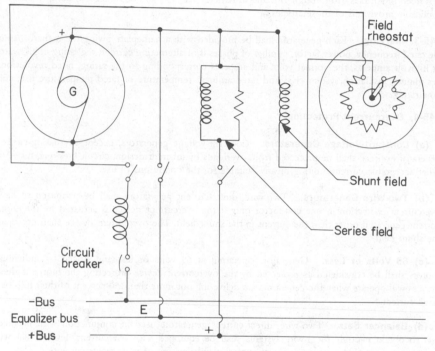

Figure 445-1. A schematic diagram of a 2-wire dc generator protected by a single-pole circuit breaker.

Section 445-4(c) indicates that generators operating at 65 V or less are to be thought of as protected by the overcurrent devices that also protect the drive-motor, providing these devices will operate when the generator delivers 150 percent of its rated full-load current.

Figure 445-2 illustrates a double-pole circuit breaker with one pole connected in each lead of the main generator and with the operating coil properly designed to be connected in the neutral lead from the balancer, and so arranged as to be operated by either one of the "A" coils or by the "B" coil. Each of the two generators used as a balancer set carries approximately one-half of the unbalanced load and, thus, is always smaller than the main generator. During an excessive imbalance of the load, the balancer set would be overloaded with no overload on the main generator, hence a double-pole circuit breaker is connected (as noted) to guard against this condition.

It should be noted that the authority having jurisdiction may judge that the generator should operate to failure rather than providing automatic means to shut it down, which, in many cases, could present a greater hazard to personnel. An overload sensing device(s) would be permitted to be connected to an annunciator or an alarm (instead of interrupting the generator) and allow operating personnel to shut down load-side equipment in a safe and orderly fashion.

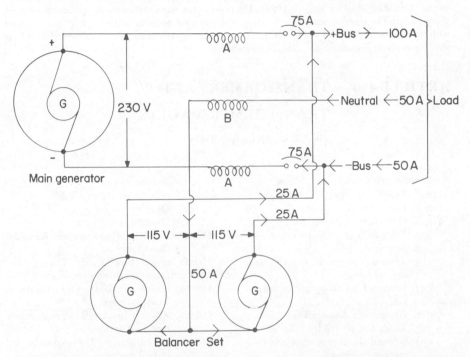

Figure 445-2. A schematic diagram of a double-pole circuit breaker (one pole connected in each lead of the main generator) with the opening coil arranged to be connected in the neutral of the balancer set.

Exception to (a) through (e): Where deemed by the authority having jurisdiction, a generator is vital to the operation of an electrical system and the generator should operate to failure to prevent a greater hazard to persons, the overload sensing device(s) is permitted to be connected to an annunciator or alarm supervised by authorized personnel instead of interrupting the generator circuit.

445-5. Ampacity of Conductors.   The ampacity of the phase conductors from the generator terminals to the first overcurrent device shall not be less than 115 percent of the nameplate current rating of the generator. It shall be permitted to size the neutral conductors in accordance with Section 220-22. Conductors which must carry ground-fault currents shall not be smaller than required by Section 250-23(b).

Exception No. 1: Where the design and operation of the generator prevent overloading, the ampacity of the conductors shall not be less than 100 percent of the nameplate current rating of the generator.

Exception No. 2: Where the generator manufacturer's leads are connected directly to an overcurrent device that is an integral part of the generator set assembly.

445-6. Protection of Live Parts. Live parts of generators operated at more than 150 volts to ground shall not be exposed to accidental contact where accessible to unqualified persons.

445-7. Guards for Attendants. Where necessary for the safety of attendants, the requirements of Section 430-133 shall apply.

445-8. Bushings. Where wires pass through an opening in an enclosure, conduit box, or barrier, a bushing shall be used to protect the conductors from the edges of an opening having sharp edges. The bushing shall have smooth, well-rounded surfaces where it may be in contact with the conductors. If used where oils, grease, or other contaminants may be present, the bushing shall be made of a material not deleteriously affected.

ARTICLE 450 — TRANSFORMERS AND
TRANSFORMER VAULTS

(Including Secondary Ties)

Contents

450-1. Scope. This article covers the installation of all transformers.

Exception No. 1: Current transformers.

Exception No. 2: Dry-type transformers that constitute a component part of other apparatus and comply with the requirements for such apparatus.

Exception No. 3: Transformers which are an integral part of an X-ray, high-frequency, or electrostatic-coating apparatus.

Exception No. 4: Transformers used with Class 2 and Class 3 circuits that comply with Article 725.

Exception No. 5: Transformers for sign and outline lighting that comply with Article 600.

Exception No. 6: Transformers for electric-discharge lighting that comply with Article 410.

Exception No. 7: Transformers used for power-limited fire protective signaling circuits that comply with Part C of Article 760.

Exception No. 8: Liquid-filled or dry-type transformers used for research, development, or testing, where effective arrangements are provided to safeguard unqualified persons from contacting high-voltage terminals or energized conductors.

Exception No. 8 permits an exemption for these transformers from the requirements of Article 450 because they are usually energized only when tests are being made, they are under constant supervision by qualified personnel, and high-voltage circuits are guarded and interlocked to protect against accidental contact by unqualified persons.

This article also covers the installation of transformers in hazardous (classified) locations as modified by Articles 501 through 503.

A. General Provisions

450-2. Location. Transformers and transformer vaults shall be readily accessible to qualified personnel for inspection and maintenance.

Exception No. 1: Dry-type transformers 600 volts, nominal, or less, located in the open on walls, columns, or structures, shall not be required to be readily accessible.

Exception No. 2: Dry-type transformers not exceeding 600 volts, nominal, and 50 kVA shall be permitted in fire-resistant hollow spaces of buildings not permanently closed in by structure and provided they meet the ventilation requirements of Section 450-8.

Unless specified otherwise in this article, the term fire resistant means a construction having a minimum fire rating of 1 hour.

See ASTM Standard E119-75; Fire Tests of Building Construction and Materials, NFPA 251-1972; and Methods of Fire Tests of Building Construction and Materials, ANSI A2.1-1972.

The location of oil-insulated transformers and transformer vaults is covered in Sections 450-26, 450-27, and 450-41; dry-type transformers in Section 450-21; and askarel-insulated transformers in Section 450-25.

450-3. Overcurrent Protection.   Overcurrent protection shall comply with (a) through (c) below. As used in this section, the word "transformer" shall mean a transformer or polyphase bank of two or three single-phase transformers operating as a unit.

(a) Transformers Over 600 Volts, Nominal.

(1) Primary.   Each transformer over 600 volts, nominal, shall be protected by an individual overcurrent device on the primary side. Where fuses are used, their continuous current rating shall not exceed 250 percent of the rated primary current of the transformer. Where circuit breakers are used, they shall be set at not more than 300 percent of the rated primary current of the transformer.

Exception No. 1: Where 250 percent of the rated primary current of the transformer does not correspond to a standard rating of a fuse, the next higher standard rating shall be permitted.

Exception No. 2: An individual overcurrent device shall not be required where the primary circuit overcurrent device provides the protection specified in this section.

Exception No. 3: As provided in (a)(2) below.

(2) Primary and Secondary.   A transformer over 600 volts, nominal, having an overcurrent device on the secondary side rated or set to open at not more than the values noted in Table 450-3(a)(2), or a transformer equipped with a coordinated thermal overload protection by the manufacturer, shall not be required to have an individual overcurrent device in the primary connection provided the primary feeder overcurrent device is rated or set to open at not more than the values noted in Table 450-3(a)(2).

Table 450-3(a)(2)
Transformers Over 600 Volts
Having Overcurrent Protection on the Primary and Secondary Sides

	Maximum Overcurrent Device				
	Primary		Secondary		
	Over 600 Volts		Over 600 Volts		600 Volts or Below
Transformer Rated Impedance	Circuit Breaker Setting	Fuse Rating	Circuit Breaker Setting	Fuse Rating	Circuit Breaker Setting or Fuse Rating
Not more than 6%	600%	300%	300%	250%	250%
More than 6% and not more than 10%	400%	300%	250%	225%	250%

(b) Transformers 600 Volts, Nominal, or Less.

(1) Primary.   Each transformer 600 volts, nominal, or less, shall be protected by an individual overcurrent device on the primary side, rated or set at not more than 125 percent of the rated primary current of the transformer.

Exception No. 1: Where the rated primary current of a transformer is 9 amperes or more and 125 percent of this current does not correspond to a standard rating of a fuse or nonadjustable circuit breaker, the next higher standard rating described in Section 240-6 shall be permitted. Where the rated primary current is less than 9 amperes, an overcurrent device rated or set at not more than 167 percent of the primary current shall be permitted.

Where the rated primary current is less than 2 amperes, an overcurrent device rated or set at not more than 300 percent shall be permitted.

Exception No. 2: An individual overcurrent device shall not be required where the primary circuit overcurrent device provides the protection specified in this section.

Exception No. 3: As provided in (b)(2) below.

(2) Primary and Secondary. A transformer 600 volts, nominal, or less, having an overcurrent device on the secondary side rated or set at not more than 125 percent of the rated secondary current of the transformer shall not be required to have an individual overcurrent device on the primary side if the primary feeder overcurrent device is rated or set at a current value not more than 250 percent of the rated primary current of the transformer.

A transformer 600 volts, nominal, or less, equipped with coordinated thermal overload protection by the manufacturer and arranged to interrupt the primary current, shall not be required to have an individual overcurrent device on the primary side if the primary feeder overcurrent device is rated or set at a current value not more than six times the rated current of the transformer for transformers having not more than 6 percent impedance, and not more than four times the rated current of the transformer for transformers having more than 6 but not more than 10 percent impedance.

Exception: Where the rated secondary current of a transformer is 9 amperes or more and 125 percent of this current does not correspond to a standard rating of a fuse or nonadjustable circuit breaker, the next higher standard rating described in Section 240-6 shall be permitted.

Where the rated secondary current is less than 9 amperes, an overcurrent device rated or set at not more than 167 percent of the rated secondary current shall be permitted.

(c) Potential (Voltage) Transformers. Potential transformers installed indoors or enclosed hall be protected with primary fuses.

Questions frequently arise as to whether the overcurrent protection required for transformers, as specified in Section 450-3, will provide satisfactory protection for the primary and secondary conductors. Where polyphase transformers are involved, these conductors will usually not be properly protected. The rules are intended to protect the transformer alone. The primary overcurrent device provides short-circuit protection for the transformer, and the secondary overcurrent device prevents it from being overloaded. The transformer is considered the point of supply, and the conductors that it supplies must be protected in accordance with their ampacity.

Exceptions to this rule are permitted under special conditions outlined in Section 230-207, and Exception No. 8 of Section 240-21.

Single-phase transformers having a 2-wire (single voltage) secondary may also omit the secondary overcurrent device if the primary overcurrent protection is provided in accordance with this section, and its rating does not exceed the value determined by multiplying the secondary conductor ampacity by the secondary to primary voltage ratio. (See Section 240-3, Exception No. 5.)

Single-phase transformers with a 3-wire secondary are not included in this

Exception because of the possibility of a severe unbalanced load which the primary protection would not recognize.

In those cases that the primary feeder to the transformer incorporates overcurrent protective devices that are rated (or set) at a level not to exceed those prescribed herein, it is not necessary to duplicate them at the transformer.

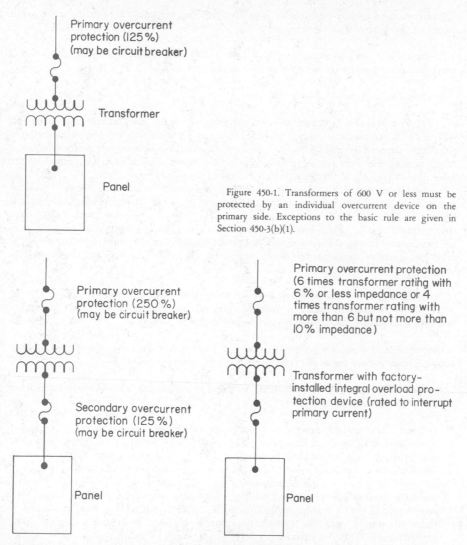

Primary overcurrent
protection (125%)
(may be circuit breaker)

Transformer

Panel

Figure 450-1. Transformers of 600 V or less must be protected by an individual overcurrent device on the primary side. Exceptions to the basic rule are given in Section 450-3(b)(1).

Primary overcurrent
protection (250%)
(may be circuit breaker)

Secondary overcurrent
protection (125%)
(may be circuit breaker)

Panel

Primary overcurrent protection
(6 times transformer rating with
6% or less impedance or 4
times transformer rating with
more than 6 but not more than
10% impedance)

Transformer with factory-
installed integral overload protection device (rated to interrupt
primary current)

Panel

Figure 450-2. Overcurrent protection on the primary and secondary sides of transformers rated 600 V or less. Exceptions to the basic rule are given in Section 450-3(b)(2).

450-4. Grounding Autotransformers. Grounding autotransformers covered in this section are zig-zag or T-connected transformers connected to 3-phase, 3-wire ungrounded systems for the purpose of creating a 3-phase, 4-wire distribution system or to provide a neutral reference for grounding purposes. Such transformers shall have a continuous per phase current rating and a continuous neutral current rating.

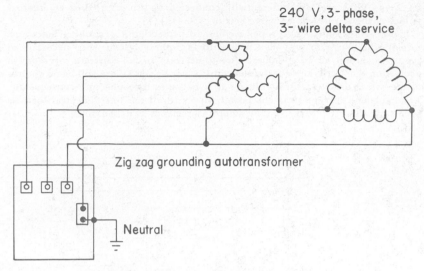

Figure 450-3. A zig-zag autotransformer used to create a 3-phase, 4-wire distribution system or to provide a neutral reference for grounding purposes.

The phase current in a grounding autotransformer is one-third the neutral current.

(a) Three-Phase, 4-Wire System.   A grounding autotransformer used to create a 3-phase, 4-wire distribution system from a 3-phase, 3-wire ungrounded system shall conform to the following:

(1) Connections.   The transformer shall be directly connected to the ungrounded phase conductors and shall not be switched or provided with overcurrent protection which is independent of the main switch and common-trip overcurrent protection for the 3-phase, 4-wire system.

(2) Overcurrent Protection.   An overcurrent sensing device shall be provided that will cause the main switch or common-trip overcurrent protection referred to in (a)(1) above to open if the load on the autotransformer reaches or exceeds 125 percent of its continuous current per phase or neutral rating. Delayed tripping for temporary overcurrents sensed at the autotransformer overcurrent device shall be permitted for the purpose of allowing proper operation of branch or feeder protective devices on the 4-wire system.

(3) Transformer Fault Sensing.   A fault sensing system that will cause the opening of a main switch or common-trip overcurrent device for the 3-phase, 4-wire system shall be provided to guard against single-phasing or internal faults.

This can be accomplished by the use of two subtractive-connected donut-type current transformers installed to sense and signal when an unbalance occurs in the line current to the autotransformer of 50 percent or more of rated current.

(4) Rating.   The autotransformer shall have a continuous neutral current rating sufficient to handle the maximum possible neutral unbalanced load current of the 4-wire system.

The donut-type current transformers in Figure 450-4 are intended to trip the main breaker if the current in any phase or the neutral conductor exceeds 125 percent of the rated current [see Section 450-4(a)(2)]. The current transformers

CT-2 and CT-3 are also differentially connected to protect against an internal failure of the autotransformer [see Section 450-4(a)(3)].

Figure 450-4 shows the proper method of protecting a grounding autotransformer where used to provide a neutral for a 3-phase system when necessary to supply a group of single-phase line-to-neutral loads. Separate overcurrent protection is not provided for the autotransformer because there will be no control of the system line-to-neutral voltages if it becomes disconnected; consequently, simultaneous interruption of the power supply to all the line-to-neutral loads is necessary whenever the grounding autotransformer is switched off.

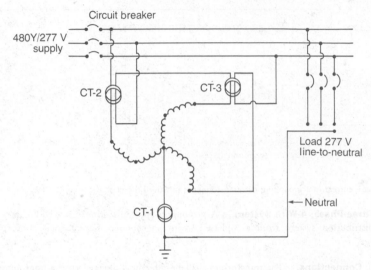

Figure 450-4. Zig-zag autotransformer for establishing a neutral connection for a 480 Y/277 V 3-phase ungrounded system to supply single-phase line-to-neutral loads. See Section 450-4(a).

CT-1 is connected to an overload relay responsive to excess neutral current being supplied. See Section 450-4(a)(2).

CT-2 and CT-3 are connected to differential-type fault-current sensing relays responsive to an unbalance of neutral current among the three phases of the grounding autotransformer (indicating an internal fault). See Section 450-4(a)(3).

All three relays are to be arranged to trip the circuit breaker located upstream of both the autotransformer and the line-to-neutral connected loads to satisfy the requirements of Section 450-4(a)(1).

(b) Ground Reference for Fault Protection Devices.   A grounding autotransformer used to make available a specified magnitude of ground-fault current for operation of a ground responsive protective device on a 3-phase, 3-wire ungrounded system shall conform to the following requirements:

(1) Rating.   The autotransformer shall have a continuous neutral current rating sufficient for the specified ground-fault current.

(2) Overcurrent Protection.   An overcurrent protective device of adequate short-circuit rating that will open simultaneously all ungrounded conductors when it operates shall be applied in the grounding autotransformer branch circuit and rated or set at a current not exceeding 125 percent of the autotransformer continuous per phase current rating or 42 percent of the continuous current rating of any series connected devices in the autotransformer neutral connection. Delayed tripping for temporary overcurrents to permit the proper operation of ground responsive tripping devices on the main system shall be permitted, but shall not exceed values which would be more than the short-time current rating of the grounding autotransformer or any series connected devices in the neutral connection thereto.

Figure 450-5 depicts a grounding autotransformer to provide a neutral reference on an ungrounded 3-phase system for protection against line-to-ground faults.

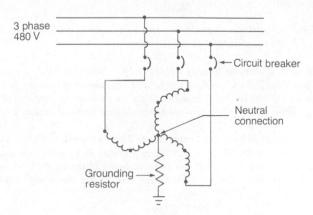

Figure 450-5. Zig-zag autotransformer for establishing a reference ground-fault current for fault-protective device operation or for damping transitory overvoltage surges. See Section 450-4(b) and (c).

The OC protective device is to have a rating (or setting) not in excess of 125 percent of the rated phase current of the autotransformer (42 percent of the neutral current rating) and not more than 42 percent of the continuous current rating of the neutral grounding resistor or other current-carrying device in the neutral connection. See Section 450-4(b)(2).

(c) Ground Reference for Damping Transitory Overvoltages. A grounding autotransformer used to limit transitory overvoltages shall be of suitable rating and connected in accordance with (a)(1) above.

For this case involving a high-resistance grounding package, the *NEC* text seems to suggest that the connections and overcurrent protection should conform with Section 450-4(a) (1), but this is not the case. The functional performance parallels that involved in Section 450-4(b), differing only in that the magnitude of available ground-fault current would likely be a lower value. It would be appropriate to employ the connections displayed on Figure 450-5, and conform with the overcurrent protection requirements prescribed in Section 450-4(b) (2).

With any of the grounding autotransformer applications covered by Sections 450-4(a), (b), or (c), it is important to emphasize the use of a ganged 3-pole switching interrupter for connecting and disconnecting the autotransformer in order to accomplish simultaneous connection (and disconnection) of the three line terminals. If at any time one or two of the line connections to the autotransformer should become "open," which could occur if the protective devices were single-pole, the grounding autotransformer ceases to function in the desired fashion and acts as a high-inductive-reactance connection between the electrical system and "ground." The latter connection is prone to create high-value transitory overvoltages, line-to-ground — a most unwanted result.

450-5. Secondary Ties. A secondary tie is a circuit operating at 600 volts, nominal, or less, between phases that connects two power sources or power supply points, such as the secondaries of two transformers. The tie may consist of one or more conductors per phase.

As used in this section, the word "transformer" means a transformer or a bank of transformers operating as a unit.

(a) Tie Circuits.   Tie circuits shall be provided with overcurrent protection at each end as required in Article 240.

Exception: Under the conditions described in (a)(1) and (a)(2) below, the overcurrent protection shall be permitted to be in accordance with (a)(3) below.

(1) Loads at Transformer Supply Points Only.   Where all loads are connected at the transformer supply points at each end of the tie and overcurrent protection is not provided in accordance with Article 240, the rated ampacity of the tie shall not be less than 67 percent of the rated secondary current of the largest transformer connected to the secondary tie system.

(2) Loads Connected Between Transformer Supply Points.   Where load is connected to the tie at any point between transformer supply points and overcurrent protection is not provided in accordance with Article 240, the rated ampacity of the tie shall not be less than 100 percent of the rated secondary current of the largest transformer connected to the secondary tie system.

Exception: As otherwise provided in (a)(4) below.

(3) Tie Circuit Protection.   Under the conditions described in (a)(1) and (a)(2) above, both ends of each tie conductor shall be equipped with a protective device that will open at a predetermined temperature of the tie conductor under short-circuit conditions. This protection shall consist of one of the following: (1) a fusible link cable connector, terminal, or lug, commonly known as a limiter, each being of a size corresponding with that of the conductor and of construction and characteristics according to the operating voltage and the type of insulation on the tie conductors, or (2) automatic circuit breakers actuated by devices having comparable current-time characteristics.

(4) Interconnection of Phase Conductors Between Transformer Supply Points.   Where the tie consists of more than one conductor per phase, the conductors of each phase shall be interconnected in order to establish a load supply point, and the protection specified in (a)(3) above shall be provided in each tie conductor at this point.

Exception: Loads shall be permitted to be connected to the individual conductors of a paralleled conductor tie without interconnecting the conductors of each phase and without the protection specified in (a)(3) above at load connection points provided the tie conductors of each phase have a combined capacity of not less than 133 percent of the rated secondary current of the largest transformer connected to the secondary tie system; the total load of such taps does not exceed the rated secondary current of the largest transformer; and the loads are equally divided on each phase and on the individual conductors of each phase as far as practicable.

(5) Tie Circuit Control.   Where the operating voltage exceeds 150 volts to ground, secondary ties provided with limiters shall have a switch at each end that, when open, will de-energize the associated tie conductors and limiters. The current rating of the switch shall not be less than the rated current of the conductors connected to the switch. It shall be capable of opening its rated current, and it shall be constructed so that it will not open under the magnetic forces resulting from short-circuit current.

(b) Overcurrent Protection for Secondary Connections.   Where secondary ties are used, an overcurrent device rated or set at not more than 250 percent of the rated secondary current of the transformers shall be provided in the secondary connections of each transformer. In addition, an automatic circuit breaker actuated by a reverse-current relay set to open the circuit at not more than the rated secondary current of the transformer shall be provided in the secondary connection of each transformer.

The rules under Section 450-5 apply specifically to network systems for power distribution that are commonly employed where the load density is high and reliability of service is important. Such a system is illustrated in Figure 450-8. This type of distribution system introduces a variety of problems not encountered in the more common radial-type distribution system and must be designed by experienced electrical engineers. The sketch shows a typical 3-phase network system for an industrial plant fed by two primary feeders, preferably from separate substations, which are energized at any standard voltage up to 34,500 V. Each of the transformers is supplied by the two primary feeders which are arranged by means of a double-throw switch at the transformer so that either feeder may supply it.

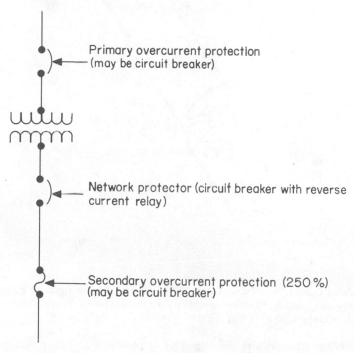

Primary overcurrent protection (may be circuit breaker)

Network protector (circuit breaker with reverse current relay)

Secondary overcurrent protection (250%) (may be circuit breaker)

Figure 450-6. Primary and secondary overcurrent protection for a transformer in a network system showing a network protector (an automatic circuit breaker actuated by a reverse-current relay).

Each of the network transformers is rated in the range of 300 kVA to 1,000 kVA and is required to be protected as illustrated in Figure 450-6. The primary and secondary protection is in accordance with Section 450-3, but an additional protective device must also be provided on the secondary side known as a network protector consisting of a circuit breaker and a reverse-power relay. This operates on reverse current to prevent power being fed back into the transformer through the secondary ties should a fault occur in the transformer or in a primary feeder. The reverse power relay is set to trip the circuit breaker at a current value not more than the rated secondary current of the transformer. The relay is not designed to trip the circuit breaker in the event of an overload on the secondary of the transformer.

The secondary ties shown in Figure 450-8 are required to be protected at each end with an overcurrent device in accordance with Section 450-5(a)(3). The overcurrent device most commonly provided for this purpose is a special type of fuse known as a current limiter (see Figure 450-7). This is a high interrupting capacity device designed to provide short-circuit protection only for the secondary ties and will open safely before temperatures damaging to the cable insulation are reached. The secondary ties form a closed loop that is equipped with switching devices so that any part of the loop may be isolated when repairs are needed or a current limiter must be replaced.

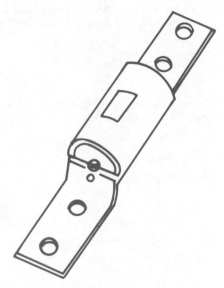

Figure 450-7. A current-limiter is a special type of high-interrupting capacity fuse.

450-6. Parallel Operation. Transformers shall be permitted to be operated in parallel and switched as a unit provided that the overcurrent protection for each transformer meets the requirements of Section 450-3 (a)(2) or (b)(2).

450-7. Guarding. Transformers shall be guarded as specified in (a) through (d) below.

(a) Mechanical Protection. Appropriate provisions shall be made to minimize the possibility of damage to transformers from external causes where the transformers are exposed to physical damage.

(b) Case or Enclosure. Dry-type transformers shall be provided with a noncombustible moisture-resistant case or enclosure that will provide reasonable protection against the accidental insertion of foreign objects.

(c) Exposed Live Parts. Transformers shall be so installed that live parts are guarded in accordance with Section 110-17.

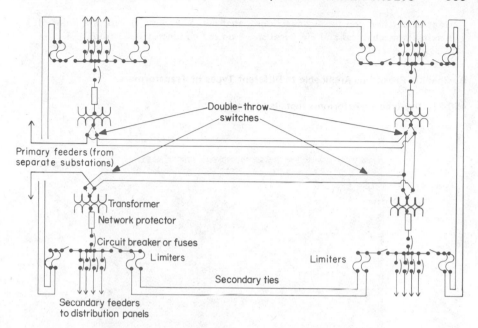

Figure 450-8. A typical 3-phase network system for an industrial plant fed by two primary feeders.

(d) Voltage Warning. The operating voltage of exposed live parts of transformer installations shall be indicated by signs or visible markings on the equipment or structures.

450-8. Ventilation. The ventilation shall be adequate to dispose of the transformer full-load losses without creating temperature rise which is in excess of the transformer rating.

See ANSI C57.12.00-1973, General Requirements for Distribution, Power, and Regulating Transformers.

450-9. Grounding. Exposed noncurrent-carrying metal parts of transformer installations, including fences, guards, etc., shall be grounded where required under the conditions and in the manner specified for electric equipment and other exposed metal parts in Article 250.

450-10. Marking. Each transformer shall be provided with a nameplate giving the name of the manufacturer; rated kilovolt-amperes; frequency; primary and secondary voltage; impedance of transformers 25 kVA and larger; and the amount and kind of insulating liquid where used. In addition, the nameplate of each dry-type transformer shall include the temperature class for the insulation system.

The information given on a transformer nameplate is necessary for determining whether the transformer is capable of carrying the load it is supplying as calculated in accordance with Article 220.

450-11. Terminal Wiring Space. The minimum wire bending space at fixed, 600 volts and below terminals of transformer line and load connections shall be as required in Section 373-6. Wiring space for pigtail connections shall conform to Table 370-6(b).

This rule is to ensure adequate wire bending space at fixed terminals of transformer line and load connections, rated 600 V or less, as this is a point of maximum mechanical and electrical stress on the conductor insulation.

B. Specific Provisions Applicable to Different Types of Transformers

450-21. Dry-type Transformers Installed Indoors.

Figure 450-9. 1,500 kVA gas-filled dry-type transformer available in ratings through 5,000 kVA, 34½ kVA for use indoors or outdoors. (*Westinghouse Electric Corp.*)

(a) Not Over 112½ kVA.   Transformers installed indoors and rated 112½ kVA or less shall have a separation of at least 12 inches (305 mm) from combustible material unless separated therefrom by a fire-resistant, heat-insulating barrier, or unless of a rating not over 600 volts and completely enclosed except for ventilating openings.

(b) Over 112½ kVA.   Transformers of more than 112½ kVA rating shall be installed in a transformer room of fire-resistant construction.

Exception No. 1 to (b): Transformers constructed with Class 80°C rise or higher insulation and separated from combustible material by a fire-resistant, heat-insulating barrier or by not less than 6 feet (1.83 m) horizontally and 12 feet (3.66 m) vertically.

Exception No. 2 to (b): Transformers constructed with Class 80°C rise or higher insulation and of completely enclosed and ventilated-type construction.

(c) Over 35,000 Volts.   Transformers rated over 35,000 volts shall be installed in a vault complying with Part C of this article.

Dry-type transformers depend on the surrounding air for adequate ventilation and where rated less than 112½ kVA are not required to be installed in a fire-resistive transformer room.

Transformers of the dry type, gas-filled, or high fire point liquid-insulated transformers (see Section 450-23) installed indoors with a primary voltage of not more than 35,000 volts are commonly used because no transformer vault is required.

For the same reason, askarel-filled transformers have been extensively used indoors in the past. However, askarel, which is a polychlorinated biphenyl, is no longer being manufactured, but acceptable substitutes that comply with Section 450-23 are now available. See Figure 450-11.

Figure 450-9 shows a 1,500 kVA gas-filled dry-type transformer available in ratings through 5,000 kVA, 34½ kV for use indoors or outdoors. These units are built using the conventional ventilated dry-type core and coils but sealed in a heavy welded steel tank and filled with fluorocarbon gas for dielectric strength as well as cooling. Since the transformers are completely hermetically sealed in a heavy gage steel tank, they are completely safe indoors and outdoors, and there is no possibility for flames or gases to escape in the event of a short circuit or transformer failure. These units are recommended for any explosive, highly combustible, or dangerous area and offer the highest resistance to fire or explosion. See Sections 501-2, 502-2, and 503-2.

Figure 450-10 shows a dry-type transformer with the outside casing in place and with the latest core and coil design for a typical dry-type power transformer rated at 1,000 kVA, 13,800 V to 480, 3-phase, 60 cycle. This transformer has a high-voltage and low-voltage flange for connection to switchgear and a high-voltage, 2-position (double-throw), 3-pole load break air switch which may be attached to the case and arranged as a selector switch for the connection of the transformer primary to either of two feeder sources.

Dry-type transformers rated less than 112½ kVA are to be separated from combustible material or rated less than 600 V and completely enclosed, except for ventilating openings. Noncombustible insulations used in transformers, such as mica, porcelain, glass, and asbestos, which can withstand high temperatures, have permitted the application of larger dry-type transformers; however, combustible materials, such as varnish, are used with those insulations, and under short-circuit conditions, flames can escape from the transformer enclosure. Hence, transformers rated under 112½ kVA are to be spaced 12 in. or separated by fire-resistive barriers from combustibles or completely enclosed. Those rated over 112½ kVA are to be located in fire-resistive transformer rooms or vaults.

450-22. Dry-type Transformers Installed Outdoors.   Dry-type transformers installed outdoors shall have a weatherproof enclosure.

Transformers exceeding 112½ kVA shall not be located within 12 inches (305 mm) of combustible materials of buildings.

450-23. High Fire Point Liquid-Insulated Transformers.   Transformers insulated with listed less-flammable liquids shall be permitted to be installed without a vault in noncombustible occupancy areas of noncombustible buildings, provided there is a liquid confinement area and the minimum clearances required by the heat release rates of the listed liquid are maintained.

Such indoor transformer installations not meeting the clearance requirements of the liquid listing, or installed in combustible buildings or combustible occupancy areas, shall be provided with an automatic fire extinguishing system or shall be installed in a vault complying with Part C of this article.

Figure 450-10. A dry-type transformer with a core and coil design rated at 1,000 kVA, 13,800 V to 480, 3-phase, 60 Hz. (*Westinghouse Electric Corp.*)

Transformers installed indoors and rated over 35,000 volts shall be installed in a vault.

Transformers installed outdoors shall comply with Section 450-27.

For purposes of this section, a less-flammable liquid is one with a fire point not less than 300°C.

For definition of "Noncombustible" as used in this section, see Types of Building Construction, NFPA 220-1979.

See definition of "Listed" in Article 100.

Figure 450-11 shows a liquid-insulated transformer filled with a listed, less flammable liquid with a fire point of at least 300°C (572°F). These may be installed indoors without a vault in noncombustible occupancy areas of noncombustible buildings provided they are not rated over 35,000 V, there is a liquid confinement area, and the minimum clearances required by the heat release rates of the listed liquid are maintained. Factory Mutual Research Corp. has listings of the "less flammable" liquids covered in this section.

450-24. Nonflammable Fluid-Insulated Transformers. Transformers insulated with a dielectric fluid identified as nonflammable shall be permitted to be installed indoors or outdoors. Such transformers installed indoors and rated over 35,000 volts shall be installed in a vault.

For the purposes of this section, a nonflammable dielectric fluid is one which does not have a flash point or fire point, and is not flammable in air.

Figure 450-11. A liquid-insulated transformer filled with a listed, less flammable liquid with a fire point of at least 300°C (572°F). (*Square D Co.*)

450-25. Askarel-Insulated Transformers Installed Indoors.   Askarel-insulated transformers installed indoors and rated over 25 kVA shall be furnished with a pressure-relief vent. Where installed in a poorly ventilated place, they shall be furnished with a means for absorbing any gases generated by arcing inside the case, or the pressure-relief vent shall be connected to a chimney or flue that will carry such gases outside the building. Askarel-insulated transformers rated over 35,000 volts shall be installed in a vault.

450-26. Oil-Insulated Transformers Installed Indoors.   Oil-insulated transformers installed indoors shall be installed in a vault constructed as specified in Part C of this article.

Exception No. 1: Where the total capacity does not exceed 112½ kVA, the vault specified in Part C of this article shall be permitted to be constructed of reinforced concrete not less than 4 inches (102 mm) thick.

Exception No. 2: Where the nominal voltage does not exceed 600, a vault shall not be required if suitable arrangements are made to prevent a transformer oil fire from igniting other materials, and the total capacity in one location does not exceed 10 kVA in a section of the building classified as combustible, or 75 kVA where the surrounding structure is classified as fire-resistant construction.

Exception No. 3: Electric furnace transformers having a total rating not exceeding 75 kVA shall be permitted to be installed without a vault in a building or room of fire-resistant construction, provided suitable arrangements are made to prevent a transformer oil fire from spreading to other combustible material.

Exception No. 4: Transformers shall be permitted to be installed in a detached building that does not comply with Part C of this article if neither the building nor its contents presents a fire hazard to any other building or property, and if the building is used only in supplying electric service and the interior is accessible only to qualified persons.

Exception No. 5: Oil-insulated transformers shall be permitted to be used without a vault in portable and mobile surface mining equipment (such as electric excavators) if each of the following conditions is met:

a. Provision is made for draining leaking fluid to the ground.

b. Safe egress is provided for personnel.

c. A minimum ¼-inch (6.35-mm) steel barrier is provided for personnel protection.

450-27. Oil-Insulated Transformers Installed Outdoors. Combustible material, combustible buildings, and parts of buildings, fire escapes, and door and window openings shall be safeguarded from fires originating in oil-insulated transformers installed on roofs, attached to, or adjacent to a building or combustible material.

Space separations, fire-resistant barriers, automatic water spray systems, and enclosures that confine the oil of a ruptured transformer tank are recognized safeguards. One or more of these safeguards shall be applied according to the degree of hazard involved in cases where the transformer installation presents a fire hazard.

Oil enclosures shall be permitted to consist of fire-resistant dikes, curbed areas or basins, or trenches filled with coarse crushed stone. Oil enclosures shall be provided with trapped drains where the exposure and the quantity of oil involved are such that removal of oil is important. Transformers installed on poles or structures or underground shall conform to the National Electrical Safety Code, ANSI C2-1977.

C. Transformer Vaults

450-41. Location. Vaults shall be located where they can be ventilated to the outside air without using flues or ducts wherever such an arrangement is practicable.

450-42. Walls, Roof and Floor. The walls and roofs of vaults shall be constructed of materials which have adequate structural strength for the conditions with a minimum fire resistance of 3 hours according to ASTM Standard E119-75; Fire Tests of Building Construction and Materials, NFPA 251-1972; and Methods of Fire Tests of Building Construction and Materials, ANSI A2.1-1972. The floors of vaults in contact with the earth shall be of concrete not less than 4 inches (102 mm) thick, but when the vault is constructed with a vacant space or other stories below it, the floor shall have adequate structural strength for the load imposed thereon and a minimum fire resistance of 3 hours.

Six-inch (152-mm) thick reinforced concrete is a typical 3-hour construction.

Exception: Where transformers are protected with automatic sprinkler, water spray, carbon dioxide, or halon, construction of 1-hour rating shall be permitted.

450-43. Doorways. Vault doorways shall be protected as follows:

(a) Type of Door. Each doorway leading into a vault from the building interior shall be provided with a tight-fitting door having a minimum fire rating of 3 hours as defined in the Standard for the Installation of Fire Doors and Windows, NFPA 80-1979 (ANSI). The authority having jurisdiction shall be permitted to require such a door for an exterior wall opening where conditions warrant.

Exception: Where transformers are protected with automatic sprinkler, water spray, carbon dioxide, or halon, construction of 1-hour rating shall be permitted.

(b) Sills. A door sill or curb of sufficient height to confine within the vault the oil from the largest transformer shall be provided, and in no case shall the height be less than 4 inches (102 mm).

(c) Locks. Entrance doors shall be equipped with locks, and doors shall be kept locked, access being allowed only to qualified persons. Locks and latches shall be so arranged that the door can be readily and quickly opened from the inside.

450-45. Ventilation Openings. Where required by Section 450-8, openings for ventilation shall be provided in accordance with (a) through (f) below.

(a) Location. Ventilation openings shall be located as far away as possible from doors, windows, fire escapes, and combustible material.

(b) Arrangement. A vault ventilated by natural circulation of air shall be permitted to have roughly half of the total area of openings required for ventilation in one or more openings near the floor and the remainder in one or more openings in the roof or in the sidewalls near the roof, or all of the area required for ventilation shall be permitted in one or more openings in or near the roof.

(c) Size. For a vault ventilated by natural circulation of air to an outdoor area, the combined net area of all ventilating openings, after deducting the area occupied by screens, gratings, or louvers, shall not be less than 3 square inches (1936 sq mm) per kVA of transformer capacity in service, and in no case shall the net area be less than 1 square foot (0.093 sq m) for any capacity under 50 kVA.

(d) Covering. Ventilation openings shall be covered with durable gratings, screens, or louvers, according to the treatment required in order to avoid unsafe conditions.

(e) Dampers. All ventilation openings to the indoors shall be provided with automatic closing fire dampers that operate in response to a vault fire. Such dampers shall possess a standard fire rating of not less than 1½ hours.

See Standard for Fire Dampers, ANSI Z233.1-1972.

(f) Ducts. Ventilating ducts shall be constructed of fire-resistant material.

450-46. Drainage. Where practicable, vaults containing more than 100 kVA transformer capacity shall be provided with a drain or other means that will carry off any accumulation of oil or water in the vault unless local conditions make this impracticable. The floor shall be pitched to the drain where provided.

450-47. Water Pipes and Accessories. Any pipe or duct system foreign to the electrical installation shall not enter or pass through a transformer vault. Piping or other facilities provided for vault fire protection, or for transformer cooling, shall not be considered foreign to the electrical installation.

450-48. Storage in Vaults. Materials shall not be stored in transformer vaults.

ARTICLE 460 — CAPACITORS

Contents

460-1. Scope.   This article covers the installation of capacitors on electric circuits.

Surge capacitors or capacitors included as a component part of other apparatus and conforming with the requirements of such apparatus are excluded from these requirements.

This article also covers the installation of capacitors in hazardous (classified) locations as modified by Articles 501 through 503.

460-2. Enclosing and Guarding.

(a) Containing More than 3 Gallons (11.36 L) of Flammable Liquid.   Capacitors containing more than 3 gallons (11.36 L) of flammable liquid shall be enclosed in vaults or outdoor fenced enclosures complying with Article 710.

(b) Accidental Contact.   Capacitors shall be enclosed, located, or guarded so that persons cannot come into accidental contact or bring conducting materials into accidental contact with exposed energized parts, terminals, or buses associated with them.

Exception: No additional guarding is required for enclosures accessible only to authorized and qualified persons.

A. 600 Volts, Nominal, and Under

460-6. Drainage of Stored Charge.   Capacitors shall be provided with a means of draining the stored charge.

(a) Time of Discharge.   The residual voltage of a capacitor shall be reduced to 50 volts, nominal, or less, within 1 minute after the capacitor is disconnected from the source of supply.

(b) Means of Discharge.   The discharge circuit shall be either permanently connected to the terminals of the capacitor or capacitor bank, or provided with automatic means of connecting it to the terminals of the capacitor bank on removal of voltage from the line. Manual means of switching or connecting the discharge circuit shall not be used.

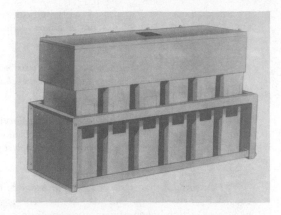

Figure 460-1. Single-tier, six-capacitor rack with prewired connections. (*Sprague Electric Co.*)

Some means must be provided to drain off the stored charge in a capacitor after the supply circuit has been opened. Otherwise, a person servicing the equipment could receive a severe shock or damage may occur to the equipment.

460-7. Power Factor Correction — Motor Circuit.

(a) Total Kilovar Rating of Capacitors. The total kilovar rating of capacitors that are connected on the load side of a motor controller shall not exceed the value required to raise the no-load power factor of the motor branch circuit to unity.

Figure 460-2(a) or (b) shows the method in which capacitors are connected in a motor circuit so that they may be switched with the motor. In either arrangement the stored charge will drain off through the windings when the circuit is opened. Figure 460-2(c) shows a third arrangement where the capacitor is permanently connected to the system. This arrangement eliminates the need for a separate switch to disconnect the capacitors.

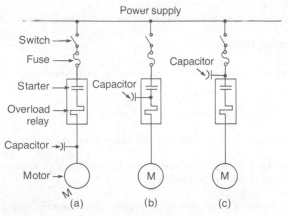

Figure 460-2. Methods of connecting capacitors in induction motor circuit for power factor correction.
Capacitors may be equipped with built-in resistors to drain off the stored charge, although this type is not needed when connected as shown in Figs. 460-2(a) and (b).

Capacitors may be equipped with built-in resistors to drain off the stored charge, although this type is not needed when connected as shown in Figures 460-2(a) and 460-2(b).

Exception: When motor ratings do not exceed 600 volts, nominal, and 50 horsepower, capacitors not exceeding 50 percent of the kVA rating of the motor input shall be permitted to be connected on the load side of the motor controller.

(b) Motor Not Subject to Unusual Switching Service.   Capacitors so connected shall be permitted only in applications where the motor is not subject to unusual switching service such as plugging, rapid reversals, reclosings or other similar operations which could generate over-voltages and over-torques.

The purpose of this rule is to prevent possible mechanical or electrical damage caused by over-voltage and also to prevent over-torques caused by induction-generator action when the motor-capacitor combination is de-energized. The words "so connected" in Section 460-7(b) refer to motors connected in accordance with the exception to 450-7(a).

460-8. Conductors.

(a) Ampacity.   The ampacity of capacitor circuit conductors shall not be less than 135 percent of the rated current of the capacitor. The ampacity of conductors that connect a capacitor to the terminals of a motor or to motor circuit conductors shall not be less than one third the ampacity of the motor circuit conductors and in no case less than 135 percent of the rated current of the capacitor.

(b) Overcurrent Protection.

(1) An overcurrent device shall be provided in each ungrounded conductor for each capacitor bank.

Exception: A separate overcurrent device shall not be required for a capacitor connected on the load side of a motor-running overcurrent device.

(2) The rating or setting of the overcurrent device shall be as low as practicable.

(c) Disconnecting Means.

(1) A disconnecting means shall be provided in each ungrounded conductor for each capacitor bank.

Exception: Where a capacitor is connected on the load side of a motor-running overcurrent device.

(2) The disconnecting means shall open all ungrounded conductors simultaneously.

Section 460-8(c)(2) has been revised in the 1981 *Code* to require simultaneous opening of all ungrounded conductors.

(3) The disconnecting means shall be permitted to disconnect the capacitor from the line as a regular operating procedure.

(4) The rating of the disconnecting means shall not be less than 135 percent of the rated current of the capacitor.

220, 440, 550, 2300 and 4000 Volt Induction Motor, 3 Phase 60 hertz.

NEMA Motor Design A or B, Normal Starting Torque, Normal Running Current

H.P. RATING	3600 RPM KVAR	3600 RPM %AR	1800 RPM KVAR	1800 RPM %AR	1200 RPM KVAR	1200 RPM %AR	900 RPM KVAR	900 RPM %AR	720 RPM KVAR	720 RPM %AR	600 RPM KVAR	600 RPM %AR
3	1.5	14	1.5	15	1.5	20	2	27	2.5	35	3.5	41
5	2	12	2	13	2	17	3	25	4	32	4.5	37
7½	2.5	11	2.5	12	3	15	4	22	5.5	30	6	34
10	3	10	3	11	3.5	14	5	21	6.5	27	7.5	31
15	4	9	4	10	5	13	6.5	18	8	23	9.5	27
20	5	9	5	10	5	11	7½	18	10	20	10	25
25	5	6	5	8	7½	11	7½	13	10	20	10	21
30	5	6	5	8	7½	11	10	15	15	22	15	25
40	7½	8	10	8	10	10	15	16	15	18	15	20
50	10	7	10	8	10	9	15	12	20	15	25	22
60	10	6	10	8	15	10	15	11	20	15	25	20
75	15	7	15	8	15	9	20	11	30	15	40	20
100	20	8	20	8	25	9	30	11	40	14	45	18
125	20	6	25	7	30	9	30	10	45	14	50	17
150	30	6	30	7	35	9	40	10	50	17	60	17
200	40	6	40	7	45	8	55	11	60	12	75	17
250	45	5	45	6	60	9	70	10	75	12	100	17
300	50	5	50	6	75	9	75	9	80	12	105	17

NEMA Motor Design C, High Starting Torque, Normal Running Current

H.P. RATING	1800 RPM KVAR	1800 RPM %AR	1200 RPM KVAR	1200 RPM %AR	900 RPM KVAR	900 RPM %AR	720 RPM KVAR	720 RPM %AR	600 RPM KVAR	600 RPM %AR
3	—	—	2	26	3	31	4	40	4.5	51
5	2	15	2.5	21	4	29	5	36	6.5	46
7½	2.5	13	3.5	18	5	27	6.5	34	8	41
10	3.5	13	4	16	6	25	8	32	9.5	39
15	5	12	5.5	14	8	21	10	28	13	36
20	6	12	6.5	13	9.5	19	12	25	17	35
25	7.5	12	8	12	11	17	14	24	20	33
30	8.5	12	9	12	13	17	16	23	23	32
40	11	11	12	11	16	16	20	22	30	30
50	13	11	16	11	20	16	25	21	35	29
60	16	11	19	11	23	15	27.5	20	40	27
75	21	11	24	11	27.5	14	35	19	45	25
100	33.3	11	33.3	11	33.3	11	33.3	11	50	12
125	33.3	10	33.3	10	33.3	11	33.3	17	66.6	18
150	33.3	9	33.3	9	33.3	10	66.6	16	66.6	17
200	45	9	45	9	45	9	75	15	75	15
250	45	8	66.6	9	45	9	—	—	—	—
300	45	6	75	9	66.6	9	—	—		

NOTES: % AR is the percentage that the running current to the motor capacitor combination is reduced by the application of the capacitor.

The capacitor size specified in the above table will increase the full load power factor to between 95 and 98%, and larger sizes should not be used without consulting the manufacturer.

Figure 460-3. Maximum size of capacitor switched with motor.

Desired Power Factor in Percentage

Original Power Factor in Percentage	80	81	82	83	84	85	86	87	88	89	90	91	92	93	94	95	96	97	98	99	1.0
50	0.982	1.008	1.034	1.060	1.086	1.112	1.139	1.165	1.192	1.220	1.248	1.276	1.306	1.337	1.369	1.403	1.440	1.481	1.529	1.589	1.732
51	0.937	0.962	0.989	1.015	1.041	1.067	1.094	1.120	1.147	1.175	1.203	1.231	1.261	1.292	1.324	1.358	1.395	1.436	1.484	1.544	1.687
52	0.893	0.919	0.945	0.971	0.997	1.023	1.050	1.076	1.103	1.131	1.159	1.187	1.217	1.248	1.280	1.314	1.351	1.392	1.440	1.500	1.643
53	0.850	0.876	0.902	0.928	0.954	0.980	1.007	1.033	1.060	1.088	1.116	1.144	1.174	1.205	1.237	1.271	1.308	1.349	1.397	1.457	1.600
54	0.809	0.835	0.861	0.887	0.913	0.939	0.966	0.992	1.019	1.047	1.075	1.103	1.133	1.164	1.196	1.230	1.267	1.308	1.356	1.416	1.559
55	0.769	0.795	0.821	0.847	0.873	0.899	0.926	0.952	0.979	1.007	1.035	1.063	1.093	1.124	1.156	1.190	1.227	1.268	1.316	1.376	1.519
56	0.730	0.756	0.782	0.808	0.834	0.860	0.887	0.913	0.940	0.968	0.996	1.024	1.054	1.085	1.117	1.151	1.188	1.229	1.277	1.337	1.480
57	0.692	0.718	0.744	0.770	0.796	0.822	0.849	0.875	0.902	0.930	0.958	0.986	1.016	1.047	1.079	1.113	1.150	1.191	1.239	1.299	1.442
58	0.655	0.681	0.707	0.733	0.759	0.785	0.812	0.838	0.865	0.893	0.921	0.949	0.979	1.010	1.042	1.076	1.113	1.154	1.202	1.262	1.405
59	0.619	0.645	0.671	0.697	0.723	0.749	0.776	0.802	0.829	0.857	0.885	0.913	0.943	0.974	1.006	1.040	1.077	1.118	1.166	1.226	1.369
60	0.583	0.609	0.635	0.661	0.687	0.713	0.740	0.766	0.793	0.821	0.849	0.877	0.907	0.938	0.970	1.004	1.041	1.082	1.130	1.190	1.333
61	0.549	0.575	0.601	0.627	0.653	0.679	0.706	0.732	0.759	0.787	0.815	0.843	0.873	0.904	0.936	0.970	1.007	1.048	1.096	1.156	1.299
62	0.516	0.542	0.568	0.594	0.620	0.646	0.673	0.699	0.725	0.754	0.782	0.810	0.840	0.871	0.903	0.937	0.974	1.015	1.063	1.123	1.266
63	0.485	0.509	0.535	0.561	0.587	0.613	0.640	0.666	0.693	0.721	0.749	0.777	0.807	0.838	0.870	0.904	0.941	0.982	1.030	1.090	1.233
64	0.451	0.474	0.503	0.529	0.555	0.581	0.608	0.634	0.661	0.689	0.717	0.745	0.775	0.806	0.838	0.872	0.909	0.950	0.998	1.068	1.201
65	0.419	0.445	0.471	0.497	0.523	0.549	0.576	0.602	0.629	0.657	0.685	0.713	0.743	0.774	0.806	0.840	0.877	0.918	0.966	1.026	1.169
66	0.388	0.414	0.440	0.466	0.492	0.518	0.545	0.571	0.598	0.626	0.654	0.682	0.712	0.743	0.775	0.809	0.846	0.887	0.935	0.995	1.138
67	0.358	0.384	0.410	0.436	0.462	0.488	0.515	0.541	0.568	0.596	0.624	0.652	0.682	0.713	0.745	0.779	0.816	0.857	0.905	0.965	1.108
68	0.328	0.354	0.380	0.406	0.432	0.458	0.485	0.511	0.538	0.566	0.594	0.622	0.652	0.683	0.715	0.749	0.786	0.827	0.875	0.935	1.078
69	0.299	0.325	0.351	0.377	0.403	0.429	0.456	0.482	0.509	0.537	0.565	0.593	0.623	0.654	0.686	0.720	0.757	0.798	0.846	0.906	1.049
70	0.270	0.296	0.322	0.348	0.374	0.400	0.427	0.453	0.480	0.508	0.536	0.564	0.594	0.625	0.657	0.691	0.728	0.769	0.817	0.877	1.020
71	0.242	0.268	0.294	0.320	0.346	0.372	0.399	0.425	0.452	0.480	0.508	0.536	0.566	0.597	0.629	0.663	0.700	0.741	0.789	0.849	0.992
72	0.214	0.240	0.266	0.292	0.318	0.344	0.371	0.397	0.424	0.452	0.480	0.508	0.538	0.569	0.601	0.635	0.672	0.713	0.761	0.821	0.964
73	0.186	0.212	0.238	0.264	0.290	0.316	0.343	0.369	0.396	0.424	0.452	0.480	0.510	0.541	0.573	0.607	0.644	0.685	0.733	0.793	0.936
74	0.159	0.185	0.211	0.237	0.263	0.289	0.316	0.342	0.369	0.397	0.425	0.453	0.483	0.514	0.546	0.580	0.617	0.658	0.706	0.766	0.909
75	0.132	0.158	0.184	0.210	0.236	0.262	0.289	0.315	0.342	0.370	0.398	0.426	0.456	0.487	0.519	0.553	0.590	0.631	0.679	0.739	0.882
76	0.105	0.131	0.157	0.183	0.209	0.235	0.262	0.288	0.315	0.343	0.371	0.399	0.429	0.460	0.492	0.526	0.563	0.604	0.652	0.712	0.855
77	0.079	0.105	0.131	0.157	0.183	0.209	0.236	0.262	0.289	0.317	0.345	0.373	0.403	0.434	0.466	0.500	0.537	0.578	0.626	0.686	0.829
78	0.052	0.078	0.104	0.130	0.156	0.182	0.209	0.235	0.262	0.290	0.318	0.346	0.376	0.407	0.439	0.473	0.510	0.551	0.599	0.659	0.802
79	0.026	0.052	0.078	0.104	0.130	0.156	0.183	0.209	0.236	0.264	0.292	0.320	0.350	0.381	0.413	0.447	0.484	0.525	0.573	0.633	0.776
80	0.000	0.026	0.052	0.078	0.104	0.130	0.157	0.183	0.210	0.238	0.266	0.294	0.324	0.355	0.387	0.421	0.458	0.499	0.547	0.609	0.750

	80	81	82	83	84	85	86	87	88	89	90	91	92	93	94	95	96	97	98	99	1.0
81		0.000	0.026	0.052	0.078	0.104	0.131	0.157	0.184	0.212	0.240	0.268	0.298	0.329	0.361	0.395	0.432	0.473	0.521	0.581	0.724
82			0.000	0.026	0.052	0.078	0.105	0.131	0.158	0.186	0.214	0.242	0.272	0.303	0.335	0.369	0.406	0.447	0.495	0.555	0.698
83				0.000	0.026	0.052	0.079	0.105	0.132	0.160	0.188	0.216	0.246	0.277	0.309	0.343	0.380	0.421	0.469	0.529	0.672
84					0.000	0.026	0.053	0.079	0.106	0.134	0.162	0.190	0.220	0.251	0.283	0.317	0.354	0.395	0.443	0.503	0.646
85						0.000	0.027	0.053	0.080	0.108	0.136	0.164	0.194	0.225	0.257	0.291	0.328	0.369	0.417	0.477	0.620
86							0.000	0.026	0.053	0.081	0.109	0.137	0.167	0.198	0.230	0.264	0.301	0.342	0.390	0.450	0.593
87								0.000	0.027	0.055	0.083	0.111	0.141	0.172	0.204	0.238	0.275	0.316	0.364	0.424	0.567
88									0.000	0.028	0.056	0.084	0.114	0.145	0.177	0.211	0.248	0.289	0.337	0.397	0.540
89										0.000	0.028	0.056	0.086	0.117	0.149	0.183	0.220	0.261	0.309	0.369	0.512
90											0.000	0.028	0.058	0.089	0.121	0.155	0.192	0.233	0.281	0.341	0.484
91												0.000	0.030	0.061	0.093	0.127	0.164	0.205	0.253	0.313	0.456
92													0.000	0.031	0.063	0.097	0.134	0.175	0.223	0.283	0.426
93														0.000	0.032	0.066	0.103	0.144	0.192	0.252	0.395
94															0.000	0.034	0.071	0.112	0.160	0.220	0.363
95																0.000	0.037	0.079	0.126	0.186	0.329
96																	0.000	0.041	0.089	0.149	0.292
97																		0.000	0.048	0.108	0.251
98																			0.000	0.060	0.203
99																				0.000	0.143
																					0.000

Example: Total KW input of load from wattmeter reading, 100 KW at a power factor of 60%. The leading reactive KVAR necessary to raise the power factor to 90% is found by multiplying the 100 KW by the factor found in the table, which is .849. Then 100 KW × 0.849 = 84.9 KVAR. Use 85 KVAR.

Figure 460-4. KW multipliers for determining capacitor kilovars.

Capacitors are rated in kilovars, which is abbreviated kVAr and means reactive kilovolt-amperes. The kVAr rating shows how many reactive kilovolt-amperes the capacitor will supply in order to cancel out the reactive kilovolt-amperes caused by inductance. For example, a 20-kVAr capacitor will cancel out 20 kVA of inductive reactive kilovolt-amperes.

The basic unit is 3-phase and delta-connected internally but single-phase and 2-phase units are also available. They are constructed with built-in fuses for short-circuit protection and discharge resistors that reduce the voltage to 50-V crest or less when disconnected from the power supply. This will occur within one minute on 600-V units and within 5 minutes for 2,400- and 4,160-V units.

The capacitor circuit conductors and disconnecting device are required to have an ampacity not less than 135 percent of the rated current of the capacitor. This is because all capacitors are manufactured with a tolerance of -0 percent to +15 percent, so that a 100-kVAr capacitor may actually draw a current equivalent to a 115-kVAr capacitor. In addition, the current drawn by a capacitor varies directly with the line voltage, and any variation in the line voltage from a pure sine wave form causes the capacitor to draw an increased current. Considering these several factors, the increased current can amount to 135 percent of the rated current of the capacitor.

The current corresponding to the kVAr rating of a 3-phase capacitor is computed from the formula

$$Ic = \frac{kVAr \times 1,000}{1.73 \times volts}.$$

The ampacity of the conductors and the switching device is then determined by multiplying Ic x 1.35. The most effective power factor correction is obtained when the individual capacitors are connected directly to the terminals of the motors, transformers, and other inductive machinery.

When connected together and operated as a unit, no complicated calculations are needed to determine the proper size capacitor to use. The capacitor manufacturers publish tables (illustrated in Figure 460-3) in which the required capacitor value is indicated by referring to the speed and hp of the motor. These values will improve the motor power factor to approximately 95 percent. To improve a plant power factor, the capacitor manufacturers also publish Figure 460-4 to assist in calculating the total kVAr rating of capacitors required to improve the power factor to any desired value. The total metered demand in kW and present power factor must first be determined. The kW demand is then multiplied by the figure that is found in the column opposite the original power factor and under the desired power factor. The result is the leading reactive kVAr required to raise the power factor to the desired value.

460-9. Rating or Setting of Motor-Running Overcurrent Device. Where a motor installation includes a capacitor connected on the load side of the motor-running overcurrent device, the rating or setting of the motor overcurrent device shall be determined in accordance with Section 430-32.

Exception: Instead of using the full-load rated current of the motor as provided in Section 430-32, a lower value corresponding with the improved power factor of the motor circuit shall be used. Section 430-22 applies with respect to the rating of the motor circuit conductors.

Where a capacitor is connected on the load side of the overload relays, as shown in Figure 460-2(a), consideration must be given to the reduction in line current due to the improved power factor when selecting the rating or setting of the motor running overcurrent device. A value lower than indicated in Section 430-32 should be used for proper protection of the motor.

460-10. Grounding.   Capacitor cases shall be grounded in accordance with Article 250.

Exception: Where the capacitor units are supported on a structure which is designed to operate at other than ground potential.

460-12. Marking.   Each capacitor shall be provided with a nameplate giving the name of the manufacturer, rated voltage, frequency, kilovar or amperes, number of phases, and, if filled with a combustible liquid, the amount of liquid in gallons. When filled with a nonflammable liquid, the nameplate shall so state. The nameplate shall also indicate if a capacitor has a discharge device inside the case.

B. Over 600 Volts, Nominal

460-24. Switching.

   (a) Load Current.   Group-operated switches shall be used for capacitor switching and shall be capable of (1) carrying continuously not less than 135 percent of the rated current of the capacitor installation; (2) interrupting the maximum continuous load current of each capacitor, capacitor bank, or capacitor installation that will be switched as a unit; (3) withstanding the maximum inrush current, including contributions from adjacent capacitor installations; (4) carrying currents due to faults on capacitor side of switch.

   (b) Isolation.

   (1) A means shall be installed to isolate from all sources of potential each capacitor, capacitor bank, or capacitor installation that will be removed from service as a unit.

   (2) The isolating means shall provide a visible gap in the electrical circuit adequate for the operating voltage.

   (3) Isolating or disconnecting switches (with no interrupting rating) shall be interlocked with the load interrupting device or shall be provided with prominently displayed caution signs in accordance with Section 710-22 to prevent switching load current.

   (c) Additional Requirements for Series Capacitors.   The proper switching sequence shall be assured by use of one of the following: (1) mechanically sequenced isolating and bypass switches; (2) interlocks; or (3) switching procedure prominently displayed at the switching location.

460-25. Overcurrent Protection.

   (a) Provided to Detect and Interrupt Fault-Current.   A means shall be provided to detect and interrupt fault current likely to cause dangerous pressure within an individual capacitor.

   (b) Single-Phase or Multiphase Devices.   Single-phase or multiphase devices shall be permitted for this purpose.

   (c) Protected Individually or in Groups.   Capacitors may be protected individually or in groups.

   (d) Protective Devices Rated or Adjusted.   Protective devices for capacitors or capacitor equipment shall be rated or adjusted to operate within the limits of the Safe Zone for individual capacitors as defined by ANSI Standard for Shunt Power Capacitors, C55.1-1968.

Exception: If the protective devices are rated or adjusted to operate within the limits of the ANSI Standard for Zone 1 or Zone 2, the capacitors shall be enclosed or isolated.

In no event shall the rating or adjustment of the protective devices exceed the maximum limit of the ANSI Standard, Zone 2.

The reference to Zones 1 and 2 of ANSI Standard C-55.1-1968 pertains to the performance of the capacitors under fault conditions. If a fault current exceeds the limit established for Zone 2, the capacitor tank may burst.

460-26. Identification.   Each capacitor shall be provided with a permanent nameplate giving the maker's name, rated voltage, frequency, kilovar or amperes, number of phases, and the amount of liquid in gallons identified as flammable, if such is the case.

460-27. Grounding.   Capacitor neutrals and cases, if grounded, shall be grounded in accordance with Article 250.

Exception: Where the capacitor units are supported on a structure which is designed to operate at other than ground potential.

460-28. Means for Discharge.

(a) Means to Reduce the Residual Voltage.   A means shall be provided to reduce the residual voltage of a capacitor to 50 volts or less within 5 minutes after the capacitor is disconnected from the source of supply.

(b) Connection to Terminals.   A discharge circuit shall be either permanently connected to the terminals of the capacitor or provided with automatic means of connecting it to the terminals of the capacitor bank after disconnection of the capacitor from the source of supply. The windings of motors, or transformers, or of other equipment directly connected to capacitors without a switch or overcurrent device interposed must meet the requirements of (a) above.

ARTICLE 470 — RESISTORS AND REACTORS

For Rheostats, see Section 430-82.

Contents

A. 600 Volts, Nominal, and Under

470-1. Scope.   This article covers the installation of separate resistors and reactors on electric circuits.

Exception: Resistors and reactors that are component parts of other apparatus.

This article also covers the installation of resistors and reactors in hazardous (classified) locations as modified by Articles 501 through 503.

470-2. Location. Resistors and reactors shall not be placed where exposed to physical damage.

470-3. Space Separation. A thermal barrier shall be required if the space between the resistors and reactors and any combustible material is less than 12 inches (305 mm).

470-4. Conductor Insulation. Insulated conductors used for connections between resistance elements and controllers shall be suitable for an operating temperature of not less than 90°C (194°F).

Exception: Other conductor insulations shall he permitted for motor starting service.

Resistors are made in many different sizes and shapes and for different purposes. They may be wire or ribbon wound, form wound, edgewise wound, cast grid, punched steel grid, or box resistors. They may be mounted in the open or in ventilated metal boxes or cabinets depending upon their use and location. Since they give off heat, they must be guarded and located a safe distance from combustible materials. When mounted on switchboards or installed in control panels, they are not required to have additional guards.

Reactors are installed in a circuit to introduce inductance for motor starting, controlling the current, and paralleling of transformers. Current-limiting reactors are installed to limit the amount of current that can flow in a circuit when a short circuit occurs. Reactors can be divided into two classes, those with iron cores and those that use no magnetic materials in the windings. Both types may be air cooled or oil immersed.

Mechanical stresses due to their external fields exist between air core reactors, and the manufacturer's recommendations should be followed in spacing and bracing between units and fastening of supporting insulators.

Saturable reactors are used for theater dimming. These have, in addition to the ac winding, an auxiliary winding conected line-to-line or line-to-ground in order to neutralize charging current and prevent a voltage rise. Those used on high voltage systems are usually oil immersed.

B. Over 600 Volts, Nominal

470-18. General.

   (a) Protected Against Physical Damage. Resistors and reactors shall be protected against physical damage.

   (b) Isolated by Enclosure or Elevation. Resistors and reactors shall be isolated by enclosure or elevation to protect personnel from accidental contact with energized parts.

   (c) Combustible Materials. Resistors and reactors shall not be installed in close enough proximity to combustible materials to constitute a fire hazard and in no case closer than within 1 foot (305 mm) of combustible materials.

   (d) Clearances. Clearances from resistors and reactors to grounded surfaces shall be adequate for the voltage involved.

See Article 710.

(e) Temperature Rise from Induced Circulating Currents. Metallic enclosures of reactors and adjacent metal parts shall be installed so that the temperature rise from induced circulating currents will not be hazardous to personnel or constitute a fire hazard.

470-19. Grounding. Resistor and reactor cases or enclosures shall be grounded in accordance with Article 250.

470-20. Oil-Filled Reactors. Installation of oil-filled reactors, in addition to the above requirements, shall comply with applicable requirements of Article 450.

ARTICLE 480 — STORAGE BATTERIES

Contents

480-1. Scope. The provisions of this article shall apply to all stationary installations of storage batteries.

There are two general types of storage cells, the lead-acid type and the alkali type.

Basically, a lead-acid cell consists of a positive plate, usually lead peroxide (a semisolid compound) mounted on a framework or grid for support, and a negative plate made of sponge lead mounted on a grid. Grids are generally made of a lead-antimony alloy and the electrolyte is usually sulfuric acid and distilled water.

In the alkali-type cell (or Edison cell), the positive plate material is nickel oxide and the negative plate material is iron oxide. The electrolyte is a solution consisting mostly of potassium hydroxide (an alkaline).

480-2. Definitions.

Storage Battery. A battery comprised of one or more rechargeable cells of the lead-acid, nickel-cadmium, or other rechargeable electrochemical types.

Sealed Cell or Battery. A sealed cell or battery is one which has no provision for the addition of water or electrolyte or for external measurement of electrolyte specific gravity. The individual cells shall be permitted to contain a venting arrangement as described in Section 480-9(b).

Nominal Battery Voltage. The voltage computed on the basis of 2.0 volts per cell for the lead-acid type and 1.2 volts per cell for the alkali type.

480-3. Wiring and Equipment Supplied from Batteries. Wiring and equipment supplied from storage batteries shall be subject to the requirements of this Code applying to wiring and equipment operating at the same voltage.

Exception: As otherwise provided for communication systems in Article 800.

480-4. Grounding. The requirements of Article 250 shall apply.

480-5. Insulation of Batteries of Not Over 250 Volts. This section shall apply to storage batteries having cells so connected as to operate at a nominal battery voltage of not over 250 volts.

(a) **Vented Lead-Acid Batteries.** Cells and multicompartment batteries with covers sealed to containers of nonconductive, heat-resistant material shall not require additional insulating support.

(b) **Vented Alkaline-type Batteries.** Cells with covers sealed to jars of nonconductive, heat-resistant material shall require no additional insulation support. Cells in jars of conductive material shall be installed in trays of nonconductive material with not more than 20 cells (24 volts, nominal) in the series circuit in any one tray.

(c) **Rubber Jars.** Cells in rubber or composition containers shall require no additional insulating support where the total nominal voltage of all cells in series does not exceed 150. Where the total voltage exceeds 150, batteries shall be sectionalized into groups of 150 volts or less and each group shall have the individual cells installed in trays or on racks.

(d) **Sealed Cells or Batteries.** Sealed cells and multicompartment sealed batteries constructed of nonconductive, heat-resistant material shall not require additional insulating support. Batteries constructed of a conducting container shall have insulating support if a voltage is present between the container and ground.

480-6. Insulation of Batteries of Over 250 Volts. The provisions of Section 480-5 shall apply to storage batteries having the cells so connected as to operate at a nominal voltage exceeding 250 volts, and, in addition, the provisions of this section shall also apply to such batteries. Cells shall be installed in groups having a total nominal voltage of not over 250 volts on any one rack. Insulation, which can be air, shall be provided between racks. Maximum protection can be secured by sectionalizing high-voltage batteries into groups.

480-7. Racks and Trays. Racks and trays shall comply with (a) and (b) below.

(a) **Racks.** Racks, as required in this article, are rigid frames designed to support cells or trays. They shall be substantial and made of:

(1) Metal, so treated as to be resistant to deteriorating action by the electrolyte and provided with nonconducting members directly supporting the cells or with continuous insulating material other than paint or conducting members; or

(2) Other construction such as fiberglass or other suitable nonmetallic materials.

(b) **Trays.** Trays are frames, such as crates or shallow boxes usually of wood or other nonconductive material, so constructed or treated as to be resistant to deteriorating action by the electrolyte.

480-8. Battery Locations. Battery locations shall conform to (a) and (b) below.

(a) **Ventilation.** Provisions shall be made for sufficient diffusion and ventilation of the gases from the battery to prevent the accumulation of an explosive mixture.

Compliance with this section is necessary to prevent classification of a battery location as a hazardous (classified) location in accordance with Article 500.

It is not the intent of Section 480-8(a) to mandate mechanical ventilation. Hydrogen disperses rapidly and requires very little air movement to prevent accumulation. Unrestricted natural air movement in the vicinity of the battery together with normal air changes for occupied spaces or heat removal will normally be sufficient. If the space is confined, mechanical ventilation may be required in the vicinity of the battery.

Mechanical ventilation can be a fan, roof ridge vent, or louvered areas.

(b) Live Parts.   Guarding of live parts shall comply with Section 110-17.

Batteries are to be located in a clean, dry room and arranged to assure sufficient work space for inspection and maintenance. Provision is to be made for adequate ventilation to prevent an accumulation of an explosive mixture of the gases from the batteries.

The fumes given off by storage batteries are very corrosive; therefore, wiring and its insulation must be of a type that will withstand corrosive action. Special precautions are necessary to ensure that all metalwork (metal raceways, metal racks, etc.) is designed or treated to be corrosion resistant. Manufacturers suggest that aluminum conduit be used to withstand the corrosive battery fumes, or, if steel conduits are used, it is recommended that they be zinc-coated and corrosion protected with a coating of an asphaltum-type paint. See Section 300-6.

Overcharging heats a battery and causes gassing and loss of water. A battery should not be allowed to reach temperatures over 110°F because heat causes a shedding of active materials from the plates that will eventually form a sediment buildup in the bottom of the case and short-circuit the plates and the cell. Because mixtures of oxygen and hydrogen are highly explosive, flame or sparks should never be allowed near a cell, especially if the filler cap is removed.

480-9. Vents.

(a) Vented Cells.   Each vented cell shall be equipped with a flame arrestor designed to prevent destruction of the cell due to ignition of gases within the cell by an external spark or flame under normal operating conditions.

(b) Sealed Cells.   Sealed battery/cells shall be equipped with a pressure-release vent to prevent excessive accumulation of gas pressure or the battery/cell shall be designed to prevent scatter of cell parts in event of a cell explosion.

5 SPECIAL OCCUPANCIES

ARTICLE 500 — HAZARDOUS (CLASSIFIED) LOCATIONS

Contents

500-1. Scope — Articles 500 Through 503. Articles 500 through 503 cover the requirements for electrical equipment and wiring for all voltages in locations where fire or explosion hazards may exist due to flammable gases or vapors, flammable liquids, combustible dust, or ignitible fibers or flyings.

Locations are classified depending on the properties of the flammable vapors, liquids or gases, or combustible dusts or fibers which may be present and the likelihood that a flammable or combustible concentration or quantity is present.

Each room, section, or area shall be considered individually in determining its classification.

Exception: Except as modified in Articles 500 through 503, all other applicable rules contained in this Code shall apply to electric equipment and wiring installed in hazardous (classified) locations.

For definitions of "approved" and "explosionproof" as used in these articles, see Article 100; "dust-ignition-proof" is defined in Section 502-1.

Equipment and associated wiring approved as intrinsically safe shall be permitted in any hazardous (classified) location for which it is approved, and the provisions of Articles 500 through 517 shall not be considered applicable to such installations. Means shall be provided to prevent the passage of gases and vapors. Intrinsically safe equipment and wiring shall not be capable of releasing sufficient electrical or thermal energy under normal or abnormal conditions to cause ignition of a specific flammable or combustible atmospheric mixture in its most easily ignitible concentration.

Abnormal conditions shall include accidental damage to any field-installed wiring, failure of electrical components, application of overvoltage, adjustment and maintenance operations, and other similar conditions.

For further information, see Intrinsically Safe Apparatus and Associated Apparatus for Use in Class I, II, and III, Division 1 Hazardous Locations, NFPA 493-1978 (ANSI) and Installation of Intrinsically Safe Instrument Systems in Class I Hazardous Locations (ANSI/ISA RP 12.6-1976).

The purpose of NFPA 493, Intrinsically Safe Apparatus and Associated Apparatus for Use in Class I, II, and III, Division 1 Hazardous Locations, is to provide requirements for the construction and testing of electrical apparatus, or parts of such apparatus, in which the circuits themselves are incapable of causing ignition in Class I, II, or III, Division 1 locations, in accordance with Articles 500, 501, 502, and 503 of the *NEC*.

This standard applies not only to apparatus or parts of apparatus in the hazardous (classified) location, but also to any parts, such as power supplies and recorders, located outside of the hazardous (classified) location, where the intrinsic safety of the electrical circuits in the hazardous (classified) location may be influenced by the design and construction of such parts. The detailed requirements apply only to apparatus for use in, or associated with, a location made hazardous by the presence of flammable gas or vapor, combustible dust, or easily ignitible fibers or flyings in air under normal atmospheric conditions. If other than normal atmospheric conditions exist, equipment approved as intrinsically safe may not be intrinsically safe. This is especially true if the atmosphere is oxygen-enriched.

In evaluating safety, all interconnected apparatus and circuits are to be considered, even though located in a Division 2 hazardous (classified) location, a nonhazardous location, or protected by other means, such as an explosionproof or purged and pressurized enclosure. They are to be examined to be sure that, under normal or fault conditions, they cannot provide a source of ignition-capable energy to the apparatus in the Divison 1 hazardous (classified) location. Associated apparatus and circuits are to conform to the requirements of the location in which the apparatus and circuits are installed.

An intrinsically safe circuit is one in which any spark or a thermal effect produced either normally or in specified fault conditions is, in the test conditions prescribed in NFPA 493, incapable of causing ignition of a specified mixture of gas or vapor in air in its most easily ignited concentration. Intrinsically safe circuits are required to be identified as intrinsically safe.

Although the scope of ANSI/RP 12.6, Installation of Intrinsically Safe Instrument Systems in Class I Hazardous Locations, is limited to instrument systems, the principles are applicable to other types of intrinsically safe systems. Precautions must be taken to ensure against intrusion of unsafe energy from nonintrinsically safe circuits, particularly in nonhazardous locations where there are fewer restrictions on the wiring methods used. Separation of intrinsically safe and nonintrinsically safe circuits is usually necessary to ensure that the circuits in the hazardous (classified) locations remain intrinsically safe.

Through the exercise of ingenuity in the layout of electrical installations for hazardous (classified) locations, it is frequently possible to locate much of the equipment in less hazardous or in nonhazardous locations and thus to reduce the amount of special equipment required. In some cases, hazards may be reduced or hazardous (classified) locations limited or eliminated by adequate positive-pressure ventilation from a source of clean air in conjunction with effective safeguards against ventilation failure. For further information, see Purged and Pressurized Enclosures for Electrical Equipment in Hazardous Locations, NFPA 496-1974 (ANSI).

NFPA 496, Purged and Pressurized Enclosures for Electrical Equipment in Hazardous Locations, covers purged enclosures for electrical equipment in Class I hazardous (classified) locations, and pressurized enclosures for electrical equipment in Class II hazardous (classified) locations.

Class I Hazardous (Classified) Locations: The object of NFPA 496 for Class I hazardous (classified) locations is to provide information for the design of purged and pressurized enclosures to eliminate or reduce within the enclosure a Class I hazardous (classified) location classification, as defined in Article 500 of the *Code*. By this means, equipment that is not otherwise acceptable for hazardous (classified) locations may be utilized in accordance with the *Code*.

Purging is defined as the process of supplying an enclosure with clean air or an inert gas, at sufficient flow and positive pressure to reduce to an acceptably safe level the concentration of any flammable gases or vapors initially present, and to maintain this safe level by positive pressure with or without continuous flow.

Type X purging reduces the classification within an enclosure from Division 1 to nonhazardous.

Type Y purging reduces the classification within an enclosure from Division 1 to Division 2.

Type Z purging reduces the classification within an enclosure from Division 2 to nonhazardous.

Class II Hazardous (Classified) Locations: The object of NFPA 496 for Class II locations is to provide information for the design of pressurized enclosures to eliminate within the enclosure a Class II hazardous location classification, as defined in Article 500 of the *Code*. By this means, equipment that is not otherwise acceptable for hazardous (classified) locations may be utilized in accordance with the *Code*. Pressurization, for the purposes of NFPA 496, may be defined as the process of supplying an enclosure with clean air or an inert gas, with or without continuous flow, at sufficient pressure to prevent the entrance of combustible dust.

It should be noted that an atmosphere made hazardous by combustible dust inside an enclosure cannot be reduced to a safe level by supplying a flow of clean air in the same manner as gases or vapors. The enclosure must be opened and the dust removed. Visual inspection can determine if the dust has been removed. Positive pressure will prevent entrance of a dust into a clean enclosure.

It is important that the authority having jurisdiction be familiar with such recorded industrial experience as well as with such standards of the National Fire Protection Association as may be of use in the classification of various areas with respect to hazard.

For further information, see Hazardous Locations Classification, NFPA 70C-1974.

For further information, see Flammable and Combustible Liquids Code, NFPA 30-1977; Drycleaning Plants, NFPA 32-1979; Manufacture of Organic Coatings, NFPA 35-1976 (ANSI); Solvent Extraction Plants, NFPA 36-1978 (ANSI); Storage and Handling of Liquefied Petroleum Gases, NFPA 58-1979; Storage and Handling of Liquefied Petroleum Gases at Utility Gas Plants, NFPA 59-1979; and Classification of Class I Hazardous Locations for Electrical Installations in Chemical Plants, NFPA 497-1975 (ANSI).

For protection against static electricity hazards, see Recommended Practice on Static Electricity, NFPA 77-1977 (ANSI).

For electrical classification of laboratory areas, see Standard for Fire Protection of Laboratories Using Chemicals, NFPA 45-1975.

All conduit referred to herein shall be threaded with a NPT standard conduit cutting die that provides ¾-inch taper per foot. Such conduit shall be made up wrenchtight to minimize sparking when fault current flows through the conduit system. Where it is impractical to make a threaded joint tight, a bonding jumper shall be utilized.

Care should be exercised if intermediate metal conduit is used, since other than National Pipe Threads may be used on the intermediate metal conduit.

500-2. Special Precaution.   Articles 500 through 503 require a form of construction of equipment and of installation that will ensure safe performance under conditions of proper use and maintenance.

It is important that inspection authorities and users exercise more than ordinary care with regard to installation and maintenance.

The explosion characteristics of air mixtures of gases, vapors, or dusts vary with the specific material involved. For Class I locations, Groups A, B, C, and D, the classification involves determinations of maximum explosion pressure, maximum safe clearance between parts of a clamped joint in an enclosure, and the minimum ignition temperature of the atmospheric mixture. For Class II locations, Groups E, F, and G, the classification involves the tightness of the joints of assembly and shaft openings, to prevent entrance of dust in the dust-ignition-proof enclosure, the blanketing effect of layers of dust on the equipment that may cause overheating, electrical conductivity of the dust, and the ignition temperature of the dust. It is necessary, therefore, that equipment be approved not only for the class, but also for the specific group of the gas, vapor, or dust that will be present.

For purposes of testing, approval, and area classification, various air mixtures (not oxygen-enriched) have been grouped on the basis of their characteristics and facilities have been made available for testing and approving equipment for use in the following atmospheric groups:

For materials which have been classified in Groups A, B, C, and D, see Table 500-2. There are other hazardous materials which have not been classified and which are not included in this table.

Determining the proper group classification for flammable gases and vapors involves a determination of explosion pressures and maximum safe clearance between parts of a clamped joint under several conditions, and comparison of the values obtained with those obtained for presently classified materials under the same test conditions. Although some work has been done on the classification of flammable materials on the basis of chemical structure, the method is not sufficiently refined or accurate to ensure proper classification of all flammable materials. For further information, see Report NMAB 353-1, Matrix of Combustion-Relevant Properties and Classifications of Gases, Vapors, and Selected Solids, published in 1979 by the National Materials Advisory Board, Commission on Sociotechnical Systems, National Research Council, National Adademy of Sciences. The report is available from the National Technical Information Service (NTIS), Springfield, VA 22151.

Group E: Atmospheres containing metal dust, including aluminum, magnesium, and their commercial alloys, and other metals of similarly hazardous characteristics having resistivity of 10^2 ohm-centimeter or less.

Group F: Atmospheres containing carbon black, charcoal, coal or coke dusts which have more than 8 percent total volatile material (carbon black per ASTM D1620, charcoal, coal and coke dusts per ASTM D271) or atmospheres containing these dusts sensitized by other materials so that they present an explosion hazard, and having resistivity greater than 10^2 ohm-centimeter but equal to or less than 10^8 ohm-centimeter.

Group G: Atmospheres containing flour, starch, grain, or combustible plastics or chemical dusts having resistivity greater than 10^8 ohm-centimeter.

For information on the proposed classification of a number of dusts, see Report NMAB 353-3, Classification of Combustible Dusts in Accordance with the *National Electrical Code*, published in 1980 by the National Materials Advisory Board, Commission on Sociotechnical Systems, National Research Council, National Academy of Sciences. The report is available from the National Technical Information Service (NTIS), Springfield, VA 22151.

1. Certain chemical atmospheres may have characteristics that require safeguards beyond those required for any of the above groups. Carbon disulfide is one of these chemicals because of its low ignition temperature, 100°C (212°F), and the small joint clearance to arrest its flame.

2. Certain metal dusts may have characteristics that require safeguards beyond those required for atmospheres containing the dusts of aluminum, magnesium, and their commercial alloys. For example, zirconium, thorium and uranium dusts have extremely low ignition temperatures [as low as 20°C (68°F)], and minimum ignition energies lower than any material classified in any of the Class I or Class II Groups.

For a complete list noting properties of flammable liquids, gases and solids, see Fire Hazard Properties of Flammable Liquids, Gases, and Volatile Solids, NFPA 325M-1977.

Report NMAB 353-2, Test Equipment for Use in Determining Classifications of Combustible Dusts, published in 1979 by the National Materials Advisory Board,

Commission on Sociotechnical Systems, National Research Council, National Academy of Sciences, includes a description of test methods to determine the ignition temperatures and electrical resistivity of combustible dusts. The report is available from the National Technical Information Service (NTIS), Springfield, VA 22151.

Table 500-2.   Chemicals by Groups

Group A Atmospheres	Chemical
Chemical	1-butanol (butyl alcohol)
acetylene	2-butanol (secondary butyl alcohol)
	n-butyl acetate
Group B Atmospheres	isobutyl acetate
acrolein (inhibited)[2]	di-isobutylene
arsine	ethane
butadiene[1]	ethanol (ethyl alcohol)
ethylene oxide[2]	ethyl acetate
hydrogen	ethyl acrylate (inhibited)
manufactured gases containing more than	ethylene diamine (anhydrous)
30% hydrogen (by volume)	ethylene dichloride
propylene oxide[2]	ethylene glycol monomethyl
propylnitrate	ether
Group C Atmospheres	gasoline
acetaldehyde	heptanes
allyl alcohol	hexanes
n-butyraldehyde	isoprene
carbon monoxide	isopropyl ether
crotonaldehyde	mesityl oxide
cyclopropane	methane (natural gas)
diethyl ether	methanol (methyl alcohol)
diethylamine	3-methyl-1-butanol (isoamyl alcohol)
epichlorohydrin	methyl ethyl ketone
ethylene	methyl isobutyl ketone
ethylenimine	2-methyl-1-propanol
ethyl mercaptan	(isobutyl alcohol)
ethyl sulfide	2-methyl-2-propanol
hydrogen cyanide	(tertiary butyl alcohol)
hydrogen sulfide	petroleum naphtha[4]
morpholine	pyridine
2-nitropropane	octanes
tetrahydrofuran	pentanes
unsymmetrical dimethyl hydrazine	1-pentanol (amyl alcohol)
(UDMH 1, 1-dimethyl hydrazine)	propane
	1-propanol (propyl alcohol)
Group D Atmospheres	2-propanol (isopropyl alcohol)
acetic acid (glacial)	propylene
acetone	styrene
acrylonitrile	toluene
ammonia[3]	vinyl acetate
benzene	vinyl chloride
butane	xylenes

[1] Group D equipment shall be permitted for this atmosphere if such equipment is isolated in accordance with Section 501-5(a) by sealing all conduit ½-inch size or larger.

[2] Group C equipment shall be permitted for this atmosphere if such equipment is isolated in accordance with Section 501-5(a) by sealing all conduit ½-inch size or larger.

[3] For classification of areas involving ammonia atmosphere, see Safety Code for Mechanical Refrigeration (ANSI/ASHRAE 15-1978) and Safety Requirements for the Storage and Handling of Anhydrous Ammonia (ANSI/CGA G2.1-1972).

[4] A saturated hydrocarbon mixture boiling in the range 20-135°C (68-275°F). Also known by the synonyms benzine, ligroin, petroleum ether, or naphtha.

(a) Approval for Class and Properties.   Equipment shall be approved not only for the class of location but also for the explosive, combustible, or ignitible properties of the specific gas, vapor, dust, fiber, or flyings that will be present. In addition, equipment shall not have exposed any surface that operates at a temperature in excess of the ignition temperature of the specific gas, vapor, dust, fiber, or flyings.

Equipment that has been approved for a Division 1 location shall be permitted in a Division 2 location of the same class and group.

Where specifically permitted in Articles 501 through 503, general-purpose equipment or equipment in general-purpose enclosures shall be permitted to be installed in Division 2 locations if the equipment does not constitute a source of ignition under normal operating conditions.

The characteristics of various atmospheric mixtures of gases, vapors, and dusts depend on the specific material involved.

(b) Marking.   Approved equipment shall be marked to show the Class, Group, and operating temperature or temperature range referenced to a 40°C ambient.

It should be noted that the marked operating temperature or temperature range is referenced to a 40°C (104°F) ambient. Unless the equipment is provided with thermally actuated sensors which limit the temperature to that marked on the equipment, operation in ambient temperatures higher than 40°C (104°F) will probably increase the operating temperature of the equipment. Many explosion-proof and dust-ignitionproof motors are equipped with thermal protectors. In a like manner, operation in ambient temperatures lower than 40°C (104°F) will usually reduce the operating temperature.

The temperature range, if provided, shall be indicated in identification numbers, as shown in Table 500-2(b).

Identification numbers marked on equipment nameplates shall be in accordance with Table 500-2(b).

Exception No. 1: Equipment of the nonheat-producing type, such as junction boxes, conduit, and fittings and equipment of the heat-producing type having a maximum temperature not more than 100°C (212°F), shall not be required to have a marked operating temperature or temperature range.

Exception No. 2: Fixed lighting fixtures marked for use in Class I, Division 2 locations only need not be marked to indicate the group.

Exception No. 3: Fixed general-purpose equipment in Class I locations, other than fixed lighting fixtures, which is acceptable for use in Class I, Division 2 locations shall not be required to be marked with the Class, Group, Division or operating temperature.

An example of such equipment is a squirrel-cage induction motor without brushes, switching mechanisms, or similar arc-producing devices. See the second paragraph of Section 501-8(b).

Exception No. 4: Fixed dust-tight equipment other than fixed lighting fixtures which are acceptable for use in Class II, Division 2 and Class III locations shall not be required to be marked with the Class, Group, Division or operating temperature.

For purposes of testing and approval, various atmospheric mixtures (not oxygen-enriched) have been grouped on the basis of their characteristics, and facilities have been made available for testing and approving equipment for use in the atmospheric groups listed in Table 500-2. Since there is no consistent relationship between explosion properties and ignition temperature, the two are independent requirements.

Table 500-2(b). Identification Numbers

Maximum Temperature Degrees C	Degrees F	Identification Number
450	842	T1
300	572	T2
280	536	T2A
260	500	T2B
230	446	T2C
215	419	T2D
200	392	T3
180	356	T3A
165	329	T3B
160	320	T3C
135	275	T4
120	248	T4A
100	212	T5
85	185	T6

(c) Temperature. The temperature marking specified in (b) above shall not exceed the ignition temperature of the specific gas or vapor to be encountered.

The ignition temperature of a solid, liquid, or gaseous substance is the minimum temperature required to initiate or cause self-sustained combustion independent of the heating or heated element.

For information regarding ignition temperatures of gases and vapors, see Fire Hazard Properties of Flammable Liquids, Gases, and Volatile Solids, NFPA 325M-1977.

Formerly the temperature limit of each Group was assumed to be the lowest ignition temperature of any material in the Group, i.e., 280°C for Group D, 180°C for Group C.

To avoid revising this limit as new gases are added (see hexane in Group D and acetaldehyde in Group C), temperature will be specified in future markings.

The ignition temperature for which equipment was approved prior to this requirement shall be assumed to be as follows:

Group A — 280°C (536°F)	Group C — 180°C (356°F)
Group B — 280°C (536°F)	Group D — 280°C (536°F)

Maximum surface temperatures for equipment in Class II locations are covered in Section 502-1.

The preceding information on ignition temperatures for Class I materials was added as a Tentative Interim Amendment to the 1968 edition of the *NEC* and has been part of the *Code* since the 1971 edition. Listed or labeled heat producing equipment, such as lighting fixtures and motors, manufactured before about 1975 may not be marked with the operating temperature or temperature range. Unless the actual operating temperatures are marked on the equipment or are otherwise known, the intent is that the operating temperatures noted above be assumed. For multiple rated equipment (e.g., Class I, Groups C and D), the lowest operating temperature [180°C (356°F)] may be assumed.

Flammable gases or vapors are separated into four different atmospheric groups: Groups A, B, C, and D (see Table 500-2). All of the listings of the four groups in Table 500-2 can result in flammable mixtures of gas or vapor atmospheres and are included in Class I locations. It is to be noted that *Code* requirements for Class I locations do not vary for different kinds of gas or vapor contained in the atmosphere. It is necessary to select equipment that is designed for use in the particular group involved; however, equipment may be listed for use in Class I, Group D or use in Class I, Group C, etc. The reason for designating the groups in this way is that explosive mixtures have different explosion pressures and maximum safe clearances between parts of a joint in an enclosure.

Underwriters Laboratories Inc. lists electrical equipment suitable for use in all groups of Class I locations and further information is available from the UL Hazardous Locations Equipment Directory. It is to be noted that "only those products bearing the appropriate Listing Mark and the company's name, trade name, trademark, or other recognized identification should be considered as covered by UL's Listing and Follow-Up Service."

Class II locations are hazardous because of the presence of combustible dust. Combustible dusts are separated into three different groups based primarily on the electrical resistivity of the dust: Groups E, F, and G (see fine print note following Section 500-2). Group E includes aluminum and magnesium metal dusts, which are electrically conductive. Group F includes nonmetallic dusts from charcoal, coal, or coke. It should be noted that Group F dusts may be considered either electrically conductive (resistivity less than 100,000 ohm-centimeters) or electrically nonconductive (resistivity equal to or greater than 100,000 ohm-centimeters). See Section 500-5(a). Group G includes nonconductive dusts from flour, starch, grain, or combustible plastics or chemicals.

As in Class I locations, equipment must be approved not only for the "class" but also for the specific "group." It is important that, in addition to the proper selection of equipment, high standards of installation be maintained for subsequent additions or alterations.

The NFPA and ANSI standards referenced in Articles 500 through 517 should be obtained for more information on specific hazardous (classified) locations.

500-3. Specific Occupancies.   Articles 510 through 517 cover garages, aircraft hangars, gasoline dispensing and service stations, bulk storage plants, finishing processes, and health care facilities.

500-4. Class I Locations.   Class I locations are those in which flammable gases or vapors are or may be present in the air in quantities sufficient to produce explosive or ignitible mixtures. Class I locations shall include those specified in (a) and (b) below.

(a) Class I, Division 1.   A Class I, Division 1 location is a location: (1) in which ignitible concentrations of flammable gases or vapors exist under normal operating conditions; or (2) in which ignitible concentrations of such gases or vapors may exist frequently because of repair or maintenance operations or because of leakage; or (3) in which breakdown or faulty operation of equipment or processes might release ignitible concentrations of flammable gases or vapors, and might also cause simultaneous failure of electric equipment.

This classification usually includes locations where volatile flammable liquids or liquefied flammable gases are transferred from one container to another; interiors of spray booths and areas in the vicinity of spraying and painting operations where volatile flammable solvents are used; locations containing open tanks or vats of volatile flammable liquids; drying rooms or compartments for the evaporation of flammable solvents; locations containing fat and oil extraction equipment using volatile flammable solvents; portions of cleaning and dyeing plants where flammable liquids are used; gas generator rooms and other portions of gas manufacturing plants where flammable gas may escape; inadequately ventilated pump rooms for flammable gas or for volatile flammable liquids; the interiors of refrigerators and freezers in which volatile flammable materials are stored in open, lightly stoppered, or easily ruptured containers; and all other locations where ignitible concentrations of flammable vapors or gases are likely to occur in the course of normal operations.

(b) Class I, Division 2.   A Class I, Division 2 location is a location: (1) in which volatile flammable liquids or flammable gases are handled, processed, or used, but in which the liquids, vapors, or gases will normally be confined within closed containers or closed systems from which they can escape only in case of accidental rupture or breakdown of such containers or systems, or in case of abnormal operation of equipment; or (2) in which ignitible concentrations of gases or vapors are normally prevented by positive mechanical ventilation, and which might become hazardous through failure or abnormal operation of the ventilating equipment; or (3) that is adjacent to a Class I, Division 1 location, and to which ignitible concentrations of gases or vapors might occasionally be communicated unless such communication is prevented by adequate positive-pressure ventilation from a source of clean air, and effective safeguards against ventilation failure are provided.

This classification usually includes locations where volatile flammable liquids or flammable gases or vapors are used, but which, in the judgment of the authority having jurisdiction, would become hazardous only in case of an accident or of some unusual operating condition. The quantity of flammable material that might escape in case of accident, the adequacy of ventilating equipment, the total area involved, and the record of the industry or business with respect to explosions or fires are all factors that merit consideration in determining the classification and extent of each location.

Piping without valves, checks, meters, and similar devices would not ordinarily introduce a hazardous condition even though used for flammable liquids or gases. Locations used for the storage of flammable liquids or of liquefied or compressed gases in sealed containers would not normally be considered hazardous unless subject to other hazardous conditions also.

Electrical conduits and their associated enclosures separated from process fluids by a single seal or barrier shall be classed as a Division 2 location if the outside of the conduit and enclosures is a nonhazardous location.

500-5. Class II Locations.   Class II locations are those that are hazardous because of the presence of combustible dust. Class II locations shall include those specified in (a) and (b) below.

(a) Class II, Division 1.   A Class II, Division 1 location is a location: (1) in which combustible dust is in the air under normal operating conditions in quantities sufficient to produce explosive or ignitible mixtures; or (2) where mechanical failure or abnormal operation of machinery or equipment might cause such explosive or ignitible mixtures to be produced, and might also provide a source of ignition through simultaneous failure of electric equipment, operation of protection devices, or from other causes; or (3) in which combustible dusts of an electrically conductive nature may be present.

Combustible dusts which are electrically nonconductive include dusts produced in the handling and processing of grain and grain products, pulverized sugar and cocoa, dried egg and milk powders, pulverized spices, starch and pastes, potato and woodflour, oil meal from beans and seed, dried hay, and other organic materials which may produce combustible dusts when processed or handled. Electrically conductive dusts are dusts with a resistivity less than 10^5 ohm-centimeter. Dusts containing magnesium or aluminum are particularly hazardous and the use of extreme precaution will be necessary to avoid ignition and explosion.

(b) Class II, Division 2.   A Class II, Division 2 location is a location in which: (1) combustible dust will not normally be in suspension in the air in quantities sufficient to produce explosive or ignitible mixtures, and dust accumulations are normally insufficient to interfere with the normal operation of electrical equipment or other apparatus, or (2) dust may be in suspension in the air as a result of infrequent malfunctioning of handling or processing equipment, and dust accumulations resulting therefrom may be ignitible by abnormal operation or failure of electrical equipment or other apparatus.

500-6. Class III Locations.   Class III locations are those that are hazardous because of the presence of easily ignitible fibers or flyings, but in which such fibers or flyings are not likely to be in suspension in the air in quantities sufficient to produce ignitible mixtures. Class III locations shall include those specified in (a) and (b) below.

(a) Class III, Division 1.   A Class III, Division 1 location is a location in which easily ignitible fibers or materials producing combustible flyings are handled, manufactured, or used.

Such locations usually include some parts of rayon, cotton, and other textile mills; combustible fiber manufacturing and processing plants; cotton gins and cotton-seed mills; flax-processing plants; clothing manufacturing plants; sawmills and other woodworking locations; and establishments and industries involving similar hazardous processes or conditions.

Easily ignitible fibers and flyings include rayon, cotton (including cotton linters and cotton waste), sisal or henequen, istle, jute, hemp, tow, cocoa fiber, oakum, baled waste kapok, Spanish moss, excelsior, sawdust, wood chips, and other materials of similar nature.

(b) Class III, Division 2.   A Class III, Division 2 location is a location in which easily ignitible fibers are stored or handled.

Exception: In process of manufacture.

Sections 500-4, 500-5, and 500-6 recognize three classes of hazardous (classified) locations with varying degrees of hazards, and each class is then subdivided into two divisions. The requirements for Division 1 of each class are more stringent than those for Division 2.

Briefly, the hazards of the three classes are defined as follows: Class I, flammable gases or vapors; Class II, combustible dust; and Class III, combustible fibers or flyings.

When a given location is classified as hazardous, it should not be difficult to determine in which of the three classes it belongs; however, when it is unknown whether a location is definitely hazardous, it would be difficult to apply rules to an area that may, because of a change in process or material, become hazardous. In this case common sense and good judgment must prevail in classifying an area that is likely to become hazardous and in determining those portions of the premises to be classed Division 1 or Division 2.

ARTICLE 501 — CLASS I LOCATIONS

Contents

501-16. Grounding, Class I, Divisions 1 and 2.
(a) Exposed Parts.
(b) Bonding.
(c) Lightning Protection.

(d) Grounded Service Conductor Connections at Service Equipment.
(e) Multiple Grounds.

501-1. General.   The general rules of this Code shall apply to the electric wiring and equipment in locations classified as Class I in Section 500-4.

Exception: As modified by this article.

The more common Class I locations are those areas involved in the handling or processing of volatile flammable liquids such as gasoline, naphtha, benzene, diethyl ether, and acetone, or flammable gases such as hydrogen, methane, and propane.

Where ignitible concentrations (concentrations within the flammable or explosive limits) of flammable gases or vapors are present, atmospheres that are explosive when ignited by an arc, a spark, or high temperature exist. NFPA 325M includes information on the explosive limits of flammable liquids, gases, and volatile solids. All electrical equipment that may cause ignition-capable arcs or sparks should be kept out of Class I locations where practicable. If this is not practicable, such apparatus must be approved for the purpose and installed properly. The arc produced at the contacts of listed or labeled intrinsically safe equipment is not ignition-capable because the energy available is insufficient to cause ignition.

Hermetic sealing of all electric equipment is impractical because equipment such as motors, switches, and circuit breakers have movable parts that must be operated through the enclosing case, that is, the lever of a switch or the shaft of a motor must have sufficient clearance to operate freely. In addition, in many cases it is necessary to have access to the inside of enclosures for installation, servicing, or alterations.

It is practically impossible to make threaded conduit joints airtight. The conduit system and apparatus enclosure "breathe" due to temperature changes, and any flammable gases or vapors in the room may slowly enter the conduit or enclosure creating an explosive mixture. Should an arc occur, an explosion could take place.

When an explosion occurs within the enclosure or conduit system, the burning mixture, or hot gases, must be sufficiently confined within the system to prevent ignition of any explosive mixture that might be present in the room. An apparatus enclosure must be designed with sufficient strength to withstand the maximum pressure that can be generated by an internal explosion in order to prevent rupture and the release of burning or hot gases. Enclosures can and have been designed to withstand such internal explosions. Such enclosures are 'explosionproof.'

It has been found that during an explosion within an enclosure gases will escape through any paths or openings that exist, but that the gases will be sufficiently cooled where carried out through an opening that is long in proportion to its width; that is, the spiral path of five fully engaged threads of a screwed-on junction box cover, as illustrated in Figure 501-1. This principle is also applied in the design of explosionproof enclosures for apparatus by providing a wide machined flange on the body of the enclosure and a similar machined flange on the cover. These machined flanges are so ground that, when the cover is seated in place, the clearance between the two surfaces will at no point exceed 0.0015 in. Thus, if an explosion occurs within the enclosure, escaping gas must travel a considerable distance through a very small opening and is, therefore, sufficiently cooled when it enters the surrounding atmosphere to prevent ignition of the external explosive mixture.

The clearance between flat surfaces may increase somewhat under explosion conditions because the internal pressures created by the explosion tend to force the surfaces apart. The amount of increase in the joint clearance depends on the "stiffness" of the enclosure parts, the size and spacing of the bolts, and the explosion pressure. See Figure 501-2. Simply measuring the joint width and clearance when there are no internal pressures will not indicate what the clearances will be under the dynamic conditions of an explosion. Actual explosion tests are usually needed to demonstrate the acceptability of the design.

501-2. Transformers and Capacitors.

(a) Class I, Division 1.   In Class I, Division 1 locations, transformers and capacitors shall comply with the following:

(1) Containing Liquid that Will Burn.   Transformers and capacitors containing a liquid that will burn shall be installed only in approved vaults that comply with Sections 450-41 through 450-48, and in addition: (1) there shall be no door or other communicating opening between the vault and the Division 1 location; and (2) ample ventilation shall be provided for the continuous removal of flammable gases or vapors; and (3) vent openings or ducts shall lead to a safe location outside of buildings; and (4) vent ducts and openings shall be of sufficient area to relieve explosion pressures within the vault, and all portions of vent ducts within the buildings shall be of reinforced concrete construction.

Figure 501-1. An explosionproof junction box with a screw-type cover.

(2) Not Containing Liquid that Will Burn.   Transformers and capactors that do not contain a liquid that will burn shall: (1) be installed in vaults complying with (a)(1) above, or (2) be approved for Class I locations.

(b) Class I, Division 2.   In Class I, Division 2 locations, transformers and capacitors shall comply with Sections 450-21 through 450-27.

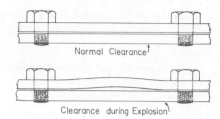

Normal Clearance

Figure 501-2. Effect of internal explosion on cover-to-body joint clearance in explosionproof enclosure. (*Underwriters Laboratories Inc.*)

Clearance during Explosion

501-3. Meters, Instruments, and Relays.

(a) Class I, Division 1.   In Class I, Division 1 locations, meters, instruments, and relays, including kilowatt-hour meters, instrument transformers, resistors, rectifiers, and thermionic tubes, shall be provided with enclosures approved for Class I, Division 1 locations.

Enclosures approved for Class I, Division 1 locations include: (1) explosionproof enclosures, and (2) purged and pressurized enclosures. See NFPA 496-1974 (ANSI), Purged and Pressurized Enclosures for Electrical Equipment in Hazardous Locations.

See the comments on purged and pressurized enclosures for electrical equipment in hazardous (classified) locations following the fine print note in Section 500-1 and the comments on explosionproof enclosures following the exception in Section 501-1.

(b) Class I, Division 2.   In Class I, Division 2 locations, meters, instruments, and relays shall comply with the following:

(1) Contacts.   Switches, circuit breakers, and make-and-break contacts of pushbuttons, relays, alarm bells, and horns shall have enclosures approved for Class I, Division 1 locations in accordance with (a) above.

Exception: General purpose enclosures shall be permitted, if current-interrupting contacts are:

a. Immersed in oil; or,

b. Enclosed within a chamber hermetically sealed against the entrance of gases or vapors; or,

There are several types of "hermetic" seals, including fusion seals such as the glass-to-metal seals in mercury tube switches, welded seals, soldered seals, and seals made with gaskets. Seals of the glass-to-metal fusion type are usually the most reliable. Soft solder seals can be relatively porous, and their effectiveness is highly dependent on workmanship. Although gasketed seals can be very effective, gasket materials are easily damaged and can deteriorate rapidly when exposed to atmospheres containing solvent vapors, depending on the gasket material used.

c. In circuits that under normal conditions do not release sufficient energy to ignite a specific ignitible atmospheric mixture; i.e., are nonincendive.

The word "nonincendive" as used here originated in publications of the Instrument Society of America (ISA), such as ISA Monogram No. 1110. It first appeared in this section and Section 501-14(b)(1) in the 1975 edition of the *Code*. It means that under the conditions specified, there is insufficient energy available to cause ignition. "Nonincendive" is similar to "intrinsically safe" as defined in Section 500-1 and NFPA 493, but does not include consideration of fault and all of the abnormal conditions inherent in the definition of "intrinsically safe." A circuit may be "nonincendive" in a Group D atmosphere, but not in a Group C atmosphere, as the minimum ignition energies for the various flammable materials differ.

(2) Resistors and Similar Equipment.   Resistors, resistance devices, thermionic tubes, rectifiers, and similar equipment that is used in or in connection with meters, instruments, and relays shall comply with (a) above.

Exception: General purpose-type enclosures shall be permitted if such equipment is without make-and-break or sliding contacts (other than as provided in (b)(1) above) and if the maximum operating temperature of any exposed surface will not exceed 80 percent of the ignition temperature in degrees Celsius of the gas or vapor involved or has been tested and found incapable of igniting the gas or vapor.

The intent of "or has been tested and found incapable of igniting the gas or vapor" is to permit approved equipment with operating temperatures higher than 80 percent of the ignition temperature. If the equipment has been tested, the "safety factor" inherent in this "80 percent rule" is not needed. The system of temperature measurement must be specified, as 80 percent of a temperature in degrees Celsius is not the same temperature as 80 percent of that temperature in degrees Fahrenheit.

(3) Without Make-or-Break Contacts.   Transformer windings, impedance coils, solenoids, and other windings that do not incorporate sliding or make-or-break contacts shall be provided with enclosures that may be of the general purpose type.

(4) General Purpose Assemblies.   Where an assembly is made up of components for which general purpose enclosures are acceptable as provided in (b)(1), (b)(2), and (b)(3) above, a single general purpose enclosure shall be acceptable for the assembly. Where such an assembly includes any of the equipment described in (b)(2) above, the maximum obtainable surface temperature of any component of the assembly shall be clearly and permanently indicated on the outside of the enclosure. Alternatively, approved equipment shall be permitted to be marked to indicate the temperature range for which it is suitable, using the identification numbers of Table 500-2(b).

(5) Fuses.   Where general purpose enclosures are permitted in (b)(1), (b)(2), (b)(3), and (b)(4) above, fuses for overcurrent protection of the instrument circuits shall be permitted to be mounted in general purpose enclosures if such fuses do not exceed a 3-ampere rating at 120 volts and if each such fuse is preceded by a switch complying with (b)(1) above.

(6) Connections.   To facilitate replacements, process control instruments shall be permitted to be connected through flexible cord, attachment plug, and receptacle, provided: (1) a switch complying with (b)(1) above is provided so that the attachment plug is not depended on to interrupt current; and (2) the current does not exceed 3 amperes at 120 volts, nominal; and (3) the power-supply cord does not exceed 3 feet (914 mm), is of a type approved for extra-hard usage or for hard usage if protected by location, and is supplied through an attachment plug and receptacle of the locking and grounding type; and (4) only necessary receptacles are provided; and (5) the receptacle carries a label warning against unplugging under load.

501-4. Wiring Methods.   Wiring methods shall comply with (a) and (b) below.

(a) Class I, Division 1.   In Class I, Division 1 locations, threaded rigid metal conduit, threaded steel intermediate metal conduit, or Type MI cable with termination fittings approved for the location shall be the wiring method employed. All boxes, fittings, and joints shall be threaded for connection to conduit or cable terminations, and shall be explosionproof. Threaded joints shall be made up with at least five threads fully engaged. Type MI cable shall be installed and supported in a manner to avoid tensile stress at the termination fittings. Where necessary to employ flexible connections, as at motor terminals, flexible fittings approved for Class I locations shall be used.

This section indicates that termination fittings used with Type MI cable are to be approved for the specific purpose. It is intended that Type MI cable fittings, approved and marked [see Section 500-2(b)] for the hazardous (classified) location class and group, be used. Type MI cable fittings have a clamp-type joint, which must be investigated to determine that it is explosionproof. Type MI cable fittings suitable for nonhazardous locations may not be suitable for Class I, Division 1 hazardous (classified) locations. Rigid metal conduit and intermediate metal conduit are to be threaded with a (NPT) standard conduit cutting die that provides ¾-in. taper per ft, and five full threads must be engaged. Each joint is to be made up tight at couplings, unions, and threaded hubs of junction boxes, device boxes, conduit bodies, etc.

Figure 501-1 shows an explosionproof junction box having three hubs and a threaded opening for the screw-type cover. Unused openings must be effectively closed by inserting threaded metal plugs engaging at least five full threads and affording protection equivalent to that of the wall of the box. Figure 501-3 shows a larger type explosionproof junction box with a bolted flanged cover.

Figure 501-4 shows a flexible fitting, which is available in lengths up to 3 ft, for use in Class I, Division 1 locations. The design of the flexible fitting consists of a deeply corrugated bronze tube with an internal fibrous tubular protective liner and an outer cover of braided fine bronze wires. A threaded fitting is securely attached to each end of the flexible tube. The flexible fitting is commonly used at motor connections, can withstand continuous vibration for long periods of time, is explosionproof, and affords maximum protection to any enclosed conductors.

Figure 501-3. Cutaway view of explosionproof junction box and bolted, flanged cover. (*Appleton Electric Co.*)

(b) Class I, Division 2.   In Class I, Division 2 locations, threaded rigid metal conduit, threaded steel intermediate metal conduit, enclosed gasketed busways, or Type PLTC cable in accordance with the provisions of Article 725, Type MI, MC, MV, TC, or SNM cable with approved termination fittings shall be the wiring method employed. Type PLTC, MI, MC, MV, TC, or SNM cable shall be permitted to be installed in cable tray systems and shall be installed in a manner to avoid tensile stress at the termination fittings. Boxes, fittings, and joints shall not be required to be explosionproof except as required by Sections 501-3(b)(1), 501-6(b)(1), and 501-14(b)(1). Where provision must be made for limited flexibility, as at motor terminals, flexible

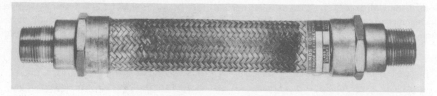

Figure 501-4. A flexible, explosionproof fitting (*Crouse-Hinds*)

metal fittings, flexible metal conduit with approved fittings, liquidtight flexible metal conduit with approved fittings, or flexible cord approved for extra-hard usage and provided with approved bushed fittings shall be used. An additional conductor for grounding shall be included in the flexible cord unless other acceptable means of grounding are provided.

Exception: Wiring, which under normal conditions cannot release sufficient energy to ignite a specific ignitible atmospheric mixture by opening, shorting or grounding, shall be permitted using any of the methods suitable for wiring in ordinary locations.

This Exception is intended to permit what have been termed "nonincendive field circuits" [see comments on "nonincendive" following Item c of the Exception in Section 501-3(b)(1)]. Many low-voltage, low-energy circuits are of this type. However, a Class 2 circuit as defined in Article 725 is not necessarily "nonincendive." There is considerable equipment listed by such testing laboratories as Factory Mutual Research Corp. and Underwriters Laboratories Inc. that have "nonincendive" circuits intended for field wiring in the various groups in Class I, Division 2 locations. Some common telephone circuits and thermocouple circuits are also "nonincendive."

In addition to the wiring method noted above, for voltages over 600 volts, nominal, and where adequately protected from physical damage, metallic shielded high voltage cable shall be accepted in cable trays when installed in accordance with Article 318.

In Class I, Division 2 locations, boxes, fittings, and joints are not required to be explosionproof at lighting outlets or at enclosures containing no arcing devices. Where general purpose enclosures are permitted by this section, rigid or intermediate metal conduit may be used with locknuts and bushings, but a bonding jumper with proper fittings [see Section 501-16(b)] is to be used between the enclosure and the raceway to assure adequate bonding from the hazardous area to the point of grounding for the service equipment. See Section 501-16(b).

Where limited flexibility is necessary and approved "fittings" are required for use with flexible metal conduit, liquidtight flexible metal conduit, extra-hard usage flexible cord, it should be noted that such approved "fittings" are not required to be specifically approved for Class I locations. Also, where flexible conduit is used, internal or external bonding jumpers with proper fittings are to be provided as required in Section 501-16(b).

This section also permits a variety of cables, cable tray systems in accordance with Section 318-2(d), and enclosed gasketed busways. The cable and cable fittings, cable trays, and busways are not required to be specifically listed or labeled for Class I locations. For example, if Type MC cable is used, neither the cable nor the fittings need to be listed for use in hazardous (classified) locations.

501-5. Sealing and Drainage.   Seals in conduit and cable systems shall comply with (a) through (f) below. Sealing compound shall be of a type approved for the conditions and use.

Sealing compound shall be used in Type MI cable termination fittings to exclude moisture and other fluids from the cable insulation.

Seals are provided in conduit and cable systems to prevent the passage of gases, vapors, or flames from one portion of the electrical installation to another through the conduit. Such communication through Type MI cable is inherently prevented by construction of the cable.

(a) Conduit Seals, Class I, Division 1.   In Class I, Division 1 locations, conduit seals shall be located as follows:

(1) In each conduit run entering an enclosure for switches, circuit breakers, fuses, relays, resistors, or other apparatus which may produce arcs, sparks, or high temperatures. Seals shall be placed as close as practicable and in no case more than 18 inches (457 mm) from such enclosures. Explosionproof unions, couplings, elbows, capped elbows and conduit bodies similar to "L," "T," and "Cross" type shall be the only enclosures or fittings permitted between the sealing fitting and the enclosure. The conduit bodies shall not be larger than the largest trade size of the conduits.

Exception: Conduit runs 1½ inches and smaller entering an explosionproof enclosure for switches, circuit breakers, fuses, relays, or other apparatus which may produce arcs or sparks need not be sealed if the current-interrupting contacts are:

a. Enclosed within a chamber hermetically sealed against the entrance of gases or vapors; or,

b. Immersed in oil in accordance with Section 501-6(b)(1)(2).

(2) In each conduit run of 2-inch size or larger entering the enclosure or fitting housing terminals, splices, or taps and within 18 inches (457 mm) of such enclosure or fitting.

See notes under Group B in Table 500-2.

(3) Where two or more enclosures for which seals are required under (a)(1) and (a)(2) above are connected by nipples or by runs of conduit not more than 36 inches (914 mm) long, a single seal in each such nipple connection or run of conduit shall be considered sufficient if located not more than 18 inches (457 mm) from either enclosure.

(4) In each conduit run leaving the Class I, Division 1 location. The sealing fitting shall be permitted on either side of the boundary of such location, but shall be so designed and installed that any gases or vapors that may enter the conduit system within the Division 1 location will not enter or be communicated to the conduit beyond the seal. There shall be no union, coupling, box, or fitting in the conduit between the sealing fitting and the point at which the conduit leaves the Division 1 location.

Exception: Metal conduit containing no unions, couplings, boxes, or fittings that passes completely through a Class I, Division 1 location with no fittings less than 12 inches (305 mm) beyond each boundary shall not be required to be sealed if the termination points of the unbroken conduit are in nonhazardous locations.

(b) Conduit Seals, Class I, Division 2.   In Class I, Division 2 locations, conduit seals shall be located as follows:

(1) For connections to explosionproof enclosures that are required to be approved for Class I locations, seals shall be provided in accordance with (a)(1), (a)(2) and (a)(3) above. All portions of the conduit run or nipple between the seal and such enclosure shall comply with Section 501-4(a).

(2) In each conduit run passing from a Class I, Division 2 location into a nonhazardous location. The sealing fitting shall be permitted on either side of the boundary of such location, but shall be so designed and installed that any gases or vapors that may enter the conduit system within the Division 2 location will not enter or be communicated to the conduit beyond the seal. Rigid metal conduit or threaded steel intermediate metal conduit shall be used between the sealing fitting and the point at which the conduit leaves the Division 2 location, and a threaded connection shall be used at the sealing fitting. There shall be no union, coupling, box, or fitting in the conduit between the sealing fitting and the point at which the conduit leaves the Division 2 location.

Exception: Unbroken metal conduit that passes completely through a Class I, Division 2 location with no fittings less than 12 inches (305 mm) beyond each boundary shall not be required to be sealed if the termination points of the unbroken conduit are in nonhazardous locations.

(c) Class I, Divisions 1 and 2. Where required, seals in Class I, Division 1 and 2 locations shall comply with the following:

(1) Fittings. Enclosures for connections or equipment shall be provided with an approved integral means for sealing, or sealing fittings approved for Class I locations shall be used. Sealing fittings shall be accessible.

(2) Compound. Sealing compound shall be approved and shall provide a seal against passage of gas or vapors through the seal fitting, shall not be affected by the surrounding atmosphere or liquids, and shall not have a melting point of less than 93°C (200°F).

(3) Thickness of Compounds. In a completed seal, the minimum thickness of the sealing compound shall not be less than the trade size of the conduit, and in no case less than ⅝ inch (16 mm).

(4) Splices and Taps. Splices and taps shall not be made in fittings intended only for sealing with compound, nor shall other fittings in which splices or taps are made be filled with compound.

(5) Assemblies. In an assembly where equipment that may produce arcs, sparks, or high temperatures is located in a compartment separate from the compartment containing splices or taps, and an integral seal is provided where conductors pass from one compartment to the other, the entire assembly shall be approved for Class I locations. Seals in conduit connections to the compartment containing splices or taps shall be provided in Class I, Division 1 locations where required by (a)(2) above.

(d) Cable Seals, Class I, Division 1. In Class I, Division 1 locations each multiconductor cable in conduit shall be considered as a single conductor if the cable is incapable of transmitting gases or vapors through the cable core. These cables shall be sealed in accordance with (a) above.

Cables with a gas/vapor-tight continuous sheath capable of transmitting gases or vapors through the cable core shall be sealed in the Division 1 location after removing the jacket and any other coverings so that the sealing compound will surround each individual insulated conductor and the outer jacket.

(e) Cable Seals, Class I, Division 2. In Class I, Division 2 locations, cable seals shall be located as follows:

(1) Cables entering enclosures which are required to be approved for Class I locations shall be sealed at the point of entrance. The sealing fitting shall comply with (b)(1) above. Multiconductor cables shall be sealed as described in (d) above.

(2) Cables with a gas/vapor-tight continuous sheath and which will not transmit gases or vapors through the cable core in excess of the quantity permitted for seal fittings shall not be required to be sealed except as required in (e)(1) above. The minimum length of such cable run shall not be less than that length which limits gas or vapor flow through the cable core to the rate permitted for seal fittings [0.007 cubic feet per hour (198 cubic centimeters per hour) of air at a pressure of 6 inches of water (1493 pascals)].

The ability of a cable to transmit gases or vapors through the core (primarily between insulated conductors) depends not only on how tightly packed the conductors are within the outer sheaths, and the location and composition of "fillers," but also on how the cable has been handled and the geometry of the cable run. If there is any question as to whether or not the cable run in question is capable of transmitting gases or vapors through the core, sealing is suggested.

See Outlet Boxes and Fittings for Use in Hazardous Locations, ANSI C33.27-1974.

The cable core does not include the interstices of the conductor strands.

This fine print note is new in the 1981 *Code*. The intent is that the conductors themselves be individually sealed, such as by dipping the ends in wax, before measuring the rate of flow. However, if this is done, the wax should be removed before making electrical connections or putting the system into service.

(3) Cables with a gas/vapor-tight continuous sheath and capable of transmitting gases or vapors through the cable core shall be sealed in the Division 2 location in such a manner as to prevent passage of gases or vapors into a nonhazardous location.

Exception: Cables with an unbroken gas/vapor-tight continuous sheath shall be permitted to pass through a Class I, Division 2 location without seals.

(4) Cables which do not have gas/vapor-tight continuous sheath shall be sealed at the boundary of the Division 2 and nonhazardous location in such a manner as to prevent passage of gases or vapors into a nonhazardous location.

The sheath mentioned in (d) and (e) above may be either metal or a nonmetallic material.

(f) Drainage.

(1) Control Equipment. Where there is a probability that liquid or other condensed vapor may be trapped within enclosures for control equipment or at any point in the raceway system, approved means shall be provided to prevent accumulation or to permit periodic draining of such liquid or condensed vapor.

(2) Motors and Generators. Where the authority having jurisdiction judges that there is a probability that liquid or condensed vapor may accumulate within motors or generators, joints and conduit systems shall be arranged to minimize entrance of liquid. If means to prevent accumulation or to permit periodic draining are judged necessary, such means shall be provided at the time of manufacture and shall be considered an integral part of the machine.

(3) Canned Pumps, Etc. For canned pumps, process connections for flow, pressure, or analysis measurement, etc., that depend upon a single seal diaphragm or tube to prevent process fluids from entering the electrical conduit system, an additional approved seal or barrier shall be provided with an adequate drain between the seals in such a manner that leaks would be obvious.

See also the last paragraph of Section 500-4(b).

Seals in conduits are used to prevent an explosion from traveling through the conduit to another enclosure, and to prevent the passage of gases or vapors from a hazardous (classified) location to a nonhazardous location. Sealing compound must be used as soon as possible on Type MI cable terminations to exclude moisture from cable insulation.

Unless specifically designed and tested for the purpose, conduit and cable seals are not intended to prevent the passage of liquids, gases, or vapors at pressures continuously above atmospheric. Even at differences in pressure across the seal equivalent to a few inches of water, there may be a slow passage of gas or vapor through a seal and through conductors passing through the seal. See Section 501-5(e)(2). Temperature extremes and highly corrosive liquids and vapors can affect the ability of seals to perform their intended function. See Section 501-5(c)(2). Attention to this is especially important if the seal is to be "the additional approved seal or barrier" required in Section 501-5(f)(3).

Where the conduit enters an enclosure containing arcing or high-temperature equipment, a sealing fitting must be placed within 18 in. of the enclosure it isolates; conduit bodies ("L," "T," etc.), couplings, unions, and elbows are the only enclosures or fittings permitted between the seal and the enclosure. See Figure 501-9 for an approved type of union. If two enclosures are spaced not more than 36 in. apart, a single seal may be placed between two connecting nipples if the seal is located not more than 18 in. from either enclosure.

In each 2-in. or larger conduit, a sealing fitting is required to be placed within 18 in. of the entrance to an explosionproof enclosure that houses terminals, splices, or taps.

A sealing fitting is required where the conduit leaves a Division 1 location or passes from a Division 2 location to a nonhazardous location. The sealing fitting is permitted on either side of the boundary, and there is to be no union, coupling, box, etc., between the seal and the boundary. It is preferable to locate the fitting on the nonhazardous location side. This sealing fitting serves two purposes. It completes the explosionproof wiring and enclosure system. Note that a ½-in. conduit connected to an explosionproof box containing only splices, even in a Division 1 location, is not required to be sealed within 18 in. of the box. The seal at the boundary of the Division 1 location serves to complete the explosionproof system. The fitting at the boundary also prevents the conduit system from serving as a pipe to transmit flammable mixtures from a Division 1 or Division 2 location to a less hazardous (classified) location.

In Class I, Division 2 locations, a seal is required in each conduit entering an enclosure that is required to be explosionproof. This is to complete the explosionproof enclosure.

Figure 501-5 illustrates the sealing of a fitting. A dam must be provided to prevent the sealing material from running out of the fitting while it is still in the liquid state. All conductors must be separated to permit the sealing material to run between them. The sealing compound must have a minimum thickness of not less than the trade size of the conduit and in no case less than ⅜ in. Conduit fittings for sealing are for use only with sealing compound supplied with the fitting and specified by the manufacturer in instructions furnished with the fitting.

Unless the additional seal or barrier, described in Section 501-5(f)(3), and interconnecting enclosures meet the performance requirements of the primary seal, the application of pressure or exposure to extreme temperatures must be prevented at the additional seal or barrier, so that the process fluid will not enter the conduit system if the primary seal fails. If the process fluid is a gas or can become a gas under ordinary atmospheric conditions (liquefied natural gas, for example), the "drain" mentioned in Section 501-5(f)(3) should be a vent.

The necessary sealing may be accomplished by a sealing fitting and compound or, to eliminate the time-consuming task of field-poured seals, a factory-sealed

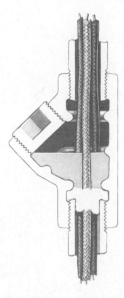

Figure 501-5. A seal fitting placed in a run of conduit to prevent the passage of gases from one portion of the electrical installation to another. (*Crouse-Hinds*)

device with the seal designed into the device is permissible. A wide selection of factory-sealed devices is available for a variety of installations in hazardous (classified) locations. Factory-sealed devices are usually marked as such. Explosionproof motors are normally factory sealed, and no other seal is required. Where a conduit terminates in a motor, however, and if the conduit is 2 in. or larger, a seal must be placed within 18 in. of the motor terminal housing.

Figure 501-7 shows a sealing fitting designed for use in a vertical run of conduit to provide drainage for any condensation of moisture trapped by the seal above an enclosure. Any accumulation of water runs over the surface of the sealing

Figure 501-6. A sealing fitting for a horizontal or vertical conduit run with a removable screw-type fitting for draining purposes. (*Appleton Electric Co.*)

Figure 501-7. A sealing fitting with an automatic drain plug. (*Appleton Electric Co.*)

Figure 501-8. A combination breather-drainage fitting. (*Appleton Electric Co.*)

Figure 501-9. An explosionproof union. (*Appleton Electric Co.*)

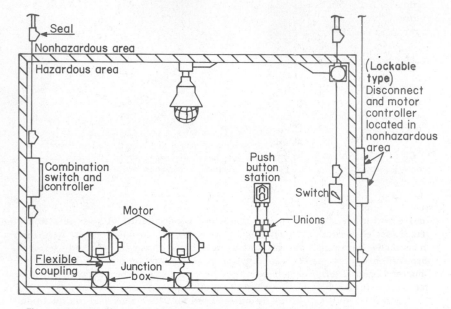

Figure 501-10. A Class I, Division 1 location where threaded metal conduits, sealing fittings, explosionproof fittings, and equipment for power and lights are used.

compound down to an explosionproof drain, through which it automatically drains. Figure 501-6 shows a sealing fitting designed for either a horizontal or vertical conduit run. Figure 501-8 shows a combination drain and breather fitting. These fittings are specially designed to serve as a water drain and an air vent while providing positive explosionproof protection. The fitting permits the escape of accumulated water through the passage of its drain, and the breather allows the continuous circulation of air, preventing condensation of any moisture that may be present. Individual drain or breather fittings are also available. It is good practice to consider the installation of drain, breather, or combination fittings in order to guard against water accumulation with subsequent insulation failures, even though prevalent conditions may not indicate a need.

Figure 501-10 illustrates a Class I, Division 1 location using threaded rigid metal conduit or threaded intermediate metal conduit and explosionproof fittings and equipment including motors, motor controllers, pushbutton stations, lighting outlets, and junction boxes. The enclosures for the disconnecting means and motor controller for the motor (right part of the drawing) are placed in a nonhazardous location and are thus not required to be explosionproof.

Each of the three conduits is sealed on the nonhazardous side before passing into the hazardous (classified) location. The pigtail leads of both motors are factory sealed at the motor-terminal housing, and, unless the size of the flexible fitting entering the motor-terminal housing is 2 in. or larger, no other seals are needed at this point. Because the pushbutton control station and the motor

controller and disconnect (left part of the drawing) are considered arc-producing devices, conduits are sealed within 18 in. of entering these enclosures. It should be noted that seals are required even though the contacts may be immersed in oil.

A seal is provided within 18 in. of the lighting switch. The design of the lighting fixture, as required by Underwriters Laboratories Inc. (UL), is such that the explosionproof chamber for the wiring must be separated or sealed from the lamp compartment, hence a separate seal is not required adjacent to UL listed lighting fixtures. The lighting fixture is suspended on a conduit stem threaded into the cover of an explosionproof ceiling box. See Section 501-9.

501-6. Switches, Circuit Breakers, Motor Controllers, and Fuses.

(a) **Class I, Division 1.**   In Class I, Division 1 locations, switches, circuit breakers, motor controllers, and fuses, including pushbuttons, relays, and similar devices, shall be provided with enclosures and the enclosure in each case, together with the enclosed apparatus, shall be approved as a complete assembly for use in Class I locations.

(b) **Class I, Division 2.**   Switches, circuit breakers, motor controllers, and fuses in Class I, Division 2 locations shall comply with the following:

(1) **Type Required.**   Circuit breakers, motor controllers, and switches intended to interrupt current in the normal performance of the function for which they are installed shall be provided with enclosures approved for Class I, Division 1 locations in accordance with Section 501-3(a), unless general purpose enclosures are provided and (1) the interruption of current occurs within a chamber hermetically sealed against the entrance of gases and vapors, or (2) the current make-and-break contacts are oil-immersed, and of the general purpose type having a 2-inch (50.8-mm) minimum immersion for power and a 1-inch (25.4 mm) minimum immersion for control.

(2) **Isolating Switches.**   General purpose-type enclosures containing no fuses shall be permitted to enclose disconnecting and isolating switches that are not intended to interrupt current.

(3) **Fuses.**   For the protection of motors, appliances, and lamps, other than as provided in (b)(4) below, standard plug or cartridge fuses shall be permitted, provided they are placed within enclosures approved for the location; or fuses shall be permitted if they are within general purpose enclosures, and if they are of a type in which the operating element is immersed in oil or other approved liquid or the operating element is enclosed within a chamber hermetically sealed against the entrance of gases and vapors.

(4) **Fuses or Circuit Breakers for Overcurrent Protection.**   Where not more than ten sets of approved enclosed fuses or not more than ten circuit breakers that are not intended to be used as switches for the interruption of current are installed for branch-circuit or feeder protection in any one room, area, or section of the Class I, Division 2 location, general purpose-type enclosures for such fuses or circuit breakers shall be permitted if the fuses or circuit breakers are for the protection of circuits or feeders supplying lamps in fixed positions only.

A set of fuses is all the fuses required to protect all the ungrounded conductors of a circuit. For example, a group of three fuses protecting an ungrounded 3-phase circuit and a single fuse protecting the ungrounded conductor of an identified 2-wire single-phase circuit is a set of fuses in each instance.

Fuses complying with (b)(3) above shall not be required to be included in counting the ten sets of fuses permitted in general-purpose enclosures.

(5) **Fuses Internal to Lighting Fixtures.**   Approved cartridge fuses filled with noncombustible granular material shall be permitted within lighting fixtures.

Figure 501-11 shows an explosionproof panelboard consisting of an assembly of branch-circuit devices enclosed in a cast-metal explosionproof housing. These panelboards are provided with bolted access covers and threaded conduit-entry hubs designed to withstand the force of any internal explosion.

Figure 501-11. An explosionproof panelboard with provisions for twelve circuits. (*Appleton Electric Co.*)

Figure 501-12. An explosionproof enclosure for a motor control starter and circuit breaker (open and closed views). (*Appleton Electric Co.*)

Figure 501-12 shows an open and closed view of a cylindrical-type combination motor controller, a motor control starter and circuit breaker, in an explosion-proof enclosure. The top and bottom covers are threaded on for quick removal for installation and servicing. Figure 501-13 shows the same type of equipment in a

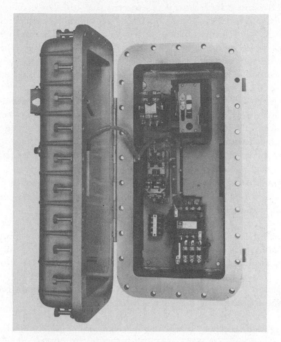

Figure 501-13. A magnetic motor starter for use in a Class I, Group D, location. Note the number of securing bolts and the width of the flange. (*General Electric Co.*)

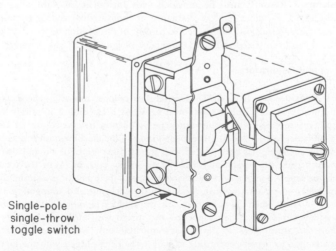

Single-pole single-throw toggle switch

Figure 501-14. A standard toggle switch in an explosionproof enclosure.

rectangular enclosure with a hinged, bolted-on cover. These types of housings are designed to accomodate a wide variety of either manually or magnetically operated across-the-line types of motor starters in a variety of ratings.

Figure 501-14 illustrates a standard toggle switch in an explosionproof enclosure.

In Class I, Division 2 locations, it is assumed that fuses or circuit breakers will seldom open the circuit when used to protect feeders or branch circuits supplying lamps in fixed positions only. Division 2 locations are not normally hazardous but may become so [see Section 500-4(b)], and since it is unlikely that the fuse or circuit breaker in such a circuit will operate simultaneously with the occurrence of an explosive mixture inside the enclosure, general purpose enclosures are permitted for such overcurrent devices.

Section 501-6(b)(5) is new in the 1981 *Code* and permits filled fuses, often used for ballast protection in high-intensity-discharge and outdoor flourescent fixtures. It does not, however, permit the common hollow glass cartridge fuse, as the ferrules of such a fuse are cemented to the glass tube, and the enclosure of the fusible element is therefore not in accordance with Section 501-6(b)(1).

501-7. Control Transformers and Resistors. Transformers, impedance coils, and resistors used as, or in conjunction with, control equipment for motors, generators, and appliances shall comply with (a) and (b) below.

(a) Class I, Division 1. In Class I, Division 1 locations, transformers, impedance coils, and resistors, together with any switching mechanism associated with them, shall be provided with enclosures approved for Class I, Division 1 locations in accordance with Section 501-3(a).

(b) Class I, Division 2. In Class I, Division 2 locations, control transformers and resistors shall comply with the following:

(1) Switching Mechanisms. Switching mechanisms used in conjunction with transformers, impedance coils, and resistors shall comply with Section 501-6(b).

(2) Coils and Windings. Enclosures for windings of transformers, solenoids, or impedance coils shall be permitted to be of the general purpose type.

(3) Resistors. Resistors shall be provided with enclosures; and the assembly shall be approved for Class I locations, unless resistance is nonvariable and maximum operating temperature, in degrees Celsius, will not exceed 80 percent of the ignition temperature of the gas or vapor involved, or has been tested and found incapable of igniting the gas or vapor.

501-8. Motors and Generators.

(a) Class I, Division 1. In Class I, Division 1 locations, motors, generators, and other rotating electric machinery shall be: (1) approved for Class I, Division 1 locations; or (2) of the totally enclosed type supplied with positive-pressure ventilation from a source of clean air with discharge to a safe area, so arranged to prevent energizing of the machine until ventilation has been established and the enclosure has been purged with at least 10 volumes of air, and also arranged to automatically de-energize the equipment when the air supply fails; or (3) of the totally enclosed inert gas-filled type supplied with a suitable reliable source of inert gas for pressuring the enclosure, with devices provided to ensure a positive pressure in the enclosure and arranged to automatically de-energize the equipment when the gas supply fails; or (4) of a type designed to be submerged in a liquid which is flammable only when vaporized and mixed with air, or in a gas or vapor at a pressure greater than atmospheric and which is flammable only when mixed with air; and the machine is so arranged to prevent energizing it until it has been purged with the liquid or gas to exclude air, and also arranged to automatically de-energize the equipment when the supply of liquid, or gas or vapor fails or the pressure is reduced to atmospheric.

Totally enclosed motors of Types (2) or (3) shall have no external surface with an operating temperature in degrees Celsius in excess of 80 percent of the ignition temperature of the gas or vapor involved. Appropriate devices shall be provided to detect and automatically de-energize the motor or provide an adequate alarm if there is any increase in temperature of the motor beyond designed limits. Auxiliary equipment shall be of a type approved for the location in which it is installed.

See ASTM Test Procedure (Designation D 2155-69).

(b) Class I, Division 2.   In Class I, Division 2 locations, motors, generators, and other rotating electric machinery in which are employed sliding contacts, centrifugal or other types of switching mechanism (including motor overcurrent, overloading and overtemperature devices), or integral resistance devices, either while starting or while running, shall be approved for Class I, Division 1 locations, unless such sliding contacts, switching mechanisms, and resistance devices are provided with enclosures approved for Class I, Division 2 locations in accordance with Section 501-3(b).

In Class I, Division 2 locations, the installation of open or nonexplosionproof enclosed motors, such as squirrel-cage induction motors without brushes, switching mechanisms, or similar arc-producing devices shall be permitted.

It is intended that the phrase "other rotating electric machinery" include electric brakes. Listed and labeled electric brakes are available for Class I, Division 1, Group C and D locations.

Figures 501-15 and 501-16 show closed and opened views of a totally enclosed fan-cooled motor approved for use in explosive atmospheres. The main frame and end-bells are designed with sufficient strength to withstand an internal explosion, and flames or hot gases are cooled while escaping because of the wide metal-to-metal joints between the frame and the end-bells and the long, close-tolerance clearance provided for the free-turn of the shaft. Air circulation outside the motor is maintained by nonsparking (aluminum, bronze or a nonstatic-generating-type plastic) fan on the end opposite the shaft end of the motor. A sheet metal housing surrounds this fan to reduce the likelihood of a person or object contacting the moving blades, and to direct the flow of air. Internal fans on the shaft circulate air around the windings.

Motors that have arcing or sparking devices, such as commutators, internal switches, or other control devices, must be explosionproof. General purpose squirrel-cage induction motors may be used in Division 2 locations.

501-9. Lighting Fixtures.   Lighting fixtures shall comply with (a) or (b) below.

(a) Class I, Division 1.   In Class I, Division 1 locations, lighting fixtures shall comply with the following:

(1) Approved Fixtures.   Each fixture shall be approved as a complete assembly for the Class I, Division 1 location and shall be clearly marked to indicate the maximum wattage of lamps for which it is approved. Fixtures intended for portable use shall be specifically approved as a complete assembly for that use.

(2) Physical Damage.   Each fixture shall be protected against physical damage by a suitable guard or by location.

(3) Pendant Fixtures.   Pendant fixtures shall be suspended by and supplied through threaded rigid metal conduit stems or threaded steel intermediate conduit stems, and threaded joints shall be provided with set-screws or other effective means to prevent loosening. For stems longer than 12 inches (305 mm), permanent and effective bracing against lateral displacement shall be provided at a level not more than 12 inches (305 mm) above the lower end of the stem, or

Figure 501-15. Terminal housing of a motor approved for use in specific hazardous locations. Note integral sealing of the motor. (*General Electric Co.*)

flexibility in the form of a fitting or flexible connector approved for the Class I, Division 1 location shall be provided not more than 12 inches (305 mm) from the point of attachment to the supporting box or fitting.

(4) Supports.   Boxes, box assemblies, or fittings used for the support of lighting fixtures shall be approved for Class I locations.

(b) Class I, Division 2.   In Class I, Division 2 locations, lighting fixtures shall comply with the following:

(1) Portable Lamps.   Portable lamps shall comply with (a)(1) above.

(2) Fixed Lighting.   Lighting fixtures for fixed lighting shall be protected from physical damage by suitable guards or by location. Where there is danger that falling sparks or hot metal from lamps or fixtures might ignite localized concentrations of flammable vapors or gases, suitable enclosures or other effective protective means shall be provided. Where lamps are of a size or type that may, under normal operating conditions, reach surface temperatures exceeding 80 percent of the ignition temperature in degrees Celsius of the gas or vapor involved, fixtures shall comply with (a)(1) above or shall be of a type which has been tested and found incapable of igniting the gas or vapor if the ignition temperature is not exceeded.

(3) Pendant Fixtures.   Pendant fixtures shall be suspended by threaded rigid metal conduit stems, threaded steel intermediate metal conduit stems or by other approved means. For rigid stems longer than 12 inches (305 mm), permanent and effective bracing against lateral displacement shall be provided at a level not more than 12 inches (305 mm) above the lower end of

Figure 501-16. View showing internal fan of motor in Figure 501-15.

the stem, or flexibility in the form of an approved fitting or flexible connector shall be provided not more than 12 inches (305 mm) from the point of attachment to the supporting box or fitting.

(4) Switches. Switches that are a part of an assembled fixture or of an individual lampholder shall comply with Section 501-6(b)(1).

(5) Starting Equipment. Starting and control equipment for electric-discharge lamps shall comply with Section 501-7(b).

Exception: A thermal protector potted into a thermally protected fluorescent lamp ballast if the lighting fixture is approved for locations of this Class and Division.

Figures 501-17 and 501-18 show typical lighting fixtures for Class I, Group C and D locations and a variety of parts of a complete lighting fixture assembly. The outlet boxes have an internally threaded opening designed to receive the cover. A pendant fixture is attached to the cover by threaded rigid metal conduit or threaded intermediate metal conduit. To prevent loosening from vibration or lamp changing, threaded joints are to be provided with set-screws. The set-screws should not interrupt the explosionproof joint. Rigid metal conduit or intermediate metal conduit stems longer than 12 in. require effective bracing or a flexible fitting approved for the purpose and placed not more than 12 in. from the point of attachment to the supporting box, cover, or fitting.

A globeholder is threaded onto the body of the fixture housing and supports a heavy glass globe, guard, and reflector. It is available in sizes suitable for lamps from 40 W through 500 W. In designing any hazardous (classified) location lighting system, operating temperatures must be considered. Therefore, if the area is Class I, Division 1, fixtures approved for this location and properly marked must be used. Generally, enclosed and gasketed fixtures (previously called vaportight fixtures) without guards, if breakage is unlikely, or fixtures approved for Class I, Division 2 locations, are required in Division 2 locations. Fixtures listed by Underwriters Laboratories Inc. (UL) for use in any of the groups under Class I, either Division 1 or 2 locations, or both, are designed to operate without causing ignition of surrounding flammable gas or vapor atmospheres, and are marked with the operating temperature or temperature range code [see Table 500-2(b)].

Figure 501-19 shows an explosionproof handlamp. It is required that lamp compartments be sealed from the terminal compartment. Provisions are to be made for the connection of 3-conductor (one, a grounding conductor), flexible, extra-hard-usage cord. See Section 501-11.

Figure 501-17. A Typical lighting fixture for use in Class I, Group C and D locations. (*Crouse-Hinds*)

501-10. Utilization Equipment.

(a) **Class I, Division 1.**   In Class I, Division 1 locations, all utilization equipment shall be approved for Class I, Division 1 locations.

(b) **Class I, Division 2.**   In Class I, Division 2 locations, all utilization equipment shall comply with the following:

(1) **Heaters.**   Electrically heated utilization equipment shall conform with either (a) or (b) below.

a. The heater shall not exceed 80 percent of the ignition temperature in degrees Celsius of the gas or vapor involved on any surface which is exposed to the gas or vapor when continuously energized at the maximum rated ambient temperature. If a temperature controller is not provided, these conditions shall apply when the heater is operated at 120 percent of rated voltage.

b. The heater shall be approved for Class I, Division 1 locations.

(2) **Motors.**   Motors of motor-driven utilization equipment shall comply with Section 501-8(b).

(3) **Switches, Circuit Breakers, and Fuses.**   Switches, circuit breakers, and fuses shall comply with Section 501-6(b).

CLASS I, DIVISION 1 — FIXTURE HANGING METHODS.

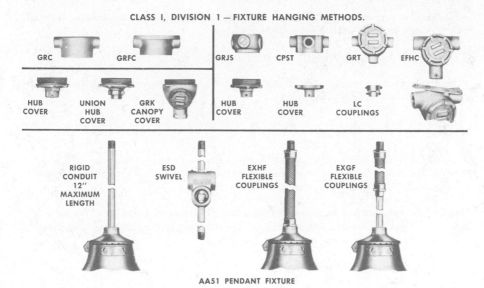

GRC   GRFC   GRJS   CPST   GRT   EFHC

HUB COVER   UNION HUB COVER   GRK CANOPY COVER   HUB COVER   HUB COVER   LC COUPLINGS

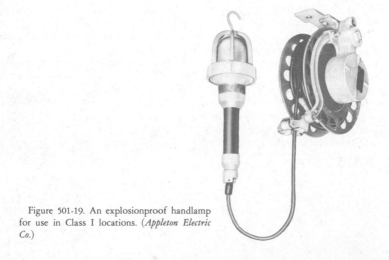

RIGID CONDUIT 12" MAXIMUM LENGTH   ESD SWIVEL   EXHF FLEXIBLE COUPLINGS   EXGF FLEXIBLE COUPLINGS

AA51 PENDANT FIXTURE

Figure 501-18. Various components used in an explosionproof lighting fixture installation. (*Appleton Electric Co.*)

Figure 501-19. An explosionproof handlamp for use in Class I locations. (*Appleton Electric Co.*)

The requirements for utilization equipment in Class I locations are virtually identical for Division 1 and 2 locations, except for heaters. Electric pipe tracing systems listed for Class I, Division 2 locations and complying with Section 501-10(b)(1)a are available.

501-11. Flexible Cords, Class I, Divisions 1 and 2. A flexible cord shall be permitted only for connection between a portable lamp or other portable utilization equipment and the fixed portion of its supply circuit; and where used shall: (1) be of a type approved for extra-hard usage; (2) contain, in addition to the conductors of the circuit, a grounding conductor complying with Section 400-23; (3) be connected to terminals or to supply conductors in an approved manner; (4) be supported by clamps or by other suitable means in such a manner that there will be no tension on the terminal connections; and (5) be provided with suitable seals where the flexible cord enters boxes, fittings, or enclosures of the explosionproof type.

Exception: As provided in Sections 501-3(b)(6) and 501-4(b).

Electric submersible pumps with means for removal without entering the wet-pit shall be considered portable utilization equipment.

See Section 501-13 for flexible cords exposed to liquids having a deleterious effect on the conductor insulation.

The second paragraph is new in the 1981 *Code*, and recognizes a wet-pit type of installation that is finding increasing acceptance for waste-water systems. Listed equipment for this use is available.

501-12. Receptacles and Attachment Plugs, Class I, Divisions 1 and 2.   Receptacles and attachment plugs shall be of the type providing for connection to the grounding conductor of a flexible cord and shall be approved for Class I locations.

Exception: As provided in Section 501-3(b)(6).

Figure 501-20 shows an explosionproof receptacle and attachment plug with an interlocking switch. The design of this device is such that when the switch is in the "on" position, the plug cannot be removed, and also the switch cannot be placed in the "on" position when the plug has been removed; that is, the plug cannot be inserted or removed unless the switch is in the "off" position. The receptacle is factory sealed with a provision for threaded-conduit entry to the switch compartment; the plug is for use with Type S or equivalent extra-hard-service flexible cord having a grounding conductor.

Figure 501-21 shows a 30-A, 4-pole receptacle and attachment plug assembly that is suitable for use without a switch. The design is such that the mating parts of the receptacle and plug are enclosed in a chamber that seals the arc and, by delayed-action construction, prevents complete removal of the plug until the arc or hot metal has cooled. The receptacle is factory sealed and the attachment plug is designed for use with a 4-conductor cord (3-conductor, 3-phase circuit with one grounding conductor) or a 3-conductor cord (two circuit conductors and one grounding conductor).

Figure 501-20. A receptacle and attachment plug of the explosionproof type with an interlocking switch. The switch must be in the off position to remove the attachment plug. (*Appleton Electric Co.*)

Figure 501-21. A four-pole (delayed action) explosionproof receptacle and attachment plug suitable for use without a switch. (*Appleton Electric Co.*)

501-13. Conductor Insulation, Class I, Divisions 1 and 2.   Where condensed vapors or liquids may collect on, or come in contact with, the insulation on conductors, such insulation shall be of a type approved for use under such conditions; or the insulation shall be protected by a sheath of lead or by other approved means.

The availability of nylon-jacketed conductors, such as Types THWN and TW, that are suitable for use where exposed to gasoline, has gained widespread acceptance because of their ease of handling, application, and economics.

An excerpt from Underwriters Laboratories Inc. (UL) Electrical Construction Materials Directory states the following: Wires, Thermoplastic

Gasoline Resistant TW — Indicates a TW conductor with a jacket of extruded nylon suitable for use in wet locations, and for exposure to mineral oil, and to liquid gasoline and gasoline vapors at ordinary ambient temperature. It is identified by tag marking and by printing on the insulation or nylon jacket with the designation "Type TW Gasoline and Oil Resistant I."

Also listed for the above use is "Gasoline Resistant THWN" with the designation "Type THWN Gasoline and Oil Resistant II."

It should be noted that other thermoplastic wires may be suitable for exposure to mineral oil; but with the exception of those marked "Gasoline and Oil Resistant," reference to mineral oil does not include gasoline or similar light-petroleum solvents.

The conductor itself must bear the marking legend designating its use as suitable for gasoline exposure; such designation on the tag alone is not sufficient.

501-14. Signaling, Alarm, Remote-Control, and Communication Systems.

(a) Class I, Division 1.   In Class I, Division 1 locations, all apparatus and equipment of signaling, alarm, remote-control, and communication systems, regardless of voltage, shall be approved for Class I, Division 1 locations, and all wiring shall comply with Sections 501-4(a) and 501-5(a) and (c).

(b) Class I, Division 2.   In Class I, Division 2 locations, signaling, alarm, remote-control, and communication systems shall comply with the following:

(1) Contacts.   Switches, circuit breakers, and make-and-break contacts of pushbuttons, relays, alarm bells, and horns shall have enclosures approved for Class I, Division 1 locations in accordance with Section 501-3(a).

Exception: General purpose enclosures shall be permitted if current interrupting contacts are:

a. Immersed in oil; or

b. Enclosed within a chamber hermetically sealed against the entrance of gases or vapors; or

See comment following Item b of exception in Section 501-3(b)(1).

c. In circuits that under normal conditions do not release sufficient energy to ignite a specific ignitible atmospheric mixture, i.e., are nonincendive.

See comment following Item c of exception in Section 501-3(b)(1).

(2) Resistors and Similar Equipment.   Resistors, resistance devices, thermionic tubes, rectifiers, and similar equipment shall comply with Section 501-3(b)(2).

(3) Protectors.   Enclosures shall be provided for lightning protective devices and for fuses. Such enclosures shall be permitted to be of the general purpose type.

(4) Wiring and Sealing.   All wiring shall comply with Sections 501-4(b) and 501-5(b) and (c).

Audible-signaling devices, such as bells, sirens and horns, other than the newer electronic types, usually involve make-and-break contacts that are capable of producing a spark of sufficient energy to cause ignition of a hazardous atmospheric mixture. Therefore, when used in Class I locations, this type of equipment is to be contained in explosionproof enclosures and wiring methods are to comply with Section 501-4 and sealing fittings are to be provided in accordance with Section 501-5. Figure 501-22 shows a signal siren for use in Class I locations.

Figure 501-22. A signal siren mounted on an explosionproof enclosure for use in hazardous areas. (*Crouse-Hinds*)

Explosionproof devices or explosionproof enclosures may prove more practical than oil-immersed contacts because maintaining the condition and level of the oil can be a problem. Hermetically sealed enclosures, such as float-operated mercury-tube switches, are available for some applications. Electronic signal devices without make-and-break contacts will usually not require explosionproof enclosures in Division 2 locations.

501-15. Live Parts, Class I, Divisions 1 and 2.   There shall be no exposed live parts.

Contact with the circuit could produce sparks that could cause an explosion in a hazardous (classified) location.

501-16. Grounding, Class I, Divisions 1 and 2.   Wiring and equipment shall be grounded as specified in (a) through (e) below.

(a) Exposed Parts.   The exposed noncurrent-carrying metal parts of equipment, such as the frames or metal exteriors of motors, fixed or portable lamps, lighting fixtures, or other utilization equipment, and cabinets, cases, and conduit, shall be grounded as specified in Article 250.

(b) Bonding.   The locknut-bushing and double-locknut types of contacts shall not be depended upon for bonding purposes, but bonding jumpers with proper fittings or other approved means shall be used. Such means of bonding shall apply to all intervening raceways, fittings, boxes, enclosures, etc., between Class I locations and the point of grounding for service equipment. Where flexible conduit is used as permitted in Section 501-4(b), internal or external bonding jumpers complying with the provisions of Section 250-79 shall be installed in parallel with the conduit.

See Section 250-78.

(c) Lightning Protection.   Each ungrounded service conductor of a wiring system in a Class I location, where supplied from an overhead line in an area where lightning disturbances are prevalent, shall be protected by a surge arrester that complies with the provisions of Article 280. The surge arresters shall be connected to the service conductors, and the arrester grounding connections shall comply with the applicable provisions of Article 250.

Surge arresters, if installed in Class I locations, shall be installed in an enclosure suitable for the location.

See Section 502-3 for surge protection.

(d) Grounded Service Conductor, Connections at Service Equipment.   Where a Class I location is supplied from an alternating-current service and the supply system is solidly grounded, the grounded service conductor shall be run to each service according to the requirements in Section 250-23(b) and shall be grounded according to the requirements in Section 250-23(a). Bonding connections to the grounded service conductor at the service equipment shall comply with Sections 250-50(a) and 250-53. Metal enclosures for service conductors and service equipment shall be bonded in accordance with the applicable provisions in Article 250, Part G.

Exception: Where the installation complies with all of the conditions specified in Section 501-16(e) and the system grounded conductor is not used as a circuit conductor, a grounded service conductor shall not be required to be run to the service equipment.

(e) Multiple Grounds.   Where, in the application of Section 250-21, it is necessary to abandon the grounding and bonding connections to the grounded service conductor that are specified in (d) above, the installation shall comply with all of the following conditions:

Figure 501-23. A fitting for the connection of an external bonding jumper used with liquidtight flexible metal conduit.

(1) The grounded service conductor shall be connected to a grounding electrode at the transformer supplying the service.

(2) A grounding conductor shall be run with the service conductors from the supply transformer to the service equipment, and shall be sized in accordance with the requirements for sizing the grounded service conductor in Section 250-23(b). The grounding conductor shall be bonded to the grounded service conductor at the transformer supplying the service and to the equipment grounding conductor(s) at the service equipment.

(3) The service equipment enclosures, the grounding conductor specified in (2) above, and the equipment grounding conductor(s) shall be bonded together and connected to a grounding electrode by a grounding electrode conductor.

Special consideration is necessary in the grounding and bonding of exposed noncurrent-carrying metal parts of equipment, such as the frames or metal exteriors of motors, fixed or portable lamps, lighting fixtures, enclosures, and conduits to ensure permanent and effective mechanical and electrical connections to prevent the possibility of arcs or sparks caused by ineffective or poor grounding methods. To be effective, proper grounding and bonding applies to all interconnected raceways, fittings, enclosures, etc., between hazardous (classified) locations and the point of grounding for service equipment. Where conduit is used in hazardous (classified) locations, it is preferable that threaded connections also be employed in the nonhazardous location.

Lightning arresters are spark-producing devices that should be connected to the service conductors outside the building and must be bonded to the service-entrance raceway system. For services less than 1,000 V, the arrester grounding conductor is connected as provided in Section 250-131.

Where the service voltage is less than 600 V, the supply system is a secondary system; thus the grounded service conductor must always be bonded to the equipment grounding conductor as required by the provisions of Article 250. Systems operating over 600 V may be permitted in a Class I, Division 2 location, but only in most unusual cases. The most common is for operation of large motors.

ARTICLE 502 — CLASS II LOCATIONS

Contents

502-1. General. The general rules of this Code shall apply to the electric wiring and equipment in locations classified as Class II locations in Section 500-5.

Exception: As modified by this article.

"Dust-ignition-proof," as used in this article, shall mean enclosed in a manner that will exclude ignitible amounts of dusts or amounts that might affect performance or rating and that, where installed and protected in accordance with this Code, will not permit arcs, sparks, or heat otherwise generated or liberated inside of the enclosure to cause ignition of exterior accumulations or atmospheric suspensions of a specified dust on or in the vicinity of the enclosure.

Equipment installed in Class II locations shall be able to function at full rating without developing surface temperatures high enough to cause excessive dehydration or gradual carbonization of any organic dust deposits that may occur.

Dust that is carbonized or excessively dry is highly susceptible to spontaneous ignition.

The maximum surface temperatures under actual operating conditions shall not exceed those indicated in Table 502-1.

Equipment and wiring of the type defined in Article 100 as explosionproof shall not be required and shall not be acceptable in Class II locations unless approved for such locations.

Where Class II, Groups E and F dusts having a resistivity less than 10^5 ohm-centimeter are present, there are only Division 1 locations.

Class II, Division 1 and 2 locations are defined in Section 500-5 as hazardous due to the presence of combustible dust. These locations are separated into three groups:

Group E, atmospheres containing metal dusts, such as aluminum and magnesium dusts having a resistivity of 100 ohm-centimeters or less;

Group F, atmospheres containing coal, coke, charcoal, or carbon black dusts having a resistivity greater than 100 ohm-centimeters but equal to or less than 100 Megohm-centimeters; and

Group G, atmospheres containing flour, starch, grain or combustible plastics or chemical dusts having a resistivity greater than 100 Meghom-centimeters.

These definitions have been revised for the 1981 *Code*, primarily to add electrical resistivity ranges and combustible chemical and plastic dusts. Note that electrically conductive dusts are now defined as those having a resistivity less than 100,000 ohm-centimeters, and a new paragraph has been added to specifically indicate that there are no Division 2 locations (only Division 1) if electrically conductive dusts are present. Also note that some Group F dusts can be considered nonelectrically conductive. See comments following the seventh and the last fine print notes in Section 500-2 for additional information. The Instrument Society of America Standard ISA-S12.10-1973, Area Classification in Hazardous Dust Locations, provides some measurements of electrical resistivity of dusts. For example, it shows that most coal dusts have resistivities greater than 100,000 ohm-centimeters. This would permit Group F, Division 2 location classifications for such areas. Prior to the 1981 *Code*, such a classification did not comply with the intent of the *Code*.

It should be noted that equipment suitable for one class and group may not necessarily be suitable for any other class and group. To protect against explosion in hazardous (classified) locations, all electrical equipment exposed to the hazardous atmospheres is required to be suitable for such locations. Look for the Underwriters Laboratories (UL) Listing Mark. Do not take for granted that equipment suitable for Class I use is also suitable for Class II use. Grain dust, for example, will ignite at a temperature lower than that of many flammable vapors.

Any one, or more, of the following four hazards may be present in a Class II location:

1. An explosive mixture of air and dust;

2. Accumulations of dust that interfere with the safe dissipation of heat from electrical equipment;

3. Accumulation of conductive dust lodging on live parts; and

4. Deposits of dust that could be ignited by arcs or sparks.

In the layout of electrical installations for hazardous (classified) locations, it is preferable to locate service equipment, switchboards, panelboards, and much of the electrical equipment in less hazardous areas, usually in a separate room.

502-2. Transformers and Capacitors.

(a) Class II, Division 1.   In Class II, Division 1 locations, transformers and capacitors shall comply with the following:

(1) Containing Liquid that Will Burn.   Transformers and capacitors containing a liquid that will burn shall be installed only in approved vaults complying with Sections 450-41 through 450-48, and in addition: (1) doors or other openings communicating with the Division 1 location shall have self-closing fire doors on both sides of the wall, and the doors shall be carefully fitted and provided with suitable seals (such as weather stripping) to minimize the entrance of dust into the vault; (2) vent openings and ducts shall communicate only with the outside air; and (3) suitable pressure-relief openings communicating with the outside air shall be provided.

Table 502-1.   Maximum Surface Temperatures

Class II Group	Equipment that Is Not Subject to Overloading		Equipment (such as Motors or Power Transformers) that May Be Overloaded			
			Normal Operation		Abnormal Operation	
	Degrees °C	Degrees °F	Degrees °C	Degrees °F	Degrees °C	Degrees °F
E	200	392	200	392	200	392
F	200	392	150	302	200	392
G	165	329	120	248	165	329

(2) Not Containing Liquid that Will Burn. Transformers and capacitors that do not contain a liquid that will burn shall: (1) be installed in vaults complying with Sections 450-41 through 450-48, or (2) be approved as a complete assembly, including terminal connections for Class II locations.

(3) Metal Dusts. No transformer or capacitor shall be installed in a location where dust from magnesium, aluminum, aluminum bronze powders, or other metals of similarly hazardous characteristics may be present.

(b) Class II, Division 2. In Class II, Division 2 locations, transformers and capacitors shall comply with the following:

(1) Containing Liquid that Will Burn. Transformers and capacitors containing a liquid that will burn shall be installed in vaults complying with Sections 450-41 through 450-48.

(2) Containing Askarel. Transformers containing askarel and rated in excess of 25 kVA shall: (1) be provided with pressure-relief vents; (2) be provided with a means for absorbing any gases generated by arcing inside the case, or the pressure-relief vents shall be connected to a chimney or flue that will carry such gases outside the building; and (3) have an air space of not less than 6 inches (152 mm) between the transformer cases and any adjacent combustible material.

(3) Dry-type Transformers. Dry-type transformers shall be installed in vaults or shall: (1) have their windings and terminal connections enclosed in tight metal housings without ventilating or other openings, and (2) operate at not over 600 volts, nominal.

At this time no dry-type or high fire point liquid-insulated transformers that are dusttight and suitable for use in a Class II location are available. It may be possible to construct a small, low-voltage, dusttight (without ventilating openings) dry-type transformer, but transformers having a primary voltage rating of over 600 V must be either high fire point liquid-insulated or installed in a vault. In almost all cases, transformers are located remote from dust atmospheres.

Capacitors used for power-factor correction of individual motors are of sealed construction but, if installed in these locations, must also be provided with dusttight terminal enclosures. The only special requirement for capacitors in Division 2 locations is that they must not contain oil or any other liquid that will burn; otherwise they are to be installed in vaults.

Capacitor and transformer oils (such as askarel) that do not burn have, in the past, contained PCBs, and production of such oil has been stopped.

Figure 502-1 illustrates suitable protection for wiring systems in Class II locations supplied from overhead transmission lines. This protection includes lightning arresters on the primary side of the transformers (within 1,000 ft of the service entrance), surge-protective capacitors connected to the supply side of the main service disconnecting means, and interconnection of all grounds. Arresters are to be of the proper voltage rating for the system to which they are connected and where protecting the primary supply should be located within 300 ft of the transformers. Surge capacitors are to protect against abrupt increases in voltage and are to be provided with automatic means for dissipating any stored charge.

Detailed information for the application of lightning arresters and surge protectors may be obtained from Mill Mutual Fire Prevention Bureau, 2 North Riverside Plaza, Chicago, Illinois 60606.

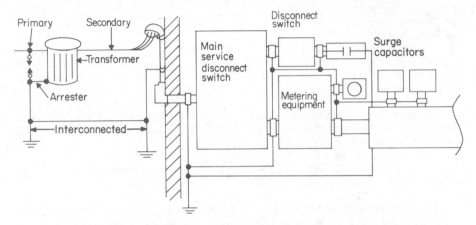

Figure 502-1. Lightning protection: arrester, interconnected grounding, and surge capacitors.

502-3. Surge Protection, Class II, Divisions 1 and 2. In geographical locations where lightning disturbances are prevalent, and where supplied by overhead services, electric systems in Class II locations shall be protected against high-voltage surges. This protection shall include surge arresters, interconnection of all grounds, and surge-protective capacitors. Surge arresters, including their installation and connections, shall comply with Article 280.

Surge arresters, if installed in Class II locations, shall be installed in an enclosure suitable for the location.

Surge-protective capacitors shall be of a type designed for the specific duty. The capacitor grounding conductors shall be connected to the grounding conductors for the surge arresters. Surge-protective capacitors shall be connected to each ungrounded service conductor at the service entrance or service equipment. The capacitors shall be protected by 30-ampere fuses of suitable type and voltage rating, or by automatic circuit breakers of suitable type and rating. Where fuse protection is provided, a disconnecting means shall be installed to disconnect the fuses from the ungrounded service conductors.

502-4. Wiring Methods. Wiring methods shall comply with (a) and (b) below.

(a) Class II, Division 1. In Class II, Division 1 locations, threaded rigid metal conduit, threaded steel intermediate metal conduit or Type MI cable with termination fittings approved for the location shall be the wiring method employed. Type MI cable shall be installed and supported in a manner to avoid tensile stress at the termination fittings.

(1) Fittings and Boxes. Fittings and boxes shall be provided with threaded bosses for connection to conduit or cable terminations, shall have close-fitting covers, and shall have no openings (such as holes for attachment screws) through which dust might enter or through which sparks or burning material might escape. Fittings and boxes in which taps, joints, or terminal connections are made, or that are used in locations where dusts are of a combustible electrically conductive nature, shall be approved for Class II locations.

(2) Flexible Connections. Where necessary to employ flexible connections, dusttight flexible connectors, liquidtight flexible metal conduit with approved fittings, or flexible cord approved for extra-hard usage and provided with bushed fittings shall be used. Where flexible cords are used and electrically conducting dusts are encountered, they shall be provided with dusttight seals at both ends. An additional conductor for grounding shall be provided in the flexible cord unless other acceptable means of grounding is provided. Where flexible connections are subject to oil or other corrosive conditions, the insulation of the conductors shall be of a type approved for the condition or shall be protected by means of a suitable sheath.

(b) Class II, Division 2. In Class II, Division 2 locations, rigid metal conduit, intermediate metal conduit, electrical metallic tubing, dusttight wireways, or Type MI, MC, or SNM cable with approved termination fittings shall be the wiring method employed.

(1) Wireways, Fittings, and Boxes. Wireways, fittings, and boxes in which taps, joints, or terminal connections are made shall be designed to minimize the entrance of dust, and: (1) shall be provided with telescoping or close-fitting covers or other effective means to prevent the escape of sparks or burning material, and (2) shall have no openings (such as holes for attachment screws) through which, after installation, sparks or burning material might escape or through which adjacent combustible material might be ignited.

(2) Flexible Connections. Where flexible connections are necessary, (a)(2) above shall apply.

Where it is necessary to use flexible connections, liquidtight flexible metal conduit or extra-hard usage flexible cord is permitted. The preferred method, however, would be to use a flexible fitting as shown in Figure 501-4. Where liquidtight flexible metal conduit is used, a bonding jumper (internal or external) must be provided around such conduit. See Section 502-16(b). An additional conductor for grounding must be provided where flexible cord is used.

In Division 1 locations, boxes containing taps, joints, or terminal connections and boxes that are used where electrically-conductive dusts (dusts with resistivities less than 100,000 ohm-centimeters) are present must be dust-ignition-proof and must be provided with threaded hubs, as shown in Figure 502-2.

To provide adequate bonding in Division 2 locations, threaded hubs, as shown in Figure 502-2, should be used. Figure 502-2 also shows a close-fitting cover as required for Class II locations. Standard pressed steel boxes are permitted where they do not contain taps, joints, or terminal connections and a bonding jumper is provided around the box.

Figure 502-2. Junction boxes with threaded hubs suitable for use in Class II, Group E hazardous atmospheres. (*Appleton Electric Co.*)

502-5. Sealing, Class II, Divisions 1 and 2. Where a raceway provides communication between an enclosure that is required to be dust-ignition-proof and one that is not, suitable means shall be provided to prevent the entrance of dust into the dust-ignition-proof enclosure through the raceway. One of the following means shall be permitted: (1) a permanent and effective seal; (2) a horizontal raceway not less than 10 feet (3.05 m) long; or (3) a vertical raceway not less than 5 feet (1.52 m) long and extending downward from the dust-ignition-proof enclosure.

Where a raceway provides communication between an enclosure that is required to be dust-ignition-proof and an enclosure in an unclassified location, seals will not be required.

Sealing fittings shall be accessible.

Where a raceway connects an enclosure that is required to be dust-ignition-proof to one that is not, this section provides three suitable ways to prevent dust from entering the dust-ignition-proof enclosure through the raceway. If sealing fittings are used, any of the fittings designed for use in Class I locations can be used. The second paragraph of Section 502-5 is new. It indicates that no sealing method is needed in the special, but not unusual, situation in which no dust can enter the raceway in the hazardous (classified) location. See Figure 502-4.

502-6. Switches, Circuit Breakers, Motor Controllers, and Fuses.

(a) Class II, Division 1. In Class II, Division 1 locations, switches, circuit breakers, motor controllers, and fuses shall comply with the following:

(1) Type Required. Switches, circuit breakers, motor controllers, and fuses, including pushbuttons, relays, and similar devices that are intended to interrupt current during normal operation or that are installed where combustible dusts of an electrically conductive nature may be present, shall be provided with dust-ignition-proof enclosures, which, together with the enclosed equipment in each case, shall be approved as a complete assembly for Class II locations.

(2) Isolating Switches. Disconnecting and isolating switches containing no fuses and not intended to interrupt current and not installed where dusts may be of an electrically conductive nature shall be provided with tight metal enclosures that shall be designed to minimize the entrance of dust, and that shall: (1) be equipped with telescoping or close-fitting covers or with other effective means to prevent the escape of sparks or burning material, and (2) have no openings (such as holes for attachment screws) through which, after installation, sparks or burning material might escape or through which exterior accumulations of dust or adjacent combustible material might be ignited.

(3) Metal Dusts. In locations where dust from magnesium, aluminum, aluminum bronze powders, or other metals of similarly hazardous characteristics may be present, fuses, switches, motor controllers, and circuit breakers shall have enclosures specifically approved for such locations.

(b) Class II, Division 2. In Class II, Division 2 locations, enclosures for fuses, switches, circuit breakers, and motor controllers, including pushbuttons, relays, and similar devices, shall be dusttight.

Figure 502-3 shows a push-button station with pilot light suitable for both Class I and Class II hazardous (classified) locations. Figure 502-5 shows a panelboard suitable for use in Class II locations only. Most, but not necessarily all, of the switches or circuit breakers approved for Class I, Division 1 locations are also approved for Class II locations, but always look for the UL Listing Mark and identification of the hazardous (classified) locations for which the listing has been given.

502-7. Control Transformers and Resistors.

(a) Class II, Division 1. In Class II, Division 1 locations, control transformers, solenoids, impedance coils, resistors, and any overcurrent devices or switching mechanisms associated with them shall have dust-ignition-proof enclosures approved for Class II locations. No control transformer, impedance coil, or resistor shall be installed in a location where dust from magnesium, aluminum, aluminum bronze powders, or other metals of similarly hazardous characteristics may be present unless provided with an enclosure approved for the specific location.

(b) Class II, Division 2. In Class II, Division 2 locations, transformers and resistors shall comply with the following:

Figure 502-3. An explosionproof and dust-tight pushbutton control station that is suitable for use in Class I, Group C and D and Class II Group E, F, and G locations. (*Appleton Electric Co.*)

(1) Switching Mechanisms. Switching mechanisms (including overcurrent devices) associated with control transformers, solenoids, impedance coils, and resistors shall be provided with dusttight enclosures.

(2) Coils and Windings. Where not located in the same enclosure with switching mechanisms, control transformers, solenoids, and impedance coils shall be provided with tight metal housings without ventilating openings.

(3) Resistors. Resistors and resistance devices shall have dust-ignition-proof enclosures approved for Class II locations.

Exception: Where the maximum normal operating temperature of the resistor will not exceed 120°C (248°F), nonadjustable resistors or resistors that are part of an automatically timed starting sequence shall be permitted to have enclosures complying with (b)(2) above.

502-8. Motors and Generators.

(a) Class II, Division 1. In Class II, Division 1 locations, motors, generators, and other rotating electrical machinery shall be:

(1) Approved for Class II, Division 1 locations, or

(2) Totally enclosed pipe-ventilated, meeting temperature limitations in Section 502-1.

It is intended that the phrase "other rotating electrical machinery" include electric brakes. Listed and labeled electric brakes are available for Class I, Group E, F, and G locations.

Although some explosionproof (Class I, Division 1) motors are also dust-ignition-proof, and approved for both Class I and II locations, this is by no means true of all motors. Always look for the marking to be sure the motor is designed and tested for the Class II location involved. If control wiring to the motor is

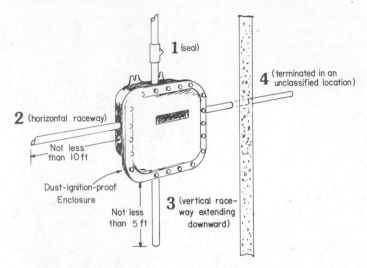

Figure 502-4. Illustrated are four methods permitted for preventing the entrance of dust into the dust-ignition-proof enclosure through the raceway.

Figure 502-5. A dust-ignition-proof panelboard for use in Class II, Group E, F, and G locations. (*Appleton Electric Co.*)

necessary (see motor installation instruction), be sure the control circuit is properly installed and connected. Most motors for Class II locations require internal thermal protection to comply with the temperature limitations in Table 502-1, and integral horsepower Class II motors may require both power and control circuit wiring from the motor controller to the motor.

(b) Class II, Division 2. In Class II, Division 2 locations, motors, generators, and other rotating electrical equipment shall be totally enclosed nonventilated, totally enclosed pipe ventilated, totally enclosed fan cooled or dust-ignition-proof for which maximum full load external temperature shall not exceed 120°C (248°F) when operating in free air (not dust blanketed) and shall have no external openings.

Exception: If the authority having jurisdiction believes accumulations of nonconductive nonabrasive dust will be moderate, and if machines can be easily reached for routine cleaning and maintenance, the following may be installed.

a. Standard open-type machines without sliding contacts, centrifugal or other types of switching mechanism (including motor overcurrent, overloading and overtemperature devices), or integral resistance devices.

b. Standard open-type machines with such contacts, switching mechanisms, or resistance devices enclosed within dusttight housings without ventilating or other openings.

c. Self-cleaning textile motors of the squirrel-cage type.

Section 502-8(b) has been revised in the 1981 *Code* to permit all types of totally enclosed motors in Class II, Division 2 locations if the external surface temperatures without a dust blanket do not exceed 120°C (248°F). Totally enclosed fan-cooled (TEFC) motors are specifically mentioned. The motor should be examined carefully to be sure there are no external openings, even though the motor may be marked "TEFC."

Figure 502-6 shows a totally enclosed pipe-ventilated motor showing intake piping through which cool, clean air is delivered to the motor from a fan or blower. The exhaust opening is connected to a pipe discharging to the outside of the building in order to prevent dust accumulation inside the motor.

Totally enclosed motors that have no special provision for cooling may be used in Class II, Division 2 locations, but to deliver the same horsepower, they must be considerably larger than an open-type, fan-cooled, or pipe-ventilated motor.

Figure 502-6. A pipe-ventilated motor that meets temperature limitations of Section 502-1. (*General Electric Co.*)

502-9. Ventilating Piping. Ventilating pipes for motors, generators, or other rotating electric machinery, or for enclosures for electric equipment, shall be of metal not lighter than No. 24 MSG, or of equally substantial noncombustible material, and shall comply with the following: (1) lead directly to a source of clean air outside of buildings; (2) be screened at the outer ends to prevent the entrance of small animals or birds; and (3) be protected against physical damage and against rusting or other corrosive influences.

Ventilating pipes shall also comply with (a) and (b) below.

(a) Class II, Division 1. In Class II, Division 1 locations, ventilating pipes, including their connections to motors or to the dust-ignition-proof enclosures for other equipment, shall be dusttight throughout their length. For metal pipes, seams and joints shall comply with one of the following: (1) be riveted and soldered; (2) be bolted and soldered; (3) be welded; or (4) be rendered dusttight by some other equally effective means.

(b) Class II, Division 2. In Class II, Division 2 locations, ventilating pipes and their connections shall be sufficiently tight to prevent the entrance of appreciable quantities of dust into the ventilated equipment or enclosure, and to prevent the escape of sparks, flame, or burning material that might ignite dust accumulations or combustible material in the vicinity. For metal pipes, lock seams and riveted or welded joints shall be permitted; and tight-fitting slip joints shall be permitted where some flexibility is necessary, as at connections to motors.

502-10. Utilization Equipment.

(a) Class II, Division 1. In Class II, Division 1 locations, all utilization equipment shall be approved for Class II locations. Where dust from magnesium, aluminum, aluminum bronze powders, or other metals of similarly hazardous characteristics may be present, such equipment shall be approved for the specific location.

(b) Class II, Division 2. In Class II, Division 2 locations, all utilization equipment shall comply with the following:

(1) Heaters. Electrically heated utilization equipment shall be approved for Class II locations.

(2) Motors. Motors of motor-driven utilization equipment shall comply with Section 502-8(b).

(3) Switches, Circuit Breakers, and Fuses. Enclosures for switches, circuit breakers, and fuses shall be dusttight.

(4) Transformers, Impedance Coils, and Resistors. Transformers, solenoids, impedance coils, and resistors shall comply with Section 502-7(b).

502-11. Lighting Fixtures. Lighting fixtures shall comply with (a) and (b) below.

(a) Class II, Division 1. In Class II, Division 1 locations, lighting fixtures for fixed and portable lighting shall comply with the following:

(1) Approved Fixtures. Each fixture shall be approved for Class II locations and shall be clearly marked to indicate the maximum wattage of the lamp for which it is approved. In locations where dust from magnesium, aluminum, aluminum bronze powders, or other metals of similarly hazardous characteristics may be present, fixtures for fixed or portable lighting and all auxiliary equipment shall be approved for the specific location.

(2) Physical Damage. Each fixture shall be protected against physical damage by a suitable guard or by location.

(3) Pendant Fixtures.   Pendant fixtures shall be suspended by threaded rigid metal conduit stems, threaded steel intermediate metal conduit stems, by chains with approved fittings, or by other approved means. For rigid stems longer than 12 inches (305 mm), permanent and effective bracing against lateral displacement shall be provided at a level not more than 12 inches (305 mm) above the lower end of the stem, or flexibility in the form of a fitting or a flexible connector approved for the location shall be provided not more than 12 inches (305 mm) from the point of attachment to the supporting box or fitting. Threaded joints shall be provided with set-screws or other effective means to prevent loosening. Where wiring between an outlet box or fitting and a pendant fixture is not enclosed in conduit, flexible cord approved for hard usage shall be used, and suitable seals shall be provided where the cord enters the fixture and the outlet box or fitting. Flexible cord shall not serve as the supporting means for a fixture.

(4) Supports.   Boxes, box assemblies, or fittings used for the support of lighting fixtures shall be approved for Class II locations.

(b) Class II, Division 2.   In Class II, Division 2 locations, lighting fixtures shall comply with the following:

(1) Portable Lamps.   Portable lamps shall be approved for Class II locations. They shall be clearly marked to indicate the maximum wattage of lamps for which they are approved.

(2) Fixed Lighting.   Lighting fixtures for fixed lighting, where not of a type approved for Class II locations, shall provide enclosures for lamps and lampholders that shall be designed to minimize the deposit of dust on lamps and to prevent the escape of sparks, burning material, or hot metal. Each fixture shall be clearly marked to indicate the maximum wattage of the lamp that shall be permitted without exceeding an exposed surface temperature of 165°C (329°F) under normal conditions of use.

(3) Physical Damage.   Lighting fixtures for fixed lighting shall be protected from physical damage by suitable guards or by location.

(4) Pendant Fixtures.   Pendant fixtures shall be suspended by threaded rigid metal conduit stems, threaded steel intermediate metal conduit stems, by chains with approved fittings, or by other approved means. For rigid stems longer than 12 inches (305 mm), permanent and effective bracing against lateral displacement shall be provided at a level not more than 12 inches (305 mm) above the lower end of the stem, or flexibility in the form of an approved fitting or a flexible connector shall be provided not more than 12 inches (305 mm) from the point of attachment to the supporting box or fitting. Where wiring between an outlet box or fitting and a pendant fixture is not enclosed in conduit, flexible cord approved for hard usage shall be used. Flexible cord shall not serve as the supporting means for a fixture.

(5) Electric-Discharge Lamps.   Starting and control equipment for electric-discharge lamps shall comply with the requirements of Section 502-7(b).

Figure 502-7 shows a fixture listed by Underwriters Laboratories Inc. as suitable for use in Groups E, F, and G of Class II locations. Lighting fixtures must be approved for use in Group E atmospheres where metal dusts are present.

Other than the requirement that the fixture is to be marked to indicate maximum lamp wattage, the only requirements for fixtures in Division 2 locations are that the lamps be enclosed in suitable glass globes to minimize dust deposits on the lamps and to prevent the escape of sparks or burning material. Guards must be provided unless, of course, globe breakage is unlikely.

Flexible cord of the hard-usage type is permitted with approved sealed connections for the wiring of chain-suspended or hook-and-eye suspended fixtures. Flexible cords are not intended to be used as a cord pendant or drop cord.

The portable handlamp shown in Figure 501-18 is approved as a complete assembly for use in Class I locations and also in any Class II, Group G location.

Figure 502-7. A typical lighting fixture for use in Class II, Division 1 locations. Where breakage is unlikely, a metal guard is not required.

502-12. Flexible Cords, Class II, Division 1 and 2.   Flexible cords used in Class II locations shall comply with the following: (1) be of a type approved for extra-hard usage; (2) contain, in addition to the conductors of the circuit, a grounding conductor complying with Section 400-23; (3) be connected to terminals or to supply conductors in an approved manner; (4) be supported by clamps or by other suitable means in such a manner that there will be no tension on the terminal connections; and (5) be provided with suitable seals to prevent the entrance of dust where the flexible cord enters boxes or fittings that are required to be dust-ignition-proof.

502-13. Receptacles and Attachment Plugs.

   (a) Class II, Division 1.   In Class II, Division 1 locations, receptacles and attachment plugs shall be of the type providing for connection to the grounding conductor of the flexible cord and shall be approved for Class II locations.

   (b) Class II, Division 2.   In Class II, Division 2 locations, receptacles and attachment plugs shall be of the type providing for connection to the grounding conductor of the flexible cord and shall be so designed that connection to the supply circuit cannot be made or broken while live parts are exposed.

502-14. Signaling, Alarm, Remote-Control, and Communication Systems, Meters, Instruments, and Relays.

   See Article 800 for rules governing the installation of communication circuits as defined in Article 100.

   (a) Class II, Division 1.   In Class II, Division 1 locations, signaling, alarm, remote-control, and communication systems; and meters, instruments, and relays shall comply with the following:

   (1) Wiring Methods.   Where accidental damage or breakdown of insulation might cause arcs, sparks, or high temperatures, the wiring method shall be rigid metal conduit, intermediate metal conduit, electrical metallic tubing, or Type MI cable with approved termination fittings. For rigid conduit, intermediate metal conduit, or electrical metallic tubing, the number of conductors shall be limited only by the requirement that the cross-sectional area of all conductors shall not exceed 40 percent of the area of the raceway. Where limited flexibility is desirable or where exposure to physical damage is not severe, flexible cord approved for extra-hard usage shall be permitted.

(2) Contacts. Switches, circuit breakers, relays, contactors, fuses and current-breaking contacts for bells, horns, howlers, sirens, and other devices in which sparks or arcs may be produced shall be provided with enclosures approved for a Class II location.

Exception: Where current-breaking contacts are immersed in oil, or where the interruption of current occurs within a chamber sealed against the entrance of dust, enclosures shall be permitted to be of the general purpose type.

(3) Resistors and Similar Equipment. Resistors, transformers, choke coils, rectifiers, thermionic tubes, and other heat-generating equipment shall be provided with enclosures approved for Class II locations.

Exception: Where resistors or similar equipment are immersed in oil, or enclosed in a chamber sealed against the entrance of dust, enclosures shall be permitted to be of the general purpose type.

(4) Rotating Machinery. Motors, generators, and other rotating electric machinery shall comply with Section 502-8(a).

(5) Combustible Electrically Conductive Dusts. Where dusts are of a combustible electrically conductive nature, all wiring and equipment shall be approved for Class II locations.

(6) Metal Dusts. Where dust from magnesium, aluminum, aluminum bronze powders, or other metals of similarly hazardous characteristics may be present, all apparatus and equipment shall be approved for the specific conditions.

(b) Class II, Division 2. In Class II, Division 2 locations, signaling, alarm, remote-control, and communication systems; and meters, instruments, and relays shall comply with the following:

(1) Contacts. Enclosures shall comply with (a)(2) above; or contacts shall have tight metal enclosures designed to minimize the entrance of dust, and shall have telescoping or tight-fitting covers and no openings through which, after installation, sparks or burning material might escape.

Exception: In circuits that under normal conditions do not release sufficient energy to ignite a dust layer, enclosures shall be permitted to be of the general purpose type.

(2) Transformers and Similar Equipment. The windings and terminal connections of transformers, choke coils, and similar equipment shall be provided with tight metal enclosures without ventilating openings.

(3) Resistors and Similar Equipment. Resistors, resistance devices, thermionic tubes, rectifiers, and similar equipment shall comply with (a)(3) above.

Exception: Enclosures for thermionic tubes, nonadjustable resistors, or rectifiers for which maximum operating temperature will not exceed 120°C (248°F) shall be permitted to be of the general purpose type.

(4) Rotating Machinery. Motors, generators, and other rotating electric machinery shall comply with Section 502-8(b).

502-15. Live Parts, Class II, Divisions 1 and 2.   Live parts shall not be exposed.

502-16. Grounding, Class II, Divisions 1 and 2.   Wiring and equipment shall be grounded in accordance with (a) through (d) below.

(a) Exposed Parts.   Exposed noncurrent-carrying metal parts of equipment, such as the frames or metal exteriors of motors, fixed or portable lamps, lighting fixtures, or other utilization equipment, or cabinets, cases, and conduit shall be grounded as specified in Article 250.

(b) Bonding.   The locknut-bushing and double-locknut type of contact shall not be depended upon for bonding purposes; but bonding jumpers with proper fittings or other approved means shall be used. Such means of bonding shall apply to all intervening raceways, fittings, boxes, enclosures, etc., between Class II locations and the point of grounding for service equipment. Where flexible conduit is used as permitted in Section 502-4, internal or external bonding jumpers complying with the provisions of Section 250-79 shall be installed in parallel with the conduit.

> Single locknuts or double locknuts and bushings are not to be depended upon for bonding purposes. Bonding jumpers or other approved means with proper fittings are required for the interconnection of all raceways, junction boxes, fittings, enclosures, etc., between the hazardous area and all the way to the grounding electrode conductor connection point at the service equipment. Where installed outside the raceway or enclosure, the grounding conductor is not to exceed 6 ft and is to be routed with the raceway or enclosure. See Section 250-79.

See Section 250-78.

(c) Grounded Service Conductor, Connections at Service Equipment.   Where a Class II location is supplied from an alternating-current service and the supply system is solidly grounded, the grounded service conductor shall be run to each service according to the requirements in Section 250-23(b) and shall be grounded according to the requirements in Section 250-23(a). Bonding connections to the grounded service conductor at the service equipment shall comply with Sections 250-50(a) and 250-53. Metal enclosures for service conductors and service equipment shall be bonded in accordance with the applicable provisions in Article 250, Part G.

Exception: Where the installation complies with all of the conditions specified in Section 502-16(d) and the system grounded conductor is not used as a circuit conductor, a grounded service conductor shall not be required to be run to the service equipment.

(d) Multiple Grounds.   Where, in the application of Section 250-21, it is necessary to abandon the grounding and bonding connections to the grounded service conductor that are specified in (c) above, the installation shall comply with all of the following conditions:

(1) The grounded service conductor shall be connected to a grounding electrode at the transformer supplying the service.

(2) A grounding conductor shall be run with the service conductors from the supply transformer to the service equipment, and shall be sized in accordance with the requirements for sizing the grounded service conductor in Section 250-23(b). The grounding conductor shall be bonded to the grounded service conductor at the transformer supplying the service, and to the equipment grounding conductor(s) at the service equipment.

(3) The service equipment enclosures, the grounding conductor specified in (2) above, and the equipment grounding conductor(s) shall be bonded together and connected to a grounding electrode by a grounding electrode conductor.

ARTICLE 503 — CLASS III LOCATIONS

Contents

503-1. General.   The general rules of this Code shall apply to electric wiring and equipment in locations classified as Class III locations in Section 500-6.

Exception: As modified by this article.

Equipment installed in Class III locations shall be able to function at full rating without developing surface temperatures high enough to cause excessive dehydration or gradual carbonization of accumulated fibers or flyings. Organic material that is carbonized or excessively dry is highly susceptible to spontaneous ignition. The maximum surface temperatures under operating conditions shall not exceed 165°C (329°F) for equipment that is not subject to overloading, and 120°C (248°F) for equipment (such as motors or power transformers) that may be overloaded.

For electric trucks, see Powered Industrial Trucks Including Type Designations, Areas of Use, Maintenance and Operation, NFPA 505-1978 (ANSI).

Class III locations usually include textile mills (cotton, rayon, etc.) where easily ignitible fibers or combustible flyings are present in the manufacturing process. Sawmills and other woodworking plants, where sawdust, wood shavings, and combustible fibers or flyings are present, may also become hazardous. If wood flour (dust) is present, the location is a Class II, Group G location, not a Class III location.

Fibers or flyings are hazardous not only because they are easily ignited, but also because flames spread through them quickly. Such fires travel with a rapidity approaching an explosion and are commonly called "flash fires."

Division 1 of Class III applies to locations where material is handled, manufactured, or used. Division 2 applies to locations where material is stored or handled, but where no manufacturing processes are performed. There are no group designations in Class III locations.

503-2. Transformers and Capacitors, Class III, Divisions 1 and 2.   Transformers and capacitors shall comply with Section 502-2(b).

503-3. Wiring Methods.   Wiring methods shall comply with (a) and (b) below.

(a) Class III, Division 1.   In Class III, Division 1 locations, the wiring method shall be threaded rigid metal conduit, threaded steel intermediate metal conduit, or approved Type MI or Type MC cable.

(1) Boxes and Fittings.   Fittings and boxes in which taps, joints, or terminal connections are made shall: (1) be provided with telescoping or close-fitting covers or other effective means to prevent the escape of sparks or burning material, and (2) shall have no openings (such as holes for attachment screws) through which, after installation, sparks or burning material might escape, or through which adjacent combustible material might be ignited.

(2) Flexible Connections.   Where flexible connections are necessary, Section 502-4(a)(2) shall apply.

(b) Class III, Division 2.   In Class III, Division 2 locations, the wiring method shall comply with (a) above.

Exception: In sections, compartments, or areas used solely for storage and containing no machinery, open wiring on insulators shall be permitted where installed in accordance with Article 320, but only on condition that protection as required by Section 320-14 be provided where conductors are not run in roof spaces and are well out of reach of sources of physical damage.

503-4. Switches, Circuit Breakers, Motor Controllers, and Fuses, Class III, Divisions 1 and 2.   Switches, circuit breakers, motor controllers, and fuses, including pushbuttons, relays, and similar devices, shall be provided with tight metal enclosures designed to minimize entrance of fibers and flyings, and which shall: (1) be equipped with telescoping or close-fitting covers or with other effective means to prevent escape of sparks or burning material, and (2) have no openings (such as holes for attachment screws) through which, after installation, sparks or burning material might escape, or through which exterior accumulations of fibers or flyings or adjacent combustible material might be ignited.

503-5. Control Transformers and Resistors, Class III, Divisions 1 and 2.   Transformers, impedance coils, and resistors used as or in conjunction with control equipment for motors, generators, and appliances shall comply with Section 502-7(b).

Exception: In Class III, Division 1 locations where these devices are in the same enclosure with switching devices of such control equipment and are used only for starting or short-time duty, the enclosure shall comply with Section 503-4.

503-6. Motors and Generators.

(a) Class III, Division 1.   In Class III, Division 1 locations, motors, generators, and other rotating electric machinery shall be totally enclosed nonventilated, totally enclosed pipe-ventilated, or totally enclosed fan-cooled.

Exception: In locations where, in the judgment of the authority having jurisdiction, only moderate accumulations of lint or flyings will be likely to collect on, in, or in the vicinity of a rotating electric machine, and where such machine is readily accessible for routine cleaning and maintenance, one of the following shall be permitted:

a. Self-cleaning textile motors of the squirrel-cage types;

b. Standard open-type machines without sliding contacts, centrifugal or other types of switching mechanism, including motor overload devices; or

c. Standard open-type machines having such contacts, switching mechanisms, or resistance devices enclosed within tight metal housings without ventilating or other openings.

(b) Class III, Division 2. In Class III, Division 2 locations, motors, generators, and other rotating electric machinery shall be totally enclosed nonventilated, totally enclosed pipe-ventilated, or totally enclosed fan-cooled.

(c) Types Not Permitted, Class III, Divisions 1 and 2. Motors, generators, or other rotating electric machinery of the partially enclosed or splashproof type shall not be installed in Class III locations.

It is intended that the phrase "other rotating electric machinery" include electric brakes. Listed and labeled electric brakes are available for Class II, Group G locations, and according to Underwriters Laboratories Inc. (UL) Hazardous Location Equipment Directory, such brakes are suitable for Class III locations.

503-7. Ventilating Piping, Class III, Divisions 1 and 2. Ventilating pipes for motors, generators, or other rotating electric machinery, or for enclosures for electric equipment shall be of metal not lighter than No. 24 MSG, or of equally substantial noncombustible material, and shall comply with the following: (1) lead directly to a source of clean air outside of buildings; (2) be screened at the outer ends to prevent the entrance of small animals or birds; and (3) be protected against physical damage and against rusting or other corrosive influences.

Ventilating pipes shall be sufficiently tight, including their connections, to prevent the entrance of appreciable quantities of fibers or flyings into the ventilated equipment or enclosure and to prevent the escape of sparks, flame, or burning material that might ignite accumulations of fibers or flyings or combustible material in the vicinity. For metal pipes, lock seams and riveted or welded joints shall be permitted; and tight-fitting slip joints shall be permitted where some flexibility is necessary, as at connections to motors.

503-8. Utilization Equipment, Class III, Divisions 1 and 2.

(a) Heaters. Electrically heated utilization equipment shall be approved for Class III locations.

(b) Motors. Motors of motor-driven utilization equipment shall comply with Section 503-6.

(c) Switches, Circuit Breakers, Motor Controllers, and Fuses. Switches, circuit breakers, motor controllers, and fuses shall comply with Section 503-4.

503-9. Lighting Fixtures, Class III, Divisions 1 and 2.

(a) Fixed Lighting. Lighting fixtures for fixed lighting shall provide enclosures for lamps and lampholders that are designed to minimize entrance of fibers and flyings and to prevent the escape of sparks, burning material, or hot metal. Each fixture shall be clearly marked to show the maximum wattage of the lamps that shall be permitted without exceeding an exposed surface temperature of 165°C (329°F) under normal conditions of use.

(b) Physical Damage.   A fixture that may be exposed to physical damage shall be protected by a suitable guard.

(c) Pendant Fixtures.   Pendant fixtures shall be suspended by stems of threaded rigid metal conduit, threaded intermediate metal conduit or threaded metal tubing of equivalent thickness. For stems longer than 12 inches (305 mm), permanent and effective bracing against lateral displacement shall be provided at a level not more than 12 inches (305 mm) above the lower end of the stem, or flexibility in the form of an approved fitting or a flexible connector shall be provided not more than 12 inches (305 mm) from the point of attachment to the supporting box or fitting.

(d) Portable Lamps.   Portable lamps shall be equipped with handles and protected with substantial guards, and lampholders shall be of the unswitched type with no exposed metal parts and without provision for receiving attachment plugs. In all other respects, portable lamps shall comply with (a) above.

503-10. Flexible Cords, Class III, Divisions 1 and 2.   Flexible cords shall comply with Section 502-12.

503-11. Receptacles and Attachment Plugs, Class III, Divisions 1 and 2.   Receptacles and attachment plugs shall comply with Section 502-13(b).

503-12. Signaling, Alarm, Remote-Control, and Local Loudspeaker Intercommunication Systems, Class III, Divisions 1 and 2.   Signaling, alarm, remote-control, and local loudspeaker intercommunication systems shall comply with Section 502-14(a).

503-13. Electric Cranes, Hoists, and Similar Equipment, Class III, Divisions 1 and 2.   Where installed for operation over combustible fibers or accumulations of flyings, traveling cranes and hoists for material handling, traveling cleaners for textile machinery, and similar equipment shall comply with (a) through (d) below.

(a) Power Supply.   Power supply to contact conductors shall be isolated from all other systems, shall be ungrounded, and shall be equipped with an acceptable recording ground detector that will give an alarm and automatically de-energize the contact conductors in case of a fault to ground, or with an acceptable ground-fault indicator that will give a visual and audible alarm, and maintain the alarm as long as power is supplied to the system and the ground fault remains.

(b) Contact Conductors.   Contact conductors shall be so located or guarded as to be inaccessible to other than authorized persons and shall be protected against accidental contact with foreign objects.

(c) Current Collectors.   Current collectors shall be so arranged or guarded as to confine normal sparking and prevent escape of sparks or hot particles. To reduce sparking, two or more separate surfaces of contact shall be provided for each contact conductor. Reliable means shall be provided to keep contact conductors and current collectors free of accumulations of lint or flyings.

(d) Control Equipment.   Control equipment shall comply with Sections 503-4 and 503-5.

In a Class III location, cranes installed over accumulations of fibers or flyings and equipped with rolling or sliding collectors making contact with bare conductors introduce two hazards:

1. Any arcing between a conductor and a collector rail may ignite combustible fibers or "lint" accumulated on or near the bare conductor. This hazard may be prevented by maintaining the proper alignment of the bare conductor, by using a collector designed so that proper contact is always maintained, and by using guards or shields to confine hot metal particles that may be caused by arcing.

2. If enough moisture is present, fibers and flyings accumulating on the insulating supports of the bare conductors may form a conductive path between the conductors, or from one conductor to ground, thereby permitting enough current to flow to ignite the fibers. Where the system is ungrounded, a current flow to ground is unlikely to start a fire. A suitable recording ground detector will give an alarm and automatically de-energize contact conductors when the insulation resistance is being lowered by an accumulation of fibers on the insulators or in case of a fault to ground. A ground-fault indicator is permitted that will maintain an alarm until the system is de-energized or the ground fault is cleared.

503-14. Storage-Battery Charging Equipment, Class III, Divisions 1 and 2.   Storage-battery charging equipment shall be located in separate rooms built or lined with substantial noncombustible materials so constructed as to adequately exclude flyings or lint and shall be well ventilated.

503-15. Live Parts, Class III, Divisions 1 and 2.   Live parts shall not be exposed.

Exception: As provided in Section 503-13.

503-16. Grounding, Class III, Divisions 1 and 2.   Wiring and equipment shall be grounded in accordance with Section 502-16.

ARTICLE 510 — HAZARDOUS (CLASSIFIED)
LOCATIONS — SPECIFIC

Contents

510-1. Scope.   Articles 511 through 517 cover occupancies or parts of occupancies that are or may be hazardous because of atmospheric concentrations of flammable liquids, gases, or vapors, or because of deposits or accumulations of materials that may be readily ignitible.

510-2. General.   The general rules of this Code shall apply to electric wiring and equipment in occupancies within the scope of Articles 511 through 517, except as such rules are modified in those articles. Where unusual conditions exist in a specific occupancy, the authority having jurisdiction shall judge with respect to the application of specific rules.

Information and copies of standards may be obtained from the National Fire Protection Association (NFPA), 470 Atlantic Avenue, Boston, MA 02210.

ARTICLE 511 — COMMERCIAL GARAGES, REPAIR
AND STORAGE

Contents

(f) Portable Lamps.

511-3. Wiring and Equipment in Class I Locations.

511-4. Sealing.

511-5. Wiring in Spaces Above Class I Locations.

(a) Fixed Wiring Above Class I Locations.

(b) Pendants.

(c) Grounded Conductor.

(d) Attachment Plug Receptacles.

511-6. Equipment Above Class I Locations.

(a) Arcing Equipment.

(b) Fixed Lighting.

511-7. Battery Charging Equipment.

511-8. Electric Vehicle Charging.

(a) Connections.

(b) Connector Design and Location.

(c) Plug Connections to Vehicles.

511-1. Scope.   These occupancies shall include locations used for service and repair operations in connection with self-propelled vehicles (including passenger automobiles, buses, trucks, tractors, etc.) in which volatile flammable liquids are used for fuel or power. Areas in which flammable fuel is transferred to vehicle fuel tanks shall conform to Article 514. Parking garages used for parking or storage and where no repair work is done except exchange of parts and routine maintenance requiring no use of electrical equipment, open flame, welding, or the use of volatile flammable liquids are not classified, but they shall be adequately ventilated to carry off the exhaust fumes of the engines.

For further information, see Parking Structures, NFPA 88A-1979, and Repair Garages, NFPA 88B-1979.

Article 100 defines "Garage" as a building or portion of a building in which one or more self-propelled vehicles carrying volatile flammable liquid for fuel or power are kept for use, sale, storage, rental, repair, exhibition, or demonstrating purposes, and all that portion of a building which is on or below the floor or floors in which such vehicles are kept and which is not separated therefrom by suitable cutoffs.

A mechanical ventilating system capable of continuously providing at least six air changes per hour is required for all enclosed, basement, and underground parking garages.

Operations involving open flame or electric arcs, including fusion gas and electric welding, are to be restricted to areas specifically provided for such purposes.

Approved suspended unit heaters may be used provided they are located not less than 8 ft above the floor and are installed in accordance with the conditions of their approval.

511-2. Class I Locations.   Classification under Article 500.

(a) Up to a Level of 18 Inches (457 mm) Above the Floor.   For each floor the entire area up to a level of 18 inches (457 mm) above the floor shall be considered to be a Class I, Division 2 location except where the enforcing agency determines that there is mechanical ventilation providing a minimum of four air changes per hour.

(b) Any Pit or Depression Below Floor Level.   Any pit or depression below floor level shall be considered to be a Class I, Division 1 location which shall extend up to said floor level, except that any pit or depression in which six air changes per hour are exhausted at the floor level of the pit shall be permitted to be judged by the enforcing agency to be a Class I, Division 2 location.

(c) Areas Adjacent to Defined Locations with Positive Pressure Ventilation.   Areas adjacent to defined locations in which flammable vapors are not likely to be released such as stock rooms, switchboard rooms, and other similar locations shall not be classified when mechanically ventilated at a rate of four or more air changes per hour or when effectively cut off by walls or partitions.

(d) Adjacent Areas by Special Permission. Adjacent areas which by reason of ventilation, air pressure differentials, or physical spacing are such that, in the opinion of the authority enforcing this Code, no ignition hazard exists shall be classified as nonhazardous.

(e) Fuel Dispensing Units. When fuel dispensing units (other than liquid petroleum gas which is prohibited) are located within buildings, the requirements of Article 514 shall govern.

When mechanical ventilation is provided in the dispensing area, the controls shall be interlocked so that the dispenser cannot operate without ventilation as prescribed in Section 500-4(b).

(f) Portable Lamps. Portable lamps shall be equipped with handle, lampholder, hook and substantial guard attached to the lampholder or handle. All exterior surfaces which might come in contact with battery terminals, wiring terminals, or other objects shall be of nonconducting material or shall be effectively protected with insulation. Lampholders shall be of unswitched type and shall not provide means for plug-in of attachment plugs. Outer shell shall be of molded composition or other suitable material. Unless the lamp and its cord are supported or arranged in such a manner that they cannot be used in the locations classified in Section 511-2 they shall be of a type approved for Class I, Division 1 locations.

Figure 511-1. This cord, which is part of a portable lamp assembly, is to be arranged so that the lamp cannot be used in a Class I location; otherwise, the lamp must be of a type approved for Class I, Division 1 hazardous locations (explosionproof). (*Appleton Electric Co.*)

Sections 511-2(a) and (b) classify Class I, Divisions 1 and 2 locations of commerical garages. Fuel dispensing units located within the garage are to be governed by the requirements of Article 514.

The Class I, Division 2 location above grade within a commercial garage extends 18 in. above the floor level unless the authority having jurisdiction determines otherwise because there is mechanical ventilation providing at least four air changes per hour.

The Class I, Division 1 location below grade extends from the floor of the pit or depression to floor level, unless the authority having jurisdiction permits the pit or depression to be classified Class I, Division 2 because ventilation providing at least six air changes per hour exhausts air at the floor level of the pit or depression.

511-3. Wiring and Equipment in Class I Locations. Within Class I locations as defined in Section 511-2, wiring and equipment shall conform to applicable provisions of Article 501. Raceways embedded in a masonry wall or buried beneath a floor shall be considered to be within the Class I location above the floor if any connections or extensions lead into or through such areas.

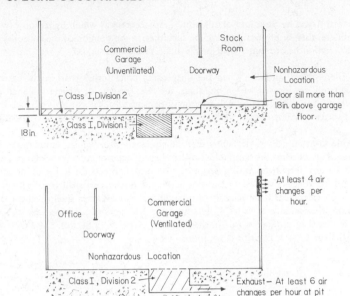

Figure 511-2. Classification of locations in commercial garages.

This section applies to raceways in walls and below floors of Class I locations in commercial garages. A raceway that is in a masonry wall or buried beneath a floor may not have any connections or extensions leading into or through a Class I, Division 1 or 2 location if it is to be considered in a nonhazardous location and not subject to the provisions of Article 501. However, any extension into a hazardous (classified) location sealed off in accordance with Section 501-5 isolates the sealed part from the unsealed part.

Article 501 applies to the raceway if any part of it is not imbedded in the wall or the wall is not masonry. Article 501 applies to the raceway if any part of it is not buried beneath the floor. The floor material is not specified.

511-4. Sealing. Approved seals conforming to the requirements of Section 501-5 shall be provided, and Section 501-5(b)(2) shall apply to horizontal as well as vertical boundaries of the defined Class I locations.

Seals are required if any part of the raceway is in, or passes through, a Class I, Division 2 location. See comments on seals, Section 501-5.

511-5. Wiring in Spaces Above Class I Locations.

(a) **Fixed Wiring Above Class I Locations.** All fixed wiring above Class I locations shall be in metallic raceways, rigid nonmetallic conduit, or shall be Type MI, TC, SNM, or Type MC cable. Cellular metal floor raceways shall be permitted to be used only for supplying ceiling outlets or extensions to the area below the floor, but such raceways shall have no connections leading into or through any Class I location above the floor. No electrical conductor shall be installed in any cell, header, or duct which contains a pipe for any service except electrical or compressed air.

(b) **Pendants.** For pendants, flexible cord suitable for the type of service and approved for hard usage shall be used.

(c) Grounded Conductor.   When a circuit which supplies portables or pendants includes a grounded conductor as provided in Article 200, receptacles, attachment plugs, connectors, and similar devices shall be of polarized type, and the grounded conductor of the flexible cord shall be connected to the screw shell of any lampholder or to the grounded terminal of any utilization equipment supplied.

(d) Attachment Plug Receptacles.   Attachment plug receptacles in fixed position shall be located above the level of any defined Class I location, or be approved for the location.

511-6. Equipment Above Class I Locations.

(a) Arcing Equipment.   Equipment that is less than 12 feet (3.66 m) above the floor level and that may produce arcs, sparks, or particles of hot metal, such as cutouts, switches, charging panels, generators, motors, or other equipment (excluding receptacles, lamps and lampholders) having make-and-break or sliding contacts, shall be of the totally enclosed type or so constructed as to prevent escape of sparks or hot metal particles.

(b) Fixed Lighting.   Lamps and lampholders for fixed lighting that is located over lanes through which vehicles are commonly driven or that may otherwise be exposed to physical damage shall be located not less than 12 feet (3.66 m) above floor level, unless of the totally enclosed type or so constructed as to prevent escape of sparks or hot metal particles.

511-7. Battery Charging Equipment.   Battery chargers and their control equipment, and batteries being charged shall not be located within locations classified in Section 511-2.

511-8. Electric Vehicle Charging.

(a) Connections.   Flexible cords and connectors used for charging shall be suitable for the type of service and approved for extra-hard usage. Their ampacity shall be adequate for the charging current.

(b) Connector Design and Location.   Connectors shall be so designed and installed that they will disconnect readily at any position of the charging cable, and live parts shall be guarded from accidental contact. No connector shall be located within a Class I location as defined in Section 511-2.

(c) Plug Connections to Vehicles.   Where plugs are provided for direct connection to vehicles, the point of connection shall not be within a Class I location as defined in Section 511-2, and where the cord is suspended from overhead, it shall be so arranged that the lowest point of sag is at least 6 inches (152 mm) above the floor. Where the vehicle is equipped with an approved plug that will disconnect readily, and where an automatic arrangement is provided to pull both cord and plug beyond the range of physical damage, no additional connector shall be required in the cable or at the outlet.

ARTICLE 513 — AIRCRAFT HANGARS

Contents

(a) Fixed Wiring.
(b) Pendants.
(c) Portable Equipment.
(d) Grounded and Grounding Conductors.
513-5. Equipment Not Within Class I Locations.
(a) Arcing Equipment.
(b) Lampholders.
(c) Portable Lamps.
(d) Portable Equipment.
513-6. Stanchions, Rostrums, and Docks.
(a) In Class I Location.
(b) Not in Class I Location.
(c) Mobile Type.

513-7. Sealing.
513-8. Aircraft Electrical Systems.
513-9. Aircraft Battery — Charging and Equipment.
513-10. External Power Sources for Energizing Aircraft.
(a) Not Less than 18 Inches Above Floor.
(b) Marking for Mobile Units.
(c) Cords.
513-11. Mobile Servicing Equipment with Electric Components.
(a) General.
(b) Cords and Connectors.
(c) Restricted Use.
513-12. Grounding.

513-1. Definition.   An aircraft hangar is a location used for storage or servicing of aircraft in which gasoline, jet fuels, or other volatile flammable liquids or flammable gases are used. It shall not include locations used exclusively for aircraft that have never contained such liquids or gases, or that have been drained and properly purged.

513-2. Classification of Locations.

(a) Below Floor Level.   Any pit or depression below the level of the hangar floor shall be classified as a Class I, Division 1 location that shall extend up to said floor level.

(b) Areas Not Cut Off or Ventilated.   The entire area of the hangar, including any adjacent and communicating areas not suitably cut off from the hangar, shall be classified as a Class I, Division 2 location up to a level 18 inches (457 mm) above the floor.

(c) Vicinity of Aircraft.   The area within 5 feet (1.52 m) horizontally from aircraft power plants or aircraft fuel tanks shall be classified as a Class I, Division 2 location that shall extend upward from the floor to a level 5 feet (1.52 m) above the upper surface of wings and of engine enclosures.

In order to properly classify the area in accordance with this section, it is necessary to obtain information on the aircraft parking patterns, the types of aircraft, and the operations to be performed in the hangar.

(d) Areas Suitably Cut Off and Ventilated.   Adjacent areas in which flammable liquids or vapors are not likely to be released, such as stock rooms, electrical control rooms, and other similar locations, shall not be classified where adequately ventilated and where effectively cut off from the hangar itself by walls or partitions.

513-3. Wiring and Equipment in Class I Locations.   All wiring and equipment that is or may be installed or operated within any of the Class I locations defined in Section 513-2 shall comply with the applicable provisions of Article 501. All wiring installed in or under the hangar floor shall comply with the requirements for Class I, Division 1 locations. Where such wiring is located in vaults, pits, or ducts, adequate drainage shall be provided; and the wiring shall not be placed within the same compartment with any service other than piped compressed air.

Attachment plugs and receptacles in Class I locations shall be approved for Class I locations or shall be so designed that they cannot be energized while the connections are being made or broken.

513-4. Wiring Not Within Class I Locations.

(a) Fixed Wiring. All fixed wiring in a hangar, but not within a Class I location as defined in Section 513-2, shall be installed in metallic raceways or shall be Type MI, TC, SNM or Type MC cable.

Exception: Wiring in nonhazardous locations as defined in Section 513-2(d) shall be of a type recognized in Chapter 3.

(b) Pendants. For pendants, flexible cord suitable for the type of service and approved for hard usage shall be used. Each such cord shall include a separate grounding conductor.

(c) Portable Equipment. For portable utilization equipment and lamps, flexible cord suitable for the type of service and approved for extra-hard usage shall be used. Each such cord shall include a separate grounding conductor.

(d) Grounded and Grounding Conductors. Where a circuit supplies portables or pendants and includes an identified grounded conductor as provided in Article 200, receptacles, attachment plugs, connectors, and similar devices shall be of the polarized type, and the grounded conductor of the flexible cord will be connected to the screw shell of any lampholder or to the grounded terminal of any utilization equipment supplied. Acceptable means shall be provided for maintaining continuity of the grounding conductor between the fixed raceway system and the noncurrent-carrying metal portions of pendant fixtures, portable lamps, and portable utilization equipment.

513-5. Equipment Not Within Class I Locations.

(a) Arcing Equipment. In locations other than those described in Section 513-2, equipment that is less than 10 feet (3.05 m) above wings and engine enclosures of aircraft and that may produce arcs, sparks, or particles of hot metal, such as lamps and lampholders for fixed lighting, cutouts, switches, receptacles, charging panels, generators, motors, or other equipment having make-and-break or sliding contacts, shall be of the totally enclosed type or so constructed as to prevent escape of sparks or hot metal particles.

Exception: Equipment in areas described in Section 513-2(d) shall be permitted to be of the general purpose type.

(b) Lampholders. Lampholders of metal-shell, fiber-lined types shall not be used for fixed incandescent lighting.

(c) Portable Lamps. Portable lamps that are used within a hangar shall be approved for the location in which they are used.

(d) Portable Equipment. Portable utilization equipment that is or may be used within a hangar shall be of a type suitable for use in Class I, Division 2 locations.

513-6. Stanchions, Rostrums, and Docks.

(a) In Class I Location. Electric wiring, outlets, and equipment (including lamps) on or attached to stanchions, rostrums, or docks that are located or likely to be located in a Class I location as defined in Section 513-2(c) shall comply with the requirements for Class I, Division 2 locations.

(b) Not in Class I Location. Where stanchions, rostrums, or docks are not located or likely to be located in a Class I location as defined in Section 513-2(c), wiring and equipment shall comply with Sections 513-4 and 513-5, except that such wiring and equipment not more than 18 inches (457 mm) above the floor in any position shall comply with (a) above. Receptacles and attachment plugs shall be of a locking type that will not readily disconnect.

(c) Mobile Type. Mobile stanchions with electric equipment complying with (b) above shall carry at least one permanently affixed warning sign to read: "WARNING — KEEP 5 FEET CLEAR OF AIRCRAFT ENGINES AND FUEL TANK AREAS."

513-7. Sealing. Approved seals shall be provided in accordance with Section 501-5. Sealing requirements specified in Section 501-5(a) (4) and (b) (2) shall apply to horizontal as well as to vertical boundaries of the defined Class I locations. Raceways embedded in a masonry floor or buried beneath a floor shall be considered to be within the Class I location above the floor where any connections or extensions lead into or through such location.

513-8. Aircraft Electrical Systems. Aircraft electrical systems shall be de-energized when the aircraft is stored in a hangar, and, whenever possible, while the aircraft is undergoing maintenance.

513-9. Aircraft Battery — Charging and Equipment. Aircraft batteries shall not be charged when installed in an aircraft located inside or partially inside a hangar.

Battery chargers and their control equipment shall not be located or operated within any of the Class I locations defined in Section 513-2, and shall preferably be located in a separate building or in an area such as defined in Section 513-2(d). Mobile chargers shall carry at least one permanently affixed warning sign to read: "WARNING — KEEP 5 FEET CLEAR OF AIRCRAFT ENGINES AND FUEL TANK AREAS." Tables, racks, trays, and wiring shall not be located within a Class I location, and, in addition, shall comply with Article 480.

513-10. External Power Sources for Energizing Aircraft.

(a) Not Less than 18 Inches (457 mm) Above Floor. Aircraft energizers shall be so designed and mounted that all electric equipment and fixed wiring will be at least 18 inches (457 mm) above floor level and shall not be operated in a Class I location as defined in Section 513-2(c).

(b) Marking for Mobile Units. Mobile energizers shall carry at least one permanently affixed warning sign to read: "WARNING — KEEP 5 FEET CLEAR OF AIRCRAFT ENGINES AND FUEL TANK AREAS."

(c) Cords. Flexible cords for aircraft energizers and ground support equipment shall be approved for the type of service and extra-hard usage and shall include an equipment grounding conductor.

513-11. Mobile Servicing Equipment with Electric Components.

(a) General. Mobile servicing equipment (such as vacuum cleaners, air compressors, air movers, etc.) having electric wiring and equipment not suitable for Class I, Division 2 locations shall be so designed and mounted that all such fixed wiring and equipment will be at least 18 inches (457 mm) above the floor. Such mobile equipment shall not be operated within the Class I location defined in Section 513-2(c) and shall carry at least one permanently affixed warning sign to read: "WARNING — KEEP 5 FEET CLEAR OF AIRCRAFT ENGINES AND FUEL TANK AREAS."

(b) Cords and Connectors. Flexible cords for mobile equipment shall be suitable for the type of service and approved for extra-hard usage, and shall include an equipment grounding conductor. Attachment plugs and receptacles shall be approved for the location in which they are installed, and shall provide for connection of the grounding conductor to the raceway system.

(c) Restricted Use. Equipment not suitable for Class I, Division 2 locations shall not be operated in locations where maintenance operations likely to release flammable liquids or vapors are in progress.

513-12. Grounding. All metal raceways and all noncurrent-carrying metal portions of fixed or portable equipment, regardless of voltage, shall be grounded as provided in Article 250.

ARTICLE 514 — GASOLINE DISPENSING
AND SERVICE STATIONS

Contents

514-1. Definition.
514-2. Class I Locations.
514-3. Wiring and Equipment Within Class I Locations.
514-4. Wiring and Equipment Above Class I Locations.

514-5. Circuit Disconnects.
514-6. Sealing.
  (a) At Dispenser.
  (b) At Boundary.
514-7. Grounding.
514-8. Underground Wiring.

514-1. Definition. A gasoline dispensing and service station is a location where gasoline or other volatile flammable liquids or liquefied flammable gases are transferred to the fuel tanks (including auxiliary fuel tanks) of self-propelled vehicles.

Other areas used as lubritoriums, service rooms, repair rooms, offices, salesrooms, compressor rooms, and similar locations shall comply with Articles 510 and 511 with respect to electric wiring and equipment.

Where the authority having jurisdiction can satisfactorily determine that flammable liquids having a flash point below 38°C (100°F), such as gasoline, will not be handled, such authority may classify that location as nonhazardous.

For further information regarding safeguards for gasoline dispensing and service stations, see Flammable and Combustible Liquids Code, NFPA 30-1977 (ANSI).

514-2. Class I Locations. Table 514-2 shall be applied where Class I liquids are stored, handled, or dispensed and shall be used to delineate and classify service stations. A Class I location shall not extend beyond an unpierced wall, roof, or other solid partition.

Section 514-2 was completely rewritten for the 1981 edition of the *Code*, and now includes classifications for indoor areas and those dispensing and service stations having vapor recovery systems. These areas were not covered in previous editions of the *Code*. Table 514-2 is new and is essentially the same as Table 7-1 in NFPA 30.

514-3. Wiring and Equipment Within Class I Locations. All electric equipment and wiring within Class I locations defined in Section 514-2 shall comply with the applicable provisions of Article 501.

Exception: As permitted in Section 514-8.

For special requirements for conductor insulation, see Section 501-13.

For "gasoline and oil resistant" insulated conductors, see the comments following Section 501-13.

Table 514-2.   Class I Locations — Service Stations

Location	Class I, Group D Division	Extent of Class I Location
Underground Tank		
Fill Opening	1	Any pit, box, or space below grade level, any part of which is within the Division 1 or 2 location.
	2	Up to 18 inches above grade level within a horizontal radius of 10 feet from a loose fill connection and within a horizontal radius of 5 feet from a tight fill connection.
Vent — Discharging Upward	1	Within 3 feet of open end of vent, extending in all directions.
	2	Space between 3 feet and 5 feet of open end of vent, extending in all directions.
Dispensing Units (except overhead type)		
Pits	1	Any pit, box, or space below grade level, any part of which is within the Division 1 or 2 location.
Dispenser	1	The space within a dispenser enclosure up to 4 feet vertically above the base except that space defined as Division 2. Any space within a nozzle boot.
	2	Spaces within a dispenser enclosure above the Division 1 location. Spaces within a dispenser enclosure isolated from Division 1 by a solid partition or a solid nozzle boot but not completely surrounded by Division 1 location. Within 18 inches horizontally in all directions from the Division 1 location located within the dispenser enclosure. Within 18 inches horizontally in all directions from the opening of a nozzle boot not isolated by a vaportight partition, except that the classified location need not be extended around a 90 degree or greater corner.
Outdoor	2	Up to 18 inches above grade level within 20 feet horizontally of any edge of enclosure.
Indoor—with Mechanical Ventilation	2	Up to 18 inches above grade or floor level within 20 feet horizontally of any edge of enclosure.
with Gravity Ventilation	2	Up to 18 inches above grade or floor level within 25 feet horizontally of any edge of enclosure.

Table 514-2 (Continued)

Location	Class I, Group D Division	Extent of Class I Location
Dispensing Units, Overhead Type	1	Within the dispenser enclosure and 18 inches in all directions from the enclosure where not suitably cut off by ceiling or wall. All electrical equipment integral with the dispensing hose or nozzle.
	2	A space extending 2 feet horizontally in all directions beyond the Division 1 location and extending to grade below this classified location.
	2	Up to 18 inches above grade level within 20 feet horizontally measured from a point vertically below the edge of any dispenser enclosure.
Remote Pump — Outdoor	1	Any pit, box, or space below grade level if any part is within a horizontal distance of 10 feet from any edge of pump.
	2	Within 3 feet of any edge of pump, extending in all directions. Also up to 18 inches above grade level within 10 feet horizontally from any edge of pump.
Remote Pump — Indoor	1	Entire space within any pit.
	2	Within 5 feet of any edge of pump, extending in all directions. Also up to 3 feet above floor or grade level within 25 feet horizontally from any edge of pump.
Lubrication or Service Room — with Dispensing	1	Any pit within any unventilated area.
	2	Any pit with ventilation.
	2	Space up to 18 inches above floor or grade level and 3 feet horizontally from a lubrication pit.
Dispenser for Class I Liquids	2	Within 3 feet of any fill or dispensing point, extending in all directions.
Lubrication or Service Room — without Dispensing	2	Entire space within any pit used for lubrication or similar services where Class I liquids may be released.
	2	Space up to 18 inches above any such pit, and extending a distance of 3 feet horizontally from any edge of the pit.

Table 514-2 (Continued)

Location	Class I, Group D Division	Extent of Class I Location
Special Enclosure Inside Building (See NFPA 30, Flammable and Combustible Liquids Code, paragraph 7-2.2.)	1	Entire enclosure.
Sales, Storage and Rest Rooms	Ordinary	If there is any opening to these rooms within the extent of a Division 1 location, the entire room shall be classified as Division 1.
Vapor Processing Systems Pits	1	Any pit, box, or space below grade level, any part of which is within a Division 1 or 2 location or which houses any equipment used to transport or process vapors.
Vapor Processing Equipment Located Within Protective Enclosures	2	Within any protective enclosure housing vapor processing equipment.
Vapor Processing Equipment Not Within Protective Enclosures (excluding piping and combustion devices)	2	The space within 18 inches in all directions of equipment containing flammable vapor or liquid extending to grade level. Up to 18 inches above grade level within 10 feet horizontally of the vapor processing equipment.
Equipment Enclosures	1	Any space within the enclosure where vapor or liquid is present under normal operating conditions.
	2	The entire space within the enclosure other than Division 1.
Vacuum Assist Blowers	2	The space within 18 inches in all directions extending to grade level. Up to 18 inches above grade level within 10 feet horizontally.

For SI units: one inch = 25.4 millimeters; one foot = 0.3048 meter.

514-4. Wiring and Equipment Above Class I Locations.   Wiring and equipment above the Class I locations defined in Section 514-2 shall comply with Sections 511-5 and 511-6.

514-5. Circuit Disconnects.   Each circuit leading to or through a dispensing pump shall be provided with a switch or other acceptable means to disconnect simultaneously from the source of supply all conductors of the circuit, including the grounded neutral, if any.

It is important to note that all conductors of a circuit, including the grounded conductor, that may be present within a dispensing device are to be provided with a switch or special-type circuit breaker to simultaneously disconnect all conductors. The intent is that no "hot" wires be in the dispenser vicinity during maintenance or alteration. Considering possible accidental reversal of the polarities of conductors at panelboards, the grounded conductor must be able to be switched to the "open" or "off" position. Grounded conductors may be present in old style pump motors, or they may pass through a dispenser as part of a circuit for the island lighting.

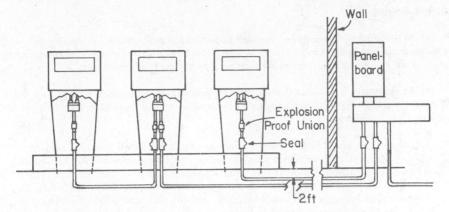

Figure 514-1. A gasoline dispensing installation indicating locations for sealing fittings.

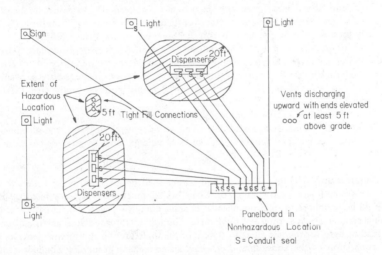

Figure 514-2. Seals are required at points marked "S." Seals are not required at the sign and two lights because conduit runs do not pass through a hazardous location.

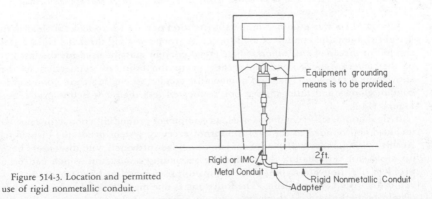

Figure 514-3. Location and permitted use of rigid nonmetallic conduit.

514-6. Sealing.

(a) At Dispenser. An approved seal shall be provided in each conduit run entering or leaving a dispenser or any cavities or enclosures in direct communication therewith. The sealing fitting shall be the first fitting after the conduit emerges from the earth or concrete.

(b) At Boundary. Additional seals shall be provided in accordance with Section 501-5. Section 501-5(a)(4) and (b)(2) shall apply to horizontal as well as to vertical boundaries of the defined Class I locations.

It should be noted that sealing fittings are required in all conduits leaving a Class I location. All conduits passing under the boundaries of the hazardous (classified) locations (20-ft radius from dispenser) or the tank fill-pipe (10-ft radius from a loose fill connection and 5-ft radius from a tight-fill connection) are considered as being in the Class I location, and the seal is to be the first fitting at the point of emergence. A seal is required to be provided in each conduit run entering or leaving a dispenser, so even though a conduit runs from dispenser to dispenser and does not leave the hazardous (classified) location, a seal is necessary when leaving and again when entering the dispenser. Panelboards are generally located in a nonhazardous room; however, any conduit coming from the dispenser, or passing under the hazardous (classified) location boundaries from the dispenser or tank fill-pipe, would require a seal at the panelboard location. Where the panelboard is located in the lube or repair room, all conduits emerging into the 18-in. hazardous (classified) location would require seals. See Figures 514-1 and 514-2.

514-7. Grounding.
Metal portions of dispensing pumps, metal raceways, and all noncurrent-carrying metal parts of electric equipment, regardless of voltage, shall be grounded as provided in Article 250.

514-8. Underground Wiring.
Underground wiring shall be installed in rigid metal conduit, threaded steel intermediate metal conduit, or, where buried under not less than 2 feet (610 mm) of earth, it shall be permitted in rigid nonmetallic conduit complying with Article 347. Where rigid nonmetallic conduit is used, threaded rigid metal conduit or threaded steel intermediate metal conduit shall be used for the last 2 feet (610 mm) of the underground run to emergence or to the point of connection to the aboveground raceway; an equipment grounding conductor shall be included to provide electrical continuity of the raceway system and for grounding of noncurrent-carrying metal parts. Refer to Exception No. 3 of Section 300-5(a).

Exception: Type MI cable shall be permitted where it is installed in accordance with Article 330.

Section 514-8 was modified in the 1981 edition of the *Code* to make it clear that, if rigid nonmetallic conduit is used for underground wiring, threaded rigid metal conduit or threaded steel intermediate metal conduit must be used for the last 2 ft of the underground run to emergence or to the point of connection to the aboveground raceway. The rigid nonmetallic conduit, including rigid nonmetallic conduit elbows and fittings, must not be located less than 2 ft below grade. See Figure 514-3.

If rigid nonmetallic conduit is used, an equipment grounding conductor must be included and bonded to the explosionproof raceway system inside the dispenser. At this writing, most explosionproof junction boxes provided with dispensers have no means for terminating the equipment grounding conductor, which can be a problem. Drilling and tapping the explosionproof junction box can destroy its explosionproof characteristics. The following is one method that has been used to terminate the grounding conductor without changing the explosionproof properties of the box or compromising its laboratory listing. Drill a blind hole from the inside surface of a threaded plug used to seal an unused conduit opening in the junction box. The hole should not be drilled all the way through the plug; there should be at least ⅛ in. of material between the bottom of the hole and the outside surface of the plug. Using a bottoming tap, tap the hole to receive a grounding screw.

ARTICLE 515 — BULK STORAGE PLANTS

Contents

515-1. Definition.   A bulk storage plant is a location where gasoline or other volatile flammable liquids are stored in tanks having an aggregate capacity of one carload or more, and from which such products are distributed (usually by tank truck).

515-2. Class I Locations.   Table 515-2 shall be applied where Class I liquids are stored, handled, or dispensed and shall be used to delineate and classify bulk storage plants. The Class I location shall not extend beyond an unpierced wall, roof, or other solid partition.

Section 515-2 has been completely rewritten for the 1981 edition of the *Code* to reference new Table 515-2, which is essentially the same as Table 6-1 in NFPA 30.

515-3. Wiring and Equipment Within Class I Locations.   All electric wiring and equipment within the Class I locations defined in Section 515-2 shall comply with the applicable provisions of Article 501.

Exception: As permitted in Section 515-5.

515-4. Wiring and Equipment Above Class I Locations.   All fixed wiring above Class I locations shall be in metallic raceways or be Type MI, TC, SNM, or Type MC cable. Fixed equipment that may produce arcs, sparks, or particles of hot metal, such as lamps and lampholders for fixed lighting, cutouts, switches, receptacles, motors, or other equipment having make-and-break or sliding contacts, shall be of the totally enclosed type or be so constructed as to prevent escape of sparks or hot metal particles. Portable lamps or other utilization equipment and their flexible cords shall comply with the provisions of Article 501 for the class of location above which they are connected or used.

515-5. Underground Wiring.

(a) Wiring Method.   Underground wiring shall be installed in rigid metal conduit, threaded steel intermediate metal conduit, or where buried under not less than 2 feet (610 mm) of earth shall be permitted in rigid nonmetallic conduit or an approved cable. Where rigid nonmetallic conduit is used, threaded rigid metal conduit or threaded steel intermediate metal conduit shall be used for the last 2 feet (610 mm) of the conduit run to emergence or to the point of connection to the

Table 515-2.   Class I Locations — Bulk Plants

Location	Class I, Group D Division	Extent of Class I Location
Tank Vehicle and Tank Car		
Loading Through Open Dome When classifying extent of space, consideration shall be given to fact that tank cars or tank vehicles may be spotted at varying points. Therefore, the extremities of the loading or unloading positions shall be used.	1	Within 3 feet of edge of dome, extending in all directions.
	2	Space between 3 feet and 15 feet from edge of dome, extending in all directions.
Loading Through Bottom Connections with Atmospheric Venting	1	Within 3 feet of point of venting to atmosphere, extending in all directions.
	2	Space between 3 feet and 15 feet from point of venting to atmosphere, extending in all directions. Also up to 18 inches above grade within a horizontal radius of 10 feet from point of loading connection.
Loading Through Closed Dome with Atmospheric Venting	1	Within 3 feet of open end of vent, extending in all directions.
	2	Space between 3 feet and 15 feet from open end of vent, extending in all directions. Also within 3 feet of edge of dome, extending in all directions.
Loading Through Closed Dome with Vapor Recovery	2	Within 3 feet of point of connection of both fill and vapor lines, extending in all directions.
Bottom Loading with Vapor Recovery or Any Bottom Unloading	2	Within 3 feet of point of connections, extending in all directions. Also up to 18 inches above grade within a horizontal radius of 10 feet from point of connection.
Pumps, Bleeders, Withdrawal Fittings, Meters and Similar Devices		
Indoors	2	Within 5 feet of any edge of such devices, extending in all directions. Also up to 3 feet above floor or grade level within 25 feet horizontally from any edge of such devices.
Outdoors	2	Within 3 feet of any edge of such devices, extending in all directions. Also up to 18 inches above grade level within 10 feet horizontally from any edge of such devices.
Storage and Repair Garage for Tank Vehicles	1	All pits or spaces below floor level.
	2	Space up to 18 inches above floor or grade level for entire storage or repair garage.
Drainage Ditches, Separators, Impounding Basins	2	Space up to 18 inches above ditch, separator, or basin. Also up to 18 inches above grade within 15 feet horizontally from any edge.

Table 515-2 (Continued)

Location	Class I, Group D Division	Extent of Class I Location
Garages for Other than Tank Vehicles	Ordinary	If there is any opening to these rooms within the extent of an outdoor Division 1 or 2 location, the entire room shall be classified the same as the area classification at the point of the opening.
Outdoor Drum Storage	Ordinary	
Indoor Warehousing Where There Is No Flammable Liquid Transfer	Ordinary	If there is any opening to these rooms within the extent of an indoor Division 1 or 2 location, the room shall be classified the same as if the wall, curb or partition did not exist.
Office and Rest Rooms	Ordinary	
Drum and Container Filling		
Outdoors, or Indoors with Adequate Ventilation	1	Within 3 feet of vent and fill opening, extending in all directions.
	2	Space between 3 feet and 5 feet from vent or fill opening, extending in all directions. Also up to 18 inches above floor or grade level within a horizontal radius of 10 feet from vent or fill opening.
Tank — Aboveground*		
Shell, Ends, or Roof and Dike Area	2	Within 10 feet from shell, ends, or roof of tank. Space inside dikes to level of top of dike.
Vent	1	Within 5 feet of open end of vent, extending in all directions.
	2	Space between 5 feet and 10 feet from open end of vent, extending in all directions.
Floating Roof	1	Space above the roof and within the shell.
Pits		
Without Mechanical Ventilation	1	Entire space within pit if any part is within a Division 1 or 2 location.
With Mechanical Ventilation	2	Entire space within pit if any part is within a Division 1 or 2 location.
Containing Valves, Fittings or Piping, and Not Within a Division 1 or 2 Location	2	Entire pit.

For SI units: one inch = 25.4 millimeters; one foot = 0.3048 meter.
* For Tanks — Underground, see Article 514-2.

aboveground raceway. Where cable is used, it shall be enclosed in rigid or threaded steel intermediate metal conduit from the point of lowest buried cable level to the point of connection to the aboveground raceway.

See comments following Section 514-8.

(b) Insulation. Conductor insulation shall comply with Section 501-13.

(c) Nonmetallic Wiring. Where rigid nonmetallic conduit or cable with a nonmetallic sheath is used, an equipment grounding conductor shall be included to provide for electrical continuity of the raceway system and for grounding of noncurrent-carrying metal parts.

515-6. Sealing.   Approved seals shall be provided in accordance with Section 501-5. Sealing requirements in Section 501-5(a)(4) and (b)(2) shall apply to horizontal as well as to vertical boundaries of the defined Class I locations. Buried raceways under defined Class I locations shall be considered to be within such locations.

515-7. Gasoline Dispensing.   Where gasoline dispensing is carried on in conjunction with bulk station operations, the applicable provisions of Article 514 shall apply.

515-8. Grounding.   All metal raceways and all noncurrent-carrying metal parts of electric equipment shall be grounded as provided in Article 250.

ARTICLE 516 — FINISHING PROCESSES

Contents

516-1. Definition.   This article covers locations where paints, lacquers, or other flammable finishes are regularly or frequently applied by spraying, dipping, brushing, or by other means; where volatile flammable solvents or thinners are used; and where readily ignitible deposits or residues from such paints, lacquers, or finishes may occur.

For further information regarding safeguards for finishing processes, such as guarding, fire protection, posting of warning signs, and maintenance, see Standard for Spray Application Using Flammable and Combustible Materials, NFPA 33-1977 (ANSI), and Standard for Dipping and Coating Processing Using Flammable or Combustible Liquids, NFPA 34-1979. For additional information regarding ventilation, see Blower and Exhaust Systems, Dust, Stock and Vapor Removal, or Conveying, NFPA 91-1973 (ANSI).

516-2. Class I Locations.   Classification is with respect to the effects of and exposure to flammable vapors, and in some cases, deposits of paint spray residue.

For deposits and residues, see Sections 516-3(b) and (c).

(a) Class I, Division 1 Locations. The following spaces shall be considered Class I, Division 1 locations.

(1) The interiors of spray booths and their exhaust ducts.

(2) Any space in the direct path of spray or any space containing dangerous quantities of air-suspended combustible residue, deposits, vapor or mists as a result of spraying operations more extensive than touch-up spraying and not conducted within spray booths.

(3) For dipping operations, all space within 5 feet (1.52 m) in any direction from the vapor source. The vapor source shall be the liquid surface in the dip tank, the wetted surface of the drain board and the surface of the dipped object over either the liquid surface or the wetted surface of the drain board and extending from these surfaces to the floor.

See Figure 516-2.

(4) Pits having an opening within Class I, Division 1 and Division 2 locations.

(b) Class I, Division 2 Locations. The following spaces shall be considered Class I, Division 2 locations unless the authority having jurisidiction judges otherwise.

(1) For extensive open spraying, all space outside of but within 20 feet (6.10 m) horizontally and 10 feet (3.05 m) vertically of the Class I, Division 1 location as defined in Section 516-2(a), and not separated from it by partitions. See Figure 1.

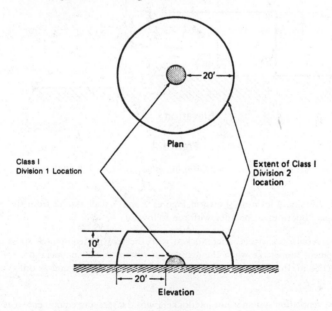

Figure 1

For SI units: one inch = 25.4 millimeters; one foot = 0.3048 meter.

(2) For spraying operations conducted within a closed top, open face, or front spray booth, the space shown in Figures 2 and 3, and the space within 3 feet (914 mm) in all directions from openings other than the open face or front.

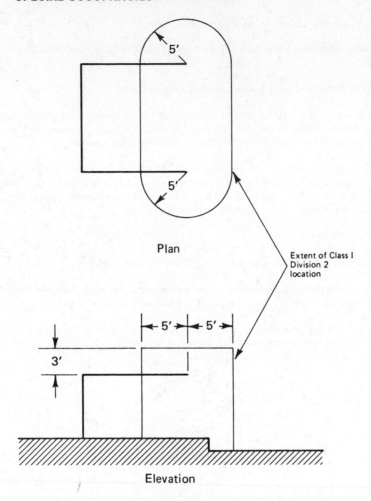

Figure 2

For SI units: one inch = 25.4 millimeters; one foot = 0.3048 meter.

The Class I, Division 2 location shown in Figures 2 and 3 shall extend from the open face o front of the spray booth in accordance with the following:

a. If the ventilation system is interlocked with the spraying equipment so as to make the spraying equipment inoperable when the ventilation system is not in operation, the space shall extend 5 feet (1.52 m) from the open face or front of the spray booth, and as otherwise shown in Figure 2.

b. If the ventilation system is not interlocked with the spraying equipment so as to make the spraying equipment inoperable when the ventilation system is not in operation, the space shall extend 10 feet (3.05 m) from the open face or front of the spray booth, and as otherwise shown in Figure 3.

(3) For spraying operations conducted within an open top spray booth, the space 5 feet (1.52 m) above the booth and within the space shown in Figure 3 as a Class I, Division 2 location adjacent to openings.

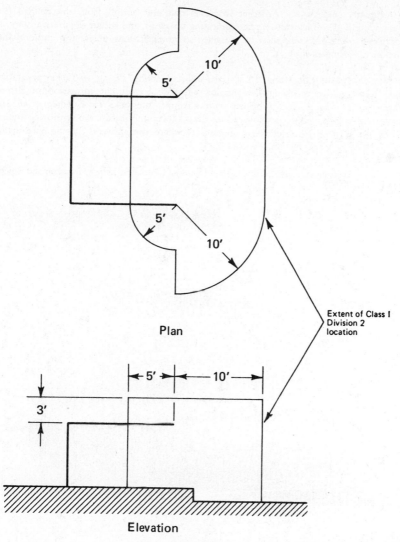

Plan

Extent of Class I
Division 2
location

Elevation

Figure 3

For SI units: one inch = 25.4 millimeters; one foot = 0.3048 meter.

(4) For spraying operations confined to an enclosed spray booth, the space within 3 feet (914 mm) in all directions from any openings in the spray booth.

See Figure 516-1.

(5) For dip tanks and drain boards, and for other hazardous operations, all space beyond the limits for Class I, Division 1 and within 8 feet (2.44 m) of the vapor source as defined in (a)(3). In addition, all space from the floor to 3 feet (914 mm) above the floor, and extending 25 feet (7.62 m) horizontally from the vapor source as defined in (a)(3).

See Figure 516-2.

(c) Adjacent Locations. Adjacent locations that are cut off from the defined Class I locations by tight partitions without communicating openings, and within which hazardous vapors are not likely to be released, shall be classified as nonhazardous unless the authority having jurisdiction judges otherwise.

(d) Nonhazardous Locations. Locations utilizing drying, curing, or fusion apparatus and provided with positive mechanical ventilation adequate to prevent formation of flammable concentrations of vapors, and provided with effective interlocks to de-energize all electric equipment (other than equipment approved for Class I locations) in case the ventilating equipment is inoperative, may be classified as nonhazardous where the authority having jurisdiction so judges.

For further information regarding safeguards, see Ovens and Furnaces, Design, Location and Equipment, NFPA 86A-1977 (ANSI).

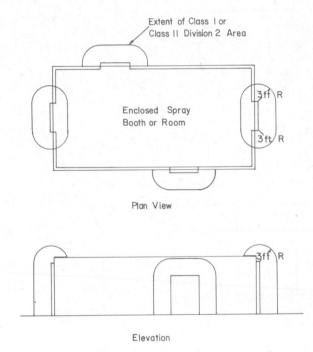

Figure 516-1. Class I or Class II, Division 2 locations adjacent to openings in an enclosed spray booth or room.

516-3. Wiring and Equipment In Class I Locations.

(a) Wiring and Equipment — Vapors. All electric wiring and equipment within the Class I location (containing vapor only—not residues) defined in Section 516-2 shall comply with the applicable provisions of Article 501.

(b) Wiring and Equipment — Vapors and Residues. Unless approved for both readily ignitible deposits and the flammable vapor location, no electric equipment shall be installed or used where it may be subject to hazardous accumulations of readily ignitible deposits or residues, as the susceptibility to spontaneous heating and ignition of some residues may be greatly increased at temperatures above normal. Type MI cable and wiring in threaded rigid metal conduit or

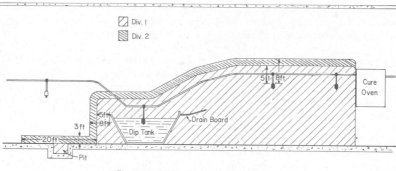

Figure 516-2. The extent of Class I, Division 1, and Class I, Division 2 hazardous (classified) locations for a paint dipping operation.

threaded steel intermediate metal conduit may be installed in such locations, if the explosionproof boxes or fittings contain no taps, splices, or terminal connections that may possibly become loose in service and thereby cause abnormal temperatures on external surfaces of boxes or fittings.

Where readily ignitible vapors and residues are present, the "only" wiring methods permitted are threaded rigid metal conduit, threaded steel intermediate metal conduit, and Type MI cable. Explosionproof boxes or enclosures used in these areas are not permitted to contain splices, taps, or terminal connections.

Electric equipment and lighting fixtures approved for Class I, Division 1 locations may be installed where not subjected to readily ignitible deposits or residues.

The authority having jurisdiction may permit an interlocked system providing adequate positive-pressure ventilation, thereby considerably reducing the possibility of hazard from vapors or residues.

(c) Illumination.   Illumination of readily ignitible areas through panels of glass or other transparent or translucent material shall be permitted only if it complies with the following: (1) fixed lighting units are used as the source of illumination; (2) the panel effectively isolates the Class I location from the area in which the lighting unit is located; (3) the lighting unit is approved for its specific location; (4) the panel is of a material or is so protected that breakage will be unlikely; and (5) the arrangement is such that normal accumulations of hazardous residue on the surface of the panel will not be raised to a dangerous temperature by radiation or conduction from the source of illumination.

The following Formal Interpretation of NFPA 33, Spray Application Using Flammable and Combustible Materials, was issued by NFPA. (See Fire News, July 1979).

"Question: Can an illumination fixture with self-contained or attached glass panel comply with Paragraph 3-9?

"Answer: Yes, provided that the glass panel accomplishes what is specified in Paragraph 3-9.

"Question: Can an illumination fixture with self-contained or attached glass panel be installed in the field or be used to replace an existing fixture?

"Answer: Yes, provided that the fixture meets the following requirements: (a) the glass panel meets the requirements of Paragraph 3-9, (b) the fixture meets the requirements of Paragraph 4-7 if applicable, and (c) the installation is done in a safe manner."

Underwriters Laboratories Inc. Hazardous Locations Equipment Directory indicates that UL listed fixtures suitable for use in hazardous (classified) locations having deposits of readily combustible paint residue are so marked.

(d) Portable Equipment.   Portable electric lamps or other utilization equipment shall not be used within a Class I location during operation of the finishing process. When such lamps or utilization equipment are used during cleaning or repairing operations, they shall be of a type approved for Class I, Group D, Division 1 locations, and all exposed metal parts shall be effectively grounded.

(e) Electrostatic Equipment.   Electrostatic spraying or detearing equipment shall be installed and used only as provided in Section 516-4.

For further information, see Standard for Spray Application Using Flammable and Combustible Materials, NFPA 33-1977 (ANSI).

516-4. Fixed Electrostatic Equipment.   This section shall apply to any equipment using electrostatically charged elements for the atomization, charging, and/or precipitation of hazardous materials for coatings on articles or for other similar purposes in which the charging or atomizing device is attached to a mechanical support and is not hand held or manipulated. Where fixed electrostatic spraying and detearing equipment is installed, such equipment shall be of an approved type and shall comply with (a) through (h) below.

(a) Power and Control Equipment.   Transformers, power packs, control apparatus, and all other electric portions of the equipment shall be installed outside of the Class I location as defined in Section 516-2 or be of a type approved for the location.

Exception: High-voltage grids, electrodes, electrostatic atomizing heads, and their connections shall be permitted within the Class I location.

(b) Electrostatic Equipment.   Electrodes and electrostatic atomizing heads shall be: (1) located in suitable noncombustible booths or enclosures provided with adequate mechanical ventilation; (2) adequately supported in permanent locations; and (3) effectively insulated from ground. Electrodes and electrostatic atomizing heads that are permanently attached to their bases, supports, or reciprocators shall be considered as complying with this section. Insulators shall be nonporous.

Fine-wire elements, where used, shall be under tension at all times and be of unkinked hardened steel or material of comparable strength.

(c) High-Voltage Leads.   High-voltage leads shall be properly insulated and protected from mechanical injury or exposure to destructive chemicals. Any exposed element at high voltage shall be effectively and permanently supported on suitable insulators and shall be effectively guarded against accidental contact or grounding. An automatic means shall be provided for grounding the electrode system when the primary of its high-voltage supply is electrically de-energized for any reason.

(d) Separation of Goods from Electrostatic Equipment.   A safe distance of at least twice the sparking distance shall be maintained between goods being painted and electrodes or electrostatic atomizing heads or conductors. A suitable sign indicating this safe distance shall be conspicuously posted near the assembly.

(e) Support of Goods.   Goods being coated using this process shall be supported on conveyors or hangers. The conveyors or hangers shall be so arranged as to assure that the parts being coated are electrically connected to ground and to maintain safe distances between goods and the electrodes or electrostatic atomizing heads at all times. Goods shall be supported to prevent such swinging or movement which would reduce the clearance to less than that specified in (d) above.

(f) Automatic Controls.   Electrostatic apparatus shall be equipped with automatic means which will rapidly de-energize the high-voltage elements under any of the following conditions: (1) stoppage of ventilating fans or failure of ventilating equipment from any cause; (2) stoppage of the conveyor carrying goods through the high-voltage field; (3) occurrence of a ground or excessive current leakage at any point in the high-voltage system; (4) reduction of clearances below that specified in (d) above.

(g) Grounding.   All electrically conductive objects within the charging influence of the electrodes except those required by the process to be at high voltage shall be adequately grounded. This requirement shall apply to paint containers, wash cans, guards, and any other electrically conductive objects or devices in the area. The equipment shall carry a prominent permanently installed warning regarding the necessity for grounding these objects.

(h) Isolation.   Safeguards such as adequate booths, fencing, railings or other means shall be placed about the equipment so that they, either by their location or character, or both, assure that a safe isolation of the process is maintained from plant storage or personnel. If mechanical guards are used, such guards shall be at least 5 feet (1.52 m) from processing equipment.

516-5. Electrostatic Hand-Spraying Equipment.   This section shall apply to any equipment using electrostatically charged elements for the atomization, charging, and/or precipitation of materials for coatings on articles, or for other similar purposes in which the atomizing device is hand held or manipulated during the spraying operation. Electrostatic hand-spraying equipment and devices used in connection with paint-spraying operations shall be of approved types and shall comply with (a) through (f) below.

(a) General.   The high-voltage circuits shall be designed so as not to produce a spark of sufficient intensity to ignite the most readily ignitible of those vapor-air mixtures likely to be encountered, nor result in appreciable shock hazard upon coming in contact with a grounded object under all normal operating conditions. The electrostatically charged exposed elements of the hand gun shall be capable of being energized only by an actuator which also controls the paint supply.

(b) Power Equipment.   Transformers, power packs, control apparatus, and all other electric portions of the equipment shall be located outside of the Class I location or be approved for the location.

Exception: The hand gun itself and its connections to the power supply shall be permitted within the Class I location.

(c) Handle.   The handle of the spraying gun shall be electrically connected to ground by a metallic connection and be so constructed that the operator in normal operating position is in intimate electrical contact with the grounded handle to prevent buildup of a static charge on the operator's body. Signs indicating the necessity for grounding other persons entering the spray area shall be conspicuously posted.

(d) Electrostatic Equipment.   All electrically conductive objects in the spraying area shall be adequately grounded. This requirement shall apply to paint containers, wash cans, and any other electrically conductive objects or devices in the area. The equipment shall carry a prominent, permanently installed warning regarding the necessity for this grounding feature.

(e) Support of Objects.   Objects being painted shall be maintained in metallic contact with the conveyor or other grounded support. Hooks shall be regularly cleaned to ensure this contact, and areas of contact shall be sharp points or knife edges where possible. Points of support of the object shall be concealed from random spray where feasible; and where the objects being sprayed are supported from a conveyor, the point of attachment to the conveyor shall be so located as to not collect spray material during normal operation.

(f) Ventilation.   The spraying operation shall take place within a spray area that is adequately ventilated to remove solvent vapors released from the operation. The electric equipment shall be interlocked with the spraying area ventilation so that the equipment cannot be operated unless the ventilating fans are in operation.

516-6. Powder Coating.   This section shall apply to processes in which combustible dry powders are applied. The hazards associated with combustible dusts are present in such a process to a degree, depending upon the chemical composition of the material, particle size, shape, and distribution.

The hazards associated with combustible dusts are inherent in this process. Generally speaking, the hazard rating of the powders employed is dependent upon the chemical composition of the material, particle size, shape, and distribution.

(a) Electric Equipment and Sources of Ignition.   Electric equipment and other sources of ignition shall comply with the requirements of Article 502. Portable electrical lamps and other utilization equipment shall not be used within a Class II location during operation of the finishing processes. When such lamps or utilization equipment are used during cleaning or repairing operations, they shall be of a type approved for Class II, Division 1 locations, and all exposed metal parts shall be effectively grounded.

(b) Fixed Electrostatic Spraying Equipment.   The provisions of Sections 516-4 and (a) above shall apply to fixed electrostatic spraying equipment.

(c) Electrostatic Hand-Spraying Equipment.   The provisions of Sections 516-5 and (a) above shall apply to electrostatic hand-spraying equipment.

(d) Electrostatic Fluidized Beds.   Electrostatic fluidized beds and associated equipment shall be of approved types. The high-voltage circuits shall be so designed that any discharge produced when the charging electrodes of the bed are approached or contacted by a grounded object shall not be of sufficient intensity to ignite any powder-air mixture likely to be encountered nor to result in an appreciable shock hazard.

(1) Transformers, power packs, control apparatus, and all other electric portions of the equipment shall be located outside the powder-coating area or shall otherwise comply with the requirements of (a) above.

Exception: The charging electrodes and their connections to the power supply shall be permitted within the powder-coating area.

(2) All electrically conductive objects within the powder-coating area shall be adequately grounded. The powder-coating equipment shall carry a prominent, permanently installed warning regarding the necessity for grounding these objects.

(3) Objects being coated shall be maintained in electrical contact with the conveyor or other support in order to ensure proper grounding. Hangers shall be regularly cleaned to ensure effective electrical contact, and areas of electrical contact shall be sharp points or knife edges where possible.

(4) The electric equipment shall be interlocked with a ventilation system so that the equipment cannot be operated unless the ventilating fans are in operation.

516-7. Wiring and Equipment Above Class I and II Locations.

(a) Wiring. All fixed wiring above the Class I and II locations shall be in metal raceways, rigid nonmetallic conduit, or shall be Type MI, TC, SNM, or Type MC cable. Cellular metal floor raceways shall be permitted only for supplying ceiling outlets or extensions to the area below the floor of a Class I or II location, but such raceways shall have no connections leading into or through the Class I or II location above the floor unless suitable seals are provided. No electric conductor shall be installed in any cell or header that contains a pipe for steam, water, air, gas, drainage, or for other than the electrical service.

(b) Equipment. Equipment that may produce arcs, sparks, or particles of hot metal, such as lamps and lampholders for fixed lighting, cutouts, switches, receptacles, motors, or other equipment having make-and-break or sliding contacts, where installed above a Class I or II location or above a location where freshly finished goods are handled, shall be of the totally enclosed type or be so constructed as to prevent escape of sparks or hot metal particles.

516-8. Grounding. All metal raceways and all noncurrent-carrying metal parts of fixed or portable equipment, regardless of voltage, shall be grounded as provided in Article 250.

NFPA 33, Spray Application Using Flammable and Combustible Materials, covers the application of flammable or combustible materials as a spray by compressed air, "airless" or "hydraulic atomization," or by steam, electrostatic methods, or any other means in continuous or intermittent processes. It also covers the application of combustible powders when applied by powder spray guns, electrostatic powder spray guns, and fluidized beds or electrostatic fluidized beds.

NFPA 33 outlines the requirements for the maintenance of safe conditions.

The proper maintenance and operation of processes and process areas where flammable and combustible materials are handled and applied are critical with respect to the protection of life and property from fire or explosion.

It has been shown that the largest fire losses and frequency of fires have occurred where the proper application of codes and standards has not been used.

Spraying Area: Any area in which dangerous quantities of flammable vapors or mists, or combustible residues, dusts, or deposits are present due to the operation of spraying processes.

A spraying area is to include the following:

(1) The interior of spray booths and rooms (with certain exceptions),

(2) The interior of ducts exhausting from spraying processes, and

(3) Any area in the direct path of spraying operations.

The authority having jurisdiction may, for the purpose of NFPA 33, define the limits of the spraying area in any specific case. The "spraying area" in the vicinity of spraying operations will necessarily vary with the design and arrangement of equipment and method of operation. When spraying operations are strictly confined to predetermined spaces provided with adequate and reliable ventilation, such as a properly constructed spray booth, the "spraying area" will ordinarily not extend beyond the booth enclosure. When spraying operations are not confined to adequately ventilated spaces, the "spraying area" may extend throughout the entire room containing spraying operations.

Spray Booth: A power-ventilated structure provided to enclose or accommodate a spraying operation, to confine and limit the escape of spray, vapor, and residue, and to conduct or direct them safely to an exhaust system. Spray booths are manufactured in a variety of forms, including automotive refinishing, downdraft, open-face, traveling, tunnel, and updraft booths.

Spray Room: A power-ventilated, fully enclosed room used exclusively for open spraying of flammable or combustible materials. The entire spray room is a spray area. A spray booth is not a spray room.

Waterwash Spray Booth: A spray booth equipped with a water washing system designed to minimize dusts or residues entering exhaust ducts and to permit the recovery of overspray finishing material.

Dry Spray Booth: A spray booth not equipped with a water washing system. A dry spray booth may be equipped with (1) distribution or baffle plates to promote an even flow of air through the booth or cause deposit of overspray before it enters exhaust duct; (2) overspray dry filters to minimize dusts or residues entering exhaust ducts; (3) overspray dry filter rolls designed to minimize dusts or residues entering exhaust ducts; or (4) powder collection systems so arranged in the exhaust to capture oversprayed material (when dry powders are sprayed).

Notes on Electrical Installations:

The safety of life and property from fire or explosion as a result of spray applications of flammable and combustible paints and finishes varies depending upon the arrangement and operation of a particular installation.

The principal hazards of spray application operations originate from flammable or combustible liquids or powders and their vapors or mists as well as from highly combustible residues or powders.

Properly constructed spray booths, with adequate mechanical ventilation, may be used to discharge vapors or powder to a safe location and reduce the possibility of an explosion. In like manner, the accumulation of overspray residues, many of which are not only highly combustible but also subject to spontaneous ignition, can be controlled.

The elimination of all sources of ignition in areas where flammable or combustible liquids, vapors, mists, or combustible residues are present, together with constant supervision and maintenance, is essential to the safe operations of spraying.

The human element necessitates careful consideration of the location of the operation and the installation of extinguishing equipment in order to reduce the possibility of fire spreading to other property and minimize the probability of damage to other property.

It is obvious that there should be no open flames or spark-producing equipment in any area where, because of inadequate ventilation, explosive vapor-air mixtures or mists are present. It is equally obvious that no open flames or spark-producing equipment should be located where highly combustible spray residues will be deposited on them. Because some residues may be ignited at very low temperatures, additional consideration must be given to operating temperatures of equipment subject to residue deposits. Many deposits may be ignited at temperatures produced by low-pressure steam pipes or by incandescent light globes, even those of explosionproof types.

It will be noted that electrical equipment is generally not permitted inside any spray booth, in the exhaust duct from a spray booth, in the entrained air of an exhaust system from a spraying operation, or in the direct path of spray, unless such equipment is specifically listed for both readily ignitible deposits and flammable vapor.

The determination of the extent of hazardous areas involved in spray application requires an understanding of the dual hazards of flammable vapors, mists, or powders, and highly combustible deposits applied to each individual installation.

When electrical equipment is installed in locations not subject to deposits of combustible residues but, due to inadequate ventilation, is subject to explosive concentrations of flammable vapors or mists, only approved explosion-proof or other type of approved Class I, Division 1-type equipment (for example, purged and pressurized or intrinsically safe) is permitted.

When spraying areas containing hazardous quantities of vapors, mists, or residues have been identified, the adjacent unpartitioned areas, safe under normal operating conditions but subject to danger as the result of accident or careless operation, should be given consideration. Equipment known to produce sparks or flames under normal operating conditions should not be installed in these adjacent unpartitioned areas.

When spraying operations are confined to adequately ventilated spray booths or rooms, there should be no dangerous concentrations of flammable vapors, mists, or dusts, or deposits of combustible residues outside the spray booth under normal operating conditions.

In the interest of safety, however, it will be noted that, unless separated by partitions, an area within a certain distance [see Section 516-2(b)] of the Class I (or II), Division 1 spraying area, depending upon the arrangement, is classified as Division 2; that is, it should contain no equipment that produces ignition-capable sparks under normal operation. Furthermore, within this distance, electric lamps must be enclosed to prevent hot particles from falling on freshly painted stock or other readily ignitible material and, if subject to mechanical injury, must be properly guarded. See Section 516-7(b).

Even though it is contemplated that areas adjacent to spray booths (particularly where coating material stocks are located) will be provided with ventilation sufficient to prevent the presence of flammable vapors or deposits, it is nevertheless advisable that electric lamps be totally enclosed to prevent the falling of hot particles in any area where there may be freshly painted stock, accidentally spilled flammable or combustible materials, readily ignitible refuse, or flammable or combustible liquid containers accidentally left open. See Section 516-7(b).

Where electric lamps are in areas subject to atmospheres of flammable vapor, lamps should be replaced when electricity is off; otherwise there may be a spark from this source.

Sufficient lighting for coating operations, booth cleaning, and booth repair work should be provided at the time the equipment is installed in order to avoid the use of "temporary" or "emergency" lamps connected to ordinary extension cords in this area. See Section 516-3(d). A satisfactory and practical method of lighting is the use of ¼-in. thick wired or tempered glass panels in the top or sides of the spray booth with electrical light fixtures outside the booth, hence not in the direct path of the spray. See Section 516-3(c).

In order to prevent sparks from the accumulation of static electricity, all electrically conductive objects, including metal parts of spray booths, exhaust ducts, piping systems conveying flammable or combustible liquids or paint, solvent tanks, and canisters should be properly grounded. See 4-9.1 of NFPA 33.

Automobile undercoating operations in garages, conducted in areas having adequate natural or mechanical ventilation, are exempt from the requirements pertaining to spray coating operations when (1) undercoating materials not more hazardous than kerosene (as classified by Underwriters Laboratories Inc. with respect to fire hazard rating 30-40) are used, or (2) undercoating materials using only solvents having a flash point in excess of 38°C (100°F) are used, and (3) no open flames are within 20 ft while such operations are conducted.

ARTICLE 517 — HEALTH CARE FACILITIES

Contents

A. General

517-1. Scope.

The provisions of this article shall apply to health care facilities.

The requirements in Parts C, D, and E apply not only to single-function buildings, but are also intended to be individually applied to their respective forms of occupancy within a multifunction building (i.e., a doctor's examining room located within a residential custodial care facility would be required to meet the provisions of Part C).

The requirements of this article are intended to apply to all types of health care facilities. The requirements for each type of health care facility are nevertheless intended to be applied in a very specific manner. An example of the application of this article could be a suite of doctors' offices within a hospital. The doctor's business office would be treated as an ordinary occupancy and would be required to meet the applicable portion of the balance of this *Code*. The examining rooms attached to the doctor's business office would be required to meet the provisions of Part C of Article 517, and a nearby X-ray unit, whether operated by a group of doctors or the hospital itself, would be required to meet the provisions of Part K of Article 517.

The scope also includes health care facilities that may be mobile or supply very limited outpatient services.

All references to other standards in this article are for advisory information only. These references are not mandatory in the enforcement of this article.

The scope of Article 517 was expanded in the 1981 *NEC* to clarify the fact that references to other standards are intended as advisory information only.

Other standards referenced in this article are Essential Electrical Systems for Health Care Facilities, NFPA 76A-1977; Life Safety Code, NFPA 101-1976; Inhalation Anesthetics, NFPA 56A-1978; Installation of Centrifugal Fire Pumps, NFPA 20-1978; and Standard for Nonflammable Medical Gas Systems, NFPA 56F-1977.

517-2. Definitions.

A number of definitions in the 1981 *NEC* were added or revised to better conform with NFPA 76A. These include "alternate power source," "critical branch," "emergency system," "essential electrical system," "health care facilities," and "selected receptacles."

The title of the definition for "patient grounding point" (1978) has been changed to "patient equipment grounding point."

Alternate Power Source.   One or more generator sets, or battery systems where permitted, intended to provide power during the interruption of the normal electrical services or the public utility electrical service intended to provide power during interruption of service normally provided by the generating facilities on the premises.

Anesthetizing Location.   Any area in which it is intended to administer any flammable or nonflammable inhalation anesthetic agents in the course of examination or treatment and includes operating rooms, delivery rooms, emergency rooms, anesthetizing rooms, corridors, utility rooms and other areas which are intended for induction of anesthesia with flammable or nonflammable anesthetizing agents.

This definition recognizes that in an emergency it may be necessary to administer an anesthetic almost anywhere in a health care facility; however, only those areas in a health care facility set aside by intent for the induction of anesthetics are required to meet the provisions of Part G of Article 517. At the present time, this definition, as well as the provisions of Part G, is not intended to apply to the administration of analgesic anesthetics such as might be employed in a dental office.

Anesthetizing-Location Receptacle.   A receptacle designed to accept the attachment plugs listed for use in such locations.

This definition requires only that the wiring device employed in an anesthetizing location be listed for such use. This means that pin and sleeve, parallel U blade, or other forms of construction are all acceptable, provided there is compliance with the applicable requirements of Part G.

Critical Branch.   A subsystem of the emergency system consisting of feeders and branch circuits supplying energy to task illumination, special power circuits, and selected receptacles serving areas and functions related to patient care, and which are connected to alternate power sources by one or more transfer switches during interruption of the normal power source.

Emergency System.   A system of feeders and branch circuits meeting the requirements of Article 700, and intended to supply alternate power to a limited number of prescribed functions vital to the protection of life and patient safety, with automatic restoration of electrical power within 10 seconds of power interruption.

Equipment System.   A system of feeders and branch circuits arranged for delayed, automatic or manual connection to the alternate power source and which serves primarily 3-phase power equipment.

Essential Electrical Systems.   A system comprised of alternate sources of power and all connected distribution systems and ancillary equipment, designed to assure continuity of electrical power to designated areas and functions of a health care facility during disruption of normal power sources, and also designed to minimize disruption within the internal wiring system.

Exposed Conductive Surfaces.   Those surfaces which are capable of carrying electric current and which are unprotected, unenclosed, or unguarded, permitting personal contact. Paint, anodizing, and similar coatings are not considered suitable insulation, unless they are listed for the use.

This definition is intended to clarify the requirements of Section 517-81. Specifically, it points out that the mere application of paint or similar coatings does not necessarily render a metallic surface nonconductive. Under the terms of this definition, the coating material must be approved as an electrical insulating medium.

Flammable Anesthetics.   Gases or vapors such as fluroxene, cyclopropane, divinyl ether, ethyl chloride, ethyl ether, and ethylene, which may form flammable or explosive mixtures with air, oxygen, or reducing gases such as nitrous oxide.

Flammable Anesthetizing Location.   Any operating room, delivery room, anesthetizing room, corridor, utility room, or any other area if intended for the application of flammable anesthetics.

Hazard Current.   For a given set of connections in an isolated system, the total current that would flow through a low impedance if it were connected between either isolated conductor and ground.

FAULT HAZARD CURRENT: The hazard current of a given isolated system with all devices connected except the line isolation monitor.

MONITOR HAZARD CURRENT: The hazard current of the line isolation monitor alone.

TOTAL HAZARD CURRENT: The hazard current of a given isolated system with all devices, including the line isolation monitor, connected.

Health Care Facilities.   Buildings or parts of buildings that contain but are not limited to hospitals, nursing homes, extended care facilities, clinics, and medical and dental offices, whether fixed or mobile.

Hospital.   A building or part thereof used for the medical, psychiatric, obstetrical or surgical care, on a 24-hour basis, of four or more inpatients. Hospital, wherever used in this Code, shall include general hospitals, mental hospitals, tuberculosis hospitals, children's hospitals, and any such facilities providing inpatient care.

Immediate Restoration of Service.   Automatic restoration of operation with an interruption of not more than 10 seconds as applied to those areas and functions served by the Emergency System, except for areas and functions for which Article 700 otherwise makes specific provisions.

Isolated Power System.   A system comprising an isolating transformer or its equivalent, a line isolation monitor, and its ungrounded circuit conductors.

Isolation Transformer.   A transformer of the multiple-winding type, with the primary and secondary windings physically separated, which inductively couples its secondary winding to the grounded feeder systems that energize its primary winding, thereby preventing primary circuit potential from being impressed on the secondary circuits.

Life Safety Branch.   A subsystem of the Emergency System consisting of feeders and branch circuits, meeting the requirements of Article 700 and intended to provide adequate power needs to ensure safety to patients and personnel, and which can be connected to alternate power sources by one or more transfer switches.

It should be noted that neither the definition nor the term "life support" is used in the *Code*. This term was deleted from the 1978 *NEC* because it was simply an arbitrary subdivision of some life safety branch functions. Its use was never mandatory, either in terms of health care facility size or in terms of electrical load.

Line Isolation Monitor.   A test instrument designed to continually check the balanced and unbalanced impedance from each line of an isolated circuit to ground and equipped with a built-in test circuit to exercise the alarm without adding to the leakage current hazard.

"Line isolation monitor" was formerly known as "ground contact indicator."

Nursing Home.   A building or part thereof used for the lodging, boarding and nursing care, on a 24-hour basis, of four or more persons who, because of mental or physical incapacity, may be unable to provide for their own needs and safety without the assistance of another person. Nursing home, wherever used in this Code, shall include nursing and convalescent homes, skilled nursing facilities, intermediate care facilities, and infirmaries of homes for the aged.

Nurses' Stations.   Areas intended to provide a center of nursing activity for a group of nurses working under one nurse supervisor and serving bed patients, where the patient calls are received, nurses are dispatched, nurses' notes written, inpatient charts prepared, and medications prepared for distribution to patients. Where such activities are carried on in more than one location within a nursing unit, all such separate areas are considered a part of the nurses' station.

Patient Equipment Grounding Point.   A jack or terminal bus which serves as the collection point for redundant grounding of electric appliances serving a patient vicinity.

Patient Vicinity.   In an area in which patients are normally cared for, the patient vicinity is the space with surfaces likely to be contacted by the patient or an attendant who can touch the patient. This encloses a space within the room 6 feet (1.83 m) beyond the perimeter of the bed in its nominal location, and extending vertically 7½ feet (2.29 m) above the floor.

> This area is limited to patients in bed. It is also limited to the bed in its nominal position, that is, the position of the bed as called for in the architect's plans, rather than the position of the bed as it may be found in daily use subject to movement by housekeeping staff or the convenience of the medical staff. It is not intended that a "halo" of electrical hazard follow the bed as it is moved about the room or the health care facility.
>
> Definitions for Hospital, Nursing Home, and Residential Custodial Care Facility are all identical to the same definitions as employed in NFPA 101, *Life Safety Code.*

Reference Grounding Point.   A terminal bus which is the equipment grounding bus or an extension of the equipment grounding bus and is a convenient collection point for grounding all electric appliances, equipment, and exposed conductive surfaces in a patient vicinity.

Residential Custodial Care Facility.   A building, or part thereof, used for the lodging or boarding of four or more persons who are incapable of self-preservation because of age, or physical or mental limitation. This includes facilities such as homes for the aged, nurseries (custodial care for children under 6 years of age), and mentally retarded care institutions. Day care facilities that do not provide lodging or boarding for institutional occupants are not classified as residential custodial care facilities.

Room Bonding Point.   A grounding terminal or group of terminals which serves as a collection point for grounding exposed metal or conductive building surfaces in a room.

Selected Receptacles.   Minimal electrical receptacles to accommodate appliances ordinarily required for local tasks or likely to be used in patient care emergencies.

Task Illumination.   Provision for the minimum lighting required to carry out necessary tasks in the described areas, including safe access to supplies and equipment, and access to exits.

Therapeutic High-Frequency Diathermy Equipment.   Therapeutic high-frequency diathermy equipment is therapeutic induction and dielectric heating equipment.

Wet Location, Health Care Facility.   A patient care area that is normally subject to wet conditions, including standing water on the floor, or routine dousing or drenching of the work area. Routine housekeeping procedures and incidental spillage of liquids do not define a wet location.

> This definition excludes such areas as laundry rooms, boiler rooms, and utility areas which, although routinely wet, are not patient care areas. The governing body of the health care facility may elect to include under this definition such areas as hydrotherapy areas, dialysis laboratories, and certain wet laboratories. No lavatories or bathrooms within a health care facility are intended to be classified as a wet location.

B. Wiring Systems — General

517-10. Wiring Methods.   Except as modified in this article, wiring methods shall comply with the applicable requirements of Chapters 1 through 4 of this Code.

517-11. Grounding.

(a) Receptacles and Fixed Electrical Equipment.   In areas used for patient care, all receptacles and all noncurrent-carrying conductive surfaces of fixed electrical equipment likely to become energized that are subject to personal contact, operating at over 100 volts, shall be grounded by an insulated copper conductor, sized in accordance with Table 250-95, installed with the branch-circuit conductors supplying these receptacles or fixed equipment.

Exception No. 1: Metal faceplates shall be permitted to be grounded by means of a metal mounting screw(s) securing the faceplate to a grounded outlet box or grounded wiring device.

Exception No. 2: An equipment grounding conductor enclosed in the sheath of a nonmetallic-sheathed cable assembly installed in accordance with the limitations of Sections 336-3 and 336-4 shall be permitted to be used in accordance with Parts C and D of this article.

This rule applies to any area used for patient care and not limited to patient rooms. Additional areas, such as therapy areas, recreational areas, solaria, and certain patient corridors, would also be included. It should be clearly understood that this section requires grounding by means of an insulated copper conductor installed with the branch-circuit conductors. The conductor can be either solid or stranded. An insulated equipment grounding conductor is not required to be run upstream from the branch-circuit panelboard with the feeder conductors in a metal raceway.

Exception No. 1 permits metallic plates to be grounded by means of the metal mounting screws rather than having a separate equipment grounding conductor run to the metal plate.

Exception No. 2 was added to recognize that the equipment grounding conductor (covered or bare) enclosed in the sheath of Types NM or NMC cable in accordance with the provisions of this section is permitted in lieu of a separate insulated grounding conductor.

(b) Equipment Connected by Cord and Plug.   Exposed, likely to become energized, noncurrent-carrying conductive parts of cord-and-plug connected equipment likely to be used in areas intended for patient care and operating at over 100 volts shall be grounded.

Exception: Listed devices protected by a system of double insulation, or its equivalent, and which have no exposed conductive surfaces. Such equipment shall be distinctively marked.

This rule differs from the general grounding rule for such equipment under Section 250-45 in that not just specific items, but all cord- and plug-connected equipment (over 100 V) is covered.

Also, in Section 250-45 listed, double-insulated equipment is permitted to have exposed conductive surfaces, whereas the Exception in Section 517-11(b) prohibits this form of construction.

517-13. Receptacles with Insulated Grounds.   Receptacles with insulated grounds as permitted in Section 250-74, Exception No. 4, shall be identified; such identification shall be visible after installation. Such receptacles shall not be installed within, or supply equipment located within, the patient vicinity of a Critical Care Area.

Note: Effective date, January 1, 1982.

This section was added to the 1981 *NEC* to prevent the indiscriminate use of such devices, and the compromising of the potential difference requirements within Critical Care Areas.

Proper identification may be by color-coding the receptacle "orange" or by other approved means. See Figure 517-1.

517-14. Ground-Fault Protection.

(a) Feeders. When ground-fault protection is provided for operation of the service disconnecting means, an additional step of ground-fault protection shall be provided in the next level of feeder downstream toward the load. Such protection shall consist of overcurrent devices and current transformers or other equivalent protective equipment which shall cause the feeder disconnecting devices to open.

(b) Selectivity. Ground-fault protection for operation of the service and feeder disconnecting means shall be fully selective such that the feeder device and not the service device shall open on ground faults on the load side of the feeder device. A six-cycle minimum separation between the service and feeder ground-fault tripping bands shall be provided. Operating time of the disconnecting devices shall be considered in selecting the time spread between these two bands to achieve 100 percent selectivity.

See Section 230-95, fine print note, for transfer of alternate source where ground-fault protection is applied.

Whenever ground-fault protective equipment is applied to the service providing power to a health care facility, whether by design or by reason of the requirements of Section 230-95, an additional level of ground-fault protection is required downstream. Under this rule, ground-fault protection must be applied to every feeder, and additional ground-fault protective devices may be applied farther downstream at the option of the governing body of the health care facility. With proper coordination, this additional ground-fault protection is intended to limit a ground fault to a single feeder and thereby prevent a total outage of the entire health care system.

However, when a health care installation, such as a doctor's office, is a part of a larger general-use facility (for example, a business office building) that has service ground-fault protection in accordance with Section 230-95, it is not intended that ground-fault protection be required on the health care facility (doctor's office) feeder since no additional protection will be achieved insofar as the doctor's office is concerned.

A fine print note to Section 230-95 calls attention to problems that may arise when ground-fault protected systems are transferred to another supply system.

C. Clinics, Medical and Dental Offices, and Outpatient Facilities

These forms of occupancy must comply with grounding requirements in accordance with Sections 517-10 and 517-11. Note Exception No. 2 to Section 517-11(a) which permits Types NM and NMC for health care areas covered in Part C.

For additional information, see Essential Electrical Systems for Health Care Facilities, NFPA 76A-1977.

517-30. General. Part C applies to those portions of clinics, medical and dental offices, and outpatient facilities wherein patients are intended to be examined or treated. It does not apply to business offices, corridors, waiting rooms, and the like.

517-31. Special Requirements.   Grounding and receptacle installations shall be in accordance with Sections 517-10 and 517-11.

D. Nursing Homes and Residential Custodial Care Facilities

For additional information, see Essential Electrical Systems for Health Care Facilities, NFPA 76A-1977.

To more properly correlate Article 517 with NFPA 76A, Part D has been extensively rewritten but still maintains the substance of Part D as it appeared in the 1978 *NEC*.

517-40. Applicability.   The requirements of Part D, Sections 517-42 through 517-47, shall apply to nursing homes and residential custodial care facilities.

Exception: Any free-standing building used for health care other than those described in Parts C and E of this article shall be exempted from the requirements of Sections 517-44 through 517-47 provided:

a. It maintains admitting and discharge policies that preclude the provision of care for any patient or resident who may need to be sustained by electrically operated or mechanical life support devices, and

b. Offers no surgical treatment requiring general anesthesia, and

c. Provides an automatic battery-operated system(s) or equipment that shall be effective for 4 or more hours and is otherwise in accordance with Section 700-12, and that shall be capable of supplying lighting for exit lights, exit corridors, stairways, nursing stations, medical preparation areas, boiler rooms and communication areas. This system shall also supply battery power to operate all alarm systems.

See *Life Safety Code*®, NFPA *101*®-1976 (ANSI).

Part D of Article 517 recognizes two classes of nursing homes or residential custodial care facilities. The smaller, less complex facility is described in the Exception to Section 517-40 and only a minimum alternate service need be furnished as indicated in Section 517-40, Exception c.

Where treatment of patients is of a more complex nature, the requirements of Sections 517-44 through 517-47 are to be applied. The branches of the Emergency System for this class of occupancy bear identical titles to their counterparts for hospital-type occupancies.

517-41. Inpatient Hospital Care Facilities.   Nursing homes and residential custodial care facilities which provide inpatient hospital care shall comply with the requirements of Part E, Hospitals.

Regardless of the name applied to the facility, the type of electrical system is dependent upon the type of patient care provided. Where such care is clearly inpatient hospital care, a hospital-type electrical system must be installed.

517-42. Facilities Contiguous with Hospitals.   Nursing homes and residential custodial care facilities which are contiguous with a hospital shall be permitted to have their Essential Electrical Systems supplied by that of the hospital.

When a hospital, nursing home, or residential custodial care facility share what is essentially the same building, the nursing home need not have its own Essential

Electrical System but may derive its supply from the hospital. It should be noted, however, that this rule applies only to the electrical supply and does not permit the sharing of transfer devices and the like.

517-43. Wiring, Grounding, and Receptacles.   Wiring, grounding, and receptacle installations shall be in accordance with Sections 517-10, 517-11, and 517-13.

517-44. Essential Electrical Systems.

   (a) General.   Essential Electrical Systems for nursing homes and residential custodial care facilities shall be comprised of two separate branches capable of supplying a limited amount of lighting and power service which is considered essential for the protection of life safety and effective operation of the institution during the time normal electrical service is interrupted for any reason. These two separate branches shall be the Life Safety Branch and the Critical Branch. The Essential Electrical Systems shall be so installed and connected to the alternate power source so that all functions specified herein shall be restored to operation after interruption of the normal source.

   (b) Transfer Switches.   The number of transfer switches to be used shall be based upon reliability, design and load considerations. Each branch of the Essential Electrical System shall be served by one or more transfer switches as shown in Diagrams 517-44(1) and 517-44(2). One transfer switch shall be permitted to serve one or more branches or systems in a small facility as shown in Diagram 517-44(3).

   Recognition has been given to the possibility of a small nursing home or residential custodial care facility functioning properly with a single transfer switch and an equivalent diagram [517-44(3)] has been added.

   See Essential Electrical Systems for Health Care Facilities, NFPA 76A-1977: Section 5-6.2, Description of Transfer Switch Operation; Section 3-2.4, Automatic Transfer Switch Features; and Section 3-2.6, Nonautomatic Transfer Device Features.

   (c) Capacity of System.   The Essential Electrical System shall have adequate capacity and rating for the operation of all functions and equipment to be served by each branch.

   (d) Separation from Other Circuits.   The Life Safety Branch shall be kept entirely independent of all other wiring and equipment and shall not enter the same raceways, boxes or cabinets with other wiring except as follows:

   (1) In transfer switches,

   (2) In exit or emergency lighting fixtures supplied from two sources, or

   (3) In a common junction box attached to exit or emergency lighting fixtures supplied from two sources.
   The wiring of the Critical Branch shall be permitted to occupy the same raceways, boxes or cabinets of other circuits that are not part of the Life Safety Branch.

517-45. Automatic Connection to Life Safety Branch.   The Life Safety Branch shall be so installed and connected to the alternate source of power that all functions specified herein shall be automatically restored to operation within 10 seconds after the interruption of the normal source. The Life Safety Branch shall supply power for the following lighting, receptacles and equipment:

   (a) Illumination of Means of Egress.   Illumination of means of egress as is necessary for corridors, passageways, stairways, landings and exit doors and all ways of approach to exits. Switching arrangement to transfer patient corridor lighting from general illumination circuits shall

MINIMUM ELECTRICAL SYSTEM – TYPICAL SMALL NURSING HOMES
AND RESIDENTIAL CUSTODIAL
CARE FACILITIES

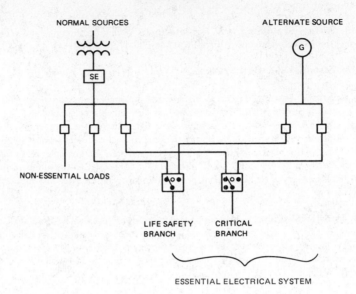

Figure 517-44(1)

be permitted providing only one of two circuits can be selected, and both circuits cannot be extinguished at the same time.

Clarification has been included regarding the illumination of means of egress in accordance with *Life Safety Code*, NFPA *101*.

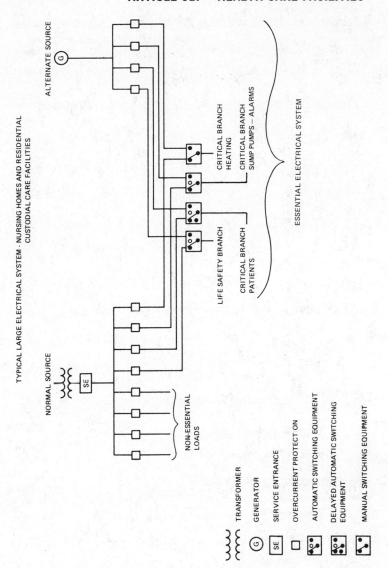

Figure 517-44(2)

See *Life Safety Code*, NFPA *101*-1976 (ANSI), Section 5-10.

(b) Exit Signs.   Exit signs and exit directional signs.

See *Life Safety Code*, NFPA *101*-1976 (ANSI), Section 5-11.

MINIMUM ELECTRICAL SYSTEM---TYPICAL SMALL NURSING HOMES
AND RESIDENTIAL CUSTODIAL
CARE FACILITIES
(SINGLE TRANSFER SWITCH)

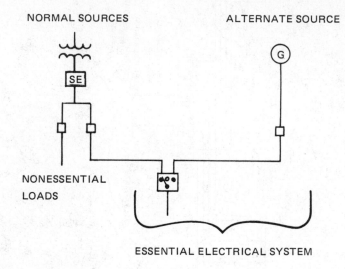

Figure 517-44(3)

(c) Alarm and Alerting Systems.   Alarm and alerting systems, including:

(1) Fire alarms activated at manual stations, electric water flow alarm devices in connection with sprinkler systems, and automatic fire or smoke or products of combustion detection devices.

See *Life Safety Code*, NFPA *101*-1976 (ANSI), Sections 6-3 and 10-136.

(2) Alarms required for systems used for the piping of nonflammable medical gases.

See Standard for Nonflammable Medical Gas Systems, NFPA 56F-1977 (ANSI).

(d) Communication Systems.   Communication systems, where used for issuing instructions during emergency conditions.

(e) Dining and Recreation Areas.   Sufficient lighting in dining and recreation areas to provide illumination to exit ways.

(f) Generator Set Location.   Task illumination and selected receptacles in the generator set location.

No function other than those listed above in (a) through (f) shall be connected to the Life Safety Branch.

517-46. Connection to Critical Branch.   The Critical Branch shall be so installed and connected to the alternate power source that the equipment listed in Section 517-46(a) shall be automatically restored to operation at appropriate time lag intervals following the restoration of the Life Safety Branch to operation. Its arrangement shall also provide for the additional connection of equipment listed in Section 517-46(b) by either delayed automatic or manual operation.

(a) Delayed Automatic Connection.   The following equipment shall be connected to the Critical Branch and shall be arranged for delayed automatic connection to the alternate power source:

(1) Patient care areas — task illumination and selected receptacles in:

a. Medication preparation areas.

b. Pharmacy dispensing areas.

c. Nurses' stations (unless adequately lighted by corridor luminaires).

(2) Sump pumps and other equipment required to operate for the safety of major apparatus and associated control systems and alarms.

(3) Elevator cab lighting and communication system.

(b) Delayed Automatic or Manual Connection.   The following equipment shall be connected to the Critical Branch and shall be arranged for either delayed automatic or manual connection to the alternate power source:

(1) Heating equipment to provide heating for patient rooms.

Exception: Heating of general patient rooms during disruption of the normal source shall not be required under any of the following conditions:

a. The outside design temperature is higher than +20°F (-6.7°C), or

b. The outside design temperature is lower than +20°F (-6.7°C) and where a selected room(s) is provided for the needs of all confined patients, then only such room(s) need be heated, or

It has become common practice in some areas of the country to install individual room heating/air conditioners rather than have a central heating/air conditioning plant. When these individual units are electrically powered, it may not be practical to apply this high demand load to the generator. When the governing body of the nursing home has full-time skilled attendants who can move people to one room(s) which will be heated when this smaller load is picked up by the generator, then the intent of the *Code* is satisfied.

It has been made clear that the provisions for limited heating during emergency conditions were based on consideration of the "outside" design temperature.

c. The facility is served by a dual source of normal power as described in Section 517-47(e).

The outside design temperature is based on the 97½ percent design values as shown in Chapter 33 of the ASHRAE Handbook of Fundamentals (1972).

(2) Elevator Service.   In instances where disruption of power would result in elevators stopping between floors, throw-over facilities shall be provided to allow the temporary operation of any elevator for the release of passengers.

The 1981 *NEC* correlates this requirement with the mandatory requirements of NFPA 76A.

(3) Additional illumination, receptacles, and equipment shall be permitted to be connected only to the Critical Branch.

517-47. Sources of Power.

(a) Two Independent Sources of Power.   Essential Electrical Systems shall have a minimum of two independent sources of power: a normal source generally supplying the entire electrical system, and one or more alternate sources for use when the normal source is interrupted.

(b) Alternate Source of Power.   The alternate source of power shall be a generator(s) driven by some form of prime mover(s), and located on the premises.

Exception No. 1: Where the normal source consists of generating units on the premises, the alternate source shall be either another generator set, or an external utility service.

Exception No. 2: Nursing homes or residential custodial care facilities meeting the requirements of the Exception to Section 517-40 shall be permitted to use a battery system or self-contained battery integral with the equipment.

(c) Utility Service Capacity.   No part of an Essential Electrical System shall be served from a utility service that does not have the capacity to serve that part of the Essential Electrical System.

(d) Location of Essential Electrical System Components.   Careful consideration shall be given to the location of the spaces housing the components of the Essential Electrical System to minimize interruptions caused by natural forces common to the area (e.g., storms, floods, earthquakes, or hazards created by adjoining structures or activities). Consideration shall also be given to the possible interruption of normal electrical services resulting from similar causes as well as possible disruption of normal electrical service due to internal wiring and equipment failures.

(e) Dual Sources of Normal Power.   Facilities whose normal source of power is supplied by two or more separate central station-fed services experience greater than normal electrical service reliability than those with only a single feed. Such a dual source of normal power shall consist of two or more electrical services fed from separate generator sets or a utility distribution network having multiple power input sources and arranged to provide mechanical and electrical separation so that a fault between the facility and the generating sources will not likely cause an interruption of more than one of the facility service feeders.

E. Hospitals

For additional information, see Essential Electrical Systems for Health Care Facilities, NFPA 76A-1977 and Installation of Centrifugal Fire Pumps, NFPA 20-1980 (ANSI).

Part E was extensively revised to correlate with NFPA 76A.

517-58. Applicability.   The requirements of Part E, Sections 517-59 through 517-65, shall apply to hospitals serving patients who are unable to provide for their own safety.

Exception: Those facilities covered by Parts C and D.

517-59. Wiring, Grounding, and Receptacles.   Wiring, grounding, and receptacle installations shall be in accordance with Sections 517-10, 517-11, and 517-13 and Parts F and G of this article.

517-60. Essential Electrical Systems.

(a) General.

(1)   Essential Electrical Systems for hospitals shall be comprised of two separate systems capable of supplying a limited amount of lighting and power service which is considered essential for life safety and effective hospital operation during the time the normal electrical service is interrupted for any reason. These two systems shall be the Emergency System and the Equipment System.

(2) The Emergency System shall be limited to circuits essential to life safety and critical patient care. These are designated the Life Safety Branch and the Critical Branch.

(3) The Equipment System shall supply major electrical equipment necessary for patient care and basic hospital operation.

(4) Wiring for each branch of the Emergency System shall be separate and independent of each other and all other wiring and equipment. The Equipment System wiring shall be permitted to be installed in raceways and boxes common with other wiring. Both systems shall be arranged for connection, within time limits specified, to an alternate source of power following a loss of the normal source.

(5) The number of transfer switches to be used shall be based upon reliability, design, and load considerations. Each branch of the Essential Electrical System shall be served by one or more transfer switches as shown in Diagrams 517-60(1) and 517-60(2). One transfer switch shall be permitted to serve one or more branches or systems in a small facility as shown in Diagram 517-60(3).

These three diagrams indicate possible electrical system connections for small and large hospitals. Diagram 517-60(2) illustrates a common situation where the expansion of the facility necessitates the addition of a normal source to that already in place. As shown in the diagram, this would not necessarily require the addition of another alternate source. Provided the alternate source has a capacity for all of the intended load, it may serve multiple services.

Recognition of a single transfer switch is given for a small hospital with an equivalent Diagram 517-60(3). A small hospital can be served by a single transfer switch that would handle the loads associated with both the emergency system and the equipment system. This, of course, is on the assumption that the transfer switch has sufficient capacity to handle the combined loads and the alternate source of power is sufficiently large to withstand the impact of the simultaneous transfer of both systems in the event of a normal power loss.

See Essential Electrical Systems for Health Care Facilities, NFPA 76A-1977: Section 3-2.4, Automatic Transfer Switch Features; Section 5-6.2, Description of Transfer Switch Operation; and Section 3-2.6, Nonautomatic Transfer Device Features.

(b) Capacity of Systems.   The Essential Electrical System shall have adequate capacity to meet the demand for the operation of all functions and equipment to be served by each system and branch.

517-61. Emergency System.

(a) General.   Those functions of patient care depending on lighting or appliances that are connected to the Emergency System shall be divided into two mandatory branches: the Life Safety Branch and the Critical Branch, described in Sections 517-62 and 517-63.

The branches of the Emergency System shall be installed and connected to the alternate power source so that all functions specified herein for the Emergency System shall be automatically restored to operation within 10 seconds after interruption of the normal source.

(b) Wiring Requirements.

(1) Separation from Other Circuits.   The Life Safety Branch and Critical Branch of the Emergency System shall be kept entirely independent of all other wiring and equipment and shall not enter the same raceways, boxes or cabinets with each other or other wiring, except as follows:

a. In transfer switches,

b. In exit or emergency lighting fixtures supplied from two sources, or

c. In a common junction box attached to exit or emergency lighting fixtures supplied from two sources.

The wiring of the Equipment System shall be permitted to occupy the same raceways, boxes or cabinets of other circuits that are not part of the Emergency System.

(2) Isolated Power Systems.   Where Isolated Power Systems are installed in any of the areas in Section 517-63(a)(1) and (a)(2), each system shall be supplied by an individual circuit serving no other load.

(3) Mechanical Protection of the Emergency System.   The wiring of the Emergency System of a hospital shall be mechanically protected by installation in metallic raceways.

Exception No. 1: Flexible power cords of appliances, or other utilization equipment, connected to the Emergency System shall not be required to be enclosed in raceways.

Exception No. 2: Secondary circuits of transformer-powered communication or signaling systems shall not be required to be enclosed in raceways unless otherwise specified by Chapter 7 or 8.

This Exception exempts nurse call, telephone, and alarm circuits from being run in metal raceways, provided they comply with their applicable articles elsewhere in the *Code*. Although this provides substantial latitude in the wiring method, it should be noted that the restrictions of Section 300-22 (ducts and plenums) still apply unless conductors listed as having adequate fire-resistant and low smoke-producing characteristics are used as required by the Exceptions under Sections 725-2(b), 760-4(d), and 800-3(d).

MINIMUM ELECTRICAL SYSTEM - TYPICAL SMALL HOSPITALS

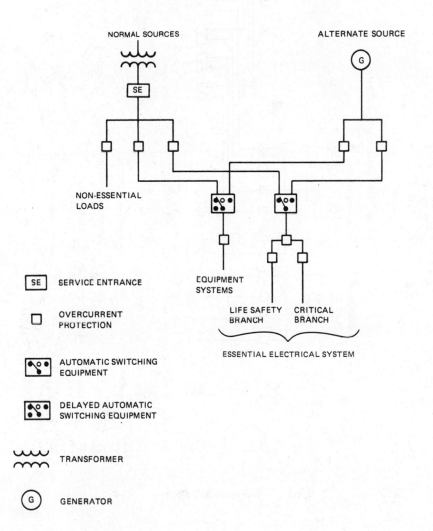

Figure 517-60(1)

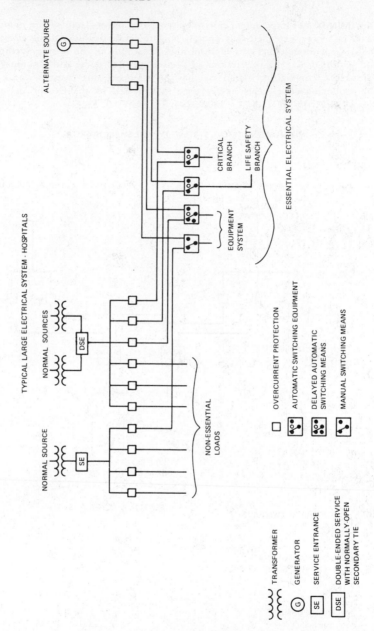

Figure 517-60(2)

517-62. Life Safety Branch. The Life Safety Branch of the Emergency System shall supply power for the following lighting, receptacles, and equipment:

(a) Illumination of Means of Egress. Illumination of means of egress, such as lighting required for corridors, passageways, stairways and landings at exit doors, and all necessary ways of approach to exits. Switching arrangements to transfer patient corridor lighting in hospitals from

MINIMUM ELECTRICAL SYSTEM---TYPICAL SMALL HOSPITALS
(SINGLE TRANSFER SWITCH)

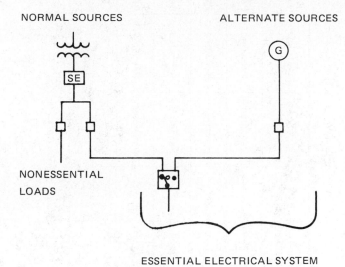

NORMAL SOURCES

ALTERNATE SOURCES

NONESSENTIAL
LOADS

ESSENTIAL ELECTRICAL SYSTEM

SE   SERVICE ENTRANCE

☐   OVERCURRENT
PROTECTION

AUTOMATIC SWITCHING
EQUIPMENT

TRANSFORMER

G   GENERATOR

Figure 517-60(3)

general illumination circuits to night illumination circuits shall be permitted provided only one of two circuits can be selected, and both circuits cannot be extinguished at the same time.

Illumination of means of egress in hospitals has been clarified and relates more properly to NFPA *101*.

See *Life Safety Code*, NFPA *101*-1976 (ANSI), Section 5-10.

	Hazardous (classified) locations	Above hazardous (classified) locations	Other than hazardous (classified) locations	Critical care areas	General care areas	All other areas
Class I, Group C	Required	Permitted	Permitted	Permitted	Permitted	Permitted
Enclosed type	—	Required	Permitted	Permitted	Permitted	Permitted
"Hospital grade"	—	—	Permitted	Permitted	Permitted	Permitted
Listed general purpose	—	—	—	Permitted	Permitted	Permitted
"EMI" type per Sec. 250-74, Exception 4	—	—	—	—	Permitted	Permitted

Figure 517-1. Plug-receptacle types required for use in specific areas of health care facilities.

(b) Exit Signs.   Exit signs and exit directional signs.

See *Life Safety Code*, NFPA *101*-1976 (ANSI), Section 5-11.

(c) Alarm and Alerting Systems.   Alarm and alerting systems including:

(1) Fire alarms, actuated at manual stations.

(2) Electric water-flow alarm devices in connection with sprinkler systems.

(3) Automatic fire or smoke or products of combustion detection devices.

See *Life Safety Code*, NFPA *101*-1976 (ANSI), Sections 10-1 and 10-2.

(4) Alarms required for systems used for the piping of nonflammable medical gases.

See Nonflammable Medical Gas Systems, NFPA 56F-1977 (ANSI).

(d) Communication Systems.   Hospital communication systems, where used for issuing instructions during emergency conditions.

(e) Generator Set Location.   Task illumination and selected receptacles at the generator set location.

No function other than those listed above in (a) through (e) shall be connected to the Life Safety Branch.

517-63. Critical Branch.

(a) Task Illumination and Selected Receptacles.   The Critical Branch of the Emergency System shall supply power for task illumination and selected receptacles serving the following areas and functions related to patient care.

The Critical Branch is intended to serve a limited number of receptacles and locations to reduce the load and to minimize the chances of a fault condition. Receptacles in general patient care area corridors are permitted on the Critical Branch, but they must be identified in some manner (color coded or labeled) as part of the Critical Branch.

(1) Anesthetizing locations — task illumination only.

(2) The isolated power systems required in anesthetizing locations and in special environments.

(3) Patient care areas — task illumination and selected receptacles in:

a. Infant nurseries,

b. Medication preparation areas,

c. Pharmacy dispensing areas,

d. Selected acute nursing areas,

e. Psychiatric bed areas (omit receptacles),

f. Ward treatment rooms, and

g. Nurses' stations (unless adequately lighted by corridor luminaires).

(4) Additional specialized patient care task illumination and receptacles, where needed.

(5) Nurse call systems.

(6) Blood, bone and tissue banks.

(7) Telephone equipment room and closets.

(8) Task illumination, receptacles, and special power circuits for:

a. Acute care beds (selected),

b. Angiographic labs,

c. Cardiac catheterization labs,

d. Coronary care units,

e. Hemodialysis rooms or areas,

f. Emergency room treatment areas (selected),

g. Human physiology labs,

h. Intensive care units, and

i. Postoperative recovery rooms (selected).

(9) Additional task illumination, receptacles and special power circuits needed for effective hospital operation.

(b) Subdivision of the Critical Branch. It shall be permitted to subdivide the Critical Branch into two or more branches.

517-64. Equipment System Connection to Alternate Power Source. The Equipment System shall be installed and connected to the alternate source, such that the equipment described in Section 517-64(a) is automatically restored to operation at appropriate time-lag intervals following the energizing of the Emergency System. Its arrangement shall also provide for the subsequent connection of equipment described in Section 517-64(b).

(a) Equipment for Delayed Automatic Connection. The following equipment shall be arranged for delayed automatic connection to the alternate power source:

(1) Central suction systems serving medical and surgical functions, including controls.

(2) Sump pumps and other equipment required to operate for the safety of major apparatus, including associated control systems and alarms.

(3) Compressed air systems serving medical and surgical functions, including controls.

The above equipment may be arranged for sequential delayed automatic action to the alternate power source to prevent overloading the generator where engineering studies indicate it is necessary.

(b) Equipment for Delayed Automatic or Manual Connection. The following equipment shall be arranged for either delayed automatic or manual connection to the alternate power source:

(1) Heating equipment to provide heating for operating, delivery, labor, recovery, intensive care, coronary care, nurseries and general patient rooms.

Exception: Heating of general patient rooms during disruption of the normal source shall not be required under any of the following conditions:

a. The outside design temperature is higher than +20°F (-6.7°C), or

b. The outside design temperature is lower than +20°F (-6.7°C) and where a selected room(s) is provided for the needs of all confined patients then only such room(s) need be heated, or

See comments following Section 517-46(b)(1), Exception b.

c. The facility is served by a dual source of normal power as described in Section 517-65(e).

The design temperature is based on the 97½ percent design value as shown in Chapter 33 of the ASHRAE Handbook of Fundamentals (1972).

(2) Elevator(s) selected to provide service to patient, surgical, obstetrical and ground floors during interruption of normal power. This shall include connection for cab lighting, control and signal systems.

In instances where interruption of normal power would result in other elevators stopping between floors, throw-over facilities shall be provided to allow the temporary operation of any elevator for the release of patients or other persons who may be confined between floors.

See comments following Section 517-46(b)(2).

(3) Supply and exhaust ventilating systems for surgical and obstetrical delivery suites, infant nurseries, infection isolation rooms, emergency treatment spaces, and laboratory fume hoods.

(4) Hyperbaric facilities.

(5) Hypobaric facilities.

(6) Automatically operated doors.

(7) Such other loads as may be deemed necessary by the hospital, subject to the approval of the authority having jurisdiction.

Careful consideration should be given to the effect of placing fire pumps on the Equipment System. In spite of the fact that manual connection of fire pumps is permitted, future additions of other equipment to the Equipment System may eventually compromise its ability to handle the fire pump load. For this reason a separate alternate source may provide the best assurance of continued capacity for the fire pump load.

(8) Minimal electrically heated autoclaving equipment shall be permitted to be arranged for either automatic or manual connection to the alternate source.

(9) Other selected equipment shall be permitted to be served by the Equipment System.

517-65. Sources of Power.

To correlate with NFPA 76A, material contained in the text of Sections 517-65 and 517-66 has been reworded and reorganized for the 1981 *NEC*.

(a) **Two Independent Sources of Power.**   Essential Electrical Systems shall have a minimum of two independent sources of power: a normal source generally supplying the entire electrical system, and one or more alternate sources for use when the normal source is interrupted.

(b) **Alternate Source of Power.**   The alternate source of power shall be a generator(s) driven by some form of prime mover(s), and located on the premises.

Exception: Where the normal source consists of generating units on the premises, the alternate source shall be either another generating set, or an external utility service.

(c) **Utility Service Capacity.**   No part of an Essential Electrical System shall be served from a utility service that does not have the capacity to serve that part of the Essential Electrical System.

(d) **Location of Essential Electrical System Components.**   Careful consideration shall be given to the location of the spaces housing the components of the Essential Electrical System to minimize interruptions caused by natural forces common to the area (e.g., storms, floods, earthquakes, or hazards created by adjoining structures or activities). Consideration shall also be given to the possible interruption of normal electrical services resulting from similar causes as well as possible disruption of normal electrical service due to internal wiring and equipment failures.

(e) **Dual Sources of Normal Power.**   Facilities whose normal source of power is supplied by two or more separate central station-fed services experience greater than normal electrical service reliability than those with only a single feed. Such a dual source of normal power shall consist of two or more electrical services fed from separate generator sets or a utility distribution network having multiple power input sources and arranged to provide mechanical and electrical separation so that a fault between the facility and the generating sources will not likely cause an interruption of more than one of the facility service feeders.

F. Patient Care Areas

The provisions of Part F apply to hospitals, nursing homes, and residential custodial care facilities that are not limited to specific services. Nursing homes and residential custodial care facilities that meet the requirements of the Exception to Section 517-40 are not covered by this part.

517-80. General.

(a) **Performance/Construction Criteria.**   It is the purpose of Part F to specify the performance criteria and/or wiring methods which will minimize electrical hazards by the maintenance of adequately low-potential differences only between exposed conductive surfaces which are likely to become energized and could be contacted by a patient.

In a health care facility, it is difficult to prevent the occurrence of a conductive or capacitive path from the patient's body to some grounded object, because that path may be established accidentally or through instrumentation directly connected to the patient. Other electrically conductive surfaces which may make an additional contact with the patient, or instruments which may be connected to the patient, then become possible sources of electric currents which can traverse the patient's body. The hazard is increased as more apparatus is associated with the patient, and therefore more intensive precautions must be taken. Control of electric shock hazard requires the limitation of electric current that might flow in an electric circuit involving the patient's body, by raising the resistance of the conductive circuit which includes the patient, or by insulating exposed surfaces which might become energized, in addition to reducing the potential difference which can appear between exposed conductive surfaces in the patient vicinity, or by combinations of these methods. A special problem is presented by the patient with an externalized direct conductive path to the heart muscle. He may be electrocuted at current levels so low that additional protection in the design of appliances, insulation of his catheter, and control of medical practice are required.

The fine print note recognizes the possibility of increased sensitivity to electric shock by patients whose body resistance may be compromised either accidentally or by a necessary medical procedure. Such diverse situations as incontinence or the insertion of a catheter may render a patient much more vulnerable to the effects of an electric current. For these reasons it is essential that those responsible for the design, installation, and maintenance of the electrical system in patient care areas be well acquainted with at least the rudiments of the hazard as explained in this note.

Since the original recognition of this hazard in the 1971 *Code*, continued clinical evaluation of the problem has provided a better understanding of the limits of the hazard, bringing about the changes in both value and wiring methods in the *Code*.

The *Code* clearly assigns designation of the types of patient care areas to the governing body of the health care facility. Both the design and inspection of a patient care area must therefore be based on the governing body's designation rather than the superficial appearance of the area.

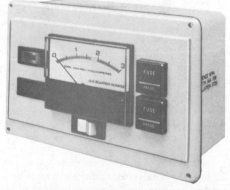

Figure 517-2. Line isolation monitor (right) for use with isolated power systems, remote indicator alarm (top left), and multiple annunciator panel (bottom left), which can monitor several operating rooms from a central location such as a nurse's station. (*Square D Co.*)

(b) Patient Care Areas.   Patient care areas, classified as follows, shall be those areas designated by the governing body of the health care facility in accordance with the type of patient care anticipated.

Green rubber handle   Copper plug

Locking pin

Figure 517-3. Grounding jack and ground-jack receptacle modules. (*Square D Co.*)

Figure 517-4. A transparent, fused attachment plug that permits constant visual check of wiring connections. It is for use with biomedical equipment. (*Daniel Woodhead Co.*)

(1) General care areas are patient bedrooms, examining rooms, treatment rooms, clinics, and similar areas in which it is intended that the patient shall come in contact with ordinary appliances such as a nurse call system, electrical beds, examining lamps, telephone, and entertainment devices. In such areas, it may also be intended that patients be connected to electromedical devices (such as heating pads, electrocardiographs, drainage pumps, monitors, otoscopes, ophthalmoscopes, peripheral intravenous lines).

(2) Critical care areas are those special care units, intensive care units, coronary care units, angiography laboratories, cardiac catheterization laboratories, delivery rooms, operating rooms, and similar areas in which patients are intended to be subjected to invasive procedures and connected to line-operated, electro-medical devices.

(3) A wet location is a patient care area that is normally subject to wet conditions including standing water on the floor or routine dousing or drenching of the work area. Routine housekeeping procedures and incidental spillage of liquids do not define a wet location.

517-81. Grounding Performance. Any two exposed conductive surfaces in the patient vicinity shall not exceed the following potential differences at frequencies of 1000 hertz or less measured across a 1000-ohm resistance.

(a) General Care Areas.   500 mV under normal operation.

(b) Critical Care Areas.   40 mV under normal operation.

Only exposed conductive surfaces (defined in Section 517-2) within the patient vicinity are required to meet the limitations of this section. The patient vicinity does not apply to ambulatory patients, only to the nominal location of the patient bed. The 1000-ohm resistance is intended to represent the patient in his nominal worst case condition.

Voltage limitations for general care areas will ordinarily be met by a reasonable level of electrical installation and maintenance. The voltage levels required for critical care areas may necessitate an additional degree of inspection and maintenance, but much of the problem can be eliminated by the use of electrical insulating or insulation-coated surfaces utilizing approved materials within the patient vicinity.

The 1981 *NEC* has been revised to indicate that a maximum potential difference between any two exposed conductive surfaces in a Critical Care Area is not to exceed 40 millivolts under normal operation.

Figure 517-5. A portable field probe used to detect leakage currents, static electricity, and improper grounds in patient care areas. (*Daniel Woodhead Co.*)

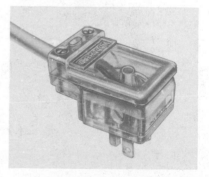

Figure 517-6. A "hospital grade" attachment plug that is designed for maximum performance in hospital environments. The plastic construction contributes to visible check of connections and toward preventing accidental energization of exposed conductive parts. (*Daniel Woodhead Co.*)

517-83. General Care Areas.

(a) Patient Bed Location Branch Circuits.   Each patient bed location where inpatient hospital care is provided shall be supplied by at least two branch circuits, at least one of which originated in a normal system panelboard; all branch circuits from the normal system shall originate in the same panelboard.

Figure 517-7. A self-contained, battery-operated, hand-held resistance meter to check ground path resistance in milliohms of the insulation on cords, which are a frequent source of electrical problems in health care facilities. (*Neurodyne-Dempsey, Inc.*)

Figure 517-8. A battery-operated precision instrument for use on all hospital electrical equipment that measures and detects line voltage and leakage current between the grounding pole of a receptacle and exposed conductive surfaces of non-electrical equipment and/or between the grounding pole and conductive surfaces of fixed or portable electrical equipment. (*Neurodyne-Dempsey, Inc.*)

Patient bed locations in this type of area are prohibited from deriving all of their branch circuits from the Emergency System. At least one branch circuit for each patient bed location must originate in a normal system panelboard. This is a reflection of the requirements stated in Section 517-63.

Exception No. 1: Branch circuits serving only special-purpose outlets or receptacles, such as portable X-ray outlets, need not be served from the same distribution panel or panels.

Exception No. 2: Clinics, medical and dental offices, outpatient facilities; nursing homes and residential custodial care facilities meeting the requirements of the Exception to Section 517-40.

This Exception has been added in the 1981 *NEC* to permit the installation of a single branch circuit in clinics, medical and dental offices, outpatient facilities and residential custodial care facilities meeting the requirements of the Exception to Section 517-40.

(b) Patient Bed Location Receptacles.   Each patient bed location shall be provided with a minimum of four single or two duplex receptacles; each receptacle shall be grounded by means of an insulated copper conductor sized in accordance with Table 250-95.

(c) Grounding and Bonding.   The equipment grounding terminal bars of the normal and Essential Electrical System panelboards shall be bonded together with an insulated continuous copper bonding jumper not smaller than No. 10.

517-84. Critical Care Areas.

(a) Patient Bed Location Branch Circuits.   Each patient bed location shall be supplied by at least two branch circuits, one or more from the Emergency System. At least one shall be an individual branch circuit. All branch circuits from the normal system shall be from a single panelboard; all branch circuits from the Emergency System shall be from a single panelboard. Emergency System receptacles shall be identified, and shall also indicate the panelboard and circuit number supplying them.

Exception: Branch circuits serving only special-purpose receptacles or equipment in Critical Care Areas shall be permitted to be served by other panelboards.

(b) Patient Bed Location Receptacles.   Each patient bed location shall be provided with a minimum of six single or three duplex receptacles, and grounded to the reference grounding point by means of an insulated copper equipment grounding conductor.

Conversely to Section 517-83, patient bed locations in critical care areas must have at least one branch circuit derived from the Emergency System. Additionally, at least one branch circuit from the Emergency System must serve only one bed location; it may not have any other receptacles serving any other bed location. Furthermore, each Emergency System receptacle must bear some form of identification indicating that it is part of the Emergency System, and a label or other appropriate means must specify the panelboard and circuit number from which it is derived. These requirements are intended to ensure that critical care patients will not be without electrical power regardless of whether the equipment, the branch circuits, or the normal system itself is at fault.

(c) Grounding and Bonding, Patient Vicinity.

(1) A patient bed location shall be permitted to have a patient equipment grounding point, grounded to the reference grounding point by means of an insulated continuous copper conductor, not smaller than No. 10, running directly to the reference grounding point or by means of a conductor permanently connected to the grounding conductor of a nearby power receptacle. The patient equipment grounding point, where supplied, shall be permitted to contain one or more jacks listed for the purpose.

(2) The equipment grounding terminal bars of the normal and Emergency System panelboards shall be bonded together with an insulated continuous copper conductor not smaller than No. 10.

(3) One or more room bonding points shall be provided, and shall be grounded to the reference point by means of an insulated continuous copper conductor not smaller than No. 10.

(4) Fixed exposed conductive surfaces in the patient vicinity likely to become energized shall be connected to the room bonding point(s) or the reference grounding point by continuous copper conductors, or conductive building structural members having conductance at least equal to AWG No. 10 copper wire. The bonding conductors, if installed, may be arranged centrically or looped as convenient.

Exception: Small wall-mounted conductive surfaces not likely to become energized, such as surface-mounted towel and soap dispensers, mirrors, and so forth, need not be connected to the room bonding point. Similarly, large metal surfaces not likely to become energized (such as window and door frames) need not be intentionally grounded by connection to the room bonding point.

Each patient bed location in a critical care area is permitted to be provided with a patient equipment grounding point that contains one or more grounding jacks listed for the purpose. It should be understood that the jack is not required to be provided. The use of grounding jumpers will be governed by the type of equipment employed at the particular location. The patient equipment grounding point is to be bonded to the reference grounding point by means of an insulated copper conductor, no smaller than No. 10. This reference grounding point may serve more than one bed location and may be located at any convenient point in the critical care area, or within the panelboard as the equipment grounding bus, if this is practical. An insulated copper conductor, not smaller than No. 10, must also bond together the equipment grounding terminal bars of both the normal and Emergency System panelboards where they serve the same bed location.

The reference grounding point is also required to supply one or more room bonding points by means of an insulated continuous copper conductor not smaller than No. 10. From the room bonding point, bonding connections are made to items such as oxygen and vacuum outlets, provided they have exposed conductive surfaces and are located within the patient vicinity. The Exception permits wall-mounted items having only a small area of conductive surface exposed to be exempt from the bonding requirement.

A suitable alternative to the use of bonding conductors to achieve the equipotential grounding intended by this requirement is the use of the conductive structural members of the building itself as the bonding means. Provided these structural members have conductance of all the components used as bonding conductors, including connections, at least equivalent to No. 10 copper wire, and are electrically and mechanically connected to the items required to be bonded, the intent of this section will be fulfilled.

All of the bonding and grounding points mentioned in this section can be combined into a single point where this is practical. Careful planning for this permissive requirement can result in a substantial savings of both labor and material costs and, at the same time, provide shorter bonding conductors, thereby minimizing voltage drop.

(5) The requirements in Section 517-84(c)(4) shall not apply to bedside stands, over-bed tables, chairs, portable IV poles, and small portable nonelectrical devices such as trays, pitchers, bedpans and the like. The requirements in Section 517-84(c)(4) shall not apply to portable appliances or furniture.

The limited mobility, as well as the tripping hazard, produced by conductors used for grounding or bonding any of the items enumerated in this section has generally outweighed the advantages of the requirements in Section 517-84(c) (4), hence their exemption from these rules.

(6) Any of the grounding and bonding points in Section 517-84(c)(1) through (c)(4) shall be permitted to be combined into a single point.

(7) One patient bed location shall not be served by more than one reference grounding point.

(d) Feeder Conduit Grounding. When a grounded electrical distribution system is used, grounding of the feeder conduit shall be assured by means of a grounding bushing, and by means of a continuous copper conductor, not smaller than No. 12, extending from the grounding bushing to the grounding bus in the panelboard.

Only the feeder conduit is required to be provided with a grounding bushing and a grounding jumper. Effective grounding of branch-circuit conduits will be accomplished by the equipment grounding conductor run with the circuit conductors as required in Section 517-11(a). It should be noted that this rule applies not only to critical care areas but also to all patient care areas.

(e) Isolated Power System Grounding. Where an isolated ungrounded power source is used and limits the first-fault current to a low magnitude, the grounding conductor associated with the secondary circuit shall be permitted to be run outside of the enclosure of the power conductors in the same circuit.

(f) Special Purpose Receptacle Grounding. The equipment grounding conductor for special purpose receptacles such as the operation of mobile X-ray equipment shall be extended to the reference grounding points for all locations likely to be served from such receptacles. When such a circuit is served from an isolated ungrounded system, the grounding conductor need not be run with the power conductors; however, the equipment grounding terminal of the special purpose receptacle shall be connected to the reference grounding point.

517-90. Additional Protective Techniques.

This Section has been expanded in the 1981 *NEC* to make reference to pediatric locations where tamperproof receptacles are to be installed. A definition of "tamperproof" is included.

An additional cross-reference has been added to call attention to material relating to therapeutic pools and tubs located in Part F of Article 680 (Swimming Pools, etc.).

(a) Critical Care Areas.

(1) Isolated power systems shall be permitted to be used for Critical Care Areas.

(2) Isolated power system equipment shall be listed for the purpose and the system so designed and installed that it meets the provisions and is in accordance with Section 517-104.

Exception: The audible and visual indicators of the line isolation monitor shall be permitted to be located at the nursing station for the area being served.

(b) Pediatric Locations. Fifteen- or 20-ampere, 125-volt receptacles intended to supply areas designated by the governing body of the health care facility as pediatric wards and/or rooms shall be tamperproof. For the purposes of this section, a tamperproof receptacle is a receptacle which by its construction, or with the use of an attached accessory, limits improper access to its energized contacts.

(c) Wet Locations. Fifteen- and 20-ampere, 125-volt, single-phase receptacles supplying wet locations shall be provided with ground-fault circuit-interrupters if interruption of power under fault conditions can be tolerated, or an isolated power system if such interruption cannot be tolerated.

In areas that the governing body of the facility designates a wet location, ground-fault circuit-interrupters are to be provided for the protection of receptacles, provided a circuit interruption can be tolerated. This rule applies only to receptacles and not to fixed, permanently wired equipment.

For requirements for installation of therapeutic pools and tubs, see Part F of Article 680.

G. Inhalation Anesthetizing Locations

For further information regarding safeguards for anesthetizing locations, see Inhalation Anesthetics, NFPA 56A-1978.

517-100. Anesthetizing Location Classifications.

(a) Hazardous (Classified) Location.

(1) In a location where flammable anesthetics are employed, the entire area shall be considered to be a Class I, Division 1 location which shall extend upward to a level 5 feet (1.52 m) above the floor. The remaining volume up to the structural ceiling is considered to be above a hazardous (classified) location.

(2) Any room or location in which flammable anesthetics or volatile flammable disinfecting agents are stored shall be considered to be a Class I, Division 1 location from floor to ceiling.

(b) Other-than-Hazardous (Classified) Location.

(1) Any location, including operating rooms, delivery rooms, anesthesia rooms, corridors, and utility rooms, intended for and permanently designated for the exclusive use of nonflammable anesthetizing agents shall be considered to be an other-than-hazardous (classified) location.

(2) Designation and confirmation of "other-than-hazardous (classified) locations" shall be accomplished by a written policy by the governing body of the health care facility prohibiting the use of flammable anesthetics in those locations, accompanied by the posting of prominently displayed notices in each location so designated. In such cases, the locations are excluded from the requirements of Sections 517-101, and 517-104(c)(2)c. and (c)(2)d. as applied to X-ray systems only.

This section divides anesthetizing locations into either a hazardous (classified) location, where flammable or nonflammable anesthetics may be interchangeably employed, or an other-than-hazardous location, where only nonflammable anesthetics may be employed. In the case of the hazardous anesthetizing location, the entire volume of the room extending upward from a level 5 ft above the floor to the surface of the structural ceiling of the room, and including the space between a drop ceiling and the structural ceiling, is considered to be above a "hazardous (classified) location."

517-101. Wiring and Equipment.

(a) Within Hazardous Anesthetizing Locations.

(1) In hazardous (classified) location(s) referred to in Section 517-100, all fixed wiring and equipment, and all portable equipment, including lamps and other utilization equipment, operating at more than 8 volts between conductors shall comply with the requirements of Sections 501-1 through 501-15 and Section 501-16(a) and (b) for Class I, Division 1 locations. All such equipment shall be specifically approved for the hazardous atmospheres involved.

(2) Where a box, fitting, or enclosure is partially, but not entirely, within a hazardous (classified) location(s), the hazardous (classified) location(s) shall be considered to be extended to include the entire box, fitting, or enclosure.

(3) Receptacles and attachment plugs in hazardous (classified) location(s) shall be listed for use in Class I, Group C hazardous (classified) locations, and shall have provision for the connection of a grounding conductor.

(4) Flexible cords used in hazardous areas for connection to portable utilization equipment, including lamps operating at more than 8 volts between conductors, shall be of a type approved for extra-hard usage in accordance with Table 400-4, and shall include an additional conductor for grounding.

(5) A storage device for the flexible cord shall be provided, and shall not subject the cord to bending at a radius of less than 3 inches (76 mm).

(b) Above Hazardous Anesthetizing Locations.

(1) Wiring above a hazardous area referred to in Section 517-100 shall be installed in rigid metal conduit, electrical metallic tubing, intermediate metal conduit, Type MI cable, or Type MC cable which employs a continuous, gas/vaportight metallic sheath.

(2) Equipment which may produce arcs, sparks, or particles of hot metal, such as lamps and lampholders for fixed lighting, cutouts, switches, receptacles, generators, motors, or other equipment having make-and-break or sliding contacts, shall be of the totally enclosed type or so constructed as to prevent escape of sparks or hot metal particles.

Plugs and receptacles used above hazardous anesthetizing locations should be of a type that precludes the escape of sparks or hot metal particles. Such devices are equipped with skirted or recessed contacts and should not be confused with a general purpose plug and receptacle, even though it may be listed as hospital grade.

(3) Surgical and other lighting fixtures shall conform to Section 501-9(b).

Exception No. 1: The surface temperature limitations set forth in Section 501-9(b)(2) shall not apply.

Exception No. 2: Integral or pendant switches which are located above and cannot be lowered into the hazardous (classified) location(s) shall not be required to be explosionproof.

(4) Approved seals shall be provided in conformance with Section 501-5, and Section 501-5(a)(4) shall apply to horizontal as well as to vertical boundaries of the defined hazardous (classified) locations.

Exception: Seals shall be permitted within 18 inches (457 mm) of the point at which a conduit emerges from a wall forming the boundary of an anesthetizing location if all of the following conditions are met:

a. The junction box, switch or receptacle contains a seal-off device between the arcing contacts and the conduit.

b. The conduit is continuous (without coupling or fitting) between the junction box and the sealing fitting within 18 inches (457 mm) of the point where the conduit emerges from the wall.

(5) Anesthetizing location receptacles and attachment plugs located above hazardous anesthetizing locations shall be listed for hospital use for services of prescribed voltage, frequency, rating, and number of conductors with provision for the connection of the grounding conductor. This requirement shall apply to attachment plugs and receptacles of the 2-pole, 3-wire grounding type for single-phase 120-volt, nominal, ac service.

(6) Plugs and receptacles for connection of 250-volt, 50-ampere and 60-ampere ac medical equipment for use above hazardous (classified) locations shall be so arranged that the 60-ampere receptacle will accept either the 50-ampere or the 60-ampere plug. Fifty-ampere receptacles shall be designed so as not to accept the 60-ampere attachment plug. The plugs shall be of the 2-pole, 3-wire design with a third contact connecting to the insulated (green or green with yellow stripe) equipment grounding conductor of the electrical system.

(c) Other-than-Hazardous Anesthetizing Locations.

(1) Wiring deemed in other-than-hazardous (classified) locations as defined in Section 517-100 shall be installed in rigid raceways or shall be in Type MI cable, or Type MC cable.

(2) Receptacles and attachment plugs installed and used in other-than-hazardous (classified) locations shall be listed for hospital use for services of prescribed voltage, frequency, rating, and number of conductors with provision for connection of the grounding conductor. This requirement shall apply to attachment plugs and receptacles of the 2-pole, 3-wire grounding type for single-phase 120-, 208-, or 240-volt, nominal, ac service.

(3) Plugs and receptacles for connection of 250-volt, 50-ampere, and 60-ampere ac medical equipment for use in other-than-hazardous (classified) locations shall be so arranged that the 60-ampere receptacle will accept either the 50-ampere or the 60-ampere plug. The 50-ampere receptacle shall be designed so as not to accept the 60-ampere attachment plug. The plug shall be of the 2-pole, 3-wire design with a third contact connecting to the insulated (green or green with yellow stripe) equipment grounding conductor of the electrical system.

Plugs and receptacles used in other-than-hazardous anesthetizing locations may be any of the types indicated in Section 517-101, or they may be of the general purpose hospital grade type. Devices that are not listed for hospital use may not be used in this class of location.

517-103. Grounding. In any anesthetizing area, all metallic raceways, and all noncurrent-carrying conductive portions of fixed or portable electric equipment shall be grounded.

Exception: Equipment operating at not more than 8 volts between conductors shall not be required to be grounded.

It should be noted that the grounding requirements for anesthetizing locations apply only to metallic raceways and electrical equipment. Carts, tables, and other nonelectrical items need not have grounding jumpers attached to them.

517-104. Circuits in Anesthetizing Locations.

This section has remained substantially unchanged in the 1981 *NEC*. To correlate with NFPA 56A, the threshold value of operation of the Line Isolation Monitor (LIM) has been changed from 2 milliamperes to 5 milliamperes under nominal line voltage conditions [see Section 517-104(b)(1)].

Also, provisions have been added to identify the third conductor in a 3-phase isolated circuit wiring system by use of yellow-color insulation. [See Section 517-104(a)(5).]

(a) Isolated Power Systems.

(1) Except as permitted in Section 517-104(c), each power circuit within, or partially within, an anesthetizing location as referred to in Section 517-100 shall be isolated from any distribution system supplying other-than-anesthetizing locations. Each isolated power circuit shall be controlled by a switch having a disconnecting pole in each isolated circuit conductor. Such isolation shall be accomplished by means of one or more transformers having no electrical connection between primary and secondary windings, by means of motor generator sets, or by means of suitably isolated batteries.

(2) Circuits supplying primaries of isolating transformers shall operate at not more than 300 volts between conductors and shall be provided with proper overcurrent protection. The secondary voltage of such transformers shall not exceed 300 volts between conductors of each circuit. All circuits supplied from such secondaries shall be ungrounded, and shall have an approved overcurrent device of proper ratings in each conductor. Circuits supplied directly from batteries or from motor generator sets shall be ungrounded, and shall be protected against overcurrent in the same manner as transformer-fed secondary circuits.

(3) The isolating transformers, motor generator sets, or batteries and battery chargers, together with their primary and/or secondary overcurrent devices, shall be installed in other-than-hazardous (classified) locations, and shall conform to the requirements of this Code for such locations. The isolated secondary circuit wiring extending into a hazardous anesthetizing location shall be installed in accordance with Section 501-4.

(4) An isolated branch circuit supplying an anesthetizing location shall supply no other location. The insulation of the branch-circuit conductors on the secondary side of the isolated power supply shall have a dielectric constant of 3.5 or less. Wire pulling compounds that increase the dielectric constant shall not be used on the secondary conductors of the isolated power supply.

(5) The isolated circuit conductors shall be identified as follows:
Isolated Conductor No. 1 — Orange
Isolated Conductor No. 2 — Brown

For three-phase systems, the third conductor shall be identified as yellow.

(b) Line Isolation Monitor.

(1) In addition to the usual control and overcurrent protective devices, each isolated power system shall be provided with a continually operating line isolation monitor that indicates possible leakage or fault currents from either isolated conductor to ground. The monitor shall be designed so that a green signal lamp, conspicuously visible to persons in the anesthetizing location, remains lighted when the system is adequately isolated from ground; an adjacent red signal lamp and an audible warning signal (remote if desired) shall be energized when the total hazard current (consisting of possible resistive and capacitive leakage currents) from either isolated conductor to ground reaches a threshold value of 5 milliamperes under nominal line voltage conditions. The line isolation monitor is not to alarm for a fault hazard current of less than 0.7 milliamperes. The line isolation monitor is not to alarm for a total hazard current of less than 1.7 milliamperes.

Exception: A system may be designed to operate at a lower threshold value of total hazard current. A line isolation monitor for such a system may be approved with the provision that the fault hazard current may be reduced but not to less than 35 percent of the corresponding threshold value of the total hazard current, and the monitor hazard current is to be correspondingly reduced to no more than 50 percent of the alarm threshold value of the total hazard current.

Such systems contribute little additional electrical safety and are used for special applications.

(2) The line isolation monitor shall be designed to have sufficient internal impedance such that when properly connected to the isolated system the maximum internal current that can flow through the line isolation monitor, when any point of the isolated system is grounded, shall be 1 milliampere.

Reduction of the monitor hazard current, provided this reduction results in an increased "not alarm" threshold value for the fault hazard current, will increase circuit capacity.

(3) An ammeter calibrated in the total hazard current of the system (contribution of the fault hazard current plus monitor hazard current) shall be mounted in a plainly visible place on the line isolation monitor with the "alarm on" zone at approximately the center of the scale. It is desirable to locate the ammeter so that it is conspicuously visible to persons in the anesthetizing location.

Exception: The line isolation monitor may be a composite unit, with a sensing section cabled to a separate display panel section on which the alarm and/or test functions are located.

(c) Grounded Power Systems.

(1) A general purpose lighting circuit connected to the normal grounded service shall be installed in each operating room.

Exception: Where connected to any alternate source permitted in Section 700-12 which is separate from the source serving the Emergency System.

The failure of the emergency circuit feeder that supplies the operating room will ordinarily plunge it into darkness. By requiring a general purpose lighting circuit supplied by a normal source feeder, the effect of this kind of failure is minimized.

(2) Branch circuits supplying only listed permanently installed X-ray equipment or fixed lighting fixtures, other than surgical lighting fixtures, above the hazardous (classified) location shall be permitted to be supplied from a normal grounded service provided:

a. Wiring for grounded and isolated circuits does not occupy the same raceways,

b. All conductive surfaces of the X-ray equipment and the lighting fixtures are grounded,

c. The X-ray equipment (except the enclosed X-ray tube and the leads to the tube) and the lighting fixtures are located at least 8 feet (2.44 m) above the floor or outside the anesthetizing location, and

d. Switches for the grounded branch circuits are located outside the hazardous (classified) location.

(3) In other-than-hazardous (classified) locations, branch circuits supplying permanently installed X-ray equipment or fixed lighting fixtures, other than surgical lighting fixtures, shall be permitted to be supplied by a normal grounded service provided:

a. Wiring for grounded and isolated circuits does not occupy the same raceways,

b. All conductive surfaces of the X-ray equipment and the lighting fixtures are grounded, and

c. The lighting fixtures are located at least 8 feet (2.44 m) above the floor.

(4) Wall-mounted remote control stations for remote control switches operating at 24 volts or less shall be permitted to be installed in any anesthetizing location.

(5) An isolated power center listed for the purpose and its grounded primary feeder shall be permitted to be located in an anesthetizing location provided it is installed above a hazardous (classified) location, or in an other-than-hazardous (classified) location.

517-105. Low-Voltage Equipment and Instruments.

(a) Equipment Requirements. Low-voltage equipment which is frequently in contact with the bodies of persons or has exposed current-carrying elements shall:

(1) Operate on an electrical potential of 8 volts or less, or

(2) Be approved as intrinsically safe or double-insulated equipment.

(3) Be moisture-resistant.

(b) Power Supplies. Power shall be supplied to low-voltage equipment from:

(1) An individual portable isolating transformer (autotransformers shall not be used) connected to an isolated power circuit receptacle by means of an appropriate cord and attachment plug, or

(2) A common low-voltage isolating transformer installed in a nonhazardous location, or

(3) Individual dry-cell batteries, or

(4) Common batteries made up of storage cells located in a nonhazardous location.

(c) Isolated Circuits. Isolating-type transformers for supplying low-voltage circuits shall:

(1) Have approved means for insulating the secondary circuit from the primary circuit, and

(2) Have the core and case grounded.

(d) Controls. Resistance or impedance devices shall be permitted to control low-voltage equipment but shall not be used to limit the maximum available voltage to the equipment.

(e) Battery-Powered Appliances. Battery-powered appliances shall not be capable of being charged while in operation unless their charging circuitry incorporates an integral isolating-type transformer.

(f) Receptacles or Attachment Plugs. Any receptacle or attachment plug used on low-voltage circuits shall be of a type which does not permit interchangeable connection with circuits of higher voltage.

Any interruption of the circuit, even circuits as low as 8 volts, either by any switch, or loose or defective connections anywhere in the circuit, may produce a spark sufficient to ignite flammable anesthetic agents. (See Section 3-5.2 of Inhalation Anesthetics, NFPA 56A-1978.)

517-106. Other Equipment.

(a) Suction, Pressure, or Insufflation Equipment. Suction, pressure, or insufflation equipment involving electrical elements, and located or used within a hazardous (classified) location shall be listed for Class I locations.

(b) X-ray Equipment. X-ray equipment installed or operated in an anesthetizing location as defined in Section 517-2 shall be provided with approved means for preventing accumulation of electrostatic charges. All X-ray control devices, switches, relays, meters, and transformers shall be totally enclosed, and, where installed or operated within a hazardous (classified) location, shall be listed for use in Class I, Group C locations. High-voltage wiring shall be effectively insulated from ground and adequately guarded against accidental contact. The entire installation shall comply with Part K.

(c) Equipment Generating High-Frequency Power. Equipment for generating high-frequency currents or voltages used in electrocautery, diathermy, television, etc., where installed or used in an anesthetizing location, shall comply with Section 517-101.

H. Communications, Signaling Systems, Data Systems, Fire Protective Signaling Systems, and Low-Voltage Systems

Part H calls attention to the fact that certain wiring methods, although appropriate to a nonhealth care facility installation, could be inappropriate in a patient care area. This part recognizes a common necessity for connecting appliances within the patient vicinity to other appliances that may be located some distance away.

517-120. Patient Care Areas. Equivalent insulation, isolation, and grounding to that required for the electrical distribution systems in patient care areas shall be provided for communications, signaling systems, data system circuits, fire protective signaling systems, and low-voltage systems.

An acceptable alternate means of providing isolation for patient/nurse call systems is by the use of nonelectrified signaling, communication or control devices held by the patient, or within reach of the patient.

For grounding requirements, see Section 250-95.

517-121. Other-than-Patient-Care Areas. See Articles 725, 760, and 800.

517-122. Signal Transmission Between Appliances.

(a) General. Permanently installed signal cabling from an appliance in a patient location to remote appliances shall employ a signal transmission system which prevents hazardous grounding interconnection of the appliances. See Section 517-81.

(b) Common Signal Grounding Wire. Common signal grounding wires (i.e., the chassis ground for single-ended transmission) shall be permitted to be used between appliances all located within the patient vicinity, provided the appliances are served from the same reference grounding point.

(c) Outdoor Signal Transmission. Outdoor signal transmission lines from appliances attached to patient shall be equipped with protection appropriate to the type of transmission line used.

J. Therapeutic High-Frequency Diathermy Equipment

517-130. Installation.

(a) Portability Not Essential. Where portability is not essential, equipment shall be permanently installed in accordance with Chapters 1 through 3.

(b) Portability Is Essential. Where portability is essential, the power-supply cord shall be a 3-conductor hard-service type with an ampacity not less than the marked ampere rating of the equipment. One insulated conductor having a continuous green color or a continuous green color with one or more yellow stripes shall be used solely for equipment grounding. The cord shall terminate in an approved grounding-type attachment plug as provided in Section 250-59(b).

517-131. Applicators for Therapeutic High-Frequency Diathermy Equipment. Applica-
tion of the high-frequency power to the patient shall be permitted by means of an electric field or an induction field. Current-carrying parts of applicators shall be so insulated or enclosed that reliable isolation of the patient will be assured.

517-132. Enclosure.
The converting apparatus, including the dc line and high-frequency electric circuits, but excluding the line cord for portable units and the output circuits, shall be contained in an enclosure of noncombustible material.

517-133. Panel Controls.
All panel controls shall be of dead-front construction.

517-134. Access to Internal Equipment.
Access shall be through panels not conveniently removable. Panels that must be removed to provide access for adjustments or to fuses, tubes, overload reset devices, internal tap switches, and the like shall be labeled to indicate danger if and when the panels are removed, or shall be provided with suitable electrical interlock devices.

K. X-ray Installations

Nothing in this part shall be construed as specifying safeguards against the useful beam or stray X-ray radiation.

Radiation safety and performance requirements of several classes of X-ray equipment are regulated under Public Law 90-602 and are enforced by the Department of Health, Education, and Welfare.

In addition, information on radiation protection by the National Council on Radiation Protection and Measurements is published as Reports of the National Council on Radiation Protection and Measurement. These reports are obtainable from NCRP Publications. P. O. Box 30175, Washington, D.C. 20014.

This part has been extensively rearranged and rewritten in the 1981 *NEC* to include all information previously obtained by cross-referencing Article 660.

In addition, a clarifying paragraph has been added under the heading "Guarding and Grounding," which indicates that grounding of noncurrent-carrying metal parts of X-ray and associated equipment (controls, tables, X-ray tube supports, transformer tanks, shielded cables, X-ray tube heads, etc.) is to be accomplished in the manner specified in Article 250, as modified by Section 517-11(a) and (b), following the criteria set forth in Section 517-81 for Critical Care Areas.

517-140. Definitions.

Long-Time Rating. A rating based on an operating interval of 5 minutes or longer.

Mobile.   X-ray equipment mounted on a permanent base with wheels and/or casters for moving while completely assembled.

Momentary Rating.   A rating based on an operating interval that does not exceed 5 seconds.

Portable.   X-ray equipment designed to be hand carried.

Transportable.   X-ray equipment to be installed in a vehicle or that may be readily disassembled for transport in a vehicle.

517-141. Connection to Supply Circuit.

(a) Fixed and Stationary Equipment.   Fixed and stationary X-ray equipment shall be connected to the power supply by means of a wiring method meeting the general requirements of this Code.

Exception: Equipment properly supplied by a branch circuit rated at not over 30 amperes shall be permitted to be supplied through a suitable attachment plug and hard-service cable or cord.

(b) Portable, Mobile, and Transportable Equipment.   Individual branch circuits shall not be required for portable, mobile, and transportable medical X-ray equipment requiring a capacity of not over 60 amperes. Portable and mobile types of X-ray equipment of any capacity shall be supplied through a suitable hard-service cable or cord. Transportable X-ray equipment of any capacity shall be permitted to be connected to its power supply by suitable connections and hard-service cable or cord.

(c) Over 600-Volt Supply.   Circuits and equipment operated on a supply circuit of over 600 volts shall comply with Article 710.

517-142. Disconnecting Means.

(a) Capacity.   A disconnecting means of adequate capacity for at least 50 percent of the input required for the momentary rating or 100 percent of the input required for the long-time rating of the X-ray equipment, whichever is greater, shall be provided in the supply circuit.

(b) Location.   The disconnecting means shall be operable from a location readily accessible from the X-ray control.

(c) Portable Equipment.   For equipment connected to a 120-volt branch circuit of 30 amperes or less, a grounding-type attachment plug and receptacle of proper rating shall be permitted to serve as a disconnecting means.

517-143. Rating of Supply Conductors and Overcurrent Protection.

(a) Diagnostic Equipment.

(1) The ampacity of supply branch-circuit conductors and the overcurrent protective devices shall not be less than 50 percent of the momentary rating or 100 percent of the long-time rating, whichever is the greater.

(2) The rated ampacity of conductors and overcurrent devices of a feeder for two or more branch circuits supplying X-ray units shall not be less than 100 percent of the momentary demand rating [as determined by (a)] of the two largest medical diagnostic X-ray apparatus plus 20 percent of the momentary ratings of other medical diagnostic X-ray apparatus.

(b) Therapeutic Equipment. Medical X-ray therapy equipment shall be calculated at 100 percent.

The ampacity of the branch-circuit conductors and the ratings of disconnecting means and overcurrent protection for X-ray equipment are usually designated by the manufacturer for the specific installation.

517-144. Wiring Terminals. X-ray equipment shall be provided with suitable wiring terminals or leads for the connection of power supply conductors of the size required by the rating of the branch circuit for the equipment.

Exception: Where provided with a permanently attached cord or a cord set.

517-145. Control Circuit Conductors.

(a) Number of Conductors in Raceway. The number of control circuit conductors installed in a raceway shall be determined in accordance with Section 300-17.

(b) Minimum Size of Conductors. Sizes No. 18 or No. 16 fixture wires as specified in Section 725-16 and flexible cords shall be permitted for the control and operating circuits of X-ray and auxiliary equipment where protected by not larger than 20-ampere overcurrent devices.

517-146. Equipment Installations. All equipment for new X-ray installations and all used or reconditioned X-ray equipment moved to and reinstalled at a new location shall be of an approved type.

517-147. Equipment Controls.

(a) Fixed and Stationary.

(1) A separate control device, in addition to the disconnecting means, shall be incorporated in the X-ray control supply or in the primary circuit to the high-voltage transformer. This device shall be a part of the X-ray equipment but shall be permitted in a separate enclosure immediately adjacent to the X-ray control unit.

(2) A protective device, which shall be permitted to be incorporated into the separate control device, shall be provided to control the load resulting from failures in the high-voltage circuit.

(b) Portable and Mobile. Portable and mobile equipment shall comply with Section 517-147(a), but the manually controlled device shall be located in or on the equipment.

517-148. Transformers and Capacitors. Transformers and capacitors that are part of an X-ray equipment shall not be required to comply with Articles 450 and 460.
Capacitors shall be mounted within enclosures of insulating material or grounded metal.

517-151. Guarding and Grounding.

(a) High-Voltage Parts. All high-voltage parts, including X-ray tubes, shall be mounted within grounded enclosures. Air, oil, gas, or other suitable insulating media shall be used to insulate the high voltage from the grounded enclosure. The connection from the high-voltage equipment to X-ray tubes and other high-voltage components shall be made with high-voltage shielded cables.

(b) Low-Voltage Cables. Low-voltage cables connecting to oil-filled units that are not completely sealed, such as transformers, condensers, oil coolers, and high-voltage switches, shall have insulation of the oil-resistant type.

(c) Noncurrent-Carrying Metal Parts. Noncurrent-carrying metal parts of X-ray and associated equipment (controls, tables, X-ray tube supports, transformer tanks, shielded cables, X-ray tube heads, etc.) shall be grounded in the manner specified in Article 250, as modified by Section 517-11(a) and (b) under the criteria set forth in Section 517-81 for critical care areas.

Exception: Battery-operated equipment.

ARTICLE 518 — PLACES OF ASSEMBLY

Contents

518-1. Scope.
518-2. Other Articles.
  (a) Hazardous (Classified) Areas.

(b) Temporary Wiring.
518-3. Wiring Methods.

518-1. Scope.   This article covers all buildings or portions of buildings or structures designed or intended for the assembly of 100 or more persons.

Places of Assembly shall include, but are not limited to:

Assembly Halls
Exhibition Halls
Armories
Dining Facilities
Restaurants
Church Chapels
Dance Halls
Mortuary Chapels
Museums
Skating Rinks
Gymnasiums
Multipurpose Rooms
Bowling Lanes
Pool Rooms
Club Rooms
Places of Awaiting Transportation
Court Rooms
Conference Rooms
Auditoriums
Auditoriums within:
  Schools
  Mercantile Establishments
  Business Establishments
  Other Occupancies.

Occupancy of any room or space for assembly purposes by less than 100 persons in a building of other occupancy, and incidental to such other occupancy, shall be classed as part of the other occupancy and subject to the provisions applicable thereto.

When any such building structures or portion thereof contain a projection booth or stage platform or area for the presentation of theatrical or musical production, either fixed or portable, the wiring for that area shall comply with all applicable provisions of Article 520.

For methods of determining population capacity, see local building code or in its absence *Life Safety Code*, NFPA *101*-1976 (ANSI).

This article applies to places of assembly designed or intended for the assembly of 100 or more persons. It would apply, for example, to a church chapel for occupancy by 100 or more persons, determined by the methods for occupancy population capacity appearing in NFPA *101*—1976, *Life Safety Code*. But the article does not apply to a supermarket, even though it may contain 100 or more persons, because a supermarket is not specifically designed or intended for the assembly of persons; nor is it an auditorium.

The following information for determining occupancy capacity is contained in NFPA *101*—1976, *Life Safety Code*.

8-1.5 Occupant Load

8-1.5.1 The occupant load permitted in any assembly building, structure, or portion thereof shall be determined by dividing the net floor area or space assigned to that use by the square feet per occupant as follows:

(a) An assembly area of concentrated use without fixed seats such as an auditorium, church, chapel, dance floor, and lodge room — 7 square feet per person.

(b) An assembly area of less concentrated use such as a conference room, dining room, drinking establishment, exhibit room, gymnasium, or lounge — 15 square feet per person.

(c) Standing room or waiting space — 3 square feet per person.

(d) Bleachers, pews, and similar bench-type seating — 18 linear inches per person.

(e) Fixed Seating. The occupant load of an area having fixed seats shall be determined by the number of fixed seats installed. Required aisle space serving the fixed seats shall not be used to increase the occupant load.

Exception: In existing places of assembly the authority having jurisdiction may permit occupancy by number of persons not to exceed that for which the existing means of egress are adequate, provided that measures are established satisfactory to the authority having jurisdiction to prevent occupancy by any greater number of persons than permitted by room area or by fixed seating.

8-1.5.2 The occupant load permitted in a building or portion thereof may be increased above that specified in 8-1.5 if the necessary aisles and exits are provided subject to the approval of the authority having jurisdiction. An approved aisle, exit, and/or seating diagram may be required by the authority having jurisdiction to substantiate an increase in occupant load.

518-2. Other Articles.

(a) Hazardous (Classified) Areas. Hazardous (classified) areas located in any assemblage occupancy shall be installed in accordance with Article 500 — Hazardous (Classified) Locations.

(b) Temporary Wiring. In exhibition halls used for display booths, as in trade shows, the temporary wiring shall be installed in accordance with Article 305 — Temporary Wiring, except that approved flexible cables and cords shall be permitted to be laid on floors where protected from contact by the general public.

518-3. Wiring Methods. The fixed wiring methods shall be metal raceways, nonmetallic raceways encased in not less than 2 inches (50.8 mm) of concrete, mineral-insulated, metal-sheathed cable, or Type MC cable.

Figure 518-1. A treadle, such as this one, can be used to protect cords from abuse where they are laid across pedestrian ways, for instance, as part of a temporary wiring scheme such as may be used in exhibition halls. (*Daniel Woodhead Co.*)

Exception No. 1: Nonmetallic-sheathed cable, Type AC cable, and rigid nonmetallic conduit shall be permitted to be installed in those buildings or portions thereof that are not required to be fire-rated construction by the applicable building code.

Exception No. 2: As provided in Article 640 — Sound Reproduction and Similar Equipment, in Article 800 — Communication Circuits, and in Article 725 for Class 2 and Class 3 remote control and signaling circuits, and in Article 760 for fire protective signaling circuits.

Fire-rated construction is the fire-resistive classification used in building codes.

ARTICLE 520 — THEATERS AND SIMILAR LOCATIONS

Contents

A. General

520-1. Scope. This article covers all buildings or that part of a building or structure designed or intended to be used for dramatic, musical, motion picture projection, or similar purposes and to areas of motion picture and television studios which incorporate assembly areas.

These special requirements apply only to that part of a building used as a theater or for a similar purpose and do not necessarily apply to the entire building. For example, they would apply to an auditorium in a school building used for dramatic or other performances. The special requirements of this chapter would be applicable to the stage, auditorium, dressing rooms, and main corridors leading to the auditorium, but not to other parts of the building that are not involved in the use of the auditorium for performances or entertainment.

520-2. Motion Picture Projectors. Motion picture equipment and its installation and use shall comply with Article 540.

520-3. Sound Reproduction. Sound-reproducing equipment and its installation shall comply with Article 640.

520-4. Wiring Methods. The fixed wiring method shall be metal raceways, nonmetallic raceways encased in at least 2 inches (50.8 mm) of concrete, mineral-insulated, metal-sheathed cable, or Type MC cable.

Exception No. 1: As provided in Article 640 for sound reproduction, in Article 800 for communication circuits, in Article 725 for Class 2 and Class 3 remote-control and signaling circuits, and in Article 760 for fire protective signaling circuits.

Exception No. 2: The wiring for stage set lighting and stage effects and other wiring that is not fixed as to location shall be permitted with approved flexible cords and cables.

Theaters and similar buildings are required to be of fire-rated construction by applicable building codes; therefore, the fixed wiring methods are limited to metal raceways such as rigid metal conduit, intermediate metal conduit, electrical metallic tubing, nonmetallic conduit encased in 2 in. of concrete, or Type MI or MC cables.

Exceptions to the rules requiring raceways are permitted for the use of communication circuits, Class 2 and 3 remote-control and signaling circuits, and fire-protective signaling circuits. Where portability, flexibility, and adjustment are necessary for stage lighting and special effects, approved cords and cables are to be permitted.

520-5. Number of Conductors in Raceway.   The number of conductors permitted in any metal conduit, rigid nonmetallic conduit as permitted in this article, or electrical metallic tubing for border or stage pocket circuits or for remote-control conductors shall not exceed the percentage fill shown in Table 1 of Chapter 9. Where contained within an auxiliary gutter or a wireway, the sum of the cross-sectional areas of all contained conductors at any cross section shall not exceed 20 percent of the interior cross-sectional area of the auxiliary gutter or wireway. The thirty-conductor limitation of Sections 362-5 and 374-5 shall not apply.

Figure 520-1. An electronic dimmer board for stage lighting. (*Packaged Lighting Systems, Inc.*)

520-6. Enclosing and Guarding Live Parts.   Live parts shall be enclosed or guarded to prevent accidental contact by persons and objects. All switches shall be of the externally operable type. Dimmers, including rheostats, shall be placed in cases or cabinets that enclose all live parts.

B. Fixed Stage Switchboard

520-21. Dead Front.   Stage switchboards shall be of the dead-front type and shall comply with Part C of Article 384 unless approved based on suitability as a stage switchboard as determined by a qualified testing laboratory and recognized test standards and principles.

520-22. Guarding Back of Switchboard.   Stage switchboards having exposed live parts on the back of such boards shall be enclosed by the building walls, wire mesh grills, or by other approved methods. The entrance to this enclosure shall be by means of a self-closing door.

520-23. Control and Overcurrent Protection of Receptacle Circuits.   Means shall be provided at a stage lighting switchboard to which load circuits are connected for individual overcurrent protection of stage lighting branch circuits and stage and gallery receptacles used for cord- and plug-connected stage equipment. Where the stage switchboard contains dimmers to control nonstage lighting, the locating of the overcurrent protective devices for these branch circuits at the stage switchboard shall be permitted.

All receptacles intended for the connection of stage lighting equipment, no matter where it is located, are covered by the term "gallery receptacles." Of necessity, the circuits supplying such receptacles must be controlled at the same location as the other stage lighting circuits.

520-24. Metal Hood.   A stage switchboard that is not completely enclosed dead-front and dead-rear or recessed into a wall shall be provided with a metal hood extending the full length of the board to protect all equipment on the board from falling objects.

Because stages are crowded and a great deal of flammable material is present, a stage switchboard must have no live parts on its front. Moreover, the space in the rear of the switchboard must be guarded to prevent entrance by unauthorized persons. One of the best methods of accomplishing this is by enclosing the space between the rear of the switchboard and the wall in a sheet steel housing with a door at one end.

Major stage switchboards are usually the remote control type. Pilot switches on the stage switchboard control the operation of remotely installed contactors in any

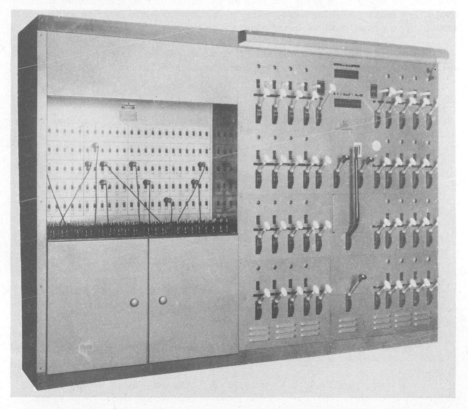

Figure 520-2. An autotransformer-type dimmer switchboard. (*Kliegl Bros.*)

conveniently located available space, such as below the stage. In turn, these contactors control the lighting circuits.

The front view of a small stage switchboard of the partial remote control type is shown in Figure 520-2. Dimmers for individual circuits are operated by the egg-shaped handles. The usual location of a stage switchboard is built into a recess in the proscenium wall. After passing through switches and dimmer, many of the main circuits must be subdivided into branch circuits so that no branch circuit will be loaded to more than 20 A (See Section 520-41). In a switchboard of the remote control type, the branch-circuit fuses are located on the same panel as the contactors. In a direct control type switchboard, and sometimes in a remote control type switchboard, branch-circuit fuses are located on special panelboards, called "magazine panels," placed in the space behind the switchboard, usually in the location of the junction box.

520-25. Dimmers.   Dimmers shall comply with (a) through (d) below.

(a) Disconnection and Overcurrent Protection.   Where dimmers are installed in ungrounded conductors, each dimmer shall have overcurrent protection not greater than 125 percent of the dimmer rating, and shall be disconnected from all ungrounded conductors when the master or individual switch or circuit breaker supplying such dimmer is in the open position.

(b) Resistance- or Reactor-type Dimmers.   Resistance- or series reactor-type dimmers may be placed in either the grounded or the ungrounded conductor of the circuit. Where designed to open either the supply circuit to the dimmer or the circuit controlled by it, the dimmer shall then comply with Section 380-1. Resistance- or reactor-type dimmers placed in the grounded neutral conductor of the circuit shall not open the circuit.

(c) Autotransformer-type Dimmers.   The circuit supplying an autotransformer-type dimmer shall not exceed 150 volts between conductors. The grounded conductor shall be common to the input and output circuits.

(d) Solid-State-type Dimmers.   The circuit supplying a solid-state dimmer shall not exceed 150 volts between conductors unless the dimmer is specifically approved for higher voltage operation. When a grounded conductor supplies a dimmer, it shall be common to the input and output circuits. Dimmer chassis shall be connected to the equipment ground conductor.

See Section 210-9 for circuits derived from autotransformers.

Figure 520-3 illustrates three branch circuits arranged to be controlled by a single switch and a single dimmer plate. A single-pole switch on the stage switchboard feeds a short bus on the magazine panel. The magazine panel is like an ordinary panelboard but branch circuits are directly connected to the bus (without switches), and the circuits are divided into several sections which contain separate feeder buses. One side of the variable resistor or dimmer plate is connected to the neutral bus at the switchboard, and the other side is connected to the neutral bus in the magazine panel. In order to avoid shunting of the dimmer, causing it to lose its control of the brightness of the lamps, the neutral bus in the magazine must be effectively insulated from ground and separate from other neutral buses in the panel.

The dimmer is permanently connected to the neutral of the wiring system, which must be effectively grounded; hence, the dimmer is essentially at ground potential.

Circuits supplying autotransformer-type dimmers are not to exceed 150 V between conductors and, by means of a movable contact, any desired voltage may be applied to the lamps from full line voltage to such a low voltage that the lamps provide no illumination. This type of dimmer produces very little heat, operates at a high efficiency, and, within its maximum rating, its dimming effect is independent of the wattage of the load.

520-26. Type of Switchboard.   Stage switchboard shall be either one or a combination of the following types:

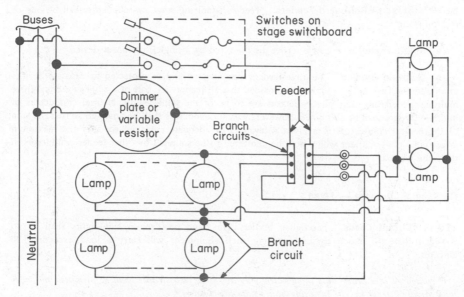

Figure 520-3. A schematic diagram of a typical stage switchboard showing connections for control switches, dimmer plate, and one section of a magazine panel showing feeder and branch-circuit connections for control of three lighting circuits.

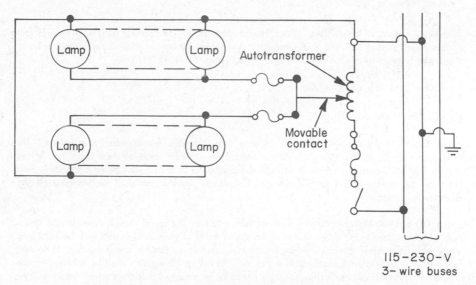

Figure 520-4. Typical connections for an autotransformer-type dimmer.

(a) Manual.   Dimmers and switches are operated by handles mechanically linked to the control devices.

(b) Remotely Controlled.   Devices are operated electrically from a pilot-type control console or panel. Pilot control panels shall either be part of the switchboard or shall be permitted to be at another location.

520-27. Stage Switchboard Feeders.   Feeders supplying stage switchboards shall be one of the following:

(a) Single Feeder.   A single feeder disconnected by a single disconnect device.

(b) Multiple Feeders.   Multiple feeders disconnected and/or protected by separate devices in an intermediate stage switchboard, provided that all feeders are part of a single system. Where multiple feeders are used, all conductors are to be of the same length. Neutral conductors of multiple feeders shall be combined; however, neutral conductors shall be arranged so that the sum of the neutral conductors in a given wireway is of adequate ampacity to carry the maximum unbalanced phase current which shall be permitted to be supplied by other feeder conductors in the same wireway.

C. Stage Equipment — Fixed

520-41. Circuit Loads.   Footlights, border lights, and proscenium side lights shall be so arranged that no branch circuit supplying such equipment will carry a load exceeding 20 amperes.

Exception: Where heavy-duty lampholders only are used, such circuits shall be permitted to comply with Article 210 for circuits supplying heavy-duty lampholders.

> Sections 210-23(b) and (c) permit 30-, 40-, or 50-A branch circuits if heavy duty lampholders, such as admedium or mogul base Edison screwshell types, are used for fixed lighting.

520-42. Conductor Insulation.   Foot, border, proscenium, or portable strip light fixtures and connector strips shall be wired with conductors having insulation suitable for the temperatures at which the conductors will be operated and not less than 125°C (257°F).

See Table 310-13 for conductor types.

520-43. Footlights.

(a) Metal Trough Construction.   Where metal trough construction is employed for footlights, the trough containing the circuit conductors shall be made of sheet metal not lighter than No. 20 MSG treated to prevent oxidation. Lampholder terminals shall be kept at least ½ inch (12.7 mm) from the metal of the trough. The circuit conductors shall be soldered to the lampholder terminals.

(b) Other-than-Metal-Trough Construction.   Where the metal trough construction specified in Section 520-43(a) is not used, footlights shall consist of individual outlets with lampholders, wired with rigid metal conduit, intermediate metal conduit, or flexible metal conduit, Type MC cable, or mineral-insulated, metal-sheathed cable. The circuit conductors shall be soldered to the lampholder terminals. Disappearing footlights shall be so arranged that the current supply will be automatically disconnected when the footlights are replaced in the recess designed for them.

accidental contact with scenery or other combustible material.

Metal troughs are commonly employed for footlights because the installation costs are less than individual outlets. Figure 520-5 illustrates a view of footlights in a typical installation.

Disappearing footlights are arranged so as to automatically disconnect the current supply when the footlights are in the closed position (see Figure 520-5), thereby preventing heat-entrapment that could cause a fire.

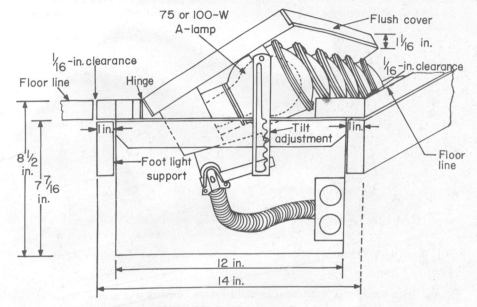

Figure 520-5. Disappearing footlights arranged to automatically disconnect the current supply when in the closed position to prevent heat-entrapment.

(b) Cables for Border Lights. Cables for supply to border lights shall be Type S, SO, ST, or STO flexible cable as provided in Table 400-4. The cables shall be suitably supported. Such cables shall be employed only where flexible conductors are necessary.

Figure 520-6 shows a modern border light installed over the stage. Figure 520-7 is a cross-sectional view of it, giving construction details. This particular border light is for 200-W lamps. Each lamp is provided with its own reflector to obtain the highest illumination efficiency. Fitted to each reflector is a glass roundel available in any color but commonly red, white, and blue are used for three-color equipment; red, white, blue, and amber are used for four-color equipment. A splice box is provided on top of the housing for enclosing connections between the cable supplying the border light and the border light's internal wiring which consists of wiring from the splice box to the lamp sockets in a trough extending the length of the border.

(partially visible text from overlapping page at left)

...sliding-contac...
the lower half enclosed by

...reens or perforated metal placed at the
...s in the wire screen or perforated metal
...e of the opening and of the material

...ampers are released by an electrical device,
...ed and shall be controlled by at least two
...d at the electrician's station and the other
...n. The device shall be designed for the full
...esistance being inserted. The device shall be
...nclosed in a suitable metal box having a tight,

...ontrolled from two externally operable
...of a normally closed circuit ensures that
...circuit opens for any reason, such as a
...ng.

...shall be supplied only from outlets provided for the
...y operable, enclosed fused switches or circuit breakers
...nt switchboard in locations readily accessible from the

...Circuits from portable switchboards directly supplying
...ps of not over 300 watts shall be protected by overcurrent
...ot over 20 amperes. Circuits for lampholders over 300 watts
...protection complies with Article 210. Other circuits shall be
...h a rating or setting not higher than the current required for

...e switchboards for use on stages shall comply with (a) through

...witchboards shall be placed within an enclosure of substantial
...ermitted to be so arranged that the enclosure is open during
...shall be completely lined with sheet metal of not less than No. 24
...zed, enameled, or otherwise properly coated to prevent corrosion or
...terial.

...shall be no exposed live parts within the enclosure.

...eplates as provided in (e) below.

To facilitate height adjustment for cleaning and lamp replacement, border lights are usually supported by steel cables. Therefore, the circuit conductors supplying the border lights must be carried to the border in a flexible cable. The size of individual conductor of the cable may be No. 14, though No. 12 is commonly used.

520-45. Receptacles. Receptacles for electrical equipment or fixtures on [...] for currents of at least 125 percent of the normal operating current for t[...] supplied by the receptacle. Conductors supplying receptacles shall be [...] 310.

This section has been revised for the 1981 *Code* t[...] previous editions) that receptacles rated at least 50 A be [...] arc lamps. Many arc lamps now available are designed fo[...] rather than dc circuits. The requirement for receptacles rate[...] of the normal operating current of the equipment supplied is a[...] *Code.*

Figure 520-6. A suspended border-light assembly for installation over a stage. (*Kliegl Bros.*)

520-46. Stage Pockets. Receptacles intended for the connection of portable stage lighting equipment shall be mounted in suitable pockets or enclosures and shall comply with Section 520-45.

Figure 520-8 shows a single-receptacle stage floor pocket for flush mounting, and Figure 520-9 shows a 3-gang floor pocket for flush mounting. Shown also is the standard-type plug which is used with either floor pockets or wall pockets of these types.

520-47. Lamps in Scene Docks. Lamps installed in scene docks shall be so located and guarded as to be free from physical damage and shall provide an air space of not less than 2 inches (50.8 mm) between such lamps and any combustible material.

520-48. Curtain Motors. Curtain motors having brushes or sliding contacts shall comply with one of the conditions in (a) through (f) below.

(a) Types. Be of the totally enclosed, enclosed-fan-cooled, or enclosed-pipe-ventilated type.

(c) Solid Metal Covers. Have the brush or sliding-contact [...] metal covers.

(d) Tight Metal Housings. Have brushes or sliding con[...] metal housings.

(e) Upper and Lower Half Enclosures. Have the uppe[...] end of the motor enclosed by a wire screen or perforated m[...] solid metal covers.

(f) Wire Screens or Perforated Metal. Have wire s[...] commutator of brush ends. No dimension of any openin[...] shall exceed .05 inch (1.27 mm), regardless of the sha[...] used.

520-49. Flue Damper Control. Where stage flue d[...] the circuit operating the device shall be normally clo[...] externally operable switches, one switch being place[...] where designated by the authority having jurisdictio[...] voltage of the circuit to which it is connected, no [...] located in the loft above the scenery and shall be e[...] self-closing door.

In addition to the flue dampers being [...] switches at different locations, the design [...] the flue dampers will release when the [...] circuit breaker tripping or a fuse blow[...]

D. Portable Switchboards on Stage

520-51. Supply. Portable switchboards [...] purpose. Such outlets shall include externa[...] mounted on the stage wall or at the perma[...] stage floor.

520-52. Overcurrent Protection. [...] equipment containing incandescent lam[...] devices having a rating or setting of n[...] shall be permitted where overcurrent [...] provided with overcurrent devices wi[...] the connected load.

520-53. Construction. Portabl[...] (i) below.

(a) Enclosure. Portable s[...] construction, which shall be [...] operation. Enclosures of wood [...] MSG and shall be well galvani[...] be of a corrosion-resistant m[...]

(b) Live Parts. There [...]

Exception: For dimmer f[...]

(b) Separa[...] noncombustible [...] a source of clean [...]

(c) **itch** **es and Circuit Breakers.** All switches and circuit breakers externally **eral** **ble**, enclosed type.

(d) Circ **Prot** **ection.** Overcurrent devices shall be provided in each conductor of e **circuit** supplied through the switchboard. Enclosures shall be provic overcurrent devic **in addition** to the switchboard enclosure.

(e) Dimmers. **termin** als of dimmers shall be provided with enclosures, and dim faceplates shall be so a **ged** **that** accidental contact cannot be readily made with the faceplat contacts.

(f) Interior Conductors. All **conductors** within the switchboard enclosure shall be stranded. Conductors shall be approved for an operating temperature at least equal to the approved operating temperature of the dimming devices used in the switchboard and in no case less than the following: (1) resistance-type dimmers 200 °C, (392 °F); or (2) reactor-type, autotransformer, and solid-state dimmers: 125 °C (257 °F).

This section has been revised for the 1981 Edition to recognize 125 °C (257 °F) insulation on conductors used within portable switchboards employing reactor-type, autotransformer-type, and solid state dimmers instead of the 200 °C (392 °F) conductors previously required. The previous requirement was based on resistance-type dimmers, which must still be wired with 200 °C (392 °F) conductors.

Each conductor shall have an ampacity at least equal to the rating of the circuit breaker, switch, or fuse which it supplies.

Exception: Conductors for incandescent lamp circuits having overcurrent protection of not over 20 amperes.

Conductors shall be enclosed in metal wireways or be securely fastened in position and shall be bushed where they pass through metal.

(g) Pilot Light. A pilot light shall be provided within the enclosure and shall be so connected to the circuit supplying the board that the opening of the master switch will not cut off the supply to the lamp. This lamp shall be on an independent circuit having overcurrent protection rated or set at not over 15 amperes.

(h) Supply Connections. The supply to a portable switchboard shall be by means of Type S, SO, ST, or STO flexible cord terminating within the switchboard enclosure or in an externally operable fused master switch or circuit breaker. The supply cable shall have sufficient ampacity to carry the total load connected to the switchboard and shall be protected by overcurrent devices.

(i) Cable Arrangement. Cables shall be protected by bushings where they pass through enclosures and shall be so arranged that tension on the cable will not be transmitted to the connections.

(j) Terminals. Terminals to which stage cables are connected shall be so located as to permit convenient access to the terminals.

E. Stage Equipment — Portable

520-61. Arc Lamps. Arc lamps shall be listed.

520-62. Portable Plugging Boxes. Portable plugging boxes shall comply with (a) through (c) below.

The connection shall be such that no current-carrying part will be

...ptacles and overcurrent Protection. Each receptacle shall have a rating of not ... amperes, and shall have overcurrent protection installed in an enclosure equipped with ...ng doors.

...c) Busbars and Terminals. Busbars shall have an ampacity equal to the sum of the ampere ...tings of all the receptacles. Lugs shall be provided for the connection of the master cable.

520-63. Bracket Fixture Wiring.

(a) Bracket Wiring. Brackets for use on scenery shall be wired internally, and the fixture stem shall be carried through to the back of the scenery where a bushing shall be placed on the end of the stem.

Exception: Externally wired brackets or other fixtures shall be permitted where wired with cords designed for hard usage that extend through scenery and without joint or splice in canopy of fixture back and terminate in an approved-type stage connector located, where practical, within 18 inches (457 mm) of the fixture.

(b) Mounting. Fixtures shall be securely fastened in place.

520-64. Portable Strips. Portable strips shall be constructed in accordance with the requirements for border lights and proscenium side lights in Section 520-44(a). The supply cable shall be protected by bushings where it passes through metal and shall be so arranged that tension on the cable will not be transmitted to the connections.

See Section 520-42 for wiring of portable strips.

520-65. Festoons. Joints in festoon wiring shall be staggered. Lamps enclosed in lanterns or similar devices of combustible material shall be equipped with guards.

Joints in festoon wiring are to be staggered and properly insulated. This ensures that connections will not be opposite to each other, which could cause sparking due to improper insulation or unraveling of insulation and, in turn, could ignite lanterns or other combustible material enclosing lamps.

520-66. Special Effects. Electrical devices used for simulating lightning, waterfalls, and the like shall be so constructed and located that flames, sparks, or hot particles cannot come in contact with combustible material.

520-67. Cable Connectors. Cable connectors for flexible conductors shall be so constructed that tension on the cord or cable will not be transmitted to the connections. The female half of the connector shall be attached to the line end of the cord or cable.

See Section 400-10 for pull at terminals.

520-68. Conductors for Portables. Flexible conductors used to supply portable stage equipment shall be Type S, SO, ST, or STO.

Exception: Reinforced cord shall be permitted to supply stand lamps where the cord is not subject to severe physical damage and is protected by an overcurrent device rated at not over 20 amperes.

520-44. Borders and Proscenium Sidelights.

(a) General. Borders and proscenium sidelights shall be: (1) constructed as specified in Section 520-43; (2) suitably stayed and supported; and (3) so designed that the flanges of the reflectors or other adequate guards will protect the lamps from mechanical injury and from accidental contact with scenery or other combustible material.

Metal troughs are commonly employed for footlights because the installation costs are less than individual outlets. Figure 520-5 illustrates a view of footlights in a typical installation.

Disappearing footlights are arranged so as to automatically disconnect the current supply when the footlights are in the closed position (see Figure 520-5), thereby preventing heat-entrapment that could cause a fire.

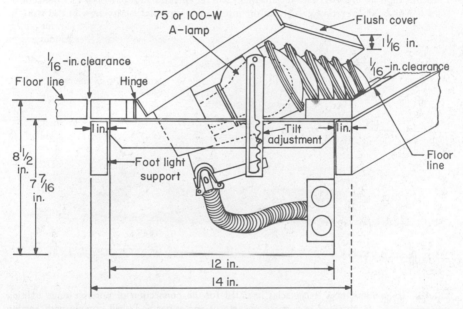

Figure 520-5. Disappearing footlights arranged to automatically disconnect the current supply when in the closed position to prevent heat-entrapment.

(b) Cables for Border Lights. Cables for supply to border lights shall be Type S, SO, ST, or STO flexible cable as provided in Table 400-4. The cables shall be suitably supported. Such cables shall be employed only where flexible conductors are necessary.

Figure 520-6 shows a modern border light installed over the stage. Figure 520-7 is a cross-sectional view of it, giving construction details. This particular border light is for 200-W lamps. Each lamp is provided with its own reflector to obtain the highest illumination efficiency. Fitted to each reflector is a glass roundel available in any color but commonly red, white, and blue are used for three-color equipment; red, white, blue, and amber are used for four-color equipment. A splice box is provided on top of the housing for enclosing connections between the cable supplying the border light and the border light's internal wiring which consists of wiring from the splice box to the lamp sockets in a trough extending the length of the border.

To facilitate height adjustment for cleaning and lamp replacement, border lights are usually supported by steel cables. Therefore, the circuit conductors supplying the border lights must be carried to the border in a flexible cable. The size of the individual conductor of the cable may be No. 14, though No. 12 is more commonly used.

520-45. Receptacles.   Receptacles for electrical equipment or fixtures on stages shall be rated for currents of at least 125 percent of the normal operating current for the equipment or fixture supplied by the receptacle. Conductors supplying receptacles shall be in accordance with Article 310.

This section has been revised for the 1981 *Code* to delete the requirement (in previous editions) that receptacles rated at least 50 A be provided for the supply of arc lamps. Many arc lamps now available are designed for lower rated ac circuits rather than dc circuits. The requirement for receptacles rated at least 125 percent of the normal operating current of the equipment supplied is also new in the 1981 *Code*.

Figure 520-6. A suspended border-light assembly for installation over a stage. (*Kliegl Bros.*)

520-46. Stage Pockets.   Receptacles intended for the connection of portable stage lighting equipment shall be mounted in suitable pockets or enclosures and shall comply with Section 520-45.

Figure 520-8 shows a single-receptacle stage floor pocket for flush mounting, and Figure 520-9 shows a 3-gang floor pocket for flush mounting. Shown also is the standard-type plug which is used with either floor pockets or wall pockets of these types.

520-47. Lamps in Scene Docks.   Lamps installed in scene docks shall be so located and guarded as to be free from physical damage and shall provide an air space of not less than 2 inches (50.8 mm) between such lamps and any combustible material.

520-48. Curtain Motors.   Curtain motors having brushes or sliding contacts shall comply with one of the conditions in (a) through (f) below.

(a) Types.   Be of the totally enclosed, enclosed-fan-cooled, or enclosed-pipe-ventilated type.

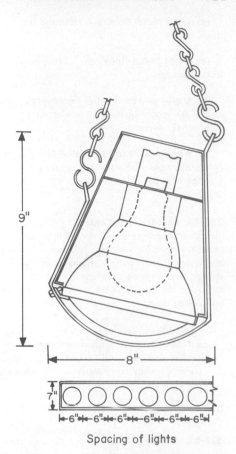

9"

8"

7"

6" 6" 6" 6" 6" 6"

Spacing of lights

Figure 520-7. A cross-sectional view of a typical light in the border assembly shown in Figure 520-6. (*Kliegl Bros.*)

Figure 520-8. A single receptacle in a stage floor pocket. (*Kliegl Bros.*)

Figure 520-9. A three-gang, three-receptacle stage floor pocket designed for flush mounting. (*Kliegl Bros.*)

(b) Separate Rooms or Housings.   Be enclosed in separate rooms or housings built of noncombustible material so constructed as to exclude flyings or lint, and properly ventilated from a source of clean air.

(c) Solid Metal Covers.   Have the brush or sliding-contact end of motor enclosed by solid metal covers.

(d) Tight Metal Housings.   Have brushes or sliding contacts enclosed in substantial, tight metal housings.

(e) Upper and Lower Half Enclosures.   Have the upper half of the brush or sliding-contact end of the motor enclosed by a wire screen or perforated metal and the lower half enclosed by solid metal covers.

(f) Wire Screens or Perforated Metal.   Have wire screens or perforated metal placed at the commutator of brush ends. No dimension of any opening in the wire screen or perforated metal shall exceed .05 inch (1.27 mm), regardless of the shape of the opening and of the material used.

520-49. Flue Damper Control.   Where stage flue dampers are released by an electrical device, the circuit operating the device shall be normally closed and shall be controlled by at least two externally operable switches, one switch being placed at the electrician's station and the other where designated by the authority having jurisdiction. The device shall be designed for the full voltage of the circuit to which it is connected, no resistance being inserted. The device shall be located in the loft above the scenery and shall be enclosed in a suitable metal box having a tight, self-closing door.

   In addition to the flue dampers being controlled from two externally operable switches at different locations, the design of a normally closed circuit ensures that the flue dampers will release when the circuit opens for any reason, such as a circuit breaker tripping or a fuse blowing.

D. Portable Switchboards on Stage

520-51. Supply.   Portable switchboards shall be supplied only from outlets provided for the purpose. Such outlets shall include externally operable, enclosed fused switches or circuit breakers mounted on the stage wall or at the permanent switchboard in locations readily accessible from the stage floor.

520-52. Overcurrent Protection.   Circuits from portable switchboards directly supplying equipment containing incandescent lamps of not over 300 watts shall be protected by overcurrent devices having a rating or setting of not over 20 amperes. Circuits for lampholders over 300 watts shall be permitted where overcurrent protection complies with Article 210. Other circuits shall be provided with overcurrent devices with a rating or setting not higher than the current required for the connected load.

520-53. Construction.   Portable switchboards for use on stages shall comply with (a) through (j) below.

(a) Enclosure.   Portable switchboards shall be placed within an enclosure of substantial construction, which shall be permitted to be so arranged that the enclosure is open during operation. Enclosures of wood shall be completely lined with sheet metal of not less than No. 24 MSG and shall be well galvanized, enameled, or otherwise properly coated to prevent corrosion or be of a corrosion-resistant material.

(b) Live Parts.   There shall be no exposed live parts within the enclosure.

Exception: For dimmer faceplates as provided in (e) below.

(c) Switches and Circuit Breakers. All switches and circuit breakers shall be of the externally operable, enclosed type.

(d) Circuit Protection. Overcurrent devices shall be provided in each ungrounded conductor of every circuit supplied through the switchboard. Enclosures shall be provided for all overcurrent devices in addition to the switchboard enclosure.

(e) Dimmers. The terminals of dimmers shall be provided with enclosures, and dimmer faceplates shall be so arranged that accidental contact cannot be readily made with the faceplate contacts.

(f) Interior Conductors. All conductors within the switchboard enclosure shall be stranded. Conductors shall be approved for an operating temperature at least equal to the approved operating temperature of the dimming devices used in the switchboard and in no case less than the following: (1) resistance-type dimmers: 200°C, (392°F); or (2) reactor-type, autotransformer, and solid-state dimmers: 125°C (257°F).

This section has been revised for the 1981 Edition to recognize 125°C (257°F) insulation on conductors used within portable switchboards employing reactor-type, autotransformer-type, and solid state dimmers instead of the 200°C (392°F) conductors previously required. The previous requirement was based on resistance-type dimmers, which must still be wired with 200°C (392°F) conductors.

Each conductor shall have an ampacity at least equal to the rating of the circuit breaker, switch, or fuse which it supplies.

Exception: Conductors for incandescent lamp circuits having overcurrent protection of not over 20 amperes.

Conductors shall be enclosed in metal wireways or be securely fastened in position and shall be bushed where they pass through metal.

(g) Pilot Light. A pilot light shall be provided within the enclosure and shall be so connected to the circuit supplying the board that the opening of the master switch will not cut off the supply to the lamp. This lamp shall be on an independent circuit having overcurrent protection rated or set at not over 15 amperes.

(h) Supply Connections. The supply to a portable switchboard shall be by means of Type S, SO, ST, or STO flexible cord terminating within the switchboard enclosure or in an externally operable fused master switch or circuit breaker. The supply cable shall have sufficient ampacity to carry the total load connected to the switchboard and shall be protected by overcurrent devices.

(i) Cable Arrangement. Cables shall be protected by bushings where they pass through enclosures and shall be so arranged that tension on the cable will not be transmitted to the connections.

(j) Terminals. Terminals to which stage cables are connected shall be so located as to permit convenient access to the terminals.

E. Stage Equipment — Portable

520-61. Arc Lamps. Arc lamps shall be listed.

520-62. Portable Plugging Boxes. Portable plugging boxes shall comply with (a) through (c) below.

(a) Enclosure. The construction shall be such that no current-carrying part will be exposed.

(b) Receptacles and Overcurrent Protection. Each receptacle shall have a rating of not less than 30 amperes, and shall have overcurrent protection installed in an enclosure equipped with self-closing doors.

(c) Busbars and Terminals. Busbars shall have an ampacity equal to the sum of the ampere ratings of all the receptacles. Lugs shall be provided for the connection of the master cable.

520-63. Bracket Fixture Wiring.

(a) Bracket Wiring. Brackets for use on scenery shall be wired internally, and the fixture stem shall be carried through to the back of the scenery where a bushing shall be placed on the end of the stem.

Exception: Externally wired brackets or other fixtures shall be permitted where wired with cords designed for hard usage that extend through scenery and without joint or splice in canopy of fixture back and terminate in an approved-type stage connector located, where practical, within 18 inches (457 mm) of the fixture.

(b) Mounting. Fixtures shall be securely fastened in place.

520-64. Portable Strips.
Portable strips shall be constructed in accordance with the requirements for border lights and proscenium side lights in Section 520-44(a). The supply cable shall be protected by bushings where it passes through metal and shall be so arranged that tension on the cable will not be transmitted to the connections.

See Section 520-42 for wiring of portable strips.

520-65. Festoons.
Joints in festoon wiring shall be staggered. Lamps enclosed in lanterns or similar devices of combustible material shall be equipped with guards.

> Joints in festoon wiring are to be staggered and properly insulated. This ensures that connections will not be opposite to each other, which could cause sparking due to improper insulation or unraveling of insulation and, in turn, could ignite lanterns or other combustible material enclosing lamps.

520-66. Special Effects.
Electrical devices used for simulating lightning, waterfalls, and the like shall be so constructed and located that flames, sparks, or hot particles cannot come in contact with combustible material.

520-67. Cable Connectors.
Cable connectors for flexible conductors shall be so constructed that tension on the cord or cable will not be transmitted to the connections. The female half of the connector shall be attached to the line end of the cord or cable.

See Section 400-10 for pull at terminals.

520-68. Conductors for Portables.
Flexible conductors used to supply portable stage equipment shall be Type S, SO, ST, or STO.

Exception: Reinforced cord shall be permitted to supply stand lamps where the cord is not subject to severe physical damage and is protected by an overcurrent device rated at not over 20 amperes.

F. Dressing Rooms

520-71. Pendant Lampholders. Pendant lampholders shall not be installed in dressing rooms.

520-72. Lamp Guards. All incandescent lamps in dressing rooms, where less than 8 feet (2.44 m) from the floor, shall be equipped with open-end guards riveted to the outlet box cover or otherwise sealed or locked in place.

> Because of the varied types of flammable materials, such as costumes, wigs, etc., present in dressing rooms, pendant lampholders are not permitted and lamps must be provided with suitable guards that are not easily removed, in order to make it difficult to circumvent their intended purpose of preventing contact between the lamps and any flammable material.

520-73. Switches Required. All lights and receptacles in dressing rooms shall be controlled by wall switches installed in the dressing rooms. Each switch controlling receptacles shall be provided with a pilot light to indicate when the receptacles are energized.

G. Grounding

520-81. Grounding. All metal raceways shall be grounded. The metal frames and enclosures of equipment, including border lights, shall be grounded.

Exception: The frames and enclosures of portable equipment on grounded circuits operating at not over 150 volts to ground and not within reach of grounded surfaces need not be grounded.

Grounding, where employed, shall be in accordance with Article 250.

ARTICLE 530 — MOTION PICTURE AND TELEVISION STUDIOS AND SIMILAR LOCATIONS

Contents

A. General

530-1. Scope.   The requirements of this article shall apply to television studios and motion picture studios using either film or electronic cameras, except as provided in Section 520-1, and exchanges, factories, laboratories, stages, or a portion of the building in which film or tape more than ⅞ inch (22 mm) in width is exposed, developed, printed, cut, edited, rewound, repaired, or stored.

For methods of protecting against cellulose nitrate film hazards, see Standard for the Storage and Handling of Cellulose Nitrate Motion Picture Film (NFPA 40-1974).

The requirements for motion picture studios and television studios are virtually the same, and are intended to apply "only" to those locations presenting special hazards. Otherwise, the conditions are similar to theater stages; therefore, the applicable provisions of Article 520 should be observed, such as for stages, dressing rooms, etc.

The special hazards are temporary structures constructed of wood or other flammable material and the presence of quantities of highly flammable film.

See NFPA 40—1974, Standard for the Storage and Handling of Cellulose Nitrate Motion Picture Film, for information on the storage and handling of this hazardous type of film.

B. Stage or Set

530-11. Permanent Wiring.   The permanent wiring shall be Type MC cable, Type MI cable, or in approved raceways.

Exception: Communication circuits, and sound recording and reproducing equipment shall be permitted to be wired as permitted by Articles 640 and 800.

530-12. Portable Wiring.   The wiring for stage set lighting, stage effects, electric equipment used as stage properties, and other wiring not fixed as to location shall be done with approved flexible cords and cables. Splices or taps shall be permitted in flexible cords used to supply stage properties when such are made with approved devices and the circuit is protected at not more than 20 amperes. Such cables and cords shall not be fastened by staples or nailing.

530-13. Stage Lighting and Effects Control.   Switches used for studio stage set lighting and effects (on the stages and lots and on location) shall be of the externally operable type. Where contactors are used as the disconnecting means for fuses, an individual externally operable switch, such as a tumbler switch, for the control of each contactor shall be located at a distance of not more than 6 feet (1.83 m) from the contactor, in addition to remote-control switches.

Exception: A single externally operable switch shall be permitted to simultaneously disconnect all the contactors on any one location board, where located at a distance of not more than 6 feet (1.83 m) from the location board.

530-14. Plugging Boxes. Each receptacle of plugging boxes shall be rated at not less than 30 amperes.

530-15. Enclosing and Guarding Live Parts.

(a) Live Parts. Live parts shall be enclosed or guarded to prevent accidental contact by persons and objects.

(b) Switches. All switches shall be of the externally operable type.

(c) Rheostats. Rheostats shall be placed in approved cases or cabinets that enclose all live parts, having only the operating handles exposed.

(d) Current-Carrying Parts. Current-carrying parts of bull-switches, location boards, spiders, and plugging boxes shall be so enclosed, guarded, or located that persons cannot accidentally come into contact with them or bring conductive material into contact with them.

530-16. Portable Lamps. Portable lamps and work lights shall be equipped with flexible cords, composition or metal-sheathed porcelain sockets, and substantial guards.

Exception: Portable lamps used as properties in a motion picture set or television stage set, on a studio stage or lot, or on location.

530-17. Portable Arc Lamps. Portable arc lamps shall be substantially constructed. The arc shall be provided with an enclosure designed to retain sparks and carbons and to prevent persons or materials from coming into contact with the arc or bare live parts. The enclosures shall be ventilated. All switches shall be of the externally operable type.

530-18. Overcurrent Protection — Short-Time Rating.*

General. Automatic overcurrent protective devices (circuit breakers or fuses) for motion picture studio stage set lighting and the stage cables for such stage set lighting shall be as given in (a) through (e) below.

Note: *Special consideration is given to motion picture studios and similar locations because filming periods are of short duration.

(a) Stage Cables. Stage cables for stage set lighting shall be protected by means of overcurrent devices set at not more than 400 percent of the values given in Tables 310-16 through 310-19 and Table 400-5.

(b) Feeders. In buildings used primarily for motion picture production, the feeders from the substations to the stages shall be protected by means of overcurrent devices (generally located in the substation) having suitable ampere rating. The overcurrent devices shall be permitted to be multipole or single-pole gang-operated. No pole or overcurrent device shall be required in the neutral conductor. The overcurrent device setting for each feeder shall not exceed 400 percent of the ampacity of the feeder, as given in Tables 310-16 and 310-18 for the kind of insulation used.

(c) Location Boards. Overcurrent protection (fuses or circuit breakers) shall be provided at the "location boards." Fuses in the "location boards" shall have an ampere rating of not over 400 percent of the ampacity of the cables between the "location boards" and the plugging boxes.

(d) Plugging Boxes.   Cables and cords supplied through plugging boxes shall be of copper. Cables and cords smaller than No. 8 shall be attached to the plugging box by means of a plug containing two cartridge fuses or a 2-pole circuit breaker. The rating of the fuses or the setting of the circuit breaker shall not be over 400 percent of the safe ampacity of the cables or cords as given in Tables 310-16 through 310-19, and 400-5 for the kind of insulation used.

> This section has been revised in the 1981 *Code* to limit cords and cables supplied through plugging boxes to copper.

(e) Lighting.   Work lights, stand lamps, and fixtures shall be connected to plugging boxes by means of plugs containing two cartridge fuses not larger than 20 amperes, or they shall be permitted to be connected to special outlets on circuits protected by fuses or circuit breakers rated at not over 20 amperes. Plug fuses shall not be used unless they are on the load side of the fuse or circuit breakers on the "location boards."

530-19. Sizing of Feeder Conductors for Television Studio Sets.

(a) General.   It shall be permissible to apply the demand factors listed in Table 530-19(a) to that portion of the maximum possible connected load for studio or stage set lighting for all permanently installed feeders between substations and stages and to all permanently installed subfeeders between the main stage switchboard and stage distribution centers or location boards.

Table 530-19(a).   Demand Factors for Stage Set Lighting

Total Stage Set Lighting Load (Wattage)	Feeder Demand Factor
First 50,000 or less at	100%
Next 50,001 to 100,000 at	75%
Next 100,001 to 200,000 at	60%
All over 200,000	50%

(b) Portable Feeders.   A demand factor of 50 percent of maximum possible connected load shall be permitted for all portable feeders.

530-20. Grounding.   Metal-clad cable, metal raceways, and all noncurrent-carrying metal parts of appliances, devices, and equipment shall be grounded as specified in Article 250. This shall not apply to pendant and portable lamps, to stage lighting and stage sound equipment, nor to other portable and special stage equipment operating at not over 150 volts to ground.

C. Dressing Rooms

530-31. Dressing Rooms.   Fixed wiring in dressing rooms shall be installed in accordance with wiring methods covered in Chapter 3. Wiring for portable dressing rooms shall be approved.

D. Viewing, Cutting, and Patching Tables

530-41. Lamps at Tables.   Only composition or metal-sheathed, porcelain, keyless lampholders equipped with suitable means to guard lamps from physical damage and from film and film scrap shall be used at patching, viewing, and cutting tables.

E. Film Storage Vaults

530-51. Lamps in Cellulose Nitrate Film Storage Vaults.   Lamps in cellulose nitrate film

storage vaults shall be rigid fixtures of the glass enclosed and gasketed type. Lamps shall be controlled by a switch having a pole in each ungrounded conductor. This switch shall be located outside of the vault and provided with a pilot light to indicate whether the switch is on or off. This switch shall disconnect from all sources of supply all ungrounded conductors terminating in any outlet in the vault.

530-52. Motors and Other Equipment in Cellulose Nitrate Film Storage Vaults. No receptacles, outlets, electric motors, heaters, portable lights, or other portable electric equipment shall be located in film storage vaults.

F. Substations

530-61. Substations. Wiring and equipment of over 600 volts, nominal, shall comply with Article 710.

530-62. Low-Voltage Switchboards. On 600 volts, nominal, or less, switchboards shall comply with Article 384.

530-63. Overcurrent Protection of DC Generators. Three-wire dc generators shall have protection consisting of overcurrent devices having an ampere rating or setting in accordance with the generator ampere rating. Single-pole or double-pole overcurrent devices shall be permitted, and no pole or overcurrent coil shall be required in the neutral lead (whether it is grounded or ungrounded).

530-64. Working Space and Guarding. Working space and guarding in permanent fixed substations shall comply with Sections 110-16 and 110-17.

For guarding of live parts on motors and generators, see Sections 430-11 and 430-14.

Exception: Switchboards of not over 250 volts dc between conductors, when located in substations or switchboard rooms accessible to qualified persons only, shall not be required to be dead-front.

530-65. Portable Substations. Wiring and equipment in portable substations shall conform to the sections applying to installations in permanently fixed substations, but, due to the limited space available, the working spaces shall be permitted to be reduced, provided that the equipment shall be so arranged that the operator can do his work safely, and so that other persons in the vicinity cannot accidentally come into contact with current-carrying parts or bring conducting objects into contact with them while they are energized.

530-66. Grounding at Substations. Noncurrent-carrying metal parts shall be grounded.

Exception: Frames of dc circuit breakers installed on switchboards.

ARTICLE 540 — MOTION PICTURE PROJECTORS

Contents

(a) Motor Generator Sets, Trans-
    formers, Rectifiers, Rheostats,
    and Similar Equipment.
(b) Switches, Overcurrent Devices,
    or Other Equipment.
540-12. Work Space.
540-13. Conductor Size.
540-14. Conductors on Lamps and Hot
        Equipment.
540-15. Flexible Cords.
540-20. Approval.

540-21. Marking.

D. Nonprofessional Projectors
540-31. Motion Picture Projection
        Room Not Required.
540-32. Approval.

E. Sound Recording and Reproduction
540-50. Sound Recording and Repro-
        duction.

A. General

540-1. Scope.   The provisions of this article apply to motion picture projection rooms, motion picture projectors, and associated equipment of the professional and nonprofessional types using incandescent, carbon arc, Xenon, or other light source equipment which develops hazardous gases, dust, or radiation.

For further information, see Storage and Handling of Cellulose Nitrate Motion Picture Film (NFPA 40-1974).

The definitions of hazardous locations in Article 500 do not classify a motion picture projection room as a hazardous location, even though some of the older types of film, such as cellulose nitrate film, barely used now, are highly flammable. In comparison, cellulose acetate film, called "safety film," a much safer film, is in wide use today. Since film is not volatile at ordinary temperatures and no flammable gases are present, the wiring installation need not be explosionproof but should be done with special care to protect against the hazards of fire.

B. Definitions

540-2. Professional Projector.   The professional projector is a type using 35- or 70-millimeter film which has a minimum width of 1⅜ inches (35 mm) and has on each edge 5.4 perforations per inch, or a type using carbon arc, Xenon, or other light source equipment which develops hazardous gases, dust, or radiation.

540-3. Nonprofessional Projector.   Nonprofessional projectors are those types other than described in Section 540-2.

C. Equipment and Projectors of the Professional Type

540-10. Motion Picture Projection Room Required.   Every professional-type projector shall be located within a projection room. Every projection room shall be of permanent construction, approved for the type of building in which the projection room is located. All projection ports, spotlight ports, viewing ports, and similar openings shall be provided with glass or other approved material so as to completely close the opening. Such rooms shall not be considered as hazardous (classified) locations as defined in Article 500.

For further information on protecting openings in projection rooms handling cellulose nitrate motion picture film, see *Life Safety Code*, NFPA *101*-1976 (ANSI).

540-11. Location of Associated Electrical Equipment.

(a) Motor Generator Sets, Transformers, Rectifiers, Rheostats, and Similar Equipment.   Motor generator sets, transformers, rectifiers, rheostats, and similar equipment for the supply or control of current to projection or spotlight equipment shall, if practicable, be located in a separate room. Where placed in the projection room, they shall be so located or guarded that arcs or sparks cannot come in contact with film, and motor generator sets shall have the commutator end or ends protected as provided in Section 520-48.

(b) Switches, Overcurrent Devices, or Other Equipment.   Switches, overcurrent devices, or other equipment not normally required or used for projectors, sound reproduction, flood or other special effect lamps, or other equipment shall not be installed in projection rooms.

Exception No. 1: Remote control switches for the control of auditorium lights or switches for the control of motors operating curtains and masking of the motion picture screen.

Exception No. 2: In projection rooms approved for use only with cellulose acetate (safety) film, the installation of appurtenant electrical equipment used in conjunction with the operation of the projection equipment and the control of lights, curtains, and audio equipment, etc., shall be permitted. In such projection rooms, a sign reading "Safety Film Only Permitted in This Room" shall be posted on the outside of each projection room door and within the projection room itself in a conspicuous location.

The plan of a projection room of a motion-picture theater is illustrated in Figure 540-1. The plan shows one stereopticon or "effect machine" "L," two spot machines "S," and three motion picture projectors "P."

A dc arc lamp is the light source in each of the six machines. The dc supply is furnished by two motor generator sets that are usually installed in soundproof areas so as not to interfere with the sound-reproducing equipment and are controlled from the generator panel in the projection room or booth. Two 500 MCM feeder cables are run from each generator to the dc panelboard.

A branch circuit consisting of two No. 2/0 cables runs from the dc panelboard to each projector "P" and to each spot machine "S." One of the two branch-circuit conductors runs directly to projector "P"; the other passes through an auxiliary gutter to the bank of resistors in the rheostat room and then to the projector. The resistors are equipped with short-circuiting switches so that the total resistance in series with each arc may be preset to a desired value.

Since the stereopticon or effect machine "L" contains two arc lamps, two circuits with No. 1 conductors are routed to this machine.

Section 540-13 requires that the conductors supplying outlets for arc and Xenon projectors of the professional type are not to be smaller than No. 8 and are to be of sufficient size for the projector employed. Hence, in each case the maximum current drawn by the lamps should be determined. In this example, when the arc lamps are adjusted for a large picture, the arc in each projector draws nearly 150 A. Four outlets, in addition to the main outlet for supplying the arc, are located at each projector for the following auxiliary circuits:

(1) Foot switches operating the shutters in front of the lenses for changing from one projector to another are supplied by Outlets F.

(2) Outlets G are for the No. 8 grounding conductor, which is connected to the projector frames and to a metal water pipe.

(3) Outlets C supply a small incandescent lamp inside the lamphouse and a lamp illuminating the turntable.

(4) Motors used to operate the projectors are supplied from Outlets M.

Two exhaust fans and two duct systems, one exhausting from the ceiling of the projection room and one connected to the arc-lamp housing of each machine, provide ventilation.

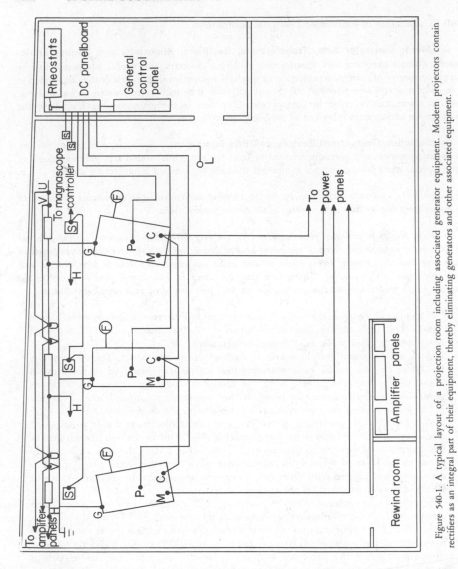

Figure 540-1. A typical layout of a projection room including associated generator equipment. Modern projectors contain rectifiers as an integral part of their equipment, thereby eliminating generators and other associated equipment.

540-12. Work Space. Each motion picture projector, floodlight, spotlight, or similar equipment shall have clear working space not less than 30 inches (762 mm) wide on each side and at the rear thereof.

Exception: One such space shall be permitted between adjacent pieces of equipment.

540-13. Conductor Size. Conductors supplying outlets for arc and Xenon projectors of the professional type shall not be smaller than No. 8 and shall be of sufficient size for the projector employed. Conductors for incandescent-type projectors shall conform to normal wiring standards as provided in Section 210-24.

540-14. Conductors on Lamps and Hot Equipment. Asbestos-covered conductors Type AA or other types of insulated conductors having a maximum operating temperature of 200°C (392°F) shall be used on all lamps or other equipment where the ambient temperature at the conductors as installed will exceed 50°C (122°F).

540-15. Flexible Cords.   Cords approved for hard usage as provided in Table 400-4 shall be used on portable equipment.

540-20. Approval.   Projectors and enclosures for arc, Xenon and incandescent lamps and rectifiers, transformers, rheostats and similar equipment shall be approved.

540-21. Marking.   Projectors and other equipment shall be marked with the maker's name or trademark and with the voltage and current for which they are designed in accordance with Section 110-21.

D. Nonprofessional Projectors

540-31. Motion Picture Projection Room Not Required.   Projectors of the nonprofessional or miniature type, when employing cellulose acetate (safety) film, shall be permitted to be operated without a projection room.

540-32. Approval.   Projection equipment shall be listed.

E. Sound Recording and Reproduction

540-50. Sound Recording and Reproduction.   Sound recording and reproduction equipment shall be installed as provided in Article 640.

ARTICLE 545 — MANUFACTURED BUILDING

Contents

A. General

545-1. Scope.   This article covers requirements for a manufactured building and/or building components as herein defined.

545-2. Other Articles.   Wherever the requirements of other articles of this Code and Article 545 differ, the requirements of Article 545 shall apply.

545-3. Definitions.

   Manufactured Building.   "Manufactured Building" means any building which is of closed construction and which is made or assembled in manufacturing facilities on or off the building site for installation, or assembly and installation on the building site, other than mobile homes or recreational vehicles.

Building Component.   "Building Component" means any subsystem, subassembly, or other system designed for use in or integral with or as part of a structure, which can include structural, electrical, mechanical, plumbing, and fire protection systems, and other systems affecting health and safety.

Building System.   "Building System" means plans, specifications, and documentation for a system of manufactured building or for a type or a system of building components, which can include structural, electrical, mechanical, plumbing, and fire protection systems, and other systems affecting health and safety, and including such variations thereof as are specifically permitted by regulation, and which variations are submitted as part of the building system or amendment thereto.

Closed Construction.   "Closed Construction" means any building, building component, assembly, or system manufactured in such a manner that all concealed parts of processes of manufacture cannot be inspected before installation at the building site without disassembly, damage, or destruction.

545-4. Wiring Methods.

(a) Methods Permitted.   All raceway and cable wiring methods included in this Code and such other wiring systems specifically intended and approved for use in manufactured building shall be permitted with approved fittings and with fittings approved for manufactured building. Where wiring devices with integral enclosures are used, sufficient length of conductor shall be provided to facilitate replacement.

(b) Securing Cables.   In closed construction, cables shall be permitted to be secured only at cabinets, boxes, or fittings where No. 10 AWG or smaller conductors are used and protection against physical damage is provided as required by Section 300-4.

545-5. Service-Entrance Conductors.   Service-entrance conductors shall meet the requirements of Article 230. Provisions shall be made to route the service-entrance conductors from the service equipment to the point of attachment of the service.

545-6. Installation of Service-Entrance Conductors.   Service-entrance conductors shall be installed after erection at the building site.

Exception: Where point of attachment is known prior to manufacture.

545-7. Service Equipment Location.   The service equipment shall be located at a readily accessible point nearest to the entrance of the conductors either inside or outside the building.

545-8. Protection of Conductors and Equipment.   Protection shall be provided for exposed conductors and equipment during processes of manufacturing, packaging, in transit, and erection at the building site.

545-9. Outlet Boxes.

(a) Other Dimensions.   Outlet boxes of dimensions other than those required in Table 370-6(a) shall be permitted to be installed when tested and approved to applicable standards.

(b) Not Over 100 Cubic Inches.   Any outlet box not over 100 cubic inches in size, intended for mounting in closed construction, shall be affixed with approved anchors or clamps so as to provide a rigid and secure installation.

545-10. Receptacle or Switch with Integral Enclosure. A receptacle or switch with integral enclosure and mounting means, when tested and approved to applicable standards, shall be permitted to be installed.

Figure 545-1. A special type of tool that is used to connect nonmetallic-sheathed cable to an approved boxless switch or receptacle. (*Amp Inc.*)

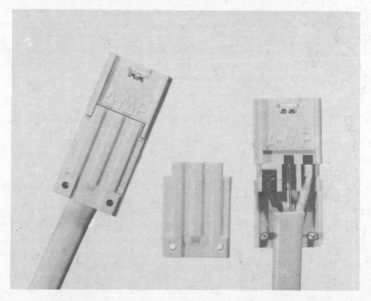

Figure 545-2. A type of nonmetallic-sheathed cable connector used for interconnecting modules in a manufacturing building. The parts are shown before mating together. (*Amp Inc.*)

545-11. Bonding and Grounding.   Prewired panels and/or building components shall provide for the bonding and/or grounding of all exposed metals likely to become energized, in accordance with Article 250, Parts E, F, and G.

545-12. Grounding Electrode Conductor.   The grounding electrode conductor shall meet the requirements of Article 250, Part J. Provisions shall be made to route the grounding electrode conductor from the service equipment to the point of attachment to the grounding electrode.

545-13. Component Interconnections.   Fittings and connectors which are intended to be concealed at the time of on-site assembly, when tested and approved to applicable standards, shall be permitted for on-site interconnection of modules or other building components. Such fittings and connectors shall be equal to the wiring method employed in insulation, temperature rise, fault-current withstand and shall be capable of enduring the vibration and minor relative motions occurring in the components of manufactured building.

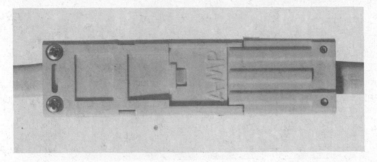

Figure 545-3. The nonmetallic-sheathed cable connector shown in Figure 545-2 after being joined together. (*Amp Inc.*)

Structural components or modules are usually constructed in manufacturing facilities and then transported over the road to a building site for complete assembly of, for instance, a dwelling unit, a motel, an office building, etc. At the on-site location, approved wiring methods are employed to interconnect two or more modules. Figures 545-2 and 545-3 show a type of nonmetallic-sheathed cable connector permitted for such interconnections.

ARTICLE 547 — AGRICULTURAL BUILDINGS

Contents

547-1. Scope.   The provisions of this article shall apply to the following agricultural buildings or that part of a building as specified in (a), (b), or (c) below.

(a) Excessive Dust and Dust With Water. Agricultural buildings where excessive dust and dust with water may accumulate. Such buildings include all areas of totally enclosed and environmentally controlled poultry and livestock confinement systems, where litter dust, feed dust, including mineral feed particles, may accumulate and enclosed areas of similar or like nature.

(b) Corrosive Atmosphere. Agricultural buildings where a corrosive atmosphere exists. Such buildings include totally enclosed and environmentally controlled areas where (1) poultry and animal excrement may cause corrosive vapors in the confinement area; (2) corrosive particles may combine with water; (3) the area is damp and wet by reason of periodic washing for cleaning and sanitizing with water and cleansing agents; (4) similar conditions exist.

(c) Other Articles. For agricultural buildings not having conditions as specified in (a) or (b), the electrical installations shall be made in accordance with the applicable articles in this Code.

547-2. General. Electrical equipment or devices installed in accordance with the provisions of this article shall be installed in a manner such that they will function at full rating without developing surface temperatures in excess of the specified normal safe operating range of the equipment or device.

547-3. Wiring Methods. In agricultural buildings as described in Section 547-1(a) and (b), Types UF, NMC, SNM, or other cables or raceways suitable for the location, with approved termination fittings, shall be the wiring methods employed. Article 320 wiring methods shall be permitted for Section 547-1(a). Buildings wired in accordance with the provisions of Article 502 shall be permitted. All cables shall be secured within 8 inches (203 mm) of each cabinet, box, or fitting.

(a) Boxes, Fittings, and Wiring Devices. All boxes in which devices are installed, where taps, joints, or terminal connections are made shall be dust- and water-tight and shall be made of corrosion-resistant material.

(b) Flexible Connections. Where necessary to employ flexible connections, dusttight flexible connectors, liquidtight flexible metal conduit, or flexible cord approved for hard usage shall be used. All shall be used with approved fittings.

547-4. Switches, Circuit Breakers, Motor Controllers, and Fuses. Switches, circuit breakers, motor controllers, and fuses, including pushbuttons, relays and similar devices, used in buildings described in Section 547-1(a) and (b), shall be provided with a weatherproof, corrosion-resistant enclosure designed to minimize the entrance of dust, water, and corrosive elements, and shall be equipped with a telescoping or close-fitting cover.

547-5. Motors. Motors and other rotating electrical machinery shall be totally enclosed or so designed as to minimize the entrance of dust, moisture, or corrosive particles.

547-6. Lighting Fixtures. Lighting fixtures installed in agricultural buildings described in Section 547-1 shall comply with the following:

(a) Minimize the Entrance of Dust. Lighting fixtures shall be installed to minimize the entrance of dust, foreign matter, moisture, and corrosive material.

(b) Exposed to Physical Damage. Any lighting fixture that may be exposed to physical damage shall be protected by a suitable guard.

(c) Exposed to Water. A fixture that may be exposed to water from condensation and/or building cleansing water or solution shall be watertight.

547-7. Grounding. Grounding shall comply with Article 250.

ARTICLE 550 — MOBILE HOMES
AND MOBILE HOME PARKS

Contents

B. Mobile Home Parks
550-21. Distribution System.
550-22. Calculated Load.
  (a) Minimum Allowable Demand Factors.
  (b) Demand Factor Shall Apply to All Lots.
  (c) Adequate Feeder Capacity.

550-23. Mobile Home Service Equipment.
  (a) Rating.
  (b) Additional Outside Electrical Equipment.
  (c) Additional Receptacles.
  (d) Location.
  (e) Grounded.

550-1. Scope.

(a) Mobile Homes and Mobile Home Parks. The provisions of this article cover the electrical conductors and equipment installed within or on mobile homes, the conductors that connect mobile homes to a supply of electricity, and the installation of electrical wiring, fixtures, equipment, and appurtenances related to electrical installations within a mobile home park up to the mobile home service-entrance conductors or, if none, the mobile home service equipment.

Wherever the requirements of other articles of this Code and Article 550 differ, the requirements of Article 550 shall apply.

(b) Mobile Home Not Intended as a Dwelling Unit. A mobile home not intended as a dwelling unit, as for example equipped for sleeping purposes only, contractor's on-site offices, construction job dormitories, mobile studio dressing rooms, banks, clinics, mobile stores, or intended for the display or demonstration of merchandise or machinery, shall not be required to meet the provisions of this article pertaining to the number or capacity of circuits required. It shall, however, meet all other applicable requirements of this article if provided with an electrical installation intended to be energized from a 115-volt or 115/230-volt ac power supply system.

(c) In Other than Mobile Home Parks. Mobile homes installed in other than mobile home parks shall comply with the provisions of this article.

(d) Connection to Wiring System. The provisions of this article apply to mobile homes intended for connection to a wiring system rated 115/230-volts, nominal, 3-wire ac, with grounded neutral.

(e) Listed or Labeled. All electrical materials, devices, appliances, fittings, and other equipment shall be listed or labeled by a qualified testing agency and shall be connected in an approved manner when installed.

The Federal Housing and Urban Development Administration (HUD) has issued the Federal Mobile Home Construction Safety Standard that has incorporated most of the provisions in the latest edition of NFPA 501B, Standard for Mobile Homes. Both the federal and NFPA standards contain requirements not only for an electrical installation, but also for body and frame design, construction, exits, interior finish, flame spread, and plumbing and heating systems. Their electrical requirements are essentially identical to those in Article 550. It is required that new mobile homes comply with the federal standard. In some cases HUD has delegated the enforcement of this standard to state and private inspection agencies and to qualified testing laboratories.

550-2. Definitions.

Appliance, Fixed. An appliance which is fastened or otherwise secured at a specific location.

Appliance, Portable.   An appliance which is actually moved or can easily be moved from one place to another in normal use.

For the purpose of this article, the following major appliances other than built-in are considered portable if cord-connected: refrigerators, gas range equipment, clothes washers, dishwashers without booster heaters, or other similar appliances.

Appliance, Stationary.   An appliance which is not easily moved from one place to another in normal use.

Distribution Panelboard.   See definition of panelboard in Article 100.

Feeder Assembly.   The overhead or under-chassis feeder conductors, including the grounding conductor, together with the necessary fittings and equipment or a power-supply cord approved for mobile home use, designed for the purpose of delivering energy from the source of electrical supply to the distribution panelboard within the mobile home.

Laundry Area.   An area containing or designed to contain either a laundry tray, clothes washer, and/or a clothes dryer.

Mobile Home.   A factory-assembled structure or structures equipped with the necessary service connections and made so as to be readily movable as a unit or units on its own running gear and designed to be used as a dwelling unit(s) without a permanent foundation.

The phrase "without a permanent foundation" indicates that the support system is constructed with the intent that the mobile home placed thereon will be moved from time to time at the convenience of the owner.

Mobile Home Accessory Building or Structure.   Any awning, cabana, ramada, storage cabinet, carport, fence, windbreak, or porch established for the use of the occupant of the mobile home upon a mobile home lot.

Mobile Home Lot.   A designated portion of a mobile home park designed for the accommodation of one mobile home and its accessory buildings or structures for the exclusive use of its occupants.

Mobile Home Park.   A contiguous parcel of land which is used for the accommodation of occupied mobile homes.

Mobile Home Service Equipment.   The equipment containing the disconnecting means, overcurrent protective devices, and receptacles or other means for connecting a mobile home feeder assembly.

Park Electrical Wiring Systems.   All of the electrical wiring, fixtures, equipment, and appurtenances related to electrical installations within a mobile home park, including the mobile home service equipment.

Definitions of fixed and stationary appliances are new in this article of the 1981 *Code.* They are the same definitions that appeared in Article 100 of the 1978 *Code.*

A. Mobile Homes

550-3. Power Supply.

(a) **Service Equipment.**   The mobile home service equipment shall be located adjacent to the mobile home and not mounted in or on the mobile home. The power supply to the mobile home shall be a feeder assembly consisting of not more than one approved 50-ampere mobile home power-supply cord with integral molded cap, or a permanently installed circuit.

Exception: A mobile home that is factory-equipped with gas or oil-fired central heating equipment and cooking appliances shall be permitted to be provided with an approved mobile home power-supply cord rated 40 amperes.

(b) Power-Supply Cord. If the mobile home has a power-supply cord, it shall be permanently attached to the distribution panelboard or to a junction box permanently connected to the distribution panelboard, with the free end terminating in an attachment plug cap.

(c) Cords. Cords with adapters and pigtail ends, extension cords, and similar items shall not be attached to, or shipped with, a mobile home.

(d) Suitable Clamp. A suitable clamp or the equivalent shall be provided at the distribution panelboard knockout to afford strain relief for the cord to prevent strain from being transmitted to the terminals when the power-supply cord is handled in its intended manner.

(e) Approved-type Cord. The cord used shall be of an approved type with four conductors, one of which shall be identified by a continuous green color or a continuous green color with one or more yellow stripes for use as the grounding conductor.

(f) Attachment Plug Cap. The attachment plug cap shall be a 3-pole, 4-wire, grounding type, rated 50 amperes, 125/250 volts with a configuration as shown in Figure 550-3(f) and intended for use with the 50-ampere, 125/250 receptacle configuration shown in Figure 550-3(f). It shall be molded of butyl rubber, neoprene, or other materials which have been found suitable for the purpose, and shall be molded to the flexible cord so that it adheres tightly to the cord at the point where the cord enters the attachment plug cap. If a right-angle cap is used, the configuration shall be so oriented that the grounding member is farthest from the cord.

Complete details of the 50-ampere plug and receptacle shown in Figure 550-3(f) can be found in ANSI Standard Dimensions of Caps, Plugs and Receptacles, C73.17-1972.

Figure 550-3(f). 50-ampere, 125/250 volt receptacle and attachment-plug-cap configurations, 3-pole, 4-wire, grounding types, used for mobile home supply cords and mobile home parks.

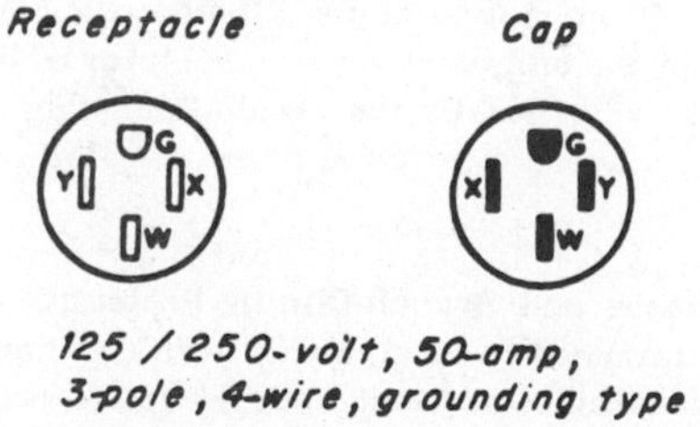

Receptacle   *Cap*

125 / 250-volt, 50-amp, 3-pole, 4-wire, grounding type

(g) Overall Length of a Power-Supply Cord. The overall length of a power-supply cord, measured from the end of the cord, including bared leads, to the face of the attachment plug cap shall not be less than 21 feet (6.4 m) and shall not exceed 36½ feet (11.13 m). The length of the cord from the face of the attachment plug cap to the point where the cord enters the mobile home shall not be less than 20 feet (6.1 m).

(h) Marking. The power-supply cord shall bear the following marking: "For use with mobile homes — 40 amperes" or "For use with mobile homes — 50 amperes."

(i) Point of Entrance. The point of entrance of the feeder assembly to the mobile home shall be in the exterior wall, floor, or roof.

> This section has been revised for the 1981 *Code* to permit the point of entrance of the power supply to the mobile home in locations other than the rear third of the mobile home. This allows greater flexibility in selecting the location of the power supply entry at the manufacturing level to fit the needs of the installation site, thus minimizing field modifications.

For location of distribution panelboard, see Section 550-4(a).

(j) Protected. Where the cord passes through walls or floors, it shall be protected by means of conduits and bushings or equivalent. The cord shall be permitted to be installed within the mobile home walls, provided a continuous raceway having a maximum size of 1¼ inches (31.8 mm) is installed from the branch-circuit panelboard to the underside of the mobile home floor.

(k) Protection Against Corrosion and Mechanical Damage. Permanent provisions shall be made for the protection of the attachment plug cap of the power-supply cord and any connector cord assembly or receptacle against corrosion and mechanical damage if such devices are in an exterior location while the mobile home is in transit.

(l) Mast Weatherhead or Metal Raceway. Where the calculated load exceeds 50 amperes or where a permanent feeder is used, the supply shall be by means of:

(1) One mast weatherhead installation installed in accordance with Article 230 containing four continuous, insulated, color-coded, feeder conductors, one of which shall be an equipment grounding conductor; or,

(2) A metal raceway from the disconnecting means in the mobile home to the underside of the mobile home with provisions for the attachment to a suitable junction box or fitting to the raceway on the underside of the mobile home [with or without conductors as in Section 550-3(l)(1)].

> In some localities mobile homes are permanently connected, as permitted in Paragraph (l) above. In this regard local requirements must be checked for the approved method of installing overhead and underground feeder assemblies.
>
> A raceway is sometimes stubbed from the distribution panelboard in the mobile home to the underside of the mobile home. Whether the feeder conductors in this raceway are pulled in by the mobile home manufacturer or by installers in the field is optional. No matter who installs the conductors, they should comprise four continuous, insulated, color-coded conductors, as indicated in Section 550-3(l)(1).

550-4. Disconnecting Means and Branch-Circuit Protective Equipment. The branch-circuit equipment shall be permitted to be combined with the disconnecting means as a single assembly. Such a combination shall be permitted to be designated as a distribution panelboard. If a fused distribution panelboard is used, the maximum fuse size for the mains shall be plainly marked, with lettering at least ¼ inch (6.4 mm) high and visible when fuses are changed.

When plug fuses and fuseholders are used, they shall be tamper-resistant, Type S enclosed in dead-front fuse panelboards. Electrical distribution panelboards containing circuit breakers shall also be dead-front type.

See Section 110-22 concerning identification of each disconnecting means and each service, feeder, or branch circuit at the point where it originated and the type marking needed.

(a) **Disconnecting Means.** A single disconnecting means shall be provided in each mobile home consisting of a circuit breaker, or a switch and fuses and its accessories installed in a readily accessible location near the point of entrance of the supply cord or conductors into the mobile home. The main circuit breakers or fuses shall be plainly marked "Main." This equipment shall contain a solderless type of grounding connector or bar for the purposes of grounding with sufficient terminals for all grounding conductors. The neutral bar termination of the grounded circuit conductors shall be insulated. The disconnecting equipment shall have a rating suitable for the connected load. The distribution equipment, either circuit breaker or fused type, shall be located a minimum of 24 inches (610 mm) from the bottom of such equipment to the floor level of the mobile home.

See Section 550-13(b) for information on disconnecting means for branch circuits designed to energize heating and/or air-conditioning equipment located outside the mobile home, other than room air conditioners.

A distribution panelboard main circuit breaker shall be rated 50 amperes and employ a 2-pole circuit breaker rated 40 amperes for a 40-ampere supply cord, or 50 amperes for a 50-ampere supply cord. A distribution panelboard employing a disconnect switch and fuses shall be rated 60 amperes and shall employ a single 2-pole, 60-ampere fuseholder with 40- or 50-ampere main fuses for 40- or 50-ampere supply cords, respectively. The outside of the distribution panelboard shall be plainly marked with the fuse size.

The distribution panelboard shall be located in an accessible location, shall not be located in a bathroom, and shall be permitted to be located just inside a closet entry if the location is such that a clear space of 6 inches (152 mm) to easily ignitible materials is maintained in front of the distribution panelboard, and the distribution panelboard door can be extended to its full open position (at least 90 degrees). A clear working space at least 30 inches (762 mm) wide and 30 inches (762 mm) in front of the distribution panelboard shall be provided. This space shall extend from floor to the top of the distribution panelboard.

(b) **Branch-Circuit Protective Equipment.** Branch-circuit distribution equipment shall be installed in each mobile home and shall include overcurrent protection for each branch circuit consisting of either circuit breakers or fuses.

The branch-circuit overcurrent devices shall be rated: (1) not more than the circuit conductors; and (2) not more than 150 percent of the rating of a single appliance rated 13.3 amperes or more which is supplied by an individual branch circuit; but (3) not more than the fuse size marked on the air conditioner or other motor-operated appliance.

A 15-ampere multiple receptacle shall be acceptable when connected to a 20-ampere laundry circuit.

(c) **Two-Pole Circuit Breakers.** When circuit breakers are provided for branch-circuit protection, 230-volt circuits shall be protected by a 2-pole common or companion trip, or handle-tied paired circuit breakers.

(d) **Electrical Nameplates.** A metal nameplate on the outside adjacent to the feeder assembly entrance shall read: "This Connection for 120/240-Volt, 3-Pole, 4-Wire, 60 Hertz, . . . Ampere Supply." The correct ampere rating shall be marked in the blank space.

550-5. Branch Circuits. The number of branch circuits required shall be determined in accordance with (a) through (c) below.

(a) **Lighting.** Based on 3 watts per square foot (0.093 sq m) times outside dimensions of the mobile home (coupler excluded) divided by 115 volts to determine the number of 15- or 20-ampere lighting area circuits, e.g.,

$$\frac{3 \times \text{Length} \times \text{Width}}{115 \times 15 \text{ (or 20)}} = \text{No. of 15- (or 20-) ampere circuits.}$$

The lighting circuits shall be permitted to serve built-in gas ovens with electric service only for lights, clocks or timers, or listed cord-connected garbage disposal units.

(b) Small Appliances.   For the small appliance load in kitchen, pantry, family room, dining room, and breakfast rooms of mobile homes, two or more 20-ampere appliance branch circuits in addition to the branch circuits specified in Section 550-5(a) shall be provided for all receptacle outlets in these rooms, and such circuits shall have no other outlets. Receptacle outlets supplied by at least two appliance receptacle branch circuits shall be installed in the kitchen.

(c) General Appliances.   (Including furnace, water heater, range, and central or room air conditioner, etc.) There shall be one or more circuits of adequate rating in accordance with the following:

(1) Ampere rating of fixed appliances not over 50 percent of circuit rating if lighting outlets (receptacles, other than kitchen, dining area, and laundry, considered as lighting outlets) are on the same circuit;

(2) For fixed appliances on a circuit without lighting outlets, the sum of rated amperes shall not exceed the branch-circuit rating. Motor loads or other continuous duty loads shall not exceed 80 percent of the branch-circuit rating;

(3) The rating of a single cord- and plug-connected appliance on a circuit having no other outlets shall not exceed 80 percent of the circuit rating;

(4) The rating of a range branch circuit shall be based on the range demand as specified for ranges in Section 550-11(b)(5).

For the laundry branch circuit, see Section 220-3(c).

For central air conditioning, see Article 440.

550-6. Receptacle Outlets.

(a) Grounding-type Receptacle Outlets.   All receptacle outlets: (1) shall be of grounding type; (2) shall be installed according to Section 210-7; and (3) except when supplying specific appliances, receptacles shall be parallel-blade, 15-ampere, 125-volt, either single or duplex.

(b) Ground-Fault Circuit-Interrupters.   All 120-volt, single-phase, 15- and 20-ampere receptacle outlets installed outdoors and in bathrooms, including receptacles in light fixtures, shall have ground-fault circuit protection for personnel. Ground-fault circuit protection for personnel shall be provided for receptacle outlets located adjacent to any lavatory. Feeders supplying branch circuits shall be permitted to be protected by a ground-fault circuit-interrupter in lieu of the provision for such interrupters specified herein.
No receptacle shall be required in the area occupied by a toilet, toilet and/or shower, or toilet and tub/shower enclosure area. If a receptacle is installed in such an area, it shall have ground-fault circuit protection for personnel.

(c) Cord-Connected Fixed Appliance.   There shall be an individual outlet of the grounding type for each cord-connected fixed appliance installed.

(d) Required Receptacle Outlets.   Receptacle outlets required in all rooms other than the bath, closet, and hall areas shall be installed so that no point along the floor line is more than 6 feet (1.83 m) measured horizontally from an outlet in that space. Countertops shall have receptacles located every 6 feet (1.83 m). The contiguous measurement of countertop and floor line shall be permitted when measured from the required receptacle in rooms requiring small appliance circuits. Receptacle outlets on small appliance circuits shall not be included in determining the spacing for receptacle outlets of other circuits.

Exception No. 1: Where the measured distance is interrupted by an interior doorway, sink, refrigerator, range, oven, or cooktop, an additional receptacle outlet shall be provided when the interrupted space is at least 2 feet (610 mm) wide at the floor line and at least 12 inches (305 mm) wide at the countertop.

Exception No. 2: Receptacles concealed by stationary appliances shall not be considered as the required outlets.

Exception No. 3: The distance along a floor line occupied by a door opened fully against that space need not be included in establishing the horizontal measurement if the door swing is limited to 90 degrees nominal by that wall space.

Exception No. 4: Receptacle requirements for bar-type counters and for fixed room dividers no more than 8 feet (2.44 m) in length shall be permitted to be provided by a receptacle outlet in the wall at the nearest point where the counter or room divider attaches to the wall.

To qualify as a "fixed room divider" the divider cannot be more than 8 feet (2.44 m) in length nor more than 4 feet (1.22 m) in height and may be attached to a wall at one end only.

(e) Outdoor Receptacle Outlets. At least one receptacle outlet shall be installed outdoors. A receptacle outlet located in a compartment accessible from the outside of the mobile home shall be considered an outdoor receptacle. Outdoor receptacle outlets shall be protected as required in Section 550-6(b).

(f) Receptacle Outlets Not Permitted. Receptacle outlets shall not be installed in or within reach [30 inches (762 mm)] of a shower or bathtub space.

(g) Heat Tape Outlet. A heat tape outlet, if installed, and if located on the underside of the mobile home at least 3 feet (914 mm) from the outside edge, shall not be considered an outdoor receptacle outlet. A heat tape outlet, if installed, shall be located within 2 feet (610 mm) of the cold water inlet.

550-7. Fixtures and Appliances.

(a) Fasten Appliances in Transit. Facilities shall be provided to securely fasten appliances when the mobile home is in transit. (See Section 550-9 for provisions on grounding.)

(1) Specifically approved pendant-type fixtures or pendant cords shall be permitted in mobile homes.

(2) Where a lighting fixture is installed over a bathtub or in a shower stall, it shall be of the enclosed and gasketed type approved for wet locations.

(3) The switch for shower lighting fixtures and exhaust fans located over a tub or in a shower stall shall be located outside the tub or shower space.

(b) Accessibility. Every appliance shall be accessible for inspection, service, repair, or replacement without removal of permanent construction.

550-8. Wiring Methods and Materials. Except as specifically limited in this section, the wiring methods and materials included in this Code shall be used in mobile homes.

(a) **Nonmetallic Outlet Boxes.**   Nonmetallic outlet boxes shall be acceptable only with nonmetallic cable.

(b) **Nonmetallic Cable Protection.**   Nonmetallic cable located 15 inches (381 mm) or less above the floor, if exposed, shall be protected from physical damage by covering boards, guard strips, or conduit. Cable likely to be damaged by stowage shall be so protected in all cases.

(c) **Metal-Clad and Nonmetallic Cable Protection.**   Metal-clad and nonmetallic cables shall be permitted to pass through the centers of the wide side of 2-inch by 4-inch studs. However, they shall be protected where they pass through 2-inch by 2-inch studs or at other studs or frames where the cable or armor would be less than 1½ inches (38 mm) from the inside or outside surface of the studs where the wall covering materials are in contact with the studs. Steel plates on each side of the cable, or a tube, with not less than No. 16 MSG wall thickness shall be required to protect the cable. These plates or tubes shall be securely held in place.

(d) **Metallic Faceplates.**   Where metallic faceplates are used, they shall be effectively grounded.

(e) **Installation Requirements.**   If the range, clothes dryer, or similar appliance is connected by metal-clad cable or flexible metal conduit, a length of free cable or conduit should be provided to permit moving the appliance. The cable or flexible metal conduit should be adequately secured to the wall. If the range, clothes dryer, or similar appliance is connected by metal-clad cable or flexible metal conduit, a length of not less than 3 feet (914 mm) of free cable or conduit shall be provided to permit moving the appliance. Type NM or Type SE cable shall not be used to connect a range or dryer. This shall not prohibit the use of Type NM or Type SE cable between the branch-circuit overcurrent protective device and a junction box or range or dryer receptacle.

This does not prohibit the use of Type NM cable between the branch-circuit overcurrent protective device and a range or dryer receptacle.

(f) **Metal Conduit.**   Threaded rigid metal conduit and intermediate metal conduit shall be provided with a locknut inside and outside the box, and a conduit bushing shall be used on the inside. Rigid nonmetallic conduit shall be permitted. Inside ends of the conduit shall be reamed.

(g) **Switches.**   Switches shall be rated as follows:

(1) For lighting circuits, switches shall have a 10-ampere, 120- 125-volt rating, or higher, if needed for the connected load.

(2) For motors or other loads, switches shall have ampere or horsepower ratings, or both, adequate for loads controlled. (An "ac general-use" snap switch shall be permitted to control a motor 2 horsepower or less with full-load current not over 80 percent of the switch ampere rating.)

(h) **Free Conductor at Each Outlet Box.**   At least 4 inches (102 mm) of free conductor shall be left at each outlet box except where conductors are intended to loop without joints.

(i) **Under-Chassis Wiring.**   (Exposed to weather.)

(1) Where outdoor or under-chassis line-voltage wiring is exposed to moisture or physical damage, it shall be protected by rigid metal conduit or intermediate metal conduit. The conductors shall be suitable for wet locations.

Exception: Electrical metallic tubing shall be permitted where closely routed against frames and equipment enclosures.

(2) The cables or conductors shall be Type NMC, TW, or equivalent.

(j) Boxes, Fittings, and Cabinets.   Boxes, fittings, and cabinets shall be securely fastened in place and shall be supported from a structural member of the home, either directly or by using a substantial brace.

Exception: Snap-in type boxes. Boxes provided with special wall or ceiling brackets and wiring devices with integral enclosures, which securely fasten to walls or ceilings and are identified for the use, shall be permitted without support from a structural member or brace. The testing and approval shall include the wall and ceiling construction systems for which the boxes and devices are intended to be used.

(k) Appliance Terminal Connections.   Appliances having branch-circuit terminal connections which operate at temperatures higher than 60°C (140°F) shall have circuit conductors as described in (1) or (2) below.

(1) Branch-circuit conductors having an insulation suitable for the temperature encountered shall be permitted to be run directly to the appliance.

(2) Conductors having an insulation suitable for the temperature encountered shall be run from the appliance terminal connection to a readily accessible outlet box placed at least 1 foot (305 mm) from the appliance. These conductors shall be in a suitable raceway which shall extend for at least 4 feet (1.22 m).

(l) Component Interconnections.   Fittings and connectors which are intended to be concealed at the time of assembly, when tested and approved to applicable standards, shall be permitted for the interconnection of building components. Such fittings and connectors shall be equal to the wiring method employed in insulation, temperature rise, fault-current withstanding, and shall be capable of enduring the vibration and shock occurring in mobile home transportation.

550-9. Grounding.   Grounding of both electrical and nonelectrical metal parts in a mobile home shall be through connection to a grounding bus in the mobile home distribution panelboard. The grounding bus shall be grounded through the green-colored insulated conductor in the supply cord or the feeder wiring to the service ground in the service-entrance equipment located adjacent to the mobile home location. Neither the frame of the mobile home nor the frame of any appliance shall be connected to the neutral conductor in the mobile home.

(a) Insulated Neutral.

(1) The grounded circuit conductor (neutral) shall be insulated from the grounding conductors and from equipment enclosures and other grounded parts. The grounded (neutral) circuit terminals in the distribution panelboard and in ranges, clothes dryers, counter-mounted cooking units, and wall-mounted ovens shall be insulated from the equipment enclosure. Bonding screws, straps, or buses in the distribution panelboard or in appliances shall be removed and discarded.

(2) Connections of ranges and clothes dryers with 115/230-volt, 3-wire ratings shall be made with 4-conductor cord and 3-pole, 4-wire, grounding-type plugs, or by Type AC cable or conductors enclosed in flexible metal conduit.

For 115-volt rated devices, a 3-conductor cord and a 2-pole, 3-wire, grounding-type plug shall be permitted.

(b) Equipment Grounding Means.

(1) The green-colored insulated grounding wire in the supply cord or permanent feeder wiring shall be connected to the grounding bus in the distribution panelboard or disconnecting means.

(2) In the electrical system, all exposed metal parts, enclosures, frames, lamp fixture canopies, etc., shall be effectively bonded to the grounding terminal or enclosure of the distribution panelboard.

(3) Cord-connected appliances, such as washing machines, clothes dryers, refrigerators, and the electrical system of gas ranges, etc., shall be grounded by means of a cord with grounding conductor and grounding-type attachment plug.

(c) Bonding of Noncurrent-Carrying Metal Parts.

(1) All exposed noncurrent-carrying metal parts that may become energized shall be effectively bonded to the grounding terminal or enclosure of the distribution panelboard. A bonding conductor shall be connected between the distribution panelboard and accessible terminal on the chassis.

(2) Grounding terminals shall be of the solderless type and approved as pressure-terminal connectors recognized for the wire size used. The bonding conductor shall be solid or stranded, insulated or bare, and shall be No. 8 copper minimum, or equal. The bonding conductor shall be routed so as not to be exposed to physical damage.

(3) Metallic gas, water, and waste pipes and metallic air-circulating ducts shall be considered bonded if they are connected to the terminal on the chassis [see Section 550-9(c)(1)] by clamps, solderless connectors, or by suitable grounding-type straps.

(4) Any metallic roof and exterior covering shall be considered bonded if (a) the metal panels overlap one another and are securely attached to the wood or metal frame parts by metallic fasteners, and (b) if the lower panel of the metallic exterior covering is secured by metallic fasteners at a cross member of the chassis by two metal straps per mobile home unit or section at opposite ends.

The bonding strap material shall be a minimum of 4 inches (102 mm) in width of material equivalent to the skin or a material of equal or better electrical conductivity. The straps shall be fastened with paint-penetrating fittings, such as screws and starwashers or equivalent.

The provisions of Section 550-3 require that the feeder assembly for a mobile home consist of four color-coded insulated conductors, one of which is the grounded conductor (white) and one of which is used for grounding purposes (green). Thus, the "grounded" and "grounding" conductors are kept independent of each other and are connected only at the service equipment (at the point of connection of the grounding electrode conductor). Grounding of both electrical and nonelectrical metal parts, including the frame of the mobile home or the frame of any appliance, is by connection to the "grounding" bus (never to the neutral bus).

Bonding screws, straps, or buses in the mobile home panelboard or in appliances (ranges, clothes dryers, etc.) are to be removed and discarded.

550-10. Testing.

(a) Dielectric Strength Test. The wiring of each mobile home shall be subjected to a 1-minute, 900-volt, dielectric strength test (with all switches closed) between live parts (including neutral) and the mobile home ground. Alternatively, the test shall be permitted to be performed at 1,080 volts for 1 second. This test shall be performed after branch circuits are complete and after fixtures or appliances are installed.

Exception: Fixtures or appliances which are approved shall not be required to withstand the dielectric strength test.

(b) Continuity and Operational Tests and Polarity Checks. Each mobile home shall be subjected to:

(1) An electrical continuity test to assure that metallic parts are properly bonded;

(2) An electrical operational test to demonstrate that all equipment, except water heaters and electric furnaces, is connected and in working order; and

(3) Electrical polarity checks to determine that connections have been properly made.

550-11. Calculations. The following method shall be employed in computing the supply-cord and distribution-panelboard load for each feeder assembly for each mobile home in lieu of the procedure shown in Article 220 and shall be based on a 3-wire, 115/230-volt supply with 115-volt loads balanced between the two legs of the 3-wire system.

(a) Lighting and Small Appliance Load:

Lighting Watts: Length times width of mobile home (outside dimensions, exclusive of coupler) times 3 watts per square foot; e.g.,
Length × width × 3 =..................lighting watts.

Small Appliance Watts: Number of circuits times 1,500 watts for each 20-ampere appliance receptacle circuit (see definition of Appliance, Portable with note) including 1,500 watts for laundry circuit; e.g.,
Number of circuits × 1,500 =..................small appliance watts.

Total: Lighting watts plus small appliance =..................total watts.

First 3,000 total watts at 100 percent plus remainder at 35 percent =..................watts to be divided by 230 volts to obtain current (amperes) per leg.

(b) Total Load for Determining Power Supply. Total load for determining power supply is the summation of:

(1) Lighting and small appliance load as calculated in Section 550-11(a).

(2) Nameplate amperes for motors and heater loads (exhaust fans, air conditioners, electric, gas, or oil heating).
Omit smaller of the heating and cooling loads, except include blower motor if used as air-conditioner evaporator motor. Where an air conditioner is not installed and a 40-ampere power supply cord is provided, allow 15 amperes per leg for air conditioning.

(3) 25 percent of current of largest motor in (2).

(4) Total of nameplate amperes for: disposal, dishwasher, water heater, clothes dryer, wall-mounted oven, cooking units.
Where number of these appliances exceeds three, use 75 percent of total.

(5) Derive amperes for free-standing range (as distinguished from separate ovens and cooking units) by dividing values below by 230 volts.

Nameplate Rating	Use
10,000 watts or less	80 percent of rating
10,001-12,500 watts	8,000 watts
12,501-13,500 watts	8,400 watts
13,501-14,500 watts	8,800 watts
14,501-15,500 watts	9,200 watts
15,501-16,500 watts	9,600 watts
16,501-17,500 watts	10,000 watts

(6) If outlets or circuits are provided for other than factory-installed appliances, include the anticipated load.

See following Example for illustration of application of this calculation.

Example

A mobile home is 70 feet × 10 feet and has two portable appliance circuits, a 1000 watt 230 volt heater, a 200 watt 115 volt exhaust fan, a 400 watt 115 volt dishwasher, and a 7000 watt electric range.

Lighting and small appliance load

Lighting 70 × 10 × 3 wts/sq ft =	2100 watts
Small appliance 1500 × 2 =	3000 watts
Laundry 1500 × 1 =	1500 watts
	6600 watts

1st 3000 watts at 100 percent 3000
Remainder (6600 — 3000 = 3600) at 35 percent 1260
                                                                                                                4260

			Amperes per leg	
			A	**B**
$\frac{4260}{230}$ = 18.5 amperes per leg		Lighting and appliances	18.5	18.5
1000 watt heater ÷ 230 =	4.4 amp	Heater (230 volt)	4	4
200 watt (fan) ÷ 115 =	1.7 amp	Fan (115 volt)	2	—
400 watt (dishwasher) ÷ 115 =	3.5 amp	Dishwasher (115 volt)	—	4
7000 watt (range) × .8 ÷ 230 =	24. amp	Range	24	24
		Totals	48.5	50.5

Based on the higher current calculated for either leg, use one 50-ampere supply cord.

(c) Optional Method of Calculation for Lighting and Appliance Load. For mobile homes, the optional method for calculating lighting and appliance load shown in Section 220-30 and Table 220-30 shall be permitted.

550-12. Wiring of Expandable Units and Dual Units.

(a) Fixed-type Wiring. Expandable or dual-unit mobile homes shall use fixed-type wiring methods and materials for connecting such units to each other.

(b) Disconnecting Means. Expandable or dual-unit mobile homes not having permanently installed feeders, and which are to be moved from one location to another, shall be permitted to have disconnecting means with branch-circuit protective equipment in each unit when so located that after assembly or joining together of units, they shall not be interconnected on either the line side or the load side, except that the grounding means shall be electrically interconnected.

550-13. Outdoor Outlets, Fixtures, Air-Cooling Equipment, Etc.

(a) Approved for Outdoor Use. Outdoor fixtures and equipment shall be approved for outdoor use. Outdoor receptacle or convenience outlets shall be of a gasketed-cover type for use in wet locations.

(b) Outside Heating and/or Air-Conditioning Equipment. A mobile home provided with a branch circuit designed to energize heating and/or air-conditioning equipment located outside the mobile home, other than room air conditioners, shall have such branch-circuit conductors terminate in a listed outlet box, or disconnecting means, located on the outside of the mobile home. A label shall be permanently affixed adjacent to the outlet box and contain the following information:

> This connection is for heating and/or air-conditioning equipment. The branch circuit is rated at not more than _____ amperes, at _____ volts, 60-Hertz, _____ conductor ampacity. A disconnecting means shall be located within sight of the equipment.

The correct voltage and ampere rating shall be given. The tag shall be not less than 0.020 inch (508 micrometers), etched brass, stainless steel, anodized or alclad aluminum or equivalent. The tag shall not be less than 3 inches (76 mm) by 1¾ inches (44.5 mm) minimum size.

B. Mobile Home Parks

550-21. Distribution System. The mobile home park secondary electrical distribution system to mobile home lots shall be single-phase, 115/230 volts, nominal. For the purpose of Part B, where the park service exceeds 240 volts, nominal, transformers and secondary distribution panelboards shall be treated as services.

See Table 550-22 for calculation of load.

Section 550-1(d) applies to mobile homes intended for connection to a wiring system nominally rated 115/230-V, 3-wire ac, with a grounded neutral; therefore, distribution systems at mobile home parks must supply 115/230 V to the mobile home lot. Because appliances and other equipment are usually installed during the manufacturing process of mobile homes and are rated 115/230 V, a 120/208-V supply derived from a 4-wire, 120/208-V wye system is unsuitable.

Section 550-22(a) requires park electrical wiring systems to be calculated on the basis of not less than 16,000 W (at 115/230 V) for each mobile home service; however, the ampacity of the feeder circuit conductors to each mobile home lot is not to be less than 100 A (at 115/230 V) according to Section 550-22(c).

550-22. Calculated Load.

(a) Minimum Allowable Demand Factors. Park electrical wiring systems shall be calculated on the basis of not less than 16,000 watts (at 115/230 volts) per each mobile home service. The demand factors which are set forth in Table 550-22 shall be considered the minimum allowable demand factors which shall be permitted in calculating load on feeders and service. No demand factor shall be allowed for any other load, except as provided in this Code.

Table 550-22
Demand Factors and Watts per Mobile Home Site (Minimum) for Feeders and Service-Entrance Conductors

Number of Mobile Homes	Demand Factor (Percent)	Watts per Mobile Home Site (Min.)
1	100	16,000
2	55	8,800
3	44	7,040
4	39	6,240
5	33	5,280
6	29	4,640
7-9	28	4,480
10-12	27	4,320
13-15	26	4,160
16-21	25	4,000
22-40	24	3,840
41-60	23	3,680
61 and over	22	3,520

(b) Demand Factor Shall Apply to All Lots. The demand factor for a given number of lots shall apply to all lots indicated.

Example: 20 lots calculated at 25 percent of 16,000 watts result in a permissible demand of 4,000 watts per lot or a total of 80,000 watts for 20 lots.

(c) Adequate Feeder Capacity. Mobile home lot feeder circuit conductors shall have adequate capacity for the loads supplied, and shall be rated at not less than 100 amperes at 115/230 volts.

See comments following Section 550-21.

550-23. Mobile Home Service Equipment.

(a) Rating. Mobile home service equipment shall be rated at not less than 100 amperes, and provision shall be made for connecting a mobile home feeder assembly by a permanent wiring method. Power outlets used as mobile home service equipment shall also be permitted to contain receptacles rated up to 50 amperes with appropriate overcurrent protection. Fifty-ampere receptacles shall conform to the configuration shown in Figure 550-3(f).

Complete details on the 50-ampere attachment plug cap configuration can be found in American National Standard Dimensions of Caps, Plugs and Receptacles, ANSI C73.17-1972.

(b) Additional Outside Electrical Equipment. Mobile home service equipment shall also contain a means for connecting a mobile home accessory building or structure or additional electrical equipment located outside a mobile home by a fixed wiring method.

(c) Additional Receptacles. Additional receptacles shall be permitted for connection of electrical equipment located outside the mobile home, and all such 120-volt, single-phase, 15- and 20-ampere receptacles shall be protected by approved ground-fault circuit protection for personnel.

(d) Location. Mobile home service equipment shall be located not more than 30 feet (9.14 m) from the point of attachment of the feeder assembly to the mobile home it serves.

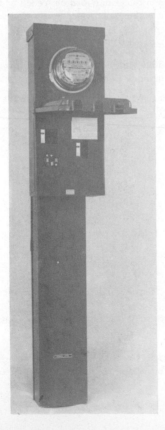

Figure 550-1. Mobile home service equipment and power outlet assembly showing metering, disconnecting means, overcurrent protective devices, and receptacle. (*Midwest*)

This section has been revised for the 1981 *Code* to specify that the mobile home service equipment is to be located not more than 30 ft from the point of attachment of the feeder assembly to the mobile home rather than from the point of entry into the mobile home. This revision recognizes use of feeder raceways external to the mobile home.

(e) Grounded.   Each mobile home service equipment shall be grounded in accordance with Article 250 for service equipment.

ARTICLE 551 — RECREATIONAL VEHICLES
AND RECREATIONAL VEHICLE PARKS

Contents

(b) Mechanical Protection.

551-52. Receptacles.

(a) 50-Ampere.

(b) 30-Ampere.

(c) 20-Ampere.

A. Recreational Vehicles

551-1. Scope.

(a) Covered. The provisions of Part A cover the electrical conductors and equipment installed within or on recreational vehicles and also the conductors that connect them to a supply of electricity. Wherever the requirements of other articles of this Code and Article 551 differ, the requirements of Article 551 shall apply.

For requirements on the installation of plumbing and heating systems in recreational vehicles, refer to Standard for Recreational Vehicles, NFPA 501C-1977 (ANSI).

(b) Not Covered. A recreational vehicle not used for the purposes as defined in Section 551-2 shall not be required to meet the provisions of Part A pertaining to the number or capacity of circuits required. It shall, however, meet all other applicable requirements of this article if the recreational vehicle is provided with an electrical installation intended to be energized from a 115- or 115/230-volt, nominal, ac power-supply system.

(c) Systems. Part A covers battery and direct-current power (12-volt or less) systems, combination electrical systems, generator installations, and 115- or 115/230-volt, nominal, systems.

Laws in some states require factory inspection performed by state inspectors. The requirements of such laws follow closely NFPA 501C, Standard for Recreational Vehicles, which contains electrical requirements identical to those in Article 551, Part A.

551-2. Definitions. (See Article 100 for other definitions.)

Air-Conditioning or Comfort-Cooling Equipment. All of that equipment intended or installed for the purpose of processing the treatment of air so as to control simultaneously its temperature, humidity, cleanliness, and distribution to meet the requirements of the conditioned space.

Appliance, Fixed. An appliance which is fastened or otherwise secured at a specific location.

Appliance, Portable. An appliance which is actually moved or can easily be moved from one place to another in normal use.

For the purpose of this article, the following major appliances other than built-in are considered portable if cord-connected: refrigerators, gas range equipment, clothes washers, dishwashers without booster heaters, or other similar appliances.

Appliance, Stationary. An appliance which is not easily moved from one place to another in normal use.

Camping Trailer. A vehicular portable unit mounted on wheels and constructed with collapsible partial side walls which fold for towing by another vehicle and unfold at the campsite to provide temporary living quarters for recreational, camping, or travel use. (See "Recreational Vehicle.")

Converter.   A device which changes electrical energy from one form to another, as from alternating current to direct current.

Dead Front.   (As applied to switches, circuit breakers, switchboards, and distribution panelboards.) So designed, constructed, and installed that no current-carrying parts are normally exposed on the front.

Disconnecting Means.   The necessary equipment usually consisting of a circuit breaker or switch and fuses, and their accessories, located near the point of entrance of supply conductors in a recreational vehicle and intended to constitute the means of cutoff for the supply to that recreational vehicle.

Receptacles used as disconnecting means shall be accessible (as applied to wiring methods) and capable of interrupting their rated current without hazard to the operator.

Distribution Panelboard.   A single panel or group of panel units designed for assembly in the form of a single panel; including buses, and with or without switches and/or automatic overcurrent protective devices for the control of light, heat, or power circuits of small individual as well as aggregate capacity; designed to be placed in a cabinet or cutout box placed in or against a wall or partition and accessible only from the front.

Low-Voltage.   An electromotive force rated nominal 24 volts, nominal, or less, supplied from a transformer, converter, or battery.

Motor Home.   A vehicular unit designed to provide temporary living quarters for recreational, camping, or travel use built on or permanently attached to a self-propelled motor vehicle chassis or on a chassis cab or van which is an integral part of the completed vehicle. (See "Recreational Vehicle.")

Power-Supply Assembly.   The conductors, including the grounding conductors, insulated from one another, the connectors, attachment plug caps, and all other fittings, grommets, or devices installed for the purpose of delivering energy from the source of electrical supply to the distribution panel within the recreational vehicle.

Recreational Vehicle.   A vehicular-type unit primarily designed as temporary living quarters for recreational, camping, or travel use, which either has its own motive power or is mounted on or drawn by another vehicle. The basic entities are: travel trailer, camping trailer, truck camper, and motor home.

Transformer.   A device, which when used, will raise or lower the voltage of alternating current of the original source.

Travel Trailer.   A vehicular unit mounted on wheels, designed to provide temporary living quarters for recreational, camping, or travel use, of such size or weight as not to require special highway movement permits when drawn by a motorized vehicle, and with a living area of less than 220 square feet (20.44 sq m), excluding built-in equipment (such as wardrobes, closets, cabinets, kitchen units or fixtures) and bath and toilet rooms. (See "Recreational Vehicle.")

Truck Camper.   A portable unit constructed to provide temporary living quarters for recreational, travel, or camping use, consisting of a roof, floor, and sides, designed to be loaded onto and unloaded from the bed of a pick-up truck. (See "Recreational Vehicle.")

551-3. Low-Voltage Systems.

(a) **Low-Voltage Circuits.**   Low-voltage circuits furnished and installed by the recreational vehicle manufacturer, other than those related to braking, are subject to this Code. Circuits supplying lights subject to federal or state regulations shall be in accordance with applicable government regulations, but shall not be lower than provided by this Code.

(b) Low-Voltage Wiring.

(1) Copper conductors shall be used for low-voltage circuits.

(2) Conductors shall conform to the requirements for Type HDT, SGT, or SGR, or Type SXL, or shall have insulation rated at least 60°C and a minimum wall thickness of 30 mils of thermoplastic insulation or equal.

See SAE Standard J1128 for Types HDT and SXL, and SAE Standard J1127 for Types SGT and SGR in the 1977 SAE Handbook.

(3) Single-wire, low-voltage conductors shall be of the stranded type.

(4) All insulated low-voltage conductors shall be surface marked at intervals no greater than 4 feet (1.22 m) as follows:

a. Listed conductors shall be marked as required by the listing agency.

b. SAE conductors shall be marked with the name or logo of the manufacturer, specification designation, and wire gage.

c. Other conductors shall be marked with the name or logo of the manufacturer, temperature rating, wire gage, conductor material, and insulation thickness.

Exception: Metal chassis or frame shall be permitted as the return path for exterior lighting. Terminals for connection to the chassis or frame shall be of the solderless type and approved for the size and type wire used. Mechanical connections to the frame or chassis shall be made secure.

(c) Low-Voltage Wiring Methods.

(1) Conductors shall be protected against physical damage and shall be secured. Where insulated conductors are clamped to the structure, the conductor insulation shall be supplemented by an additional wrap or layer of equivalent material, except that jacketed cables need not be so protected. Wiring shall be routed away from sharp edges, moving parts, or heat sources.

(2) Conductors shall be spliced or joined with approved splicing devices or by brazing, welding, or soldering with a fusible metal or alloy. Soldered splices shall first be so spliced or joined as to be mechanically and electrically secure without solder and then soldered. All splices, joints, and free ends of conductors shall be covered with an insulation equivalent to that on the conductors.

(3) Battery and direct-current circuits shall be physically separated by at least a ½-inch (12.7-mm) gap or other approved means from circuits of a different power source. Acceptable methods shall be by clamping, routing, or equivalent means which ensure permanent total separation. Where circuits of different power sources cross, the external jacket of the nonmetallic-sheathed cables shall be deemed adequate separation.

(4) Ground terminals shall be accessible for service. The surface on which ground terminals make contact shall be cleaned and free from oxide or paint, or shall be electrically connected through use of a cadmium, tin, or zinc plated external toothed lockwasher or lockring terminals. Ground terminal attaching screws, rivets or bolts, nuts and lockwashers shall be cadmium, tin or zinc plated, except rivets shall be permitted to be unanodized aluminum when attaching to aluminum structures.

(5) The chassis-grounding terminal of the battery shall be bonded to the vehicle chassis with a No. 8 AWG copper conductor minimum or equivalent.

Subsection 551-3(c)(5) is new in the 1981 *Code*. It has been added to require one terminal of the battery to be bonded to the vehicle chassis with a No. 8 AWG copper conductor minimum or equivalent. This will minimize the possibility of low-voltage circuit fault current paths through the ac panelboard bonding conductor and the grounding conductor of the combination ac/dc appliance and then through the negative dc conductor feeding the appliance which may be also bonded to the external metal cover of the appliance. The ac grounding conductor of the appliance may not have sufficient ampacity to safely conduct the dc fault current. This will necessitate installation of the battery bonding conductor, although in some present constructions one side of the battery circuit is already bonded to the frame by a No. 8 AWG copper or larger conductor.

(d) Battery Installations.   Storage batteries subject to the provisions of this Code shall be securely attached to the vehicle and installed in an area vaportight to the interior and ventilated directly to the exterior of the vehicle. When batteries are installed in a compartment, the compartment shall be ventilated with openings having a minimum area of 1.7 square inches (1.1 sq mm) at both the top and at the bottom. Batteries shall not be installed in a compartment containing spark or flame producing equipment except that they shall be permitted to be installed in the engine generator compartment if the only charging source is from the engine generator.

(e) Overcurrent Protection.

(1) Low-voltage circuit wiring shall be protected by overcurrent protective devices rated not in excess of the ampacity of copper conductors, as follows:

Wire Size	Ampacity	Wire Type
18	6	Stranded only
16	8	Stranded only
14	15	Stranded or Solid
12	20	Stranded or Solid
10	30	Stranded or Solid

(2) Circuit breakers or fuses shall be of an approved type, including automotive types. Fuseholders shall be clearly marked with maximum fuse size and shall be protected against shorting and physical damage by a cover or equivalent means.

The requirement for protection by a cover or equivalent means is new in the 1981 *Code* and is intended to reduce the possibility of the low-voltage system shorting to ground.

For further information, see Society of Automotive Engineers (SAE) Standard J554-1973, and Standard for Electric Fuses, ANSI C118.1-1973, and Underwriters Laboratories Inc. Standard for Automotive Glass Tube Fuses, UL 275b-1973.

(3) Higher current-consuming, direct-current appliances such as pumps, compressors, heater blowers, and similar motor-driven appliances shall be installed in accordance with the manufacturer's instructions.

Motors which are controlled by automatic switching or by latching-type manual switches shall be protected in accordance with Section 430-32(c).

(4) The overcurrent protective device shall be installed in an accessible location on the vehicle within 18 inches (457 mm) of the point where the power supply connects to the vehicle circuits. If located outside the recreational vehicle, the device shall be protected against weather and physical damage.

Exception: External low-voltage supply shall be permitted to be fused within 18 inches (457 mm) after entering the vehicle or after leaving a metal raceway.

(f) Switches.   Switches shall have a direct-current rating not less than the connected load.

(g) Lighting Fixtures.   All low-voltage interior lighting fixtures shall be approved.

(h) Cigarette Lighter Receptacles.   Twelve-volt receptacles that will accept and energize cigarette lighters shall be installed in a noncombustible outlet box.

Twelve-V systems for running and signal lights, similar to those in a conventional automobile, are covered in Sections 551-3, 551-4, and 551-5. In many recreational vehicles, 12-V systems are also used for interior lighting and other small loads. The 12-V system is often supplied from an onboard battery or through a transfer switch from a 120/12-V transformer in conjunction with a full-wave rectifier.

551-4. Combination Electrical Systems.

(a) General.   Vehicle wiring suitable for connection to a battery or direct-current supply source shall be permitted to be connected to a 115-volt source provided that the entire wiring system and equipment are rated and installed in full conformity with Part A requirements covering 115-volt electrical systems. Circuits fed from alternating-current transformers shall not supply direct-current appliances.

(b) Voltage Converters (115-Volt Alternating Current to Low-Voltage Direct Current).   The 115-volt alternating current side of the voltage converter shall be wired in full conformity with Part A requirements for 115-volt electrical systems.

Exception: Converters supplied as an integral part of an approved appliance shall not be subject to the above.

All converters and transformers shall be listed for use in recreation vehicles and designed or equipped to provide over-temperature protection. To determine the converter rating the following formula shall be applied to the total connected load, including average battery charging rate, of all 12-volt equipment:
The first 20 amperes of load at 100 percent; plus
The second 20 amperes of load at 50 percent; plus
All load above 40 amperes at 25 percent.

Exception: A low-voltage appliance which is controlled by a momentary switch (normally "open") which has no means for holding in the "closed" position shall not be considered as a "connected load" when determining the required converter rating. Momentarily energized appliances shall be limited to those used to prepare the vehicle for occupancy or travel.

This exception is new in the 1981 *Code.*

(c) Bonding Voltage Converter Enclosures.   The noncurrent-carrying metal enclosure of the voltage converter shall be bonded to the frame of the vehicle with a No. 8 AWG copper conductor minimum or equivalent. The grounding conductor for the battery and the metal enclosure may be the same conductor.

This section is new in the 1981 *Code*. It requires that the metal enclosure of a voltage converter be bonded to the frame of the vehicle by a No. 8 AWG copper conductor minimum or equivalent. The grounding conductor for the battery, required by new Section 551-3(c)(5), and for the metal enclosure may be the same conductor. This is intended to reduce the possibility of damage to the power supply cord by large dc fault currents finding their way back to the vehicle frame or the battery over the ac grounding conductor of the converter. Metal enclosures of UL listed converters are provided with an external pressure terminal connector for this purpose.

(d) Dual-Voltage Fixtures or Appliances.   Fixtures or appliances having both 115-volt and low-voltage connections shall be approved for dual voltage.

In such fixtures, barriers must separate the 115-V and the 12-V wiring connections.

(e) Autotransformers.   Autotransformers shall not be used.

(f) Receptacles and Plug Caps.   Where a recreational vehicle is equipped with a 120-volt or 120/240-volt alternating-current system and/or a low-voltage system, receptacles and plug caps of the low-voltage system shall differ in configuration from those of the 120- or 120/240-volt system. When a vehicle equipped with a battery or direct-current system has an external connection for low-voltage power, the receptacle shall have a configuration that will not accept 120-volt power.

551-5. Generator Installations.

(a) Mounting.   Generators shall be mounted in such a manner as to be effectively bonded to the recreational vehicle chassis.

(b) Generator Protection.   Approved equipment shall be installed to ensure that the current-carrying conductors from the engine generator and from an outside source are not connected to a vehicle circuit at the same time. The generator field shall be protected by appropriately rated, approved equipment.

(c) Installation of Storage Batteries and Generators.   Storage batteries and internal-combustion-driven generator units (subject to the provisions of this Code) shall be secured in place to avoid displacement from vibration and road shock.

(d) Ventilation of Generator Compartments.   Compartments accommodating internal-combustion-driven generator units shall be provided with approved ventilation in accordance with instructions provided by the manufacturer of the generator unit.

(e) Supply Conductors.   The supply conductors from the engine generator shall terminate in (1) a junction box with a blank cover, or (2) a panelboard mounted on the outside of the generator compartment wall.
Supply conductors from the generator(s) to their first termination shall be of the stranded type installed in flexible metal conduit.

551-6. 115- or 115/230-Volt, Nominal, Systems.

(a) General Requirements.   The electrical equipment and material of recreational vehicles indicated for connection to a wiring system rated 115 volts, nominal, 2-wire with ground, or a wiring system rated 115/230 volts, nominal, 3-wire with ground, shall be approved and installed in accordance with the requirements of Part A.

(b) Materials and Equipment. Electrical materials, devices, appliances, fittings, and other equipment installed, intended for use in, or attached to the recreational vehicle shall be listed. All products shall be used only in the manner in which they have been tested and found suitable for the intended use.

551-7. Receptacle Outlets Required.

(a) Spacing. Receptacle outlets shall be installed at wall spaces 2 feet (610 mm) wide or more so that no point along the floor line is more than 6 feet (1.83 m), measured horizontally, from an outlet in that space.

Exception No. 1: Bath and hall areas.

Exception No. 2: Wall spaces occupied by kitchen cabinets, wardrobe cabinets, built-in furniture, behind doors which may open fully against a wall surface, or similar facilities.

(b) Location. Receptacle outlets shall be installed:

(1) Adjacent to counter tops in the kitchen [at least one on each side of the sink if counter tops are on each side and are 12 inches (305 mm) or over in width].

(2) Adjacent to the refrigerator and gas range space, except when a gas-fired refrigerator or cooking appliance, requiring no external electrical connection, is factory-installed.

(3) Adjacent to counter top spaces of 12 inches (305 mm) or more in width which cannot be reached from a receptacle required in Section 551-7(b) (1) by a cord of 6 feet (1.83 m) without crossing a traffic area, cooking appliance, or sink.

(c) Ground-Fault Circuit Protection. Where provided, each 120-volt, single-phase, 15- or 20-ampere receptacle outlet shall have ground-fault circuit protection for personnel in the following locations:

(1) Adjacent to a bathroom lavatory. [The receptacle outlet shall be a minimum of 24 inches (610 mm) from the compartment floor.]

This section has been revised for the 1981 *Code* to reduce the minimum height from 30 inches to 24 inches. This revision permits mounting of a bathroom receptacle in the side of a lavatory cabinet when installation of a receptacle is not possible in a thin wall.

(2) Adjacent to any lavatory.

(3) In the area occupied by a toilet, toilet and/or shower, or toilet and tub-shower enclosure.

(4) On the exterior of the vehicle.

The receptacle outlet shall be permitted in a listed lighting fixture. A receptacle outlet shall not be installed in a tub or combination tub-shower compartment.

(d) Face-Up Position. A receptacle shall not be installed in a face-up position in any counter top or similar horizontal surfaces within the living area.

551-8. Branch Circuits Required. The branch circuits required in a recreational vehicle shall conform to Section 551-19 and be determined in accordance with subparagraphs (a), (b), (c) or (d) below. When provisions are made to facilitate future installations of an electrical appliance, the anticipated load of such appliance shall be counted in the total rating of fixed appliances (e.g., air-conditioning prewiring).

(a) Not More than Eight Outlets. Recreational vehicles with not more than eight lighting and receptacle outlets combined shall have either:

(1) One 15-ampere general-purpose branch circuit to supply these outlets, provided the total rating of fixed appliances connected to this circuit does not exceed 600 watts, or

(2) One 20-ampere general-purpose branch circuit to supply these outlets, provided the total rating of fixed appliances connected to this circuit does not exceed 1,000 watts.

Vehicles wired in accordance with (a)(1) or (a)(2) above shall not be equipped with electrical heating or cooking appliances.

(b) More than Eight Outlets. Recreational vehicles with more than eight lighting and receptacle outlets combined shall have a minimum of two 15- or 20-ampere branch circuits.

(c) Panelboard and Feeder Assembly. Recreational vehicles having a distribution panelboard and a feeder assembly rated not less than 30 amperes shall be permitted to serve two or more 15- or 20-ampere branch circuits.

See Section 210-23(a) for permissible loads.

See Section 551-11(c) for main disconnect and overcurrent protection requirements.

(d) Calculations for Lighting and Appliance Load. When Section 551-8(b) (relative to recreational vehicles with more than eight lighting and receptacle outlets combined) is not applied, the following method shall be employed in computing the power-supply assembly and distribution panelboard load for the recreational vehicle:

A. Lighting. Length times width of vehicle (outside dimensions, exclusive of hitch and cab) times 3 watts per square foot, e.g.,

Length $\times$ width $\times$ 3 = _____ lighting watts.

B. Small Appliance. Number of circuits times 1,500 watts for each 20-ampere appliance receptacle circuit, e.g.,

Number of Circuits $\times$ 1,500 = _____ small appliance watts.

C. Total. Lighting watts plus small appliance watts = _____ total watts.

D. First 3,000 total watts at 100 percent plus remainder at 35 percent = _____ watts to be divided by voltage to obtain current (amperes) per leg.

Amperes per Leg	
A	*B*

Lighting and small appliance current (amperes) per leg
(from D above) =

E. Add nameplate amperes for motors and heater loads (exhaust fans, air conditioners*, electric, gas, or oil heating*) =
    *Omit smaller of these two except include
    any motor common to both functions.

F. Add 25 percent of amperes of largest motor in E = _____

G. Add nameplate amperes for:**   _____
Disposal   ____ ____
Water Heater   ____ ____
Wall-Mounted Ovens   ____ ____
Cooking Units   ____ ____

TOTAL   ____ ____ = _____
**When number of appliances is four or
more, use 75 percent of total.

H. Add amperes for free-standing range as distinguished from separate ovens and cooking units. Derive from following table by dividing watts by 230 volts.

Range	Nameplate Rating (watts)	Use (watts)
(Freestanding range as	10,000 or less	80 percent of rating
distinguished from separate	10,001-12,500	8,000
oven and cooking units)	12,501-13,500	8,400
	13,501-14,500	8,800
	14,501-15,500	9,200
	15,501-16,500	9,600
	16,501-17,500	10,000

	Amperes per Leg
	A *B*

I. If outlets or circuits are provided for other than factory-installed major appliances, the anticipated load shall be added for each.

TOTAL = _____

When the total for Legs A and B are unequal, use the larger to determine the distribution panelboard and supply cord rating. (Service amperes shall not exceed supply cord rating. See Section 551-10.)

551-9. Branch-Circuit Protection.

(a) Rating.   The branch-circuit overcurrent devices shall be rated:

(1) Not more than the circuit conductors; and

(2) Not more than 150 percent of the rating of a single appliance rated 13.3 amperes or more and supplied by an individual branch circuit; but

(3) Not more than the fuse size marked on an air conditioner or other motor-operated appliances.

(b) Protection for Smaller Conductors.   A 20-ampere fuse or circuit breaker shall be considered adequate protection for fixture leads, cords, or small appliances, and No. 14 tap conductors, not over 6 feet (1.83 m) long for recessed lighting fixtures.

(c) 15-Ampere Receptacle Considered Protected by 20 Amperes.   If more than one outlet or load is on a branch circuit, a 15-ampere receptacle shall be considered protected by a 20-ampere fuse or circuit breaker.

551-10. Power-Supply Assembly.

(a) 15-Ampere Main Power-Supply Assembly.   Recreational vehicles wired in accordance with Section 551-8(a)(1) shall use an approved 15-ampere, or larger, main power-supply assembly.

(b) 20-Ampere Main Power-Supply Assembly.   Recreational vehicles wired in accordance with Section 551-8(a)(2) shall use an approved 20-ampere, or larger, main power-supply assembly.

(c) 30-Ampere Main Power-Supply Assembly.   Recreational vehicles wired in accordance with Section 551-8(b) or (c) shall use an approved 30-ampere, or larger, main power-supply assembly.

(d) 40- or 50-Ampere Power-Supply Assembly.   In accordance with Section 551-8(c), any recreational vehicle with a rating in excess of 30 amperes, 115 volts, shall use an approved 40-ampere or 50-ampere, 115/230-volt power-supply assembly.

Exception No. 1: When the calculated load of the recreational vehicle exceeds 30 amperes, 115 volts, a second power-supply cord shall be permitted. Where a two-cord supply system is installed, they shall not be interconnected on either the line side or the load side. The grounding circuits and grounding means shall be electrically interconnected.

Exception No. 2: For a dual-supply source consisting of a generator and a power-supply cord, see Section 551-12.

551-11. Distribution Panelboard.

(a) Listed and Appropriately Rated.   A listed and appropriately rated distribution panelboard or other equipment specifically listed for the purpose shall be used. The distribution panelboard shall be of the insulated neutral type, with the grounding bar attached to the metal frame of the panelboard or other approved grounding means.

(b) Location.   The distribution panelboard shall be installed in a readily accessible location. Working clearance for the panelboard shall be no less than 24 inches (610 mm) wide and 30 inches (762 mm) deep.

Exception: Where the panelboard cover is exposed to the inside aisle space, then one of the working clearance dimensions shall be permitted to be reduced to a minimum of 22 inches (559 mm). A panelboard is considered exposed where the panelboard cover is within 2 inches (50.8 mm) of the aisle's finished surface.

This section has been revised for the 1981 *Code* to indicate working clearances in front of a distribution panelboard. Smaller dimensions than those indicated in Section 110-16 are permitted. While recognizing the limited space in recreational vehicles, this revision maintains a minimum working space needed for proper examination of a live panelboard.

(c) Dead-Front Type.   The distribution panelboard shall be of the dead-front type and shall consist of one or more circuit breakers or Type S fuseholders. A main disconnecting means shall be provided where fuses are used or where more than two circuit breakers are employed. A main overcurrent protective device not exceeding the power-supply assembly rating shall be provided where more than two branch circuits are employed.

551-12. Dual-Supply Source.

(a) Dual-Supply System.   Where a dual-supply system, consisting of a generator and a power-supply cord is installed, the feeder from the generator shall be protected by an overcurrent protective device. Installation shall be in accordance with Section 551-5(a) and (b).

(b) Calculation of Loads. Calculation of loads shall be in accordance with Section 551-8(d).

(c) Two Supply Sources Capacity. The two supply sources shall not be required to be of the same capacity.

(d) AC Generator Exceeding 30 Amperes. If the ac generator source exceeds 30 amperes, 115 volts, nominal, it shall be permissible to wire either as a 115-volt, nominal, system or a 115/230-volt, nominal, system, providing an overcurrent protective device of the proper rating is installed in the feeder.

(e) Power-Supply Assembly Not Less than 30 Amperes. The external power-supply assembly shall be permitted to be less than the calculated load but not less than 30 amperes and shall have overcurrent protection not greater than the capacity of the external power-supply assembly.

551-13. Means for Connecting to Power Supply.

(a) Assembly. The power-supply assembly or assemblies shall be factory-supplied or factory-installed when of the permanently connected type as specified herein:

(1) Separable. Where a separable power-supply assembly consisting of a cord with a female connector and molded attachment plug cap is provided, the vehicle shall be equipped with a permanently mounted, approved flanged surface inlet (male-recessed-type motor-base receptacle) wired directly to the distribution panelboard by an approved wiring method. The attachment plug cap shall be of an approved type.

(2) Permanently Connected. Each power-supply assembly shall be connected directly to the terminals of the distribution panelboard or conductors within an approved junction box and provided with means to prevent strain from being transmitted to the terminals. The ampacity of the conductors between each junction box and the terminals of each distribution panelboard shall be at least equal to the ampacity of the power-supply cord. The supply end of the assembly shall be equipped with an attachment plug of the type described in Section 551-13(c). Where the cord passes through the walls or floors, it shall be protected by means of conduit and bushings or equivalent.

(b) Cord. The cord exposed usable length shall be measured from the point of entrance to the recreational vehicle or the face of the flanged surface inlet (motor-base attachment plug) to the face of the attachment plug at the supply end.

The cord exposed usable length shall be a minimum of 20 feet (6.1 m) or the distance as measured between the point of entrance and the front of the recreational vehicle, whichever is greater.

See Section 551-13(e).

A revision to this section for the 1981 *Code* has deleted the 26½-ft maximum length restriction for vehicle power supply cords in the 1978 *Code*. The *Code* now requires that the exposed usable length of the cord be a minimum of 20 ft for the distance as measured between the point of entrance and the front of the recreational vehicle, whichever is greater. For vehicles longer than 26½ ft and having the cord attached to the rear of the vehicle, this revision will require the use of a cord longer than 26½ ft.

(c) Attachment Plugs.

(1) Recreational vehicles having only one 15-ampere branch circuit as permitted by Section 551-8(a)(1) shall have an attachment plug which shall be 2-pole, 3-wire, grounding type, rated 15 amperes, 125 volts, conforming to the configuration shown in Figure 551-13(c).

Complete details of this configuration can be found in American National Standard ANSI C73.11-1972.

(2) Recreational vehicles having only one 20-ampere branch circuit as permitted in Section 551-8(a)(2) shall have an attachment plug which shall be 2-pole, 3-wire, grounding type, rated 20 amperes, 125 volts, conforming to the configuration shown in Figure 551-13(c).

Complete details of this configuration can be found in American National Standard ANSI C73.12-1972.

(3) Recreational vehicles wired in accordance with Section 551-8(b) or (c) shall have an attachment plug which shall be 2-pole, 3-wire, grounding type, rated 30 amperes, 125 volts, conforming to the configuration shown in Figure 551-13(c) intended for use with units rated at 30 amperes, 125 volts.

Complete details of this configuration can be found in American National Standard Dimensions of Caps, Plugs and Receptacles, ANSI C73.13-1972.

(4) Recreational vehicles having a power-supply assembly rated 40 amperes or 50 amperes as permitted by Section 551-8(c) shall have a 3-pole, 4-wire, grounding-type attachment plug rated 50 amperes, 125/250 volts, conforming to the configuration shown in Figure 551-13(c).

Complete details of this configuration can be found in American National Standard Dimensions of Caps, Plugs and Receptacles, ANSI C73.17-1972.

Figure 551-13(c).   Configurations for grounding-type receptacles and attachment plug caps used for recreational vehicle supply cords and recreational vehicle lots.

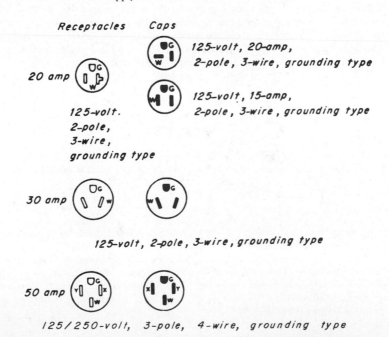

(d) Labeling at Electrical Entrance. Each recreational vehicle shall have permanently affixed to the exterior skin at or near the point of entrance of the power-supply cord(s) a label 3 inches (76 mm) by 1¾ inches (44.5 mm) minimum size, made of etched, metal-stamped or embossed brass, stainless steel, anodized or alclad aluminum not less than 0.020 inch (508 micrometers) thick, or other approved material [e.g., 0.005-inch (127-micrometers) plastic laminates], which reads, as appropriate, either:

"This connection is for 110-125 volt ac, 60 Hz ___ ampere supply," or
"This connection is for 120/240 volt ac, 3-pole, 4-wire 60 Hz ___ ampere supply."
The correct ampere rating shall be marked in the blank space.

(e) Location. The point of entrance of a power-supply assembly shall be located within 15 feet (4.57 m) of the rear, on the left (road) side or at the rear, left of the longitudinal center of the vehicle, within 18 inches (457 mm) of the outside wall.

Exception: A recreational vehicle equipped with only a listed flexible drain system or a side-vent drain system shall be permitted to have the electrical point of entrance located on either side provided the drain(s) for the plumbing system is (are) located on the same side.

551-14. Wiring Methods.

(a) Permitted. Electrical metallic tubing, flexible metal conduit, metal-clad cable, and nonmetallic-sheathed cable with a grounding conductor shall terminate by means of listed fittings, clamps, or connectors. Flexible metal conduit shall be permitted as a grounding means where installed in accordance with the requirements of Section 350-5.

(b) Double Locknuts and Bushings. Rigid metal conduit and intermediate metal conduit shall be provided with a locknut inside and outside the box, and a conduit bushing shall be used on the inside. Inside ends of the conduit shall be reamed.

(c) Nonmetallic Outlet Boxes. Nonmetallic outlet boxes shall be acceptable only with nonmetallic-sheathed cable.

(d) Outlet Boxes. In walls and ceilings constructed of wood or other combustible material, outlet boxes and fittings shall be flush with the finished surface or project therefrom.

(e) Wall and Ceiling Outlets. Wall and ceiling outlets shall be mounted in accordance with Article 370.

Exception No. 1: Snap-in type boxes or boxes provided with special wall or ceiling brackets that securely fasten boxes in walls or ceilings shall be permitted.

Exception No. 2: A wooden plate providing a 1½-inch (38-mm) minimum width backing around the box and of a thickness of ½ inch (12.7 mm) or greater (actual) glued to the wall panel shall be considered as approved means for mounting outlet boxes.

This new exception in the 1981 *Code* permits mounting of outlet boxes by screws to a wooden backer plate secured by adhesive to the back of the wall panel. The wooden backer plate is required to be not less than ½ in. thick, and it has to extend at least 1½ in. around the box. This revision recognizes the construction of recreational vehicle walls, in many of which it is quite difficult or impossible to attach an outlet box to a structural member as required in Section 370-13.

(f) Sheath or Armor. The sheath of nonmetallic cable or the armor of metal-clad cable shall be continuous between outlet boxes and other enclosures.

(g) Protected.   Metal-clad and nonmetallic cables shall be permitted to pass through the centers of the wide side of 2-inch by 4-inch studs. However, they shall be protected where they pass through 2-inch by 2-inch studs or at other studs or frames where the cable would be less than 1½ inches (38 mm) from the inside or outside surface. Steel plates on each side of the cable, or a steel tube, with not less than No. 16 MSG wall thickness, shall be installed to protect the cable. These plates or tubes shall be securely held in place.

(h) Bends.   No bend shall have a radius of less than five times the cable diameter.

(i) Cable Supports.   When connected with cable connectors or clamps, cables shall be supported within 12 inches (305 mm) of outlet boxes, distribution panelboards, and splice boxes on appliances. Supports shall be provided every 4½ feet (1.37 m) at other places.

(j) Nonmetallic Box Without Cable Clamps.   Nonmetallic-sheathed cables shall be supported within 8 inches (203 mm) of a nonmetallic outlet box without cable clamps.

Exception: Where approved devices of insulating material are employed with a loop of extra cable to permit future replacement of the device, the cable loop shall be considered as an integral portion of the device.

(k) Physical Damage.   Where subject to physical damage, exposed nonmetallic cable shall be protected by covering boards, guard strips, or conduit.

(l) Metallic Faceplates.   Metallic faceplates shall be of ferrous metal not less than 0.030 inch (762 micrometers) in thickness or of nonferrous metal not less than 0.040 inch (1.02 mm) in thickness. Nonmetallic faceplates shall be of an approved type.

(m) Metallic Faceplates Effectively Grounded.   Where metallic faceplates are used, they shall be effectively grounded.

(n) Moisture or Physical Damage.   Where outdoor or underchassis wiring is 115 volts, nominal, or over and is exposed to moisture or physical damage, the wiring shall be protected by rigid metal conduit, intermediate metal conduit, or by electrical metallic tubing that is closely routed against frames and equipment enclosures.

(o) Component Interconnections.   Fittings and connectors which are intended to be concealed at the time of assembly, when tested and approved to applicable standards, shall be permitted for the interconnection of components. Such fittings and connectors shall be equal to the wiring method employed in insulation, temperature rise, fault-current withstanding, and shall be capable of enduring the vibration and shock occurring in recreational vehicles.

551-15. Conductors and Outlet Boxes.

(a) Maximum Number of Conductors.   The maximum number of conductors permitted in outlet and junction boxes shall be in accordance with Section 370-6.

The exception permitting smaller boxes, which appeared in the 1978 *Code*, has been deleted in the 1981 *Code*.

(b) Free Conductor at Each Outlet Box.   At least 4 inches (102 mm) of free conductor shall be left at each outlet box except where conductors are intended to loop without joints.

551-16. Grounded Conductors.   The identification of grounded conductors shall be in accordance with Section 200-6.

551-17. Connection of Terminals and Splices. Conductor splices and connections at terminals shall be in accordance with Section 110-14. If splices of the grounding wire in nonmetallic-sheathed cable are made in outlet boxes, the splices shall be insulated.

551-18. Switches.   Switches shall be rated as follows:

(a) Lighting Circuits.   For lighting circuits, switches shall be rated not less than 10 amperes, 120-125 volts and in no case less than the connected load.

(b) Motors or Other Loads.   For motors or other loads, switches shall have ampere or horsepower ratings, or both, adequate for loads controlled. (An ac general-use snap switch shall be permitted to control a motor 2 horsepower or less with full-load current not over 80 percent of the switch ampere rating.)

551-19. Receptacles.   All receptacle outlets shall be: (1) of the grounding type, and (2) installed in accordance with Sections 210-7 and 210-21.

551-20. Lighting Fixtures.

(a) General.   Any combustible wall or ceiling finish exposed between the edge of a fixture canopy, or pan and the outlet box, shall be covered with noncombustible material of either metal equal to the thickness of the fixture or asbestos of 1/16 inch (1.59 mm).

(b) Shower Fixtures.   If a lighting fixture is provided over a bathtub or in a shower stall, it shall be of the enclosed and gasketed type and approved for the type of installation.
The switch for shower lighting fixtures and exhaust fans, located over a tub or in a shower stall, shall be located outside the tub or shower space.

(c) Outdoor Outlets, Fixtures, Air-Cooling Equipment, Etc.   Outdoor fixtures and other equipment shall be approved for outdoor use.

551-21. Grounding.   (See also Section 551-23 on bonding of noncurrent-carrying metal parts.)

(a) Power-Supply Grounding.   The grounding conductor in the supply cord or feeder shall be connected to the grounding bus or other approved grounding means in the distribution panelboard.

(b) Distribution Panelboard.   The distribution panelboard shall have a grounding bus with sufficient terminals for all grounding conductors or other approved grounding means.

(c) Insulated Neutral.

(1) The grounded circuit conductor (neutral) shall be insulated from the equipment grounding conductors and from equipment enclosures and other grounded parts. The grounded (neutral) circuit terminals in the distribution panelboard and in ranges, clothes dryers, counter-mounted cooking units, and wall-mounted ovens shall be insulated from the equipment enclosure. Bonding screws, straps, or buses in the distribution panel board or in appliances shall be removed and discarded.

(2) Connection of electric ranges and electric clothes dryers utilizing a grounded (neutral) conductor, if cord-connected, shall be made with 4-conductor cord and 3-pole, 4-wire, grounding-type plug caps and receptacles.

551-22. Interior Equipment Grounding.

(a) Exposed Metal Parts. In the electrical system, all exposed metal parts, enclosures, frames, lighting fixture canopies, etc., shall be effectively bonded to the grounding terminals or enclosure of the distribution panelboard.

(b) Equipment Grounding Conductors. Bare wires, green-colored wires, or green wires with yellow stripe(s) shall be used for equipment grounding conductors only.

(c) Grounding of Electrical Equipment. Where grounding of electrical equipment is specified, it shall be permitted as follows:

(1) Connection by metallic raceway (conduit or electrical metallic tubing) or the sheath of metal-clad cable to metallic outlet boxes.

(2) A connection between the one or more grounding conductors and a metallic box by means of a grounding screw, which shall be used for no other purpose, or an approved grounding device.

(3) The grounding wire in nonmetallic-sheathed cable shall be permitted to be secured under a screw threaded into the fixture canopy other than a mounting screw or cover screw, or attached to an approved grounding means (plate) in a nonmetallic outlet box for fixture mounting (grounding means shall also be permitted for fixture attachment screws).

(d) Grounding Connection in Nonmetallic Box. A connection between the one or more grounding conductors brought into a nonmetallic outlet box shall be so arranged that a connection can be made to any fitting or device in that box that requires grounding.

(e) Grounding Continuity. Where more than one equipment grounding conductor of a branch circuit enters a box, all such conductors shall be in good electrical contact with each other, and the arrangement shall be such that the disconnection or removal of a receptacle, fixture, or other device fed from the box will not interfere with or interrupt the grounding continuity.

(f) Cord-Connected Appliances. Cord-connected appliances, such as washing machines, clothes dryers, refrigerators, and the electrical system of gas ranges, etc., shall be grounded by means of an approved cord with grounding conductor and grounding-type attachment plug.

551-23. Bonding of Noncurrent-Carrying Metal Parts.

(a) Required Bonding. All exposed noncurrent-carrying metal parts that may become energized shall be effectively bonded to the grounding terminal or enclosure of the distribution panelboard.

(b) Bonding Chassis. A bonding conductor shall be connected between any distribution panelboard and an accessible terminal on the chassis. Aluminum or copper-clad aluminum conductors shall not be used for bonding if such conductors or their terminals are exposed to corrosive elements.

Exception: Any recreational vehicle which employs a unitized metal chassis-frame construction to which the distribution panelboard is securely fastened with a bolt(s) and nut(s) or by welding or riveting shall be considered to be bonded.

(c) Bonding Conductor Requirements. Grounding terminals shall be of the solderless type and approved as pressure terminal connectors recognized for the wire size used. The bonding conductor shall be solid or stranded, insulated or bare, and shall be No. 8 copper minimum, or equal.

(d) Metallic Roof and Exterior Bonding.   The metallic roof and exterior covering shall be considered bonded where:

(1) The metal panels overlap one another and are securely attached to the wood or metal frame parts by metallic fasteners, and

(2) The lower panel of the metallic exterior covering is secured by metallic fasteners at each cross member of the chassis, or the lower panel is bonded to the chassis by a metal strap.

(e) Gas, Water, and Waste Pipe Bonding.   The gas, water, and waste pipes shall be considered grounded if they are bonded to the chassis.

See Section 551-23(b) for chassis bonding.

(f) Furnace and Metallic Air Duct Bonding.   Furnace and metallic circulating air ducts shall be bonded.

551-24. Appliance Accessibility.   Every appliance shall be accessible for inspection, service, repair, and replacement without removal of permanent construction.

551-25. Factory Tests (Electrical).   Each recreational vehicle shall be subjected to the following tests:

(a) Circuits of 115 Volts or 115/230 Volts.   Each recreational vehicle designed with a 115-volt or a 115/230-volt electrical system shall withstand the applied potential without electrical breakdown of a 1-minute, 900-volt dielectric strength test, or a 1-second, 1080-volt dielectric strength test, with all switches closed, between current-carrying conductors, including neutral, and the recreational vehicle ground. During the test, all switches and other controls shall be in the "on" position. Fixtures and permanently installed appliances shall not be required to withstand this test.

Each recreational vehicle shall be subjected to: (1) a continuity test to assure that all metallic parts are properly bonded; (2) operational tests to demonstrate that all equipment is properly connected and in working order; and (3) polarity checks to determine that connections have been properly made.

(b) Low-Voltage Circuits.   Low-voltage circuit conductors in each recreational vehicle shall withstand the applied potential without electrical breakdown of a 1-minute, 500-volt or a 1-second, 600-volt dielectric strength test. The potential shall be applied between live and grounded conductors.

The test shall be permitted on running light circuits before the lights are installed provided the vehicle's outer covering and interior cabinetry has been secured. The braking circuit shall be permitted to be tested before being connected to the brakes, provided the wiring has been completely secured.

B. Recreational Vehicle Parks

551-40. Application and Scope.   Part B covers electrical systems on recreational vehicle parks. It does not apply to the electrical systems of recreational vehicles or the conductors that connect them to the park electrical supply facilities. Wherever the requirements of other articles of this Code and Article 551 differ, the requirements of Article 551 shall apply.

551-41. Definitions.

Power-Supply Assembly.   The conductors, including the grounding conductors, insulated from one another, the connectors, attachment plug caps, and all other fittings, grommets, or devices installed for the purpose of delivering energy from the source of electrical supply to the distribution panelboard within the recreational vehicle.

Recreational Vehicle Park.   A plot of land upon which two or more recreational vehicle sites are located, established, or maintained for occupancy by recreational vehicles of the general public as temporary living quarters for recreation or vacation purposes.

Recreational Vehicle Site.   A plot of ground within a recreational vehicle park intended for the accommodation of either a recreational vehicle, tent, or other individual camping unit on a temporary basis.

Recreational Vehicle Site Feeder Circuit Conductors.   The conductors from the park service equipment to the recreational vehicle site supply equipment.

Recreational Vehicle Site Supply Equipment.   The necessary equipment, usually a power outlet, consisting of a circuit breaker or switch and fuse and their accessories, located near the point of entrance of supply conductors to a recreational vehicle site and intended to constitute the disconnecting means for the supply to that site.

Recreational Vehicle Stand.   That area of a recreational vehicle site intended for the placement of a recreational vehicle.

551-42. Type Receptacles Provided.   A minimum of 75 percent of all recreational vehicle sites with electrical supply shall each be equipped with a 30-ampere, 125-volt receptacle conforming to Figure 551-13(c). This supply shall be permitted to include additional receptacle configurations conforming to Section 551-52. The remainder of all recreational vehicle sites with electrical supply shall be equipped with one or more of the receptacle configurations conforming to Section 551-52.

All 15- and 20-ampere, 125-volt receptacles shall have approved ground-fault circuit protection for personnel. Additional receptacles shall be permitted for the connection of electric equipment outside the recreational vehicle and all such 125-volt, single-phase, 15- and 20-ampere receptacles shall have approved ground-fault circuit-interrupters.

551-43. Distribution System.   The recreational vehicle park secondary electrical distribution system to recreational vehicle sites shall be derived from a single-phase 120/240-volt, 3-wire system.

See comments in the first paragraph following Section 550-21.

551-44. Calculated Load.

(a) **Basis of Calculations.**   Electrical service and feeders shall be calculated on the basis of not less than 3,600 watts per site equipped with both 20-ampere and 30-ampere supply facilities and 2,400 watts per site equipped with only 20-ampere supply facilities. The demand factors set forth in Table 551-44 shall be the minimum allowable demand factors that shall be permitted in calculating load for service and feeders.

(b) **Transformers and Secondary Distribution Panelboards.**   For the purpose of this Code, where the park service exceeds 240 volts, transformers and secondary distribution panelboards shall be treated as services.

(c) **Demand Factors.**   The demand factor for a given number of sites shall apply to all sites indicated. For example: twenty sites calculated at 26 percent of 3,600 watts result in a permissible demand of 936 watts per site or a total of 18,720 watts for twenty sites.

Table 551-44

Demand Factors for Feeders and Service-Entrance Conductors for Park Sites

Number of Recreational Vehicle Sites	Demand Factor (percent)	Number of Recreational Vehicle Sites	Demand Factor (percent)
1	100	10-12	29
2	100	13-15	28
3	70	16-18	27
4	55	19-21	26
5	44	22-40	25
6	39	41-100	24
7-9	33	101 and over	23

(d) **Feeder Circuit Capacity.** Recreational vehicle site feeder circuit conductors shall have adequate ampacity for the loads supplied, and shall be rated at not less than 30 amperes.

551-45. Overcurrent Protection. Overcurrent protection shall be provided in accordance with Article 240.

551-46. Grounding. All electrical equipment and installations in recreational vehicle parks shall be grounded as required by Article 250.

551-47. Recreational Vehicle Site Supply Equipment.

(a) **Location.** Where provided, the recreational vehicle site electrical supply equipment shall be located on the left (road) side of the parked vehicle, on a line which is 9 feet (2.74 m), ±1 foot (0.3 m), from the longitudinal centerline of the stand and shall be located at any point on this line from the rear of the stand to 15 feet (4.57 m) forward of the rear of the stand.

(b) **Disconnecting Means.** A disconnecting switch or circuit breaker shall be provided in the site supply equipment for disconnecting the power supply to the recreational vehicle.

(c) **Access.** All site supply equipment shall be accessible by an unobstructed entrance or passageway not less than 2 feet (610 mm) wide and 6½ feet (1.98 m) high.

(d) **Mounting Height.** Site supply equipment shall be located not less than 2 feet (610 mm) nor more than 6½ feet (1.98 m) above the ground.

(e) **Working Space.** Sufficient space shall be provided and maintained about all electric equipment to permit ready and safe operation, in accordance with Section 110-16.

551-48. Grounding, Recreational Vehicle Site Supply Equipment.

(a) **Exposed Noncurrent-Carrying Metal Parts.** Exposed noncurrent-carrying metal parts of fixed equipment, metal boxes, cabinets, and fittings, which are not electrically connected to grounded equipment, shall be grounded by a continuous grounding conductor run with the circuit conductors from the service equipments or from the transformer of a secondary distribution system. Equipment grounding conductors shall be sized in accordance with Section 250-95.

(b) **Secondary Distribution System.** Each secondary distribution system shall be grounded at the transformer.

(c) Neutral Conductor Not to Be Used as an Equipment Ground.   The neutral conductor shall not be used as an equipment ground for recreational vehicles or equipment within the recreational vehicle park.

(d) No Connection on the Load Side.   No connection to a grounding electrode shall be made to the neutral conductor on the load side of the service disconnecting means or transformer distribution panelboard.

551-49. Protection of Outdoor Equipment.

(a) Wet Locations.   All switches, circuit breakers, receptacles, control equipment, and metering devices located in wet places or outside of a building shall be rainproof equipment.

(b) Meters.   If secondary meters are installed, meter sockets without meters installed shall be blanked-off with an approved blanking plate.

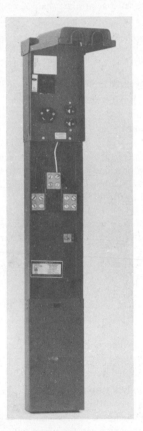

Figure 551-1. Recreational vehicle site supply equipment in accordance with Section 551-42. (*Midwest*)

551-50. Overhead Conductors.

(a) Vertical Clearance.   Open conductors of not over 600 volts, nominal, shall have a vertical clearance of not less than 18 feet (5.49 m) in all areas subject to recreational vehicle movement. In all other areas, vertical clearances shall conform to Section 225-18.

For clearance of conductors of over 600 volts, nominal, see National Electrical Safety Code (ANSI C2-1976).

(b) Horizontal Clearance. The horizontal clearance from structures and recreational vehicles for overhead conductors shall be not less than 3 feet (914 mm) for 600 volts, nominal, or less.

551-51. Underground Service, Feeder, Branch-Circuit and Recreational Vehicle Site Feeder Circuit Conductors.

(a) General. All direct-burial conductors, including the equipment grounding conductor if of aluminum, shall be insulated and identified for the use. All conductors shall be continuous from fitting to fitting. All splices shall be made in approved junction boxes.

(b) Mechanical Protection. Where underground conductors enter or leave a building or trench, they shall have mechanical protection in the form of rigid metal conduit, intermediate metal conduit, rigid nonmetallic conduit Schedule 80, electrical metallic tubing, or other approved mechanical means, extending a minimum of 18 inches (457 mm) into the trench from the finished grade.

See Section 300-5 and Article 339 for conductors or Type UF cable used underground or in direct burial in earth.

551-52. Receptacles. A receptacle to supply electric power to a recreational vehicle shall be one of the configurations shown in Figure 551-13(c) in the following ratings:

(a) 50 Ampere. 125/250 volts, 50-ampere, 3-pole, 4-wire, grounding type for 115/230-volt systems.

(b) 30 Ampere. 125-volt, 30-ampere, 2-pole, 3-wire, grounding type for 115-volt systems.

(c) 20 Ampere. 125-volt, 20-ampere, 2-pole, 3-wire, grounding type for 115-volt systems.

Complete details of these configurations can be found in American National Standard Dimensions of Caps, Plugs and Receptacles, ANSI C73.17-1972; ANSI C73.13-1972; and C73.12-1972.

ARTICLE 555 — MARINAS AND BOATYARDS

Contents

555-1. Scope. This article covers the installation of wiring and equipment in the areas comprising fixed or floating piers, wharfs, docks, and other areas in marinas, boatyards, boat basins, and similar establishments that are used, or intended for use, for the purpose of repair, berthing, launching, storage, or fueling of small craft and the moorage of floating dwelling units.

See Part B for Floating Dwelling Units.

A. Marinas and Boatyards

555-2. Application of Other Articles. Wiring and equipment for marinas and boatyards shall comply with this article and also with the applicable provisions of other articles of this Code.

See notes following Sections 210-19(a) and 215-2(c) for voltage drop on branch circuits and feeders respectively.

For disconnection of auxiliary power from boats, see Motor Craft, NFPA 302-1972 (ANSI).

555-3. Receptacles. Receptacles that provide shore power for boats shall be rated not less than 20 amperes and shall be single and of the locking and grounding types.

Fifteen- and 20-ampere, single-phase, 120-volt receptacles other than those supplying shore power to boats located at piers, wharfs, and other locations shall be protected by ground-fault circuit-interrupters.

For various configurations and ratings of locking- and grounding-type receptacles and caps, see Dimensions of Caps, Plugs, and Receptacles (ANSI C73-1972).

Receptacles that provide shore power for boats are to be single and of the locking and grounding types. See Figure 555-1 and also Figure 210-7 for a complete chart of locking and grounding configurations.

Each single receptacle that supplies shore power to boats is to be supplied from an individual branch circuit, and locking- and grounding-type receptacles and attachment caps are required to ensure proper connections to prevent unintentional disconnection of onboard equipment such as bilge pumps, refrigerators, etc. Fifteen- and 20-A, single-phase, 120-V receptacles, other than those supplying shore power to boats, that are used for maintenance or other purposes at piers, wharves, etc., may be general purpose nonlocking and nongrounding types and are to be protected by ground-fault circuit-interrupters.

555-4. Branch Circuits. Each single receptacle that supplies shore power to boats shall be supplied from a power outlet or panelboard by an individual branch circuit of the voltage class and rating corresponding to the rating of the receptacle.

555-5. Feeders and Services. The load for each ungrounded feeder and service conductor supplying receptacles that supply shore power for boats shall be calculated as follows:

For 1 to 4 receptacles	100% of the sum of the rating of the receptacles					
For 5 to 8	90%	"	"	"	"	" "
For 9 to 13	80%	"	"	"	"	" "
For 14 to 30	70%	"	"	"	"	" "
For 31 to 50	50%	"	"	"	"	" "
For 50 to 100	40%	"	"	"	"	" "
For over 100	30%	"	"	"	"	" "

555-6. Wiring Methods. The wiring method shall be one or more of the following identified as suitable for use where exposed to the weather or water: (1) rigid nonmetallic conduit; (2) mineral-insulated, metal-sheathed cable; (3) nonmetallic cable; (4) corrosion-resistant rigid metal

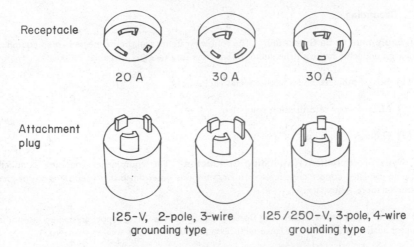

Receptacle

20 A   30 A   30 A

Attachment
plug

125-V, 2-pole, 3-wire   125/250-V, 3-pole, 4-wire
    grounding type   grounding type

Figure 555-1. Typical configurations for single, locking- and grounding-type receptacles and attachment plug caps used to provide shore power for boats in marinas and boatyards.

Figure 555-2. Power outlet assembly suitable for use at docks, wharfs, piers, and other locations that provide shore power to boats. (*Hubbell*)

conduit; (5) corrosion-resistant intermediate metal conduit; (6) underground wiring that complies with the requirements of this Code; (7) Type MC cable.

Exception No. 1: Where flexibility is required, other types identified for the purpose.

Exception No. 2: Open wiring shall be permitted by special permission.

In granting special permission, major factors include possible contact of open wires with masts, cranes, or similar structures or equipment.

For further information on wiring methods for various locations, see Fire Protection Standard for Marinas and Boatyards, NFPA 303-1975.

555-7. Grounding.

(a) **Equipment to Be Grounded.** The following items shall be connected to an equipment grounding conductor run with the circuit conductors in a raceway or cable:

(1) Boxes, cabinets, and all other metal enclosures.

(2) Metal frames of utilization equipment.

(3) Grounding terminals of grounding-type receptacles.

(b) **Type of Equipment Grounding Conductor.** The equipment grounding conductor shall be an insulated copper conductor with a continuous outer finish that is either green or green with one or more yellow stripes.

(c) **Size of Equipment Grounding Conductor.** The insulated copper equipment grounding conductor shall be sized in accordance with Section 250-95 but not smaller than No. 12.

(d) **Branch-Circuit Equipment Grounding Conductor.** The insulated equipment grounding conductor for branch circuits shall terminate at a grounding terminal in a remote panelboard or the grounding terminal in the main service equipment.

(e) **Feeder Equipment Grounding Conductors.** Where a feeder supplies a remote panelboard, an insulated equipment grounding conductor shall extend from a grounding terminal in the service equipment to a grounding terminal in the remote panelboard.

The purpose of Section 555-7 is to provide an insulated grounding conductor that will ensure a high integrity grounding circuit. Because of corrosive conditions in marinas and boatyards, metal raceways and boxes are not allowed to serve as equipment grounding conductors.

555-8. Wiring Over and Under Navigable Water. Wiring over and under navigable water shall be subject to approval by the authority having jurisdiction.

Some federal and local agencies have specific authority over navigable waterways; therefore, their approval of any proposed installation over or under such a waterway should be obtained.

555-9. Gasoline Dispensing Stations — Hazardous (Classified) Locations.

(a) **Class I, Division 1 Location.** The following spaces shall be considered a Class I, Division 1 location:

(1) The space within the dispenser from its base to a level measured 4 feet (1.22 m) vertically from its base.

(2) The space outside the dispenser for a distance measured 4 feet (1.22 m) horizontally from all points of the dispenser and measured vertically upwards for a distance of 18 inches (457 mm) from the base of the dispenser.

(3) The entire space between the base of the dispenser and the lowest water surface for a distance of 4 feet (1.22 m) measured horizontally from any point on the outside of the dispenser.

(b) Class I, Division 2 Location.   In an outside location, the following space shall be considered a Class I, Division 2 location (spaces which are Class I, Division 1 as defined above are excluded. Buildings within the following space which are not suitably cut off shall be included.) This space shall include the entire volume enveloped within the following limits:

(1) A horizontal limit of 20 feet (6.1 m) from all points on the exterior enclosure of a dispenser.

(2) An upper limit of 18 inches (457 mm) measured vertically from the base of the dispenser.

(3) A lower limit which shall be the lowest water surface.

For further information, see Marinas and Boatyards, NFPA 303-1975.

NFPA 303 includes requirements pertaining to gasoline dispensing stations.

555-11. Sealing.

(a) At Dispenser.   An approved seal shall be provided in each conduit run entering or leaving a dispenser or any cavities or enclosures in direct communication therewith.

(b) At Boundary.   Additional seals shall be provided in accordance with Section 501-5. Section 501-5(a)(4) and (b)(2) shall apply to horizontal as well as to vertical boundaries of the defined hazardous (classified) locations.

B. Floating Dwelling Units (FDU)

555-20. General.   This part covers floating dwelling units and services and feeders to the associated pier, dock, or wharf to which they are moored.

555-21. Application of Other Articles.   Wiring and equipment for floating dwelling units shall comply with this article, and also with the applicable provisions of other articles of this Code.

555-22. Services.   Overhead service wiring shall be installed so that changes in water level will not result in unsafe clearances.

555-23. Connection of Service and Feeders.   Flexibility of the wiring system shall be maintained between the floating dwelling units and the supply conductors.

555-24. Grounding.   Ground continuity shall be assured between an earth ground on the shore, the floating dwelling unit and the incoming electric distribution system.

Part B is new in the 1981 *Code*. It specifically subjects floating dwelling units, such as houseboats, to the requirements of the *Code*.

6 SPECIAL EQUIPMENT

ARTICLE 600 — ELECTRIC SIGNS AND
OUTLINE LIGHTING

Contents

(b) Tube Connections Other than with Receptacles.
(c) Receptacles.
(d) Bushings.
(e) Show Windows.
(f) Receptacles and Bushing Seals.
(g) Enclosures of Metal.
(h) Enclosures of Insulating Material.
(i) Live Parts.
600-35. Switches on Doors.
600-36. Fixed Outline Lighting and Skeleton-type Signs for Interior Use.

(a) Tube Support.
(b) Transformers.
(c) Supply Conductors.
(d) High-Tension Conductors.
600-37. Portable Gas Tube Signs for Show Windows and Interior Use.
(a) Location.
(b) Transformer.
(c) Supply Conductors.
(d) High-Voltage Conductors.
(e) Grounding.
(f) Support.

A. General

600-1. Scope. This article covers the installation of conductors and equipment for electric signs and outline lighting as defined in Article 100.

600-2. Disconnect Required. Each outline lighting installation, and each sign of other than the portable type, shall be controlled by an externally operable switch or breaker which will open all ungrounded conductors.

(a) In Sight of Sign. The disconnecting means shall be within sight of the sign or outline lighting which it controls.

Exception: Signs operated by electronic or electromechanical controllers located external to the sign shall have a disconnecting means located within sight from the controller location. The disconnecting means shall disconnect the sign and the controller from all ungrounded supply conductors and shall be so designed that no pole can be operated independently. The disconnecting means shall be permitted to be in the same enclosure with the controller. The disconnecting means shall be capable of being locked in the open position.

Disconnect means must be located in a direct line of sight from the sign or outline lighting which it controls. This requirement, obviously, is for the protection of a worker who can keep the disconnecting means within his view while working on the sign. The Exception permits disconnecting means capable of being locked in the "open" position to be located elsewhere.
See Figure 600-1.

(b) Control Switch Rating. Switches, flashers, and similar devices controlling transformers shall be either rated for controlling inductive load(s) or have an ampere rating not less than twice the ampere rating of the transformer.

Exception: For other than motors, ac general-use snap switches shall be permitted to be used on alternating-current circuits to control inductive loads not exceeding the ampere rating of the switch.

See Section 380-14 for rating of snap switches.

A switching device that controls the primary circuit of a transformer supplying a luminous gas tube encounters unusually severe arcing of its contacts. Therefore, the switch or flasher must be a general-use ac snap switch or have a current rating of at least twice the rating of the transformer it controls.

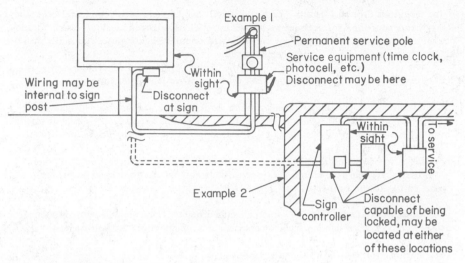

Figure 600-1. Example 1 depicts the disconnecting means placement which satisfies the requirements of Section 600-2(a). Example 2 illustrates the location of a disconnecting means as permitted by the Exception to Section 600-2(a).

600-3. Enclosures as Pull Boxes.   The wiring method used to supply signs and outline lighting shall terminate in the sign or transformer enclosures.

Exception: Such signs and transformer boxes shall be permitted to be used as pull or junction boxes for conductors supplying other adjacent signs, outline lighting systems and floodlights that are part of signs provided the conductors extending from the equipment are protected by an overcurrent device rated 20 amperes or less.

600-4. Listing Required.   Every electric sign of any type, fixed or portable, shall be listed and installed in conformance with that listing, unless otherwise permitted by special permission.

Section 600-4 requires every electric sign of any type to be listed, unless otherwise permitted by special permission. The "special permission" exception is new in the 1981 *Code*. Many times signs of large dimensions are transported, in several parts, from the manufacturer to a location site where they are assembled. It is at this time that an inspection authority must be present to ensure that the components are assembled in conformance with their listing.

600-5. Grounding.   Signs, troughs, tube terminal boxes, and other metal frames shall be grounded in the manner specified in Article 250.

Exception No. 1: Insulated and Inaccessible. Where they are insulated from ground and from other conducting surfaces and are inaccessible to unauthorized persons, they need not be grounded.

Exception No. 2: Isolated Parts. Isolated noncurrent-carrying metal parts of outline lighting may be bonded by No. 14 conductors, protected from physical damage, and grounded in accordance with Article 250.

600-6. Branch Circuits.

(a) Rating.   Circuits which supply lamps, ballasts, and transformers, or combinations, shall be rated not to exceed 20 amperes. Circuits containing electric-discharge lighting transformers exclusively shall not be rated in excess of 30 amperes.

(b) Required Branch Circuit. Each commercial building and each commercial occupancy with ground floor footage accessible to pedestrians shall be provided at an accessible location outside the occupancy, with at least one outlet for sign or outline lighting use. This outlet shall be supplied by an individual 20-ampere branch circuit.

Exception: Interior hallways or corridors shall not be considered outside the occupancy.

A commercial occupancy with ground floor footage and with an entrance for pedestrians from a sidewalk, street, enclosed mall, etc., is required to have at least one outlet for sign or outline lighting use supplied by an individual 20-A branch circuit.

Signs for commercial occupancies are usually in use for three hours or longer and are therefore considered continuous loads and are not to exceed 80 percent of the rating of the branch circuit (16 A).

(c) Computed Load. The load for the required branch circuit installed for the supply of exterior signs or outline lighting shall be computed at a minimum of 1200 volt-amperes.

This section is new in the 1981 *Code.*

600-7. Marking.

(a) Signs. Signs shall be marked with the maker's name; and, for incandescent lamp signs, with the number of lampholders; and, for electric-discharge-lamp signs, with input amperes at full load and input voltage. The marking of the sign shall be visible after installation.

(b) Transformers. Transformers shall be marked with the maker's name; and transformers for electric-discharge-lamp signs shall be marked with the input rating in amperes or volt-amperes, the input voltage, and the open-circuit output voltage.

600-8. Enclosures.

(a) Conductors and Terminals. Conductors and terminals in sign boxes, cabinets, and outline troughs shall be enclosed in metal or other noncombustible material.

Exception: The supply leads shall not be required to be enclosed.

(b) Cutouts, Flashers, etc. Cutouts, flashers, and similar devices shall be enclosed in metal boxes, the doors of which shall be arranged so they can be opened without removing obstructions or finished parts of the enclosure.

(c) Strength. Enclosures shall have ample strength and rigidity.

(d) Material. Signs and outline lighting shall be constructed of metal or other noncombustible material. Wood shall be permitted for external decoration if placed not less than 2 inches (50.8 mm) from the nearest lampholder or current-carrying part.

Exception: Portable signs of the indoor type shall not be required to meet this requirement.

(e) Minimum Thickness — Enclosure Metal. Sheet copper shall be at least 20 ounce [0.028 inch (711 micrometers)]. Sheet steel shall be of No. 28 MSG.

Exception: For outline lighting and for electric-discharge signs, sheet steel shall be of No. 24 MSG if not ribbed, corrugated, or embossed over its entire surface and of No. 26 MSG if it is so ribbed, corrugated, or embossed.

(f) Protection of Metal.   All steel parts of enclosures shall be galvanized or otherwise protected from corrosion.

(g) Enclosures Exposed to Weather.   Enclosures for outdoor use shall be weatherproof and shall have an ample number of drain holes, each not larger than ½ inch (12.7 mm) or smaller than ¼ inch (6.35 mm). Wiring connections shall not be made through the bottoms of nonraintight enclosures exposed to the weather.

600-9. Portable Signs.   Portable signs, letters, fixtures, symbols, and similar displays used in conjunction with fixed outdoor signs shall only be used when in compliance with all applicable provisions of this Code and, in addition, shall meet all of the following requirements:

(a) Weatherproof Receptacle and Attachment Plug.   A weatherproof receptacle and attachment plug having one pole for grounding shall be provided for each individual letter, fixture, or sign.

(b) Cords.   All cords shall be Type S, SJ, SJO, SJT, SJTO, SO, or ST, 3-conductor, with one conductor grounded as provided in the foregoing.

(c) Cord from Ground Level.   No cord shall be less than 10 feet (3.05 m) from the ground level directly underneath.

600-10. Clearances.

(a) Vertical and Horizontal.   Signs and outline system enclosures shall have not less than the vertical and horizontal clearances from open conductors specified in Article 225.

(b) Elevation.   The bottom of sign and outline lighting enclosures shall not be less than 16 feet (4.88 m) above areas accessible to vehicles.

Exception: The bottom of such enclosures may be less than 16 feet (4.88 m) above areas accessible to vehicles where such enclosures are protected from physical damage.

600-11. Outdoor Portable Signs.   The internal wiring of an outdoor sign that is portable or mobile and is readily accessible shall be supplied from, and protected by, ground-fault circuit interrupters identified for use with portable electric signs installed within or on the sign, thereby providing protection for personnel. Conductive supports of signs covered by this section shall be considered part of the sign.

Exception: This requirement shall become effective January 1, 1982.

This section is new in the 1981 *Code*. The GFCI will not provide protection for faults on the line (supply) side of the GFCI, so inspection of the extension cords used for supplying portable outdoor signs is desirable. GFCI protection for faults within the sign should contribute to greater safety in view of the difficulty in inspecting such signs because of their often short-term use.

B. 600 Volts, Nominal, or Less

600-21. Installation of Conductors.

(a) Wiring Method.   Conductors shall be installed in rigid metal conduit, intermediate metal conduit, rigid nonmetallic conduit subject to the installation provisions of Chapter 3, flexible metal conduit, liquidtight flexible metal conduit, electrical metallic tubing, metal-clad cable, metal troughing, and mineral-insulated, metal-sheathed cable.

(b) Insulation and Size. Conductors shall be of a type approved for general use and shall not be smaller than No. 14.

Exception No. 1: Conductors not smaller than No. 18 of a type listed in Table 402-3 shall be permitted:

a. In portable signs.

b. As short leads permanently attached to lampholders or electric-discharge ballasts.

c. As leads not more than 8 feet (2.44 m) long permanently attached to electric-discharge lampholders or electric-discharge ballasts if the leads are enclosed in wiring channels.

d. For signs with multiple incandescent lamps requiring one conductor from a control to one or more lamps whose total load does not exceed 250 watts, if in an approved cable assembly of two or more conductors.

Exception No. 2: Conductors not smaller than No. 20 shall be permitted as short leads permanently attached to synchronous motors.

(c) Exposed to Weather. Conductors in raceways, metal-clad cable, or enclosures exposed to the weather shall be of the lead-covered type or other type specially approved for the conditions.

Exception: This shall not apply when rigid metal conduit, intermediate metal conduit, electrical metallic tubing, or enclosures are made raintight and arranged to drain.

(d) Number of Conductors in Raceway. The number of conductors in a raceway for sign fixtures shall be in accordance with Table 1 of Chapter 9.

(e) Conductors Soldered to Terminals. Where the conductors are fastened to lampholders other than of the pin type, they shall be soldered to the terminals or made with wire connectors, and the exposed parts of conductors and terminals shall be treated to prevent corrosion. Where the conductors are fastened to pin-type lampholders that protect the terminals from the entrance of water, and that have been found acceptable for sign use, the conductors shall be of the stranded type but shall not be required to be soldered to the terminals.

> Conductors are required to be sized No. 14 or larger (note Exceptions) and are to be installed in the specified raceways or metal-clad cables. Unless raceways or enclosures exposed to the weather are made raintight and arranged to drain, conductors are to be lead-covered or approved for wet locations. See Table 310-13.

600-22. Lampholders. Lampholders shall be of the unswitched type having bodies of suitable insulating material and shall be so constructed and installed as to prevent turning. Miniature lampholders shall not be employed for outdoor signs and outline lighting. The screw-shell contact of all sign lampholders in grounded circuits shall be connected to the grounded conductor of the circuit.

600-23. Conductors Within Signs and Troughs. Wires within the sign and outline lighting troughs shall be installed as to be mechanically secure.

600-24. Protection of Leads. Bushings shall be employed to protect wires feeding through enclosures.

C. Over 600 Volts, Nominal

600-31. Installation of Conductors.

(a) **Wiring Method.** Conductors shall be installed as concealed conductors on insulators, in rigid metal conduit, in intermediate metal conduit, in rigid nonmetallic conduit, in flexible metal conduit, in liquidtight flexible metal conduit, or in electrical metallic tubing, or as Type MC cable.

This section has been revised in the 1981 *Code* to permit rigid nonmetallic conduit.

(b) **Insulation and Size.** Conductors shall be of a type identified for voltage not less than the voltage of the circuit and shall not be smaller than No. 14.

Exception: Conductors not smaller than No. 18 shall be permitted:

a. As leads not more than 8 feet (2.44 m) long permanently attached to electric-discharge lampholders or electric-discharge ballasts if the leads are enclosed in wiring channels.

b. In show window displays or small portable signs, as leads not more than 8 feet (2.44 m) long that run from the line ends of the tubing to the secondary windings of transformers if the leads are permanently attached within the transformer enclosure.

(c) **Bends in Conductors.** Sharp bends in the conductors shall be avoided.

(d) **Concealed Conductors on Insulators — Indoors.** Concealed conductors on insulators shall be separated from each other and from all objects other than the insulators on which they are mounted by a spacing of not less than 1½ inches (38 mm) for voltages above 10,000 and not less than 1 inch (25.4 mm) for voltages of 10,000 or less. They shall be installed in channels lined with noncombustible material and used for no other purpose, except that the primary circuit conductors shall be permitted to be in the same channel. The insulators shall be of noncombustible, nonabsorbent material. Concealed conductors on insulators shall not be allowed outside the sign enclosure.

(e) **Conductors in Raceways.** Where the conductors are covered with lead or other metal sheathing, the covering shall extend beyond the end of the raceway, and the surface of the cable shall not be injured where the covering terminates.

(1) In damp or wet locations, the insulation on all conductors shall extend beyond the metal covering or raceway not less than 4 inches (102 mm) for voltages over 10,000, 3 inches (76 mm) for voltages over 5000 but not exceeding 10,000, and 2 inches (50.8 mm) for voltages of 5000 or less.

(2) In dry locations the insulation shall extend beyond the end of the metal covering or raceways not less than 2½ inches (64 mm) for voltages over 10,000, 2 inches (50.8 mm) for voltages over 5000 but not exceeding 10,000, and 1½ inches (38 mm) for voltages of 5000 or less.

(3) For conductors at grounded midpoint terminals, no spacing shall be required.

(4) A metal raceway containing a single conductor from one secondary terminal of a transformer shall not exceed 20 feet (6.1 m) in length.

(f) **Show Windows and Similar Locations.** Conductors that hang freely in the air, away from combustible material, and where not subject to physical damage, as in some show window displays, shall not be required to be otherwise protected.

(g) Between Tubing and Grounded Midpoint.   Conductors shall be permitted to be run from the ends of tubing to the grounded midpoint of transformers specifically designed for the purpose and provided with terminals at the midpoint. Where such connections are made to the transformer grounded midpoint, the connections between the high-voltage terminals of the transformer and the line ends of the tubing shall be as short as possible.

600-32. Transformers.

(a) Voltage.   The transformer secondary open-circuit voltage shall not exceed 15,000 volts with an allowance on test of 1000 volts additional. For end-grounded transformers, the secondary open-circuit voltage shall not exceed 7500 volts with an allowance on test of 500 volts additional.

(b) Type.   Transformers shall be of a type identified for use with electrical-discharge tubing and shall be limited in rating to a maximum of 4500 volt-amperes.

Open core-and-coil-type transformers shall be limited to 5000 volts with an allowance on test of 500 volts and to indoor applications in small portable signs.

Transformers for outline lighting installations shall have secondary current ratings not more than 30 milliamperes.

Exception: Where the transformers and all wiring connected to them are installed in accordance with Article 410 for electric-discharge lighting of the same voltage.

(c) Exposed to Weather.   Transformers used outdoors shall be of the weatherproof type or shall be protected from the weather by enclosure in the sign body or in a separate metal box.

(d) Transformer Secondary Connections.   The high-voltage windings of transformers shall not be connected in parallel or in series.

Exception No. 1: Two transformers each having one end of its high-voltage winding connected to the metal enclosure shall be permitted to have their high-voltage windings connected in series to form the equivalent of a midpoint-grounded transformer. The grounded ends shall be connected by insulated conductors not smaller than No. 14.

Exception No. 2: Transformers for small portable signs, show windows, and similar locations that are equipped with leads permanently attached to the secondary winding within the transformer enclosure and that do not extend more than 8 feet (2.44 m) beyond the enclosure for attaching to the line ends of the tubing shall not be smaller than No. 18.

(e) Accessibility.   Transformers shall be located where accessible and shall be securely fastened in place.

(f) Working Space.   A work space at least 3 feet (914 mm) high and measuring at least 3 feet (914 mm) by 3 feet (914 mm) horizontally shall be provided about each transformer or its enclosure where not installed in a sign.

(g) Attic Locations.   Transformers may be located in attics provided there is a passageway at least 3 feet (914 mm) in height and at least 2 feet (610 mm) in width, provided with a suitable permanent fixed walkway or catwalk at least 12 inches (305 mm) in width extending from the point of entry into the attic to each transformer.

It is intended that Article 600 provide the necessary safeguards for personnel who are required to perform maintenance on signs and outline lighting by requiring a disconnecting means, by requiring that the use of open wiring be permitted "only" as concealed wiring on insulators within a sign enclosure, and by further requiring that transformers be located in a safe, accessible location.

600-33. Electric-Discharge Tubing.

(a) Design. The tubing shall be of such length and design as not to cause a continuous overvoltage on the transformer.

(b) Support. Tubing shall be adequately supported on noncombustible, nonabsorbent supports. Tubing supports shall, where practicable, be adjustable.

(c) Contact with Flammable Material and Other Surfaces. The tubing shall be free from contact with flammable material and shall be located where not normally exposed to physical damage. Where operating at over 7500 volts, the tubing shall be supported on noncombustible, nonabsorbent insulating supports that maintain a spacing of not less than ¼ inch (6.35 mm) between the tubing and the nearest surface.

600-34. Terminals and Electrode Receptacles for Electric-Discharge Tubing.

(a) Terminals. Terminals of the tubing shall be inaccessible to unqualified persons and isolated from combustible material and grounded metal or shall be enclosed. Where enclosed, they shall be separated from grounded metal and combustible material by noncombustible, nonabsorbent insulating material or by not less than 1½ inches (38 mm) of air. Terminals shall be relieved from stress by the independent support of the tubing.

(b) Tube Connections Other than with Receptacles. Where tubes do not terminate in receptacles designed for the purpose, all live parts of tube terminals and conductors shall be supported so as to maintain a separation of not less than 1½ inches (38 mm) between conductors or between conductors and any grounded metal.

(c) Receptacles. Electrode receptacles for the tubing shall be of noncombustible, nonabsorbent insulating material.

(d) Bushings. Where electrodes enter the enclosure of outdoor signs or of an indoor sign operating at a voltage in excess of 7500 volts, bushings shall be used unless receptacles are provided. Electrode terminal assemblies shall be supported not more than 6 inches (152 mm) from the electrode terminals.

(e) Show Windows. In the exposed type of show-window signs, terminals shall be enclosed by receptacles.

(f) Receptacles and Bushing Seals. A flexible, nonconducting seal shall be permitted to close the opening between the tubing and the receptacle or bushing against the entrance of dust or moisture. This seal shall not be in contact with grounded conductive material and shall not be depended upon for the insulation of the tubing.

(g) Enclosures of Metal. Enclosures of metal for electrodes shall not be less than No. 24 MSG sheet metal.

(h) Enclosures of Insulating Material. Enclosures of insulating material shall be noncombustible, nonabsorbent, and suitable for the voltage of the circuit.

(i) Live Parts. Live parts shall be enclosed or suitably guarded to prevent contact.

Electric-discharge tubing is to be of such length and design as not to cause a continuous overload on the transformer. A tube too long in length and/or too small in diameter increases the impedance of the load and, thus, would burden the transformer. Generally, primary voltages of transformers are 115 V, and proper installation and maintenance of transformers and high-voltage secondary conductors will minimize the possibility of injury or fire. Precautions should be taken to ensure that secondary conductors are properly terminated to the tube electrodes, and that these connections are protected from contact by unauthorized persons or by any flammable or combustible material. Broken tubes should be replaced or de-energized.

600-35. Switches on Doors. Doors or covers giving access to uninsulated parts of indoor signs or outline lighting exceeding 600 volts, nominal, and accessible to the general public shall either be provided with interlock switches that on the opening of the doors or covers disconnect the primary circuit, or shall be so fastened that the use of other than ordinary tools will be necessary to open them.

600-36. Fixed Outline Lighting and Skeleton-type Signs for Interior Use.

(a) Tube Support. Gas tubing shall be supported independently of the conductors by means of insulators of noncombustible, nonabsorptive materials such as glass or porcelain or by suspension from suitable wires or chains.

(b) Transformers. Transformers shall be installed in metal enclosures and as near as practicable to the gas tubing system.

(c) Supply Conductors. The supply conductors for the transformers shall be enclosed in grounded metallic raceway or rigid nonmetallic conduit where installed in accordance with the requirements of Article 347.

(d) High-Tension Conductors. High-tension conductors shall be insulated for the voltage of the circuit and shall be enclosed in grounded metallic raceway.

Exception: Conductors not exceeding 4 feet (1.22 m) in length between gas tubing and adjacent metallic enclosures shall be permitted to be enclosed in continuous glass or other insulating sleeves.

600-37. Portable Gas Tube Signs for Show Windows and Interior Use. This section shall apply to the installation and use of portable gas tube signs.

(a) Location. Portable gas tube signs shall be for indoor use only.

(b) Transformer. The transformer shall be of the window type or shall be within a metal enclosure.

(c) Supply Conductors. Supply conductors shall consist of hard or extra-hard usage-type cord containing a grounding conductor. The cord shall not exceed more than 10 feet (3.05 m) in length.

(d) High-Voltage Conductors. High-voltage conductors shall not be more than 6 feet (1.83 m) long and shall be located where not subject to mechanical injury, and shall be insulated for the voltage of the circuit and be protected by continuous glass or other insulating sleeves or tubing.

(e) Grounding. Transformers and attached noncurrent-carrying metal parts shall be grounded in accordance with Article 250.

(f) Support. Portable indoor signs shall be held in place by not more than two open hooks attached to the transformer case.

ARTICLE 604 — MANUFACTURED WIRING SYSTEMS

Contents

604-1. Scope.
604-2. Definition.
604-3. Uses Permitted.
604-4. Uses Not Permitted.

604-5. Other Articles.
604-6. Construction.
604-7. Unused Outlets.

604-1. Scope. The provisions of this article apply to field-installed wiring using off-site manufactured subassemblies for branch circuits, signaling circuits, and communication circuits in accessible areas.

This article is new in the 1981 *Code* and introduces the concept of factory-made (prefabricated) wiring systems.

604-2. Definition.

Manufactured Wiring System. A system containing component parts that are assembled in the process of manufacture and cannot be inspected at the building site without damage or destruction to the assembly.

604-3. Uses Permitted. The manufactured wiring systems shall be permitted in accessible and dry locations and in plenums and spaces used for environmental air, when listed for this application, and installed in accordance with Section 300-22.

Exception: In concealed spaces, one end of tapped cable shall be permitted to extend into hollow walls for direct termination at switch and outlet points in an approved manner.

604-4. Uses Not Permitted. Where conductors or cables are limited by the provisions in Articles 333 and 334.

604-5. Other Articles. Installations shall conform with, but not be limited only to, applicable sections of the following articles: 110, 200, 210, 220, 250, 300, 310, 333, 334, 350, 410, 545, 640, 700, 725 and 800.

604-6. Construction.

(a) Cable Types. Cable shall be listed Type AC or MC nominal 600V No. 12 AWG copper insulated conductors with a bare No. 12 AWG copper bonding conductor or listed flexible metal conduit with 600V No. 12 AWG copper insulated conductors with an insulated No. 12 AWG copper ground conductor. Each section shall be marked to identify the type cable.

(b) Receptacles and Connectors. Receptacles and connectors shall be locking type, uniquely polarized and identified for the purpose and shall be part of a listed assembly for the appropriate system.

(c) Other Component Parts. Other component parts shall be listed for the appropriate system.

604-7. Unused Outlets. All unused outlets shall be capped to effectively close the connector openings.

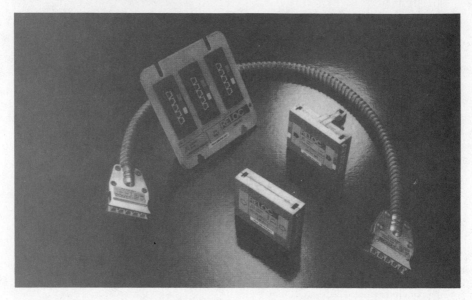

Figure 604-1. Components of a manufactured wiring system. (*RELOC a div. of Lithonia Lighting*)

ARTICLE 610 — CRANES AND HOISTS

Contents

F. Control
610-51. Separate Controllers.
610-53. Overcurrent Protection.
610-55. Limit Switch.

610-57. Clearance.

G. Grounding
610-61. Grounding.

A. General

610-1. Scope. This article covers the installation of electric equipment and wiring used in connection with cranes, monorail hoists, hoists, and all runways.

For further information, see Safety Code for Cranes, Derricks, Hoists, Jacks, and Slings (ANSI B-30).

610-2. Special Requirements for Particular Locations.

(a) Hazardous (Classified) Locations. All equipment which operates in a hazardous (classified) location shall conform to Article 500.

(1) Equipment used in locations which are hazardous because of the presence of flammable gases or vapors shall conform to Article 501.

(2) Equipment used in locations which are hazardous because of combustible dust shall conform to Article 502.

(3) Equipment used in locations which are hazardous because of the presence of easily ignitible fibers or flyings shall conform to Article 503.

(b) Combustible Materials. Where a crane, hoist, or monorail hoist operates over readily combustible material, the resistors shall be placed in a well-ventilated cabinet composed of noncombustible material so constructed that it will not emit flames or molten metal.

Exception: Resistors shall be permitted to be located in a cage or cab constructed of noncombustible material which encloses the sides of the cage or cab from the floor to a point at least 6 inches (152 mm) above the top of the resistors.

(c) Electrolytic Cell Lines. See Section 668-32.

Section 610-2(c) is new in the 1981 *Code*. Special precautions are necessary on electrolytic cell lines to prevent introduction of exposed grounded parts, as described in Section 668-32.

B. Wiring

610-11. Wiring Method. Conductors shall be enclosed in raceways or be Type MC cable, or Type MI cable.

Exception No. 1: Contact conductors.

Exception No. 2: Short lengths of open conductors at resistors, collectors, and other equipment.

Exception No. 3: Where flexible connections are necessary to motors and similar equipment, flexible stranded conductors shall be installed in flexible metal conduit, liquidtight flexible metal conduit, multiconductor cable, or an approved nonmetallic enclosure.

Exception No. 4: Where multiconductor cable is used with a suspended pushbutton station, the station shall be supported in some satisfactory manner that protects the electric conductors against strain.

Figure 610-1. A suitable grip for strain relief with a suspended pushbutton station. (*Hubbell, Kellems Div.*)

Use of short lengths of "open" wiring is a permitted wiring method on cranes and hoists where a separately bushed hole from a box or fitting is provided for each conductor and the method is used for the connection of resistors, collectors, or similar equipment. In addition to other types of raceways, flexible metal conduit and liquidtight flexible metal conduit are permissible in lengths of not more than 3 ft where flexibility is necessary.

610-12. Raceway Terminal Fittings.   Conductors leaving raceways shall comply with one of the following:

(a) Separately Bushed Hole.   A box or terminal fitting having a separately bushed hole for each conductor shall be used wherever a change is made from rigid metal conduit, intermediate metal conduit, electrical metallic tubing, nonmetallic-sheathed cable, metal-clad cable, or mineral-insulated cable or surface raceway wiring to open wiring. A fitting used for this purpose shall contain no taps or splices and shall not be used at fixture outlets.

(b) Bushing in Lieu of a Box.   A bushing shall be permitted to be used in lieu of a box at the end of a rigid metal conduit, intermediate metal conduit or electrical metallic tubing where the raceway terminates at dc split frame motors, unenclosed controls, or similar equipment including contact conductors, collectors, resistors, brakes, and power circuit limit switches.

610-13. Types of Conductors.   Conductors shall comply with Table 310-13.

Exception No. 1: Conductor(s) exposed to external heat or connected to resistors shall have a flame-resistant outer covering or be covered with flame-resistant tape individually or as a group.

Exception No. 2: Contact conductors along runways, crane bridges, and monorails shall be permitted to be bare, and shall be copper, aluminum, steel, or other alloys or combinations thereof in the form of hard drawn wire, tees, angles, tee rails, or other stiff shapes.

Exception No. 3: Flexible conductors shall be permitted to be used to convey current and, where practicable, cable reels or take-up devices shall be employed.

610-14. Rating and Size of Conductors.

(a) **Ampacity.** The allowable ampacities of conductors shall be as shown in Table 610-14(a).

For the ampacities of conductors between controllers and resistors, see Section 430-23.

Table 610-14(a). Ampacities of Insulated Conductors up to Four Conductors in Raceway or Cable** Used with Short-Time Rated Crane and Hoist Motors

Size AWG MCM	75°C Type MTW, RH, RHW, THW, THWN, XHHW		90°C Type AVB, FEP, FEPB, PFA, PFAH, RHH, SA, TA, THHN, XHHW*, Z		110°C Type AVA	
	60 min	30 min	60 min	30 min	60 min	30 min
16	10	12	..	..	..	..
14	25	26	31	32	38	40
12	30	33	36	40	45	50
10	40	43	49	52	60	65
8	55	60	63	69	73	80
6	76	86	83	94	93	105
5	85	95	95	106	109	121
4	100	117	111	130	126	147
3	120	141	131	153	145	168
2	137	160	148	173	163	190
1	143	175	158	192	177	215
0	190	233	211	259	239	294
00	222	267	245	294	275	331
000	280	341	305	372	339	413
0000	300	369	319	399	352	440
250	364	420	400	461	447	516
300	455	582	497	636	554	707
350	486	646	542	716	616	809
400	538	688	593	760	666	856
450	600	765	660	836	740	930
500	660	847	726	914	815	1004

Other insulations shown in Table 310-13 and approved for the temperatures and location shall be permitted to be substituted for those shown in Table 610-14(a). The allowable ampacities of conductors used with 15-minute motors shall be the 30-minute ratings increased by 12 percent.   *For dry locations only. See Table 310-13.   **For 5 or more simultaneously energized power conductors in raceway or cable, the ampacity of each power conductor shall be reduced to a value of 80 percent of that shown in the table.

(b) Secondary Resistor Conductors.   Where the secondary resistor is separate from the controller, the minimum size of the conductors between controller and resistor shall be calculated by multiplying the motor secondary current by the appropriate factor from Table 610-14(b) and selecting a wire from Table 610-14(a).

Table 610-14(b).   Secondary Conductor Rating Factors

Time in Seconds		Ampacity of Wire in Percent of Full-Load Secondary Current
On	**Off**	
5	75	35
10	70	45
15	75	55
15	45	65
15	30	75
15	15	85
Continuous Duty		110

(c) Minimum Size.   Conductors external to motors and controls shall not be smaller than No. 16.

Exception No. 1: No. 18 wire in multiple conductor cord shall be permitted for control circuits at not over 7 amperes.

Exception No. 2: Wires not smaller than No. 20 shall be permitted for electronic circuits.

(d) Contact Conductors.   Contact wires shall have an ampacity not less than that required by Table 610-14(a) for 75°C wire, and in no case shall they be smaller than the following:

Distance Between End Strain Insulators or Clamp-type Intermediate Supports	Size of Wire
0-30 feet	No. 6
30-60 feet	No. 4
Over 60 feet	No. 2

For SI units: one foot = 0.3048 meter.

(e) Calculation of Motor Load.

(1) For one motor, use 100 percent of motor nameplate full-load ampere rating.

(2) For multiple motors on a single crane or hoist, the minimum circuit ampacity of the power supply conductors on a crane or hoist shall be the nameplate full-load ampere rating of the largest motor or group of motors for any single crane motion, plus 50 percent of the nameplate full-load ampere rating of the next largest motor or group of motors, using that column of Table 610-14(a) which applies to the longest time-rated motor.

(3) For multiple cranes and/or hoists supplied by a common conductor system, compute the motor minimum ampacity for each crane as defined in Section 610-14(e), add them together, and multiply the sum by the appropriate demand factor from Table 610-14(e).

(f) Other Loads.   Additional loads, such as heating, lighting, and air conditioning, shall be provided for by application of the appropriate sections of this Code.

Table 610-14(e).   Demand Factors

Number of Cranes or Hoists	Demand Factor
2	0.95
3	0.91
4	0.87
5	0.84
6	0.81
7	0.78

(g) Nameplate.   Each crane, monorail, or hoist shall be provided with a visible nameplate marked with the maker's name, the rating in volts, frequency, number of phases, and circuit ampacity as calculated in Section 610-14(e) and (f).

610-15. Common Return.   Where a crane or hoist is operated by more than one motor, a common-return conductor of proper ampacity shall be permitted.

C. Contact Conductors

610-21. Installation of Contact Conductors.   Contact conductors shall comply with (a) through (h) below.

(a) Locating or Guarding Contact Conductors.   Runway contact conductors shall be guarded and bridge contact conductors shall be located or guarded in a manner that persons cannot inadvertently touch energized current-carrying parts.

(b) Contact Wires.   Wires that are used as contact conductors shall be secured at the ends by means of approved strain insulators and shall be so mounted on approved insulators that the extreme limit of displacement of the wire will not bring the latter within less than 1½ inches (38 mm) from the surface wired over.

(c) Supports Along Runways.   Main contact conductors carried along runways shall be supported on insulating supports placed at intervals not exceeding 20 feet (6.1 m).

Exception: Supports for grounded rail conductors as provided in (f) below shall not be required to be of the insulating type.

Such conductors shall be separated not less than 6 inches (152 mm) other than for monorail hoists where a spacing of not less than 3 inches (76 mm) shall be permitted. Where necessary, intervals between insulating supports shall be permitted to be increased up to 40 feet (12.2 m), the separation between conductors being increased proportionately.

(d) Supports on Bridges.   Bridge wire contact conductors shall be kept at least 2½ inches (64 mm) apart, and where the span exceeds 80 feet (24.4 m), insulating saddles shall be placed at intervals not exceeding 50 feet (15.2 m).

(e) Supports for Rigid Conductors.   Conductors along runways and crane bridges, which are of the rigid type specified in Section 610-13, Exception No. 2, and not contained within an approved enclosed assembly, shall be carried on insulating supports spaced at intervals of not more than eighty times the vertical dimension of the conductor, but in no case greater than 15 feet (4.57 m), and spaced apart sufficiently to give a clear electrical separation of conductors or adjacent collectors of not less than 1 inch (25.4 mm).

(f) Track as Circuit Conductor. Monorail, tramrail, or crane-runway tracks shall be permitted as a conductor of current for one phase of a 3-phase, alternating-current system furnishing power to the carrier, crane, or trolley, provided all of the following conditions are met:

(1) The conductors supplying the other two phases of the power supply are insulated.

(2) The power for all phases is obtained from an insulating transformer.

(3) The voltage does not exceed 300 volts.

(4) The rail serving as a conductor is effectively grounded at the transformer and also shall be permitted to be grounded by the fittings used for the suspension or attachment of the rail to a building or structure.

Crane-runway tracks are permitted as a current-carrying conductor where part of a 3-phase ac system is furnishing power to the crane. Figure 610-2 illustrates a 3-phase isolated delta secondary with one phase grounded (at the transformer and is also permitted to be grounded through the metal supporting means attached to the metal frame of a building).

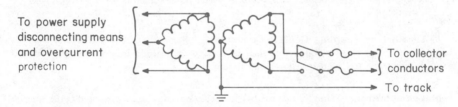

Figure 610-2. Three-phase delta isolating transformer.

(g) Electrical Continuity of Contact Conductors.   All sections of contact conductors shall be mechanically joined to provide a continuous electrical connection.

(h) Not to Supply Other Equipment.   Contact conductors shall not be used as feeders for any equipment other than the crane or cranes which they are primarily designed to serve.

610-22. Collectors.   Collectors shall be so designed as to reduce to a minimum sparking between them and the contact conductor; and where operated in rooms used for the storage of easily ignitible combustible fibers and materials, they shall comply with Section 503-13.

D. Disconnecting Means

610-31. Runway Conductor Disconnecting Means.   A disconnecting means having a continuous ampere rating not less than that computed in Section 610-14(e) and (f) shall be provided between the runway contact conductors and the power supply. Such disconnecting means shall consist of a motor circuit switch or circuit breaker. This disconnecting means shall be readily accessible and operable from the ground or floor level, shall be arranged to be locked in the open position, shall open all ungrounded conductors simultaneously, and shall be placed within view of the crane or hoist and the runway contact conductors.

610-32. Disconnecting Means for Cranes and Monorail Hoists.   A motor circuit switch or circuit breaker arranged to be locked in the open position shall be provided in the leads from the runway contact conductors or other power supply on all cranes and monorail hoists.

Exception: Where a monorail hoist or hand-propelled crane bridge installation meets all of the following, the disconnect shall be permitted to be omitted.

a. The unit is floor controlled.

b. The unit is within view of the power supply disconnecting means.

c. No fixed work platform has been provided for servicing the unit.

Where the disconnecting means is not readily accessible from the crane or monorail hoist operating station, means shall be provided at the operating station to open the power circuit to all motors of the crane or monorail hoist.

Many crane installations are not arranged so that the unit is within view of the power supply disconnecting means, hence the requirement that a disconnecting means (lock-open type) be provided in the contact conductors. However, personnel should be aware that while servicing one crane, another unit on the same system could remain energized and could be run in to the person performing maintenance on the locked-out unit.

610-33. Rating of Disconnecting Means. The continuous ampere rating of the switch or circuit breaker required by Section 610-32 shall not be less than 50 percent of the combined short-time ampere rating of the motors, nor less than 75 percent of the sum of the short-time ampere rating of the motors required for any single motion.

E. Overcurrent Protection

610-41. Feeders, Runway Conductors. The runway supply conductors and main contact conductors of a crane or monorail shall be protected by an overcurrent device(s) which shall not be greater than the largest rating or setting of any branch-circuit protective device, plus the sum of the nameplate ratings of all the other loads with application of the demand factors from Table 610-14(e).

610-42. Branch-Circuit Protection. Branch circuits shall be protected as follows:

(a) Fuse or Circuit Breaker Rating. Crane, hoist, and monorail hoist motor branch circuits shall be protected by fuses or inverse-time circuit breakers having a rating in accordance with Table 430-152. Taps to control circuits shall be permitted to be taken from the load side of a branch-circuit protective device, provided each tap and piece of equipment is properly protected.

Exception No. 1: When two or more motors operate a single motion, the sum of their nameplate current ratings shall be considered as a single motor current in the above calculations.

Exception No. 2: Two or more motors shall be permitted to be connected to the same branch circuit if no tap to an individual motor has an ampacity less than one-third that of the branch circuit and if each motor is protected for running overcurrent according to Section 610-43.

(b) Taps to Brake Coils. Taps to brake coils do not require separate overcurrent protection.

610-43. Motor Running Overcurrent Protection. Each motor shall be protected from running overcurrent by one of the following means:

(1) A single motor shall be considered as protected when the branch-circuit overcurrent device meets the rating requirements of Section 610-42.

(2) Overload relay elements in each ungrounded circuit conductor, with all relay heaters protected from short circuit by the branch-circuit protection.

(3) Thermal sensing device(s), sensitive to motor temperature or to temperature and current which are thermally in contact with the motor winding(s). A hoist or trolley is considered to be protected if the sensing device is connected in the hoist's upper limit switch circuit so as to prevent further hoisting during an overcurrent condition of either motor.

Exception No. 1: If the motor is manually controlled, with spring return controls, the running overcurrent protective device need not protect the motor against stalled rotor conditions.

Exception No. 2: Where two or more motors drive a single trolley, truck, or bridge and are controlled as a unit by a single set of running overcurrent devices with a rating equal to the sum of their rated full-load currents. A hoist or trolley is considered to be protected if the sensing device is connected in the hoist's upper limit switch circuit so as to prevent further hoisting during an overtemperature condition of either motor.

Exception No. 3: Hoists and monorail hoists and their trolleys which are not used as part of an overhead traveling crane do not require individual motor running overcurrent protection provided the largest motor does not exceed 7½ horsepower and all motors are under manual control of the operator.

F. Control

610-51. Separate Controllers.   Each motor shall be provided with an individual controller.

Exception No. 1: Where two or more motors drive a single hoist, carriage, truck, or bridge, they shall be permitted to be controlled by a single controller.

Exception No. 2: One controller shall be permitted to be switched between motors provided,

a. The controller shall have a horsepower rating which shall not be lower than the horsepower rating of the largest motor.

b. Only one motor is operated at one time.

610-53. Overcurrent Protection.   Conductors of control circuits shall be protected against overcurrent. Control circuits shall be considered as protected by overcurrent devices that are rated or set at not more than 300 percent of the ampacity of the control conductors.

Exception No. 1: Taps to control transformers shall be considered as protected when the secondary circuit is protected by a device rated or set at not more than 200 percent of the rated secondary current of the transformer and not more than 200 percent of the ampacity of the control circuit conductors.

Exception No. 2: Such conductors shall be considered as being properly protected by the branch-circuit overcurrent devices where the opening of the control circuit would create a hazard, as for example, the control circuit of a hot metal crane.

610-55. Limit Switch.   A limit switch or other device shall be provided to prevent the load block from passing the safe upper limit of travel of all hoisting mechanisms.

610-57. Clearance.   The dimension of the working space in the direction of access to live parts which are likely to require examination, adjustment, servicing, or maintenance while alive shall be a minimum of 2½ feet (62 mm). Where controls are enclosed in cabinets, the door(s) shall either open at least 90 degrees or be removable.

G. Grounding

610-61. Grounding. All exposed metal parts of cranes, monorail hoists, hoists and accessories including pendant controls shall be metallically joined together into a continuous electrical conductor so that the entire crane or hoist will be grounded in accordance with Article 250. Moving parts, other than removable accessories or attachments having metal-to-metal bearing surfaces, shall be considered to be electrically connected to each other through the bearing surfaces for grounding purposes. The trolley frame and bridge frame shall be considered as electrically grounded through the bridge and trolley wheels and its respective tracks unless local conditions, such as paint or other insulating material, prevent reliable metal-to-metal contact. In this case a separate bonding conductor shall be provided.

ARTICLE 620 — ELEVATORS, DUMBWAITERS, ESCALATORS, AND MOVING WALKS

Contents

K. Overspeed

620-91. Overspeed Protection for Elevators.

620-92. Motor-Generator Overspeed Device.

620-101. Emergency Power.
  (a) Other Building Loads.
  (b) Disconnecting Means.

A. General

620-1. Scope.   This article covers the installation of electric equipment and wiring used in connection with elevators, dumbwaiters, escalators, and moving walks.

For further information, see Safety Code for Elevators, Dumbwaiters, Escalators and Moving Walks (ANSI A17.1-1978).

This article is also applicable to similar equipment, such as moving theater stages. The fine print note is necessary to provide for lighting requirements for and about the equipment, including workspace areas.

620-2. Voltage Limitations.   The nominal voltage used for elevator, dumbwaiter, escalator, and moving-walk operating control and signaling circuits, operating equipment, driving machine motors, machine brakes, and motor-generator sets shall not exceed the following:

(a) 300 Volts.   For operating control and signaling circuits and related equipment, including door operator motors: 300 volts.

Exception: Higher potentials shall be permitted for frequencies of 25-through 60-hertz alternating current or for direct current provided the current in the system cannot, under any conditions, exceed 8 milliamperes for alternating current or 30 milliamperes for direct current.

(b) 600 Volts.   Driving machine motors, machine brakes, and motor-generator sets: 600 volts.

Exception: Higher potentials shall be permitted for driving motors of motor-generator sets.

620-3. Live Parts Enclosed.   All live parts of electric apparatus in the hoistways, at the landings, or in or on the cars of elevators and dumbwaiters or in the wellways or the landings of escalators or moving walks shall be enclosed to protect against accidental contact.

B. Conductors

620-11. Insulation of Conductors.   The insulation of conductors installed in connection with elevators, dumbwaiters, escalators, and moving walks shall comply with (a) through (d) below.

(a) Control Panel Wiring.   Conductors from panels to main circuit resistors shall be flame-retardant and suitable for a temperature of not less than 90°C (194°F). All other wiring on control panels shall be flame-retardant and moisture-resistant.

(b) Traveling Cables.   Traveling cables used as flexible connections between the elevator or dumbwaiter car and the raceway shall be of the types of elevator cable listed in Table 400-4 or other approved types.

(c) Other Wiring.   All conductors in raceways; in or on the cars of elevators and dumbwaiters; in the wellways of escalators and moving walks; and in the machine room of elevators, dumbwaiters, escalators, and moving walks shall have flame-retardant and moisture-resistant insulation.

(d) Thickness of Insulation. The thickness of the insulation of all conductors shall be suitable for the voltage to which the conductors are subjected.

Conductors from control panels to main circuit resistors are to be suitable for temperatures not less than 90°C (194°F). All other control panel wiring and all other wiring associated with elevators, dumbwaiters, escalators, and moving walks are to be flame-retardant and moisture-resistant. See Table 310-13 for conductor application and insulation. See also Table 310-16.

See Table 400-4 for approved types of elevator cables to be used in hazardous and nonhazardous locations. See also Notes 4 and 6 to Table 400-4. A characteristic equally important with respect to safety is the prevention of twisting of cables during their rise and fall with the elevator or dumbwaiter.

620-12. Minimum Size of Conductors. The minimum size of conductors used for elevator, dumbwaiter, escalator, and moving-walk wiring, other than conductors that form an integral part of control equipment, shall be as follows:

(a) Traveling Cables.

(1) For lighting circuits: No. 14.

Exception: No. 20 or larger conductors shall be permitted in parallel provided the ampacity is equivalent to at least that of No. 14 wire.

(2) Operating control and signaling circuits: No. 20.

(b) Other Wiring. All operating control and signaling circuits: No. 24.

More extensive use of electronics with corresponding lower required currents permits the use of smaller wire sizes, hence conductors of elevator cables may be sized as small as No. 20 AWG conforming to the description in Table 400-4. Operating control and signal circuits in other than traveling cables may be as small as No. 24 AWG. In the 1978 *Code* these were limited to No. 20 AWG minimum.

620-13. Motor Circuit Conductors. Conductors supplying elevator, dumbwaiter, escalator or moving-walk motors shall have an ampacity in accordance with (a), (b), and (c) below based on the nameplate current rating of the motors. With generator field control, the ampacity shall be based on the nameplate current rating of the driving motor of the motor-generator set which supplies power to the elevator motor.

The heating of conductors depends on root-mean-square current values which, with generator field control, are reflected by the nameplate current rating of the motor-generator set driving motor rather than by the rating of the elevator motor, which represents actual but short-time and intermittent full-load current values.

(a) Conductors Supplying Single Motor. Conductors supplying a single motor shall have an ampacity in conformance with Section 430-22, and Table 430-22(a) Exception.

(b) Conductors Supplying Several Motors. Conductors supplying two or more motors shall have an ampacity of not less than 125 percent of the nameplate current rating of the highest rated motor in the group plus the sum of the nameplate current ratings of the remainder of the motors in the group.

(c) Feeder Demand Factor. Feeder conductors of less ampacity than required by (b) above shall be permitted subject to the requirements of Section 430-26.

C. Wiring

620-21. Wiring Methods.   Conductors located in hoistways, in escalator and moving-walk wellways, in or on cars, and in machine and control rooms, not including the traveling cables connecting the car and hoistway wiring, shall be installed in rigid metal conduit, intermediate metal conduit, electrical metallic tubing, wireways, or be Type MC cable or Type MI cable.

Exception No. 1: Flexible metal conduit or Type AC cable shall be permitted in hoistways and in escalator and moving-walk wellways between risers and limit switches, interlocks, operating buttons, and similar devices. Low-voltage cables (24 volts or less) shall be permitted to be installed between risers and signal fixtures.

Exception No. 2: Short runs of flexible metal conduit or Type AC cable shall be permitted on cars where so located as to be free from oil and if securely fastened in place.

Exception No. 3: Type S, SO, STO, or ST cords shall be permitted as flexible connections between the fixed wiring on the car and the switches on car doors or gates. Such cords shall be permitted as flexible connections for the top-of-car operating device or the car top work light. These devices or fixtures shall be grounded by means of a grounding conductor run with the circuit conductors.

Exception No. 4: Conductors between control panels and machine motors, machine brakes, and motor-generator sets, not exceeding 6 feet (1.83 m) in length, shall be permitted to be grouped together and taped or corded without being installed in a raceway provided the taping or cording is painted with an insulating paint. Such cable groups shall be supported at intervals of not more than 3 feet (914 mm) and so located as to be free from physical damage.

Where motor-generators and machine motors are located adjacent to or underneath control equipment and are provided with extra length terminal leads not exceeding 6 feet (1.83 m) in length, such leads shall be permitted to be extended to connect directly to controller terminal studs without regard to the carrying-capacity requirements of Articles 430 and 445. Auxiliary gutters shall be permitted in machine and control rooms between controllers, starters, and similar apparatus.

Section 620-21 has been revised in the 1981 *Code* to make it clear that the rigid conduit required in the first paragraph is rigid *metal* conduit. Rigid nonmetallic conduit is not permitted.

620-22. Car Light Source.   On multicar installations, a separate branch circuit shall supply the car lights for each elevator.

D. Installation of Conductors

620-31. Raceway Terminal Fittings.   Conductors shall comply with Section 300-16(b). In locations where conduits project from the floor and terminate in other than a wiring enclosure, they shall extend at least 6 inches (152 mm) above the floor.

620-32. Wireways.   Section 362-5 shall not apply to wireways. The sum of the cross-sectional area of the individual conductors in a wireway shall not be more than 50 percent of the interior cross-sectional area of the wireway.

Vertical runs of wireways shall be securely supported at intervals not exceeding 15 feet (4.57 m) and shall have not more than one joint between supports. Adjoining wireway sections shall be securely fastened together to provide a rigid joint.

620-33. Number of Conductors in Raceways. The sum of the cross-sectional area of the operating and control circuit conductors in raceways shall not exceed 40 percent of the interior cross-sectional area of the raceway.

Exception: In wireways as permitted in Section 620-32.

620-34. Supports. Supports for cables or raceways in a hoistway or in an escalator or moving-walk wellway shall be securely fastened to the guide rail or to the hoistway or wellway construction.

620-35. Auxiliary Gutters (Wiring Troughs). Auxiliary gutters shall not be subject to the restrictions of Section 374-2 as to length or of Section 374-5 as to number of conductors.

620-36. Different Systems in One Raceway or Traveling Cable. Conductors for operating, control, power, signaling, and lighting circuits of 600 volts or less shall be permitted to be run in the same traveling cable or raceway system if all conductors are insulated for the maximum voltage found in the cables or raceway system and if all live parts of the equipment are insulated from ground for this maximum voltage. Such a traveling cable or raceway shall also be permitted to include a pair of telephone conductors for the car telephone, provided such conductors are insulated for the maximum voltage found in the cable or raceway system.

With the use of greater numbers of individual cables and the use of much longer cables in tall buildings, there is a possibility of intertwisting cable loops. In order to eliminate the practice of tying a cable to the traveling cable with its proper operation, one elevator cable or raceway is permitted to enclose all the conductors of power, control, lighting, video, and communication circuits where all conductors are insulated for the maximum voltage of any conductor within the cable or raceway.

620-37. Wiring in Hoistways. Main feeders for supplying power to elevators and dumbwaiters shall be installed outside the hoistway. Only such electric wiring, conduit, and cable used directly in connection with the elevator or dumbwaiter, including wiring for signals, for communication with the car, for lighting and ventilating the car, and wiring for fire-detecting systems for the hoistways, shall be permitted inside the hoistway.

Exception: In existing structures, feeders for elevators or other purposes shall be permitted within a hoistway by special permission provided no conductors are spliced within the hoistway.

620-38. Electric Equipment in Garages and Similar Occupancies. Electric equipment and wiring used for elevators, dumbwaiters, escalators, and moving walks in garages shall comply with the requirements of Article 511. Wiring and equipment located on the underside of the car platform shall be considered as being located in the hazardous area.

620-39. Sidewalk Elevators. Sidewalk elevators with sidewalk doors located exterior to the building shall have all electric wiring in rigid metal conduit, intermediate metal conduit, liquidtight flexible metal conduit or electrical metallic tubing and all electrical outlets, switches, junction boxes, and fittings shall be weatherproof.

E. Traveling Cables

620-41. Suspension of Traveling Cables. Traveling cables shall be so suspended at the car and hoistways' ends as to reduce the strain on the individual copper conductors to a minimum. Traveling cables shall be supported by one of the following means: (1) by its steel supporting fillers; (2) by looping the cables around supports for unsupported lengths less than 100 feet (30.5 m); (3) by suspending from the supports by a means that automatically tightens around the cable when tension is increased.

620-42. Hazardous (Classified) Locations.   In hazardous (classified) locations, traveling cables shall be of a type approved for hazardous (classified) locations and shall be secured to explosionproof cabinets as provided in Section 501-11.

620-43. Location of and Protection for Cables.   Traveling cable supports shall be so located as to reduce to a minimum the possibility of damage due to the cables coming in contact with the hoistway construction or equipment in the hoistway. Where necessary, suitable guards shall be provided to protect the cables against damage.

F. Control

620-51. Disconnecting Means.   Elevators, dumbwaiters, escalators, and moving walks shall have a single means for disconnecting all ungrounded main power supply conductors for each unit.

On single- and multi-car installations where a separate power supply is used for signals or lights or other equipment (multicar) common to the group, additional separate disconnecting means shall be provided to disconnect all such ungrounded conductors for these power supplies.

Where interconnections between control panels are necessary for operation of the system on multicar installations that remain energized from a source other than the disconnecting means, a warning sign shall be mounted on or adjacent to the disconnecting means. The sign shall be clearly legible and shall read "Warning — Parts of the control panel are not de-energized by this switch."

   (a) Type.   The disconnecting means shall be an enclosed externally operable fused motor circuit switch or circuit breaker arranged to be locked in the open position. No provision shall be made to close this disconnecting means from any other part of the premises, nor shall circuit breakers be opened automatically by a fire alarm system.

   (b) Location.   The disconnecting means shall be located where it is readily accessible to qualified persons. Where practicable, the disconnecting means shall be located adjacent to the door of the machine room or enclosure.

   (1) On ac control and rheostatic controlled elevators, the disconnecting means shall be located in the vicinity of the controller. When the machine is not in the vicinity of the controller, an additional manually operated switch shall be provided at the machine, connected in the control circuit to prevent starting.

   (2) On elevators with generator field control, the disconnecting means shall be located within sight of the motor starter for the driver motor of the motor-generator set. When the disconnecting means is not within sight of the hoist machine, the control panel, or the motor-generator set, an additional manually operated switch shall be installed adjacent to the remote equipment, connected in the control circuit to prevent starting.

620-53. Phase Protection.

   (a) Electric Elevators.   Electric elevators driven by polyphase alternating-current motors shall be provided with a means to prevent starting of the elevator motor when: (1) the phase rotation is in the wrong direction, or (2) there is a failure in any phase.

If the motor rotation were in the wrong direction, the elevator car would also travel in the wrong direction, hence the use of a reverse-phase relay which would prevent the controller from energizing the motor. This condition is possible when a workman unintentionally crosses two conductor leads of the motor circuit during maintenance or replacement.

(b) Hydraulic Elevators. Hydraulic elevators powered by a polyphase alternating-current motor shall be provided with the means to prevent overheating of the drive system (pump and motor) due to phase rotation reversals or failure.

The requirement in Section 620-53(b) is new in the 1981 *Code*. Although phase reversal will not result in the car traveling in the wrong direction if the elevator is hydraulically operated, phase reversal can cause overheating of the drive system because the pump will run backwards.

G. Overcurrent Protection

620-61. Overcurrent Protection. Overcurrent protection shall be provided as follows:

(a) Control and Operating Circuits. Control and operating circuits and signaling circuits shall be protected against overcurrent in accordance with the requirements of Section 725-12.

(b) Motors.

(1) Duty on elevator and dumbwaiter driving machine motors and driving motors of motor-generators used with generator field control shall be classed as intermittent. Such motors shall be protected against overcurrent in accordance with Section 430-33.

(2) Duty on escalator and moving-walk driving machine motors shall be classed as continuous. Such motors shall be protected against overcurrent in accordance with Section 430-32.

(3) Escalator and moving-walk driving machine motors and driving motors of motor-generator sets shall be protected against running overcurrent as provided in Table 430-37.

H. Machine Room

620-71. Guarding Equipment. Elevator, dumbwaiter, escalator, and moving-walk driving machines, motor-generator sets, controllers, auxiliary control equipment, and disconnecting means shall be installed in a room or enclosure set aside for that purpose. The room or enclosure shall be secured against unauthorized access.

Exception: Dumbwaiter, escalator, or moving-walk controllers shall be permitted outside the spaces herein specified, provided they are enclosed in cabinets with doors or removable panels capable of being locked in the closed position and the disconnecting means is located adjacent to the controller. Such cabinets shall be permitted in the balustrading on the side away from the moving steps or moving treadway.

620-72. Clearance Around Control Panels. Sufficient clear working space shall be provided around control panels to provide safe and convenient access to all live parts of the equipment necessary for maintenance and adjustment. The minimum clear working space about live parts on control panels shall not be less than specified in Section 110-16.

Exception: Where an escalator or moving-walk control panel is mounted in the same space as the escalator or moving-walk drive machine and the clearances specified cannot be provided, the clearance requirements of Section 110-16 shall be permitted to be waived where the entire panel is arranged so that it can be readily removed from the machine space and is provided with flexible leads to all external connections.

Where control panels are not located in the same space as the drive machine, they shall be located in cabinets with doors or removable panels capable of being locked in the closed position. Such cabinets shall be permitted in the balustrading on the side away from the moving steps or moving treadway.

J. Grounding

620-81. Metal Raceways Attached to Cars. Conduit, Type MC cable, or Type AC cable attached to elevator cars shall be bonded to grounded metal parts of the car with which they come in contact.

620-82. Electric Elevators. For electric elevators, the frames of all motors, elevator machines, controllers, and the metal enclosures for all electric devices in or on the car or in the hoistway shall be grounded.

620-83. Nonelectric Elevators. For elevators other than electric having any electric conductors attached to the car, the metal frame of the car, where normally accessible to persons, shall be grounded.

620-85. Inherent Ground. Equipment mounted on members of the structural metal frame of a building shall be considered to be grounded. Metal car frames supported by metal hoisting cables attached to or running over sheaves or drums of elevator machines shall be considered to be grounded where the machine is grounded in accordance with Article 250.

K. Overspeed

620-91. Overspeed Protection for Elevators. Under overhauling load conditions a means shall be provided on the load side of each elevator power disconnecting means to prevent the elevator from attaining a speed equal to the governor tripping speed or a speed in excess of 125 percent of the elevator rated speed, whichever is the lesser.

Overhauling load conditions shall include all loads up to rated elevator loads for freight elevators and all loads up to 125 percent of rated elevator loads for passenger elevators.

620-92. Motor-Generator Overspeed Device. Motor-generators driven by direct-current motors and used to supply direct current for the operation of elevator machine motors shall be provided with speed-limiting devices as required by Section 430-89(c) that will prevent the elevator from attaining at any time a speed of more than 125 percent of its rated speed.

620-101. Emergency Power. An elevator can be powered by an emergency power system provided that when operating on such emergency power there is conformance with Section 620-91.

Exception: Where the emergency power system is designed to operate only one elevator at a time, the energy absorption means, if required, shall be permitted on the power side of the disconnecting means, provided all other requirements of Section 620-91 are conformed to when operating any of the elevators the system might serve.

(a) Other Building Loads. Other building loads, such as power and light that can be supplied by the emergency power system, shall not be considered as means of absorbing the regenerated energy for the purpose of conforming to Section 620-91 unless such loads are using their normal power from the emergency power system when it is activated.

(b) Disconnecting Means. The disconnecting means required by Section 620-51 shall disconnect the emergency power service and the normal power service.

ARTICLE 630 — ELECTRIC WELDERS

Contents

A. General

630-1. Scope. This article covers electric arc welding, resistance welding apparatus, and other similar welding equipment that is connected to an electric supply system.

    The two general types of electric welding are resistance welding and arc welding. Resistance welding or "spot" welding is the process of joining or fusing together electrically two or more metal sheets or parts without any preparation of stock. The metal parts are placed between two electrodes, or welding points, and a heavy current at a low voltage is passed through the electrodes. The metal parts offer a great resistance to the flow of current so that they heat to a molten state and a weld is made.

    Arc welding is the "butting" of two metal parts to be welded and striking an arc at this joint with a metal electrode (a flux coated wire rod). The electrode, itself, is melted and supplies the extra metal necessary for joining the metal parts.

    A transformer supplies current for one ac arc welder and a generator supplies current for one or more dc arc welders.

B. AC Transformer and DC Rectifier Arc Welders

630-11. Ampacity of Supply Conductors. The ampacity of conductors for ac transformer and dc rectifier arc welders shall be as follows:

(a) Individual Welders. The rated ampacity of the supply conductors shall not be less than the current values determined by multiplying the rated primary current in amperes given on the welder nameplate and the following factor based upon the duty cycle or time rating of the welder.

Duty Cycle

Duty Cycle (percent)	100	90	80	70	60	50	40	30	20 or less
Multiplier	1.00	.95	.89	.84	.78	.71	.63	.55	.45

For a welder having a time rating of 1 hour, the multiplying factor shall be 0.75.

(b) Group of Welders. The rated ampacity of conductors that supply a group of welders shall be permitted to be less than the sum of the currents, as determined in accordance with (a) above, of the welders supplied. The conductor rating shall be determined in each case according to the welder loading based on the use to be made of each welder and the allowance permissible in the event that all the welders supplied by the conductors will not be in use at the same time. The load value used for each welder shall take into account both the magnitude and the duration of the load while the welder is in use.

Conductor ratings based on 100 percent of the current, as determined in accordance with (a) above, of the two largest welders, 85 percent for the third largest welder, 70 percent for the fourth largest welder, and 60 percent for all the remaining welders, can be assumed to provide an ample margin of safety under high-production conditions with respect to the maximum permissible temperature of the conductors. Percentage values lower than those given are permissible in cases where the work is such that a high-operating duty cycle for individual welders is impossible.

Even under high-production conditions the loads on transformer arc welders are considered intermittent; therefore, it is permissible to reduce the ampacity of feeder conductors supplying several transformers (three or more) to the allowable percentages described in the fine print note. It is obvious that intermittent transformer arc welder loads would be considerably less than a continuous load equal to the sum of the full-load current ratings of all the transformers. See also Section 630-31(b).

630-12. Overcurrent Protection. Overcurrent protection for ac transformer and dc rectifier arc welders shall be as provided in (a) and (b) below. Where the nearest standard rating of the overcurrent device used is under the value specified in this section, or where the rating or setting specified results in unnecessary opening of the overcurrent device, the next higher rating or setting shall be permitted.

(a) For Welders. Each welder shall have overcurrent protection rated or set at not more than 200 percent of the rated primary current of the welder.

Exception: An overcurrent device shall not be required for a welder having supply conductors protected by an overcurrent device rated or set at not more than 200 percent of the rated primary current of the welder.

(b) For Conductors. Conductors that supply one or more welders shall be protected by an overcurrent device rated or set at not more than 200 percent of the conductor rating.

Some arc-welding machines have a so-called welding-range involving an excess secondary-current output capacity beyond that indicated by the marked secondary rating on the machines. This excess capacity (generally not more than 150 percent of the marked output capacity) is usually supplied by means of one or more secondary taps in addition to the tap, or taps, intended for normal output current; and the higher currents thus available are intended to provide for heavier welding work, including the use of larger size electrodes. This excess capacity is somewhat analogous to the inherent overload capacity of motors and transformers, and it is not covered at present by any definite requirements and is not investigated by Underwriters Laboratories Inc. However, the abuse of this excess current capacity — the overloading of a welding machine, except for relatively short periods of time — may be hazardous and should receive careful consideration by all those concerned.

630-13. Disconnecting Means. A disconnecting means shall be provided in the supply for each ac transformer and dc rectifier arc welder which is not equipped with a disconnect mounted as an integral part of the welder.

The disconnecting means shall be a switch or circuit breaker, and its rating shall not be less than that necessary to accommodate overcurrent protection as specified under Section 630-12.

630-14. Marking. A nameplate shall be provided for ac transformer and dc rectifier arc welders giving the following information: name of manufacturer; frequency; number of phases; primary voltage; rated primary current; maximum open-circuit voltage; rated secondary current; basis of rating, such as the duty cycle or time rating.

C. Motor-Generator Arc Welders

630-21. Ampacity of Supply Conductors. The ampacity of conductors for motor-generator arc welders shall be as follows:

(a) Individual Welders. The rated ampacity of the supply conductors shall not be less than the current values determined by multiplying the rated primary current in amperes given on the welder nameplate and the following factor based upon the duty cycle or time rating of the welder.

Duty Cycle (percent)	100	90	80	70	60	50	40	30	20 or less
Multiplier	1.00	.96	.91	.86	.81	.75	.69	.62	.55

For a welder having a time rating of 1 hour, the multiplying factor shall be 0.80.

(b) Group of Welders. The rated ampacity of conductors that supply a group of welders shall be permitted to be less than the sum of the currents, as determined in accordance with (a) above, of the welders supplied. The conductor rating shall be determined in each case according to the welder loading based on the use to be made of each welder and the allowance permissible in the event that all the welders supplied by the conductors will not be in use at the same time. The load value used for each welder shall take into account both the magnitude and the duration of the load while the welder is in use.

Conductor ratings based on 100 percent of the current, as determined in accordance with (a) above, of the two largest welders, 85 percent for the third largest welder, 70 percent for the fourth largest welder, and 60 percent for all the remaining welders, can be assumed to provide an ample margin of safety under high-production conditions with respect to the maximum permissible temperature of the conductors. Percentage values lower than those given are permissible in cases where the work is such that a high-operating duty cycle for individual welders is impossible.

The ampacity of supply conductors for a welder that is not wired for a specific function, that is, one that is operated at varying intervals for different applications such as dissimilar metals or thicknesses, is permitted to be 70 percent of the rated primary current for automatically fed welders and 50 percent of the rated primary current for manually operated welders.

Rated primary current = kVA x 1,000 ÷ rated primary voltage (using values given on nameplate)

Where the "actual" primary current and duty cycle are known, such as for a welder wired for a specific operation, the ampacity of the supply conductors is not to be less than the product of the actual primary current (current drawn during weld operation) and the multiplier [as given in (a)(2)] for the duty cycle at which the welder will be operated. For example, a spot welder is specifically set to perform 300 welds per hour on a 60-Hz system. Each weld draws current for 16 cycles. During the one-hour period, the welder draws current for 4,800 cycles (300 x 16). There are 216,000 cycles per hour (60 x 60 x 60).

$$\frac{4,800}{216,000} \times 100 \text{ percent} = 2.2 \text{ percent (duty cycle)}$$

or, a seam welder draws current for 3 cycles and is off for 4 cycles during every 7-cycle period.

$$\frac{3}{7} \times 100 \text{ percent} = 42.9 \text{ percent (duty cycle)}$$

An ammeter capable of measuring current impulses for 3 cycles ($\frac{1}{20}$th of a second), as per the example, is required to measure the actual primary current. The duty cycle is set for a specific operation by adjusting the controller for the welder. When sizing supply conductors, voltage drop should be limited to a value permissible for the satisfactory performance of the welder.

630-22. Overcurrent Protection.   Overcurrent protection for motor-generator arc welders shall be as provided in (a) and (b) below. Where the nearest standard rating of the overcurrent device used is under the value specified in this section, or where the rating or setting specified results in unnecessary opening of the overcurrent device, the next higher rating or setting shall be permitted.

   (a) For Welders.   Each welder shall have overcurrent protection rated or set at not more than 200 percent of the rated primary current of the welder.

   Exception: An overcurrent device shall not be required for a welder having supply conductors protected by an overcurrent device rated or set at not more than 200 percent of the rated primary current of the welder.

   (b) For Conductors.   Conductors that supply one or more welders shall be protected by an overcurrent device rated or set at not more than 200 percent of the conductor rating.

630-23. Disconnecting Means.   A disconnecting means shall be provided in the supply connection of each motor-generator arc welder.

   The disconnecting means shall be a circuit breaker or motor-circuit switch, and its rating shall not be less than that necessary to accommodate overcurrent protection as specified under Section 630-22.

630-24. Marking.   A nameplate shall be provided for each motor-generator arc welder giving the following information: name of manufacturer; rated frequency; number of phases; input voltage; input current; maximum open-circuit voltage; rated output current; basis of rating, such as duty cycle or time rating.

D. Resistance Welders

630-31. Ampacity of Supply Conductors. The ampacity of the supply conductors for resistance welders necessary to limit the voltage drop to a value permissible for the satisfactory performance of the welder is usually greater than that required to prevent overheating as prescribed in (a) and (b) below.

(a) Individual Welders. The rated ampacity for conductors for individual welders shall comply with the following:

(1) The rated ampacity of the supply conductors for a welder that may be operated at different times at different values of primary current or duty cycle shall not be less than 70 percent of the rated primary current for seam and automatically fed welders, and 50 percent of the rated primary current for manually operated nonautomatic welders.

(2) The rated ampacity of the supply conductors for a welder wired for a specific operation for which the actual primary current and duty cycle are known and remain unchanged shall not be less than the product of the actual primary current and the multiplier given below for the duty cycle at which the welder will be operated.

Duty Cycle

(percent)	50	40	30	25	20	15	10	7.5	5.0 or less
Multiplier	.71	.63	.55	.50	.45	.39	.32	.27	.22

(b) Groups of Welders. The rated ampacity of conductors that supply two or more welders shall not be less than the sum of the value obtained in accordance with (a) above for the largest welder supplied, and 60 percent of the values obtained for all the other welders supplied.

Explanation of Terms. (1) The rated primary current is the rated kVA multiplied by 1000 and divided by the rated primary voltage, using values given on the nameplate. (2) The actual primary current is the current drawn from the supply circuit during each welder operation at the particular heat tap and control setting used. (3) The duty cycle is the percentage of the time during which the welder is loaded. For instance, a spot welder supplied by a 60-hertz system (216,000 cycles per hour) making four hundred 15-cycle welds per hour would have a duty cycle of 2.8 percent (400 multiplied by 15, divided by 216,000, multiplied by 100). A seam welder operating 2 cycles "on" and 2 cycles "off" would have a duty cycle of 50 percent.

630-32. Overcurrent Protection. Overcurrent protection for resistance welders shall be as provided in (a) and (b) below. Where the nearest standard rating of the overcurrent device used is under the value specified in this section, or where the rating or setting specified results in unnecessary opening of the overcurrent device, the next higher rating or setting shall be permitted.

(a) For Welders. Each welder shall have an overcurrent device rated or set at not more than 300 percent of the rated primary current of the welder.

Exception: An overcurrent device shall not be required for a welder having a supply circuit protected by an overcurrent device rated or set at not more than 300 percent of the rated primary current of the welder.

(b) For Conductors. Conductors that supply one or more welders shall be protected by an overcurrent device rated or set at not more than 300 percent of the conductor rating.

Conductors of resistance welders and arc welders are provided with overcurrent protection against short circuits. Proper application and operation of the welder will safeguard against overload conditions. See comments following Section 630-12(b).

630-33. Disconnecting Means.   A switch or circuit breaker shall be provided by which each resistance welder and its control equipment can be isolated from the supply circuit. The ampere rating of this disconnecting means shall not be less than the supply conductor ampacity determined in accordance with Section 630-31. The supply circuit switch shall be permitted as the welder disconnecting means where the circuit supplies only one welder.

630-34. Marking.   A nameplate shall be provided for each resistance welder giving the following information: name of manufacturer; frequency; primary voltage rated kVA at 50 percent duty cycle; maximum and minimum open-circuit secondary voltage; short-circuit secondary current at maximum secondary voltage; and specified throat and gap setting.

ARTICLE 640 — SOUND-RECORDING AND
SIMILAR EQUIPMENT

Contents

640-1. Scope.   This article covers equipment and wiring for sound-recording and reproduction, centralized distribution of sound, public address, speech-input systems, and electronic organs.

Such equipment includes amplifiers, public address (PA) and centralized sound systems such as are utilized in schools, factories and similar locations, intercommunication devices and systems, and devices used for recording and reproducing voice or music.

640-2. Application of Other Articles.

 (a) Wiring to and Between Devices.   Wiring and equipment from source of power to and between devices connected to the interior wiring systems shall comply with the requirements of Chapters 1 through 4, except as modified by this article.

 (b) Wiring and Equipment.   Wiring and equipment for public-address, speech-input, radio-frequency and audio-frequency systems, and amplifying equipment associated with radio receiving stations in centralized distribution systems shall comply with Article 725.

Chapters 1 through 4 apply generally to branch-circuit wiring that supplies power to sound systems and to wiring that supplies power between components of the system, unless modified by this Article (see Sections 640-3 and 640-4, Exceptions).

Wiring and equipment with electrical power limitations that differentiate them from light and power circuits are to comply with Article 725 (see Section 640-5).

Radio equipment is to comply with Article 810 unless specifically referenced therein, such as Section 810-2.

640-3. Number of Conductors in Raceway.   The number of conductors in a conduit or other raceway shall comply with Tables 1 through 7 of Chapter 9.

Exception No. 1: Special permission may be granted for the installation of two 2-conductor lead-covered cables in ¾-inch conduit, provided the cross-sectional area of each cable does not exceed .11 square inch.

Exception No. 2: Special permission may be granted for the installation of two 2-conductor No. 19 lead-covered cables in ½-inch conduit, provided the sum of the cross-sectional areas of the cables does not exceed 32 percent of the internal cross-sectional area of the conduit.

640-4. Wireways and Auxiliary Gutters.   Wireways shall comply with the requirements of Article 362, and auxiliary gutters shall comply with the requirements of Article 374.

Exception: Where used for sound-recording and reproduction, the following shall be complied with:

a. Conductors in wireways or gutters shall not fill the raceway to more than 75 percent of its depth.

b. Where the cover of auxiliary gutters is flush with the flooring and is subject to the moving of heavy objects, it shall be of steel at least ¼ inch (6.35 mm) in thickness; where not subject to moving of heavy objects, as in the rear of patch or other equipment panels, the cover shall be at least No. 10 MSG.

c. Wireways shall be permitted in concealed places provided they are run in a straight line between outlets or junction boxes. Covers of boxes shall be accessible. Edges of metal shall be rounded at outlet or junction boxes and all rough projections smoothed to prevent abrasion of insulation or conductors. Wireways made of sections shall be bonded and grounded as specified in Section 250-76.

d. Wireways and auxiliary gutters shall be grounded in accordance with the requirements of Article 250. Where the wireway or auxiliary gutter does not contain power-supply wires, the grounding conductor shall not be required to be larger than No. 14 copper or its equivalent. Where the wireway or auxiliary gutter contains power-supply wires, the grounding conductor shall not be smaller than specified in Section 250-95.

640-5. Conductors.   Amplifier output circuits carrying audio-program signals of 70 volts or less and whose open-circuit voltage will not exceed 100 volts shall be permitted to employ Class 2 or Class 3 wiring as covered in Article 725.

The above is based on amplifiers whose open-circuit voltage will not exceed 100 volts when driven with a signal at any frequency from 60 to 100 hertz sufficient to produce rated output (70.7 volts) into its rated load. This also accepts the known fact that the average program material is 12 db below the amplifier rating — thus the average rms voltage for an open-circuit 70-volt output would be only 25 volts.

640-6. Grouping of Conductors. Conductors of different systems grouped in the same conduit or other metal enclosure or in portable cords or cables shall comply with (a) through (c) below.

(a) Power-Supply Conductors. Power-supply conductors shall be properly identified and shall be used solely for supplying power to the equipment to which the other conductors are connected.

(b) Leads to Motor-Generator or Rotary Converter. Input leads to a motor-generator or rotary converter shall be run separately from the output leads.

(c) Conductor Insulation. The conductors shall be insulated individually, or collectively in groups, by insulation at least equivalent to that on the power supply and other conductors.

Exception: Where the power supply and other conductors are separated by a lead sheath or other continuous metallic covering.

640-7. Flexible Cords. Flexible cords and cables shall be of Type S, SJ, ST, SJO, or SJT or other approved types. The conductors of flexible cords, other than power-supply conductors, shall be permitted to be of a size not smaller than No. 26, provided such conductors are not in direct electrical connection with the power-supply conductors and are equipped with a current-limiting means so that the maximum power under any condition will not exceed 150 watts.

640-8. Terminals. Terminals shall be marked to show their proper connections. Terminals for conductors other than power-supply conductors shall be separated from the terminals of the power-supply conductors by a spacing at least as great as the spacing between power-supply terminals of opposite polarity.

Branch-circuit wiring that supplies power to sound systems and their components is usually 115-V or 230-V power circuit and is not considered to be a part of the sound system and therefore is kept separate from sound system cables or conductors. It is permitted in the same enclosure, however, where terminals are spaced according to this section.

640-9. Storage Batteries. Storage batteries shall comply with (a) and (b) below.

(a) Installation. Storage batteries shall be installed in accordance with Article 480.

(b) Conductor Insulation. Storage-battery leads shall be rubber-covered or thermoplastic-covered.

640-10. Circuit Overcurrent Protection. Overcurrent protection shall be provided as follows:

(a) Heater or Filament (Cathode). Circuits to the heater or filament (cathode) of an electronic tube shall have overcurrent protection not exceeding 15 amperes where supplied by lighting branch circuits, or by storage batteries exceeding 20 ampere-hour capacity.

(b) Plate (Anode-Positive). Circuits to the plate (anode-positive) and to the screen grid of an electronic tube shall have overcurrent protection not exceeding 1.0 ampere.

(c) Control Grid. Circuits to the control grid of an electronic tube shall have overcurrent protection not exceeding 1.0 ampere where supplied by lighting branch circuits or by storage batteries exceeding 20 ampere-hour capacity.

(d) Location. Overcurrent devices shall be located as near as practicable to the source of power supply.

Overcurrent protection is to be located at the point where the conductor to be protected receives its supply from a battery or other power source. The three circuits are defined for clarity to assure proper application and value of overcurrent devices.

640-11. Amplifiers and Rectifiers — Type.

(a) Approved Type. Amplifiers and rectifiers shall be of an approved type and shall be suitably housed.

(b) Readily Accessible. Amplifiers and rectifiers shall be so located as to be readily accessible.

(c) Ventilation. Amplifiers and rectifiers shall be so located as to provide sufficient ventilation to prevent undue temperature rise within the housing.

640-12. Hazardous (Classified) Locations. Equipment used in hazardous (classified) locations shall comply with Article 500.

640-13. Protection Against Physical Damage. Amplifiers, rectifiers, loudspeakers, and other equipment shall be so located or protected as to guard against physical damage, such as might result in fire or personal hazard.

ARTICLE 645 — DATA PROCESSING SYSTEMS

For further information, see Standard for the Protection of Electronic Computer/Data Processing Equipment, NFPA 75-1976 (ANSI).

Contents

645-1. Scope. This article covers equipment, power-supply wiring, equipment interconnecting wiring, and grounding of data processing systems, including data communications equipment used as a terminal unit in a data processing room.

This section has been revised for the 1981 *Code* to make it clear that Article 645 includes only equipment and wiring *in the data processing room*. Small terminals, such as remote telephone terminal units and cash registers in supermarkets, are not covered by Article 645.

645-2. Supply Circuits and Interconnecting Cables.

(a) Branch-Circuit Conductors. The branch-circuit conductors to which one or more units of a data processing system are connected to a source of supply shall have an ampacity not less than 125 percent of the total connected load.

(b) Connecting Cables. The data processing system shall be permitted to be connected by means of computer cable or flexible cord and an attachment plug cap or cord-set assembly specifically approved as a part of the data processing system. Separate units shall be permitted to be interconnected by means of flexible cords and cables specifically approved as part of the data processing system. When run on the surface of the floor, they shall be protected against physical damage.

(c) Under Raised Floors.   The power and communications supply cables and interconnecting cables shall be permitted under a raised floor provided:

(1) The raised floor is of suitable construction.

See Electronic Computer/Data Processing Equipment, NFPA 75-1976 (ANSI).

(2) The branch-circuit supply conductors to receptacles are in rigid metal conduit, intermediate metal conduit, electrical metallic tubing, metal wireway, metal surface raceway with metal cover, flexible metal conduit, liquidtight flexible metal conduit, mineral-insulated, metal-sheathed cable, metal clad cable, or Type AC cable.

This section has been revised for the 1981 *Code* to make it clear that the rigid conduit is rigid *metal* conduit and to permit type AC cable under raised floors.

(3) Ventilation in the underfloor area is used for the data processing equipment and data processing area only.

645-3. Disconnecting Means.   A disconnecting means shall be provided to disconnect the power to all electronic equipment in the computer room. This disconnecting means shall be controlled from locations readily accessible to the operator at the principal exit doors. There shall also be a similar disconnecting means to disconnect the air-conditioning system serving this area.

This section has been revised for the 1981 *Code* to delete requirements for "general building areas" and to specify that a disconnecting means is to be provided in a computer room to disconnect the power to all electronic equipment, but not necessarily to other electrical equipment in the room. A similar disconnecting means is also to be provided for the air-conditioning system serving the computer room.

645-4. Grounding.   All exposed noncurrent-carrying metal parts of a data processing system shall be grounded in accordance with Article 250.

645-5. Marking.   Each unit of a data processing system that is intended to be supplied by a branch circuit shall be provided with a manufacturer's nameplate, which shall also include the rating in volts, the operating frequency, and the total load in amperes.

ARTICLE 650 — ORGANS

Contents

650-1. Scope.   This article covers those electric circuits and parts of electrically operated organs which are employed for the control of the sounding apparatus and keyboards. Electronic organs shall comply with the appropriate provisions of Article 640.

650-2. Source of Energy.   The source of energy shall have a potential of not over 15 volts and shall be a self-excited generator, a two-coil transformer-type rectifier, or a battery.

650-3. Insulation — Grounding.   The generator shall be effectively insulated from ground and from the motor driving it, or both the generator and the motor frames shall be grounded in the manner specified in Article 250.

The energy source required to power electrically operated organs has a potential of less than 15 V and is generally supplied by a motor-driven generator, although a rectifier or a battery may be used.

Usually the motor and generator are mounted on the same metal frame and are effectively grounded. However, if this is not the case, the generator is to be effectively insulated from the motor and from ground. If the motor and generator were not grounded and the generator was not effectively insulated, then a motor-winding fault could energize the motor housing and also the generator housing to a potential of 115 V or 230 V (depending on the motor branch-circuit) and damage to the generator windings or the organ circuit conductors could result.

650-4. Conductors.   Conductors shall comply with (a) through (d) below.

(a) Size.   No conductor shall be smaller than No. 26, and the common-return conductor shall not be smaller than No. 14.

(b) Insulation.   Conductors shall have rubber, thermoplastic, asbestos, cotton, or silk insulation.

Exception: The common-return conductors shall be rubber-covered, thermoplastic, or asbestos-covered (Type AA, AI, or AIA).

The cotton or silk shall be permitted to be saturated with paraffin if desired.

(c) Conductors to Be Cabled.   Except the common-return conductor and conductors inside the organ proper, the organ sections and the organ console conductors shall be cabled. The common-return conductor shall be permitted under an additonal covering enclosing both cable and return conductor, or shall be permitted as a separate conductor and shall be permitted to be in contact with the cable.

(d) Cable Covering.   The cable shall be provided with one or more braided outer coverings, or a tape shall be permitted in place of an inner braid. Where not installed in metal raceways, the outer braid shall be flame-retardant or shall be covered with a closely wound fireproof tape.

The common-return conductor carries the full voltage (usually about 10 V) of the control system and must be sized No. 14 or larger. The other wires of the control system may be as small as No. 26 and, being of the same polarity and potential, are not required to be overly protected from each other as they are to be effectively insulated from the common-return conductor.

650-5. Installation of Conductors.   Cables shall be securely fastened in place and shall be permitted to be attached directly to the organ structure without insulating supports. Cables shall not be placed in contact with other conductors.

Insulating supports are not required for such a low-voltage system; however, conductors that are required to be cabled are to have a flame-retardant outer covering or are to be run in metal raceways. Measures should be taken to prevent contact between cables and conductors of other systems.

650-6. Overcurrent Protection. Circuits shall be so arranged that all conductors shall be protected from overcurrent by an overcurrent device rated at not over 15 amperes.

Exception: The main supply conductors and the common-return conductor.

The two conductors that are run from the generator to the point of connection to the common-return conductor and to the many circuit conductors necessary for the system are the "main supply conductors" and do not require overcurrent protection. The common-return conductor also does not require overcurrent protection; however, the circuit conductors are to be arranged to be protected by a 15-A overcurrent device at their connection point to the main supply conductor.

ARTICLE 660 — X-RAY EQUIPMENT

Contents

A. General

660-1. Scope. This article covers all X-ray equipment operating at any frequency or voltage for industrial or other nonmedical or nondental use.

See Article 517 for medical and dental X-ray.

Nothing in this article shall be construed as specifying safeguards against the useful beam or stray X-ray radiation.

Radiation safety and performance requirements of several classes of X-ray equipment are regulated under Public Law 90-602 and are enforced by the Department of Health, Education, and Welfare.

In addition, information on radiation protection by the National Council on Radiation Protection and Measurements are published as Reports of the National Council on Radiation Protection and Measurement. These reports are obtainable from NCRP Publications, P.O. Box 30175, Washington, D.C. 20014.

660-2. Definitions.

Long-Time Rating.   A rating based on an operating interval of 5 minutes or longer.

Mobile.   X-ray equipment mounted on a permanent base with wheels and/or casters for moving while completely assembled.

Momentary Rating.   A rating based on an operating interval that does not exceed 5 seconds.

Portable.   X-ray equipment designed to be hand carried.

Transportable.   X-ray equipment to be installed in a vehicle or that may be readily disassembled for transport in a vehicle.

660-3. Hazardous (Classified) Locations.   Unless approved for the location, X-ray and related equipment shall not be installed or operated in hazardous (classified) locations.

See Article 517, Part G.

X-ray equipment in use in industrial establishments or similar locations is usually for the purpose of inspection of a process or product. This method permits testing without dismantling or applying stress to detect cracks, flaws, or structural details. Welded joints are frequently inspected with X-ray equipment to detect hidden defects that may cause failure under stress.

Among the industrial applications of X-rays, the most common is radiography where shadow pictures of the subject matter are produced on photographic film. The type and thickness of the material involved governs the voltage to be employed and may range from a few thousand volts (kilovolts) to millions of volts (megavolts). It is possible to X-ray metal objects that are 20 in. thick.

Fluoroscopy is another X-ray technique that is used for industrial or commercial applications. This method is similar to radiography, but operates at a much lower voltage range (less than 250 kilovolts) and, instead of producing a film, a shadow picture is projected upon a screen such as is used for security checks of luggage at airport terminals. Fluoroscopy is capable of detecting extremely minute flaws or defects.

660-4. Connection to Supply Circuit.

(a) Fixed and Stationary Equipment.   Fixed and stationary X-ray equipment shall be connected to the power supply by means of a wiring method meeting the general requirements of this Code.

Exception: Equipment properly supplied by a branch circuit rated at not over 30 amperes shall be permitted to be supplied through a suitable attachment plug cap and hard-service cable or cord.

(b) Portable, Mobile, and Transportable Equipment.   Individual branch circuits shall not be required for portable, mobile, and transportable medical X-ray equipment requiring a capacity of not over 60 amperes. Portable and mobile types of X-ray equipment of any capacity shall be supplied through a suitable hard-service cable or cord. Transportable X-ray equipment of any capacity shall be permitted to be connected to its power supply by suitable connections and hard-service cable or cord.

(c) Over 600 Volts, Nominal. Circuits and equipment operated at more than 600 volts, nominal, shall comply with Article 710.

660-5. Disconnecting Means. A disconnecting means of adequate capacity for at least 50 percent of the input required for the momentary rating or 100 percent of the input required for the long-time rating of the X-ray equipment, whichever is greater, shall be provided in the supply circuit. The disconnecting means shall be operable from a location readily accessible from the X-ray control. For equipment connected to a 120-volt, nominal, branch circuit of 30 amperes or less, a grounding-type attachment plug cap and receptacle of proper rating shall be permitted to serve as a disconnecting means.

660-6. Rating of Supply Conductors and Overcurrent Protection.

(a) Branch-Circuit Conductors. The ampacity of supply branch-circuit conductors and the overcurrent protective devices shall not be less than 50 percent of the momentary rating or 100 percent of the long-time rating, whichever is the greater.

(b) Feeder Conductors. The rated ampacity of conductors and overcurrent devices of a feeder for two or more branch circuits supplying X-ray units shall not be less than 100 percent of the momentary demand rating [as determined by (a)] of the two largest X-ray apparatus plus 20 percent of the momentary ratings of other X-ray apparatus.

The ampacity of the branch-circuit conductors and the ratings of disconnecting means and overcurrent protection for X-ray equipment are usually designated by the manufacturer for the specific installation.

660-7. Wiring Terminals. X-ray equipment shall be provided with suitable wiring terminals or leads for the connection of power supply conductors of the size required by the rating of the branch circuit for the equipment.

Exception: Where provided with a permanently attached cord or a cord set.

660-8. Number of Conductors in Raceway. The number of control circuit conductors installed in a raceway shall be determined in accordance with Section 300-17.

660-9. Minimum Size of Conductors. Sizes No. 18 or 16 fixture wires as specified in Section 725-16 and flexible cords shall be permitted for the control and operating circuits of X-ray and auxiliary equipment where protected by not larger than 20-ampere overcurrent devices.

660-10. Equipment Installations. All equipment for new X-ray installations and all used or reconditioned X-ray equipment moved to and reinstalled at a new location shall be of an approved type.

B. Control

660-20. Fixed and Stationary Equipment.

(a) Separate Control Device. A separate control device, in addition to the disconnecting means, shall be incorporated in the X-ray control supply or in the primary circuit to the high-voltage transformer. This device shall be a part of the X-ray equipment, but shall be permitted in a separate enclosure immediately adjacent to the X-ray control unit.

(b) Protective Device. A protective device, which shall be permitted to be incorporated into the separate control device, shall be provided to control the load resulting from failures in the high-voltage circuit.

660-21. Portable and Mobile Equipment. Portable and mobile equipment shall comply with Section 660-20, but the manually controlled device shall be located in or on the equipment.

660-23. Industrial and Commercial Laboratory Equipment.

(a) **Radiographic and Fluoroscopic Types.** All radiographic- and fluoroscopic-type equipment shall be effectively enclosed or shall have interlocks that de-energize the equipment automatically to prevent ready access to live current-carrying parts.

(b) **Diffraction and Irradiation Types.** Diffraction- and irradiation-type equipment shall be provided with a positive means to indicate when it is energized. The indicator shall be a pilot light, readable meter deflection, or equivalent means.

Exception: Equipment or installations effectively enclosed or provided with interlocks to prevent access to live current-carrying parts during operation.

660-24. Independent Control. Where more than one piece of equipment is operated from the same high-voltage circuit, each piece or each group of equipment as a unit shall be provided with a high-voltage switch or equivalent disconnecting means. This disconnecting means shall be constructed, enclosed, or located so as to avoid contact by persons with its live parts.

A control device provides means for initiating and terminating X-ray exposures and automatically times their duration.

C. Transformers and Capacitors

660-35. General. Transformers and capacitors that are part of an X-ray equipment shall not be required to comply with Articles 450 and 460.

High-ratio step-up transformers that are an integral part of an X-ray are not required to comply with Article 450 and are generally used to provide the high voltage necessary for X-ray tubes. There is a lesser degree of fire hazard due to the low primary voltage; therefore, X-ray transformers are not required to be installed in fire-resistant vaults.

660-36. Capacitors. Capacitors shall be mounted within enclosures of insulating material or grounded metal.

D. Guarding and Grounding

660-47. General.

(a) **High-Voltage Parts.** All high-voltage parts, including X-ray tubes, shall be mounted within grounded enclosures. Air, oil, gas, or other suitable insulating media shall be used to insulate the high voltage from the grounded enclosure. The connection from the high-voltage equipment to X-ray tubes and other high-voltage components shall be made with high-voltage shielded cables.

(b) **Low-Voltage Cables.** Low-voltage cables connecting to oil-filled units that are not completely sealed, such as transformers, condensers, oil coolers, and high-voltage switches, shall have insulation of the oil-resistant type.

Grounded enclosures are to be provided for all high-voltage X-ray equipment, including X-ray tubes. High-voltage shielded cables must be used to connect high-voltage equipment to X-ray tubes, and the shield is to be grounded as provided in Section 660-48.

660-48. Grounding. Noncurrent-carrying metal parts of X-ray and associated equipment (controls, tables, X-ray tube supports, transformer tanks, shielded cables, X-ray tube heads, etc.) shall be grounded in the manner specified in Article 250. Portable and mobile equipment shall be provided with an approved grounding-type attachment plug cap.

Exception: Battery-operated equipment.

ARTICLE 665 — INDUCTION AND DIELECTRIC HEATING EQUIPMENT

Contents

A. General

665-1. Scope. This article covers the construction and installation of induction and dielectric heating equipment and accessories for industrial and scientific applications, but not for medical or dental applications, appliances, or line frequency pipelines and vessels heating.

See Article 517 for medical and dental therapeutic equipment.

See Article 422 for appliances.

See Article 427, Part E for line frequency pipelines and vessels heating.

To prevent spurious radiation caused by induction and dielectric heating equipment and to ensure that the frequency spectrum is utilized equitably, the Federal Communications Commission (FCC) has established rules (Code of Federal Regulations, Title 47, Part 18) that govern the use of industrial heating equipment of this type operating above 10 kHz.

665-2. Definitions.

Dielectric Heating.   Dielectric heating is the heating of a nominally insulating material due to its own dielectric losses when the material is placed in a varying electric field.

Heating Equipment.   The term "heating equipment" as used in this article includes any equipment used for heating purposes whose heat is generated by induction or dielectric methods.

Induction Heating.   Induction heating is the heating of a nominally conductive material due to its own I^2R losses when the material is placed in a varying electromagnetic field.

Induction and dielectric heating are used for ovens, furnaces, and industrial equipment where pieces of material are heated by a rapidly alternating magnetic or electric field. For further information on electric heating systems using an induction heater or a dielectric heater on ovens and furnaces, see NFPA 86A, Ovens and Furnaces, and NFPA 86D, Industrial Furnaces Using Vacuum as an Atmosphere.

Theory of Operation — Solid State Converter Power Circuit
The circuit consists of three sections: the rectifier section, the inverter section, and the tank circuit which includes the load coil located on the outside. The rectifier section input power is 480 V ac nominal, 3-phase, 60 Hz. See Figure 665-1. The output of the rectifier section is most generally a fixed 600-V dc nominal. This feeds the inverter section which is a tuned variable frequency switching network that converts the dc power to single-phase nominal, 180 Hz, 1 kHz, 3 kHz, or 10 kHz square wave or sinusoidal power. The operating frequency is determined by the control section. The single-phase output drives the tank circuit which consists of a load coil and tuning capacitors.

Variable output power is achieved by frequency variation of the inverter section. Since the tank circuit is a tuned load, as the output approaches the frequency of the tank circuit, the power into the load approaches the maximum output. At minimum frequency the output power is very low. As the frequency increases, the power increases until a maximum is reached. This is the resonant frequency of the tank circuit.

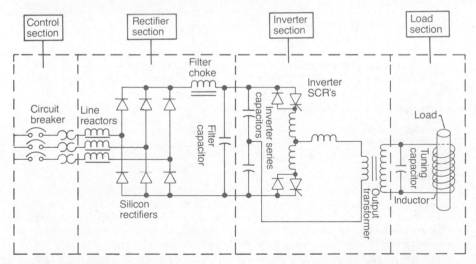

Figure 665-1. Simplified diagram of the components of a solid-state converter used for induction heating. (*Tocco Div. Park Ohio Industries*)

Most induction heating loads exhibit a dynamic change as the work piece passes through the Curie temperature point (where the work load changes from the magnetic to the nonmagnetic state). The converter automatically adjusts to maintain a constant output power during this dynamic load change. If this maximum power is below the operator power setting, the converter unit will automatically limit at this maximum power point.

Induction Heating

Induction heating is accomplished with the aid of a current-carrying conductor that induces the transfer of electrical energy to the work by an eddy current. Induction heating, in general, involves frequencies ranging from 3 to about 500 kHz, and power outputs from a few hundred watts to several thousand kilowatts.

When induction heating is employed, a nominally conductive material is placed in an inductor coil. The effective intensity of inductance is caused by a current flow in the coil at a high frequency which produces a rapidly alternating magnetic field, thereby inducing a voltage in the material to be heated and causing a current to flow through the resistance of the material (I^2R loss), producing induction heating. See Figure 665-2.

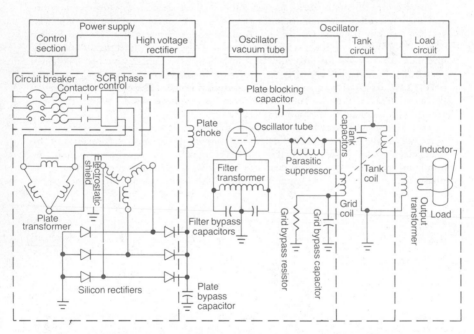

Figure 665-2. Simplified diagram of the components of a vacuum-tube generator used for induction heating. (*Tocco Div. Park Ohio Industries*)

Dielectric Heating

Dielectric heating equipment is similar to induction heating equipment; however, the frequencies are generally higher (in the order of 3 MHz or more) than those in induction heating. This type of heater is useful for heating materials that are commonly thought of as being nonconductive, for instance, heating plastic preforms before molding, curing glue and plywood, drying rayon cakes, and for many similar applications. Frequencies for this type of equipment range from 1 to 200 MHz, especially in the 1 to 50 MHz range. Vacuum tube generators are used exclusively to supply dielectric heating power, and outputs range from a few hundred watts to several hundred kilowatts.

A typical wiring diagram of a vacuum tube generator is shown in Figure 665-3. Whereas induction heating uses a varying magnetic field, dielectric heating employs a varying electric field. This is done by placing the material to be heated between a pair of metal plates, called electrodes, in the output circuit of the generator. When high-frequency voltage is applied to the electrodes, a rapidly alternating electric field is set up between them, passing through the material to be heated. Because of the electrical charges within the molecules of this material, the field causes the molecules to vibrate in proportion to its frequency. This internal molecular action generates the heat used for dielectric heating.

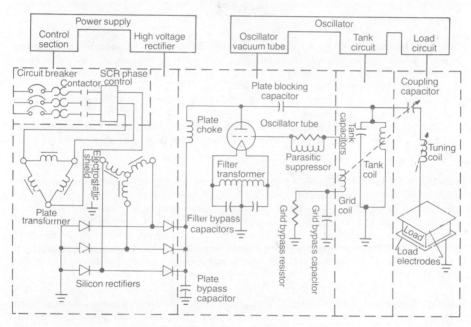

Figure 665-3. Simplified diagram of the components of a vacuum-tube generator used for dielectric heating. (*Tocco Div. Park Ohio Industries*)

665-3. Other Articles.   Wiring from the source of power to the heating equipment shall comply with Chapters 1 through 4. Circuits and equipment operated at more than 600 volts, nominal, shall comply with Article 710.

665-4. Hazardous (Classified) Locations.   Induction and dielectric heating equipment shall not be installed in hazardous (classified) locations as defined in Article 500.

Exception: Where the equipment and wiring are designed and approved for the hazardous (classified) locations.

B. Guarding, Grounding, and Labeling

665-20. Enclosures.   The converting apparatus (including the dc line) and high-frequency electric circuits (excluding the output circuits and remote-control circuits) shall be completely contained within an enclosure or enclosures of noncombustible material.

665-21. Panel Controls.   All panel controls shall be of dead-front construction.

665-22. Access to Internal Equipment.   Doors or detachable panels shall be employed for internal access. Where doors are used giving access to voltages from 500 to 1000 volts ac or dc, either door locks shall be provided or interlocking shall be installed. Where doors are used giving access to voltages of over 1000 volts ac or dc, either mechanical lockouts with a disconnecting means to prevent access until voltage is removed from the cubicle, or both door interlocking and mechanical door locks shall be provided. Detachable panels not normally used for access to such parts shall be fastened in a manner that will make them inconvenient to remove.

665-23. Warning Labels.   "Danger" labels shall be attached on the equipment, and shall be plainly visible even when doors are open or panels are removed from compartments containing voltages of over 250 volts ac or dc.

665-24. Capacitors.   Where capacitors in excess of 0.1 microfarad are used in dc circuits, either as rectifier filter components or suppressors, etc., having circuit voltages of over 240 volts to ground, bleeder resistors or grounding switches shall be used as grounding devices. The time of discharge shall be in accordance with Section 460-6(a).

Where capacitors are individually switched out of a circuit, a bleeder resistor or automatic switch shall be used as a discharge means.

Where auxiliary rectifiers are used with filter capacitors in the output for bias supplies, tube keyers, etc., bleeder resistors shall be used even though the dc voltage may not exceed 240 volts.

665-25. Work Applicator Shielding.   Protective cages or adequate shielding shall be used to guard work applicators other than induction heating coils. Induction heating coils shall be permitted to be protected by insulation and/or refractory materials. Interlock switches shall be used on all hinged access doors, sliding panels, or other easy means of access to the applicator. All interlock switches shall be connected in such a manner as to remove all power from the applicator when any one of the access doors or panels is open. Interlocks on access doors or panels shall not be required if the applicator is an induction heating coil at dc ground potential or operating at less than 150 volts ac.

665-26. Grounding and Bonding.   Grounding and/or inter-unit bonding shall be used wherever required for circuit operation, for limiting to a safe value radio frequency potentials between all exposed noncurrent-carrying parts of the equipment and earth ground, between all equipment parts and surrounding objects, and between such objects and earth ground. Such grounding and bonding shall be installed in accordance with Article 250.

Bonding presents special problems at radio frequencies due to stray currents flowing between units of the equipment or to ground. These special bonding requirements are especially needed at dielectric heating frequencies (100 to 200 MHz) due to the differences in radio-frequency potential that can exist between the equipment and surrounding metal units or other units of the installation. Satisfactory bonding can be accomplished by placing all of the units of the equipment on a flooring or base consisting of a copper or aluminum sheet and thoroughly bonded where necessary by soldering, welding, or bolting.

By such special bonding, the radio-frequency resistance and reactance between units is held to a minimum and any stray circulating currents flowing through this bonding will not cause a dangerous voltage drop.

It is necessary to provide operator protection from high radio-frequency potentials by shielding at dielectric heating frequencies. Interference with radio communication systems at such high frequencies may be eliminated by totally enclosing all components of the circuiting in a shielding of copper or aluminum.

665-27. Marking.   Each heating equipment shall be provided with a nameplate giving the manufacturer's name and model identification and the following input data: line volts, frequency, number of phases, maximum current, full-load kVA, and full-load power factor.

665-28. Control Enclosures.   Direct current or low-frequency ac shall be permitted in the control portion of the heating equipment. This shall be limited to not over 150 volts. Solid or stranded wire No. 18 or larger shall be used. A step-down transformer with proper overcurrent protection shall be permitted in the control enclosure to obtain an ac voltage of less than 150 volts. The higher-voltage terminals shall be guarded to prevent accidental contact. 60-hertz components shall be permitted to control high frequency where properly rated by the induction heating equipment manufacturer. Electronic circuits utilizing solid-state devices and tubes shall be permitted printed circuits or wires smaller than No. 18.

C. Motor-Generator Equipment

665-40. General.   Motor-generator equipment shall include all rotating equipment designed to operate from an ac or dc motor or by mechanical drive from a prime mover, producing an alternating current of any frequency for induction and/or dielectric heating.

665-41. Ampacity of Supply Conductors.   The ampacity of supply conductors shall be determined in accordance with Article 430.

665-42. Overcurrent Protection.   Overcurrent protection shall be provided as specified in Article 430 for the electric supply circuit.

665-43. Disconnecting Means.   The disconnecting means shall be provided as specified in Article 430.

A readily accessible disconnecting means shall be provided by which each heating equipment can be isolated from its supply circuit. The ampere rating of this disconnecting means shall not be less than the nameplate current rating of the equipment. The supply circuit disconnecting means shall be permitted as a heating equipment disconnecting means where the circuit supplies only one equipment.

665-44. Output Circuit.   The output circuit shall include all output components external to the generator, including contactors, transformers, busbars, and other conductors, and shall comply with (a) and (b) below.

  (a) Generator Output.   The output circuit shall be isolated from ground.

  Exception No. 1: Where the capacitive coupling inherent in the generator causes the generator terminals to have voltages from terminal to ground that are equal.

  Exception No. 2: Where a vacuum or controlled atmosphere is used with a coil in a tank or chamber, the center point of the coil shall be grounded to maintain an equal potential between each terminal and ground.

Where rated at over 500 volts, the output circuit shall incorporate a dc ground protector unit. The dc impressed on the output circuit shall not exceed 30 volts and shall not exceed a current capability of 5 milliamperes.

An isolating transformer for matching the load and the source shall be permitted in the output circuit if the output secondary is not at dc ground potential.

  (b) Component Interconnections.   The various components required for a complete induction heating equipment installation shall be connected by properly protected multiconductor cable, busbar, or coaxial cable. Cables shall be installed in nonferrous raceways. Busbars shall be protected, where required, by nonferrous enclosures.

665-47. Remote Control.

(a) **Selector Switch.** Where remote controls are used for applying power, a selector switch shall be provided and interlocked to provide power from only one control point at a time.

(b) **Foot Switches.** Switches operated by foot pressure shall be provided with a shield over the contact button to avoid accidental closing of a switch.

D. Equipment Other than Motor-Generator

665-60. General. Equipment other than motor-generators shall consist of all static multipliers and oscillator-type units utilizing vacuum tubes and/or solid-state devices. The equipment shall be capable of converting ac or dc to an ac frequency suitable for induction and/or dielectric heating.

665-61. Ampacity of Supply Conductors. The ampacity of supply conductors shall be determined in accordance with (a) and (b) below.

(a) **Nameplate Rating.** The ampacity of the circuit conductors shall not be less than the nameplate current rating of the equipment.

Figure 665-4. An 80-kW oscillator used to harden the exhaust valve seats of an automotive engine. (*Tocco Div. Park Ohio Industries*)

(b) **Two or More.** The ampacity of conductors supplying two or more equipments shall not be less than the sum of the nameplate current ratings on all equipments.

Exception: If simultaneous operation of two or more equipments supplied from the same feeder is not possible, the ampacity of the feeder shall not be less than the sum of the nameplate ratings for the largest group of machines capable of simultaneous operation, plus 100 percent of the stand-by currents of the remaining machines supplied.

665-62. Overcurrent Protection. Overcurrent protection shall be provided as specified in Article 240 for the equipment as a whole. This overcurrent protection shall be provided separately or as a part of the equipment.

665-63. Disconnecting Means. A readily accessible disconnecting means shall be provided by which each heating equipment can be isolated from its supply circuit. The rating of this disconnecting means shall not be less than the nameplate rating of the equipment. The supply circuit disconnecting means shall be permitted for disconnecting the heating equipment where the circuit supplies only one equipment.

665-64. Output Circuit. The output circuit shall include all output components external to the converting device, including contactors, transformers, busbars, and other conductors and shall comply with (a) and (b) below.

(a) Converter Output. The output circuit shall be isolated from ground.

Exception: Where a dc voltage can exist at the terminals because of an internal component failure, then the output circuit (direct or coupled) shall be at dc ground potential.

(b) Converter and Applicator Connection. Where the connections between the converter and the work applicator exceed 2 feet (610 mm) in length, the connections shall be enclosed or guarded with nonferrous, noncombustible material.

665-66. Line Frequency in Converter Equipment Output. Commercial frequencies of 25- to 60-hertz alternating-current output shall be permitted to be coupled for control purposes, but shall be limited to not over 150 volts during periods of circuit operation.

665-67. Keying. Where high-speed keying circuits dependent on the effect of "oscillator blocking" are employed, the peak radio-frequency output voltage during the blocked portion of the cycle shall not exceed 100 volts in units employing radio-frequency converters.

665-68. Remote Control.

(a) Selector Switch. Where remote controls are used for applying power, a selector switch shall be provided and interlocked to provide power from only one control point at a time.

(b) Foot Switches. Switches operated by foot pressure shall be provided with a shield over the contact button to avoid accidental closing of the switch.

ARTICLE 668 — ELECTROLYTIC CELLS

Contents

668-1. Scope. The provisions of this article apply to the installation of the electrical components and accessory equipment of electrolytic cells, electrolytic cell lines and process power supply for the production of aluminum, cadmium, chlorine, copper, fluorine, hydrogen peroxide, magnesium, sodium, sodium chlorate and zinc.

Not covered by this article are cells used as a source of electric energy and for electroplating processes and cells used for the production of hydrogen.

In general, any cell line or group of cell lines operated as a unit for the production of a particular metal, gas, or chemical compound may differ from any other cell line or group of cell lines producing the same product because of variations in the particular raw materials used, output capacity, use of proprietary methods or process practices, or other modifying factors to the extent that detailed Code requirements become overly restrictive and do not accomplish the stated purpose of this Code.

For further information, see IEEE Standard for Electrical Safety Practices in Electrolytic Cell Line Working Zones: IEEE Std. 463-1977.

An electrolytic cell line and its dc process power supply circuit, both within a cell line working zone, constitute and are treated as an individual machine supplied from a single source, even though they may cover acres of space, have a load current in excess of 400,000-A dc, or a circuit voltage in excess of 1,000-V dc. The cell line process current passes through each cell in a series connection, and the load current cannot be subdivided, as it can, for example, in the heating circuit of a resistance-type electric furnace.

Because a cell line is supplied by its individual dc rectifier system, the rectifier or the entire cell line circuit is de-energized by removing its source of primary power.

In some electrolytic cell systems, the terminal voltage of the process supply can be appreciable. The voltage-to-ground of exposed live parts from one end of a cell line to the other is variable between the limits of the terminal voltage. Hence, operating and maintenance personnel and their tools are required to be insulated from ground.

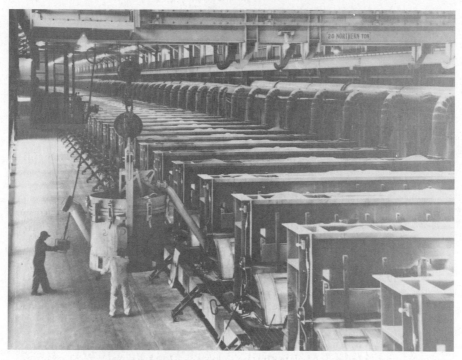

Figure 668-1. A typical potroom in an aluminum reduction plant. (*Alcoa*)

668-2. Definitions.

Cell Line.   An assembly of electrically interconnected electrolytic cells supplied by a source of direct-current power.

Cell Line Attachments and Auxiliary Equipment.   As applied to Article 668, cell line attachments and auxiliary equipment include, but are not limited to: auxiliary tanks; process piping; duct work; structural supports; exposed cell line conductors; conduits and other raceways; pumps, positioning equipment and cell cutout or by-pass electrical devices. Auxiliary equipment includes tools, welding machines, crucibles, and other portable equipment used for operation and maintenance within the electrolytic cell line working zone.

In the cell line working zone, auxiliary equipment includes the exposed conductive surfaces of ungrounded cranes and crane-mounted cell-servicing equipment.

Electrolytic Cell.   A receptacle or vessel in which electrochemical reactions are caused by applying electrical energy for the purpose of refining or producing usable materials.

Electrolytic Cell Line Working Zone.   The cell line working zone is the space envelope wherein operation or maintenance is normally performed on or in the vicinity of exposed energized surfaces of electrolytic cell lines or their attachments.

668-3. Other Articles.

(a) Lighting, Ventilating, Material Handling.   Chapters 1 through 4 shall apply to service feeders, branch circuits, and apparatus for supplying lighting, ventilating, material handling, and the like, which are outside the electrolytic cell line working zone.

(b) Systems Not Electrically Connected.   Those elements of a cell line power-supply system that are not electrically connected to the cell supply system, such as the primary winding of a two-winding transformer, the motor of a motor-generator set, feeders, branch circuits, disconnecting means, motor controllers, and overload protective equipment shall be required to comply with all applicable provisions of this Code.

For the purpose of this section, "electrically connected" shall mean connection capable of carrying current as distinguished from connection through electromagnetic induction.

(c) Electrolytic Cell Lines.   Electrolytic cell lines shall comply with the provisions of Chapters 1, 2, 3, and 4.

Exception No. 1: The electrolytic cell line conductors shall not be required to comply with the provisions of Articles 110, 210, 215, 220, and 225. (See Section 668-11.)

Exception No. 2: Overcurrent protection of electrolytic cell dc process power circuits shall not be required to comply with the requirements of Article 240.

Exception No. 3: Equipment located or used within the electrolytic cell line working zone or associated with the cell line dc power circuits shall not be required to comply with the provisions of Article 250.

Exception No. 4: The electrolytic cells, cell line attachments and the wiring of auxiliary equipments and devices within the cell line working zone shall not be required to comply with the provisions of Articles 110, 210, 215, 220, and 225. (See Section 668-30.)

See Section 668-15 on equipment, apparatus, and structural component grounding.

668-10. Cell Line Working Zone.

(a) Area Covered.   The space envelope of the cell line working zone shall encompass any space:

(1) Within 96 inches (2.44 m) above energized surfaces of electrolytic cell lines or their energized attachments.

(2) Below energized surfaces of electrolytic cell lines or their energized attachments, provided the head room in the space beneath is less than 96 inches (2.44 m).

(3) Within 42 inches (1.07 m) horizontally from energized surfaces of electrolytic cell lines or their energized attachments or from the space envelope described in Section 668-10(a)(1) or (a)(2).

(b) Area Not Covered.   The cell line working zone shall not be required to extend through or beyond walls, floors, roofs, partitions, barriers, or the like.

668-11. DC Cell Line Process Power Supply.

(a) Not Grounded.   The dc cell line process power supply conductors shall not be required to be grounded.

(b) Metal Enclosures Grounded.   All metal enclosures of dc cell line process power supply apparatus operating at a power supply potential between terminals of over 50 volts shall be grounded:

(1) Through protective relaying equipment, or

(2) By No. 2/0 AWG minimum copper grounding conductor or a conductor of equal ampacity.

(c) Grounding Requirements. The grounding connections required by Section 668-11(b) shall be installed in accordance with Sections 250-112, 250-113, 250-115, 250-117, and 250-118.

668-12. Cell Line Conductors.

(a) Insulation and Material. Cell line conductors shall be either bare, covered, or insulated and of copper, aluminum, copper-clad aluminum, steel, or other suitable material.

(b) Size. Cell line conductors shall be of such cross-sectional area that the temperature rise under maximum load conditions and at maximum ambient shall not exceed the safe operating temperature of the conductor insulation or the material of the conductor supports.

(c) Connections. Cell line conductors shall be joined by bolted, welded, clamped, or compression connectors.

668-13. Disconnecting Means.

(a) More than One Process Power Supply. Where more than one dc cell line process power supply serves the same cell line, a disconnecting means shall be provided on the cell line circuit side of each power supply to disconnect it from the cell line circuit.

(b) Removable Links or Conductors. Removable links or removable conductors shall be permitted to be used as the disconnecting means.

668-14. Shunting Means.

(a) Partial or Total Shunting. Partial or total shunting of cell line circuit current around one or more cells shall be permitted.

(b) Shunting One or More Cells. The conductors, switches, or combination of conductors and switches used for shunting one or more cells shall comply with the applicable requirements of Section 668-12.

668-15. Grounding. For equipment, apparatus, and structural components which are required to be grounded by provisions of Article 668, the provisions of Article 250 shall apply.

Exception No. 1: A water pipe electrode shall not be required to be used.

Exception No. 2: Any electrode or combination of electrodes described in Sections 250-81 and 250-83 shall be permitted.

668-20. Portable Electrical Equipment.

(a) Portable Electrical Equipment Not to Be Grounded. The frames and enclosures of portable electrical equipment used within the cell line working zone shall not be grounded.

Exception No. 1: Where the cell line circuit voltage does not exceed 200 volts dc these frames and enclosures shall be permitted to be grounded.

Exception No. 2: These frames and enclosures shall be permitted to be grounded where guarded.

(b) Isolating Transformers. Electrically powered, hand-held, cord-connected portable equipment with ungrounded frames or enclosures used within the cell line working zone shall be connected to receptacle circuits having only ungrounded conductors such as a branch circuit supplied by an isolating transformer with an ungrounded secondary.

Exception: Where frames and enclosures of such equipments are grounded as permitted in Section 668-20(a), Exception No. 1.

(c) **Marking.** Ungrounded portable electrical equipment shall be distinctively marked and shall employ plugs and receptacles of a configuration which prevents connection of this equipment to grounding receptacles and which prevents inadvertent interchange of ungrounded and grounded portable electrical equipments.

668-21. Power Supply Circuits and Receptacles for Portable Electrical Equipment.

(a) **Isolated Circuits.** Circuits supplying power to ungrounded receptacles for hand-held, cord-connected equipments shall be electrically isolated from any distribution system supplying areas other than the cell line working zone and shall be ungrounded. Power for these circuits shall be supplied through isolating transformers. Primaries of such transformers shall operate at not more than 600 volts between conductors and shall be provided with proper overcurrent protection. The secondary voltage of such transformers shall not exceed 300 volts between conductors, and all circuits supplied from such secondaries shall be ungrounded and shall have an approved overcurrent device of proper rating in each conductor.

(b) **Noninterchangeability.** Receptacles and their mating plugs for ungrounded equipment shall not have provision for a grounding conductor and shall be of a configuration which prevents their use for equipment required to be grounded.

(c) **Marking.** Receptacles on circuits supplied by an isolating transformer with an ungrounded secondary shall be a distinctive configuration, distinctively marked, and shall not be used in any other location in the plant.

668-30. Fixed and Portable Electrical Equipment.

(a) **Electrical Equipment Not Required to Be Grounded.** AC systems supplying fixed and portable electrical equipments within the cell line working zone shall not be required to be grounded.

(b) **Exposed Conductive Surfaces Not Required to Be Grounded.** Exposed conductive surfaces, such as electrical equipment housings, cabinets, boxes, motors, raceways, and the like that are within the cell line working zone shall not be required to be grounded.

(c) **Wiring Methods.** Auxiliary electrical devices such as motors, transducers, sensors, control devices, and alarms, mounted on an electrolytic cell or other energized surface, shall be connected by any of the following means:

(1) Multiconductor hard usage cord;

(2) Wire or cable in suitable raceways;

(3) Exposed metal conduit, cable tray, armored cable, or similar metallic systems installed with insulating breaks such that they will not cause a potentially hazardous electrical condition.

(d) **Circuit Protection.** Circuit protection shall not be required for control and instrumentation that are totally within the cell line working zone.

(e) **Bonding.** Bonding of fixed electrical equipment to the energized conductive surfaces of the cell line, its attachments or auxiliaries shall be permitted. Where fixed electrical equipment is mounted on an energized conductive surface it shall be bonded to that surface.

668-31. Auxiliary Nonelectric Connections.   Auxiliary nonelectric connections, such as air hoses, water hoses, and the like, to an electrolytic cell, its attachments, or auxiliary equipments shall not have continuous conductive reinforcing wire, armor, braids and the like. Hoses shall be of a nonconductive material.

668-32. Cranes and Hoists.

(a) Conductive Surfaces to Be Insulated From Ground.   The conductive surfaces of cranes and hoists that enter the cell line working zone shall not be required to be grounded. The portion of an overhead crane or hoist which contacts an energized electrolytic cell or energized attachments shall be insulated from ground.

(b) Hazardous Electrical Conditions.   Remote crane or hoist controls which may introduce hazardous electrical conditions into the cell line working zone shall employ one or more of the following systems:

(1) Insulated and ungrounded control circuit in accordance with Section 668-21(a);

(2) Nonconductive rope operator;

(3) Pendant pushbutton with nonconductive supporting means and having nonconductive surfaces or ungrounded exposed conductive surfaces;

(4) Radio.

668-40. Enclosures.   General purpose electrical equipment enclosures shall be permitted where a natural draft ventilation system prevents the accumulation of gases.

ARTICLE 669 — ELECTROPLATING

Contents

669-1. Scope.   The provisions of this article apply to the installation of the electrical components and accessory equipment that supply the power and controls for electroplating, anodizing, electropolishing, and electrostripping. For purposes of this article the term electroplating shall be used to identify any or all of these processes.

This article is new in the 1981 *Code*. Because of the extremely high currents and low voltages normally involved, conventional wiring methods cannot be used in electroplating, anodizing, electropolishing, and electrostripping processes. Note the permission to use bare conductors even in systems exceeding 50 V dc. See Figures 669-1 and 669-2. Some systems in the aluminum anodizing process have potentials up to 240 V. Warning signs are required to be posted to indicate the presence of bare conductors.

669-2. Other Articles.   Except as modified by this article, wiring and equipment used for electroplating processes shall comply with the applicable requirements of Chapters 1 through 4.

669-3. General. Equipment for use in electroplating processes shall be identified for such service.

669-5. Branch-Circuit Conductors. Branch-circuit conductors supplying one or more units of equipment shall have an ampacity of not less than 125 percent of the total connected load. The ampacities for busbars shall be in accordance with Section 374-6.

669-6. Wiring Methods. Conductors connecting the electrolyte tank equipment to the conversion equipment shall be as follows:

(a) Systems Not Exceeding 50 Volts DC. Insulated conductors shall be permitted to be run without insulated support provided they are protected from physical damage. Bare copper or aluminum conductors shall be permitted where supported on insulators.

(b) Systems Exceeding 50 Volts DC. Insulated conductors shall be permitted to be run on insulated supports provided they are protected from physical damage. Bare copper or aluminum conductors shall be permitted where supported on insulators and guarded against accidental contact in accordance with Section 110-17.

Exception: Unguarded bare conductors shall be permitted at the terminals.

Figure 669-1. A typical electroplating line.

669-7. Warning Signs. Warning signs shall be posted to indicate the presence of bare conductors.

669-8. Disconnecting Means.

(a) More than One Power Supply. Where more than one power supply serves the same dc system a disconnecting means shall be provided on the dc side of each power supply.

Figure 669-2. Bare busbar to supply an electro-plating tank.

(b) Removable Links or Conductors. Removable links or removable conductors shall be permitted to be used as the disconnecting means.

669-9. Overcurrent Protection. DC conductors shall be protected from overcurrent by one or more of the following: (1) fuses or circuit breakers; (2) a current sensing device which operates a disconnecting means; or (3) other approved means.

ARTICLE 670 — METALWORKING MACHINE TOOLS

For further information, see Electrical Metalworking Machine Tools, NFPA 79-1977 (ANSI).

Contents

<table>
<tr><td>670-1. Scope.</td><td>(a) Circuit Conductors.</td></tr>
<tr><td>670-2. Definition.</td><td>(b) Single Unit.</td></tr>
<tr><td>670-3. Machine Tool Nameplate Data.</td><td>(c) Overcurrent Protection.</td></tr>
<tr><td>670-4. General.</td><td></td></tr>
</table>

670-1. Scope. This article covers the size and overcurrent protection of supply conductors to metalworking machine tools and the nameplate data required on each such tool.

670-2. Definition.

Metalworking Machine Tool. A power-driven machine not portable by hand, used to shape or form metal by cutting, impact, pressure, electrical techniques, or a combination of these processes.

It should be noted that these requirements do not apply to any motor-driven machine not covered by this definition. Thus, these provisions do not apply to plastic or woodworking machine tools nor to a machine or tool that can be carried from place to place by hand and is not normally used in a fixed location.

670-3. Machine Tool Nameplate Data. A permanent nameplate listing supply voltage, phase, frequency, full-load currents (see notes below), ampere rating of largest motor, short-circuit interrupting capacity of the machine overcurrent protective device if furnished, and diagram number shall be attached to the control equipment enclosure or machine where plainly visible after installation.

NOTE 1. The full-load current shall not be less than the sum of the full-load currents required for all motors and other equipment which may be in operation at the same time under normal conditions of use. Where unusual type loads, duty cycles, etc., require oversized conductors, the required capacity shall be included in the marked "full-load current."

NOTE 2. Where more than one incoming supply circuit is to be provided, the nameplate shall state the above information for each circuit.

670-4. General.

(a) Circuit Conductors.   The supply circuit conductors shall have an ampacity of not less than the marked full-load current rating plus 25 percent of the full-load current rating of the highest rated motor as indicated on the nameplate.

For the protection of supply conductors to the machine tool, see Section 240-3.

(b) Single Unit.   A machine tool complying with NFPA 79-1977 (ANSI) shall be considered an individual unit equipment. It shall be provided with a disconnecting means and shall be permitted to be supplied by branch circuits protected by either fuses or circuit breakers.

(c) Overcurrent Protection.   The disconnecting means shall not be required to incorporate overcurrent protection. Where the machine tool nameplate is marked "Overcurrent protection provided at machine supply terminals," the supply conductors shall be considered either as feeders or taps as covered by Section 240-21.

"Overcurrent protection provided at machine supply terminals" means that provision has been made in the machine tool for each set of supply conductors to terminate in a single circuit breaker or set of fuses.

NFPA 79 states: "The center of the grip of the operating handle of the disconnecting means, when in its highest position, shall not be more than 6½ ft above the floor. A permanent operating platform, readily accessible by means of a permanent stair or ladder, shall be considered as the floor for the purpose of this requirement. The operating handle shall be capable of being locked only in the 'off' position."

ARTICLE 675 — ELECTRICALLY DRIVEN OR
CONTROLLED IRRIGATION MACHINES

Contents

A. General

675-1. Scope.   The provisions of this article apply to electrically driven or controlled irrigation machines, and to the branch circuits and controllers for such equipment.

Electric pump motors used to supply water to irrigation machines are governed by the general requirements of the *Code*, not by Article 675.

675-2. Definitions.

Center Pivot Irrigation Machines.   A center pivot irrigation machine is a multimotored irrigation machine which revolves around a central pivot and employs alignment switches or similar devices to control individual motors.

Collector Rings.   A collector ring is an assembly of slip rings for transferring electrical energy from a stationary to a rotating member.

Irrigation Machines.   An irrigation machine is an electrically driven or controlled machine, with one or more motors, not hand portable, and used primarily to transport and distribute water for agricultural purposes.

675-3. Other Articles.   These provisions are in addition to, or amendatory of, the provisions of Article 430 and other articles in this Code which apply except as modified in this article.

The requirements of this section apply to special equipment for a particular condition to supplement or modify the general rules. See Section 90-3, Code Arrangement.

675-4. Irrigation Cable.

(a) Construction.   The cable used to interconnect enclosures on the structure of an irrigation machine shall be an assembly of stranded, insulated conductors with nonhygroscopic filler in a core of moisture- and flame-resistant, nonmetallic material overlaid with a metallic covering and jacketed with a moisture-, corrosion- and sunlight-resistant nonmetallic material.
The conductor insulation shall be of a type listed in Table 310-13 for an operating temperature of 75°C and for use in wet locations. The core insulating material thickness shall not be less than 30 mils and the metallic overlay thickness shall not be less than 8 mils. The jacketing material thickness shall not be less than 50 mils.
A composite of power, control, and grounding conductors in the cable shall be permitted.

(b) Alternate Wiring Methods.   Other cables listed for the purpose.

(c) Supports.   Irrigation cable shall be secured by approved straps, hangers, or similar fittings so designed and installed as not to injure the cable. Cable shall be supported at intervals not exceeding 4 feet (1.22 m).

(d) Fittings.   Fittings shall be used at all points where irrigation cable terminates. The fittings shall be designed for use with the cable and shall be suitable for the conditions of service.

675-5. More than Three Conductors in a Raceway or Cable.   The signal and control conductors of a raceway or cable shall not be counted for the purpose of derating the conductors as required in Note 8 of Tables 310-16 through 310-19.

675-6. Marking on Main Control Panel.   The main control panel shall be provided with a nameplate which shall give the following information: (1) the manufacturer's name, the rated voltage, the phase, and the frequency; (2) the current rating of the machine; and (3) the rating of the main disconnecting means and size of overcurrent protection required.

675-7. Collector Rings.

(a) Ampacity.   Collector rings shall have an ampacity not less than 125 percent of the full-load current of the largest device served plus the full-load current of all other devices served.

(b) Grounding.   Collector rings used for grounding shall be of the same ampacity as the largest collector ring in the assembly.

(c) Protection.   Collector rings shall be protected from the expected environment and from accidental contact by means of a suitable enclosure.

675-8. Grounding.   The following equipment shall be grounded: (1) all electrical equipment on the irrigation machine; (2) all electrical equipment associated with the irrigation machine; (3) metallic junction boxes and enclosures; and (4) control panels or control equipment that supply or control electrical equipment to the irrigation machine.

Exception: Grounding shall not be required on machines where all of the following provisions are met:

a. The machine is electrically controlled but not electrically driven.

b. The control voltage is 30 volts or less.

c. The control or signal circuits are current-limited as specified in Section 725-31.

675-9. Methods of Grounding.   Machines which require grounding shall have a noncurrent-carrying equipment grounding conductor provided as an integral part of each cord, cable, or raceway. This grounding conductor shall be equal in size to the supply conductors, but not smaller than No. 14 copper. Feeder circuits supplying power to irrigation machines shall have an equipment grounding conductor sized according to Table 250-95.

The last sentence in this section is new in the 1981 *Code*. It was added to make it clear that the feeder equipment grounding conductor does not have to be sized in the same manner as the equipment grounding conductors to various components of the machine.

675-10. Bonding.   Where electrical grounding is required on an irrigation machine, the metallic structure of the machine, metallic conduit, or metallic-sheath of cable shall be bonded to the grounding conductor. Metal-to-metal contact with a part which is bonded to the grounding conductor and the noncurrent-carrying parts of the machine shall be considered as an acceptable bonding path.

675-11. Lightning Protection.   If an irrigation machine has a stationary point, a driven ground rod shall be connected to the machine at the stationary point for lightning protection.

Where the electrical power supply to irrigation machine equipment is a service, provisions in Sections 250-81 and 250-83 would require a made electrode, specifically a driven ground rod. Consideration should be given to Section 250-86 and NFPA 78, Lightning Protection Code, in areas where lightning protection is critical.

675-12. Energy from More than One Source.   Equipment within an enclosure receiving electrical energy from more than one source shall not be required to have a disconnecting means for the additional source, provided that its voltage is 30 volts or less and meets the requirements of Section 725-31.

675-13. Connectors.   External plugs and connectors on the equipment shall be of the weatherproof type.
Unless provided solely for the connection of circuits meeting the requirements of Section 725-31, external plugs and connectors shall be constructed as specified in Section 250-99(a).

B. Center Pivot Irrigation Machines

675-21. General.   The provisions of Part B are intended to cover additional special requirements which are peculiar to center pivot irrigation machines. See Section 675-2 for definition of Center Pivot Irrigation Machines.

Figure 675-1. A center pivot irrigation machine. (*Lockwood Corp.*)

675-22. Equivalent Current Ratings.   In order to establish ratings of controllers, disconnecting means, conductors, and the like, for the inherent intermittent duty of center pivot irrigation machines, the following determination shall be used:

The ratings of electrical components of any circuit should be selected so as to avoid extensive damage to the equipment during a short-circuit or a ground-fault condition. Section 675-22 gives the requirements for establishing ratings of components of special equipment for inherent intermittent duty. Also see comments following Sections 110-10 and 430-52.

(a) Continuous-Current Rating.   The equivalent continuous-current rating for the selection of branch-circuit conductors and branch-circuit devices shall be equal to 125 percent of the motor nameplate full-load current rating of the largest motor plus 60 percent of the sum of the motor nameplate full-load current ratings of all remaining motors on the circuit.

(b) Locked-Rotor Current.   The equivalent locked-rotor current rating shall be equal to the numerical sum of two times the locked-rotor current of the largest motor plus 80 percent of the sum of the motor nameplate full-load current ratings of all the remaining motors on the circuit.

675-23. Disconnecting Means.

(a) Main Controller.   A controller which is used to start and stop the complete machine shall meet all of the following requirements:

(1) An equivalent continuous current rating not less than specified in Section 675-22(a).

(2) A horsepower rating not less than the value from Table 430-151 based on the equivalent locked-rotor current specified in Section 675-22(b).

(b) Main Disconnecting Means.   The main disconnecting means for the machine shall be at the point of connection of electrical power to the machine or shall be visible and not more than 50 feet (15.2 m) from the machine and shall be readily accessible and capable of being locked in the open postition. This disconnecting means shall have the same horsepower and current ratings as required for the main controller.

> A change in this section in the 1981 *Code* permits the main disconnecting means to be up to 50 ft from the machine if readily accessible and capable of being locked in the open position. This change will eliminate one set of overcurrent protective devices and one disconnecting means when the circuit originates at the motor control panel for the irrigation pump and this panel is within 50 ft of the center pivot machine. It will also alleviate some potential problems with machines designed to be towed to a second site.

(c) Disconnecting Means for Individual Motors and Controllers.   A disconnecting means shall be provided for each motor and controller and shall be located as required by Article 430, Part H. The disconnecting means shall not be required to be readily accessible.

> Article 430, Part H, provides for safety during maintenance and inspection shutdown periods. See comments following Section 430-103.

675-24. Branch-Circuit Conductors.   The branch-circuit conductors shall have an ampacity not less than specified in Section 675-22(a).

675-25. Several Motors on One Branch Circuit.

> Section 430-53 provides for motor branch-circuit short-circuit and ground-fault protection for several motors on one branch circuit. A combination of these requirements, which are more or less stringent for this special equipment application, is found in Section 675-25.

(a) Protection Required.   Several motors, each not exceeding 2-horsepower rating, shall be permitted to be used on an irrigation machine circuit protected at not more than 30 amperes at 600 volts, nominal, or less, provided all of the following conditions are met:

(1) The full-load rating of any motor in the circuit shall not exceed 6 amperes.

(2) Each motor in the circuit shall have individual running overcurrent protection in accordance with Section 430-32.

(3) Taps to individual motors shall not be smaller than No. 14 copper and not more than 25 feet (7.62 m) in length.

(b) Individual Protection Not Required. Individual branch-circuit short-circuit protection for motors and motor controllers shall not be required where the requirements of Section 675-25(a) are met.

675-26. Collector Rings.

(a) Transmitting Current for Power Purposes. Collector rings transmitting current for power purposes shall have an ampacity not less than specified in Section 675-22(a)

(b) Control and Signal Purposes. Collector rings for control and signal purposes shall have an ampacity not less than 125 percent of the full-load current of the largest device served plus the full-load current of all other devices served.

(c) Grounding. The collector ring used for grounding shall be of the same ampacity as the largest collector ring in the assembly.

ARTICLE 680 — SWIMMING POOLS, FOUNTAINS, AND SIMILAR INSTALLATIONS

Contents

A. General

680-1. Scope. The provisions of this article apply to the construction and installation of electric wiring for and equipment in or adjacent to all swimming, wading, therapeutic, and decorative pools, fountains, hot tubs, and spas, whether permanently installed or storable, and to metallic auxiliary equipment, such as pumps, filters, and similar equipment.

The 1981 *NEC* added requirements to clarify the appropriate application of Article 680 to spas and hot tubs (Part D); to therapeutic pools and tubs in health care facilities (Part F); and to deck area heating (Section 680-27).

See Section 517-90(c) fine print note referencing therapeutic pools and tubs as covered in Part F of Article 680.

The term "pool" as used in the balance of this article shall include swimming, wading, and permanently installed therapeutic pools. The term "fountain" as used in the balance of this article shall include fountains, ornamental pools, display pools, and reflection pools.

This article applies to swimming pools and similar installations, indoors or outdoors, permanent or storable, and whether or not served by any electrical circuits of any nature. Studies conducted by Underwriters Laboratories, various manufacturers and others indicate that a person in a swimming pool can receive a severe electric shock by reaching over and touching the energized casing of a faulty appliance, such as a radio, hair dryer, etc., as his body establishes a conductive path through the water and pool to earth; and, also, a person not in contact with a faulty appliance or any grounded object may receive an electric shock and be rendered immobile by a potential gradient in the water itself. Accordingly, requirements of this article covering effective bonding and grounding, installation of receptacles and lighting fixtures, use of ground-fault circuit-interrupters, modified wiring methods, etc., apply not only to the installation of the pool, but also to installations and equipment adjacent to, or associated with, the pool.

680-2. Approval of Equipment.   All electric equipment installed in the water, walls, or decks of pools, fountains, and similar installations shall comply with the provisions of this article.

680-3. Other Articles.   Except as modified by this article, wiring and equipment in or adjacent to pools and fountains shall comply with the applicable requirements of Chapters 1 through 4.

See Section 370-13 for junction boxes, Section 347-3 for rigid nonmetallic conduit, and Article 720 for low-voltage lighting.

Note that Section 370-13 specifies the requirements for the support of boxes, and Section 347-3(b) does not permit equipment to be supported by rigid nonmetallic conduit. See Figure 680-1.

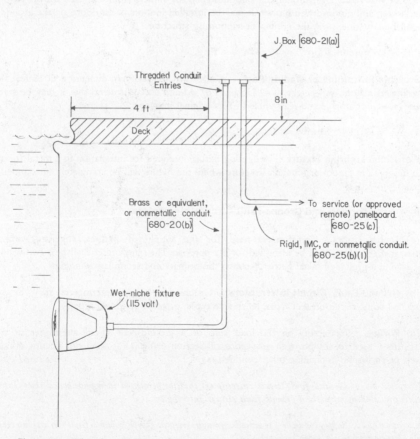

Figure 680-1. Where boxes are supported according to the provisions of Section 370-13, as above, additional supporting means may be required where nonmetallic conduit is used. See Section 347-3(b).

680-4. Definitions.

Dry-Niche Lighting Fixture.   A lighting fixture intended for installation in the wall of a pool or fountain in a niche that is sealed against the entry of pool water.

Forming Shell.   A metal structure designed to support a wet-niche lighting fixture assembly and intended for mounting in a pool or fountain structure.

Permanently Installed Decorative Fountains and Reflection Pools.   Those that are constructed in the ground, on the ground, or in a building in such a manner that the fountain cannot be readily disassembled for storage and are served by electrical circuits of any nature. These units are primarily constructed for their aesthetic value and not intended for swimming or wading.

Permanently Installed Swimming, Wading, and Therapeutic Pools.   Those that are constructed in the ground, on the ground, or in a building in such a manner that the pool cannot be readily disassembled for storage, whether or not served by electrical circuits of any nature.

See comments following Part F, heading.

Spa or Hot Tub.   A hydromassage pool designed for immersion of users and usually having a filter, heater, and motor-driven blower. It may be installed indoors or outdoors, on the ground or supporting structure, or in the ground or supporting structure.

See comments following Part D, heading.

Storable Swimming or Wading Pool.   A pool with a maximum dimension of 18 feet (5.49 m) and a maximum wall height of 42 inches (1.07 m) and so constructed that it may be readily disassembled for storage and reassembled to its original integrity.

See comments following Section 680-31.

Wet-Niche Lighting Fixture.   A lighting fixture intended for installation in a metal forming shell mounted in a pool or fountain structure where the fixture will be completely surrounded by water.

680-5. Transformers and Ground-Fault Circuit-Interrupters.

(a) Transformers.   Transformers used for the supply of fixtures, together with the transformer enclosure, shall be identified for the purpose. The transformer shall be a two-winding type having a grounded metal barrier between the primary and secondary windings.

(b) Ground-Fault Circuit-Interrupters.   Ground-fault circuit-interrupters shall be self-contained units, circuit-breaker types, receptacle types, or other approved types.

(c) Wiring.   Conductors on the load side of a ground-fault circuit-interrupter or of a transformer, used to comply with provisions of Section 680-20(a)(1), shall not occupy conduit, boxes, or enclosures containing other conductors.

Exception No. 1: Ground-fault circuit-interrupters shall be permitted in a panelboard that contains circuits protected by other than ground-fault circuit-interrupters.

Exception No. 2: Supply conductors to a feed-through, receptacle-type, ground-fault circuit-interrupter shall be permitted in the same enclosure.

680-6. Receptacles, Lighting Fixtures, and Lighting Outlets.

(a) Receptacles.

(1) Receptacles on the property shall be located at least 10 feet (3.05 m) from the inside walls of a pool.

Exception: A receptacle that provides power for a recirculating pump motor for a permanently installed pool, as permitted in Section 680-7, shall be permitted not less than 5 feet (1.52 m) from the inside walls of the pool and shall be single and of the locking and grounding types. A receptacle supplied by 120 volts shall be protected by a ground-fault circuit-interrupter.

(2) Where a permanently installed pool is installed at a dwelling unit(s), at least one 120-volt convenience receptacle shall be installed a minimum of 10 feet (3.05 m) from and not more than 15 feet (4.57 m) from the inside wall of the pool.

(3) All 120-volt receptacles located within 15 feet (4.57 m) of the inside walls of a pool shall be protected by a ground-fault circuit-interrupter. See Section 210-8(a)(3).

Section 680-6(a) has been revised to make it clear that a 120-V receptacle for the recirculating motor pump permitted not less than 5 ft from the inside walls of the pool is to be protected by a GFCI. This change makes it clear that all 120-V receptacles located within 15 ft [outdoors or indoors, dwelling unit(s) or commerical] are to be protected by GFCIs.

If the recirculating pump motor is rated more than 120 V (i.e., 230 V), GFCI protection is not required. The same applies to other receptacles.

See Figure 680-2.

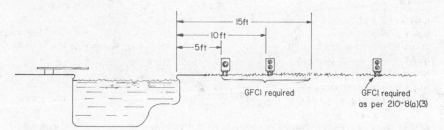

Figure 680-2. For permanently installed pools at dwelling unit(s), it is mandatory to install a 120-V receptacle between 10 and 15 ft from the inside wall of the pool.

In determining the above dimensions, the distance to be measured is the shortest path the supply cord of an appliance connected to the receptacle would follow without piercing a floor, wall, or ceiling of a building or other effective permanent barrier.

See Figure 680-3.

(b) Lighting Fixtures and Lighting Outlets.

(1) Lighting fixtures and lighting outlets shall not be installed over the pool or over the area extending 5 feet (1.52 m) horizontally from the inside walls of a pool unless 12 feet (3.66 m) above the maximum water level.

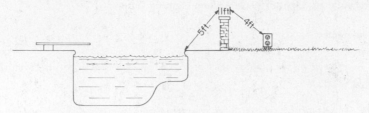

Figure 680-3. This figure illustrates the shortest path a supply cord of an appliance connected to the receptacle would follow without piercing the wall.

Exception: Existing lighting fixtures and lighting outlets located less than 5 feet (1.52 m) measured horizontally from the inside walls of a pool shall be at least 5 feet (1.52 m) above the surface of the maximum water level and shall be rigidly attached to the existing structure.

The 1981 *NEC* deletes the provision that "existing" lighting fixtures and lighting outlets located less than 5 ft horizontally from and 5 ft above the pool are to be protected by ground-fault circuit-interrupters. See Figure 680-4.

(2) Lighting fixtures and lighting outlets installed in the area extending between 5 feet (1.52 m) and 10 feet (3.05 m) horizontally from the inside walls of a pool shall be protected by a ground-fault circuit-interrupter unless installed 5 feet (1.52 m) above the maximum water level and rigidly attached to the structure adjacent to or enclosing the pool.

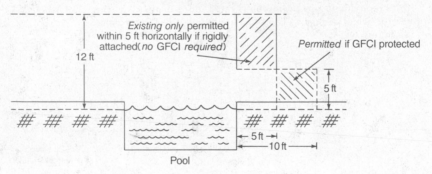

Figure 680-4. The requirements for ground-fault circuit-interrupter protection for lighting fixtures and lighting outlets over pools.

(3) Cord-connected lighting fixtures shall meet the same specifications as other cord- and plug-connected equipment as set forth in Section 680-7 when installed within 16 feet (4.88 m) of any point on the water surface, measured radially.

680-7. Cord- and Plug-Connected Equipment. Fixed or stationary equipment rated 20 amperes or less, other than an underwater lighting fixture for a permanently installed pool, shall be permitted to be connected with a flexible cord to facilitate the removal or disconnection for maintenance or repair. For other than storable pools, the flexible cord shall not exceed 3 feet (914 mm) in length and shall have a copper equipment grounding conductor not smaller than No. 12 with a grounding-type attachment plug.

See Section 680-25(e) for connection with flexible cords.

In some geographic areas, it is preferable to disconnect the filter pump for a permanent pool during the cold weather months, and a 3-ft cord is allowed to facilitate the removal of fixed or stationary equipment for maintenance and storage.

The 3-ft cord limitation does not apply to cord- and plug-connected filter pumps used with storable-type pools, covered in Part C of this article, since these pumps are neither fixed nor stationary. Listed filter pumps for use with storable pools are considered portable and permitted to be equipped with cords longer than 3 ft.

680-8. Overhead Conductor Clearances.   The following parts of pools shall not be placed under existing service-drop conductors or any other open overhead wiring; nor shall such wiring be installed above the following: (1) pools and the area extending 10 feet (3.05 m) horizontally from the inside of the walls of the pool; (2) diving structure; or (3) observation stands, towers, or platforms.

Exception No. 1: Structures listed in (1), (2), and (3) above shall be permitted under utility-owned, -operated and -maintained supply lines or service drops where such installations provide the following clearances:

The clearance dimension chart and the diagram for Figure 680-8, Exception No. 1 have been revised in the 1981 *NEC* by adding dimension "C" to establish a horizontal limit of clearance measured from the inside of the pool of 10 ft, and the limit for extending the radii "A" and "B" in the diagram is to extend to the outer limit of the structures, but not less than 10 ft.

The diagram as shown in the 1978 *NEC* incorrectly illustrated radii "A" and "B" extending to the ground. The 1981 *NEC* limits the horizontal distance of concern to 10 ft and is a clarification.

	Insulated supply or service drop cables, 0-750 volts to ground, supported on and cabled together with an effectively grounded bare messenger	All other supply or service drop conductors	
		Voltage to Ground	
		0-15 kV	**15-50 kV**
A. Clearance in any direction to the water level, edge of water surface, base of diving platform or permanently-anchored raft	18 feet (5.49m)	25 feet (7.62m)	27 feet (8.23m)
B. Clearance in any direction to the diving platform or tower	14 feet (4.27m)	16 feet (4.88m)	18 feet (5.49m)
C. Horizontal limit of clearance measured from inside wall of the pool.	This limit shall extend to the outer edge of the structures listed in (1) and (2) above but not less than 10 feet (3.05m).		

Exception No. 2: Utility-owned, -operated, and -maintained communication conductors, community antenna system coaxial cables complying with Article 820, and the supporting messengers shall be permitted at a height of not less than 10 feet (3.05 m) above swimming and wading pools, diving structures and observation stands, towers or platforms.

The 1981 *NEC* adds Exception No. 2 to permit communication wires at a height of not less than 10 ft over pools and structures.

See Sections 225-18 and 225-19 for clearances for conductors not covered by this section.

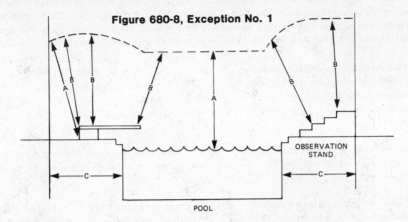

Figure 680-8, Exception No. 1

680-9. Electric Pool Water Heaters.   All electric pool water heaters shall have the heating elements subdivided into loads not exceeding 48 amperes and protected at not more than 60 amperes.

680-10. Underground Wiring Location.   Underground wiring shall not be permitted under the pool or under the area extending 5 feet (1.52 m) horizontally from the inside wall of the pool.

Previous editions of the *NEC* covered the requirements for overhead conductors. The 1981 *NEC* also provides installation requirements for underground wiring around or under pools.

Exception No. 1: Wiring necessary to supply pool equipment permitted by this article shall be allowed within this area.

Exception No. 2: When space limitations prevent wiring from being routed 5 feet (1.52 m) or more from the pool, such wiring shall be permitted when installed in rigid metal conduit, intermediate metal conduit, or a nonmetallic raceway system. All metallic conduit shall be corrosion-resistant and suitable for the location. The Exceptions to Section 300-5(a) shall not apply.

680-11. Equipment Rooms.   Electric equipment shall not be installed in rooms which do not have adequate drainage to prevent water accumulation during normal operation or filter maintenance.

The text of Section 680-11 was relocated from Section 680-47 (1978 *NEC*) to be included with sections of Part A General, thereby making this requirement applicable to all of Article 680.

B.   Permanently Installed Pools

680-20. Underwater Lighting Fixtures.

(a) General.   Paragraphs (a) through (c) of this section apply to all lighting fixtures installed below the normal water level of the pool. All lighting fixtures shall be installed for operation at 150 volts or less between conductors.

(1) The design of an underwater lighting fixture supplied from a branch circuit either directly or by way of a transformer meeting the requirements of Section 680-5(a) shall be such that, when the fixture is properly installed without a ground-fault circuit-interrupter, there is no shock hazard with any likely combination of fault conditions during normal use (not relamping).

In addition, a ground-fault circuit-interrupter shall be installed in the branch circuit supplying fixtures operating at more than 15 volts, so that there is no shock hazard during relamping. The installation of the ground-fault circuit-interrupter shall be such that there is no shock hazard with any likely fault-condition combination that involves a person in a conductive path from any ungrounded part of the branch circuit or the fixture to ground.

Compliance with this requirement shall be obtained by the use of an approved underwater lighting fixture and by installation of an approved ground-fault circuit-interrupter in the branch circuit.

(2) No lighting fixtures shall be installed for operation at over 150 volts between conductors.

(3) Lighting fixtures mounted in walls shall be installed with the top of the fixture lens at least 18 inches (457 mm) below the normal water level of the pool. A lighting fixture facing upward shall have the lens adequately guarded to prevent contact by any person.

Exception: Lighting fixtures identified for use at a depth of not less than 4 inches (102 mm) below the normal water level of the pool shall be permitted.

(4) Fixtures that depend on submersion for safe operation shall be inherently protected against the hazards of overheating when not submerged.

The 1981 *NEC* revised (a)(4) to require fixtures that depend on submersion for safe operation to be inherently protected against the hazards of overheating when not submerged, for instance, during a relamping process.

The 1978 *NEC* required that fixtures that depend on submersion for safe operation (cooling) be protected for overheating by a low-water cutoff or other approved means. This has been changed to make it clear that the protection against overheating be built into or be a part of the fixture. A remotely located low-water cutoff switch would not provide the intended protection.

(b) Wet-Niche Fixtures.

(1) Approved metal forming shells shall be installed for the mounting of all wet-niche underwater fixtures and shall be equipped with provisions for threaded conduit entries. Rigid metal conduit or intermediate metal conduit of brass or other approved corrosion-resistant metal or rigid nonmetallic conduit shall extend from the forming shell to a suitable junction box or other enclosure located as provided in Section 680-21. Where rigid nonmetallic conduit is used, a No. 8 insulated, solid copper conductor shall be installed in this conduit with provisions for terminating in the forming shell, junction box or transformer enclosure, or ground-fault circuit-interrupter enclosure. The termination of the No. 8 conductor in the forming shell shall be covered with, or encapsulated in, a suitable potting compound to protect such connection from the possible deteriorating effect of pool water. Metal parts of the fixture and forming shell in contact with the pool water shall be of brass or other approved corrosion-resistant metal.

(2) The end of the flexible-cord jacket and the flexible-cord conductor terminations within a fixture shall be covered with, or encapsulated in, a suitable potting compound to prevent the entry of water into the fixture through the cord or its conductors. In addition, the grounding connection within a fixture shall be similarly treated to protect such connection from the deteriorating effect of pool water in the event of water entry into the fixture.

(3) The fixture shall be bonded to and secured to the forming shell by a positive locking device that assures a low-resistance contact and requires a tool to remove the fixture from the forming shell.

(c) Dry-Niche Fixtures.   A dry-niche lighting fixture shall be provided with: (1) provision for drainage of water, and (2) means for accommodating one equipment grounding conductor for each conduit entry.

Approved rigid metal conduit, intermediate metal conduit, or rigid nonmetallic conduit shall be installed from the fixture to the service equipment or panelboard. A junction box shall not be required, but if used shall not be required to be elevated or located as specified in Section 680-21(a)(4) if the fixture is specifically identified for the purpose.

Underwater lighting fixtures of either dry-niche or wet-niche types operating at more than 15 V require ground-fault circuit-interrupter protection.

Branch-circuit conductors for dry-niche fixtures are required to be run in rigid metal conduit, intermediate metal conduit, or rigid nonmetallic conduit from the fixture to an approved panelboard or to the service equipment. Branch-circuit conductors for wet-niche fixtures leaving the pool junction box are to be enclosed in rigid metal conduit, intermediate metal conduit, or rigid nonmetallic conduit, except in or on buildings where the conductors may be protected by electrical metallic tubing as permitted by Exception No. 1 to Section 680-25(b)(1). However, unlike wet-niche fixtures, a junction box is not required for dry-niche fixtures, but, if used, is not required to be elevated or located as specified in Section 680-21(a)(4). See Figures 680-1 and 680-5.

It should be noted that where rigid nonmetallic conduit is used between a forming shell for a wet-niche fixture and a junction box or other enclosure, a No. 8 insulated, solid copper bonding conductor is to be installed within this conduit to provide electrical continuity between the forming shell and the junction box or other enclosure. Section 310-3, Exception No. 2 references this permitted use of a No. 8 solid conductor within a raceway. It is advisable to ensure that the rigid nonmetallic conduit is sized to enclose both the No. 8 insulated solid bonding conductor and the approved flexible cord that supplies the wet-niche fixture to facilitate easy withdrawal and insertion of the conductor and the cord.

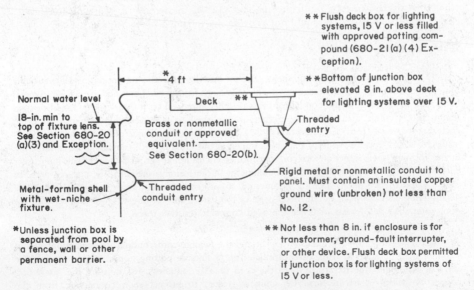

Figure 680-5. Installation requirements for wet-niche forming shell and deck box.

680-21. Junction Boxes and Enclosures for Transformers or Ground-Fault Circuit-Interrupters.

(a) Junction Boxes. A junction box connected to a conduit that extends directly to a forming shell shall be:

(1) Equipped with provisions for threaded conduit entries; and

(2) Of copper, brass, suitable plastic, or other approved corrosion-resistant material; and

(3) Provided with electrical continuity between every connected metal conduit and the grounding terminals by means of copper, brass, or other approved corrosion-resistant metal that is integral with the box; and

(4) Located not less than 8 inches (203 mm), measured from the inside of the bottom of the box, above the ground level, pool deck, or maximum pool water level, whichever provides the greatest elevation, and located not less than 4 feet (1.22 m) from the inside wall of the pool unless separated from the pool by a solid fence, wall, or other permanent barrier.

Exception: On lighting systems of 15 volts or less, a flush deck box shall be permitted provided:

a. An approved potting compound is used to fill the box to prevent the entrance of moisture; and

b. The flush deck box is located not less than 4 feet (1.22 m) from the inside wall of the pool.

(b) Other Enclosures. An enclosure for a transformer, ground-fault circuit-interrupter, or a similar device connected to a conduit that extends directly to a forming shell shall be:

(1) Equipped with provisions for threaded conduit entries; and

(2) Provided with an approved seal, such as duct seal at the conduit connection, that prevents circulation of air between the conduit and the enclosures; and

(3) Provided with electrical continuity between every connected metal conduit and the grounding terminals by means of copper, brass, or other approved corrosion-resistant metal that is integral with the enclosures; and

(4) Located not less than 8 inches (203 mm), measured from the inside bottom of the enclosure to the ground level, pool deck, or maximum pool water level, whichever provides the greatest elevation, and located not less than 4 feet (1.22 m) from the inside wall of the pool unless separated from the pool by a solid fence, wall, or other permanent barrier.

(c) Protection. Junction boxes and enclosures mounted above the grade of the finished walkway around the pool shall not be located in the walkway unless afforded additional protection, such as by location under diving boards, adjacent to fixed structures, and the like.

(d) Grounding Terminals. Junction boxes, transformer enclosures, and ground-fault circuit-interrupter enclosures connected to a conduit which extends directly to a forming shell shall be provided with a number of grounding terminals that shall be at least one more than the number of conduit entries.

(e) Strain Relief. The termination of a flexible cord of an underwater lighting fixture within a junction box, transformer enclosure, ground-fault circuit-interrupter, or other enclosure shall be provided with a strain relief.

680-22. Bonding.

(a) Bonded Parts.   The following parts shall be bonded together:

(1)   All metallic parts of the pool structure, including the reinforcing metal of the pool shell, coping stones, and deck.

(2)   All forming shells.

(3)   All metal fittings within or attached to the pool structure.

(4)   Metal parts of electric equipment associated with the pool water circulating system, including pump motors.

(5)   Metal conduit, metal piping, and all fixed metal parts that are within 5 feet (1.52 m) of the inside walls of the pool and that are not separated from the pool by a permanent barrier.

Exception No. 1: The usual steel tie wires shall be considered suitable for bonding the reinforcing steel together, and welding or special clamping shall not be required.

Exception No. 2: Structural reinforcing steel or the walls of bolted or welded metal pool structures shall be permitted as a common bonding grid for nonelectrical parts where connections can be made in accordance with Section 250-113.

Exception No. 3: Isolated parts which are no more than 4 inches (102 mm) in any dimension and do not penetrate into the pool structure more than 1 inch (25.4 mm) shall not require bonding.

(b) Common Bonding Grid.   These parts shall be connected to a common bonding grid with a solid, copper conductor, insulated, covered, or bare, not smaller than No. 8. Connection shall be made by pressure connectors or clamps of brass, copper, or copper alloy. The common bonding grid may be any of the following:

(1)   The structural reinforcing steel of a concrete pool where the reinforcing rods are bonded together by the usual steel tie wires or the equivalent; or,

(2)   The wall of a bolted or welded metal pool; or,

(3)   A solid, copper conductor, insulated, covered, or bare, not smaller than No. 8.

This section has been revised to provide safety by requiring a suitable corrosion-resistant material for the ground clamp. The need for brass, copper, or copper alloy was substantiated by field problems where bonding has failed due to corrosion.

(c) Pool Water Heaters.   For pool water heaters rated at more than 50 amperes which have specific instructions regarding bonding and grounding, only those parts designated to be bonded shall be bonded, and only those parts designated to be grounded shall be grounded.

It is important to know the difference between the terms "bonding" and "grounding" as they apply to this article. As defined in Article 100, "Bonding" is the permanent joining of metallic parts to form an electrically conductive path that will ensure electrical continuity and the capacity to conduct safely any current likely to be imposed.

This section indicates the metal parts that must be "bonded" together, including all metal parts of electric equipment associated with the pool water circulating system, all metal parts of the pool structure, and all fixed metal parts, which include conduit and piping within 5 ft of the inside walls of the pool and not separated by a permanent barrier (see Exception No. 3). It should be noted that the "bonding together of these parts" does not mean that they must be connected to each other; it means that they must be connected to a common bonding grid with an insulated, covered, or bare solid copper conductor not smaller than No. 8 (see Figures 680-6 and 680-7). Connections must be made by pressure connectors, clamps, or other approved means in accordance with Section 250-113. It is not required to run the No. 8 conductor back to the panelboard.

The reason for connecting metal parts (ladders, hand-rails, water-circulating equipment, forming shells, diving boards, etc.) to a common bonding grid (pool reinforcing steel, pool metal wall, or a No. 8 solid conductor) is to ensure that all such metal parts will be at the same electrical potential. This will reduce any possible shock hazard created by stray currents in the ground or piping connected to the swimming pool, including plastic piping, because water containing salt or chemicals could have a low resistance, thereby permitting dangerous currents to flow.

Since corrosion is normally associated with the wet conditions of swimming pool areas, wiring and connections should be checked periodically, especially bonding connections between the No. 8 copper conductor and, for instance, an aluminum (or other dissimilar metal) ladder.

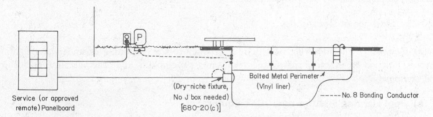

Figure 680-6. Illustrated is a metal (i.e., steel, aluminum) perimeter pool with bolted (may be welded) sections. The metal perimeter serves as the common bonding grid to which the metal ladder, the metal diving board, the dry-niche fixture, and pump motor are connected. Note that the pump motor is connected to a receptacle as per Sections 680-6 and 680-7.

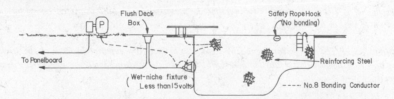

Figure 680-7. Illustrated is a poured concrete pool. The structural reinforcing steel serves as the common bonding grid to which all metal appurtenances associated with the pool are connected. Safety rope hooks are not required to be bonded as per Section 680-22(a), Exception No. 3. The flush deck box meets the provisions of Section 680-21(a), Exception.

680-23. Underwater Audio Equipment.   All underwater audio equipment shall be identified for the purpose.

(a) Speakers.   Each speaker shall be mounted in an approved metal forming shell, the front of which is enclosed by a captive metal screen, or equivalent, that is bonded to and secured to the forming shell by a positive locking device that assures a low resistance contact and requires a tool to open for installation or servicing of the speaker. The forming shell shall be installed in a recess in the wall or floor of the pool.

(b) Wiring Methods.   Rigid metal conduit or intermediate metal conduit of brass or other identified corrosion-resistant metal or rigid nonmetallic conduit shall extend from the forming shell to a suitable junction box or other enclosure as provided in Section 680-21. Where rigid nonmetallic conduit is used, a No. 8 insulated, solid copper conductor shall be installed in this conduit with provisions for terminating in the forming shell and the junction box. The termination of the No. 8 conductor in the forming shell shall be covered with, or encapsulated in, a suitable potting compound to protect such connection from the possible deteriorating effect of pool water.

(c) Forming Shell and Metal Screen.   The forming shell and metal screen shall be of brass or other approved corrosion-resistant metal.

680-24. Grounding.   The following equipment shall be grounded: (1) wet-niche underwater lighting fixtures; (2) dry-niche underwater lighting fixtures; (3) all electric equipment located within 5 feet (1.52 m) of the inside wall of the pool; (4) all electric equipment associated with the recirculating system of the pool; (5) junction boxes; (6) transformer enclosures; (7) ground-fault circuit-interrupters; (8) panelboards that are not part of the service equipment and that supply any electric equipment associated with the pool.

680-25. Methods of Grounding.

(a) General.   The following provisions shall apply to the grounding of underwater lighting fixtures, junction boxes, metal transformer enclosures, panelboards, and other electrical enclosures and equipment.

(b) Pool Lighting Fixtures and Other Equipment.

(1) Wet-niche lighting fixtures shall be connected to an equipment grounding conductor sized in accordance with Table 250-95 but not smaller than No. 12. It shall be an insulated copper conductor and shall be installed with the circuit conductors in rigid metal conduit, intermediate metal conduit, or rigid nonmetallic conduit.

Exception No. 1: Electrical metallic tubing shall be permitted to be used to protect conductors where installed on or within buildings.

Exception No. 2: The equipment grounding conductor between the wiring chamber of the secondary winding of a transformer and a junction box shall be sized in accordance with the overcurrent device in this circuit.

(2) The junction box, transformer enclosure, or other enclosure in the supply circuit to a wet-niche lighting fixture and the field-wiring chamber of a dry-niche lighting fixture shall be grounded to the equipment grounding terminal of the panelboard. This terminal shall be directly connected to the panelboard enclosure. The equipment grounding conductor shall be installed without joint or splice.

Exception No. 1: Where more than one underwater lighting fixture is supplied by the same branch circuit, the equipment grounding conductor, installed between the junction boxes, transformer enclosures, or other enclosures in the supply circuit to wet-niche fixtures or between the field-wiring compartments of dry-niche fixtures, shall be permitted to be terminated on grounding terminals.

Exception No. 2: Where the underwater lighting fixture is supplied from a transformer, ground-fault circuit-interrupter, or clock-operated switch which is located between the panelboard and a junction box connected to the conduit that extends directly to the underwater lighting fixture, the equipment grounding conductor shall be permitted to terminate on grounding terminals on the transformer, ground-fault circuit-interrupter, or clock-operated switch enclosure.

(3) Wet-niche lighting fixtures that are supplied by a flexible cord or cable shall have all exposed noncurrent-carrying metal parts grounded by an insulated copper equipment grounding conductor that is an integral part of the cord or cable. This grounding conductor shall be connected to a grounding terminal in the supply junction box, transformer enclosure, or other enclosure. The grounding conductor shall not be smaller than the supply conductors and not smaller than No. 16.

(c) Panelboards.   A panelboard, not part of the service equipment, shall have an equipment grounding conductor installed between its grounding terminal and the grounding terminal of the service equipment. This conductor shall be sized in accordance with Table 250-95 but not smaller than No. 12. It shall be an insulated conductor and shall be installed with the feeder conductors in rigid metal conduit, intermediate metal conduit, or rigid nonmetallic conduit. The equipment grounding conductor shall be connected to an equipment grounding terminal of the panelboard.

The insulated equipment grounding conductor may be aluminum or copper and installed in a raceway. It is to be noted that for an "existing" remote panelboard, Exception No. 1 permits an approved cable assembly with an insulated "or covered" aluminum or copper equipment grounding conductor. See Figure 680-8.

Exception No. 1: The equipment grounding conductor between an existing remote panelboard and the service equipment shall not be required to be in conduit if the interconnection is by means of an approved cable assembly with an insulated or covered equipment grounding conductor.

Exception No. 2: Electrical metallic tubing shall be permitted to be used to protect conductors where installed on or within the building.

See Section 348-1.

(d) Other Equipment.   Electrical equipment other than the underwater lighting fixture shall be grounded in accordance with Article 250 and connected by wiring methods of Chapter 3.

Equipment, other than underwater lighting fixtures, is permitted to be connected by wiring methods of Chapter 3 and grounded in accordance with Article 250. For example, equipment such as a motor filter pump is permitted to be wired with Type UF cable (Article 339 - Chapter 3) containing an insulated or bare conductor for equipment grounding purposes. See Figure 680-8.

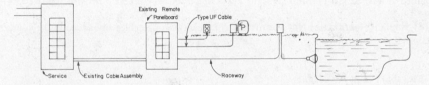

Figure 680-8. Circuits for pool requirements may be derived from an existing remote panelboard that is supplied by an approved cable assembly as specified in Section 680-25(c). Section 680-25(d) permits Type UF cable to be used for the filter pump, the receptacle required by Section 680-6(a)(2), and other equipment; but circuit conductors for underwater lighting must be run in raceways.

(e) Cord-Connected Equipment.   Where fixed or stationary equipment is connected with a flexible cord to facilitate removal or disconnection for maintenance, repair, or storage as provided in Section 680-7, the equipment grounding conductors shall be connected to a fixed metal part of the assembly. The removable part shall be mounted on or bonded to the fixed metal part.

When the provisions of Sections 680-24 and 680-25 are considered, the difference between "bonding" and "grounding" becomes apparent. As required in these sections, "grounding" is the connection of noncurrent-carrying metal parts of "electric" equipment associated with the pool (or located within 5 ft of the inside wall of the pool) to the grounding terminal bus of an approved panelboard [see Section 680-25(c)] or to the grounding terminal of the service equipment. This "equipment grounding conductor" provides a path of low impedance that limits the voltage to ground and facilitates the operation of the circuit overcurrent protective device. Furthermore, this "grounding" conductor must be an insulated copper conductor not smaller than No. 12 (see Exceptions), and for underwater lighting it must be run with the circuit conductors in rigid metal conduit, intermediate metal conduit, rigid nonmetallic conduit, or, where installed in or on buildings, it may be protected by electrical metallic tubing. Also, all equipment grounding conductors must terminate at an equipment grounding terminal located within lighting fixtures, junction boxes, transformer enclosures, panelboards, service equipment, etc.

Bonding conductors, however, may be insulated, covered, or bare, and must be No. 8 copper or larger. They may be direct buried, and, where connected to metal parts of the pool structure or metal parts of electric equipment, they may be externally clamped or attached and need not be accessible. All of these parts form a common bonding grid that establishes an equipotential grounding system, and they do not have to be run to the equipment grounding terminals of panelboards or service equipment.

680-27. Deck Area Heating.   The provisions of this section apply to all pool deck areas, including a covered pool, where electrically operated comfort heating units are installed within 20 feet (6.1 m) of the inside wall of the pool.

Only unit heaters and permanently connected radiant heaters are permitted in the area extending 5 to 20 ft horizontally from the inside walls of a pool. Radiant heat cables embedded in the deck are not permitted.

(a) Unit Heaters.   Unit heaters shall be rigidly mounted to the structure and shall be of the totally enclosed or guarded types. Unit heaters shall not be mounted over the pool or over the area extending 5 feet (1.52 m) horizontally from the inside walls of a pool.

(b) Permanently Wired Radiant Heaters.   Radiant electric heaters shall be suitably guarded and securely fastened to their mounting device(s). Heaters shall not be installed over a pool or over the area extending 5 feet (1.52 m) horizontally from the inside walls of the pool and shall be mounted at least 12 feet (3.66 m) vertically above the pool deck unless otherwise approved.

(c) Radiant Heat Cables Not Permitted.   Radiant heating cables embedded in the concrete deck shall not be permitted.

C. Storable Pools

680-30. Pumps.   A cord-connected pool filter pump shall incorporate an approved system of double insulation or its equivalent, and shall be provided with means for grounding only the internal and nonaccessible noncurrent-carrying metal parts of the appliance.

The means for grounding shall be an equipment grounding conductor run with the power-supply conductors in the flexible cord that is properly terminated in a grounding-type attachment plug having a fixed grounding contact member.

680-31. Ground-Fault Circuit-Interrupters Required.   All electric equipment, including power supply cords, used with storable pools shall be protected by ground-fault circuit-interrupters.

A storable pool may be readily disassembled and has a maximum dimension of 18 ft and a maximum wall height of 42 in. See definition, Section 680-4. This type of pool, and its associated equipment, does not require "bonding" conductors. However, the filter pump is to be double insulated or equivalent, and "grounding" means consisting of an equipment grounding conductor that is an integral part of the flexible cord is to be provided. There are portable filter pumps for use with storable pools listed by Underwriters Laboratories Inc.

The storable pool is to be located at least 10 ft from any receptacle [see Section 680-6(a)], and all electric equipment is to have a ground-fault circuit-interrupter for personnel protection. See Figure 680-9.

When flexible cords are used, see Section 400-4.

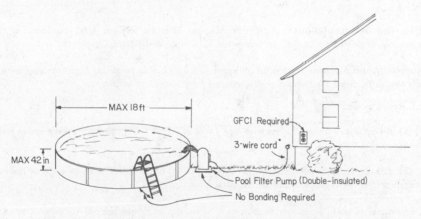

Figure 680-9. Illustrated are the requirements for a storable-type pool. Metal appurtenances are not required to be bonded. The 3-wire cord* may be longer than 3 ft. (Some listed filter pumps are equipped with cords 25 ft long.) The GFCI-protected receptacle need not be on a separate circuit.

D. Spas and Hot Tubs

The requirements of this part are divided into two categories: outdoor installations and indoor installations.

Outdoor installations are subjected to Parts A and B of Article 680 with three exceptions:

1. Metal bands or hoops used to secure wooden staves need not be bonded.

2. Listed packaged units may be cord connected and must be protected by a GFCI.

3. Bonding by metal-to-metal mounting on a common frame or base is permitted.

Indoor installations are subjected to basically the same requirements, but take into consideration the more restricted confines of an indoor location.

Receptacles, wall switches, and electrical devices and controls not associated with a spa or hot tub are to be located at least 5 ft away. Receptacles within 20 ft and those providing power to a spa or hot tub must be protected by a GFCI.

Lighting fixtures located over a spa or hot tub or within 5 ft horizontally must be protected by a GFCI.

Bonding and grounding requirements are similar to Parts A and B of Article 680, except that metal-to-metal mounting on a common frame or base is an acceptable bonding method.

Listed packaged units may be cord connected.

680-40. Outdoor Installations.   A spa or hot tub installed outdoors shall comply with the provision of Parts A and B.

Exception No. 1: Metal bands or hoops used to secure wooden staves are exempt from Section 680-22.

Exception No. 2: Listed packaged units may be cord connected with a cord no longer than 15 feet (4.57 m) and shall be protected by a ground-fault circuit-interrupter.

Exception No. 3: Bonding by metal-to-metal mounting on a common frame or base shall be permitted.

680-41. Indoor Installations.   A spa or hot tub installed indoors shall conform to the requirements of this part and shall be connected by wiring methods of Chapter 3.

Exception: Listed packaged units rated 20 amperes or less shall be permitted to be connected with a flexible cord to facilitate the removal or disconnection for maintenance and repair.

(a) Receptacles.

(1) Receptacles on the property shall be located at least 5 feet (1.52 m) from the inside walls of the spa or hot tub.

(2) 120-volt receptacles located within 20 feet (6.1 m) of the inside walls of a spa or hot tub shall be protected by a ground-fault circuit-interrupter.

In determining the above dimensions, the distance to be measured is the shortest path the supply cord of an appliance connected to the receptacle would follow without piercing a floor, wall, or ceiling of a building or other effective permanent barrier.

(3) Receptacles that provide power for a spa or hot tub shall be ground-fault circuit-interrupter protected.

(b) Lighting Fixtures and Lighting Outlets.

(1) Lighting fixtures and lighting outlets located over the spa or hot tub or within 5 feet (1.52 m), measured horizontally, from the inside walls shall be ground-fault circuit-interrupter protected.

(2) Underwater lighting fixtures shall comply with the provisions of Part B of this article.

(c) Wall Switches.   Switches shall be located at least 5 feet (1.52 m), measured horizontally, from the inside walls of the spa or hot tub.

(d) Bonding.   The following parts shall be bonded together:

(1) All metal fittings within or attached to the spa or hot tub structure.

(2) Metal parts of electric equipment associated with the spa or hot tub water circulating system, including pump motors.

(3) Metal conduit and metal piping within 5 feet (1.52 m) of the inside walls of the spa or hot tub and that are not separated from the spa or hot tub by a permanent barrier.

(4) All metal surfaces that are within 5 feet (1.52 m) of the inside walls of the spa or hot tub and not separated from the spa or hot tub area by a permanent barrier.

(5) Electrical devices and controls not associated with the spas or hot tubs shall be located a minimum of 5 feet (1.52 m) away from such units or be bonded to the spa or hot tub system.

(e) Methods of Bonding. All metallic parts associated with the spa or hot tub shall be bonded by any of the following methods: the interconnection of threaded metallic piping and fittings, metal-to-metal mounting on a common frame or base, or by the provisions of a copper bonding jumper, insulated, covered, or bare, not smaller than No. 8 solid.

(f) Grounding. The following equipment shall be grounded:

(1) All electric equipment located within 5 feet (1.52 m) of the inside wall of the spa or hot tub.

(2) All electric equipment associated with the circulating system of the spa or hot tub.

(g) Methods of Grounding.

(1) All electrical equipment shall be grounded in accordance with Article 250 and connected by the wiring methods of Chapter 3.

(2) Where equipment is connected with a flexible cord, the equipment grounding conductor shall be connected to a fixed metal part of the assembly.

E. Fountains

680-50. General. The provisions of Part E shall apply to all fountains as defined in Section 680-1. Fountains which have water common to a pool shall comply with the pool requirements of this article.

Exception: Self-contained, portable fountains no larger than 5 feet (1.52 m) in any dimension are not covered by Part E.

680-51. Lighting Fixtures, Submersible Pumps, and Other Submersible Equipment.

(a) Ground-Fault Circuit-Interrupter. A ground-fault circuit-interrupter shall be installed in the branch circuit supplying fountain equipment.

Exception: Ground-fault circuit-interrupters shall not be required for equipment operating at 15 volts or less and supplied by a transformer complying with Section 680-5(a).

(b) Operating Voltage. All lighting fixtures shall be installed for operation at 150 volts or less between conductors. Submersible pumps and other submersible equipment shall operate at 300 volts or less between conductors.

(c) Lighting Fixture Lenses.   Lighting fixtures shall be installed with the top of the fixture lens below the normal water level of the fountain unless approved for above water locations. A lighting fixture facing upward shall have the lens adequately guarded to prevent contact by any person.

(d) Overheating Protection.   Electric equipment which depends on submersion for safe operation shall be protected against overheating by a low-water cut-off or other approved means if the water level drops below normal.

(e) Wiring.   Equipment shall be equipped with provisions for threaded conduit entries or be provided with a suitable flexible cord. The maximum length of exposed cord in the fountain shall be limited to 10 feet (3.05 m). Cords extending beyond the fountain perimeter shall be enclosed in approved wiring enclosures. Metal parts of equipment in contact with water shall be of brass or other approved corrosion-resistant metal.

(f) Servicing.   All equipment shall be removable from the water for relamping or normal maintenance. Fixtures shall not be permanently imbedded into the fountain structure so that the water level must be reduced or the fountain drained for relamping, maintenance, or inspection.

(g) Stability.   Equipment shall be inherently stable or be securely fastened in place.

680-52. Junction Boxes and Other Enclosures.

(a) General.   Junction boxes and other enclosures used for other than underwater installation shall comply with Section 680-21(a) (1), (2), (3); and (b), (c), and (d).

(b) Underwater Junction Boxes and Other Underwater Enclosures.   Junction boxes and other underwater enclosures shall be watertight and (1) be equipped with provisions for threaded conduit entries or compression glands or seals for cord entry; (2) be of copper, brass, or other approved corrosion-resistant material; (3) be filled with an approved potting compound to prevent the entry of moisture; and (4) be firmly attached to the supports or directly to the fountain surface and bonded as required. When the junction box is supported only by the conduit the conduit shall be of copper, brass, or other approved corrosion-resistant metal. When the box is fed by nonmetallic conduit, it shall have additional supports and fasteners of copper, brass, or other approved corrosion-resistant material.

680-53. Bonding.   All metallic piping systems associated with the fountain shall be bonded to the equipment grounding conductor of the branch circuit supplying the fountain.

See Section 250-95 for sizing of these conductors.

680-54. Grounding.   The following equipment shall be grounded: (1) all electric equipment located within 5 feet (1.52 m) of the inside wall of the fountain; (2) all electric equipment associated with the recirculating system of the fountain; (3) panelboards that are not part of the service equipment and that supply any electric equipment associated with the fountain.

680-55. Methods of Grounding.

(a) Applied Provisions.   The following provisions of Section 680-25 shall apply: Paragraph (a) and (c) excluding Exceptions.

(b) Supplied by a Flexible Cord.   Electric equipment that is supplied by a flexible cord shall have all exposed noncurrent-carrying metal parts grounded by an insulated copper equipment grounding conductor that is an integral part of this cord. This grounding conductor shall be connected to a grounding terminal in the supply junction box, transformer enclosure, or other enclosure.

680-56. Cord- and Plug-Connected Equipment.

(a) Ground-Fault Circuit-Interrupter. All electric equipment, including power supply cords, shall be protected by ground-fault circuit-interrupters.

(b) Cord Type. Flexible cord immersed in or exposed to water shall be a water-resistant Type SO or ST.

(c) Sealing. The end of the flexible cord jacket and the flexible cord conductor termination within equipment shall be covered with or encapsulated in a suitable potting compound to prevent the entry of water into the equipment through the cord or its conductors. In addition, the ground connection within equipment shall be similarly treated to protect such connections from the deteriorating effect of water which may enter into the equipment.

(d) Terminations. Connections with flexible cord shall be permanent, except that grounding-type attachment plugs and receptacles shall be permitted to facilitate removal or disconnection for maintenance, repair, or storage of fixed or stationary equipment not located in any water-containing part of a fountain.

F. Therapeutic Pools and Tubs in Health Care Facilities

Portable therapeutic appliances are covered by the provisions of Article 422. They must be protected by a GFCI unless protected by an approved system of double insulation.

Permanently installed therapeutic pools that cannot be readily disassembled must comply with Parts A and B of Article 680. The limitations regarding lighting fixtures over and around a swimming pool do not apply to therapeutic pools and tubs if the lighting fixtures are totally enclosed.

Therapeutic tubs not easily moved are subjected to basically the same requirements.

Bonding and grounding are similar to Parts A and B of Article 680, except that metal-to-metal mounting on a common frame or base is acceptable. Where equipment is connected by a flexible cord, the equipment grounding conductor is to be connected to a fixed metal part of the assembly.

680-60. General.
The provisions of Part F include therapeutic pools and tubs in health care facilities. See Section 517-2 for definition of Health Care Facilities. Portable therapeutic appliances shall comply with Article 422.

680-61. Permanently Installed Therapeutic Pools.
Therapeutic pools which are constructed in the ground, on the ground, or in a building in such a manner that the pool cannot be readily disassembled shall comply with Parts A and B of this article.

Exception: The limitations of Section 680-6(b)(1) and (2) shall not apply where all lighting fixtures are of the totally enclosed type.

680-62. Therapeutic Tubs (Hydrotherapeutic Tanks).
Therapeutic tubs, used for the submersion and treatment of patients, which are not easily moved from one place to another in normal use or which are fastened or otherwise secured at a specific location including associated piping systems shall conform to this part.

(a) Ground-Fault Circuit-Interrupter. A ground-fault circuit-interrupter shall protect all therapeutic equipment.

Exception: Portable therapeutic appliances shall comply with Section 250-45.

(b) Bonding.   The following parts shall be bonded together:

(1) All metal fittings within or attached to the tub structure.

(2) Metal parts of electric equipment associated with the tub water circulating system, including pump motors.

(3) Metal conduit and metal piping that are within 5 feet (1.52 m) of the inside walls of the tub and not separated from the tub by a permanent barrier.

(4) All metal surfaces that are within 5 feet (1.52 m) of the inside walls of the tub and not separated from the tub area by a permanent barrier.

(5) Electrical devices and controls not associated with the therapeutic tubs shall be located a minimum of 5 feet (1.52 m) away from such units or be bonded to the therapeutic tub system.

(c) Methods of Bonding.   All metallic parts associated with the tub shall be bonded by any of the following methods: the interconnection of threaded metallic piping and fittings; metal-to-metal mounting on a common frame or base; connections by suitable metallic clamps; or by the provisions of a copper bonding jumper, insulated, covered, or bare, not smaller than No. 8 solid.

(d) Grounding.   The following equipment shall be grounded:

(1) All electric equipment located within 5 feet (1.52 m) of the inside wall of the tub.

(2) All electric equipment associated with the circulating system of the tub.

(e) Methods of Grounding:

(1) All electric equipment shall be grounded in accordance with Article 250 and connected by wiring methods of Chapter 3.

(2) Where equipment is connected with a flexible cord, the equipment grounding conductor shall be connected to a fixed metal part of the assembly.

(f) Receptacles.   All receptacles within 5 feet (1.52 m) of a therapeutic tub shall be protected by a ground-fault circuit-interrupter.

680-63. Lighting Fixtures.   All lighting fixtures used in therapeutic pool areas shall be of the totally enclosed type.

ARTICLE 685 — INTEGRATED ELECTRICAL SYSTEMS

Contents

A. General

685-1. Scope. This article covers integrated electrical systems, other than unit equipment, in which orderly shutdown is necessary to ensure safe operation. An integrated electrical system as used in this article is a unitized segment of an industrial wiring system where all of the following conditions are met: (1) an orderly shutdown is required to minimize personnel hazard and equipment damage; (2) the conditions of maintenance and supervision assure that qualified persons will service the system; and (3) effective safeguards, acceptable to the authority having jurisdiction, are established and maintained.

> This article is new in the 1981 *Code*. Integrated electrical systems are commonly used in large industrial establishments where the electrical system and equipment are designed and installed (supervised) by engineering work forces. The control equipment, including overcurrent devices, is located to be accessible to qualified personnel, but may not be "readily accessible" as defined in Article 100.

685-2. Application of Other Articles. In other articles applying to particular cases of installation of conductors and equipment, there are orderly shutdown requirements that are in addition to those of this article or are modifications of them:

	Section
Protection of Conductors	240-3, Exception No. 8
Electrical System Coordination	240-12
Grounding ac Systems of 50 to 1000 Volts	250-5(b), Exception No. 3
Orderly Shutdown	430-44
Disconnection	430-74, Exceptions No. 1 and 2
Disconnecting Means in Sight from Controller	430-102, Exception No. 2
Energy from More than One Source	430-113, Exception

B. Orderly Shutdown

685-10. Location of Overcurrent Devices In or On Premises. Location of overcurrent devices which are critical to integrated electrical systems shall be permitted to be accessible with mounting heights allowed to assure security from operation by nonqualified personnel.

685-12. Direct-Current System Grounding. Two-wire direct-current circuits shall be permitted to be ungrounded.

685-14. Ungrounded Control Circuits. Where operational continuity is required, control circuits of 150 volts or less from separately derived systems shall be permitted to be ungrounded.

7 SPECIAL CONDITIONS

ARTICLE 700 — EMERGENCY SYSTEMS

Contents

A. General

700-1. Scope. The provisions of this article apply to the installation, operation, and maintenance of emergency systems consisting of circuits and equipment intended to supply, distribute, and control electricity for illumination and/or power to required facilities when the normal electrical supply or system is interrupted.

The provisions of this article apply to the installation of emergency systems where such systems are legally required by municipal, state, federal, or other codes or governmental agency having jurisdiction.

Except for health care facilities (Article 517), this *Code* does not determine whether emergency systems are required or the location of emergency or exit lights. This function is covered in NFPA *101-1976, Life Safety Code.*

Emergency systems are those systems legally required and classed as emergency by municipal, state, federal, or other codes, or by any governmental agency having jurisdiction. These systems are intended to automatically supply illumination and/or power to critical areas and equipment in the event of failure of the normal supply or in the event of accident to elements of a system intended to supply, distribute, and control power and illumination essential for safety to human life.

For further information regarding wiring and installation of emergency systems in health care facilities, see Article 517.

For further information regarding performance and maintenance of emergency systems in health care facilities, see Essential Electric Systems for Health Care Facilities, NFPA 76A-1977.

Emergency systems are generally installed in places of assembly where artificial illumination is required for safe exiting and for panic control in buildings subject to occupancy by large numbers of persons, such as hotels, theaters, sports arenas, health care facilities, and similar institutions. Emergency systems may also provide power for such functions as ventilation when essential to maintain life, fire detection and alarm systems, elevators, fire pumps, public safety communication systems, industrial processes where current interruption would produce serious life safety or health hazards, and similar functions.

For specification of locations where emergency lighting is considered essential to life safety, see *Life Safety Code*, NFPA *101*-1976 (ANSI).

Emergency systems are designed to maintain a specific degree of illumination or provide power for essential equipment, such as fire pumps, operating room equipment, etc., in the event of failure of the normal power supply.

Where authorities determine that emergency lighting, including the proper placement of exit signs, is required for safe egress from various classes of buildings, or parts of buildings, sufficient illumination is to be provided for corridors, passageways, stairways, lobbies, etc.

700-2. Application of Other Articles.   Except as modified by this article, all applicable articles of this Code shall apply.

700-3. Equipment Approval.   All equipment shall be approved for use on emergency systems.

700-4. Tests and Maintenance.

(a) **Conduct or Witness Test.**   The authority having jurisdiction shall conduct or witness a test on the complete system upon installation and periodically afterward.

(b) **Tested Periodically.**   Systems shall be tested periodically on a schedule acceptable to the authority having jurisdiction to assure their maintenance in proper operating condition.

(c) **Battery Systems Maintenance.**   Where battery systems or unit equipments are involved, including batteries used for starting or ignition in auxiliary engines, the authority having jurisdiction shall require periodic maintenance.

(d) **Written Record.**   A written record shall be kept of such tests and maintenance.

(e) **Testing Under Load.**   Means for testing any emergency lighting or power system under load shall be provided.

700-5. Capacity.

(a) **Capacity and Rating.**   An emergency system shall have adequate capacity and rating for the emergency operation of all equipment connected to the system.

It is essential that the emergency system be designed with adequate capacity and rating to carry the entire emergency connected load safely. The emergency operation of the equipment may be something less than the nameplate rating. Further, some equipment may be "spared," and with both normal and spare, it may be necessary for the emergency system to be sized for both to operate at the same time. The emergency system must be capable of restarting emergency loads that may have stopped.

Where such equipment is connected, in the event of a loss of normal power supply, emergency systems must be capable of supplying power to emergency lights for the illumination of specific areas, exit signs, and paths of egress, or for the operation of elevators, alarm systems, essential refrigeration, breathing apparatus or ventilation when essential to maintain life, fire pumps, public address systems, or other equipment.

The alternate power source in hospital facilities must be capable of supplying power to illuminate all exit signs and ways of approach to exits, alarm systems, communication systems, task illumination, as well as for illumination of operating rooms and power for elevators, heating for specific areas, and special equipment such as inhalators, incubators, etc. See Sections 517-61 through 517-64. For nursing homes and residential custodial care facilities, see Sections 517-44 through 517-46.

(b) Selective Load Pickup and Load Shedding.   The alternate power source may supply emergency, legally required standby, and optional standby system loads where automatic selective load pickup and load shedding is provided as needed to assure adequate power to (1) the emergency circuits; (2) the legally required standby circuits; and (3) the optional standby circuits, in that order of priority.

This recognizes the use of a generator to serve more than one level of emergency, standby, and other loads. It also permits the use of a generator for load peak shaving, supplying backup power, and other uses. However, there must be assurance that priority loads will be properly and reliably served. Such systems must be maintained and tested periodically to provide the necessary assurance.

A portable or temporary alternate source shall be available whenever the emergency generator is out of service for major maintenance or repair.

The added use that may result from serving other loads may necessitate major maintenance of emergency generator sets. The requirement for a portable or temporary alternate source is to provide emergency power when the generator set is out of service for a prolonged period of time. A major maintenance or repair procedure is one that keeps the generator set out of service for more than a few hours.

700-6. Transfer Equipment.   Transfer equipment shall be automatic and identified for emergency use or approved by the authority having jurisdiction. Transfer equipment shall be designed and installed to prevent the inadvertent interconnection of normal and emergency sources of supply in any operation of the transfer equipment. See Section 230-83.

700-7. Signals.   Audible and visual signal devices shall be provided, where practicable, for the following purposes:

(a) Derangement.   To indicate derangement of the emergency source.

(b) Carrying Load.   To indicate that the battery or generator set is carrying load.

(c) Not Functioning.   To indicate that the battery charger is not functioning.

(d) Prime Mover.   To indicate derangement of the prime mover starting equipment.

Improper or lack of testing, inadequate maintenance, and negligence by attendants to observe visual signals indicating a malfunction of battery-charging equipment are the major causes of emergency equipment failures.

Signal devices should be located in an area where they will be readily visible to or heard by attendants or other personnel familiar with the operation of the emergency equipment.

It should be noted that, in locations such as theaters or assembly halls, audible signal bells or horns should be located where they will not cause panic.

Battery-operated unit equipments generally have test switches to simulate a failure of the normal system and an indicating light that glows bright while charging and dim when ready. Transparent plastic cases are to be provided for lead acid batteries for easy viewing of electrolyte levels.

A storage battery system is capable of delivering 12 V, 24 V, 32 V, or 120 V and consists of monitoring and distribution cabinets and console with battery and charger. It generally includes audio, visual, and remote signal devices, a test switch, and may provide a trouble bell and silence switch.

B. Circuit Wiring

700-9. Wiring, Emergency System.   Wiring from emergency source or emergency source distribution overcurrent protection to emergency loads shall be kept entirely independent of all other wiring and equipment and shall not enter the same raceway, cable, box, or cabinet with other wiring.

Exception No. 1: In transfer equipment enclosures.

Exception No. 2: In exit or emergency lighting fixtures supplied from two sources.

Exception No. 3: In a common junction box attached to exit or emergency lighting fixtures supplied from two sources.

Exception No. 4: Wiring of two or more emergency circuits supplied from the same source shall be permitted in the same raceway.

Exception No. 5: In a common junction box attached to a unit equipment, and which contains only the branch circuit supplying the unit equipment and the emergency circuit supplied by the unit equipment.

Emergency circuit wiring is not to enter the same raceway, cable, box, or cabinet with the regular or normal wiring of the building concerned. Wiring for the emergency circuits must be completely independent of all other wiring and equipment, thus ensuring that any fault on the normal wiring circuits will not affect the performance of the emergency wiring or equipment.

To effect an immediate throw-over from one system to the other, it is necessary for both the normal source and the emergency source to be present within a transfer switch enclosure as per Exception No. 1.

Exceptions No. 2 and 3 permit the use of two-lamp exit or two-lamp emergency fixtures where one lamp is connected to the normal supply and one lamp is connected to the alternate supply. It is to be noted that both lamps may be illuminated as part of the regular lighting operation.

C. Sources of Power

700-12. Emergency Systems.   Current supply shall be such that in the event of failure of the normal supply to, or within, the building or group of buildings concerned, emergency lighting, emergency power, or both will be available within the time required for the application but not to exceed 10 seconds. The supply system for emergency purposes, in addition to the normal services to the building, shall be permitted to comprise one or more of the types of systems described in (a) through (e) below. Unit equipments in accordance with Section 700-12(f) shall satisfy the applicable requirements of this article.

In selecting an emergency source of power, consideration shall be given to the type of service to be rendered, whether of short-time duration, as for exit lights of a theater, or long duration, as for supplying emergency power and lighting due to a long period of current failure from trouble either inside or outside the building, as in the case of a hospital.

Consideration shall be given to the location and/or design of all equipment to minimize the hazards that might cause complete failure due to floods, fires, icing, and vandalism.

Assignment of degree of reliability of the recognized emergency supply system depends upon the careful evaluation of the variables at each particular installation.

(a) Storage Battery.   A storage battery of suitable rating and capacity to supply and maintain at not less than 87½ percent of system voltage the total load of the circuits supplying emergency lighting and emergency power for a period of at least 1½ hours.

Batteries, whether of the acid or alkali type, shall be designed and constructed to meet the requirements of emergency service and shall be compatible with the charger for that particular installation.

For a sealed battery, the container shall not be required to be transparent. However, for the lead acid battery which requires water additions, transparent or translucent jars shall be furnished. Automotive-type batteries shall not be used.

An automatic battery charging means shall be provided.

(b) Generator Set.

(1)   A generator set driven by a prime mover acceptable to the authority having jurisdiction and sized in accordance with Section 700-5. Means shall be provided for automatically starting the prime mover on failure of the normal service and for automatic transfer and operation of all required electrical circuits. A time delay feature permitting a 15-minute setting shall be provided to avoid retransfer in case of short-time reestablishment of the normal source.

(2)   Where internal combustion engines are used as the prime mover, an on-site fuel supply shall be provided with an on-premise fuel supply sufficient for not less than 2 hours full-demand operation of the system.

(3)   Prime movers shall not be solely dependent upon a public utility gas system for their fuel supply or municipal water supply for their cooling systems. Means shall be provided for automatically transferring from one fuel supply to another where dual fuel supplies are used.

Exception: Where acceptable to the authority having jurisdiction, the use of other than on-site fuels shall be permitted when there is a low probability of a simultaneous failure of both the off-site fuel delivery system and power from the outside electrical utility company.

(4)   Where the means of starting the prime mover is a storage battery, it shall be suitable for the purpose and shall be equipped with an automatic charging means.

(5)   Generator sets which require more than 10 seconds to develop power are acceptable providing an auxiliary power supply will energize the emergency system until the generator can pick up the load.

See Section 700-4 for test and maintenance requirements.

(c) Uninterruptible Power Supplies. Uninterruptible power supplies used to provide power for emergency systems shall comply with the applicable provision of Section 700-12(a) and (b).

(d) Separate Service. Where acceptable to the authority having jurisdiction, a second service shall be permitted. This service shall be in accordance with Article 230, with separate service drop or lateral, widely separated electrically and physically from the normal service to minimize the possibility of simultaneous interruption of supply.

(e) Connection Ahead of Service Disconnecting Means. Where acceptable to the authority having jurisdiction, connections ahead of, but not within, the main service disconnecting means shall be permitted. The emergency service shall be sufficiently separated from the normal main service disconnecting means to prevent simultaneous interruption of supply through an occurrence within the building or groups of buildings served.

When designing emergency systems, whether for lighting, power, or both, consideration is to be given to the type of service rendered, for instance, short-time duration for hospitals.

Supply systems for emergency systems can be one or more of the following:

1. One, or a group of storage batteries, provided with an automatic battery-charging means. See also Article 480 and paragraph (e) of this section.

2. A generator set driven by a prime mover, acceptable to the authority having jurisdiction, and with adequate capacity to carry its connected load. Prime movers may be internal-combustion engines, steam turbines, or other approved types. A storage battery used to start the prime mover is to be provided with an automatic battery-charging means. An on-site fuel supply sufficient to operate internal-combustion engines at full load for 2 hours is to be available.

Off-site fuel supplies may be used where experience has demonstrated their reliability. Off-site fuel supplies may also be used where they will provide greater reliability than gasoline engines or in isolated areas where maintenance or refueling could be a problem.

Some types of drivers, particularly large ones, may take longer than 10 seconds to accelerate and develop voltage. Gas and steam turbines and large internal-combustion engines may have prolonged starting times. Depending on the specific loads, short-time supply could be provided by an uninterrupted power supply; a generator shared with other loads; or a generator with limited emergency supply, such as an expander, steam turbine, or waste heat system.

3. Two services, overhead or underground, widely separated electrically and physically, and preferred by some authorities to be completely independent of each other; that is, separate service locations, separate transformers, and supplied from separate utility substations where practical.

4. Uninterrupted power supplies (UPS) generally include a rectifier, storage battery, and inverter to AC. These may be very complex systems with redundant components and high-speed solid-state switching. It is common practice to include an automatic bypass for UPS malfunction and to permit maintenance.

5. The use of a separate service or connection ahead of the service disconnect requires a judgment by the authority having jurisdiction. Such judgment should be based on the nature of the emergency loads and the expected reliability of the other available sources.

See Section 230-82 for equipment permitted on the supply side of a service disconnecting means.

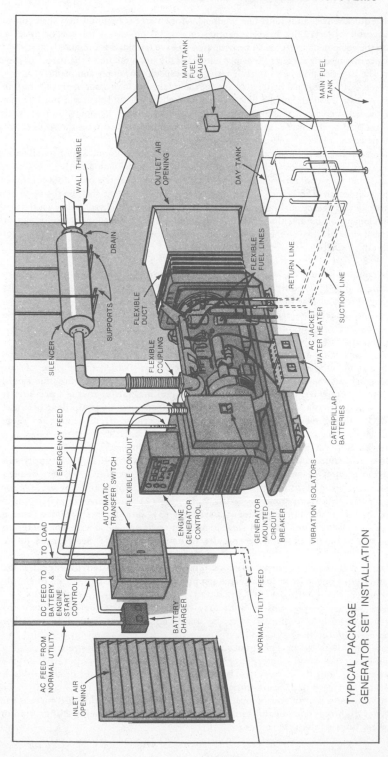

MAIN TANK FUEL GAUGE

MAIN FUEL TANK

WALL THIMBLE

OUTLET AIR OPENING

DAY TANK

DRAIN

FLEXIBLE FUEL LINES

RETURN LINE

SUPPORTS

FLEXIBLE DUCT

SILENCER

FLEXIBLE COUPLING

SUCTION LINE

AC JACKET WATER HEATER

CATERPILLAR BATTERIES

EMERGENCY FEED

VIBRATION ISOLATORS

AUTOMATIC TRANSFER SWITCH

FLEXIBLE CONDUIT

ENGINE GENERATOR CONTROL

GENERATOR MOUNTED CIRCUIT BREAKER

TO LOAD

DC FEED TO BATTERY & ENGINE START CONTROL

NORMAL UTILITY FEED

AC FEED FROM NORMAL UTILITY

BATTERY CHARGER

INLET AIR OPENING

TYPICAL PACKAGE
GENERATOR SET INSTALLATION

Figure 700-1. A typical generator installation supplying standby power in ratings from 55 kW to 930 kW, 60 Hz. (*Caterpillar*)

(f) Unit Equipment. Individual unit equipment for emergency illumination shall consist of: (1) a rechargeable battery; (2) a battery charging means; (3) provisions for one or more lamps mounted on the equipment and/or shall be permitted to have terminals for remote lamps; and (4) a relaying device arranged to energize the lamps automatically upon failure of the supply to the unit equipment. The batteries shall be of suitable rating and capacity to supply and maintain at not less than 87½ percent of the nominal battery voltage for the total lamp load associated with the unit for a period of at least 1½ hours, or the unit equipment shall supply and maintain not less than 60 percent of the initial emergency illumination for a period of at least 1½ hours. Storage batteries, whether of the acid or alkali type, shall be designed and constructed to meet the requirements of emergency service.

Unit equipment shall be permanently fixed in place (i.e., not portable) and shall have all wiring to each unit installed in accordance with the requirements of any of the wiring methods in Chapter 3. Flexible cord- and plug-connection shall be permitted provided that the cord does not exceed 3 feet (914 mm) in length. The branch circuit feeding the unit equipment shall be the same branch circuit as that serving the normal lighting in the area and connected ahead of any local switches. Emergency illumination fixtures that obtain power from a unit equipment and are not part of the unit equipment shall be wired to the unit equipment as required by Section 700-9 and by one of the wiring methods of Chapter 3.

Unit equipment may be wired with a flexible cord- and plug-connection (not exceeding 3 ft). This equipment must be permanently fixed in place, usually by mounting screws accessible only from within the unit. One or more lamps may be mounted on, or remote from, the unit which must be located where it can be readily checked or tested for proper performance.

Unit equipment is intended to provide illumination for the area where it is installed. For instance, if a unit is located in a corridor, it must be connected to the branch circuit supplying the normal corridor lights (on the line side of any switching arrangements), and in the event of loss of normal power, the unit would automatically energize the unit lamps, restoring illumination to the corridor. It ·should be noted that a separate circuit is not required for unit equipment because, if applied to the above case, failure of the normal corridor circuit would not affect the unit equipment and the corridor would remain in darkness.

Notes on General Requirements for Emergency Lighting Systems

At least two sources of power are to be provided, that is, one normal supply and one or more types of emergency systems described in Section 700-6(a) through (d). The sources may be (1) two services, one normal supply and one emergency supply (preferably from separate utility stations); (2) one normal service and a storage battery (or unit equipment) system; (3) one normal service and a generator set; or (4) one normal service and one emergency service connected to the line side of the normal service (usually at the weatherhead). See Figures 700-3, 700-4, and 700-5.

A transfer means (or throw-over switch) is to be provided to energize the emergency equipment from the alternate supply when the normal source of supply is interrupted. See Figure 700-3.

Where two services are used, both may operate normally, but equipment for emergency lighting and power is to be arranged to be energized from either service. See Figure 700-4.

Where the alternate or emergency source of supply is a storage battery or a generator set, the single emergency system would usually be operated on the normal service, and the battery (or batteries) or generator would operate only if the normal service failed. See Figure 700-5.

Two or more separate and complete systems may be used to provide current for emergency lighting, but means are to be provided for energizing either system upon the failure of the other.

It should be noted that provisions for disconnecting means and overcurrent protection (see Figures 700-3, 700-4, and 700-5) are to be provided for emergency systems as required by Article 230. See also Section 230-83.

Figure 700-2. Self-contained fully automatic unit equipment to operate emergency lighting located on the unit or for remotely located exit signs or lighting heads. (*Dual-Lite Inc.*)

D. Emergency System Circuits for Lighting and Power

700-15. Loads on Emergency Branch Circuits.   No appliances and no lamps, other than those specified as required for emergency use, shall be supplied by emergency lighting circuits.

700-16. Emergency Illumination.   Emergency illumination shall include all required exit lights and all other lights specified as necessary to provide required illumination.

Emergency lighting systems shall be so designed and installed that the failure of any individual lighting element, such as the burning out of a light bulb, cannot leave in total darkness any space which requires emergency illumination.

700-17. Circuits for Emergency Lighting.   Branch circuits which supply emergency lighting shall be installed to provide service from a source complying with Section 700-12 when the normal supply for lighting is interrupted. Such installations shall provide either one of the following: (1) an emergency lighting supply, independent of the general lighting supply, with provisions for automatically transferring the emergency lights upon the event of failure of the general lighting system supply, or (2) two or more separate and complete systems with independent power supply, each system providing sufficient current for emergency lighting purposes. Unless both systems are used for regular lighting purposes and are both kept lighted, means shall be provided for automatically energizing either system upon failure of the other. Either or both systems shall be permitted to be a part of the general lighting system of the protected occupancy if circuits supplying lights for emergency illumination are installed in accordance with other sections of this article.

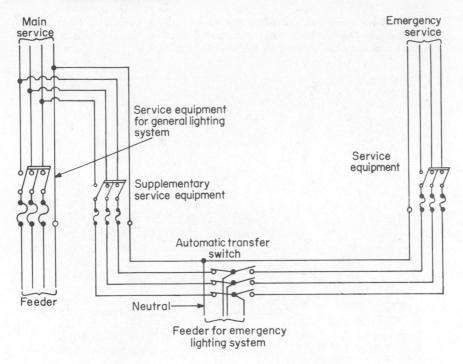

Figure 700-3. Small emergency load arranged to be supplied from the normal service or, under emergency conditions, the emergency service.

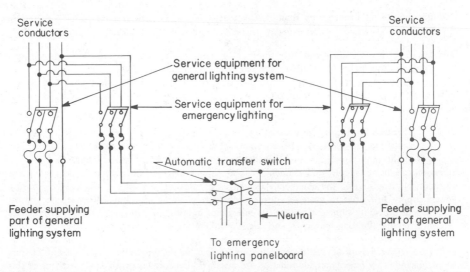

Figure 700-4. Emergency load arranged to be supplied by two widely separated services. Upon the failure of one service, the emergency load will be transferred automatically to the other service.

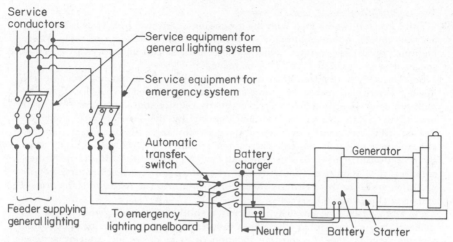

Figure 700-5. Emergency load arranged to be supplied from the normal service or from a generator (or storage battery).

1. General Considerations for Transfer Switches

Automatic transfer switches of double-throw construction are primarily used for emergency and standby power generation systems rated 600 V and less. These transfer switches do not normally incorporate overcurrent protection and are designed and applied in accordance with the *Code*, particularly Articles 700 and 750. They are available in ratings from 30 to 3,000 A. For reliability, most automatic transfer switches rated above 100 A are mechanically held and electrically operated from the power source to which the load is to be transferred.

An automatic transfer switch is usually located in the main or secondary distribution bus which feeds the branch circuits. Because of its location in the system, the abilities which must be designed into the transfer switch are unique and extensive as compared with the design requirements for other branch-circuit devices. For example, special consideration should be given to the following characteristics of an automatic transfer: (1) its ability to close against high in-rush currents, (2) its ability to carry full-rated current continuously from normal and emergency sources, (3) its ability to withstand fault currents, and (4) its ability to interrupt six times the full-load currents. In addition to considering each of the above characteristics individually, it is also necessary to consider the effect each has upon the other.

In arrangements to provide protection against failure of the utility service, consideration should also be given to (1) an open circuit within the building area on the load side of the incoming service, (2) overload or fault condition, and (3) electrical or mechanical failure of the electric power distribution system within the building. It, therefore, is desirable to locate transfer switches close to the load and have the operation of the transfer switches independent of overcurrent protection. It is often desirable to use multiple transfer switches of lower current located near the load rating rather than one large transfer switch at the point of incoming service.

2. Location of Overcurrent Devices

The location of overcurrent devices for both normal and emergency power is covered by Section 240-21 and is not affected by the installation of an automatic transfer switch. Transfer switches should be rated for continuous duty and have low contact temperature rise.

3. Solid Neutral on AC and DC Systems

Solid neutrals can be used with the grounding connections made as required in Section 250-23 where automatic ac to ac transfer switches are used. Where multiple grounding creates objectionable ground-current, corrective action specified in Section 250-21(b) is to be made.

Section 230-95 requires ground-fault protection of equipment. Because the normal source and emergency source are typically grounded at their locations, the multiple neutral-to-ground connections usually require some additional means or devices to assure proper ground-fault sensing by the ground-fault protection device. Additional means or devices are generally required because the normal alterations to stop objectionable current per Section 250-21(b) do not apply when the objectionable current is a ground-fault current. See Section 250-21(c). Rather, solutions such as an overlapping neutral transfer pole or conventional fourth pole are often added to the transfer switch. Other solutions are isolation transformers and special ground-fault circuits.

On ac to dc automatic transfer switches, a solid neutral tie between the ac and dc neutrals is not permitted where both sources of supply are exterior distribution systems. Section 250-22 regarding location of grounds for dc exterior systems clearly specifies that the dc system can be grounded only at the supply station.

Where the dc system is an interior isolated system, such as a storage battery, solid neutral connection between the ac system neutral and the dc source is acceptable.

On an ac to dc automatic transfer switch where the neutral must be switched, the size of the neutral switching pole must be considered. A 4-pole, double-throw switch must be used where a 3-phase, 4-wire normal source and a 2-wire dc emergency source are transferred. Due to the neutral being switched, a 4-pole, double-throw transfer switch would be required. In this instance, one pole of the dc emergency source would carry three times the current of the other poles.

4. Close Differential Voltage Supervision of Normal Source

Most often the normal source is an electric utility company whose power is transmitted many miles to the point of utilization. The automatic transfer switch control panel continuously monitors the voltage of all phases. (Because utility frequency is, for all practical purposes, constant, only the voltage need be monitored.) For single-phase power systems, the line-to-line voltage is monitored. For 3-phase power systems, all three line-to-line voltages should be monitored to provide full-phase protection.

In addition, monitoring protects against operation at reduced voltage, such as brownouts, which can damage loads. Since the voltage sensitivity of loads vary, the pickup (acceptable) voltage setting, and dropout (unacceptable) voltage setting of the monitors should be adjustable. Typical range of adjustment for the pickup is 85 percent to 100 percent of nominal, while the dropout setting, which is a function of the pickup setting, is 75 percent to 98 percent of the pickup selected. Usual settings for most loads are 95 percent of nominal for pickup and 85 percent of nominal for dropout (90 percent of pickup).

Consideration must be given to voltage supervision at closer differential for many installations where the load circuits are critical to voltage.

Starter-type fluorescent lighting is extremely voltage sensitive, and at voltages below 105 V it becomes uncertain as to whether the fluorescent lamp will burn. Therefore, a closer differential of transfer and retransfer is required for this type of lighting.

Electronic equipment load is frequently voltage critical. These installations include patient care equipment in health care facilities, television stations, microwave communications, telephone communications, computer centers, and similar applications.

Polyphase motors operating at low load have a tendency to single phase, despite the loss of voltage in one phase, leading to burnup of the motor. A close differential of voltage supervision should be applied to automatic transfer switches for motor installations of the polyphase type. Differential voltage relays with a close adjustment of 2 percent for transfer and retransfer values will aid in the detection of phase outages and provide protection from single phasing.

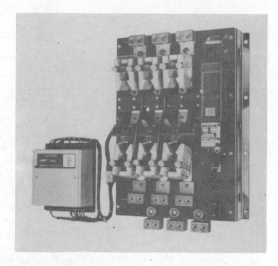

Figure 700-6. Automatic emergency transfer switch and control panel. (*Automatic Switch Co.*)

5. Automatic Transfer Switches with Emergency Source on Automatically Started Power Plant

In these installations the normal source is usually a utility power line, and the emergency source is an automatically started engine generator set which starts upon failure of the normal source. To ensure maximum reliability, a minimum installation should be arranged to:

1. Initiate engine starting of the power plant from a contact on the automatic transfer switch control panel (see Figure 700-7),

2. Sustain connection of load circuits to the normal source during the starting period to provide utilization of any existing service on the normal source,

3. Measure output voltage and frequency of emergency source through the use of voltage-frequency-sensitive monitor (see Figure 700-7) and effect transfer of the load circuits to the power plant only when both voltage and frequency of the power plant are approximately normal. Sensing of the emergency source need only be single phase since most applications involve an on-site engine generator with a relatively short line run to the ATS. In addition to monitoring voltage, the emergency source's frequency should also be monitored. Unlike the utility power, the engine generator frequency can vary during startup. Frequency monitoring will avoid overloading the engine generator while it is starting and can thus avoid stalling the engine. Combined frequency and voltage monitoring will protect against transferring loads to an engine generator set with an unacceptable output, and

4. Provide visual signal and auxiliary contact for remote indication when power plant is feeding the load per Section 700-7(b).

6. Time-Delay Devices on Automatic Transfer Switches

Time delays are provided to program operation of the automatic transfer

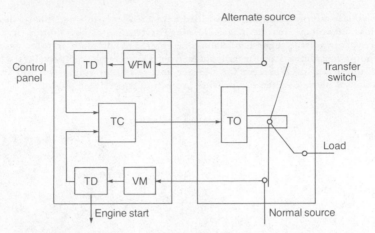

Figure 700-7. Diagram of connections of the automatic transfer switch shown in Figure 700-6. TD, Time Delay; TO, Transfer; TC, Transfer Controls; V/FM, Voltage Frequency Monitor; VM, Voltage Monitor. (*Automatic Switch Co.*)

switch. To avoid unnecessary starting and transfer to the alternate supply, a nominal one-second time delay, adjustable up to six seconds, can override momentary interruptions and reductions in normal source voltage but allow starting and transfer if the reduction or outage is sustained. See Figure 700-7. The advantages of this feature are realized in all types of automatic transfer installations. In standby plant installations the reduced number of false starts is especially important to minimize wear on the starting gear, battery, and associated equipment. This delay is generally set at one second, but may be set higher if reclosers on the high lines take longer to operate or if momentary power dips exceed one second. If longer delay settings are used, care must be taken to ensure that sufficient time remains to meet ten-second power restoration requirements.

Once the load is transferred to the alternate source, another timer delays retransfer to the normal source until that source has time to stabilize. This timer is required by Section 700-6(b)(1) and is controlled by the preferred source voltage monitors. The timer is adjustable from 0 to 30 minutes and is normally set at 30 minutes. Another important function of this retransfer timer is to allow an engine generator to operate under load for a preselected minimum time to ensure continued good performance of the set and its starting system. This delay should be automatically nullified if the alternate source fails and the normal source is available as determined by the voltage monitors.

Engine generator manufacturers often recommend a cool-down period for their sets which allows them to run unloaded after the load is retransferred to the normal source. A third time delay, usually five minutes, is provided for this purpose. Running an unloaded engine for more than five minutes is neither necessary nor recommended since it can cause deterioration in engine performance.

It is sometimes prescribed to purposely sequence transfer of the loads to the alternate source where more than one automatic transfer switch is connected to the same engine generator. Utilization of such a sequencing scheme can reduce starting kVA capacity requirements of the generator. A fourth timer, adjustable from 0 to five minutes, will delay transfer to emergency for this and other similar requirements.

700-18. Circuits for Emergency Power.   For branch circuits that supply equipment classed as emergency, there shall be an emergency supply source to which the load will be transferred automatically upon the failure of the normal supply.

E. Control — Emergency Lighting Circuits

700-20. Switch Requirements.   The switch or switches installed in emergency lighting circuits shall be so arranged that only authorized persons will have control of emergency lighting.

Exception No. 1: Where two or more single-throw switches are connected in parallel to control a single circuit, at least one of these switches shall be accessible only to authorized persons.

Exception No. 2: Additional switches that act only to put emergency lights into operation but not disconnect them are permissible.

Switches connected in series or 3- and 4-way switches shall not be used.

700-21. Switch Location.   All manual switches for controlling emergency circuits shall be in locations convenient to authorized persons responsible for their actuation. In places of assembly, such as theaters, a switch for controlling emergency lighting systems shall be located in the lobby or at a place conveniently accessible thereto.

700-22. Exterior Lights.   Those lights on the exterior of a building that are not required for illumination when there is sufficient daylight shall be permitted to be controlled by an automatic light-actuated device.

F. Overcurrent Protection

700-25. Accessibility.   The branch-circuit overcurrent devices in emergency circuits shall be accessible to authorized persons only.

700-26. Ground-Fault Protection of Equipment.   The alternate source for emergency systems shall not be required to have ground-fault protection of equipment.

This is an exception to the general ground-fault protection requirement of Article 230-95 for protective devices set to, or rated at, 1,000 amperes or more. It permits the designer to exercise judgment in risking equipment damage in order to keep emergency circuits in operation as long as they will continue to function.

ARTICLE 701 — LEGALLY REQUIRED
STANDBY SYSTEMS

Contents

701-6. Capacity and Rating.
701-7. Transfer Equipment.
701-8. Signals.
   (a) Derangement.
   (b) Carrying Load.
   (c) Not Functioning.
   (d) Prime Mover.

B. Circuit Wiring
701-9. Wiring Legally Required Standby Systems.

C. Sources of Power
701-10. Legally Required Standby Systems.

   (a) Storage Battery.
   (b) Generator Set.
   (c) Uninterruptable Power Supplies.
   (d) Separate Service.
   (e) Connection Ahead of Service Disconnecting Means.
   (f) Unit Equipment.

D. Overcurrent Protection
701-15. Accessibility.
701-17. Ground-Fault Protection of Equipment.

A. General

701-1. Scope. The provisions of this article apply to the installation, operation, and maintenance of legally required standby systems consisting of circuits and equipment intended to supply, distribute, and control electricity to required facilities for illumination and/or power when the normal electrical supply or system is interrupted.

The systems covered by this article shall be permanently installed in their entirety including power source.

For additional information, see Article 517 and NFPA 76A-1977, Essential Electrical Systems for Health Care Facilities.

This article was added to the 1981 *NEC* to treat separately the requirements for legally required standby systems. In earlier editions of the *Code*, these requirements were included with the requirements for optional standby systems in Article 750, which tended to obscure an important level of standby systems.

Legally required standby systems are intended to provide electric power to aid in fire fighting, rescue operations, control of health hazards, and similar operations. In comparison, emergency systems (Article 700) are those which are essential for safety to human life. Optional standby systems are those whose failure could cause such effects as physical discomfort, serious interruption of an industrial process, damage to process equipment, or disruption of business.

Legally required standby systems have much the same needs as emergency systems; however, there are some differences in requirements. Upon loss of normal power, legally required systems must be able to supply standby power in 60 seconds or less instead of the 10 seconds or less required of emergency systems. Wiring for legally required standby systems may occupy the same raceways, cables, boxes, and cabinets as other general wiring. Wiring for emergency systems must be kept entirely independent of other wiring. Legally required standby systems take second order priority to emergency systems where they are involved in sharing an alternate supply and/or load shedding schemes.

The 1981 *NEC* contains expanded requirements for legally required standby systems to give the regulating authority assurance that the standby electrical system will be available and reliable when needed.

701-2. Legally Required Standby Systems. Legally required standby systems are those systems required and so classed as legally required standby by municipal, state, federal, or other codes or by any governmental agency having jurisdiction. These systems are intended to automatically supply power to selected loads (other than those classed as emergency systems) in the event of failure of the normal source.

Legally required standby systems are typically installed to serve loads, such as heating and refrigeration systems, communication systems, ventilation and smoke removal systems, sewerage disposal, lighting systems and industrial processes, that, when stopped during any interruption of the normal electrical supply, could create hazards or hamper rescue or fire fighting operations.

701-3. Application of Other Articles.   Except as modified by this article, all applicable articles of this Code shall apply.

701-4. Equipment Approval.   All equipment shall be approved for the intended use.

701-5. Tests and Maintenance for Legally Required Standby Systems.

  (a) Conduct or Witness Test.   The authority having jurisdiction shall conduct or witness a test on the complete system upon installation.

  (b) Tested Periodically.   Systems shall be tested periodically on a schedule and in a manner acceptable to the authority having jurisdiction to assure their maintenance in proper operating condition.

  (c) Battery Systems Maintenance.   Where batteries are used for starting or ignition of prime movers the authority having jurisdiction shall require periodic maintenance.

  (d) Written Record.   A written record shall be kept on such tests and maintenance.

  (e) Testing under Load.   Means for testing legally required standby systems under load shall be provided.

701-6. Capacity and Rating.   A legally required standby system shall have adequate capacity and rating for the supply of all equipment intended to be operated at one time.
  The alternate power source may supply legally required standby and optional standby system loads when automatic selective load pickup and load shedding is provided as needed to assure adequate power to the legally required standby circuits.

701-7. Transfer Equipment.   Transfer equipment shall be automatic and identified for standby use or approved by the authority having jurisdiction. Transfer equipment shall be designed and installed to prevent the inadvertent interconnection of normal and alternate sources of supply in any operation of the transfer equipment.

701-8. Signals.   Audible and visual signal devices shall be provided, where practicable, for the following purposes:

  (a) Derangement.   To indicate derangement of the standby source.

  (b) Carrying Load.   To indicate that the standby source is carrying load.

  (c) Not Functioning.   To indicate that the battery charger is not functioning.

  (d) Prime Mover.   To indicate derangement of the prime mover starting equipment.

B. Circuit Wiring

701-9. Wiring Legally Required Standby Systems.   The legally required standby system wiring shall be permitted to occupy the same raceways, cables, boxes and cabinets with other general wiring.

C. Sources of Power

701-10. Legally Required Standby Systems. Current supply shall be such that in event of failure of the normal supply to, or within, the building or group of buildings concerned, legally required standby power will be available within the time required for the application but not to exceed 60 seconds. The supply system for legally required standby purposes, in addition to the normal services to the building, shall be permitted to comprise one or more of the types of systems described in (a) through (e) below. Unit equipment in accordance with Section 701-10(f) shall satisfy the applicable requirements of this article.

In selecting a legally required standby source of power, consideration shall be given to the type of service to be rendered whether of short-time duration or long duration.

Consideration shall be given to the location and/or design of all equipment to minimize the hazards that might cause complete failure due to floods, fires, icing, and vandalism.

Assignment of degree of reliability of the recognized legally required standby supply system depends upon the careful evaluation of the variables at each particular installation.

(a) Storage Battery. A storage battery of suitable rating and capacity to supply and maintain at not less than 87½ percent of system voltage the total load of the circuits supplying legally required standby power for a period of at least 1½ hours.

Batteries, whether of the acid or alkali type, shall be designed and constructed to meet the service requirements of emergency service and shall be compatible with the charger for that particular installation.

For a sealed battery, the container shall not be required to be transparent. However, for the lead acid battery which requires water additions, transparent or translucent jars shall be furnished. Automotive-type batteries shall not be used.

An automatic battery charging means shall be provided.

(b) Generator Set.

(1) A generator set driven by a prime mover acceptable to the authority having jurisdiction and sized in accordance with Section 701-6. Means shall be provided for automatically starting the prime mover on failure of the normal service and for automatic transfer and operation of all required electrical circuits. A time delay feature permitting a 15-minute setting shall be provided to avoid retransfer in case of short-time reestablishment of the normal source.

(2) Where internal combustion engines are used as the prime mover, an on-site fuel supply shall be provided with an on-premise fuel supply sufficient for not less than 2 hours full-demand operation of the system.

(3) Prime movers shall not be solely dependent upon a public utility gas system for their fuel supply or municipal water supply for their cooling systems. Means shall be provided for automatically transferring one fuel supply to another where dual fuel supplies are used.

Exception: Where acceptable to the authority having jurisdiction, the use of other than on-site fuels shall be permitted when there is a low probability of a simultaneous failure of both the off-site fuel delivery system and power from the outside electrical utility company.

(4) Where the means of starting the prime mover is a storage battery, it shall be suitable for the purpose and shall be equipped with an automatic charging means.

See Section 701-5 for test and maintenance requirements.

(c) Uninterruptible Power Supplies. Uninterruptible power supplies used to provide power for legally required standby systems shall comply with the applicable provision of Section 701-10(a) and (b).

(d) Separate Service. Where acceptable to the authority having jurisdiction, a second service shall be permitted. This service shall be in accordance with Article 230 with separate service drop or lateral widely separated electrically and physically from the normal service to minimize the possibility of simultaneous interruption of supply.

(e) Connection Ahead of Service Disconnecting Means. Where acceptable to the authority having jurisdiction, connections ahead of, but not within, the main service disconnecting means shall be permitted. The legally required standby service shall be sufficiently separated from the normal main service disconnecting means to prevent simultaneous interruption of supply through an occurrence within the building or groups of buildings served.

See Section 230-82 for equipment permitted on the supply side of a service disconnecting means.

(f) Unit Equipment. Individual unit equipment for legally required standby illumination shall consist of (1) a rechargeable battery; (2) a battery charging means; (3) provisions for one or more lamps mounted on the equipment and/or shall be permitted to have terminals for remote lamps; and (4) a relaying device arranged to energize the lamps automatically upon failure of the supply to the unit equipment. The batteries shall be of suitable rating and capacity to supply and maintain at not less than 87½ percent of the nominal battery voltage for the total lamp load associated with the unit for a period of at least 1½ hours, or the unit equipment shall supply and maintain not less than 60 percent of the initial legally required standby illumination for a period of at least 1½ hours. Storage batteries, whether of the acid or alkali type, shall be designed and constructed to meet the requirements of emergency service.

Unit equipment shall be permanently fixed in place (i.e., not portable) and shall have all wiring to each unit installed in accordance with the requirements of any of the wiring methods in Chapter 3. Flexible cord-and plug-connection shall be permitted provided that the cord does not exceed 3 feet (914 mm) in length. The branch circuit feeding the unit equipment shall be the same branch circuit as that serving the normal lighting in the area and connected ahead of any local switches. Legally required standby illumination fixtures that obtain power from a unit equipment and are not part of the unit equipment shall be wired to the unit equipment by one of the wiring methods of Chapter 3.

D. Overcurrent Protection

701-15. Accessibility. The branch-circuit overcurrent devices in legally required standby circuits shall be accessible to authorized persons only.

701-17. Ground-Fault Protection of Equipment. The alternate source for legally required standby systems shall not be required to have ground-fault protection of equipment.

ARTICLE 702 — OPTIONAL STANDBY SYSTEMS

Contents

A. General

702-1. Scope.   The provisions of this article apply to the installation and operation of optional standby systems.

The systems covered by this article consist only of those that are permanently installed in their entirety, including prime movers.

702-2. Optional Standby Systems.   Optional standby systems are intended to protect private business or property where life safety does not depend on the performance of the system. Optional standby systems are intended to supply on-site generated power to selected loads either automatically or manually.

Optional standby systems are typically installed to provide an alternate source of electric power for such facilities as industrial and commercial buildings, farms, and residences, and to serve loads such as heating and refrigeration systems, data processing and communications systems, and industrial processes that, when stopped during any power outage, could cause discomfort, serious interruption of the process, damage to the product or process, or the like.

702-3. Application of Other Articles.   Except as modified by this article all applicable articles of this Code shall apply.

702-4. Equipment Approval.   All equipment shall be approved for the intended use.

702-5. Capacity.   An optional standby system shall have adequate capacity and rating for the supply of all equipment intended to be operated at one time.

702-6. Transfer Equipment.   Transfer equipment shall be suitable for the intended use and so designed and installed as to prevent the inadvertent interconnection of normal and alternate sources of supply in any operation of the transfer equipment.

702-7. Signals.   Audible and visual signal devices shall be provided, where practicable, for the following purposes:

(a) Derangement.   To indicate derangement of the optional standby source.

(b) Carrying Load.   To indicate that the optional standby source is carrying load.

B. Circuit Wiring

702-8. Wiring Optional Standby Systems.   The optional standby system wiring shall be permitted to occupy the same raceways, cables, boxes and cabinets with other general wiring.

ARTICLE 710 — OVER 600 VOLTS, NOMINAL

GENERAL

Contents

A. General

710-1. Scope. This article covers the general requirements for all circuits and equipment operated at more than 600 volts, nominal. For specific installations, see the articles referred to in Section 710-2.

710-2. Other Articles. Provisions applicable to specific types of installations are included in Article 225, Outside Branch Circuits and Feeders; Article 230, Services; Article 318, Cable Trays; Article 326, Medium Voltage Cable; Article 345, Intermediate Metal Conduit; Article 346, Rigid Metal Conduit; Article 347, Rigid Nonmetallic Conduit; Article 364, Busways; Article 365, Cablebus; Article 410, Lighting Fixtures, Lampholders, Lamps, Receptacles, and Rosettes; Article 427, Fixed Electric Heating Equipment for Pipelines and Vessels; Article 430, Motors, Motor Circuits, and Controllers; Article 450, Transformers and Transformer Vaults; Article 460, Capacitors; Article 600, Electric Signs and Outline Lighting; Article 660, X-ray Equipment; Article 665, Induction and Dielectric Heating Equipment; and for construction and ampacities of high-voltage conductors, see Article 310.

710-3. Wiring Methods.

(a) Aboveground Conductors. Aboveground conductors shall be installed in rigid metal conduit, in intermediate metal conduit, in rigid nonmetallic conduit, in cable trays, as busways, as cablebus, in other suitable raceways, or as open runs of metal-clad cable suitable for the use and purpose.

Rigid nonmetallic conduit and busways were added as wiring methods in the 1981 *Code.*

In locations accessible to qualified persons only, open runs of nonmetallic-sheathed cable, bare conductors and bare busbars shall also be permitted.

(b) Underground Conductors. Underground conductors shall be suitable for the voltage and conditions under which they are installed.

Direct burial cables shall comply with the provisions of Section 310-7.

The reference to Section 310-7 is new in the 1981 *Code.*

Underground cables shall be permitted to be direct buried or installed in raceways identified for the use and shall meet the depth requirements of Table 710-3(b).

Nonshielded cables shall be installed in rigid metal conduit, in intermediate metal conduit, or in rigid nonmetallic conduit encased in not less than 3 inches (76 mm) of concrete.

Exception No. 1: Type MC cable with nonshielded conductor where the metallic sheath is grounded through an effective grounding path meeting the requirements of Section 250-51.

Exception No. 2: Lead sheath cable with nonshielded conductor where the lead sheath is grounded through an effective grounding path meeting the requirements of Section 250-51.

Exception Nos. 1 and 2 are new in the 1981 *Code.*

Table 710-3(b)

Minimum Cover Requirements
(Cover Means the Distance in Inches Between the Top
Surface of Cable or Raceway and the Grade)

Circuit Voltage	Direct Buried Cables	Rigid Nonmetallic Conduit Approved for Direct Burial*	Rigid Metal Conduit and Intermediate Metal Conduit
Over 600-22kV	30	18	6
Over 22kV-40kV	36	24	6
Over 40kV	42	30	6

For SI units: one inch = 25.4 millimeters.

* Listed by a qualified testing agency as suitable for direct burial without encasement. All other nonmetallic systems shall require 2 inches (50.8mm) of concrete or equivalent above conduit in addition to above depth.

Exception No. 1: The above minimum cover requirements shall be permitted to be reduced 6 inches (152 mm) for each 2 inches (50.8 mm) of concrete or equivalent above the conductors.

Exception No. 2: Areas subject to heavy vehicular traffic, such as thoroughfares or commercial parking areas, shall have a minimum cover of 24 inches (610 mm).

Exception No. 3: Lesser depths are permitted where cables and conductors rise for terminations or splices or where access is otherwise required.

Exception No. 4: In airport runways, including adjacent defined areas where trespass is prohibited, cable shall be permitted to be buried not less than 18 inches (457 mm) deep and without raceways, concrete enclosement, or equivalent.

Exception No. 5: Raceways installed in solid rock shall be permitted to be buried at lesser depth when covered by 2 inches (50.8 mm) of concrete which may extend to the rock surface.

(1) Protection from Damage. Conductors emerging from the ground shall be enclosed in approved raceway. Raceways installed on poles shall be of rigid metal conduit, intermediate metal conduit, PVC Schedule 80 or equivalent extending from the ground line up to a point 8 feet (2.44 m) above finished grade. Conductors entering a building shall be protected by an approved enclosure from the ground line to the point of entrance. Metallic enclosures shall be grounded.

(2) Splices. Direct burial cables shall be permitted to be spliced or tapped without the use of splice boxes provided they are installed using materials suitable for the application. The taps and splices shall be watertight and protected from mechanical injury. Where cables are shielded, the shielding shall be continuous across the splice or tap.

(3) Backfill. Backfill containing large rock, paving materials, cinders, large or sharply angular substance, or corrosive materials shall not be placed in an excavation where materials can damage raceways, cables, or other substructures or prevent adequate compaction of fill or contribute to corrosion of raceways, cables, or other substructures.

(4) Raceway Seal. Where a raceway enters from an underground system the end within the building shall be sealed with suitable compound so as to prevent the entrance of moisture or gases, or it shall be so arranged to prevent moisture from contacting live parts.

In switch rooms, transformer vaults, and similar areas that are restricted to qualified personnel, any suitable wiring method may be used. Open wiring using bare or insulated conductors on insulators is commonly employed, as is rigid metal conduit and rigid nonmetallic conduit.

(c) Busbars. Busbars shall be permitted to be either copper or aluminum.

Section 710-3(c) is new in the 1981 *Code.*

710-4. Braid-Covered Insulated Conductors — Open Installation. Open runs of braid-covered insulated conductors shall have a flame-retardant braid. If the conductors used do not have this protection, a flame-retardant saturant shall be applied to the braid covering after installation. This treated braid covering shall be stripped back a safe distance at conductor terminals, according to the operating voltage. This distance shall not be less than 1 inch (25.4 mm) for each kilovolt of the conductor-to-ground voltage of the circuit, where practicable.

710-6. Insulation Shielding.   Metallic and semiconducting insulation shielding components of shielded cables shall be removed for a distance dependent on the circuit voltage and insulation. Stress reduction means shall be provided at all terminations of factory applied shielding.

Metallic shielding components such as tapes, wires or braids, or combinations thereof and their associated conducting or semiconducting components shall be grounded.

Special kits are now available from several manufacturers that permit a quick and easy means of providing the required stress reductions when terminating solid dielectric cables.

710-7. Grounding.   Wiring and equipment installations shall be grounded in accordance with the applicable provisions of Article 250.

710-8. Moisture or Mechanical Protection for Metal-Sheathed Cables.   Where cable conductors emerge from a metal sheath and where protection against moisture or physical damage is necessary, the insulation of the conductors shall be protected by a cable termination.

710-9. Protection of Service Equipment, Metal-Enclosed Switchgear, and Industrial Control Assemblies.   Pipes or ducts foreign to the electrical installation which require periodic maintenance or whose malfunction would endanger the operation of the electrical system shall not be located in the vicinity of the service equipment, metal-enclosed power switchgear, or industrial control assemblies. Protection shall be provided where necessary to avoid damage from condensation leaks and breaks in such foreign systems.

B. Equipment — General Provisions

710-11. Indoor Installations.   See Section 110-31(a).

710-12. Outdoor Installations.   See Section 110-31(b).

710-13. Metal-Enclosed Equipment.   See Section 110-31(c).

710-14. Oil-Filled Equipment.   Installation of electrical equipment, other than transformers, covered in Article 450, containing more than 10 gallons (37.85 L) of flammable oil per unit shall meet the requirements of Parts B and C of Article 450.

C. Equipment — Specific Provisions

See also references to specific types of installations in Section 710-2.

710-20. Overcurrent Protection.   Overcurrent protection shall be provided for each ungrounded conductor by one of the following:

(a) Overcurrent Relays and Current Transformers.   Circuit breakers used for overcurrent protection of ac 3-phase circuits shall have a minimum of three overcurrent relays operated from three current transformers.

Exception No. 1: On 3-phase, 3-wire circuits, an overcurrent relay in the residual circuit of the current transformers shall be permitted to replace one of the phase relays.

Exception No. 2: An overcurrent relay, operated from a current transformer which links all phases of a 3-phase, 3-wire circuit, shall be permitted to replace the residual relay and one of the phase conductor current transformers.

(b) Fuses. A fuse shall be connected in series with each ungrounded conductor.

710-21. Circuit-Interrupting Devices.

(a) Circuit Breakers.

(1) Indoor installations shall consist of metal-enclosed units or fire-resistant cell-mounted units.

Exception: Open mounting of circuit breakers shall be permitted in locations accessible to qualified persons only.

(2) Circuit breakers used to control oil-filled transformers shall be either located outside the transformer vault or be capable of operation from outside the vault.

(3) Oil circuit breakers shall be so arranged or located that adjacent readily combustible structures or materials are safeguarded in an approved manner.

(4) Circuit breakers shall have the following equipment or operating characteristics:

a. An accessible mechanical or other approved means for manual tripping, independent of control power.

b. Be release free (trip free).

c. If capable of being opened or closed manually while energized, the main contacts shall operate independently of the speed of the manual operation.

d. A mechanical position indicator at the circuit breaker to show the open or closed position of the main contacts.

e. A means of indicating the open and closed position of the breaker at the point(s) from which they may be operated.

f. A permanent and legible nameplate showing manufacturer's name or trademark, manufacturer's type or identification number, continuous current rating, interrupting rating in MVA or amperes, and maximum voltage rating. Modification of a circuit breaker affecting its rating(s) shall be accompanied by an appropriate change of nameplate information.

For the control and protection of feeders leaving a substation, Figure 710-1 shows a typical example of modern, metal-enclosed switchgear. This industrial unit substation includes a high-voltage disconnect switch, transformer, and low-voltage switchgear with a full functioning ground-fault relay protection system.

Indicating instruments, such as voltmeters, ammeters, wattmeters and protective relays, may be mounted on the panel doors as desired. This switchgear affords a high degree of safety because all live parts are metal enclosed, and interlocks are provided for safe operation. It is also available with air circuit breakers which eliminate the fire hazard associated with oil breakers.

Figure 710-1. An assembly of metal-enclosed switchgear. (*Federal Pacific Electric Co.*)

(5) The continuous current rating of a circuit breaker shall be not less than the maximum continuous current through the circuit breaker.

(6) The interrupting rating of a circuit breaker shall not be less than the maximum fault current the circuit breaker will be required to interrupt, including contributions from all connected sources of energy.

(7) The closing rating of a circuit breaker shall not be less than the maximum asymmetrical fault current into which the circuit breaker can be closed.

(8) The momentary rating of a circuit breaker shall not be less than the maximum asymmetrical fault current at the point of installation.

(9) The rated maximum voltage of a circuit breaker shall not be less than the maximum circuit voltage.

(b) Power Fuses and Fuseholders.

(1) Use.   Where fuses are used to protect conductors and equipment a fuse shall be placed in each ungrounded conductor. Two power fuses shall be permitted to be used in parallel to protect the same load, if both fuses have identical ratings, and both fuses are installed in an identified common mounting with electrical connections that will divide the current equally.

(2) Interrupting Rating.   The interrupting rating of power fuses shall not be less than the maximum fault current the fuse will be required to interrupt, including contributions from all connected sources of energy.

(3) Voltage Rating. The maximum voltage rating of power fuses shall not be less than the maximum circuit voltage. Fuses having a minimum recommended operating voltage shall not be applied below this voltage.

(4) Identification of Fuse Mountings and Fuse Units. Fuse mountings and fuse units shall have permanent and legible nameplates showing the manufacturer's type or designation, continuous current rating, interrupting current rating, and maximum voltage rating.

(5) Fuses. Fuses that expel flame in opening the circuit shall be so designed or arranged that they will function properly without hazard to persons or property.

(6) Fuseholders. Fuseholders shall be designed or installed so that they will be de-energized while replacing a fuse.

Exception: Fuse and fuseholder designed to permit fuse replacement by qualified persons using equipment designed for the purpose without de-energizing the fuseholder.

(7) High-Voltage Fuses. Metal-enclosed switchgear and substations that utilize high-voltage fuses shall be provided with a gang-operated disconnecting switch. Isolation of the fuses from the circuit shall be provided by either connecting a switch between the source and the fuses or providing roll-out switch and fuse type of construction. The switch shall be of the load-interrupter type, unless mechanically or electrically interlocked with a load-interrupting device arranged to reduce the load to the interrupting capability of the switch.

(c) Distribution Cutouts and Fuse Links — Expulsion Type.

(1) Installation. Cutouts shall be so located that they may be readily and safely operated and re-fused, and so that the exhaust of the fuses will not endanger persons. Distribution cutouts shall not be used indoors, underground, or in metal enclosures unless identified for the use.

(2) Operation. Where fused cutouts are not suitable to interrupt the circuit manually while carrying full load, an approved means shall be installed to interrupt the entire load. Unless the fused cutouts are interlocked with the switch to prevent opening of the cutouts under load, a conspicuous sign shall be placed at such cutouts reading, "WARNING — DO NOT OPEN UNDER LOAD."

(3) Interrupting Rating. The interrupting rating of distribution cutouts shall not be less than the maximum fault current the cutout will be required to interrupt, including contributions from all connected sources of energy.

(4) Voltage Rating. The maximum voltage rating of cutouts shall not be less than the maximum circuit voltage.

(5) Identification. Distribution cutouts shall have on their body, door, or fuse tube a permanent and legible nameplate or identification showing the manufacturer's type or designation, continuous current rating, maximum voltage rating, and interrupting rating.

(6) Fuse Links. Fuse links shall have a permanent and legible identification showing continuous current rating and type.

(7) Structure Mounted Outdoors. The height of cutouts mounted outdoors on structures shall provide safe clearance between lowest energized parts (open or closed position) and standing surfaces, in accordance with Section 110-34(e).

(d) Oil-Filled Cutouts.

(1) Continuous Current Rating.   The continuous current rating of oil-filled cutouts shall not be less than the maximum continuous current through the cutout.

(2) Interrupting Rating.   The interrupting rating of oil-filled cutouts shall not be less than the maximum fault current the oil-filled cutout will be required to interrupt, including contributions from all connected sources of energy.

(3) Voltage Rating.   The maximum voltage rating of oil-filled cutouts shall not be less than the maximum circuit voltage.

(4) Fault Closing Rating.   Oil-filled cutouts shall have a fault closing rating not less than the maximum asymmetrical fault current that can occur at the cutout location, unless suitable interlocks or operating procedures preclude the possibility of closing into a fault.

(5) Identification.   Oil-filled cutouts shall have a permanent and legible nameplate showing the rated continuous current, rated maximum voltage, and rated interrupting current.

(6) Fuse Links.   Fuse links shall have a permanent and legible identification showing the rated continuous current.

(7) Location.   Cutouts shall be so located that they will be readily and safely accessible for re-fusing, with the top of the cutout not over 5 feet (1.52 m) above the floor or platform.

(8) Enclosure.   Suitable barriers or enclosures shall be provided to prevent contact with nonshielded cables or energized parts of oil-filled cutouts.

(e) Load Interrupters.   Load-interrupter switches shall be permitted if suitable fuses or circuit breakers are used in conjunction with these devices to interrupt fault currents. Where these devices are used in combination, they shall be so coordinated electrically that they will safely withstand the effects of closing, carrying, or interrupting all possible currents up to the assigned maximum short-circuit rating.

710-22. Isolating Means.   Means shall be provided to completely isolate an item of equipment. The use of isolating switches shall not be required where there are other ways of de-energizing the equipment for inspection and repairs, such as drawout-type metal-enclosed switchgear units and removable truck panels.

Isolating switches not interlocked with an approved circuit-interrupting device shall be provided with a sign warning against opening them under load.

A fuseholder and fuse, designed for the purpose, shall be permitted as an isolating switch.

710-23. Voltage Regulators.   Proper switching sequence for regulators shall be assured by use of one of the following: (1) mechanically sequenced regulator bypass switch(es); (2) mechanical interlocks; or (3) switching procedure prominently displayed at the switching location.

710-24. Metal-Enclosed Power Switchgear and Industrial Control Assemblies.

(a) Scope.   This section covers assemblies of metal-enclosed power switchgear and industrial control, including but not limited to switches, interrupting devices and their control, metering, protection and regulating equipment, where an integral part of the assembly, with associated interconnections and supporting structures. This section also includes metal-enclosed power switchgear assemblies that form a part of unit substations, power centers, or similar equipment.

Figure 710-2. A 300-kVA, 15-kV pad-mounted transformer integral unit containing a primary hook-stick operated switch with a limited number of secondary breakers or switches. (*Square D Co.*)

(b) Arrangement of Devices in Assemblies.   Arrangement of devices in assemblies shall be such that individual components can safely perform their intended function without adversely affecting the safe operation of other components in the assembly.

(c) Guarding of High-Voltage Energized Parts Within a Compartment.   When access for other than visual inspection is required to a compartment that contains energized high-voltage parts, barriers shall be provided as follows:

(1) To prevent accidental contact with energized parts.

Exception No. 1: Fuse and fuseholder designed to permit fuse replacement by qualified persons using equipment designed for the purpose without de-energizing the fuseholder.

Exception No. 2: Exposed live parts shall be permitted within the compartment where accessible to qualified persons only.

(2) To prevent tools or other equipment from being dropped on energized parts.

(d) Guarding of Low-Voltage Energized Parts Within a Compartment.   Energized bare parts mounted on doors shall be guarded where the door must be opened for maintenance of equipment or removal of drawout equipment.

(e) Clearance for Cable Conductors Entering Enclosure.   The unobstructed space opposite terminals or opposite conduits or other raceways entering a switchgear or control assembly shall be adequate for the type of conductor and method of termination.

(f) Accessibility of Energized Parts.

(1) Doors which would provide nonqualified persons access to high-voltage energized parts shall be locked.

Figure 710-3. A 1,500-kVA, 15-kV unit substation transformer or power center type which is adaptable to a line-up of a high-voltage switch, transformer, and low-voltage secondary. (*Square D Co.*)

(2) Low-voltage control equipment, relays, motors, and the like shall not be installed in compartments with exposed high-voltage energized parts or high-voltage wiring unless the access door or cover is interlocked with the high-voltage switch or disconnecting means to prevent door or cover from being opened or removed unless the switch or disconnecting means is in its isolating position.

Exception No. 1: Instrument or control transformers connected to high voltage.

Exception No. 2: Space heaters.

(g) Grounding.   Frames of switchgear and control assemblies shall be grounded.

(h) Grounding of Devices.   Devices with metal cases and/or frames, such as instruments, relays, meters, and instrument and control transformers, located in or on switchgear or control, shall have the frame or case grounded.

(i) Door Stops and Cover Plates.   External hinged doors or covers shall be provided with stops to hold them in the open position. Cover plates intended to be removed for inspection of energized parts or wiring shall be equipped with lifting handles and shall not exceed 12 square feet (1.11 sq m) in area or 60 pounds (27.22 kg) in weight, unless they are hinged and bolted or locked.

(j) Gas Discharge from Interrupting Devices.   Gas discharged during operating of interrupting devices shall be so directed as not to endanger personnel.

(k) Inspection Windows.   Windows intended for inspection of disconnecting switches or other devices shall be of suitable transparent material.

(l) Location of Devices.   Control and instrument transfer switch handles or pushbuttons shall be in a readily accessible location at an elevation not over 78 inches (1.98 m).

Exception No. 1: Operating handles requiring more than 50 pounds (22.68 kg) of force shall not be higher than 66 inches (1.68 m) in either the open or closed position.

Exception No. 2: Operating handles for infrequently operated devices, such as drawout fuses, fused potential or control transformers and their primary disconnects, and bus transfer switches, shall not be required to be readily accessible, where they are otherwise safely operable and serviceable from a portable platform.

(m) Interlocks — Interrupter Switches.   Interrupter switches equipped with stored energy mechanisms shall have mechanical interlocks to prevent access to the switch compartment unless the stored energy mechanism is in the discharged or blocked position.

(n) Stored Energy for Opening.   The stored energy operator may be left in the uncharged position after the switch has been closed if a single movement of the operating handle charges the operator and opens the switch.

(o) Fused Interrupter Switches.

Figure 710-4. (left) Group-operated interrupter-switch and power-fuse combination rated at 13.8 kV, 600 A continuous and interrupting, 40,000 A momentary, 40,000 A fault closing. Figure 710-5 (right). Components of the indoor solid-material (SM) power fuseholder (boric-acid arc-extinguishing type) with a 14.4 kV, 400 E A max, 40,000 A RMS asym. interrupting rating. Shown here are the spring and cable assembly, refill unit, holder, and snuffler. (*S & C Electric Co.*)

(1) Fused interrupter switches shall be so installed that all supply terminals shall be at the top of the switch enclosure.

Exception: Supply terminals shall not be required to be at the top of the switch enclosure if barriers are installed to prevent persons from accidentally contacting energized parts or dropping tools or fuses into energized parts.

(2) Where fuses can be energized by backfeed, a sign shall be placed on the enclosure door reading, "WARNING — FUSES MAY BE ENERGIZED BY BACKFEED."

(p) Interlocks — Circuit Breakers.

(1) Circuit breakers equipped with stored energy mechanisms shall be designed to prevent the release of the stored energy unless the mechanism has been fully charged.

(2) Mechanical interlocks shall be provided in the housing to prevent the complete withdrawal of the circuit breaker from the housing when the stored energy mechanism is in the fully charged position.

Exception: Where a suitable device is provided that prevents the complete withdrawal of the circuit breaker unless the closing function is blocked.

D. Installations Accessible to Qualified Persons Only

710-31. Enclosure for Electrical Installations. See Section 110-31.

710-32. Circuit Conductors. Circuit conductors shall be permitted to be installed in raceways, in cable trays, as metal-clad cable, as bare wire, cable, and busbars, or as nonmetallic-sheathed cables, or conductors as provided in Sections 710-3 through 710-6. Bare live conductors shall conform with Sections 710-33 and 710-34.

Insulators, together with their mounting and conductor attachments, where used as supports for wires, single-conductor cables, or busbars, shall be capable of safely withstanding the maximum magnetic forces that would prevail when two or more conductors of a circuit were subjected to short-circuit current.

Open runs of insulated wires and cables having a bare lead sheath or a braided outer covering shall be supported in a manner designed to prevent physical damage to the braid or sheath. Supports for lead-covered cables shall be designed to prevent electrolysis of the sheath.

710-33. Minimum Space Separation. In field-fabricated installations, the minimum air separation between bare live conductors and between such conductors and adjacent grounded surfaces shall not be less than the values given in Table 710-33. These values shall not apply to interior portions or exterior terminals of equipment designed, manufactured, and tested in accordance with accepted national standards.

710-34. Work Space and Guarding. See Section 110-34.

E. Mobile and Portable Equipment

710-41. General.

(a) Covered. The provisions of this part shall apply to installations and use of high-voltage power distribution and utilization equipment which is portable and/or mobile, such as substations and switch houses mounted on skids, trailers, or cars, mobile shovels, draglines, cranes, hoists, drills, dredges, compressors, pumps, conveyors, underground excavators, and the like.

(b) Other Requirements. The requirements of this part shall be additional to, or amendatory of, those prescribed in Articles 100 through 725 of this Code. Special attention shall be paid to Article 250.

(c) Protection. Adequate enclosures and/or guarding shall be provided to protect portable and mobile equipment from physical damage.

Table 710-33.   Minimum Clearance of Live Parts*

Nominal Voltage Rating, kV	Impulse Withstand, B.I.L. kV		Minimum Clearance of Live Parts, in Inches			
			Phase-to-Phase		Phase-to-Ground	
	Indoors	Outdoors	Indoors	Outdoors	Indoors	Outdoors
2.4-4.16	60	95	4.5	7	3.0	6
7.2	75	95	5.5	7	4.0	6
13.8	95	110	7.5	12	5.0	7
14.4	110	110	9.0	12	6.5	7
23	125	150	10.5	15	7.5	10
34.5	150	150	12.5	15	9.5	10
	200	200	18.0	18	13.0	13
46		200		18		13
		250		21		17
69		250		21		17
		350		31		25
115		550		53		42
138		550		53		42
		650		63		50
161		650		63		50
		750		72		58
230		750		72		58
		900		89		71
		1050		105		83

For SI units: one inch = 25.4 millimeters.

* The values given are the minimum clearance for rigid parts and bare conductors under favorable service conditions. They shall be increased for conductor movement or under unfavorable service conditions, or wherever space limitations permit. The selection of the associated impulse withstand voltage for a particular system voltage is determined by the characteristics of the surge protective equipment.

710-42. Overcurrent Protection.   Motors driving single or multiple dc generators supplying a system operating on a cyclic load basis do not require running overcurrent protection, provided that the thermal rating of the ac drive motor cannot be exceeded under any operating condition. However, the branch-circuit protective device(s), which may be external to the equipment, shall provide short-circuit and locked-rotor protection.

710-43. Enclosures.   All energized switching and control parts shall be enclosed in effectively grounded metal cabinets or enclosures. These cabinets or enclosures shall be marked "WARNING — HIGH VOLTAGE" and shall be locked so that only authorized and qualified persons can enter. Circuit breakers and protective equipment shall have the operating means projecting through the metal cabinet or enclosure so these units can be reset without opening locked doors. With doors closed, reasonable safe access for normal operation of these units shall be provided.

710-44. Collector Rings.   The collector ring assemblies on revolving-type machines (shovels, draglines, etc.) shall be guarded to prevent accidental contact with energized parts by personnel on or off the machine.

710-45. Power Cable Connections to Mobile Machines.   A metallic enclosure shall be provided on the mobile machine for enclosing the terminals of the power cable. The enclosure shall include provisions for a solid connection for the ground wire(s) terminal to effectively ground the machine frame. Ungrounded conductors shall be attached to insulators or terminated in approved high-voltage cable couplers (which include ground wire connectors) of proper voltage and ampere rating. The method of cable termination used shall prevent any strain or pull on the cable from stressing the electrical connections. The enclosure shall have provision for locking so only authorized and qualified persons may open, and shall be marked "WARNING — HIGH VOLTAGE."

710-46. High-Voltage Portable Cable for Main Power Supply.   Flexible high-voltage cable supplying power to portable or mobile equipment shall comply with Article 250 and Article 400, Part C.

710-47. Grounding.   Mobile equipment shall be grounded in accordance with Article 250.

F. Tunnel Installations

710-51. General.

   (a) Covered.   The provisions of this part shall apply to installation and use of high-voltage power distribution and utilization equipment which is portable and/or mobile, such as substations, trailers, or cars, mobile shovels, draglines, hoists, drills, dredges, compressors, pumps, conveyors, underground excavators, and the like.

   (b) Other Articles.   The requirements of this part shall be additional to, or amendatory of, those prescribed in Articles 100 through 710 of this Code. Special attention shall be paid to Article 250.

   (c) Protection Against Physical Damage.   Conductors and cables in tunnels shall be located above the tunnel floor and so placed or guarded to protect them from physical damage.

710-52. Overcurrent Protection.   Motor-operated equipment shall be protected from overcurrent in accordance with Article 430. Transformers shall be protected from overcurrent in accordance with Article 450.

710-53. Conductors.   High-voltage conductors in tunnels shall be installed in (1) metal conduit or other metal raceway; (2) Type MC cable; or (3) other approved multiconductor cable. Multiconductor portable cable shall be permitted to supply mobile equipment.

710-54. Bonding and Equipment Grounding Conductor.

   (a) Grounded and Bonded.   All nonenergized metal parts of electric equipment and all metal raceways and cable sheaths shall be effectively grounded and bonded to all metal pipes and rails at the portal and at intervals not exceeding 1000 feet (305 m) throughout the tunnel.

   (b) Equipment Grounding Conductor.   An equipment grounding conductor shall be run with circuit conductors inside the metal raceway or inside the multiconductor cable jacket. The equipment grounding conductor shall be permitted to be insulated or bare.

710-55. Transformers, Switches, and Electric Equipment.   All transformers, switches, motor controllers, motors, rectifiers, and other equipment installed below ground shall be protected from physical damage by location or guarding.

710-56. Energized Parts.   Bare terminals of transformers, switches, motor controllers, and other equipment shall be enclosed to prevent accidental contact with energized parts.

710-57. Ventilation System Controls.   Electrical controls for the ventilation system shall be so arranged that the air flow can be reversed.

710-58. Disconnecting Means.   A switching device meeting the requirements of Article 430 or 450 shall be installed at each transformer or motor location for disconnecting the transformer or motor. The switching device shall open all ungrounded conductors of a circuit simultaneously.

710-59. Enclosures.   Enclosures for use in tunnels shall be dripproof, weatherproof, or submersible as required by the environmental conditions. Switch or contactor enclosures shall not be used as junction boxes or raceways for conductors feeding through or tapping off to other switches, unless special designs are used to provide adequate space for this purpose.

710-60. Grounding.   Tunnel equipment shall be grounded in accordance with Article 250.

G. Electrode-type Boilers

710-70. General.   The provisions of this part shall apply to boilers operating over 600 volts, nominal, in which heat is generated by the passage of current between electrodes through the liquid being heated.

710-71. Electric Supply System.   Electrode-type boilers shall be supplied only from a 3-phase, 4-wire solidly grounded wye system, or from isolating transformers arranged to provide such a system. Control circuit voltages shall not exceed 150 volts, shall be supplied from a grounded system, and shall have the controls in the ungrounded conductor.

710-72. Branch Circuit Requirements.

   (a) Rating.   Each boiler shall be supplied from an individual branch circuit rated not less than 100 percent of the total load.

   (b) Common-Trip Fault Interrupting Device.   The circuit shall be protected by a 3-phase common-trip fault interrupting device, which shall be permitted to automatically reclose the circuit upon removal of an overload condition but shall not reclose after a fault condition.

   (c) Phase Fault Protection.   Phase fault protection shall be provided in each phase, consisting of a separate phase overcurrent relay connected to a separate current transformer in the phase.

   (d) Ground Current Detection.   Means shall be provided for detection of the sum of the neutral and ground currents and shall trip the circuit interrupting device if the sum of those currents exceeds the greater of 5 amperes or 7½ percent of the boiler full-load current for 10 seconds or exceeds an instantaneous value of 25 percent of the boiler full-load current.

   Section 710-22(d) has been revised in the 1981 *Code* to permit the sum of the neutral and ground currents to reach more than the 5-A neutral current permitted in the 1978 *Code*, under the conditions specified.

   (e) Grounded Neutral Conductor.   The grounded neutral conductor shall:

   (1) Be connected to the pressure vessel containing the electrodes.

   (2) Be insulated for not less than 600 volts.

   (3) Have not less than the ampacity of the largest ungrounded branch-circuit conductor.

   (4) Be installed in the same raceway or cable tray with the ungrounded conductors.

   (5) Not be used for any other circuit.

710-73. Pressure and Temperature Limit Control.   Each boiler shall be equipped with a means to limit the maximum temperature and/or pressure by directly or indirectly interrupting all current flow through the electrodes. Such means shall be in addition to the temperature and/or pressure regulating systems and pressure relief or safety valves.

710-74. Grounding. All exposed noncurrent-carrying metal parts of the boiler and associated exposed grounded structures or equipment shall be bonded to the pressure vessel or to the neutral conductor to which the vessel is connected, in accordance with Section 250-79, except the ampacity of the bonding jumper shall be not less than the ampacity of the neutral conductor.

ARTICLE 720 — CIRCUITS AND EQUIPMENT
OPERATING AT LESS THAN 50 VOLTS

Contents

720-1. Scope. This article covers installations operating at less than 50 volts, direct current or alternating current.

Exception: As covered in Articles 650, 725, and 760.

720-2. Hazardous (Classified) Locations. Installations coming within the scope of this article and installed in hazardous (classified) locations shall also comply with the appropriate provisions of Articles 500 through 517.

It should be noted that low voltage alone does not make a circuit incapable of igniting flammable atmospheres. Under some conditions, even ordinary flashlights using two 1½ V "D" cells can be a source of ignition in hazardous (classified) locations.

720-4. Conductors. Conductors shall not be smaller than No. 12 copper or equivalent. Conductors for appliance branch circuits supplying more than one appliance or appliance receptacle shall not be smaller than No. 10 copper or equivalent.

720-5. Lampholders. Standard lampholders having a rating of not less than 660 watts shall be used.

720-6. Receptacle Rating. Receptacles shall have a rating of not less than 15 amperes.

720-7. Receptacles Required. Receptacles of not less than 20-ampere rating shall be provided in kitchens, laundries, and other locations where portable appliances are likely to be used.

720-8. Overcurrent Protection. Overcurrent protection shall comply with Article 240.

720-9. Batteries. Installations of storage batteries shall comply with Article 480.

720-10. Grounding. Grounding shall comply with Sections 250-5(a) and 250-45.

ARTICLE 725 — CLASS 1, CLASS 2, AND CLASS 3
REMOTE-CONTROL, SIGNALING, AND
POWER-LIMITED CIRCUITS

Contents

A. Scope and General

725-1. Scope.   This article covers remote-control, signaling, and power-limited circuits that are not an integral part of a device or appliance.

The circuits described herein are characterized by usage and electrical power limitations which differentiate them from light and power circuits and, therefore, special consideration is given with regard to minimum wire sizes, derating factors, overcurrent protection, and conductor insulation requirements.

725-2. Locations and Other Articles.   Circuits and equipment shall comply with (a), (b), (c), (d), and (e) below.

(a) Prevention of Spread of Fire or Products of Combustion.   Section 300-21.

(b) Ducts or Plenums.   Section 300-22 where installed in ducts or plenums.

Exception to (b): Single and multiconductor cables of Class 2 and Class 3 circuits listed as having adequate fire-resistant and low-smoke producing characteristics shall be permitted for ducts, hollow spaces used as ducts, and plenums other than those described in Section 300-22(a).

(c) Hazardous (Classified) Locations.   Articles 500 through 516, and Article 517, Part G where installed in hazardous (classified) locations.

(d) Cable Trays.   Article 318 where installed in cable tray.

(e) Motor Control Circuits.   Article 430, Part F where tapped from the load side of the motor branch-circuit protective device(s) as specified in Section 430-72(a).

725-3. Classifications.   A remote-control, signaling, or power-limited circuit is the portion of the wiring system between the load side of the overcurrent device or the power-limited supply and all connected equipment, and shall be Class 1, Class 2, or Class 3 as defined in (a) and (b) below.

(a) Class 1 Circuits.   Circuits that comply with Part B of this article and in which the voltage and power limitations are in accordance with Section 725-11.

(b) Class 2 and Class 3 Circuits.   Circuits that comply with Part C of this article and in which the voltage and power limitations are in accordance with Section 725-31.

Due to their power limitations, both Class 2 and 3 circuits consider safety from a fire initiation standpoint. In addition, Class 2 circuits provide acceptable protection from electric shock. However, since Class 3 circuits permit higher allowable levels of voltage and current, additional safeguards are specified to provide protection against the electric shock hazard that could be encountered.

725-4. Safety-Control Equipment.   Remote-control circuits to safety-control equipment shall be Class 1 if the failure of the equipment to operate introduces a direct fire or life hazard. Room thermostats, water temperature regulating devices, and similar controls used in conjunction with electrically controlled household heating and air conditioning shall not be considered safety-control equipment.

725-5. Communication Cables.   Class 1 circuits shall not be run in the same cable with communication circuits. Class 2 and Class 3 circuit conductors shall be permitted in the same cable with communication circuits, in which case the Class 2 and Class 3 circuits shall be classified as communication circuits and shall meet the requirements of Article 800.

B. Class 1 Circuits

725-11. Power Limitations for Class 1 Circuits.

(a) Class 1 Power-Limited Circuits.   These circuits shall be supplied from a source having a rated output of not more than 30 volts and 1000 volt-amperes. The source shall be protected by overcurrent devices rated at not more than 167 percent of the volt-ampere rating of the source divided by the rated voltage. The overcurrent devices shall not be interchangeable with overcurrent devices of higher ratings. The overcurrent device shall be permitted to be an integral part of the power supply.

(1) Transformers.   Transformers used to supply power-limited Class 1 circuits shall comply with Article 450.

(2) Other Power Sources.   To comply with the 1000 volt-ampere limitation, power sources other than transformers shall not exceed a maximum power output of 2500 volt-amperes, and the product of the maximum current and maximum voltage shall not exceed 10,000 volt-amperes with the overcurrent protection bypassed.

(b) Class 1 Remote-Control and Signaling Circuits.   Class 1 remote-control and signaling circuits shall not exceed 600 volts; however, the power output of the source shall not be required to be limited.

725-12. Overcurrent Protection.

(a) Conductors Larger than No. 14.   Conductors larger than No. 14 shall be protected against overcurrent in accordance with the ampacities given in Tables 310-16 through 310-19.

(b) Conductors of Nos. 18, 16, and 14.   Conductors of Nos. 18, 16, and 14 shall be considered as protected by overcurrent devices of not over 20 amperes rating.

Exception No. 1 for (a) and (b): Where other articles of this Code permit or require other overcurrent protection.

See Section 430-72 for motors and Section 620-61 for elevators, escalators, and moving walks.

Exception No. 2 for (a) and (b): Transformer Secondary Conductors. Class 1 circuit conductors supplied by the secondary side of a single-phase transformer having only a 2-wire (single-voltage) secondary shall be considered as protected by overcurrent protection provided on the primary (supply) side of the transformer, provided this protection is in accordance with Section 450-3 and does not exceed the value determined by multiplying the secondary conductor ampacity by the secondary-to-primary transformer voltage ratio. Transformer secondary conductors other than 2-wire shall not be considered to be protected by the primary overcurrent protection.

Exception No. 2, completely revised for the 1981 *Code*, correlates with Section 240-3, Exception No. 5 and Section 430-72(b), Exception No. 3.

Exception No. 3 for (a) and (b): Class 1 circuit conductors No. 14 and larger which are tapped from the load side of the overcurrent protective device(s) of the controlled light and power circuit shall be considered to be protected by the branch-circuit overcurrent protective device(s) where the rating of the protective device(s) is not more than 300 percent of the ampacity of the Class 1 circuit conductor.

Exception No. 3, new in the 1981 *Code*, correlates with Section 240-3, Exception No. 4.

(c) Transformers.   Transformers shall be protected in accordance with Section 450-3.

725-13. Location of Overcurrent Devices.   Overcurrent devices shall be located at the point where the conductor to be protected receives its supply.

Exception: Where the overcurrent device protecting the larger conductor also protects the smaller conductor.

725-14. Wiring Method.   Installations of Class 1 circuits shall be in accordance with the appropriate articles in Chapter 3.

Exception No. 1: As provided in Sections 725-15 through 725-17.

Exception No. 2: Where other articles of this Code permit or require other methods.

725-15. Conductors of Different Circuits in Same Enclosure, Cable, or Raceway.   Class 1 circuits shall be permitted to occupy the same enclosure, cable, or raceway without regard to whether the individual circuits are alternating current or direct current, provided all conductors are insulated for the maximum voltage of any conductor in the enclosure, cable, or raceway. Power supply and Class 1 circuit conductors shall be permitted in the same enclosure, cable, or raceway only where the equipment powered is functionally associated.

725-16. Conductors.

(a) Sizes and Use.   Conductors of Nos. 18 and 16 shall be permitted to be used provided they supply loads that do not exceed the ampacities given in Section 402-5 and are installed in a raceway or a listed cable. Conductors larger than No. 16 shall not supply loads greater than the ampacities given in Tables 310-16 through 310-19. Flexible cords shall comply with Article 400.

(b) Insulation.   Insulation on conductors shall be suitable for 600 volts. Conductors larger than No. 16 shall comply with Article 310. Conductors in sizes No. 18 and 16 shall be Type RFH-2, FFH-2, TF, TFF, TFN, TFFN, PF, PFF, PGF, PGFF, PTF, PTFF, SF-2, SFF-2, PAF, PAFF, ZF, ZFF, KF-2, or KFF-2. Conductors with other types and thicknesses of insulation shall be permitted if listed for Class 1 circuit use.

725-17. Number of Conductors in Raceways, Cable Trays, and Cables, and Derating.

(a) Class 1 Circuits.   Where only Class 1 circuits are in a raceway, the number of conductors shall be determined in accordance with Section 300-17. The derating factors given in Note 8 to Tables 310-16 through 310-19 shall apply only if such conductors carry continuous loads.

(b) Power-Supply Conductors and Class 1 Circuit Conductors.   Where power-supply conductors and Class 1 circuit conductors are permitted in a raceway in accordance with Section 725-15, the number of conductors shall be determined in accordance with Section 300-17. The derating factors given in Note 8 to Tables 310-16 through 310-19 shall apply as follows:

(1) To all conductors when the Class 1 circuit conductors carry continuous loads and where the total number of conductors is more than three.

(2) To the power-supply conductors only, when the Class 1 circuit conductors do not carry continuous loads and where the number of power-supply conductors is more than three.

(c) Class 1 Circuit Conductors in Cable Trays.   Where Class 1 circuit conductors are installed in cable trays they shall comply with the provisions of Sections 318-8 through 318-10.

725-18. Physical Protection.   Where damage to remote-control circuits of safety control equipment would introduce a hazard, as covered in Section 725-4, all conductors of such remote-control circuits shall be installed in rigid metal conduit, intermediate metal conduit, rigid nonmetallic conduit, electrical metallic tubing, Type MI cable, Type MC cable, or be otherwise suitably protected from physical damage.

Rigid nonmetallic conduit was added in the 1981 *Code.*

725-19. Circuits Extending Beyond One Building.   Class 1 circuits that extend aerially beyond one building shall also meet the requirements of Article 225.

725-20. Grounding.   Class 1 circuits and equipment shall be grounded in accordance with Article 250.

C. Class 2 and Class 3 Circuits

725-31. Power Limitations of Class 2 and Class 3 Circuits.   As specified in Table 725-31(a) for ac circuits and Table 725-31(b) for dc circuits, the power for Class 2 and Class 3 circuits shall be either inherently limited requiring no overcurrent protection or limited by a combination of a power source and overcurrent protection.

725-32. Interconnection of Power Supplies.   Class 2 or Class 3 power supplies shall not be paralleled or otherwise interconnected unless listed for such interconnection.

725-34. Marking.   A Class 2 or Class 3 power supply unit shall be durably marked where plainly visible to indicate the class of supply and its electrical rating.

725-35. Overcurrent Protection.   Where overcurrent protection is required, the overcurrent protective devices shall not be interchangeable with devices of higher ratings. The overcurrent device shall be permitted as an integral part of the power supply.

725-36. Location of Overcurrent Devices.   Overcurrent devices shall be located at the point where the conductor to be protected receives its supply.

725-37. Wiring Methods on Supply Side.   Conductors and equipment on the supply side of overcurrent protection, transformers, or current-limiting devices shall be installed in accordance with the appropriate requirements of Chapter 3. Transformers or other devices supplied from light or power circuits shall be protected by an overcurrent device rated not over 20 amperes.

Exception: The input leads of a transformer or other power source supplying Class 2 and Class 3 circuits shall be permitted to be smaller than No. 14, but not smaller than No. 18 if they are not over 12 inches (305 mm) long and if they have insulation that complies with Section 725-16(b).

725-38. Wiring Methods on Load Side.   Conductors on the load side of overcurrent protection, transformers, and current-limiting devices shall be insulated at not less than the requirements of Section 725-40 and shall comply with (a) and (b) below.

(a) Separation from Light, Power, and Class 1 Conductors.

(1) Open Conductors.   Conductors of Class 2 and Class 3 circuits shall be separated at least 2 inches (50.8 mm) from conductors of any light, power, or Class 1 circuits.

Exception No. 1: Where the light or power, and Class 1 circuit conductors are in a raceway or in metal-sheathed, metal-clad, nonmetallic-sheathed, or Type UF cables.

Exception No. 2: Where the conductors are permanently separated from the conductors of the other circuits by a continuous and firmly fixed nonconductor, such as porcelain tubes or flexible tubing in addition to the insulation on the wire.

(2) In Enclosures, Raceways, Cable Trays, and Cables.   Conductors of Class 2 and Class 3 circuits shall not be placed in any enclosure, raceway, cable tray, cable, compartment, outlet box, or similar fitting with conductors of light, power, and Class 1 circuits.

Table 725-31(a). Power Limitations for Alternating Current (Class 2 and Class 3 Circuits)

Circuit	Inherently Limited Power Source (Overcurrent protection not required)				Not Inherently Limited Power Source (Overcurrent protection required)			
	Class 2		Class 3		Class 2		Class 3	
Circuit Voltage V_{max} (Note 1)	0-20†	Over 20-30†	0-150	Over 30-100	0-20†	Over 20-30†	Over 30-100	Over 100-150
Power Limitation $(VA)_{max}$ (Note 1) (Volt-Amps)	—	—	—	—	250 (see Note 3)	250	250	N.A.
Current Limitation I_{max} (Note 1) (Amps)	8.0	8.0	0.005	$150/V_{max}$	$1000/V_{max}$	$1000/V_{max}$	$1000/V_{max}$	1.0
Maximum Over-current Protection (Amps)	—	—	—	—	5.0	$100/V_{max}$	$100/V_{max}$	1.0
Power Source Maximum Name-plate Ratings — VA (Volt-Amps)	$5.0 \times V_{max}$	100	$0.005 \times V_{max}$	100	$5.0 \times V_{max}$	100	100	100
Power Source Maximum Name-plate Ratings — Current (Amps)	5.0	$100/V_{max}$	0.005	$100/V_{max}$	5.0	$100/V_{max}$	$100/V_{max}$	$100/V_{max}$
Supply Conductors and Cables	See Section 725-37							
Circuit Conductors and Cables	See Section 725-40							

† Voltage ranges shown are for sinusoidal ac in indoor locations or where wet contact is not likely to occur. For nonsinusoidal or wet contact conditions, see Note 2.

Table 725-31(b). Power Limitations for Direct Current (Class 2 and Class 3 Circuits)

Circuit	Inherently Limited Power Source (Note 4) (Overcurrent protection not required)					Not Inherently Limited Power Source (Overcurrent protection required)			
	Class 2			Class 3		Class 2			Class 3
Circuit Voltage V_{max} (Note 1)	0-20††	Over 20-30††	Over 30-60††	0-150	Over 60-100	0-20††	Over 20-60††	Over 60-100	Over 100-150
Power Limitation $(VA)_{max}$ (Note 1) (Volt-Amps)	—	—	—	—	—	250 (see Note 3)	250	250	N.A.
Current Limitation I_{max} (Note 1) (Amps)	8.0	8.0	$150/V_{max}$	0.005	$150/V_{max}$	$1000/V_{max}$	$1000/V_{max}$	$1000/V_{max}$	1.0
Maximum Overcurrent Protection (Amps)	—	—	—	—	—	5.0	$100/V_{max}$	$100/V_{max}$	1.0
Power Source Maximum Nameplate Ratings VA (Volt-Amps)	$5.0 \times V_{max}$	100	100	$0.005 \times V_{max}$	100	$5.0 \times V_{max}$	100	100	100
Current (Amps)	5.0	$100/V_{max}$	$100/V_{max}$	0.005	$100/V_{max}$	5.0	$100/V_{max}$	$100/V_{max}$	$100/V_{max}$
Supply Conductors and Cables	See Section 725-37					See Section 725-40			

Circuit Conductors and Cables

†† Voltage ranges shown are for continuous dc in indoor locations or where wet contact is not likely to occur. For interrupted dc or wet contact conditions, see Note 5.

Notes for Tables 725-31(a) and (b)

Note 1. V_{max}: Maximum output voltage regardless of load with rated input applied. I_{max}: Maximum output after 1 minute of operation under any noncapacitive load, including short circuit, and with overcurrent protection bypassed if used. VA_{max}: Maximum volt-ampere output regardless of load and overcurrent protection bypassed if used. Note 2. For nonsinusoidal ac, V_{max} shall be not greater than 42.4 volts peak. Where wet contact (immersion not included) is likely to occur, Class 3 wiring methods shall be used or V_{max} shall be not greater than: 15 volts for sinusoidal ac: 21.2 volts peak for nonsinusoidal ac. Note 3. If the power source is a transformer, $(VA)_{max}$ is 350 or less when V_{max} is 15 or less. Note 4. A dry cell battery shall be considered an inherently limited power source provided the voltage is 30 volts or less and the capacity is equal to or less than that available from series connected No. 6 carbon zinc cells. Note 5. For dc interrupted at a rate of 10 to 200 Hz, V_{max} shall not be greater than 24.8 volts. Where wet contact (immersion not included) is likely to occur, Class 3 wiring methods shall be used or V_{max} shall not be greater than: 30 volts for continuous dc; 12.4 volts for dc that is interrupted at a rate of 10 to 200 Hz.

Exception No. 1: Where the conductors of the different circuits are separated by a partition.

Exception No. 2: Conductors in outlet boxes, junction boxes, or similar fittings, or compartments where power-supply conductors are introduced solely for supplying power to the equipment connected to Class 2 or Class 3 circuits to which the other conductors in the enclosure are connected.

An example would be power circuit and Class 2 circuit conductors in the same motor starter enclosure where the Class 2 conductors are functionally associated with the motor starter. In such an installation, the Class 2 conductor insulation is not required to have the same voltage rating as the insulation on the power conductors in the same enclosure.

(3) In Shafts.   Class 2 or Class 3 conductors run in the same shaft with conductors for light, power, or Class 1 circuits shall be separated by not less than 2 inches (50.8 mm) from the light, power, and Class 1 conductors.

Exception No. 1: Where the conductors of either the light, power, or Class 1 circuits or the Class 2 or Class 3 circuits are encased in noncombustible tubing.

Exception No. 2: Where the light, power, or Class 1 circuit conductors are in a raceway, or are in metal-sheathed, metal-clad, nonmetallic-sheathed, or Type UF cables.

(4) In Hoistways.   Class 2 or Class 3 conductors shall be installed in rigid conduit, intermediate metal conduit, or electrical metallic tubing in hoistways.

Exception: As provided for in Section 620-21, Exceptions No. 1 and 2 for elevators and similar equipment.

(b) Vertical Runs.   Conductors in a vertical run in a shaft or partition shall have a fire-resistant covering capable of preventing the carrying of fire from floor to floor.

Exception: Where conductors are encased in noncombustible tubing or other outer covering of noncombustible materials or are located in a fireproof shaft having fire stops at each floor.

725-39. Conductors of Different Class 2 and Class 3 Circuits in Same Cable, Enclosure, or Raceway.

(a) Two or More Class 2 Circuits.   Conductors of two or more Class 2 circuits shall be permitted within the same cable, enclosure, or raceway provided all conductors in the cable, enclosure, or raceway are insulated for the maximum voltage of any conductor.

(b) Two or More Class 3 Circuits.   Conductors of two or more Class 3 circuits shall be permitted within the same cable, enclosure, or raceway.

(c) Class 2 Circuits With Class 3 Circuits.   Conductors of one or more Class 2 circuits shall be permitted within the same cable, enclosure, or raceway with conductors of Class 3 circuits provided that the insulation of the Class 2 circuit conductors in the cable, enclosure, or raceway is at least that required for Class 3 circuits.

725-40. Conductors.

(a) Class 2 Circuits.   The conductor material size and insulation shall be suitable for the particular application.

The conductor insulation is not specified in further detail as reliance is placed on Class 2 power supplies which limit voltage and current to safe values.

Exception: Where installed in cable tray or in hazardous (classified) locations, or both, conductors shall comply with (b) (3) below except conductors used for thermocouple circuits shall be permitted to be any of the materials used for thermocouple extension wire.

(b) Class 3 Circuits.   Conductors shall comply with (1), (2), (3), or (4) below.

Exception: Where installed in cable tray or in hazardous (classified) locations, or both, conductors shall comply with (3) below.

(1) Single conductors shall not be smaller than No. 18 and shall be insulated in accordance with Section 725-16(b).

(2) Conductors of a multiconductor cable shall be of solid or stranded copper not smaller than No. 22, and shall have thermoplastic insulation of not less than 12 mils nominal (10 mils minimum) thickness. The cable conductors shall have an overall thermoplastic jacket having a nominal thickness of not less than 35 mils (30 mils minimum). Where the number of conductors in a cable exceeds four, the thickness of the thermoplastic jacket shall be increased so as to provide equivalent performance characteristics. Similarly, where the size of conductors in a cable exceeds No. 16, the thickness of the conductor insulation shall be increased so as to provide equivalent performance characteristics.

Exception No. 1: Cables with smaller conductors and other types and thicknesses of insulations and jackets shall be permitted, if listed for this use.

Exception No. 2: Two conductors assembled in a flat parallel construction with a 30-mil nominal integral insulation-jacket and a 47-mil minimum web shall be permitted.

(3) Type PLTC nonmetallic-sheathed, power-limited tray cable shall be a factory assembly of two or more insulated conductors under a nonmetallic jacket. The insulated conductors shall be a No. 22 through 16. The conductor material shall be copper (solid or stranded). Insulation on conductors shall be suitable for 300 volts. The cable core shall be either (1) two or more parallel conductors; (2) one or more group assemblies of twisted or parallel conductors; or (3) a combination thereof. A metallic shield or a metallized foil shield with drain wire(s) shall be permitted to be applied either over the cable core, over groups of conductors, or both. The outer jacket shall be a flame-retardant, sunlight- and moisture-resistant nonmetallic material. The cable shall be marked in accordance with Section 310-11. Where the use of PLTC cable is permitted in Section 501-4(b), the cable shall be installed in cable trays, in raceways, supported by messenger wires, or directly buried where the cable is listed for this use.

Exception: Where a smooth metallic sheath, welded and corrugated metallic sheath, or interlocking tape armor is applied over the nonmetallic jacket, an overall nonmetallic jacket shall not be required. On metallic-sheathed cable without an overall nonmetallic jacket, the information required in Section 310-11 shall be located on the nonmetallic jacket under the sheath.

(4) Approved power-limited (low-energy) circuit cable, Class 3 circuit cable, or other equivalent cable.

General Discussion of Remote-Control, Signaling, and Power-Limited Circuits
The wiring methods required by Chapters 1 through 4 of the *Code* apply to remote-control, signaling, and power-limiting circuits, except as amended by Article 725 for the particular conditions.
A remote-control, signaling, or power-limited circuit is the portion of the wiring system between the load side of the overcurrent device or the power-limited supply and all connected equipment, and is separated into Class 1, Class 2, and Class 3 circuits.
Class 1 circuits are not to exceed 600 V. A remote-control circuit to safety

control equipment is to be a Class 1 circuit, if the failure of the safety control introduces a hazard to life or property. Room thermostats and water-temperature regulating devices used in conjunction with household heating and air-conditioning systems are not considered safety-control equipment. In many cases, Class 1 circuits are extensions of power systems and are subject to the requirements of the power systems, except for the following: (1) conductors sized Nos. 16 and 18 may be used for special applications and Nos. 14, 16, and 18 are considered protected by overcurrent devices rated not over 20 A; (2) where damage to the circuit would introduce a hazard, the circuit is to be suitably protected (metal raceway, Type MI or MC cable, or other suitable means); (3) the derating factors of Note 8 to Tables 310-16 through 310-19 are to apply only if such conductors carry a continuous load (see Section 725-17).

Class 1 remote-control circuits are commonly used to operate motor-controllers in conjunction with moving equipment or mechanical processes, elevators, conveyors, and such equipment where it is necessary to control the equipment from one or more locations to prevent a hazard to life.

Another example of a Class 1 circuit is a hospital nurses call system where it is intended to use the system for issuing instructions during emergency conditions.

Class 1 signaling circuits often operate at 115 V with 20-A overcurrent protection, though not limited to these values, and are often used for alarm and security systems.

Conductors and equipment on the supply side of overcurrent protection, a transformer, or current-limiting devices of Class 2 and Class 3 circuits are to be installed according to the applicable requirements of Chapter 3. Load-side conductors and equipment are to comply with Article 725 and must be separated from, and are not to occupy the same, raceways, cable trays, cables, or enclosures with light, power, and Class 1 conductors [see Section 725-38(a)(2), Exceptions].

Primary batteries are satisfactory with respect to current limitations provided the voltage is 30 or less and the capacity is equal to or less than that available from series connected No. 6 carbon zinc cells.

Where dry cells are used, the requirements of Note 4 to Tables 725-31(a) and 725-31(b) must be met for inherent power limitation.

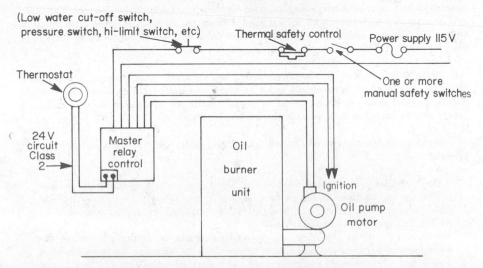

Figure 725-1. Typical installation of an automatic oil burner unit.

Figure 725-1 illustrates a simplified diagram of an automatic domestic oil burner unit. A thermostat is supplied by a current-limiting transformer at 24 V and the opening and closing of the thermostat contacts controls a relay that operates the oil burner ignition and pump motor. Failure of the thermostat would not introduce a hazard. Assume that the thermostat failed in the closed-contact position thereby energizing the ignition and motor. The Class 1 circuit, in this case an extension of the power circuit, would operate and open the circuit, that is the high-limit control (forced warm air) or pressure switch control (circulating hot water or steam). Therefore the safety controls and ignition circuit would be considered a Class 1 circuit and the thermostat circuit would be considered a Class 2 circuit.

725-41. Circuits Extending Beyond One Building. Class 2 or Class 3 circuits that extend beyond one building and are so run as to be subject to accidental contact with light or power conductors operating at over 300 volts to ground shall also meet the requirements of Sections 800-2, 800-11, and 800-12 for communication circuits.

725-42. Grounding. Class 2 and Class 3 circuits and equipment shall be grounded in accordance with Article 250.

ARTICLE 760 — FIRE PROTECTIVE SIGNALING SYSTEMS

Contents

760-28. Wiring Methods and Materials on Load Side.
 (a) Nonpower-Limited Wiring Methods and Materials.
 (b) Power-Limited Wiring Methods and Materials.
760-29. Separation of Conductors.
 (a) Separation from Light, Power, Class 1 and Nonpower-Limited Fire Protective Signaling Circuits.
 (b) Conductors of Different Power-Limited Fire Protective Signaling Circuits and Class 2 and Class 3 Circuits in Same Cable, Enclosure, or Raceway.

760-30. Conductors and Cables.
 (a) Conductor Material.
 (b) Sizes.
 (c) Insulation-Multiconductor Cables.
 (d) Insulation-Single Conductors.
 (e) Ratings.
 (f) Coaxial Cables.
760-31. Current-Carrying Continuous Line-type Fire Detectors.
 (a) Application.
 (b) Insulation.
 (c) Installation.

A. Scope and General

760-1. Scope. This article covers the installation of wiring and equipment of fire protective signaling systems operating at 600 volts, nominal, or less.

For further information for fire alarm, guard tour, sprinkler waterflow, and sprinkler supervisory systems, refer to the following:

NFPA 71-1977 — Central Station Signaling Systems.
NFPA 72A-1979 — Local Protective Signaling Systems.
NFPA 72B-1979 — Auxiliary Protective Signaling Systems.
NFPA 72C-1975 — Remote Station Protective Signaling Systems.
NFPA 72D-1979 — Proprietary Protective Signaling Systems.
NFPA 72E-1978 — Automatic Fire Detectors.
NFPA 74-1978 — Household Fire Warning Equipment.

Class 1, 2 and 3 circuits are defined in Article 725.

NFPA 71, Central Station Signaling Systems. This standard covers the installation, maintenance, and use of central station signaling systems. These systems include the central station physical plant, exterior communication channels, satellite stations, and the signaling facilities located at the protected premises.

This standard is intended to apply primarily to supervisory and alarm service furnished by operators constantly in attendance at a central station, manually or automatically controlled, with the required maintenance, inspection, and testing force and runner service readily available. Central station companies customarily follow this standard for maintenance, testing, and inspection with respect to other classes of contract service that they furnish.

Such systems are controlled and operated by a person, firm, or corporation whose principal business is the furnishing and maintaining of supervised signaling service.

NFPA 72A, Local Protective Signaling Systems. The provisions of this standard contemplate supervised systems providing fire alarm or supervisory signals within the protected premises. These systems are primarily for the protection of life by indicating the necessity for building evacuation and secondarily for the protection of property.

NFPA 72B, Auxiliary Protective Signaling Systems. An auxiliary alarm system provides protection to an individual occupancy or building or to a group of buildings of a single occupancy and utilizes municipal fire alarm facilities in order to transmit an alarm to the fire department.

Alarms from an auxiliary system are received at municipal fire alarm headquarters on the same equipment and by the same methods as alarms transmitted from municipal fire alarm boxes located on streets.

An auxiliary alarm system is maintained and supervised by a responsible person or corporation. The auxiliary alarm system deals with equipment and circuits in the protected property which, of themselves, are insufficient for notifying the fire department in the event of fire, but which, in combination with a suitable municipal fire alarm system, are arranged to summon fire department response when operated.

NFPA 72C, Remote Station Protective Signaling Systems. The provisions of this standard contemplate a system of electrically supervised circuits employing a direct circuit connection between signaling devices at the protected premises and signal-receiving equipment in a remote station (where someone is always on duty), such as a municipal fire alarm headquarters, a fire station, or other location acceptable to the authority having jurisdiction.

NFPA 72D, Proprietary Protective Signaling Systems. The provisions of this standard apply to a system supervised by competent and experienced personnel in a central supervising station at the property protected. The system is to include equipment and other facilities required to permit the operators to test and operate the system and, upon receipt of a signal, to take such action as is required under the rules established for their guidance by the authority having jurisdiction. The system is to be maintained and tested by owner personnel or an organization satisfactory to the authority having jurisdiction.

NFPA 72E, Automatic Fire Detectors. The purpose of this standard is to provide basic minimum requirements for performance of automatic fire detectors to ensure timely warning for the purposes of life safety and property protection.

This standard is intended for use by persons knowledgeable in fire protection. It covers minimum performance, location, mounting, testing, and maintenance requirements of automatic fire detectors for the protection of the occupant, building, space, structure, area, or object in accordance with the stated purpose.

This standard is intended to be used with other NFPA standards that deal specifically with fire alarm, extinguishment, or control. Automatic fire detectors add to fire protection by initiating emergency action but only when used in conjunction with other equipment.

NFPA 1221, Public Fire Service Communications. This standard covers the installation, maintenance, and use of all public fire service communication facilities. These facilities include a municipal fire alarm system, telephone facilities, and fire department radio facilities, all of which fulfill two principal functions: receiving fire alarms or other emergency calls from the public and retransmitting these alarms and emergency calls to fire companies and other interested agencies.

NFPA 74, Household Fire Warning Equipment. This standard is primarily concerned with life protection, not with the protection of property. It contemplates that the family has an exit plan and covers the requirements for the proper selection, installation, operation, and maintenance of fire warning equipment for use within family living units.

A control and associated equipment, single or multiple station alarm device(s), or any combination thereof, may be used to form a household fire warning system.

Detection and alarm systems covered by this standard are solely for the use of the protected household. If the alarm is extended to any other location, such as the fire department, the system is then considered to be one of the aforementioned systems (as applicable), except that the requirements of detector location and spacing, as they apply to home warning systems, would continue to be followed.

760-2. Classifications.   Fire protective signaling circuits shall be classified as nonpower limited or power limited. All fire protective signaling circuits shall comply with Part A and, in addition, nonpower-limited circuits shall comply with Part B and power-limited circuits with Part C.

760-3. Identification.   Fire protective signaling circuits shall be identified at terminal and junction locations, in a manner which will prevent unintentional interference with the signaling circuit during testing and servicing.

760-4. Location and Other Articles.   Circuits and equipment shall comply with (a), (b), (c), and (d) below.

   (a) Prevention of Spread of Fire or Products of Combustion.   Section 300-21.

   (b) Hazardous (Classified) Locations.   Articles 500 through 516 and Article 517, Part G where installed in hazardous (classified) locations.

   (c) Corrosive, Damp, or Wet Locations.   Sections 110-11, 300-6 and 310-9 where installed in corrosive, damp, or wet locations.

   (d) Ducts or Plenums.   Section 300-22 where installed in ducts or plenums.

   Exception to (d): Single and multiconductor cables covered under Part C and listed as having adequate fire-resistant and low-smoke producing characteristics shall be permitted for ducts, hollow spaces used as ducts, and plenums other than those described in Section 300-22(a).

760-5. Signaling Line Circuits Extending Beyond One Building.   Fire protective signaling line circuits that extend aerially beyond one building shall either meet the requirements of Article 800 and be classified as communications circuits, or shall meet the requirements of Article 225.

760-6. Grounding.   Fire protective signaling circuits and equipment shall be grounded in accordance with Article 250.

   Exception: DC power-limited fire protective signaling circuits having a maximum current of 0.030 amperes.

760-7. Supervision.   The circuit shall be electrically supervised so that a trouble signal shall indicate the occurrence of a single open or a single ground fault on any installation wiring circuit that would prevent proper alarm operation.

   Exception: Interconnecting circuits of household fire warning equipment wholly within a dwelling unit.

   For additional information, see NFPA 74-1978, Household Fire Warning Equipment.

   See articles on electrical supervision in NFPA 71, 72A, 72B, 72C, and 72D for more information about electrical supervision.

B. Nonpower-Limited Fire Protective Signaling Circuits

760-11. Power Limitations.   The power supply of nonpower-limited fire protective signaling circuits shall comply with Chapters 1 through 4 and the output voltage shall not be more than 600 volts, nominal.

760-12. Overcurrent Protection.

(a) Conductors Larger than No. 14. Conductors larger than No. 14 shall be protected against overcurrent in accordance with the ampacities given in Tables 310-16 through 310-19.

(b) Conductors of Nos. 18, 16, and 14. Conductors of Nos. 18, 16, and 14 shall be considered as protected by overcurrent devices of not over 20 amperes rating.

Exception for (a) and (b) above: Where other articles of this Code require other overcurrent protection.

760-13. Location of Overcurrent Devices. Overcurrent devices shall be located at the point where the conductor to be protected receives its supply.

Exception: Where the overcurrent device protecting the larger conductor also protects the smaller conductor.

760-14. Wiring Method. Wiring installation shall be in accordance with the appropriate articles in Chapter 3.

Exception No. 1: As provided in Sections 760-15 through 760-18.

Exception No. 2: Where other articles of this Code require other methods.

760-15. Conductors of Different Circuits in Same Enclosure, Cable, or Raceway. Class 1 and nonpower-limited fire protective signaling circuits shall be permitted to occupy the same enclosure, cable, or raceway without regard to whether the individual circuits are alternating current or direct current, provided all conductors are insulated for the maximum voltage of any conductor in the enclosure or raceway. Power supply and fire protective signaling circuit conductors shall be permitted in the same enclosure, cable, or raceway only when connected to the same equipment.

760-16. Conductors.

(a) Sizes and Use. Conductors of Nos. 18 and 16 shall be permitted to be used provided they supply loads that do not exceed the ampacities given in Table 402-5 and are installed in a raceway or a listed cable. Conductors larger than No. 16 shall not supply loads greater than the ampacities given in Tables 310-16 through 310-19.

(b) Insulation. Insulation on conductors shall be suitable for 600 volts. Conductors larger than No. 16 shall comply with Article 310. Conductors in sizes Nos. 18 and 16 shall be Type RFH-2, FFH-2, TF, TFF, TFN, TFFN, PF, PGF, PFF, PGFF, PTF, PTFF, SF-2, SFF-2, PAF, PAFF, ZF, ZFF, KF-2, or KFF-2. Conductors with other type and thickness of insulation shall be permitted if listed for nonpower-limited fire protective signaling circuit use.

For application provisions, see Table 402-3.

760-17. Multiconductor Cable for Circuits Operating at 150 Volts or Less. A multiconductor cable of two or more No. 16 or 18 solid or stranded (maximum of 7 strands) copper conductors listed for this use shall be permitted to be used on fire protective signaling circuits operating at 150 volts or less. The multiconductor cable shall be installed in a raceway or exposed in accordance with the requirements of Chapter 3 except that surface-mounted cable shall not be permitted within 7 feet (2.13 m) of the floor.

760-18. Number of Conductors in Raceways, Cable Trays, and Cables, and Derating.

(a) Nonpower-Limited Fire Protective Signaling Circuits and Class 1 Circuits.   Where only nonpower-limited fire protective signaling circuits and Class 1 circuits are in a raceway, the number of conductors shall be determined in accordance with Section 300-17. The derating factors given in Note 8 to Tables 310-16 through 310-19 shall apply if such conductors carry continuous loads.

(b) Power-Supply Conductors and Fire Protective Signaling Circuit Conductors.   Where power-supply conductors and fire protective signaling circuit conductors are permitted in a raceway in accordance with Section 760-15, the number of conductors shall be determined in accordance with Section 300-17. The derating factors given in Note 8 to Tables 310-16 through 310-19 shall apply as follows:

(1) To all conductors when the fire protective signaling circuit conductors carry continuous loads and where the total number of conductors is more than three.

(2) To the power-supply conductors only, when the fire protective signaling circuit conductors do not carry continuous loads and where the number of power-supply conductors is more than three.

(c) Cable Trays.   Where fire protective signaling circuit conductors are installed in cable trays, they shall comply with Sections 318-8 through 318-10.

C. Power-Limited Fire Protective Signaling Circuits

760-21. Power Limitations.   As specified in Table 760-21(a) for ac circuits and Table 760-21(b) for dc circuits, the power for power-limited fire protective signaling circuits shall be either inherently limited requiring no overcurrent protection or limited by a combination of a power source and overcurrent protection.

760-22. Supervision.   In addition to the requirements of Section 760-7, either a trouble or alarm signal shall indicate the occurrence of a multiple ground fault or any short-circuit fault that would prevent proper alarm operation.

Exception: Interconnecting circuits of household fire warning equipment wholly within a dwelling unit.

For additional information see Household Fire Warning Equipment, NFPA 74-1978.

760-23. Marking.   The circuit shall be durably marked where plainly visible at terminations to indicate that it is a power-limited fire protective signaling circuit.

760-25. Overcurrent Protection.   Where overcurrent protection is required, the overcurrent protective devices shall not be interchangeable with devices of higher ratings. The overcurrent device shall be permitted as an integral part of the power supply.

760-26. Location of Overcurrent Device.   Overcurrent devices shall be located at the point where the conductor to be protected receives its supply.

760-27. Wiring Methods on Supply Side.   Conductors and equipment on the supply side of overcurrent protection, transformers, or current-limiting devices shall be installed in accordance with the appropriate requirements of Part B and Chapter 3. Transformers or other devices supplied from power-supply conductors shall be protected by an overcurrent device rated not over 20 amperes.

Exception: The input leads of a transformer or other power source supplying power-limited fire protective signaling circuits shall be permitted to be smaller than No. 14 but not smaller than No. 18, if they are not over 12 inches (305 mm) long and if they have insulation that complies with Section 760-16(b).

760-28. Wiring Methods and Materials on Load Side. Circuits on the load side of overcurrent protection, transformers, and current-limiting devices shall be permitted to use wiring methods and materials in accordance with (a) and (b) below.

(a) Nonpower-Limited Wiring Methods and Materials. The appropriate articles of Chapter 3 including Section 300-17 shall apply.

Exception No. 1: Conductors and multiconductor cables described in and installed in accordance with Sections 760-16 and 760-17 shall be permitted.

Exception No. 2: The derating factors given in Note 8 to Tables 310-16 through 310-19 shall not apply.

(b) Power-Limited Wiring Methods and Materials. Power-limited circuit conductors and cables described in Section 760-30 shall be installed as follows:

(1) In raceway or exposed on surface of ceiling and sidewalls or "fished" in concealed spaces. Cable shall be adequately supported and terminated in approved fittings and installed in such a way that maximum protection against physical injury is afforded by building construction such as baseboards, door frames, ledges, etc. When located within 7 feet (2.13 m) of the floor, cable shall be securely fastened in an approved manner, such as insulated stapling at intervals of not more than 18 inches (457 mm).

(2) In metal raceway or rigid nonmetallic conduit when passing through a floor or wall to a height of 7 feet (2.13 m) above the floor unless adequate protection can be afforded by building construction such as detailed in (1) above, or unless an equivalent solid guard is provided.

(3) In rigid conduit, intermediate metal conduit or electrical metallic tubing when installed in hoistways.

Exception: As provided for in Section 620-21, Exceptions No. 1 and 2 for elevators and similar equipment.

(4) Encased in noncombustible tubing or other outer covering of noncombustible materials or located in a fireproof shaft having fire stops at each floor when installed in a vertical run in a shaft or partition.

Exception: Power-limited circuit conductors and cables listed as having a fire-resistant covering capable of preventing the carrying of fire from floor to floor.

760-29. Separation of Conductors. Conductors and cables on the load side of overcurrent protection, transformers, and current-limiting devices shall comply with (a) and (b) below.

(a) Separation from Light, Power, Class 1 and Nonpower-Limited Fire Protective Signaling Circuits.

(1) Power-limited circuits shall be separated at least 2 inches (50.8 mm) from open conductors of any light, power, Class 1, or nonpower-limited fire protective signaling circuits.

Exception No. 1: Where the light, power, Class 1, or nonpower-limited fire protective signaling circuit conductors are in raceway or in metal-sheathed, metal-clad, nonmetallic-sheathed, or Type UF cables.

Table 760-21(a).   Power Limitations for Alternating-Current Fire Protective Signaling Circuits

	Inherently Limited Power Source (Overcurrent protection not required)			Not Inherently Limited Power Source (Overcurrent protection required)		
	0-20	Over 20-30	Over 30-100	0-20	Over 20-100	Over 100-150
Power Source Maximum Nameplate Ratings						
Circuit Voltage V_{max} (Note 1)						
Power Limitation $(VA)_{max}$ (Note 1) (Volt-Amps)	—	—	—	250 (see Note 2)	250	N.A.
Current Limitation I_{max} (Note 1) (Amps)	8.0	8.0	$150/V_{max}$	$1000/V_{max}$	$1000/V_{max}$	1.0
Maximum Over-current Protection (Amps)	—	—	—	5.0	$100/V_{max}$	1.0
VA (Volt-Amps)	$5.0 \times V_{max}$	100	100	$5.0 \times V_{max}$	100	100
Current (Amps)	5.0	$100/V_{max}$	$100/V_{max}$	5.0	$100/V_{max}$	$100/V_{max}$
Supply Conductors and Cables	See Section 760-27					
Circuit Conductors and Cables	See Section 760-30					

Table 760-21(b).   Power Limitations for Direct-Current Fire Protective Signaling Circuits

	Inherently Limited Power Source (Note 4) (Overcurrent protection not required)				Not Inherently Limited Power Source (Overcurrent protection required)		
Circuit Voltage V_{max} (Note 1)	0-20	Over 20-30	Over 30-100	Over 100-250	0-20	Over 20-100	Over 100-150
Power Limitation $(VA)_{max}$ (Note 1) (Volt-Amps)	—	—	—	—	250 (see Note 2)	250	N.A.
Current Limitation I_{max} (Note 1) (Amps)	8.0	8.0	$150/V_{max}$	0.030	$1000/V_{max}$	$1000/V_{max}$	1.0
Maximum Over-current Protection (Amps)	—	—	—	—	5.0	$100/V_{max}$	1.0
Power Source Maximum Name-plate Ratings — VA (Volt-Amps)	$5.0 \times V_{max}$	100	100	$0.030 \times V_{max}$	$5.0 \times V_{max}$	100	100
Power Source Maximum Name-plate Ratings — Current (Amps)	5.0	$100/V_{max}$	$100/V_{max}$	0.030	5.0	$100/V_{max}$	$100/V_{max}$
Supply Conductors and Cables	See Section 760-27						
Circuit Conductors and Cables	See Section 760-30						

Notes for Tables 760-21(a) and (b)

Note 1. V_{max}: Maximum output voltage regardless of load with rated input applied.

I_{max}: Maximum output current after one minute of operation under any noncapacitive load, including short circuit, and with overcurrent protection bypassed if used.

VA_{max}: Maximum volt-ampere output regardless of load and overcurrent protection bypassed if used.

Note 2. If the power source is a transformer, $(VA)_{max}$ is 350 or less when V_{max} is 15 or less.

Exception No. 2: Where the power-limited circuit conductors are permanently separated from the conductors of the other circuits by a continuous and firmly fixed nonconductor, such as porcelain tubes or flexible tubing in addition to the insulation on the wire.

(2) Power-limited circuits shall not be placed in any enclosure, raceway, cable, compartment, outlet box, or similar fitting containing conductors of light, power, Class 1, or nonpower-limited fire protective signaling circuits.

Exception No. 1: Where the conductors of the different systems are separated by a partition.

Exception No. 2: Conductors in outlet boxes, junction boxes, or similar fittings or compartments where power-supply conductors are introduced solely for supplying power to the power-limited fire protective signaling system to which the other conductors in the enclosure are connected.

(3) Power-limited circuits shall be separated by not less than 2 inches (50.8 mm) from light, power, Class 1, or nonpower-limited fire protective signaling circuit conductors run in the same shaft.

Exception No. 1: Where the conductors of either the light, power, Class 1, the nonpower-limited fire protective signaling circuits, or the power-limited fire protective signaling circuits are encased in noncombustible tubing.

Exception No. 2: Where the light, power, Class 1, or the nonpower-limited fire protective signaling circuit conductors are in a raceway or are in metal-sheathed, metal-clad, nonmetallic-sheathed, or Type UF cables.

(b) Conductors of Different Power-Limited Fire Protective Signaling Circuits and Class 2 and Class 3 Circuits in Same Cable, Enclosure, or Raceway.

(1) Cables and conductors of two or more power-limited fire protective signaling circuits or Class 3 circuits shall be permitted in the same cable, enclosure, or raceway.

(2) Conductors of one or more Class 2 circuits shall be permitted within the same cable, enclosure, or raceway with conductors of power-limited fire protective signaling circuits provided that the insulation of the Class 2 circuit conductors in the cable, enclosure, or raceway is at least that required by the power-limited fire protective signaling circuits.

760-30. Conductors and Cables.   Conductors and cables for use with power-limited fire protective signaling circuits installed in accordance with Section 760-28(b) shall be listed for this use and shall meet or exceed the requirements of (a) through (e) or where coaxial cable is used, the requirements of (f) below.

(a) Conductor Materials.   Conductors shall be solid copper or bunch-tinned (bonded) stranded copper.

Exception: Stranded copper with a maximum of 7 strands for sizes No. 18 and larger shall be permitted.

(b) Sizes.   Conductors shall be not smaller than No. 16 for single conductor, No. 19 for two or three conductor and No. 22 for four or more conductor multiconductor cables.

(c) Insulation — Multiconductor Cables.   Conductors of multiconductor cables shall be covered by approved thermoplastic insulation of not less than 12 mils nominal (10 mils minimum) thickness. The cable conductor shall have an overall thermoplastic jacket having a nominal thickness of not less than 35 mils (30 mils minimum). Where the number of conductors in a cable exceeds four, the thickness of the thermoplastic jacket shall be increased so as to provide equivalent performance characteristics. Similarly, where the size of conductors in a cable exceeds No. 16, the thickness of the conductor insulation shall be increased so as to provide equivalent performance characteristics.

Exception No. 1: Two conductors assembled in a flat parallel construction with a 30 mils nominal integral insulation-jacket and a 47 mils minimum web shall be permitted.

Exception No. 2: Other types and thicknesses of insulation and jackets shall be permitted if listed for this use.

Exception No. 3: Where a smooth metallic sheath, welded and corrugated metallic sheath, or interlocking tape armor is applied over the nonmetallic jacket, an overall nonmetallic jacket shall not be required.

(d) Insulation — Single Conductors.   Single conductors shall be covered by approved thermoplastic insulation of not less than 30 mils nominal (28 mils minimum) thickness.

Exception: Other types and thicknesses of insulation shall be permitted if listed for this use.

(e) Ratings.   The cable shall have a voltage rating of not less than 300 volts and the jacket compound shall have a high degree of abrasion resistance.

(f) Coaxial Cables.   Coaxial cables shall have a minimum No. 22 AWG copper or 30 percent minimum conductivity copper covered steel center conductor, an overall insulation rated at 300 volts, an overall metallic shield covered by a flame retardant nonmetallic jacket having a minimum thickness not less than 35 mils nominal (30 mils minimum), and they shall have a high degree of abrasion resistance.

760-31. Current-Carrying Continuous Line-type Fire Detectors.

(a) Application.   Listed continuous line-type fire detectors, including insulated copper tubing of pneumatically operated detectors, employed for both detection and carrying signaling currents shall be permitted to be used in circuits having power-limiting characteristics in accordance with Section 760-21.

(b) Insulation.   Continous line-type fire detectors shall be insulated in accordance with Section 760-30(c) through (e), or with an equivalent type of insulation.

(c) Installation.   Continuous line-type fire detectors shall be installed in accordance with Sections 760-22 through 760-29.

8 COMMUNICATION SYSTEMS

ARTICLE 800 — COMMUNICATION CIRCUITS

Contents

A. General

800-1. Scope. This article covers telephone, telegraph (except radio), district messenger, outside wiring for fire alarm and burglar alarms, and similar central station systems; and telephone systems not connected to a central station system but using similar types of equipment, methods of installation, and maintenance.

For further information for fire alarm, sprinkler, supervisory, or watchman systems, see Article 760.

Section 90-3, "Code Arrangement," states that Chapter 8, which includes Articles 800, 810, and 820, covers communication systems and is independent of the other chapters, except where they are specifically referenced therein. For instance, Section 800-2(b) references Article 500, Section 800-3(d) references Section 300-22, Section 800-11(a)(3) references Section 225-14(d), etc.

B. Protection

800-2. Protective Devices. A listed protector shall be provided on each circuit run partly or entirely in aerial wire or aerial cable not confined within a block. Also, a listed protector shall be

917

provided on each circuit, aerial or underground, so located within the block containing the building served as to be exposed to accidental contact with light or power conductors operating at over 300 volts to ground.

The word "block" as used in this article means a square or portion of a city, town, or village enclosed by streets and including the alleys so enclosed but not any street.

The word "exposed" as used in this article means that the circuit is in such a position that, in case of failure of supports or insulation, contact with another circuit may result.

(a) Location.   The protector shall be located in, on, or immediately adjacent to the structure or building served and as close as practicable to the point at which the exposed conductors enter or attach.

(b) Hazardous (Classified) Locations.   The protector shall not be located in any hazardous (classified) location as defined in Article 500, nor in the vicinity of easily ignitible material.

(c) Protector Requirements.   The protector shall consist of an arrester connected between each line conductor and ground in an appropriate mounting. Protector terminals shall be marked to indicate line and ground as applicable.

(1) Fuseless-type protectors shall be permitted under any of the following conditions:

a. Where circuits enter a building through metallic-sheathed cable or through a nonmetallic-sheathed cable having a metallic grounding shield between the sheath and the conductor assembly, if the metallic sheath or shield of the cable is effectively grounded, and if the conductors in the cable safely fuse on all currents greater than the current-carrying capacity of the protector, and the ampacity of the protector grounding conductor.

b. Where insulated conductors in accordance with Section 800-11(c)(1) or (c)(2) are used to extend circuits to a building from a metallic-sheathed cable or from a nonmetallic-sheathed cable having a metallic grounding shield between the sheath and the conductor assembly, if the metallic sheath or shield is effectively grounded and if the conductors in the cable or cable stub, or the connections between the insulated conductors and the exposed plant safely fuse on all currents greater than the current-carrying capacity of the protector, and the ampacity of the associated insulated conductors and the protector grounding conductor.

c. Where insulated conductors in accordance with Section 800-11(c)(1) or (c)(2) are used to extend circuits to a building from other than a grounded metallic-sheathed or shielded cable, if (1) the protector is listed for this purpose, and (2) the connections of the insulated conductors to the exposed plant or the conductors of the exposed plant safely fuse on all currents greater than the current-carrying capacity of the protector, and the ampacity of the associated insulated conductors and the protector grounding conductor.

d. Where insulated conductors in accordance with Section 800-11(c)(1) or (c)(2) are used to extend circuits aerially to a building from an unexposed buried or underground circuit.

Effectively grounded means intentionally connected to earth through a ground connection or connections of sufficiently low impedance and having sufficient current-carrying capacity to prevent the buildup of voltages which may result in undue hazard to connected equipment or to persons.

e. Where insulated conductors in accordance with Section 800-11(c)(1) or (c)(2) are used to extend circuits to a building from an effectively grounded metallic-sheathed or shielded cable, and if (1) the combination of the protector and insulated conductors is listed for this purpose, and (2) the insulated conductors safely fuse on all currents greater than the current-carrying capacity of the protector and the ampacity of the protector grounding conductor.

(2) Where the requirements listed under (c)(1)a, (1)b, (1)c, or (1)d above are not met, fused-type protectors shall be used. Fused-type protectors shall consist of an arrester connected between each line conductor and ground, a fuse in series with each line conductor, and an appropriate mounting arrangement. Protector terminals shall be marked to indicate line, instrument, and ground, as applicable.

800-3. Installation of Conductors. Conductors from the protector to the equipment or, where no protector is required, conductors attached to the outside or inside of the building shall comply with (a) through (d) below.

(a) Separation from Other Conductors.

(1) Open Conductors. Conductors shall be separated at least 2 inches (50.8 mm) from conductors of any light or power circuits or Class 1 circuits.

Exception No. 1: Where the light or power or Class 1 circuit conductors are in a raceway or in metal-sheathed, metal-clad, nonmetallic-sheathed, or Type UF cables.

Exception No. 2: Where the conductors are permanently separated from the conductors of the other circuit by a continuous and firmly fixed nonconductor, such as porcelain tubes or flexible tubing, in addition to the insulation on the wire.

(2) In Raceways and Boxes. Communication conductors shall not be placed in any raceway, compartment, outlet box, junction box, or similar fitting with conductors of light or power circuits or Class 1 circuits.

Exception No. 1: Where the conductors of the different systems are separated by a partition.

Exception No. 2: Conductors in outlet boxes, junction boxes, or similar fittings or compartments where such conductors are introduced solely for power supply to communication equipment or for connection to remote-control equipment.

(3) In Shafts. Conductors run in the same shaft with conductors of light or power shall be separated from light or power conductors by not less than 2 inches (50.8 mm).

Exception No. 1: Where the conductors of either system are encased in noncombustible tubing.

Exception No. 2: Where the light or power conductors are in a raceway, or in metal-sheathed, metal-clad, nonmetallic-sheathed, or Type UF cables.

(b) Vertical Runs. Conductors bunched together in a vertical run in a shaft shall have a fire-resistant covering capable of preventing the carrying of fire from floor to floor.

Exception: Where conductors are encased in noncombustible tubing or are located in a fireproof shaft having fire stops at each floor.

(c) Spread of Fire or Products of Combustion. Installations in hollow spaces, vertical shafts, and ventilation or air-handling ducts shall be so made that the possible spread of fire or products of combustion will not be substantially increased. Openings around penetrations through fire resistance rated walls, partitions, floors, or ceilings shall be firestopped using approved methods.

(d) Location. Circuits and equipment installed in ducts and plenums shall also comply with Section 300-22 as to wiring methods.

Exception to (d): Single and multiconductor cables listed as having adequate fire-resistant and low-smoke producing characteristics shall be permitted for ducts, hollow spaces used as ducts, and plenums other than those described in Section 300-22(a).

The conductors referred to in this section would ordinarily be insulated, but the kind of insulation is not specified as reliance is placed on the protective device to stop all dangerous voltages and currents.

C. Outside Conductors

800-11. Overhead Conductors.   Overhead conductors entering buildings shall comply with (a) through (c) below.

(a) On Poles.   Where communication conductors and light or power conductors are supported by the same pole, the following conditions shall be met:

(1) Relative Location.   Where practicable, the communications conductors shall be located below the light or power conductors.

(2) Attachment to Crossarms.   Conductors shall not be attached to a crossarm that carries light or power conductors.

(3) Climbing Space.   The climbing space through communication conductors shall comply with the requirements of Section 225-14(d).

(b) On Roofs.   Conductors passing over buildings shall be kept at least 8 feet (2.44 m) above any roof that may be readily walked upon.

Exception: Auxiliary buildings, such as garages and the like.

(c) Circuits Requiring Protectors.   Circuits that require protectors as provided in Section 800-2 shall comply with the following:

(1) Insulation, Single or Paired Conductors.   Each conductor from the last outdoor support to the protector shall have 30-mil rubber insulation, except that where such conductors are entirely within a block the insulation on the conductor may be less than 30 mils, but not less than 25 mils in thickness. In addition, the conductor, either individually or over the pair, shall be covered with a substantial fibrous covering or equivalent protection. Listed conductors having rubber insulation of a thickness less than specified above, or having other kinds of insulation, shall be permitted.

(2) Insulation, Cables.   Conductors within a cable of the metal-sheathed type or within a cable having a rubber sheath of at least 30-mil thickness and covered with a substantial fibrous covering shall be permitted to have paper or other suitable insulation. Where the metal or rubber sheath is omitted, each conductor shall be insulated as required in (c)(1) above, and the bunched conductors shall be covered with a substantial fibrous covering or equivalent covering.

(3) On Buildings.   Open conductors shall be separated at least 4 inches (102 mm) from light or power conductors not in conduit or cable, or be permanently separated from conductors of the other system by a continuous and firmly fixed nonconductor in addition to the insulation on the wires, such as porcelain tubes or flexible tubing. Open conductors exposed to accidental contact with light and power conductors operating at over 300 volts to ground and attached to buildings shall be separated from woodwork by being supported on glass, porcelain, or other insulating material.

Exception: Separation from woodwork shall not be required where fuses are omitted as provided for in Section 800-2(c)(1), or where conductors are used to extend circuits to a building from a cable having a grounded metal sheath.

(4) Entering Buildings.   Where a protector is installed inside the building, the conductors shall enter the building either through a noncombustible, nonabsorbent insulating bushing, or through a metal raceway. The insulating bushing shall not be required where the entering conductors (1) are in metal-sheathed cable; (2) pass through masonry; (3) meet the requirements of (c)(1) above and fuses are omitted as provided in Section 800-2(c)(1); or (4) meet the requirements of (c)(1) above and are used to extend circuits to a building from a cable having a grounded metal sheath. Raceways or bushings shall slope upward from the outside or, where this cannot be done, drip loops shall be formed in the conductors immediately before they enter the building. Raceways shall be equipped with an approved service head. More than one conductor shall be permitted to enter through a single raceway or bushing. Conduits or other metal raceways located ahead of the protector shall be grounded.

800-12. Lightning Conductors.   Where practicable, a separation of at least 6 feet (1.83 m) shall be maintained between open conductors of communication systems on buildings and lightning conductors.

D. Underground Circuits

800-21. Underground Circuits Entering Buildings.   Underground conductors of communication circuits entering buildings shall comply with (a) and (b) below.

(a) With Electric Light or Power Conductors.   Underground conductors in a duct, handhole, or manhole containing electric light or power conductors shall be in a section separated from such conductors by means of brick, concrete, or tile partitions.

(b) Underground Block Distribution.   Where the entire street circuit is run underground and the circuit within the block is so placed as to be free from likelihood of accidental contact with electric light or power circuits of over 300 volts to ground, the insulation requirements of Section 800-11(c)(1) and (c)(4) shall not apply, insulating supports shall not be required for the conductors, and bushings shall not be required where the conductors enter the building.

E. Grounding

800-31. Grounding.   Equipment shall be grounded as specified in (a) and (b) below.

(a) Cable Sheath.   Where exposed to contact with electric light or power conductors, the metal sheath of aerial cables entering buildings shall be grounded or shall be interrupted close to the entrance to the building by an insulating joint or equivalent device.

(b) Protector Ground.   The protector ground shall comply with the following:

(1) Insulation.   The grounding conductor shall have a 30-mil rubber insulation and shall be covered by a substantial fibrous covering. Conductors listed for this use having less than 30-mil rubber insulation or having other kinds of insulation shall be permitted.

(2) Size.   The grounding conductor shall not be smaller than No. 18 copper or equivalent.

(3) Run in Straight Line. The grounding conductor shall be run to the grounding electrode in as straight a line as practicable.

(4) Physical Damage. Where necessary, the grounding conductor shall be guarded from physical damage.

(5) Electrode. The grounding conductor shall be connected as follows:

a. To the nearest accessible location on the building or structure grounding electrode system as covered in Section 250-81; or

b. To the metallic power service conduit, service-equipment enclosure, or grounding electrode conductor where the grounded conductor of the power service is connected to the grounding electrode system; or

c. If the building or structure served has no grounding means as described in (5)a or (5)b, to the grounding electrode, grounding electrode conductor, metallic service conduit, or service-equipment enclosure of the power service, where the service is grounded in accordance with Article 250, Part H; or

d. If the building or structure served has no grounding means as described in (5)a, (5)b, or (5)c, to any one of the individual electrodes described in Section 250-81; or

e. If the building or structure served has no grounding means as described in (5)a, (5)b, (5)c, or (5)d, to: (1) an effectively grounded metal structure; or (2) a continuous and extensive underground gas piping system where acceptable to both the serving gas supplier and to the authority having jurisdiction; or (3) to a ground rod or pipe driven into permanently damp earth. Steam or hot water pipes or lightning-rod conductors shall not be employed as electrodes for protectors.

(6) Electrode Connection. The grounding conductor shall be attached to a pipe electrode by means of a bolted clamp to which the conductor is connected in an effective manner. Where a gas pipe electrode is used, connection shall be made between the gas meter and the street main. In every case the connection to the grounding electrode shall be made as close to the earth as practicable. Connectors, clamps, fittings, or lugs used to attach grounding conductors and bonding jumpers to grounding electrodes or to each other which are to be concrete-encased or buried in the earth shall be suitable for its application.

(7) Bonding of Electrodes. A bonding jumper not smaller than No. 6 copper or equivalent shall be connected between the communication and the power grounding electrodes where the requirements of (5) above result in the use of separate electrodes. Bonding together of all separate electrodes shall be permitted.

See Section 250-86 for use of lightning rods.

Bonding together of all separate electrodes will limit potential differences between them and between their associated wiring systems.

ARTICLE 810 — RADIO AND TELEVISION EQUIPMENT

Contents

B. Receiving Equipment — Antenna Systems

810-11. Material.

810-12. Supports.

810-13. Avoidance of Contacts with Conductors of Other Systems.

810-14. Splices.

810-15. Grounding.

810-16. Size of Wire-Strung Antenna — Receiving Station.
   (a) Size of Antenna Conductors.
   (b) Self-Supporting Antennas.

810-17. Size of Lead-in — Receiving Station.

810-18. Clearances — Receiving Stations.
   (a) On Outside of Buildings.
   (b) Antennas and Lead-ins — Indoors.

810-19. Electric Supply Circuits Used in Lieu of Antenna — Receiving Stations.

810-20. Antenna Discharge Units — Receiving Stations.
   (a) Where Required.
   (b) Location.
   (c) Grounding.

810-21. Grounding Conductors — Receiving Stations.
   (a) Material.
   (b) Insulation.
   (c) Supports.
   (d) Mechanical Protection.
   (e) Run in Straight Line.

   (f) Electrode.
   (g) Inside or Outside Building.
   (h) Size.
   (i) Common Ground.

C. Amateur Transmitting and Receiving Stations — Antenna Systems

810-51. Other Sections.

810-52. Size of Antenna.

810-53. Size of Lead-in Conductors.

810-54. Clearance on Building.

810-55. Entrance to Building.

810-56. Protection Against Accidental Contact.

810-57. Antenna Discharge Units — Transmitting Stations.

810-58. Grounding Conductors — Amateur Transmitting and Receiving Stations.
   (a) Other Sections.
   (b) Size of Protective Grounding Conductor.
   (c) Size of Operating Grounding Conductor.

D. Interior Installation — Transmitting Stations

810-70. Clearance from Other Conductors.

810-71. General.
   (a) Enclosing.
   (b) Grounding of Controls.
   (c) Interlocks on Doors.
   (d) Audio-Amplifiers.

A. General

810-1. Scope. This article covers radio and television receiving equipment and amateur radio transmitting and receiving equipment, but not equipment and antennas used for coupling carrier current to power line conductors.

The requirements for Article 810 are similar to the requirements for Article 800. See Section 800-11 for the provisions that cover outside conductor location, clearances, and insulation. It should be noted that 30-mil insulation is required except where such conductors are entirely within a block; that is, where conductors are run separately from light and power conductors, such as between buildings or from building to building, not less than 25-mil insulation is permitted.

See Section 800-21 for underground circuits. Note, particularly, the provisions of paragraph (b) regarding minimum permitted insulation.

810-2. Other Articles. Wiring from the source of power to and between devices connected to the interior wiring system shall comply with Chapters 1 through 4 other than as modified by Sections 640-3, 640-4, and 640-5. Wiring for radio-frequency and audio-frequency equipment and loud speakers shall comply with Article 640.

810-3. Community Television Antenna.   The antenna shall comply with this article. The distribution system shall comply with Article 820.

810-4. Radio Noise Suppressors.   Radio interference eliminators, interference capacitors, or noise suppressors connected to power-supply leads shall be of a listed type. They shall not be exposed to physical damage.

B. Receiving Equipment — Antenna Systems

810-11. Material.   Antennas and lead-in conductors shall be of hard-drawn copper, bronze, aluminum alloy, copper-clad steel or other high-strength, corrosion-resistant material.

Exception: Soft-drawn or medium-drawn copper shall be permitted for lead-in conductors where the maximum span between points of support is less than 35 feet (10.67 m).

810-12. Supports.   Outdoor antennas and lead-in conductors shall be securely supported. The antennas shall not be attached to the electric service mast. They shall not be attached to poles or similar structures carrying electric light or power wires or trolley wires of over 250 volts between conductors. Insulators supporting the antenna conductors shall have sufficient mechanical strength to safely support the conductors. Lead-in conductors shall be securely attached to the antennas.

810-13. Avoidance of Contacts with Conductors of Other Systems.   Outdoor antennas and lead-in conductors from an antenna to a building shall not cross over electric light or power circuits and shall be kept well away from all such circuits so as to avoid the possibility of accidental contact. Where proximity to electric light or power service conductors of less than 250 volts between conductors cannot be avoided, the installation shall be such as to provide a clearance of at least 2 feet (610 mm).

Where practicable, antenna conductors shall be so installed as not to cross under electric light or power conductors.

One of the leading causes of electrical hazard and electrocution, according to statistical reports, is the accidental contact of radio and television receiving antennas and equipment, and amateur radio transmitting and receiving antennas and equipment with light or power conductors. Extreme caution should therefore be exercised during this type of installation, and periodic visual inspections should be conducted thereafter.

810-14. Splices.   Splices and joints in antenna spans shall be made mechanically secure with approved splicing devices or by such other means as will not appreciably weaken the conductors.

Conductor spans from antennas should be of sufficient size and strength to maintain clearances and avoid possible contact with light or power conductors. Splices and joints should be made with approved connectors or other means providing sufficient mechanical strength so as not to weaken appreciably the conductors.

810-15. Grounding.   Masts and metal structures supporting antennas shall be grounded in accordance with Section 810-21.

810-16. Size of Wire-Strung Antenna — Receiving Station.

(a) Size of Antenna Conductors.   Outdoor antenna conductors for receiving stations shall be of a size not less than given in Table 810-16(a).

Table 810-16(a)

Size of Receiving-Station Outdoor Antenna Conductors

Material	Minimum Size of Conductors		
	When Maximum Open Span Length is		
	Less than 35 feet	35 feet to 150 feet	Over 150 feet
Aluminum alloy, hard-drawn copper	19	14	12
Copper-clad steel, bronze, or other high-strength material	20	17	14

For SI units: one foot = 0.3048 meter.

(b) Self-Supporting Antennas.   Outdoor antennas, such as vertical rods or dipole structures, shall be of noncorrodible materials and of strength suitable to withstand ice and wind loading conditions, and shall be located well away from overhead conductors of electric light and power circuits of over 150 volts to ground, so as to avoid the possibility of the antenna or structure falling into or making accidental contact with such circuits.

810-17. Size of Lead-in — Receiving Station.   Lead-in conductors from outside antennas for receiving stations shall, for various maximum open span lengths, be of such size as to have a tensile strength at least as great as that of the conductors for antennas as specified in Section 810-16. Where the lead-in consists of two or more conductors that are twisted together, are enclosed in the same covering, or are concentric, the conductor size shall, for various maximum open span lengths, be such that the tensile strength of the combination will be at least as great as that of the conductors for antennas as specified in Section 810-16.

810-18. Clearances — Receiving Stations.

(a) On Outside of Buildings.   Lead-in conductors attached to buildings shall be so installed that they cannot swing closer than 2 feet (610 mm) to the conductors of circuits of 250 volts or less between conductors, or 10 feet (3.05 m) to the conductors of circuits of over 250 volts between conductors, except that in the case of circuits not over 150 volts between conductors, where all conductors involved are supported so as to ensure permanent separation, the clearance shall be permitted to be reduced but shall not be less than 4 inches (102 mm). The clearance between lead-in conductors and any conductor forming a part of a lightning rod system shall not be less than 6 feet (1.83 m) unless the bonding referred to in Section 250-86 is accomplished.

(b) Antennas and Lead-ins — Indoors.   Indoor antennas and indoor lead-ins shall not be run nearer than 2 inches (50.8 mm) to conductors of other wiring systems in the premises.

Exception No. 1: Where such other conductors are in metal raceways or cable armor.

Exception No. 2: Where permanently separated from such other conductors by a continuous and firmly fixed nonconductor, such as porcelain tubes or flexible tubing.

810-19. Electric Supply Circuits Used in lieu of Antenna — Receiving Stations.   Where an electric supply circuit is used in lieu of an antenna, the device by which the radio receiving set is connected to the supply circuit shall be listed.

The approved device is usually a small fixed condenser connected between the antenna terminal of the receiving set and one wire of the lighting circuit. As is the case with most receiving sets, the condenser should be designed for operation at not less than 300 V and mica should be used as the dielectric. This ensures a high degree of safety and minimizes the possibility of a breakdown in the condenser thereby avoiding a short circuit to ground through the antenna coil of the set.

810-20. Antenna Discharge Units — Receiving Stations.

(a) Where Required. Each conductor of a lead-in from an outdoor antenna shall be provided with a listed antenna discharge unit.

Exception: Where the lead-in conductors are enclosed in a continuous metallic shield that is either permanently and effectively grounded, or is protected by an antenna discharge unit.

(b) Location. Antenna discharge units shall be located outside the building or inside the building between the point of entrance of the lead-in and the radio set or transformers, and as near as practicable to the entrance of the conductors to the building. The antenna discharge unit shall not be located near combustible material nor in a hazardous (classified) location as defined in Article 500.

A lightning arrester is not required where the lead-in conductors are enclosed in a continuous metal shield such as rigid or intermediate metal conduit, or electrical metallic tubing, or any other metal shielded cable that is effectively grounded. A lightning discharge will take the path of lower impedance and jump from the lead-in conductors to the metal shield rather than take the path through the antenna coil of the receiving set.

(c) Grounding. The antenna discharge unit shall be grounded in accordance with Section 810-21.

810-21. Grounding Conductors — Receiving Stations. Grounding conductors shall comply with (a) through (i) below.

(a) Material. The grounding conductor shall be of copper, aluminum, copper-clad steel, bronze, or similar corrosion-resistant material.

(b) Insulation. Insulation on grounding conductors shall not be required.

(c) Supports. The grounding conductors shall be securely fastened in place and shall be permitted to be directly attached to the surface wired over without the use of insulating supports.

Exception: Where proper support cannot be provided, the size of the grounding conductors shall be increased proportionately.

(d) Mechanical Protection. The grounding conductor shall be protected where exposed to physical damage, or the size of the grounding conductors shall be increased proportionately to compensate for the lack of protection.

(e) Run in Straight Line. The grounding conductor for an antenna mast or antenna discharge unit shall be run in as straight a line as practicable from the mast or discharge unit to the grounding electrode.

(f) Electrode. The grounding conductor shall be connected as follows:

(1) To the nearest accessible location on the building or structure grounding electrode system as covered in Section 250-81; or

(2) To the metallic power service conduit, service-equipment enclosure, or grounding electrode conductor where the grounded conductor of the power service is connected to the grounding electrode system; or

(3) If the building or structure served has no grounding means as described in (f)(1) or (f)(2), to the grounding electrode, grounding electrode conductor, metallic service conduit, or service-equipment enclosure of the power service, where the service is grounded in accordance with Article 250, Part H; or

(4) If the building or structure served has no grounding means as described in (f)(1), (f)(2), or (f)(3), to any one of the individual electrodes described in Section 250-81; or

(5) If the building or structure served has no grounding means as described in (f)(1), (f)(2), (f)(3), or (f)(4), to: (1) an effectively grounded metal structure; or (2) a continuous and extensive underground gas piping system where acceptable to both the serving gas supplier and to the authority having jurisdiction; or (3) to a ground rod or pipe driven into permanently damp earth. Steam or hot water pipes or lightning-rod conductors shall not be employed as electrodes for protectors.

Exception: At a penthouse or similar location, the grounding conductor shall be permitted to be connected to a grounded water pipe, rigid metal conduit, or intermediate metal conduit.

(g) Inside or Outside Building. The grounding conductor shall be permitted to be run either inside or outside the building.

(h) Size. The grounding conductor shall not be smaller than No. 10 copper or No. 8 aluminum or No. 17 copper-clad steel or bronze.

(i) Common Ground. A single grounding conductor shall be permitted for both protective and operating purposes.

The requirements for grounding are in accordance with the provisions of Article 250. It is required that antenna masts be grounded to the same grounding electrode used for the electrical system of the building. In many cases masts are wrongly grounded to conveniently located vent pipes, metal gutters, and down spouts that could create potential differences between various metal parts located in or on buildings and lead-in conductors.

C. Amateur Transmitting and Receiving Stations — Antenna Systems

810-51. Other Sections. In addition to complying with Part C, antenna systems for amateur transmitting and receiving stations shall also comply with Sections 810-11 through 810-15.

810-52. Size of Antenna. Antenna conductors for transmitting and receiving stations shall be of a size not less than given in Table 810-52.

Table 810-52
Size of Amateur Station Outdoor Antenna Conductors

Material	Minimum Size of Conductors	
	Where Maximum Open Span Length is	
	Less Than 150 feet	Over 150 feet
Hard-drawn copper	14	10
Copper-clad steel, bronze or other high-strength material	14	12

For SI units: one foot = 0.3048 meter.

810-53. Size of Lead-in Conductors.   Lead-in conductors for transmitting stations shall, for various maximum span lengths, be of a size at least as great as that of conductors for antennas as specified in Section 810-52.

810-54. Clearance on Building.   Antenna conductors for transmitting stations, attached to buildings, shall be firmly mounted at least 3 inches (76 mm) clear of the surface of the building on nonabsorbent insulating supports, such as treated pins or brackets equipped with insulators having not less than 3-inch (76-mm) creepage and airgap distances. Lead-in conductors attached to buildings shall also comply with these requirements.

Exception: Where the lead-in conductors are enclosed in a continuous metallic shield that is permanently and effectively grounded, they shall not be required to comply with these requirements. Where grounded, the metallic shield shall also be permitted to be used as a conductor.

The creepage distance is measured from the conductor, across the face of the supporting insulator, to the building surface. The airgap distance is measured from the conductor (at its closest point) across the air space to the surface of the building. The exception covers coaxial cable with the shield permanently and effectively grounded.

810-55. Entrance to Building.   Except where protected with a continuous metallic shield that is permanently and effectively grounded, lead-in conductors for transmitting stations shall enter buildings by one of the following methods: (1) through a rigid, noncombustible, nonabsorbent insulating tube or bushing; (2) through an opening provided for the purpose in which the entrance conductors are firmly secured so as to provide a clearance of at least 2 inches (50.8 mm); or (3) through a drilled window pane.

810-56. Protection Against Accidental Contact.   Lead-in conductors to radio transmitters shall be so located or installed as to make accidental contact with them difficult.

810-57. Antenna Discharge Units — Transmitting Stations.   Each conductor of a lead-in for outdoor antennas shall be provided with an antenna discharge unit or other suitable means that will drain static charges from the antenna system.

Exception No. 1: Where protected by a continuous metallic shield that is permanently and effectively grounded.

Exception No. 2: Where the antenna is permanently and effectively grounded.

Where a lightning arrester is not installed at a transmitting station, protection against lightning may be provided by a switch that connects the lead-in to ground during the time the station is not in operation.

810-58. Grounding Conductors — Amateur Transmitting and Receiving Stations.   Grounding conductors shall comply with (a) through (c) below.

(a) Other Sections.   All grounding conductors for amateur transmitting and receiving stations shall comply with Section 810-21(a) through (g).

(b) Size of Protective Grounding Conductor.   The protective grounding conductor for transmitting stations shall be as large as the lead-in, but not smaller than No. 10 copper, bronze, or copper-clad steel.

(c) Size of Operating Grounding Conductor.   The operating grounding conductor for transmitting stations shall not be less than No. 14 copper or its equivalent.

D. Interior Installation — Transmitting Stations

810-70. Clearance from Other Conductors.   All conductors inside the building shall be separated at least 4 inches (102 mm) from the conductors of any lighting or signaling circuit.

Exception No. 1: As provided in Article 640.

Exception No. 2: Where separated from other conductors by conduit or some firmly fixed nonconductor, such as porcelain tubes or flexible tubing.

810-71. General.   Transmitters shall comply with (a) through (d) below.

(a) Enclosing.   The transmitter shall be enclosed in a metal frame or grille, or separated from the operating space by a barrier or other equivalent means, all metallic parts of which are effectively connected to ground.

(b) Grounding of Controls.   All external metal handles and controls accessible to the operating personnel shall be effectively grounded.

(c) Interlocks on Doors.   All access doors shall be provided with interlocks that will disconnect all voltages of over 350 volts between conductors when any access door is opened.

(d) Audio-Amplifiers.   Audio-amplifiers that are located outside the transmitter housing shall be suitably housed and shall be so located as to be readily accessible and adequately ventilated.

ARTICLE 820 — COMMUNITY ANTENNA TELEVISION
AND RADIO DISTRIBUTION SYSTEMS

Contents

A. General

820-1. Scope.   This article covers coaxial cable distribution of radio frequency signals typically employed in community antenna television (CATV) systems. Where the wiring system employed is other than coaxial, Article 800 shall apply.

The coaxial cable shall be permitted to deliver low-energy power to equipment directly associated with this radio frequency distribution system if the voltage is not over 60 volts and if the current supply is from a transformer or other device having energy-limiting characteristics.

820-2. Material.   Coaxial cable used for radio frequency distribution systems shall be suitable for the application.

B. Protection

820-7. Ground of Outer Conductive Shield of a Coaxial Cable.   Where coaxial cable is exposed to lightning or to accidental contact with lightning arrester conductors or power conductors operating at a potential of over 300 volts to ground, the outer conductive shield of the coaxial cable shall be grounded at the building premises as close to the point of cable entry as practicable.

(a) Shield Grounding.   Where the outer conductive shield of a coaxial cable is grounded, no other protective devices shall be required.

(b) Shield Protective Devices.   Grounding of a coaxial drop cable shield by means of a protective device that does not interrupt the grounding system within the premises shall be permitted.

Section 820-7(b) is new in the 1981 *Code*. It was added to permit the use of a shield protective device which does not interrupt the grounding system within the premises. This permits protection against overheating for the CATV service drop cable. Overheating can occur due to neutral fault currents in the power and lighting system.

C. Installation of Cable

820-11. Outside Conductors.   Coaxial cables, prior to the point of grounding, as defined in Section 820-7, shall comply with (a) through (e) below.

(a) On Poles.   Where practicable, conductors on poles shall be located below the light or power conductors and shall not be attached to a cross-arm that carries light or power conductors.

(b) Lead-in Clearance.   Lead-in or aerial-drop cables from a pole or other support, including the point of initial attachment to a building or structure, shall be kept away from electric light or power circuits so as to avoid the possibility of accidental contact.

Exception: Where proximity to electric light or power service conductors cannot be avoided, the installation shall be such as to provide clearances of not less than 12 inches (305 mm) from light or power service drops.

(c) Over Roofs.   Cables passing over buildings shall be at least 8 feet (2.44 m) above any roof that is accessible for pedestrian traffic.

(d) Between Buildings.   Cables extending between buildings and also the supports or attachment fixtures shall be acceptable for the purpose and shall have sufficient strength to withstand the loads to which they may be subjected.

Exception: Where a cable does not have sufficient strength to be self-supporting, it shall be attached to a supporting messenger cable that, together with the attachment fixtures or supports, shall be acceptable for the purpose and shall have sufficient strength to withstand the loads to which they may be subjected.

(e) On Buildings. Where attached to buildings, cables shall be securely fastened in such a manner that they will be separated from other conductors as follows:

(1) Light or Power. The coaxial cable shall have a separation of at least 4 inches (102 mm) from light or power conductors not in conduit or cable, or be permanently separated from conductors of the other system by a continuous and firmly fixed nonconductor in addition to the insulation on the wires.

(2) Other Communication Systems. Coaxial cable shall be installed so that there will be no unnecessary interference in the maintenance of the separate systems. In no case shall the conductors, cables, messenger strand, or equipment of one system cause abrasion to the conductors, cable, messenger strand, or equipment of any other system.

(3) Lightning Conductors. Where practicable, a separation of at least 6 feet (1.83 m) shall be maintained between any coaxial cable and lightning conductors.

820-13. Conductors Inside Buildings. Beyond the point of grounding, as defined in Section 820-7, the cable installation shall comply with (a) through (d) below.

(a) Light or Power. Coaxial cable shall be separated at least 2 inches (50.8 mm) from conductors of any light or power circuits or Class 1 circuits.

Exception No. 1: Where the light or power or Class 1 circuit conductors are in a raceway, or in metal-sheathed, metal-clad, nonmetallic-sheathed, or Type UF cables.

Exception No. 2: Where the conductors are permanently separated from the conductors of the other circuit by a continuous and firmly fixed nonconductor, such as porcelain tubes or flexible tubing, in addition to the insulation on the wire.

(b) In Raceways and Boxes. Coaxial cable shall not be placed in any raceway, compartment, outlet box, junction box, or other enclosures with conductors of light or power circuits or Class 1 circuits.

Exception No. 1: Where the conductors of the different systems are separated by a permanent partition.

Exception No. 2: Conductors in outlet boxes, junction boxes, or similar fittings or compartments where such conductors are introduced solely for power supply to the coaxial cable system distribution equipment or for power connection to remote-control equipment.

(c) In Shafts. Coaxial cable installed in the same shaft with conductors for light or power shall be separated from the light or power conductors by not less than 2 inches (50.8 mm).

Exception No. 1: Where the conductors of either system are encased in noncombustible tubing.

Exception No. 2: Where the light or power conductors are in a raceway, or in metal-sheathed, metal-clad, nonmetallic-sheathed, or Type UF cables.

(d) Vertical Runs.   Coaxial cables bunched together in a vertical run in a shaft shall have a fire-resistant covering capable of preventing the carrying of flame from floor to floor.

Exception: Where cables are encased in noncombustible tubing or are located in a fireproof shaft having fire stops at each floor.

There is no specific separation requirement between Class 2 or Class 3 circuits, wired distribution system cables, and communication cables or conductors, other than the clearance necessary to prevent conflict or abrasion.

820-14. Spread of Fire or Products of Combustion.   Installations in hollow spaces, vertical shafts, and ventilation or air-handling ducts shall be so made that the possible spread of fire or products of combustion will not be substantially increased. Openings around penetrations through fire resistance rated walls, partitions, floors, or ceilings shall be firestopped using approved methods.

820-15. Location.   Circuits and equipment installed in ducts and plenums shall also comply with Section 300-22 as to wiring methods.

Exception: Coaxial cables listed as having adequate fire-resistant and low-smoke producing characteristics shall be permitted for ducts, hollow spaces used as ducts, and plenums other than those described in Section 300-22(a).

D. Underground Circuits

820-18. Entering Buildings.   Underground coaxial cables in a duct, pedestal, handhole, or manhole containing electric light or power conductors shall be in a section permanently separated from such conductors by means of a suitable barrier.

E. Grounding

820-22. Cable Grounding.   Coaxial cable shall be grounded as specified in (a) through (h) below.

(a) Insulation.   The grounding conductor shall have a rubber or other suitable kind of insulation.

(b) Material.   The grounding conductor shall be copper or other corrosion-resistant conductive material, stranded or solid.

(c) Size.   The grounding conductor shall not be smaller than No. 18; it shall have an ampacity approximately equal to that of the outer conductor of the coaxial cable.

(d) Run in Straight Line.   The grounding conductor shall be run to the grounding electrode in as straight a line as practicable.

(e) Physical Protection.   Where necessary, the grounding conductor shall be guarded from physical damage.

(f) Electrode.   The grounding conductor shall be connected as follows:

(1) To the nearest accessible location on the building or structure grounding electrode system as covered in Section 250-81; or

(2) To the metallic power service conduit, service-equipment enclosure, or grounding electrode conductor where the grounded conductor of the power service is connected to the grounding electrode system; or

(3) If the building or structure served has no grounding means as described in (f)(1) or (f)(2), to the grounding electrode, grounding electrode conductor, metallic service conduit or service-equipment enclosure of the power service, where the service is grounded in accordance with Article 250, Part H; or

(4) If the building or structure served has no grounding means as described in (f)(1), (f)(2), or (f)(3), to any one of the individual electrodes described in Section 250-81; or

(5) If the building or structure served has no grounding means as described in (f)(1), (f)(2), (f)(3), or (f)(4), to: (1) an effectively grounded metal structure; or (2) a continuous and extensive underground gas piping system where acceptable to both the serving gas supplier and to the authority having jurisdiction; or (3) to a ground rod or pipe driven into permanently damp earth. Steam or hot water pipes or lightning-rod conductors shall not be employed as electrodes.

(g) Electrode Connection. Connections to grounding electrodes shall comply with Section 250-115. Where a gas pipe electrode is used, connection shall be made between the gas meter and the street main. In every case the connection to the grounding electrode shall be made as close to the earth as practicable.

(h) Bonding of Electrodes. A bonding jumper not smaller than No. 6 copper or equivalent shall be connected between the antenna systems and the power grounding electrodes where the requirements of (f) above result in the use of separate electrodes. Bonding together of all separate grounding electrodes shall be permitted.

See Section 250-86 for use of lightning rods.

820-23. Equipment Grounding. Unpowered equipment and enclosures or equipment powered by the coaxial cable shall be considered grounded where connected to the metallic cable shield.

9

Tables and Examples

Contents

A. Tables

Notes to Tables

1. Tables 3A, 3B and 3C apply only to complete conduit or tubing systems and are not intended to apply to short sections of conduit or tubing used to protect exposed wiring from physical damage.

2. Equipment grounding conductors, when installed, shall be included when calculating conduit or tubing fill. The actual dimensions of the equipment grounding conductor (insulated or bare) shall be used in the calculation.

3. When conduit nipples having a maximum length not to exceed 24 inches (610 mm) are installed between boxes, cabinets, and similar enclosures, the nipple shall be permitted to be filled to 60 percent of its total cross-sectional area, and Note 8 of Tables 310-16 through 310-19 does not apply to this condition.

4. For conductors not included in Chapter 9, such as compact or multiconductor cables, the actual dimensions shall be used.

5. See Table 1 for allowable percentage of conduit or tubing fill.

Table 1 is based on common conditions of proper cabling and alignment of conductors where the length of the pull and the number of bends are within reasonable limits. It should be recognized that for certain conditions a larger size conduit or a lesser conduit fill should be considered.

Tables 3A, 3B, and 3C provide for the maximum allowable number of conductors (new work or rewiring) that may be enclosed in complete systems of conduit or tubing, based on the percentage fill of Table 1, and do not apply to short sections of conduit or tubing used for the physical protection of conductors and cables. Cables are commonly protected from physical damage by conduit or tubing sleeves sized to enable the cable to be passed through with relative ease without injuring or abrading the protective jacket of the cable.

Conduit nipples, not exceeding 24 in. in length, may be filled to 60 percent of their capacity and the derating factors of Note 8 to Tables 310-16 through 310-19 need not be applied.

All conductors occupy space in a raceway, and they must therefore all be counted, including equipment grounding conductors (insulated or bare) and neutral or grounded conductors (insulated or bare). The only exception to this rule is the addition of a bare grounding conductor permitted within short lengths (not more than 72 in.) of ⅜-in. flexible metal conduit (see fine print note to Table 350-3). The dimensions of bare conductors are given in Table 8.

For conductors not included in Chapter 9, such as high-voltage types, the cross-sectional area may be calculated in the following manner, using the actual dimensions of each conductor:

D = outside diameter of a conductor (including insulation)

CM = circular mils

1 in. = 1,000 mils (1 mil = 0.001 in.)

CM = [π(3.1416) ÷ 4] = 0.7854 of a square mil

Diameter in mils squared × 0.7854 = cross-sectional area

Table 1. Percent of Cross Section of Conduit and Tubing for Conductors

(See Table 2 for Fixture Wires)

Number of Conductors	1	2	3	4	Over 4
All conductor types except lead-covered (new or rewiring)	53	31	40	40	40
Lead-covered conductors	55	30	40	38	35

Note 1. See Tables 3A, 3B, and 3C for number of conductors all of the same size in trade sizes of conduit ½ inch through 6 inch.

Note 2. For conductors larger than 750 MCM or for combinations of conductors of different sizes, use Tables 4 through 8, Chapter 9, for dimensions of conductors, conduit and tubing.

Note 3. Where the calculated number of conductors, all of the same size, includes a decimal fraction, the next higher whole number shall be used where this decimal is 0.8 or larger.

Note 4. When bare conductors are permitted by other sections of this Code, the dimensions for bare conductors in Table 8 of Chapter 9 shall be permitted.

Note 5. A multiconductor cable of two or more conductors shall be treated as a single conductor cable for calculating percentage conduit fill area. For cables that have elliptical cross section, the cross-sectional area calculation shall be based on using the major diameter of the ellipse as a circle diameter.

Example: Three 15-kV single conductors are to be installed in conduit. The outside diameter of each conductor measures 1⅝ in. (1⅝ in. = 1.62 in.).

$$1.62 \times 1.62 \times .7854 \times 3 = 6.18 \text{ sq in.}$$

Table 1 allows 40 percent conduit fill for three or more conductors. Table 4 indicates that 40 percent of a 4½-in. conduit is 6.38 sq in., thus accommodating three 15-kV single conductors.

The percentage fills of Table 1 for conduit and tubing are to be used where any conflict occurs in Tables 3A, 3B, or 3C and also when various conductor sizes are to be installed in the same conduit.

An example of computing the conduit size for various conductor sizes follows:

Number	Wire size and type	Table 5 cross-sectional area (ea.)	Subtotal cross-sectional area
4	12 THWN	0.0117	0.0468
3	8 TW	0.0471	0.1413
3	6 THW	0.0819	0.2457
		Total cross-sectional area	0.4338

The 40 percent column (three or more conductors) of Table 4 indicates that 40 percent of a 1¼-in. conduit is 0.60 sq in., the required conduit size for these ten conductors.

An example based on Note 3 (decimal fractions) would be to determine how many No. 12 THWN conductors are permitted in a ¾-in. conduit. Table 1 permits a 40 percent fill (three or more conductors), hence, from Table 4, 40 percent of a ¾-in. conduit is 0.21 sq in., and, from Table 5, the cross-sectional area of a No. 12 THWN conductor is 0.0117 sq in.

$$0.21 \div 0.0117 = 17.9$$

Eighteen such conductors are permitted in a ¾-in. conduit. [Since the decimal (0.9) is more than 0.8, it is increased to the next higher whole number. If the decimal had been less than 0.8, the decimal would have been dropped.]

Table 2. Maximum Number of Fixture Wires in Trade Sizes of Conduit or Tubing

(40 Percent Fill Based on Individual Diameters)

Conduit Trade Size (Inches) → Wire Types ↓	½					¾					1					1¼					1½					2				
	18	16	14	12	10	18	16	14	12	10	18	16	14	12	10	18	16	14	12	10	18	16	14	12	10	18	16	14	12	10
PTF, PTFF, PGFF, PGF, PFF, PF, PAF, PAFF, ZF, ZFF	23	18	14			40	31	24			65	50	39			115	90	70			157	122	95			257	200	156		
TFFN, TFN	19	15				34	26				55	43				97	76				132	104				216	169			
SF-1	16					29					47					83					114					186				
SFF-1, FFH-1	15					26					43					76					104					169				
CF	13	10	8	4	3	23	18	14	7	6	38	30	23	12	9	66	53	40	21	16	91	72	55	29	22	149	118	90	48	37
TF	11	10				20	18				32	30				57	53				79	72				129	118			
RFH-1	11					20					32					57					79					129				
TFF	11	10				20	17				32	27				56	49				77	66				126	109			
AF	11	9	7	4	3	19	16	12	7	5	31	26	20	11	8	55	46	36	19	15	75	63	49	27	20	123	104	81	44	34
SFF-2	9	7	6			16	12	10			27	20	17			47	36	30			65	49	42			106	81	68		
SF-2	9	8	6			16	14	11			27	23	18			47	40	32			65	55	43			106	90	71		
FFH-2	9	7				15	12				25	19				44	34				60	46				99	75			
RFH-2	7	5				12	10				20	16				36	28				49	38				80	62			
KF-1, KFF-1, KF-2, KFF-2	36	32	22	14	9	64	55	39	25	17	103	89	63	41	28	182	158	111	73	49	248	216	152	100	67	406	353	248	163	110

Table 3A.   Maximum Number of Conductors in Trade Sizes of Conduit or Tubing

(Based on Table 1, Chapter 9)

Type Letters	Conductor Size AWG, MCM	½	¾	1	1¼	1½	2	2½	3	3½	4	4½	5	6
TW, T, RUH, RUW, XHHW (14 thru 8)	14	9	15	25	44	60	99	142	171	176				
	12	7	12	19	35	47	78	111	131					
	10	5	9	15	26	36	60	85						
	8	2	4	7	12	17	28	40	62	84	108			
RHW and RHH (without outer covering), THW	14	6	10	16	29	40	65	93	143	192				
	12	4	8	13	24	32	53	76	117	157				
	10	4	6	11	19	26	43	61	95	127	163			
	8	1	3	5	10	13	22	32	49	66	85	106	133	
TW, T, THW, RUH (6 thru 2), RUW (6 thru 2)	6	1	2	4	7	10	16	23	36	48	62	78	97	141
	4	1	1	3	5	7	12	17	27	36	47	58	73	106
	3	1	1	2	4	6	10	15	23	31	40	50	63	91
	2		1	2	4	5	9	13	20	27	34	43	54	78
	1		1	1	3	4	6	9	14	19	25	31	39	57
FEPB (6 thru 2), RHW and RHH (without outer covering)	0		1	1	2	3	5	8	12	16	21	27	33	49
	00		1	1	1	3	5	7	10	14	18	23	29	41
	000		1	1	1	2	4	6	9	12	15	19	24	35
	0000			1	1	1	3	5	7	10	13	16	20	29
	250			1	1	1	2	4	6	8	10	13	16	23
	300				1	1	2	3	5	7	9	11	14	20
	350				1	1	1	3	4	6	8	10	12	18
	400				1	1	1	2	4	5	7	9	11	16
	500					1	1	1	3	4	6	7	9	14
	600					1	1	1	3	4	5	6	7	11
	700					1	1	1	2	3	4	5	7	10
	750					1	1	1	2	3	4	5	6	9

Table 3B.   Maximum Number of Conductors in Trade Sizes of Conduit or Tubing

(Based on Table 1, Chapter 9)

Type Letters	Conductor Size AWG, MCM	½	¾	1	1¼	1½	2	2½	3	3½	4	4½	5	6
THWN,	14	13	24	39	69	94	154	164						
	12	10	18	29	51	70	114	104	160					
	10	6	11	18	32	44	73	51	79	106				
	8	3	5	9	16	22	36				136			
THHN,	6	1	4	6	11	15	26	37	57	76	98	125	154	
FEP (14 thru 2),	4	1	2	4	7	9	16	22	35	47	60	75	94	137
FEPB (14 thru 8),	3	1	1	3	6	8	13	19	29	39	51	64	80	116
PFA (14 thru 4/0),	2	1	1	3	5	7	11	16	25	33	43	54	67	97
PFAH (14 thru 4/0),	1		1	1	3	5	8	12	18	25	32	40	50	72
Z (14 thru 4/0)	0		1	1	3	4	7	10	15	21	27	33	42	61
XHHW (4 thru 500MCM)	00		1	1	2	3	6	8	13	17	22	28	35	51
	000		1	1	1	3	5	7	11	14	18	23	29	42
	0000			1	1	2	4	6	9	12	15	19	24	35
	250			1	1	1	3	4	7	10	12	16	20	28
	300			1	1	1	3	4	6	8	11	13	17	24
	350			1	1	1	2	3	5	7	9	12	15	21
	400					1	1	3	5	6	8	10	13	19
	500				1	1	1	2	4	5	7	9	11	16
	600				1	1	1	1	3	4	5	7	9	13
	700					1	1	1	3	4	5	6	8	11
	750					1	1	1	2	3	4	6	7	11
XHHW	6	1	3	5	9	13	21	30	47	63	81	102	128	185
	600				1	1	1	1	3	4	5	7	9	13
	700					1	1	1	3	4	5	6	7	11
	750					1	1	1	2	3	4	6	7	10

Table 3C.   Maximum Number of Conductors in Trade Sizes of Conduit or Tubing

(Based on Table 1, Chapter 9)

Type Letters	Conductor Size AWG, MCM	½	¾	1	1¼	1½	2	2½	3	3½	4	4½	5	6
RHW,	14	3	6	10	18	25	41	58	90	121	155			
	12	3	5	9	15	21	35	50	77	103	132			
	10	2	4	7	13	18	29	41	64	86	110	138		
	8	1	2	4	7	9	16	22	35	47	60	75	94	137
RHH	6	1	1	2	5	6	11	15	24	32	41	51	64	93
	4	1	1	1	3	5	8	12	18	24	31	39	50	72
(with	3	1	1	1	3	4	7	10	16	22	28	35	44	63
outer	2		1	1	3	4	6	9	14	19	24	31	38	56
covering)	1		1	1	1	3	5	7	11	14	18	23	29	42
	0		1	1	1	2	4	6	9	12	16	20	25	37
	00			1	1	1	3	5	8	11	14	18	22	32
	000			1	1	1	3	4	7	9	12	15	19	28
	0000			1	1	1	2	4	6	8	10	13	16	24
	250				1	1	1	3	5	6	8	11	13	19
	300				1	1	1	3	4	5	7	9	11	17
	350				1	1	1	2	4	5	6	8	10	15
	400				1	1	1	1	3	4	6	7	9	14
	500				1	1	1	1	3	4	5	6	8	11
	600					1	1	1	2	3	4	5	6	9
	700						1	1	1	3	3	4	6	8
	750						1	1	1	3	3	4	5	8

Tables 4 through 8, Chapter 9.   Tables 4 through 8 give the nominal size of conductors and conduit or tubing for use in computing size of conduit or tubing for various combinations of conductors. The dimensions represent average conditions only, and variations will be found in dimensions of conductors and conduits of different manufacture.

Table 4.   Dimensions and Percent Area of Conduit and of Tubing

Areas of Conduit or Tubing for the Combinations of Wires Permitted in Table 1, Chapter 9.

Trade Size	Internal Diameter Inches	Total 100%	Not Lead Covered			1 Cond. 55%	Lead Covered			
			2 Cond. 31%	Over 2 Cond. 40%	1 Cond. 53%		2 Cond. 30%	3 Cond. 40%	4 Cond. 38%	Over 4 Cond. 35%
½	.622	.30	.09	.12	.16	.17	.09	.12	.11	.11
¾	.824	.53	.16	.21	.28	.29	.16	.21	.20	.19
1	1.049	.86	.27	.34	.46	.47	.26	.34	.33	.30
1¼	1.380	1.50	.47	.60	.80	.83	.45	.60	.57	.53
1½	1.610	2.04	.63	.82	1.08	1.12	.61	.82	.78	.71
2	2.067	3.36	1.04	1.34	1.78	1.85	1.01	1.34	1.28	1.18
2½	2.469	4.79	1.48	1.92	2.54	2.63	1.44	1.92	1.82	1.68
3	3.068	7.38	2.29	2.95	3.91	4.06	2.21	2.95	2.80	2.58
3½	3.548	9.90	3.07	3.96	5.25	5.44	2.97	3.96	3.76	3.47
4	4.026	12.72	3.94	5.09	6.74	7.00	3.82	5.09	4.83	4.45
4½	4.506	15.94	4.94	6.38	8.45	8.77	4.78	6.38	6.06	5.56
5	5.047	20.00	6.20	8.00	10.60	11.00	6.00	8.00	7.60	7.00
6	6.065	28.89	8.96	11.56	15.31	15.89	8.67	11.56	10.98	10.11

Area — Square Inches

Table 5. Dimensions of Rubber-Covered and Thermoplastic-Covered Conductors

Size AWG MCM	Types RFH-2, RH, RHH,*** RHW,*** SF-2		Types TF, T, THW,† TW, RUH,** RUW**		Types TFN, THHN, THWN		Types**** FEP, FEPB, FEPW, TFE, PF, PFA, PFAH, PGF, PTF, Z, ZF, ZFF		Type XHHW, ZW††		Types KF-1, KF-2, KFF-1, KFF-2	
	Approx. Diam. Inches	Approx. Area Sq. In.	Approx. Diam. Inches	Approx. Area Sq. In.	Approx. Diam. Inches	Approx. Area Sq. In.	Approx. Diam. Inches	Approx. Area Sq. Inches	Approx. Diam. Inches	Approx. Area Sq. In.	Approx. Diam. Sq. In.	Approx. Area Sq. In.
Col. 1	Col. 2	Col. 3	Col. 4	Col. 5	Col. 6	Col. 7	Col. 8	Col. 9	Col. 10	Col. 11	Col. 12	Col. 13
18	.146	.0167	.106	.0088	.089	.0064	.081	.0052	....	....	.065	.0033
16	.158	.0196	.118	.0109	.100	.0079	.092	.0066	....	....	.070	.0038
14	30 mils .171	.0230	.131	.0135	.105	.0087	.105 .105	.0087 .0087	....	....	.083	.0054
14	45 mils .204*	.0327*	.162†	.0206†	....	....	....	....	.129	.0131	....	....
12	30 mils .188	.0278	.148	.0172	.122	.0117	.121 .121	.0115 .0115	....	....	.102	.0082
12	45 mils .221*	.0384*	.179†	.0251†	....	....	....	....	.146	.0167	....	....
10	.242	.0460	.168	.0224	.153	.0184	.142 .142	.0159 .0159	.166	.0216	.124	.0121
10	....	....	.199†	.0311†	....	....	....	....	....	....	....	....
8	.328	.0854	.245	.0471	.218	.0373	.206 .186	.0333 .0272	.241	.0456	....	....
8	....	....	.276†	.0598†	....	....	....	....	....	....	....	....
6	.397	.1238	.323	.0819	.257	.0519	.244 .302	.0467 .0716	.282	.0625	....	....
4	.452	.1605	.372	.1087	.328	.0845	.292 .350	.0669 .0962	.328	.0845	....	....
3	.481	.1817	.401	.1263	.356	.0995	.320 .378	.0803 .1122	.356	.0995	....	....
2	.513	.2067	.433	.1473	.388	.1182	.352 .410	.0973 .1316	.388	.1182	....	....
1	.588	.2715	.508	.2027	.450	.1590	.420	.1385	.450	.1590	....	....
0	.629	.3107	.549	.2367	.491	.1893	.462	.1676	.491	.1893	....	....
00	.675	.3578	.595	.2781	.537	.2265	.498	.1974	.537	.2265	....	....
000	.727	.4151	.647	.3288	.588	.2715	.560	.2463	.588	.2715	....	....
0000	.785	.4840	.705	.3904	.646	.3278	.618	.2999	.646	.3278	....	....

Table 5 (Continued)

Size AWG MCM	Types RFH-2, RH, RHH,*** RHW,*** SF-2		Types TF, T, THW,† TW, RUH,** RUW**		Types TFN, THHN, THWN		Types**** FEP, FEPB, FEPW, TFE, PF, PFA, PFAH, PGF, PTF, Z, ZF, ZFF		Type XHHW, ZW††	
	Approx. Diam. Inches	Approx. Area Sq. In.	Approx. Diam. Inches	Approx. Area Sq. In.	Approx. Diam. Inches	Approx. Area Sq. In.	Approx. Diam. Inches	Approx. Area Sq. Inches	Approx. Diam. Inches	Approx. Area Sq. In.
Col. 1	Col. 2	Col. 3	Col. 4	Col. 5	Col. 6	Col. 7	Col. 8	Col. 9	Col. 10	Col. 11
250	.868	.5917	.788	.4877	.716	.4026	. . . .	. . . .	.716	.4026
300	.933	.6837	.843	.5581	.771	.4669	. . . .	. . . .	.771	.4669
350	.985	.7620	.895	.6291	.822	.5307	. . . .	. . . .	.822	.5307
400	1.032	.8365	.942	.6969	.869	.5931	. . . .	. . . .	.869	.5931
500	1.119	.9834	1.029	.8316	.955	.7163	. . . .	. . . .	.955	.7163
600	1.233	1.1940	1.143	1.0261	1.058	.8792	. . . .	. . . .	1.073	.9043
700	1.304	1.3355	1.214	1.1575	1.129	1.0011	. . . .	. . . .	1.145	1.0297
750	1.339	1.4082	1.249	1.2252	1.163	1.0623	. . . .	. . . .	1.180	1.0936
800	1.372	1.4784	1.282	1.2908	1.196	1.1234	. . . .	. . . .	1.210	1.1499
900	1.435	1.6173	1.345	1.4208	1.259	1.2449	. . . .	. . . .	1.270	1.2668
1000	1.494	1.7531	1.404	1.5482	1.317	1.3623	. . . .	. . . .	1.330	1.3893
1250	1.676	2.2062	1.577	1.9532	. . . .	. . . .	. . . .	. . . .	1.500	1.7672
1500	1.801	2.5475	1.702	2.2748	. . . .	. . . .	. . . .	. . . .	1.620	2.0612
1750	1.916	2.8895	1.817	2.5930	. . . .	. . . .	. . . .	. . . .	1.740	2.3779
2000	2.021	3.2079	1.922	2.9013	. . . .	. . . .	. . . .	. . . .	1.840	2.6590

* The dimensions of Types RHH and RHW.
** No. 14 to No. 2.
† Dimensions of THW in sizes No. 14 to No. 8. No. 6 THW and larger is the same dimension as T.
*** Dimensions of RHH and RHW without outer covering are the same as THW No. 18 to No. 10, solid; No. 8 and larger, stranded.
**** In Columns 8 and 9 the values shown for sizes No. 1 thru 0000 are for TFE and Z only. The right-hand values in Columns 8 and 9 are for FEPB, Z, ZF, and ZFF only.
†† No. 14 to No. 2.

Table 6. Dimensions of Lead-Covered Conductors

Types RL, RHL, and RUL

Size AWG-MCM	Single Conductor		Two Conductor		Three Conductor	
	Diam. Inches	Area Sq. In.	Diam. Inches	Area Sq. In.	Diam. Inches	Area Sq. In.
14	.28	.062	.28 × .47	.115	.59	.273
12	.29	.066	.31 × .54	.146	.62	.301
10	.35	.096	.35 × .59	.180	.68	.363
8 sol.	.41	.132	.41 × .71	.255	.82	.528
8 str.	.43	.145	.43 × .75	.282	.86	.581
6	.49	.188	.49 × .86	.369	.97	.738
4	.55	.237	.54 × .96	.457	1.08	.916
2	.60	.283	.61 × 1.08	.578	1.21	1.146
1	.67	.352	.70 × 1.23	.756	1.38	1.49
0	.71	.396	.74 × 1.32	.859	1.47	1.70
00	.76	.454	.79 × 1.41	.980	1.57	1.94
000	.81	.515	.84 × 1.52	1.123	1.69	2.24
0000	.87	.593	.90 × 1.64	1.302	1.85	2.68
250	.98	.754	....	.....	2.02	3.20
300	1.04	.85	....	.....	2.15	3.62
350	1.10	.95	....	.....	2.26	4.02
400	1.14	1.02	....	.....	2.40	4.52
500	1.23	1.18	....	.....	2.59	5.28

The above cables are limited to straight runs or with nominal offsets equivalent to not more than two quarter bends.

Note — No. 14 to No. 10, solid conductors; No. 8, solid or stranded conductors; No. 6 and larger, stranded conductors.

Table 7.   Dimensions of Asbestos-Varnished-Cambric
Insulated Conductors

Types AVA, AVB, and AVL

Size AWG, MCM	Type AVA		Type AVB		Type AVL	
	Approx. Diam. Inches	Approx. Area Sq. In.	Approx. Diam. Inches	Approx. Area Sq. In.	Approx. Diam. Inches	Approx. Area Sq. In.
14	.245	.047	.205	.033	.320	.080
12	.265	.055	.225	.040	.340	.091
10	.285	.064	.245	.047	.360	.102
8 sol.	.310	.075	.270	.057	.390	.119
8 str.	.325	.083	.285	.064	.390	.119
6	.395	.122	.345	.094	.430	.145
4	.445	.155	.395	.123	.480	.181
2	.505	.200	.460	.166	.570	.255
1	.585	.268	.540	.229	.620	.300
0	.625	.307	.580	.264	.660	.341
00	.670	.353	.625	.307	.705	.390
000	.720	.406	.675	.358	.755	.447
0000	.780	.478	.735	.425	.815	.521
250	.885	.616	.855	.572	.955	.715
300	.940	.692	.910	.649	1.010	.800
350	.995	.778	.965	.731	1.060	.885
400	1.040	.850	1.010	.800	1.105	.960
500	1.125	.995	1.095	.945	1.190	1.118
550	1.165	1.065	1.135	1.01	1.265	1.26
600	1.205	1.140	1.175	1.09	1.305	1.34
650	1.240	1.21	1.210	1.15	1.340	1.41
700	1.275	1.28	1.245	1.22	1.375	1.49
750	1.310	1.35	1.280	1.29	1.410	1.57
800	1.345	1.42	1.315	1.36	1.440	1.63
850	1.375	1.49	1.345	1.43	1.470	1.70
900	1.405	1.55	1.375	1.49	1.505	1.78
950	1.435	1.62	1.405	1.55	1.535	1.85
1000	1.465	1.69	1.435	1.62	1.565	1.93

Note: No. 14 to No. 10, solid; No. 8, solid or stranded; No. 6 and larger, stranded; except AVL where all sizes are stranded.

Varnished-Cambric Insulated Conductors
Type V

The insulation thickness for varnished-cambric conductors, Type V, is the same as for rubber-covered conductors, Type RHH, except for No. 8 which has 45-mil insulation for varnished-cambric, and 60-mil insulation for rubber-covered conductors. See Table 310-13. Therefore, Table 3C shall be permitted to be used for the number of varnished-cambric insulated conductors in a conduit or tubing.

Table 8.   **Properties of Conductors**

Size AWG, MCM	Area Cir. Mils	Concentric Lay Stranded Conductors		Bare Conductors		DC Resistance Ohms/M Ft. At 25°C, 77°F.		
		No. Wires	Diam. Each Wire Inches	Diam. Inches	*Area Sq. Inches	Copper		Alumi-num
						Bare Cond.	Tin'd. Cond.	
18	1620	Solid	.0403	.0403	.0013	6.51	6.79	10.7
16	2580	Solid	.0508	.0508	.0020	4.10	4.26	6.72
14	4110	Solid	.0641	.0641	.0032	2.57	2.68	4.22
12	6530	Solid	.0808	.0808	.0051	1.62	1.68	2.66
10	10380	Solid	.1019	.1019	.0081	1.018	1.06	1.67
8	16510	Solid	.1285	.1285	.0130	.6404	.659	1.05
8	16510	7	.0486	.1458	.0167	.653	.679	1.07
6	26240	7	.0612	.184	.027	.410	.427	.674
4	41740	7	.0772	.232	.042	.259	.269	.424
3	52620	7	.0867	.260	.053	.205	.213	.336
2	66360	7	.0974	.292	.067	.162	.169	.266
1	83690	19	.0664	.332	.087	.129	.134	.211
0	105600	19	.0745	.372	.109	.102	.106	.168
00	133100	19	.0837	.418	.137	.0811	.0843	.133
000	167800	19	.0940	.470	.173	.0642	.0668	.105
0000	211600	19	.1055	.528	.219	.0509	.0525	.0836
250	250000	37	.0822	.575	.260	.0431	.0449	.0708
300	300000	37	.0900	.630	.312	.0360	.0374	.0590
350	350000	37	.0973	.681	.364	.0308	.0320	.0505
400	400000	37	.1040	.728	.416	.0270	.0278	.0442
500	500000	37	.1162	.813	.519	.0216	.0222	.0354
600	600000	61	.0992	.893	.626	.0180	.0187	.0295
700	700000	61	.1071	.964	.730	.0154	.0159	.0253
750	750000	61	.1109	.998	.782	.0144	.0148	.0236
800	800000	61	.1145	1.030	.833	.0135	.0139	.0221
900	900000	61	.1215	1.090	.933	.0120	.0123	.0197
1000	1000000	61	.1280	1.150	1.039	.0108	.0111	.0177
1250	1250000	91	.1172	1.289	1.305	.00863	.00888	.0142
1500	1500000	91	.1284	1.410	1.561	.00719	.00740	.0118
1750	1750000	127	.1174	1.526	1.829	.00616	.00634	.0101
2000	2000000	127	.1255	1.630	2.087	.00539	.00555	.00885

* Area given is that of a circle having a diameter equal to the overall diameter of a stranded conductor.

The values given in the table are those given in Handbook 100 of the National Bureau of Standards except that those shown in the 8th column are those given in Specification B33 of the American Society for Testing and Materials, and those shown in the 9th column are those given in Standard No. S-19-81 of the Insulated Power Cable Engineers Association and Standard No. WC3-1969 of the National Electrical Manufacturers Association.

The resistance values given in the last three columns are applicable only to direct current. When conductors larger than No. 4/0 are used with alternating current, the multiplying factors in Table 9 compensate for skin effect.

Table 9.   Multiplying Factors for Converting DC
Resistance to 60 Hertz AC Resistance

| Size | Multiplying Factor | | | |
| | For Nonmetallic-Sheathed Cables in Air or Nonmetallic Conduit | | For Metallic-Sheathed Cables or all Cables in Metallic Raceways | |
	Copper	Aluminum	Copper	Aluminum
Up to 3 AWG	1.	1.	1.	1.
2	1.	1.	1.01	1.00
1	1.	1.	1.01	1.00
0	1.001	1.000	1.02	1.00
00	1.001	1.001	1.03	1.00
000	1.002	1.001	1.04	1.01
0000	1.004	1.002	1.05	1.01
250 MCM	1.005	1.002	1.06	1.02
300 MCM	1.006	1.003	1.07	1.02
350 MCM	1.009	1.004	1.08	1.03
400 MCM	1.011	1.005	1.10	1.04
500 MCM	1.018	1.007	1.13	1.06
600 MCM	1.025	1.010	1.16	1.08
700 MCM	1.034	1.013	1.19	1.11
750 MCM	1.039	1.015	1.21	1.12
800 MCM	1.044	1.017	1.22	1.14
1000 MCM	1.067	1.026	1.30	1.19
1250 MCM	1.102	1.040	1.41	1.27
1500 MCM	1.142	1.058	1.53	1.36
1750 MCM	1.185	1.079	1.67	1.46
2000 MCM	1.233	1.100	1.82	1.56

B. Examples

Selection of Conductors. In the following examples, the results are generally expressed in amperes. To select conductor sizes, refer to Tables 310-16 through 310-19 and the Notes that pertain to such tables.

Voltage. For uniform application of the provisions of Articles 210, 215 and 220, a voltage of 115 and 230 volts shall be used in computing the ampere load on the conductor.

Fractions of an Ampere. Except where the computations result in a major fraction of an ampere (larger than 0.5), such fractions may be dropped.

Ranges. For the computation of the range loads in these examples, Column A of Table 220-19 has been used. For optional methods, see Columns B and C of Table 220-19.

SI Units: For SI units: one square foot = 0.093 square meter; one foot = 0.3048 meter.

In the following examples loads are assumed to be properly balanced on the system. Where loads are not properly balanced, additional feeder capacity may be required.

Example No. 1.   Single-Family Dwelling

Dwelling has a floor area of 1500 square feet exclusive of unoccupied cellar, unfinished attic, and open porches. It has a 12-kW range.

Computed Load [see Section 220-10(a)]:
General Lighting Load:
1500 sq. ft. at 3 watts per sq. ft. = 4500 watts.

Minimum Number of Branch Circuits Required (see Section 220-3):
General Lighting Load:
4500 ÷ 115 = 39.1 amperes: or three 15-ampere 2-wire circuits; or two 20-ampere 2-wire circuits
Small Appliance Load: Two 2-wire 20-ampere circuits [Section 220-3(b)]
Laundry Load: One 2-wire 20-ampere circuit [Section 220-3(c)]

Minimum Size Feeders Required [see Section 220-10(a)]:
Computed Load

General Lighting	4500 watts
Small Appl. Load	3000 watts
Laundry	1500 watts
Total (without range)	9000 watts
3000 watts at 100%	3000 watts
9000 − 3000 = 6000 watts at 35% =	2100 watts
Net computed load (without range)	5100 watts
Range Load (see Table 220-19).............................	8000 watts
Net computed load (with range)	13,100 watts

For 115/230-volt 3-wire system feeders, 13,100 W ÷ 230 V = 57 amperes

Net computed load exceeds 10 kW, so service conductors shall be 100 amperes [see Section 230-41(b)(2)].

Reduced size neutral shall be permitted, usually two trade sizes smaller than the ungrounded conductors.

Feeder and Service Neutral

Lighting and small appliance load	5100 watts
Range load 8000 watts at 70%	5600 watts
Total..	10,700 watts

10,700 W ÷ 230 V = 46.5 = 46 amperes

(Example 1 Continued Next Page.)

Example No. 1 (Continued)

The general lighting and general-use receptacle load is computed from the outside dimensions of the building, apartment, or other area involved. For dwelling unit(s), the computed floor area is not to include open porches, garages, or unused or unfinished spaces unadaptable for future use. See Section 220-2(b).

Example: A two-story dwelling measures 30 ft × 30 ft for the first floor and 30 ft × 20 ft for the second floor.

$$30 \text{ ft} \times 30 \text{ ft} = \ \ 900 \text{ sq ft (first floor)}$$
$$30 \text{ ft} \times 20 \text{ ft} = \ \underline{600} \text{ sq ft (second floor)}$$
$$\text{Total area} = 1,500 \text{ sq ft}$$

The air-conditioning load in Example No. 1(c) is counted at 100 percent, and this load is calculated separately in order to comply with the requirements of Section 220-30(5) and Table 220-30.

Example No. 1(a).   Single-Family Dwelling

Same conditions as Example No. 1, plus addition of one 6-ampere 230-volt room air-conditioning unit and three 12-ampere 115-volt room air-conditioning units.* See Article 440, Part G.

From Example No. 1, feeder current is 57 amperes (3 wire, 230 volt)

Line A	Neutral	Line B	
57	46	57	amperes from Example No. 1
6	—	6	one 230-volt air cond. motor
12	12	12	two 115-volt air cond. motors
—	12	12	one 115-volt air cond. motor
3	3	3	25% of largest motor (Section 430-24)
78	73	90	amperes per line

* For feeder neutral, use load of one air cond. motor for unbalanced condition.

Example No. 1(b).   Single-Family Dwelling
Optional Calculation for Single-Family Dwelling

(See Section 220-30.)

Dwelling has a floor area of 1500 square feet exclusive of unoccupied cellar, unfinished attic, and open porches. It has a 12-kW range, a 2.5-kW water heater, a 1.2-kW dishwasher, 9 kW of electric space heating installed in five rooms, a 5-kW clothes dryer, and a 6-ampere 230-volt room air-conditioning unit.

Air conditioner kW is 6 × 230 ÷ 1000 = 1.38 kW

1.38 kW is less than the connected load of 9 kW of space heating; therefore, the air conditioner load need not be included in the service calculation (see Section 220-21).

1500 sq. ft. at 3 watts	4.5 kW
Two 20-amp. appliance outlet circuits at 1500 watts each	3.0 kW
Laundry circuit	1.5 kW
Range (at nameplate rating)	12.0 kW
Water heater	2.5 kW
Dishwasher	1.2 kW
Space heating	9.0 kW
Clothes dryer	5.0 kW
	38.7 kW

First 10 kW at 100% = 10.00 kW
Remainder at 40% (28.7 kW × .4) = 11.48 kW

Calculated load for service size 21.48 kW = 21,480 watts
21,480 W ÷ 230 V = 93 amperes

Therefore, this dwelling may be served by a 100-ampere service.

(Example 1(b) Continued Next Page.)

Example No. 1(b) (Continued)

Feeder Neutral Load, per Section 220-22:

1500 sq. ft. @ 3 watts	4500 watts
Three 20-amp. circuits @ 1500 watts	4500 watts
Total	9000 watts
3000 watts @ 100%	3000 watts
9000 W—3000 W = 6000 watts @ 35%	2100 watts
	5100 watts
Range—8 kW @ 70%	5600 watts
Dishwasher	1200 watts
Total	11,900 watts

11,900 W ÷ 230 V = 51.7 = 52 amp.

Example No. 1(c). Single-Family Dwelling
Optional Calculation for Single-Family Dwelling

(See Section 220-30.)

Dwelling has a floor area of 1500 square feet exclusive of unoccupied cellar, unfinished attic, and open porches. It has two 20-ampere small appliance circuits, one 20-ampere laundry circuit, two 4-kW wall-mounted ovens, one 5.1-kW counter-mounted cooking unit, a 4.5-kW water heater, a 1.2-kW dishwasher, a 5-kW combination clothes washer and dryer, six 7-ampere 230-volt room air-conditioning units, and a 1.5-kW permanently installed bathroom space heater.

Air Conditioning kW Calculation:

Total amperes 6 × 7 = 42.00 amperes

42 × 230 ÷ 1000 = 9.7 kW of air-conditioned load

Load Included at 100%:

Air conditioning	9.7 kW
Space heater (omit, see Section 220-21)	

Other Load:

	kW
1500 sq. ft. at 3 watts	4.5
Two 20-amp. small appliance circuits at 1500 watts	3.0
Laundry circuit	1.5
2 ovens	8.0
1 cooking unit	5.1
Water heater	4.5
Dishwasher	1.2
Washer/dryer	5.0
Total other load	32.8
1st 10 kW at 100%	10.0 kW
Remainder at 40% (22.8 kW × .4)	9.12 kW
Total calculated load	28.82 kW = 28,820 watts

28,820 W ÷ 230 V = 125 amperes (service rating)

Feeder Neutral Load, per Section 220-22:

(It is assumed that the 2-4 kW wall-mounted ovens are supplied by one branch circuit, the 5.1 kW counter-mounted cooking unit by a separate circuit.)

1500 sq. ft. @ 3 watts	4500 watts
Three 20-amp. circuits @ 1500 watts	4500 watts
Total	9000 watts
3000 watts @ 100%	3000 watts
9000 W—3000 W = 6000 watts @ 35%	2100 watts
	5100 watts

(Example 1(c) Continued Next Page.)

Example No. 1(c) (Continued)

Two 4-kW ovens = 8000 watts @ 65% =	
5200 watts @ 70% (for neutral load)	3640 watts
One 5.1-kW cooking unit @ 80% =	
4080 watts @ 70% (for neutral load)	2856 watts
(See Table 220-19, Note 3)	
Dishwasher	1200 watts
Total	12,796 watts

12,796 W ÷ 230 V = 55.6 = 56 amperes

Example No. 2.   Small Roadside Fruitstand with No Show Windows

A small roadside fruitstand with no show windows has a floor area of 150 square feet. The electrical load consists of general lighting and a 1000-watt flood light. There are no other outlets.

Computed Load [Section 220-10(a)]:
    * General Lighting
        150 sq. ft. at 3 watts/sq. ft. × 1.25 = 562 watts
        (3 watts/sq. ft. for stores)
        562 watts ÷ 115 = 4.88 amperes
            One 15-ampere 2-wire branch circuit required (Section 220-3)

Minimum Size Service Conductor Required [Section 230-41(b), Exception No. 1]:

Computed load	562 watts
Floodlight load (1000 watts × 1.25)	1250 watts
Total load	1812 watts

1812 W ÷ 115 V = 15.76 amperes
Use No. 8 service conductor [Section 230-41(b), Exception No. 1]
Use a 30-ampere service switch or breaker [Section 230-79(b)]

Example No. 3.   Store Building

A store 50 feet by 60 feet, or 3000 square feet, has 30 feet of show window. There are a total of 80 duplex receptacles.

Computed Load [Section 220-10(b)]:

* General lighting load:	
3000 sq. ft. at 3 watts per sq. ft. × 1.25	11,250 watts
** Show window lighting load:	
30 feet at 200 watts per foot	6000 watts
Receptacles (Section 220-13)	
80 receptacles at 180 VA = 14,400 VA	
10,000 @ 100% (Table 220-13)	= 10,000 watts
14,400—10,000 = 4,400 @ 50%	= 2,200 watts
Outside sign circuit [600-6(c)]	
1,200 volt-amperes	= 1,200 watts
	Total = 30,650 watts

Minimum Number of Branch Circuits Required (Section 220-3):
    *** General lighting load: 11,250 W ÷ 230 V = 49 amperes for 3-wire, 115/230 volts; or 98 amperes for 2-wire, 115 volts:
        Three 30-ampere, 2-wire and one 15-ampere, 2-wire circuits; or
        Five 20-ampere, 2-wire circuits; or
        Three 20-ampere, 2-wire and three 15-ampere, 2-wire circuits; or
        Seven 15-ampere, 2-wire circuits; or
        Three 15-ampere, 3-wire and one 15-ampere, 2-wire circuits.

(Example 3 Continued Next Page.)

Example No. 3 (Continued)

Special lighting load (show window): [Sections 220-2(c), Exception No. 3 and 220-12]: 6000 W ÷ 230 V = 26 amperes for 3-wire, 115/230 volts; or 52 amperes for 2-wire, 115 volts:
Four 15-ampere, 2-wire circuits; or
Three 20-ampere, 2-wire circuits; or
Two 15-ampere, 3-wire circuits.

Receptacle load: 14,400 watts ÷ 115 volts = 125 amperes for 2-wire, 115 volts:
125 amperes ÷ (15 × .8) = Eleven 15-ampere, 2-wire circuits; or
125 amperes ÷ (20 × .8) = Eight 20-ampere, 2-wire circuits.

Minimum Size Feeders (or Service Conductors) Required (Section 215-2):

For 115/230-volt, 3-wire system:
30,650 watts ÷ 230 volts = 133 amperes (Section 220-2)
For 115-volt, 2-wire system:
30,650 watts ÷ 115 volts = 267 amperes (Section 220-2)

* The above examples assume that the entire general lighting is a continuous load and the load is therefore increased by 25 percent in accordance with Section 220-10(b). The 25 percent increase is not applicable to any portion of the load that is not continuous.

** If show window load is computed as per Section 220-2, the unit load per outlet shall be increased 25 percent.

*** The load on each general lighting branch circuit shall not exceed 80 percent of the branch-circuit rating [Sections 210-22(c) and 220-2(a)].

Example No. 4. Multifamily Dwelling

Multifamily dwelling having a total floor area of 32,000 square feet with 40 dwelling units.

Meters in two banks of 20 each and individual subfeeders to each dwelling unit.

One-half of the dwelling units are equipped with electric ranges of not exceeding 12 kW each.

Area of each dwelling unit is 800 square feet.

Laundry facilities on premises available to all tenants. Add no circuit to individual dwelling unit. Add 1500 watts for each laundry circuit to house load and add to the example as a "house load."

Computed Load for Each Dwelling Unit (Article 220):

General lighting load:	
800 sq. ft. at 3 watts per sq. ft.	2400 watts
Special appliance load:	
Electric range	8000 watts

Minimum Number of Branch Circuits Required for Each Dwelling Unit (Section 220-3):

General lighting load: 2400 ÷ 115 = 21 amperes or two 15-ampere, 2-wire circuits; or two 20-ampere, 2-wire circuits.

Small appliance load: Two 2-wire circuits of No. 12 wire. [See Section 220-3(b).]

Range circuit: 8,000 ÷ 230 = 35 amperes or a circuit of two No. 8's and one No. 10 as permitted by Section 210-19(b).

Minimum Size Subfeeder Required for Each Dwelling Unit (Section 215-2):

Computed load (Article 220):	
General lighting load	2400 watts
Small appliance load, two 20-ampere circuits....................................	3000 watts
Total computed load (without ranges)	5400 watts
Application of Demand Factor:	
3000 watts at 100%	3000 watts
2400 watts at 35%	840 watts
Net computed load (without ranges)	3840 watts
Range load	8000 watts
Net computed load (with ranges)	11,840 watts

(Example 4 Continued Next Page.)

Example No. 4 (Continued)

For 115/230-volt, 3-wire system (without ranges):
    Net computed load, 3840 ÷ 230 = 16.7 amperes.
    Size of each subfeeder (see Section 215-2).
For 115/230-volt, 3-wire system (with ranges):
    Net computed load, 11,840 ÷ 230 = 51.5 amperes.

Subfeeder Neutral:
Lighting and small appliance load	3840 watts
Range load, 8000 watts at 70% (see Section 220-22)	5600 watts
Net computed load (neutral)..	9440 watts

              9440 W ÷ 230 V = 41 amperes

Minimum Size Feeders Required from Service Equipment to Meter Bank

(For 20 Dwelling Units — 10 with Ranges):

Total Computed Load:
Lighting and small appliance load, 20 × 5400	108,000 watts

Application of Demand Factor:
3000 watts at 100%	3000 watts
105,000 watts at 35%	36,750 watts
Net computed lighting and small appliance load...........................	39,750 watts
Range load, 10 ranges (less than 12 kW; Col. A, Table 220-19)	25,000 watts
Net computed load (with ranges)	64,750 watts

For 115/230-volt, 3-wire system:
    Net computed load, 64,750 W ÷ 230 V = 282 amperes.

Feeder Neutral:
Lighting and small appliance load	39,750 watts
Range load: 25,000 watts at 70% (see Section 220-22)	17,500 watts
Computed load (neutral)	57,250 watts

           57,250 W ÷ 230 V = 249 amperes.

Further Demand Factor (Section 220-22):
200 amperes at 100%	= 200 amperes
49 amperes at 70%	= 34 amperes
Net computed load (neutral)...................................234 amperes	

Minimum Size Main Feeder (or Service Conductors) Required

(For 40 Dwelling Units — 20 with Ranges):

Total Computed Load:
Lighting and small appliance load, 40 × 5400	216,000 watts

Application of Demand Factor:
3000 watts at 100%	3000 watts
117,000 watts at 35%	40,950 watts
96,000 watts at 25%	24,000 watts
Net computed lighting and small appliance load.........................	67,950 watts
Range load, 20 ranges (less than 12 kW, Col. A, Table 220-19)	35,000 watts
Net computed load	102,950 watts

For 115/230-volt, 3-wire system:
        Net computed load, 102,950 W ÷ 230 V = 448 amperes.

Feeder Neutral:
Lighting and small appliance load	67,950 watts
Range load, 35,000 watts at 70% (see Section 220-22)	24,500 watts
Computed load (neutral)	92,450 watts

           92,450 W ÷ 230 V = 402 amperes.

Further Demand Factor (see Section 220-22):
200 amperes at 100%	= 200 amperes
202 amperes at 70%	= 141 amperes
Net computed load (neutral)...................................341 amperes	

    See Tables 310-16 through 310-19, Notes 8 and 10.

Example No. 4(a).   Optional Calculation for Multifamily Dwelling

Multifamily dwelling equipped with electric cooking and space heating or air conditioning and having a total floor area of 32,000 square feet with 40 dwelling units.

Meters in two banks of 20 each plus house metering and individual subfeeders to each dwelling unit.

Each dwelling unit is equipped with an electric range of 8-kW nameplate rating, four 1.5-kW separately controlled 230-volt electric space heaters, and a 2.5-kW 230-volt electric water heater.

A common laundry facility is available to all tenants [Section 210-52(e), Exception No. 1].

Area of each dwelling unit is 800 square feet.

Computed Load for Each Dwelling Unit (Article 220):

General Lighting Load:

800 sq. ft. at 3 watts per sq. ft.	2400 watts
Electric range	8000 watts
Electric heat 6 kW	6000 watts
(or air conditioning if larger)	
Electric water heater	2500 watts

Minimum Number of Branch Circuits Required for Each Dwelling Unit:

General lighting load 2400 watts ÷ 115 = 21 amperes or two 15-ampere 2-wire circuits or two 20-amp 2-wire circuits.

Small appliance loads: Two 2-wire circuits of No. 12 [see Section 220-3(b)].

Range circuit 8000 watts × 80% ÷ 230 = 28 amperes on a circuit of three No. 10 as permitted in Column C of Table 220-19

Space Heating 6000 watts ÷ 230 = 26 amperes

No. of Circuits (see Section 220-3)

Minimum Size Sub-Feeder Required for Each Dwelling Unit (Section 215-2):

Computed Load (Article 220):

General lighting load	2400 watts
Small appliance load, two 20-amp circuits	3000 watts
Total computed load (without range and space heating)	5400 watts

Application of Demand Factor:

3000 watts at 100%	3000 watts
2400 watts at 35%	840 watts
Net computed load (without range and space heating)	3840 watts
Range load	6400 watts
Space heating, Section 220-15	6000 watts
Water heater	2500 watts
Net computed load for individual dwelling unit	18,740 watts

For 115/230-volt 3-wire system

Net computed load 18,740 W ÷ 230 V = 81 amperes

Subfeeder Neutral (Section 220-22)

Lighting and small appliance load	3840 watts
Range load 6400 watts at 70% (see Section 220-22)	4480 watts
Space and water heating (no neutral) 230 volt	0 watts
Net computed load (neutral)	8320 watts

8320 W ÷ 230 V = 36 amperes

Minimum Size Feeder Required from Service Equipment to Meter Bank for 20 Dwelling Units:

Total Computed Load:

Lighting and small appliance load 20 × 5400	108,000 watts
Water and space heating load 20 × 8500	170,000 watts
Range load 20 × 8000	160,000 watts
Net computed load (20 dwelling units)	438,000 watts

(Example 4(a) Continued Next Page.)

Example No. 4(a) (Continued)

Net computed load using Optional Calculation (Table 220-32)
  438,000 × .38 .... 166,440 watts

  166,440 W ÷ 230 V = 724 amperes

Minimum Size Mains Feeder Required (less house load)

(For 40 Dwelling Units):
  Total Computed Load:
    Lighting and small appliance load 40 × 5400 .... 216,000 watts
    Water and space heating 40 × 8500 .... 340,000 watts
    Range load 40 × 8000 .... <u>320,000</u> watts
  Net computed load (40 dwelling units).. 876,000 watts

  Net computed load using Optional Calculation (Table 220-32)
    876,000 × 28% .... 245,280 watts

  245,280 W ÷ 230 V = 1066 amperes

Feeder Neutral Load for Feeder from Service Equipment to Meter Bank for 20 Dwelling Units:

Lighting and small appliance load
  20 × 5400 watts   = 108,000 watts
  1st 3000 watts @ 100%   =   3000 watts
  105,000 watts @   35%   =   36,750 watts

    Subtotal .... 39,750 watts
20 Ranges = 35,000 watts @ 70% .... <u>24,500</u> watts
  (See Table 220-19 and Section 220-22.)
    Total .... 64,250 watts
  64,250 W ÷ 230 V = 279 amperes
Further Demand Factor (Section 220-22)
  First 200 amperes @ 100%   = 200 amperes
  Balance: 79 amperes @ 70%   = 55 amperes
    Total .... 255 amperes

Feeder Neutral Load for Mains Feeder (less house load) for 40 Dwelling Units:

Lighting and small appliance load
  40 × 5400 watts .... 216,000 watts
  1st 3000 watts @ 100% ....   3000 watts
  120,000 watts—3000 watts = 117,000 watts @ 35%......................   40,950 watts
  216,000 watts—120,000 watts = 96,000 watts @ 25% .... <u>24,000</u> watts
                                                                                67,950 watts

  40 Ranges = 55,000 watts @ 70% .... <u>38,500</u> watts
  (See Table 220-19 and Section 220-22.)
    Total .... 106,450 watts
  106,450 W ÷ 230 V = 462.8 = 463 amperes
Further demand factor (Section 220-22)
First 200 amp. @ 100%   = 200 amperes
Balance: 263 amperes @ 70%   = <u>184</u> amperes
    Total .... 384 amperes

Example No. 5   Calculation of Feeder Neutral

(See Section 220-22.)

The following example illustrates the method of calculating size of a feeder neutral for the computed load of a 5-wire, 2-phase system, where it is desired to modify the load in accordance with provisions of Section 220-22.

An installation consisting of a computed load of 250 amperes connected between the feeder neutral and each ungrounded feeder conductor.

Feeder Neutral (maximum unbalance of load 250 amp. × 140% = 350 amperes):
  200 amperes (first) at 100%   = 200 amperes
  150 amperes (excess) at 70%   = <u>105</u> amperes
    Computed load...105 amperes

Example No. 6.   Maximum Demand for Range Loads

Table 220-19, Column A applies to ranges not over 12 kW. The application of Note 1 to ranges over 12 kW (and not over 27 kW) is illustrated in the following examples:

A. Ranges all of same rating.

Assume 24 ranges each rated 16 kW.

From Column A the maximum demand for 24 ranges of 12 kW rating is 39 kW.
16 kW exceeds 12 kW by 4.
5% × 4 = 20% (5% increase for each kW in excess of 12).
39 kW × 20% = 7.8 kW increase.
39 + 7.8 = 46.8 kW: value to be used in selection of feeders.

B. Ranges of unequal rating.

Assume 5 ranges each rated 11 kW.
2 ranges each rated 12 kW.
20 ranges each rated 13.5 kW.
3 ranges each rated 18 kW

$$\begin{array}{rl} 5 \times 12 & = \ \ 60 \text{ Use 12 kW for range rated less than 12.} \\ 2 \times 12 & = \ \ 24 \\ 20 \times 13.5 & = 270 \\ \underline{3 \times 18} & = \ \underline{54} \\ 30 & \ \ \ 408 \text{ kW} \end{array}$$

408 ÷ 30 = 13.6 kW (average to be used for computation)

From Column A the demand for 30 ranges of 12 kW rating is 15 + 30 = 45 kW.
13.6 exceeds 12 by 1.6 (use 2).
5% × 2 = 10% (5% increase for each kW in excess of 12).
45 kW × 10% = 4.5 kW increase.
45 + 4.5 = 49.5 kW = value to be used in selection of feeders.

Example No. 7.   Ranges on a 3-Phase System

(See Section 220-19.)

Thirty ranges rated at 12 kW each are supplied by a 3-phase, 4-wire, 120/208-volt feeder, 10 ranges on each phase.

As there are 20 ranges connected to each ungrounded conductor, the load should be calculated on the basis of 20 ranges (or in case of unbalance, twice the maximum number between any two-phase wires), since diversity applies only to the number of ranges connected to adjacent phases and not the total.

The current in any one conductor will be one-half the total watt load of two adjacent phases divided by the line-to-neutral voltage. In this case, 20 ranges, from Table 220-19, will have a total watt load of 35,000 watts for two phases; therefore, the current in the feeder conductor would be:

17,500 ÷ 120 = 146 amperes.

On a 3-phase basis the load would be:

3 × 17,500 = 52,500 watts

and the current in each feeder conductor —

$$\frac{52,500}{208 \times 1.73} = 146 \text{ amperes}$$

Example No. 8.   Motors, Conductors, Overload,
and Short-Circuit and Ground-Fault Protection

(See Sections 430-6, 430-7, 430-22, 430-24, 430-32, 430-34, 430-52, 430-62, and Tables 430-150 and 430-152.)

Determine the conductor size, the motor overload protection, the branch-circuit short-circuit and ground-fault protection, and the feeder protection, for one 25-horsepower squirrel-cage induction motor (full-voltage starting, service factor 1.15, Code letter F), and two 30-horsepower wound-rotor induction motors (40°C rise), on a 460-volt, 3-phase, 60-Hertz supply.

(Example 8 Continued Next Page.)

Example No. 8 (Continued)

Conductor Loads

The full-load current of the 25-horsepower motor is 34 amperes (Table 430-150). A full-load current of 34 amperes × 1.25 = 42.5 amperes (Section 430-22). The full-load current of the 30-horsepower motor is 40 amperes (Table 430-150). A full-load current of 40 amperes × 1.25 = 50 amperes (Section 430-22).

The feeder ampacity will be 125 percent of 40 plus 40 plus 34, or 124 amperes (Section 430-24).

Overload and Short-Circuit and Ground-Fault Protection

Overload. Where protected by a separate overload device, the 25-horsepower motor, with full-load current of 34 amperes, must have overload protection of not over 42.5 amperes [Sections 430-6(a) and 430-32(a)(1)]. Where protected by a separate overload device, the 30-horsepower motor, with full-load current of 40 amperes, must have overload protection of not over 50 amperes [Sections 430-6(a) and 430-32 (a)(1)]. If the overload protection is not sufficient to start the motor or to carry the load, it may be increased according to Section 430-34. For a motor marked "thermally protected", overload protection is provided by the thermal protector [See Sections 430-7(a)(12) and 430-32(a)(2)].

Branch-Circuit Short-Circuit and Ground-Fault. The branch circuit of the 25-horsepower motor must have branch-circuit short-circuit and ground-fault protection of not over 300 percent for a nontime-delay fuse (Table 430-152) or 3.00 × 34 = 102 amperes. The next smaller standard size fuse is 100 amperes and is not sufficient for the starting current of the motor. The fuse size may be increased to 110 or 125 amperes (Section 430-52, Exception).

For the 30-horsepower motor, the branch-circuit short-circuit and ground-fault protection is 150 percent (Table 430-152) or 1.50 × 40 = 60 amperes. Where the maximum value of branch-circuit short-circuit and ground-fault protection is not sufficient to start the motor, the value for a nontime-delay fuse may be increased to 400 percent [Section 430-52, Exception a.].

Feeder Circuit. The maximum rating of the feeder short-circuit and ground-fault protection device is based on the sum of the largest branch-circuit protective device (110-ampere fuse) plus the sum of the full-load currents of the other motors or 110 plus 40 plus 40 = 190 amperes. The nearest standard fuse which does not exceed this value is 175 amperes [Section 430-62(a)].

Appendix

The following rules on Tentative Interim Amendments and Formal Interpretations are excerpted from the NFPA Regulations Governing Committee Projects as adopted by the Board of Directors on June 17, 1980.

Section 15. Tentative Interim Amendments

15-1. **Authorization.** A Tentative Interim Amendment to any existing Standard, Code, Recommended Practice, Manual, or Guide may be processed if the Tentative Interim Amendment is of an emergency nature requiring prompt action and has the endorsement of a member of the involved Technical Committee.

15-2. **Determination of Compliance.** A proposed Tentative Interim Amendment shall be submitted to the Council Secretary who, after consultation with the appropriate Committee Chairmen, shall determine compliance with 15-1.

15-3. **Processing.** If such compliance is determined, the Council Secretary shall submit the proposed Tentative Interim Amendment to the responsible Committee and it shall be processed in the following manner:

(a) The text of a proposed Tentative Interim Amendment, as submitted, shall not be changed by the Committee except to correct obviously incorrect references.

(b) A proposed Tentative Interim Amendment which meets the provisions of 15-1 shall be published by the Association in *Fire News* and other appropriate media with a notice that the proposed Tentative Interim Amendment has been forwarded to the responsible Technical Committee for processing and that anyone interested may respond to the proposed Tentative Interim Amendment within the time period established and published.

(c) Committees shall process a proposed Tentative Interim Amendment within sixty days; such time to be measured from the closing date for responses (see 15-3(b)) to submittal to the Council for approval for release.

(d) The proposed Tentative Interim Amendment shall be submitted to letter ballot of the Technical Committee and at least three-quarters of the members shall have voted in favor of the Tentative Interim Amendment.

NOTE: In calculating the three-fourths majority, those who have expressed in writing valid reasons for not having voted, and those who after a second request fail to return their ballots within the specified time limit, are omitted from the calculations. In no event will an affirmative vote by less than a simple majority of the total members of the Technical Committee eligible to vote satisfy the requirement that there be a three-fourths majority.

(e) The proposed Tentative Interim Amendment shall be reviewed by the Correlating Committee, if any, which shall make a recommendation to the Council with respect to the disposition of the Tentative Interim Amendment.

(f) All Committee actions on the proposed Tentative Interim Amendment shall be reported to the Council for action in accordance with 15-4.

15-4. **Action of the Council.** The Council shall:

(a) review the Committee action,

(b) accept or reject the Committee action,

(c) direct a different action,

(d) authorize release of the proposed Tentative Interim Amendment, if approved.

15-5. **Publication of Tentative Interim Amendment.** The Association shall publish in one of its publications sent to all members notice of the issuance of each Tentative Interim Amendment, shall issue a news release to applicable and interested technical journals, and shall also include in any subsequent distribution of the document to which the Tentative Interim Amendment applies the text of the Tentative Interim Amendment in a manner judged most feasible to accomplish the desired objectives. The tentative character of the Tentative Interim Amendment shall be clearly indicated in the publication and release.

15-6. **Subsequent Processing of Tentative Interim Amendments.** The Technical Committee concerned shall process the subject matter of any Tentative Interim Amendment through normal Technical Committee procedures (see Sections 11 and 12) at the next meeting of the Association to which the Technical Committee reports.

15-7. **Exception.** When the Board of Directors authorizes other procedures for the processing and/or issuance of Tentative Interim Amendments, the provisions of this Section shall not apply.

Section 16. Formal Interpretations Procedure

16-1. **General.** The following formal interpretation procedure is for the purpose of providing formal explanations of the meaning or intent of any specific provision or provisions of any document.

NOTE: This formal interpretation procedure does not prevent any Committee Chairman, member of any Committee, or the Staff Liaison from expressing an opinion on the meaning or intent of any provision of any such document, provided that the opinion is clearly identified as not being a Formal Interpretation of the Committee or of the Association.

16-2. **Nature of Formal Interpretations.** Two general forms of Formal Interpretations are recognized:

(a) those making an interpretation of the literal text, and

(b) those making an interpretation of the intent of the Technical Committee when the particular text was adopted.

16-3. **Editions to be Interpreted.** Interpretations shall be rendered on the text of the latest adopted document and any text of earlier editions which is identical to the text in the latest document. Interpretations may be rendered to the requester on text of an outdated document where such has been revised in or deleted from later editions. If possible, the requester should be informed why the text was revised or deleted.

16-4. **Method of Requesting Formal Interpretations.** A request for a Formal Interpretation shall be directed to the Council Secretary, at the National Fire Protection Association Headquarters. The request shall include a statement in which shall appear specific references to a single problem and identifying the portion (article, section, paragraph, etc.) of the document and edition of the document on which an interpretation is requested. Such a request shall be in writing and shall indicate the business interest of the requester. A request involving an actual field situation shall so state and all parties involved shall be named and notified.

16-5. **Qualifications for Processing.** A request for an interpretation may be processed if it:

(a) complies with 16-2 and 16-4,

(b) does not involve a determination of compliance of a design, installation, or product or equivalency of protection,

(c) does not involve a review of plans or specifications, or require judgment or knowledge that can only be acquired as a result of on-site inspection,

(d) does not involve text that clearly and decisively provides the requested information.

16-6. **Determination of Qualification.** The Council Secretary, after consultation with the appropriate Committee Chairmen, shall determine the qualification in accordance with 16-5.

16-7. **Editing of Interpretation Request.** A request for an interpretation may be rephrased. The rephrased version and any pertinent background information shall be sent to the requester and all parties named in the request for agreement. A deadline for receipt of agreement shall be established.

16-8. **Establishment of Interpretations Subcommittee.** If accepted for consideration, each request shall then be submitted to letter ballot of an Interpretations Subcommittee made up of five or more members or alternates of the Technical Committee(s) or Subcommittee having primary jurisdiction of the document or portion thereof covering the subject under consideration. The members shall be selected by the Committee Chairmen or the Council Secretary, if the Chairmen are not available. No member or alternate shall be eligible for appointment to an Interpretations Subcommittee if he or she is directly involved in the particular case prompting the request for the interpretation. The Interpretations Subcommittee should include Committee members or alternates representing the same interest categories as the requester and the other parties involved, as well as representatives of other parties. The personnel of Interpretations Subcommittees may be varied for each request.

16-9. **Voting on Interpretations.** In any case where more than twenty percent of the Subcommittee members disagree on the interpretation, the request for interpretation shall be referred to the Technical Committee(s). Under these conditions, a Formal Interpretation requires a two-thirds majority agreement of the Technical Committee(s) as tallied in accordance with 12-4. Where the necessary agreement is not received, the item shall be placed on the docket for regular processing by the Technical Committee(s) for subsequent possible action.

16-10. **Publication of Interpretation.** If the required agreement is secured from the Interpretations Subcommittee(s) or from the Technical Committee, the requester and all named parties shall be informed by the Staff Liaison and the interpretation shall be published by the Association in one of its publications sent to all members and announced in an Association news release to other media.

Interpretations of text of an outdated document which has been revised in or deleted from later editions shall not be published by the Association but shall be sent to the requester and all parties named in the request.

16-11. **Action Following Issuance of Formal Interpretations.** Any Technical Committee(s) whose document has been the subject of a Formal Interpretation shall review the item on which the interpretation has been issued to determine whether any change may be desired to the text of the document on which the interpretation has been rendered. If such a change is indicated, the Technical Committee(s) shall process such change in conformance with procedures set forth in Sections 10, 11 and 12.

16-12. **Applicability of Formal Interpretations.** Any Formal Interpretation issued shall apply to the edition of the document for which the interpretation is made and to any other edition of the document if the text is identical to the text of the edition of which the Formal Interpretation was rendered.

Time Schedule for the
1984 *National Electrical Code*

Nov. 30, 1981	Final date for receipt of proposals from the public for revision of the 1981 *National Electrical Code* preparatory to the issuance of the 1984 edition. Proposals should be forwarded to the Vice President—Standards, National Fire Protection Association.
Jan. 4–22, 1982	Code-Making Panels Preliminary Meeting to consider proposals for *Code* changes.
April 26–30, 1982	Correlating Committee reviews the Preliminary Report submitted by the Code-Making Panels. Establishes that no conflicts exist, that satisfactory correlation is achieved among the recommendations of the Code-Making Panels, and that the Committee's activities have been conducted in accordance with the Regulations Governing Committee Projects and any approved Operating Procedures.
June 7, 1982	Preprint of the Proposed Amendments (TCR) for the 1984 *National Electrical Code* published for distribution to the *National Electrical Code* Committee and other interested parties.
June 7– Nov. 1, 1982	Period of study by interested parties and submittal of recommendations for modifying report to the Vice President—Standards, NFPA.
Nov. 1, 1982	Closing date for comments.
Nov. 29– Dec. 10, 1982	Code-Making Panels meet to act on public comments.
Feb. 28– Mar. 4, 1983	Correlating Committee meeting to review the Code-Making Panel action on comments (Technical Committee Documentation).
April 1, 1983	NFPA prints and distributes the 1983 NFPA Technical Committee Documentation and the proposed 1984 *National Electrical Code* to members of the *National Electrical Code* Committee and to all other parties who file requests therefor.
May 16–19, 1983	Official action by NFPA Annual Meeting. Submitted by NFPA to American National Standards Institute for approval as ANSI Standard.
September 1983	Publication of the 1984 *National Electrical Code*.

INDEX

Tentative Interim Amendment 70-81-1

to the

National Electrical Code®

NFPA 70-1981

Pursuant to Section 15 of the NFPA Regulations Governing Committee Projects, the National Fire Protection Association has issued the following Tentative Interim Amendment to the 1981 edition of the *National Electrical Code*, NFPA 70, effective November 14, 1980.

A Tentative Interim Amendment is tentative because it has not been processed through the entire standards-making procedures. It is interim because it is effective only between editions of the standard. A TIA automatically becomes a Proposal of the proponent for the next edition of the standard; as such, it then is subject to all the procedures of the standards-making process.

1. Revise 450-23 as follows:

450-23. High Fire Point Liquid-Insulated Transformers. Transformers insulated with less-flammable liquids shall be permitted to be installed without a vault in noncombustible occupancy areas of noncombustible buildings, provided there is a liquid confinement area and the liquid is listed as having a fire point of not less than 300°C.

Such indoor transformer installations in combustible buildings or combustible occupancy areas shall be provided with an automatic fire extinguishing system or shall be installed in a vault complying with Part C of this article.

Transformers installed indoors and rated over 35,000 volts shall be installed in a vault.

Transformers installed outdoors shall comply with Section 450-27.

For definition of "Noncombustible" as used in this section, see Types of Building Construction, NFPA 220-1979.

See definition of "Listed" in Article 100.

Tentative Interim Amendment 70-81-2

to the

National Electrical Code®

NFPA 70-1981

Pursuant to Section 15 of the NFPA Regulations Governing Committee Projects, the National Fire Protection Association has issued the following Tentative Interim Amendment to the 1981 edition of the *National Electrical Code*, NFPA 70.

A Tentative Interim Amendment is tentative because it has not been processed through the entire standards-making procedures. It is interim because it is effective only between editions of the standard. A TIA automatically becomes a Proposal of the proponent for the next edition of the standard; as such, it then is subject to all the procedures of the standards-making process.

1. Add an Exception to Section 380-18 to read as follows:

Exception: Table 373-6(a) spacings shall be permitted if the switch is designed and constructed for wiring using only one single 90 degree bend for each conductor including the neutral and the wiring diagram shows and specifies the method of wiring that must be used.

Tentative Interim Amendment 70-81-3

to the

National Electrical Code®

NFPA 70-1981

Pursuant to Section 15 of the NFPA Regulations Governing Committee Projects, the National Fire Protection Association has issued the following Tentative Interim Amendment to the 1981 edition of the *National Electrical Code*, NFPA 70.

A Tentative Interim Amendment is tentative because it has not been processed through the entire standards-making procedures. It is interim because it is effective only between editions of the standard. A TIA automatically becomes a Proposal of the proponent for the next edition of the standard; as such, it then is subject to all the procedures of the standards-making process.

1. Add an Exception to Section 384-25 to read as follows:

Exception No. 3: The top and bottom wire bending space shall be permitted to be sized in accordance with Table 373-6(a) spacings if the panelboard is designed and constructed for wiring using only one single 90 degree bend for each conductor including the neutral and the wiring diagram shows and specifies the method of wiring that must be used.

Tentative Interim Amendment 70-81-4

to the

National Electrical Code®

NFPA 70-1981

Pursuant to Section 15 of the NFPA Regulations Governing Committee Projects, the National Fire Protection Association has issued the following Tentative Interim Amendment to the 1981 edition of the *National Electrical Code®*, NFPA 70. The TIA was processed by the National Electrical Code Committee and was approved for release by the Standards Council on April 2, 1981.

A Tentative Interim Amendment is tentative because it has not been processed through the entire standards-making procedures. It is interim because it is effective only between editions of the standard. A TIA automatically becomes a Proposal of the proponent for the next edition of the standard; as such, it then is subject to all the procedures of the standards-making process.

1. Change the first sentence of the Fine Print Note following the first paragraph of Section 501-5 to read:

Seals are provided in conduit and cable systems to minimize the passage of gases and vapors and prevent the passage of flames from one portion of the electrical installation to another through the conduit.

2. Add the following sentences to the Fine Print Note following the first paragraph of Section 501-5:

Unless specifically designed and tested for the purpose, conduit and cable seals are not intended to prevent the passage of liquids, gases or vapors at a continuous pressure differential across the seal. Even at differences in pressure across the seal equivalent to a few inches of water, there may be a slow passage of gas or vapor through a seal, and through conductors passing through the seal. See Section 501-5(e)(2). Temperature extremes and highly corrosive liquids and vapors can affect the ability of seals to perform their intended function. See Section 501-5(c)(2).

3. Change the second sentence of Section 501-5(a)(4) to read:

The sealing fitting shall be permitted on either side of the boundary of such location but shall be so designed and installed to minimize the amount of gas or vapor which may have entered the conduit system within the Division 1 location from being communicated to the conduit beyond the seal.

4. Change the second sentence to Section 501-5(b)(2) to read:

The sealing fitting shall be permitted on either side of the boundary of such location but shall be so designed and installed to minimize the amount of gas or vapor which may have entered the conduit system within the Division 2 location from being communicated to the conduit beyond the seal.

5. Change the heading of Section 501-5(f)(3) to "**Canned Pumps, Process Connections, Etc.**"

6. Change Section 501-5(f)(3) to read:

For canned pumps, process connection for flow, pressure, or analysis measurement, etc., that depend on a single seal diaphragm or tube to prevent process fluids from entering the electrical conduit system an additional approved seal, barrier or other means shall be provided to prevent the process fluid from entering the conduit system beyond the additional devices or means, if the primary seal fails.

The additional approved seal or barrier and interconnecting enclosure shall meet the pressure and temperature requirements of the primary seal unless other approved means are provided to accomplish the purpose above.

Drains, vents or other devices shall be provided so that primary seal leakage will be obvious.

7. At the end of the Fine Print Note to Section 501-5(f)(3), delete the period and add "and Fine Print Note to Section 501-5."